D1685907

FLORA OF
NORTH
LANCASHIRE

FLORA OF NORTH LANCASHIRE

ERIC GREENWOOD

Credits

Photographs

Anne Ancell: Plate 2.59
Professor Malcolm Edmunds: Plate 2.49
Jon Hickling: Plates 2.10, 2.23, 2.25, 2.30, 2.31, 2.32, 2.34, 2.38, 2.39, 2.40 & 2.57
John Lamb: Plates 2.3, 2.11, 2.19, 2.44, 2.47, 2.52, & 2.71
Tim Mitcham: Plates 2.64 & 2.76
Dr Jennifer Newton: Plates 2.1, 2.42, 2.46 & 2.72
Graeme Skelcher: Plates 2.60 & 2.61
Jason Smalley: Plate 2.24
Lancashire Wildlife Trust: Plate 2.73
All other Plates E.F. and/or B.D. Greenwood.

Maps

Species distribution maps in chapter 3 are produced with MapMate® using digitised map data copyright© HarperCollinsBartholmew 2010. Data overlays copyright Botanical Society of the British Isles 2011.
All other distribution maps produced in DMAP© Alan Morton.

First published in the UK in 2012 by

Palatine Books, an imprint of
Carnegie Publishing Ltd
Carnegie House,
Chatsworth Road,
Lancaster LA1 4SL
www.carnegiepublishing.com

for
The Lancashire Wildlife Trust
The Barn,
Berkeley Drive,
Bamber Bridge,
Preston PR5 6BY
www.wildlifetrust.org.uk/lancashire

ISBN 978-1-874181-89-7

Copyright © E.F. Greenwood

Designed and typeset by Carnegie Book Production
Printed and bound by 1010 Printing International

Contents

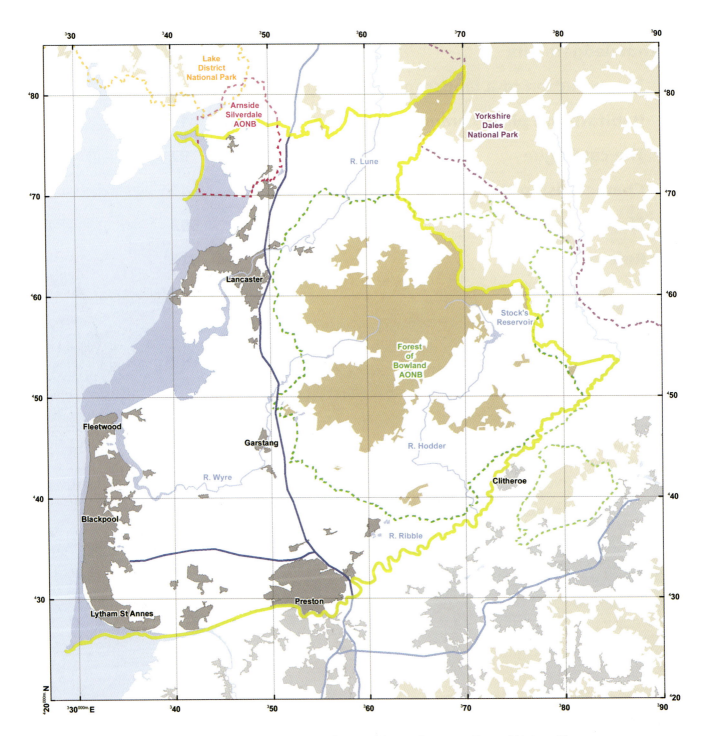

North Lancashire (map prepared with the assistance of Lancashire Environment Record Network).

Introduction

When the *Atlas of the British Flora* was published in 1962, I and members of Preston Scientific Society were surprised to find that many common species were not recorded from the Preston area. Correspondence with the late Dr Franklyn Perring revealed that for northern Lancashire the editors had relied on old publications, notably Wheldon and Wilson's *Flora of West Lancashire* (1907) and brief visits by non-resident members of the Botanical Society of the British Isles (B.S.B.I.). Dr Perring suggested I might like to become vice-county recorder for VC 60 and perhaps compile a supplement to Wheldon and Wilson's Flora.

After taking further advice from Dr Perring, the late Dr John Dony and others, I agreed to become VC 60 recorder and with members of the Preston Scientific Society embarked upon a systematic survey at the tetrad level of the vice-county. However after a few years it became clear that major changes had occurred over the previous 60 years and that these were so great only a completely new Flora could do the area justice. It also became clear that with only a small number of dedicated recorders and our botanical inadequacies it would take many years to satisfactorily survey the area. It became a 'learning on the job' exercise.

Then, in 1974, local government reorganisation added a large part of VC 64, Mid-west Yorkshire, to the administrative county of Lancashire. At the same time my personal circumstances changed resulting in less time for fieldwork. However in his retirement the late Len Livermore and his wife Pat embarked on a systematic survey of Lancaster District culminating in a series of publications and reports in the 1980s and 1990s.

By the late 1990s I realised that VC 60 was not a viable area for a Flora but on retirement in 1998 I had more time for fieldwork. Accordingly with the agreement of Phyl Abbott, vice-county recorder for Mid-west Yorkshire, I decided to include Lancashire VC 64 north of the R. Ribble with the intention of publishing a Flora of North Lancashire. In the meantime Phyl published her Plant Atlas for the whole of VC 64 in 2005. The addition of this part of Yorkshire to Lancashire considerably extended the area to be covered and included most of the Forest of Bowland Area of Outstanding Natural Beauty (A.O.N.B.), a distinct phytogeographical upland area little known to either botanists or tourists. Until Phyl's work the only previous publications of any significance in this area were by Joseph Pickard 100 years earlier.

Over the years extensive literature and archive sources were used in compiling the present work. The region has benefited from extensive and detailed palaeontological research, much of it instigated by a lack of archaeological evidence to support an understanding of human impact in the area. By incorporating the results of this research a much better understanding was achieved of vegetational and floristic changes since the retreat of the ice some 12,000 years ago.

Today the pace of change is as rapid as ever. Some may say it is faster than ever but that is to ignore, for example, the enclosure of commons 200 or more years ago. However northern Lancashire is a varied region. The Arnside & Silverdale and Forest of Bowland A.O.N.B.s are mostly within the area. Also the region borders the Yorkshire Dales National Park and there are proposals to extend it to include parts of Leck. The Lake District National Park borders the Arnside and Silverdale A.O.N.B. Hawes Water and Gait Barrows National Nature Reserve is within northern Lancashire as is a small part of the Ribble Estuary National Nature Reserve. Despite the crowded coastal resort towns and two cities (Lancaster and Preston) much of the Forest of Bowland and Leck is remote and known to relatively few visitors. The diversity of the region is reflected in its flora, which is one of the most floristically diverse in England.

Acknowledgements

Whilst I am solely responsible for the text it is impossible to produce a book of this kind without an enormous amount of help from others. I am very grateful to all the recorders, listed in Table 3.2 and in the text, for the data they provided over many years and to Lancashire Environment Record Network for access to its data. I am also grateful to the many referees who have validated many of the difficult to identify plants. They are listed in Table 3.3. In the course of the research for the Flora, specimens in several herbaria were consulted and I am very grateful to the curators for allowing access and for the loan of material. Similarly I am grateful to various archivists who allowed me access to consult original documents in their care. Much of the recording was done from public rights of way but until recently many areas required permission for access from landowners and tenants. I am most grateful to them for giving this access but where sites are mentioned there is no implication for public access.

Finding suitable photographs to illustrate the Flora was difficult and I am grateful to those people who kindly allowed me to use their work (see credits on page iv).

Working on the northern Lancashire flora has been a life-long activity giving me a great deal of pleasure and a deep love of the region. I am grateful to the late Franklyn Perring for persuading me to take up the challenge and to my mother who thought it was a 'good idea'.

Many thanks go to Professor Malcolm Edmunds for reading a first draft, to Dr Geoff Morries for helpful suggestions and to several major recorders for reading later versions of chapter 3. However special thanks go to my wife, Barbara, for her forbearance, encouragement, IT skills, for detailed proofing of later versions of the text and for help in compiling the index to species.

In bringing the book to fruition I am grateful to Bob Ellis (B.S.B.I. Volunteers Officer), Anna Goddard & Lucy Frontani of Carnegie Publishing and Tim Mitcham (Head of Conservation, Wildlife Trust for Lancashire, Manchester and North Merseyside).

In order to bring the retail price to under £60 per copy it has been necessary to obtain considerable financial support. Most of this has come from a legacy from my brother, the late Dr Duncan J. Greenwood. I would also like to thank further contributions from Steve Palmer, The Wildflower Society, The Botanical Society of the British Isles, Liverpool Botanical Society, Preston Bird Watching & Natural History Society (formerly part of Preston Scientific Society), Wildlife Trust for Lancashire, Manchester and North Merseyside and grants from the Sustainable Development Funds of the Arnside and Silverdale and Forest of Bowland Areas of Outstanding Natural Beauty.

E.F. Greenwood
July 2011

With special thanks to the following people for their support

Malcolm Edmunds
Emma Greenwood
Peter Jepson
Sheila Grey
Peter Gateley
Peter Tipping
John Crowder
Ken and Ann Kitchen

Francis Fitzherbert-Brockholes
Susan Bowden
Phil Dykes
Dorothy M. Bates
Bowland Ecology
Stephen Ross
Jennifer Newton
Barry Dyson

Lancashire Moth Group
Jeremy Steeden
Lancashire Biodiversity Partnership
Maurice Jones
Dr Philip H. Smith
Mr R. Copson
Mrs Muriel Lord

1. The evolution of a landscape and its flora

Introduction

Increasingly floristic studies in the British Isles are focussing on change. The 'New Atlas' (Preston, et al., 2002) focused strongly on changes in the British and Irish flora and the factors driving change during the second half of the twentieth century. Similarly at the local level recent studies have recorded the changing floras and postulated reasons for change (Preston, 2000; Greenwood, 2003). However data for these studies relies on observations made by botanists over relatively short and recent time periods.

On the other hand palaeoecological studies have demonstrated the main landscape and vegetation changes over the much longer time scale of the postglacial period but necessarily lack the details of species composition. Frequently there is very little information covering the first millennium AD. Nevertheless detailed archaeological and local history research has revealed for more recent periods an increasingly accurate picture of the usually human induced changes in the British landscape. From the middle of the nineteenth century there is an abundance of written information but at the local level it may remain unpublished or published in local history papers and books. These large-scale changes are reflected in the composition of the flora and whilst the general picture is increasingly well-known floristic changes at the level of a few kilometres are much less well understood.

A wide range of resources were used here to achieve a better understanding of how the present composition and distribution of the flora has changed in northern Lancashire often in response to human influences.

Location

Northern Lancashire is situated in the centre of Great Britain and lies between the R. Ribble in the south and Cumbria to the north. The eastern half of the area is formed by Leck Fell and the Bowland hills rising to 628m on Leck Fell and to 561m in Bowland and covered in blanket bog overlying acid millstone grit. More strictly the ancient Forest of Bolland comprises the upland area based on the drainage catchments of the middle and upper reaches of the R. Hodder but extending southwards to the villages bordering the R. Ribble between Grindleton and Great Mitton. The hills are incised with numerous river valleys radiating out from the centre. To the west there is a plain covered in boulder clay deposited by the retreating ice of the last glaciation and more recent organic deposits. Carboniferous limestone exposures occur in the north and in parts of the Ribble valley with extensive limestone pavements in the Silverdale – Warton area, on Dalton Crags and to a lesser extent on Leck Fell. There is a long coast line fringed by sand dunes, mostly developed as towns or converted into golf courses, and by salt marshes extending several kilometres inland on river estuaries. It is a varied but compact area measuring some 50 × 50km.

This diverse and often attractive landscape gave rise to the designation of two Areas of Outstanding Natural Beauty: Arnside – Silverdale A.O.N.B. on the limestone at the head of Morecambe Bay and Bowland A.O.N.B. covering the Bowland Fells. In addition Leck adjoins the Yorkshire Dales National Park.

Similarly many areas are designated in some way for their wildlife interest including the Ribble Estuary and Hawes Water – Gait Barrows National Nature Reserves.

Changes in vegetation – the impact of humans

Although the broad sequences of change are well-known (Atkinson and Houston, 1993; Greenwood, 1999) an enormous amount of research was carried out during the second half of the twentieth century in northern Lancashire to elucidate on the one hand the changes in the coastline and the vegetation associated with it and on the other the changes in the vegetation further inland since the retreat of the last ice-age some 12,000 years ago to the present day

The coastline and coastal habitats

Until Tooley's research (1978) the changes on the coast since the retreat of the ice some 12,000 years ago had puzzled many people. However his work demonstrated that the position of the coastline had oscillated over the years. He revealed a complex picture but that the final episodes on the Lancashire coast took place some 4,000 to 2,400 years ago and again during the twelfth and thirteenth centuries. Thus the sand dunes that were formerly so extensive on the Fylde coast are of relatively recent origin. Similarly today's salt marshes, which like the sand dunes have lined the coast for millennia, are of recent or very recent origin.

However the coast remained largely free of major development until the mid nineteenth century. Small communities were established from the earliest times and their inhabitants grazed their animals on the coastal grasslands, marshes and heaths. It is difficult to know how many animals were grazed in coastal areas but some information survives for Cockersand Abbey founded between 1180 and 1184. In an inventory for 1536 Marshall (2001) records that the Abbey had 87 sheep and lambs on the Pilling marshes but it is believed their cattle comprising 24 draught oxen, 58 milkers, 30 heifers, 42 stirks and 3 bulls were kept on arable and grazing lands within the township rather than on the shore. The Cockersand Abbey Chartulary (compiled 1267–1268) shows that 100 sheep were kept at Middleton (Farrer, 1905). However for most of the coast there is little information although the sand dunes at Fleetwood were used as a rabbit warren and Rothwell (1974) refers to sheep and horses in 1585.

Blackpool started to become a seaside resort in the late eighteenth century but it was not until the middle of the nineteenth century that serious development of the whole coast between Lytham and Fleetwood began. Peter Hesketh started development at Fleetwood in the 1830s (the railway arrived in 1840) and Thomas Clifton and his agents started developments on the sand dunes at Lytham at about the same time although it was not until the end of the century before St Anne's could be fully developed as a seaside resort (Rogers, 1996; Crosby, 1998).

However, preceding the building of towns and seaside resorts, Parliamentary Enclosure of commons had often resulted in the drainage of land and using the reclaimed land for more intensive agricultural purposes. Nevertheless many areas retained their wild, semi-natural vegetation and continued to be used for rough grazing as they had been for millennia (Table 1.1).

Together these developments transformed the Fylde coast into what is seen today as a more or less urban landscape with fragments of the former coastal habitats. Further north a similar situation occurred at Morecambe and Heysham but here development was delayed until the late nineteenth century. Although Irish ferry services operated from Morecambe from 1851 (Archer, 1999) with the resort developing later, the Port of Heysham and industrial development did not start until 1904 (Clague, 2004).

Although reclamation of the sand dunes was largely delayed until the nineteenth century small scale enclosure of salt marshes had occurred from the earliest times. Towards the end of the eighteenth century ideas for larger scale enclosures were considered and in 1820 Edward Dawson reclaimed 166 acres of Aldcliffe Marsh on the Lune estuary (Hewitson, 1900). Elsewhere the development and enclosure of salt marshes on the Ribble estuary had been charted (Berry, 1967; Holden, 2010). It has long been appreciated that in Morecambe Bay the extent of salt marshes at any one locality fluctuates in a cyclical manner (Marshall, 1967; Gray and Scott, 1987) and in a series of diagrams Gray (1972) showed how from a very small area the marshes on the Keer estuary developed from 1845–1862 into the extensive ones recorded in 1967.

Inland habitats

The research carried out on the coast is matched by work further inland and the relationship between the lowland bogs and the changing coastline further explored. In the Bowland fells Tallis and his colleagues (Mackay, 1993; Mackay and Tallis, 1994) provided a detailed understanding of the changes that occurred whilst the lowland part of the region was covered by the North West Wetlands Survey (Middleton, et al., 1995), initiated largely because so little was known of the ancient landscape, palaeoecology and archaeology of lowland Lancashire and other lowland areas of north-western England.

Pre-history

Middleton, et al. (1995) described the vegetation changes in lowland northern Lancashire in the postglacial period. These followed a familiar pattern for north-western England with the vegetation influenced by climatic variation, marine incursions (Tooley, 1978) and increasing human influence. However human influences and settlement always seemed to be low compared with other parts of the country. By the Neolithic period (6,000–5,000BP) much of Lancashire was covered by an oak and alder forest interspersed with wetter and more open areas and in these the lowland raised bogs were developing as long as 8000 years ago. The forest probably extended over the tops of the Bowland Fells if only as scrubby woodland and west of the present coastline. Within the 'wildwood' there were possibly clearer areas of 'wood pasture' created or maintained perhaps by large herbivores (Vera, 2000). The extent of these clearances and the role of large herbivores is debatable (Mitchell, 2005). The presence of large herbivores is not doubted as footprints off Formby confirmed their presence (Plater, et al., 1999; Lewis, 2010). A small number of humans exploited these resources and introduced the first crops and with them the first weeds (Jones, 1988; Preston, et al., 2004).

However at some point a vegetation pattern was reached upon which human influence largely determined the future vegetation and its floristic composition. This seems to be sometime in the first millennium BC but at that time there also appears to have been an abrupt change to much wetter surface conditions with *Sphagnum imbricatum* complex dominating lowland mire surfaces. In particular the sub-fossil remains of the hyperoceanic temperate *Sphagnum austinii*, part of the *S. imbricatum* complex (Smith, 2004), are a major component of raised bog peat in many parts of the British Isles but it is long extinct in Lancashire. This probably relates to a wetter climate but more controversially it is suggested that human influences may have inadvertently aided the spread of bogs. This is particularly true where blanket bog developed in the Bowland Fells. Nevertheless Middleton, et al. (1995) consider that the evidence for human influence, at least in lowland areas, is weak. Clearly the vegetation and the species forming it owe their origins to the flora that had previously colonised the region including any archaeophytes that might have been brought in by humans. However these changes to a wet, soggy landscape provided poor grazing and even more problems for cultivating crops. Yet the former wooded landscape remained in a broad belt around the Bowland Fells, extending up the valleys, westwards along boulder clay ridges and on better drained areas elsewhere. The coast remained fringed with sand dunes and salt marshes. Nevertheless the picture that emerges is one of retrenchment of human activity in the early – mid Iron Age and with woodland probably covering only a third of the landscape.

Towards the end of the Iron Age and in the early Romano-British period a radical change occurred with woodland, although still plentiful, less extensive with tree/shrub accounting for perhaps only 25% of pollen. However sampling sites were either in the uplands or in the lowland raised bogs (Dark, 2000). Nevertheless woodland was still extensive in boulder clay areas. Thus, 2000 years ago it is envisaged that the landscape was one of extensive blanket bogs covering the fells and wherever drainage was poor at lower levels there were numerous small bogs. In addition in the low-lying areas in the west raised bogs covered large parts of the Fylde and Over Wyre. On the better drained land and in the steep sided valleys the forest still dominated but with an increasing number of clearings and a retreating forest from higher altitudes. In places, but especially in the west where drainage was impeded, there were extensive fens but few areas of open water. However there were probably more areas of open water than can be appreciated today. Apart from Hawes Water in the north and Marton Mere near Blackpool a number of small water bodies were also probably found. They included a series of shallow lakes behind the sand dunes (the Leaches) and small tarns elsewhere, e.g. near Garstang where Greenhalgh Castle built in 1490 (Hewitson, 1900) was more or less surrounded by water and fen and where a fragment remains today, whilst there were bog pools in the lowland raised mosses, e.g. Cockerham Great Tarn and on the fell tops where small tarns and pools are still present, e.g. Brennand Tarn.

With this background humans largely transformed the landscape, its vegetation and the species that grew there. Yet for the following 1000 years palaeoecological and archaeological evidence for what happened is scanty and it is only from Domesday Book (Williams and Martin, 2003) and the increasing development of written records that a picture of the changes that took place emerges. This picture has been researched by an increasing number of local historians working on original documents.

The landscape from medieval times to the sixteenth century

There are a number of seminal works on the making of the English landscape including those of Hoskins, *The making of the English Landscape* (1955) and Rackham, *The History of the Countryside* (1997). Domesday Book (Williams and Martin, 2003) is unhelpful. Whereas in other parts of England it gives an assessment of woodland and habitation, Lancashire woodlands are not mentioned and most of the villages are described as waste. It seems that the 'Harassment of the North' had more or less destroyed many of them. At that time the R. Ribble formed the border between the ancient Kingdoms of Northumbria and Mercia and was therefore a border region. Local historians have turned to place names to provide evidence for woodlands in the centuries before 1300AD. Winchester (1993) showed that names derived from Old English and Old Norse terms for wood form a pattern in the boulder clay areas east of a line between Preston and Lancaster and surrounding the Bowland Fells including the Ribble valley. In contrast the plain in the west (the Fylde) is devoid of names derived from wood. Indeed the name 'Fylde' is derived from an Old English word meaning open country. This contrast between unwooded and wooded country can be found in two names based on Plumpton. Near Lytham in the Fylde there are two places called Great and Little Plumpton. However in the nineteenth century they were known as Little and Great Field or Fylde Plumpton whilst further east on the edge of the woodland zone there was and still is Woodplumpton. The deeds and papers of the de Hoghton family also show that in the thirteenth and fourteenth centuries woodland was an important part of the local economy in the lower Ribble valley (e.g. in Alston, Dilworth, Grimsargh, Hothersall, Ribchester etc.) and possibly even on the Wyre estuary at Staynall and Preesall (Lumby, 1936).

In addition to these two zones of non-wooded or open country in the west and wooded zone to the east there was an upland area comprising Leck Fell and the Bowland Fells, including the Forest of Bowland. Following the Norman Conquest much of the area and indeed many other parts of the County were made a Royal Forest and preserved for hunting (Shaw, 1956; Harrison, 1901). These were not necessarily wooded but contained important reserves of pasture and 'empty' land awaiting exploitation and settlement. However as early as the thirteenth century vaccaries (commercial cattle farms) and pastures were established for the rearing of draught oxen (Porter, 1974; Winchester, 2000) and whilst sheep farming occurred from at least the thirteenth century it may have been associated particularly with abbey estates, e.g. at Cockerham, Ellel and Claughton (Farrer, 1898–1905) or in the extreme east of Bowland as part of the Kirkstall Abbey Estates (Greenwood and Bolton, 2000). Nevertheless extensive sheep walks

do not seem to have been a feature of the northern Lancashire landscape and perhaps the monastic sheep walks in Yorkshire and elsewhere were not as influential as once thought (Rackham, 1999). Yet overall wool was a major monastic product requiring the maintenance of many thousand sheep (Simmons, 2003). On the coast the inventory of the Pilling Estate of Cockersand Abbey made on the dissolution of the monasteries in 1536 showed that even here cattle were more important than sheep (Sobee, 1997; Marshall, 2001). The remarkable feature of the inventory is the small area of Pilling that was cultivated, most being bog (Table 1.1). The sheep probably grazed the salt marshes whilst the cattle were found on the inland pastures.

Table 1.1   Crops grown at Pilling, 1536 (From Marshall, 2001)

Crop	Area in acres
Wheat	3
Barley	10
Oats	32
Peas	2
TOTAL	47
Animals	Numbers
Pigs	18
Sheep	87
Horses	10
Domestic cattle	157
Wild cattle	18

Total farmed area = 1000 acres, total area of Pilling = 6000 acres

Using archaeological, palaeoecological and documentary sources a more detailed picture of the mediaeval landscape can be developed. Much of the treeless lowland landscape in the west of northern Lancashire was still covered in bog, especially north of the R. Wyre and near Lytham. Elsewhere in the vicinity of Marton Mere and slow moving streams etc. there were extensive fens and carrs with alder and willow. On many parts of the coast there were shifting sand dunes with oscillations of accretion and erosion of salt marshes. There were also shingle banks in some places, e.g. between Blackpool and Fleetwood, behind

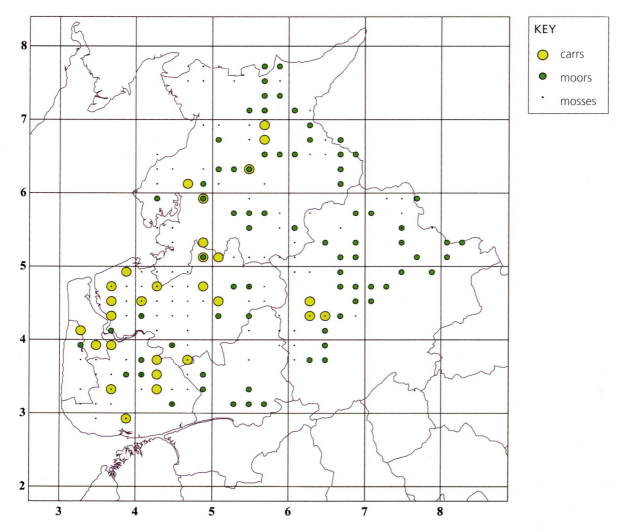

Map 1.1   Distribution of 'moors', 'carrs' and 'mosses' derived from place name evidence. Note that the three terms are largely complementary to each other. In the uplands only the wettest bogs were called mosses.
Sources: Various Ordnance Survey maps; Jeffery's map of Yorkshire, 1771; Middleton, *et al.* (1995) and Porter (1994)

which there were further fens and possibly bogs before the salt marshes of the Wyre estuary were reached. Also behind the dunes there was an area of dune heath in which the shallow lakes or Leaches were found. Today it is difficult to be sure of the exact location and extent of these features. Organic remains, especially peat, were exploited and in many places they were completely removed leaving only the underlying boulder clay. Some idea of the extent of the former peat mosses can be gained by mapping the name moss derived from place names (Map 1.1) but as this data is derived from information assembled in the last 200 years or so it is likely that bogs and fens were even more extensive than Map 1.1 suggests.

This was an inhospitable region for human habitation. Small religious houses developed in coastal areas at Heysham, Cockersand and Lytham with access largely from the sea. Inland settlements developed on higher land on drumlins and on other boulder clay features, e.g. Preesall, Poulton-le-Fylde and on the terminal moraine running westward from Preston through Kirkham to the coast near Blackpool.

These settlements were small with open fields in their vicinity, which can be identified today by strip-like fields resulting from the piecemeal enclosure of open fields and common meadows. Beyond lay the common grazing of the 'waste', often bog, which provided a supply of fuel. At some stage in the first millennium AD or earlier the woodlands that existed on these higher 'islands' of boulder clay were cleared but how or when is not certain. The old Welsh element 'pres' in the village names of Preesall and Preece meaning 'brushwood' implies that even in the British period before the Anglo-Saxons arrived Fylde woodland was scrubby brushwood rather than high forest. Even today landscape features remain that identify these early cultivated areas and can be traced as ancient enclosures following the former forest zone extending into the Fylde on boulder clay ridges and drumlins etc. (Ede and Darlington, 2002). Similarly the remains of this former woodland can be traced, at least to some extent, by the present distribution of some woodland species, e.g. *Anemone nemorosa, Dryopteris affinis, Primula vulgaris* and *Viola riviniana* that survive in hedgerows in the boulder clay areas of the Fylde.

There is also little evidence for the regular division of the fields into two, three or four cropping units (i.e. the 'Midland System'), rather the north-western open fields, which appear to be more akin to the Scottish 'infield' nucleus of intensively cropped ploughland.

The waste beyond the settlements was often given names that accurately described their vegetation. Moor (Map 1.1) was the driest and provided grazing for livestock especially in the summer. This was probably often heath, with dwarf ericaceous shrubs as well as heathy grassland, e.g. on Preston Moor (Hunt, 1992b). The name was also used to describe heaths in the Bowland Fells etc. Carr (from the Norse 'kjarr', a marsh overgrown with brushwood) was wet fenland with alder/ willow scrub whilst Moss described raised bogs in the lowlands but the term was also used to describe wet bogs in the Bowland Fells. Carrs (Map 1.1) were found mostly in the lowland west of northern Lancashire, sometimes close to mosses but usually alongside slow moving streams and occasionally elsewhere as in the Lune valley. All these terms suggest that in mediaeval times much of northern Lancashire was devoid of forest and was often some form of wetland.

Nevertheless in the woodland zone there was a wooded landscape with numerous trees, dispersed hamlets and farmsteads set in a patchwork of small, enclosed fields. As time passed clearances became larger and more numerous with some open fields by the fourteenth century. The scale of the landscape was small and intimate. There were small nuclei of open field arable land set in a patchwork of small enclosures,

which had been created by grubbing up of woodland in the twelfth and thirteenth centuries. Nevertheless in the Forest of Bowland by the mid-sixteenth, century despite concerns at the deterioration of the oak forest, there were still plenty of large oak and ash trees but also much scrub with holly, hawthorn, hazel and crab apple. There was also an abundance of alder growing in carrs and marshes and this was cherished as a useful forest product (Porter, 1994). Also by the mid-sixteenth century Bowland was still thinly populated.

In the forest upland zone the fell tops had long been covered in peat with active bog development. Woodland remained on the slopes especially in valleys or cloughs but thinning towards the fell tops. Also in hollows or more level ground there were numerous small bogs. Farms were often developed along spring lines on the valley sides.

Although much of northern Lancashire was designated a Royal Forest after the Norman Conquest and managed for deer hunting, after the mid fourteenth century special deer parks were enclosed for that purpose (e.g. Leagram and Radholme) (Porter, 1980; Winchester, 1993), and whilst the Forest zone was used for hunting large areas were divided into vaccaries or cattle farms. This implies that much of the area was grassland but some form of heath is more likely before the bogs of the tops were reached. Out of the thirteenth and fourteenth century cattle ranching economy emerged a landscape of small pastorally based hamlets each with a small area of arable land with traces of the strips still visible today (e.g. at Slaidburn). Porter (1978) shows this as a mosaic of nucleated and dispersed settlements in eastern Bowland. In the north of the County many of the woods were used for charcoal burning (Mourholme Local History Society, 1998) and in some places this was almost on an industrial scale as at Crag Wood, Caton-with-Littledale (Hudson, 1997).

Changes 1500–1750

During the succeeding period to about 1750 the north Lancashire landscape changed dramatically, perhaps in response to an expanding population, which gradually became wealthier. Through a process of small scale enclosure (Porter, 1974, 1980) the landscape became devoid of trees except for the steeper river valleys fringing the Bowland Fells. The deer parks gradually fell into disrepair and were disemparked during the sixteenth century. Timber remained an important building material but by the seventeenth century was scarce (Porter, 1994). The needs of Lancaster had exhausted the supply from Quernmore to the southeast and similarly Preston had used the timber from Preston Moor and Fulwood (Hunt, 1992b). During the seventeenth and especially in the eighteenth century stone and brick replaced the wattle, daub and thatch of earlier times with many quarries being opened (Hudson, 2000).

Historically woodland was used for fuel and despite many restrictions on its use remained valuable until it became a scarce commodity. In upland areas it was always scarce. An alternative fuel was peat and this was plentiful in most parts of northern Lancashire. However it too could be exploited until it became scarce (Winchester, 2000; Chipping Local History Society, 2000). It is likely that all the peat of Chipping Moss was removed for fuel and even on the tops of the Bowland Fells the large number of tracks leading up to the tops probably demonstrate the need for access to the peat beds as well as a means of getting animals up to summer grazing. Today the distinction between areas, which were cleared of peat and original bog surfaces, can sometimes be seen clearly. On Dunsop Fell the cleared areas are now well vegetated but the bog vegetation is species poor as compared with the original bog surfaces. In particular some of the rarer species, e.g. *Andromeda polifolia*, have not colonised the cleared areas although peat removal may have ceased 200 years ago. Middleton, *et al.* (1995) described the importance of peat, largely for fuel, in lowland Lancashire. There is no doubt that peat cutting both in lowland and upland areas of the region over many centuries profoundly altered the landscape. Nevertheless, although peat digging continued, sometimes on a small but commercial scale into the mid twentieth century, it gradually declined, as coal became a more readily available fuel. Coal was probably used from Roman times but it was not until the early nineteenth century that it was used as the fuel of choice (Hudson, 1998).

Whilst the woodlands were cleared of trees and converted to a mixed farming regime with grazing animals (cattle predominating) the wetlands of the Fylde remained largely undrained until late in the eighteenth century. The Fylde became known as the granary of Lancashire with oats the main crop grown on the boulder clay areas. A picture of an increasing population emerges but for whatever reason (disease, poor climate or crop failure) there were setbacks and

reclaimed land reverted to waste and scrub from time to time. Nevertheless by the middle of the seventeenth century the cruck framed, wattle and daub houses with thatched roofs were being replaced with stone buildings – a process that accelerated with rising wealth in the eighteenth century (Watson and McClintock, 1979). By that time there were still many common and unenclosed lands. It is also clear that the practice of clearing the forest for a pastoral economy as well as for fuel and building purposes had, through a process of grazing and leaching over hundreds of years, created both wet and dry heaths. Thus Fulwood to the north of Preston became Fulwood Moor to adjoin Preston Moor to the south as dry heaths whilst to the east they became the wetter Ribbleton Moor.

Towards the end of the period detailed contemporary documents and diaries survive giving an accurate picture of the landscape, its people and economy. It is largely a subsistence economy and Hunt (1992b) illustrates how the land was farmed in the vicinity of Preston. In the town centre the Burgesses had plots in strips running down from their houses to the common fields beyond. Here the farming practice was of half-year lands with a rotation of crops and fallow but with winter grazing. Further away still lay the common, its use often referred to as grazing of the 'waste'. The crops grown in the common fields and other arable areas were predominantly oats with some barley and in more favoured areas wheat. Peas and beans and, in the eighteenth century potatoes, were also grown. Later and in the nineteenth century potatoes became common. However common fields only appear to have existed in the immediate vicinity of townships and much of the enclosure resulted in a patchwork of small fields attached to individual holdings. Many of these were less than 10 acres, which usually required some other form of livelihood, especially in the uplands. Larger farms were also formed; 40 acres was as much as one household could manage. Until the nineteenth century crops were sown broadcast, not drilled and cereals harvested with a sickle and not a scythe. Weeds were a problem and they were controlled by hand weeding in early summer and by a system of fallowing (Ford and Fuller-Maitland, 1931).

Various systems of rotation existed but all too often the land was cropped to exhaustion then, in the eighteenth century, marling (extraction and spreading of calcareous boulder clay on the fields, but leaving behind ponds), and the use of farmyard manure became more prevalent. The rotation often involved a fallow grassland phase of 6 years or longer period. Grass was rarely sown but the gleanings from a hay crop might be used as seed. Thus meadows and pastures were rarely permanent, i.e. in the sense that they had never been cultivated. Permanent grasslands only seem to have existed in inaccessible places and on especially thin soils. Even in the sixteenth century fields were cultivated at an altitude of 200m in Leagram Park and for the next 200–300 years cultivation of poor hill soils continued perhaps at even higher levels (Holt, 1795) where only the poorest of crops could have been harvested bearing in mind the climate was often cooler than it is today (Porter, 1978, 1994; Anon, 1971). Overall crops and grasslands were poor and weed infested.

1750 to the present day

By the end of the eighteenth century increasing wealth, an increasing population with a town based economy and various wars (American wars of independence, Napoleonic wars etc.) all argued for higher productivity and improved farming methods culminating in Holt's review (1795). It was also the Age of Enlightenment with exploration of distant lands and numerous inventions (see for example Uglow, 2002), which were to transform the nation's rural economy to one that was industrially and urban-based. It also allowed for leisure time. In the twenty-first century the landscape and its flora were to be transformed. Yet much of the original flora that migrated into the county following the retreat of the last ice age remained but it was augmented by an influx of new species reflecting the interests of a nation of gardeners.

Towards the end of the eighteenth century and into the nineteenth century many of the remaining common lands were enclosed (Tate, 1978; Whyte, 2003; Table 1.2) and drainage of the lowland bogs accelerated as new technologies became available. Many landowners sought to extend or improve their land by reclaiming land from the sea (e.g. salt marsh enclosures on the Ribble estuary (Berry, 1967; Shakeshaft, 2001; Holden, 2010), at Aldcliffe near Lancaster (Hewitson, 1900) etc.) whilst other attempts at reclamation involved reclaiming land from stony wastes, e.g. following enclosure of common land in 1778 at Yealand Conyers and Yealand Redmayne. Improved agricultural practices included drilling for sowing seeds, the use of clovers introduced from Holland, hence 'Dutch Cover', the seeding of grasslands, horses replacing oxen and a diversification of

crops. However oats continued as the main cereal crop and both cattle and horses remained the most important animals. Most farmers had a few pigs for personal use along with a few sheep. Whilst sheep were always present until recently they were not an important crop. Historically sheep farming was important from medieval times at least on the coastal salt marshes (Marshall, 1967; Ford and Fuller-Maitland, 1931) but in the fells, with a few exceptions, farms kept only a small flock of perhaps 10 animals that were largely left on their own. The flock of about 10 animals kept by Peter Walkden in 1733 (Chipping Local History Society, 2000) on his farm on the north side of Longridge Fell was typical. In general farms were mixed with arable predominating in the west and pastoral in the east.

Table 1.2   Common Land Enclosures

Place names	Year of enclosure	Possible habitats
Aighton, Bailey, Chaigley, Thornley and Ribchester	1812	Heath
Barnacre Moor	1772	Heath
Borwick Moor	1819	Heath
Carnforth marsh & wastes	1864	Salt marsh
Claughton Moor, nr Lancaster	1806	Heath/Mire
Dalton Crags	1815	Limestone pavement
Ellel Moor	1757	Heath
Forton Green, Forton Moss, Cook Green, Cross Hill	1786	
Fulwood & Cadley Moors	1817	Heath
Grindleton, West Bradford, Waddington, Bashall Eaves	1819	Heath/Mire
Halton Moor	1800	Heath
Howarth Moor, Wilkinson's Green, Claughton Moor, Alias High Moor, Claughton nr Garstang	1731	
Lancaster	c. 1795	Heath
Layton Hawes	1769	Sand dunes, Heath Fresh water

Place names	Year of enclosure	Possible habitats
Leck Fell, Cantsfield Green, Tunstall Green	1826	Heath/ Mire/ Grassland
Lytham Hawes (Pre Parliamentary enclosure)	1607	Heath/sand dunes
Nether Kellet Moor	1815	
Over Kellet Moor	1805	
Pilling Moss	1867	Mire
Quernmore Moor	1817	Heath
Rawcliffe Moss, Stalmine Moss	1833	Mire
Ribbleton Moor	1870	Heath
Scotforth & Bailrigg Moors	1809	Heath
Silverdale Common	1817	Limestone scrub and pavement?
Tatham Common, Bank Common, Barn Moor Common, Oak Bank Waites	1858	Heath/Mire
Thornton Marsh	1799	Marsh/Fen/ Mire?
Warton Crag, Lindeth Common, The Myers	1817	Limestone pavement and Crags
Whit Moor, Arkholme Moor, Gressingham Moor	1804	Heath/Mire
Whitmoor, Rushy Lee & Otter Gear, Caton	1818	
Whittington Moor, Newton Moor, Docker Moor, Whittington Common etc.	1817	Heath/Mire
Yealand Redmayne Common, Storrs Moss, Yealand Conyers Common, Waitham Moss, Hilderstone Moss etc.	1778	Limestone scrub/ Mire

The landscape was, however, devoid of woodlands except in the steep sided river valleys of the Bowland fringe. These remaining woodlands are today identified as ancient woodlands (Map 4.19). In addition there were also hedgerow trees in the early years of the eighteenth century. Even before that new hedges with a mixture of species were planted but by the end of the century they were mostly of quickthorn or hawthorn (*Crataegus monogyna*). But the century also saw the development of large estates and the first new plantings for amenity and sport. The copses found in the west of the county, e.g. Shelley Wood at Catterall (Winckley of Preston) and some of the higher-level conifer woods, e.g. above Marshaw, Over Wyresdale (Anon, 1821) date from the late eighteenth and early nineteenth centuries. Amenity planting to create landscaped parks also occurred from the eighteenth century and references (Peel, A., 1913) can be found to the species introduced, e.g. Scots Pine (*Pinus sylvestris*).

During the first 50 years of the nineteenth century agricultural improvements accelerated (Garnett, 1849) and more land was reclaimed from the mosses although old and poor land management systems persisted in many areas. Amongst the improvements were the use of tile drains and lime, e.g. taken from Thornley quarries for use around Broughton (Hewitson, 1900), guano from Peru and night soil from the towns and in rural villages, e.g. in Chipping up until the early years of the twentieth century (Fletcher, 2003/4) as fertilizers. Garnett (1849) also refers to large flocks of Black Face Sheep on the moors in contrast to Holt's (1795) earlier assertion that there were very few.

From the middle of the nineteenth century agriculture entered a long period of recession but increasing mechanisation, use of fertilizers and the development of cleaner seed marked continued progress (Salisbury, 1961). However from the mid nineteenth century a number of developments took place that give an increasingly accurate picture of change. In the 1840s tithe returns provide a guide to the area under different crops whilst the 1841 census provided details of the population (earlier census returns were less detailed). Together these show that the predominant crop remained oats and that some arable land remained in the upland fringe. Here as elsewhere there was a tendency for farm holdings to amalgamate. For example Saddle Side farm, Chipping comprised 260 acres, had eight tenants in 1574 and was divided amongst seven holdings in 1841 – an average of 37 acres each or close to the maximum size that an individual farm unit could manage. Ten years later seven dwellings were still occupied but the number of separate farm holdings had fallen to five. By 1971 there was just one farm (Anon, 1971).

Another development in the mid nineteenth

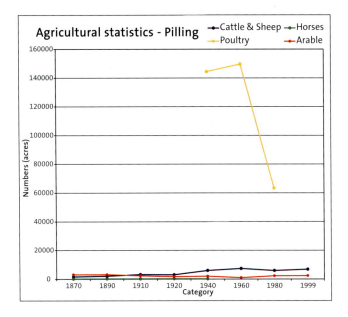

Agricultural statistics - Pilling

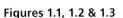

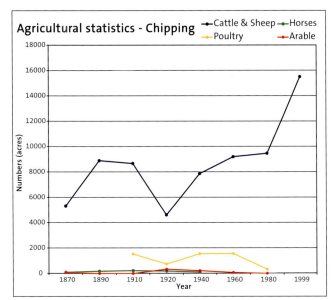

Agricultural statistics - Chipping

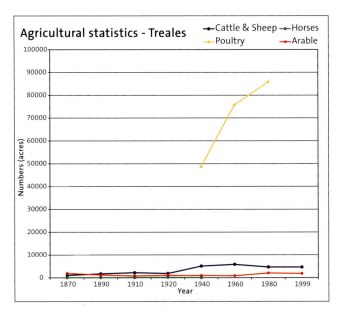

Agricultural statistics - Treales

Figures 1.1, 1.2 & 1.3

Three contrasting parishes in northern Lancashire were selected to demonstrate the differences between them and the changes in agriculture at each in the period 1870–1999. Earlier and later comparable statistics are not available.

century was the invention of the breach-loading gun in 1853 (Vesey-Fitzgerald, 1946). This was to have profound consequences for the management of the uplands. From about 1870 onwards they were managed primarily as sporting estates for grouse shoots (Simmons, 2003) or as water catchment grounds to supply the rapidly growing towns and cities or both. An ancillary function was as sheep walks but management included regular moor burning in spring. This form of management was reflected in the appearance of sheepfolds and shooting butts on Ordnance Survey maps.

From the 1870s the Ministry of Agriculture collected annual agricultural statistics based on civil parishes (Coppock, 1964). These continued until 1999 but thereafter the statistics were based on local authority administrative units and are not comparable with earlier returns. As examples of agricultural practice and the changes that took place in the period 1870–1999 three parishes were selected for analysis and summaries of their statistics are shown in Figures 1.1, 1.2 and 1.3 (Agricultural Statistics, No Date).

Chipping is an upland area with uncultivated hills and lower ground with pastoral farming. Pilling is a parish with extensive grazed salt marshes and lowland areas with both pasture and arable land with small amounts of un-reclaimed mossland. Treales is a lowland parish with boulder clay soils. All three parishes have small numbers of horses until 1940 with a peak in 1920. They were used on farms until mechanisation took over about 1950. They were also bred for use in towns and cities. Although not shown in the figures poultry were first kept in substantial numbers in lowland areas in the 1920s and 1930s reaching huge numbers between 1940 and 1960 although at Treales the peak was in 1980. Until the 1950s most poultry were kept in free-range conditions. At Chipping small numbers were kept throughout most of the period. Numbers of cattle and sheep vary but minor peaks occurred about 1910 before a steady rise took place from 1940 onwards. At Chipping both the rate of increase and the numbers increased greatly in 1999. In the lowland parishes arable land showed only relatively small variation during the whole period whilst at Chipping it was never important.

The figures show considerable differences in farming practice between the upland Chipping parish and the two lowland parishes. All three parishes show a response to demands for increased productivity, especially from 1940, but the most remarkable response was the huge increase in animal numbers at Chipping no doubt in response to subsidies based on numbers. Almost certainly the numbers achieved were unsustainable for the pasture available and damaging to the moors.

Despite problems in using the statistics (Best and Coppock, 1962) a number of conclusions can be reached for the period 1870–1930.

1. Farming practises vary enormously from parish to parish, making county compilations of little relevance to more local landscape and vegetation studies.
2. In the early years farming continued in much the same way as in the previous 50 years or so. Oats was the main cereal but all farms were mixed with a predominance of arable in the west and animal husbandry in the east.
3. Root crops, especially potatoes in parishes with soils reclaimed from peat were important and turnips introduced earlier in the seventeenth century were often grown for winter fodder.
4. In the Bowland Fells sheep were important as were cattle and to a lesser extent horses. Earlier in the nineteenth century many dairy cows were exported to the towns and cities to provide fresh milk and similarly horses were bred for use in the towns and cities.
5. Most farms had a few pigs.
6. In the western half of the county in the second half of the nineteenth century the stiff boulder clay soils, the light sandy soils near the coast and peaty soils derived from the reclaimed peat mosses were all cultivated.
7. Further east meadows and 'permanent' grasslands dominated the landscape but permanent meant grassland over 5 years old. In practice

there was little grassland that by the end of the nineteenth century had not been ploughed at some time (Coppock, 1964).

By 1900 a few unploughed grasslands remained, identified by characteristic mesotrophic grassland species, e.g. *Platanthera chlorantha*, etc. (Wheldon and Wilson, 1907) usually located on stony ground or in inaccessible places.

During the 100 years from 1850 to 1950 agricultural improvement was slow. Reclamation of the mosses, salt marshes and further reclamation of natural or semi-natural woodland fragments continued but perhaps at a slower pace. However in both World Wars, but especially between 1939 and 1945, land rarely if ever cultivated was ploughed in an effort to maximise home produced food, e.g. Carr House Green Common was converted to arable farmland from common grazing. Where not reclaimed for agriculture the mosses were also further cut over for peat leaving little or nothing of the original peat surface so that today none of the mosses survive in a natural condition.

Between the wars major changes occurred. Clean seed was introduced with the seed acts of the 1920s and almost all the boulder clay areas in the west were converted to grassland leaving arable farming to the reclaimed peat mosses. Where not built over by expanding towns or converted to golf courses, market gardens developed on the lighter coastal soils and occasionally elsewhere, e.g. in the Eaves Brook valley north of Preston and on Marton Moss near Blackpool. Often considerable areas of glasshouses were used in these enterprises. In the hilly areas of the east arable farming almost ceased. However the largest impact was the development of poultry farming. Egg production based on free-range husbandry remained an important aspect of Lancashire farming well into the 1960s and extended eastwards into the Bowland uplands. Poultry keeping also impinged on the mosses where peat cutting was mechanised to provide 'moss litter' for poultry houses. Overall the numbers of cattle, sheep and pigs (also free-range) increased greatly. A consequence of this change was that some of the few remaining grasslands that had escaped ploughing now succumbed to eutrophication through use as poultry (France, 1931) or pig runs. It was in this way that one of the finest limestone pastures at Trowbarrow, Silverdale was destroyed in the late 1960s. Horses also continued to be important and it was not until 1940 that tractors began to feature.

Indeed mechanisation was slow even though reapers were introduced from the late nineteenth century replacing scythes for cutting hay and harvesting cereals.

During the nineteenth century marling ceased and was replaced by the regular use of lime (leaving a legacy of abandoned lime kilns) and farmyard manure but from 1889 basic slag, rich in phosphates was used ubiquitously. It was produced in steel making and its effect was to promote the growth of *Trifolium repens*, which in turn increased nitrogen levels (Moore, 1966; Duffey, *et al.*, 1974). There can be no doubt that basic slag and other fertilizers hastened the decline of floriferous grasslands in Lancashire. In some areas, e.g. in market gardens, offal from slaughterhouses was used as manure.

The second half of the twentieth century saw dramatic changes to farming practices. Mechanisation, use of fertilizers, herbicides, pesticides and European Union (EU) subsidies based on production levels transformed farming. Drainage and land reclamation continued especially in upland areas even at the highest levels where attempts were made to drain the blanket bogs. The amalgamation of farms continued to form larger farming units, which with continued mechanisation, could be run with less labour. Arable cropping changed with a greater emphasis on autumn sown wheat and barley and whilst oil seed rape was not a popular crop, from the 1990s an increasing amount of maize was grown for silage. Oats became a minor crop. Rye grasses were grown in the grasslands like any other arable crop and with new cultivars and the use of fertilizers etc. up to four crops a year could be harvested for silage or haylage.

EU subsidies based on the number of animals increased their numbers in the county with sheep levels reaching almost certainly unsustainable levels, particularly in the uplands. Whilst it is difficult to translate the total numbers of sheep counted on census day in the annual parish statistics into figures for grazing intensity, some indication is possible by converting the figures to number of ewes/ha. In Whitendale in about 2000 there were approximately 1 or more ewes/ha (pers. comm.). For a farm at Chipping the figure was 2 ewes/ha in 1971 (Anon, 1971) whilst in a study in the northern Pennines where the altitude was up to 300m higher than in Bowland (Rawes and Welch, 1964) there was an average of 0.7 ewes/ha. It was pointed out that this masked considerable variation in the intensity of

grazing pressure for any locality or vegetation type. Using direct observational techniques it was found that on *Calluna-Eriophorum* vegetation there were only 0.1 sheep/ha but on *Agrostis-Festuca* grassland there were as many as 8 sheep/ha (Rawes and Welch, 1969). However these figures are for sheep so converting the figures to ewes they could be halved. Also grazing was limited to April to October. Extrapolating from the figures for Bowland using the annual parish statistics it seems that a rough average across the moorland areas was about 0.5 ewes/ha in 1870 rising to as many as 1.4 ewes/ha in the 1990s but in some places grazing intensity could have been much higher. At Chipping in 1971 for every ewe there was at least one lamb but the number of sheep grazing the fell varied with the time of year. No doubt similar patterns existed elsewhere in Bowland but on sporting estates at least there were periods when the moor was not grazed. Thus it is exceptionally difficult to know from available data what kind of grazing pressure existed on a particular moor. Yet if the number of sheep in 1870 equates to 0.5 ewes/ha and this was already high by historical standards, stocking rates to provide sustainable levels of mire and heath vegetation with some woodland in upland cloughs would possibly be in the region of 0.1 to 0.5 ewes/ha. The realisation in the post war period that productivity could be increased in moorland areas with increased drainage and fertilizer applications led, with appropriate subsidies, to more moorland heaths being converted to grassland and to drains (grips) being dug across mire surfaces in the hope that they too could be converted to grassland to improve sheep productivity.

Horses disappeared rapidly from the 1930s and poultry similarly from the 1970s. However arable farming returned to the boulder clay areas as well as on the reclaimed mosses whilst much animal husbandry was intensive. Interestingly there was little hedge removal. High productivity meant high and costly inputs. Overall farming was less diverse, tending towards monocultures leaving little room for the flora (and fauna) that had been associated with the farmed landscape for centuries. However towards the end of the twentieth century ideas of the countryside being a valuable amenity resource gained ground (Marren, 2002). Areas were set aside as nature reserves and in places were managed as much for amenity as for agriculture but diffuse pollution, especially nitrogen, continued to take its toll of many native species. Nevertheless by the beginning of the present century some areas such as the Silverdale – Warton area of the county where not built over were largely managed for amenity and elsewhere especially in the hills the first steps were being taken to reduce stocking levels. Also to the surprise of many the landscape, as elsewhere, had become much more wooded (Ziegler, 1999) not through the creation of large coniferous plantations, which were relatively small in Lancashire, but through a more ill-defined policy of simply letting tree saplings grow in hedges or through small scale deciduous plantings. Despite some of the deciduous plantations being over 200 years old none has achieved a diverse flora in anyway approaching that of ancient woodland. Atkinson, *et al.* (1999) reported that fewer than 21 species of flowering plant were found in plantation woodlands in the Mersey Basin whereas ancient woodlands in the Ribble valley often have over 120 species. Nevertheless some coniferous woods were planted. Amongst the larger plantations were ones in the Lune valley and on Longridge Fell but the largest was the planting of Gisburn Forest near Slaidburn in the 1930s (Mitchell, 2004). Furthermore in 2005 the grant schemes changed to provide farmers with payments for looking after their land in a more sympathetic way for wildlife. However it remains to be seen if these latest measures are too little too late to reverse the declining diversity of the native flora.

Towns

The industrial revolution during the nineteenth century heralded a period of urbanisation and rapid population growth. Most of the growing population was housed in the towns but in northern Lancashire this was largely confined to Preston and Lancaster. Nevertheless as on the coast with the developing seaside resorts, land was taken from the countryside and interesting semi-natural habitats were lost, e.g. Lancaster and Ribbleton Moors. The expansion of towns continues today but the development of towns required servicing. Transport links involving canals, railways, new and improved roads etc. whilst destroying old established habitats created new ones. At Tewitfield the building of the Lancaster Canal created an interesting small mire only to be destroyed by the building of the M6 motorway. To service the towns water was required in addition to food and this was provided by reservoirs built from the 1830s onwards. Similarly to build new towns, quarries, clay and gravel pits were formed but on their abandonment they often became reservoirs for wildlife.

Vegetation changes

Changes in farming practices and land use over the last two millennia have shaped the rural landscape in Lancashire as it is seen today. Four main phases of agricultural development and land use can be identified.

1. A general expansion of farming into the more or less natural wetland and woodland landscape with little or no mechanisation. This phase lasted from Neolithic times until the eighteenth century and whilst its impact on the landscape was huge it is unlikely that any vegetation type or species were lost by human intervention. On the other hand species were introduced as weeds or escaped from cultivation (especially from medicinal and herb plants grown in gardens (e.g. *Myrrhis, Aegopodium, Ribes* spp. (Allen and Hatfield, 2004; Mabey, 1996)).

2. From the eighteenth to mid nineteenth century agricultural development was still largely unmechanised but wars and the developing towns required more food, mostly home produced. Improved techniques for drainage, manuring and seed sowing (drilling) were introduced. The remaining forests were largely cleared, common lands were enclosed, most wetlands were drained and farming extended up into the hills to 150–230m above sea level. During this period land that could be ploughed was ploughed. Much 'permanent' grassland was lost although 'permanent' often referred to long leys. During this period marl pits and the Lancaster Canal replaced many of the former wetlands. Woodland cover also increased with the planting of copses and small plantations but they were, and continue to be, largely devoid of the diverse flora typical of natural woods.

3. From the mid nineteenth to mid twentieth centuries agriculture suffered a major recession but despite this, two world wars put pressure on farmers to produce more home-grown food in the second half of this period. Nevertheless changes occurred as mechanisation was gradually introduced (e.g. reapers replaced scythes), manuring and new fertilizers (basic slag) were introduced and the Clean Seed Acts ensured that only clean seed was used. These measures started the slow permanent

enrichment of agricultural soils and reduced the diversity of weeds. However new habitats started to be produced with the appearance of abandoned pits and quarries, spoil heaps and the construction of reservoirs. Only a few large coniferous woodlands were planted in northern Lancashire of which Gisburn Forest was the most important. Following the failure of the pumping engine Warton Moss was flooded to form Leighton Moss and the largest reed bed in north-western England developed.

4. The final fifty years of the twentieth century saw the most profound changes with the retreat of natural vegetation to discrete enclosures (nature reserves and similar) with only the toughest nitrophilous vegetation and species surviving in the countryside as a whole. This was caused by extensive mechanisation and the use of fertilizers, pesticides and herbicides to maximise productivity enabling large farms to be managed by a small labour force. The era of factory farming and big agribusiness had arrived. On the other hand new habitats were created with the development of the urban landscape and the creation of post-industrial habitats, e.g. gravel pits, some of which have been retained as nature reserves as at Brockholes near Preston. In the early twenty-first century further changes are taking place. With a change in the method of paying agricultural subsidies animal numbers are being reduced, especially in the uplands and in the Fylde the water table has been lowered drying out ditches following the installation of an improved pumping station at Lytham.

2. Habitats and plant communities

Introduction

Wheldon and Wilson (1907) described West Lancashire in terms of three divisions and eight districts based on broad landscape characteristics. Their eight districts are similar to the Natural Areas summarised by Hickling (2004). There are six Natural Areas partly or wholly in northern Lancashire:

Cumbria Fells and Dales
Forest of Bowland
Yorkshire Dales
Lancashire Plain and Valleys
Morecambe Bay
Liverpool Bay.

Cumbria Fells and Dales

Only part of this area is in northern Lancashire but includes the limestone areas of Silverdale – Warton and Dalton Crag as well as the upland areas north of the R. Lune where there are extensive upland pastures, some valley woodlands, conifer plantations and heaths. It covers districts 1 and 2 of Wheldon and Wilson's North Division.

Forest of Bowland

This covers much of Wheldon and Wilson's Eastern Division. It consists of rounded hills with extensive bogs in the fells, heather moorland (heath), wooded valleys and grasslands. Some conifer plantations are also present and there are reservoirs in some of the valleys.

Yorkshire Dales

Leck Fell in the northeast of the region is topographically part of the Craven area of Yorkshire. There are extensive bogs and heather moorland but the presence of upland limestone grassland, potholes and gorges provides a range of habitats not seen elsewhere. Deciduous woodland is found by the Leck Beck and downstream towards Leck. It coincides with District 1 of Wheldon and Wilson's Northern Division.

Lancashire Plain and Valleys

This covers the whole of Wheldon and Wilson's Western Division but extends up the Ribble valley to the south of Longridge Fell. In the west it comprises a mixture of arable and pastoral farming with a few remnant raised bogs. The pastoral farming is concentrated on the boulder clay ridges and towards the east where the numerous marl pits, lanes and old hedges give character to the landscape.

Morecambe and Liverpool Bays

Parts of these essentially similar areas fall within northern Lancashire. They are coastal areas with extensive salt marshes and other coastal habitats.

Natural Area descriptions provide a general ecological description but do not provide any detail of the habitats that might be found within them. However describing habitats is also difficult and precise meanings vary from author to author. In this account the vegetation of northern Lancashire is described in terms of wide habitat groups and the plant communities that are found within them.

Whilst the pioneering work of Sir Arthur Tansley (Tansley, 1911, 1939) and others wrote authoritative descriptions of British vegetation there was no objectively derived framework for the whole country until *British Plant Communities* was published (Rodwell, 1991–2000).

Elsewhere in Europe, particularly under the leadership of Braun-Blanquet (1928) and Tüxen (1937), an objective system based on the concept of plant communities was developed. This phytosociological method was adopted widely in Europe but not in Britain so that British vegetation could not be compared with that in Europe. The problem was rectified when the then Nature Conservancy Council commissioned a project to draw together existing data, undertake new surveys and publish the results according to standard phytosociological techniques. The contract was awarded to Lancaster University under the leadership of Dr John Rodwell with sub-contracts awarded to the Universities of Cambridge, Exeter and Manchester.

The phytosociological methods used to describe vegetation are described by Rodwell (1991–2000) but in summary depend upon the concept of dominance, constant and characteristic species. Furthermore to provide the data it was important that in the field plots (usually of 2 × 2m) of apparently homogeneous vegetation were identified. From the many thousands of plots analysed across the country it was possible to prepare descriptions of British plant communities – the National Vegetation Classification (NVC). Often it was clear that these were the same as communities described elsewhere although new ones were also described. The NVC provides a reference to the first description of a plant community with synonymy. Furthermore the name of a plant community reflects the species (often only one but sometimes up to three) that are most abundant or more strictly provide the greatest cover in the vegetation. Associated constant species further define the community. Sometimes whilst the general character of a community seems clear other species achieve prominence to give rise to sub-communities and very occasionally one of the dominant species in the name of the community is missing. To provide further clarity the NVC gives a unique code letter and number to every plant community.

In this section the vegetation of northern Lancashire is described in eight major habitat groups. The descriptions follow the NVC system but depart from it in providing separate sections for arable farmland and urban & industrial sites whilst omitting a section on open habitats. Most of the NVC open habitats describe communities of arable farmland, some urban and industrial sites and a few wetland sites. Table 2.1 provides a summary of the major habitats and NVC plant communities whilst Table 4.7 (pp. 561–566) provides a concordance of Broad Habitats, UK BAP priority habitats and NVC communities. (Note the taxonomy and nomenclature of NVC plant communities is not revised in line with Stace (2010)).

Table 2.1 Summary of major North Lancashire habitat groups and NVC Communities

HABITAT GROUP	NVC HABITAT & COMMUNITY (Volume name and Numbers refer to Rodwell, 1991–2000)
1. Woodland and scrub. Trees and shrubs dominate the communities. Also included is a note about conifer plantations not covered by NVC.	*Woodlands and scrub.* Community numbers prefixed W (vol. 1).
2. Mires. Mires, bogs, wet heaths, fens, flushes, springs and soakaways where the ground is kept permanently or periodically waterlogged by high atmospheric humidity, a high ground water-table or lateral water flow.	*Mires and heaths* (vol.2). Mire community numbers prefixed M.
3. Heaths. Lowland and upland communities where sub-shrubs, e.g. *Calluna vulgaris*, play the most important structural role.	*Mires and heaths* (vol. 2). Heath community numbers prefixed H.
4. Grasslands. Mesotrophic: vegetation dominated by grasses on neutral soils Calcicolous: vegetation dominated by grasses on calcareous soils Calcifugous: vegetation dominated by grasses on acid soils but also includes montane communities poorly represented in N. Lancashire.	*Grasslands and montane communities* (vol. 3). Mesotrophic grassland communities prefixed MG Calcicolous grassland communities prefixed CG Calcifugous grasslands and montane communities prefixed U.
5. Arable weeds. Communities found as weeds in arable farmland but also in any area where cultivated plants in open communities are grown.	*Maritime communities and vegetation of open habitats* (vol. 5). Community descriptions prefixed OV.
6. Wetlands. Aquatic communities including vegetation of standing and moving waters. Vegetation dominated by emergent, often tall species frequently characteristic of open water transitions with permanently or seasonally submerged substrates. It includes fens that are sometimes loosely described as 'marshes' – a term best reserved informally for vegetation of any wet ground.	*Aquatic communities, swamps and tall-herb fens* (vol. 4). Aquatic communities prefixed A Swamps and tall-herb fens prefixed S Open communities of habitats with fluctuating water levels are prefixed OV in *Maritime communities and vegetation of open habitats* (vol. 5).

HABITAT GROUP	NVC HABITAT & COMMUNITY (Volume name and Numbers refer to Rodwell, 1991–2000)
7. Coastal habitats. Shingle, strandline and sand dune – habitats often open and mobile. Salt marsh vegetation, which is subjected to tidal inundation. Maritime cliff communities – vegetation of coastal rocky and clay cliffs.	*Maritime communities and vegetation of open habitats* (vol. 5). Shingle, strandline and sand dune communities prefixed SD Salt marsh communities prefixed SM Rocky maritime cliff communities prefixed MC but communities on clay cliffs are likely to be described as grasslands or occasionally woodland.
8. Urban and post-industrial sites. These areas embrace a wide range of habitats and communities that have developed in urban and post-industrial areas.	There is no NVC volume devoted to the urban and post-industrial environment. Many of the communities that develop are aquatic, swamps and tall-herb fens; grasslands and occasionally woodland. However the communities found in urban and post-industrial sites were poorly surveyed but those that were included were mostly of open habitats (*Maritime communities and vegetation of open habitats*, vol. 5).

1. Woodland and scrub

Introduction

Since the majority of northern Lancashire woodlands were cleared before 1700 what remained of the natural and semi-natural woodland was confined to the steep sided valleys draining the Bowland Fells, including the Lune, Wyre, Hodder and Ribble valleys and on the limestone in the Silverdale area. None were left in the low-lying land west of the M6 where, in any case, much of the land was formerly covered in bogs and fens. Nevertheless even here the former

extent of woodland can be traced today through the occurrence of relic woodland species in hedgerows on boulder clay soils, e.g. *Anemone nemorosa, Dryopteris affinis, Primula vulgaris, Viola riviniana* etc.

In addition to planted deciduous woodlands established from the end of the eighteenth century coniferous woodlands were also planted, especially in the twentieth century. The most notable of these is Gisburn Forest planted in the 1920s. Whilst little new broad-leaved woodland was planted more broad-leaved and mixed woodland, much of it ancient, was cleared, amounting to 17% of Lancashire's 1945 stock (Morries, 1986). In 1988 the then Nature Conservancy Council compiled an inventory of Lancashire's ancient woodland (Backmeroff, *et al.*, 1988).

In this account only the vegetation and flora of natural or semi-natural woodland is described. Much of it is ancient but a number of communities that have colonized other habitats are described and some of these, particularly the scrub communities, may be short lived.

Classifying woodlands has proved problematical and a number of schemes have been devised (e.g. Peterken, 1981). Although there is a consensus on the major groupings there is considerable variation in detail. Only the NVC provides detailed descriptions of the plant communities represented in them. In northern Lancashire the types of woodland represented and their composition is as complex as anywhere yet familiarity with them suggests that essentially ancient woods can be grouped into those of Silverdale, the Lune valley, the Wyre valley and the Ribble valley (Morries, 1986). Similarly the Regional Biodiversity Steering Group for North West England (1999) provided a further regional approach to describing woodlands. However, other than location, defining what makes these woodlands different from each other is much more difficult.

Rodwell (1991a) reviews the factors governing the composition of woodlands and their distribution. The relationships of six mixed deciduous oak-birch woodlands based on soils and climate is particularly instructive. The distribution maps accompanying his analysis show that northern Lancashire is on the boundary of woodlands that are either predominantly north-western or south-eastern in their distribution within Great Britain.

The underlying rocks where these are near the surface and drift deposits (primarily boulder clay) determine soil characteristics. Thus in the Silverdale and Warton areas, by the upper Leck Beck and Ease Gill and in the Hodder valley outcropping limestone gives rise to highly calcareous soils, but even here there are pockets of drift where leaching has produced acid soils. Underlying most of the Bowland Fells the acid millstone grit outcrops in places and gives rise to acid soils but in the steep sided valleys there are bands of shale and these produce neutral to base-rich substrates. However overlying much of the millstone grit there is a deep layer of drift or boulder clay. This produces, after leaching, neutral to acid soils but it is often inherently calcareous and these more calcareous soils are found on drumlins south of Lancaster and particularly near Preston where the R. Ribble erodes the clay forming steep, unstable slopes of wet calcareous clay. However within any one wood soils vary over short distances from wet to dry and from acid to calcareous as well as varying in altitude from the top to bottom of the wooded valley. Thus within one extended wood many different community types may be present.

Climatically northern Lancashire straddles the rough divide of the 26°C mean annual maximum isotherm (Conolly and Dahl, 1970) separating the cooler, cloudier and shorter summers of the north and west from the warmer, sunnier and longer summers of the south and east of Britain. To the northwest of this isotherm conditions are more oceanic but adversely affect the sexual reproduction of more southern species. These climatic factors influence the species composition of woodlands, especially those on calcareous substrates, and therefore help to define the plant communities of different woodlands.

In addition to these natural variables management of woodlands has altered the species composition. Clear and selective felling together with coppice with standards management over many centuries, at least in the north of the area, has had a major impact. Unfortunately detailed records for most woods are not available. Similarly details of miscellaneous plantings of non-native trees are not available although estate and other records may contain some details. *Acer pseudoplatanus* is classed as a neophyte (Preston, et al., 2004) although it may have been planted near Liverpool as early as the late 15th century (Innes, 1992). By the twentieth century it was common everywhere and often formed an important constituent of many woodlands.

Finally the presence or absence of *Quercus robur* and *Q. petraea* is often regarded as an important determinant of woodland types (e.g. Tansley, 1939; Rackham, 2003) yet taxonomically they pose immense identification problems (Rich and Jermy, 1998). Although *Q. robur* and *Q. petraea* are mapped separately it is best to regard identification on which these maps are based as referring to *Q. petraea*-like or *Q. robur*-like and probably represent forms of the hybrid *Q. × rosacea*. Certainly there is no evidence today that *Q. petraea* is a more upland species and *Q. robur* is a more lowland plant. However many oaks on the limestone around Morecambe Bay seem to be *Q. petraea* or near to this species.

Also taxonomically difficult is the range of intermediates between *Betula pubescens* and *B. pendula*. Hybrids occur but seem to be rare (Rich and Jermy, 1998) and most plants are referable to *B. pubescens*. This is the native species of Lancashire woodlands but the picture is confused through numerous and often recent plantings of *B. pendula*. However on the limestone around Morecambe Bay *B. pendula* may be a native constituent of the oak–birch woodlands, although this is by no means certain. Also in the upper reaches of the clough woodlands, e.g. Black Clough, Marshaw Fell, Over Wyresdale, *Betula pubescens* seems to be ssp. *tortuosa* or close to it.

This confused taxonomic picture, described well for Cumbria (Halliday, 1997) adds even more complexity to an already complex situation.

Given the problems, and in the absence of detailed survey, only a summary of woodlands in northern Lancashire can be given. However the range of soils and geographical position gives rise to all six mixed

Plate 2.1 The Lune valley looking north over the river to the mixed deciduous Lawsons and Burton woods (Lancashire Wildlife Trust nature reserves) clothing southeast facing hill slopes.

Plate 2.2 Bluebell (*Hyacinthoides non-scripta*) carpeting the floor of Springs Wood, Leck. The mixed deciduous woodland is coppiced.

Plate 2.3 Ramsons (*Allium ursinum*) growing on calcareous clay in a Silverdale woodland, a mixed deciduous oak-birch woodland.

deciduous oak–birch woodlands occurring in the area, and often many community types can be found in the same woodland complex. This gives richness and diversity that can only be found on the boundary between north-western and south-eastern communities, i.e. in Lancashire, Yorkshire and the Welsh borders. The valley woodlands of the Bowland Fells can be particularly complex. Essentially these woods tend to be dry and acidic at the top of the valley side and wet and basic towards the stream at the bottom. Woodlands in the Lune valley tend to contain species with a more northerly distribution, e.g. *Prunus padus*, *Circaea × intermedia*, whilst in the Ribble valley species with a more southerly distribution are found, e.g. *Lamiastrum galeobdolon* ssp. *montanum*. The oceanic character of woodlands is exemplified by the presence of other species, e.g. *Polystichum setiferum*, *Ilex aquifolium*. Higher up the valleys upland woodlands are poorly represented and usually peter out with *Sorbus aucuparia*, *Betula pubescens* and *Quercus* spp. However the greatest concentration of more southerly species is found on the limestone around Morecambe Bay.

Whilst these phytosociological features are useful in characterising woodlands a visitor to the region will be impressed by the broad sweep of woods on the north bank of the R. Ribble seen to advantage travelling north on the M6 motorway. In spring these can be especially impressive with the bold patches of white flowering Wild Cherry (*Prunus avium*). Similarly the woods on the bank of the R. Lune at Caton, immortalised by Turner's romanticized painting following his tour of 1816, are equally impressive. Many of Lancashire's woodlands are carpeted in early May with a blue mist of Bluebell (*Hyacinthoides non-scripta*) and on the wetter soils the blue is replaced by a white carpet of Ramsons (*Allium ursinum*) filling the air with an onion-like fragrance. In addition there are often small patches of red provided by Red Campion (*Silene dioica*) and in the wet oxbows in the valley floor the large leaves and extended 'female' inflorescences of Butterbur (*Petasites hybridus*) are a feature. In some woods, especially in the Ribble valley, *Carex pendula* can provide a fine spectacle. Other species that can make a woodland colourful include *Crepis paludosa*, *Stellaria nemorum* and *Cardamine amara* whilst *Chrysosplenium alternifolium* is also typical of many woods. These species give the author a 'feel' for Lancashire woodlands but they do not necessarily feature in NVC phytosociological descriptions that follow. However the warmth of early spring, before the trees come into leaf, allows the colourful woodland floor vegetation to provide a spectacle rarely seen on a world scale. The light shading and light litter fall of the oceanic species found in western Britain further encourage this herbaceous layer.

Woods on calcareous soils

Fraxinus-Acer-Mercurialis (W8) woodlands occur on calcareous soils and reach their north-western limit on the limestone around Morecambe Bay. Key species are *Acer campestre*, *Fraxinus excelsior* in the tree layer with *Corylus avellana* amongst the shrubs. *Mercurialis*

Plate 2.4   Developing woodland on limestone pavement, Dalton Crags.

perennis and *Rubus* spp. are important components, as is the presence of more southerly-distributed species, e.g. *Euonymus europaeus*, *Rhamnus catharticus*, *Tilia cordata* and *Lamiastrum galeobdolon* ssp. *montanum* (only in the Ribble valley). However this community has at least five sub-communities and these tend to reflect geographical variation. In addition to the limestone pavement communities in the Silverdale, Yealand and Warton areas and on Dalton Crags the community is found in the Lune, Ribble and Hodder valleys. However a key component of the community, *Acer campestre*, is absent apart from the Ribble valley where it is often no more than a rare component. Frequently it is replaced by *Ulmus glabra* that, in the Redscar – Tunbrook Woods in the Ribble valley near Preston, was especially abundant before Dutch Elm disease took its toll of mature trees. It is still abundant but at this stage of its regeneration it is more of an understorey rather than a canopy tree. The absence of *Acer campestre* from the woodlands in the Silverdale area is at first puzzling yet it remains frequent in old hedges. It is likely that most of the woodlands are secondary ones and for some reason in the regenerating process *Acer campestre* was a poor competitor.

Throughout the distribution of this community oak is frequent with *Quercus robur* particularly important towards the southeast of England. In Lancashire the taxonomic complexity of oak suggests that most trees are *Q.* × *rosacea* but on the limestone in the Silverdale, Yealand and Warton areas *Q. petraea* or *Q. petraea*-like plants are more usual. Amongst the sub-communities *Anemone nemorosa* is common with an abundance of *Hyacinthoides non-scripta*. The *Allium ursinum* sub-community, which carpets many woodland floors, is also common. The *Geranium robertianum* sub-community, where *Fraxinus excelsior*, *Acer pseudoplatanus* and *Ulmus glabra* are prominent is also found in northern Lancashire. However, although not recorded by Rodwell (1991a) the south-eastern *Deschampsia cespitosa* sub-community may be common except that in northern Lancashire *D. cespitosa* is represented by *D. cespitosa* ssp. *parviflora*. The north-western *Teucrium scorodonia* sub-community has not been definitely recorded in northern Lancashire being largely confined to the southern Pennines. In many of the north-western sub-communities *Acer pseudoplatanus* is common, and although a neophyte, lends character to these woodlands. In many of the woodlands an almost continuous cover of *Mercurialis perennis* dominates the ground floor vegetation.

The *Fraxinus-Acer-Mercurialis* woodland (W8) is home to a number of rare Lancashire species. These include *Lathraea squamaria*, *Neottia nidus-avis*, *Daphne mezereum*, *Daphne laureola*, *Ophrys insectifera* (in clearings and on disturbed ground), *Carex digitata* (in the Silverdale, Yealand and Warton areas only), *Paris quadrifolia*, *Rubus saxatilis*, *Gagea lutea*, and in the Ribble woods, *Lamiastrum galeobdolon* ssp. *montanum*.

In the north of the area many of these woodlands overlie limestone pavement and in dense shade few vascular plants are found. Often the shade is made darker by *Taxus baccata*. In these situations a mat of bryophytes may cover the rocks. However, where the grykes are few or in the presence of grazing, the

Plate 2.5   This photograph was taken at the top of an Ash woodland in Ease Gill, Leck. The calcareous soils are confined to the steep slopes of the valley whilst on the more acid soils of the valley floor fine plants of Golden-scaled Male fern (*Dryopteris affinis* ssp. *affinis*) are found.

trees and shrubs give way to bare limestone and open communities in the grykes with only the odd stunted tree and shrub. These include *Juniperus communis*, *Taxus baccata*, *Fraxinus excelsior*, *Salix cinerea* ssp. *oleifolia*, *Rhamnus catharticus*, *Sorbus lancastriensis*, *Sorbus rupicola* and *Sorbus aria*, which is possibly self-sown from old introductions. Very occasionally, as on the Silverdale cliffs and in Eaves Wood, *Sorbus torminalis* occurs. Within the grykes a number of nationally rare or scarce plants can be found including *Dryopteris submontana*, *Gymnocarpium robertianum*, *Polygonatum odoratum*, *Galium boreale* (only at Gait Barrows), *Melica nutans* and *Thalictrum minus* (Dalton Crags) whilst *Convallaria majus* can be a conspicuous feature of many grykes. Interestingly this list of species is a mixture of plants with both northerly and more southern distributions in Europe coming together in Lancashire in a predominantly south-eastern plant community.

The north-westerly counterpart to W8 *Fraxinus-Acer-Mercurialis* woodland is W9 *Fraxinus excelsior-Sorbus aucuparia-Mercurialis perennis* woodland. *Mercurialis* is still a major component of the herb layer along with *Geum urbanum*, *Circaea lutetiana*, *Sanicula europaea*, *Viola reichenbachiana*, *Arum maculatum* and *Brachypodium sylvaticum*. Similarly *Fraxinus excelsior* and *Corylus avellana* are key features of the canopy but *Acer campestre* is absent. On the other hand *Betula pubescens* and *Sorbus aucuparia* are common and *Alnus glutinosa* may occur in wetter places. Also present are *Ulmus glabra*, *Quercus* sp. and *Acer pseudoplatanus*.

Ferns are also prominent with an abundance of *Athyrium filix-femina* together with both *Dryopteris filix-mas* and *D. affinis*. Amongst the rare species are *Dryopteris submontana* and *Gymnocarpium robertianum*. Other characteristic ferns on more rocky substrates include *Asplenium trichomanes* ssp. *quadrivalens*, *A. ruta-muraria*, *A. adiantum-nigrum*, *A. viride*, *Cystopteris fragilis* and *Polystichum aculeatum*.

The herb layer is often grassy with, in addition to *Brachypodium sylvaticum*, *Deschampsia cespitosa* ssp. *parviflora*, *Poa trivialis*, occasional stands of *Bromopsis ramosa*, *Festuca altissima*, *Schedonorus giganteus*, *Melica uniflora*, *Milium effusum* etc. In wetter patches *Crepis paludosa* may be present or even abundant and rarer species may include *Rubus saxatilis*, *Actaea spicata*, *Trollius europaeus* and *Cirsium heterophyllum*.

Rodwell (1991a) shows this community as occurring in the Lune valley and around Morecambe Bay, but in these situations it will grade into its southern counterpart, W8 *Fraxinus-Acer-Mercurialis* woodland.

However W9 is particularly characteristic of damp ravines in the central Pennines and high level limestone pavements. In this context probably some of the best examples to be found in Lancashire are in the wooded limestone gorge of upper Leck Beck and Ease Gill, Artle Dale and other more calcareous woodlands of the Bowland Fells including Park Wood in Gisburn Forest in the east of the area.

In describing W8 woodlands, the occurrence of species with a more northerly distribution was mentioned. Conversely in W9 species with a more southerly distribution may be present in small quantity, e.g. *Tilia cordata*, *Rhamnus catharticus* and *Carpinus betulus*, which may be native in some locations, e.g. in some of the Lune valley woodlands.

Woods on neutral soils

Woodlands on neutral, brown earth soils may be found in the same woods as those of more calcareous soils but on higher slopes away from the river at the bottom of the valley. The north-western *Quercus-Betula-Oxalis* woodland (W11) is common throughout the area. It is generally species poor with in Lancashire *Betula pubescens*, *Quercus × rosacea*, *Oxalis acetosella*, *Deschampsia flexuosa*, *Galium saxatile*, *Holcus mollis*, *Pteridium aquilinum*, *Anthoxanthum odoratum*, *Corylus avellana* and *Viola riviniana* frequent. Other frequent species often becoming sufficiently abundant to merit sub-community status include *Dryopteris dilatata*, *Blechnum spicant*, *Anemone nemorosa*, *Stellaria holostea* and *Hypericum pulchrum*.

Plate 2.6 A steep sided woodland on the left of the photograph with a landslip in the distance taken in the Brock valley.

The south-eastern counterpart to W11 is *Quercus-Pteridium-Rubus* woodland (W10) usually found in lowland areas. Here oak, *Quercus × rosacea*, is the dominant tree and the woodland appears to be restricted in northern Lancashire to the western edge of the Bowland Fells. It usually has an abundance of *Dryopteris dilatata*, *Rubus* spp. *Lonicera periclymenum* and *Pteridium aquilinum*. Several sub-communities have been identified but in northern Lancashire the most frequent is the south-western *Dryopteris dilatata* sub-community. However other sub-communities are present. The most noteworthy is the nationally rare and north-western *Blechnum spicant* sub-community, which occurs in Littledale (Steward, *et al.*, 1993). It is probably unique to the British Isles (Averis, *et. al.*, 2004). Other sub-communities that have been identified in northern Lancashire include *Anemone nemorosa*, *Holcus lanatus*, often in disturbed woodlands, *Acer pseudoplatanus-Oxalis acetosella* and *Hedera helix* (Rodwell, 1991a).

Neither W11 nor W10 seem to be associated with any particularly noteworthy species in northern Lancashire except perhaps *Phegopteris connectilis* in W10.

Woods on acid soils

Woodlands on acidic podzolic soils are divided into two groups. On the one hand there are warm, dry lowland *Quercus-Betula-Deschampsia* woodlands (W16) characteristic of south-eastern Britain, and on the other there is *Quercus-Betula-Dicranium* woodland (W17) characteristic of the cool north-western sub-montane zone. The former is only rarely encountered in northern Lancashire but may occur on level ground above the steep sided Brock valley. It is characterised by the presence of *Quercus × rosacea* and *Betula pubescens* in the canopy layer with a ground layer of *Deschampsia flexuosa* and less abundantly *Pteridium aquilinum*. *Rubus* spp. and *Lonicera periclymenum* may be present; also *Vaccinium myrtillus* and *Calluna vulgaris*. The presence of *Erica cinerea* in a few places on the western sides of the Bowland Fells, e.g. near Nicky Nook, may suggest remnants of this type of woodland.

At Holdron Castle in the Langden Brook valley oak woodland, not marked on older Ordnance Survey maps, appears to have developed during the twentieth century. No doubt a few relic trees of an ancient woodland survived and from these the present woodland developed. Most of the woodland is between 240 and 300m altitude on steep, dry

Plate 2.7 The oak woodland that has developed in the last 100 years or so close to the 300m contour in the Langden valley.

south facing grit boulder scree but it extends into nearby small cloughs. In a visit in 2005 the trees were low growing and appeared quite young. The trees seemed to be *Quercus × rosacea*, especially at lower levels, and *Quercus petraea*. No other tree species were found. The herb layer was limited to *Vaccinium myrtillus*, often growing to a height of 1m but dominating many areas. Associated species included *Deschampsia flexuosa*, *Pteridium aquilinum* (dominant on nearby slopes in U20, *Pteridium aquilinum-Galium saxatile* community), *Blechnum spicant*, *Juncus effusus*, *Calluna vulgaris*, *Dryopteris dilatata* and *Oxalis acetosella*. Although surrounding hillsides were grazed by sheep the steep slopes and large boulders limited grazing in the woodland where oak regeneration was occurring.

This is an example of *Quercus* spp.-*Betula* spp.-*Deschampsia flexuosa* woodland (W16), *Vaccinium myrtillus-Dryopteris dilatata* sub-community characteristic of the warm, dry south-eastern lowland zone. It is therefore unusual to find this community at a relatively high altitude in one of the wettest parts of Lancashire where *Quercus petraea-Betula pubescens-Dicranum majus* woodland (W17), characteristic of the cool and wet, north-western, sub-montane zone, might be expected. However the ground is well-drained and dry receiving maximum insolation from the south facing aspect. Rodwell (1991a) suggests that this type of community may be typical of secondary woodland and that in the Pennine fringes atmospheric pollution suppressed the development of bryophytes, which are a major feature of W17. It is also surprising that *Betula pubescens* is absent, but it

appears that during the twentieth century there was a decrease in the numbers of sheep grazing the area, perhaps because it was an important water catchment area. Whatever the reason for its development this is an interesting secondary woodland.

At higher altitudes in clough woodlands a few remnants of *Quercus-Betula-Dicranum* woodland (W17) persist. The best of these, approaching 300m altitude, is found in Black Clough on Marshaw Fell, Over Wyresdale. *Betula pubescens* ssp. *tortuosa* and *Quercus × rosacea* dominate the tree layer with some *Ilex aquifolium* and *Crataegus monogyna* as understorey shrubs. *Sorbus aucuparia* is also present and this is often the only surviving tree at the highest level of some cloughs. *Populus tremula* may be present in this community but only in Foxdale does it achieve any prominence and here on dry grit cliffs it is the dominant tree. Also here is the rare northern Lancashire species *Asplenium trichomanes* ssp. *trichomanes*. In the ground layer, often on rocky steep sided slopes, *Deschampsia flexuosa* and *Pteridium aquilinum* may be found but in Black Clough above the wooded valley *Pteridium aquilinum* is dominant while higher up still the moorland heath is dominated by *Calluna vulgaris*. This Bracken dominated community, *Pteridium aquilinum-Galium saxatile* community (U20) is probably derived from woodland through grazing pressure but it provides the habitat in its only remaining Lancashire station for *Trientalis europaea*. Characteristic of the rocky slopes in these woodlands are *Vaccinium myrtillus* and *Calluna vulgaris*.

Plate 2.8 Many of the higher-level deciduous woodlands in the Bowland valleys are on acid soils. At the top of oak woodland in Rotten Clough, Littledale, Juniper (*Juniperus communis*) survives in one of its few remaining Bowland localities.

Also often present are *Luzula pilosa, Luzula sylvatica, Oxalis acetosella, Lonicera periclymenum, Galium saxatile, Potentilla erecta, Teucrium scorodonia, Digitalis purpurea, Solidago virgaurea, Blechnum spicant, Corylus avellana, Viola riviniana* and *Oreopteris limbosperma*. *Quercus petraea-Betula pubescens-Oxalis acetosella* woodland is an oceanic and northern community near its southern climatic limit in Lancashire (Steward, *et al.*, 1993).

In Lancashire the clough woodlands of the Bowland Fells pass imperceptibly from W11 *Quercus-Betula-Oxalis* woodland into W17 *Quercus-Betula-Dicranum*

Plate 2.9 Although above the present day tree line the cliffs and block screes of the south facing Hell and Thorn Crags, Over Wyresdale support the remains of an oceanic woodland flora. Where sheep are unable to graze seedlings of Holly (*Ilex aquifolium*), Downy Birch (*Betula pubescens*) and Rowan (*Sorbus aucuparia*) may occur. In the deep recesses of the scree, filmy ferns (*Hymenophyllum* spp. and Hay-scented Buckler-fern (*Dryopteris aemula*) survive.

woodland as altitude is gained and rainfall increases. Between them they share some interesting species. On the drier soils, especially to the north of Clougha, *Ceratocapnos claviculata* and *Melampyrum pratense* are particularly frequent although according to Rodwell (1991a) *Ceratocapnos* is more characteristic of W10 and W16. *Phegopteris connectilis* is found in many clough woods and on occasion ascends higher than the present tree line where it is found by moorland streams, e.g. Tarnbrook Wyre, Over Wyresdale. On humid and shady rocks *Gymnocarpium dryopteris* is also found. However Lancashire clough woodlands remain a retreating feature of the landscape, probably through grazing pressure from sheep. Until comparatively recently (*c.* eighteenth century) *Juniperus communis* was a common Bowland plant. By 1900 it was already rare and by the 1960s only small numbers remained by high level, moorland streams. Today a few bushes remain in woods and hillsides on the north side of the Bowland Fells but no regeneration is taking place. Its disappearance is probably due to sheep grazing pressure but it is interesting to speculate that at one time some of the hillsides in the upper valleys could have been covered in *Juniperus communis* ssp. *communis-Oxalis acetosella* woodland (W19). This is a northern and boreal community still found in the northern Pennines and upland areas, mostly in eastern Scotland. None of the more interesting species associated with this community have survived in Bowland.

Apart from most of these acidic woodlands showing northern affinities a striking feature is the presence of relic oceanic or sub-oceanic species sometimes found above the present tree line. These include *Trichomanes speciosum* (gametophyte only), *Hymenophyllum* spp., *Dryopteris aemula* and *Dryopteris oreades*. Some of these are sensitive to extreme cold and are found in consistently humid but possibly largely frost free situations.

Other woodlands

In addition to this matrix of six mixed deciduous woodlands where climate and base status are inextricably mixed a number of other special situation woodlands are found.

Yew woods

Throughout Lancashire *Taxus baccata* is found as a hedgerow tree or in association with churches and more rarely in mixed deciduous woodland on base-rich soils. In all of these situations it is either planted

Plate 2.10 In the absence of grazing yew woods develop on limestone pavements. Under the dense shade of the evergreen trees mosses may be the only plants growing on the limestone as here in a Silverdale wood.

Plate 2.11 Inside the mixed deciduous Tunbrook Wood (a Lancashire Wildlife Trust nature reserve), near Preston. The wet calcareous clay on the steep sides of the valley frequently slump into the stream uprooting young trees. In the wettest parts of the wood near the stream the trees are usually Alder (*Alnus glutinosa*). Also near the stream seepage areas often support Opposite-leaved Golden-saxifrage (*Chrysosplenium oppositifolium*).

(sometimes centuries ago) or self-sown. However on the limestone around Morecambe Bay *Taxus baccata* forms a prominent feature in *Fraxinus-Acer-Mercurialis* woodland (W8). Generally it does not become the dominant woodland tree as it does on the chalk downs of southern England. Nevertheless in places, e.g. part of Cringlebarrow and near Burton Well, Silverdale, it forms a yew wood and with few associated species represents a northern outlier of W13 *Taxus baccata* woodland.

Wet woodlands

Along some of the valley bottoms of mixed deciduous woodland around the Bowland Fells the ground is very wet and swampy. There is often slumping of

ground from above but generally conditions are mesotrophic. In these situations, as in Tunbrook Wood near Preston, the stream sides are lined by *Alnus glutinosa-Fraxinus excelsior-Lysimachia nemorum* woodland (W7) and this often merges into the drier *Fraxinus-Sorbus-Mercurialis* woodland (W9). *Alnus glutinosa-Fraxinus excelsior-Lysimachia nemorum* woodland is characterised by the presence of these species and in the canopy layer *Betula pubescens* and *Acer pseudoplatanus* may be present whilst in the shrub layer *Corylus avellana*, *Crataegus monogyna* and *Salix cinerea* ssp. *oleifolia* may also occur. In addition to *Lysimachia nemorum*, the following herbs can be found: *Ranunculus repens*, *Filipendula ulmaria*, *Poa trivialis*, *Holcus mollis*, *Athyrium filix-femina* and *Carex remota*. Where water seeps

Plate 2.12 Spring lines arise at the base of steep sided valley woodlands giving rise to swampy areas and rivulets draining into the main stream or river in the valley. Here, in the Brock valley, a swampy area is colonised by Marsh-marigold (*Caltha palustris*).

across the surface extensive mats of *Chrysosplenium oppositifolium* may occur especially in the *Urtica dioica* sub-community. More rarely *Chrysosplenium alternifolium* is found whilst *Caltha palustris*, *Cardamine amara* and *Allium ursinum* can provide patches of colour in wet woodlands, especially in the Ribble and western valleys draining the Bowland Fells. In slightly drier areas, and perhaps where the wet woodland merges with the drier W9 woods *Deschampsia cespitosa* ssp. *parviflora* can achieve prominence.

Much more rarely W7 *Alnus glutinosa-Fraxinus excelsior-Lysimachia nemorum* woodland can be found on its own on gently sloping ground, as near Galgate but in these situations it seems to be secondary woodland.

A further *Alnus glutinosa* dominated woodland is W6 *Alnus glutinosa-Urtica dioica* woodland. Rodwell (1991a) admits to it being a rather ill defined community that brings together a variety of canopies dominated by *Alnus glutinosa*, *Salix* spp. and *Betula pubescens* with a species poor herb community below, usually with *Urtica dioica* prominent. Steward, *et al.*, (1993) show it occurring in northern Lancashire, but it is a rather nondescript community that has not been recorded often. Yet *Urtica dioica* dominates patches in wet valley woodlands throughout the area, e.g. in parts of the Brock valley.

Another much rarer *Alnus glutinosa* woodland in northern Lancashire is *Alnus glutinosa-Carex paniculata* woodland (W5). There are a few possible examples of this around Morecambe Bay and perhaps the best is the alder woodland surrounding Little Hawes Water. Typically the *Alnus glutinosa-Carex paniculata* woodland is found on wet or waterlogged organic soils, base-rich and moderately eutrophic, in mires dependant on rainfall or ground water. It is associated with fen peats in open water transitions where there is a strong influence of calcareous ground water. These are the conditions surrounding Little Hawes Water today, but in 1902 (Petty, 1902) contemporary botanists describe the pool as being surrounded by a bog dominated by *Myrica gale*. Whether the current woodland was always present and the more acid conditions suggested by the presence of *Myrica* surrounded it or whether the alder wood replaced *Myrica* is not clear. Nevertheless Rodwell (1991a) suggests that either alder woodland in these transitional situations eventually gives way to a *Sphagnum* dominated mire or that *Sphagnum* dominated communities might be a natural climax of swamp-carr in small inland basins in the British Isles. Given the history of Little Hawes Water this latter seems a likely situation. However today the alder is intermixed and in places it is replaced by *Salix cinerea* ssp. *oleifolia* whilst the ground flora is characterised by *Carex paniculata*, *Carex elata*, *Galium palustre* and *Rubus* spp. Other *Carex* spp. include *C. pseudocyperus* and *C. rostrata*, which forms a *C. rostrata* mire in places. Similarly *C. nigra* dominates some areas.

Salix pentandra-Carex rostrata woodland (W3) is not known from northern Lancashire although both species occur. However in Little Bowland, one of the small valleys on the south side of the Bowland Fells, contains a grove of *Salix pentandra*. There are few associated species here but in the vicinity are found many of the associated species of this community including *Salix cinerea* ssp. *oleifolia*, *Angelica sylvestris*, *Cardamine pratensis*, *Caltha palustris*, *Filipendula ulmaria* and *Valeriana dioica* but *Carex rostrata* is absent. A similar

Plate 2.13 In a few hill cloughs where drainage is impeded mixed deciduous woodland is replaced by Bay Willow (*Salix pentandra*) rather than by Alder (*Alnus glutinosa*) as might be expected. This view is taken near Chipping.

grove of *S. pentandra* occurs in Fielding Clough, Bowland Forest Low.

The fens to the south of Hawes Water and at Leighton Moss have developed during the last 100 years or so. It is possible that the mire at Hawes Water was never fully reclaimed and in any case the lake has always been surrounded by fen and scrubby woodland. This is now invading the species rich and largely *Phragmites* dominated fen to the south. At Leighton Moss, formerly Warton Moss, however, the raised bog was completely reclaimed for arable farming and it was only after the failure of the pump in 1917 (Peter, 1994) that maintained the drainage system that the area became flooded. Today the mire is a mosaic of a species poor *Phragmites* swamp (S4) and open water with scrub invasion occurring in some places. A similar situation also occurs around parts of Marton Mere, Blackpool. It is possible that these scrub communities are referable to W2 *Salix cinerea-Betula pubescens-Phragmites australis* woodland. This community is found mainly in East Anglia and in the low lying areas of Shropshire and Cheshire. The fen woodland at Hawes Water in particular seems to have affinities with East Anglia through the presence of *Salix cinerea* ssp. *cinerea* as well as *S. cinerea* ssp. *oleifolia* and many intermediates. Also present are *Rhamnus catharticus* and *Frangula alnus*.

Finally in this review of wet woodlands fragments of W1 *Salix cinerea-Galium palustre* woodland are found throughout northern Lancashire. It is characteristically found fringing wide, wet roadside verges where associated shrubs may include *Crataegus monogyna*, *Salix purpurea*, *Corylus avellana* and saplings of *Alnus glutinosa*, *Quercus × rosacea* and *Betula pubescens*. The field layer is generally species poor but may include *Mentha aquatica*, *Juncus effusus*, *Angelica sylvestris*, *Ranunculus repens*, *Epilobium palustre*, *Filipendula ulmaria*, *Cirsium palustre* and *Rumex sanguineus*.

Moss woodlands

When raised bogs become drier through drainage etc. the characteristic wet mire plants die out leaving *Molinia caerulea* to become dominant. In due course the mire is colonised by trees, principally *Betula pubescens*. In Lancashire many old mosses are now covered by *Betula pubescens-Molinia caerulea* woodland (W4). It is an acidic, species poor woodland seen well on the Winmarleigh, Cockerham and Heysham Mosses and elsewhere on old mosslands in the western half of northern Lancashire. Occasionally *Alnus glutinosa* and *Quercus × rosacea* may occur, usually where the peat is thin. However the striking feature of these woodlands apart from *Betula pubescens* is the ground cover of *Molinia caerulea*. Often there are few other species but *Dryopteris dilatata* and more occasionally *D. carthusiana* with which it hybridises and *Rubus* spp. may be present (*Dryopteris dilatata-Rubus fruticosus* sub-community). Two species are particularly associated with these woodlands. A few plants of *Osmunda regalis* survive in this community on the edges of Cockerham and Winmarleigh Mosses where *Rhododendron groenlandicum* also occurs, but the status of the latter species is unclear. On wetter surfaces *Sphagnum* spp. may be prominent to form the *Sphagnum* spp. sub-community. However *Betula pubescens-Molinia caerulea* woodland may occur in a completely different situation. Here the *Juncus effusus* sub-community is often found in association with acid oak-birch woodlands. This is a rare vegetation type nationally but is found in parts of Littledale.

Scrub

A number of scrub communities are best described under woodlands. Most of these are rarely home to more interesting species but rather reflect neglect or abandonment of former habitats. A major exception to this is the development of scrub and woodland communities on coastal clay cliffs. Here erosion causes cliffs to collapse and the bare clay surfaces are colonised first by open herb communities followed by forms of grassland. If further erosion does not take place the grasslands become colonised by scrub and woodland. These are amongst the most natural of all plant communities having arisen naturally and remaining unmanaged.

Ulex europaeus-Rubus fruticosus scrub (W23) is perhaps one of the more interesting communities. It is widespread, often where drier grasslands have been neglected or on the edges of woodland. It is particularly fine on the M6 motorway embankment at Lancaster where initially *Ulex gallii* was also abundant. This latter species is more characteristic of oceanic heaths but occasionally it can form a scrub community in its own right. This has occurred on the river gravels of the River Dunsop where it is the dominant shrub over a considerable distance near Dunsop Bridge. On the 6 inch to 1 mile Ordnance Survey map 'furze' is often marked and in places it remains today, e.g. on parts of the Whittington Estate.

Another scrub community, *Prunus spinosa-Rubus fruticosus* scrub (W22) is found throughout northern Lancashire on neutral to base-rich soils but is especially prevalent in the Silverdale and Warton areas and on coastal clay cliffs. It is also found on the wide verges of some lanes in the Bowland Fells.

Crataegus monogyna-Hedera helix scrub (W21) is often found around woodland margins and on coastal clay banks whilst *Rubus fruticosus-Holcus lanatus* underscrub (W24) is found in lowland areas especially in association with waste ground. W25 *Pteridium aquilinum-Rubus fruticosus* underscrub is similarly associated with waste ground but it is more particularly associated with woodlands, which it replaced or from which it may have spread. It is found less frequently on heaths. It is characteristic of deeper and generally free draining neutral to acidic soils in lowland areas. In northern Lancashire a particularly fine example covers Arm Hill, Barnaby's Sands, Preesall-with-Hackensall. Here the community forms an impenetrable scrub with few associated species except *Dryopteris dilatata*.

Roadside verges and hedges

In lowland areas the strip of land between a field and the adjacent road usually comprises a hedge and verge dominated by shrubs and grasses. In addition there is very often a ditch between the hedge and verge.

Together these linear habitats are characteristic of much of the countryside. Some of the verges and hedgerows have a diverse and rich flora whilst others are species poor. In general terms the older hedges and adjacent verges are richer than those planted more recently. Thus the hedges and roadside verges in former mossland areas in the west of the region and areas north of the R. Lune that were planted following eighteenth and nineteenth century enclosures are species poor. On the other hand the hedges and verges surrounding the Bowland Fells are much richer. These are essentially woodland edge habitats and in some cases may have originated from woodland. Rackham (1999) discusses these habitats in his *The history of the countryside* whilst Greenwood (2003) shows how their flora in northern Lancashire has changed in recent years. Plates 2.14–2.16 illustrate three Bowland roadside verges.

Nevertheless not all roadside verges support woodland edge vegetation. In constructing the M6 motorway minor roads were often carried over the motorway on bridges and to do this embankments were built on their approaches. These were usually sown with grass species or a mix of grasses and herbs. However near Carnforth natural colonisation also occurred producing a herb-rich calcareous grassland. (Plate 2.17).

Coniferous plantations

Native pinewoods do not occur in northern Lancashire but coniferous plantations dominate the landscape in a few places, e.g. Gisburn Forest. These are composed of several species but mostly *Picea abies* and *Picea sitchensis*. The trees were planted close together and the dense shade that this provides ensures that there is little ground flora. However if a little light penetrates to the woodland floor one of the first species to appear is *Dryopteris dilatata*. Plantations were usually developed on acidic upland soils, and where a little more light penetrates the canopy, as in firebreaks or on the edge of the plantation a few other species occur. These include *Agrostis capillaris, Agrostis stolonifera, Blechnum spicant, Deschampsia flexuosa* and *Molinia caerulea*. Unusually *Lycopodium clavatum*, rare in northern Lancashire, was found in the shade of a plantation on Longridge Fell and in similar situations in Gisburn Forest. The vegetation of coniferous plantations was not considered by the NVC but Hill, *et al.* (2004) recognise it as part of Broad Habitat 2 Coniferous woodland.

Plate 2.14   A feature of many Bowland roadsides in May is the profusion of white flowered Apiaceae. On this roadside near Slaidburn the verge is dominated by Sweet Cicely (*Myrrhis odorata*).

Plate 2.15   Another roadside verge dominated by white flowered Apiaceae. This time by Cow Parsley (*Anthriscus sylvestris*) on a roadside near Whitewell.

Plate 2.16   A herb-rich verge with ditch and ancient boundary hedge taken in 1988. In the following twenty years nutrient enrichment caused significant loss of species diversity.

Plate 2.17 A herb-rich south facing embankment of a minor road as it crosses the M6 motorway near Carnforth. Oxeye Daisy (*Leucanthemum vulgare*) and Common Spotted-orchid (*Dactylorhiza fuchsii*) are conspicuous but Bee Orchid (*Ophrys apifera*) was also plentiful. The photograph was taken in 2007.

Plate 2.18 The planted coniferous Gisburn Forest has little of botanical interest amongst the trees. However the mixed deciduous Park Wood, limestone exposures, flushes and the sides of tracks through the forest support a rich flora. Many of the tracks are surfaced with limestone chips and this has attracted a particularly rich flora with spectacular displays of Common Spotted-orchid (*Dactylorhiza fuchsii*).

2. Mires

Introduction

Northern Lancashire has a rich assemblage of mire habitats. These include the raised bogs, usually called mosses in lowland areas and the blanket bogs of the summit plateaux of the fells in the east and north of the region. In between these areas there is a range of bogs where, as elsewhere, the vegetation has formed peat. However in addition to these habitats mires include wet heaths, some fens, flushes, springs and soakways or anywhere where the ground is kept permanently or periodically waterlogged by high atmospheric humidity, a high ground water table or lateral water flow. Thus mire vegetation includes communities not only growing on peat but also on mineral soils, and whilst most are acidic and nutrient poor, species diversity increases where base status and/or nutrient levels are enhanced. They then merge into communities considered under wetlands.

Rodwell (1991b) and Averis, *et al.* (2004) provide comprehensive descriptions of mire communities and detailed analysis of how the different communities are related to each other as well as indicating how management and environmental factors affect distribution and occurrence. Thus, as with most communities, intermediates between the main types occur frequently.

Bog and wet heath communities

These are communities of damp to waterlogged, acidic and nutrient poor (oligotrophic) peats. They occur most commonly in the north and west of Britain where rainfall and humidity are such that peat building *Sphagnum* spp. have built up peat deposits that blanket the landscape (ombrogenous deposits). They occur on level ground as well as on gentle slopes. Peat deposits may also be initiated in areas with impeded drainage giving rise to raised bogs or mosses in the lowlands and in valleys (valley bogs). Northern Lancashire has a range of these bogs but those characteristic of the most oceanic conditions are absent (at least at the present time), and many have been severely modified or eroded, sometimes exposing extensive areas of bare peat or even stony surfaces. It is thought that these modifications were caused by a variety of factors, some natural and others man-induced, but often the relationship between cause and effect is not known. The factors include changes in climate, grazing regime, drainage, peat

Plate 2.19　Blanket bog (M19 *Calluna vulgaris-Eriophorum vaginatum* blanket mire) on the summit of Gragareth, Leck.

cutting, intentional and accidental moor burning and air pollution. For a general discussion of the problems see Tallis (1997a, b, 1999) and for Bowland Mackay and Tallis (1994, 1996).

On deep peat, such as is found on the fell tops, probably the most nearly natural plant community is M19 *Calluna vulgaris-Eriophorum vaginatum* blanket mire. In wetter places *Eriophorum angustifolium* bog pool community (M3) is present, e.g. at Dunsop Head and in some of the bog pools or small tarns, e.g. on Fairsnape and Lythe Fells, a *Carex rostrata-Sphagnum recurvum* mire (M4) is found. Both these bog pool communities have few associated species. However in the blanket bog itself the tussocks of *Calluna vulgaris* and *Eriophorum vaginatum* interspersed with shoots of *Vaccinium myrtillus* and *Eriophorum angustifolium* are characteristic of the better-managed moors. Here the peat is often at least 2m deep. Also present amongst the carpet of *Sphagnum* spp. between the tussocks can be found an abundance of *Vaccinium oxycoccus*, often with *Erica tetralix*. *Empetrum nigrum* is also often present and occasionally *Andromeda polifolia* and *Rubus chamaemorus* are found on old undisturbed bog surfaces. *Rubus chamaemorus* often flowers freely but rarely produces any fruit.

However Bowland has suffered from erosion and sometimes this is sufficiently severe to leave islands of dried out bog surrounded by bare peat or bedrock devoid of vegetation. The erosion on Fairsnape Fell was illustrated by Wheldon and Wilson (1907) and can be seen today on Ward's Stone. It is not clear what causes the erosion but old turbary activity or may be deep burning fires are implicated. Radley (1965) in his work in the southern Pennines drew attention to the importance of fires but suggested that after five years or so re-colonization of the bare surfaces could take place. However in a detailed study on the North York Moors, Maltby, *et al.* (1990) suggested that re-colonisation was much slower and incomplete, and after eight years 30% was still largely unvegetated. Mackay and Tallis (1996) working on Fairsnape Fell also believed that a catastrophic burn, probably in 1921, was one of the causal agents of erosion. On Tarnbrook Fell it is believed that a deep peat fire in 1947 caused considerable damage leaving almost a desert of blowing peat. This area and surrounding fells is home to a large gull colony that started to colonize the area in 1949 – shortly after the fire. The species nesting there are Herring Gull (*Larus argentatus*), Lesser Black-backed Gull (*Larus fuscus graellsii*) and a few Great Black-backed Gulls (*Larus marinus*) (Pyefinch and Golborn, 2001). The development of the gull colony is possibly one of the consequences of the fire and with many thousand pairs of breeding birds they continue to influence the habitat and prevent significant re-colonization. In addition the colony has expanded on to adjacent areas causing damage to the vegetated surfaces. However, historical evidence shows that erosion on the Bowland Fells has been taking place for at least 100 years, probably for centuries. Over a

Plate 2.20 Bog pool on the top of Burnslack Fell, possibly formed from old peat workings.

Plate 2.21 Common Cottongrass (*Eriophorum angustifolium*) in a bog pool (M3 *Eriophorum angustifolium* bog pool community) on Dunsop Fell, Slaidburn.

Plate 2.22 Eroding blanket bog on the top of Ward's Stone, Over Wyresdale.

Plate 2.23 Hare's-tail Cottongrass (*Eriophorum vaginatum*) forming a M20 *Eriophorum vaginatum* blanket and raised mire community on Staple Oak Fell, Bowland Forest High.

period of several hundred years large areas of peat on the fell tops were probably removed for fuel and this may have left islands of peat, which wind would erode. It is also possible that fires may have initiated erosion over a long timescale but during the last 100 years erosion is more certainly associated with deep burning moorland fires, e.g. following the dry summers of 1921 and 1947.

Derived from *Calluna vulgaris-Eriophorum vaginatum* blanket bog, probably through increased grazing pressure from sheep and perhaps atmospheric pollution in more southerly parts of Bowland, is M20 *Eriophorum vaginatum* blanket and raised mire. In its most typical form, characteristic of the southern Pennines, there are few associated species and the waving silky white heads of cottongrass are an attractive sight in early summer. In northern Lancashire a good example is found on Waddington Fell. Not only is this heavily grazed but, like the southern Pennines, it received considerable smoke pollution from the former cotton towns to the south in the nineteenth and twentieth centuries.

The effects of management on blanket bog vegetation can be seen on the summit plateaux of the fells marking the watershed between the Brennand (R. Hodder) and the Wyre valleys, which was also the old boundary between Lancashire and Yorkshire. Today there is a fence that marks the boundary between two different ownerships and it is probable that for

centuries a different management regime occurred on either side of the fence. On the Lancashire side the vegetation is characteristic of M19 *Calluna vulgaris-Eriophorum vaginatum* blanket mire but on the former Yorkshire side *Calluna vulgaris* has almost disappeared. This leaves behind a community dominated by *Eriophorum vaginatum* and *Vaccinium myrtillus*, which falls within the description of M20 *Eriophorum vaginatum* blanket and raised mire. Unlike the community on Waddington Fell this one is relatively species rich with patches of *Empetrum nigrum* and in the wetter areas *Eriophorum angustifolium*. The grasses *Agrostis canina*, *Deschampsia flexuosa* and *Nardus stricta* are present. *Vaccinium oxycoccus* is abundant and perhaps surprisingly *Andromeda polifolia* and *Drosera rotundifolia* are more frequent here than in M19 on the other side of the fence.

In lowland areas raised bogs covered much of the landscape. Their distribution, archaeology and palaeoecology are described by Middleton, *et al.* (1995) (see Map 1.1) and the significance of remaining fragments is discussed by Middleton (1995). A much dried out fragment survives at Fenton's Cottage, Out Rawcliffe and it is the only one with a complete stratigraphy. All the other surviving bogs suffer to some extent from the effects of grazing, drainage, turf cutting and burning. Despite these influences fragments of M18 *Erica tetralix-Sphagnum papillosum* raised and blanket mire survive at Cockerham and

Plate 2.24 Heysham Moss (a Lancashire Wildlife Trust nature reserve) with remnants of M18 *Erica tetralix-Sphagnum papillosum* raised and blanket mire.

Plate 2.25 Winmarleigh Moss with remnants of M18 *Erica tetralix-Sphagnum papillosum* raised and blanket mire.

Winmarleigh Mosses and at Heysham Moss. Amongst the species found are *Andromeda polifolia, Calluna vulgaris, Drosera rotundifolia, Erica tetralix, Eriophorum angustifolium, Molinia caerulea, Myrica gale, Narthecium ossifragum, Rhynchospora alba* and *Vaccinium oxycoccus.* Formerly there was an abundance of *Carex limosa* and *Drosera anglica* but both probably succumbed to peat cutting and drying out of the bog surface around 1900. These bogs deteriorate into *Molinia caerulea* dominated grasslands (M25 *Molinia caerulea-Potentilla erecta* mire) and later *Betula pubescens-Molinia caerulea* woodlands (W4). In the latter at Cockerham Moss *Rhododendron groenlandicum* became established by natural spread sometime between the 1920s and 1960.

Molinia caerulea-Potentilla erecta mire also occurs in Bowland at lower levels usually below the summit plateaux blanket bogs. In these situations it often forms large tussocks with few associated species although between the tussocks *Sphagnum* spp. are often found. This community is indicative of the cool and wet northwest of Britain. Examples are on Champion and Marl Hill Moors. (See calcifugous grasslands and Plate 2.45)

Between the lowland raised bogs and the summit plateaux there were formerly a range of ombrogenous bogs occupying level or gentle slopes below the steep slopes of the fells and above the farmed land of the valley sides. These bogs have been the targets for reclamation for two hundred years or more. Good examples are on Tarnbrook Fell immediately above the hamlet and on Catshaw and Fellside Fells, Over Wyresdale. However the bog on the side of Peacock Hill was reclaimed in the last 30 years whilst similar bogs in Bowland-with-Leagram were reclaimed during the last 50 years.

Trying to assign the remaining bogs to an NVC community is not easy because they have changed over the years. It is believed that they were M18 *Erica tetralix-Sphagnum papillosum* raised and blanket mire and an apparently not too badly modified community survives on the lowest slopes of Catshaw Fell, but it lacks most of the rarer species typical of this community. Another example survives on the lower slopes of Tarnbrook Fell but here Wheldon and Wilson (1901a, 1907) were able to record two of the rarer species: *Myrica gale* and *Rhynchospora alba.* Similarly another of the rarer species, *Andromeda polifolia,* was seen at Dinckling Green Hey before it was drained in the late 1960s. Nearby at Ginney Hey and Stanley *Molinia caerulea* and *Trichophorum germanicum* or *Molinia caerulea* and *Eriophorum vaginatum* are co-dominant. Both are developing into M25 *Molinia caerulea-Potentilla erecta* mires. It is likely that both are derived from M18 *Erica tetralix-Sphagnum papillosum* raised and blanket mire and in 2005 *Andromeda polifolia* was found at Ginney Hey. However the abundance of *Trichophorum germanicum* suggests that perhaps the oceanic M17 *Trichophorum germanicum-Eriophorum vaginatum* blanket mire might have occurred. Yeo (1997) suggests that this might have been commoner than it is today in Wales and that many *Molinia caerulea* dominated grasslands on peat were developed from this community.

Although raised bogs may have developed, especially in the lowlands, from sites with impeded drainage and former fen communities their later development depended upon ombrogenous conditions with high levels of rainfall and humidity. Other mire communities depend upon continued impeded drainage either in hollows, basins or in valleys with water flowing slowly through the system.

Basin mires are rare in northern Lancashire and only two are known to survive. They are White Moss SSSI, Gisburn Forest and a bog at Whittington. Outfield Moss, another former bog at Whittington, was also a basin mire described both by Wheldon and Wilson (1907) and in the old SSSI description (it was later descheduled). However in the 1960s and 1970s the surrounding fields were improved and the fertilizers drained into the bog causing eutrophication. Then, in the 1970s, the bog was blown up to form a duck pond. Nevertheless the former description suggests that the plant community involved was M9 *Carex rostrata-Calliergonella cuspidata/Calliergon giganteum* mire, recently found in another basin mire at Whittington. This surviving mire is surrounded by unimproved grassland, M25 *Molinia caerulea-Potentilla erecta* mire and gorse scrub (W23 *Ulex europaeus-Rubus fruticosus* scrub). As a consequence it retains much of its interest although there is a drainage outlet, and with the fields and drainage outlets downstream of the bog improved in the late 1960s some lowering of the bog surface may have occurred. It is also too dangerous to be grazed and it is therefore fenced off from the surrounding farmland. It is characterised by a grey-green sward of *Carex rostrata* and *Eriophorum angustifolium* interspersed with *Galium palustre, Menyanthes trifoliata, Comarum palustre,* patches of *Narthecium ossifragum,* and in pools, *Potamogeton polygonifolius.* There are drier hummocks with *Calluna vulgaris, Deschampsia flexuosa, Eriophorum vaginatum, Festuca ovina* and *Vaccinium myrtillus.* Throughout *Drosera rotundifolia, Erica tetralix, Molinia caerulea* and *Vaccinium oxycoccus* are frequent. In places the plant assemblage is further enriched with *Angelica sylvestris, Caltha palustris, Carex nigra, Dactylorhiza fuchsii, Silene flos-cuculi, Mentha aquatica, Myosotis secunda* and *Valerianella dioica* etc. Occasional shrubs of *Salix cinerea* ssp. *oleifolia* and *Betula pubescens* are found but overall the bog is very wet with deep pools and the infant

River Keer meandering through it. It is also home to a number of rare northern Lancashire species including *Carex diandra, Salix repens* ssp. *repens* and *Scutellaria minor.* Livermore and Livermore (1987) claim to have found *Carex lasiocarpa* here and there is no reason to believe that it is not still present. At Outfield Moss *Utricularia minor* (Wheldon and Wilson, 1925) was recorded growing with the moss *Hamatocaulis vernicosus* but both are now believed extinct (Wigginton, 1995). It is possible that with further study *Carex lasiocarpa* and the key bryophyte species may be found at the surviving mire. Also growing at Outfield Moss was *Calliergon giganteum* and Wigginton (1995) suggests that his 1978 record for this was from the same locality. However by that time Outfield Moss had been destroyed and whilst it is possible he found it there it seems more likely that he visited the 'recently discovered' site at Whittington. Nevertheless it is probable that the species assemblage at the 'new site' belongs to the *Carex diandra-Calliergon giganteum* sub-community.

Another mire of this type is at White Moss on the Yorkshire border in Gisburn Forest. According to the SSSI description the Moss is somewhat truncated and was partly used for peat extraction. However unlike the 'newly discovered' mire at Whittington *Myrica gale* is present but *Carex diandra* and *Scutellaria minor* were not noted. At the time of the site's last revision in 1991 it was thought to be the best example of its type in Lancashire and it is possible that further searches for the rarer species of this habitat could be rewarding although on a recent visit it appeared to be suffering from nutrient enrichment.

Sometimes at the higher levels of Bowland rivers drainage is impeded and oligotrophic mires form by their side or near their source. In upper Whitendale a *Carex rostrata – Sphagnum recurvum* mire (M4) has formed by the side of the river with few associated species. These include *Agrostis canina, Carex nigra, Equisetum fluviatile, Potamogeton polygonifolius* where there is some water movement and *Potentilla erecta.* This community is surrounded by M23 *Juncus effusus/acutiflorus – Galium palustre* rush-pasture with *Juncus acutiflorus* dominating the vegetation on the wetter inside and adjacent to the M4 community.

Another high-level *Carex rostrata* community believed to be M4 may have occurred in upper Roeburndale at the head of the R. Roeburn. Here however the most frequent species was *Carex canescens* with *Carex rostrata, Carex nigra, Eriophorum angustifolium, Juncus effusus* and *Menyanthes trifoliata.* However by 2010 it is believed that it was this mire where drains had been cut across it drying it out and leaving a species poor *Carex rostrata* mire.

Valley mires are a feature of many parts of Bowland and merge into a variety of flushes and soakways. At one extreme are acidic, nutrient poor flushes dominated by *Sphagnum* spp. A particularly fine example is at Arbour in the Calder valley. Here there are few associated species but they include *Drosera rotundifolia, Erica tetralix, Eriophorum angustifolium, Narthecium ossifragum* and *Vaccinium oxycoccus* and, as the edges are reached, *Calluna vulgaris* and *Molinia caerulea* appear. This probably belongs to M21 *Narthecium ossifragum-Sphagnum papillosum* valley mire. It is thinly distributed in Bowland but a *Narthecium ossifragum* rich series of valley mires occurs on Docker Moor where they alternate with ridges of M25 *Molinia caerulea-Potentilla erecta* mire. It also occurs over an extensive area above Burnslack, Chipping.

Springs, flushes and soakways

Draining the Bowland Fells are many flushes where spring water soaks down the hillside to streams below. The nature of the vegetation in these flushes depends upon whether or not the spring water is enriched with bases and the ground over which it flows is stony or peaty. Most are acidic, peaty flushes belonging to one of the sub-communities of M6 *Carex echinata-Sphagnum recurvum/auriculatum* mire. The *Carex echinata* sub-community is particularly widespread with *Carex nigra* and *Carex panicea* also usually

Plate 2.26 Valley bog (M21 *Narthecium ossifragum-Sphagnum papillosum* valley mire) on Docker Moor.

present along with *Carex demissa*. A *Sphagnum* moss carpet is extensive but amongst other species that may be found are *Agrostis canina, Drosera rotundifolia, Erica tetralix, Eriophorum angustifolium, Juncus bulbosus, Molinia caerulea, Narthecium ossifragum, Potentilla erecta* and *Viola palustris*.

The *Carex nigra-Nardus stricta* sub-community was not identified but may well occur. On the other hand the *Juncus effusus* sub-community is often found instead of the *Carex echinata* sub-community. Averis, *et al.* (2004) show a sketch of an upland valley where the *Carex echinata-Sphagnum recurvum/auriculatum* mire might be found. In addition to flushes it is also found in wet level ground on the valley floor and along the edges of streams and pools and here the *Juncus effusus* sub-community is especially common. This is often a very impoverished sub-community with few associated species yet in the Whitendale valley one of the sites for *Wahlenbergia hederacea* is in this sub-community. In many places *Juncus acutiflorus* replaces *Juncus effusus* but both sub-communities may occur close by each other with *J. acutiflorus* occupying the wetter ground. These sub-communities are often found on river terraces by upland streams.

With more basic spring water a series of flushes with more interesting or rare species occur. They belong to M10 *Carex dioica-Pinguicula vulgaris* mire, which is itself variable. In northern Lancashire the more acidic, less base-rich flushes belong to the *Carex viridula* ssp. *oedocarpa-Juncus bulbosus* sub-community, which is widespread in Bowland and also occurs rarely in Leck. In addition to *Carex dioica, Carex demissa* and *Juncus bulbosus, Carex flacca, Carex hostiana, Carex nigra, Carex panicea, Carex pulicaris, Carex lepidocarpa* and *Eleocharis quinquiflora* may be found. Near Newton-in-Bowland a small patch of the *Eleocharis quinquiflora* variant of this sub-community is found where this species achieves dominance at a springhead. It is also home to a small patch of *Epipactis palustris*. Another variant is *Carex hostiana-Ctenidium molluscum* with an increased abundance of *Carex hostiana, Carex panicea* and *Carex pulicaris*. *Drosera rotundifolia, Erica tetralix* and *Narthecium ossifragum* may also occur in this sub-community but conspicuous by its absence in northern Lancashire is *Pinguicula vulgaris*, yet this once common Bowland species must surely have occurred in this community. However where flushes are stonier and the habitat is more open it can still be found.

The more base-rich and less acidic *Briza media-Primula farinosa* sub-community is only rarely found

Plate 2.27 An acidic flush with M6 *Carex echinata-Sphagnum recurvum/auriculatum* mire with heather moor behind. Langden valley, Bowland Forest High.

Plate 2.28 Upper reaches of Marshaw Wyre, Over Wyresdale bordered by flushes dominated by Soft-rush (*Juncus effusus*)

in northern Lancashire but examples can be found in the Slaidburn area. Associated species include *Anagallis tenella* (also found in some flushes of the *Carex viridula* ssp. *oedocarpa-Juncus bulbosus* sub-community), *Carex hostiana*, *Carex pulicaris*, *Carex lepidocarpa*, *Linum catharticum* with small shoots of *Molinia caerulea*. Other species characteristic of neutral grasslands, e.g. *Bellis perennis*, *Euphrasia* spp., *Scorzoneroides autumnalis*, *Prunella vulgaris*, *Thymus polytrichus* and *Trifolium repens* may also occur. At Leck *Selaginella selaginoides* still occurs but is absent elsewhere whilst *Parnassia palustris*, once widespread in Bowland, has not been seen in this community for some years. It is believed that *Eriophorum latifolium* is found in flushes of this sub-community on Marshaw Fell where it is probably part of the *Molinia caerulea-Eriophorum latifolium* variant. Also found here is *Valeriana dioica*, which may occur in the other sub-communities and variants as well.

The *Carex dioica-Pinguicula vulgaris* mire in all its variants is an important constituent of the vegetation in Bowland and Leck. It is complex and it is difficult to understand the factors determining its composition. However drainage, grazing, moor burning and atmospheric pollution (e.g. smoke, sulphur dioxide, nitrogen etc.) are all factors to be considered. Whatever the causal agencies it is clear that the more base-rich flushes, home to *Parnassia palustris*, *Pinguicula vulgaris* and *Primula farinosa*, have changed sufficiently for these species to become much rarer over the last 100 years.

Averis, *et al.* (2004) show that M32 *Philonotis fontana-Saxifraga stellaris* springs occur in Bowland, yet *Saxifraga stellaris* does not occur in Lancashire. Wigginton (1995) on the other hand shows that the moss *Philonotis fontana* is common in Bowland and Leck. It is found in mesotrophic springs with *Chrysosplenium oppositifolium* and *Montia fontana* where it forms the *Montia fontana-Chrysosplenium oppositifolium* sub-community. Bryophytes are a major feature of this community but in Bowland the striking features are the mats of *Montia fontana* (both sspp. *fontana* and *variabilis*) and *Chrysosplenium oppositifolium*. The few associated species include *Cardamine pratensis*, *Cerastium fontanum*, *Equisetum palustre*, *Epilobium palustre* and *Ranunculus flammula*. Amongst the grasses and sedges associates include *Anthoxanthum odoratum*, *Carex echinata*, *Carex nigra*, *Carex panicea*, *Carex demissa*, *Festuca rubra*, *Festuca ovina* and *Poa trivialis*. Typically only a selection of these species will be present in any one flush and usually at very low cover levels. The *Montia fontana-Chrysosplenium oppositifolium* sub-community is not noted for rare species but it is home to the scarce *Myosotis stolonifera*, which is found throughout Bowland. Unfortunately it is easily confused with small or depauperate *Myosotis secunda*, which also occurs frequently. Much of the dubious material is sterile and it is believed these are hybrids

The typical *Philonotis fontana-Saxifraga stellaris* springs sub-community is more characteristic of flushes at higher levels than occur in Lancashire and whilst a form of this may occur at Leck it has not been confirmed. In the Pennines many of the rarer species are found in this community.

At lower altitudes M32 *Philonotis fontana-Saxifraga stellaris* spring communities are replaced by M35 *Ranunculus omiophyllus-Montia fontana* rills. In contrast to M32, which is associated with a cool, wet climate in the north and west of Britain, M35 is more characteristic of warmer oceanic environments in the uplands of south-western England, Wales and the Pennines. It is a common community in northern Lancashire and shares many of the associated species with M32. However the delicate white flowers of *Ranunculus omiophyllus* appearing out of a floating mat of leaves is typical. Associated species may include *Agrostis stolonifera, Callitriche stagnalis, Equisetum palustre, Galium palustre, Glyceria fluitans, Hydrocotyle vulgaris, Isolepis setacea, Juncus bufonius, Juncus bulbosus, Juncus articulatus, Lotus pedunculatus, Myosotis secunda, Potamogeton polygonifolius, Ranunculus flammula, Ranunculus repens* and *Stellaria alsine.*

As one approaches the lowlands with more woodland cover the spring and rill vegetation becomes floristically richer. The communities represented are grouped together as M36 Lowland springs and stream banks of shaded situations. Amongst the species found here are *Achillea ptarmica, Ajuga reptans, Angelica sylvestris, Cirsium palustre, Dactylorhiza fuchsii, Deschampsia cespitosa, Galium palustre, Juncus acutiflorus, Lysimachia nemorum, Silene flos-cuculi* and *Valeriana dioica.* More rarely *Galium uliginosum* may be found whilst in the

absence of grazing the wet flushes and marshes are readily colonized by *Alnus glutinosa*, the forerunner of these communities becoming wet woodland.

One of the commonest spring and rill species is *Potamogeton polygonifolius*, which is often dominant, but neither Rodwell (1995) nor Averis, *et al.* (2004) recognise this as a distinct community. Rather it is associated with other communities, e.g. M35 *Ranunculus omiophyllus-Montia fontana* rill. These communities are brought together in the ill-defined M30 related vegetation of seasonally inundated habitats. Some of these could be considered derivatives of M29 *Hypericum elodes-Potamogeton polygonifolius* soakway. Certainly the description of this community fits many of the *Potamogeton polygonifolius* dominated communities in Bowland but today the co-dominant *Hypericum elodes* is missing in Bowland as is *Eleocharis multicaulis*, which is also sometimes present in the community. Nevertheless *Eleocharis multicaulis* was found on the north side of Clougha in 1988 in a site that has not been re-found and *Hypericum elodes* was probably present in this community as late as the 1940s on the north side of Nicky Nook, Nether Wyresdale. It was also found on Ribbleton Moor, Preston and here the rare *Pilularia globulifera*, an interesting associate, was also found. Thus it seems that the oceanic M29 *Hypericum elodes-Potamogeton polygonifolius* soakway extended eastwards as far as Lancashire but that only remnants survive today.

M37 *Crataneuron commutatum-Festuca rubra* spring community is characteristic of base-rich, calcareous

Plate 2.29 Lowland mesotrophic flushes with an abundance of rushes (*Juncus* spp.) by the R. Hodder, Bowland Forest Low.

Plate 2.30 A mesotrophic flush in Bowland with Ragged-Robin (*Silene flos-cuculi*) in the foreground.

but generally oligotrophic waters in the oceanic, western uplands. It is common in the Craven Fells of the Pennines and, although not confirmed in northern Lancashire, it probably occurs by the Ease Gill, Leck. According to Wigginton (1995) the moss *Crataneuron commutatum* is found in a wide range of habitats including open springs and flushes. Vascular species are generally sparse but associates include *Agrostis canina, Carex flacca, Carex panicea, Carex demissa, Pinguicula vulgaris* and *Saxifraga hypnoides*.

Other mire communities

A particularly rare community in northern Lancashire is M26 *Molinia caerulea – Crepis paludosa* mire. This occurs on flushed hill slopes in Bowland where the spring water is slightly calcareous. In some respects it is similar to M10 *Carex dioica – Pinguicula vulgaris* mire and supports many of the same species. However the vegetation is taller with besides *Molinia caerulea, Juncus acutiflorus, Juncus × surrejanus* (abundant), *Juncus articulatus, Succisa pratensis, Sanguisorba officinalis, Serratula tinctoria* and *Trollius europaeus*. Also present are *Dactylorhiza purpurella* and very rarely *Gymnadenia borealis*. Rodwell (1991b) shows the community to be a variant of M25 *Molinia caerulea – Potentilla erecta* mire but this is a species poor grassland, often found on peat but described here as a grassland.

One of the commonest yet least well recorded communities is M27 *Filipendula ulmaria-Angelica sylvestris* tall-herb fen. Wherever there are periodically waterlogged conditions on mesotrophic soils, e.g. marshes by springs, streams or in poorly drained fields especially in the Bowland Fells, this community is found. It tends to be overlooked but the creamy patches of sweet scented flowers of *Filipendula ulmaria* and the large white flower heads of *Angelica sylvestris* are a feature of the Bowland countryside. Associated species include *Achillea ptarmica, Alchemilla glabra, Caltha palustris, Cirsium palustre, Crepis paludosa, Equisetum fluviatile, Galium uliginosum, Iris pseudacorus, Lotus pedunculatus, Silene flos-cuculi, Lythrum salicaria, Mentha aquatica, Oenanthe crocata, Rumex acetosa, Sanguisorba officinalis* and *Valeriana officinalis*. Many of these species are characteristic of the *Valeriana officinalis-Rumex acetosa* sub-community where, as in the *Urtica dioica-Vicia cracca* sub-community, they are rare or absent. Instead *Urtica dioica* and *Vicia cracca* with *Centaurea nigra, Cirsium arvense, Epilobium hirsutum* and *Eupatorium cannabinum* are commoner. In the *Juncus effusus-Holcus lanatus* sub-community *Juncus effusus*

Plate 2.31 A north facing hillside near Slaidburn with Globeflower (*Trollius europaeus*) in a M26 *Molinia caerulea-Crepis paludosa* mire.

and *Holcus lanatus* are more frequent with *Agrostis canina, Agrostis stolonifera, Anthoxanthum odoratum, Juncus acutiflorus, Molinia caerulea* and *Poa trivialis* often present.

Elsewhere in northern England *Cirsium heterophyllum* and *Trollius europaeus* are found in this community but in northern Lancashire this does not seem to be the case today.

At the head of Hawes Water, Silverdale, there is one of the most unusual of Lancashire's habitats and communities. On a deposit of shell marl M13 *Schoenus nigricans-Juncus subnodulosus* mire has developed. The substrate is highly calcareous but it is slowly drying out as the adjacent lake level and water table is at an historically low level. *Schoenus nigricans* is abundant along with *Molinia caerulea* and *Sesleria caerulea* more typical of CG9 *Sesleria caerulea-Galium sterneri* grassland, but *Juncus subnodulosus* is rare and in small quantity. It is therefore probably best to consider most of the vegetation as belonging to CG9. Rodwell (1991b) records M13 in the appropriate 10 km square, SD47, and presumably refers to this site but does so with the *Festuca rubra-Juncus acutiflorus* sub-community. However the floristically rich assemblage of species, often rare in northern Lancashire, is more characteristic of the *Briza media-Pinguicula vulgaris* sub-community. It is possible that *Myrica gale*, formerly found abundantly around the nearby Little Hawes Water, also occurred on the margins of this community, as does *Eupatorium cannabinum* today.

Plate 2.32 A meadow near Slaidburn with an abundance of Meadowsweet (*Filipendula ulmaria*) in a M27 *Filipendula ulmaria-Angelica sylvestris* mire.

Plate 2.33 The northern end of Hawes Water (part of a National Nature Reserve) where a deposit of shell marl supports a rich calcicole mire flora.

More apparently out of place in the community is *Calluna vulgaris* growing on drier tussocks but indicative of leaching.

This is an unusual community so far north for this normally southern mire that favours a warmer climate. However the calcareous mire at Hawes Water and the warmer climate at the head of Morecambe Bay provide a suitable localised environment for this community, while also providing a suitable habitat for a series of more montane species characteristic of the Pennines, e.g. *Epipactis atrorubens*, *Galium sterneri*, *Primula farinosa* and *Sesleria caerulea*. However the lowered water table is detrimental to the long-term survival of some of the rare species and *Pinguicula vulgaris* and *Selaginella selaginoides* seem especially vulnerable.

Crag Bank SSSI, Carnforth is one of the more remarkable northern Lancashire sites. It is only 3.5ha yet encompasses a range of habitats. Most of the site consists of poorly drained ground situated between two calcareous, boulder clay ridges containing limestone boulders. They are covered in W21 *Crataegus monogyna-Hedera helix* scrub. Attempts at draining the poorly drained areas have been made and two active ditches remain. The area is divided into two sections, the dividing line probably corresponding to an old ditch, with differing plant communities. However these communities have changed over the years and to appreciate their present composition it is necessary to know the probable history of the area. According to John Lucas (Ford and Fuller-Maitland, 1931) in the eighteenth century the poorly drained area was some kind of peat bog known as Lang-Haas Moss and was used primarily as fuel for Carnforth. It suffered from periodic inundation from the sea and presumably at some time previously it had been a saline lagoon. This probably became a *Phragmites* reed-bed before the peat developed. At this stage there may have been an intermediate community between the mire and coastal communities with *Molinia caerulea* and *Schoenus nigricans*. A remnant of this persisted by a track on the Keer estuary until the community was destroyed by road works in the 1970s. It is believed that almost all the peat was removed at Crag Bank and the area drained to provide a damp pasture. It is not known when this happened but the 1840 Ordnance Survey map shows the area as drained farmland. Wheldon and Wilson (1907) did not mention any botanical interest in the area and it is thought it remained as pasture until sometime after the Second World War. Nevertheless by the 1960s local naturalists reported that following a lack of maintenance most of the low-lying areas south of Carnforth had become a *Phragmites australis* swamp and reed-bed (S4). By the early 1970s local naturalists again reported that the whole area had become botanically interesting and that the reed-beds were confined to the low lying areas to the south of the present SSSI created in 1979.

At this time the southern half of the site was floristically less diverse than the northern half and was dominated by *Juncus subnodulosus*, probably forming the typical community of a *Juncus subnodulosus-Cirsium palustre* fen-meadow (M22) (Rodwell, 1991b). This community occurs in places at the highest part of salt marshes around Morecambe Bay and occasionally elsewhere. It is a lowland community typically found in southern Britain.

In the 1970s the vegetation in the northern half of the site was much less coarse and *Molinia caerulea* was dominant. However defining the community that was present is not easy, and Rodwell (1991b) suggests that defining *Molinia caerulea* dominated communities can be difficult. At Crag Bank the species rich flora suggested that it belonged to either the southerly-distributed *Molinia caerulea-Cirsium dissectum* fen-meadow (M24) or the northern or montane *Molinia caerulea-Crepis paludosa* mire (M26), but neither of the co-dominants of these communities were present at Crag Bank. Nevertheless many of the constant and associated species of both community types were present, e.g. *Carex nigra, Carex panicea, Equisetum palustre, Filipendula ulmaria, Lotus pedunculatus, Potentilla erecta, Ranunculus acris, Succisa pratensis* and *Valerianella dioica,* but without any of the rarer species associated with these communities occurring. On the other hand the rich assemblage of other species present included *Anagallis tenella, Caltha palustris, Carex hostiana, Carex otrubae, Carex pulicaris, Carex spicata, Carex demissa, Carex lepidocarpa, Dactylorhiza fuchsii, Dactylorhiza incarnata*, Epipactis palustris*, Silene flos-cuculi, Mentha aquatica, Menyanthes trifoliata*, Pedicularis palustre, Pinguicula vulgaris, Ranunculus flammula* and *Senecio aquatilis.* By the late 1990s those marked with an * had disappeared and *Parnassia palustris* and *Pinguicula vulgaris* were present in very small quantity. On the other hand a few spikes of *Dactylorhiza purpurella* had appeared. Overall by the 1990s the site's interest seemed to be decreasing.

The changes that have taken place at Crag Bank over a long period of time are remarkable. Whilst the general sequence of vegetation change has been elucidated the detailed causes for the changes are not fully understood but peat extraction, drainage, subsequent neglect of the drains and changes in grazing regime must all be important influences but how, when and what these have been are not known for certain although horse (rather than cattle) grazing may be responsible for the latest changes.

Although the upland M26 *Molinia caerulea-Crepis paludosa* mire does not occur at Crag Bank it is found in two SSSIs in Bowland. Near Slaidburn the rich assemblage of species present in the calcareous flushes includes *Primula farinosa, Trollius europaeus, Valeriana dioica, Parnassia palustris, Dactylorhiza purpurella, Gymnadenia borealis* and *Sanguisorba officinalis.* However there is some suggestion that rushes and in particular the hybrid jointed rush *Juncus × surrejanus* is becoming more abundant and crowding out the rarer species.

Mires with an abundance of *Juncus effusus* or *Juncus acutiflorus* are often confusing. In upland areas sites irrigated by spring water often belong to M6 *Carex echinata-Sphagnum* mire or where flushes are calcareous to the M26 *Molinia caerulea-Crepis paludosa* mire both discussed above. However in northern Lancashire rush-pastures occur in neglected grasslands, by streams and on more or less level ground in upland areas. These communities lack both *Molinia* and *Sphagnum* spp. and are referable to M23 *Juncus effusus/acutiflorus-Galium palustre* rush-pasture. They are often derived from MG10 *Holcus lanatus-Juncus effusus* rush-pasture or other species poor, slightly mesotrophic pastures where grassland management lapses and drainage is impeded. They are found in western parts of the British Isles where high rainfall and more oceanic conditions prevail. The related M22 *Juncus subnodulosus-Cirsium palustre* fen meadow described above is more characteristic of the warmer and dryer conditions of south-eastern Britain.

The floristically rich and rare M26 *Molinia caerulea-Crepis paludosa* mire may revert to M23 if open flushed habitats are not maintained despite their flushing with base-rich water. It is believed adjustment of the type and level of grazing controls the type of community present but at the remaining localities where M26 occurs conversion to M23 may be occurring. However only occasionally noted in the literature many stands of *Juncus acutiflorus* may in fact be the vigorous and largely sterile *Juncus × surrejanus,* which is difficult to identify until late summer. The presence of this hybrid may have significance in terms of its ecology and palatability for stock.

Stands of M23 *Juncus effusus/acutiflorus-Galium palustre* rush-pasture have not often been identified in northern Lancashire but a large area of low lying land near Chipping is dominated by this community. Here the site was once a peat bog but all the peat was removed long ago and the land drained and improved as rough pasture. It probably once supported MG10 *Holcus lanatus-Juncus effusus* rush-pasture, which remains on better-drained parts of the site, or similar acid grassland but as the drains became blocked *Juncus effusus* and *Juncus acutiflorus* (or hybrid) came to dominate the area with the latter growing in the wettest places. Large stands of this community have also been seen in Easington near Slaidburn and in Tatham.

3. Heaths

Introduction

In the early twenty-first century it is difficult to imagine the impact of humans on the semi-natural vegetation and flora of the intensively farmed landscape of northern Lancashire. By the eighteenth century human influence was such that it gave rise to anthropogenically-derived habitats with vegetation types and flora that today often receive the highest conservation priority. These are heaths (especially in the lowlands), grasslands and arable farmland.

Arguably all heaths where low growing ericaceous shrubs dominate the vegetation were derived from other habitats largely through grazing. Typically they occur on podsols or peaty podsols but without significant peat development. However they often merge with wetter areas to form mires with peat formation (Webb, 1986). Thousands of hectares of *Calluna* dominated heath remain in the Bowland Fells where it is managed through a regime of sheep grazing and moor burning. Many of the upland heaths belong to sporting estates used for grouse shooting.

In some upland areas where common land survived there was much heavier grazing pressure and here the heather gave way to other vegetation. These alternative heaths may be dominated by *Vaccinium myrtillus* (Clougha) or *Molinia caerulea* (parts of Tarnbrook) or in some places where heather was removed suddenly, e.g. after heather beetle attack, the vegetation became dominated by *Deschampsia flexuosa* (e.g. parts of Leck Fell).

Lowland Heaths

In the lowlands almost all trace of heath vegetation has disappeared. The heaths in the western Fylde, especially those on wind blown sand behind the sand dunes at Lytham St Anne's, were possibly the only natural heaths to survive into the Neolithic and later periods but they were amongst the first areas to be reclaimed for agriculture. By the early nineteenth century if not earlier they had disappeared leaving only a trace of their former existence, e.g. in small patches on both the Royal Lytham & St Anne's and the St Anne's Old Links Golf Courses.

Further inland heaths were once numerous and in most instances were clearly derived from former woodland, e.g. Preston, Fulwood and Ribbleton Moors, which provided ideal terrain for the Civil War Battle of Preston in 1648 (Hunt, 1992b). Map 1.1 shows that by plotting the use of the word Moor found on old maps, heaths occurred all round the Bowland Fells and covered extensive areas of Lonsdale north of the R. Lune, which was mostly common land until the early nineteenth century (Whyte, 2003). Although it is assumed that they were formed by woodland clearance and grazing over many centuries it is not clear how their distinctive flora developed. Furthermore the inland heaths could be roughly divided into wet and dry heaths (Thompson, *et al.*, 1995) of which fragments of both survived into the twentieth centuries. Wet heaths were a mosaic of wet and dry areas but it is the wetland species that are of most interest. This habitat survives, albeit in a degraded form, just beyond the Lancashire border at Keasden, near Bentham, where a characteristic species of this habitat, *Gentiana pneumonanthe* can still be found. Dry heaths were dominated by *Calluna vulgaris* and/or *Ulex gallii*. Using various sources it has been possible to reconstruct a list of perhaps the rarer and possibly typical species of these two Broad Habitats. Ribbleton Moor was an example of a wet heath and this survived in a much-reduced form until the early twentieth century before being reclaimed for farming and later housing, mostly in the 1930s. Other examples existed, e.g. at Poulton (the village out of which the coastal resort known as Morecambe developed), Claughton near Garstang and possibly Melling Moor. Dry heaths may have been more common, e.g. parts of Lancaster Moor. This was reclaimed in the mid nineteenth century after some areas of the Moor had already been destroyed by a quarry that was used in rebuilding the city in stone some hundred or so years earlier. Today the prominent Williamson Memorial marks the area. Enclosed in 1756 Ellel Moor was described as being covered in furze with, perhaps surprisingly, alder, suggesting wetter areas. Garnett (1849) provided a detailed account of how the moor was 'improved' at Newlands in the 1840s where the vegetation seemed to consist of a mosaic of rushes, gorse, alder and heather. Even as late as the 1960s a remnant covered in *Ulex gallii* remained but was lost as quarrying finally destroyed the area. Table 2.2 provides a list of the species known to have occurred on the wet heath at Ribbleton Moor.

Table 2.2 Species recorded from Ribbleton Moor (heath and habitats immediately adjoining) prior to 1900

Apium inundatum	Hydrocotyle vulgaris
Baldellia ranunculoides	Hydrocharis morsus-ranae
Calluna vulgaris	Hypericum elodes
Carex dioica	Lemna gibba
Carex demissa	Limosella aquatica
Chrysosplenium alternifolium	Lythrum portula
Comarum palustre	Menyanthes trifoliata
Drosera rotundifolia	Pilulifera globulifera
Erica tetralix	Ranunculus hederaceus
Eriophorum angustifolium	Veronica officinalis
Galium saxatile	Veronica scutellata
Genista anglica	Viola palustris
Gentiana pneumonanthe	

This lists suggests that these heaths were forms of oceanic heath. At Ribbleton this was probably a habitat dominated by M16 *Erica tetralix-Sphagnum compactum* wet heath community. The drier heaths were possibly H8 *Calluna vulgaris-Ulex gallii* heath characteristic of western Britain. However intensive grazing or reclamation for grassland suggests that once lost it takes centuries for heaths of this kind to re-establish themselves. This is clearly seen at Port Erin, Isle of Man where arable fields were reclaimed from the heath in the nineteenth century or earlier and converted to a golf course before abandonment in 1938. Since then, despite being surrounded by a *Calluna vulgaris–Ulex gallii* heath the old golf course has not reverted to heath. Terry, *et al.* (2004) suggest that in upland areas, once lost, natural reversion to a heather moor may be a long process.

Evidence for wetter heaths comes from the records of wet heath species. Table 2.3 shows a selection of heath species found on the moors on the former commons that extended from near Carnforth to Kirkby Lonsdale to the north of the R. Lune. The records are abstracted from Wheldon and Wilson (1907) and neither the species nor the localities are comprehensive, but the list gives a good idea of the wealth of heath species still growing nearly 100 years after enclosure. Some of the species survived until the twenty-first century on the fragments of mire still extant (notably at Whittington and Docker Moor) but many are now extinct.

Table 2.3 Heath and mire species recorded on the moors to the north of the R. Lune prior to 1900

Species	Locality
Anagallis tenella	Arkholme Moor
Andromeda polifolia	Whittington Moor, Outfield Moss
Carex binervis	Arkholme Moor, Whittington Moor
Carex canescens	Whittington Moor, Outfield Moss, Lord's Lot
Carex diandra	Outfield Moss
Carex dioica	Outfield Moss
Carex disticha	Outfield Moss
Carex hostiana	Whittington Moor
Centunculus minimus	Arkholme Moor
Dactylorhiza incarnata	Outfield Moss
Dactylorhiza purpurella	Gressingham Moor
Drosera rotundifolia	Arkholme Moor, Whittington Moor, Gressingham Moor, Outfield Moss
Dryopteris carthusiana	Whittington Moor
Empetrum nigrum	Whittington Moor
Eriophorum angustifolium	Lord's Lot
Eriophorum vaginatum	Outfield Moss
Genista anglica	Outfield Moss
Genista tinctoria	Gressingham Moor, Outfield Moss
Isolepis setacea	Arkholme Moor
Jasione montana	Arkholme Moor
Juniperus communis	Arkholme Moor
Melampyrum pratense	Lord's Lot
Myrica gale	Arkholme Moor, Lord's Lot
Narthecium ossifragum	Arkhome Moor, Outfield Moss, Whittington Moor
Pedicularis palustris	Outfield Moss, Whittington Moor
Platanthera bifolia	Gressingham Moor, Whittington Moor, Mire nr. Redwell Inn
Radiola linoides	Arkholme Moor

Species	Locality
Ranunculus omiophyllus	Nr Lord's Lot, Whittington Moor
Scutellaria minor	Arkholme Moor, Whittington Moor
Ulex gallii	Gressingham Moor
Vaccinium oxycoccus	Arkholme Moor, Outfield Moss
Viola palustris	Arkholme Moor, Gressingham Moor, Whittington Moor

If heaths have an anthropogenic origin, however ancient, a question arises as to how these native, characteristic wet heath species colonized sites in the former woodland zone. It is possible that some natural heaths have existed continuously since late glacial times in coastal areas where a shifting coastline, exposure to storms, grazing animals and later human intervention kept habitats open and suitable for heath vegetation. A similar situation may have occurred inland where large herbivores and later humans maintained woodland clearances. Some evidence for coastal refugia comes from the former presence of *Gentiana pneumonanthe* and *Hypericum elodes* at Poulton where there was a wet heath between the sandy coastal areas and the extensive raised bogs in the Heysham and Torrisholme areas.

Upland Heaths

The boundary between community types is often not clear and one community may merge into another. Similarly with increasing altitude the distinction between lowland and upland heaths is not clear. However it is possible that the large areas of common land in the Lune valley were more characteristic of dry upland heaths than lowland ones. Here in a cooler and wetter climate the occurrence of *Ulex gallii* was less common and even *Erica cinerea* was rarer to be replaced by *Vaccinium myrtillus*. These heaths may have been dominated by H9 *Calluna vulgaris-Deschampsia flexuosa* heath. Fragments of this remain in the Bowland fringe and it is likely that its formation and maintenance is related to the intensity of moor burning and perhaps atmospheric pollution. Also on some moors, e.g. Leck, that have suffered severe heather beetle attacks this community seems to have developed from H12 *Calluna vulgaris- Vaccinium myrtillus* heath. However with rising altitude and on more stony ground with less intensive

burning but heavily grazed, H9 is replaced by H18 *Vaccinium myrtillus-Deschampsia flexuosa* heath. This is a common Bowland community, e.g. on Clougha, which is probably derived from H12 *Calluna vulgaris-Vaccinium myrtillus* heath. On Clougha a fence separates common land with its long history of common and probably more intensive grazing from a less intensively grazed heather moor. The common land is H18 whilst the heather moor is H12.

However the most important upland dry heath community in northern Lancashire is H12 *Calluna vulgaris-Vaccinium myrtillus* heath. This covers thousands of hectares of the drier moors merging in wetter areas with various mire communities. On some slopes, e.g. Fairsnape Fell, and high level valley edges, e.g. by the Tarnbrook Wyre, other shrubby species such as *Empetrum nigrum* and *Vaccinium vitis-idaea* are important constituents of what can otherwise be almost a pure stand of two co-dominant species. Despite it being highly characteristic of parts of northern Britain, it is of limited occurrence elsewhere in Europe and it is, therefore, of high conservation value (Averis, *et al.*, 2004). Nevertheless it is a community that has arisen by thousands of years of management (grazing and moor burning), which is maintained today in the same way with grazing sheep. The resultant heather moor is of considerable economic value to sporting estates for grouse shooting, e.g. at Abbeystead (Pyefinch and Golborn, 2001; Simmons, 2003). However to obtain optimum heather productivity and therefore grouse numbers requires careful and subtle management. With especially heavy atmospheric nitrogen deposits threatening to damage or even eradicate *Calluna vulgaris*, management techniques become even more critical (de Smidt, 1995; Terry, *et al.*, 2004).

Woodland survives in some places, especially in upland valleys or cloughs, to over 300m. An important constituent of some of these woodlands is Bracken, *Pteridium aquilinum*, that survives in the absence of tree cover and may then become a vigorous monoculture spreading over the hillsides and invading calcifugous grasslands or *Calluna vulgaris-Vaccinium myrtillus* heath. Bracken covered hillsides of this kind probably belong to U20 *Pteridium aquilinum-Galium saxatile* community and may be derived from W11 *Quercus petraea-Betula pubescens-Oxalis acetosella* woodland. In the absence of tree cover Bracken may act as a low growing 'tree' sheltering early flowering species.

Plate 2.34 Heather moor (H12 *Calluna vulgaris-Vaccinium heath*) on Beatrix Fell near Dunsop Bridge, Bowland Forest High.

Plate 2.35 An M6 *Carex echinata-Sphagnum recurvum/paniculatum* mire arising from a hillside covered in Bracken (*Pteridium aquilinum*) and Heather (*Calluna vulgaris*), Calder valley near Oakenclough, Bleasdale.

A small number of rarer species are associated with communities dominated by *Calluna vulgaris* and where these merge with Bracken and upland woodland. These include *Neottia cordata* and *Trientalis europaea* in Wyresdale, and, although more widespread, *Melampyrum pratense* is particularly fine on the lower slopes of Clougha, Quernmore.

The most natural of the upland heath communities is the oceanic H21 *Calluna vulgaris-Vaccinium myrtillus-Sphagnum capillifolium* heath (Averis, *et al.*, 2004; A.B.G. Averis, pers. comm.). This community is characterised by a deep, richly coloured cover of bryophytes of which *Sphagnum capillifolium* is the most important. Through this carpet of bryophytes emerge the principal vascular plants of *Calluna vulgaris*, *Erica cinerea* and *Vaccinium myrtillus* with *Potentilla erecta*. It is found on steep slopes usually facing north or northeast where grazing and moor burning is slight or absent. In Lancashire it is represented by H21a *Calluna vulgaris-Pteridium aquilinum* sub-community characterised by the presence of *Pteridium aquilinum* and the absence of the hyper oceanic bryophytes found in H21b *Mastigophora woodsii-Herbertus aduncus* ssp. *hutchinsiae* sub-community. Other species associated with this community are *Blechnum spicant*, *Molinia caerulea* and *Empetrum nigrum*. The near naturalness of this community on the south-eastern edge of its British range makes this an important feature of Lancashire's vegetation. Where grazing occurs H21a gives way to a similar community without *Calluna vulgaris*.

In Lancashire the *Calluna vulgaris-Vaccinium myrtillus-Sphagnum capillifolium* community appears to be confined to the upper reaches of the Langden Brook and elsewhere on steep sided valleys or cliffs in eastern Bowland. It is probably a near natural community of high elevation in north-western Scotland but in Lancashire it is probably derived from woodland.

Plate 2.36 Raven Scar, Langden valley, Bowland Forest High supporting the oceanic H21 *Calluna vulgaris-Vaccinium myrtillus-Sphagnum capillifolium* heath.

4. Grasslands

Introduction

There is a tendency to think that in the early twenty-first century all grasslands are highly eutrophic and dominated by recently sown *Lolium* species and culti-vars. This is an over simplification of the present situation and what is present today was derived from something else. The something else is difficult to define but using the scanty data from the early nineteenth century (mostly rarer nineteenth century grassland species) and the dynamic relation-ship of grassland communities developed by Rodwell (1992), it is possible to postulate the kinds of vegeta-tion from which the present grasslands and flora were developed.

Holt (1795) provides the earliest references to the floristic composition of Lancashire grasslands and the way farming methods created them. The Oldham Botanical Society provided a short list of grasses found in hay meadows and pastures presumably recorded from nearby upland areas in the east of South Lancaster (VC 59). It is difficult to give correct names to the ones recorded in 1795 but the following species give an idea of what was present. In hay meadows *Anthoxanthum*, **Alopecurus*, *Dactylis*, **Poa*, *Festuca*, **Bromus*, *Avena* and *Holcus* were recorded where those marked with * were abundant. In pastures *Aira (Deschampsia flexuosa?)*, *Agrostis* and *Lolium* were very common but *Secale (Elytrigia?)* and *Arundo* were not common. These indicate that they were meso-trophic grasslands but non-grasses were not included. However, Holt also indicates that in the Fylde pastures were often created from exhausted land supporting little vegetation. The land was left to recuperate but for many years only 'weeds' were present. Sometimes White Clover, *Trifolium repens*, was sown.

More active measures were taken to create grass-lands for hay. After a few crops were taken, often barley and oats sometimes undersown with clover (unspecified species), the land was cleaned (weeded) and dunged (farmyard manure spread on the fields). It was then sown with hay seed gathered from seed that had fallen off hay fed to stock. Red Clover, trefoil and occasionally Chicory were added. Rye grass was used occasionally at the end of the eighteenth century but it was not considered useful. The main hay grasses were *Alopecuris pratensis* and *Festuca pratensis* along with trefoil (*Lotus corniculatus*?) and 'rib-grass' (*Plantago lanceolata*). Dock and knotgrass (unspecified species) were common weeds controlled by lime along with 'couch-grass' (*Elytrigia repens*). These comments suggest that even by 1795 the better grasslands were moderately eutrophic.

Twenty years later Dickson (1815) provides another much more complete list of species typical of good meadows often found by rivers (Table 2.4). These are clearly mesotrophic grasslands but it is impos-sible to be more precise. Where grasslands were wet and overgrazed or poached by cattle, rush-pasture developed. In mesotrophic communities these would be dominated by *Juncus effusus* or more rarely *J. inflexus* (possibly MG10 *Holcus lanatus-Juncus effusus* rush-pasture) but in more upland and acidic areas the rush-pasture was dominated by *Juncus acutiflorus* (M23 *Juncus effusus/acutiflorus-Galium palustre* rush-pasture) with *J. effusus* and *Galium palustre*. No doubt these were the pastures referred to by Garnett (1849). Rush-pastures are found frequently today where mesotrophic grasslands become neglected.

Table 2.4 Grasses and flowering plants recorded in Lancashire grasslands by Dickson (1815)

Meadow Species	Other flowering plants
Alopecurus agrestis*	Achillea millefolium
Alopecurus bulbosus*	Centaurea nigra
Alopecurus pratensis*	Cirsium dissectum (C. arvense?)
Anthoxanthum odoratum*#	Cirsium palustre
Arrhenatherum elatius*	Cirsium vulgare
Cynosurus cristatus#	Lathyrus pratensis
Dactylis glomerata	Lotus corniculatus
Festuca duriuscula (=F. rubra?)	Medicago lupulina
Festuca pratensis*	Plantago lanceolata
Holcus lanatus	Plantago major
Phleum nodosum*	Ranunculus acris
Poa annua	Ranunculus bulbosus
Poa compressus	Rhinanthus minor
Poa palustris	Rumex acetosa
Poa pratensis#	Rumex acetosella
Poa trivialis*	Rumex crispus
	Senecio jacobaea
	Trifolium hybridum
	Trifolium medium
	Trifolium repens
	Vicia sativa

Notes: * = most frequent on moist soils; # = most frequent on dry soils

Rodwell provides a good description of grassland communities and it is possible using his descriptions, and especially the dynamic interrelationships of the different communities, to determine the main grassland communities that probably existed in the eighteenth century and their evolution into what can be found today. Similarly many of the communities are discussed by Averis, *et al.*, (2004) and, whilst rather old, Taylor's survey (1986) provides localities for some of the Lancashire communities identified.

Mesotrophic grasslands

In the nineteenth century and earlier much of the permanent grassland, at least at lower levels, was probably MG5 *Cynosurus cristatus-Centaurea nigra* grassland, which was mown annually in July and grazed in the autumn and winter. It was manured by stock. This kind of management has almost disappeared but some pastures survive. However by 1900 some grasslands were fertilized with basic slag and this probably eliminated some species from an otherwise colourful meadow.

With the advent of fertilizers MG5 grasslands became MG6 *Lolium perenne-Cynosurus cristatus* grassland where grazing took place throughout the year and the fields were chemically fertilized, in addition to farmyard manure and herbicides being applied. Additionally they were often re-sown. This is a common grassland today but increasingly it is being replaced by MG7, *Lolium perenne* leys and related grasslands. This is an intensively managed grassland, sown as swards, chemically fertilized, treated with herbicides and increasingly used for silage with at least four crops taken each year. There are few if any associated species but *Cerastium glomeratum* may be found with occasional plants of *Rumex obtusifolius*. Occasionally when these grasslands were neglected patches of nettles and thistles became established to form OV25 *Urtica dioica-Cirsium arvense* community. However this community is also found frequently on roadside verges, waste ground and in woodland clearings.

Of these grasslands much the most floristically diverse were MG5 *Cynosurus cristatus-Centaurea nigra* grassland and its northern derivative MG3, *Anthoxanthum odoratum-Geranium sylvaticum* grassland. The former occurred on clay soils throughout the county and in the west of the county one of the rarer species found was *Anacamptis morio*, e.g. at Heysham, Pilling, Cottam, Lea, Bolton-le-Sands, Poulton (Morecambe) and in the Lune valley near Caton. East of the M6 variants supported the butterfly orchids, *Platanthera bifolia* and *Platanthera chlorantha*, of which the latter was frequent in Wyresdale, and *Silaum silaus* at Cantsfield. Other species probably belonging to this community include *Pimpinella major* largely confined to the Ribble valley and *Pimpinella saxifraga*. Examples of MG5 meadows are the Tarnbrook Meadows SSSI, Over Wyresdale; Dale Head Church Yard, Hammerton Mere, other meadows in the Slaidburn area and grasslands in the flood plain of the R. Lune, Melling.

However in the meadows in the Bowland Fells

MG5 probably merged into MG3 grasslands perhaps better known as northern hay meadows so characteristic of meadows in northern Pennine valleys. Characteristic rarer species include *Geranium sylvaticum, Trollius europaeus, Cirsium heterophyllum, Gymnadenia conopsea* (extinct in this community in Lancashire) and *Lathyrus linifolius* all characteristic of typical woodland edge communities from which this grassland community is derived. No meadows typical of this community survive, but fragments similar to this occur at Clear Beck Meadow in Hindburndale and in the Slaidburn area e.g. Myttons, Bell Sykes and Field Head Meadows SSSIs.

Where drainage is impeded, wetter grasslands occur. Amongst the more colourful is MG8 *Cynosurus cristatus-Caltha palustris* grassland, which is dominated by *Caltha palustris*. This was once a common community found within MG5 grasslands or on their edge by streams etc. It was often the community where *Trollius europaeus, Crepis paludosa, Geum rivale* and

perhaps *Dactylorhiza purpurella* were found. However places where this community is found can be readily drained yet small patches survive as for example in the Tarnbrook Meadows SSSI, Over Wyresdale. Two grasslands, which are typical of poorly drained pastures, have probably arisen through neglect of formerly well-drained pastures. These are species poor communities comprising MG9 *Holcus lanatus-Deschampsia cespitosa* grassland and MG10 *Holcus lanatus-Juncus effusus* rush-pasture. They are found on neutral to acid soils and differ largely through the dominance of either *Deschampsia cespitosa* or *Juncus effusus*. In MG10 *Juncus effusus* may be replaced by *Juncus inflexus* in more base rich areas or by *Iris pseudacorus*. All these community types may be found but MG10 with *Juncus effusus* is much the most frequent

Amongst the derivations of MG3 and MG5, probably via MG6, are three grasslands dominated by *Bromus hordeaceus, Taraxacum* spp. or *Ranunculus acris*. Rodwell shows *Bromus hordeaceus* ssp. *hordeaceus*

Plate 2.37 A view across the Newton Fells looking west. Fields close to the farm have been 'improved' to provide better grazing for sheep and cattle and are probably MG7 *Lolium perenne* leys or MG6 *Lolium perenne-Cynoglossum cristatus* grasslands. Beyond are upland calcifugous grasslands.

Plate 2.38 This meadow near Slaidburn is a herb-rich northern hay meadow probably supporting a form of MG3 *Anthoxanthum odoratum-Geranium sylvaticum* grassland. Melancholy Thistle (*Cirsium heterophyllum*) is in the foreground.

Plate 2.39 Another herb-rich meadow near Slaidburn supporting a rich grassland flora, which is probably a form of MG3 *Anthoxanthum odoratum-Geranium sylvaticum* grassland.

sub-community as a variant of MG3 *Anthoxanthum odoratum-Geranium sylvaticum* community. In some areas of Bowland this is almost certainly the case but in the Wyresdale Meadows SSSI at Tarnbrook the southern *Bromus racemosus* is found. In the Fylde this sub-community may be derived from MG5 but here it is often the recently described *Bromus hordeaceus* ssp. *longipedicillatus* or *Bromus commutatus* that dominates the meadow, e.g. at Pilling.

Frequently, however, in well-drained meadows and pastures *Ranunculus acris,* often with *Alopecurus pratensis,* dominates the community but in wetter meadows, especially ones poached by cattle, vigorous species of *Taraxacum* dominate the grassland. Both these types were frequent in the grasslands to the north of Preston in the Grimsargh and Goosnargh areas. Neither of them is specifically mentioned by Rodwell.

Two communities that are recognised by the NVC occur in similar mesotrophic grasslands but are periodically inundated to form patches of distinctly different vegetation to the neighbouring communities. These are OV28 *Agrostis stolonifera-Ranunculus repens* community and OV29 *Alopecurus geniculatus-Rorippa palustris* community. The former community is especially common in a variety of situations. The latter is also frequent with *Alopecurus geniculatus* dominating the vegetation and *Rorippa palustris* taking a

less prominent role or even being absent. Both these communities are illustrated by Rodwell (2000, p.429) as constituents of the mosaic of wetland and grassland communities found in the R. Lune oxbows at Melling. Another community associated with periodically inundated mesotrophic grassland is the almost ubiquitous MG13 *Agrostis stolonifera-Alopecurus geniculatus* grassland, e.g. on Newton Marsh SSSI.

A further community found in mesotrophic grasslands is OV12 *Poa annua-Myosotis arvensis* community. Typically it is found in habitats where trampling, dunging by animals or other activities have opened up the sward. Associated species are *Agrostis stolonifera, Poa trivialis* and *Polygonum aviculare s.l.* In northern Lancashire it is widespread in lowland areas but not often noted – possibly because the constituent species are very common.

Of the remaining mesotrophic grasslands described by Rodwell the species poor MG1 *Arrhenatherum elatius* grassland is frequent on roadside verges, railway banks and on coastal clay banks where in several places *Arrhenatherum elatius* is replaced by *Calamagrostis epigejos.*

On reservoir banks at Grimsargh and Alston there are species-rich mesotrophic grasslands, which were established from the mid nineteenth century. Since then the banks have been mown once a year in summer. They are probably a form of MG1

Plate 2.40 A buttercup meadow at Hammerton Mere near Slaidburn.

Plate 2.41 A pasture near Chipping with an abundance of dandelions (*Taraxacum* spp.) mostly section *Ruderalia*.

Arrhenatherum elatius grassland but the species composition with an abundance of *Alopecurus pratensis* and *Sanguisorba officinalis* is reminiscent of MG4 *Alopecurus pratensis – Sanguisorba officinalis* grassland identified by Taylor (1986) as occurring in Hindburndale. However this is a southern form of mesotrophic grassland or meadow that is seasonally flooded in winter. Furthermore a feature of the reservoir embankments is the abundance of *Orchis mascula* and at Alston of *Ophioglossum vulgatum*. It is difficult, therefore, to assign these grasslands to one of the community types described by Rodwell. However fragments of MG4 *Alopecurus pratensis-Sanguisorba officinalis* grasslands, which are seasonally flooded, can be found especially by the side of some streams in the vicinity. It is possible that this was a more widespread community and could have provided the source of some of the species on the Grimsargh and Alston reservoir banks.

Calcifugous Grasslands

On Leck Fell and on the Bowland Fells two types of calcifugous grassland cover extensive areas especially on hill slopes. These are U4 *Festuca ovina-Agrostis capillaris-Galium saxatile* grassland and U5 *Nardus stricta-Galium saxatile* grassland. U4 is generally found on drier slopes and U5 on wetter ones. Both were once derived from woodland and in the absence of grazing can revert to woodland or heath. On lower slopes particularly U4 can be improved agriculturally to MG6, and many grasslands of this type have been found on upland farms. On mineral soils the *Vaccinium myrtillus-Deschampsia flexuosa* sub-community is sometimes found especially where grazing pressure is greater. In other places, where disturbance is greater, e.g. following heather beetle attack or severe moor burning of *Calluna* heath, U2 *Deschampsia flexuosa* grassland develops. In more natural conditions the *Vaccinium myrtillus* sub-community develops perhaps derived from upland birch woodland where both *Vaccinium myrtillus* and *Deschampsia flexuosa* were prominent in the herb layer. It is perhaps in these communities that *Trientalis europaea*, now confined to upland oak-birch woodland edge communities and often growing under Bracken in Black Clough, Over Wyresdale (see upland heaths) occurs.

Bracken dominated hill slopes are common in Bowland and belong to U20 *Pteridium aquilinum-Galium saxatile* community. They are derived from former woodland communities and developed following woodland clearance. During the last twenty years or so many Bracken covered hill slopes have been treated with the herbicide Asulam. This kills the Bracken but unfortunately it often leaves a bare hillside that is subject to erosion and restoration to grassland or heath is problematical (Averis, *et al.*, 2004).

On damp and rather peaty soils or gleyed podsols on flat or gently sloping ground, both U4 *Festuca ovina-Agrostis capillaris-Galium saxatile* and U5 *Nardus stricta-Galium saxatile* grasslands can merge into U6 *Juncus squarrosus-Festuca ovina* grassland. Here *Juncus squarrosus* becomes much more prominent. Sometimes the *Agrostis capillaris-Luzula multiflora* sub-community forms an intermediate stage between U6 and U4. In general there is a gradient from *Festuca ovina-Agrostis capillaris-Galium saxatile* grassland on mineral soils on steep free-draining slopes through *Nardus stricta-Galium saxatile* grassland on moister, peat-topped soils on somewhat gentler slopes to *Juncus squarrosus-Festuca ovina* grassland on wet, peaty level or gently sloping hillsides. All these communities are seen on Leck Fell and elsewhere in Bowland.

In between limestone outcrops around Morecambe Bay the drift is often leached to produce acid soils. Formerly these areas were grazed and U4 *Festuca ovina-Agrostis capillaris-Galium saxatile* grassland developed often with a little *Calluna* suggesting that in time heath would develop. However in the absence of grazing these grasslands become colonised by scrub and develop into woodlands.

On steep sheltered banks with moist, base-poor, peaty soils in the wetter parts of Britain U19 *Oreopteris limbosperma-Blechnum spicant* community develops.

Both species are common in northern Lancashire but rarely achieve dominance. It is believed, however, that it occurs in the upper part of the Whitendale valley, which was once wooded. Associated species are few but include *Galium saxatile*, *Oxalis acetosella* and *Potentilla erecta* but it is the dominance of *Oreopteris limbosperma* with a scattering of *Blechnum spicant* that is striking.

At the highest levels on Leck Fell small areas of a heath similar to U7 *Nardus stricta-Carex bigelowii* grass-heath have developed with *Carex bigelowii* at its only Lancashire locality. It is typically a community that only develops where there is a long snow-lie above 600m but on Leck Fell the community is closer to U5 *Nardus stricta-Galium saxatile* grassland. However nearby there is an abundance of *Trichophorum germanicum*, and the hybrid *T. × foersteri* also grows in the vicinity.

Finally, associated with acid block screes on Casterton Fell and formerly elsewhere U21 *Cryptogramma crispa-Deschampsia flexuosa* communities develop. *Cryptogramma crispa* is probably susceptible

Plate 2.42   The summit ridge of Gragareth, Leck supporting a U5 *Nardus stricta-Galium saxatile* grassland.

to both grazing and air pollution and today only remnants of the community flourishing as late as the 1960s remain. However formerly it flourished throughout Bowland, on Waddington Fell, where it was probably lost through quarrying and more surprisingly at low levels on Lancaster Moor. Notable species found in nearby rocky habitats on Casterton Fell include *Dryopteris oreades* and *Gymnocarpium dryopteris*.

Another grass dominated community is M25, *Molinia caerulea-Potentilla erecta* mire dominated by *Molinia caerulea*. Rodwell describes this under mires as it occurs on or creates a thin peat. It may be derived from mesotrophic grassland, especially MG10 *Holcus lanatus-Juncus effusus* rush-pasture or the mire M23 *Juncus effusus/acutiflorus-Galium palustre* rush-pasture. These changes may occur through long neglect of a waterlogged pasture, from other mire vegetation, e.g. with deeper peats, that have dried out following peat removal and drainage or have been subject to frequent burning. The former derivation may have occurred with the *Molinia* dominated hill pastures north of Tarnbrook, Over Wyresdale, but the community occurs elsewhere in Bowland, e.g. Champion Moor, Grindleton. On the other hand *Molinia* dominated grasslands on or surrounding old drying out Fylde Mosses are derived from former raised bogs, e.g. M18 *Erica tetralix-Sphagnum papillosum* raised and blanket mire. Examples can be found surrounding Cockerham and Winmarleigh Mosses and at Out Rawcliffe.

Calcareous Grasslands

A feature of the carboniferous limestone areas of the Craven Pennines and Morecambe Bay is the abundance of calcareous grasslands often dominated by *Sesleria caerulea*. Except at the highest levels and on the most windswept coastal areas, where the climate might limit woodland development, they are all probably derived from woodland. However centuries of grazing eradicated woodland cover and created or maintained the conditions necessary for these grasslands. By 1800 grazing had created an almost treeless landscape and the calcareous grasslands provided a habitat for a number of rare or localised species. From 1900 grazing diminished and today it is absent at many sites with a consequent encroachment of scrub and woodland. Indeed the small breeds of goats and sheep responsible for the former grazing regime are extinct (Mourholme Local History Society, 1998). Peter (1994) and Wright (1998/9) describe the history

Plate 2.43 A view of the Langden valley, Bowland Forest High from Langden Castle looking downstream. This photograph shows a mosaic of plant communities on acid soils including ones dominated by Heather (*Calluna vulgaris*), Bilberry (*Vaccinium myrtillus*), Bracken (*Pteridium aquilinum*) and U4 *Festuca ovina-Agrostis capillaris-Galium saxatile* grassland.

Plate 2.44 A scree slope on Leck Fell supporting little but Fir Clubmoss (*Huperzia selago*) and Broad Buckler-fern (*Dryopteris dilatata*). Similar screes nearby support U21 *Cryptogramma crispa-Deschampsia flexuosa* community.

Plate 2.45 An upland grassland on Marl Hill Moor, Bowland Forest Low supporting a M25 *Molinia caerulea-Potentilla* mire with tussock forming clumps of Purple Moor-grass (*Molinia caerulea*) photographed in early spring.

of land use for Eaves Wood, Silverdale where the grassland on the top of Castlebarrow was almost eliminated and replaced by woodland and scrub. However the National Trust has cleared the scrub in recent years enabling the grassland to become re-established.

Rodwell describes two types of *Sesleria* grassland. Of these only CG9 *Sesleria caerulea-Galium sterneri* grassland is found in VC 60, West Lancaster. It occurs in the Silverdale, Yealand and Warton areas, on Dalton Crags and formerly probably on the limestone in the Hodder valley. However it does not appear to have ever been present at Leck where surprisingly *Sesleria* has not been recorded. Rodwell provides a detailed account of this community around Morecambe Bay. Amongst the rare species that have been found here are *Carex ericetorum*, *Epipactis atrorubens*, *Hippocrepis comosa*, *Minuartia verna* and *Potentilla tabernaemontani*

whilst *Thalictrum minus* occurs on Dalton Crags. It is possible that former colonies of *Antennaria dioica* were part of this community. Often, however, *Sesleria caerulea* occurs as an extensive monoculture, e.g. on Dalton Crags.

Newman (1988), who surveyed calcareous grasslands in Lancashire, also includes in CG9 the grasslands by Hawes Water that developed on shell marl. There are a number of rare species growing here including *Carex lepidocarpa*, *Epipactis atrorubens*, *Galium sterneri*, *Gymnadenea conopsea* ssp. *conopsea*, *Juniperus communis*, *Lithospermum officinale*, *Minuartia verna*, *Parnassia palustris*, *Primula farinosa*, *Selaginella selaginoides* and *Viola hirta* together with an abundance of *Schoenus nigricans* and *Molinia caerulea*. Formerly *Anagallis tenella*, *Dactylorhiza incarnata*, *Dactylorhiza purpurella*, *Gentianella amarella* and *Viola canina* grew here possibly with *Epipactis palustris*. At the southern end of the shell marl area a patch of *Calamagrostis epigejos* dominates the vegetation forming an un-named community with few associated species. The shell marl area is a unique habitat that was clearly wetter when the lake levels were higher and although *Sesleria caerulea* and other grasses are often abundant it may be more appropriate to consider part of the vegetation as a form of mire (see M13 *Schoenus nigricans-Juncus subnodulosus* mire). It is unfortunate that despite being part of a National Nature Reserve the floristic interest of the site is declining quite rapidly, as many of the losses have occurred during the last 50 years.

Also in the Silverdale area, especially on pastures close to the sea, there are a few stands of CG2 *Festuca ovina-Avenula pratensis* grassland. This is part of the lowland European and Continental group of calcicolous grasslands. Generally it is more characteristic of more southerly limestone and chalk with only a few examples of the *Dicranium* sub-community found around Morecambe Bay. In Lancashire it seems to favour south facing slopes. However the community supports a number of rare Lancashire species including *Carex ericetorum*, *Gentianella campestris* (now gone), *Gentianella amarella*, *Spiranthes spiralis*, *Hippocrepis comosa* and *Anacamptis morio*. The extinct *Neotinea ustulata*, *Coeloglossum viride* and *Veronica spicata* may also have been components of this community. This community is also present in the Hodder valley on reef limestone knolls, but there are no rare species associated with the grasslands here. However in VC 59 South Lancaster the similar but more extensive CG2 and CG9 communities on Warsaw Hill are floristically richer. In the Hodder valley the woodland origins are clearly seen with scrub and woodland on some of the hillsides with *Euonymus europaeus* and *Rhamnus catharticus*.

However a recently discovered plant community near Whitewell is CG1 *Festuca ovina-Carlina vulgaris* grassland found on a steep and rocky south facing slope. This is an oceanic community occurring on warm, well-drained rocky slopes in areas with a high rainfall. It is found in western Britain as far north as the North Wales coast so that the present locality is a significant northward extension of its British range.

Towards the summit of Green Hill, Leck, at approximately 600m there are outcrops of limestone as there are also by the Leck Beck. On Green Hill the limestone supports a grassland flora currently (2003) heavily

Plate 2.46 Limestone crags and grassland on Warton Crag Local Nature Reserve supporting a CG9 *Sesleria albicans-Galium sterneri* grassland. Blue Moorgrass (*Sesleria caerulea*) often dominates the community to such an extent that there are few associated species.

grazed by sheep. This probably belongs to the northern montane CG10 *Festuca ovina-Agrostis capillaris-Thymus polytrichus* grassland, probably the *Trifolium-Luzula* sub-community found in the Pennines. Whilst *Galium sterneri* is present *Sesleria caerulea* is absent. Other rare and localised Lancashire species include *Draba incana*, *Cochlearia pyrenaica*, *Minuartia verna*, and *Saxifraga hypnoides*. It is also possible that the extinct *Antennaria dioica* was found in this community. It is perhaps only the complete absence of *Sesleria caerulea* that distinguishes this community occurring at over 600m from the *Saxifraga hypnoides-Cochlearia pyrenaica* sub-community of CG9 *Sesleria caerulea-Galium sterneri* grassland found elsewhere in the Pennines. CG10 also occurs at lower levels on Leck Fell in the absence of *Cochlearia pyrenaica* and *Saxifraga hypnoides*. As with other grasslands this community was probably derived from thin scrubby woodland.

The Inland Broad Rock Habitat (BH16) includes limestone pavements and calcareous and acidic cliffs (see Table 4.7, pp. 561–566). The vegetation found in these habitats was described under woodland, from which most of the present day communities were probably derived. However in the limestone gorge of Ease Gill above Ease Gill Kirk, Leck there are carboniferous limestone cliffs supporting calcareous grassland as well as remains of woodland. Further up the valley there are further limestone cliffs in the vicinity of Long Gill Foot. At the lower levels of Ease Gill the limestone rocks support OV38 *Gymnocarpium robertianum-Arrhenatherum elatius* community. This is a local community in Britain and favours unwooded, sunny slopes. *Brachypodium sylvaticum* and *Geranium robertianum* are often present. Further up the valley in shaded limestone rock crevices OV40 *Asplenium viride-Cystopteris fragilis* community is found. This is a very rare Lancashire community only found here in limited quantity but it is much more common further north in the northern Pennines, Lake District and Scottish Highlands. The crevices in which the community occurs are damp and irrigated by fresh water.

Grassland Summary

Lancashire grasslands are all derived from other habitats and plant communities but the composition of any given community depends upon a complex inter-relationship of geology and soils, climate and land management. Some of the communities, especially MG7 *Lolium perenne* leys and related grasslands, were created in the last 50 years or so and depend upon intensive management and re-sowing to maintain them. On the other hand species-rich calcicolous and mesotrophic grasslands have arisen through centuries or longer periods of grazing and meadow management techniques. This is also true of the upland pastures, but here there is a complex of management practices that links the meadows and grasslands of the valley bottoms, the enclosed hill pastures and the unenclosed grazings higher up the fells in Bowland and Leck. However cultivation of the valley bottoms was limited to the last 200–300 years. Before that they were bogs and fens, too wet to cultivate but were used for rough grazing etc. These practices are described by Winchester (2000) who points out how these developed and evolved over a thousand years into the management techniques practiced in the last 100 years. In understanding these processes it is important to appreciate that most of Bowland was managed as a Royal Forest in medieval times, cattle grazing (vaccaries) was developed between the sixteenth and nineteenth centuries but sheep farming only became important, at least in western Bowland, from the first half of the nineteenth century. This history and the development of grouse shooting in the mid nineteenth century with regular moor burning and a shorter moorland grazing period probably ensured the

Plate 2.47   Limestone crags and grassland with some scrub development at Jack Scout, Silverdale (National Trust). The grassland is CG2 *Festuca ovina-Avenula pratensis* grassland with a rich assemblage of associated species including Rare Spring-sedge (*Carex ericetorum*) and Autumn Lady's-tresses (*Spiranthes spiralis*). Until recently Green-winged Orchid (*Anacamptis morio*) and Field Gentian (*Gentianella campestris*) also occurred in this grassland.

survival of heather moorland in Bowland in contrast to the largely grassy sheep walks of the Cheviots and Southern Uplands.

Thus increasingly intensive management with fertilizers, herbicides, re-seeding and drainage has led to the loss of most species characteristic of species-rich grasslands in lowland Lancashire including those in Bowland where some highly modified mesotrophic grasslands survive, notably at Tarnbrook, Over Wyresdale; Hindburndale and in the Slaidburn area.

However the question remains as to how the species-rich grasslands evolved if the landscape was covered in woodland or wetlands 5,000–7,000 years ago. Throughout the wooded period open spaces and clearings must have survived from the earlier more open post-glacial periods and before Neolithic Man created ever-larger clearings. It has been suggested that grasslands, essentially woodland edge communities, were maintained as wood pasture in clearings created and maintained by large herbivores (Vera, 2000) although this theory has been challenged (Mitchell, 2005).

5. Arable weeds

Introduction

Arable weeds are plants growing in cultivated ground where humans have planted crops. They may be in arable farmland, market gardens, allotments and gardens. Management is aimed at maximising production of crops and in so doing eliminating or attempting to eliminate weeds. Until recently the technology to do this did not exist and in pre-history the difference between weeds and crops was sometimes blurred (Jones, 1988).

Archaeological studies provide some information on pre-history weed floras but in this account of the weed flora of northern Lancashire reliance is made on documentary evidence covering only the last 200 years or so. Although there is an extensive literature on weeds in arable crops this is mostly based on control measures and observations made in midland and southern counties of England (Kay, 2000; Lockton, 2004). Since Neolithic times crops have been cultivated throughout the British Isles but no comprehensive survey and analysis of weed floras has been published although it is known that they vary from region to region (Preston, *et al.*, 2002). However many weed species are threatened with extinction as control measures become increasingly effective. Although this account draws on observations over the whole survey period from 1964 it was becoming increasingly clear that by 2010 herbicide treatments were so efficient that few weeds were left in arable farmland and weeds, if they were present at all, were largely confined to field edges.

The weed flora

In northern Lancashire there was very little data on the composition of the arable or garden weed flora until comparatively recently. Holt (1795) refers to the detrimental effects of weeds on crop production but only mentions couch (*Elytrigia repens*) and dock (*Rumex* spp.). Jenkinson (1775) scarcely mentions them and it is not until the Fieldings' work of the 1830s (Fielding MS) that a better picture emerges of the weed flora. However no systematic survey of the weed flora was undertaken until 1970/71 when 50 fields were examined, and in 1998 when 21 fields were explored. In these surveys the species were recorded until no more could be found in individual fields west of the M6. In addition to the location the type of crop growing was also noted. All the fields were surveyed in late August and early September after the harvest of cereal crops.

During the surveys approximately 175 weed species were recorded growing in arable fields in northern Lancashire of which 59 (34%) were introduced and archaeophytes (see Preston, *et al.*, 2004) accounted for 45 or (or 26% of the total number of species recorded). Of the remaining introduced species (neophytes) four were recent introductions and 10 were relics of cultivation although some, e.g. *Linum usitatissimum*, were very rare by 2000 reflecting the abandonment of flax as a crop plant at least 150 years earlier (Winterbotham, 1986).

Many of the archaeophytes were plants typically associated with cereal crops, which gave fields a show of colour now no longer seen. They included *Papaver* spp., *Glebionis segetum*, *Galeopsis speciosa*, *Agrostemma githago* and *Centaurea cyanus*. Unfortunately it is not possible to define the characteristic weed flora of the eighteenth century but it is likely that many less colourful species were generally common. This was suggested by Holt (1795) referring to couch and docks. By 2000 typical weeds, if present, were generally low growing and inconspicuous.

The changing flora

Despite the lack of data it is probable that in the nineteenth century (and earlier) archaeophytes were proportionately commoner than in the second half of the twentieth century as several species, including some conspicuous ones, had become extinct or nearly so. These include *Agrostemma githago*, *Centaurea cyanus*, *Euphorbia exigua*, *Lithospermum arvense*, *Papaver argemone*, *Ranunculus arvensis*, *Scandix pectin-veneris*, *Sinapis alba* and *Valerianella dentata*. Others, e.g. *Valerianella locusta*, *Papaver rhoeos* and *Papaver dubium* are no longer found as arable weeds but are found as ruderals. The Fieldings considered many of these serious problems but others were rare even in the 1830s, e.g. *Scandix pectin-veneris* and *Valerianella dentata*. A further group of colourful species were perhaps found a little more frequently but were never plentiful so that individual localities were recorded. These included *Agrostemma githago* and *Centaurea cyanus* whilst *Papaver argemone* was confined to sandy soils at Lytham St Anne's and *Ranunculus arvensis* was possibly no more than a casual. Overall of the 47 archaeophytes recorded prior to 1970, 11 were not seen again.

Then, as now, a number of weeds were relics of cultivation. These included grassland species, e.g.

Sanguisorba officinalis (1830) and *Trifolium hybridum* (from 1971). However apart from a few crop species there are very few neophytes in the Lancashire weed flora. These include *Veronica persica* recorded by Hall in 1862 and only recorded in the wild for the first time in Britain in 1825, *Veronica polita, Lepidium didymum* and *Matricaria discoidea*.

Perhaps the most interesting weed species in Lancashire is *Fumaria purpurea*. It is endemic to the British Isles with centres of distribution in southwest England, the Isle of Man and parts of Scotland as well as Lancashire. However in VC 60 it is more commonly found as a ruderal in urban areas, especially in and near Lancaster.

Characterising arable weed species by their Ellenberg values (Hill, *et al.* 2004) gives some indication of change (Table 2.5). This suggests that weed species are light demanding and characteristic of neutral soils. However whilst weeds in the nineteenth century were typically from well-drained soils of intermediate fertility, late twentieth century weeds seem to prefer slightly wetter more fertile soils.

Table 2.5   Average Ellenberg values for arable weeds prior to 1870 and in 1998

Period	Average Ellenberg Values			
	Light	Moisture	Base status	Fertility
Prior to 1870	7.3	4.3	6.7	5.0
1998	7.1	5.5	6.6	6.4
Change	-0.2	+1.2	-0.1	+1.4

In general recorded changes between 1971/2 and 1998 were slight but if the Ellenberg values for species recorded in 1971/2 but not in 1998 were compared with species newly recorded in 1998 some differences emerge (Table 2.6). Although changes are small the differences suggest that increasing soil fertility was taking place, which is in line with statistics for increased use of fertilizers. A summary of these changes is given by Greenwood (2003).

Between 1971/2 and 1998 the commonest weed species remained the same. These were *Stellaria media, Poa annua, Persicaria maculosa, Plantago major* and *Polygonum aviculare s.l.* Other common species recorded in both surveys (over 20% frequency of occurrence) included *Elytrigia repens, Matricaria chamomilla, Taraxacum* spp. *Matricaria discoidea, Glebionis segetum, Chenopodium album, Fallopia convolvulus, Lolium perenne, Senecio vulgaris* and *Veronica persica*. In 1971/2 *Ranunculus repens* was also common whilst in 1998 *Galium aparine* and *Myosotis arvensis* joined this group. More subjectively further changes appeared to be taking place. Weeds were commonly found in fields of root crops in 1971/2 but not in 1998. In both surveys few weeds were found in the growing area of cereal crops (almost none in maize crops) so that weeds were largely confined to the uncultivated edges of fields. Increasingly herbicides are so efficient that within the cultivated areas weeds are eliminated. In 2010 in response to a belief that *Glebionis segetam* was suffering a marked and recent decline an unsuccessful search was made for it in the Fylde, suggesting that the decline was real.

Table 2.6   Changes in Ellenberg values for weeds found in 1971/2 and 1998

Year of survey	Average Ellenberg values			
	Light	Moisture	Base status	Fertility
Species recorded 1971/2 but not 1998	7.0	5.3	5.9	4.9
Species newly recorded 1998	7.0	5.8	6.4	6.0
Change	0	+0.5	+0.5	+1.1

Almost all recent records for arable weeds have been made in lowland Lancashire west of the M6. This has been the main area for arable farming for 150 years. However before then there were arable fields in all areas and some ploughed fields occur today east of the M6. Maize and turnips are often grown here and where fields have been laid to grass for many years dormant arable weed seeds may germinate.

Long-term changes in arable farming were outlined in chapter 2 but general accounts of arable farming were given by Thompson (1933) for the 1930s and by Coppock (1964) for the 1950s. Unfortunately although there have been many changes, both in the location and kinds of crops grown, there is insufficient evidence to link these changes to changes in weed flora. However areas where cultivation has been practiced longest have the potential for the largest seed bank. This implies that till soils, particularly to the west of the M6 but also near villages in the east, and in the Bowland valleys should have the richest weed flora when cultivated but this does not seem to be the case. For the last 200 years arable farming has been concentrated until recently on the reclaimed mossland soils. Here spectacular displays of weeds occurred, especially with *Glebionis segetum* and *Galeopsis speciosa* but more recently efficient herbicide treatments have probably reduced the seed bank.

Phytosociology of arable weed communities

Rodwell (2000) reviewed the phytosociological literature of weed communities and points out that until recently it was largely ignored in England. Drawing on the work of others as well as his own survey teams he divides the communities into three groups. Arable weed and track-side communities of light, less fertile soils; arable weed and wasteland communities of fertile loams and clays and arable weed communities of light limey soils. Also considered here are gateway, trackside and courtyard vegetation, which, whilst not strictly characteristic of arable weeds, may be found at entrances to fields, along tracksides and in the urban environment. Several communities are described within each group and whilst there are no distribution maps a general description of their distribution in Britain is given.

The field surveys of arable weeds carried out in VC 60 during 1971/2 and 1998 did not assign the vegetation to NVC communities. Therefore, the following account is a preliminary assessment of the plant communities that may be found in the western part of the vice-county.

Communities of light, less-fertile, acid soils.

OV1 *Viola arvensis-Aphanes australis* community. This is characterised by the presence of *Aphanes australis, Poa annua, Rumex acetosella* and *Viola arvensis*. It is a local community of southern and eastern Britain north to Angus. In VC 60 all the key species were found on the light peaty soils of reclaimed mosslands at Out Rawcliffe in 1971/2 and they may have been sufficiently abundant to form this community.

OV4 *Glebionis segetum–Spergula arvensis* community is widely distributed, especially in the west of Britain.

Plate 2.48 A typical arable field at Singleton in the Fylde. There are few or no weeds in the cultivated area, here growing potatoes (*Solanum tuberosum*). The few weeds that are present are typical of open communities, e.g. Annual Meadow-grass (*Poa annua*) or Common Field-speedwell (*Veronica persica*) and are confined to the edges of the cultivated area or the field entrance. Rough grassland with Common Couch (*Elytrigia repens*) often occurs between the boundary hedge and the cultivated area.

It was probably this community that was until recently characteristic of reclaimed mosslands and more occasionally in some of the boulder clay areas. However a characteristic feature of many fields, in addition to an abundance of *Glebionis segetum*, was an abundance of *Galeopsis speciosa*.

Communities of fertile loams and clays.

OV7 *Veronica persica–Veronica polita* community is found mostly in southern and eastern England and around the coast elsewhere. *Veronica persica* is a common Lancashire weed and the community is probably widespread in the county.

OV9 *Tripleurospermum inodorum–Stellaria media* community is widespread in Britain and is probably very common in Lancashire. This community was found in a fallow field at Great Plumpton in 2003 where the field was made white by *Tripleurospermum inodorum*. It was still present in 2010.

OV10 *Poa annua–Senecio vulgaris* community occurs throughout Britain but it appears to be rare in Lancashire.

OV11 *Poa annua–Stachys arvensis* community is largely confined to south-western England and Wales. It occurs in Lancashire but seems to be found on lighter soils, especially near the coast.

OV13 *Stellaria media – Capsella bursa-pastoris* community is found throughout lowland Britain where it is often associated with root and vegetable crops. This is a common Lancashire community especially where market garden crops are grown.

Communities of light, limey soils

Neither of the two communities described by Rodwell in this group could be identified with assemblages in Lancashire. Some of the species, e.g. *Kickxia* spp, that give the communities their character do not occur as far north as Lancashire. However, when 50% of farmed land was arable, i.e. before 1830, similar communities might have existed on the limestone soils around Morecambe Bay where one of the key species, *Euphorbia exigua*, was recorded as an arable weed. It is now only known as a rare ruderal of open habitats in the area.

Communities of gateways, track sides and courtyards

The NVC groups a number of plant communities here but two are especially characteristic of rural areas and may dominate the vegetation of fields, which are left fallow for a year.

OV18 *Polygonum aviculare-Matricaria discoidea* community is characteristic of moderately trampled path sides and gateways. A number of species are associated with the community including *Capsella bursa-pastoris*, *Tripleurospermum inodorum* and *Lolium perenne*. In addition *Sisymbrium officinale* and *Plantago major* may become prominent. This is a ubiquitous community throughout the country and may be found at the entrance to any field in northern Lancashire. Frequently it extends into the cropped area of the field.

Very similar to OV18 is OV19 *Poa annua-Tripleurospermum inodorum* community, which is found in similar situations but Rodwell suggests that *Tripleurospermum inodorum* is more sensitive to trampling than *Matricaria discoidea*. It is more common in fallow fields and in urban areas. Associated species may include *Elytrigia repens*, *Senecio squalidus* (in urban areas), *Lolium perenne*, *Atriplex prostrata*, *Chenopodium album* and *Plantago major*. Where *Atriplex patula* and *Chenopodium album* are abundant, as in some potato fields, an *Atriplex prostrata-Chenopodium album* sub community is recognised. In Lancashire potatoes and turnips are important crops and until recently weeds were left to grow, once the main growth had ceased, until harvesting. Consequently from late August to October they were often full of weeds and amongst these *Chenopodium album* was often dominant. Indeed in 2004 a turnip field at Bleasdale was dominated by this species. More recently herbicides have been used to kill all weeds and the top growth of root crops so that at harvesting there is no surface vegetation.

6. Wetlands

Introduction

In chapter 1 it was explained that wetlands of some kind have historically covered large areas of Lancashire. However the kinds of wetlands and where they were found has varied over the millennia. Following the so-called climatic optimum when woodland covered most of the area, fens and open water areas became more extensive in the lowlands, but in time raised bogs or mosses succeeded many of these. By the Bronze Age acidic mires covered large parts of the county both in upland and lowland areas. Many of these survived until the eighteenth century or later.

Today the county still has many wetlands but only a few are remnants of the pre Bronze Age landscape. Many were created by agricultural and industrial developments during the last 200 years.

The resultant matrix is complex and dynamic as succession and change imposed by a variety of factors cause one plant community to become another. Thus many plant communities are linked to others, and although Rodwell (1991b, 1995) describes all the important ones, what is found on the ground does not always fit the published descriptions.

In this account wetlands are simply habitats that are waterlogged permanently or for a large part of each year. They vary from open water communities to acidic, oligotrophic blanket bogs on the summit plateaux of the fells. In between there are numerous types of flushed and marshy areas containing a multitude of different plant communities in addition to small water bodies and running water. In this account only the more distinct communities, excluding mires, are described leaving aside the more ephemeral, ruderal and perhaps recently created habitats where wetland species are also found.

Aquatic habitats

Running water bodies

In addition to the main rivers there are numerous streams most of which in the lowlands have marginal vegetation of some kind. In the uplands few if any species are associated with the swift flowing acidic waters draining the fells but numerous springs and soakways are associated with the valley sides (see mires, above). As the streams flow through the lowlands most have been canalised and what are now highly eutrophic waters also have few associated species. However in a few places aquatic species may be found. These include *Myriophyllum spicatum, Elodea* spp. and *Potamogeton pectinatus.*

Of the larger rivers both the R. Ribble and the R. Lune have specialised communities associated with them. In the R. Ribble where the river flows moderately quickly beds of *Ranunculus penicillatus* ssp. *pseudofluitans* (but probably all *R. × bachii*) form large patches. If the river levels are low in June they form conspicuous white patches. These communities belong to A17 *Ranunculus penicillatus* ssp. *pseudofluitans* community. It is found in base-rich and moderately fertile waters but in the R. Ribble it has flourished despite changes in nutrient status as effluent discharges from industry, sewage works and agriculture have varied. There are few associated species although *Myriophyllum spicatum*, *Potamogeton pectinatus* and *Potamogeton crispus* are sometimes found nearby, but the water-crowfoot usually forms a monoculture. *Ranunculus penicillatus* is also found in the canalised R. Brock and R. Wyre but only in the R. Wyre does it become sufficiently abundant to form the A17 community. Also present in the R. Wyre are both *Myriophyllum spicatum* and *M. alterniflorum*, this latter being sufficiently abundant in places to form a *Myriophyllum alterniflorum* (A14) community.

In the R. Lune there are few species associated with the river itself. However beds of *Carex* spp fringe the banks of the river near Lancaster. The identity of the taxa involved proved difficult to resolve but *Carex acuta, Carex acutiformis* and the hybrid between them, *C. × subgracilis*, are involved. The resulting fringing sedge beds have few associated species. Rodwell (1995) suggests that *C. acuta* is rarely the overwhelming dominant species (although a Fylde pond was dominated by this species) and does not describe a community dominated by it. However he describes a *Carex acutiformis* swamp (S7) and perhaps the Lune sedge beds are most closely allied to this community.

Still waters

Only a few natural open water bodies and their fringing vegetation remain. Hawes Water is by far the most important and is the least modified while the nearby Little Hawes Water that drains into the larger lake may have been influenced by adjacent agricultural changes. Marton Mere bears little resemblance to the natural lake that was formerly present having been largely drained and its banks landscaped. However Cinderbarrow Tarn on the Cumbrian border and Greenhalgh Tarn near Garstang are little known fragments of natural waters. When Greenhalgh Castle was built in 1490 (Hewitson, 1900) it was more or less surrounded by open water and swamps of which the present pool is all that remains.

Other natural or semi-natural pools that remain include the oxbows of the R. Lune between Kirkby Lonsdale and Halton and the shallow pools on Newton Marsh on the Ribble estuary. Newton Marsh was enclosed from a tidal salt marsh by an embankment before 1800 but its drainage was hampered by difficulty in maintaining the sluices (Shakeshaft, 2001) and it was probably not until the twentieth century that the old creeks lost any salt water influence. Today the old creeks form a matrix of freshwater pools and marshes.

In the flood plain of the R. Lune the river naturally changes its course from time to time so that the main channel varied in response to flood events. This however gave no permanence to the fertile pastures that developed and thus presented logistical difficulties to owners and tenants. As a consequence by the twentieth century the river channel was increasingly kept to a single permanent river course. Some of these changes can be traced in successive editions of the Ordnance Survey maps from the middle of the nineteenth century. Today the main channel of the early mid nineteenth century is left as a series of pools, some a metre or so deep, and marshes. These form some of the most important freshwater habitats in northern Lancashire.

Wholly man-made wetlands are numerous and diverse. Marling is an ancient practice but during the eighteenth and early nineteenth centuries when the benefits of marling were better appreciated (Holt, 1795) numerous pits were dug, approximately one to every field. However the pits soon filled with water and ever since have become a refuge for wildlife in the intensively farmed landscape of the boulder clay areas of the county. The flora associated with these

Plate 2.49   River Ribble at Sawley.

Plate 2.50   *Ranunculus × bachii* near Preston. This large flowered, fine-leaved Water-crowfoot is particularly characteristic of the R. Ribble.

Plate 2.51   Hawes Water (part of a National Nature Reserve) is a calcareous lake with a deposit of shell marl at one end. The lake is fringed with reed beds and the shell marl supports a diverse calcicole flora.

pits was described by Day, *et al.* (1982) and their significance and distribution discussed by Boothby and Hull (1999) and Boothby (1997, 2000). Unfortunately many ponds have been lost. Thus in the 10km square SD43 approximately 733 ponds or 39% were lost between 1951 and 2000 (desk study comparing maps).

In the eighteenth and nineteenth centuries many water-powered mills were built each with one or more millponds serviced by mill leets. These have largely gone or are silted up to form marshy areas. However before they were lost *Potamogeton alpinus* was found at Brock Bottoms and *Groenlandia densa* dominated the Thurnham Mill leet.

The building of the Lancaster Canal at the end of the eighteenth century and in the early nineteenth century introduced further freshwater habitats, which unlike the marl pits, was a very slow moving river rather than a still water body. The history of plant colonization, subsequent loss and significance of plant life in the canal and on its banks was described by Greenwood (2005).

In the second half of the nineteenth century

reservoirs were built to provide clean water for the rapidly expanding industrial and seaside resort towns. One of the earliest of these was at Grimsargh completed in 1835 (Hindle, 2002) and the largest, Stocks near Slaidburn, was completed in 1932 (Mitchell, 2004). Many of the reservoirs have interesting habitats associated with them but where water levels fluctuate particularly important communities develop.

Mineral workings of various kinds also leave wetland habitats. Abandoned clay pits, e.g. at Cottam near Preston or Peel in the Fylde, develop a range of base-rich communities. Similarly the limestone quarries at Lundsfield, Carnforth and Arbour, Thornley-with-Wheatley, provide an interesting range of habitats. Many of these were active in the second half of the nineteenth century and continued working well into the twentieth century before abandonment. Similarly other small scale reservoirs, tanks and mill lodges were formed at this time but few survive.

However in the second half of the twentieth century the post war building boom and motorway

Plate 2.52 From Kirkby Lonsdale to Caton the R. Lune meanders through a flood plain creating oxbows as the river channel alters course from time to time. Most of these have been filled in. This photograph shows a surviving oxbow at Melling with deep water supporting submerged aquatics and fringing marsh vegetation.

Plate 2.53 Marl pits were numerous in the Fylde and many still survive. This pit at Grange Park, Preston has been colonised by Water Fern (*Azolla filiculoides*) creating a vivid splash of colour in late summer.

construction work required large quantities of gravel. As a consequence a line of gravel pits developed alongside the M6 motorway. In 2005 the latest of these, at Brockholes, Preston, was due for abandonment and became a nature reserve of the Wildlife Trust for Lancashire, Manchester and North Merseyside in 2009.

Whether natural, semi-natural or wholly man-made there is a wide and complex range of wetland plant communities associated with the habitats provided by these features. The complexity of aquatic communities is explained by Rodwell (1995) and because of this together with the ephemeral nature of some communities and insufficient samples he has not mapped their distribution. Similarly in northern Lancashire many of the plant communities seem to come and go whilst the rapidly changing nature of fresh waters means that a number of once widespread species seem to be disappearing, e.g. *Ceratophyllum demersum*, *Potamogeton perfoliatus* and *Zannichellia palustris*.

The NVC divides aquatic communities into six general groups.

1. Surface and sub-surface duckweed and frogbit vegetation of moderately rich to eutrophic standing waters.
2. Free floating or rooted and submerged pondweed vegetation.
3. Rooted water-lily and pondweed vegetation with floating leaves.
4. Water-crowfoot and starwort vegetation of running waters.
5. Submerged swards of quillworts and hairgrass.
6. Free floating vegetation of impoverished base-poor standing waters.

Representatives or similar communities of all these groups are found in northern Lancashire but it is often difficult to adhere strictly to his scheme especially in respect of R. Lune oxbow communities. In addition it is felt that a seventh group, inundation communities, is best considered here.

1. Surface and sub-surface duckweed and frogbit vegetation of moderately rich to eutrophic standing waters

The first of these is A1 *Lemna gibba* community, which appears to be very rare in northern Lancashire. *Lemna gibba* occurs widely in the lowlands but rarely achieves dominance. It also fluctuates in abundance from year to year and on a few occasions in the mid 1970s it became so abundant in the Lancaster Canal that this community was probably represented at that time.

On the other hand A2 *Lemna minor* community is found frequently in marl pits and in other small water bodies. *Lemna trisulca* may be sufficiently abundant submerged beneath more open mats of *L. minor* to form a sub-community. Interestingly *L. trisulca* only just extends into Cumbria (Halliday, 1997). *Lemna miniscula* has only recently arrived in northern Lancashire but when it was found in the main drain of Lytham Moss it had replaced *L. minor* as the dominant species. Also in this group of communities is *Azolla filiculoides*, another recently arrived species. It is another species with fluctuating levels of abundance and in favourable circumstances can completely cover a pond's surface in a few weeks. This was the situation in 1998 on one of the ponds adjoining Pope Lane, Grange Park, Preston (Plate 2.53).

A3 *Spirodela polyrhiza-Hydrocharis morsus-ranae* community may not now be present in northern Lancashire. This community probably occurred in ditches at Cockerham and in the Fylde where *Hydrocharis morsus-ranae* grew but in its remaining

locality at Pope Lane, Preston it hardly achieves dominance. On the other hand *Spirodela polyrhiza* seems to be becoming more abundant in Fylde marl pits where it occasionally achieves dominance. Associated species may include *Apium nodiflorum*, *Berula erecta*, *Elodea canadensis*, *Glyceria fluitans*, *Lemna gibba*, *L. minor* and *L. trisulca*.

Similar to A3 *Spirodela polyrhiza-Hydrocharis morsus-ranae* community is A4 *Hydrocharis morsus-ranae-Stratiotes aloides* community where the description is largely based on East Anglian examples. However *Stratiotes aloides* was recorded from marl pits in northern Lancashire from the first half of the nineteenth century and still occurs in a few places. When it is present it usually dominates the pond's vegetation. For a few years this also occurred on the Lancaster Canal (Greenwood, 2005). However the community description does not fit the situation in Lancashire. Many of the constant species occur and a rare associate, *Myriophyllum verticillatum*, is found in a pond near Blackpool whilst *Hottonia palustris*, another rare

Plate 2.55 Stocks Reservoir near Slaidburn looking upstream to where the R. Hodder enters the reservoir. The shallow water in this part of the reservoir supports marshes, fens and willow carr.

Plate 2.54 The Lancaster Canal at Garstang in 1967 before herbicide treatments and before an increase in pleasure boating disturbed the plant communities. This photograph shows fringing reed beds often dominated by Yellow Iris (*Iris pseudacorus*) and Sweet-flag (*Acorus calamus*) with the floating leaves of Yellow Water-lily (*Nuphar lutea*) beyond.

Plate 2.56 The fluctuating water levels of reservoirs provides a specialised habitat for some species to colonise the banks when water levels drop. This photograph of Grizedale Reservoir, Nether Wyresdale taken when it was drained for repairs shows the banks covered in OV35 *Lythrum portula-Ranunculus flammula* community supporting an abundance of Shoreweed (*Littorella uniflora*) and Small Water-pepper (*Persicaria minor*).

7. Inundation communities

These are not included by the NVC as wetland communities but are included as vegetation of open habitats. However it is felt they are best considered here for whilst the communities are open they are found in wetlands.

Alopecurus geniculatus-Rorippa palustris community (OV29) is described in the context of mesotrophic grasslands and the upper levels of salt marshes but it can also occur on reservoir shores where water levels fluctuate.

OV31 *Rorippa palustris-Gnaphalium uliginosum* community favours organic, muddy margins of ponds but also occurs on reservoir margins. On nitrogen enriched muds this community is replaced by OV32 *Myosotis scorpioides-Ranunculus sceleratus* community, which is possibly becoming commoner in lowland areas of northern Lancashire. In the R. Lune oxbows at least one drying out pond was dominated by the rare northern Lancashire species *Ranunculus circinatus* forming possibly a variant of OV32

Perhaps the most interesting of the communities subject to the fluctuating water levels of reservoirs is OV35 *Lythrum portula-Ranunculus flammula* community. Besides these two species other rare plants are found here including *Alopecurus aequalis, Limosella aquatica,*

Littorella uniflora and *Persicaria minor*. Closely associated with this community is one dominated by *Juncus filiformis*. The NVC suggests that this is a rare species associated with A10 *Persicaria amphibia* community, which also occurs on reservoir banks. However *Juncus filiformis* is more usually associated with Cumbrian lakes. *Lythrum portula-Ranunculus flammula* community was found in the 1990s at Grizedale Reservoir, Nether Wyresdale but it occurs most abundantly and often in association with *Juncus filiformis* on the shores of Stocks Reservoir. It is perhaps interesting to reflect that reservoirs have provided habitats and refuges for rare species and communities that would otherwise not occur in northern Lancashire. In some cases interesting habitats were lost by their construction, e.g. the reservoirs on Barnacre Moor destroyed a tarn and associated mire habitats with *Wahlenbergia hederacea*, but in most it is not thought that much of botanical significance was lost.

Swamps and tall-herb fens

Swamps and tall-herb fens present another confusing series of communities. Despite a long history of wetland drainage, nutrient rich, waterlogged areas are common. Where drainage attempts failed land became flooded, and where new wetland habitats were created the succession of open water through fens to woodland or bog is often at an early stage of development. Also the availability of propagules and other factors means that it was often a matter of chance what species became established. However many of the species concerned are tall and competitive so that many of the communities are monocultures. The exception to this may be the fen at Hawes Water, which appears to have been a raised bog and/or fen in the seventeenth century. Drainage attempts were made and in addition to the main dyke draining the lake there are traces of the subsidiary dykes. The moss was cut for its peat (Middleton, *et al.*, 1995) but it seems likely that it never provided more than rough grazing following its attempted drainage. It is perhaps this incomplete drainage that allowed the present unusually species-rich fen to develop, which often shows a mosaic of individual tall herbs achieving local dominance.

In addition to communities dominated by tall competitive herbs a number of water-margin and even ephemeral wetland habitats contain a variety of water loving species. These are often species-rich. The communities are found in a wide variety of places including ponds, ditches, recently man-made habitats in gravel and clay pits etc. The following account follows the communities described by Rodwell (1995).

Carex elata is a rare north Lancashire species but occasionally it achieves dominance. This occurred around an outflow of the Tewitfield Locks on the Lancaster Canal but was destroyed by the building of the M6 motorway. Perhaps the only remaining example is the sedge bed surrounding Greenhalgh Tarn near Garstang. The community is described as S1 *Carex elata* sedge-swamp. There are few if any associated species.

Cladium mariscus only occurs around Hawes Water and Little Hawes Water and in places it forms a monoculture, but usually it is part of a more species-rich, tall-herb vegetation (see S25 *Phragmites australis-Eupatorium cannabinum* tall-herb fen). However where dominance is achieved it may form S2 *Cladium mariscus* swamp and sedge-beds. This is a rare community benefiting from warm summers and absence of hard frosts, and is best developed in calcareous basin mires – a rare feature in Britain.

Phragmites australis occurs commonly in lowland Lancashire and at Leighton Moss forms one of the largest reed beds in the country. This developed during the twentieth century following the failure of the pumping engine that enabled the drained Warton and Storrs Mosses to become productive arable land. Today the reed beds are managed by the RSPB to maintain their important nature reserve. There are few associated species. *Phragmites australis* occurs as a dominant feature in many other places, e.g. on the Lancaster Canal. It occasionally dominates marl pits and in recent years extensive reed beds have developed at the top of salt marshes. One of the largest has formed at Burrows Marsh on the Wyre estuary and extends upstream towards Shard Bridge. In all these places the community developed is S4 *Phragmites australis* swamp and reed-bed.

Schoenoplectus lacustris is uncommon in northern Lancashire but in parts of the fen at Hawes Water it forms an S8 *Schoenoplectus lacustris* swamp.

Glyceria maxima is a rare and possibly non-native component of the northern Lancashire flora. However a single clump appeared in 1968 on the Ribble estuary at Warton and by 2000 this had developed into an extensive S5 *Glyceria maxima* swamp.

Carex acuta and *Carex acutiformis* have been discussed earlier in relation to the sedge beds fringing the R. Lune near Lancaster. However *Carex acuta* is much the

rarer of the two species in Lancashire and was only once found as a dominant in a pond at Little Marton, Blackpool. *Carex acutiformis* sometimes dominates the vegetation, e.g. by the Lancaster Canal near Galgate, in the Hodder valley near Newton-in-Bowland and in the R. Lune oxbows to form S7 *Carex acutiformis* swamps. Also in the Lune valley at least one of the oxbows is dominated by *Carex riparia* to form a *Carex riparia* swamp (S6). This, like the more widespread *Carex acutiformis* swamp, is a lowland community but occurs in southern Britain. In the eighteenth century Silverdale Moss was a raised bog. Subsequently it was drained to form wet pasture. However the pasture was difficult to keep drained and by the 1990s it had become flooded supporting a *Carex acutiformis* swamp with *Carex riparia* in places. In 2003 the RSPB acquired the moss and deepened many of the drainage dykes. It remains to be seen how this will affect the vegetation.

Carex rostrata is one of the few species that occurs in both lowland and upland situations. It occurs in shallow, moderately deep, mesotrophic to oligotrophic, standing waters with organic substrates. When it achieves dominance it forms S9 *Carex rostrata* swamp with few associated species. Some of the R. Lune oxbows form a suitable habitat for this community as do the flushes at The Heaning near Newton-in-Bowland. On the tops of the Bowland Fells occasional tarns form a contrasting habitat for this community.

Plate 2.57 Leighton Moss (Royal Society for the Protection of Birds nature reserve) showing reed beds dominated by Common Reed (*Phragmites australis*). Wooded limestone hills are in the background.

In the R. Lune oxbows, pools adjacent to ones dominated by *Carex rostrata* may be dominated by *Equisetum fluviatile* to form S10 *Equisetum fluviatile* swamp. This is, however, a much more widespread community and is found in many marl pits and other marshy areas. It also fringes the shallow end of some reservoirs, e.g. at Longridge, whilst in some places the community is dominated by its hybrids with *Equisetum arvense* (*E. × litorale*) or in one place on the Lancaster Canal with *E. telmateia* (*E. × willmotii*).

Both S12 *Typha latifolia* and S13 *Typha angustifolia* swamps are found in marl pits and by the Lancaster Canal. *Typha latifolia* swamps, however, are much commoner and may be found anywhere in lowland areas with standing or slow-moving mesotrophic to eutrophic waters.

Sparganium erectum is common in lowland Lancashire and becomes sufficiently abundant to dominate the margins of some ponds and parts of the Lancaster Canal. There are few associated species but *Alisma plantago-aquatica*, *Butomus umbellatus*, *Mentha aquatica* and *Myosotis scorpioides* may be locally abundant. Closely associated with this community on the Lancaster Canal is S15 *Acorus calamus* swamp and occasionally it becomes co-dominant with *Sparganium erectum*. *Iris pseudacorus* is a common associated species.

Eleocharis palustris is one of the commonest wetland species and may dominate standing and slow moving waters anywhere from the sand dunes to upland fringe areas. Where it achieves dominance it forms S19 *Eleocharis palustris* swamp.

Schoenoplectus lacustris is a rare Lancashire species but was occasionally recorded erroneously for the much more frequent *Schoenoplectus tabernaemontani*. This is a lowland species found mostly at the top of salt marshes or in coastal freshwater marshes, ponds and lakes. In all of these situations it dominates the vegetation to form S20 *Schoenoplectus tabernaemontani* swamp. Examples can be found around the salt subsidence pools at Preesall, on the salt marsh at Bolton-le-Sands and in Lundsfield Quarry at Carnforth. Closely associated with this community in northern Lancashire are stands of *Juncus subnodulosus*, which at Bolton-le-Sands and in Lundsfield Quarry form monocultures.

Another coastal community is S21 *Bolboschoenus maritimus* swamp. *Bolboschoenus maritimus* is one of the commonest components of the upper salt marsh communities but it extends inland to adjacent brackish or fresh waters. An example occurs for some distance along the lowest section of the Glasson Branch of the Lancaster Canal although by 2010 it was much reduced.

Glyceria fluitans is one of the commonest fresh water species and is characteristic of shallow, standing or sluggish mesotrophic waters. It frequently achieves dominance in wet hollows around ponds to form S22 *Glyceria fluitans* water-margin vegetation.

In similar habitats and occasionally co-dominant with *Glyceria fluitans* is *Alopecurus geniculatus*, which may form the *Alopecurus geniculatus* sub-community. Other taxa that may be confused with *Glyceria fluitans* are *Glyceria notata* and *Glyceria × pedicellata*, and whilst both occur in lowland areas it is not known if they achieve dominance anywhere although Boothby (2000) suggests that *Glyceria notata* at least replaces *Glyceria fluitans* in some ponds. However the blue-green *Glyceria declinata* has also been confused with *Glyceria fluitans* and this dominates the margins of some ponds and damp areas especially in and around the Bowland Fells.

One of the most characteristic assemblages of marshy vegetation in lowland Lancashire is a heterogeneous collection of species with no particular dominants except very locally, and no especially constant species. Typical species include *Alisma plantago-aquatica*, *Apium nodiflorum*, *Galium palustre*, *Mentha aquatica*, *Myosotis scorpioides*, *Ranunculus sceleratus*, *Nasturtium microphyllum*, *Nasturtium officinale*, *Solanum dulcamara*, *Stachys palustris* and *Veronica beccabunga*. More rarely *Berula erecta*, *Veronica anagallis-aquatica* and *Veronica catenata* may be found. Amongst the grasses *Catabrosia aquatica* is sometimes found especially in the northern half of the Lancaster Canal whilst *Callitriche platycarpa*, *Callitriche stagnalis* and *Juncus bufonius* can be seen frequently amongst marshy vegetation. These communities can be found in and around the pools on Newton Marsh, in many ponds, ditches, marl pits and in the R. Lune oxbows or indeed anywhere where there are small water bodies. No doubt because of their heterogeneity Rodwell (1995) grouped them together under S23 water-margin vegetation.

Amongst the tall herb communities S28 *Phalaris arundinacea* tall-herb community is the most common and widespread. It is found throughout the lowland areas and occurs wherever drainage is impeded and in generally mesotrophic to eutrophic conditions. There are generally few associated species but an

Epilobium hirsutum-Urtica dioica sub-community has been described in which both species may occur. *Epilobium hirsutum* may become dominant to form its own community especially in ditches and in some waste ground situations. It then forms OV26 *Epilobium hirsutum* community, widespread throughout the Lancashire lowlands.

At the southern end of Hawes Water the extensive fen contains a few shrubs of which the most notable is *Salix cinerea* ssp. *cinerea* suggesting an affinity with East Anglian fens. *Phragmites australis* dominates large areas forming an S4 *Phragmites australis* reed-bed, but especially characteristic of the area is a more species-rich fen. The presence of *Cladium mariscus* also provides an affinity with East Anglia but this community is S25 *Phragmites australis-Eupatorium cannabinum* tall-herb fen. All three of the sub-communities recognised by Rodwell (1995) are present: *Phragmites australis, Carex paniculata* and *Cladium mariscus* sub-communities. Noteworthy species in the fen include *Carex pseudocyperus, Carex vesicaria, Juncus subnodulosus, Rumex hydrolapathum,* and *Schoenoplectus lacustris.*

Conclusion

It is often difficult to be precise about assigning any given stand of wetland vegetation to a particular plant community and it is often better to regard the community descriptions as a guide. In northern Lancashire, as elsewhere, aquatic communities vary and change over time merging from one to another through inter-mediates. On the coast they merge with brackish and saltwater habitats, in others with fens and mineral flushes whilst in more acidic and oligotrophic conditions with mires, especially in the uplands. Similarly aquatic habitats adjoin and merge with swamp and tall-herb fens.

7. Coastal Communities

Introduction

Northern Lancashire has a long coastline extending for about 165km from Silverdale to the estuary of the R. Ribble at Preston. It is a varied coastline with lime-stone cliffs at Silverdale, sandstone cliffs at Heysham, numerous clay cliffs and many salt marshes in the estuaries, and around Morecambe Bay. Shingle ridges and beaches were once more widespread and the formerly extensive sand dunes are limited to a few fragments particularly in Lytham St Anne's. Almost the whole coastline is modified by human interference

yet parts remain wild and remote and, apart from the built up coasts at Blackpool, Fleetwood, Heysham and Morecambe, most of the coast provides suitable habitats for a wide variety of plant communities and species. Whilst the present sand dunes and salt marshes are of relatively recent origin they are the successors to habitats that have fronted the oscillating position of the coastline for millennia.

Shingle, strandline and sand dune communities

The once extensive shingle habitats at Rossall, Barnaby's Sands on the Wyre estuary and on the coast north of Morecambe have either become stabi-lized by vegetation or replaced by massive sea defence works (as at Rossall). Nevertheless fragments remain and at Carnforth on the Keer estuary slag from the former iron works acts as a man-made shingle habitat.

Rodwell (2000) describes only one shingle community and elements of this can be seen around Cockerham and north of Morecambe. This is SD1 *Rumex crispus-Glaucium flavum* shingle commu-nity with *Rumex crispus* ssp. *littoreus* and more rarely *Glaucium flavum* and *Crambe maritima.* Other species that may be found include *Atriplex glabriuscula, Atriplex laciniata, Atriplex prostrata, Beta vulgaris* ssp. *maritima, Elytrigia juncea, Honckenya peploides, Sonchus arvensis* and *Tripleurospermum maritimum.* Probably only the typical sub-community is represented. However at Barnaby's Sands, where the shingle is largely covered in grassland, the community that has developed may be MG1 *Arrhenatherum elatius* grassland, *Centaurea nigra* sub-community and within that it may be the *Pimpinella saxifraga* variant reflecting its presence here.

Shingle communities often merge with strandline vegetation. In particular communities attributable to SD2 *Honckenya peploides-Cakile maritima* strandline community are found. In these sandier substrates *Cakile maritima* and *Honckenya peploides* are more prom-inent but *Atriplex* spp. are also common. Occasional plants of *Silene uniflora, Sonchus arvensis* and *Elytrigia juncea* can be seen but more interestingly *Polygonum oxyspermum* ssp. *raii* is found here.

Closely similar to SD2 is SD3 *Tripleurospermum maritimum-Galium aparine* strandline community in which *Tripleurospermum maritimum* and *Galium aparine* are more prominent along with *Stellaria media.* This strandline vegetation can also merge with salt marsh communities where *Glaux maritima* is an important constituent.

Plate 2.58 The shore at Bolton-le-Sands showing strandline vegetation (probably SD2 *Honckenya peploides-Cakile maritima* strandline community) in the middle of the photograph with salt marsh vegetation to the left and stabilized shingle to the right with Lyme-grass (*Leymus arenarius*).

Plate 2.59 Mobile sand dunes at St Anne's dominated by Marram (*Ammophila arenaria*).

All these shingle and strandline communities are ephemeral and their appearance at any locality changes from year to year. Their appearance is also greatly influenced by beach cleaning activities at Lytham St Anne's and at Fleetwood where in many years they are not permitted to develop. On the landward side they merge into fore dune communities. However for fore dune and mobile dune communities to develop the strandlines must be colonized by dune forming species. These can tolerate, or need the build up of blown sand through which their shoots can grow.

In northern Lancashire the strandlines are usually colonized by *Elytrigia juncea* ssp. *boreoatlantica* and, where beach cleaning activities allow, SD4 *Elytrigia juncea* ssp. *boreoatlantica* fore dune communities develop. In favourable years these develop at Lytham St Anne's and Fleetwood along with SD2 *Honkenya peploides-Cakile maritima* strandline community. *Eryngium maritimum*, *Polygonum oxyspermum* and *Salsola kali* are some of the rarer associates of these communities.

Eventually the fore dunes are colonized by *Leymus arenarius* and *Ammophila arenaria*. The vegetation on the mobile dunes nearest the sea at both Lytham St Annes and Fleetwood usually belongs to SD5 *Leymus arenarius* mobile dune community. This is often a monoculture

but *Elytrigia juncea* may also be present to form the *Elytrigia juncea* sub-community. In some places *Festuca rubra* becomes important to form a *Festuca rubra* sub-community, as was reported by Radley (1994).

Most of the Lancashire mobile dunes are dominated by *Ammophila arenaria*. This is the major sand binding plant and requires the shifting coastal sands to grow well, building dunes up to 10m high. It forms SD6 *Ammophila arenaria* mobile dunes community and often there are few associated species but some of these give rise to sub-communities. In particular on the more mobile, seaward side of the dunes *Elytrigia juncea* and *Leymus arenarius* may be sufficiently prominent to form the *Elytrigia juncea*, *Elytrigia juncea-Leymus arenarius* or *Leymus arenarius* sub-communities. Where the sand is especially mobile *Ammophila arenaria* may form a monoculture, which is the typical sub-community. Although not mentioned by Rodwell (2000) or Radley (1994), *Euphorbia paralias* is not always an occasional associate, as they suggest, but may dominate large areas particularly on the landward side of mobile dunes, e.g. near Squires Gate. This is a striking feature of the dunes and merits sub-community rank. On the other hand the closely similar *Euphorbia portlandica* favours more stabilized mobile dunes. Also found on the landward side of mobile dunes are *Coincya monensis* ssp. *monensis* and *Raphanus raphanistrum* ssp.

maritimus. More usually as the mobile dunes become stabilized *Festuca rubra* becomes prominent to form the *Festuca rubra* sub-community. *Poa humilis* is a common associate of the more stabilized dunes and can form a *Poa pratensis* sub-community, but this has not been identified in northern Lancashire. On the other hand the *Carex arenaria* sub-community occurs in several places on the Lytham St Anne's dunes.

As stability increases on dunes further inland *Ammophila arenaria* and other species favouring more mobile conditions become less vigorous and whilst *Ammophila arenaria* especially may persist other species become established. Amongst these is *Festuca rubra*, to give rise to SD7 *Ammophila arenaria-Festuca rubra* semi-fixed dune community. In the heavily human modified northern Lancashire dune system the communities may not be typical of more natural situations. Nevertheless the community is widespread. Typical species include *Anthyllis vulneraria, Blackstonia perfoliata, Carlina vulgaris, Cerastium fontanum, Erodium cicutarium, Euphrasia* spp. *Galium verum, Geranium sanguineum, Hypochaeris radicata, Leontodon saxatilis, Lotus corniculatus, Luzula campestris, Ononis repens, Orobanche minor, Pilosella officinarum, Ranunculus bulbosus, Rhinanthus minor, Rubus caesius, Scorzoneroides autumnalis, Sedum acre, Taraxacum* Section *Erythrosperma, Thalictrum minus, Thymus polytrichus, Viola canina* and *Viola tricolor* ssp. *curtisii.* Very often *Salix repens* ssp. *argentea* encroaches up the side of the dunes and in its shelter the rare *Epipactis dunensis* and *Epipactis phyllanthes* var. *pendula* can be found along with *Monotropa hypopitys.* Other orchids include *Anacamptis pyramidalis* and *Ophrys apifera.* *Calystegia soldanella* is often found in this community but in northern Lancashire its only sand dune habitat is now at Fleetwood.

In some places the SD7 community becomes rather open following disturbance with bare sand showing, yet the dune is not subject to much mobility. Early in the year this is the habitat for a variety of early flowering dune annuals. These form SD19 *Phleum arenarium-Arenaria serpyllifolia* dune annual community. Other annuals include *Aira praecox, Centaurium erythraea, Cerastium diffusum, Cerastium semidecandrum, Erophila verna, Erophila glabrescens, Geranium molle, Myosotis ramosissima* and *Vicia lathyroides.* In slightly more mobile conditions and perhaps more appropriately assigned to one of the semi-fixed dune communities, is *Vulpia fasciculata*, which can become especially abundant or locally dominant.

Plate 2.60 Mobile and fixed sand dunes at St Anne's. On the left a salt marsh is developing in front of the sand dunes whilst to the right in the distance the sand dunes have been levelled to form amenity grassland.

Further inland the dunes become predominantly grassy and in northern Lancashire SD8 *Festuca rubra-Galium verum* fixed dune grassland can be found on the older dunes many of which are now part of golf courses. In this community the dominant grass is *Festuca rubra* with an abundance of *Galium verum* that forms a low growing and closed community. Species diversity is reduced from SD7 but many species found there persist. However in northern Lancashire it is not noted for any special rarities and with the development of the seaside resorts much of this community has gone. Nevertheless *Polypodium vulgare* and formerly *Rosa spinosissima* were probably associated with SD8.

Many fixed dune species, especially those belonging to the Fabaceae, fix atmospheric nitrogen and with other nutrients possibly brought in with former human disturbance the vegetation of older dunes can become lush and taller. *Festuca rubra* and *Ammophila arenaria* may be still present but the striking feature of these grasslands is the large tussocks of *Arrhenatherum elatius.* On the landward side of Lytham St Anne's Local Nature Reserve close to the railway there is a large area dominated by this community (SD9 *Ammophila arenaria-Arrhenatherum elatius* dune grassland). There are few associated species but other coarse grasses, e.g. *Dactylis glomerata*, are also present.

Still further inland, on the landward side of the

railway, golf courses were built on links dunes in the second half of the nineteenth century. The sand here is level and overlies former peat bogs, but further inland it thins out until the now drained peat bogs are reached. Formerly a line of shallow lakes or leaches occurred on the link dunes. Unfortunately there are no records of the flora of this habitat or from similar habitats that were found in Sefton south of the R. Ribble. Today the golf courses contain a mosaic of habitats ranging from the intensively managed greens to the more natural fixed dunes and dune heath with occasional recently made ponds and slacks.

The dune heath is of considerable interest for its rarity and occurs in two forms, a *Calluna vulgaris* dominated community and acidic grassland. Of these two, acidic grassland is seen best at Royal Lytham St Anne's and is the most puzzling. The most likely grassland is SD12 *Carex arenaria-Festuca ovina-Agrostis capillaris* dune grassland, but both *Ammophila arenaria* and *Carex arenaria* are rare. In many ways it best fits U4 *Festuca ovina-Agrostis capillaris-Galium saxatilis* grassland although it is no doubt derived from SD12. The key features of this grassland are the dominance of *Festuca filiformis* (rather than *Festuca ovina*) with *Anthoxanthum odoratum, Aphanes australis, Carex leporina, Danthonia decumbens, Deschampsia flexuosa, Galium saxatile, Luzula multiflora* ssp. *multiflora* and *Ornithopus perpusillus*. In wetter patches *Carex nigra, Juncus squarrosus* and *Nardus stricta* are present suggesting this is a U5 *Nardus stricta-Galium saxatile* grassland. Other species present include *Campanula rotundifolia, Dryopteris carthusiana, Hieracium umbellatum, Polypodium vulgare, Thymus polytrichus* and *Trisetum flavescens*.

At the Old Links Golf Course, there is a fine patch of H11 *Calluna vulgaris-Carex arenaria* dune heath. This is found as the typical community with few other species or as the *Empetrum nigrum* sub-community. The few associated species include *Anthoxanthum odoratum, Carex pilulifera, Danthonia decumbens, Equisetum arvense, Galium saxatile, Hieracium umbellatum, Hypochaeris radicata, Juncus conglomeratus, Juncus squarrosus, Nardus stricta, Pilosella officinarum, Polygala serpyllifolia, Salix repens* and *Sanguisorba officinalis*. A single plant of *Pyrola rotundifolia* was also found amongst the heather in 2002 and until at least 1976 *Osmunda regalis* was also present.

Almost all the dune slack or wet hollow communities between the drier dunes were created relatively recently by sand removal. At Fairhaven the remains of a saline lagoon was largely converted into a boating lake and then cut off from it by a pumping station and is drying out, as are the hollows in the Lytham St Anne's Local Nature Reserve. Similarly the hollows on the western side of Clifton Drive created when sand was removed to lessen the incidence of wind blown sand crossing the road are also drying out and no new hollows are being formed. Because so many of the slacks have a recent man-made origin, as indeed have many of the semi-fixed and fixed dunes, the bryophyte flora is poorly represented. As a consequence it is difficult to describe the plant communities that are present in NVC terms. Perhaps the most difficult is the permanently wet slack on the Lytham St Anne's Local Nature Reserve. Various parts of this slack are dominated by *Phalaris arundinacea* (S28 *Phalaris arundinacea* tall-herb fen), *Eriophorum angustifolium* and *Eleocharis palustris* (S19 *Eleocharis palustris* swamp), but part of the slack is dominated by the hybrid *Juncus balticus* × *Juncus inflexus*. This was first seen in 1966.

Bearing in mind the absence of diagnostic bryophytes, there are few if any examples of the most open and immature dune slack communities, e.g. SD13 *Sagina nodosa-Bryum pseudotriquetrum* dune slack community. *Salix repens* dominates many of the slacks and these are no doubt related to SD14 *Salix repens-Campylum stellatum*, SD15 *Salix repens-Calliergon cuspidatum*, and SD16 *Salix repens-Holcus lanatus* dune slack communities. SD14 is the youngest of these

Plate 2.61 A view looking north across the large dune slack at Lytham St Anne's Local Nature Reserve with fixed dunes beyond with developing scrub on some of them.

communities and floods regularly in winter, whilst SD16 is an older, drier community. In addition SD17 *Potentilla anserina-Carex nigra* dune slack community also occurs: this indicates an older community and characteristic of more northern dune systems where heavier rainfall enhances leaching but also keeps the vegetation from drying out in summer.

These dune slack communities are home to a range of rare species. In the younger slacks are *Carex oederi* and *Equisetum variegatum*. However it is in the intermediately aged slacks where some of the most interesting species occur. These include *Anagallis tenella, Centaurium littorale, Dactylorhiza fuchsii, Dactylorhiza incarnata* (mostly sspp. *coccinea* and *incarnata*), *Dactylorhiza praetermissa, Dactylorhiza purpurella* and *Epipactis palustris* together with numerous *Dactylorhiza* hybrids. Also present in an artificially created slack on the St Anne's Old Links Golf Course is *Parentucellia viscosus*, and *Blysmus compressus* occurs in an old slack at Fairhaven. In some of the wet hollows *Hydrocotyle vulgaris* and *Mentha aquatica* are present whilst in drier places *Agrostis stolonifera, Carex flacca, Festuca rubra, Holcus lanatus* and *Lotus corniculatus* are abundant.

As the dunes mature shrubs invade the semi-fixed and fixed dunes as well as dune slacks. SD18 *Hippophae rhamnoides* dune scrub *Urtica dioica-Arrhenatherum elatius* sub-community was recognised by Radley (1994). *Hippophae rhamnoides* was not known from the

northern Lancashire sand dunes until 1956 and it is still not abundant. In this sub-community the dune vegetation is obliterated and occasional nitrophilous species such as *Urtica dioica* and *Solanum dulcamara* are found. However a range of other shrubs and small trees form localised communities in which *Acer pseudoplatanus* is the most important but patches of *Populus* spp., *Rosa multiflora* and *Rosa rugosa* scrub also occur. Most importantly the dunes carry populations of *Salix* taxa. The species include *Salix alba, Salix cinerea* ssp. *oleifolia, Salix caprea, Salix fragilis, Salix pentandra,* and *Salix viminalis*. More interestingly a range of rare hybrids occur including *Salix × multinervis (S. aurita × S. cinerea* ssp. *oleifolia), Salix × holosericea (S. cinerea × S. viminalis), Salix × reichardtii (S. caprea × S. cinerea), Salix × subserica (S. cinerea × S. repens), Salix × friesiana (S. viminalis × S. repens)* and *Salix × angusensis (S. viminalis × S. cinerea × S. repens)* and some of these form dense thickets. The presence of *Salix × multinervis* is interesting as one parent, *Salix aurita,* has not been seen on the dunes yet it must once have been common in a zone between the sand dunes and the mosses further inland.

In addition to the observations of Radley (1994) the unpublished surveys of Nissenbaum (1989) and University of Liverpool Environmental Research and Consultancy (2005) have been consulted. Nissenbaum's work was completed before the NVC sand dune accounts were fully available and her records for SD10 *Carex arenaria* dune community from the Lytham St Anne's Local Nature Reserve may be erroneous. Whilst *Carex arenaria* can be dominant locally, the rare associates of this East Anglian community, *Astragalus danicus* and *Corynephorus canescens,* do not occur in northern Lancashire. However it is noteworthy that *Corynephorus canescens* is found on the Sefton dunes in VC 59.

The University of Liverpool also identified SD10 and additionally SD11 *Carex arenaria-Cornicularia aculeata* dune community as occurring on the Fylde coast. This is also an East Anglian community. Other communities they recorded were MC9 *Festuca rubra-Holcus lanatus* maritime grassland, MG1 *Arrhenatherum elatius* grassland and OV23 *Lolium perenne-Dactylis glomerata* community. MC9 is a maritime cliff community and whilst something similar may have been found a sand dune habitat is not suitable for it. Both MG1 and OV23 are likely to occur, the former on mature dunes and OV23 in more disturbed areas of older dunes.

Plate 2.62 Common Cord-grass (*Spartina anglica*) colonising mud flats at Middleton. Mud flats may also be colonised by Glassworts (*Salicornia* spp.). Both form the lowest zones of salt marshes.

Salt marshes

Introduction

The salt marsh habitat is readily definable but Rodwell (2000) suggests that it is difficult to define the communities that make up the vegetation. There is considerable variation from marsh to marsh and whilst the best known and perhaps best studied are on the north Norfolk coast, salt marshes are distributed all round the coasts of the British Isles. In Lancashire they extend at intervals along the whole coast and many of them are extensive wild areas, which have received detailed study. The Morecambe Bay marshes were studied by Adam (2000) who refers to earlier work by Gray (1972) and Robinson and Pringle (1987). On the Wyre estuary Horwood (2003) carried out detailed surveys for Canatxx Gas Storage Ltd. These studies show that Lancashire salt marshes are as diverse as any in the country.

The NVC describes salt-marsh communities under four headings.
1. Eel-grass and tassel-weed communities of tidal flats, pools and ditches
2. Lower salt-marsh communities
3. Middle salt-marsh communities
4. Upper salt-marsh communities.

In addition there are transitional communities where the vegetation is more characteristic of inland habitats but which also occur at the highest levels of salt marshes and are perhaps inundated by the highest spring tides.

1. Eel-grass and tassel-weed communities

There are three communities recognised in this group only one of which occurs in northern Lancashire. Typically at the lowest levels of a muddy shore *Zostera* spp. are found but whilst there are records to the north and south of VC 60 no *Zostera* spp. have been found in the vice-county.

However *Ruppia maritima* has been found at various times in permanently water-filled pans on salt marshes from the Ribble estuary to Morecambe Bay. In recent years it has been recorded in pools and ditches at Middleton, Bolton-le-Sands and Warton but its occurrence varies from year to year. In 2003 it dominated an artificial pool at Warton to form SM2 *Ruppia maritima* salt-marsh community. Also until the recent population explosion of wildfowl this community was seen regularly at Fairhaven Marine Lake.

2. Lower salt-marsh communities

The distinctions between the low- mid- and upper-salt-marsh communities are often indistinct with one merging into another. By far the commonest plant community is one dominated by *Spartina anglica*. This occurs on all the Lancashire salt marshes having been planted on the Ribble estuary in 1932, and ten years later it was found on the Wyre Estuary (Hubbard and Stebbings, 1967). The first records for *Spartina anglica* on marshes further north were in the Overton and Sunderland areas where it was planted in 1955 (Garlick 1957a) and at Bolton-le-Sands also in 1955 (Garlick, 1957b). By the late 1960s *Spartina* marshes were extensive along the whole coastline where the muddy conditions it prefers were present. These marshes are attributable to SM6 *Spartina anglica* salt-marsh community. This community seems to develop rapidly in the initial years following colonization but then tends to die back in some places. There are few associated species.

Also found as pioneers of bare mud at the lowest levels of salt marshes as well as in pans and other bare areas higher up the marsh are communities dominated by *Salicornia* spp., *Suaeda maritima* and *Puccinellia maritima*. SM8 Annual *Salicornia* salt-marsh community tends to occur as patches rather than in extensive zones. Its extent was possibly reduced by the spread of *Spartina anglica* communities in the lowest parts of salt marshes that are inundated by the tide for extensive periods each day. *Salicornia* spp. are difficult to identify (Stace, 2010) but it might be possible to distinguish sub-communities based on different species. In Lancashire all the species currently recognised within *Salicornia europaea* agg. (diploid species) and *Salicornia procumbens* agg. (tetraploid species) occur. According to Stace (2010) the distinctive and common *S. dolichostachya* (tetraploid) is found mainly on the lower parts of salt marshes whilst *S. ramosissima* (diploid) is typically found at middle and upper levels and *S. europaea* (diploid) may be found at any level. Whilst these distinctions may be true overall it is felt that in Lancashire all species may be found within the same extended communities. The annual *Salicornia* salt-marsh community is found in suitable places on all the marshes and although not now so popular, *Salicornia* is still harvested to provide a Lancashire delicacy.

SM9 *Suaeda maritima* salt-marsh community is generally found as strips or patches on mud often along the top of creek edges or in pans. It is found

Plate 2.63 A salt marsh on the Wyre estuary characteristic of the mid zones of an ungrazed salt marsh.

on most of the marshes, often as a monoculture but sometimes with *Salicornia* spp. and less frequently with other species.

SM10 Transitional low-marsh vegetation with *Puccinellia maritima*, annual *Salicornia* species and *Suaeda maritima* is species poor. It occurs in similar places to SM8 and SM9 but is probably transitional between 'Salicornia' rich SM9 and SM13 *Puccinellia maritima* salt-marsh community. It probably occurs on several of the Lancashire marshes and Rodwell (2000) shows that marshes in Morecambe Bay are a particular stronghold.

Aster tripolium is a common component of Lancashire salt marshes. Most plants are ligulate and belong to var. *tripolium* but var. *flosculosus*, without ligulate flowers, is also present (Sell and Murrell, 2006). *A. tripolium* var. *tripolium* is abundant alongside some creeks on lower salt marshes and here may form a distinct community as tentatively suggested by Rodwell (2000), but it does not achieve the dominance that *A. tripolium* var. *flosculosus* does on East Anglian marshes.

3. Middle salt-marsh communities

With less tidal inundation the low salt marsh communities gradually merge into the mid and upper marsh communities.

As the name suggests SM13 *Puccinellia maritima* salt-marsh community is usually dominated by *Puccinellia maritima* but several sub-communities are recognised depending upon the presence and abundance of associated species. Grazing pressure in turn influences these. Generally Lancashire salt marshes were thought to be all grazed by cattle or sheep or used for turf cutting. Undoubtedly the long history of grazing has influenced the vegetation but some salt marshes have only been grazed lightly or not at all, e.g. on the north bank of the Wyre estuary at Barnaby's Sands and Burrows Marsh. However over the last 40 years or so grazing seems to have become less prevalent and turf cutting has ceased altogether. As a consequence the sub-communities associated with SM13 show considerable variation.

Vegetation dominated by *Puccinellia maritima* is extensive and widespread on mid zones of salt marsh in the British Isles. This is especially true in Lancashire where it is particularly associated with grazing marshes. It is often a monoculture but *Salicornia* spp., *Suaeda maritima*, *Triglochin maritimum*, *Plantago maritima* and *Aster tripolium* may be associates.

Associated with grazing marshes is a sub-community where *Glaux maritima* is abundant. It is often found higher up the marsh in hollows or, as at Hest Bank and Bolton-le-Sands, where public pressure has lowered the surface at the back of the marsh to create a lower marsh community. On the Wyre estuary, where there is little or no grazing, this sub-community is rare.

A feature of the ungrazed Burrows Marsh and Barnaby's Sands is the presence of *Limonium vulgare-Armeria maritima* sub-community. In July and August this provides one of the most colourful spectacles in Lancashire's landscape covering large areas of the marsh in a purple carpet. The colour is provided largely by an abundance of *Limonium vulgare, Limonium humile* and hybrids between them. Also present is *Aster tripolium* and *Armeria maritima* but the latter flowers earlier and does not provide such a colourful display. Other species present are *Triglochin maritima, Plantago maritima Atriplex portulacoides* (in a low growing form), *Salicornia* spp., *Suaeda maritima* and *Spergularia media. Puccinellia maritima* is not abundant and towards the inland or higher parts of the marsh *Festuca rubra* and *Juncus gerardii* are more important.

This *Limonium vulgare-Armeria maritima* sub-community is seen elsewhere on ungrazed or lightly grazed marshes on the Lune estuary and on the marshes from Sunderland Point to Middleton, but as *Limonium* spp. are particularly sensitive to grazing it does not achieve the dominance found on the Wyre marshes. However at Granny's Bay, Fairhaven, a new ungrazed marsh has developed over the last 40 years. Here a single plant of *Limonium vulgare* became established and although sterile, this plant has spread vegetatively as a single clone to form a *Limonium vulgare-Armeria maritima* sub-community. More recently *Limonium vulgare* has been joined by *Limonium humile*. Whilst the community at Granny's Bay has been identified as belonging to SM13 *Puccinellia maritima* salt-marsh community a nearby more recently developed salt marsh with *Limonium* spp. has been identified as belonging to SM6 *Spartina anglica* salt-marsh community. Also *Limonium* spp. appeared for the first time on the salt marshes on the south side of the Ribble estuary in 2008 (Smith and Greenwood, 2009). These observations suggest that given suitable conditions both *Limonium vulgare* and *L. humile* readily colonise ungrazed salt marshes even at an early stage of their development.

The *Plantago maritima-Armeria maritima* sub-community occurs around Morecambe Bay and less frequently on the Wyre estuary. *Limonium* spp. and *Atriplex portulacoides* are absent and *Puccinellia maritima* is present but with low cover. The sub-community seems to be associated more with grazed marshes.

Another feature of many salt marshes is the presence of the grey shrub *Atriplex portulacoides*. This occurs as large hemispherical bushes or patches or, as on the Wyre estuary where it is especially abundant, as large zones fringing the tops of the creeks. In these situations it forms a conspicuous feature of the marsh. Although it is not grazed it is sensitive to trampling so that this is another community found mostly on ungrazed or lightly grazed marshes. The community formed is SM14 *Atriplex portulacoides* salt-marsh which is particularly widespread in south-eastern England.

Juncus maritimus generally does not dominate Lancashire salt marshes but Rodwell (2000) records SM15 *Juncus maritimus-Triglochin maritimum* salt-marsh from the Wyre and Lune estuaries. This is dominant at Cockerham although recent sea defence works may have restricted its presence.

On the grazed salt marshes of the west coast SM13 *Puccinellia maritima* salt-marsh community typical sub-community passes directly into a *Festuca rubra* dominated zone – SM16 *Festuca rubra* salt-marsh

Plate 2.64 Sea-lavenders (*Limonium vulgare* and *L. humile*) provide a colourful spectacle in summer at Barnaby's Sands (a Lancashire Wildlife Trust reserve) on the Wyre estuary.

Plate 2.65 Meandering through the mid marsh zones of a salt marsh are deep creeks. Very often the lips of the creeks are fringed by a zone of Sea-purslane (*Atriplex portulacoides*), which may extend further into the marsh as here to form SM14 *Atriplex portulacoides* salt-marsh community.

community with few associated species. There may be a transitional zone between the two communities where both dominant species intermingle – *Festuca rubra* salt-marsh *Puccinellia maritima* sub-community. However the range of vegetation types within SM16 is complex and related to the amount of tidal inundation and grazing pressure. On the most heavily grazed marshes, e.g. on the Ribble estuary and parts of Morecambe Bay, a fine short turf is produced with *Festuca rubra* and, towards the upper reaches, *Agrostis stolonifera* becomes increasingly prominent. *Plantago maritima*, *Glaux maritima*, *Triglochin maritimum* and *Armeria maritima* may all be present to a varying extent in less intensively grazed marshes although *Glaux maritima* is often the most important giving rise to the *Festuca rubra-Glaux maritima* sub-community. Where grazing ceases this sub-community often develops into a tall *Festuca rubra* dominated vegetation – tall *Festuca rubra* sub-community, e.g. on the south side of the Wyre estuary near Fleetwood.

Three other sub-communities are also present. Nearly always within SM16 there are large patches of *Juncus gerardii* forming a *Juncus gerardii* sub-community. This is found on all the salt marshes, grazed or ungrazed, and is usually found at the higher levels. Similarly two other sub-communities are found at the higher levels. *Trifolium repens* is found in both, but in the *Leontodon autumnalis* sub-community *Scorzoneroides (Leontodon) autumnalis* and *Potentilla anserina* are frequent. Also perhaps belonging here is *Plantago major* often as ssp. *intermedia*. However the *Leontodon autumnalis* sub-community is often more floristically rich, especially on marshes that are ungrazed or lightly grazed by cattle, e.g. at Middleton. Species that might be present include *Bromus hordeaceus*, *Carex distans*, *Cynosurus cristatus*, *Elytrigia repens*, *Centaurium* spp., *Lolium perenne*, *Poa pratensis*, *Odontites verna* and *Trifolium fragiferum*, these latter two often associated with fresh water seepage. Also associated with fresh water seepage are *Apium graveolens*, *Carex disticha*, *Carex otrubae*, *Eleocharis quinqueflora*, *Juncus ranarius*, *Myosotis laxa*, *Ranunculus baudotii* (but not seen recently on salt marshes), *Ranunculus sceleratus*, *Samolus valerandi* and *Triglochin palustre*. In places *Scorzoneroides autumnalis* is replaced by patches of *Carex flacca* to form a *Carex flacca* sub-community. From the Wyre estuary northwards and especially in the vicinity of Bolton-le-Sands and Carnforth, particularly where there is some fresh water seepage, 'Juncus compressus like' can be found, often forming patches with, but usually

Plate 2.66 On the shores of Morecambe Bay the salt marshes have been grazed by sheep and cattle for centuries. In this photograph of the grazing marsh at Warton near Carnforth a dense sward of Red Fescue (*Festuca rubra* ssp. *litoralis*) dominates the vegetation to form SM16 *Festuca rubra* salt marsh community.

slightly above *Juncus gerardii* zones. The presence of this on salt marshes was not appreciated until recently and doubts exist as to its identity.

Although not mentioned by Rodwell (2000) *Carex extensa* can be frequent. Also present in both SM13 and SM16 communities are *Cochlearia anglica* and *Plantago coronopus*, the latter more especially in the upper reaches of SM16 whilst the former occurs throughout both communities. There is some doubt about the identity of salt marsh *Cochlearia* (Halliday, 1997) but it is now believed that most plants are *C. atlantica*. *Cochlearia officinalis* probably does not occur.

Rodwell (2000, Figure 9, p.75) provides a detailed description of the plant communities present at Bolton-le-Sands. In particular he shows how the sub-communities of SM16 are related to each other and how these merge into other mid-marsh and upper-marsh communities.

During the last 40 years or so *Artemisia maritima* seems to have increased in abundance, probably in response to a reduction in grazing pressure. On the Wyre estuary it is abundant at Barnaby's Sands especially on the ridges on the inside of the spit extending from the end of Arm Hill. There are few other species but it may occur with *Festuca rubra*, *Atriplex portulacoides* and *Plantago maritima*. When *Artemisia maritima* dominates the vegetation it is referred to SM17 *Artemesia maritima* salt-marsh community.

Artemesia maritima occurs in two communities. It forms a sub-community in the lower marsh, SM15 *Juncus maritimus-Triglochin maritimum* salt-marsh community, but it also occurs more abundantly higher up the marsh as SM18 *Juncus maritimus* salt-marsh community. This latter occurs to some extent on all the Lancashire salt marshes and is distinguished from SM15 communities by the presence of upper marsh species, e.g. *Agrostis stolonifera, Festuca rubra, Glaux maritima* and *Juncus gerardii*. One of the characteristic species associated with this taller vegetation is *Oenanthe lachenalii* giving rise to the *Oenanthe lachenalii* sub-community. The community is resistant to some grazing, e.g. at Middleton, but whilst *Juncus maritimus* is unpalatable it is susceptible to trampling. This community is mostly found on the west coast of Britain and is especially characteristic of Lancashire salt marshes.

Along the shores of Morecambe Bay *Blysmus rufus* forms characteristic patches often alternating with *Juncus gerardii* (SM16 *Festuca rubra* salt-marsh community *Juncus gerardii* sub-community). It also occurs on the Wyre estuary but many of its former stations have been swamped by taller growing vegetation. Where *Blysmus rufus* forms extensive patches it forms a species poor SM19 *Blysmus rufus* salt-marsh community. This is a northern type of salt marsh community.

Also a northern community is SM20 *Eleocharis uniglumis* salt-marsh community. Rodwell (2000) records this from Bolton-le-Sands but it has occurred occasionally on other salt marshes from the Wyre estuary northwards.

Two further species occur on drier but often stabilized stony surfaces, especially at Arm Hill, Barnaby's Sands on the Wyre estuary. Here the boulder clay spit of Arm Hill extends southwards into the estuary with a series of spit laterals often only distinguished from the salt marsh vegetation by forming slightly higher ridges supporting mesotrophic grassland, MG1 *Arrhenatherum elatius* grassland. In East Anglia similar lateral spits support SM21 *Suaeda vera-Limonium binervosum* salt-marsh but Lancashire is far away from the natural distribution of *Suaeda vera*. Nevertheless there is one large patch of *Limonium britannicum* ssp. *celticum* (formerly identified as *L. binervosum*), which might properly be referred to this community. *Limonium britannicum* was formerly much more widespread but today it is confined to the Wyre estuary where it is more frequently found on old sea walls. Also found in the drier parts of marshes is *Parapholis strigosa* which can dominate small areas of this drier zone, especially on the Wyre marshes. Except when it is in flower or fruit it is easily overlooked. It might possibly belong to SM27 Ephemeral salt-marsh vegetation with *Sagina maritima*. *Sagina maritima* is a common coastal species often found in cracks in pavements and sea walls as well as in open habitats on salt marshes.

4. Upper salt-marsh communities

Only a few salt marshes preserve the uppermost zones intact; usually they have been truncated by reclamation schemes. However the uppermost zones can be found in places notably on the estuary of the R. Conder and as the tidal influences decrease upstream on other river estuaries, e.g. R. Lune and R. Wyre.

Uppermost salt marsh zones, which themselves merge into brackish communities, are often dominated by extensive areas of *Elytrigia* taxa. Rodwell (2000) describes these as SM24 *Elytrigia atherica* and SM28 *Elytrigia repens* salt-marsh communities and shows both as occurring in Lancashire. The identification of salt marsh *Elytrigia* has long been a problem but only recently has the difficulty been resolved (Greenwood, 2004). Although *Elytrigia atherica* dominated zones almost certainly existed this species is now extinct in Lancashire. Nevertheless hybrids with *Elytrigia repens* (*E. × drucei*) and *Elytrigia juncea* (*E. × acuta*) are found, as is the hybrid between *Elytrigia juncea* and *Elytrigia repens* (*E. × laxa*). All three hybrids are difficult to identify and to distinguish from glaucous forms of *Elytrigia repens*.

So far as can be ascertained *Elytrigia × drucei* is much the commonest taxon and dominates extensive areas of the upper salt marsh along the whole coast. It often forms a monoculture and can extend as a strip 10–20m wide for long stretches, e.g. for nearly 2km alongside Freckleton Pool on the Ribble estuary. It usually occupies a zone that is flooded by most tides.

In several places, e.g. at Barnaby's Sands on the Wyre estuary and on the coast at Bolton-le-Sands etc. sandy or gravelly areas occur in close association with salt marshes and often support *Elytrigia juncea*. Where salt marshes meet these habitats a zone dominated by *Elytrigia × acuta* can occur on its own or occupying a zone above *Elytrigia × drucei* where the marsh is perhaps not inundated quite so frequently. *Elytrigia × laxa* has not been found to dominate salt marshes

Plate 2.67 At the highest levels of many salt marshes the vegetation is dominated by Couches. In northern Lancashire this is usually the hybrid *Elytrigia × drucei* with *E. repens* at the highest levels where it is rarely inundated even by the highest spring tides. These communities are variants of SM24 *Elytrigia atherica* salt-marsh community.

and is usually found as clumps in drier or sandy areas, although on the south bank of the Ribble estuary at Crossens it does form a distinct salt marsh zone. Finally, as Rodwell rightly indicates, *Elytrigia repens* can dominate the highest parts of salt marshes but in a position that is rarely inundated by seawater. This zone can be found at Lytham and on most marshes on the Wyre estuary. The transition from *Elytrigia × drucei* dominated salt marsh to one dominated by *Elytrigia repens* can be seen upstream from Cartford Bridge. Salt marshes dominated by *Elytrigia repens* are referred to SM28 *Elymus repens* salt-marsh community and seem to be confined to the west coast of Britain.

Associated with these upper marsh communities are *Atriplex* spp. Occasionally they dominate the vegetation as on parts of the Ribble estuary or at Conder Green. There can be a confusing complex of taxa but *Atriplex prostrata* is the most commonly encountered taxon with *Atriplex littoralis* much less frequent. However, hybrids with the very rare Lancashire species, *Atriplex longipes*, also occur. *Atriplex longipes* is a northern species typically found at the highest levels of salt marshes, mostly reclaimed for agriculture, but in Lancashire the only records are from Conder Green and Lea on the Ribble estuary. *Atriplex prostrata × A. longipes* (*A. × gustafssoniana*) is frequent and may be

found on any of the Lancashire salt marshes. It is a fertile annual that produces abundant seed.

Where fresh water seeps into the upper salt marsh zones, perhaps from springs in clay banks backing the marsh, a number of swamp communities occur in addition to the shorter herb dominated communities described earlier. S4 *Phragmites australis* swamp and reedbed is a developing feature and these have extended rapidly upstream from Burrows Marsh on the Wyre estuary. In so doing they have obliterated the more open and lower growing plant communities characterised by such species as *Blysmus rufus, Centaurium littorale, Triglochin palustre, Samolus valerandi* etc. Nevertheless the taller and more competitive *Thalictrum flavum* still survives along with *Apium graveolens*, which also occurs in upper salt marsh zones elsewhere. Although only rarely inundated by salt water some of the reed beds, often in ditches, behind the sea walls at Conder Green and Cockerham support the beautiful pink-flowered, oceanic *Calystegia sepium* ssp. *roseata*.

Another frequent community at the top of salt marshes is S21 *Bolboschoenus maritimus* swamp and this too can develop into extensive zones on some marshes. Likewise although much less frequent is S20 *Schoenoplectus tabernaemontani* swamp, which dominates parts of the Bolton-le-Sands marsh.

At Warton on the Ribble estuary a single clump of *Glyceria maxima* became established sometime in the mid 1960s. This is a very rare north Lancashire species and is probably introduced in most locations. However at Warton the single clump has developed into an extensive S5 *Glyceria maxima* swamp. Similarly a small clump of *Carex divisa* established itself nearby and this too now forms an extensive community in the marsh.

It is not known why these tall herb communities should have developed so much in recent years but it may relate to the decrease in grazing pressure and the cessation of dredging in the Ribble channel following the closure of the Port of Preston. Increased nitrogen pollution may also be a factor favouring these communities.

Although not frequent MG12 *Festuca arundinacea* grassland is sometimes found at the top edge of salt marshes. In the *Oenanthe lachenalii* sub-community an array of salt marsh species, e.g. *Oenanthe lachenalii, Juncus gerardii, Glaux maritima, Juncus maritimus* and *Triglochin maritimum* may be found. At Hambleton on the Wyre estuary *Thalictrum flavum* is also present.

Also often found in this community are the large yellow flowers of *Sonchus arvensis*. It frequently grows on detritus left by the highest spring tides along with *Atriplex prostrata*, *Hypochaeris radicata*, and *Scorzoneroides autumnalis*.

Other grasslands backing salt marshes in northern Lancashire include MG1 *Arrhenatherum elatius*, MG6 *Lolium perenne-Cynosurus cristatus*, MG11 *Festuca rubra-Agrostis stolonifera-Potentilla anserina* and MG13 *Agrostis stolonifera-Alopecurus geniculatus* grasslands. MG11 is particularly important and backs many of the Lancashire salt marshes. It occurs in its typical form with *Potentilla anserina* often dominant but in the *Atriplex prostrata* sub-community *A. prostrata* is abundant with *Tripleurospermum maritimum*, *Polygonum aviculare* and less commonly *Oenanthe lachenalii* and *Silene vulgaris*. The *Lolium perenne* sub-community is also frequent and here *Lolium perenne* is often co-dominant with *Agrostis stolonifera* together with varying amounts of *Festuca rubra* and *Potentilla anserina*.

Amongst the transitional communities to wetland vegetation, often found in ditches behind the salt marsh, may be found S28 *Phalaris arundinacea* tall-herb fen or S26 *Phragmites australis-Urtica dioica* tall-herb fen *Oenanthe crocata* sub-community with *Oenanthe crocata* usually present. Also often found in these tall herb communities is *Iris pseudacorus*.

Conclusion

The vegetation of Lancashire salt marshes is complex and varied. It is unfortunate that so many of the marshes are truncated by sea walls as further variety with transition zones to raised bogs are missing. Nevertheless complete transects across salt marshes from low to upper marsh zones can be seen at several places often ending with clay banks, which indicate that at some time they were eroded by the sea at a time when no salt marsh existed in front of them. More remarkably on the Wyre estuary the same vegetational sequences from low to upper marsh zones can be seen at the riverside level as one travels up the estuary from its mouth to some distance above Cartford Bridge where the saltwater influence finally dissipates towards St Michael's on Wyre.

There is still much to learn about the dynamics of salt marshes and the causal influences for change. Plant identification problems, with many hybrids, add to the complexity but this also suggests that in this Broad Habitat evolution of new species is actively taking place.

The Lancashire salt marshes are generally characterised as typical of the west coast but this is possibly based on the grazing marshes of Morecambe Bay and the Ribble estuary with their low growing grassy swards of *Puccinellia maritima* and *Festuca rubra*. However the plant communities of the ungrazed Wyre marshes are reminiscent of East Anglia. Yet the juxtaposition of northern, southern and oceanic species suggests that befitting this central location in the British Isles they are simply unique and amongst the most diverse and interesting in the British Isles if not western Europe.

Coastal cliffs

Introduction

Despite Lancashire's long coastline there are only a few limestone and sandstone rocky coastal cliffs, but there are numerous boulder clay cliffs, mostly with salt marshes in front of them. Unfortunately the vegetation associated with them has received little attention and none were surveyed by Rodwell (2000). Furthermore, whilst he recognised the importance of earth cliffs in eastern and southern England he admitted that even there they had received little attention. This presents some difficulty in assigning this group of habitats to any recognised scheme. With the exception of woodland communities Rodwell (2000) covers most of the communities found in northern Lancashire in his chapter on maritime cliff communities. Yet despite being almost completely ignored clay cliffs are a conspicuous feature of the coast from northern Wales to Cumbria and along other Irish Sea coasts.

Limestone cliffs

These occur at Silverdale but they too have received little attention. Most are covered in open communities of CG9 *Sesleria caerulea-Galium sterneri* grassland but with increasing shelter they support forms of W8 *Fraxinus excelsior-Acer campestre-Mercurialis perennis* woodland although *Acer campestre* is absent. However amongst the trees the rare *Sorbus torminalis*, *S. rupicola* and *S. lancastriensis* are found. These features are perhaps best seen in the vicinity of Jack Scout round to Cow's Mouth. Towards the Cumbrian border at Silverdale Cove some of the cliffs have become colonised by garden escapes of which *Erysimum cheiri*,

Plate 2.68 At Silverdale the coast is bordered by a line of limestone cliffs as here at Jack Scout (a National Trust property). These support a variety of grasslands, scrub and woodland. Amongst the trees found on the cliffs are Lancastrian Whitebeam (*Sorbus lancastriensis*) and Wild Service-tree (*Sorbus torminalis*), both often in a stunted form.

first recorded in 1864 (Ashfield, 1864), is perhaps the most noteworthy. Some species have become extinct including *Asplenium marinum* seen by Simpson (1843) but apparently lost by 1864 (Ashfield, 1864). *Antennaria dioica* and *Veronica spicata*, both now gone from Silverdale, also grew on or near the cliffs.

Sandstone cliffs

At Heysham there is an exposure of sandstone with a maritime cliff flora irrigated by fresh water from above. Here there is an interesting assemblage including *Asplenium marinum, Calluna vulgaris, Carex arenaria, Carex distans, Cochlearia officinalis, Danthonia decumbens, Festuca rubra* ssp. *juncea, Hyacinthoides non-scripta, Osmunda regalis, Polypodium vulgare* agg., *Sedum telephium, Senecio sylvatica, Silene uniflora, Teucrium scorodonia,* and *Viola riviniana*.

Boulder clay cliffs

The boulder clay cliffs that outcrop at intervals from the Ribble estuary to Carnforth support vegetation that is related to the degree of erosion and proximity to the sea. Unfortunately there are no detailed surveys of this vegetation and only a paragraph was ever written about them (Greenwood, 1972).

The most exposed cliffs occur at North Shore, Blackpool but these have all been stabilized and made into promenade gardens etc. Nevertheless the maritime nature of the flora that formerly existed was still seen in 1968 with the presence of *Armeria maritima, Aster tripolium, Atriplex littoralis, Atriplex portulacoides, Carex arenaria, Carex distans, Catapodium marinum, Crambe maritima, Glaux maritima, Honckenia peploides, Puccinellia maritima, Salicornia* spp., *Silene uniflora* and *Spergularia marina*.

Plate 2.69 The only sandstone cliffs in northern Lancashire are at Half Moon Bay, Heysham. Amongst the rarer plants found on them are Royal Fern (*Osmunda regalis*), Sea Spleenwort (*Asplenium marinum*), Orpine (*Sedum telephium*) and Common Scurvygrass (*Cochlearia officinalis*).

However most cliffs are more sheltered, although still subject to varying degrees of erosion according to the extent of their exposure. Also they are largely ungrazed by domestic stock. On the cliffs at Bolton-le-Sands there is a form of MG1 *Arrhenatherum elatius* grassland but varying from open to closed communities. In contrast to this ubiquitous community so common on roadsides and other inland habitats, these coastal clay cliff communities can be floristically diverse and in these situations are unusually little affected by human impact. Because these cliff communities have not previously been studied it is not possible to detail the sub-communities. Nevertheless there is considerable variation in the vegetation influenced by the nature of the clay although most are calcareous. Also the presence of springs not only affects water status but cliff stability.

In addition to *Arrhenatherum elatius* other grasses include *Agrostis capillaris, Agrostis stolonifera, Anthoxanthum odoratum, Brachypodium sylvaticum, Bromus hordeaceus, Cynosurus cristatus, Dactylis glomerata, Festuca rubra, Lolium perenne*, and *Poa pratensis s.l.* Much more rarely *Calamagrostis epigejos* is found, e.g. on the Wyre estuary and at Conder Green. Calcicole species include *Carlina vulgaris, Centaurium erythraea, Clinopodium vulgare* and *Linum catharticum* whilst in marshy areas *Achillea ptarmica, Angelica sylvestris, Carex flacca, Carex nigra, Carex panicea, Filipendula ulmaria, Juncus articulatus, Juncus acutiformis, Juncus effusus, Juncus inflexus, Pulicaria dysenterica* and *Scutellaria galericulata* may be present. Other scarce species include *Ononis repens, Ononis spinosa* (very rare) and *Dipsacus fullonum. Helminthotheca echioides* and *Blackstonia perfoliata* have also been found occasionally.

On some of the clay cliffs from the Wyre estuary northwards grasslands dominated by *Festuca arundinacea* forming MG12 *Festuca arundinacea* grassland occur. *Agrostis stolonifera* and *Festuca rubra* are common associates. This community also occurs at the top of salt marshes in the same area.

Over the years species lists were compiled for eleven clay cliffs with over 220 species recorded, but on more stable cliffs in sheltered situations scrub and woodland develops although these vegetation types are species poor. *Crataegus monogyna* is an early colonizer along with *Rosa* spp. Other shrubs include *Corylus avellana, Ilex aquifolium, Prunus spinosa, Rubus* spp., *Salix cinerea* ssp. *oleifolia, Sambucus nigra, Ulex europaeus*, and *Viburnum opulus*. On the most stable slopes low growing woodland becomes established, e.g. by the R. Ribble and Freckleton Pool, with *Acer pseudoplatanus, Alnus glutinosa, Fraxinus excelsior, Malus* spp., *Salix alba, Salix fragilis* and *Salix viminalis* amongst the species present. *Quercus* spp. are rare. The ground flora is usually sparse but often includes *Arum maculatum, Athyrium filix-femina, Dryopteris dilatata, Dryopteris filix-mas, Geranium robertianum, Hedera helix, Hyacinthoides non-scripta, Silene dioica, Asplenium scolopendrium, Poa trivialis* and *Rumex sanguineus*.

Most of these clay cliff woodlands have become established in their present position only in the last 100 years or so and their species diversity and composition contrast markedly with ancient woodlands found inland. The relative importance of *Acer pseudoplatanus*

Plate 2.70   Clay cliffs border many of the estuaries and these may have open grassland, scrub or woodland communities. This photograph taken at Barnaby's Sands on the Wyre estuary (a Lancashire Wildlife Trust nature reserve) shows grassland and scrub on the clay and gravel bank with a stony salt marsh in front.

and rarity of *Quercus* spp. reflects the greater competitiveness of the former whilst the paucity of species probably reflects the lack of woodlands in the immediate vicinity to provide a seed source. Nevertheless these woodlands and other communities found on coastal clay cliffs are as natural as any in northern Lancashire.

Sea walls

The only other coastal 'cliffs' or hard surfaces are sea walls. Recently built walls with smooth unbroken surfaces support little vegetation but where crevices appear they are soon colonized by salt tolerant species, e.g. *Armeria maritima, Catapodium marinum,*

Cochlearia danica, Plantago coronopus, Sagina maritima and *Tripleurospermum maritimum* etc. However in some places, e.g. on the R. Wyre at Knott End *Crithmum maritimum* is found whilst on older walls made out of stone blocks *Limonium humile, Limonium vulgare* and *Festuca rubra* ssp. *juncea* occur. Much more rarely along the Wyre estuary *Limonium britannicum* grows on the oldest walls. The communities involved are probably forms of MC1 *Crithmum maritimum-Spergularia rupicola* maritime rock-crevice community although *Spergularia rupicola* does not occur. Sometimes grassy vegetation covers the whole wall and perhaps the communities should then be referred to MC8 *Festuca rubra-Armeria maritima* maritime grassland.

Urban and post-industrial sites

Introduction

Previous sections showed that there are few if any habitats that are not profoundly influenced by human activities, not just in recent years but also over millennia. Although there have been successive waves of human influence many of the habitats and plant communities seen in the early years of the twenty-first century were ones that, in many instances, had survived for a very long time. Nevertheless each successive wave left its mark although usually it is the most recent activities that have the greatest effect on the habitats and plant communities that are seen today.

The urban and industrial landscape is constantly changing. Little is known of the habitats and plant communities inhabiting the urban landscape from the Roman period to the eighteenth century. Here and there, there are snippets of information. Archaeological work reveals a few of the plants that grew in the Roman forts and settlements. Similarly there are a few records from the early years of the industrial revolution. Unfortunately detailed ecological and floristic studies are largely limited to the second half of the twentieth century.

Many of the plant communities found in urban and industrial areas have been described in previous sections, as few are unique to this landscape, e.g. the flora and plant communities associated with reservoirs and millponds are covered under wetlands. Often urban and industrial plant communities represent stages in a seral succession that is generally not allowed, for various reasons, to reach a climax or, in some places, the plant communities that became established are so interesting that current management is aimed at arresting further plant succession.

The first comprehensive account of the ecology of urban habitats was by Gilbert (1989) who reviewed the existing literature, often from continental Europe or elsewhere, and described the situation in this country. Here he relied heavily on his own work in Sheffield. Since then there have been several detailed studies on different aspects of the urban and industrial environment but providing a comprehensive description of the plant communities has proved difficult.

Tucker, *et al.* (2005) reviewed the current extent of knowledge, defined what is meant by urban habitats and provided a concordance table showing the relationships between Broad Habitats, Gilbert types (i.e.

Plate 2.71 If left undisturbed abandoned limestone quarries develop a rich calcicole flora often forming a refuge for rare species. Trowbarrow quarry, Yealand Redmayne shown here was not abandoned until 1965 but even then it was known for its rare plants including Fly Orchid (*Ophrys insectifera*). It is now a Local Nature Reserve.

as described by Gilbert, 1989), Phase 1 types and NVC types (Rodwell, 1991–2000). They also provided an analysis of the plant communities (as defined by NVC) found within the urban environment. Overall however Rodwell (1991–2000) described few of the plant communities that are only found in the urban environment.

In northern Lancashire little attention has been given to the urban and industrial landscape and in this account only a brief review highlighting particular features of interest is given.

Mineral extraction

From earliest times stone, clay and gravel etc. have been extracted from the ground leaving behind a variety of holes, heaps and quarries. These were eventually abandoned often then providing a refuge for the local wildlife.

Amongst the earliest holes to be dug were marl pits and the flora associated with these conspicuous features of the boulder clay landscape has been considered under wetlands. Similarly quarries were opened to provide stone for building, or in the case of limestone, to provide lime for agriculture. They have received little attention in northern Lancashire yet some of the abandoned limestone quarries have proved of botanical interest. They support a calcicolous flora with calcareous grassland and scrub on the quarry floor although in places this may be sufficiently wet to provide marsh, aquatic or even mire conditions, e.g. this occurred in an abandoned quarry at Thornley near Chipping. Some of the rare species associated with limestone quarries include *Carex diandra*, *Carex lepidocarpa*, *Clinopodium acinos*, *Clinopodium vulgare*, *Gentianella amarella*, *Ophrys insectifera* and *Potamogeton alpinus*. The quarry faces forming cliffs were not explored but *Brassica oleracea* has colonised the quarry face at Warton whilst *Dryopteris submontana* has been found in a Bowland quarry.

Much more widespread in Bowland are old grit quarries but few were explored. Heathy vegetation colonizes the rocky surfaces including *Calluna vulgaris*, *Deschampsia flexuosa*, *Dryopteris dilatata* and *Vaccinium myrtillus*. However very occasionally some of the rarest calcifugous species have colonised them. Most remarkable was the colonisation of the quarries on Lancaster Moor, possibly in the eighteenth century or earlier, and at Waddington by *Cryptogramma crispa* (gone at both localities). Other grit quarries that have become important refugia for rare species are in the Lune valley. At Backsbottom in Roeburndale *Neottia nidus-avis* was found in the slate quarry in 1965 and again in 1988. This quarry was used in the building of Wray in the seventeenth century and later. It was known to be active in the early nineteenth century (Hudson, 2000) and remained operational until the early twentieth century (Kenyon, 2008). Not far away by Dale Beck on Botton Head Fell another slate quarry was probably abandoned by 1844 when the survey was undertaken for the first edition of the Ordnance Survey maps. It was probably used in building local farms and a date stone at Botton Head Farm is dated 1666. Here a number of ferns find a refuge including, unusually for an acid grit stone quarry, *Cystopteris fragilis*. In recent years *Lycopodium clavatum* has also colonised old grit quarries but of greatest interest is the colonisation by *Diphasiastrum alpinum* of a recently abandoned quarry in Gisburn Forest. The nearest source of spores for this latter species is possibly North Wales, some 90km to the southwest. Also found in a quarry in Croasdale is *Dryopteris oreades* whilst *Huperzia selago* is another rare colonizer of grit quarries.

In areas where stone was scarce clay was used to make bricks and tile drains. As a consequence many brick pits were opened but most of these were eventually reclaimed for various purposes. At Peel and Cottam two remained abandoned and these became havens for wildlife. Perhaps not dissimilar to brick pits was a gravel pit and quarry at Carnforth. This was quarried for the abundance of limestone found in drift deposits. All three sites are similar in so far as there is a matrix of wet and dry areas within the context of sticky calcareous clay. In all three the plant communities are a mixture of calcareous to mesotrophic grasslands, scrub, marsh and aquatic communities all of which have been described elsewhere. Probably many of the communities found in the wet or marshy areas belong to S23 Other

Plate 2.72 Until recently it was not appreciated that the acid rocks in abandoned quarries in Bowland could provide a refuge for rare calcifuge species. Little is known about Dale Beck quarry in Hindburndale but it must have been abandoned at least 100 years ago. Today there are a number of rare species in the quarry and on its tipped spoil including Parsley Fern (*Cryptogramma crispa*). This photograph shows the quarry spoil overlooking Dale Beck.

Plate 2.73 Abandoned gravel and clay pits provide a refuge for many species. Marsh orchids (*Dactylorhiza* spp.) can be particularly plentiful. One of the more recently abandoned gravel pits is Brockholes near Preston, which is now a Lancashire Wildlife Trust nature reserve. This photograph shows one of the ponds with Boilton Wood behind.

water-margin vegetation. However the particular significance of these sites is the abundance of orchids. Old abandoned clay pits were first recognised as important refuges for marsh orchids by Richardson (1957) who described the flora that had colonised clay pits in Co. Durham. In Lancashire marsh orchids have colonised clay pits in several places in south Lancashire as well as further north, but all share essentially the same flora. *Dactylorhiza fuchsii* is always present and usually either *Dactylorhiza praetermissa* or *Dactylorhiza purpurella* but rarely both. Hybrids between the marsh orchids and Common Spotted-orchid invariably occur and together these orchids can dominate the clay pit floor. *Neottia ovata* is also often present. More rarely *Anacamptis pyramidalis*, *Dactylorhiza incarnata* ssp. *coccinea*, *Epipactis palustris* and *Ophrys apifera* complete the assemblage of orchids.

One such assemblage was found on Leblanc waste in South Lancashire (Gilbert, 1989; Ash, 1999). There are few habitats where such a rich orchid flora can be seen in northern Lancashire. At a Carnforth quarry other rare species were found. Of particular note was a colony of *Equisetum variegatum* and another of *Juncus subnodulosus* that was sufficiently abundant in one area to form its own community similar to those found at the top of some salt marshes, e.g. at Bolton-le-Sands located only a few kilometres to the west.

Towards the end of the twentieth century an enormous demand for gravel developed to meet the needs of the construction industry and especially motorway building, so a line of gravel pits was opened near to what was to become the M6 motorway. In particular there are flooded pits in the Wyre valley around Scorton and to the north of Carnforth. Older abandoned pits were found at Knott End and Preesall where some salt subsidence pools were formed and indeed are still being formed. Apart from a flooded gravel pit at Scorton, a pit at Claughton near Garstang and the recently abandoned Brockholes complex at Preston, now a nature reserve, the gravel pit flora has not been studied.

A flooded gravel pit near Scorton was formed between 1961 and 1964 and the first plant records were made in 1967. At that time many parts of the banks supported open communities with many bare areas and it was noted that the pH of the clay and gravel was 6.8. Round the edges there were many shallow areas and small reed beds with *Typha latifolia* abundant (probably S12 *Typha latifolia* swamp). Other areas were dominated by *Elodea canadensis* (A15 *Elodea canadensis* community) with *Myriophyllum spicatum* and *Potamogeton berchtoldii*. The only other detailed records were made in 1971 when 141 species were recorded from the lake and its surrounding banks. Marshy areas probably belonged to S23 Other water-margin vegetation, but amongst the aquatics *Potamogeton crispus*, *Potamogeton pusillus*, *Potamogeton natans* and *Callitriche hermaphroditica* were recorded. This latter species came to dominate the shallow waters of some of the gravel pits for a period shortly after they were formed.

At Claughton, near Garstang, observations of the changing flora were made at intervals between 1967, one year after the pit was dug, and 2006. The pit had few shallow areas and the banks sloped steeply to a depth of about 9.6m. The exposed boulder clay on the banks of the pit was highly calcareous with a pH of 8.3. By 1969 there was a zone of *Potamogeton natans* 3–4m wide (A9 *Potamogeton natans* community) at the sheltered south-western corner of the pit together with a zone less than a metre wide of *Glyceria × pedicellata*. A narrower zone of submerged aquatics extended all the way round the pit with *Elodea canadensis*, *Myriophyllum spicatum*, *Potamogeton crispus* and *Potamogeton berchtoldii* (probably A15 *Elodea canadensis* community). In subsequent years there were changes in detail but the pattern set in the early years remained with individual species disappearing and others colonizing. However two noteworthy early colonizers, *Ruppia maritima* and *Ranunculus circinatus*, did not persist. Both were unusual. *Ruppia maritima* is a species of brackish water on the coast and *Ranunculus circinatus* is a rare species of mesotrophic to eutrophic water and at that time grew in a nearby marl pit. As there was no inflow of

water to the gravel pit from surface streams all the plants colonizing the pit came either from wind born propagules or were brought in by animals. Gulls of various species used the lake as a resting place and they may have been responsible for the introduction of some species particularly *Ruppia maritima*.

One year after the pit was formed 40 species had colonized its waters and banks. After five years there were still only 42 species although there had been changes in the species composition. In subsequent years more species arrived and others disappeared. By 1991, 25 years later, 90 species were recorded and 37 of the original colonizers were still present. However after a further 15 years, 40 years from when the pit was abandoned, only 74 species were recorded and 26 of these had been found in the first five years. Altogether a total of 131 species were recorded over the 40-year time-span. These figures are only a guide as to what has happened, as the recording method was simple being based on a single visit in summer. Inevitably species were missed. Also the fishing club and/or owners may have introduced species and other unknown management practices will have been undertaken, e.g. the pit is stocked with different species of fish. Nevertheless the observed changes suggest that for the first 25 years plant diversity increased but species both came and went. Perhaps surprisingly the floating leaf communities dominated by *Potamogeton natans* and *Persicaria amphibia* disappeared, perhaps deliberately removed. Then, between 1991 and 2006, species diversity decreased. By this time the pit was surrounded by marginal vegetation and for the first time *Alisma plantago-aquatica* and *Sparganium erectum* made their appearance in 2006. Both are characteristic of pond marginal vegetation. Also of interest in the 2006 list is the replacement of *Elodea canadensis* by *E. nuttallii* and *Potamogeton berchtoldii* by *P. pusillus*, both in line with changes occurring nationally. Furthermore the decrease in species diversity noted in 2006 is consistent with the development of mature communities. Clearly succession was not straightforward.

Bradshaw (1999) discussed succession in the context of urban wastelands (see below) and suggested three models for colonization. In the *facilitation* model early colonizers 'improve' the habitat allowing subsequent species to colonize and grow and he argued that this is what happens in urban wastelands. In the *tolerance* model changes in succession are driven more by accident of arrival combined with speed of growth.

Plate 2.74 Iron slag from the Carnforth iron works, which closed in 1929 (Price, 1983), was tipped on the nearby Warton salt marsh. It weathers very slowly but provides a refuge for several calcicole species found on the adjacent limestone hills.

Finally in the *inhibition* model later species may not be able to invade because the site is already occupied. This may well be true for older more mature habitats with closed communities (e.g. on sand dunes) but at Claughton there were still plenty of opportunities for further colonization in 1991 but perhaps not by 2006. At Claughton it seems that both the *facilitation* model (perhaps applicable to the clay banks only) and the *tolerance* model were operating. What is clear is that plant colonization was complex involving species coming and going, and whilst chance is important, vectors, such as birds (especially gulls), humans (who fish the lake from stock they have introduced) and other animals are all important in ensuring a continuing supply of propagules that may colonize the pit and its surrounding banks providing a suitable niche is available.

The complex of gravel pits at Brockholes, Preston was abandoned in 2006 and the first survey of the flora was undertaken that year. Colonization of the pits was well under way but much of the area was in the early pioneer stages of colonization. Nevertheless 166 taxa were recorded on a single visit in July and although a number of local species were noted the only rare species seen was *Rorippa islandica*. Also recorded for the first time in northern Lancashire was the hybrid bulrush *Typha × glauca*. The old gravel workings are now a nature reserve of the Wildlife

Trust for Lancashire, Manchester and N. Merseyside. Hopefully it will be possible to follow the colonization process as the site matures.

Mining operations often produce spoil heaps but fortunately in northern Lancashire coalmines were small operations and have left little trace. Metal ores were extracted in parts of Bowland but they too have left few interesting spoil heaps. Nevertheless at Warton there are banks of iron slag extending south-westwards across the salt marsh and then turning north-westwards for a total distance of approximately 2.25km. They are the remains of the iron smelting industry developed at Carnforth in 1864 but closed in 1929. The industry depended on coal (coke) mined in Co. Durham, iron ore in Cumbria and limestone quarried locally (Price, 1983). As a waste product of the process calcium oxide (from the limestone) reacted with siliceous earth material from the ore to form a fusible slag containing mainly silicates. This cools to form a hard, chemically fairly stable material that under the influence of acid rain weathers slowly (P.N. Reed, pers. comm.). Over the years it provides a habitat for some calcicolous species. However there are few nutrients for plant growth so that today the vegetation is sparse, even on the oldest heaps.

However this inhospitable habitat supports nearly 100 taxa of vascular plants. Most are plants favouring open, nutrient poor habitats with basic soils, whilst the maritime location ensures that a number of coastal taxa are present. Many of the taxa are rare or localised in northern Lancashire.

Notable coastal species include the hybrid grass *Elytrigia × acuta*, *Rumex crispus* ssp. *littoreus*, *Raphanus raphanistrum* ssp. *maritimus* and *Glaucium flavum*. A few are confined to the limestone around Morecambe Bay, e.g. *Clinopodium acinos*, *Euphorbia exigua*, or more widely distributed on limestone, e.g. *Galium sterneri* and *Helianthemum nummularia*. A further group are found in coastal localities usually on limestone or sand dunes. These include *Cerastium semidecandrum*, *Carlina vulgaris*, *Erigeron acer*, *Euphrasia tetraquetra* (or hybrids), *Inula conyzae* and *Myosotis ramosissima*. They are particularly adapted to the dry conditions either by completing their life cycle before the onset of summer drought (dune annuals) or have deep rooting systems. Finally *Poa angustifolia* was also found on the slag and this rare species seems to be confined to limestone soils or railway ballast, perhaps a relic of the ballast that was used to support the tramway that brought the slag from the iron works.

The iron slag heaps are remarkable for the highly specialist maritime and basic habitats they provide, which just happen to match the requirements of a number of Lancashire's rarest species. Here they find a refuge whilst a variety of environmental forces threaten their more natural habitats.

Although ephemeral landfill sites were formerly rewarding for their alien flora, today tipped material is quickly covered and the seeds from a variety of sources found in waste material do not have an opportunity to germinate, grow and flower. Blackpool tip especially produced a number of interesting records in the 1960s.

Table 2.7   Species recorded from a Claughton Gravel Pit

Species	1967	1969	1971	1979	1991	2006
Acer pseudoplatanus	-	-	-	-	-	+
Achillea millefolium	+	-	-	-	+	+
Agrostis capillaris	+	+	-	-	+	+
Agrostis stolonifera	+	+	+	+	+	+
Alnus glutinosa	-	-	+	+	+	+
Alopecurus geniculatus	+	+	+	+	-	-
Alopecurus pratensis	-	-	-	-	+	-
Angelica sylvestris	-	-	-	+	+	+
Anthriscus sylvestris	-	-	-	-	+	+
Arrhenatherum elatius	-	-	-	-	-	+
Betula pendula	-	-	-	-	-	+
Betula pubescens	-	-	+	+	+	+
Carex hirta	-	+	+	+	+	+
Carex leporina	-	-	+	-	-	-
Carex nigra	-	-	-	-	+	-
Carex remota	-	-	-	-	+	+
Cerastium fontanum	+	+	-	+	+	+
Chamerion angustifolium	-	-	-	-	+	-
Chenopodium album	-	-	+	-	-	-
Cirsium arvense	+	+	+	+	+	+
Cirsium palustre	-	-	-	-	-	+
Cirsium vulgare	-	-	-	-	+	+

Species	1967	1969	1971	1979	1991	2006
Cotoneaster simonsii	-	-	-	-	+	+
Crepis capillaris	-	-	-	-	+	+
Cynosurus cristatus	-	-	-	-	+	-
Cytisus scoparius	-	-	-	-	+	+
Dactylis glomerata	-	+	+	+	-	+
Dactylorhiza fuchsii	-	-	-	-	+	+
Dryopteris affinis	-	-	-	-	+	-
Dryopteris filix-mas	-	-	-	-	-	+
Eleocharis palustris	-	-	+	+	+	+
Elodea canadensis	-	+	+	+	-	-
Elodea nuttallii	-	-	-	-	-	+
Elytrigia repens	-	-	-	+	-	+
Epilobium ciliatum	-	-	-	-	+	-
Epilobium hirsutum	+	+	+	+	+	+
Epilobium montanum	-	-	-	-	+	-
Epilobium palustre	-	+	-	+	+	-
Equisetum arvense	+	+	+	+	+	-
Equisetum palustre	-	-	-	+	-	-
Festuca pratensis	-	-	-	-	+	-
Festuca rubra	-	-	-	-	+	+
Fraxinus excelsior	-	-	-	-	+	+
Galium aparine	-	-	-	-	+	+
Glyceria declinata	+	+	+	-	+	-
Glyceria fluitans	+	+	+	+	-	-
Glyceria × pedicellata	-	-	+	-	-	-
Callitriche spp.	+	-	-	-	-	-
Heracleum sphondyllium	-	-	-	-	+	-
Holcus lanatus	+	+	+	+	+	-
Holcus mollis	-	-	-	-	-	+
Iris pseudacorus	-	-	-	+	+	+
Isolepis setacea	-	+	-	-	-	-
Juncus acutiflorus	+	-	+	-	+	-
Juncus articulatus	+	+	+	+	+	+
Juncus bufonius	+	+	+	+	+	+
Juncus conglomeratus	+	+	+	+	-	-
Juncus effusus	+	+	+	+	+	+
Juncus inflexus	-	-	+	+	+	+
Larix decidua	-	-	-	-	-	+

Species	1967	1969	1971	1979	1991	2006
Lathyrus pratensis	-	-	-	-	+	+
Lemna minor	-	+	-	-	-	-
Lolium perenne	+	+	-	+	+	+
Lotus corniculatus	-	-	-	-	+	-
Lotus pedicillatus	-	-	-	-	+	+
Lycopus europaeus	-	-	-	-	+	+
Mentha aquatica	-	-	-	-	+	+
Mentha arvensis	-	-	-	-	+	-
Montia fontana	+	-	-	-	-	-
Myosotis laxa	-	+	-	-	+	+
Myriophyllum spicatum	+	+	+	+	+	+
Persicaria amphibia	+	-	+	-	-	-
Persicaria maculosa	+	+	+		+	-
Phalaris arundinacea	+	+	+	+	+	+
Phleum pratense	+	+	+	+	+	+
Plantago lanceolata	-	-	-	-	+	+
Plantago major	+	+	+	+	+	+
Poa annua	-	-	-	-	+	-
Polygonum aviculare s.l.	+	+	+	+	-	-
Populus nigra s.l.	-	-	-	+	+	+
Potamogeton berchtoldii	+	+	+	+	+	-
Potamogeton crispus	+	+	+	+	+	+
Potamogeton natans	+	+	+	+	-	-
Potamogeton pusillus	-	-	-	-	-	+
Potentilla anglica	-	-	-	-	+	-
Potentilla × suberecta	-	-	-	+	-	-
Prunella vulgaris	-	-	-	-	+	+
Pulicaria dysenterica	-	-	-	+	+	+
Ranunculus acris	-	-	-	+	+	-
Ranunculus aquatilis	+	-	-	+	+	-
Ranunculus repens	+	+	+	+	+	-
Ranunculus sceleratus	+	-	-	-	-	-

Species	1967	1969	1971	1979	1991	2006
Ranunculus circinatus	+	-	-	-	-	-
Rubus spp.	-	-	-	+	+	+
Rumex acetosella	-	-	-	-	-	+
Rumex acetosa	-	-	-	-	+	+
Rumex conglomeratus	-	-	-	-	-	+
Rumex crispus	-	-	-	-	-	+
Rumex obtusifolius	-	-	-	-	+	-
Rumex sanguineus	-	-	+	-	-	-
Ruppia maritima	-	+	-	-	-	-
Salix alba	-	-	-	+	+	+
Salix cinerea	-	+	+	+	+	+
Sambucus nigra	-	-	-	-	+	+
Scorzoneroides autumnalis	-	-	-	+	-	+
Scrophularia nodosa	-	-	-	-	+	-
Sedum album	-	-	-	-	-	-
Senecio aquaticus	-	-	+	-	+	-
Senecio jacobaea	-	-	-	-	+	+
Senecio vulgaris	+	+	+	-	-	-
Solanum dulcamara	-	-	-	-	-	+
Sonchus arvensis	-	-	-	-	+	+
Sonchus asper	-	-	-	-	+	+
Sparganium erectum	-	-	-	-	-	+
Stachys sylvatica	-	-	-	-	+	+
Stellaria graminea	-	-	-	-	+	-
Stellaria media	-	-	-	-	+	-
Taraxacum spp.	+	+	+	+	+	-
Trifolium hybridum	-	+	+	-	-	-
Trifolium medium	-	-	-	-	+	-
Trifolium pratense	+	+	-	+	+	+
Trifolium repens	+	-	+	+	+	+
Tussilago farfara	+	+	+	+	+	+
Typha latifolia	-	-	-	-	+	+
Urtica dioica	+	-	-	+	+	+
Veronica beccabunga	+	-	-	+	-	-
Vicia cracca	-	-	+	-	+	+
Vicia hirta	-	-	-	+	+	-
Vicia sativa s.l.	-	-	-	-	+	-
Vicia sepium	-	-	-	-	+	+
Total numbers of species recorded	40	39	42	50	90	74

Plate 2.75   After the ballast has been removed from abandoned railways the gravely substrate (cest) provides a habitat for a few rare introductions and native species. This photograph shows an open habitat with an abundance of Common Bird's-foot-trefoil (*Lotus corniculatus*). However these communities may not last long before development takes place.

Plate 2.76   At Heysham Harbour a nuclear power station was built on old railway sidings but part of the area was left undeveloped. This photograph shows the diverse flora that colonised the area and now forms a Lancashire Wildlife Trust nature reserve.

Transport routes

The flora associated with transport routes has largely been considered in relation to other habitats. Most of the communities associated with roads, railways and canals have been described under grasslands, wetlands and woodland edge communities.

However, in a few instances a distinct flora has developed in association with railways. When railways are constructed the rails and sleepers are laid on a bed of ballast made up of rock chippings. This in turn is laid on a bed of cest (the material on which the chippings are placed) formerly often made up of old boiler ash. During the 1960s many railways and particularly sidings were abandoned and at a later date the rails, sleepers and ballast were removed leaving behind the cest. This well-drained and often basic substrate is a harsh environment for most plants but provided suitable open habitats for some species. No systematic recording has been carried out but it

has become apparent that some species are particularly associated with this habitat. In particular the old sidings at Heysham (located on reclaimed land when the harbour was built but now occupied by two nuclear power stations), Fleetwood and Middleton were especially rewarding for these plants. Although not exclusively found on cest the following species seemed to thrive on the ash: *Chaenorhinum minus*, *Corrigiola litoralis*, *Echium vulgare*, *Filago vulgaris*, *Descurania sophia*, *Diplotaxis erucoides*, *Diplotaxis tenuifolia*, *Illecebrum verticillatum*, *Oenothera* spp., *Orobanche minor*, *Poa compressa*, *Senecio viscosus* and *Sisymbrium orientale*.

Another species that seemed to like the cest environment was *Agrostis scabra*. This was first seen in the 1960s on cest and other open habitats in the vicinity of the old Fishergate Hill station, Preston that was for many years used as a goods station particularly for the import of grain. The railway premises were eventually developed but *Agrostis scabra* escaped into the surrounding areas and is still seen from time to time in the built up areas of Preston.

Other habitats associated with former and existing railways were not explored. Problems of safety have also caused difficulties for others but Sargent (1984) published an account of *Britain's railway vegetation* based on her work on rural or semi-rural lines throughout the country, which included sampling sites in northern Lancashire.

Transport routes are also believed to provide a corridor facilitating the spread of plants across the country. The colonisation of the Lancaster Canal was discussed by Greenwood (2005), where it was shown how some species spread along the canal, e.g. *Acorus calamus, Butomus umbellatus, Sagittaria sagittifolia* and more recently *Nymphoides peltata*, whilst railways were believed to be important in the spread of *Senecio squalidus* (Grime, *et al.*, 2007). More recently motorways and trunk roads have been shown to be important for salt tolerant species (Preston, *et al.*, 2002). In northern Lancashire in addition to *Cochlearia danica, Puccinellia distans* and *Spergularia marina* non-salt tolerant *Hordeum jubatum, Lactea serriola* and *Lepidium ruderale* also appear to be spreading along motorways and other roads.

The built landscape

The built, urban landscape provides a surprising number of habitats for plants and animals. It comprises a variety of hard surfaces interspersed with cracks and more open spaces. These latter might be extensive consisting of parks, gardens, cemeteries and allotments with arable, grassland and wooded areas. Also within the built landscape are areas of derelict land where buildings have been demolished and left before further development at some future date. These are often referred to as urban commons (Gilbert, 1989). Whilst these habitats provide a haven for wildlife, the plants are often garden escapes or species that have been accidentally introduced with other materials. Until relatively recently these areas were ignored by botanists but in the last 50 years or so much more attention has been given to them. In northern Lancashire there has been no systematic survey of these habitats but their flora has been noted in the course of general recording.

Rodwell (2000, p. 402) illustrates diagrammatically the kinds of habitats that might be found in a suburban street and the plant communities that might be found in them. These habitats comprise pavements with a mown grassy verge, walls and gardens, and within this small area he notes six major plant communities and several sub-communities. He could have noted several more. Yet of these habitats only walls have received much attention nationally.

Mortared walls of stone or brick are found in rural as well as urban areas but the flora that they may support is similar. Their flora has been recorded in many places in this country and elsewhere and the paper by Payne (1978) describing his work in south-eastern Essex provides references to other work. More recently Edgington (2003) has pointed out the significance of walls as a habitat for ferns in London. In northern Lancashire little time was devoted to recording the flora of walls but in 1980 the flora of a blue brick wall at Poulton-le-Fylde station was noted. It supported the following species:

Arrhenatherum elatius	*Hypochaeris radicata*
Asplenium ruta-muraria	*Medicago lupulina*
Athyrium filix-femina	*Polypodium vulgare s.l.*
Asplenium scolopendrium	*Pteridium aquilinum*
Asplenium trichomanes	*Rubus* sp.
Calystegia silvatica	*Rumex acetosa*
Chamerion angustifolium	*Sagina procumbens*
Cymbalaria muralis	*Sambucus nigra*
Dactylis glomerata	*Senecio jacobaea*
Dryopteris filix-mas	*Senecio vulgaris*
Epilobium montanum	*Sonchus* sp.
Festuca rubra	*Taraxacum* spp.
Hieracium vagum	

A number of other species are also associated with walls. These include *Antirrhinum majus, Asplenium ceterach, Asplenium adiantum-nigrum, Campanula poscharskyana, Centranthus ruber* (especially near the coast), *Erinus alpinus, Parietaria diffusa*, and *Pseudofumaria lutea*. In some places where nearby substrates are calcareous *Saxifraga tridactylites* is commonly found on walls and more unusually *Osmunda regalis* grew on the walls of Lancaster Castle whilst a fine colony of *Dryopteris submontana* was found on another wall in Lancaster. In contrast a nearby wall was colonised by *Dryopteris dilatata*. Amongst the garden plants *Erinus alpinus*, although unusual, has been known from walls for many years as has *Rumex scutatus* (at Staynall), but increasingly other garden plants are found on walls including *Fallopia baldschuanica* and *Parthenocissus* spp. both extensively used to provide screens and to cover walls.

The NVC recognises a number of discrete plant communities on walls. OV39 *Asplenium trichomanes-A. ruta-muraria* community is widespread and in addition to the dominant species *Asplenium adiantum-nigrum* and *Asplenium ceterach* may be present. It is particularly characteristic of calcareous habitats, i.e. mortared walls, but also occurs on limestone rocks.

OV41 *Parietaria diffusa* community is widespread on walls but also in rocky places. It is often the only species present but may be associated with *Hedera helix*. It also occurs in rocky places such as the cliffs at Silverdale. However it is often found in association with OV42 *Cymbalaria muralis* community.

In the urban landscape there is usually a pavement or at least a paved area at the base of a wall. Here there may be a strip of soil separating the wall from the pavement, and in the pavement itself there are invariably cracks sometimes formed by the paved area being composed of stone sets. At the base of the wall OV22 *Poa annua-Taraxacum officinale* community is often found. *Poa annua* and *Taraxacum* spp., usually of Section *Ruderalia*, are the sole constants but this means that many different *Taraxacum* species can be found here, often introductions. Other species that may be present include *Plantago major* and *Senecio vulgaris* giving rise to the *Senecio vulgaris* sub-community. Also present here may be found *Cerastium fontanum*, *Tripleurospermum inodorum* and *Holcus lanatus*. Sometimes coarse herbs such as *Cirsium vulgare*, *Cirsium arvense*, *Rumex obtusifolius*, *Rumex crispus* and *Chenopodium album* along with the smaller *Stellaria media* and *Trifolium repens* occur giving rise to the *Cirsium vulgare-Cirsium arvense* sub-community. In this sub-community *Lolium perenne*, *Matricaria discoidea*, *Poa annua* and *Taraxacum* spp. are always present. This habitat also provides a home for annual species of willowherb: *Epilobium montanum*, *Epilobium ciliatum* and hybrids between them are particularly prevalent. Other species include *Plantago major*, *Sonchus oleraceus*, *Poa trivialis*, *Trifolium dubium*, *Cardamine hirsuta*, *Lepidium didymum* and *Capsella bursa-pastoris*, but in some parts of the country *Crepis vesicaria* occurs along with *Epilobium ciliatum* to give rise to the *Crepis vesicaria-Epilobium ciliatum* sub-community.

Pavements, cobbles, stone sets or flags have many cracks where plants can become established, at least temporarily. The plant communities formed belong to OV20 *Poa annua-Sagina procumbens* community.

In addition to *Poa annua* and *Sagina procumbens* other species may include *Capsella bursa-pastoris*, *Plantago major*, *Agrostis stolonifera*, *Stellaria media* and *Medicago lupulina*. In the typical sub-community *Arenaria serpyllifolia*, *Juncus bufonius*, *Polygonum aviculare s.l.* and *Sagina apetala* can also occur, and occasionally but increasingly *Oxalis* spp. are found here. If the pavements are neglected and the plants are allowed to grow richer vegetation develops to form the *Lolium perenne-Matricaria discoidea* sub-community. Here *Lolium perenne* and *Matricaria discoidea* are both always present and *Plantago major*, *Agrostis stolonifera*, and *Dactylis glomerata* are frequent whilst *Ranunculus repens* is occasional.

Very often in suburban areas a mown grassy verge separates the pavement from a kerbstone adjoining the carriageway of the road itself. This grassy verge is usually a form of OV23 *Lolium perenne-Dactylis glomerata* community. Other species usually present include *Plantago lanceolata* and *Taraxacum* spp. but *Achillea millefolium*, *Plantago major*, *Trifolium pratense*, *Agrostis stolonifera*, *Hypochaeris radicata* and *Potentilla reptans* might also occur. In the *Plantago major-Trifolium repens* sub-community *Poa annua* and *Holcus lanatus* are frequent with *Ranunculus repens* and *Rumex crispus* occasional. It is also in this community that *Veronica filiformis* is becoming established in some places and where it does so it can dominate the community.

Where there is heavier pedestrian pressure on the grassy verge OV23 gives way to OV21 *Poa annua-Plantago major* community and especially the *Lolium perenne* sub-community. *Lolium perenne* is a constant associate but *Capsella bursa-pastoris*, *Polygonum aviculare s.l.*, *Trifolium repens*, *Ranunculus repens*, *Agrostis stolonifera* and *Taraxacum* spp. may also be found – all species that can take advantage of more open vegetation subject to heavy trampling.

Also found in the urban environment, especially on wasteland where houses have been demolished and land awaits development, are OV18 *Polygonum aviculare-Matricaria discoidea* and OV19 *Poa annua-Tripleurospermum inodorum*. These are found elsewhere as arable weeds.

Within gardens two further habitats should be mentioned but because gardens are private little is known about the species and communities present. Most suburban gardens contain a lawn and if this is well maintained cultivars of *Lolium perenne*, *Agrostis vinealis* and *Festuca rubra* are found. With less maintenance but regular cutting communities found on the mown verge outside become established including *Bellis perennis* on clay soils. Sometimes however, especially where the soils become less nutrient rich, some interesting species may be found including *Hypericum humifusum*, *Trifolium micranthum* and *Montia fontana* ssp. *chondrosperma*. Most gardens contain cultivated areas, as do allotments and here plants characteristic of arable cultivation may be found including *Trifolium media*, *Veronica persica*, *Veronica hederifolia*, *Senecio vulgaris*, *Euphorbia peplus*, *Euphorbia helioscopia* and *Poa annua*. Perennial herbs can become established and sometimes they are difficult to eradicate. They include *Elytrigia repens*, *Cirsium arvense*, *Equisetum arvense*, *Calystegia sepium*, *Calystegia silvatica*, and *Ranunculus repens* (especially on wet clay soils).

Many of these communities can be found elsewhere in the urban environment especially in parks, gardens, allotments and cemeteries. However in many towns and cities buildings are demolished, and before the land is re-developed the ground is left as wasteland. Brick rubble is a major component of the soil along with other building materials, but although initially devoid of plants they soon invade the vacant ground. It is to some extent a matter of chance what species invade the wasteland or for how long the succession process is allowed to proceed, but in some places dormant seed from the demolished houses or factories germinates and this can provide added interest to urban commons. The general sequence in which colonization proceeds is well documented. Initially annual species predominate but from the outset perennials including woody species are present. Gilbert (1989) refers to this as the Oxford Ragwort stage and in Sheffield recorded *Epilobium ciliatum*, *Poa annua*, *Buddleja davidii*, *Tussilago farfara*, *Salix caprea*, *Senecio vulgaris*, *Polygonum aviculare s.l.*, *Senecio squalidus*, *Chamerion angustifolium* and *Lolium perenne* amongst 41 species that had colonized bare ground in the city within a year of it having become derelict. This list is typical of what might be found anywhere in similar situations in England. In northern Lancashire *Epilobium montanum* is common as well as *Epilobium ciliatum* and hybrids between the two species are generally present. In time tall herbs come to dominate such sites. Often these form large patches and amongst the most common are *Fallopia japonica*, *Chamerion angustifolium*, *Aster* spp. (Michaelmas-daisies) and *Solidago* spp. (goldenrods). The NVC recognises communities dominated by *Chamerion angustifolium*

as OV27 *Chamerion angustifolium* community. There are few associated species and in August large patches of this species lives up to one of its common names: Fireweed. This native species is still found in its natural habitat of upland rocky places, but today it is found dominating habitats ranging from dried out and/or fire damaged lowland mosses to urban commons and railway banks.

Often scrambling over taller vegetation or fences etc. *Calystegia silvatica* forms a colourful feature in late summer. In other places a tall herb community develops with *Urtica dioica* and *Galium aparine* co-dominant to form OV24 *Urtica dioica-Galium aparine* community. In the typical sub-community there are few associated species although *Cirsium arvense* and *Anisantha sterilis* may be present. In the *Arrhenatherum elatius-Rubus fruticosus* agg. sub-community these species together with *Heracleum sphondylium*, *Chenopodium album*, *Artemisia vulgaris*, *Taraxacum* spp. *Lolium perenne*, *Dactylis glomerata*, *Bromus hordeaceus*, *Achillea millefolium* and *Potentilla reptans* may be present whilst *Hedera helix* can form a patchy ground carpet. Although not seen so much in towns, wasteland can support large stands of *Conium maculatum*. Grassland can also develop with coarser species, e.g. *Arrhenatherum elatius* and *Dactylis glomerata* predominating (MG1 *Arrhenatherum elatius* grassland) but in other places *Lolium perenne*, *Festuca rubra*, *Holcus lanatus*, *Elytrigia repens*, and *Agrostis* spp. are common. Eventually if the site is not developed scrubby woodland becomes established, but in northern Lancashire this does not often happen. In this phase typical species include *Buddleja davidii*, *Salix cinerea*, *Salix caprea*, *Betula pubescens*, *Malus domestica*, *Acer pseudoplatanus*, *Rubus* spp. and *Sorbus* spp. especially *S. intermedia* and *S. aria*. Factors controlling the establishment and development of vegetation on urban commons are discussed by Bradshaw (1999).

Very occasionally earlier land-use may determine the initial colonizers. In these special situations species from elsewhere in the world may predominate. This was the situation in Preston when the Victorian houses and factories in the vicinity of North Road were demolished in the mid 1960s. Table 2.8 lists the species that were found on the wasteland in 1966 after the buildings were demolished and before subsequent development took place. Many are from the Mediterranean region or southern Europe generally and it is interesting to speculate on their origin. However, as the later years of the cotton industry in the area used imports from Egypt it is possible that many of the species originated as impurities in the cotton. North American species were occasionally found and no doubt some cotton originated in the USA, but if North American cotton was used generally more North American species would be expected. Other sources are possible, e.g. birdseed or impurities in grain imports.

Table 2.8 Species recorded on demolition sites near North Road, Preston in 1966 based on records supplied by Mrs E. Hodgson

Alopecurus geniculatus	*Melilotus officinalis*
Alopecurus myosuroides	*Papaver somniferum*
Anagallis arvensis ssp.	*Phleum bertolonii*
foemina	*Polygonum patulum*
Arenaria serpyllifolia	*Raphanus raphanistrum* ssp.
Atriplex prostrata	*maritimus*
Avena fatua	*Rapistrum rugosum*
Brassica juncea	*Rorippa palustris*
Bupleurum subovatum	*Senecio squalidus*
Catapodium marinum	*Senecio viscosus*
Chaenorhinum minus	*Silene gallica*
Chenopodium berlandieri	*Silene latifolia*
Chenopodium ficifolium	*Silene muscipula*
Chenopodium opulifolium	*Sisymbrium altissimum*
Coriandrum sativum	*Sisymbrium orientale*
Crepis capillaris	*Trachyspermum ammi*
Festuca pratensis	*Trifolium arvense*
Hirschfeldia incana	*Trifolium lappaceum*
Malva parviflora	*Trigonella glabra*
Medicago polymorpha	*Vaccaria hispanica*
Melilotus indicus	

Although not strictly an urban common, a similar influx of aliens was noted by Bailey (1902, 1907 and 1910) at Lytham St Anne's. The sites were located in two areas in what is now the centre of St Anne's, the first bounded by Richmond Road, Park Road, St Thomas's Road and Orchard Road (*c.* SD325285), and the second bounded by Beach Road, St Andrew's Road North, St Leonard's Road and North Drive (now Clifton Drive North, *c.* SD317293). When the resort was being developed it was the practice to use the sand dunes for chicken runs. It is possible that many of the dunes were already levelled as Bailey locates the chicken runs within areas laid out for building with roads. Reworking his lists it appears that some 95 species were associated with the chicken runs. A few were common native species or aliens that had already become established by the early years of the

twentieth century. Overall 77% originated in Europe and Asia with many from the Mediterranean region and 23% from North America. However Bailey noticed that there was a difference between his first lists (from SD325285) and his later list from north of the present day Ashton Gardens. In the first list of 43 species 33% were from North America but in the second list of 50 species only 14% were from the New World. He suggested that the dunes had been used from time to time over many years for chickens and that they were fed using imported grain. The early years of the twentieth century marked the start of a considerable expansion in chicken farming using imported grain, often the cleanings from the holds of ships or grain warehouses. The grain was probably full of impurities. The chickens only used one area of the dunes for a short while before building started, however there was probably enough time for the impurities to grow after the chickens left but before building commenced. Overall 11% of the species introduced with chicken feed became established even if two of them, *Ambrosia trifida* and *Ambrosia psilostachya*, eventually became extinct. This is in line with the 'Tens rule' where it is suggested that 10% of introductions become established (Williamson, 1996). However only one species became established from the second list whilst 9 (or 29%) of the aliens from the first list became naturalised. The 'Tens rule' also postulates that of the introduced species that become established 10% of these will become invasive but so far none of the introductions at St Anne's has become a nuisance.

Analogous to the situation at St Anne's was that at Newton-in-Bowland although here it is difficult to imagine a more rural situation. In 1911 a farmer in an effort to get his cattle to eat coarse grass in a poor and 'benty' field top-dressed it with screenings of wheat obtained from corn-millers. In the following summer Peel (1913) recorded 18 introduced species but it is not clear if any became established.

Most aliens introduced with imported goods cannot survive in the Lancashire climate. They grow for one season only but a few are able to flourish and it is possible to see that on the coast at St Anne's the chicken farms using imported grain contributed a significant number of species to the present Lancashire flora. However the lists at both Newton and St Anne's demonstrate the considerable contamination of grain that occurred before laws existed to ensure clean grain. Yet also notable is the absence of *Papaver* spp. Overall it is clear that grain crops, grown here or elsewhere, would have been full of weeds.

In both urban and rural areas landscaping schemes have taken place in a variety of places ranging from roadside verges to the rehabilitation of post-industrial sites. In some of these schemes it is difficult to know when a planted species has become wild, e.g. with *Cotoneaster* spp. However other species have appeared, which may be accidentally or deliberately introduced. Those that have been noted include *Lathyrus nissolia, Lotus corniculatus* var. *sativus, Medicago sativa* ssp. *varia, Primula veris, Salvia verbenaca, Poterium sanguisorba* ssp. *balearica* and *Vicia tetrasperma*.

Conclusion

Urban and post-industrial habitats may not be the first choice for many botanists to explore yet they provide fascinating problems for the ecologist to solve and for planners to change into something else. The something else may be a new built landscape, open space or even a nature reserve.

However they are of interest for other reasons. Some sites provide a refuge, at least temporarily, for species otherwise rare in the region (Richardson, 1957; Greenwood and Gemmell, 1978). Many of the species are aliens from elsewhere in the world, and whilst fascinating in their own right for those who like to find new species for the locality, some become established and form an important component of the local flora. Some, e.g. *Fallopia japonica*, become pests. The new and unstable habitats bring together species that might not normally meet but are sufficiently closely related to hybridise. Good examples are the dactyl orchids amongst native species whilst the North American *Epilobium ciliatum* hybridises readily with the native *Epilobium montanum*. Occasionally a new species is produced, e.g. *Senecio cambrensis* arose first in North Wales from the hybrid between *Senecio squalidus* and *Senecio vulgaris,* and then it appeared again in Midlothian, Scotland (Preston, *et al.,* 2002). Thus urban and post-industrial sites are important for studies in plant evolution.

3. The catalogue

Introduction

The account for each species or sub-species follows a standard pattern, starting with a statement of the floristic element to which the taxon belongs (Preston, *et al.*, 2002). Where this is not known a general indication of its world distribution is provided. All taxa are presumed to be native in northern Lancashire unless otherwise stated.

Following the introductory comments an account of the taxon's occurrence in northern Lancashire is given with reference to appropriate Broad Habitats (BH) (see Table 4.7, pp. 561–566) ending with comments on changes in its frequency and distribution in the region and nationally. A map showing the distribution of the taxon in northern Lancashire is shown for most species that have been found in six or more tetrads since 1964 (see below). The base map used for the distribution maps shows the following features:

- Coastline and major rivers, solid blue line
- Canals, dotted blue line
- County and unitary authority boundaries, solid green line
- Vice-county boundaries (approximate), solid black line
- 10km squares, thin grey line
- Contours at 50m intervals 0–200 then at 100m intervals.

Nomenclature

The sequence of families, genera and species as well as Latin and English names follows Stace (2010) unless indicated otherwise and corrections published on BSBI web site in 2011.

Status

Introduced species may be archaeophytes or neophytes. Species are assumed to be established but if they are clearly planted or appear to be occurring casually this is indicated. For a discussion of these terms see Preston, *et al.* (2002).

Herbaria

Many herbaria were consulted. References to them follow the abbreviations, where available, used in Kent and Allen (1984).

Distribution

Maps show the tetrad distribution of most species, which have been found in six or more tetrads since 1964. Different symbols are used for pre (white dots) and post 1964 (black dots) records to illustrate change where known. However as older records are not always localised some of the tetrad records are approximations. For very rare species (found in five or fewer tetrads) locality details are given to at least the level of the civil parish (as shown on 1964 Ordnance Survey maps) together with the appropriate tetrad notation using the convention of figures and letters (see Figure 3.1). However for old records it is not always possible to give a grid reference.

E	J	P	U	Z
D	I	N	T	Y
C	H	M	S	X
B	G	L	R	W
A	F	K	Q	V

Figure 3.1 Tetrad notation within a 2 × 2km square.

Frequency

Data was not collected on the size of populations but an indication of frequency of occurrence is given in the following table (Table 3.1).

Table 3.1 Species frequency

Frequency category	No. of tetrads in which a taxon was recorded	Approx. % frequency of occurrence
Extinct	0	0
Very rare	1–5	<1
Rare	6–14	1–3
Occasional	15–69	4–15
Frequent	70–231	16–50
Common	232–347	51–75
Very common	348–466	>75

Following the statement of a species frequency the number of tetrads in which a species was found in the period 1964–2009 inclusive is given in parenthesis. However it is important to realise that at any one time a species may not occur in all the tetrads indicated in the maps.

Recorders

The names of recorders (using initials in the text) are given for very rare species (Table 3.2). In some cases records are attributed to Anon. In these instances the recorder is either not known or wishes to remain anonymous.

Table 3.2   Recorders

Initials	Name
P.P.A.	Abbott, Mrs P.P.
P.A.	Adam, P.
A.A.	Aldridge, A.
M.B.	Baecker, Mrs M.
C.B.	Bailey, Charles
H.B.	Beesley, H.
P.B.	Bentley, P.
T.B.	Blockeel, T.
B.R.C.	Biological Records Centre, Centre for Ecology and Hydrology
J.T.I.B.	Boswell-Syme, J.T.I.
B.S.B.I.	Botanical Society of the British Isles
J.B.	Bradley, J.
C.J.B.	Bruxner, C.J.
S.B.	Bungard, S.
H.E.B.	Bunker, H.E.
B.B.	Burrow, B.
J.C.	Cadbury, J.
A.J.C.	Campbell, A.J.
A.E.C.	Cannell, A.E
P.C.	Carah, P.
M.C.	Chappell, Mrs Marion
M.Cl.	Clapham, M.
J.Cl.	Clarke, Mrs Julie
C.C. & J.O'R	Coleman, C. & O'Reilly, J.
A.C.	Conolly, Dr A.
R.C.	Copson, R.
C.C.	Cornish, C
A.A.D.	Dallman, A.A.
J.E.D.	Dandy, J.E.
J.D.	Ducket, J.
D.P.E.	Earl, D.P.
D.P. & J.E.	Earl, D.P & J.
M.E.	Edmunds, Prof., M.
H.B.F.	Fielding, H.B.
L.R.F.	Fitzgerald, Lady R.
M.J.Y.F.	Foley, M.J.Y.
R.S.F.	France, R. Sharpe
J.N.F.	Frankland, J.N.
J.B.F.	Frankton, J.B.
J. Fr.	Fraser, J.
J.F.	Fryer, Mrs J.
V.G.	Gordon, V.
H.E.G.	Green, H.E.
P.G.	Green, Paul
T.G.	Greenlees, T.
E.F.G.	Greenwood, E.F. (including B.D.G. née B.D.W., B.D. Walker)
E.J.H.	Harling, Miss E.J.

R.M.H.	Harley, Dr. R.M.
W.H.	Hall, W.
G.H.	Halliday, Dr G.
W.P.H.	Hiern, W.P.
A.H.	Hitchin, Arthur
E.H.	Hodgson, Mrs E.
J.H.	Hodgson, Dr J.
N.T.H.H.	Holmes, N.T.H.
J.M.H.	Hopkinson, J.M.
W.E.H.	Hughes, W. E.
J.I.	Innes, J.
P.J.	Jepson, Peter
M.J.	Jones, M.
V.J.	Jones, V.
C.J.-P.	Jones-Parry, Mrs C.
G.M.K.	Kay, G.M.
J.K.	Killick, J.
F.C.K.	King, F.C.
G.K.	Kitchener, G.
R.L.	Leatham, R. (Bob)
F.A.L.	Lees, F.A.
W.R.L.	Linton, W.R.
L.A.L.	Livermore, L.A. (including P.D.L.)
N.F.McM.	McMillan, Mrs N.F.
J.M.	Maudsley, Jean
J.N.M.	Mills, Prof. J.N.
M.	Moon, Dr
J.Mo.	Moss, J.
A.N.	Newton, A.
J.M.N.	Newton, Dr J.M.
J.O'R.	O'Reilly, J.
E.P.	Pearce, Mrs E.
J.Pe.	Pearson, J.
R.P.-J.	Petley-Jones, R
C.D.P.	Pigott, Prof. C.D.
J.F.P	Pickard, J.F.
J.P.	Poingdestre, J.
R.P.	Pollock, Ruth
M.P.	Porter, M.
K.R.	Raistrick, K.
A.E.R.	Ratcliffe, Miss A.E.
D.R.	Redmore, D.
T.C.G.R.	Rich, Dr T.C.G.
C.S.	Sargent, C
M.Sh.	Sherlock, M.
H.S.	Shorrock, H.
S.S.	Simpson, S.
P.H.S.	Smith, Dr P.H.
G.S.	Stabler, George
C.F. & N.J.S.	Steeden, C.F. & N.J. (known as Derek and Jeremy Steeden)
O.S.	Stewart, Mrs O.
M.S.	Sutcliffe, M.
C.S.	Swindells, C.
P.M.T.	Taschereau, Dr P.M.
B.A.T.	Tregale, B.A.
A.U.	Underhill, A.
J.W.	Ward, J.
S.D.W.	Ward, S.D.
A.Wa.	Watson, A.
C.B.W.	Webb, C. Bromley
J.W.	Webb, Jill
A.W.W.	Westrup, A.W.
M.J.W.	Wigginton, M.J.
J.A.W.	Wheldon, J.A.
M.W.	Wilcox, M.
G.W.	Wilmore, G.
A.W.	Wilson, Albert
J.Wi.	Wilson, Joan
R.W.	Wilson, R.
N.W.	Woods, N.

Referees

Over the years many plants have been sent to B.S.B.I. referees who have kindly named many gatherings. This help is enormously valuable and I am greatly indebted to them for their expertise. The following table (Table 3.3) lists the referees and the area of their expertise.

Table 3.3   Referees

Referee	Area of expertise
Akroyd, J.R.	*Polygonum, Rumex*
Allen, D.E.	*Rubus*
Bowra, J.C.	*Oenothera*
Bradshaw, M.	*Alchemilla*
Brenan, J.P.M.	*Chenopodium*
Clement, E.	Introductions
Conolly, A.P.	*Fallopia*
Cope, T.A.	*Elytrigia, Juncus*
Cullen, J.	*Rhododendron*
David, R.W.	*Carex*
Dudman, A.A.	*Taraxacum*
Edees, E.S.	*Rubus*
Elkington, T.T.	*Erophila*
Earl, D.P.	*Rubus*
Ferguson, I.K.	*Salicornia*
Fryer, J.	*Cotoneaster*
Graham, G.G.	*Rosa*
Green, P.R.	*Allium*
Harley, R.M.	*Mentha*
Haworth, C.C.	*Taraxacum*
Holmes, N.T.H.	*Potamogeton, Batrachium Ranunculus*
Jermy, C.	*Carex, Dryopteris*
Kent, D.H.	*Ononis,* various
Kitchener, G.	*Epilobium*
Lansdown, R.V.H.	*Callitriche, Batrachium Ranunculus*
Lousley, J.E.	Various
McAllister, H.A.	Various
McCosh, D.	*Hieracium*
McClintock, D.	Introductions
Maskew, R.	*Rosa*
Meikle, R.D.	*Salix*
Melville, R.	*Rosa*
Mills, J.N.	*Hieracium*
Mullen, M.	*Chenopodium*
Newton, A.	*Rubus*
Page, C.N.	*Equisetum*
Pennington, T.D.	*Epilobium*
Perring, F.H.	*Arctium*
Preston, C.D.	*Potamogeton*
Primavesi, A.L.	*Rosa*
Rich, T.C.G.	Brassicaceae and various
Richards, A.J.	*Taraxacum*
Robson, N.K.B.	*Hypericum*
Rumsey, F.J.	*Asplenium*
Savidge, J.P.	*Callitriche*
Sell, P.D.	*Hieracium*
Silverside, A.J.	*Euphrasia*
Stace, C.A.	*Juncus,* hybrids, *Festuca* spp.
Styles, B.	*Polygonum*
Swan, G.A.	*Trichophorum*
Taschereau, P.M.	*Atriplex*
Thomas, P.L.	X*Festulpia hubbardii*
Tutin, T.G.	*Salicornia*
Walker, T.	*Euphorbia*
Walters, S.M.	*Alchemilla, Montia*
Webb, D.A.	*Saxifraga*
Welch, D.	*Myosotis*
Yeo, P.F.	*Aster, Euphrasia*

Dates

The year of first introduction into the British Isles is given for neophytes and unless otherwise indicated is taken from Preston, *et al.* (2002).

The date of the first record in northern Lancashire is noted for neophytes, some archaeophytes and for species recorded for the first time since 1964. The date of the last known record for presumed extinct species is also given. However some presumed extinct species were re-found after long absences. This may be due to periods of long dormancy, e.g. some annuals, rediscovery of an old site or recent spread into the region.

Change

A description of change in distribution or frequency is given for northern Lancashire and related to the national situation by reference to the 'New Atlas' (Preston, *et al.*, 2002) and 'Local Change' (Braithwaite, *et al.*, 2006).

Old Records

Former records in VC 60 are largely attributable to Wheldon and Wilson (1907) and in VC 64 to the work of J.F. Pickard whose herbarium is at LDS. Some notes of his are in the F.A. Lees collection at KGY and his principal publications are 'Some rarer plants of Bowland' and 'Additions to the Bowland flora' (Pickard, 1901; 1902). References are given in the text to other records.

Herbaria were consulted widely, especially those at YRK containing the collection of A. Wilson and NMW containing the collection of J.A. Wheldon. Since 1964 voucher specimens have been deposited at LIV. However H.E. Bunker's collection was consulted shortly after he died at his former home in Preston. Some years later it was transferred to LIV but by then it appears a number of specimens had been lost. If specimens had been seen before the transfer took place, but have not been traced at LIV, they are referred to as herb. Bunker.

Doubtful Records

Sometimes species have been recorded in error or there is some doubt about their occurrence and in these circumstances the account is given in square brackets. On the other hand there are species that it is felt might occur in northern Lancashire having been recorded just beyond the region's borders and notes about these have also been included in square brackets.

LYCOPHYTES

Clubmosses and Quillworts

LYCOPODIACEAE   CLUBMOSS FAMILY

Huperzia selago (L.) Bernh. ex Schrank & C. Mart. ssp. **selago**

Fir Clubmoss

Circumpolar Boreo-arctic Montane element.

Fir Clubmoss occurs on acid rocks (BH16) and occasionally in acid grassland in upland areas of the British Isles and occasionally in lowland areas.

Occasional (18). In northern Lancashire it is confined to Leck and the Bowland Fells where it occurs on grit rocks and occasionally in acid grassland by hill streams.

The present distribution is similar to that recorded formerly except that lowland localities near Garstang and Hurst Green seem to have gone. The situation in northern Lancashire is in agreement with the 'New Atlas' and 'Local Change'.

Lycopodium clavatum L.   Stag's-horn Clubmoss

Circumpolar Boreo-arctic Montane element.

Nationally it is found in dwarf shrub heaths (BH10) in upland areas of the British Isles and occasionally in lowland areas.

Rare (10). In northern Lancashire it favours acid stony places with open communities or open acid grasslands. It was found on Longridge Fell and scattered throughout Bowland and the Lune valley uplands. Formerly, although always rare, it seems to have occurred more widely with localities in Leck, on Warton Crag, Grindleton and in Whitendale. However there is evidence that individual colonies may only be present for a few years. The 'New Atlas' suggests that populations tend to be transient nationally and that losses were mostly from lowland areas pre 1930. 'Local Change' suggests that there has been little change in recent years.

Diphasiastrum alpinum (L.) Holub   Alpine Clubmoss

Circumpolar Arctic-montane element.

This is found on acidic and often stony montane habitats (BH15) throughout most of the British Isles.

Very rare (1), extinct in VC 60. Only found in a disused grit quarry in Gisburn Forest (SD75N) in 1998 (P.J.). It was still present in a nearby quarry with *Lycopodium clavatum* in 2007. However in 2011 it could not be found in the quarry, which had become overgrown with *Picea* sp. Formerly it occurred on Gragareth and in upper Ease Gill, Leck where it was last seen in 1900. The appearance of this species in a quarry in Gisburn Forest is remarkable, as old Lancashire and Yorkshire colonies have gone suggesting that long distance dispersal from colonies in the Lake District or northern Wales about 100km or more away was involved. Many losses nationally were prior to 1962 ('New Atlas') although most montane habitat species show a significant recent decrease ('Local Change').

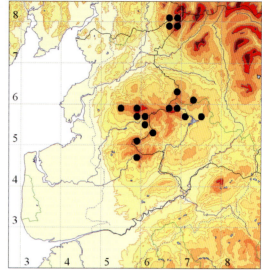
Huperzia selago

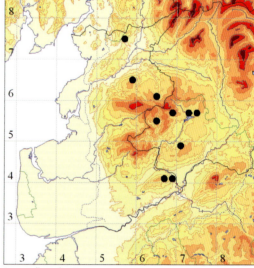
Lycopodium clavatum

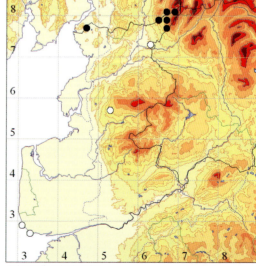
Selaginella selaginoides

SELAGINELLACEAE — LESSER CLUBMOSS FAMILY

Selaginella selaginoides (L.) P. Beauv.   Lesser Clubmoss

Circumpolar Boreal-montane element.

Nationally it occurs in calcareous grassland (BH7), fens, marshes and swamps including flushes (BH11) in upland areas in much of the British Isles.

Rare (6). In northern Lancashire Lesser Clubmoss is confined to calcareous flushes in Leck and Ireby and on shell marl, Hawes Water, Silverdale. Former records were from the same areas, where it is found today, but additionally it was found on the Lytham St Anne's sand dunes, near Damas Gill Head, Quernmore and in the gorge of the R. Greta. It has not been recorded from Lancashire VC 64. The 'New Atlas' suggests losses occurred nationally before 1930 and 'Local Change' confirms that there has been no recent decline although many calcareous grassland (BH7) species showed a significant decrease since 1987.

[ISOETACEAE — QUILLWORT FAMILY

Isoetes sp.   Quillwort

There are no historical records but an *Isoetes* sp. was recorded from various places in postglacial pollen records (Middleton, *et al.*, 1995). It is not known when it last occurred in northern Lancashire but suitable habitats have not been present for a long time.]

EUSPORANGIATE FERNS

Adder's-tongues & Moonworts

OPHIOGLOSSACEAE — ADDER'S-TONGUE FAMILY

Ophioglossum vulgatum L.   Adder's-tongue

Circumpolar Temperate element.

It occurs in dune slacks, neutral and calcareous grasslands (BH6, 7, 19) in most of the British Isles although it is rare in northern and eastern Scotland.

Frequent (71). In northern Lancashire Adder's-tongue is found scattered throughout the area. However there is qualitative evidence suggesting that during the last twenty years or so this species has declined markedly and by 2000 may have become rare. Its former habitats were usually in short turf at the margins of fields and on roadside verges and in many of these habitats it appears that eutrophication has caused much lusher and taller vegetation to develop (Greenwood, 2003). The 'New Atlas' confirms that a decline took place in lowland areas between 1962 and 2000 but 'Local Change' did not observe any further significant decline.

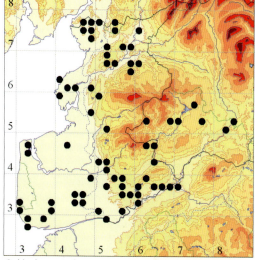
Ophioglossum vulgatum

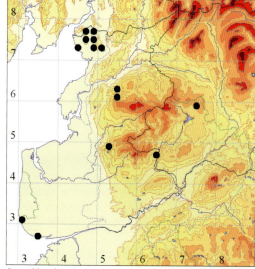
Botrychium lunaria

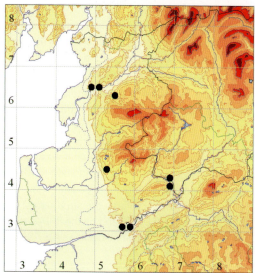
Equisetum hyemale

Botrychium lunaria (L.) Sw.   Moonwort

Circumpolar Boreo-temperate element.

This is found in calcareous pastures and sand dunes (BH7, 19) in much of the British Isles but it is rare in most of Ireland and south-eastern England.

Rare (14). In northern Lancashire Moonwort is found mostly in the Silverdale and Warton areas but also in Bowland and Lytham St Anne's. Since 2000 the only records have been from Warton Crag (SD47W) and Little Bowland (SD64N). There are no recent records from Lancashire VC 64. Although always rare it was formerly more widespread in Bowland including three localities near Newton-in-Bowland in VC 64. Despite it having declined over the last 100 years the appearance of individual colonies was always erratic. The 'New Atlas' reports losses nationally since 1962 and 'Local Change' suggests further losses since 1987 may be continuing.

CALAMOPHYTES

Horsetails

EQUISETACEAE   HORSETAIL FAMILY

Equisetum hyemale L.   Rough Horsetail

Circumpolar Boreo-temperate element.

This is found in heavy, wet soils in woodlands (BH1), often by streams in many parts of the British Isles.

Rare (8). In northern Lancashire Rough Horsetail is found in ancient woodlands by rivers and streams, notably the Rivers Lune, Calder, Hodder and Ribble. In addition there are former records from near Wray and Wennington. The 'New Atlas' records that there were losses nationally before 1930 but 'Local Change' noted no recent losses.

Equisetum variegatum Schleich. ex F. Weber & D. Mohr
                                                   Variegated Horsetail

Circumpolar Boreo-arctic Montane element.

Variegated Horsetail occurs in a variety of habitats including dune-slacks, river shingle and base-rich upland flushes (BH11, 19). It is found mostly in western and northern parts of the British Isles.

Rare (7). In northern Lancashire it has been found in open habitats in dune-slacks at Lytham St Anne's and in damp, base-rich places elsewhere. It has the capacity to colonize man-made sites, e.g. an old railway at Great Plumpton; Lundsfield Quarry, Carnforth, but soon disappears if closed communities develop. In Lancashire VC 64 it grows by the R. Dunsop with *Carex arenaria* and it is possible that it was introduced here in connection with water catchment works. In addition to the post 1964 records it was also found on damp sand at Sunderland Point, Overton (Garlick, 1957b). By 2005 its known localities were at Lytham St Anne's (SD33A), Lundsfield Quarry, Carnforth (SD46Z) and by the R. Dunsop (SD65K). The 'New Atlas' is not clear if there is any real decline since 1962 as losses seem to be balanced by gains.

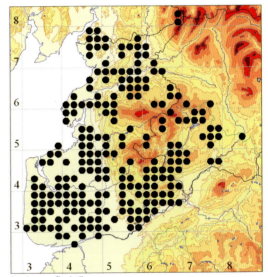
Equisetum variegatum

Equisetum fluviatile

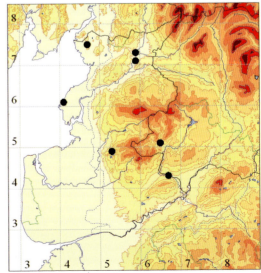
Equisetum × litorale

Equisetum fluviatile L.   Water Horsetail

Circumpolar Boreo-temperate element.

This is found in a variety of fens, marshes and swamps (BH11) throughout the British Isles.

Frequent (228). It occurs throughout northern Lancashire but it does not occur on peat bogs. There is no evidence of any change in frequency in northern Lancashire and this is reflected nationally for most of the country.

Equisetum fluviatile × E. arvense

(**E. × litorale** Kühlew. ex Rupr.)   Shore Horsetail

This is the commonest horsetail hybrid nationally but maps of its distribution in the British Isles show recorder bias indicating that it is likely to be overlooked.

Rare (7). Similarly it is probably under recorded in northern Lancashire where it occurs in fens, marshes and swamps (BH11) scattered throughout the area. It was first recorded in northern Lancashire from Leighton Moss in 1977 (P.J.).

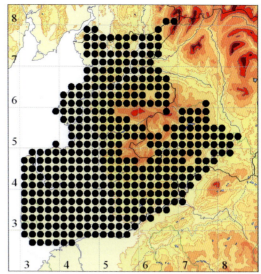
Equisetum arvense

Equisetum fluviatile × E. telmateia (**E. × willmotii** C.N. Page)

This hybrid is endemic to the British Isles and was first described from a colony in Co. Cavan, Ireland in 1984.

Very rare (2). First recorded in northern Lancashire from a passing bay on the Lancaster Canal at Yealand Redmayne (SD57C) in 1988 (L.A.L.). A second colony was found in a roadside ditch at Chipping (SD64C) in 2005 (E.F.G.). Morphologically the two colonies in northern Lancashire are dissimilar probably reflecting different directions of the cross.

Equisetum arvense L.   Field Horsetail

Circumpolar Wide-boreal element.

This occurs throughout the British Isles in a wide variety of habitats especially roadside verges, grasslands and disturbed places generally (BH3, 4).

Very common (413). Field Horsetail occurs in most of northern Lancashire but it is not found in wet places or in the upland heaths and mires of Bowland. There is no evidence for spread or decline of this species in northern Lancashire or nationally.

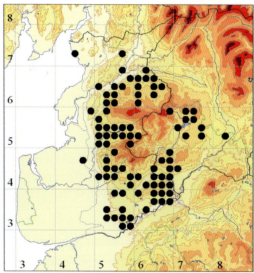
Equisetum sylvaticum

Equisetum arvense × E. palustre (**E. × rothmaleri** C.N. Page)

This hybrid was first recognised from the Isle of Skye in 1971. Since then it has been found in a few scattered places mostly in northern Britain. It is intermediate between the parents and is sterile. It is easily overlooked and may be more frequent than current records suggest.

Very rare (1). In northern Lancashire *E. × rothmaleri* was found at Brockholes Wetlands Nature Reserve (SD53V) in 2008 (M.J.Y.F.). Unfortunately before the identity of the colony was confirmed the visitor centre was built on top of it.

Equisetum sylvaticum L.   Wood Horsetail

Circumpolar Boreo-temperate element.

Wood Horsetail favours damp places in ancient woodland (BH1) or in more open areas by streams where it is probably a relic of a former woodland flora. It is found in the north and west of the British Isles.

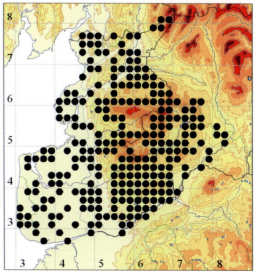
Equisetum palustre

Frequent (91). This woodland species is found in the east of northern Lancashire where populations appear stable but decline in British lowlands was noted in 1962 and since ('New Atlas').

Equisetum palustre L.   Marsh Horsetail

Circumpolar Boreo-temperate element.

Marsh Horsetail is found throughout the British Isles in fens, marshes and swamps (BH11).

Common (263). It is found in most of northern Lancashire where there is no evidence for spread or decline but the most recent national survey ('Local Change') reports a significant decrease.

Equisetum palustre × E. telmateia (E. × font-queri Rothm.)

This hybrid is found in scattered localities in western Britain.

Very rare (3). All three localities in northern Lancashire, in an abandoned brick pit at Preston (SD53A), where it was first seen in 2003, in a flush on Marshaw Fell (SD55B) and in a marshy area by the R. Dunsop (SD65K), were discovered by P.J.

Equisetum telmateia Ehrh.   Great Horsetail

European Southern-temperate element.

Great Horsetail occurs in fens, marshes and swamps (BH11) rather than woodland in many parts of the British Isles although it is absent from parts of northern and eastern Scotland.

Frequent (88). Typically this is found in wet ancient woodlands (BH1) in Bowland especially in the Ribble and Hodder river valleys, perhaps reflecting its more southerly distribution in Britain and Europe. However it can also be found in non-wooded and flushed areas by streams or on roadsides. There is no evidence for a change in its distribution in northern Lancashire or nationally.

Equisetum arvense × E. telmateia (E. × robertsii T.D. Dines)

This hybrid was first described from Anglesey (Dines and Bonner, 2002).

Very rare (3). In northern Lancashire this hybrid was first found by the Lancaster Canal at Cabus (SD44Y) in 2001 and probably further south by the canal at Catterall (SD54B) in 2003. However the identity of these plants has been questioned subsequently and they may only be forms of *E. arvense*. A sterile hybrid believed to be this was found in a hedge bottom on the boundary between Middleton and Overton (SD45J) in 2002. All records E.F.G.

Equisetum hybrids

Many horsetail hybrids have only been described relatively recently. They are often difficult to distinguish from their parents with which they may or may not occur. Most are thought to be rare but in recent years, as the ability to recognise them improves, they are proving to be more widespread and perhaps more frequent than at first thought. However once a hybrid has arisen colonies are likely to be long-lived although for hybrids to form the parents must be in close contact with each other. This implies that at formation there was considerable habitat disturbance even if this was hundreds of years ago (C.N. Page pers. comm.). This is probably the case for colonies of *E. × robertsii* on the Lancaster Canal, which was built

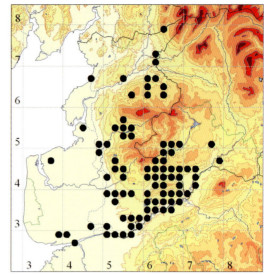
Equisetum telmateia

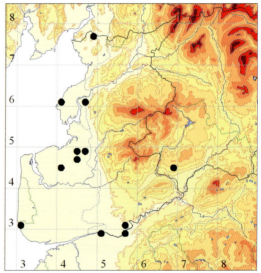
Osmunda regalis

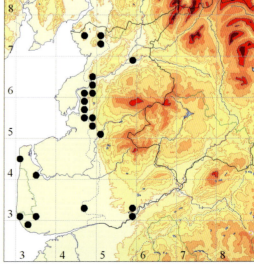
Azolla filiculoides

in 1795 and for *E. × willmotii* at Chipping where the colony is found in a roadside ditch adjoining what was a major military encampment at the end of the nineteenth century (Mrs M. Lord, pers. comm.). On the other hand the recent discovery of *E. × rothmaleri* at Brockholes is clearly a recent hybrid. Thus, even though habitats for *Equisetum* hybrids today may appear stable their presence probably reflects major disturbance at some time in the past.

LEPTOSPORANGIATE FERNS

True Ferns

OSMUNDACEAE   ROYAL FERN FAMILY

Osmunda regalis L.   Royal Fern

Suboceanic Southern-temperate element.

Royal Fern is found mostly in the west of the British Isles in neutral or acid habitats varying from fens and mires to woodlands (BH1, 11).

Rare (12). Formerly it was confined to the edges of lowland raised bogs (mosses), heaths, coastal sandstone cliffs and wet ancient woodlands. By 1907 Wheldon and Wilson (1907) thought it almost extinct but in recent years it has colonized railway cuttings and the walls of Lancaster Castle. In Lancashire VC 64 it was planted in the grounds of Browsholme Hall. In general after suffering greatly from collecting in the nineteenth century there may be signs of recovery although it seems to have gone recently from the dune heath at Lytham St Anne's. These recent changes are reflected nationally in the 'New Atlas' although 'Local Change' suggests further losses may still be occurring in its woodland and wetland habitats.

HYMENOPHYLLACEAE   FILMY-FERN FAMILY

Hymenophyllum tunbrigense (L.) Sm.

Tunbridge Filmy-fern

Oceanic Temperate element.

This is found in very sheltered and humid rocky places (BH16) mostly in the west of the British Isles.

Very rare (3). *H. tunbrigense* was recorded from the western side of Clougha (G.S. in Wheldon and Wilson, 1907) and not seen again here (SD56F) until 2006 (P.G.). However a specimen collected from Thorn Crag (SD55Y) in 2000 (E.F.G.) was identified in 2006 as also this species and in 2007 (P.G.) a further colony was found to the west of Ward's Stone summit (SD55Z). In most localities it occurs in small quantity in deep recesses of grit rocks but nevertheless there is a slight extension of its range in northern Lancashire. Nationally populations are stable.

Hymenophyllum wilsonii Hook.   Wilson's Filmy-fern

Oceanic Boreo-temperate element.

H. wilsonii is found in sheltered, shaded and rocky habitats (BH16) in the west of the British Isles.

Very rare (1). This is only found in small quantity in deep recesses of grit rock (BH16) on Thorn Crag (SD55Y). The notes by Wheldon and Wilson (1907), other publications and herbarium specimens indicate it was formerly more widespread on both sides of Ward's Stone and on Clougha (SD56F, 65D and 55Z) whilst Samuel Simpson reports it as occurring commonly near Lancaster (Newman, 1854). It would appear that there may have been substantial losses in the nineteenth century and whilst further losses may have occurred it manages to survive in the vicinity of Ward's Stone. The 'New Atlas' similarly reports a stable situation nationally. However, whilst not statistically significant 'Local Change' suggests it is decreasing. As this species is at the southern and eastern limits of its distribution in England any environmental changes, especially a decrease in oceanicity, are likely to be detrimental to its continued survival.

Trichomanes speciosum Willd. (Gametophyte)

Killarney Fern

Oceanic Temperate element.

This occurs in damp shaded places (BH16) mostly in the west of the British Isles.

Very rare (3). The fronds of the sporophyte form have not been recorded in northern Lancashire and it was not until recently that the filaments of the gametophyte form were recognised as occurring in western Britain. However they remain difficult to recognise and it is probably more widespread than the three records (all recorded by C.S. in 1999) known today from damp woodland ravines (Dutton, SD63N; Hurst Green, SD63Y and Caton-with-Littledale, SD56L) in western Bowland suggest. It is evident from recent research that environmental conditions are critical for the sporophyte to develop yet historically it must have occurred in Lancashire. *Trichomanes speciosum* is internationally endangered (it is listed in Annex 2 of the *European Communities Directive 92/43/EEC, on the conservation of national habitats and of wild fauna and flora*) and ecological, biological, physiological and genetic research is being carried out by Conservatoire Botanique National de Brest (Loriot and Magnanon, 2006).

MARSILEACEAE   PILLWORT FAMILY

Pilularia globulifera L.   Pillwort

Suboceanic Temperate element.

Pillwort has been found in non-calcareous ponds, lakes and reservoirs, often where there is a fluctuating water level, in many parts of the British Isles.

Extinct, formerly very rare (1). Only known from a specimen gathered on Ribbleton Moor, Preston by an anonymous collector in 1825 (MANCH). At that time Ribbleton Moor was a wet heath and remained so for another 50 years before the moor was finally reclaimed for agriculture in the late nineteenth and early twentieth centuries.

SALVINIACEAE   WATER FERN FAMILY

Azolla filiculoides Lam.   Water Fern

Neophyte. This is a native of North and South America but it is widely naturalized in temperate and southern Europe and elsewhere. It was first recorded in Britain in 1883.

Occasional (22). Water Fern was not reported from northern Lancashire until it was seen in the Lancaster Canal at Tewitfield (SD57B) in 1985 (G.H.). Since then it has been recorded in several places in the Lancaster Canal and occasionally elsewhere in ponds and ditches. In some years it becomes abundant and can completely cover a pond surface (see Plate 2.53). Since 1962 it has spread considerably in the southern half of the British Isles ('New Atlas').

DENNSTAEDTIACEAE   BRACKEN FAMILY

Pteridium aquilinum   Bracken

Circumpolar Temperate element.

Bracken is found on a variety of acidic or neutral substrates but mainly in woodlands (BH1) and on hillsides where it may dominate large areas (BH9). However it also occurs in limestone areas where substrates overlying the limestone become leached, on dried out lowland raised bogs (mosses), on fixed dunes and old buildings and walls. It is absent from aquatic habitats and mires. It is found throughout the British Isles.

Common (341). It occurs in most of northern Lancashire but its apparent absence from parts of eastern Bowland seems anomalous. There is no evidence for a change of status in northern Lancashire and the 'New Atlas' supports this nationally but 'Local Change' suggests that it may have declined since 1987 in its woodland habitat and in some areas of arable farmland.

PTERIDACEAE   RIBBON FERN FAMILY

Cryptogramma crispa (L.) R. Br. ex Hook.   Parsley Fern

European Boreal-montane element.

This is found on acid rocks and upland heaths (BH10, 15, 16) in montane areas of North Wales, northern England, Scotland and in the north of Ireland.

Very rare (4). Since 1964 this fern has only been seen on grit rocks at Fell End Crag (SD67U), and in apparently man-made hollows on Gragareth (SD67Z) both in Leck. Another colony was found in Dale Beck, Wray-with-Botton (SD65U) in 2008 (P.G.). It was also found in rocks in a stream on Whiteray Fell (SD66Q) in 1965 (E.F.G.) probably washed down from a colony higher up the valley. However this colony was not found until 2010

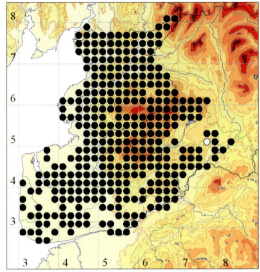

Pteridium aquilinum

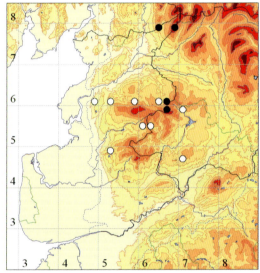

Cryptogramma crispa

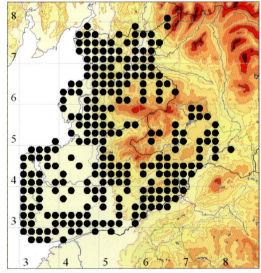

Asplenium scolopendrium

(P.G.). Formerly Parsley Fern was found more widely on grit rocks (BH16) in Bowland and near Lancaster where the Williamson Memorial is situated today. The loss from Lancaster was caused by quarrying and building works whilst quarrying probably caused its extinction at Waddington. However its loss, probably in the early twentieth century, from other sites in Bowland is not understood. Its loss from sites in the southern Pennines was widespread but further losses between 1962 and 2000 did not seem to occur ('New Atlas') and 'Local Change' suggests that there might have been a slight increase after 1987. Whilst the cause for the loss in the southern Pennines in the first half of the twentieth century is not known it is possible that smoke pollution, which badly affected the region, could be responsible.

ASPLENIACEAE   SPLEENWORT FAMILY

Asplenium scolopendrium L   Hart's-tongue

European Temperate element.

This occurs on base-rich banks, walls, and rocks and in woodlands (BH1, 16, 17) throughout the British Isles although it is rare in northern Scotland.

Common (268). Hart's-tongue occurs throughout northern Lancashire wherever there are basic substrates. It particularly favours damp wooded banks, grykes in limestone pavement, hedgerows and old buildings and walls. It seems to be absent from large areas of Bowland, the intensively farmed lowland areas and lowland mosses. There is no evidence that its status in northern Lancashire has changed, a situation reflected nationally in the 'New Atlas'. However 'Local Change' reports a significant increase in its frequency in woodlands and inland rock habitats.

Asplenium adiantum-nigrum L.   Black Spleenwort

European Temperate element.

A. adiantum-nigrum is primarily a species of walls and hedge banks (BH3). It occurs throughout the British Isles.

Frequent (98). Although this species is widespread in northern Lancashire, particularly towards the coast, it is less frequent in Lancashire VC 64. There is no evidence of changing status in the region and nationally it appears stable.

Asplenium marinum L.   Sea Spleenwort

Suboceanic Southern-temperate element.

Sea Spleenwort is found on rocks (BH18) around the coasts of the British Isles except eastern England.

Very rare (1). There are very few rocky sea cliffs in northern Lancashire available for this species. At Heysham (SD46A) there is a continuous record for its presence following its discovery there in April 1685 by Thomas Lawson (Raven, 1942). However Samuel Simpson reported it from Silverdale (Simpson, 1843) but Ashfield (1864) thought it had been eradicated by collectors. Petty (1902) thought the locality was Cow's Mouth (SD458737). Following losses before 1930 populations nationally seem stable ('New Atlas') but although the sample was small 'Local Change' suggests that since 1987 there has been a significant increase in the number of tetrads in which the species occurs.

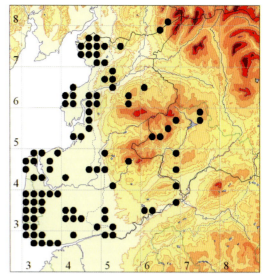
Asplenium adiantum-nigrum

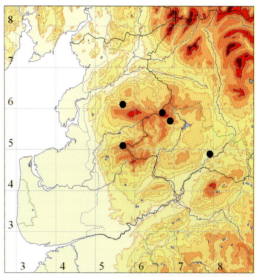
Asplenium trichomanes ssp. *trichomanes*

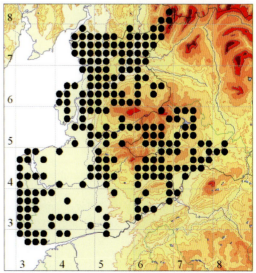
Asplenium trichomanes ssp. *quadrivalens*

Asplenium trichomanes L. ssp. **trichomanes**

Maidenhair Spleenwort

Circumpolar Temperate element.

The subspecies of *Asplenium trichomanes* were not recognised until recently. However *A. trichomanes* ssp. *trichomanes* occurs on acid rocks (BH16) in Wales and northern Britain.

Very rare (5). In northern Lancashire it has been confirmed growing in Foxdale (SD56Q) in 2004 (E.F.G. & J.M.N.); in Hawthornthwaite Greeve, Nether Wyresdale (SD55Q) in 2005 (E.F.G.); quarry, Wray-with-Botton (SD65U) in 2007 (J.M.N.); Croasdale, Bowland Forest High (SD65Y) in 2006 (E.F.G.) and in woodland at Bolton-by-Bowland (SD74Z) in 2006 (E.F.G.). It is not possible to assess any change in status locally or nationally but as it occurs in small quantity it must be vulnerable to any changes to the climate or environment.

Asplenium trichomanes L. ssp. **quadrivalens** D.E. Mey

Circumpolar Southern-temperate element.

This is characteristic of basic substrates of limestone rocks or mortared walls (BH3, 16, 17) throughout the British Isles.

Common (238). It is assumed that records for *Asplenium trichomanes sensu lato* belong to this subspecies There is no evidence for a change of status in northern Lancashire or nationally.

Asplenium viride Huds.

Green Spleenwort

Circumpolar Boreal-montane element.

This species occurs on limestone rocks and calcareous shale (BH16) in upland areas of the British Isles.

Rare (8). In northern Lancashire most colonies are found in Leck and Ireby whilst the colony at Silverdale was last seen in 1983. In Bowland it occurs on shale cliffs in Artle and Fox Dales. Formerly it occurred in Buckbanks Wood, Little Bowland on limestone (SD64H) where it was lost after a flood at the end of the nineteenth century (J. Weld, c. 1888) and from an unknown locality at the head of the Brennand valley in 1901 (Pickard, 1902). There is also a 1958 record (Henderson, 1962) from Dalton Crags (SD57N). This species is at its climatic limits in Lancashire requiring cool, humid summers and whilst a slow decline can be detected over the last 100 years national populations are thought to be stable ('New Atlas') although there is a possibility that further decline might be taking place since 1987 ('Local Change').

Asplenium ruta-muraria L.

Wall-rue

Circumpolar Temperate element.

This species occurs on basic rocks and mortared walls (BH3, 17, 18) throughout the British Isles.

Common (268). It is also found throughout northern Lancashire. There is no evidence for a change in its frequency or abundance in northern Lancashire although the 'New Atlas' suggests that there were some losses nationally since 1950 but 'Local Change' reports no change since 1987.

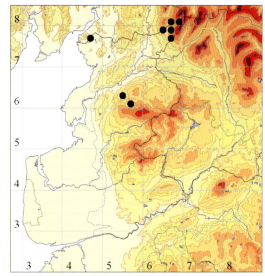

Asplenium viride

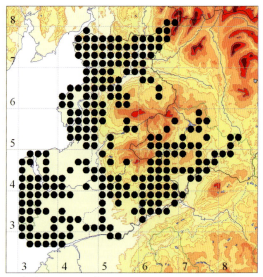

Asplenium ruta-muraria

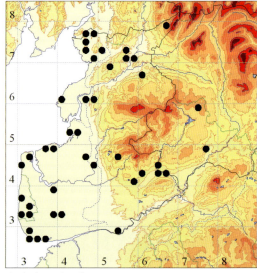

Asplenium ceterach

Asplenium ceterach L   Rustyback

Submediterranean-Subatlantic element.

Rustyback occurs on calcareous rocks and walls (BH3, 16, 17) in western parts of the British Isles.

Occasional (43). It is scattered throughout northern Lancashire. Although overall there is little evidence for any change in its distribution in northern Lancashire there have been minor changes. Petty (1902) had difficulty in finding it in Silverdale where today there are several sites whilst Weld (c. 1888) knew it at the end of the nineteenth century from the mill dam, Chipping from where it has been reported at intervals ever since. The 'New Atlas' suggests that it has become more frequent and 'Local Change' reports that this is possible.

THELYPTERIDACEAE   MARSH FERN FAMILY

[Thelypteris palustris Schott   Marsh Fern

Although this fern has not been recorded in northern Lancashire it is possible that it occurs as it was recorded in Cumbria on the border with Lancashire (SD47S) in 1994 (Halliday, 1997)].

Phegopteris connectilis (Michx.) Watt   Beech Fern

Circumpolar Boreo-temperate.

Beech Fern occurs primarily in ancient woodland (BH1) but it is also found in rocky places in the uplands (BH16), probably former woodland.

Occasional (56). In northern Lancashire it is found in the north and east of the area. However whilst populations are stable overall, it is capable of colonizing new places, e.g. on mill ruins in Duddel Wood on the south side of Longridge Fell. On the other hand it seems to have gone or has not been rediscovered in others, e.g. in woods about Newton-in-Bowland where J.F. Pickard described it as common at the end of the nineteenth century. The 'New Atlas' also considers it to be stable, a situation confirmed by 'Local Change'.

Oreopteris limbosperma (All.) Holub   Lemon-scented Fern

European Temperate element.

This fern is found on peaty or humus-rich soils in woodlands (BH1) and by streams and ditches mostly in western Britain and coastal parts of Ireland.

Frequent (166). It is a characteristic species of acidic Bowland woods and upland stream sides with occasional occurrences elsewhere. Occasionally it achieves dominance as in upper Whitendale. It seems to have gone in recent years from some of its more lowland sites but generally it appears stable. Similarly the 'New Atlas' suggests that there were losses in lowland areas but largely before 1930. However whilst 'Local Change' also shows populations to be largely stable it is included in a group of woodland species and species of inland rock habitats (BH16) that are showing a significant decrease.

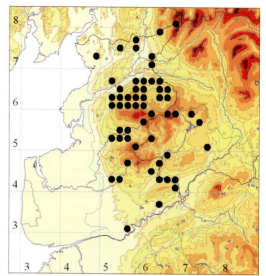

Phegopteris connectilis

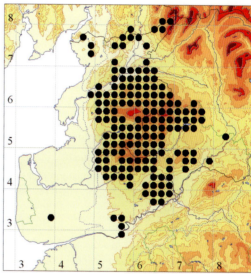

Oreopteris limbosperma

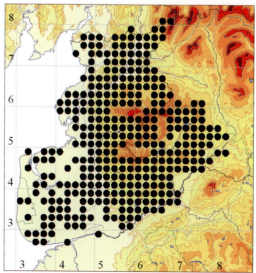

Athyrium filix-femina

WOODSIACEAE   LADY-FERN FAMILY

Athyrium filix-femina (L.) Roth   Lady-fern

Circumpolar Boreo-temperate element

This common fern occurs in woodland (BH1), beside streams, in hedge-rows (BH3) and occasionally on old buildings (BH17) throughout the British Isles.

Common (341). Although of no taxonomic significance two striking forms occur with many intermediates. One has narrow fronds with pinnae well spaced out on a reddish rachis. The other has broader, paler green fronds with pinnae crowded together on a green rachis. In northern Lancashire there is no evidence for any changes in its distribution, a situation reflected nationally.

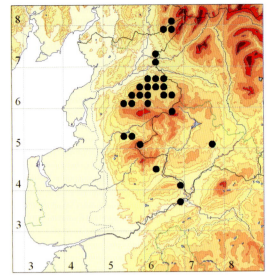

Gymnocarpium dryopteris

Gymnocarpium dryopteris (L.) Newman   Oak Fern

Circumpolar Boreo-temperate element.

This delicate fern grows in acid, rocky places generally in shady parts of ancient woodland (BH1) but sometimes in more exposed situations (BH16) in Wales and northern Britain and very rarely in the north of Ireland.

Occasional (28). In northern Lancashire Oak Fern grows in western Bowland and Leck. There may have been some losses towards the east and south of the area, which is consistent with its reported loss from the edges of its British range ('New Atlas'), but 'Local Change' suggests the evidence for further losses since 1987 is weak.

Gymnocarpium robertianum (Hoffm.) Newman   Limestone Fern

Circumpolar Boreo-temperate element.

This attractive fern is found on limestone rocks and grykes of limestone pavements (BH16) and in woodland (BH1) in parts of England and Wales but rarely elsewhere.

Rare (7). In northern Lancashire it is found on the limestone in the north of the area but it also occurs in woodland on dripping tufa by the side of the R. Wyre in an area otherwise devoid of basic rocks. It has not been found in Lancashire VC 64. Its distribution is stable both locally and nationally.

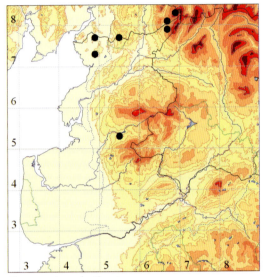

Gymnocarpium robertianum

Cystopteris fragilis (L.) Bernh.   Brittle Bladder-fern

Circumpolar Wide-boreal element.

This is found on basic rocks and mortared walls (BH3, 16, 17) in western parts of the British Isles.

Frequent (73). In northern Lancashire C. fragilis is found mostly in the north and east of the area. There is no evidence for decline and it is possible that over the last 100 years it has become more frequent although the 'New Atlas', shows that there have been some losses nationally since 1962. This is confirmed by 'Local Change' that suggests that most losses are from mortared walls in lowland areas.

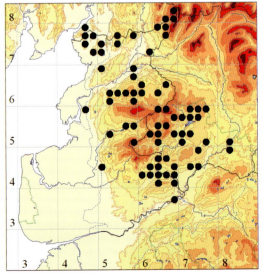

Cystopteris fragilis

BLECHNACEAE   HARD-FERN FAMILY

Blechnum spicant (L.) Roth   Hard-fern

European Temperate element.

Hard-fern is a calcifuge growing in woodland, hedgerows and in moorland areas (BH1, 3, 16) throughout the British Isles but it is rare in south-eastern England.

Frequent (201). In northern Lancashire this is found in acid woodlands, hedgerows, by streams especially in the hills and on rocks. There is no evidence for change in northern Lancashire and losses nationally were before 1950 ('New Atlas').

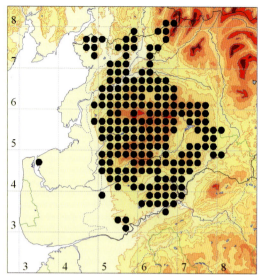
Blechnum spicant

ONOCLEACEAE   SENSITIVE FERN FAMILY

Matteuccia struthiopteris (L.) Tod.   Ostrich Fern

Neophyte. This is a European species introduced into Britain in 1760 and cultivated in gardens.

Very rare (1). It was reported growing outside cottages at Silverdale (Tipping, 2001).

Onoclea sensibilis L.   Sensitive Fern

Neophyte. A North American and eastern Asian fern cultivated in gardens.

Very rare (1). Recorded as well established in an old garden site at Melling (SD57V) in 1967 (E.H., LANC).

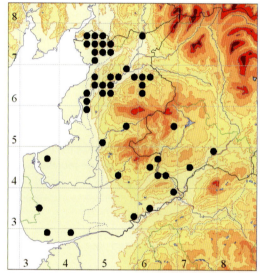
Polystichum setiferum

DRYOPTERIDACEAE   BUCKLER-FERN FAMILY

Polystichum setiferum (Forssk.) T. Moore ex Woyn. Soft Shield-fern

Submediterranean-Subatlantic element.

This fern occurs in damp ancient woodland (BH1) on clay soils but also in hedgerows and roadsides (BH3) in Ireland and western Britain.

Occasional (46). *P. setiferum* is found scattered in northern Lancashire but it is rare in the Fylde and Lancashire VC 64. It is possible that this fern was overlooked by Wheldon and Wilson (1907), who cited only two records, one of which had been lost by 1900. However some of the recent records are from new hedgerow sites suggesting that the observed increase in this species' abundance is real. However whilst the 'New Atlas' observes an increased abundance nationally between 1962 and 2000 it is suggested that this is due to better recording and that populations are stable. On the other hand 'Local Change' notes significantly increased abundance since 1987 (like other woodland ferns) and suggests that it might have benefited from milder winters or increased shading in some woodlands in recent decades.

[**Polystichum setiferum × P. aculeatum**
(**P. × bicknellii** (H. Christ) Hahne)

This is an overlooked but common, sterile hybrid often found in disturbed habitats. The parents may sometimes be recorded in error for this hybrid and it is likely that it is found in the north of the region where both parents grow.]

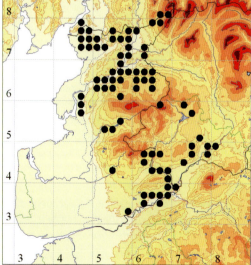
Polystichum aculeatum

Polystichum aculeatum (L.) Roth   Hard Shield-fern

Eurasian Temperate element.

This fern is found on basic rocks, mortared walls, and woodland banks (BH1, 3, 16) throughout the British Isles.

Frequent (79). In northern Lancashire it is found in the east and north of the area. There is no evidence for any change in its distribution or frequency in northern Lancashire. A similar situation occurs nationally although some decrease is noted in south-eastern England ('New Atlas', 'Local Change').

Dryopteris oreades Fomin   Mountain Male-fern

Suboceanic Boreal-montane element.

D. oreades is found in rocky places (BH15, 16) in the mountains of Britain.

Very rare (4). It has only been found in very small quantity at four sites. A single plant was found on the county boundary at Leck (SD67P) in 2000 (E.F.G.) and it was also found in eastern Bowland (Abbott, 2005; SD65K), Trough of Bowland (SD65F) in 2007 (P.G.) and in Croasdale, Bowland Forest High (SD65Y) in 2007 (E.F.G.). All are new records following an improved ability to recognise the species. Nationally populations are stable or possibly declining ('New Atlas').

Dryopteris filix-mas (L.) Schott   Male-fern

Circumpolar Temperate element.

This is a common fern of woodland and hedgerows (BH1, 3) in the British Isles.

Very common (412). The map shows the distribution of *Dryopteris filix-mas sensu lato*. It is a very common fern found in a wide variety of habitats in northern Lancashire and possibly only absent from salt marshes, arable farmland and wet peat covered mires. However it hybridises with *D. affinis* and as this is at least partially fertile it back crosses with either parent sometimes making identification of individual plants difficult. Its distribution is stable both locally and nationally.

Dryopteris affinis *sensu lato*   Golden-scaled Male-ferns

European Temperate element.

D. affinis sensu lato is found in woodlands and hedge banks (BH1, 3) throughout the British Isles.

Frequent (218). This beautiful group of ferns are characteristic of ancient woodland, stream sides in upland areas and hedge banks but they are absent from most lowland areas of northern Lancashire. They are also found in a variety of forms but the delimitation of species and subspecies is problematic and this variation together with the presence of hybrids with *D. filix-mas* makes identification difficult. There is no evidence for a change in their distribution in northern Lancashire or nationally ('New Atlas') but 'Local Change' suggests that they have become more frequent in woodlands (BH1) and inland rock habitats (BH16) since 1987.

During the last twenty years or so specimens of Golden-scaled Male-ferns have been collected in northern Lancashire, especially in Lancaster District by L.A. and P.D. Livermore. Following the publication of a revision of the group (Fraser-Jenkins, 2007) a tentative account of the species found in northern Lancashire is given here.

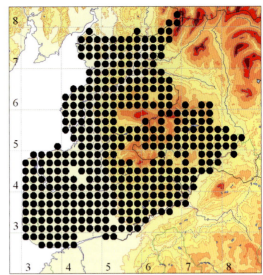

Dryopteris filix-mas s.l.

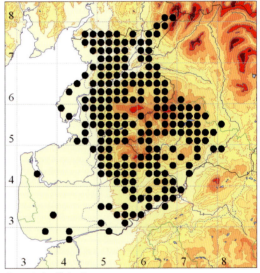

Dryopteris affinis s.l.

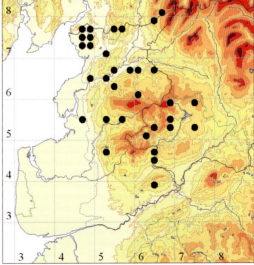

Dryopteris affinis s.s.

Dryopteris affinis (R. Lowe) Fraser-Jenk.

This occurs throughout the range of the group but in the British Isles it is often associated with more upland and western areas. Fraser-Jenkins (2007) recognises several subspecies but it is believed only *D. affinis* ssp. *affinis* and *D. affinis* ssp. *paleaceolobata* (T. Moore) Fraser-Jenk. occur in northern Lancashire.

Frequent (33). In northern Lancashire the golden colour of the unfurling fronds make this fern a beautiful feature of upland stream banks in spring (see Plate 2.5). It is however found in woods and hedges as well as in more open areas beside streams in northern areas and in Bowland.

Dryopteris cambrensis (Fraser-Jenk.) Beitel & W. Buck

D. cambrensis has an oceanic distribution and although several subspecies are recognised only *D. cambrensis* ssp. *cambrensis* occurs in northern Lancashire.

Very rare (3). Fraser-Jenkins (2007) did not list this as occurring in northern Lancashire but specimens (LIV) from Nether Wyresdale (SD55F) collected in 1991 (E.F.G.); Barnacre-with-Bonds (SD54D) in 1991 (E.F.G.) and Caton-with-Littledale (SD56R) in 1997 (A. Pigott) were identified as this species. L.A. and P.D. Livermore also gathered specimens in Lancaster District, which they thought were this species but most if not all are *D. affinis*.

Dryopteris borreri (Newm.) Newm. ex Oberh. & Tavel

This is the most widespread of the *D. affinis sensu lato* species in Europe and in the British Isles. It is found in woodlands, woodland edge and hedgerow habitats.

Occasional (53). In northern Lancashire the distribution of *D. borreri* is probably that of *D. affinis sensu lato*. However whilst it is the most frequent of the *D. affinis sensu lato* species it does not appear to extend as high up the valleys as *D. affinis* but tends to occur more frequently than *D. affinis* in lowland areas.

Hybrids

The cytotypes of *D. affinis* × *D. filix-mas* hybrids are tetraploid or pentaploid whereas the species are diploid or triploid. Several hybrids have been recognised but they are all difficult to identify. They often occur as single plants and may be found wherever the parents grow in close proximity.

In northern Lancashire a specimen (LIV) found in Caton-with-Littledale (SD56R) in 1997 (A. Pigott) was identified as *D. affinis* × *D. filix-mas* (*D. × complexa* Fraser-Jenk.). However Fraser-Jenkins (2007) cites a record of *D. borreri* × *D. filix-mas* (*D. × critica* (Fraser-Jenk.) Fraser-Jenk.) as occurring in VC 60. It is likely that these records are based on the same plant and the voucher specimen at LIV looks as if one of the parents is *D. borreri* rather than *D. affinis*.

Another specimen (LIV) from Over Wyresdale (SD55M) collected in 1991 (E.F.G.) was tentatively identified as a hybrid between *D. borreri* and *D. oreades*. This seems unlikely as *D. oreades* is very rare in northern Lancashire and Fraser-Jenkins (2007) comments that plants attributed to this hybrid have not been confirmed. It is therefore likely that the Over Wyresdale plant belongs to another taxon.

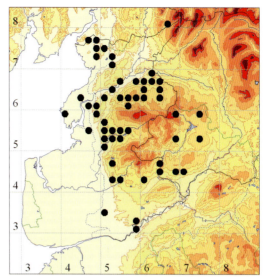

Dryopteris borreri

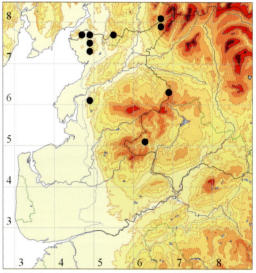

Dryopteris submontana

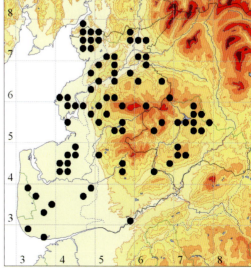

Dryopteris carthusiana

Dryopteris aemula (Aiton) Kuntze

Hay-scented Buckler-fern

Oceanic Temperate element.

D. aemula is found on acidic substrates in woodland and rocky places (BH1, 16) in western Britain and Ireland.

Very rare (1). Only found in one locality in deep recesses of grit rocks on Thorn Crag, Over Wyresdale (SD55Y) in 1985 and 2007 (E.F.G.). This is a hyperoceanic species and its VC 60 locality is at its climatic limit in Britain. Populations in the British Isles are thought to be stable.

Dryopteris submontana (Fraser-Jenk. & Jermy) Fraser-Jenk.

Rigid Buckler-fern

Mediterranean-montane element.

Typically this is found on limestone rocks and pavements (BH16) in northern England and occasionally elsewhere.

Rare (10). In northern Lancashire it is characteristic of limestone rocks and pavement in the north. However it has been found on mortared walls near Garstang in 1954 (V.G. & A.H.), Lancaster in 2000 (B.S.B.I. Recorders' Conference) and unusually on grit rocks on Lythe Fell (C.C. & J.O'R.) in 2004. There is no evidence for a change in its distribution or frequency in northern Lancashire and generally it is stable nationally.

Dryopteris carthusiana (Vill.) H.P. Fuchs

Narrow Buckler-fern

Eurosiberian Boreo-temperate element.

This is found in wet acidic and often peaty places in woodlands (BH1), hedgerows (BH3), by the side of streams and on raised bogs in all parts of the British Isles.

Frequent (80). Although *D. carthusiana* is never abundant it is found in most of northern Lancashire and there is no evidence for a change in its status. It declined nationally before 1962 but further decline has not occurred.

Dryopteris carthusiana × D. dilatata
(**D. × deweveri** (J.T. Jansen) Jansen & Wacht.)

This hybrid fern occurs on fairly acid substrates in many parts of the British Isles wherever the distribution of the parents overlaps.

Very rare (3). It is often found with the parents and so far localities have been on the edge of peat mires at Arkholme (SD57K) in 1999 (J.M.N.); Yealand Storrs (SD47Y) in 2002 (R.C.) and Out Rawcliffe (SD44C) in 2004 (E.F.G.) It is almost certainly overlooked.

Dryopteris dilatata (Hoffm.) A. Gray   Broad Buckler-fern

European Temperate element.

This occurs in almost all habitats (e.g. BH1, 3) and throughout the British Isles.

Very common (429). Broad Buckler-fern occurs throughout northern Lancashire. On grit rocks at high levels in Leck and in the Bowland Fells there is a small form that is often without sporangia or if sporangia are produced, usually late in the season, they appear to be sterile. This is probably var. *nana* Newman mentioned by Wheldon and Wilson (1907) but not now recognised. There is no evidence for change locally or nationally.

[**Dryopteris expansa** (C. Presl) Fraser-Jenk. & Jermy

Northern Buckler-fern

Circumpolar Boreal-montane element.

It is possible that this occurs in the Bowland Fells or in Leck but so far none of the material gathered has proved to be this. One or two sterile plants from Thorn Crag, Over Wyresdale might be *D. expansa* but for certain identification fertile material is required. If it occurs it will be at the limits of its climatic range.]

POLYPODIACEAE   POLYPODY FAMILY

Polypodium vulgare L.   Polypody

European Boreo-temperate element.

Polypody occurs throughout the British Isles mostly in woodlands.

Common (264). *Polypodium vulgare sensu lato* occurs throughout northern Lancashire in woodlands (BH1), on walls (BH3), rocky places (BH16) and on sand dunes (BH19). However recorders rarely noted *P. vulgare sensu stricto* and it is only recently that a determined effort has been made to distinguish the individual taxa of the group, which can only be done by microscopical examination of the sporangia and spores. This shows that *P. interjectum* and the hybrid *P. × mantoniae* may be as frequent as or even more frequent than *P. vulgare*. It would appear however that *P. vulgare* is a woodland plant occurring on trees or on fixed sand dunes. The 'New Atlas' suggests that there was no change in its distribution since 1962 whilst 'Local Change' suggests *P. vulgare sensu lato* could be increasing.

Polypodium vulgare × P. interjectum
(**P. × mantoniae** Rothm. & U. Schneid.)

This is a frequent hybrid and probably occurs throughout the range of the parents in the British Isles.

Occasional (17) but almost certainly more frequent. However as it can only certainly be recognised microscopically few recorders have attempted identification. Most records are post 1998. It occurs in a wide range of habitats although it has not been found on sand dunes and it seems to favour walls and hedge banks (BH3). It is sometimes found with one or other of the parents but often in the absence of both. There is no information on any changes in its distribution or frequency locally or nationally.

Polypodium interjectum Shivas   Intermediate Polypody

Suboceanic Temperate element.

P. interjectum occurs on base-rich substrates in woodlands (BH1) in most parts of the British Isles.

Occasional (50). Although likely to have been overlooked in northern Lancashire it favours base-rich substrates, especially in the north of the region where it grows on limestone rocks and pavements around Morecambe Bay (BH16). However it is also found on walls (BH3) and calcareous banks in woodlands. It is not known if there is any change in its distribution and frequency locally or nationally.

Polypodium interjectum × P. cambricum (P. × shivasiae Rothm.)

This is a rare hybrid found in scattered places in Ireland and western Britain.

Very rare (1). This has only been recorded from a limestone cliff at Warton (SD47W) where it was found in 1976 (W.E.H. at LANC). It could occur elsewhere in the Silverdale to Warton areas but it can only be identified microscopically.

Polypodium vulgare × P. cambricum (P. × font-queri Rothm.)

This rare hybrid is found in scattered localities in western Britain north to southern Scotland

Very rare (1). There is a single record from limestone rocks in a woodland in the Yealand Conyers, Yealand Redmayne area (Livermore and Livermore, 1987; SD47X). It can only be identified microscopically.

Polypodium cambricum L.   Southern Polypody

Mediterranean-Atlantic element.

This occurs in woodlands and on basic rocks and walls (BH1, 16) in Ireland and western Britain

Rare (7) but possibly overlooked. It is confined to limestone rocks and pavement, sometimes in woodlands, in the Silverdale to Warton areas and on Dalton Crags. It is not known if there is any change in its distribution or frequency locally or nationally.

GYMNOSPERMS

Conifers

PINACEAE   PINE FAMILY

Abies grandis (Douglas ex D. Don) Lindl.   Giant Fir

Neophyte. A native of western North America introduced into the British Isles in 1831 for amenity and forestry but not recorded as self-sown until 1961 (Davies, 1961).

Very rare (1). Only recorded from the Hodder valley and Longridge Fell (SD64V) in 1998 (E.F.G.) but probably planted elsewhere on estates and in plantations.

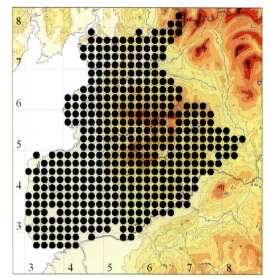
Dryopteris dilatata

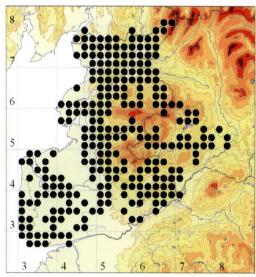
Polypodium vulgare s.l.

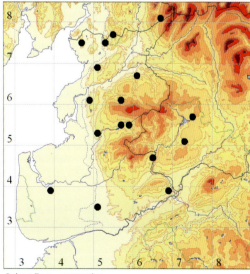
Polypodium × mantoniae

Abies delavayi Franch.   Delavay's Silver-fir

Neophyte. A native of China grown in large gardens and estates for amenity. There are several varieties all introduced into the British Isles about 100 years ago.

Very rare (1). Reported as planted in woodland at Silverdale (SD47S; Livermore and Livermore, 1987).

Pseudotsuga menziesii (Mirb.) Franco   Douglas Fir

Neophyte. A native of western North America introduced into Britain for amenity purposes in 1826.

Very rare (3). Found planted at Aughton (SD56N) in 1985 (J.M.N.), Tatham (SD66D) in 1987 and Over Wyresdale (SD55N; Livermore and Livermore, 1987). It is regenerating from seed at some sites.

Tsuga heterophylla (Raf.) Sarg.   Western Hemlock-spruce

Neophyte. A native of western North America planted largely for amenity in a few scattered localities. First introduced into Britain in 1852 but not recorded from the wild until 1959.

Rare (7). In northern Lancashire it is found scattered in parkland and woodland. It was first recorded by Livermore and Livermore (1987).

Picea sitchensis (Bong.) Carrière   Sitka Spruce

Neophyte. A native of western North America widely planted for timber production. Introduced into Britain in 1832 but not reported from the wild until 1957.

Occasional (45). In northern Lancashire it forms a major constituent of plantations and often regenerates. It was first reported from the Brock valley in 1964.

Picea abies (L.) H. Karst.   Norway Spruce

Neophyte. A native of Europe and western Asia found planted widely throughout Britain. It is not known when it was first introduced into Britain but it was not reported from the wild until 1927.

Occasional (52). In northern Lancashire it is found in plantations, woodlands and gardens and often regenerates. It was first recorded in 1964.

Picea smithiana (Wall.) Boiss   Morinda Spruce

Neophyte. This is a native of the Himalayas. It was introduced into Britain in 1818 (Mitchell, 1974) and occasionally planted in gardens and parkland.

Very rare (1). In northern Lancashire it was found planted at Silverdale (SD47S) by Livermore and Livermore (1987).

Picea orientalis (L.) Link   Oriental Spruce

Neophyte. Oriental Spruce is a native species of Turkey and the Caucasus. It was introduced into Britain in 1839 and is widely grown in gardens and parks.

Very rare (1). In northern Lancashire *Picea orientalis* was recorded from estate parkland at Silverdale (SD47S) in 2000 (C.B.W.).

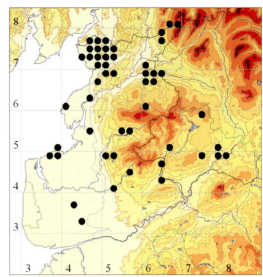

Polypodium interjectum

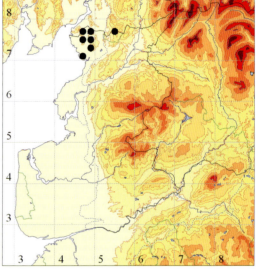

Polypodium cambricum

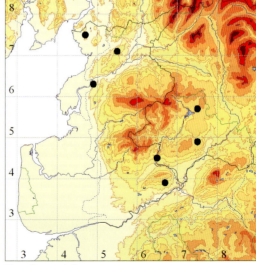

Tsuga heterophylla

Larix decidua Mill.   European Larch

Neophyte. This is a native of the mountains of central Europe and has been planted widely for amenity and in plantations for forestry. It had been introduced into Britain by 1629 but was not reported from the wild until 1886.

Frequent (180). In northern Lancashire it is also found in plantations and sometimes as single trees in hill pastures in the Bowland fells. Wheldon and Wilson (1907) reported it as frequently planted. Larch regenerates in suitable conditions.

Larix decidua × L. **kaempferi** (L. × **marschlinsii Coaz**)   Hybrid Larch

Neophyte. This was first noticed at Dunkeld, Perthshire in 1904 (Stace, 2010) but not reported from the wild until 1983. It is a vigorous hybrid and is planted widely, mostly for forestry.

Occasional (18). It was first reported in northern Lancashire from a plantation on Beacon Fell (M.J.W.) in 1978 but occurs scattered throughout the area.

Larix kaempferi (Lamb.) Carrière   Japanese Larch

Neophyte. This was introduced into Britain in 1861 and reported from the wild by 1957. It is mostly found in forestry plantations.

Occasional (18). In northern Lancashire it is found scattered in plantations. It was first recorded from Leagram, near Chipping in about 1960 (ms at SYT). Both this and *L.* × *marschlinsii* are probably under recorded and confused with each other and with *L. decidua*.

Cedrus libani A. Rich.   Cedar-of-Lebanon

Neophyte. This is a native of the Middle East between Lebanon and Turkey. It was first introduced into Britain in 1638–9. It is found in large gardens and parks.

Very rare (3). In northern Lancashire it was recorded from the Borwick area (SD57G) by Livermore and Livermore (1987) and from Ribbleton, Preston (SD53Q and T) in 1992 (R.L.). It is almost certainly planted elsewhere in parks and gardens.

Cedrus atlantica (Endl.) Carrière   Atlas Cedar

Neophyte. This is a native of the Atlas Mountains of northern Africa and was introduced into Britain in about 1840. It is found in large gardens and parks.

Very rare (1). In northern Lancashire it was reported from Silverdale (SD47S) by Livermore and Livermore (1987) but it is likely to be planted elsewhere.

Pinus sylvestris L.   Scots Pine

Boreal-montane element

It is native in parts of Scotland where it is characteristic of the Caledonian Pinewoods (BH2) but it is probably an archaeophyte in northern Lancashire where it has been planted for amenity and timber.

Common (248). It is found throughout the area, often as single trees or in small groups and in plantations.

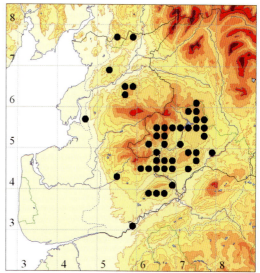

Picea sitchensis

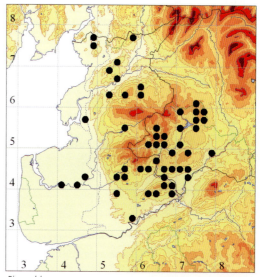

Picea abies

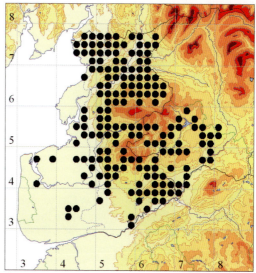

Larix decidua

Pinus nigra J.F. Arnold

A native of central and south-eastern Europe.

Pinus nigra ssp. **nigra**   Austrian Pine

Pinus nigra ssp. **laricio** Maire   Corsican Pine

A native of Corsica, Sicily and southern Italy.

Both subspecies are neophytes with *P. nigra* ssp. *laricio* being introduced into Britain in 1814 and *P. nigra* ssp. *nigra* in 1835. Both are found in forestry plantations and as amenity trees with *P. nigra* ssp. *laricio* found particularly in coastal areas and on sand dunes.

Occasional (63). In northern Lancashire the subspecies were not recorded separately. The species was first recognised from Wrayton in 1967 but it is believed single trees were planted for amenity long before this.

Pinus contorta Douglas ex Loudon   Lodgepole Pine

Neophyte. A native of western North America, which was introduced into Britain in 1851. It is grown as a timber tree and has been widely planted in the last fifty years.

Rare (7). It was first recognised in northern Lancashire in 1987 (C.J.B.) from a shelterbelt at Myerscough. However most records are from forestry plantations, e.g. Gisburn Forest.

Pinus pinaster Aiton   Maritime Pine

Neophyte. This is a native of the Mediterranean and south-western Europe introduced into Britain before 1596 and subsequently planted in coastal areas, especially in southern and western England and Wales.

Very rare (3). In northern Lancashire it was recorded by from Silverdale (SD47S) in 1978 (J.M.N.) and from Fleetwood (SD34D) and Thistleton (SD43D), both in 1998 (E.F.G.).

Pinus strobus L.   Weymouth Pine

Neophyte. A native of central and eastern North America first introduced into Britain for amenity purposes in 1605.

Very rare (1). Only reported from Silverdale (SD47S) by Livermore and Livermore (1987).

ARAUCARIACEAE   MONKEY-PUZZLE FAMILY

Araucaria araucana (Molina) K.Koch   Monkey-puzzle

Neophyte. Monkey-puzzle is a distinctive tree found as a native in the mountains of the southern Andes in South America. It was introduced into Britain in 1795 and was planted widely throughout the British Isles. It has been inconsistently recorded.

Very rare (1). No doubt because it is an obviously planted tree in Lancashire parklands and more occasionally in woodlands it was not recorded until 2005 (Anon) where it was noted in Ellel Grange Wood (SD45W). *A. araucana* flourishes in Lancashire, where the climate is similar to that of its native South America and produces seed readily. It is possibly only a matter of time before seedlings and regeneration occurs.

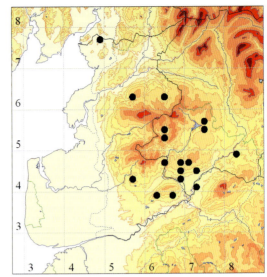

Larix × marschlinsii

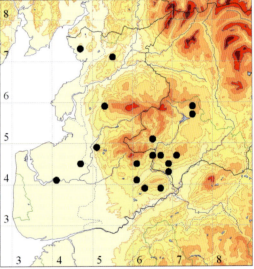

Larix kaempferi

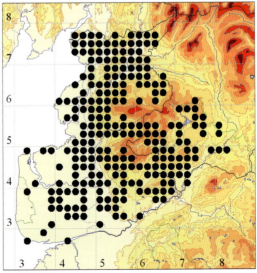

Pinus sylvestris

TAXACEAE   YEW FAMILY

Taxus baccata L.   Yew

European Temperate element.

As a native tree Yew occurs on basic substrates in woodlands (BH1) but it is widely planted. It is found throughout the British Isles.

Frequent (102). Probably only native on the limestone around Morecambe Bay and on Dalton Crags but it occurs widely, often as single trees, throughout northern Lancashire. Yew is especially associated with church-yards and perhaps other sites of religious significance where some trees may be over 1000 years old (Mabey, 1996). However no Yew trees are known to be particularly old in northern Lancashire. Both the 'New Atlas' and 'Local Change' suggest Yew may be becoming slightly more frequent, possibly by deliberate planting as well as by natural spread and this is probably the situation in Lancashire.

CUPRESSACEAE   JUNIPER FAMILY

Sequoia sempervirens (D. Don) Endl.   Coastal Redwood

Neophyte. A native of the Californian coast of North America first intro-duced into Britain in 1844 for amenity purposes.

Very rare (1). Only recorded in northern Lancashire from Silverdale (SD47S) in 1978 (Livermore and Livermore, 1987).

Sequoiadendron giganteum (Lindl.) Buchholz   Wellingtonia

Neophyte. A native of western North America first introduced into Britain in 1853 for amenity purposes. Today it is found in scattered localities in the British Isles but especially in south-western England.

Rare (6). Recorded as planted trees in northern Lancashire from Hornby (SD56Z) in 1986 (J.M.N.), Littledale (SD56R) in 1997 (B.S.B.I.), Silverdale (SD47S, X) in 1999 (C.B.), near Newton-in-Bowland (SD64Z) in 2009 (E.F. & B.D.G) and forming an avenue between Dunsop Bridge and Thorneyholme Hall (SD65Q) in 2008 (E.F. & B.D.G).

Cupressus macrocarpa Hartw. ex Gordon   Monterey Cypress

Neophyte. A native of California, North America introduced into Britain for ornamental purposes in 1838 and now found in many places in the British Isles but especially in south and western Britain.

Very rare (4). Recorded in northern Lancashire from Barnacre-with-Bonds (SD54D) in 1989 (B.S.B.I.), Upper Rawcliffe-with-Tarnacre (SD44L) in 1996 (C.J.B.), Hurst Green (SD63U) in 1999 (E.F.G.) and Waddington (SD74G) by E.F.G. (Abbott, 2005).

Chamaecyparis lawsoniana (A. Murray bis) Parl.   Lawson's Cypress

Neophyte. A native of western North America introduced into Britain in 1854 for amenity purposes and to form shelterbelts. It is also found in forestry plantations. It occurs throughout the British Isles

Rare (11). First recorded in northern Lancashire from Out Rawcliffe in 1902 (M. Harrison of St Michael's School). More recent records

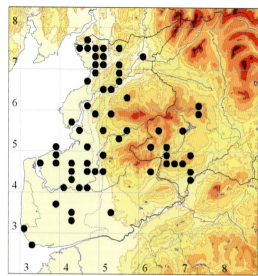

Pinus nigra

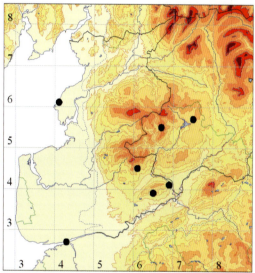

Pinus contorta

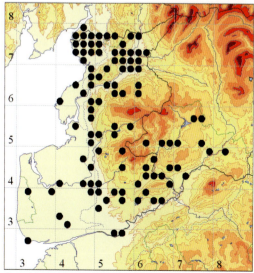

Taxus baccata

are from Silverdale (SD47S) in 1978 (Livermore and Livermore, 1987), Winmarleigh (SD44T) in 1995 (C.J.B.), Upper Rawcliffe-with-Tarnacre (SD44Z) in 1996 (C.J.B.), Nether Wyresdale (SD54E) in 1999 (E.F.G.), Dilworth (SD63J) in 2004 (E.F.G.) and Newton-in-Bowland (SD64Z) in 2008 (E.F. & B.D.G.)

Thuja plicata Donn ex D. Don   Western Red-cedar

Neophyte. A native of western North America introduced into Britain in 1853 for amenity but it is also found in forestry plantations. It is found throughout the British Isles.

Very rare (3). Planted for amenity purposes at Silverdale (SD47S; Livermore and Livermore, 1987), Winmarleigh (SD44T) in 1995 and from near Whitewell (SD64N; Abbott, 2005).

Thuja occidentalis L.   Northern White-cedar

Neophyte. Northern White-cedar is a native species of eastern North America and has probably been grown in British gardens and parks since the sixteenth century. However local flora writers have rarely recorded it.

Very rare (1). In northern Lancashire saplings of *Thuja occidentalis* were seen in parkland at Bashall Eaves (SD64X; Abbott, 2005).

Juniperus communis L. ssp. communis   Common Juniper

Eurosiberian Boreo-temperate element.

Common Juniper is found on chalk in southern England and on limestone elsewhere as well as in moorland areas of upland Britain (BH7, 10, 15, 16).

Occasional (19). This occurs on the limestone in the Silverdale to Warton area and on Dalton Crags. However it also occurs in small quantity on the north side of the Bowland Fells (see Plate 2.8). Except for some of the populations on limestone regeneration is not taking place and over the last fifty years there has been a slow decline of known localities. It is believed that this was once a common species in all the Bowland valleys but by the early years of the twentieth century it was almost extinct in the southern half of the region with the last remaining colonies seen on Tarnbrook Fell, Over Wyresdale and in Whitendale (Pickard, 1902) although there is an unconfirmed report from Whin Fell (SD65L) in 1985 (Lancashire County Council database). Even by the early nineteenth century the pollen record suggests it was rare in the vicinity of Fairsnape Fell (Mackay, 1993). Seed is produced plentifully but no regeneration seems to be taking place in Bowland and on the limestone it is rare. Recent losses are probably due to a combination of over grazing by sheep, moor burning and at least one colony was lost by the Wray flood in 1967 (Garnett, 2002). As part of conservation measures being undertaken in the early twenty-first century (N. Pilling, pers. comm.) Juniper was planted at Hareden (SD65F) and Langden (SD65A). Whilst both the 'New Atlas' and 'Local Change' suggest that Juniper is declining the recorded decrease is not significant, possibly because the decline is slow for this long-lived species.

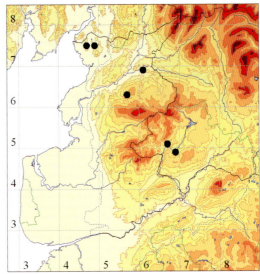
Sequoiadendron giganteum

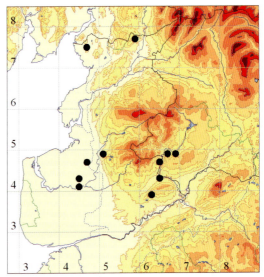
Chamaecyparis lawsoniana

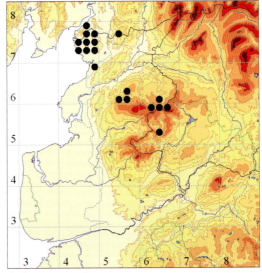
Juniperus communis

ANGIOSPERMS

Flowering Plants

PRE-DICOTS

Primitive Angiosperms

NYMPHAEACEAE   WATER-LILY FAMILY

Nymphaea alba L. ssp. **alba**   White Water-lily

European Temperate element.

It is found scattered in ponds, lakes and other large, still water bodies (BH13) throughout the British Isles.

Occasional (32). In northern Lancashire White Water-lily is found in ponds, the Lancaster Canal, Hawes Water, Silverdale and Little Hawes Water, Yealand Redmayne but there are no records for Lancashire VC 64. Over the last 100 years this species has spread from the six sites listed by Wheldon and Wilson (1907). However it may have been introduced into some locations. These observations are in line with the 'New Atlas' and 'Local Change'.

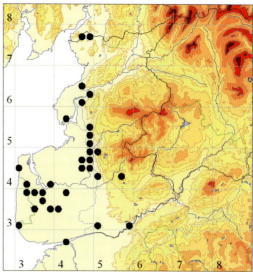
Nymphaea alba

Nuphar lutea (L.) Sm.   Yellow Water-lily

Eurosiberian Boreo-temperate element.

Yellow Water-lily is found in ponds, lakes and slow moving water bodies (BH13) throughout the British Isles but it is rare in much of Scotland, north-eastern and south-western England and southern Ireland.

Occasional (57). It is found scattered in ponds throughout VC 60 and in the Lancaster Canal. It is not found in Lancashire VC 64. Whilst its occurrence in ponds is probably unchanged there has been a marked extension in its distribution in the Lancaster Canal (Greenwood, 2005). There has been little change in its distribution nationally since 1962.

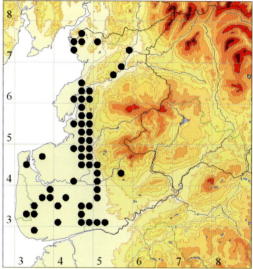
Nuphar lutea

ARISTOLOCHIACEAE   BIRTHWORT FAMILY

Asarum europaeum L.   Asarabacca

Neophyte. A European temperate species known as a medicinal plant in British gardens since at least 1200 but it was not known in the wild until 1640. It was found scattered in Britain but only a few localities remain.

Very rare (1). Old northern Lancashire records date from the early nineteenth century when it was seen near Preston. Other records were from Barton and Ribby Hall, Kirkham (Wheldon and Wilson, 1907) and from Hest Bank in 1932 (Whiteside, no date). More recently there was a report in 1963 that it grew in woods downstream from Calder Vale but the only localised record is from Dalton Hall (SD57M) where it persisted until at least the 1970s (Halliday, 1997).

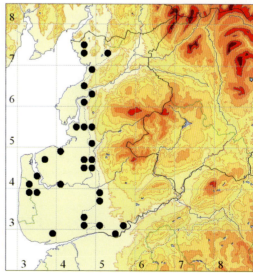
Ceratophyllum demersum

Aristolochia clematitis L.   Birthwort

Neophyte. This is probably a native of south-eastern Europe, northern Turkey and the Caucasus. It is not known when it was introduced into gardens for medicinal purposes but it was not recorded growing wild until 1645 and is mostly found today in south-eastern England. As its name suggests it was used in pregnancy to speed up childbirth and also as an abortifacient (Mabey, 1996).

In northern Lancashire the only record is from a field at Warton by the road to Lytham (Ashfield, 1860).

EU-DICOTS

True Dicotyledons

CERATOPHYLLACEAE   HORNWORT FAMILY

Ceratophyllum demersum L.   Rigid Hornwort

Circumpolar Southern-temperate element.

C. demersum is found in still, eutrophic waters (BH13) mostly in midland and southern England.

Occasional (30). This species is found in ponds and the Lancaster Canal but is confined in northern Lancashire to areas west of the M6. The record from the River Hodder in 1891 (Anon, 1891) was an error for *Myriophyllum alterniflorum* (STY). The first confirmed record (E.H.) was from the Lancaster Canal (SD44T) in 1964 and shortly afterwards it proved to be common in the waterway. However by 2000 it could not be found in the Canal. The causes of its spread into northern Lancashire and its subsequent decline are not known. Preston and Croft (1997) suggest that fluctuations in its abundance may be related to nutrient status. The 'New Atlas' suggests that it may have increased in abundance since 1962 and 'Local Change' confirms that it may still be extending its range.

Ceratophyllum submersum L.   Soft Hornwort

Eurosiberian Temperate element.

C. submersum occurs in still, eutrophic waters (BH13) mostly in the Severn Valley and eastern England.

Rare (6). It was first reported from the Lancaster Canal at Borwick (SD57G) in 1966 (E.F.G.) and from a pond at Fleetwood (SD34D) also in 1966 (E.J.H.), which was subsequently filled in. Later records were from various places in the Lancaster Canal and from the dyke at Crag Foot, Warton. *C. submersum* became much more frequent after 1962 ('New Atlas') but 'Local Change' provided no further comment.

PAPAVERACEAE   POPPY FAMILY

Papaver pseudoorientale (Fedde) Medw.   Oriental Poppy

Neophyte. This is a native of south-western Asia introduced

into cultivation by 1714 but not recorded in the wild until 1927. It is an imposing and popular garden plant.

Very rare (4). It was recorded from a quarry at Dalton (SD57N) in 2007 (G.H.), sand dunes at Lytham-St Anne's (SD32I) in 1999 and (SD32N) in 2009 (both E.F.G.) and from Fleetwood (SD34J) in 2001 (E.F.G.).

Papaver atlanticum (Ball) Coss.   Atlas Poppy

Neophyte. This is a native of Morocco introduced into cultivation in 1889 and recorded in the wild by 1928.

Very rare (2). It was recorded from the River Ribble banks at Preston (SD52J) in 1997 (P.J.) and from Lytham (SD32Y) in 2007 (J.Cl.).

Papaver somniferum L. ssp. **somniferum**   Opium Poppy

Archaeophyte. Probably a native of the eastern Mediterranean region but extensively cultivated throughout the world. It has been found in Bronze Age deposits and frequently from the Iron Age onwards. It is found in disturbed habitats (BH3, 4, 17) throughout the British Isles although it is rare in upland areas and most of Ireland.

Frequent (96). Opium Poppy was first recorded in northern Lancashire from Roman deposits at Ribchester (Huntley and Hillam, 2000) and then not until it was found at Caton in 1941 (J.N.F.). Today it occurs widely throughout VC 60 in disturbed situations (BH3, 4, 17) but there are only two records from Lancashire VC 64. However it was probably present in the wild long before this and C.B. reports that it was self-sown in his garden at St Anne's in 1903 (MANCH).

Papaver rhoeas L.   Common Poppy

Archaeophyte. European Southern-temperate element.

This is characteristically found in disturbed habitats (BH3, 4) throughout most of the British Isles except in upland areas.

Occasional (54). Formerly Common Poppy was a common weed of cereal and other arable crops in northern Lancashire but today it occurs on waste ground, on newly made roadside verges and in other areas where works create newly exposed bare earth. It is mostly found in the west of the area. Its distribution appears largely stable.

Papaver dubium L.   Long-headed Poppy

Archaeophyte. European Southern-temperate element.

This has a similar history and distribution and often occurs in similar situations (BH3, 4) to *P. rhoeas* with which it frequently occurs.

Frequent (89). In northern Lancashire it is perhaps more closely associated with coastal areas but extends up both the Lune and Ribble valleys. Its distribution in northern Lancashire is stable. However the 'New Atlas' suggests it has declined in Britain since 1962 but 'Local Change' suggests it is now extending its range.

Papaver lecoqii Lamotte   Yellow-juiced Poppy

Archaeophyte. European Southern-temperate element.

This annual is an arable weed or is found in other disturbed places (BH4) and is found mostly in south-eastern England and eastern Ireland.

Rare (13). All the records for this taxon in northern Lancashire are from disturbed calcareous soil between Silverdale and Lancaster. These range from old railway tracks, coastal shingle and waste ground to open ground in quarries. It was not recognised 100 years ago and the first record was not made until 1942 (Whellan, 1942). It is not known if populations are stable either locally or nationally.

[Papaver hybridum L.   Rough Poppy

Archaeophyte. Submediterranean-Subatlantic element.

This was recorded by France (1931) from a meadow to the northwest of Marton Mere but as a voucher specimen has not been seen it could be an identification error.]

Papaver argemone L.   Prickly Poppy

Archaeophyte. European Southern-temperate element.

This is found as a weed in arable fields and in other disturbed places on light soils (BH4). It is found mostly in eastern Britain and Ireland.

Very rare (2). In northern Lancashire the only recent records are from Lytham St Anne's (SD32J) recorded sometime between 1964 and 1970 (A.E.R.), and in 1973 (C.F. & N.J.S.) from Bryning-with-Warton (SD32Z). This was always a rare species but H.B.F. in the 1830s said 'it flourished in much perfection in the light sandy soils at Lytham'. Other records from the area were from Blackpool (Thornber, 1837), Lytham (Preston Scientific Society, 1903) and St Anne's (Wheldon, 1898 in Wheldon and Wilson, 1907). In addition to these records for the Fylde coast it was also recorded from Silverdale in 1881 (LDS) and in 1961 (V.G. in database for Stewart, *et al.*, 1994).

Papaver nudicaule L.   Iceland Poppy

Neophyte. This is a native species of northern subarctic regions and has been grown in British gardens for over 100 years. It occasionally escapes into the wild.

Very rare (1). Found on disturbed ground near partly constructed houses at Torrisholme (SD46M) in 1974 (A.E.C.).

Meconopsis cambrica (L.) Vig.   Welsh Poppy

Oceanic Boreo-temperate element. It is believed to be native in parts of Ireland and Wales but elsewhere it is widely naturalised from plants originating in gardens. It is found in woodlands (BH1), hedgerows, on walls (BH3) and in ruderal habitats (BH17).

Frequent (131). This occurs throughout northern Lancashire. Wheldon and Wilson (1907) knew of three records of which the earliest was an introduction by the R. Hodder near Whitewell (Ashfield, 1862). It is probably still extending its range both locally and nationally.

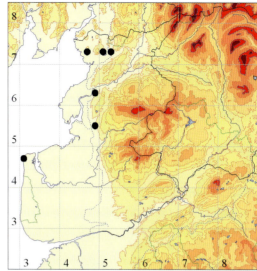

Ceratophyllum submersum

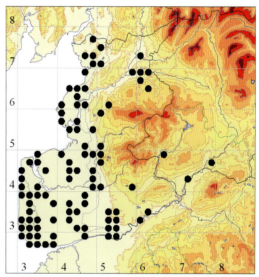

Papaver somniferum

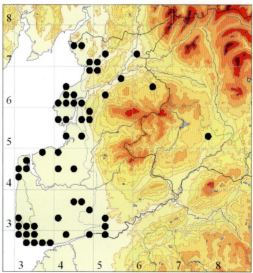

Papaver rhoeas

Glaucium flavum Crantz   Yellow Horned-poppy

Mediterranean-Atlantic element.

This occurs on coastal shingle and more rarely on fore-dunes (BH19) mostly on English and Welsh coasts as well as eastern Scotland.

Occasional (17). In northern Lancashire Yellow Horned-poppy is found at Lytham St Anne's but most populations are found around the Lune estuary and between Morecambe and Warton. It is particularly fine on iron slag heaps at Warton. It seems to have gone from the Wyre estuary (Ashfield, 1860) but otherwise its present distribution reflects the historic records. Similarly little change has been observed in its distribution nationally.

Chelidonium majus L.   Greater Celandine

Archaeophyte. Eurasian Temperate element but widely naturalised elsewhere. It has been known in Britain since Roman times and grown for medicinal purposes (Mabey, 1996). It is found in hedge banks and roadsides (BH3) usually near houses in southern and eastern parts of the British Isles.

Frequent (129). In northern Lancashire it is found mostly in the west of the area but extends up the Lune and Ribble valleys. It is rare in Lancashire VC 64. The 'New Atlas' suggests it has declined at the edges of its 1962 range but 'Local Change' reports no further decline.

Eschscholzia californica Cham.   Californian Poppy

Neophyte. This is a native of North America but widely grown in gardens since 1826 from which it escapes. It was first recorded in the wild in 1864.

Very rare (2). It was recorded from St Anne's as a garden weed in 1967 (A.E.R.) and on a nearby golf course (SD33A) in 2003 (C.F. & N.J.S.).

Corydalis solida (L.) Clairv.   Bird-in-a-bush

Neophyte. A Eurosiberian Boreo-temperate species but absent as a native species from much of western Europe. It was cultivated in Britain by 1596 but not recorded in the wild until 1796.

Very rare (3). First recorded in northern Lancashire by a stream below Caton (J.N.F.) in 1941. More recent records were by the R. Wenning (SD56Z) in the 1970s but gone by 1985 (J.M.N.), on a roadside north of Carr House Green Common (SD43T) in 1969 (C.F. & N.J.S.) and by a wall, Granny's Bay, Lytham St Anne's (SD32N; C.F. & N.J.S.) in c. 1980. Probably a short-lived garden escape.

Pseudofumaria lutea (L.) Borkh.   Yellow Corydalis

Neophyte. This is a native of the southern foothills of the south-western and central Alps but widely naturalised elsewhere in Europe. It was grown in Britain by 1596 and was first recorded in the wild in 1796. By the 1800s it was widespread.

Occasional (58). This was first recorded in northern Lancashire as a garden weed at Garstang (Ashfield, 1860) and Wheldon and Wilson (1907) only added two more localities, at Little Singleton and Barton. Today it is found scattered throughout the area often growing on walls. The 'New Atlas' and 'Local Change' both show that it is still spreading.

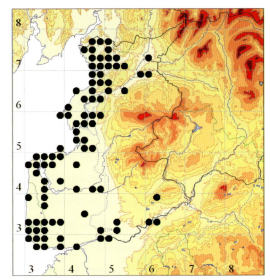

Papaver dubium

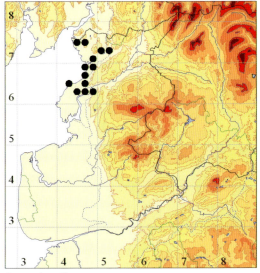

Papaver lecoqii

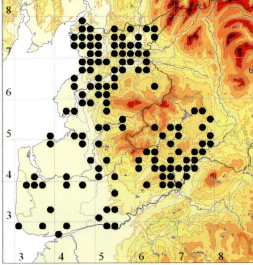

Meconopsis cambrica

Ceratocapnos claviculata (L.) Lidén   *Climbing Corydalis*

Oceanic Temperate element.

This is found on well-drained acidic soils in woodland and heaths, often under Bracken where it is easily overlooked (BH1, 9, 10) and occurs throughout Britain but in Ireland only in the east.

Occasional (42). Climbing Corydalis is found in suitable habitats throughout northern Lancashire. It is not thought that there has been any change in its distribution locally or nationally.

Fumaria capreolata L. ssp. **babingtonii** (Pugsley) P.D. Sell
                                             White Ramping-fumitory

Submediterranean-Subatlantic element.

It occurs as an arable and garden weed as well as in other disturbed habitats (BH3, 4, 17) mostly in coastal areas of the British Isles.

Occasional (20). Apart from one specimen from Hornby material has not been critically determined. Nevertheless it is assumed that all records from Lancashire belong to the endemic *F. capreolata* ssp. *babingtonii* as only this subspecies has been found in mainland Britain. It is found scattered mostly in the west of northern Lancashire but also in the Lune valley. There were too many localities for Wheldon and Wilson (1907) to mention them and the impression is that since 1964 it has become increasingly rare. The last records were from Rossall (SD34D; C.J.B.) in 1998 and Trowbarrow Quarry (SD46S, J.M.N.) in 1981. The 'New Atlas' suggests populations have declined inland but are stable on the coast. The decline of this endemic taxon is of serious conservation concern.

Fumaria bastardii Boreau   *Tall Ramping-fumitory*

Mediterranean-Atlantic element.

It is found scattered as a weed in arable and cultivated land and in disturbed places (BH4) in the west of the British Isles.

Rare (13). In northern Lancashire *F. bastardii* is also found mostly in the west and north of the area. It was never common and Wheldon and Wilson (1907) only knew it from near Little Eccleston. Its distribution is stable both locally and nationally.

Fumaria muralis Sond. ex W.D.J. Koch ssp. **boroei** (Jord.) Pugsley
                                             Common Ramping-fumitory

Oceanic Southern-temperate element.

Common Ramping-fumitory is found in cultivated and disturbed land (BH4) and hedgerows (BH3) mostly in the west of Britain but also in eastern Ireland, eastern Scotland and south-eastern England.

Frequent (91). In northern Lancashire *F. muralis* is found mostly in the west of the area. Little change in its distribution was noted in northern Lancashire or by the 'New Atlas' but 'Local Change' reported that it had extended its range in some areas possibly by exploiting hedgerows whilst at the same time declining as a weed in arable farmland.

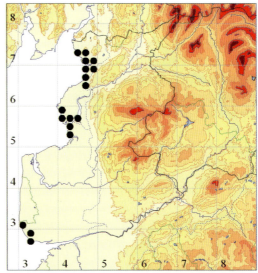
Glaucium flavum

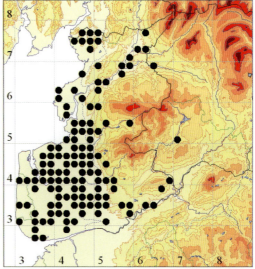
Chelidonium majus

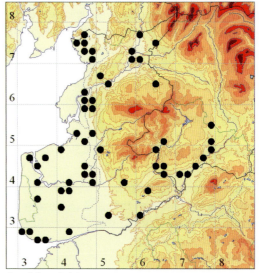
Pseudofumaria lutea

Fumaria purpurea Pugsley   Purple Ramping-fumitory

Endemic to the British Isles with particular concentrations of populations centred in the Orkney Islands, south-eastern Scotland, Lancashire and south-western England. It occurs in disturbed ground (BH3, 17).

Occasional (41). In northern Lancashire most records were in the north-west of the area centred on Lancaster. A few records were from sites on either side of the mouth of the Wyre estuary and from Lytham St Anne's. Only a few records were from arable fields (BH4). There is no evidence for a decline of this species in Lancashire although its appearance is erratic and it seems to exploit new sites if the habitat is appropriate whilst disappearing from others, at least for a time. This seems to be characteristic of its national distribution ('New Atlas').

Fumaria officinalis L.   Common Fumitory

Archaeophyte. This has a European Southern-temperate distribution but it is widely naturalised in cultivated and waste ground (BH3, 17) throughout most of the British Isles.

Frequent (84). *F. officinalis* occurs mostly in the west of northern Lancashire. Both *F. officinalis* L. ssp. *officinalis* and ssp. *wirtgenii* (W.D.J. Koch) Arcang. occur (Livermore and Livermore, 1987) but there has been no systematic recording of the subspecies. It is believed populations are stable locally and nationally.

BERBERIDACEAE   BARBERRY FAMILY

Berberis vulgaris L.   Barberry

European Temperate element. Its status in the British Isles is doubtful. It was recorded in Neolithic deposits in Norfolk and cultivated in mediaeval times and later planted in hedges.

It is found today in hedges, coppices and waste ground (BH1, 3) in most of Britain but it is rare in Ireland.

Rare (14). Wheldon and Wilson (1907) recorded Barberry in only three places in VC 60. One of these was Silverdale where there is a concentration of records today. It is scattered elsewhere in northern Lancashire, often in hedges and scrub. Whilst there are a few more records than 100 years ago it seems all records owe their origins to introductions.

Berberis darwinii Hook.   Darwin's Barberry

Neophyte. A native of Chile and Argentina first cultivated in 1849 and reported from the wild in 1928. Today it occurs in scattered localities throughout much of the British Isles.

Very rare (3). First recorded from Silverdale (Livermore and Livermore, 1987) as a garden escape where it still occurs (SD47R) and near Heald Brow (SD47S) in 2000 (Arnside Naturalists). It was also recorded from Poulton-le-Fylde (SD33P) in 2008 (D.P.E.).

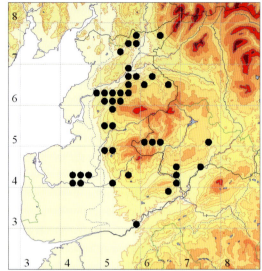

Ceratocapnos claviculata

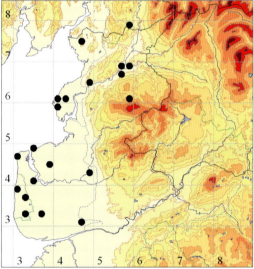

Fumaria capreolata

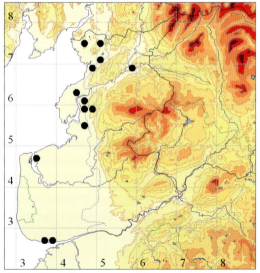

Fumaria bastardii

Berberis aggregata C.K. Schneid. × **B. wilsoniae** Hemsl.

Neophyte. A commonly planted garden plant that occasionally escapes into the wild.

Very rare (1). The only record (P.J. & J.Cl.) is from beside a path at Warton in 2001 (SD47W).

Berberis darwinii Hook. × **B. empetrifolia** Lam.
(**B. × stenophylla** Lindl.) Hedge Barberry

Neophyte. This hybrid arose in a garden around 1860 and is frequently grown for amenity purposes. It was first reported in the wild in 1925.

Very rare (2). In northern Lancashire the only records are from the Borwick area (SD57G; Livermore and Livermore, 1987) and from a hedge bordering Fleetwood Golf Course (SD34D) in 1998 (E.F.G.).

Mahonia aquifolium (Pursh) Nutt. Oregon-grape

Neophyte. A native of western North America introduced into Britain in 1823 and then frequently planted, often for game cover. It was known from the wild in 1874.

Occasional (17). It is scattered throughout northern Lancashire, often in hedges and scrub (BH1, 3). It is naturalised on the limestone around Morecambe Bay but the first records were from Warton (SD47) and Claughton, near Garstang both by E.F.G. in 1967. The 'New Atlas' suggests it has increased its range in Britain since 1962 probably through plantings and escape from cultivation.

RANUNCULACEAE BUTTERCUP FAMILY

Caltha palustris L. Marsh-marigold

Circumpolar Wide-boreal element.

Marsh-marigold is a common plant of wet habitats (BH11) throughout the British Isles.

Common (297). This species is widespread in wetland areas except in the more intensively cultivated parts in the west and upland areas of Bowland (see Plate 2.12). The 'New Atlas' did not report any decline since 1962 but 'Local Change' found that there were considerable recent losses in the south and east of England. In northern Lancashire it is thought that losses may be occurring but for a common species this is not yet reflected in tetrad distribution maps.

Trollius europaeus L. Globeflower

European Boreal-montane element.

This is an attractive meadow and woodland edge species (BH11, 16) of Wales, northern England, Scotland and northern Ireland.

Rare (12). Globeflower is confined to one site at Silverdale and to a few Bowland valley woodlands and pastures. Although Pickard (1901) thought it was frequent in moist meadows and woods on limestone in the Hodder valley (VC 64) Wheldon and Wilson (1907) considered it rare in VC 60 giving details of the sites where they knew it. When the pre 1964 records are mapped together with the post 1964 data the overall distribution has not changed but clearly *Trollius europaeus* has become much rarer. This

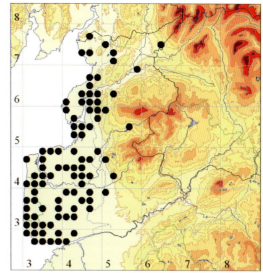
Fumaria muralis

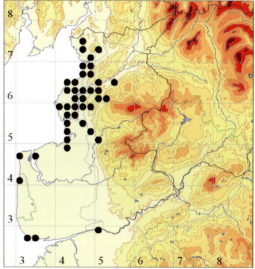
Fumaria purpurea

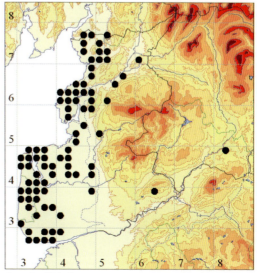
Fumaria officinalis

decline is noted in the 'New Atlas', particularly on the fringes of its range, and 'Local Change' reports further recent decline throughout its range in Britain. In northern Lancashire its decline since 1907 was probably due to agricultural improvement of pastures, but more recently general eutrophication of habitats and increased shading in woodland locations, where some non-flowering populations survive, are probably the causal agents. Most populations of this attractive species are small and endangered.

Helleborus foetidus L. — Stinking Hellebore

Suboceanic Southern-temperate element.

The native range of Stinking Hellebore is obscured by numerous naturalised introductions. However it is thought to be native in parts of England and Wales. Presumed native populations are usually found in woodland edge habitats (BH3).

Rare (10). It is generally regarded as a neophyte in northern England but it could be native in the limestone woodlands (BH1) around Morecambe Bay and possibly in the Ribble valley. However, it is grown in gardens and naturalised plants occur, e.g. at Barton (Wheldon and Wilson, 1907) and Preston in 2000 (P.J.). It was first recorded from Gait Barrows in 1901 (Wheldon and Wilson, 1907), where it still occurs. Neither the 'New Atlas' nor 'Local Change' is able to comment on changes to its distribution.

Helleborus viridis L. — Green Hellebore

Suboceanic Temperate element.

This is another species where it is difficult to know its status. It is generally regarded as native in limestone woodlands (BH1) around Morecambe Bay and in other English woodlands but it is a naturalized escape from cultivation elsewhere.

Rare (8). In northern Lancashire and in the British Isles generally it was used for medicinal and veterinary purposes (Halliday, 1977) and one of its sites in Silverdale is an old orchard. The 'New Atlas' suggests it is declining but 'Local Change' makes no comment.

Helleborus argutifolius Viv. — Corsican Hellebore

Neophyte. This is a native of Corsica and Sardinia but it is grown in gardens from where it sometimes escapes into the wild.

Very rare (1). It was recorded from Silverdale (SD47S) by Livermore and Livermore (1987).

Eranthis hyemalis (L.) Salisb. — Winter Aconite

Neophyte. This is a native of southern Europe grown widely in gardens, estates and churchyards.

Rare (6). In northern Lancashire it was first recorded from Caton (SD56H) in 1973 (L.A.L.). Further records followed from Silverdale (SD47M) in 1974 (L.A.L.), Peel (SD33K) in c. 1980 (C.F. & N.J.S.), near Ellel (SD45W; Livermore and Livermore, 1987), Lytham (SD32T) in 1997 (C.F. & N.J.S.) and Blackpool (SD33I) in 2001 (C.F. & N.J.S.).

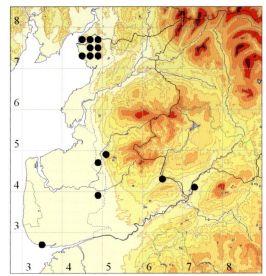

Berberis vulgaris

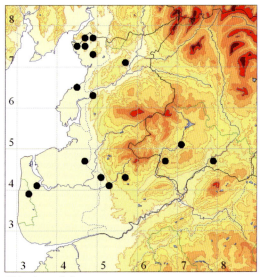

Mahonia aquifolium

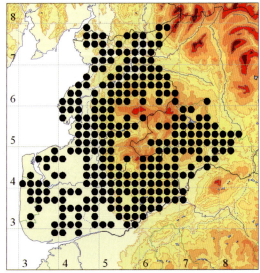

Caltha palustris

Nigella damascena L. — Love-in-a-mist

Neophyte. A native of southern Europe that is often cultivated in gardens. It is found occasionally, usually as a casual on waste ground and rubbish tips.

Very rare (2). The only records for northern Lancashire are as casuals on Lytham tip (SD32) in c. 1966 (A.E.R.) and on disturbed ground, Lytham St Anne's (SD33A) in 2004 (C.F. & N.J.S.).

Aconitum napellus *sensu lato* — Monk's-hood

Neophyte. European Temperate element. It is regarded as native in parts of England and Wales but most plants are escapes from cultivation and records may be for *Aconitum napellus* L. × *A. variegatum* L. (*A.* × *stoerkianum* Rchb.). It was not recorded in the wild in Britain until 1821.

Rare (14). In northern Lancashire the first records were from Bailey Hall Wood (SD63T) in 1886 (Anon, 1891) and from the Holden Clough area in 1892 (Milne-Redhead, 1870s). Today it is found scattered on the edges of woodlands and on roadsides.

Aconitum lycoctonum L. — Wolf's-bane

Neophyte. A European species grown in gardens, which occasionally escapes into the wild.

Very rare (1). The only record is from a roadside at Dutton (SD63P) in 1991 (E.F.G.).

Aconitum napellus × A. variegatum L.
(A. × stoerkianum Rchb.) — Hybrid Monk's-hood

Neophyte. This is a naturally occurring hybrid in Europe and south-western Asia. Hybrid Monk's-hood was in British cultivation by 1752 and has been known in the wild since at least 1905. It is usually found in damp soils often in woodlands and marginal habitats and is found in scattered localities in Britain.

Very rare (1). In northern Lancashire it was found in woodland at Bashall Eaves (SD64X; Abbott, 2005).

Consolida ajacis (L.) Schur — Larkspur

Neophyte. It is probably a native of southern Europe and south-western Asia but grown in British gardens since 1573. It was first recorded from the wild in 1650.

In northern Lancashire it was first found on waste ground at St Anne's in 1902 (C.B. at MANCH). C.B. found further plants on the sand dunes at St Anne's in 1908 and it was recorded from Blackpool tip in 1963 (A.E.R.).

Consolida hispanica (Willk. ex Costa) Greuter & Burdet — Eastern Larkspur

Neophyte. This is a European plant formerly grown in gardens.

In northern Lancashire it was found as a casual at St Anne's in 1907 (C.B.; MANCH).

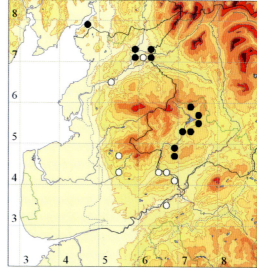
Trollius europaeus

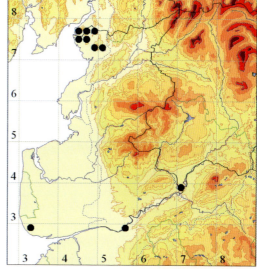
Helleborus foetidus

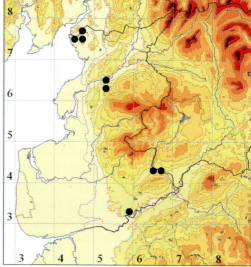
Helleborus viridis

Consolida regalis Gray   Forking Larkspur

Neophyte. This is a European species formerly grown in gardens.

It was recorded from Blackpool tip (SD33I) in 1964 (A.E.R.; Wildflower diary, copy at LIV). This may also have been recorded from Lytham (Anon, 1829).

Actaea spicata L.   Baneberry

Circumpolar Boreal-montane element.

This is only found from limestone rocks (BH16) in northern England.

Very rare (2). Baneberry was recorded from limestone rocks in Ease Gill, Leck (SD68Q) and from a pothole on Leck Fell (SD67U). The last records by L.A.L. are from the 1980s but there is no reason to believe that it is not extant at both localities. There is also a record from Silverdale in 1954 (H.E.G.) although this might refer to an Arnside locality (Halliday, 1997). The 'New Atlas' suggests the long-lived plants are maintaining the historic distribution. 'Local Change' makes no comment.

Anemone nemorosa L.   Wood Anemone

Eurosiberian Temperate element.

This is a common woodland species (BH1) found throughout the British Isles.

Frequent (206). Wood Anemone is found in woodlands throughout northern Lancashire. It is largely absent from much of upland Bowland and the intensively cultivated areas in the west. The 'New Atlas' suggests its distribution is stable but the more recent 'Local Change' records a significant decline. It is believed its distribution in northern Lancashire is unchanged.

Anemone apennina L.   Blue Anemone

Neophyte. A Mediterranean species grown in gardens but it is found in woodlands, churchyards and parkland etc. It has been recorded in the wild in Britain since 1724.

Very rare (2). It was first found in northern Lancashire in 1941 (LIV) where it was found at Silverdale. It was found at Silverdale (SD47M) again in 1974 and from Slyne (SD46T) in 1990 (Livermore and Livermore, 1990a).

Anemone ranunculoides L.   Yellow Anemone

Neophyte. A European plant grown in gardens since 1596 and was first found growing wild in 1778.

In northern Lancashire the only record is from Redscar, Preston in 1900 (Wheldon and Wilson, 1907).

Anemone hupehensis (Lemoine) Lemoine × **A. vitifolia**
Buch.-Ham. ex DC. (**A. × hybrida** Paxton)   Japanese Anemone

Neophyte. Japanese Anemone is a perennial hybrid of garden origin. It has been in cultivation since 1848 and was first recorded in the wild by *c.* 1900. Today it is found on waste ground and as a relic of cultivation, mostly in southern England and the Isle of Man.

Very rare (1). In northern Lancashire *A. × hybrida* was found on waste land near a former railway line at Fleetwood (SD34I) in 2010 (N.J.S.)

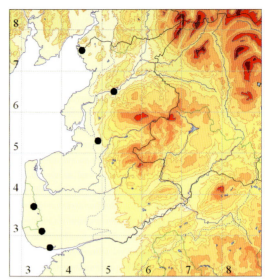

Eranthis hyemalis

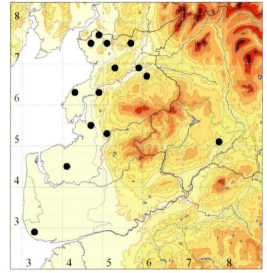

Aconitum napellus

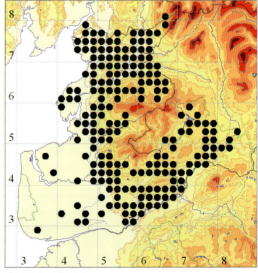

Anemone nemorosa

Clematis vitalba L.   Traveller's-joy

European Temperate element but a neophyte in northern Lancashire.

Occasional (19). Although Halliday (1997) regards this species as native on the limestone around Morecambe Bay it was not recorded in northern Lancashire until 1899 (Wheldon and Wilson, 1907) when it was thought to have been planted. Since 1899 it has spread more widely in hedgerows and woodlands on the limestone in the Silverdale to Warton area with a few scattered localities elsewhere in VC 60.

Ranunculus acris L.   Meadow Buttercup

Eurasian Wide-boreal element.

This is a herb of damp meadows and pastures as well as other habitats (e.g. BH3, 6, 7, 17) and is found all over the British Isles.

Very common (430). Meadow Buttercup is found throughout northern Lancashire in a wide variety of habitats except in some of the Bowland Fells. Little change has been detected in its distribution in northern Lancashire or in Britain as a whole.

Ranunculus repens L.   Creeping Buttercup

Eurasian Boreo-temperate element.

This has a wide ecological tolerance and is found in a variety of habitats (e.g. BH3, 6) in the British Isles.

Very common (449). Creeping Buttercup is found in a variety of generally wet habitats, except peat bogs, throughout northern Lancashire. It has a stable distribution locally and nationally.

Ranunculus bulbosus L.   Bulbous Buttercup

European Southern-temperate element.

This is characteristic of well-drained, neutral or calcareous grassland and sand dunes (BH6, 7, 19) in most of the British Isles.

Common (234). It occurs in calcareous and neutral grasslands, including sand dunes, throughout northern Lancashire. The 'New Atlas' and Abbott (2005) suggest that it might be overlooked and this accounts for a slight decline in its distribution towards the west and north of the British Isles. 'Local Change' does not support this view and suggests it may be increasing. In northern Lancashire, with the continuing loss of old calcareous and neutral grasslands, it might be thought to be decreasing in the region but as yet there is no evidence for this.

Ranunculus sardous Crantz   Hairy Buttercup

European Temperate element.

This is mostly a coastal species of open habitats (BH3, 6, 17) in damp grassland in England and Wales.

Rare (13). In northern Lancashire Hairy Buttercup is confined to coastal grasslands and waste places from Freckleton to Fleetwood but most records are from Rossall to Fleetwood. During the twentieth century this species was lost from most inland areas of Britain ('New Atlas') but further losses seem minimal. In northern Lancashire Wheldon and Wilson (1907) knew it only from Ashton but from 1916 it was recorded from several places between Blackpool and Fleetwood (Wheldon and Wilson, 1925). However H.B.F. suggested in the 1830s that it was one of the more

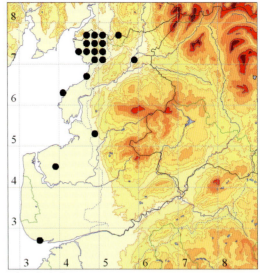
Clematis vitalba

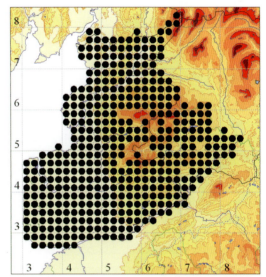
Ranunculus acris

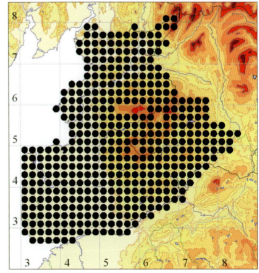
Ranunculus repens

common species but under recorded for *Ranunculus bulbosus* and gave a 'newly laid down field at Stodday' near Lancaster as a habitat and locality. It was also recorded in 1862 from Heaton Marsh near Lancaster (W.H. at LIV) and H.E.B. found it at Overton Marsh, also near Lancaster in 1937. This confusing picture suggests that it was formerly more widespread with a concentration of records in the Lancaster area from where it has now gone. Overall it appears that the distribution of this species has become more restricted and the paucity of post 1990 records suggests that it is declining further.

Ranunculus arvensis L.   Corn Buttercup

Archaeophyte. Eurosiberian Southern-temperate element.

Very rare (1). This is probably only a casual in northern Lancashire. Records are from a cornfield near Garstang in 1914 (A.J.C.), a garden at Poulton-le-Fylde (Stalker, 1960), Blackpool tip (SD33I) in 1963 (Miss Willis) and a plantation in Preston (SD53A) in 1992 (R.L.).

Ranunculus auricomus L.   Goldilocks Buttercup

European Boreo-temperate element.

This is found in woodlands and hedgerows (BH1, 3) in many parts of the British Isles.

Occasional (56). *R. auricomus* is a morphologically variable species and a large number of taxa have been named and many are apomicts (Clapham, *et al.*, 1987). Further study may reveal a number of different species but this variation has not been studied in northern Lancashire. It has an unusual disjunct distribution and is confined to old woodlands and hedge-rows in the north of the county, in the Ribble and Hodder valleys and in a line running north to south between Lancaster and Catterall. The 'New Atlas' suggests the range of *R. auricomus* is stable but 'Local Change' records a clear decline in the last few years and this may be the position in northern Lancashire.

Ranunculus sceleratus L.   Celery-leaved Buttercup

Circumpolar Boreo-temperate element.

This species of wet, eutrophic habitats (BH11, 13, 14) occurs in most of the British Isles but it is rare in many parts of Scotland (except between Glasgow and Edinburgh).

Frequent (174). In northern Lancashire *R. sceleratus* is a common wetland (BH11, 13, 14) species in lowland areas west of the M6 and less commonly in the lower Lune and Ribble valleys. It favours eutrophic marshes but it also occurs in brackish conditions at the top of salt marshes. The 'New Atlas' and 'Local Change' suggest its distribution is stable. However in VC 60 Wheldon and Wilson (1907) thought it 'rather uncommon' and noted about 20 sites. Thus it appears that over the last 100 years *R. sceleratus* has become commoner, probably in response to nutrient enrichment of lowland wetlands.

Ranunculus lingua L.   Greater Spearwort

Eurosiberian Temperate element.

This is a species of ponds, fens and marshes (BH11) throughout much of the British Isles although it is rare in most of Scotland. Its native distribution is obscured by escapes from cultivation.

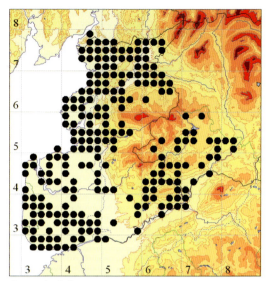
Ranunculus bulbosus

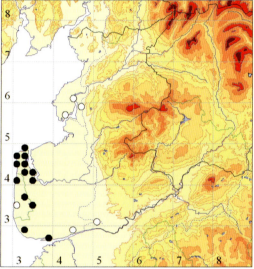
Ranunculus sardous

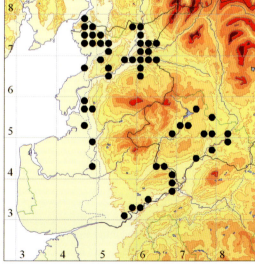
Ranunculus auricomus

Occasional (18). The status of this species in northern Lancashire is uncertain. It was first recorded by Ashfield (1858) but by none of the other early botanists. However by 1925 (Wheldon and Wilson, 1925) a few localities in coastal ditches had been found. Today it still occurs in ponds and ditches in coastal areas but also occasionally inland and in at least some of these it is planted. However in the Heysham peninsula natural spread is taking place. The 'New Atlas' suggests that up to 1962 its native distribution was declining but since then through its popularity as a garden plant its range has expanded making it impossible to distinguish between native and introduced populations. 'Local Change' suggests it may still be expanding its range.

Ranunculus flammula L. ssp. flammula Lesser Spearwort

European Temperate element.

This is a common wetland (BH11) species found throughout the British Isles.

Common (275). In northern Lancashire Lesser Spearwort is found in wetlands throughout the region but occurs less frequently in the intensively farmed lowland areas in the west. Apart from south-eastern England, where *R. flammula* has become less frequent, the 'New Atlas' reports no changes in its distribution and this situation is confirmed by 'Local Change'. As northern Lancashire is well to the northwest of the decline in south-eastern England it is not thought that there has been any change in its distribution.

Ranunculus hederaceus L. Ivy-leaved Crowfoot

Suboceanic Southern-temperate element.

This is found at the edges of small water bodies (BH11, 13) in many parts of the British Isles but it is rare in northern Scotland, south-eastern England and central Ireland.

Frequent (111). Ivy-leaved Crowfoot is found scattered in wet places throughout northern Lancashire but it never extends far into the uplands. The 'New Atlas' reports a long and continuous decline in its distribution in arable farming areas but 'Local Change' suggests there is little recent change in its distribution. The latter situation seems to appertain in northern Lancashire.

Ranunculus omiophyllus Ten. Round-leaved Crowfoot

Suboceanic Southern-temperate element.

This is found at the edge of small water bodies (BH11) and in upland flushes in England, Wales, southern Scotland and southern Ireland.

Frequent (102). *R. omiophyllus* is characteristic of upland flushes in northern Lancashire, which are irrigated with some nutrients and whilst it avoids the most acidic situations it nevertheless favours mesotrophic to oligotrophic conditions. It is found mostly in the Bowland Fells and on Longridge Fell. The 'New Atlas' reports a continuing decline in its distribution but 'Local Change' considers the recent distribution unchanged, which seems to be the situation in northern Lancashire.

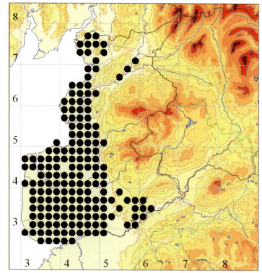
Ranunculus sceleratus

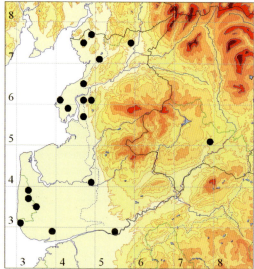
Ranunculus lingua

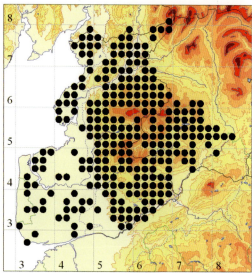
Ranunculus flammula

Ranunculus baudotii Godr.   Brackish Water-crowfoot

European Southern-temperate element.

This is a species of brackish (BH13) coastal marshes around the British Isles

Rare (11). In northern Lancashire *R. baudotii* is confined to coastal marshes including an inland brackish pool at Preesall. However whilst this was never a common plant it appears to have declined in recent years and since 1990 it has only been seen at Fleetwood, Middleton, Silverdale and possibly at Peel. This decline is reflected in an apparent decline shown by the 'New Atlas' elsewhere on western coasts of Britain but because of identification difficulties it is not clear if this is due to under recording or is a real decline.

Ranunculus trichophyllus Chaix   Thread-leaved Water-crowfoot

Circumpolar Wide-boreal element.

This is found in small water bodies (BH11) in much of the British Isles but especially in south-eastern England.

Occasional (24). *R. trichophyllus* is found in ponds, largely in the west of northern Lancashire. Because of identification difficulties it is not clear if all the old records for *Ranunculus drouettii* F. Schultz should be referred here or if some should be included within *R. aquatilis*. Nevertheless it is clear that from the relatively small number of records for either *R. trichophyllus* or *R. aquatilis* 100 years ago (Wheldon and Wilson, 1907) this was never a common species. Unfortunately identification difficulties continue. Most post 1964 records were based on identifications using the shape of the nectar-pit and absence of laminar leaves as diagnostic features but recent work suggests that the shape of the nectar-pit is unreliable (B.S.B.I. Recorders' Conference, 2006). Thus it is likely that some post 1964 records are also errors for *R. aquatilis*. Furthermore there are few recent records. It was recorded at Thwaite House Moss, Carnforth (SD46Z) in 1991 (P.J.), Silverdale (SD47S) in 2000 (C.B.W.) and in the R. Lune oxbows, Melling (SD57V) in 2009 and 2010 (E.F.G.). It is difficult to explain the recent decline of this species as although the 'New Atlas' shows a decline in Britain it is thought that the concentration of pre 1970 records is due to misidentification for other species. 'Local Change' does not report any change in its distribution.

Ranunculus aquatilis L.   Common Water-crowfoot

European Temperate element.

R. aquatilis is found in ponds (BH11) in most of the British Isles.

Frequent (85). Despite confusion with *Ranunculus trichophyllus* this is the commonest of the small flowered water-crowfoots occurring in ponds in lowland areas mostly in the west of northern Lancashire but it also occurs in the Lune valley. There is no doubt that this species has increased in frequency and extended its range during the last 100 years. However because of identification problems the 'New Atlas' and 'Local Change' are not able to give an opinion for Britain as a whole.

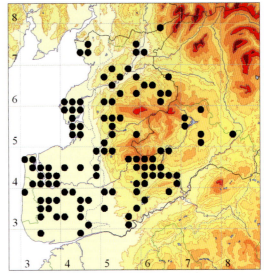
Ranunculus hederaceus

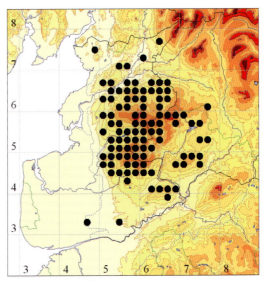
Ranunculus omiophyllus

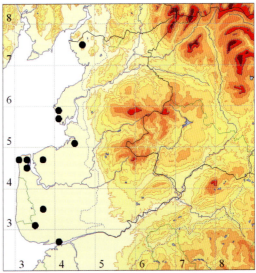
Ranunculus baudotii

Ranunculus peltatus Schrank   Pond Water-crowfoot

European Wide-temperate element.

This is found in slow-moving rivers and ponds (BH11) in England, Wales, Ireland and southern and eastern Scotland.

Rare (6). There were at least ten former localities for *R. peltatus* in ponds, ditches and canals with clusters of records for the Lune valley, around Silverdale, in the Heysham peninsula and near Blackpool and Lytham. Additional records were from Grimsargh, Thornley and Garstang. More recently there have been records from Leighton Moss in 1980 (Arnside Naturalists), Warton near Lytham in 1964 (A.E.R.) and Gressingham in 1968 (E.F.G.). However the only post 1990 records are from R. Lune oxbow pools in the Melling area. Although never common this species has declined over the last 100 years and this decline is continuing. Unfortunately because of identification difficulties it has not been possible to assess change in Britain as a whole.

Ranunculus penicillatus (Dumort.) Bab. ssp. **pseudofluitans** S.D. Webster var. **pseudofluitans**   Stream Water-crowfoot

Ranunculus fluitans × **R. aquatilis** and **R. fluitans** × **R. trichophyllus** (The two hybrids can only be distinguished cytologically and are known as **R. × bachii** Wirtg.)

Ranunculus fluitans Lam.   River Water-crowfoot

European Temperate element and or Suboceanic Temperate element.

These taxa are found in moderately flowing or slow-moving rivers (BH11) in most of the British Isles except western Scotland.

Occasional (20). Identification of these taxa relies on the account by Webster and Rich (1998) but recent studies on this most difficult group have shown that it is perhaps impossible to distinguish between them (except cytologically). In northern Lancashire the situation is complicated by a puzzling history. The first definite records were from the R. Ribble at Preston in 1914 and 1916 (Wheldon and Wilson, 1925), later identified as the sterile *R. × bachii*, yet it seems inconceivable that this large flowered water-crowfoot would not have been recorded in the nineteenth century had it been present. The only earlier records for the Ribble catchment are from the Settle millrace (this was probably at Gildersleets near Giggleswick Station then known as Settle Station) some time before 1870 but where it seems to have gone shortly afterwards (Lees, 1888) and near Hurst Green and Mitton (Anon, 1891) where it was not flowering. Thus although it may have been present in the nineteenth century it was rare but by the mid-twentieth century is was common from above Hellifield to Preston (Savidge, *et al.*, 1963). Although some records have been attributed to *R. fluitans* all material seen by myself, Lees (1888) and Savidge, *et al.* (1963) is morphologically similar with submerged, long, five times divided leaf segments and hispid receptacles. This suggests that the same taxon occurs throughout the catchment and fits the description for *R. penicillatus* ssp. *pseudofluitans* or *R. × bachii*. Thus River Water-crowfoot probably arrived in the river either naturally or was introduced deliberately sometime in the second half of the nineteenth century, perhaps in the Settle area from where it spread downstream (see Plate 2.50).

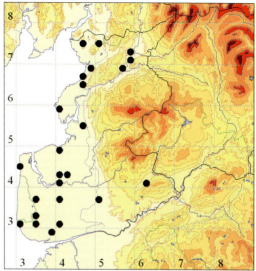

Ranunculus trichophyllus

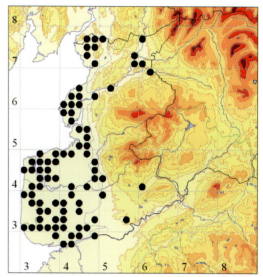

Ranunculus aquatilis

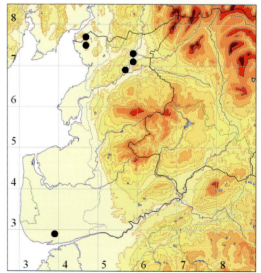

Ranunculus peltatus

Greenhalgh (2009) maintains a distinction between *R. fluitans* and *R. penicillatus* ssp. *pseudofluitans* and suggests that above Sawley the vegetation was dominated by the latter taxon and in the lower reaches, especially below the confluence with the polluted R. Calder, by the more pollution tolerant *R. fluitans*. However, after about 1983 the River Water-crowfoot populations in the upper river were decimated by pollution and an abundance of *Cladophera* spp. but that the more pollution tolerant *R. fluitans* was largely unaffected in the river's lower reaches. The decimation of the River Water-crowfoot populations in response to pollution certainly occurred and whilst still present it is no longer abundant in the upper reaches. The differences in susceptibility to pollution by *R. fluitans* and *R. penicillatus* ssp. *pseudofluitans* are supported by Preston and Croft (1977). However to my knowledge only a plant fitting the description of *R. penicillatus* ssp. *pseudofluitans* has been found in the lower reaches of the river since 1964 and its abundance varies from year to year according to weather conditions and possibly other factors. It is possible that different genetic entities have different susceptibilities to pollution but it is believed that overall *R. penicillatus* ssp. *pseudofluitans* is tolerant of nutrient rich waters although if eutrophication becomes too great direct or indirect effects may cause its loss, as does scouring from floods. In addition to eutrophication various chemicals have polluted the river from time to time and on occasions their effects may have been catastrophic.

Water-crowfoot was absent from the Rivers Brock and Wyre until 1986 but there is also a record from Silverdale in 1936 (CGE), which was identified as var. *vertumnus* C.D.K. Cook.

For convenience it is probably best to regard all river water-crowfoots with long, branched capillary leaves and no laminar leaves as *R. penicillatus* ssp. *pseudofluitans* or *R. × bachii*. Nevertheless some material is close to the description of *R. fluitans*.

The sterile *R.× bachii* was recorded from near Preston in 1914 and from near Hellifield probably in the 1960s (Webster, 1990). In 2010 material was taken from the R. Ribble near Paythorne and grown on in a dish. The material lost its long linear segmented leaves and developed small leaves similar to *R. trichophyllus* but divided five times. The receptacles were hairy and the petals were intermediate in size between *R. trichophyllus* and *R. penicillatus*. The plant was sterile. Presumably this plant was *R. × bachii*. Thus the water-crowfoots in the R. Ribble present a confusing taxonomic picture with an interesting history based on at least one introduction in the mid nineteenth century. However, Webster (1990) suggested that *R. × bachii*, one of whose parents is *R. fluitans*, gave rise to *R. penicillatus* ssp. *pseudofluitans*.

More recent research into water-crowfoots in the R. Eden and R. Itchen (Lansdown, pers. comm., 2010) suggests all material is of hybrid origin whether fertile or not and that the genetic origins of the plants in the two river systems are different although they are morphologically similar. Furthermore it is thought that in any river there may be many different genetic entities. These do not correspond to identifiable morphological characters and each river system contains a different assemblage of genetic entities. It is therefore difficult to understand the separate accounts for *R. fluitans*, *R. penicillatus* ssp. *pseudofluitans* and *R. × bachii* in many national and local accounts of these taxa.

With this complicated situation it seems prudent that even where plants seem to fit the description of *R. penicillatus* ssp. *pseudofluitans* it is probably best to refer all northern Lancashire material to *R. × bachii* (Lansdown, pers. comm., 2010). *R. fluitans* is unlikely to occur.

Ranunculus circinatus Sibth.   Fan-leaved Water-crowfoot
Eurasian Temperate element.

This is found in ponds (BH11) mostly in midland and southern England with localities in Ireland, Wales and eastern Scotland.

Very rare (4). Since 1964 *R. circinatus* has been found in a pond at Claughton, near Garstang (SD54B) in 1965 (J.H. & E.F.G.) but it had gone by 1999 and in oxbows of the R. Lune (SD56U & 67B) by Livermore and Livermore (1987) and J.M.N. who last saw it in 1999. However it was re-found in two R. Lune oxbow ponds (SD57W) in 2010 (Endangered Plants Group). Formerly it was found extensively in the Lancaster Canal and in a ditch near Marton Mere. Eutrophication probably caused its loss from the Lancaster Canal and from the pond at Claughton. The 'New Atlas' also reports a decline in Britain through eutrophication and habitat loss.

Ficaria verna Huds.   Lesser Celandine
Recent molecular research has shown that *Ranunculus ficaria* should be treated as a separate genus (Stace, 2010). This perennial herb is found all over the British Isles in woodlands, hedgerows and other marginal habitats (BH1, 3).

Very common (393). Lesser Celandine occurs throughout northern Lancashire in woodlands hedgerows and other marginal habitats. In addition to native populations it is also grown in gardens and it is likely that in some areas it has escaped from cultivation. The 'New Atlas' and 'Local Change' report little change in its distribution in Britain, which is probably the situation in Lancashire. For many years data on the distribution of subspecies was not gathered but more recently data has accumulated that suggests that there are differences in the distribution of *Ficaria verna* ssp. *fertilis* and *Ficaria verna* ssp. *verna*.

Ficaria verna Huds. ssp. **fertilis**
(Lawralrée ex Laegaard) Stace

Suboceanic Southern-temperate element

This is usually a woodland or hedgerow plant found less commonly in the intensively farmed lowland areas in the west than elsewhere in northern Lancashire.

Ficaria verna Huds. ssp. **verna**

European Temperate element.

This is found in woodlands, hedgerows and marginal habitats, often in the lowland intensively farmed areas of the west but it is also common in the Lune, Ribble and other river valleys. It is possible that at least some populations in marginal habitats are escapes from cultivation. However as more data is received it seems increasingly likely that this is a native subspecies characteristic of river valley woodlands.

Myosurus minimus L.   Mousetail

European Temperate element.

This is found mostly in south-eastern England in nutrient rich, damp and disturbed places (BH4).

It was reported from near Slyne in the 1850s where it was probably a casual (Wheldon and Wilson, 1907).

Adonis annua L.   Pheasant's-eye

Archaeophyte. This is a native of southern Europe but it is known from Iron Age deposits in Britain. It is an arable weed that suffered from improved agricultural methods.

In northern Lancashire it was found near Blackpool (Thornber, 1837) and from waste ground near Bare (Lees, 1899).

Adonis aestivalis L.   Summer Pheasant's-eye

Neophyte. *A. aestivalis* is a native of Eurasia and northern Africa. It is a rare casual in Britain.

In northern Lancashire it was found as a casual at St Anne's (Bailey, 1910).

Aquilegia vulgaris L.   Columbine

European Temperate element.

Native populations are found in calcareous woodlands (BH1) in England and Wales but it is also found as a naturalised garden escape throughout the British Isles.

Occasional (53). Columbine is scattered throughout northern Lancashire. However, whilst this was probably native in woodland on limestone around Morecambe Bay and perhaps also in some of the woodlands in the Brock, Hodder and Ribble valleys most populations today are derived from garden plants. It is possible that plants with small and intensely blue flowers are derived from native populations whilst large multi-coloured flowered plants are clearly derived from gardens. This species has increased its range considerably in Britain during the last 50 years ('New Atlas') probably almost entirely through garden escapes. Already by 1907 Wheldon and Wilson were recording garden escapes in VC 60 and a modest increase in records across the area has occurred since then.

Thalictrum flavum L.   Common Meadow-rue

Eurosiberian Boreo-temperate element.

This is found in fens, ditches and marshes (BH11) in England, Wales and Ireland.

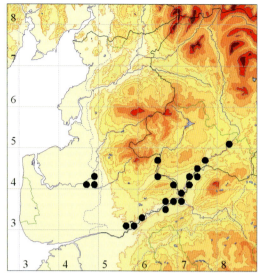
Ranunculus × bachii

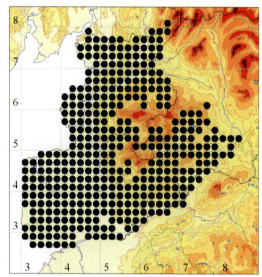
Ficaria verna

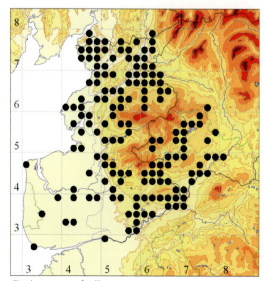
Ficaria verna ssp. *fertilis*

Occasional (32). Common Meadow-rue is a characteristic species of fens, usually near the coast and the brackish upper parts of salt marshes where it occurs with other tall vegetation, and it even survives amongst *Phragmites* reed beds. In northern Lancashire it is reaching the northern limits of its British distribution. According to the 'New Atlas' it has declined since 1930 but recent changes are not significant ('Local Change') and this appears to be the situation in northern Lancashire. However an inland locality at Newton (SD75V) discovered by Pickard (1901) seems to have gone.

Thalictrum minus L.   Lesser Meadow-rue

Eurasian Boreo-temperate element.

This is found in base-rich heaths, grasslands and sand dunes (BH16, 19) in many parts of the British Isles but in midland and southern England especially many populations are garden escapes. These are referred to as *T. flexuosum* Bernh. by Chater (2010).

Occasional (21). Lesser Meadow-rue is a morphologically variable but little understood species and various subspecies have been recognised. Until the taxonomy is better understood all forms are considered part of a variable species. Wheldon and Wilson (1907) found it on Dalton Crags, by the River Wenning and from Lytham where it has not been seen recently. Today it occurs in coastal situations from Silverdale to St Anne's, on Dalton Crags and occasionally elsewhere but the increase in the species' distribution is almost certainly due to the escape of garden plants. Presumed native populations on the sand dunes at Lytham St Anne's and on Dalton Crags are very small – perhaps fewer than 50 plants. The 'New Atlas' reports a similar situation for Britain but 'Local Change' reports no significant recent changes.

PLATANACEAE   PLANE FAMILY

Platanus occidentalis L. × P. orientalis L.
(Platanus × hispanica Mill. ex Münchh.)   London Plane

This is of uncertain horticultural origin but apparently arose in the seventeenth century and has been recorded in the wild since 1939. It is a long-lived hardy tree tolerant of pollution and widely planted in towns and cities. It is recorded from England, especially in the south east, Wales, Ireland and central Scotland.

It is recorded from northern Lancashire (Preston, *et al.*, 2002; Stace, *et al.*, 2003) but the records for VC 60 are based on those of Livermore and Livermore (1991), which are believed to be of planted trees in urban Lancaster. It has also been recorded from Grimsargh (SD53W) in 2008 (Anon.).

BUXACEAE   BOX FAMILY

Buxus sempervirens L.   Box

Submediterranean-Subatlantic element but a neophyte in northern Lancashire.

Although Box is probably native on some of the chalk downs in southern England it has been widely cultivated since Roman times. It is common

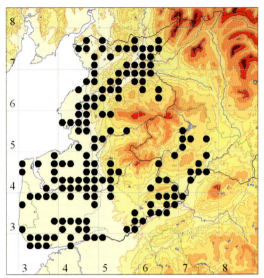

Ficaria verna ssp. *verna*

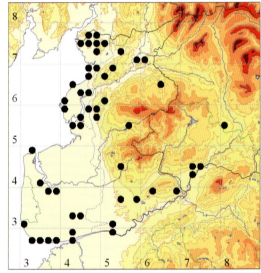

Aquilegia vulgaris

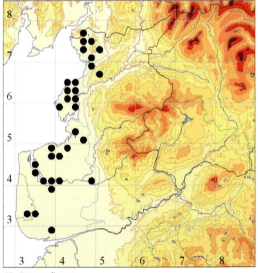

Thalictrum flavum

in the southern half of Britain but it is much rarer further north and in Ireland. It is found in woodland, scrub and in parks.

Rare (11). Box was first found at St Michael's (SD44Q) in 1902 (St Michael's School) and has been found in scattered localities in northern Lancashire since then.

PAEONIACEAE   PEONY FAMILY

Paeonia officinalis L.   Garden Peony

Neophyte. This species was cultivated in Britain by 1548 and was recorded in the wild in 1650. It is a native of southern Europe.

Very rare (4). In northern Lancashire it was recorded as a garden escape at Morecambe (SD46M; Livermore and Livermore, 1987), by the canal, Lancaster (SD46V; Livermore and Livermore, 1989) and from an old railway line near Morecambe (SD46L; Livermore and Livermore, 1990b). It was also recorded from a roadside bank at Lytham St Anne's (SD33A) in 2009 (E.F.G.).

GROSSULARIACEAE   GOOSEBERRY FAMILY

Ribes rubrum L.   Red Currant

Suboceanic Temperate element but widely naturalised outside its native range.

It occurs throughout the British Isles in woodlands (BH1) and fens but its status is unclear. Small-fruited plants may be native but most plants are large-fruited derived from cultivation. It was first recorded in 1568.

Frequent (125). It is found throughout northern Lancashire but especially in the north of the area and in the Wyre and Ribble valleys. It is thought that most records are derived from garden plants. There has been a considerable increase since Wheldon and Wilson (1907) recorded Red Currant from seven localities. It has also increased nationally.

Ribes spicatum E. Robson   Downy Currant

European Boreo-temperate element.

This is a shrub of limestone woods and streamside (BH1, 16) in northern England and Scotland. However its native distribution is obscured by garden escapes.

Very rare (1). The status of this species in northern Lancashire is unclear, as it may have been confused with *R. rubrum*. However it was recorded by Wheldon and Wilson (1907) from near Docker and by the R. Lune below Kirkby Lonsdale and from the Silverdale area in 1956 (V.G.). The only recent record is from the Hodder valley near Whitewell (SD64N; Abbott, 2005).

Ribes nigrum L.   Black Currant

Neophyte. This has a Eurosiberian Boreo-temperate distribution but it is widely naturalised outside its native range. It is a shrub of damp woods, hedgerows and shaded stream sides and is found throughout the British Isles. It was first cultivated in Britain shortly after 1600

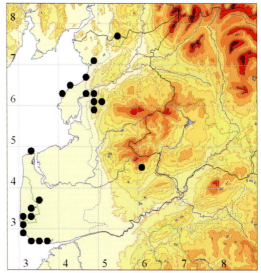
Thalictrum minus

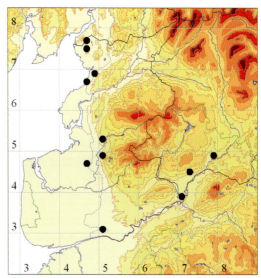
Buxus sempervirens

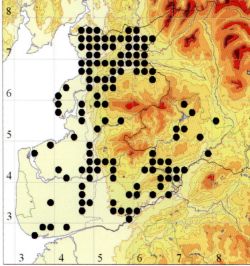
Ribes rubrum

when plants were imported from Holland and it was found in the wild in 1660.

Frequent (88). Black Currant was first recorded in northern Lancashire from the Salwick Brook (Ashfield, 1858) and today occurs throughout the area. This is a considerable expansion of its range since 1907 when Wheldon and Wilson knew it from only eight localities.

Ribes sanguineum Pursh   Flowering Currant

Neophyte. This is a native of western North America and was introduced into Britain in 1826. It is a common garden plant and was first recorded in the wild in 1916. It occurs throughout the British Isles and whilst it may be common in some, mostly urban areas, it is rare in others. It is found in a variety of wasteland and woodland edge habitats.

Occasional (48). It is not known when *R. sanguineum* first grew wild in northern Lancashire but it was sometime before 1964. Today it occurs scattered throughout the area.

Ribes alpinum L.   Mountain Currant

European Boreal-montane element but its native distribution is obscured by garden escapes. It is found in calcareous woodland (BH1) in many parts of Britain but its native distribution is thought to be limited to the Pennines and northern England.

Rare (7). This is probably a garden escape or planted as most records are from hedges or old gardens, e.g. in the Brock valley and from between Longridge and Chipping. There is also a record from Storth, Newton-in-Bowland (SD64Z; Pickard, 1901). Today it is found scattered throughout northern Lancashire but it is possibly under recorded as non-flowering bushes in hedges are easily missed.

Ribes odoratum H.L. Wendl.   Buffalo Currant

Neophyte. This is a native of North America introduced into cultivation in Britain in 1812. It was recorded in the wild in 1975 and today occurs in scattered localities in Britain. It is found as a garden escape, on waste ground and in hedgerows.

Very rare (2). In northern Lancashire it was found in a hedge at Forton (SD45V) in 1998 (E.F.G.) and at Heysham Power Station (SD45E) in 1999 (J.M.N.).

Ribes uva-crispa L.   Gooseberry

Neophyte. This has a European Temperate distribution but it is widely naturalised outside of its native range. It has been grown in British gardens since the thirteenth century but it was not recorded in the wild until 1763. Today it is found in most parts of the British Isles on waste ground, in woodlands and in hedges.

Common (239). Whilst *R. uva-crispa* occurs throughout much of northern Lancashire it is rare or absent from most of Bowland and in the east it is most often found in the Hodder and Ribble valleys.

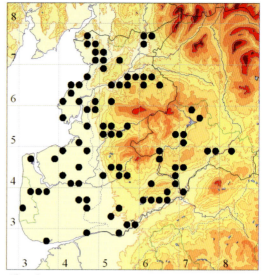

Ribes nigrum

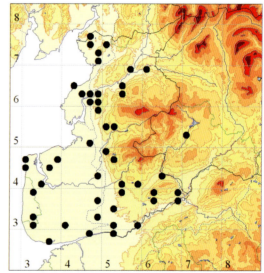

Ribes sanguineum

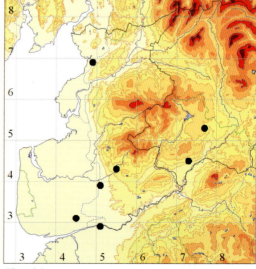

Ribes alpinum

SAXIFRAGACEAE   SAXIFRAGE FAMILY

Astilbe chinensis (Maxim.) Franch. & Sav.   Tall False-buck's-beard

Neophyte. This is a native of Nepal grown occasionally in British gardens since 1825. It was recorded growing wild in Roxburghshire in 1906 but not again until it was found by a river in Kintyre in 1987.

Very rare (1). A buck's-beard was found naturalised in riverside woodland at Halton (SD56C) in 1970 (E.F.G.) when it was identified as *A. japonica* (C. Morren & Decne.) A. Gray but the voucher specimen at LIV appears to be *A. chinensis*. Unidentified *Astilbe* spp. were recorded from waste ground between Lancaster and Morecambe and by a river bank in the Halton area (SD46L, SD56C; Livermore and Livermore, 1987).

Astilbe chinensis × A. japonica (Morren & Decne.) A. Gray
(**Astilbe × arendsii** Arends)   Red False-buck's-beard

Neophyte. This is a clump forming perennial herb that originated in cultivation and was first seen in Britain in 1907. It is found as a garden escape on waste ground and in damp places. *Astilbe × arendsii* was first recorded in the wild in 1979 but it is now found in scattered localities throughout Britain.

Very rare (1). Red False-buck's-beard was recorded in northern Lancashire from the edge of an old gravel pit at Warton (SD57B) in 2009 (E.F.G.).

Bergenia sp.   Elephant-ears

Livermore and Livermore (1987) recorded this as a garden escape from tetrad SD46T and thought it might be *B. cordifolia* (Haw.) Sternb., although *B. crassifolia* (L.) Fritsch is the more usual introduction found in parts of England and the Isle of Man. *Bergenia crassifolia × B. ciliata* (Haw.) Sternb. (*B. × schmidtii* (Regel) Silva Tar.) is thought to be the commonest taxon in cultivation and was found on the sand dunes at Lytham St Anne's (SD33A) in 2010 (M.W.).

Darmera peltata (Torr. ex Berth.) Voss ex Post & Kuntze
                                        Indian-rhubarb

Neophyte. This is a native of western North America and was introduced into cultivation in Britain about 1873. It was known from the wild by about 1920 and occurs in many parts of the British Isles.

Very rare (3). Indian-rhubarb was first recorded in northern Lancashire from near Lytham in 1959 (V.G.; LIV) and Holden Clough in 1961 (V.G.; LIV). More recently it was seen naturalised in woodland at Halton (SD56C) in 1970 (E.F.G.) and subsequently from near Lancaster (SD45Z; Livermore and Livermore, 1987) and Lytham Hall Wood (SD32P) in 1988 (C.F. & N.J.S.), this latter probably confirming the 1959 record from near Lytham.

Saxifraga cymbalaria L.   Celandine Saxifrage

Neophyte. This is a native of south-western Asia, northern Africa and Romania. It was introduced into cultivation in 1880 and was known from the wild by 1908. Today it is recorded from scattered localities in many parts of the British Isles.

Very rare (2). It was recorded in northern Lancashire from a path in Silverdale (SD47S) in 1996 (A.U.) and from tetrad SD47M where it was found at the base of, and on the top of, a path-side wall in 2007 (E.F. & B.D.G.).

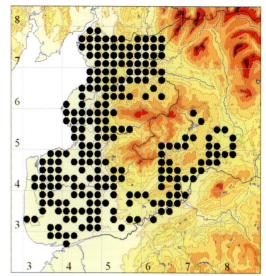

Ribes uva-crispa

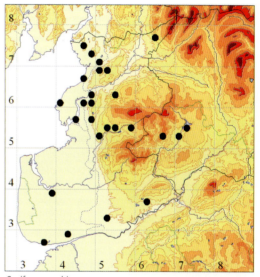

Saxifraga × urbium

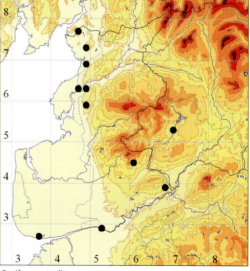

Saxifraga × polita

Saxifraga umbrosa L. × **S. spathularis** Brot.
(S. × urbium D.A. Webb) Londonpride

Neophyte. A popular garden plant that was known in Britain before 1700. It was reported from the wild in 1837 and is now found throughout the British Isles although it is rare in some parts.

Occasional (26). Londonpride was first recorded in northern Lancashire near Botton, Wray-with-Botton in 1899 (Wheldon and Wilson, 1900) although it was recorded in a garden at St Michael's as early as 1815 (Herb. Fleetwood Museum). Today it is found as a garden escape throughout the area although it appears to be most frequent in the north of the region.

Saxifraga hirsuta L. Kidney Saxifrage

Oceanic Temperate element but a neophyte in northern Lancashire.

This only occurs as a native plant in south-western Ireland but occurs as a garden escape and is naturalised in some parts of the British Isles including parts of the Pennines and southern Lakeland. However it is difficult to distinguish from hybrids with *S. umbrosa* and *S. spathularis*. The accounts of this and its hybrids are therefore tentative.

Very rare (3). Kidney Saxifrage was recorded from Hurst Green (SD63Y; LIV) in 1999 (E.F.G.) and in VC 64 from near Doeford Bridge (SD64L) and Browsholme Hall (SD64X), both in the Hodder valley (Abbott, 2005). A voucher specimen at LIV from near Hawes Water (SD47T) collected in 1959 (H.E.B.) also appears to be *S. hirsuta* although other material collected in 1989 from presumably the same site (see below) suggests at least some of the plants in the colony were *S. × polita*. Also it is possible that *S. hirsuta* recorded by Ashfield (1858, 1860) from near Lower Lea, Over Wyresdale was *S. × polita*..

Saxifraga spathularis × **S. hirsuta**
(S. × polita (Haw.) Link) False Londonpride

Native in north-western Spain and south-western Ireland but a neophyte elsewhere. It backcrosses with both parents making identification difficult and uncertain.

It is grown in gardens and has escaped into the wild especially in north-western England and parts of Scotland where it occurs in damp shady places.

Rare (11). This was first recorded in northern Lancashire from near Hawes Water, Silverdale (SD47T) in 1973 (L.A.L.) although there is some doubt about the identity and some plants were close to if not *S. hirsuta*. Most other records are from localities in the north west of the area, in the Hodder valley and at Lytham St Anne's.

Saxifraga umbrosa × **S. hirsuta** (**S. × geum** L.)
Scarce Londonpride

Neophyte. This hybrid was cultivated in Britain by 1754 and was recorded from the wild in 1854. However it is an uncommon garden plant and occurs in only a few places in damp shady places in the British Isles. It is easily confused with *S. hirsuta* and *S. × polita*.

Very rare (3). This was first confirmed in northern Lancashire from tetrad SD66I in 1987 (L.A.L.). It was also found in Quernmore (SD55E) in 1998 (E.F.G.) and near Slaidburn (SD75B) in c. 2005 (P.P.A.). *S. × geum* was recorded from near Newton-in-Bowland (SD65W) in 1899 and from below Whitewell SD64N in 1902 (both J.F.P.; LDS) but without critical determination these records could be for *S. × polita* or *S. hirsuta*.

Saxifraga granulata L. Meadow Saxifrage

European Temperate element.

This is a plant of moist well-drained grasslands and woodland edge habitats (BH1, 6, 7) and occurs throughout Britain and more rarely in eastern Ireland. However it also occurs as an escape from cultivation in some areas.

Occasional (35). Meadow Saxifrage grows in damp woodlands and grasslands in the Lune, Hodder and Ribble valleys and occasionally elsewhere where it is probably a garden escape. It has increased its range considerably over the last 100 years since Wheldon and Wilson recorded it from only four localities. However nationally losses noted by the 'New Atlas' have continued ('Local Change').

Saxifraga hypnoides L. Mossy Saxifrage

Oceanic Boreal-montane element.

This is a plant of moist, often rocky places and flushes (BH7, 15, 16) in upland areas of the British Isles. It also occurs occasionally as a garden escape but these plants may be complex hybrids.

Very rare as a native plant (5) and rare including garden escapes (7). As a native species this is found in damp and often rocky places and in flushes usually on limestone in the upland parts of Leck and Ireby. It is likely that these plants are tetraploid (2n = 52) in contrast to diploid cytotypes (2n = 26) found more commonly in areas to the south west of Lancashire (Parker, 1979). It was also found as a garden escape by the Lancaster Canal at Lancaster (SD46V) in 1971 (E.F.G.) and on the Lytham St Anne's Local Nature Reserve (SD33A) in 1985 (M.J.) where it persisted for several years. There has been no change in its distribution locally or nationally.

Saxifraga tridactylites L.   Rue-leaved Saxifrage

European Southern-temperate element.

Rue-leaved Saxifrage is a winter annual flowering early in the year in dry open habitats, e.g. sand dunes, limestone rocks and on walls (BH3, 16, 19). It occurs in England, Wales and Ireland but more rarely in Scotland.

Frequent (71). In northern Lancashire this is a common species in the north of the area especially on calcareous rocks and also on the Fylde coast. There are occasional records elsewhere especially on calcareous substrates in the east. There has been no change in its distribution in northern Lancashire but the 'New Atlas' reports a widespread decline in southern and eastern England since 1950 but no further decline was noted by 'Local Change'.

Heuchera sanguinea Engelm   Coralbells

Neophyte. Coralbells is a native of southern North America and Mexico and occurs as a naturalised garden escape in Britain. It has been cultivated in Britain since 1882 and was recorded in the wild in 1967.

Very rare (1). Livermore and Livermore (1990) recorded it from Lancaster (SD46Q).

Tolmiea menziesii (Pursh) Torr. & A. Gray   Pick-a-back-plant

Neophyte, a native of western North America. It was introduced in 1812 and grown as a houseplant and in gardens. It was recorded from the wild by 1928 and it occurs in many parts of the British Isles, especially between Glasgow and Edinburgh in Scotland. It is naturalised in a few areas.

Rare (10). This was first recorded in northern Lancashire from woodland at Bartle Hall (SD43W) in 1964 (E.H.; LANC) and from an old garden site at Blackpool (SD33I) in 1965 (E.H.). However it has become naturalised in wooded tributaries of the R. Ribble on the south side of Longridge Fell where it was first seen by the Dean Brook, Hurst Green (SD63Z) in 1967 (V.G.) and by the R. Ribble itself downstream to Preston.

Tellima grandiflora (Pursh) Douglas ex Lindl.   Fringecups

Neophyte. This is a native of western North America and was introduced into British cultivation in 1826. It was recorded from the wild by 1908 and occurs in many parts of the British Isles.

Occasional (15). In northern Lancashire it was first recorded from Heysham (SD46A) in 1975 (A.E.C.). Subsequently it has been recorded from scattered localities throughout the region. It is established in woodlands in the Ribble valley, where it is probably under recorded, and perhaps elsewhere.

Chrysosplenium oppositifolium L.

Opposite-leaved Golden-saxifrage

Suboceanic Temperate element.

This spring flowering plant is found on wet ground by springs in woodlands, hedgerows and in upland areas in flushes and by small streams (BH1, 14). It is found throughout the British Isles although it is rare in parts of eastern England and central Ireland.

Common (240). In northern Lancashire Opposite-leaved Golden-saxifrage is a common species in the east and north of the area. There has been no change in its distribution locally or nationally.

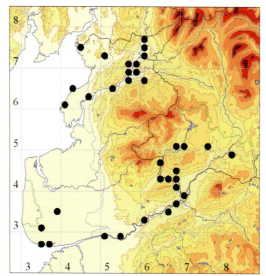

Saxifraga granulata

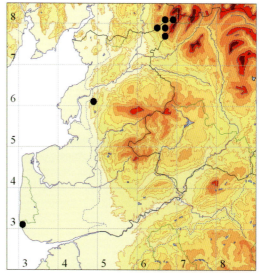

Saxifraga hypnoides

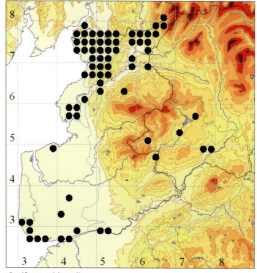

Saxifraga tridactylites

Chrysosplenium alternifolium L.   Alternate-leaved Golden-saxifrage

Circumpolar Wide-boreal element.

This occurs in similar habitats to *C. oppositifolium* but it is more restricted to shaded situations (BH1, 14). It occurs in much of Britain but it is rare or absent from northern Scotland, western Wales, south-western and eastern England. It is not found in Ireland.

Frequent (95). In northern Lancashire it has a more restricted distribution than *C. oppositifolium* being apparently absent from much of central Bowland. However it seems especially frequent in the Ribble, Hodder and Brock valleys. There has been no change in its distribution in northern Lancashire and although there were losses in East Anglia and parts of the English Midlands before 1930 populations nationally seem to have stabilised since then.

CRASSULACEAE   STONECROP FAMILY

Crassula helmsii (Kirk) Cockayne   New Zealand Pigmyweed

Neophyte. This is a native of Australia and New Zealand and was first cultivated in Britain in 1927. It was found in the wild in 1956 (Greensted, Essex) and since the late 1970s has spread rapidly north and west. It grows submerged in ponds and shallow lakes or as an emergent on damp ground. Today it is found in much of England and Wales but it is still rare in Scotland and Ireland.

Rare (11). This was first recorded from the Lowther Gardens, Lytham (SD32N) in 1984 (C.F. & N.J.S.) from where it was removed. The next record was from a pond on the St Anne's Old Links Golf Course (SD33A) in 1998 (P. B.). Since then it has been recorded from other localities on the Fylde coast and occasionally inland. In 2009 the Lancashire Wildlife Trust Endangered Plant Group found it in the R. Lune Oxbows, Melling-with-Wrayton (SD57V). No doubt this invasive aquatic will spread further in future years.

Umbilicus rupestris (Salisb.) Dandy   Navelwort

Mediterranean-Atlantic element but status in northern Lancashire unclear.

Navelwort is a perennial herb growing on walls and in rock crevices usually on acidic substrates (BH3, 16) in western Britain and in Ireland. However it occurs further east as an introduction.

Very rare (2). Navelwort was first found at the base of a limestone wall in Silverdale (SD47M) in 2006 (Jill Webb) where it still grows and again on an old sandstone wall in a lane at Bailrigg, Scotforth (SD45Z) in 2008 (E.F. & B.D.G). At this site it was associated with *Saxifraga* × *polita* and probably *Polypodium* × *mantoniae*. Although private gardens were not far away the plant community on the wall gave the impression of having been established for a very long time. It seems that it reached both sites by natural spread or at Bailrigg as a garden throw out many years ago from old gardens in the nearby hamlet. However although *U. rupestris* had not been reported in VC 60 prior to these records the vice-county is within the overall area of its native distribution in Britain.

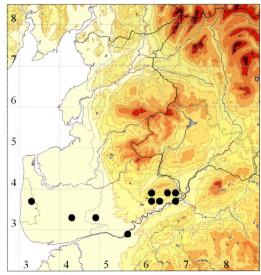
Tolmiea menziesii

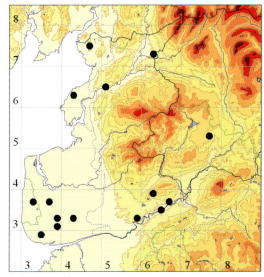
Tellima grandiflora

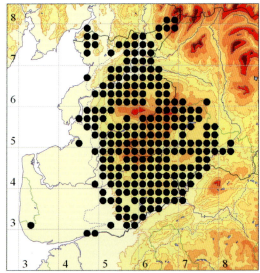
Chrysosplenium oppositifolium

Chiastophyllum oppositifolium (Ledeb.) Stapf ex A. Berger

Lamb's-tail

Neophyte. This is a native of the Caucasus and was introduced into Britain as a garden plant. It is now a popular garden species and was recorded in the wild from near Matlock (Anon, 1933) but it has only been found subsequently in a few places.

Very rare (3). In northern Lancashire Lamb's-tail was found at Slaidburn (SD75B) in 2005 (P.P.A.), on a wall in Silverdale (SD47M) in 2008 (J.Cl.) and near Dale Head Church, Easington (SD75H) in 2011 (E.F.G.).

Sempervivum tectorum L.

House-leek

Neophyte. This is a native of central and southern Europe more or less naturalised on roofs and old walls. It has been grown in gardens since 1200 and was known in the wild by 1629. Individual colonies are long-lived.

Very rare (5). This was first recorded in northern Lancashire from Aldcliffe in the 1830s (Fielding MS). Other early records were from Blackpool (Thornber, 1837), Leck (Petty, 1893), Holden Clough area, Bolton-by-Bowland (Milne-Redhead, 1870s) and Wheldon and Wilson (1907) also noted records from Preesall, both sides of the R. Wyre near St Michael's and at Tarnbrook, Over Wyresdale. It was still present on a roof at Tarnbrook (SD55X) in 2006 (E.F.G.) and other post 1964 records are from Heysham (SD46A) in 1975 (A.E.C.), Lancaster (SD46Q; Livermore and Livermore, 1991), Mallowdale, Roeburndale (SD66A) in 2004 (E.F.G. & J.M.N.) and near Dale Head Church, Easington (SD75H) in 2011 (E.F.G.)..

Sedum rosea (L.) Scop.

Roseroot

Circumpolar Arctic-montane element but a neophyte in northern Lancashire.

This is found as a native plant on sea cliffs and on mountains of the British Isles.

Very rare (1). In northern Lancashire there is an unattributed record for the 10km square SD32 from 1972 (B.R.C.) but otherwise the only record is from Lancaster (Livermore and Livermore, 1991).

Sedum spectabile Boreau

Butterfly Stonecrop

Neophyte. This is a native of China and Japan that was first cultivated in Britain in 1868. It was recorded in the wild in Wiltshire in 1930 and today occurs in woodlands, roadsides and on waste ground throughout England, Wales, and the Isle of Man but much more rarely in Scotland and Ireland.

Rare (7). *S. spectabile* was first recorded from Lancaster (SD46L; Livermore and Livermore, 1987; SD46W, 46Q, Livermore and Livermore, 1991) and has since been found in a few other localities in VC 60.

Sedum telephium L.

Orpine

Eurasian Temperate element.

This is found in wood-borders, hedgerows, on rocky banks and on limestone pavement (BH1, 3, 16). It is found in England, Wales and in much of Scotland except in the north and west. It was introduced into Ireland and the Isle of Man and in Britain many colonies may be derived from garden plants.

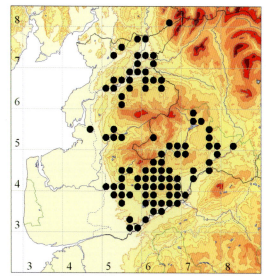

Chrysosplenium alternifolium

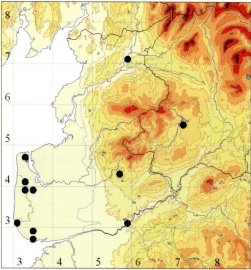

Crassula helmsii

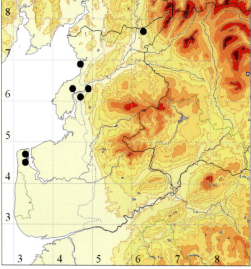

Sedum spectabile

Occasional (23). Orpine is found in several places in VC 60 but in most cases it is impossible to determine its status. It occurs on limestone near Slaidburn (SD75A) where it was first seen by J.F. Pickard (1901) and more recently in 2007 (P.G.). However the colonies on limestone in the Silverdale area and at Slaidburn and on the cliffs at Heysham are likely to be native although Wheldon and Wilson (1907) did not record it at the latter site. There has been a modest increase in the number of sites in northern Lancashire over the last 100 years, probably due to the recording of garden escapes but nationally there is a confused picture. The 'New Atlas' shows a decrease in the distribution in England but considers that the problem of garden escapes obscures what is happening to its native distribution whilst 'Local Change' suggests that there is no significant change.

Sedum spurium M. Bieb. — Caucasian-stonecrop

Neophyte. This native of the Caucasus is widely naturalised in temperate Europe. It was introduced into cultivation in 1816 and was recorded in the wild by 1910. It is found throughout the British Isles but it is rare in parts of Scotland and Ireland.

Occasional (35). This was first recorded on a sea wall at Knott End (SD34P) in 1967 (J.H.) and subsequently from several sites in northern Lancashire. There seems to be a concentration of records in the Lancaster – Morecambe – Bolton-le-Sands region in the northwest of the area.

Sedum rupestre L. — Reflexed Stonecrop

A neophyte with a European Temperate distribution but cultivated in Britain since the seventeenth century. It was known in the wild by 1666 and occurs today on old walls, rock outcrops, roadside banks and on waste ground throughout the British Isles although it is rare in parts of Ireland and Scotland.

Occasional (20). This was first recorded from stone walls in Heysham in the 1830s (Fielding MS) but not seen again until it was found at St Anne's in 1968 (A.E.R.). Today it is mostly found near the coast of VC 60 with a single record in the Bowland area of VC 64.

Sedum fosterianum Sm. — Rock Stonecrop

Oceanic Southern-temperate element but a neophyte in northern Lancashire.

Rock Stonecrop is found in open well-drained habitats in Wales and south-western England but it occurs elsewhere in the British Isles as a garden escape.

Very rare (5). This was first recorded from an old wall at Bailrigg (SD45Y) in 1862 (W.H.; LIV). Post 1964 records are from Overton (SD45J) in 1975 (A.E.C.), Heysham (SD46A, 46F; Livermore and Livermore, 1987), Hest Bank (SD46T; Livermore and Livermore, 1989) and near Whitewell in the Hodder valley (SD64M; Abbott, 2005).

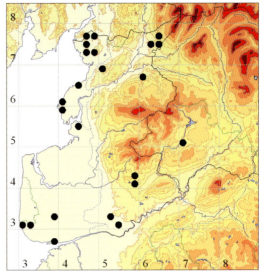
Sedum telephium

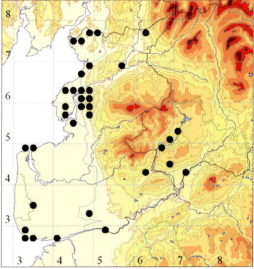
Sedum spurium

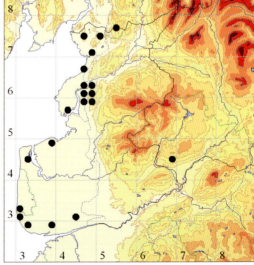
Sedum rupestre

Sedum acre L.   Biting Stonecrop

European Temperate element.

This is found on undisturbed but open habitats or on skeletal, stony and sandy substrates (BH16) throughout most of the British Isles.

Frequent (190). Biting Stonecrop is found throughout northern Lancashire but it is especially common in coastal areas. Although Wheldon and Wilson (1907) reported this as common in northern VC 60 they only recorded eight other localities suggesting an expansion of the range of the species over the last 100 years. Nationally its distribution is stable.

Sedum sexangulare L.   Tasteless Stonecrop

Neophyte with a European Temperate distribution.

It was first recorded in the wild in Britain by 1763. It was formerly more widespread as a garden plant but it is now infrequently cultivated. It occurs in scattered localities in the southern half of the British Isles.

In northern Lancashire the only records are from Silverdale (Petty, 1902; A.J.C. in 1915; LSA).

Sedum album L.   White Stonecrop

Archaeophyte with a Submediterranean-Suboceanic distribution.

This occurs on thin soils, stony or cindery substrates in open habitats throughout the British Isles although it is rare in north-eastern Scotland.

Frequent (80). In northern Lancashire this was first recorded from Chaigley and Chipping (Anon, 1891) but today it is found throughout the area. It is especially frequent in the north of VC 60 and at Lytham St Anne's. This increase in its distribution is reflected nationally.

Sedum anglicum Huds.   English Stonecrop

Oceanic Temperate element.

This is a plant of base-poor substrates, on rocks, sand dunes and shingle (BH16, 18) mostly in western coastal areas of Britain and around the coasts of Ireland.

Very rare (1). Formerly this grew on banks near Sunderland, Overton (SD45I; Ashfield, 1860) and on the Far Naze cliffs, Heysham (SD36V; Wheldon and Wilson, 1907), which were destroyed when Heysham Harbour was built in 1904 (Clague, 2004). It was also introduced to Higher Island in the R. Hodder (SD64V; Anon, 1891) and in 2007 it was found at Lytham St Anne's (SD32J), possibly a garden escape (P.G.).

Sedum confusum Hemsley   Lesser Mexican-stonecrop

Neophyte. This is a native of Mexico and was first found as a garden escape in Cornwall in 1976.

Very rare (1). In northern Lancashire the only record is from Overton (SD45I) in 2000 (E.F.G.) when it was found growing on a wall with *S. spurium*.

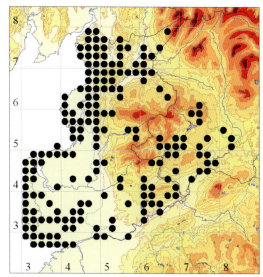
Sedum acre

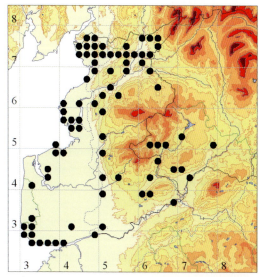
Sedum album

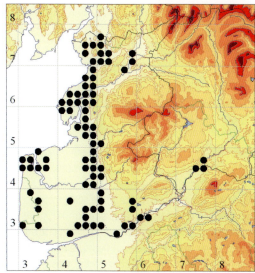
Myriophyllum spicatum

HALORAGACEAE WATER-MILFOIL FAMILY

Myriophyllum verticillatum L. Whorled Water-milfoil

Circumpolar Temperate element.

Whorled Water-milfoil grows in still or slow moving, calcareous waters (BH13, 14) in England, Wales and Ireland.

Very rare (1). The only records in northern Lancashire are from Ashton Marsh (SD52E; Ashfield, 1858) and in ponds at Staining, Blackpool (SD33M) where it was first recorded in 1965 (A.E.R.). However as ponds have been filled in it has been transplanted into neighbouring ponds where it was still found in 2000 (M.S.). There has been a considerable decline in its distribution in the British Isles, especially in England.

Myriophyllum aquaticum (Vell.) Verdc. Parrot's-feather

Neophyte. This is a native of central South America and has been grown in British water gardens since 1878. It was first recorded in the wild in 1960 in Surrey but it has spread northwards as far as southern Scotland. It is also found in Ireland and in the Isle of Man. Only female plants are known in Britain and it spreads when plant fragments are introduced into ponds either accidentally or deliberately when surplus plants from water gardens are dumped in them or by other means.

Very rare (3). Parrot's-feather was first found in two ponds at Poulton-le-Fylde (SD33J, N) some time in the 1990s but it had gone from both by 1998 (M.S.). It was also found in a pond in an industrial estate at Bispham, Blackpool (SD34F) in 2003 (M.S.)

Myriophyllum spicatum L. Spiked Water-milfoil

Eurasian Temperate element.

This grows in a wide range of mesotrophic to eutrophic and often calcareous waters (BH13, 14) throughout the British Isles.

Frequent (83). Spiked Water-milfoil has been recorded from many parts of northern Lancashire where it occurs in ponds, the Lancaster Canal and in the Rivers Lune and Ribble. There has been no change in its distribution locally or nationally.

Myriophyllum alterniflorum DC. Alternate Water-milfoil

Suboceanic Boreo-temperate element.

This is found in less nutrient rich waters than *M. spicatum* and often in swift flowing rivers (BH13, 14). It is found mostly in western parts of the British Isles but including the whole of Scotland whilst it is rare or absent from much of England.

Occasional (21). Sometimes *M. alterniflorum* can be confused with *M. spicatum* and occasionally it may have been recorded in error for the latter species. It is much less common than *M. spicatum* and whilst there are scattered records from the north and east of the area its stronghold is the River Lune and its oxbows where Wheldon and Wilson (1907) also recorded it. However in recent years it has spread to the R. Wyre in the vicinity of Garstang. Nationally there was a substantial decline in England largely before 1930 ('New Atlas').

VITACEAE GRAPE-VINE FAMILY

Vitis vinifera L. Grape-vine

Neophyte. A native of southern and central Europe, northern Africa and south-western Asia. It is a scrambling woody perennial naturalised in hedges in southern Britain and occurs occasionally elsewhere.

Very rare (2). Grape-vine was recorded from Roman deposits at Ribchester (Huntley and Hillam, 2000). More recently it was reported from near the R. Ribble at Preston (SD52) in 1966 (A.E.R.) and from an overgrown tip near Marton Mere, Blackpool (SD33M) in 2000 (M.J.) where it had been known for several years.

Parthenocissus quinquefolia (L.) Planch. Virginia-creeper

Neophyte. This is a native of North America and was introduced into cultivation before 1629. It was recorded in the wild by 1972 and occurs in scattered localities in southern Britain, especially in southern England and Ireland.

Very rare (3). Early records of this in northern Lancashire were recorded as 'Virginia-creeper' and may not necessarily have referred to this species. Nevertheless the unlocalised and unattributed record for Preston (SD52J) made in 1965, is almost certainly this species. It was confirmed as growing on a tunnel entrance of the Dock Railway in 1984 and 2007 (E.F.G.; LIV) but it had been known here for many years before 1984. Virginia-creeper was also found nearby close to the R. Ribble in 2006 (Anon). Other records are from Fleetwood (SD34I) in 1995 and South Shore, Blackpool (SD33B) in 2007 (both C.F. & N.J.S.). It is likely that the 1965 record is the first for *P. quinquefolia* growing wild in Britain.

Parthenocissus vitacea (Knerr) Hitchc.

False Virginia-creeper

Neophyte. This scrambling woody climber is a native of North America and was introduced into cultivation before 1824 but it is often confused with *P. quinquefolia*. It was recorded in the wild by 1948 and is found today in scattered localities in southern Britain.

Very rare (3). In northern Lancashire False Virginia-creeper was recorded from the Lancaster Canal at Lancaster (SD46X; Livermore and Livermore, 1989). It was also found scrambling on hedges and walls in Silverdale (SD47T, S) in 2000 and 2003 (E.F.G.).

Parthenocissus tricuspidata (Siebold & Zucc.) Planch.

Boston-ivy

Neophyte. Boston-ivy is a native of China and Japan and was introduced into British cultivation in about 1862. It was recorded from the wild by 1928 but it is not as popular in gardens as *P. quinquefolia*. It has been recorded in scattered localities in southern Britain and occasionally elsewhere.

Very rare (2). The only records in northern Lancashire are from Preston (SD52J, 53F) in 1984 (E.F.G.).

FABACEAE   PEA FAMILY

Robinia pseudoacacia L.   False-acacia

Neophyte. This deciduous tree, a native of eastern North America, was introduced into Britain in the 1630s. It was known from the wild by at least 1888 and it is extensively planted for amenity. Most records are from England and Wales.

Very rare (2). The only records in northern Lancashire are from woodland in Morecambe (SD46M) in 1975 (A.E.C.) and from Borwick (SD57B) in 2009 (E.F.G).

Colutea arborescens L.   Bladder-senna

Neophyte. A deciduous shrub introduced into Britain by 1568 but it has only become naturalised in the wild since 1900, initially spreading along railways. It is a native of southern Europe and occurs mostly in midland and south-eastern counties of England.

Very rare (2). In northern Lancashire it was recorded from a tip at Lytham (SD32Y) in 1966 (J.H.) and from near Fairhaven Lake, Lytham St Anne's (SD32I) in 1995 (C.F. & N.J.S.).

Onobrychis viciifolia Scop.   Sainfoin

Eurosiberian Temperate element but introduced into northern Lancashire.

Agricultural varieties of Sainfoin were introduced in the seventeenth century obscuring its probable native distribution on chalk grassland in southern England. It continued to be used as a fodder plant until the nineteenth century and today it is often found in wild flower mixes used in amenity planting.

Very rare (3). Sainfoin was first recorded from Carleton (St Michael's School, 1902). Subsequent records are from Marton Moss (c. SD33G) in the period 1948–1955 (M. Quinn), sand dunes at St Anne's (SD32E) in 1966 and 1969 (A.E.R.), a roadside bank at St Anne's (SD32I) in 1966 (A.E.R.) and near Lancaster railway station (SD46Q) in 1984 (D.P.E.).

Anthyllis vulneraria L.   Kidney Vetch

European Boreo-temperate element.

This is found on free draining, usually calcareous soils in open communities, often on sand dunes and in calcareous grassland (BH7, 19). It is found throughout the British Isles.

Occasional (51). In northern Lancashire Kidney Vetch is found in coastal areas and more rarely inland. Where material has been critically examined most records are for ssp. *vulneraria*. Whilst the distribution of Kidney Vetch has remained unchanged or has possibly extended its range in northern Lancashire 'Local Change' reported a decline nationally.

Anthyllis vulneraria L. ssp. lapponica (Hyl.) Jalas

European Boreal-montane element.

This subspecies is found on sand dunes, coastal cliffs and inland in rocky places but it also occurs in ruderal habitats. Most records are from northern coasts of the British Isles.

Very rare (2). In northern Lancashire A. *vulneraria* ssp. *lapponica* was found on old railways at Lancaster (SD46R) and Quernmore (SD46X) by Livermore and Livermore (1990b). It is probably a casual in the region.

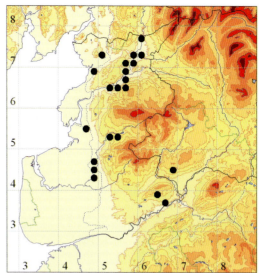

Myriophyllum alterniflorum

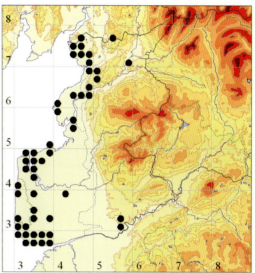

Anthyllis vulneraria

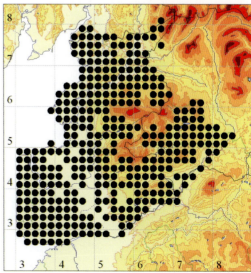

Lotus corniculatus

Lotus tenuis Waldst. & Kit. ex Willd.   Narrow-leaved Bird's-foot-trefoil

European Southern-temperate element.

This is a species of coastal grazing marshes and rough grassland inland (BH3, 6, 7). It is found mostly in south-eastern England.

Very rare (1). The only record in northern Lancashire is from a coastal hedge bank at Overton (SD45J) in 1974 (A.E.C.). It is not clear whether or not there has been a change in its distribution nationally.

Lotus corniculatus L.   Common Bird's-foot-trefoil

Eurasian Southern-temperate element.

This is a common species found throughout the British Isles in neutral to calcareous grasslands (BH6, 7).

Very common (375). Common Bird's-foot-trefoil is found throughout northern Lancashire. Var. *sativus* Hyl. was recorded from a car park at Bolton-le-Sands (SD46T) in 1997 (B.S.B.I.), Lytham (SD32Z) in 1995 (C.F. & N.J.S.), by the M6, Broughton (SD53M) in 2005 (C.F. & N.J.S.) and near Dalton (SD57N) in 2006 (G.H.). It may occur elsewhere as it is probably introduced in amenity landscaping schemes. There has been no change in the distribution of *L. corniculatus* locally or nationally.

Lotus pedunculatus Cav.   Greater Bird's-foot-trefoil

European Temperate element.

L. pedunculatus is found in wet meadows, marshes and by rivers, ponds and lakes (BH11) throughout the British Isles.

Very common (370). Greater Bird's-foot-trefoil is found throughout northern Lancashire. There has been no change in its distribution locally or nationally.

Ornithopus perpusillus L.   Bird's-foot

Suboceanic Temperate element.

This is a winter annual of short open grassland (BH8) on free draining acidic soils in England, Wales, southern and eastern Scotland and eastern Ireland.

Rare (11). In northern Lancashire Bird's-foot is found on sandy soils at Blackpool and Lytham St Anne's, Overton, Silverdale and Fleetwood. It may have become slightly more frequent over the last 100 years as old records were confined to Moss Side, St Michael's (SD44L; St Michael's School, 1902) and Aldcliffe in 1862 (W.H.; LIV). Its distribution nationally is unchanged.

Hippocrepis emerus (L.) Lassen   Scorpion Senna

Neophyte. Scorpion Senna is a native species in central and eastern Europe and south-western Asia. It was cultivated in Britain by 1596 and is widely grown in gardens. It was reported from the wild in East Sussex in 1937 and today most records are from south-eastern England.

Very rare (1). Although it is believed to have become naturalised on coastal cliffs at Silverdale (SD47M) in the 1970s the first confirmed record from this locality was in 2003 (C.B.W.).

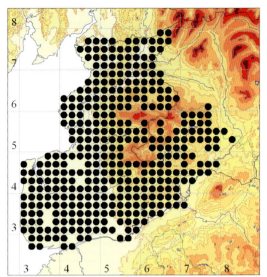

Lotus pedunculatus

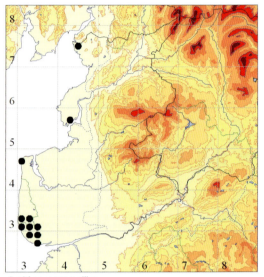

Ornithopus perpusillus

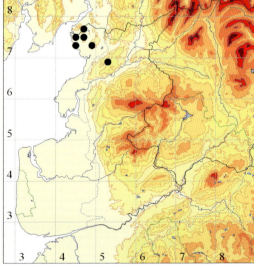

Hippocrepis comosa

Hippocrepis comosa L.   Horseshoe Vetch

European Temperate element.

This perennial herb is found on dry, sunny grasslands on calcareous soils (BH7) in southern Britain and occasionally elsewhere.

Rare (6). In northern Lancashire Horseshoe Vetch is found on limestone around Morecambe Bay. Although there is little change in its distribution locally it has declined nationally.

Securigera varia (L.) Lassen   Crown Vetch

Neophyte. *S. varia* is a native of central and southern Europe and was introduced into British gardens by 1597 but it was not recorded from the wild until 1843. Most occurrences are escapes from gardens in England, Wales and southern Scotland. There are also a few records from Ireland.

In northern Lancashire a single plant was reported from the sand dunes at St Anne's (Bailey, 1910). However the voucher specimen at MANCH is in poor condition and it is difficult to be sure of the identification.

Scorpiurus muricatus L.   Caterpillar-plant

Neophyte. This is a native of the Mediterranean region and south-western Asia. *S. muricatus* was cultivated in Britain by 1640 and reported from the wild in 1859. It is found in ruderal habitats in scattered localities in England and Wales.

In northern Lancashire *S. muricatus* was found on a tip at Marton, Blackpool (SD33H) in 1961 (A.E.R.; LIV).

Vicia cracca L.   Tufted Vetch

Eurasian Boreo-temperate element.

This is a scrambling perennial plant found in hedgerows, scrub and woodland edge habitats (BH3, 11) throughout the British Isles.

Very common (363). Tufted Vetch is found in most parts of northern Lancashire but it is absent or rare in upland areas. Its distribution locally and nationally is unchanged.

[**Vicia sylvatica** L.   Wood Vetch

Although there are no historical records for this Eurosiberian Boreo-temperate species it occurs in the pollen record for Little Hawes Water (SD47T) at *c.* 8,600; 8,400 and 5,000 years BP (J.I. pers. comm.).]

Vicia villosa Roth   Fodder Vetch

Neophyte. This is a Eurosiberian Temperate species but it is found in much of north-western Europe. It was first grown in Britain in 1815 but arose in the wild as a grain contaminant in 1857. It is found in scattered localities in the British Isles but most records are from the London area.

In northern Lancashire the only records are from Fleetwood Docks in 1900 (Wheldon and Wilson, 1907) and from several localities on sand dunes at St Anne's in 1902 and 1906 (C.B.; MANCH).

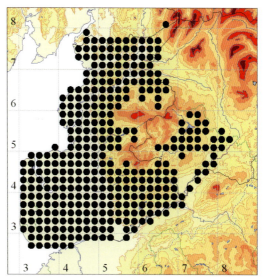

Vicia cracca

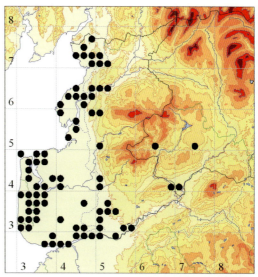

Vicia hirsuta

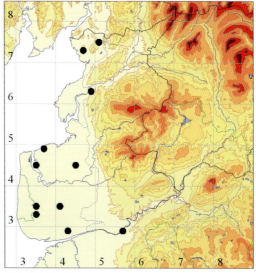

Vicia tetrasperma

Vicia hirsuta (L.) Gray — Hairy Tare

European Temperate element.

This is a scrambling annual plant of hedgerows, scrub and disturbed ground (BH3, 6), and although it is found throughout the British Isles it is rare in much of Ireland and northern Scotland.

Frequent (81). Hairy Tare is found mostly near the coast and in southern parts of northern Lancashire with occasional records from elsewhere. As Wheldon and Wilson (1907) recorded *V. hirsuta* from only ten localities it appears that it has extended its range in the area over the last 100 years. The 'New Atlas' refers to Hairy Tare as being a troublesome arable weed in the nineteenth century and reports that since 1962 its distribution is stable, 'Local Change' also notes no change since 1987.

Vicia tetrasperma (L.) Schreb. — Smooth Tare

European Temperate element.

This is a scrambling annual of hedgerows, woodland edge habitats and rough grassland (BH3, 4, 6). It is found as a native species in southern Britain but it is thought to be introduced further north in Scotland and in Ireland.

Rare (11). There are old records for a turnip field at Halton (Wheldon and Wilson, 1907), Brock in 1898 (T.G.; BON) and Long Pad, Pilling (Heathcote, 1923). Recent records are from scattered localities in VC 60. Whilst this is a rare plant there is probably little change in its distribution in northern Lancashire. However although the 'New Atlas' reports losses 'Local Change' suggests its distribution is unchanged nationally since 1987.

Vicia sepium L. — Bush Vetch

Eurosiberian Boreo-temperate element.

Bush Vetch is found scrambling over vegetation in hedgerows, rough grassland and in woodland edge habitats (BH3, 6) throughout the British Isles.

Very common (381). *V. sepium* is found throughout northern Lancashire except on the fells. There has been no change in its distribution locally or nationally between 1962 and 1987 ('New Atlas') but 'Local Change' reports a decline after 1987.

Vicia pannonica Crantz — Hungarian Vetch

Neophyte. This is a native of central and southern Europe, the Mediterranean region and south-western Asia. It was recorded in the wild in 1902 but most occurrences are of rare casuals in England and Wales.

Very rare (1). In northern Lancashire it was found on the sand dunes at Lytham St Anne's in 1907 (Bailey, 1910; MANCH), on a tip at Blackpool (SD33H) in the 1960s (A.E.R.) and from Preston in 1964 (A.E.R.; LIV).

Vicia sativa L. ssp. nigra (L.) Ehrh. — Common Vetch

V. sativa sensu lato has a European Southern-temperate distribution but the wider distribution of the subspecies is uncertain. Only *V. sativa* ssp. *nigra* is thought to be native in the British Isles and until 1991 most if not all records for *V. sativa* were referred to ssp. *nigra*. However because of identification difficulties, accounts here of *V. sativa* subspecies are tentative. *V. sativa* ssp. *nigra* is found in rough grassland, waste places and woodland edge habitats (BH6) throughout the British Isles.

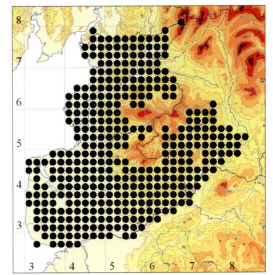

Vicia sepium

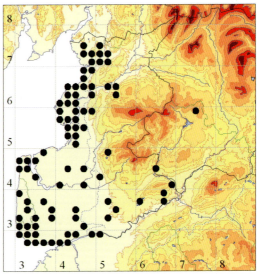

Vicia sativa ssp. *nigra*

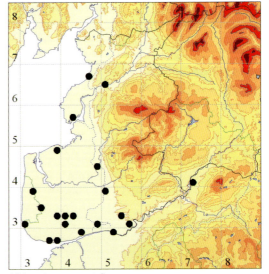

Vicia sativa ssp. *segetalis*

Frequent (87). This is found throughout northern Lancashire but most records are from coastal areas. It is not known if there has been any change in its distribution locally or nationally.

Vicia sativa L. ssp. **segetalis** (Thuill.) Gaudin

Archaeophyte. This was formerly grown for fodder but today it has become the most frequent of the subspecies and it is found in most parts of the British Isles although it is rare or absent in parts of Ireland and northern Scotland. It occurs in rough grassland and waste places.

Occasional (21). *V. sativa* ssp. *segetalis* occurs in scattered localities in northern Lancashire.

Vicia sativa L. ssp. **sativa**

Archaeophyte. This was formerly grown for fodder and was recorded from the wild by 1660. However the area of farmland grown with 'vetches and tares' decreased by 91% between 1891 and 1958 and the incidence of this subspecies in the wild has similarly fallen. It is found growing in grassy and waste places throughout the British Isles.

Frequent (105). *V. sativa* ssp. *sativa* is found mostly in the west of the area with a few records from the Lune and Ribble valleys. It is probably over recorded in error for ssp. *segetalis*.

Vicia lathyroides L.   Spring Vetch

European Temperate element.

This is an annual of open habitats on sand dunes and well-drained coastal grassland (BH8, 19). It is found on many coasts of the British Isles except parts of western Scotland and Ireland.

Rare (7). In northern Lancashire Spring Vetch is confined to sandy ground at Pilling, Blackpool and Lytham St Anne's. There has been no change in its distribution locally or nationally between 1962 and 1987 ('New Atlas') but since 1987 it has declined nationally ('Local Change').

Vicia lutea L.   Yellow-vetch

Submediterranean-Subatlantic element but a neophyte in Lancashire.

This annual species is a native plant in coastal localities of southern England and on cliffs in south-western Scotland. It is found elsewhere as a casual in ruderal habitats.

Very rare (1). In northern Lancashire it persisted on waste land at Lytham St Anne's (SD33F) between 2000 and 2008 (C.F. & N.J.S.).

Vicia bithynica (L.) L.   Bithynian Vetch

Mediterranean-Atlantic element but a neophyte in northern Lancashire.

This occurs in coastal grasslands and waste ground, mostly in southern England.

Very rare (1). In northern Lancashire Bithynican Vetch was found on rough ground on the east side of the A6 at Lancaster (SD45Z) in 1981 (A.E.C.).

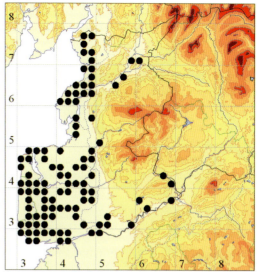

Vicia sativa ssp. *sativa*

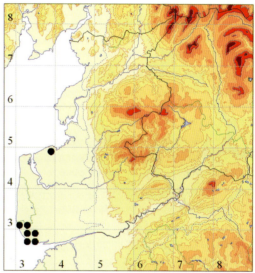

Vicia lathyroides

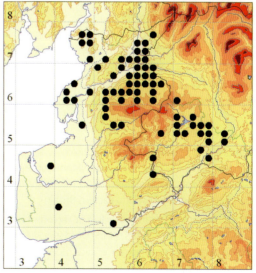

Lathyrus linifolius

Vicia faba L.   Broad Bean

Neophyte. The origins of this crop plant are unknown but it was cultivated in the Middle East eight thousand years ago, later spreading to western Europe where seeds from the Iron Age have been found at Glastonbury. It may occur as a relic of cultivation anywhere in the British Isles but most records are from south-eastern England.

Very rare (4). The first report for *Vicia faba* in northern Lancashire was from Roman deposits at Ribchester where it was no doubt cultivated (Huntley and Hillam, 2000). Broad Bean was then not recorded again until it was found on a tip at Blackpool (SD33H) in c. 1966 (A.E.R.). Other post 1964 records are from a potato field at Inskip-with-Sowerby (SD43U) in 1970 (E.F.G.), Lancaster (SD45Z; Livermore and Livermore, 1991) and by the R. Lune, Heaton-with-Oxcliffe (SD46K; Livermore and Livermore, 1990a).

Lathyrus linifolius (Reichard) Bässler   Bitter-vetch

European Temperate element.

Bitter-vetch is found in moist, infertile heathy meadows and woodland edge habitats (BH8, 16) in many parts of the British Isles but it is rare or absent from some lowland areas including Lancashire, eastern England and central Ireland.

Frequent (72). In northern Lancashire *L. linifolius* is found mostly in the north and east of the area. Its distribution is unchanged locally but losses since 1950 were reported by the 'New Atlas' although those noted by 'Local Change' since 1987 were not significant.

Lathyrus pratensis L.   Meadow Vetchling

Eurosiberian Boreo-temperate element.

This is found on fertile soils on roadsides, waste ground and in unimproved grasslands (BH6) throughout the British Isles.

Very common (384). Meadow Vetchling is found all over northern Lancashire except on the higher fells. The distribution of *L. pratensis* is stable locally and nationally.

Lathyrus grandiflorus Sm.   Two-flowered Everlasting-pea

Neophyte. This scrambling perennial herb is a native of the central Mediterranean region. It was introduced into cultivation in 1814 and was known in the wild by 1908. *L. grandiflorus* occurs in many parts of the British Isles as a garden escape.

Very rare (1). In northern Lancashire it was found in a lane near the works for Trowbarrow quarry, Silverdale (SD47S) in 1965 (M.J. & H.S.).

Lathyrus latifolius L.   Broad-leaved Everlasting-pea

Neophyte. This is a European Southern-temperate species planted as a garden plant since the 15th century and recorded in the wild since 1670. It is found in coastal localities and on waste ground throughout the British Isles but especially in south-eastern Britain.

Occasional (16). *L. latifolius* was first recorded in northern Lancashire from a roadside sand dune at St Anne's in 1965 (A.E.R.). Subsequent records are from scattered coastal localities and more occasionally inland.

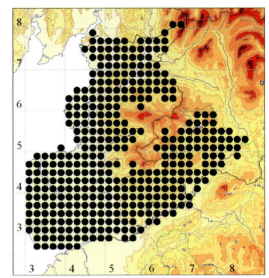

Lathyrus pratensis

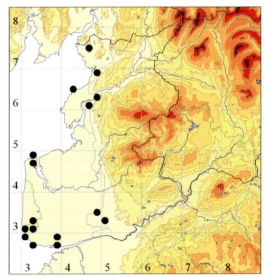

Lathyrus latifolius

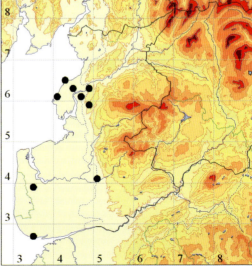

Pisum sativum

Lathyrus hirsutus L.   Hairy Vetchling

Neophyte. Hairy Vetchling has a European Southern-temperate distribution and was discovered in Essex in 1666 where it was thought at one time to be native. Today it has been recorded from scattered localities in England, Wales, Ireland and southern Scotland where it is usually of casual occurrence.

Very rare (2). This was found on a building site in Preston in 1965 (E.H.; LANC) and in the same year from Fleetwood (SD53G; E.H.).

Lathyrus nissolia L.   Grass Vetchling

European Temperate element but a neophyte in northern Lancashire.

This is found on grassy banks and waste ground (BH3, 6, 7) in southern Britain extending northwards as a neophyte to southern Scotland.

Very rare (5). In northern Lancashire Grass Vetchling has been found in rough grassland in Lancaster (SD45Z; Livermore and Livermore, 1991), Freckleton (SD42J) in 1999 (C.F. & N.J.S.), Blackpool (SD33I) in 2000 (M.S.), near Marton Mere, Blackpool (SD33M) in 2005 (C.F. & N.J.S.) and at Brockholes Quarry, Preston (SD53V) in 2008 (G. Wilmore & M.Cl.). In most of these localities it is believed it has been introduced as seed in amenity plantings.

[Lathyrus saxatilis (Vent.) Vis.

In northern Lancashire it was believed it was found on the sand dunes at Lytham St Anne's in 1908 (Bailey, 1910; MANCH). However the voucher specimen is *Medicago* ssp. *falcata*.]

Pisum sativum L.   Garden Pea

Archaeophyte. In the Middle East this was a crop plant from *c.* 7000BC and was present in Britain 2000 years ago. However it was first recorded from the wild in 1888. Today it is grown commercially on a large scale and widely cultivated in gardens and allotments. In the wild it is found as a casual on field margins and on waste ground throughout the British Isles.

Rare (9). In northern Lancashire the first record was from a tip at Blackpool (SD33H) in *c.* 1966 (A.E.R.). Subsequent records are from scattered localities in the area although most are from Lancaster and Morecambe. It is probably under recorded.

Ononis spinosa L.   Spiny Restharrow

Eurosiberian Southern-temperate element.

This is found in rough grassland and scrub on calcareous soils (BH6, 7) in the southern half of Britain.

Rare (14). In northern Lancashire this is found on coastal embankments, sometimes created artificially, e.g. bordering the Ribble estuary, from Preston to Carnforth. Whilst Spiny Restharrow has been lost from inland localities its coastal distribution in northern Lancashire remains unchanged. Nevertheless it may have been recorded in error for spiny forms of *O. repens* in some places. Nationally *O. spinosa* is probably declining.

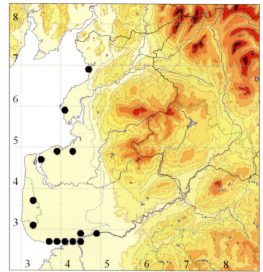

Ononis spinosa

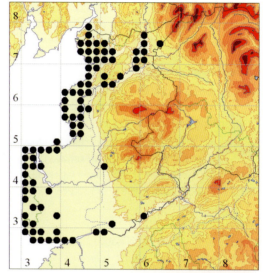

Ononis repens

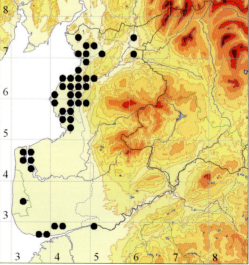

Melilotus altissimus

Ononis repens L.   Common Restharrow

European Temperate element.

This occurs in base-rich grasslands and on sand dunes (BH7, 19) in much of the British Isles although it is rare or absent in western and central Ireland and in upland areas generally.

Frequent (87). Common Restharrow is a coastal species in northern Lancashire with a few inland records, especially in the Lune and Ribble valleys. There has been no change in its distribution locally or nationally.

Melilotus altissimus Thuill.   Tall Melilot

Archaeophyte with a European Temperate distribution but its native range is obscured by introductions. It has been known in Britain since the sixteenth century. It occurs in disturbed grassland and waste places (BH3, 17) in England and Wales, parts of Scotland and Ireland but it is absent from most upland areas.

Occasional (42). Tall Melilot was first found in northern Lancashire at Lytham and near Freckleton on the Ribble estuary (Ashfield, 1858). Today it has a disjunct distribution with records on the Ribble estuary between Lytham and Preston, on the Wyre estuary and at Blackpool but most records are from the north-west of the area and in the Lune valley.

Melilotus albus Medik.   White Melilot

Neophyte. This is probably a native of southern Europe, western and central Asia and was recorded in the wild in Britain in 1822. It is a species of wasteland and urban areas wherever these occur in the British Isles.

Occasional (20). In northern Lancashire White Melilot was first recorded from a grassy bank by the side of Fairhaven Lake, Lytham St Anne's in 1901 (A.A.D.) shortly after the lake was created. Today it is found in coastal localities from Preston to Morecambe.

Melilotus officinalis (L.) Pall.   Ribbed Melilot

Neophyte. This is probably native in central and southern Europe extending eastwards to central Asia. *M. officinalis* came to Britain as seed impurity with clover imported from America and was first recorded in 1835. It occurs in grassy and waste places mostly in urban areas of the British Isles.

Occasional (39). It was first recorded from northern Lancashire on sand dunes at Lytham St Anne's in 1904 (Wheldon and Wilson, 1907). Today Ribbed Melilot is found in coastal areas with an occasional inland record especially around Preston.

Melilotus indicus (L.) All.   Small Melilot

Neophyte. This is a native of southern Europe, northern Africa, south-western and central Asia but first came to Britain with South American clover seed. Although it had been cultivated in Britain in 1680 it did not spread from this source. It was recorded in the wild in 1852 and today there are records from scattered localities in the British Isles.

Rare (6). The first record in northern Lancashire was from Fleetwood Docks in 1900 (Wheldon and Wilson, 1901a). Subsequent records were from Preston Docks (Preston Scientific Society, 1903), St Anne's (Wheldon and Wilson, 1907), Warton near Lytham (Wallace, 1948) and Poulton-le-Fylde in 1959 (Stalker, 1960). Recent records are from Heysham (SD45E) in 1965

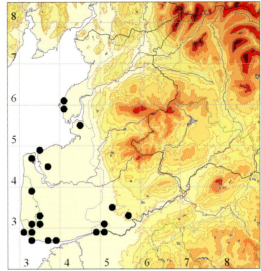

Melilotus albus

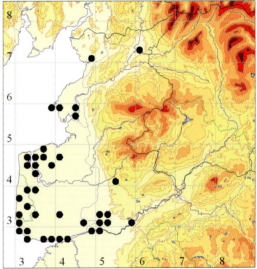

Melilotus officinalis

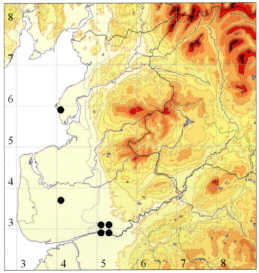

Melilotus indicus

(E.F.G.), Fleetwood in 1965 (A.E.R.), Greenhalgh-with-Thistleton (SD43D) in 1964 (J. and E.H.), Preston Dock (SD52E) in 1999 (C.F. & N.J.S.) and Preston (SD52J, 53A, F) in 1965 (J.H. & E.H.). The lack of post 1970 records reflects a similar decline observed nationally ('New Atlas').

Trigonella corniculata (L.) L.   Sickle-fruited Fenugreek

Neophyte. This is a native of the European Mediterranean region and only occurs as a rare casual on waste ground and on tips. It was grown in Britain by 1597 but it was not recorded in the wild until 1874.

The only record in northern Lancashire was from the sand dunes at Lytham St Anne's (Wheldon and Wilson, 1907).

Trigonella glabra Thunb.   Egyptian Fenugreek

Neophyte. This is a native of northern Africa and south-western Asia and is a rare casual in the British Isles.

Very rare (2). In northern Lancashire it was found on waste land at Fulwood in 1965 (E.H.; RNG) and on a demolition site in Preston (SD53F) in 1966 and 1968 (E.H.; RNG).

Trigonella polyceratia L.

Neophyte. This is a native of the western Mediterranean region and occurs as a rare grain casual in Britain.

In northern Lancashire it was recorded from the sand dunes at Lytham St Anne's (Wheldon and Wilson, 1907; MANCH).

Medicago lupulina L.   Black Medick

Eurosiberian Temperate element.

This occurs in grassland and waste places (BH7, 17) in most of the British Isles but it is rare or absent from many upland areas.

Frequent (226). In northern Lancashire Black Medick occurs throughout the area but it is much more common in the west than elsewhere. Its distribution is stable both locally and nationally.

Medicago sativa L. ssp. falcata (L.) Arcang.   Sickle Medick

Eurosiberian Boreo-temperate element but a neophyte in northern Lancashire.

Although a native of sandy heaths in East Anglia this is found on waste ground and in sandy areas elsewhere.

Very rare (2). The only northern Lancashire records are from Lytham St Anne's in 1908 (C.B.; MANCH, originally identified as *Lathyrus saxatilis*); in 1915 (A.J.C.; LSA) and again in 1946 (Whellan, 1954). It was also recorded from dredgings from the R. Ribble tipped on Lea Marsh (SD42Z) in 1964 (E. & J.H.) and one plant was found at Fleetwood (SD34I) in 1995 (C.F. & N.J.S.).

Medicago sativa L. ssp. sativa   Lucerne

Neophyte. This is a cultivated species of obscure origin. It was first cultivated in Britain for fodder and green manure in the seventeenth century and recorded from the wild by 1804. It is found in many parts of the British Isles but it is rare or absent from much of Scotland and Ireland.

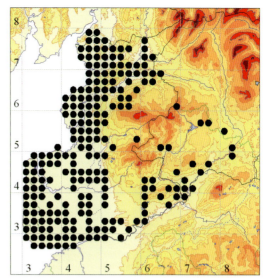

Medicago lupulina

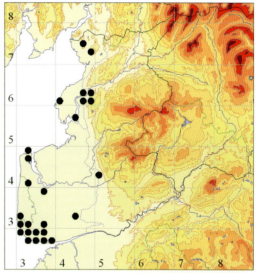

Medicago sativa ssp.sativa

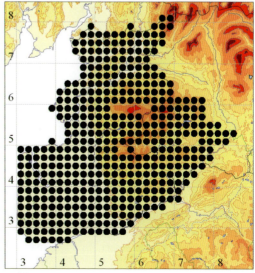

Trifolium repens

Occasional (26). The first records in northern Lancashire, c. 1900, were from Silverdale, Fleetwood and Ashton (Wheldon and Wilson, 1907). Since 1964 it has been found in scattered localities in the west of the area but particularly at Lytham St Anne's where it appears naturalised.

Medicago sativa L. nothossp. **varia** (Martyn) Arcang.
Sand Lucerne

Sand Lucerne is a spontaneous fertile hybrid between *M. sativa* ssp. *sativa* and *M. sativa* ssp. *falcata*. It is a native plant in East Anglia and is widespread in Europe but it also occurs in many, mostly urban areas of the British Isles.

Very rare (1). In northern Lancashire Sand Lucerne was found on levelled dunes north of St Anne's (SD32E) in 1997 (C.F. & N.J.S.).

Medicago polymorpha L.
Toothed Medick

Submediterranean-Subatlantic element but a neophyte in northern Lancashire.

Although this is regarded as a native species of southern coastal areas of England, further north it is a casual of waste land and tips.

Very rare (2). In northern Lancashire it was first found in St Mary's Hall gardens, Stonyhurst (SD63Z) in 1886 (SYT). Later it was recorded from a waste heap at Lytham St Anne's in 1915 (A.J.C.; LSA) whilst more recent records are confined to waste heaps in Haslam Park, Preston (SD53A) in 1965 (E.H.) and demolition sites in Preston (SD53F) in 1966 (J.H & E.H.).

Medicago arabica (L.) Huds.
Spotted Medick

Submediterranean-Subatlantic element but a neophyte in northern Lancashire.

Spotted Medick is a winter annual of sandy and gravely soils, especially near the coast. However it also occurs as a weed in short turf and in ruderal habitats. It is thought to be native in many southern areas of England and Wales but introduced further north.

Very rare (1). In northern Lancashire *M. arabica* was found on the miniature golf course at St Anne's (SD32J) in 2002 (C.F. & N.J.S.)

Trifolium ornithopodioides L.
Bird's-foot Clover

Suboceanic Southern-temperate element.

This inconspicuous annual clover is found in open habitats on acidic sands (BH8) in southern and western coastal areas of Britain, the Isle of Man and eastern Ireland. It occurs in disturbed ground as a casual inland and in Scotland.

Very rare (1). The only record for northern Lancashire is from a golf course at Fleetwood (SD34J) in 1999 (C.F. & N.J.S.; LIV) but an unsuccessful search for it was made in 2001. The Fleetwood site represents its northernmost locality in England. It may be declining nationally ('New Atlas').

Trifolium repens L.
White Clover

Eurosiberian Boreo-temperate element.

This common clover is found in grasslands (BH6) and also in some flushes in upland areas. There are numerous cultivars, some of which have been imported from elsewhere, and it has been extensively planted in grasslands since at least the eighteenth century.

Very common (443). This is one of the commonest species in northern Lancashire occurring in all but a few tetrads in the uplands. There has been no change to its distribution locally or nationally.

Trifolium hybridum L.
Alsike Clover

Neophyte. Native subspecies are found in southern Europe and south-western Asia but British material belongs to the cultivated ssp. *hybridum*. It is grown as a forage crop and was known in the wild by 1762. It is found in agricultural grass-lands and on waste ground throughout much of the British Isles.

Frequent (160). In northern Lancashire this was first recorded from Hacking Boat by the R. Ribble (SD73D) in 1887 (Anon, 1891) and Wheldon and Wilson (1907) only knew of a further eight localities in VC 60. Today it occurs in most lowland areas in the west of northern Lancashire and occasionally elsewhere.

[**Trifolium suffocatum** L.
Suffocated Clover

Mediterranean-Atlantic element.

This is a winter annual found on sandy or rocky coasts (BH8) in southern and south-eastern England with a single record in the Isle of Man

In northern Lancashire Ashfield (1860) reported this from the beach at Lytham but in 1865 suggested this was an error but qualified his remark by saying that 'at any rate I have not been able to meet with it there for several years'.]

Trifolium strictum L.
Upright Clover

Submediterranean-Subatlantic element but a neophyte in northern Lancashire.

This is a rare plant of open habitats on serpentine and other rock outcrops in Cornwall and in Wales but it also occurs as a rare casual elsewhere.

Very rare (1). The only northern Lancashire record was from newly sown grassland at Carleton Cemetery, Blackpool (SD33J) in 2003 (E.F.G. & M.S.; LIV).

Trifolium fragiferum L.
Strawberry Clover

Eurosiberian Southern-temperate element.

This is often a coastal species found at the top of salt marshes (BH21) and in other brackish places, but in south-eastern England it occurs in damp pastures (BH6). It is very rare in Scotland but it also occurs on the coast of Ireland.

Occasional (28). In northern Lancashire it is found at the top of salt marshes in VC 60. Its distribution locally and nationally is unchanged.

Trifolium resupinatum L. — Reversed Clover

Neophyte. This is apparently native in south-western Asia and perhaps south-eastern Europe but it has been cultivated for fodder since 1713. It was first recorded in the wild in 1830 and has been found in scattered localities in England and eastern Wales, usually in ruderal habitats.

Very rare (1). In northern Lancashire it was recorded from a tip at Blackpool (SD33I) between 1962 and 1966 (A.E.R.).

Trifolium aureum Pollich — Large Trefoil

Neophyte. A European Temperate species introduced into Britain in 1815 and recorded in the wild in 1838. It is found in ruderal habitats in scattered localities in the British Isles.

Very rare (3). In northern Lancashire it was found at the edge of an arable field in Pilling (SD44M) in 1964 (E.F.G. & J.H.), Fairhaven golf course, Lytham St Anne's (SD32P) in 2001 (C.F. & N.J.S.) and from Brockholes Quarry, Preston (SD53V) in 2005 (P.H.S. & M.W.).

Trifolium campestre Schreb. — Hop Trefoil

Eurosiberian Southern-temperate element.

This is an annual of grassland habitats on dry, infertile, neutral to base-rich soils (BH3, 16, 19). It is found in many parts of the British Isles although it is rare in upland areas, north-western Scotland and western Ireland.

Frequent (70). In northern Lancashire Hop Trefoil is found in coastal areas and occasionally inland in Lancashire VC 64. In northern Lancashire it may have become less frequent in inland localities over the last 100 years, which is consistent with the decline noted by the 'New Atlas' and 'Local Change'.

Trifolium dubium Sibth. — Lesser Trefoil

European Temperate element.

Lesser Trefoil is a grassland species and also occurs in waste places (BH6). It is found throughout the British Isles.

Common (272). *T. dubium* is found throughout northern Lancashire but it is especially common in western parts of the area. There has been no change in its distribution locally and whilst the 'New Atlas' also reports no change 'Local Change' notes that there has been an increase since 1987.

Trifolium micranthum Viv. — Slender Trefoil

Submediterranean-Subatlantic element.

This is found in coastal grassland, in open sandy ground and inland in dry grasslands but it is also found on lawns where it thrives on close cutting (BH8, 17). It is found in many parts of southern Britain but it is also found as an introduction as far north as the Moray Firth in Scotland.

Occasional (18). In northern Lancashire this is predominantly a coastal species but it seems to have spread recently to localities in the Brennand valley and Gisburn Forest in Lancashire VC 64. Although not recorded by Wheldon and Wilson (1907) it was found at Morecambe (T.G.) in 1891 (BON). There is also an unlocalised record for the 10km square SD67

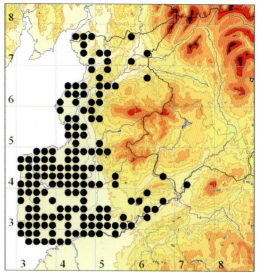

Trifolium hybridum

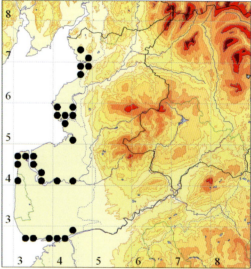

Trifolium fragiferum

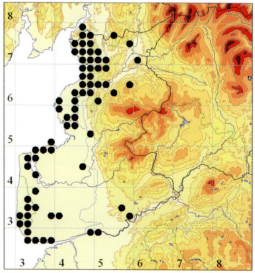

Trifolium campestre

(Perring and Walters, 1962). Despite probably having been overlooked Slender Trefoil has extended its range northwards into and within northern Lancashire during the last 100 years. However most records are post 1990. Both the 'New Atlas' and 'Local Change' also reported this spread nationally.

Trifolium pratense L.   Red Clover

Eurosiberian Temperate element.

This is a common plant of grassland and waste land (BH6, 7) and is found throughout the British Isles. It is also a common agricultural species and occurs in various cultivars.

Very common (405). Red Clover is found throughout northern Lancashire only being absent from the higher fells. There has been no change in its distribution locally or nationally.

Trifolium medium L.   Zigzag Clover

Eurosiberian Boreo-temperate element.

Zigzag Clover is found in neutral grassland and ruderal habitats (BH6). It is found in many parts of the British Isles but it is often rare or absent from the Scottish Highlands, much of Ireland and parts of East Anglia.

Frequent (181). Whilst this is found in many parts of northern Lancashire its distribution is either coastal or corresponds to pastoral areas on heavy clay soils and in river valleys. Wheldon and Wilson (1907) considered Zigzag Clover to be very frequent but less common than Red Clover, and whilst this is true today there is a possibility that its abundance if not its range is decreasing. The 'New Atlas' reported a marked decline in southern and eastern England since 1962 but 'Local Change' did not note further decline.

Trifolium striatum L.   Knotted Clover

European Southern-temperate element.

This is a winter annual of open communities on thin infertile and drought prone soils (BH8) in many localities in England, Wales, eastern Ireland, southern and eastern Scotland.

Rare (12). This occurs on sandy soils in Preston, Lytham St Anne's and Blackpool and on limestone soils in the northwest of VC 60. Although often overlooked this species has extended its range in the south of the area over the last 100 years whilst the records from the limestone area around Morecambe Bay are new. However nationally the 'New Atlas' reported losses since 1962 but 'Local Change' did not note further decline since 1987.

Trifolium lappaceum L.   Bur Clover

Neophyte. This is a native of the Mediterranean region and south-western Asia. It was cultivated in Britain in 1787 and recorded from the wild by 1862. It has been recorded casually on tips and waste ground in a few localities scattered across Britain.

Very rare (2). In northern Lancashire it was found on a tip at Blackpool (SD33I) in 1966 (A.E.R. & J.H.) and from a demolition site in Preston (SD53F) also in 1966 (E.H.).

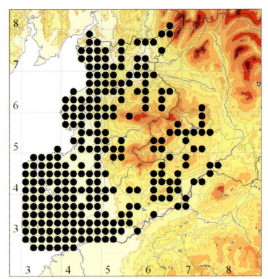

Trifolium dubium

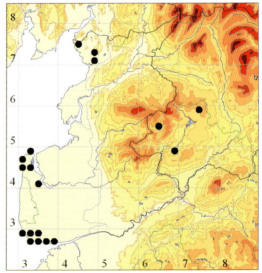

Trifolium micranthum

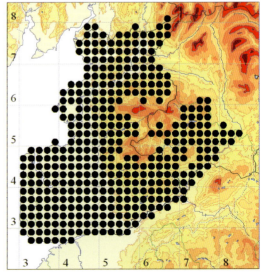

Trifolium pratense

Trifolium arvense L.   Hare's-foot Clover

Eurosiberian Southern-temperate element.

This occurs in sandy habitats, on sand dunes and in ruderal habitats (BH8) throughout much of Britain but seems to be mostly a coastal species in Ireland.

Occasional (41). Hare's-foot Clover is found in coastal areas of northern Lancashire from Preston to Bolton-le-Sands. Wheldon and Wilson (1907) recorded only four localities indicating that in northern Lancashire *T. arvense* has extended its range considerably. However nationally there has been a widespread decline since 1950 in south-eastern England and possibly elsewhere ('New Atlas') with further decline reported since 1987 ('Local Change').

[Trifolium purpureum Lois   Purple Clover

Neophyte. This is a very rare introduction from the Mediterranean region.

What is believed to be this species was found at Fleetwood Nature Park (SD34M) in 2005 (P.J. & D.P.E.).]

Lupinus arboreus Sims   Tree Lupin

Neophyte. This is a native of western North America first introduced into British cultivation in 1793 but not recorded from the wild until 1945. However it was well established by 1962. Today it is found in many parts of the British Isles.

Very rare (4). In northern Lancashire Tree Lupin was recorded from Lytham tip (SD32Y) in 1966 (J.H.), St Anne's (SD32I) in the 1960s (A.E.R.), Thornton (SD34K) in 1966 (Anon) and Blackpool Airport (SD33A) in 1988 (C.F. & N.J.S.).

Lupinus polyphyllus Lindl.   Garden Lupin

Neophyte. This is a native of western North America and was introduced into cultivation in 1826 and was known in the wild by 1900. It has been found in many parts of the British Isles but it has been confused with *L. nootkatensis* Donn ex Sims found in the British Isles only in Scotland and *L. × regalis* as well as other garden hybrids. However *L. polyphyllus* is rarely grown in gardens today having been superseded by *L. × regalis*.

The status of this species in northern Lancashire is unclear but the record of *L. nootkatensis* from railway banks between Salwick and Kirkham reported by Wheldon in 1899 (Wheldon and Wilson, 1902) and still present thirty years later (France, 1931) is probably this species.

Lupinus arboreus × L. polyphyllus (L. × regalis Bergmans)
                                                               Russell Lupin

Neophyte. This hybrid was first cultivated in 1937 after many years of experiments with other *Lupinus* species and hybrids, and was recorded in the wild in 1955. It is a popular garden plant and is found mostly in urban areas throughout the British Isles.

Rare (11). All post 1964 records are included here although most were recorded as *L. polyphyllus*. Indeed the first record from a railway line at Heysham Harbour (SD46A) in 1974 (A.E.C.) could be this species. However most records from scattered localities in VC 60 are almost certainly this and other garden hybrids.

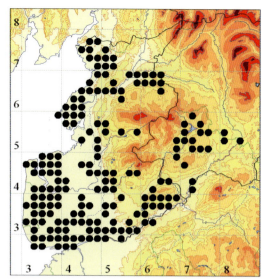
Trifolium medium

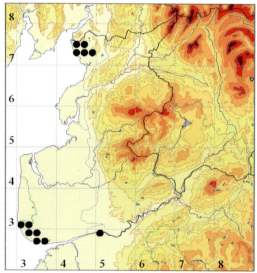
Trifolium striatum

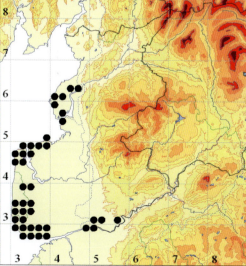
Trifolium arvense

Lupinus luteus L.   Yellow Lupin

Neophyte. An annual, which is a native of the eastern Mediterranean region. It is found very rarely as a casual in the British Isles.

In northern Lancashire it was found on the sand dunes at St Anne's (Bailey, 1910).

Laburnum anagyroides Medik.   Laburnum

Neophyte. Laburnum is a native of the mountains of central Europe and was introduced into British cultivation before 1596. It was known from the wild by 1879. It is a popular garden tree and has been used in hedges in western Britain. It sets seed readily and occurs in ruderal habitats throughout the British Isles.

Occasional (23). In northern Lancashire the first records were noted by Livermore and Livermore (1987) but it was probably found in the wild long before this. Recorders ignored its presence possibly because it was such an obvious garden plant. Today it is found in scattered localities throughout the area.

Laburnum anagyroides × L. alpinum (Mill.) J. Presl (L. × watereri (Wettst.) Dippel)

Neophyte. A partially sterile hybrid of garden origin brought into cultivation in Britain by 1864. It was recorded from the wild in 1970 and although it is possibly under recorded, as it is confused with both parents, most records will be of planted trees. It occurs in scattered localities in Britain.

Very rare (1). In northern Lancashire it was recorded from Singleton (SD33Z) in c. 1965 (E.P.).

Cytisus scoparius (L.) Link ssp. scoparius   Broom

European Temperate element.

This shrub of heaths, banks and scrubby places on acidic soils (BH3) is found throughout the British Isles. It is also planted in some places.

Frequent (100). Broom is found in scattered localities in northern Lancashire. Its distribution locally is unchanged and whilst the 'New Atlas' also reported an unchanged distribution 'Local Change' noted a decline since 1987.

Spartium junceum L.   Spanish Broom

Neophyte. Spanish Broom is a native of the Mediterranean region and was introduced into British gardens in 1845. It is frequently grown for its sweetly scented flowers and was known from the wild by 1905, but it was little noticed until the 1950s. Today it is often used in amenity planting schemes but most records of it in the wild are from south-eastern England.

Very rare (1). The only record in northern Lancashire is from an old garden at Blackpool (SD33I) in 1965 (A.E.R. & E.H.) but it almost certainly occurs elsewhere, probably where new roads have been constructed in urban and suburban areas.

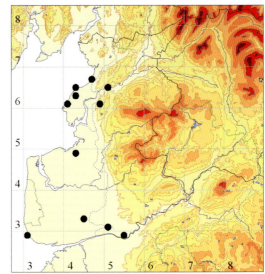
Lupinus x regalis

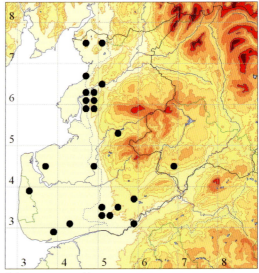
Laburnum anagyroides

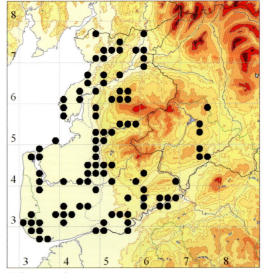
Cytisus scoparius

Genista tinctoria L. ssp. **tinctoria**   Dyer's Greenweed

European Temperate element.

This is a species of rough pastures, old meadows and grassy banks (BH6) and it is found in England, Wales and southern Scotland.

Occasional (30). Most records of Dyer's Greenweed are from the Lune valley but single and groups of tetrad records are scattered throughout northern Lancashire. A comparison of *G. tinctoria's* distribution 100 years ago with that noted since 1964 suggests that there has been little change. However it belongs to a group of species that were thought to be too frequent for individual post 1964 sites to be noted (*cf. Parnassia palustris, Pinguicula vulgaris*) yet anecdotal evidence suggests a considerable decline in recent years. The 'New Atlas' reports a considerable decline nationally since the 1940s. A further decline since 1987 was not noted by 'Local Change' but again anecdotal evidence suggests it is still declining.

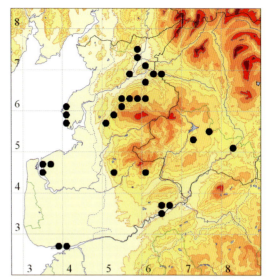
Genista tinctoria

Genista anglica L.   Petty Whin

Oceanic Temperate element.

This is a small spiny shrub found on heaths (BH10) and occurs throughout England, Wales, and Scotland.

Extinct. This was always rare with former records from Ribbleton Moor (SD53Q; Ashfield, 1858), a bog near Docker (probably Outfield Moss, SD57X; Wheldon and Wilson, 1902) last seen 1978 (M.J.W.), Melling Moor (SD67A) last seen 1990 (B.B.), Robert Hall Moor (SD66J) last seen 1983 (A.E.C.) and from a roadside between Grindleton and Harrop (Anon, 1891). The 'New Atlas' reports a considerable decline but no further loss since 1987 was noted by 'Local Change'.

Genista hispanica L.   Spanish Gorse

Neophyte. Spanish Gorse is a native of south-western Europe. It has been cultivated in Britain since 1759 and although a common garden plant it was not recorded in the wild until 1927. Today it occurs in scattered localities, mostly in southern Britain.

Very rare (1). In northern Lancashire it was found near Stanah (SD34L) in 1997 (C.F. & N.J.S.).

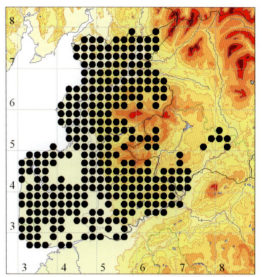
Ulex europaeus

Ulex europaeus L.   Gorse

Oceanic temperate element.

This is found in hedges, woodland edge habitats and scrub (BH10) throughout the British Isles. Formerly it was often planted and used as bedding for cattle etc.

Common (319). Gorse is a common species in most parts of northern Lancashire but it does not occur in some areas. It is absent from the higher fells, the peat covered areas of western VC 60 and, perhaps more surprisingly, large parts of Lancashire VC 64. There has been no change in its distribution locally or nationally.

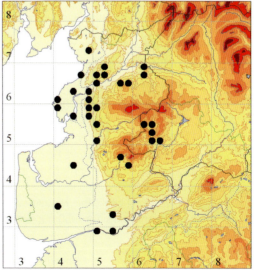
Ulex gallii

Ulex gallii Planch.   Western Gorse

Oceanic temperate element.

Western Gorse is found on heaths and as scrub on acidic soils (BH10) mostly in western parts of the British Isles as far north as southern Scotland.

Occasional (33). Western Gorse is found in scattered localities mostly in the north and east of northern Lancashire. It was formerly common on what was once Ellel Common but most of the scrub seen in the 1960s was lost to quarrying. However this area of scrub probably provided the seed source for colonizing the M6 embankments near Lancaster, but over time *U. europaeus* has tended to out-compete *U. gallii*. Nevertheless the river gravels on the R. Dunsop, Forest of Bowland, support fine stands of Western Gorse. However its future here depends on the extent of future works to the river channel. At one time this was probably a common plant of dry heaths in northern Lancashire and its abundance was probably already reduced 100 years ago. Further losses have continued since then. Neither the 'New Atlas' nor 'Local Change' considers that there has been a significant decrease in its distribution nationally.

POLYGALACEAE   MILKWORT FAMILY

Polygala vulgaris L. ssp. **vulgaris**   Common Milkwort

European Temperate element.

This small perennial herb grows in infertile, neutral to basic grasslands, including sand dunes (BH7), and is found throughout the British Isles.

Occasional (59). In northern Lancashire Common Milkwort is found in suitable places in many localities but it is largely absent from western areas. It is particularly associated with calcareous grassland. Whilst it is possible that *P. vulgaris* is more frequent than 100 years ago in northern Lancashire, the 'New Atlas' shows a decline nationally since 1950 and 'Local Change' noted further decline.

Polygala vulgaris L. ssp. **collina** (Rchb.) Borbás

Very rare (2). The distribution of this subspecies is uncertain.

In northern Lancashire it is confined to the Fylde coast sand dunes where it was recorded in SD32I in 1999 (E.F.G.) and in SD33A in 2003 (E.F.G.).

Polygala serpyllifolia Hosé   Heath Milkwort

Suboceanic Temperate element.

This is found on acidic soils in grasslands and heaths (BH8, 10, 12) throughout most of the British Isles but it is rare in many parts of midland and eastern England.

Frequent (112). In northern Lancashire Heath Milkwort is mostly found in the hilly areas of the east and north of the area with only occasional localities elsewhere. Its distribution in northern Lancashire is probably unchanged. However nationally the 'New Atlas' shows a considerable decline in southern England since 1950 but further decline since 1987 was not noted by 'Local Change'.

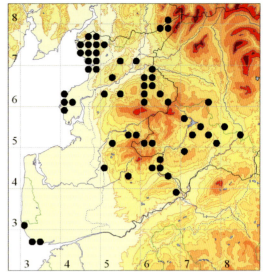
Polygala vulgaris

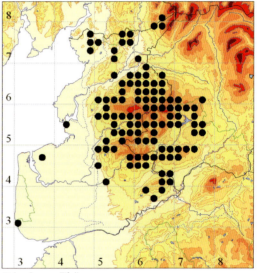
Polygala serpyllifolia

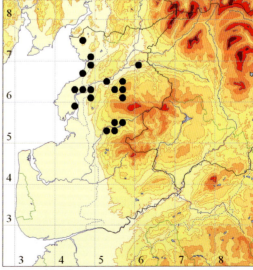
Spiraea × billardii

ROSACEAE   ROSE FAMILY

Sorbaria sorbifolia (L.) A. Braun   Sorbaria

Neophyte. This is a vigorously suckering shrub from northern Asia. It was cultivated in Britain by 1759 and today it is found growing wild in hedges, mostly in southern and eastern England.

Very rare (1). Sorbaria was confirmed from a roadside hedge north of Carnforth (SD57A) in c. 2004 and was still present in 2011 (A.M. Boucher). Another plant, possibly this species was found by the Lancaster Canal (SD46W; Livermore and Livermore, 1989) whilst there is an unlocalised record for the 10km square SD42 ('New Atlas' CD) but this could be in VC 59.

Spiraea L.   Brideworts

Brideworts comprise a group of taxa introduced into gardens and elsewhere, often as hedging plants. Today they are a feature of many recently planted hedges. Also until recently most records were of *S. salicifolia* and although the 'New Atlas' shows a distribution map for this species it is thought that whilst very early records may be correct it is now extinct in the British Isles (Rich and Jermy, 1998). Because of identification difficulties this is a tentative account of *Spiraea* spp.

[Spiraea salicifolia L.   Bridewort

Neophyte. This is a native of Eurasia and was introduced into cultivation in Britain by 1665. It is shown in the 'New Atlas' scattered throughout the British Isles.

Rare (14). Records are from the Fylde with a few localities elsewhere but it is thought that all sightings are for one or more of the following taxa.]

Spiraea alba Du Roi × S. douglasii (S. × billardii Hérincq)
                                              Billard's Bridewort

Neophyte. This is a hybrid of garden origin that has been in cultivation since 1854 and known in the wild since 1964. It is found in much of Britain but it is thought to be over recorded for *S. × pseudosalicifolia*.

Occasional (19). *S. × billardii* was first recorded in northern Lancashire by Livermore and Livermore (1987) who recorded it in several localities in the Lancaster area. Most subsequent records are also from the north of northern Lancashire but subsequent re-appraisal of a few voucher specimens suggest that some records are for *S. × pseudosalicifolia*.

Spiraea douglasii Hook.   Steeple-bush

Neophyte. This is a native of western North America and has been cultivated in Britain since 1827. It has been known in the wild since 1910 and records are apparently grouped around the Glasgow area, Lancashire, the Severn valley and the London area as well as occurring in scattered places elsewhere. It may have been over recorded through confusion with its hybrids or the disjunct distribution may be real. It is found in hedges and sometimes in extensive patches on waste ground.

Rare (14). Steeple-bush occurs mostly in the north of northern Lancashire, where it was first recorded on the banks of the Gressingham Beck (SD56U) in 1970 (J.M.N.) and on the western side of Bowland.

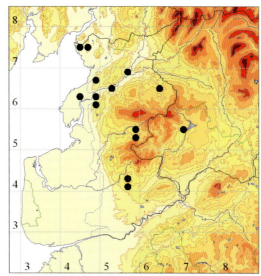
Spiraea douglasii

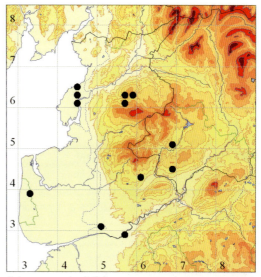
Spiraea × pseudosalicifolia

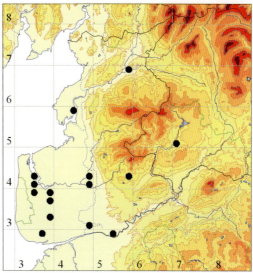
Prunus cerasifera

Spiraea douglasii × S. salicifolia
(S. × pseudosalicifolia Silverside)   Confused Bridewort

Neophyte. This is a hybrid of garden origin cultivated in Britain since about 1850 but not recorded in the wild until 1984. It occurs in hedges and in thickets on waste ground throughout the British Isles. It is probably under recorded and mistaken for other taxa.

Rare (12). *S. × pseudosalicifolia* was first recognised in northern Lancashire from St Anne's in 1963 (A.E.R.; LIV) and is found scattered throughout the area.

Spiraea japonica L. f.   Japanese Spiraea

Neophyte. This species was introduced into cultivation in Britain about 1850 and is found scattered in the British Isles as a relic of cultivation. It was recorded in the wild in 1909.

Very rare (1). In northern Lancashire it was recorded as naturalised on the banks of the R. Brock at Myerscough (SD44V) in 1987 (C.J.B.).

Spiraea thunbergii Sieb. ex Blume × S. multiflora Zabel
(S. × arguta Zabel)   Bridal-spray

Neophyte. This is a hybrid shrub of garden origin first cultivated in Britain *c.* 1884. It is a popular garden plant and was recorded in the wild by 1967. It is found in a few places on waste land in Britain.

Very rare (2). It is probably under recorded in northern Lancashire but it was found on railway ballast at Great Plumpton (SD33W) in 2003 (E.F.G.) and on sand dunes at Lytham (SD32N) in 2010 (E.F.G.).

Aruncus dioicus (Walter) Fernald   Buck's-beard

Neophyte. A large perennial herb first cultivated in Britain by 1633 but not seen in the wild until 1950. It was planted in estate gardens and usually occurs as single-sex clones that spread by means of rhizomatous growth. It is found scattered in Britain.

Very rare (1). A single plant was found in Artle Dale, Caton-with-Littledale (SD56G) in 2005 (E.F.G. & J.M.N.).

Prunus cerasifera Ehrh.   Cherry Plum

Neophyte. This is a native of south-eastern Europe, south-western and central Asia and was known in cultivation in Britain in the sixteenth century. However it was also found in Roman deposits at Ribchester (Huntley and Hillam, 2000) but it was not recorded in the wild until the twentieth century by which time it was known to be frequent in many areas. It is likely that it was overlooked, possibly because Cherry Plum flowers in February.

Rare (15). In northern Lancashire *P. cerasifera* was first recorded from a hedge near Beacon Fell (SD54W) in 1965 (E.F.G.). Today it is found in scattered localities throughout the area.

Prunus spinosa L.   Blackthorn

European Temperate element.

Blackthorn is a common plant of hedgerows and scrub (BH3) in the British Isles except in northern Scotland. However the taxonomy of *P. spinosa* and *P. domestica* is complex and sometimes it is difficult to identify individual

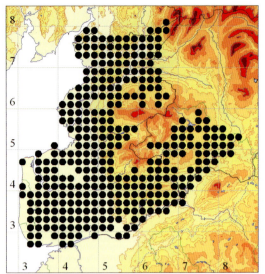
Prunus spinosa

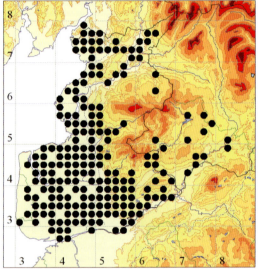
Prunus domestica

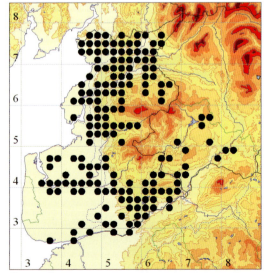
Prunus avium

bushes (Rich and Jermy, 1998). In north-western England some plants may be almost spineless (Halliday, 1997) and in northern Lancashire some bushes, whilst flowering profusely, fail to produce fruit. Some or all of these plants may be *P. spinosa* × *P. domestica*. This complexity has not been studied in northern Lancashire and plants have been assigned to a particular species on a 'best' fit basis.

Very common (351). Blackthorn is found throughout northern Lancashire except on the higher ground of Bowland and Leck. Its distribution locally and nationally is stable.

Prunus spinosa × P. domestica (P. × fruticans Weihe)

This is a small tree or shrub found in hedges, scrub and on railway banks. The hybrid is fertile and often difficult to distinguish from forms of *P. domestica* but see above for the account for *P. spinosa*. The distribution map in the 'New Atlas' suggests that when recorders are able to recognise it *P. × fruticans* is probably common.

Very rare (2). The only records from northern Lancashire are from Dutton (SD63J) in 2003 (E.F.G.) and from Preston (SD52U) in 2007 (Anon).

Prunus domestica L. — Wild Plum

Archaeophyte. This species has been grown in gardens since at least 995 and known from the wild since 1777. It is found in woodland edge and urban habitats (BH3, 17). It is apparently derived from hybrids of *P. cerasifera* and *P. spinosa* but has been considerably modified in cultivation. There is a great deal of variation within the species with two or three subspecies sometimes recognised: ssp. *domestica* (Plum), ssp. *insititia* (L.) Bonnier & Layens (Bullace, Damson) and ssp. × *italica* (Borkh.) Gams ex Hegi (Greengage). All three subspecies probably occur in northern Lancashire but as there are many intermediates they are difficult to distinguish. Halliday (1997) gives an account of these problems, which probably also refer to northern Lancashire.

Frequent (213). Wild Plum is found throughout northern Lancashire but most records are from the west of the area. Ssp. *domestica* and *insititia* have been distinguished in a few places. Surprisingly *P. domestica* was not recorded by Wheldon and Wilson (1907).

Prunus avium (L.) L. — Wild Cherry

European Temperate element.

Wild Cherry is found in most of the British Isles but it is rare in western Ireland and north-western Scotland. It is found in woodlands (BH1).

Frequent (174). *P. avium* is found in most of northern Lancashire but it is rare or absent in the Fylde and in eastern and upland parts of the area. Travelling north on the M6 in spring it makes a particularly fine show in the woodlands on the north bank of the R. Ribble where it is especially frequent.

In northern Lancashire its distribution is stable but nationally it appears to have extended its range possibly due to escapes from cultivation.

Prunus cerasus L. — Dwarf Cherry

Archaeophyte. Dwarf Cherry is a native of south-western Asia and is found in many localities in England, Wales and Ireland but it is absent from most of Scotland.

Occasional (21). This was first found in northern Lancashire in the Holden Clough area, Bolton-by-Bowland (Milne-Redhead, 1870s) and in Boilton Wood, Preston (SD53Q) in 1965 (H.E.B.). Today it is found in scattered localities throughout northern Lancashire in old gardens, plantations and hedgerows but as it does not always produce flowers it is easily overlooked.

Prunus padus L. — Bird Cherry

Eurasian Boreo-temperate element.

This is a native shrub or small tree in northern Britain and Wales and perhaps in Norfolk but is found elsewhere as an introduction. It is found in woodland and hedgerows (BH1, 3).

Frequent (165). Bird Cherry is a characteristic feature of woodlands and hedgerows in the north and east of northern Lancashire but also occurs occasionally elsewhere where it may be an escape from cultivation. Its native distribution in northern Lancashire is probably unchanged but since 1987 it appears to have spread nationally ('Local Change'), possibly due to escapes from cultivation.

Prunus lusitanica L. — Portugal Laurel

Neophyte. Portugal Laurel is a native of the Iberian Peninsula but it is frequently planted in parks and gardens. It was cultivated in Britain by 1648 and was found in the wild by 1927. Portugal Laurel is found in many places in the British Isles but especially in southern England and around Edinburgh and Glasgow.

Rare (9). In northern Lancashire Livermore and Livermore (1987) recorded it from old plantings in tetrads SD45W, Y, 47T, 56H and 66E. It has also been recorded from a wood at Lea (SD43V) in 2006 and from Thornton (SD34L) in 2008, both D.P.E.

Prunus laurocerasus L. — Cherry Laurel

Neophyte. This is a native of the Balkan Peninsula and is found in many parts of the British Isles although it is rare or absent from many rural areas. It was cultivated in Britain by 1629 and reported from the wild by 1886.

Occasional (19). Cherry Laurel was first recorded in northern Lancashire from Morecambe (SD46H) in 1975 (A.E.C.) and now occurs in scattered localities throughout the area.

Pyrus communis L.   Pear

Archaeophyte. Pears have been grown in gardens since at least 995 but
the pear found today in many parts of the British Isles embraces a number
of taxa of complex hybrid origin. *P. pyraster* (L.) Burgsd., Wild Pear, is
probably a native of central and southern Europe, south-west and central
Asia. This may occur in the British Isles but as there are many intermediates
it is sometimes difficult to distinguish from *P. communis*.

Occasional (20). Pear was first recorded in northern Lancashire from
Staynall (SD34R) by Ashfield (1860) and today it occurs in scattered localities in VC 60. Most records are of trees with typically pear shaped fruits.
However in the old orchards attached to eighteenth or possibly seventeenth century farms the fruits are more rounded or obovoid. They have
small, hard and often bitter fruit. Furthermore on the edge of Brockholes
Wood, Preston a tree with oval fruits was found in 2001 that could be
P. pyraster. Wheldon and Wilson (1907) knew three localities for Pear
suggesting a modest increase in the species locally. It is not clear if there
has been an increase nationally.

Malus sylvestris *sensu lato*   Apples

Distinguishing between the native *M. sylvestris* and the cultivated *M.
pumila* Mill. and its numerous cultivars can be difficult as they readily
hybridise giving rise to many intermediates. *Malus sylvestris sensu lato*
(including *M. sylvestris* and *M. pumila*) is found in most of the British Isles
except northern Scotland.

Common (272). This is found throughout northern Lancashire, mostly
in hedgerows (BH3) and more occasionally on waste ground (BH17) and
where care has been taken to examine trees critically they are mostly *M.
pumila*. This is more frequent than *M. sylvestris* locally and nationally and
has probably extended its range considerably in northern Lancashire over
the last 100 years but Wheldon and Wilson (1907) recorded *M. sylvestris*
as the more frequent species.

Malus sylvestris (L.) Mill.   Crab Apple

European Temperate element.

Nationally the distribution of this species has not been mapped separately
from *M. sylvestris sensu lato*.

Occasional (41). In northern Lancashire this is found in woodlands and
hedgerows (BH1, 3) mostly in the woodland belt in the north and east of
the area. It is occasionally cultivated and some records may be of garden
escapes. Interestingly both Livermore and Livermore (1987) and Halliday
(1997) regarded *M. sylvestris* as more frequent than *M. pumila* and it is
possible that where ancient woodland is more prevalent this is the case
whereas in other areas, particularly in urban and suburban places, *M.
pumila* becomes the more frequent species. Relative frequencies of the
two species may correlate with the relative abundance of seed sources and
the prevalence of apple cores that are thrown into hedgerows etc. It is not
known if there is any change in the distribution of Crab Apple locally or
nationally.

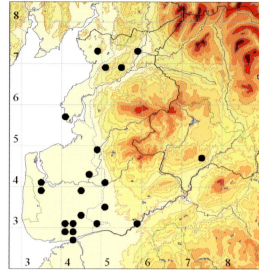
Prunus cerasus

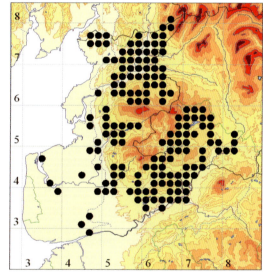
Prunus padus

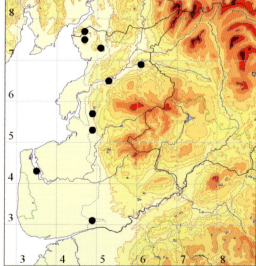
Prunus lusitanica

Sorbus

There are four native *Sorbus* species in Lancashire. *S. aucuparia* is common and widespread but the three other species are very rare and one is endemic to the Morecambe Bay area.

In their monograph Rich, *et al.* (2010) provide an explanation of the origin of apomictic species in the British Isles. In Lancashire *S. aucuparia* and *S. torminalis* are ancestral sexual species whilst *S. rupicola* is an ancient hybrid involving *S. aria* and is apomictic. All the species migrated into Britain from Europe sometime after the retreat of ice following the last Ice Age. *S. aucuparia* and *S. rupicola* were the most rapid to spread into Britain and both had reached western Scotland by at least 6500–6000 BP. It is not known when *S. torminalis* arrived but it is believed it was after the land bridge with Europe was severed *c.* 7500BP.

However the origins of the endemic *S. lancastriensis* are more interesting and involve another native British species. This is *S. aria*, which it is believed also arrived in Britain after the continental land bridge was severed. By the time it arrived the landscape was largely wooded but with clearings and as a native tree it is thought that it spread north only as far as the southern midland counties of England and Wales.

S. aria is an ancestral sexual species but somewhere in the Wye valley area of south-western Britain it hybridised with *S. rupicola* to form the apomictic and endemic *S. porrigentiformis* E.F. Warb. However, it appears that apomictic species sometimes hybridise with sexual species and this seems to have happened with *S. porrigentiformis*, which hybridised further with *S. aria* to give rise to a series of closely related endemic apomictic species found mostly in southern Britain but extending northwards to North Wales. *S. lancastriensis* is probably derived from one of these species and is therefore of comparatively recent origin.

The other Lancashire *Sorbus* species are introductions of Eurasian hybrid origin.

Sorbus aucuparia L.   Rowan

Eurasian Boreo-temperate element.

Rowan is a well-known small tree found in upland woodlands, hedges and on waste ground (BH1, 2, 16) throughout the British Isles.

Common (338). This tree often reaches the highest levels in clough woodlands where it may appear as single trees. Although it may be found throughout northern Lancashire it is scarce west of the M6 south of Lancaster. There appears to be an increase in its distribution in the British Isles, including northern Lancashire, but this is probably due to amenity planting.

Sorbus aucuparia × S. aria (S. × thuringiaca (Nyman) Schönach)
German Service-tree

This hybrid occurs where the parents grow together and is found in scattered localities in Britain. It is sometimes planted.

Very rare (1). *S.* × *thuringiaca* was found on a roadside at Whittington (SD57S) in 1983 (L.A.L.). This may have been previously recorded as *S. aucuparia* × *S. intermedia* (L.A. and P.D. Livermore, 1987).

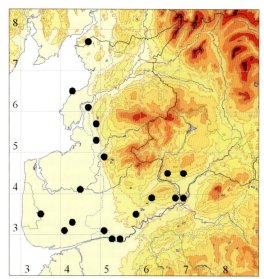

Prunus laurocerasus

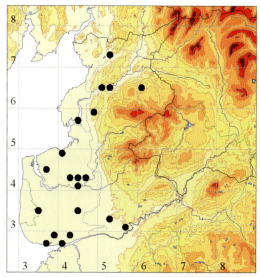

Pyrus communis

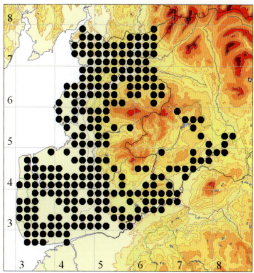

Malus sylvestris s.l.

Sorbus intermedia (Ehrh.) Pers.   Swedish Whitebeam

Neophyte. Swedish Whitebeam was introduced into cultivation in 1789 and is now widely planted as an ornamental tree. It was known from the wild by 1908 and is found in many parts of the British Isles but particularly in and near urban areas.

Occasional (37). It was first recorded in northern Lancashire from Myerscough (SD53E) in 1967 (E.H.) but was probably established in the wild before this. Today it is found in scattered localities in VC 60, especially near the coast, but there is only one record from Lancashire VC 64.

Sorbus aria (L.) Crantz   Common Whitebeam

European Temperate element.

Whilst this is commonly planted in hedges and woodlands it occurs as a native tree on chalk and limestone in southern England (BH1). It also occurs on limestone in northern England around Morecambe Bay, where it appears to be native (Halliday, 1997).

Occasional (59). Common Whitebeam is found throughout northern Lancashire but there are clusters of records on the limestone, especially around Morecambe Bay and in the urban areas centred on Lancaster and Morecambe. Most occurrences of this tree in northern Lancashire clearly originate from introductions. Forma *incisa* (Rchb.) Jáv. was found at Hest Bank (SD46T) in 2010 (M.W.). It is not known if its distribution has changed locally or nationally.

Sorbus lancastriensis E.F. Warb.   Lancastrian Whitebeam

Endemic.

This small tree is restricted to woodland and scrub on limestone (BH16) around Morecambe Bay.

Rare (7). This whitebeam is found in woodlands and scrub on limestone in the northwest of northern Lancashire. Within a limited area it is frequent. Rich, *et al.* (2010) give a total population in Britain of *c.* 2300 trees in 46 sites.

Sorbus rupicola (Syme) Hedl.   Rock Whitebeam

Suboceanic Boreal-montane element.

This has a widely disjunct distribution in the British Isles but is usually found on limestone or basic rocks (BH16) and often as single trees. It is absent from south-eastern England.

Very rare (2). There have been a number of misidentifications of this species and only those seen by Dr T. Rich are accepted. Although it may occur elsewhere it has only been recorded from Warton Crag (SD47W) in 1984 (T.C.G.R.) and from Jack Scout, Silverdale (SD47L) in 1983 (M.B. and T.C.G.R.).

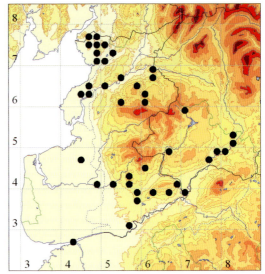
Malus sylvestris s.s.

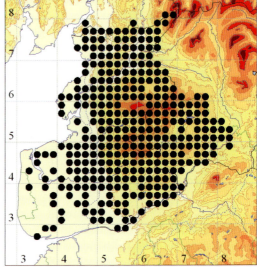
Sorbus aucuparia

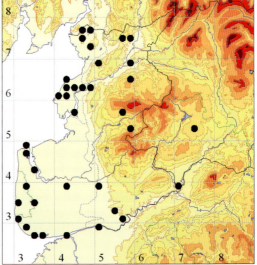
Sorbus intermedia

Sorbus croceocarpa P.D. Sell   Orange Whitebeam

Neophyte. This species has possibly been cultivated in Britain since 1874. It is widely planted and also regenerates freely from seed. It had been collected in the wild by 1909 but it was not described as a distinct species until 1989. Prior to that date many records for *S. latifolia* probably refer to this species. It is found in scattered localities in Britain.

Rare (8). It was first recorded from Warton Crag (SD47W) in 1983 (M.B. and T.C.G.R.) and today occurs on the limestone around Morecambe Bay where it is naturalised and as planted trees in the Lancaster area.

Sorbus torminalis (L.) Crantz   Wild Service-tree

European Temperate element.

This is often regarded as an indicator of ancient woodland (BH1) and occurs in many places in southern Britain and on limestone around Morecambe Bay.

Very rare (4). Wild Service-tree is easily overlooked and was not recorded until 1969 (Pigott, 1974) when it was found in Eaves Wood, Silverdale (SD47T). It was also found on coastal cliffs at Silverdale (SD47L) in 1984 (D.R.) and at SD47R in 2003 (C.B.W.) as well as at Warton (SD47W) in 1992 (M. Evans).

Amelanchier lamarckii F.G. Schroed.   Juneberry

Neophyte. This is a native of North America but it is widely naturalised in north-western Europe. It was introduced into cultivation in 1746 and was recorded in the wild in 1887.

Very rare (3). In northern Lancashire Juneberry has been recorded from Beacon Fell (SD54R) in 2006 (Anon), Preston (SD52J) in 2007 (Anon) and from Doe Barn Wood, Bowland Forest Low (SD64L; Abbott, 2005).

Cotoneaster Medik.   Cotoneasters

This is an extremely difficult genus of mostly apomictic species and as a consequence small morphological differences separate the species. However sexual species also occur and these give rise to hybrids. The genus is distributed widely in the northern hemisphere in Europe, North Africa and Asia. Many species make attractive garden plants and these are escaping into the wild. So far about 70 species have been found growing wild in the British Isles and some of them have spread rapidly. In this account nomenclature follows the recently published monograph (Fryer and Hylmö, 2009) that describes *c.* 460 taxa. Recording in northern Lancashire has been haphazard and several identifications are doubtful so that it is possible that some plants have been wrongly named. This account is therefore tentative.

Cotoneaster frigidus Wall. ex Lindl.   Tree Cotoneaster

Neophyte. This is a native of the Himalayas and has been cultivated in Britain since 1824 but it was not recorded from the wild until 1918. It occurs in scattered localities throughout the British Isles.

Very rare (1). Tree Cotoneaster was recorded from a disused railway at Lancaster (SD46R; Livermore and Livermore, 1990b).

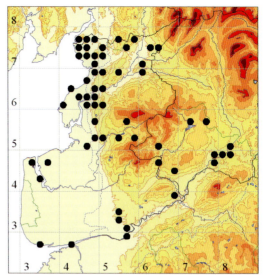

Sorbus aria

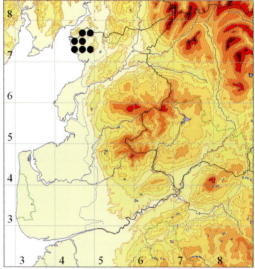

Sorbus lancastriensis

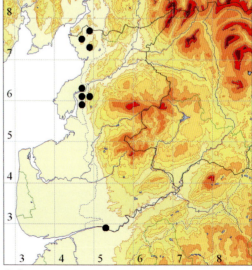

Sorbus croceocarpa

Cotoneaster frigidus × C. salicifolius Franch. or **× C. henryanus**
(C.K. Schneid.) Rehder & E.H. Wilson (**C. × watereri** Exell.)

Waterer's Cotoneaster

Neophyte. This is a variable hybrid first raised in 1928 and recorded in the wild in 1968. It is found in scattered localities throughout the British Isles.

Rare (7). Waterer's Cotoneaster was first recorded in northern Lancashire from Lancaster (SD46Q; Livermore and Livermore, 1989). Subsequently it has been found in a few localities mostly in the north of the region. It is probably under recorded and could be frequent in urban and suburban areas.

Cotoneaster lacteus W.W. Sm.   Late Cotoneaster

Neophyte. This is a native of China grown in gardens since 1913 and recorded from the wild by 1976. It is now naturalised in ruderal habitats in scattered localities in the British Isles.

Very rare (2). It was recorded from Lancaster (SD46R) by Livermore and Livermore (1991) and from Poulton-le-Fylde (SD33P) in 2008 (D.P.E.).

Cotoneaster Series **microphylli** T.T. Yu   Small-leaved Cotoneasters

Neophyte. There are nine species in this series, which are natives of northern India, the Himalayas and China. They were first cultivated in Britain by 1824 and were found in the wild by 1892. Today they are found frequently throughout the British Isles although it is likely that most records refer to **C. integrifolius** (Roxb.) G. Klotz, Entire-leaved Cotoneaster.

Rare (14). It is likely that all records in northern Lancashire recorded as *C. microphyllus* are for *C. integrifolius*, which was first recorded from Burton Well, Silverdale (Petty, 1902). Today it is common on the limestone around Morecambe Bay but otherwise it is confined to the Lancaster area and very rarely elsewhere.

Cotoneaster dammeri C.K. Schneid.   Bearberry Cotoneaster

Neophyte. This native of central China was introduced into cultivation in Britain in 1900 and was recorded from the wild in 1976.

Very rare (3). Bearberry Cotoneaster was recorded from the disused Carnforth iron works (SD57A) in 1990 (J.M.N.; Clement and Foster, 1994), Silverdale in 2003 (J.Cl.) and from Lancaster (SD46V; Livermore and Livermore, 1991).

Cotoneaster dammeri × C. conspicuus C. Marquand
(**C. × suecicus** G. Klotz) and other *C. dammeri* hybrids

Swedish Cotoneaster

Neophyte. These hybrids originated in cultivation and sometimes escape into the wild.

Very rare (4). There are records for these hybrids planted in Lancaster (SD46R, V, 45Z; Livermore and Livermore, 1991) and from an old railway at Caton-with-Littledale (SD56H; Livermore and Livermore, 1990b).

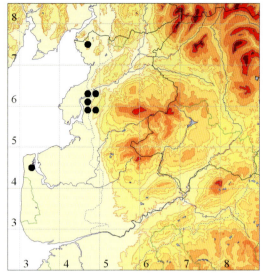

Cotoneaster × watereri

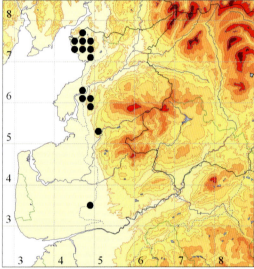

Cotoneaster integrifolius

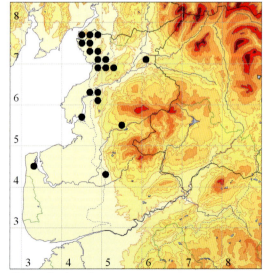

Cotoneaster simonsii

Cotoneaster conspicuus J.B. Comber ex C. Marquand

Tibetan Cotoneaster

Neophyte. This taxon is one of the species of *C. microphyllus* agg. and has probably been overlooked. It is a native of Tibet and was cultivated in Britain by 1925. It has been recorded in the wild since 1984.

Very rare (1). Tibetan Cotoneaster has probably been overlooked in northern Lancashire and some records for *C. microphyllus* on the limestone around Morecambe Bay may be of this species. However the only record is for a self-seeded plant on a wall in Preston (SD52J) found in 2005 (M.W.).

Cotoneaster simonsii Baker

Himalayan Cotoneaster

Neophyte. This is a native of the Himalayas, was introduced into Britain in 1865 and was recorded from the wild by 1910. It is a popular garden plant and occurs throughout the British Isles.

Occasional (20). In northern Lancashire it was first recorded from Silverdale (SD47S) in 1973 (L.A.L.). Today it is found mostly in the northwest of the area with only occasional records from elsewhere.

Cotoneaster horizontalis Decaisne

Wall Cotoneaster

Neophyte. This is a native of western China and was introduced into cultivation in Britain around 1879. It was recorded in the wild by 1940 and is a popular garden plant occurring throughout the British Isles.

Occasional (34). In northern Lancashire Wall Cotoneaster was first recorded from Silverdale (SD47S) in 1967 (A.E.R.). Today it is found throughout the area particularly on the limestone around Morecambe Bay and in the Lancaster area.

Cotoneaster hjelmqvistii Flinck & B. Hylmö

Hjelmqvist's Cotoneaster

Neophyte. *C. hjelmqvistii* is a native of western China, which has been cultivated in Britain since 1954 and was recorded from the wild by 1983. It is found naturalised in ruderal habitats in many parts of Britain and appears to be spreading.

Very rare (3). In northern Lancashire it was found by the Lancaster Canal in Lancaster (SD46Z; Livermore and Livermore, 1989), from sand dunes at Lytham St Anne's (SD33A) in 2010 (M.W.) and from landscaped land in Preston (SD52J) in 2005 (M.W.).

Cotoneaster ascendens Flinck & B. Hylmö

Ascending Cotoneaster

Neophyte. This is a native of central China but its first date of cultivation and escape into the wild are unknown. The 'New Atlas' CD shows only two records in central Scotland and south-eastern England but omits what may be the first record in VC 60 (Stace, 1997).

Very rare (1). The only record for *C. ascendens* in northern Lancashire is from Eaves Wood, Silverdale (SD47S or T) where it was found in 1995 (O.S. and J.F.). It was still there in 2003 (M.W.).

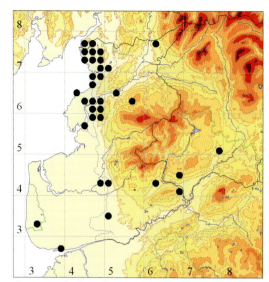

Cotoneaster horizontalis

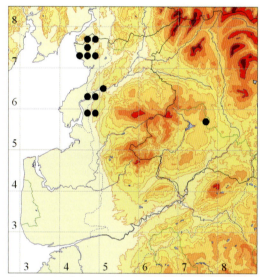

Cotoneaster bullatus

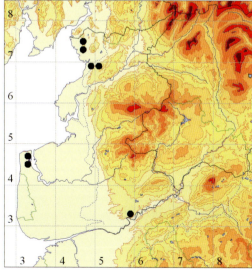

Cotoneaster rehderi

Cotoneaster divaricatus Rehder & E.H. Wilson
Spreading Cotoneaster

Neophyte. Spreading Cotoneaster is a native of western China, which was introduced into cultivation in 1907. It was recorded in the wild by 1983 and today is found in scattered localities in Britain.

Very rare (5). The only records in northern Lancashire are from Silverdale (SD47S) in 2009 (M.J.Y.F. & M.P.) and from the Lancaster area (SD45Z, 46Q, R, W; Livermore and Livermore, 1991).

Cotoneaster villosulus (Rehder & E.H. Wilson) Flinck & Hylmö
Lleyn Cotoneaster

Neophyte. This deciduous shrub is a native of central China and was introduced into British gardens in 1900. It was first recorded in the wild in 1983 but it remains a very rare garden escape.

Very rare (1). It was originally recorded as *C. foveolatus* Rehder & E.H. Wilson when it was first found in Eaves Wood, Silverdale (Clement and Foster, 1994). Preston, *et al.* (2002) refer to it as *C. moupinensis* Franch. but Mrs J. Fryer confirmed the record as *C villosulus* (pers. comm., 2007).

Cotoneaster bullatus Bois
Hollyberry Cotoneaster

Neophyte. This native of western China was introduced into cultivation in 1898 and was recorded from the wild in 1957. It is now widely planted in gardens and in roadside amenity schemes. It is found throughout the British Isles but may be over recorded for *C. rehderi*.

Rare (12). *C. bullatus* was probably recorded first from Eaves Wood, Silverdale (although recorded as Waterslack, SD47S) in c. 1981 (National Trust). Today it is found in several localities in the northwest of the area and in Gisburn Forest in Lancashire VC 64. However at least some of the records are likely to be of *C. rehderi*.

Cotoneaster rehderi Pojark.
Bullate Cotoneaster

Neophyte. *C. rehderi* is a native of western China and was brought into British cultivation in 1908 but was not recorded in the wild until 1986, possibly because it was confused with *C. bullatus*. Today it is found in scattered localities in the British Isles.

Rare (7). This was not recognised as occurring in northern Lancashire until 1999 (C.J.B.) when it was found on an old railway at Fleetwood (SD34N). Other records are from Silverdale (SD47L, S) in 2001 (P.J.), Carnforth (SD46Z) in 2003 (E.F.G.), Fleetwood (SDI & H) in 2006 (D.P.E.) and Grimsargh (SD53W) in 2008 (D.P.E.).

Cotoneaster franchetii Bois
Franchet's Cotoneaster

Neophyte. This is a native of south-western China, which was introduced into Britain about 1895 and first recorded from the wild in 1977. It is now found in scattered localities in the British Isles.

Very rare (2). In northern Lancashire this was recorded from Lancaster (SD46R; Livermore and Livermore, 1991) and Warton (SD47W) in 2009 (M.J.Y.F. & M.P.).

Cotoneaster induratus J. Fryer & B. Hylmö
Hardy Cotoneaster

Neophyte. This is a very hardy Cotoneaster found as a native species in China. It was introduced into cultivation by George Forrest in the first half of the twentieth century and occasionally escapes into the wild. However it was not named until 1997.

Very rare (1). In northern Lancashire a single plant of Hardy Cotoneaster was found in an old quarry at Carnforth (SD56E) in 2009 (M.J.Y.F. & M.P.).

Cotoneaster dielsianus E. Pritz. ex Diels
Diels' Cotoneaster

Neophyte. This native of China is a popular garden species first cultivated in Britain in 1900 and recorded from the wild in 1965. It now occurs throughout Britain but it is easily confused with *C. franchetii* and *C. tengyuehensis*.

Very rare (5). This was recorded in northern Lancashire from Lancaster (SD46R, W; L.A. & P.D. Livermore, 1991) and Carnforth (SD57A) in 2001 (E.F.G.) and in 2009 (M.J.Y.F. & M.P.) in tetrads SD56E and 47V. There is also a record from Silverdale, which appears different and may be *C. tengyuehensis*.

Pyracantha coccinea M. Roem.
Firethorn

Neophyte. This popular garden plant is a native of southern Europe and south-western Asia. It was first cultivated in Britain by 1629 and reported from the wild by 1905.

In northern Lancashire the only record is from the bank of the R. Ribble near Freckleton (Wheldon and Wilson, 1906).

Crataegus coccinea L.
Pear-fruited Cockspurthorn

Neophyte. This is a native of eastern North America and was introduced into cultivation in 1683 but was not reported from the wild until 1982. It is found in a few localities in Britain.

Very rare (2). *C. coccinea* was only recorded as planted by the Lancaster Canal at Lancaster (SD46W, V; Livermore and Livermore, 1989).

Crataegus persimilis Sarg.   Broad-leaved Cockspurthorn

Neophyte. The origin of this shrub is unknown; it has been cultivated in Britain since 1791 but it was not recorded from the wild until 1934. It is a popular garden plant and is used in amenity plantings. Although it is found in many localities in southern Britain it may be overlooked.

Very rare (4). This was recorded as planted in Lancaster (SD46R, W, Q, 45U; Livermore and Livermore, 1991).

Crataegus monogyna Jacq.   Hawthorn

European Temperate element.

This deciduous shrub or tree is found in hedges, woodland edge and scrub habitats (BH1, 3) and occurs throughout the British Isles. *Crataegus rhipidophylla* Gand. has recently been recognised as occurring in scattered localities in Britain where it is increasingly planted in hedges. However it is easily mistaken for *C. monogyna* and is probably under recorded. So far it has not been found in northern Lancashire.

Very common (427). Hawthorn is found throughout northern Lancashire being absent only from the higher hills. It has been planted in hedges for hundreds of years and is the commonest hedgerow shrub. Its distribution has probably remained unchanged locally and nationally.

Crataegus monogyna × C. laevigata (C. × media Bechst.)

This hybrid is frequent where the parents grow together but it is also found as an introduction elsewhere. It grows in hedgerows and woodland edge habitats in many parts of the British Isles but especially in south-eastern England, where it is regarded as native.

Very rare (4). The only records in northern Lancashire are from Cottam (SD53G) in 1965 (A.E.R., E.H.), Fulwood (unlocalised) in 1965 (A.E.R.) and possibly in hedges in Upper Rawcliffe-with-Tarnacre & Inskip-with-Sowerby (SD43U) and Salwick (SD43S) in 2010 (E.F.G.). It is possible that some of the records for *C. laevigata* are this taxon.

Crataegus laevigata (Poir.) DC.   Midland Hawthorn

European Temperate element.

This is a common native plant in hedgerows, woodlands and woodland edge habitats (BH1, 3) in midland and south-eastern England but it occurs as an introduction elsewhere in England, Wales, Ireland and southern Scotland.

Rare (13). It is assumed that in northern Lancashire Midland Hawthorn is an introduction usually being found in hedges. Whilst Wheldon and Wilson (1907) knew it from two localities, probably both in hedges, they also recognised it from 1100ft (330m) on Mallowdale Fell, perhaps at the highest levels in one of the formerly wooded cloughs. Such a locality might suggest native status although this seems unlikely. Today it is recorded from hedgerows in scattered localities in western VC 60 but some of these may be *C. × media*.

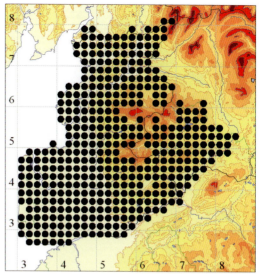
Crataegus monogyna

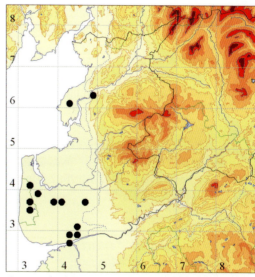
Crataegus laevigata

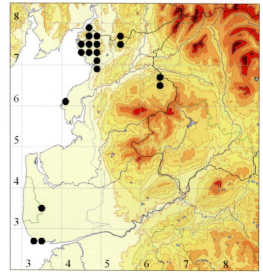
Filipendula vulgaris

Filipendula vulgaris Moench   Dropwort

Eurosiberian Temperate element.

Dropwort is found on calcareous grassland (BH7) in most of England, northern Wales, the Burren in Ireland and occasionally in southern Scotland. It is also frequently planted in churchyards in western Wales.

Occasional (19). In northern Lancashire it is mostly found on limestone around Morecambe Bay and on Dalton Crags. However there are occasional records elsewhere. Wheldon and Wilson (1907) only recorded Dropwort from five localities in the Silverdale area indicating that it has extended its range somewhat over the last 100 years. Its distribution nationally has probably remained unchanged.

Filipendula ulmaria (L.) Maxim.   Meadowsweet

Eurasian Boreo-temperate element.

This is a characteristic herb of damp or wet habitats (BH11) throughout the British Isles.

Very common (395). In northern Lancashire Meadowsweet is found throughout the area being absent only from the higher parts of Bowland (see Plate 2.32). Its distribution is stable both locally and nationally.

Kerria japonica (L.) DC.   Kerria

Neophyte. This is a native of China introduced into cultivation in 1804 for its yellow flowers but not recorded from the wild until 1965. It is found in scattered localities in the British Isles but there is a concentration of records near London.

Very rare (4). In northern Lancashire Kerria was found in Kit Bill Wood, Over Kellet (SD56E) in 1998 (E.F.G.), Yealand Redmayne (SD47U) in 2000 (C.B.W.) and in Silverdale (SD47S) in 2002 (Arnside Naturalists) and in tetrad SD47M in 2007 (J.W.).

Rubus L.

The genus *Rubus* consists of a number of subgenera some of which are further divided into sections and series. In this account, which follows Stace (2010), the subgenera and the sections or species assigned to them are:

Chamaemorus (Hill) Focke – includes *R. chamaemorus*

Dalibardastrum Focke – includes *R. tricolor*

Cylactis (Raf.) Focke – includes *R. saxatilis*

Anoplobatus Focke – includes *R. odoratus, R. parviflorus*

Idaeobatus Focke – includes *R. idaeus, R. spectabilis*

Rubus includes sections:

    Rubus

    Glandulosus Wimm. & Grab.

    Corylifolii Lindl.

    Caesii Lej. & Courtois

In this account *Rubus fruticosus sensu lato* covers all the species included in subgenus **Rubus.**

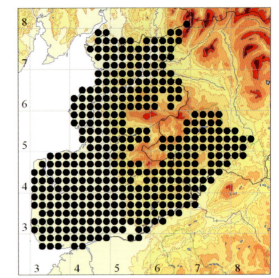

Filipendula ulmaria

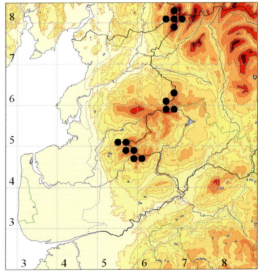

Rubus chamaemorus

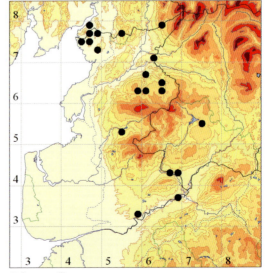

Rubus saxatilis

Subgenus **Chamaemorus** (Hill) Focke

Rubus chamaemorus L.   Cloudberry

Circumpolar Boreal-montane element.

This is found in Britain on heaths and blanket bogs (BH10, 12) from northern Wales and the southern Pennines northwards. There is a single record from Northern Ireland.

Occasional (15). Cloudberry is found on the higher and undisturbed surfaces of blanket bogs in the Bowland and Leck Fells. It rarely sets fruit. Its distribution locally and nationally is stable.

Subgenus **Dalibardastrum** Focke

Rubus tricolor Focke   Chinese Bramble

Neophyte. This is a native of China first cultivated in Britain in 1908 and reported in the wild in 1976. It is found in scattered localities in the British Isles.

Very rare (4). Chinese Bramble was first recorded in northern Lancashire from an old quarry in Lancaster (SD46V) in 1989 (V.G.). It was also recorded from a disused railway platform at Lytham (SD32T) in 1999 (C.F. & N.J.S.), the Lancaster Canal, Preston (SD53F) in 2006 (D.P.E.) and from Dunsop Bridge (SD65Q; Abbott, 2005).

Subgenus **Cylactis** (Raf.) Focke

Rubus saxatilis L.   Stone Bramble

Eurasian Boreo-temperate element.

Stone Bramble is found on basic substrates in woodland and rocky places (BH1, 16, 17) in northern England, Wales, Scotland and Ireland.

Occasional (20). In northern Lancashire it is found on limestone in the north of the area and in woodland valleys in the east. Although there were some losses before 1930 ('New Atlas') it is believed its distribution locally and nationally is stable.

Subgenus **Anoplobatus** Focke

Rubus parviflorus Nutt.   Thimbleberry

Neophyte, a native of North America introduced into cultivation in Britain in 1818 and first found growing wild in 1913. It is only infrequently grown but it is known in the wild from a few British localities.

Very rare (1). In northern Lancashire it is known from a wood at Yealand Conyers (SD57C) where it was first recorded c. 1975 (P.J.).

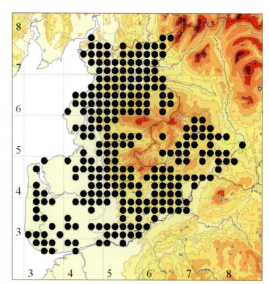

Rubus idaeus

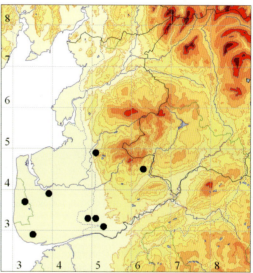

Rubus spectabilis

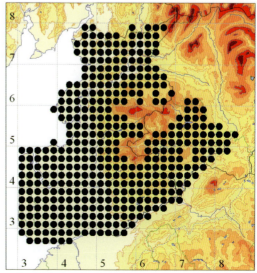

Rubus fruticosus agg.

Subgenus **Idaeobatus** Focke

Rubus idaeus L.   Raspberry

Circumpolar Boreo-temperate element.

This is found in woodland and woodland edge habitats (BH1) throughout the British Isles.

Common (272). Raspberry is a common northern woodland species but it also occurs on waste ground in most parts of Lancashire. Some populations are garden escapes. Its distribution in northern Lancashire and nationally up to 1987 was stable ('New Atlas') but 'Local Change' showed it to have declined nationally since 1987.

Rubus spectabilis Pursh   Salmonberry

Neophyte. This is a native of western North America, which was first introduced into Britain in 1827. It was found in the wild in 1899 and today is found scattered throughout the British Isles but with a concentration of records in parts of Scotland and Northern Ireland.

Rare (8). In northern Lancashire Salmonberry was first found at Bartle Hall (SD43W) in 1964 (E. & J.H.), where it is naturalised. Since then it has been found in a few scattered localities in the south of the region.

Subgenus **Idaeobatus** × **Rubus**

Rubus loganobaccus L.H. Bailey   Loganberry

Neophyte. A hexaploid hybrid species discovered in California in 1881 and introduced into British gardens in 1897. It was first found in the wild in 1938 and occurs today as a garden escape in scattered localities in Britain.

Very rare (2). In northern Lancashire it was recorded from an abandoned allotment in the Carnforth area (SD47V; Livermore and Livermore, 1987) and from Lytham Dock (SD32Y) in 1994 (D.P.E.).

Subgenus **Rubus**

Rubus fruticosus agg.   Brambles

European Southern-temperate element.

This is a taxonomically complex aggregate of over 320 species in **Rubus** subgenus **Rubus.** The species occur in a wide variety of habitats but they are especially frequent in woodlands, woodland edge habitats (including hedgerows) and on heaths and heath margins as well as on waste ground (BH1, 3) on neutral and rather acid soils. Map 3.1 shows the distribution of critically determined species and by comparing this map with Map 4.19, showing the distribution of semi-ancient woodland, it can be seen that there is a correlation between the two. However the distribution of brambles is also associated with heaths and wasteland and avoids the

calcareous soils in the Silverdale area. Furthermore, with only a few recorders, there is probably some bias in the records towards where recorders have worked. This is mitigated by the thorough surveys of the Earls but perhaps the paucity of records in the upper Lune valley and north Bowland valleys reflects this bias.

Brambles occur throughout the British Isles except the Northern Isles and very few occur in the Outer Hebrides.

Very common (405). Brambles are found throughout northern Lancashire and the distribution of the aggregate is stable locally and nationally.

A total of 59 species or nearly 18% of the total recorded in the British Isles have so far been recognised as occurring in northern Lancashire. Of these 22 (36%) are endemic and confined to the British Isles. However there are a number of taxa that have either not been named or are unidentified and it is likely that the numbers for the British Isles and northern Lancashire will both increase as further research is carried out. Further, it is known that *R. caesius* hybridises with other species, especially with those in section **Corylifolii**, giving rise to plants with a few large drupelets. Several hybrid taxa are widespread in northern Lancashire particularly on waste ground, but they are not covered in this account.

In general the number of species found in the British Isles decreases from south to north and a total of nearly 60 species in northern Lancashire represents a relatively rich bramble flora for northern England. Comments on the national distribution of species follows Newton and Randall (2004) but whilst the overall patterns are relatively well-known the density of records still reflects areas where most work by bramble specialists has been carried out. Ireland is especially under recorded whilst Lancashire is one of the better-known areas.

Wheldon and Wilson (1907) took a keen interest in brambles. Since their day considerable advances have taken place in bramble taxonomy, and during the last 40 years the northern Lancashire bramble flora has been studied in some detail. In the 1970s a number of gatherings were made and identified by the late Eric Edees. In the 1980s Len and Pat Livermore studied the brambles in the City of Lancaster and Alan Newton checked their gatherings. However from the 1990s to date Dave Earl has made a comprehensive survey of the area. This account has only been possible through the efforts of these botanists but it is the work of Dave Earl that makes it possible to provide meaningful tetrad distribution maps. With the exception of *R. ulmifolius* all records have been checked by E. Edees, A. Newton or D.P. Earl and occasionally by other specialists. In compiling this account Dave Earl's draft Bramble Flora of Lancashire has been made available to the author.

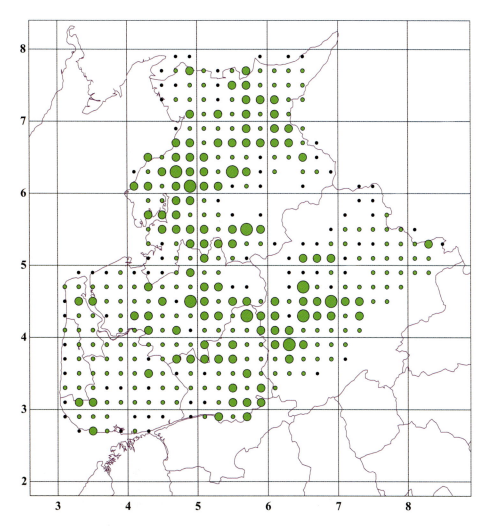

KEY

- ● Tetrads with 16 or more species
- ● Tetrads with 11–15 species
- · Tetrads with 6–10 species
- · Tetrads with 1–5 species.

Map 3.1 Map showing the distribution of *Rubus* subgenus *Rubus* spp. and their relative abundance

In this account the order of the species follows Edees and Newton (1988) who provided keys and detailed descriptions of the species. A useful account with keys of northern brambles is also provided by Halliday (1997) whilst comments on the distribution of brambles in the British Isles rely on Newton and Randall (2004).

Section **Rubus**

Rubus bertramii G. Braun

This is widespread in damp woods and heath margins in western Europe. It occurs in western Britain as far north as Cumbria.

Very rare (4). This was recorded from Abbeystead (SD55) in 1901 (J.A.W.; LIV) and in 1966 from tetrads SD43H, 44G and 53L (D.P.E.) and in 1997 from tetrad SD54E (D.P. & J.E.).

Rubus nessensis W. Hall

Chiefly a plant of damp wooded riversides in north-western Europe, which is found in many parts of the British Isles.

Very rare (2). This was recorded from Botton, Hindburndale (SD66) in 1901 and 1902 (A.W., J.A.W.; NMW), from Over Kellet (SD57F) in 1997 (D.P. & J.E.) and Roeburndale (SD56W) in 1998 (D.P. & J.E.).

Rubus plicatus Weihe & Nees

This is a species of heaths and moors, often on dry sandy soils, in central and north-western Europe and occurs in suitable places throughout the British Isles.

Rare (8). *R. plicatus* is found on the edge of mosslands in the west of northern Lancashire.

Rubus scissus W.C.R. Watson

This is found at the margins of heaths and moors, in peaty areas and in birch woods in north-western Europe. It is frequent in upland areas of Britain but much scarcer elsewhere.

Occasional (40). *R. scissus* is found in upland areas as well as in a few lowland areas on the edge of mosslands in northern Lancashire.

Section **Glandulosus** Wimm. & Grab.

Series **Sylvatici** (P.J. Mueller) Focke

Rubus albionis W.C.R. Watson

Endemic but widespread in south-western and western Britain as far north as Lancashire and also in Ireland. It occurs in woodland edge habitats and on the margins of heaths and moors.

Very rare (1). What is believed to be this species was found in a neglected garden at Blackpool (SD33B) in 1996 (D.P.E.).

Rubus calvatus Lees ex Bloxam

Endemic to the north of Ireland, England and Wales but it is particularly characteristic of the Pennine foothills. It is found in woodland edge habitats and on the margins of heaths and moors.

Rare (12). Apart from a 1886 record from Sale Wheel (SD65S) on the banks of the R. Ribble (BM) and a record from tetrad SD43H in 1996 (D.P.E.) all records are from eastern Bowland in the Hodder and Ribble valleys.

Rubus cumbrensis Newton

This endemic species was described from a plant gathered at Abbeystead in 1971 (CGE) and is confined to north-western England, the Isle of Man and Dumfries. It is found on the margins of woods, moors and heaths.

Frequent (79). *R. cumbrensis* is found throughout northern Lancashire but records are centred in western Bowland.

Rubus errabundus W.C.R. Watson

Endemic but with a disjunct distribution in the British Isles. Most records are from southern England, north-western England and south-western Scotland, between Glasgow and Edinburgh and in the Isle of Man. It is found in woodland edge habitats, heaths and moorland roadsides.

Frequent (115). *R. errabundus* occurs throughout northern Lancashire but especially in Bowland. It is one of the commonest Lancashire brambles (Newton and Randall, 2004).

Rubus gratus Focke

This is widespread in north-western Europe but in Britain it has a disjunct distribution with groups of localities scattered across England, Wales and Scotland. It is found on heaths and peaty soils especially in Norfolk and on the lower ground of Lancashire and Cheshire.

Very rare (1). In northern Lancashire *R. gratus* was found in a hedgerow in the Ribble valley at West Bradford (SD74M) in 1999 (D.P. & J.E.; Abbott, 2005).

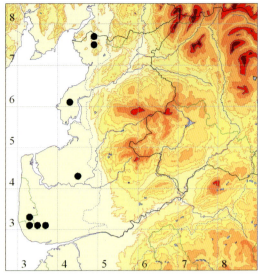

Rubus plicatus

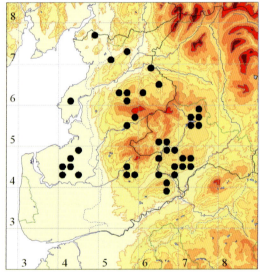

Rubus scissus

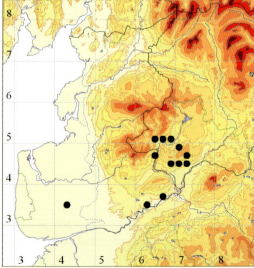

Rubus calvatus

Rubus laciniatus Willd.

This distinctive species with its dissected leaflets is of horticultural origin and is widespread in north-western Europe. It is found in gardens and allotments and has become naturalised in various habitats.

Rare (9). In northern Lancashire *R. laciniatus* was first recorded from Layton Cemetery, Blackpool (SD33I) in 1985 (C.F. & N.J.S.). Other records are scattered in VC 60.

Rubus leptothyrsos G. Braun

Most of the records in the British Isles are from lowland areas in Scotland with only occasional records elsewhere. It is found in hedgerows and on the margins of moorland pastures. It is widespread in north-western Europe.

Very rare (2). *R. leptothyrsos* was found at Tosside, Gisburn Forest (SD75S) and Paythorne Moor (SD85G) both in 1999 (D.P. & J.E.).

Rubus lindleianus Lees

R. lindleianus is widespread in north-western Europe and lowland parts of the British Isles. It is typically a late flowering hedgerow plant with large white flowers.

Common (239). This is found throughout northern Lancashire except in moorland areas and it is rare in the western Fylde and eastern Bowland.

Rubus robiae (W.C.R. Watson) Newton

An endemic species found mainly on the western side of the central Pennines but with localities in eastern England, Wales, southern Scotland and Ireland. It is characteristic of woodland edge and hedgerow habitats.

Frequent (219). This is found throughout northern Lancashire except in high moorland areas and it is less frequent in VC 64 than in VC 60.

Rubus sciocharis (Sudre) W.C.R. Watson

This is widespread in north-western Europe and is found scattered in England with a few Welsh and Scottish records. It is found in woodland edge and hedgerow habitats.

Very rare (5). *R. sciocharis* has only been found in the Hodder valley (SD64 L, M, N, S; D.P.E.; Abbott, 2005) and in the vicinity of Beacon Fell (SD54R; D.P.E.).

Rubus silurum (Ley) Ley

An endemic species found in western England, and Wales in woodland edge habitats or on mossland margins.

Occasional (31). Records for this species are concentrated in the valleys of northern Bowland and to a lesser extent in eastern Bowland.

Series **Rhamnifolii** (Bab.) Focke

Rubus cardiophyllus Lef. & P.J. Mueller

This is widespread in north-western Europe and in lowland areas of the British Isles southwest of a line from south-western Scotland to East Anglia with only a few records northeast of this line. It is a species of woodland margins.

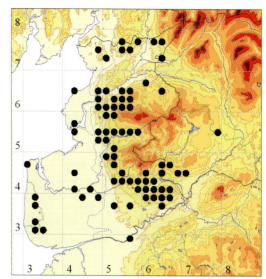

Rubus cumbrensis

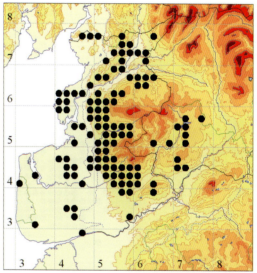

Rubus errabundus

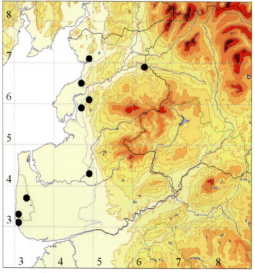

Rubus laciniatus

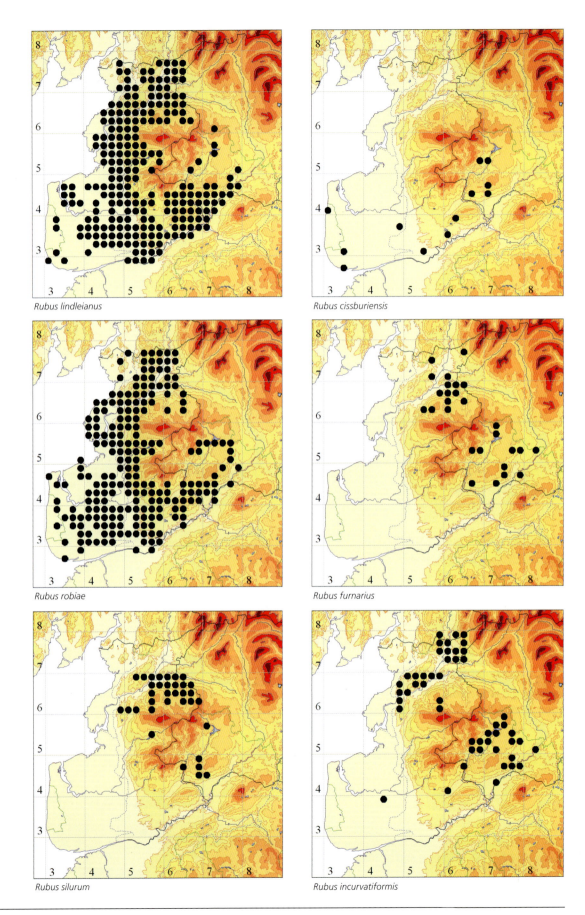

Rubus lindleianus

Rubus cissburiensis

Rubus robiae

Rubus furnarius

Rubus silurum

Rubus incurvatiformis

Very rare (4). There is an 1899 record for *R. cardiophyllus* from Pilling Moss (SD44; J.A.W.; NMW), a 1902 record from Elston Wood (SD53N; J.A.W.; CGE) and a pre 1988 record for the 10km square SD34 (Newton and Randall, 2004). Recent records include an unlocalised record for Longridge Fell (SD63) in 1972 (A.N.), Fulwood (SD53B, L) in 1996 (D.P.E.) and White Lund, near Morecambe (SD46L) in 2007 (D.P.E.).

Rubus cissburiensis W.C. Barton & Riddelsd.

This occurs in south-eastern England where it is thought to be endemic (Edees and Newton, 1988) and as an introduction in north-western England. It is found on heaths and in woodland edge habitats.

Rare (12). *R. cissburiensis* is found in scattered localities in the southern half of northern Lancashire.

Rubus elegantispinosus (A. Schum.) H. Weber

A species of horticultural origin naturalised in woods and ruderal habitats especially in suburban areas in scattered localities in Britain.

Very rare (1). This was found in a shrubbery in central Preston (SD52J) in 1996 (D.P.E.).

Rubus furnarius W.C. Barton & Riddelsd.

This is an endemic species of woodland and moor margins largely confined to north-western England.

Occasional (26). There are old records from Elston Wood in 1902 (SD53W; BM) and near Nicky Nook in 1888 (SD54E; A.W., YRK) but otherwise records are confined to the north and east of northern Lancashire.

Rubus incurvatiformis Edees

This is another endemic species largely confined to woodland margins and upland heaths in north-western England and northern Wales.

Occasional (49). *R. incurvatiformis* is found mainly in the north and east of northern Lancashire with occasional localities elsewhere.

Rubus lindebergii P.J. Mueller

R. lindebergii is an upland species widespread in north-western Europe and in Britain occurs in southern Scotland, England and Wales. It is found in woodland and moor margins often on calcareous substrates.

Frequent (89). This occurs mostly in the north and east of northern Lancashire but especially in the Hodder and Ribble valleys. There are a few records elsewhere.

Rubus nemoralis P.J. Mueller

This is widespread in north-western Europe and is found in most parts of the British Isles. It occurs on heaths, moors and woodland margins.

Frequent (190). *R. nemoralis* occurs throughout VC 60 except in the higher moorland areas of Leck and Bowland. However it appears to be rare in Lancashire VC 64 and may possibly be under recorded.

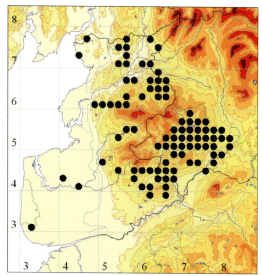

Rubus lindebergii

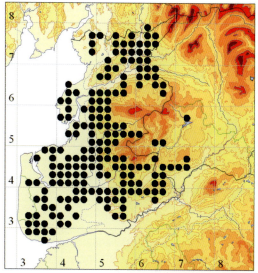

Rubus nemoralis

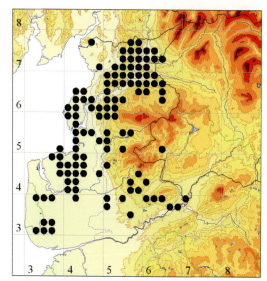

Rubus polyanthemus

Rubus pistoris W.C. Barton & Riddelsd.

R. pistoris is apparently a dwarf form of *R. nemoralis* and occurs in scattered localities in England, Scotland and Ireland.

The only northern Lancashire record is from Claughton Moor (SD56) in 1905 (A.W.; YRK).

Rubus polyanthemus Lindeb.

This is found in north-western Europe and occurs in many parts of the British Isles. It favours woodland edge habitats and heaths.

Frequent (113). *R. polyanthemus* is a common bramble in the north and west of northern Lancashire but appears to be much rarer in the south and east.

Rubus rhombifolius Weihe ex Boenn.

This is widespread in north-western Europe and is found in scattered localities in the British Isles. It occurs in woodland edge habitats and on heaths.

Rare (10). *R. rhombifolius* occurs in the Lune valley and occasionally elsewhere.

Rubus rubritinctus W.C.R. Watson

This distinctive endemic, red-stemmed species of hedgebanks and heath margins is found in south-western England, southern Wales, Lancashire and occasionally elsewhere.

Frequent (116). *R. rubritinctus* is a common bramble south of Lancaster and west of the M6 with only occasional records elsewhere in northern Lancashire.

Series **Sprengeliani** Focke

Rubus sprengelii Weihe

This is widespread in central and northern Europe but in the British Isles it is found mostly southwest of a line from southwest Scotland to East Anglia with a concentration of records in the central and southern Pennines. It is found on sandy or gravely soils in woodland and on heaths.

Frequent (86). *R. sprengelii* is found in western and southern Bowland with a few records elsewhere in northern Lancashire.

Series **Discolores** (P.J. Müll.) Focke

Rubus armeniacus Focke   Himalayan Giant

Himalayan Giant is a common garden blackberry but its origins are uncertain. It has been in cultivation in Germany since the nineteenth century and it is possible that it was exported from there to the USA before being exported back to Europe. During the Second World War it was grown widely in British gardens and allotments from where it has escaped into the wild. Today it is found widely in Britain, especially in suburban areas. It is a very vigorous species.

Frequent (114). In northern Lancashire *R. armeniacus* is found in most of the area but records are concentrated in the more urbanised areas around Lancaster and the Heysham peninsula, the Fylde coast and in the Preston area.

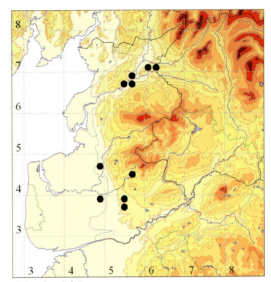
Rubus rhombifolius

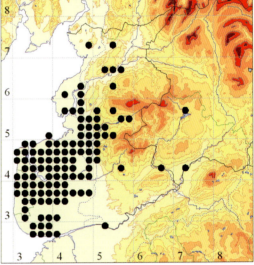
Rubus rubritinctus

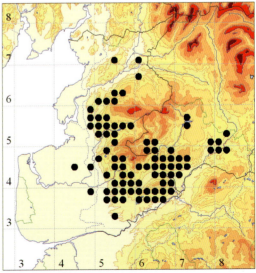
Rubus sprengelii

Rubus ulmifolius Schott

This distinctive species with chalky white undersides to the leaves is widespread in western Europe and whilst it occurs in eastern and southern Scotland it is ubiquitous in Britain south of the Lake District and Yorkshire except on higher ground and on wet acid soils. It is under recorded in Ireland. It is found in hedgerows but it is intolerant of shade and is rarely found in woodlands.

Frequent (137). In northern Lancashire *R. ulmifolius* is found mostly in the west of the area with occasional records elsewhere.

Series **Vestiti** (Focke) Focke

Rubus bartonii Newton

This is an endemic species found in western Britain from Lancashire to south-western England as well as in Ireland and the Isle of Man. It has also been taken into cultivation and some records may be garden escapes. It is found in woods and hedgerows.

Very rare (4). *R. bartonii* was found in Wyresdale in the Dolphinholme area (SD55B, G) in 1997 (D.P. & J.E.), on the dock estate Preston (SD52E) in 2010 (D.P.E.) and in Moor Park, Preston (SD53K) in 2011 (D.P.E.).

Rubus criniger (E.F. Linton) Rogers

An endemic species with a disjunct distribution centred on Lancashire and central and southern England. It is found in woodland edge habitats.

Rare (6). There are old records from Caton and Claughton Moors (SD56R) in 1905 (A.W.; NMW, YRK) and Claughton, near Garstang (SD54G) in 1904 (A.W. & J.A.W.; YRK). This latter locality is close to present-day records from Barnacre-with-Bonds (SD54H, I) in 1996 (D.P. & J. E.). It has also been recorded in the Preston to Longridge area. (SD52J, 53R, W, X) between 2006 and 2009 (D.P.E.).

Rubus painteri Edees

An endemic species found in woodland edge habitats in the western foothills of the central and southern Pennines.

Occasional (16). *R. painteri* occurs in the Bowland foothills as far north as Abbeystead in the west and Gisburn Forest in the east.

Rubus vestitus Weihe

This is widespread in central and western Europe but in the British Isles, whilst it is common in much of England and Wales, it is found only occasionally in Scotland. It also occurs in Ireland. It is found in woodland edge habitats and is often abundant on calcareous or clay soils.

Frequent (88). In northern Lancashire *R. vestitus* has a disjunct distribution occurring mainly in the north of the area and in the Ribble and Hodder valleys with only occasional records elsewhere.

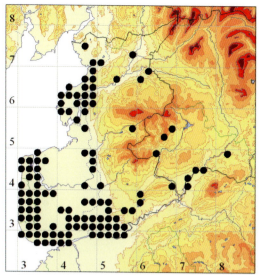
Rubus armeniacus

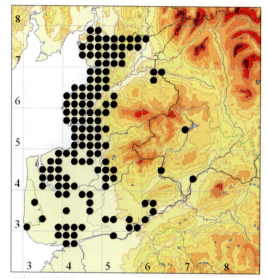
Rubus ulmifolius

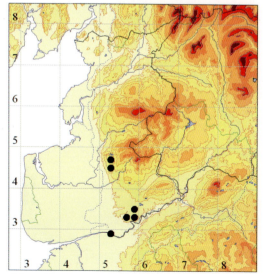
Rubus criniger

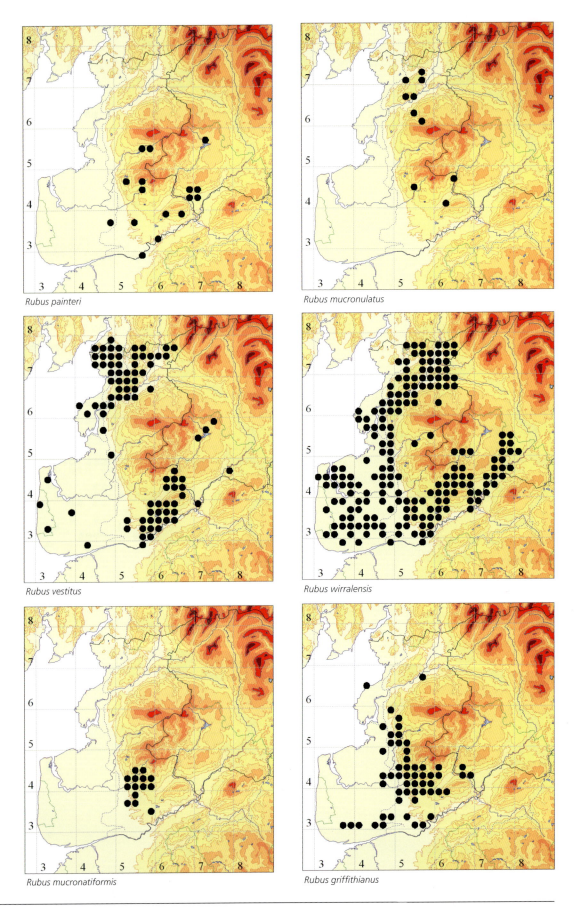

Rubus painteri

Rubus mucronulatus

Rubus vestitus

Rubus wirralensis

Rubus mucronatiformis

Rubus griffithianus

Series **Mucronati** (Focke) H.E. Weber

Rubus mucronatiformis (Sudre) W.C.R. Watson

Endemic and until recently it was thought to be confined to localities in southern England with only scattered occurrences elsewhere. It is now believed to be more widespread.

Rare (14). In northern Lancashire *R. mucronatiformis* appears to be confined to an area around Goosnargh in VC 60.

Rubus mucronulatus Boreau

This is widespread in north-western Europe but in the British Isles it is a northern species with southern limits in East Anglia and the southern midlands of England. It is found in woodland edge habitats.

Rare (10). In northern Lancashire *R. mucronulatus* is found around the western edges of Bowland.

Rubus wirralensis Newton

This endemic species is found mainly in western parts of the British Isles but it also occurs in north-eastern England. It is particularly frequent in Lancashire and Cheshire where it is found in woodland edge habitats especially on clay soils.

Frequent (189). In northern Lancashire it occurs in most areas although it is absent from much of Bowland.

Series **Micantes** Sudre ex Bouvet

Rubus diversus W.C.R. Watson

Apart from localities in the Netherlands this species is found in scattered localities from Lancashire southwards. It can form dense thickets in woodlands.

Very rare (2). This was found amongst planted shrubs in Preston (SD52J) in 2003. It may also have been found in another Preston locality (SD52E) in 2010 (both D.P.E.).

Rubus griffithianus Rogers

An endemic species found in Lancashire, Cheshire and northern Wales with further records in central England and Ireland. It occurs in woodland edge habitats.

Occasional (56). In northern Lancashire *R. griffithianus* is found mostly in central and southern parts of VC 60 especially in the 10km square SD54 north of Preston.

Rubus newbouldii Bab.

An endemic species found in a limited area on either side of the central Pennines where it is often prolific in hedges and wood borders.

Frequent (11). In northern Lancashire *R. newbouldii* is particularly abundant in the south of VC 60 but occurs in the west as far north as Warton and is found in scattered localities further east in Lancashire VC 64.

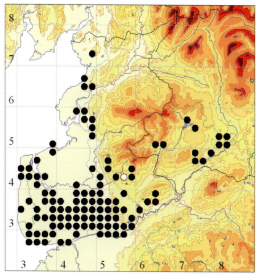

Rubus newbouldii

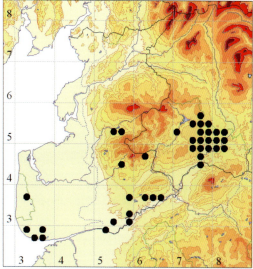

Rubus anisacanthos

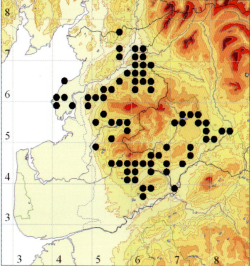

Rubus infestus

Rubus raduloides (Rogers) Sudre

This is widespread in north-western Europe and is scattered in southern Britain and Ireland but with clusters of records in some other areas, e.g. around Glasgow and Bristol. It is a species of woodland margins.

Very rare (1). In northern Lancashire *R. raduloides* has only been recorded from Lytham St Anne's (SD32N) in 1996 (D.P.E.).

Series **Anisacanthi** H.E. Weber

Rubus anisacanthos G. Braun

This is widespread in north-western Europe and is found in eastern England and Scotland but its distribution extends to the west coast in northern England and southern Scotland. It is also found in Ireland. It is a species of woodland edges and moorland.

Occasional (38). As might be expected of a species with a largely eastern distribution in Britain most records for *R. anisacanthos* are from eastern Bowland in VC 64 with only occasional records further west from VC 60.

Rubus infestus Weihe ex Boenn.

This is widespread in north-western Europe and in the British Isles, it is found from central Scotland southwards to the English Midlands with only a few localities elsewhere. It occurs in wood, heath and moor margins.

Frequent (72). In northern Lancashire *R. infestus* is found in the north of the area and in Bowland.

Series **Radulae** (Focke) Focke

Rubus adenanthoides Newton

An endemic species found mostly in northern England, Ireland and the Isle of Man. It occurs in woodland edge habitats and on the margins of heaths and moors

Occasional (26). In northern Lancashire *R. adenanthoides* is mostly found in the north of VC 60 with a few records in the Fylde.

Rubus echinatoides (Rogers) Dallman

An endemic species found in many parts of the British Isles but particularly in Lancashire and Yorkshire. It occurs on the margins of woods, heaths and moors.

Occasional (28). In northern Lancashire *R. echinatoides* is found in the southeast of the area in the Ribble valley and in VC 64 with only occasional localities elsewhere.

Rubus echinatus Lindley

This is widespread in west central Europe and is mostly found in England as far north as Lancashire with a few records from Wales and Ireland. It is a species of woodland edge habitats and heaths.

Very rare (1). The only records in northern Lancashire are from near Cockerham (SD45R) in 1904 (A.W.; YRK) and from Sandholme Mill, Claughton (SD54B) in 1971 (A.N.).

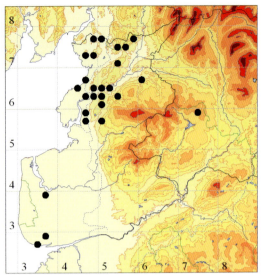

Rubus adenanthoides

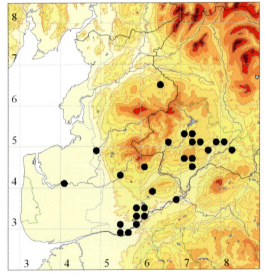

Rubus echinatoides

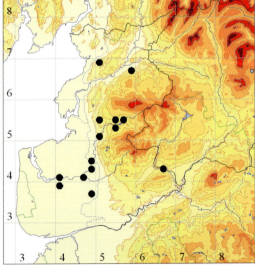

Rubus radula

Rubus pallidus Weihe

This is a widespread bramble in north-western Europe and occurs in woods and thickets in England and Wales as far north as the Lake District and northern Yorkshire. There are two localities in Ireland.

Very rare (3). In northern Lancashire this has been found at Lytham St Anne's (SD32N) in 1996 (D.P.E.), Oakenclough (SD54I; D.P.E.) and near Whittington (SD57S) in 1998 (D.P. & J.E.).

Rubus radula Weihe ex Boenn.

This is widespread in western and central Europe and occurs in most of Britain and more rarely in Ireland. It is found in wood, heath and moor margins.

Rare (14). In northern Lancashire R. radula is found in scattered localities in VC 60 with a single Lancashire VC 64 locality in the Hodder valley.

Rubus rudis Weihe

A species widespread in north-western and central Europe and found mostly in southern Britain with occasional localities elsewhere including Lancashire. It is found in woodland edge habitats and on heaths.

Very rare (2). In northern Lancashire R. rudis was found near Abbeystead (SD55S) in 1998 (D.P. & J.E.) and in the Ribble valley (SD84J; Abbott, 2005).

Rubus rufescens Lef. & P.J. Mueller

This species is widespread in western Europe and in the British Isles is found mostly from Lancashire southwards with only occasional records from Scotland and Ireland. It is a woodland species often forming large thickets.

Rare (9). Most records in northern Lancashire are from the Wyre valley in the Dolphinholme area but there are records from near Lancaster and Lytham St Anne's.

Rubus subtercanens W.C.R. Watson

This has a widespread but disjunct distribution in Europe extending from Ireland to north-eastern France. In Britain it is particularly frequent in the vicinity of Ormskirk in VC 59. It is a woodland edge species.

Rare (7). In northern Lancashire localities are clustered around Preston in VC 60 and in the Ribble valley near Bolton-by-Bowland in VC 64.

Series **Hystrices** Focke

Rubus dasyphyllus (Rogers) E. Marshall

A widespread species in the British Isles except southern Ireland, highland Scotland and a few areas in eastern and south-western England. Elsewhere in Europe it occurs in north-western Germany. It is abundant in many habitats including woods, hedges, heaths and moors on acid soils.

Common (292). R. dasyphyllus occurs throughout northern Lancashire except on the higher parts of the Bowland Fells and some lowland areas in the west. It is one of the commonest Lancashire brambles.

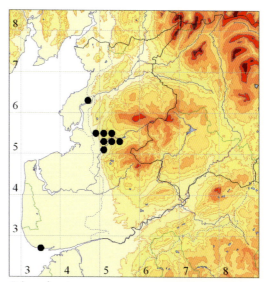

Rubus rufescens

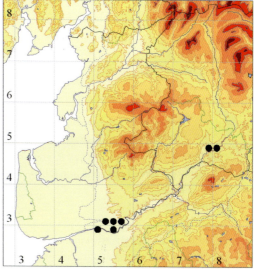

Rubus subtercanens

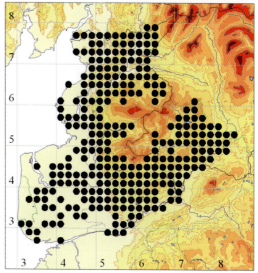

Rubus dasyphyllus

Rubus hylocharis W.C.R. Watson

An endemic species with a predominantly western distribution in Britain but with a large presence in Norfolk. It is found in woods.

Occasional (46). This is largely confined to woodland valleys in western Bowland.

Rubus phaeocarpus W.C.R. Watson.

This is a widespread species of south-eastern England and northern France where it is found on heaths and in woodland margins.

Very rare (2). The records from Gisburn Forest in Lancashire VC 64 (SD75T; Abbott, 2005 and SD75P; D.P. & J.E. in 1998 (BON)) are a long way north of the main centre of its British distribution and it is possible that it was introduced when the forest was planted.

Section **CORYLIFOLII** Lindley

Rubus conjungens (Bab.) Rogers

This species is confined to hedgerows and banks in Belgium and the British Isles where it is mostly found in south-eastern England.

Very rare (3). In northern Lancashire what is believed to be this species was found in the Conder Green to Galgate area (SD45S) in 1996 and at Fleetwood (SD34H, I) in 2006 (all D.P.E.).

Rubus eboracensis W.C.R. Watson

An endemic species found mostly in an area from southern Scotland south to a line between Bristol and Essex. It is found in woodland edge habitats.

Frequent (89). In northern Lancashire *R. eboracensis* is found throughout the area but especially in the Lune and Ribble valleys.

Rubus intensior Edees

This endemic species is found largely in an area extending from Lancashire and Yorkshire to Warwickshire with a few isolated localities elsewhere. It is found in hedges and on waste ground.

Very rare (1). In northern Lancashire the only record for *R. intensior* is from near Dunsop Bridge (SD65K; Abbott, 2005).

Rubus latifolius Bab.

An endemic species found in the British Isles from Lancashire northwards and in Northern Ireland. It is often a coastal species and occurs on banks and in hedges.

Occasional (57). Apart from an occasional record elsewhere this is a coastal species in northern Lancashire.

Rubus pruinosus Arrh.

This is widespread in north-western Europe and occurs over much of England, Wales and Ireland. It is found in woodland edge habitats and on heaths.

Frequent (131). *R. pruinosus* is found in most of northern Lancashire except in the higher ground of central Bowland.

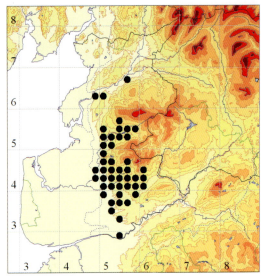

Rubus hylocharis

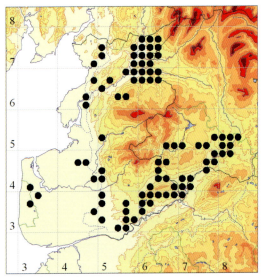

Rubus eboracensis

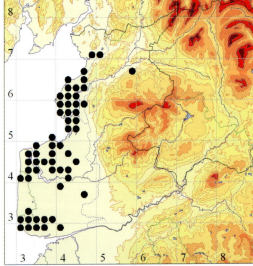

Rubus latifolius

Rubus tuberculatus Bab.

This is found in north-western Germany and the British Isles where it occurs in woodland edge habitats and waste ground mostly in the west of Britain from Morecambe Bay southwards. In Scotland it is associated with railways.

Frequent (224). In northern Lancashire *R. tuberculatus* is found mostly in western areas but there are also localities further east in the Lune and Ribble valleys.

Rubus warrenii Sudre

An endemic species, which is locally abundant in Lancashire, Yorkshire and the southern Pennines with occasional records elsewhere including a series of localities coinciding with the former Great Central Railway. It is found in woodland edge habitats.

Occasional (46). In northern Lancashire *R. warrenii* is found most frequently in the south of the area and in the Ribble valley with only occasional records elsewhere.

Section CAESII Lej. & Courtois

Rubus caesius L.   Dewberry

Eurosiberian Temperate element.

Dewberry is found in England, Wales, southern Scotland and Ireland. It is a deciduous shrub found on basic soils in woodland edge habitats, fen carr and on fixed sand dunes. A number of hybrids with *R.caesius* have been found but their distribution is not described here.

Frequent (105). In northern Lancashire this is a coastal species but it also occurs in the Lune, Hodder and Ribble valleys.

Potentilla fruticosa L.   Shrubby Cinquefoil

Neophyte with a Circumpolar Boreal-montane distribution. This is a native species on basic rocks in northern England but it is believed all records in northern Lancashire are escapes from cultivation.

Very rare (4). It was first recorded in northern Lancashire from Nether Kellet in 1870 (Wheldon and Wilson, 1907). Other records are from near Carnforth (SD57A; Livermore and Livermore, 1987), Lancaster (SD46V; Livermore and Livermore, 1991), Preston (SD52J) in 2005 (M.W.) and from near Doeford Bridge (SD64L) in VC 64 (Abbott, 2005).

Potentilla anserina L.   Silverweed

Circumpolar Boreo-temperate element.

Silverweed is found throughout the British Isles except in parts of northern Scotland and occurs in open habitats on damp ground and on waste ground (BH6).

Very common (393). *P. anserina* is found all over northern Lancashire except the higher parts of Bowland and Leck. There has been no change in its distribution locally but since 1987 there has been a decline nationally ('Local Change').

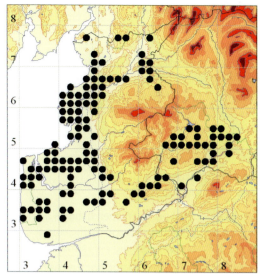

Rubus pruinosus

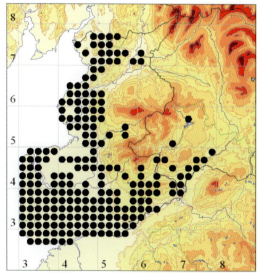

Rubus tuberculatus

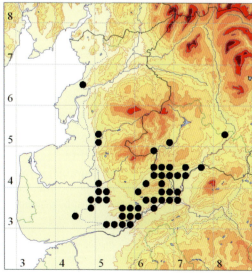

Rubus warrenii

Potentilla indica (Jacks.) Wolf   Yellow-flowered Strawberry

Neophyte. This is probably a native of southern and eastern Asia but it is widely naturalised elsewhere. It was cultivated in Britain by 1805 and recorded in the wild by 1879. It is mostly found in south-eastern England with occasional records from elsewhere.

Very rare (4). In northern Lancashire *P. indica* was found on shingle by the R. Wenning at Hornby (SD56Z) in 1999 (J.M.N.), from Avenham Park, Preston (SD52J) in 2001 (P.J.) and from two sites at Silverdale (SD47M & S) in 2007 (J.W.).

Potentilla argentea L.   Hoary Cinquefoil

Eurosiberian Temperate element.

Hoary Cinquefoil occurs in open habitats on dry sandy and often base-rich soils. It is regarded as native in many parts of south-eastern Britain as far north as Fifeshire in Scotland but in some areas it may be an introduction.

Very rare (2). In northern Lancashire it has only been recorded by Livermore and Livermore (1987) from sandy limestone at Warton (SD47W) and on slag heaps at Carnforth (SD57A) where it was also seen in 2008 (J.M.N.). Nationally it is probably declining.

Potentilla recta Vill.   Grey Cinquefoil

Neophyte. *P. recta* has a European Boreo-temperate distribution and was introduced into Britain by 1648. Today it is found scattered in Britain but especially in central and south-eastern England. Wild populations, often found on waste ground, originate from gardens or as a contaminant of grass seed.

Rare (6). In northern Lancashire most records are from Lytham St Anne's, where it was found in 1962 (A.E.R.) and also in 1962 from Holden Clough, Bolton-by-Bowland (V.G.; LIV). Other records are from Blackpool, Heysham and Hornby.

Potentilla norvegica L.   Ternate-leaved Cinquefoil

Neophyte with a Circumpolar Boreo-temperate distribution but naturalised or found as a casual in western Europe. It occurs on waste ground in scattered localities in mid- and southern Scotland, England, Wales and the north of Ireland.

In northern Lancashire *P. norvegica* was recorded from near Halton Station (SD56C) in 1941 (J.N.F.) and there is an unlocalised, unattributed record for the 10km square SD47 (B.R.C.).

Potentilla crantzii (Crantz) Beck ex Fritsch   Alpine Cinquefoil

Eurosiberian Boreo-arctic Montane element.

This occurs on basic rocks (BH7, 16) in the mountains of Scotland, the Lake District, Pennines and northern Wales.

Extinct. This grew on Great Dunnow Cliff between Newton-in-Bowland and Slaidburn, VC 64 (SD75A), where it was found in 1896 (Pickard, 1901; LDS). However increasing shade cast by planted pines caused its extinction by 1909 (T. S[heppard], 1909).

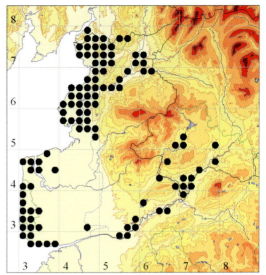

Rubus caesius

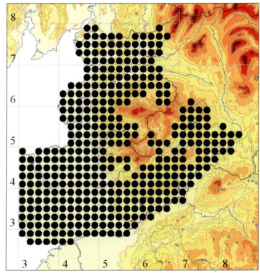

Potentilla anserina

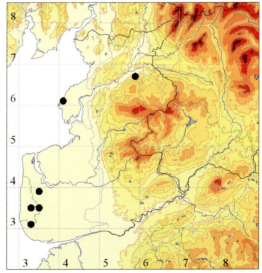

Potentilla recta

Potentilla tabernaemontani Asch.   Spring Cinquefoil

European Temperate element.

This is a species of undisturbed, dry, basic open habitats (BH7, 18) found in scattered localities in Britain.

Rare (10). Spring Cinquefoil is a characteristic plant of open habitats on limestone around Morecambe Bay. It was also found at Knowle Green, near Longridge (SD63J) in the early 1900s (NMW) or even earlier (Ashfield, 1858). This is an unlikely locality but the voucher specimens are correctly identified. It has also been found on limestone on New Laund Hill (SD64N) in 2006 (P.G.). Although there have been losses in southern England ('New Atlas') populations in northern Lancashire appear stable.

Potentilla erecta (L.) Raeusch.   Tormentil

Eurosiberian Boreo-temperate element.

This is a common plant of heaths (BH8) throughout the British Isles.

Common (304). *P. erecta* ssp. *erecta* and ssp. *strictissima* (Zimmeter) A.J. Richards were not distinguished in northern Lancashire until 2007 when it was found that both subspecies occur. However it appears that ssp. *erecta* is much more common than ssp. *strictissima*. Tormentil is common in most of the area but it is rare or absent in lowland areas of the Fylde in VC 60. Locally its distribution is stable but nationally it shows a decline on the fringes of its distribution, especially in south-eastern England.

Potentilla anglica Laichard   Trailing Tormentil

European Temperate element.

This is found on heaths, dry banks and woodland edges (BH6) mostly in western Britain and Ireland. However it is probably over recorded for *P. × mixta*.

Frequent (150). In northern Lancashire localities are scattered throughout the area. Wheldon and Wilson (1907) only recorded eight localities indicating an apparent increase in its distribution but they may have overlooked it. Populations are probably stable locally but the 'New Atlas' indicates considerable losses since 1950 in eastern Britain and in Ireland but further losses since 1987 were not noted by 'Local Change'.

Potentilla hybrids

P. erecta and *P. reptans* are well-known but *P. anglica* and its hybrids with *P. reptans* and *P. erecta* are less well-known and extremely difficult to distinguish from one another. However they are largely sterile. In recent years efforts have been made to identify the hybrids but this account remains tentative.

Potentilla erecta × P. anglica (**P. × suberecta** Zimmeter)

This is apparently widespread in temperate regions of Europe and probably occurs throughout the British Isles where the parents grow together. Because of identification difficulties the map in the 'New Atlas' probably shows the distribution of recorders rather than that of the hybrid. It is found on heaths and woodland edges.

Rare (8). In northern Lancashire it has been found in a few scattered localities including Marton Moss (SD33G) where it was first gathered in the period 1948–1955 (M. Quinn).

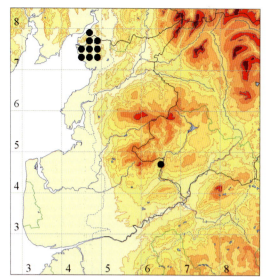

Potentilla tabernaemontani

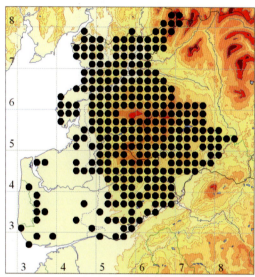

Potentilla erecta

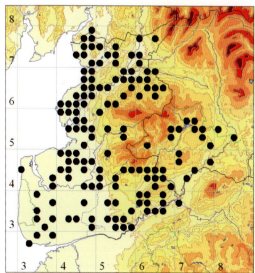

Potentilla anglica

Potentilla anglica × P. reptans & P. reptans × P. erecta
(**P. × mixta** Nolte ex Rchb.)   Hybrid Cinquefoils

These two hybrids are extremely difficult if not impossible to identify in the field. However it is believed that *P. reptans × P. erecta* is very rare. The hybrids are common in Europe including the British Isles and occur on roadsides, in hedge banks and in waste places but are rare in most of Scotland. They are likely to be very much under recorded.

Occasional (31). The hybrids are scattered throughout northern Lancashire.

Potentilla reptans L.   Creeping Cinquefoil

Eurasian Southern-temperate element.

This is found in woodland edge habitats, roadsides and waste ground (BH6) throughout the British Isles but it is thought to be an introduction in northern Scotland where it is rare.

Common (313). In northern Lancashire Creeping Cinquefoil is found in most areas although it is absent from much of Bowland and Leck. Its distribution is thought to be stable both locally and nationally.

Potentilla sterilis (L.) Garcke   Barren Strawberry

Suboceanic Temperate element.

P. sterilis is found in woodland edge habitats (BH1) in many parts of the British Isles being absent only from the Outer Hebrides, the Northern Isles or where its habitats have been lost or are absent. However it can persist in hedgerows long after native woodland has gone from the area.

Common (249). In northern Lancashire Barren Strawberry occurs in the former woodland belt around the Bowland Fells and in the north of the area but it is only found in the intensively farmed lowland areas in the west on clay soils where woodland edge habitats remain in hedgerows. Nationally the 'New Atlas' reported its distribution was stable but since 1987 there has been a decline ('Local Change'). Its distribution in northern Lancashire is thought to be unchanged.

Comarum palustre L.   Marsh Cinquefoil

Circumpolar Boreo-temperate element.

This is found throughout most of the British Isles although it is rare or absent in many parts of south-eastern Britain. Marsh Cinquefoil grows in permanently flooded swamps and mires in nutrient poor but slightly to moderately base-rich water (BH11).

Frequent (84). In northern Lancashire it occurs scattered throughout the area and although apparently more frequent than the 13 localities noted by Wheldon and Wilson (1907) there has been a marked decline in recent years. This decline was noted nationally by the 'New Atlas' but not confirmed since 1987 by 'Local Change'.

Fragaria vesca L.   Wild Strawberry

Eurosiberian Temperate element.

This is found throughout the British Isles in open communities, often on basic soils in woodland edge habitats and in post-industrial sites (BH1, 7).

Frequent (220). Wild Strawberry occurs throughout northern Lancashire but it is especially common in the north of the area and in the Ribble and Hodder valleys. Its distribution is stable in northern Lancashire but

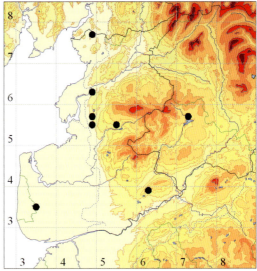

Potentilla × suberecta

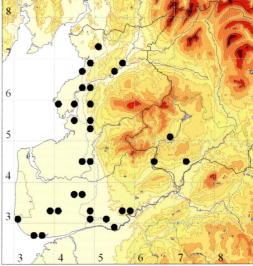

Potentilla × mixta

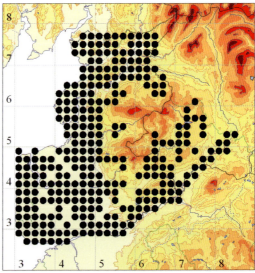

Potentilla reptans

nationally the 'New Atlas' reported a decline although further decline since 1987 was not significant ('Local Change').

Fragaria ananassa (Duchesne) Duchesne   Garden Strawberry

Neophyte. This is believed to be derived from a hybrid between two American species developed in France in the eighteenth century. It has been grown in Britain since 1806 and was known in the wild by 1900. However many early records for *F. moschata* (Duchesne) Weston were probably this. Today it is found as an escape from cultivation and often naturalised in ruderal habitats in many urban and suburban areas of the British Isles.

Rare (11). Garden Strawberry was first recorded in northern Lancashire at St Anne's (C.B.) in 1906 (Wheldon and Wilson, 1907) where it was originally recorded as *F. moschata* (MANCH). Today it occurs in scattered localities in VC 60.

Geum rivale L.   Water Avens

Eurosiberian Boreo-temperate element.

This is found in wet places in shaded or open habitats (BH1, 16) throughout most of the British Isles.

Frequent (122). In northern Lancashire Water Avens is typically a plant of wooded river valleys, especially the Lune and Ribble and their tributaries and only found occasionally elsewhere. Although its distribution locally is probably stable there have been extensive losses since 1950 in central and southern England ('New Atlas') although further losses since 1987 were not confirmed ('Local Change').

Geum rivale × **G. urbanum** (**G.** × **intermedium** Ehrh.)

This is a highly fertile and variable hybrid that occurs frequently where the habitats of the parents overlap. It occurs throughout Europe, including the British Isles and western Asia.

Occasional (25). In northern Lancashire *G.* × *intermedium* appears to be more frequent in Lancashire VC 64 than in VC 60. It usually occurs in areas where both parents are found.

Geum urbanum L.   Wood Avens

Eurosiberian Temperate element.

This occurs in free draining soils in woodlands, woodland edges and waste ground (BH1, 17) throughout the British Isles.

Common (324). Wood Avens is found in most of northern Lancashire except the higher parts of Bowland. Its distribution locally and nationally is stable.

Agrimonia eupatoria L.   Agrimony

Eurosiberian Southern-temperate element.

Agrimony is found on basic and neutral soils in woodland edge habitats, roadsides, grasslands and waste ground (BH6) in most of the British Isles but it is rare over much of Scotland.

Frequent (81). In northern Lancashire it is found in scattered localities in most of the area but it is most frequent in coastal areas and more rarely in the Hodder and Ribble valleys. Whilst its distribution in northern Lancashire appears unchanged, nationally losses were reported by the 'New Atlas' and since 1987 these have continued ('Local Change').

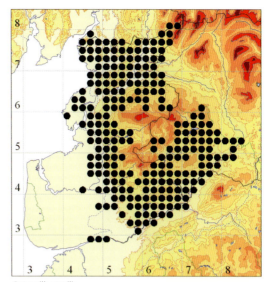

Potentilla sterilis

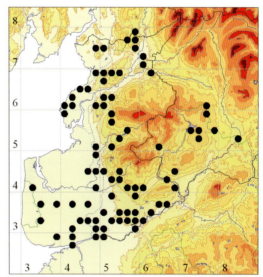

Comarum palustre

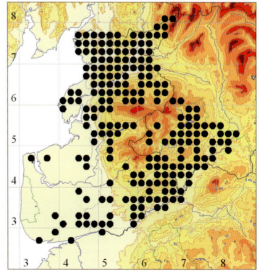

Fragaria vesca

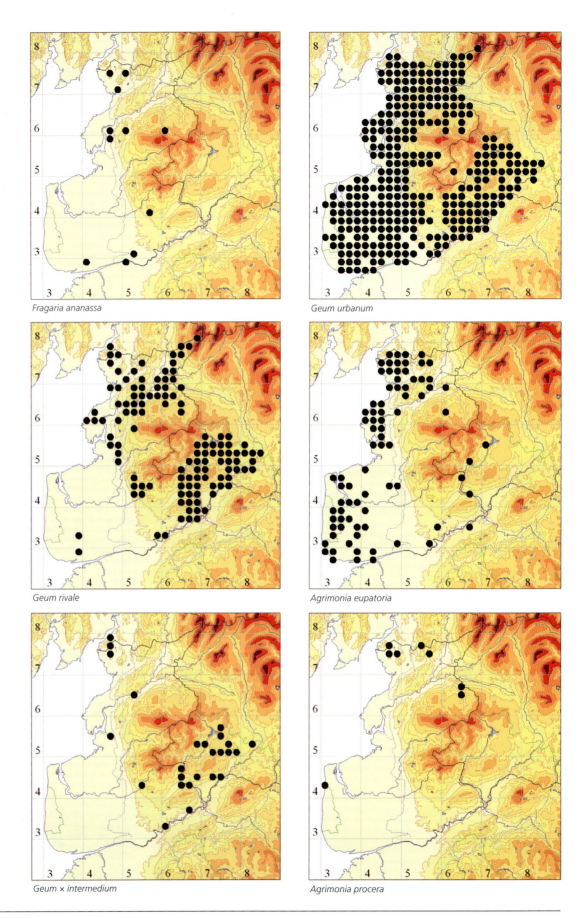

Fragaria ananassa

Geum urbanum

Geum rivale

Agrimonia eupatoria

Geum × intermedium

Agrimonia procera

Agrimonia procera Wallr.   Fragrant Agrimony

European Temperate element.

This occurs in similar habitats (BH6) to *A. eupatoria* but its localities are much more thinly scattered across the British Isles. However it is possible that it is under recorded having been confused with *A. eupatoria*.

Rare (8). Wheldon and Wilson (1907) recorded Fragrant Agrimony from three sites in the Lune valley and apart from a site on the Fylde coast all recent records are from the same area. Its distribution in northern Lancashire is probably stable and nationally the increased number of localities noted by the 'New Atlas' is likely to be through better recording. 'Local Change' reported its distribution unchanged.

Sanguisorba officinalis L.   Great Burnet

Circumpolar Boreo-temperate element.

This is found in neutral grassland often occurring in damp situations as well as in dryer places (BH6). It occurs in southern Scotland, England and Wales but more rarely in Ireland.

Frequent (132). In northern Lancashire Great Burnet is distributed in two main areas. It occurs in the north of the area, particularly in the Lune valley and in the south in the Ribble and Hodder valleys with only occasional localities elsewhere. The absence of records in central areas of northern Lancashire might suggest some decline in its distribution and the 'New Atlas' also suggests that losses have occurred nationally but 'Local Change' did not confirm further losses since 1987.

Poterium sanguisorba L. ssp. **sanguisorba**   Salad Burnet

Temperate Europe.

This perennial herb is almost confined to dry, infertile grassland on calcareous soils and rocks (BH7). It is found in southern Scotland, England, Wales and Ireland.

Occasional (44). In northern Lancashire most records are from the limestone and calcareous soils around Morecambe Bay, in the Hodder valley and more occasionally elsewhere. A cluster of records near Preston may be misidentifications. Its distribution in northern Lancashire and nationally is stable although 'Local Change' suggests it may be declining.

Poterium sanguisorba L.
ssp. **balearicum** (Bourg. ex Nyman) Stace   Fodder Burnet

Neophyte. This is a native of southern Europe and was introduced as a fodder plant in 1803 and was recorded in the wild by 1849. It occurs today as a relic of cultivation but it is also used in amenity planting. Fodder Burnet is found in Scotland, England and Wales.

Rare (6). Fodder Burnet was first found in northern Lancashire on an old railway at Lancaster (SD46R) in 1989 (Livermore and Livermore, 1990b) and subsequently in other parts of Lancaster (SD46V, 45Z; Livermore and Livermore, 1991). It was also found in newly sown roadside verges near Ashton (SD52E) in 1994 (C.F. & N.J.S.), at Freckleton (SD42J) in 1996 (C.F. & N.J.S.) and on newly sown sand dunes at Lytham St Anne's (SD32I) in 1998 (C.F. & N.J.S.).

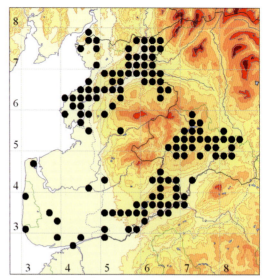
Sanguisorba officinalis

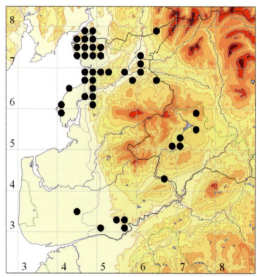
Poterium sanguisorba ssp. sanguisorba

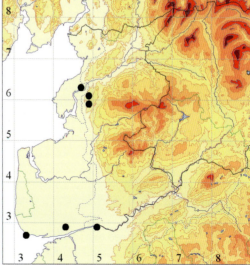
Poterium sanguisorba ssp. balearicum

Alchemilla conjuncta Bab.   Silver Lady's-mantle

Neophyte, a native of the Jura and south-western Alps introduced into Britain as a rockery plant c. 1800. It was first recorded in the wild in 1837 and it is found in scattered localities in Britain.

Very rare (2). Silver Lady's-mantle was recorded from Warton Crag (SD47W), where it was first seen in 1983 (A.E.C.) and where it appears naturalised, and from woodland near Dalton (SD57N) in 2009 (A. McLay).

[Alchemilla glaucescens Wallr.   Silky Lady's-mantle

This was recorded from Green Hill, Leck (SD78A) in 1991 (B.B.) but subsequent searches have failed to refind it. Until it is rediscovered it is a doubtful VC 60 species.]

Alchemilla xanthochlora Rothm.   Pale Lady's-mantle

European Temperate element.

This Lady's-mantle is found in neutral grasslands (BH6, 7) mostly in north-western parts of the British Isles with only a few records from south-east of a line between the Severn estuary and the Wash.

Frequent (205). *A. xanthochlora* occurs throughout northern Lancashire but it is less frequent in western and central areas than elsewhere. Its distribution in northern Lancashire appears unchanged but nationally both the 'New Atlas' and 'Local Change' report losses.

Alchemilla filicaulis Buser ssp. **filicaulis**   Slender Lady's-mantle

European Boreal-montane element.

This occurs in grassland and flushed areas (BH7, 15, 16) in upland areas of England, Wales and Scotland.

Very rare (2). This probably occurs on limestone and flushed areas of Green Hill, Leck (SD68V) where it may have been seen in 2002 (E.F.G. & J.M.N.) but it is difficult to distinguish from large plants of *A. minima*. There is also a doubtful record from Ease Gill, Leck (SD68Q) recorded in 1968 (E.F.G.).

Alchemilla filicaulis Buser ssp. **vestita** (Buser) M.E. Bradshaw
Hairy Lady's-mantle

European Boreal-montane element.

This is found in neutral grasslands, roadsides and mountain flushes (BH7, 15, 16) in most parts of the British Isles.

Occasional (58). In northern Lancashire most records for *A. filicaulis* ssp. *vestita* are from the north of the area and in the Ribble and Hodder valleys. Its distribution is probably stable but losses were noted by the 'New Atlas'. However further losses since 1987 were not confirmed by 'Local Change'.

Alchemilla minima Walters   Least Lady's-mantle

Endemic. This very rare species was not recognised until 1947 and is confined to flushes and calcareous grassland (BH7) in a small area of the Craven area of Yorkshire and Lancashire. However recent taxonomic studies suggest it should be regarded as a variety of *A. filicaulis* (S.M. Walters, pers. comm.).

Very rare (1). This is confined to a small flush on Green Hill, Leck (SD68V) where it was found in 2000 and 2002 E.F.G. & J.M.N.; LIV).

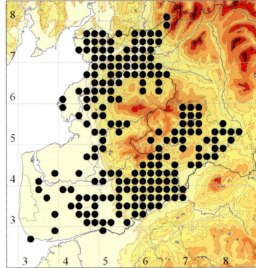

Alchemilla xanthochlora

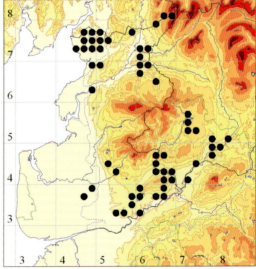

Alchemilla filicaulis ssp. vestita

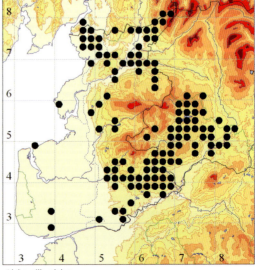

Alchemilla glabra

Alchemilla wichurae (Buser) Stefánsson   Rock Lady's-mantle

European Boreal-montane element.

This is found in calcareous grasslands (BH7) in upland areas of England and Scotland.

Very rare (1). It was found near Stocks Reservoir, Easington (SD75I; Abbott, 2005) and may have been introduced with limestone chippings used in surfacing tracks in Gisburn Forest. It was first found in 2002 and was still present in 2010 (P.G.).

Alchemilla glabra Neygenf.   Smooth Lady's-mantle

This occurs in upland grassland habitats and on mountain ledges (BH6, 15, 16) in suitable upland areas of the British Isles except southern Ireland and south-western England.

Frequent (125). *A. glabra* is found mostly in the north of northern Lancashire and the valleys of the R. Ribble and R. Hodder and their tributaries and only occasionally elsewhere. It is likely that its distribution locally is unchanged but nationally losses were noted by both the 'New Atlas' and 'Local Change'.

Alchemilla mollis (Buser) Rothm.   Soft Lady's-mantle

Neophyte. This is a native of south-eastern Europe and south-western Asia that was first cultivated in Britain in 1874 and recorded in the wild in 1948. Today it occurs throughout Britain and the north of Ireland.

Occasional (45). In northern Lancashire it was first recorded from Freckleton (SD42J) in 1981 (C.F. & N.J.S.) and today localities are scattered throughout the area. It is a robust plant and readily escapes from gardens into the wild.

Aphanes arvensis L.   Parsley-piert

European Temperate element.

This is a winter or spring germinating annual of dry and usually basic soils in open habitats or bare patches in grasslands, roadsides, heaths, waste places and woodland edges (BH4, 16) and is found throughout the British Isles.

Occasional (46). In northern Lancashire Parsley-piert is found in scattered localities throughout the area but with a concentration of sites on the limestone around Morecambe Bay and on the sand dunes at Lytham St Anne's. However in the latter area some of the records may refer to *A. australis*. Because distinguishing between *A. arvensis* and *A. australis* is difficult it is not known if there has been any change in the distribution of these two species.

Aphanes australis Rydb.   Slender Parsley-piert

Temperate element.

Slender Parsley-piert is very similar to *A. arvensis* and has a similar distribution but it is characteristic of acidic, sandy soils and rocks (BH8, 16).

Rare (10). In northern Lancashire this has been found in the north of the area but most records are from dune heaths at Lytham St Anne's and Fleetwood and as an arable weed on peat soils at Pilling.

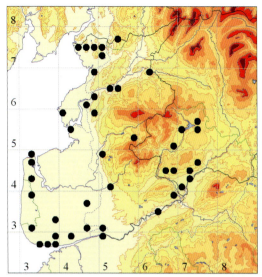
Alchemilla mollis

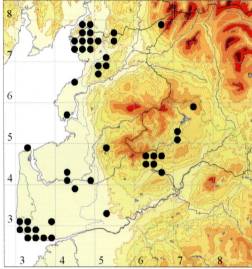
Aphanes arvensis

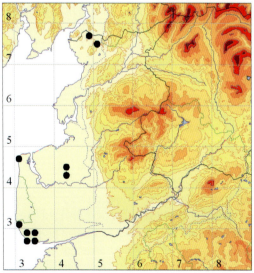
Aphanes australis

Rosa L.   Roses

The taxonomy of this genus is exceptionally complex and until the publication of *Roses of Great Britain and Ireland* (Graham and Primavesi, 1993) there was considerable uncertainty in naming roses. Until then identification had relied on the work of Wolley-Dod (1931) and where voucher specimens existed they had to be re-evaluated. Unfortunately roses do not press well and often this was not possible. Furthermore synonymy between the names given by Wolley-Dod and Graham and Primavesi was uncertain. Although there are relatively few native species the morphology of some, particularly *R. canina*, is variable and an unusual breeding system gives rise to numerous fertile hybrids. In view of these problems this account is tentative and it is often impossible to assess if distributions have changed.

Rosa multiflora Thunb.   Many-flowered Rose

Neophyte. This is a native of eastern Asia and has been cultivated since 1804 although it only became a popular garden plant after its reintroduction in 1862. It has been known in the wild since 1930 and today occurs in scattered localities in the British Isles.

Very rare (5). Many-flowered Rose was first found in northern Lancashire at Blackpool (SD33I) as a relic of cultivation in 1965 (A.E.R.). Further records are from Lytham St Anne's (SD32E, 33A) in 1994 (B.S.B.I.) and 1999 (E.F.G.) where it is naturalised, Carleton (SD33J) in 2003 (M.S.) and Heysham (SD45E) in 2006 (E.F.G. & J.M.N.).

Rosa arvensis Huds.   Field-rose

European Temperate element.

This is a common plant of woodland edge habitats and hedgerows (BH3) in England, Wales and Ireland but only as an introduction in Scotland.

Frequent (215). Field-rose is a characteristic feature of hedgerows in the southern half of VC 60 extending northwards into the Lune Valley. It is much less frequent elsewhere in northern Lancashire. It is not thought that the distribution of *R. arvensis* has changed locally or nationally.

Rosa arvensis × R. canina (**R. × irregularis** Déségl. & Guillon)

This hybrid is found in woodland edge habitats throughout the range of *R. arvensis* but it may occur in the absence of one or both parents. Where *R. arvensis* is the female parent it is one of the more easily recognisable hybrids. Nevertheless it is very much under recorded.

Very rare (1). Old records are from Caton where it was found in 1900 (J.A.W.; E, OXF) and Longridge where it was also found in 1900 (J.A.W.; BM). The only recent record is from Lees (SD64S) in VC 64 (Abbott, 2005).

Rosa spinosissima L.   Burnet Rose

European Temperate element.

This low suckering deciduous shrub is found on sand dunes, sea cliffs and in scrubby places, usually on calcareous substrates (BH10, 16, 19) in most parts of the British Isles. However its native distribution is confused by the introduction of cultivars that have escaped into the wild.

Occasional (17). In northern Lancashire Burnet Rose is confined as a native plant to coastal areas of north-western VC 60, including the limestone area around Morecambe Bay together with a record from tipped clay forming an embankment by the R. Ribble at Lea Marsh. Other records are

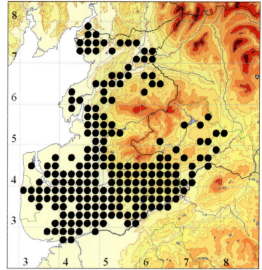
Rosa arvensis

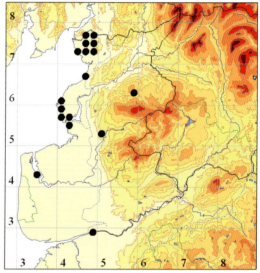
Rosa spinosissima

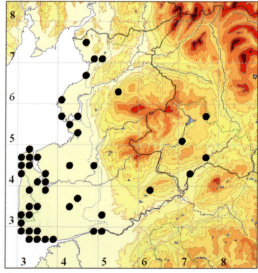
Rosa rugosa

likely to be escapes from cultivation and the record for Thornton (SD34L) was a robust cultivar. However it no longer occurs at St Anne's (Wheldon and Wilson, 1907). Apart from the loss from the Fylde coast sand dunes the distribution of *R. spinosissima* appears stable in northern Lancashire. The 'New Atlas' reported losses from inland localities in the British Isles before 1930 but otherwise its national distribution also appears stable.

[Rosa spinosissima × R. sherardii (R. × involuta Sm.)

Preston Scientific Society (Anon, 1903) reported this from a hedge at Kirkham but in the absence of a voucher specimen or later records this is very doubtful.]

Rosa rugosa Thunb.   Japanese Rose

Neophyte. This vigorous rose is a native of eastern Asia and was brought into cultivation in Britain in 1796 but it was not successfully grown until its reintroduction in 1845. It was first recorded in the wild in 1927 but it is becoming increasingly common as it escapes into the wild following its use in amenity plantings.

Occasional (46). In northern Lancashire *R. rugosa* was recorded from the sand dunes at St Anne's in 1946 (Whellan, 1954). It is now common in coastal areas especially on the Fylde coast sand dunes but it occurs throughout the area.

Rosa virginiana Mill (non Herrm.)   Virginian Rose

Neophyte. Virginian Rose is a native of eastern North America and has been grown in British gardens for many years. It was first recorded in the wild in 1888. Today it is found in a few British localities but once established it persists.

Very rare (1). In northern Lancashire *R. virginiana* was planted around the car park at Dunsop Bridge (SD65Q) where it was found to be growing vigorously in 2007 (E.F.G.).

Rosa × alba L.   White Rose (of York)

Neophyte. This hybrid of garden origin, but of unknown parentage (Stace, 2010), was cultivated in Britain by 1597 but it is now rarely grown. It was known in the wild by 1905 and today it is a rare but persistent or naturalised garden escape in a few English localities and in the Isle of Man.

Very rare (1). This was found at Bartle Hall (SD43W) in 1964 (Hodgson, 1965).

Rosa ferruginea Vill.   Red-leaved Rose

Neophyte. Red-leaved Rose is a native of the mountains of central and southern Europe. It is a popular garden plant and has been in cultivation since before 1830. It occurs in scattered localities throughout the British Isles.

Very rare (1). In northern Lancashire it was found on waste ground at Lytham (SD32T) in 2005 (C.F. & N.J.S.).

Rosa canina L.   Dog-rose

European Temperate element.

The Dog-rose is a shrub of well-drained calcareous to moderately acid soils and is found in a variety of habitats but especially woodland edges and hedges (BH1, 3). Unfortunately recorders have 'lumped' a variety of species

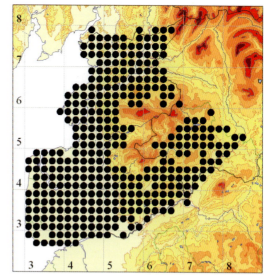

Rosa canina

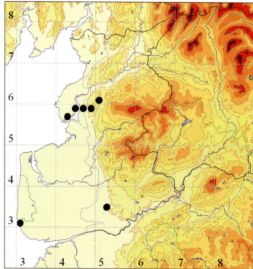

Rosa × rothschildii

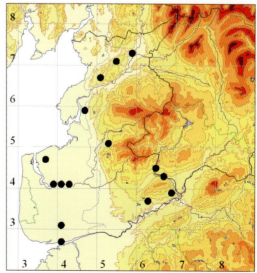

Rosa caesia ssp. *caesia*

and hybrids into this species so that there is an under recording of true *R. canina*, which is itself morphologically variable. However it is likely that *R. canina* occurs throughout the British Isles and is one of the commonest roses in most localities.

Very common (368). Only *R. canina sensu lato* was recorded systematically in northern Lancashire and it occurs throughout the area except in the higher parts of Bowland. To cover the morphological variation within *R. canina* Graham and Primavesi (1993) recognised four groups: **'Lutetianae'**, **'Dumales'**, **'Transitoriae'** and **'Pubescentes'** but pointed out that there was no evidence yet that any one group had a different ecological niche or geographical distribution in the British Isles. All four groups are represented in northern Lancashire. It is not thought that there has been any change in the distribution of *R. canina* locally or nationally.

Rosa canina × R. obtusifolia (R. × dumetorum Thuill.)

This fertile hybrid occurs in woodland edge habitats and hedges, usually in areas where both species occur. It is found in England and Wales from Lancashire and Yorkshire southwards and in Ireland.

Very rare (3). This hybrid was first recorded in northern Lancashire from Fulwood in 1873 (W.R. Linton; LIV). Other records are from Ashton-with-Stodday (SD45T) in 1988 (Livermore and Livermore, 1989), Aighton, Bailey and Chaigley (SD64V) in 1968 (E.F.G.; LIV) and near Browsholme Hall in VC 64 (SD64X; Abbott, 2005).

Rosa canina × R. sherardii (R. × rothschildii Druce)

This occurs in woodland edge habitats and hedges in many parts of the British Isles but it is mostly absent from south-eastern England.

Rare (7). This has been found in a few scattered localities in northern Lancashire and is no doubt under recorded.

Rosa canina × R. mollis (R. × molletorum Hesl.-Harr.)

This is a rare hybrid of woodland edge and hedge habitats in Scotland and northern England.

Very rare (3). This has only been found at Tarnbrook, Over Wyresdale (SD55X) in 1997 (E.F.G.), Ellel (SD55C) in 1967 (E.F.G.) and near Grindleton (SD74N; Abbott, 2005).

Rosa caesia Sm. ssp. **caesia**   Hairy Dog-rose

European Temperate element.

This is a deciduous shrub that grows on a wide range of well-drained, calcareous to mildly acid soils in woodland edge habitats and hedges (BH1, 3) in Britain mostly north of a line between Bristol and the Wash.

Occasional (15). This has been found in scattered localities in VC 60 but not in Lancashire VC 64. It is probably under recorded.

Rosa caesia Sm. ssp. **vosagiaca** (N.H.F. Desp.) D.H. Kent
Glaucous Dog-rose

European Temperate element.

Glaucous Dog-rose grows in similar habitats to Hairy Dog-rose and has a similar distribution but appears to be more common.

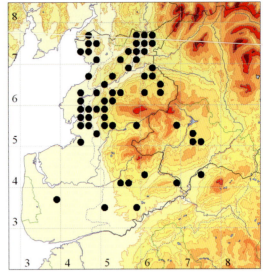
Rosa caesia ssp. *vosagiaca*

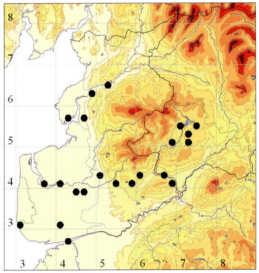
Rosa × *dumalis*

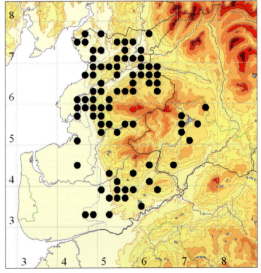
Rosa sherardii

Occasional (60). In northern Lancashire it appears to be more frequent that *R. caesia* ssp. *caesia* and whilst it occurs throughout the area it is more common in the north of VC 60 than elsewhere. It is probably under recorded.

Rosa caesia × R. canina (R. × dumalis Bechst.)

This robust and common hybrid of woodland edge and hedge habitats occurs throughout the British Isles.

Occasional (22). *R. × dumalis* is found in scattered localities throughout northern Lancashire.

[Rosa caesia × R. sherardii

There are scattered localities for this hybrid from the English midlands northwards and in Ireland.

Very rare (1). There is a doubtful record for this from near Slaidburn (SD75F) in 2002 (E.F.G. in Abbott, 2005).]

Rosa obtusifolia Desv.   Round-leaved Dog-rose

European Temperate element.

This rose of woodland edge and hedge habitats (BH1, 3) is found in the southern half of the British Isles. However because of identification difficulties it is likely to be under recorded.

Very rare (5). There is an old record from Preston in 1874 (W.R.L.; BM) but recent records are confined to Ashton-with-Stodday (SD45T) in 1988 (L.A.L.), Hothersall and Ribchester areas (SD63C, I) in 1988/9 (E.F.G.), at Middle Lees (SD64S) and Bashall Eaves (SD64W), both Abbott (2005). It is not thought that there has been any change in its distribution locally or nationally.

[Rosa tomentosa Sm.   Harsh Downy-rose

European Temperate element.

Harsh Downy-rose is found in woodland edge habitats and in hedges. It can be easily confused with other downy-roses and hybrids and occurs in the south of the British Isles.

Very rare (3). In northern Lancashire *R. tomentosa* was recorded from Silverdale in 1967 (A.E.R.), Dutton (SD63T) in 1968 (E.F.G.) and in tetrad SD67B in 1985 (Anon). However, none of these records has been confirmed and, whilst it could occur in the region, northern Lancashire is some distance north of the nearest confirmed locality. Until confirmed all records are doubtful.]

Rosa sherardii Davies   Sherard's Downy-rose

European Temperate element.

This is found in woodland edge and hedge habitats (BH1, 3, 16) mostly north west of a line between Devon and the Wash.

Frequent (85). Sherard's Downy-rose is found mostly in the east and north of northern Lancashire but it is surprisingly rare in Lancashire VC 64 and this may be due to under recording. Its distribution is probably unchanged in northern Lancashire but there have been losses nationally, especially towards the south-east of its range ('New Atlas').

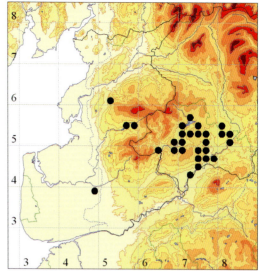

Rosa mollis

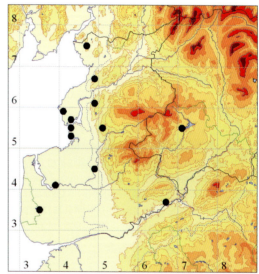

Rosa rubiginosa

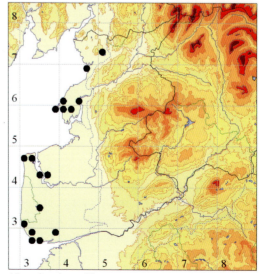

Hippophae rhamnoides

Rosa sherardii × R. mollis (R. × perthensis Rouy)

This hybrid is found in a few scattered localities in Scotland and northern England, Wales and Ireland. It is difficult to identify and it is probably under recorded.

Very rare (5). There is an unattributed and probably old record from between Emmetts and Abbeystead, Over Wyresdale (SD55; NMW). Livermore and Livermore (1987) also recorded it from the Scotforth and Quernmore area (SD55E) and in the Wray-with-Botton and Tatham area (SD66I). In Lancashire VC 64 it was recorded from Newton-in-Bowland (SD65V) in 2006 (E.F. & B.D.G.), Slaidburn (SD75C) in 2007 (E.F.G.) and Easington (SD75M) in 2007 (E.F.G.). The records for 2006 and 2007 were in localities where both the parents are found.

Rosa sherardii × R. rubiginosa (R. × suberecta (Woods) Ley)

There are a number of localities for this hybrid scattered across the British Isles.

Very rare (1). The only record in northern Lancashire is from a roadside hedge in the Caton-with-Littledale area (SD65F) in 1987 (L.A.L.).

Rosa mollis Sm.   Soft Downy-rose

European Boreo-temperate element.

This distinctive rose is found in woodland edge and hedgerow habitats (BH1, 3, 16) north west of line between the Severn estuary and the Humber.

Occasional (28). Soft Downy-rose is found mostly in Bowland with occasional records elsewhere in northern Lancashire. However there has been confusion between *R. mollis* and *R. sherardii* and their hybrids and it is possible that it is over recorded. Thus Livermore and Livermore (1987) recorded *R. mollis* frequently in Lancaster District whereas subsequent work in the area suggests that it is rare being found mostly in the Tarnbrook Wyre valley. The distribution locally and nationally is probably stable.

Rosa villosa L.   Apple Rose

Neophyte. Apple Rose is a native of northern Europe and south-western Asia introduced as a garden plant by 1771 but now rarely found in gardens. It was reported from the wild in a few localities before 1930. It should not be confused with *R. mollis*, which was referred to as *R. villosa* until recently.

In northern Lancashire there is a record from Alston Rake quarry, near Chaigley (SD64V?); Preston Scientific Society, 1903).

Rosa rubiginosa L.   Sweet-briar

European Temperate element.

Although Sweet-briar is a native species found in scrub and hedgerows (BH3, 7) on calcareous soils in many parts of the British Isles it is also widely introduced and is frequently used in amenity plantings.

Rare (13). The status of this fragrant rose in northern Lancashire is unclear. It was recorded from the slopes of Warton Crag in 1906 (NMW, LIV), where Wheldon and Wilson (1907) were doubtful of its native status and at Far Arnside in Cumbria (Halliday, 1997). It is possible or perhaps likely

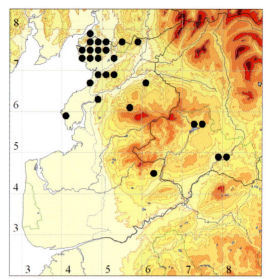

Rhamnus cathartica

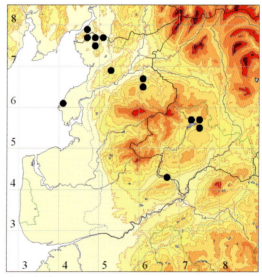

Frangula alnus

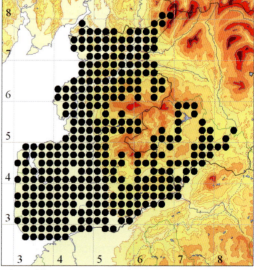

Ulmus glabra

that in these limestone areas and on the calcareous soils of the Heysham peninsula it is native but most records are likely to have arisen from recent introductions. It is not known if its native distribution is changing but it is becoming more frequent in the British Isles through introductions.

Rosa micrantha Borrer ex Sm.   Small-flowered Sweet-briar
European Temperate element.

This rose is found in woodland, scrub and hedgerows (BH1, 3, 7) in southern parts of the British Isles with a few records reaching as far north as south-eastern Scotland. It is most frequent on well-drained calcareous soils.

Extinct. In northern Lancashire E.S. Pickard described it as frequent at Silverdale in the period 1877–81 (Wheldon and Wilson, 1907). However this was considered doubtful as no further records were made for the limestone areas around Morecambe Bay, but in 1991 several bushes were found not far away in south facing scrub at Far Arnside in Cumbria (Halliday, 1997). Accordingly searches should be made for *R. micrantha* in VC 60 as it may have been overlooked.

ELAEAGNACEAE   SEA-BUCKTHORN FAMILY

Hippophae rhamnoides L.   Sea-buckthorn
European Boreo-temperate element but a neophyte in northern Lancashire.

Sea-buckthorn is thought to be a native species on the east coast of England but introduced elsewhere. It occurs throughout the British Isles, especially in coastal areas where it can form dense thickets on sand dunes.

Occasional (17). Although recorded from post-glacial deposits around Morecambe Bay in north-western England (Godwin, 1975) it did not persist until historical times. Groves (1958) described the then current distribution and first vice-county records for the British Isles. It was first recorded in VC 60 in 1905 when J.G. Wilkinson recorded Sea-buckthorn at Silverdale (SHD, LDS). Further records were not made until the middle of the twentieth century and today it is found in coastal areas of VC 60. It is abundant in some places on the sand dunes at Lytham St Anne's, where it was first found at Fairhaven in 1956 (J.M.H.).

Elaeagnus macrophylla Thunb.
(or **E. × submacrophylla** Servett.)   Broad-leaved Oleaster
Neophyte. This is a native of Korea and Japan and was brought into British cultivation in 1879. It was recorded from the wild in 1984 and today it has been recorded from a few places in southern Britain. However there is considerable uncertainty over the plants found in the wild. The common garden plant, with which it can be easily confused, is *E. pungens* Thunb., whilst it is thought that most records are for the hybrid between *E. macrophylla* and *E. pungens* (*E. × submacrophylla*).

Very rare (2). In northern Lancashire Broad-leaved Oleaster was found near Squires Gate railway station, Blackpool (SD33A) in 1994 (C.F. & N.J.S.) and in an old hedge bordering Fleetwood Golf Course (SD34D) in 1998 (E.F.G.). It is likely to occur planted in other coastal hedges.

RHAMNACEAE   BUCKTHORN FAMILY

Rhamnus cathartica L.   Buckthorn
Eurosiberian Temperate element.

This shrub is found on calcareous soils in woodland edge habitats and in fen carr (BH1, 3). Buckthorn is found throughout England, Wales and Ireland and as an introduction in Scotland and in a few places elsewhere.

Occasional (27). In northern Lancashire this is found mostly on the limestone around Morecambe Bay and more occasionally elsewhere, where it may have been planted in a few localities. Although Wheldon and Wilson (1907) did not find Buckthorn in the Ribble and Hodder valleys it was known to Pickard (1901) in Lancashire VC 64. The 'New Atlas' thought there had been some decline between 1962 and 2000 nationally but further decline was not noted by 'Local Change'.

Frangula alnus Mill.   Alder Buckthorn
Eurosiberian Temperate element.

This shrub is found on a wide range of soils in habitats varying from fen peat to scrub and woodland edge habitats (BH1) but avoids waterlogged soils. It occurs in England, Wales and Ireland but the few records from Scotland are thought to be introductions. It is also sometimes planted elsewhere.

Rare (13). In northern Lancashire Alder Buckthorn is found mostly on the limestone around Morecambe Bay and more occasionally in Bowland valley woodlands. The cluster of records in Gisburn Forest is probably from introduced plants, especially as it was not known to J.F. Pickard 100 years ago. It was introduced at Heysham. Its distribution nationally is believed to be stable.

ULMACEAE   ELM FAMILY

Ulmus glabra Huds.   Wych Elm
European Temperate element.

This is a common hedgerow and woodland tree (BH1, 3), especially on basic soils and is found throughout the British Isles.

Very common (352). It occurs in most of northern Lancashire but it does not extend up to the higher levels of the Bowland valleys. Despite Dutch Elm disease it does not seem to have declined although most large trees were killed. This seems to reflect the national situation.

Ulmus minor *sensu lato*   Elm

The description and classification of elms in the British Isles causes many problems because of the considerable variation between different taxa and within an individual taxon. Richens (1983) included all English or common elms under *Ulmus minor* Mill., but this ignored variation. Nevertheless *Ulmus minor sensu lato* was known to Wheldon and Wilson (1907) who considered it 'not very common' and found it often planted in hedges and parks. Coleman (2009) suggests recent molecular research indicates that there are just two species: *Ulmus glabra* and *Ulmus minor* but that the latter has given rise to a number of distinct clones and that extensive hybridisation has taken place. Stace (1997) provides a workable solution but because of the difficulties the following account is tentative. The taxa covered are: *U. procera*, *U. minor*, *U. plotii*, *U.* × *vegeta*, *U.* × *elegantissima* and *U.* × *hollandica*.

Ulmus procera Salisb.   English Elm

Archaeophyte, European Temperate element. Recent research (Gil, *et al.*, 2004) shows that English Elm was almost certainly introduced by the Romans from Italy via Spain. It is found in hedgerows (BH3), plantations and parks mostly in England, Wales, Ireland and southern Scotland.

Frequent (94). It is found throughout northern Lancashire. Morphologically it is variable with vegetative features varying greatly between hedging plants and mature trees, which suffered badly from Dutch Elm disease. Its distribution is probably stable both locally and nationally.

Ulmus minor Mill. ssp. **minor**   Small-leaved Elm

Neophyte. European Temperate element and regarded as native in southern England and Wales. A very variable species.

Rare (8). It is scattered across the area but always planted. It was first recorded from Lytham in 1964 (A.E.R.).

Ulmus plotii Druce   Plot's Elm

Neophyte, endemic. It is found mostly in central England but as a mature tree its distinctive narrow shape makes it attractive for amenity planting. However it is very susceptible to Dutch Elm disease.

Very rare (2). In northern Lancashire it was found at Little Carleton (SD32J) in 2003 (E.F.G. & M.S.) and near Lancaster (SD46K) in 2004 (E.F.G.).

Ulmus glabra × U. minor (U. × **vegeta** (Loudon) Ley)
                                                        Huntingdon Elm

Neophyte. It is a natural hybrid but planted in hedgerows and for amenity. Stace (1997) distinguishes between *U. glabra* × *U. minor* and *U.* × *vegeta* which has the same parents but where the cultivar, Huntingdon Elm, is distinctive. However no distinction is made here between the two taxa.

Very rare (4). This hybrid was first recorded in northern Lancashire from tetrad SD44F (J.H.) in the 1960s and subsequently it was found planted by a car park at Silverdale (SD47S) in 1987 (L.A.L.), in a copse at Lytham (SD32Z) in 1998 (E.F.G.) and from Carleton Cemetery, Blackpool (SD33J) in 2003 (E.F.G. & M.S.).

Ulmus glabra × U. plotii (U. × **elegantissima** L.)

Neophyte. This is a common British hybrid in central England.

Very rare (1). Only confirmed in northern Lancashire from Conder Green (SD45M) in 1983 (L.A.L.).

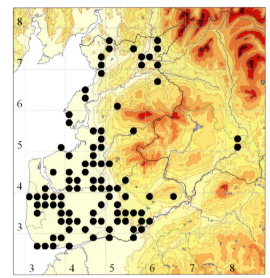
Ulmus procera

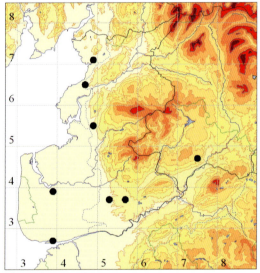
Ulmus minor ssp. *minor*

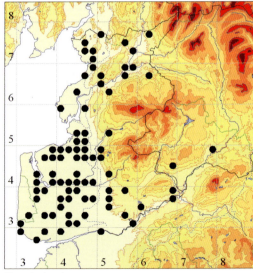
Humulus lupulus

Ulmus × hollandica Mill   Dutch Elm

(A hybrid involving *U. glabra*, *U. minor* and *U. plotii*)

Neophyte. This is a natural hybrid native in southern Britain but it is also frequent in western Europe.

Very rare (4). In northern Lancashire it was found planted at Weeton-with-Preese (SD33X), Scorton Picnic site, Nether Wyresdale (SD55A), by a motorway at Broughton (SD53M) and near Hurst Green (SD63U) all recorded by E.F.G. in 1998 and 1999. As all the records are of young plants it is likely that this is more frequent than the records suggest and that it has been used recently in hedging and possibly for amenity planting.

Ulmus laevis Pallas   European White-elm

Neophyte. This is a native of central and eastern Europe.

Very rare (2). This was found in a copse near Winmarleigh (SD44M) in 1980 (C.F. & N.J.S.) and in Nether Wyresdale (SD54E) in 2006 (R.C.).

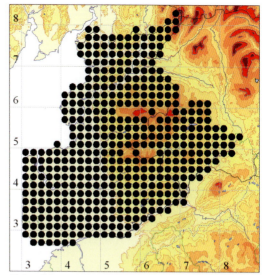

Urtica dioica

CANNABACEAE   HOP FAMILY

Cannabis sativa L.   Hemp

Archaeophyte but always a casual. It is probably a native of south-western and central Asia but it was cultivated from ancient times. It has been grown in British gardens since at least 1304 and was cultivated as a fibre crop up to the eighteenth century. It was grown for fibre in Lancashire but more recently it was a constituent of birdseed mixtures and it is probably from this source that recent records have originated.

Very rare (4). It was first recorded from Blackpool tip (SD33I) between 1961 and 1963 (A.E.R.). Subsequent records were from Lytham St Anne's, near Peel (SD33K and SD32J) in 1973 and 2005 respectively (C.F. & N.J.S.), Out Rawcliffe (SD44A) in 1985 (C.F. & N.J.S.) and Heysham (SD46A) in 1995 (B.S.B.I.).

Humulus lupulus L.   Hop

Eurosiberian Temperate element.

This is thought to be native in midland and southern Britain but it is also a naturalised introduction and is found as such in northern England, Scotland and Ireland. It is usually found in hedges (BH3).

Frequent (83). Scattered throughout northern Lancashire but especially in the west and north of the area. It is found largely in hedgerows and often near houses suggesting that most populations are derived from cultivation. It has been used for flavouring and beer making for a long time but its history in Lancashire is not known. Its distribution is thought to be stable both locally and nationally.

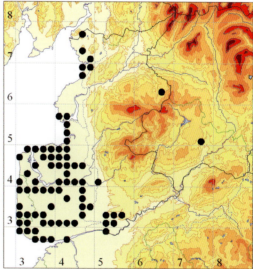

Urtica urens

MORACEAE   MULBERRY FAMILY

Ficus carica L.   Fig

Neophyte. A native of the eastern Mediterranean region and south-western Asia but cultivated and naturalised throughout the Mediterranean region for thousands of years. Figs were imported into Britain by the Romans and cultivated since at least the 10th century. It was first recorded

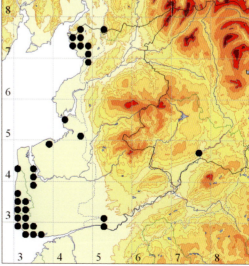

Parietaria judaica

in the wild in 1918 but today plants often arise from discarded fruit or sewage waste.

Very rare (5). In northern Lancashire it was first reported from Roman horse dung at Lancaster (Wilson, 1979) and from Roman deposits at Ribchester (Huntley and Hillam, 2000). Recent records are from an old garden at Singleton (SD33Z) in 1968 (M.J.). Livermore and Livermore (1987) reported it from tetrads SD46Q and 57A while in 1988 L.A.L. recorded it from the canal at Lancaster (SD46Y) and in 1971 from an old iron works at Carnforth (SD47V) where it was re-found in 2005 (J.M.N.).

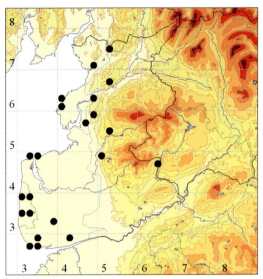

Soleirolia soleirolii

URTICACEAE   NETTLE FAMILY

Urtica pilulifera L.   Roman Nettle

This is a native of southern Europe and was formerly reported as a casual from several places in Britain.

In northern Lancashire it was reported from pastures near the sea, near Lytham (Buckley, 1842).

Urtica dioica L. ssp. **dioica**   Common Nettle

Eurosiberian Boreo-temperate element.

This is found in nutrient rich habitats (e.g. BH3, 14, 17) throughout the British Isles

Very common (444). Common Nettle occurs throughout northern Lancashire. Because it is such a common species it is not clear if Common Nettle is spreading or not.

Urtica dioica L. ssp. **galeopsifolia** (Wierzb. ex Opiz) Chrtek
Stingless Nettle

Attention was drawn to the presence of this taxon in the British Isles by Geltman (1992). It occurs throughout temperate Europe and probably elsewhere but its distribution is imperfectly known. It occurs in wet woodlands, especially in association with *Alnus glutinosa*, on riverbanks and in eutrophic fens. It is similar to *Urtica dioica* ssp. *dioica* but has longer, narrower and more regularly dentate leaves but strikingly almost completely lacks stinging hairs. Key identification features are illustrated by Rich and Jermy (1998). It is a diploid species whereas *U. dioica* ssp. *dioica* is tetraploid. Despite being clearly distinct from *U. dioica* ssp. *dioica* its taxonomic status is doubted (Stace, 1997). Nevertheless since its discovery at Wicken Fen (Geltman, 1992) it has been recorded from widely separated localities in the British Isles.

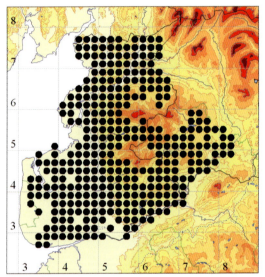

Fagus sylvatica

However what was probably this taxon was well known to British botanists 100 years ago. It was known as '*Urtica dioica* b. *angustifolia* Wimm. & Grab'. (Hanbury, 1908) and specimens were circulated by members of the *Botanical Exchange Club and Society*.

In northern Lancashire Wheldon and Wilson (1907) refer to it as *U. dioica* var. *angustifolia* Blytt. and give records from shady woods by the R. Lune between Caton and Aughton, Damas Gill near Dolphinholme, near Abbeystead and Knowle Green. A voucher specimen (LIV) collected by J.A.W. in 1901 from Dolphinholme is clearly ssp. *galeopsifolia* and no doubt some at least of Wheldon and Wilson's other records are this subspecies.

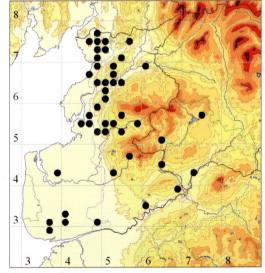

Castanea sativa

It is remarkable that a taxon well known to botanists 100 years ago has been overlooked in recent years and although not likely to be common it is possible that *U. dioica* ssp. *galeopsifolia* is present in wet woodlands in the east of northern Lancashire and may well be an indicator of ancient woodland. However some plants may appear intermediate and it is probable that these are hybrids.

Urtica urens L. — Small Nettle

Archaeophyte with a Eurosiberian Southern-temperate distribution.

This is found in cultivated (BH4) and waste ground (BH17) throughout most of the British Isles.

Frequent (77). In northern Lancashire Small Nettle is found mostly in the west of the area. There has been little change in its distribution locally or nationally.

Parietaria judaica L. — Pellitory-of-the-wall

Submediterranean-Subatlantic element.

Pellitory-of-the-wall is found in cracks in rocks and walls (BH14, 17) in much of the British Isles but it is rare or absent in most of western and northern Scotland.

Occasional (32). In northern Lancashire it is largely confined to the Fylde coast around Lytham St Anne's and in the northwest of the area around Morecambe Bay with only occasional records elsewhere. This species favours a mild damp climate and its distribution in northern Lancashire reflects this preference. Wheldon and Wilson (1907) knew only six localities for this species and none were on the Fylde coast although Thornber (1837) and Buckley (1842) had recorded it at Blackpool and Lytham respectively. Thus there has been considerable expansion of its range locally, at least since 1907, but nationally there was little change between 1962 and 2000 ('New Atlas') although 'Local Change' shows that *P. judaica* has increased and that it belongs to a group of plants found on walls that have increased significantly.

Soleirolia soleirolii (Req.) Dandy — Mind-your-own-business

Neophyte. This is a native of the western Mediterranean islands. It has been cultivated in Britain since 1905 and was recorded in the wild by 1917.

Occasional (22). This was first recorded on a cinder path inside and outside greenhouses in Nether Wyresdale (SD56H) in 1965 (E.F.G.). Subsequently records were made from ruderal habitats (BH3, 17) scattered across northern Lancashire but especially in coastal areas. Nationally it has increased considerably since 1962 and appears to be still extending its range.

NOTHOFAGACEAE — SOUTHERN BEECH FAMILY

Nothofagus Blume — Southern Beeches

Neophyte. Increasingly during the last 30 years or so southern beeches have been planted for forestry and amenity. *N. obliqua* (Mirb.) Blume was confirmed as growing in Britain in 1902 and reported from the wild in 1956 whilst *N. alpina* (Poepp. & Endl.) Oerst. was introduced in 1910 and reported from the wild in 1956. Both are natives of Chile and western Argentina.

Very rare (1). In northern Lancashire Livermore and Livermore (1990) recorded planted *N. obliqua* and *N. alpina* by the disused railway at Caton (SD56H). As both species regenerate freely in the British Isles it is likely that they will become common in the area.

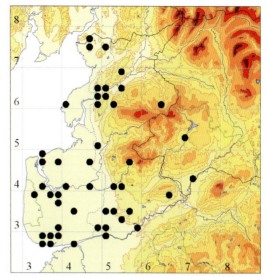

Quercus cerris

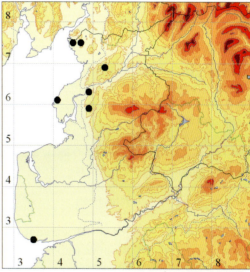

Quercus ilex

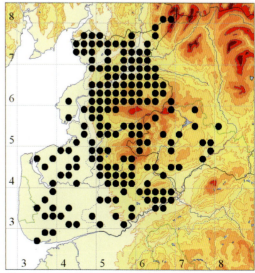

'Quercus petraea like'

FAGACEAE   BEECH FAMILY

Fagus sylvatica L.   Beech

European Temperate element but probably a neophyte in northern Lancashire.

Beech is found throughout most of the British Isles but it is thought to be native only in southern England and Wales.

Common (346). It occurs in hedgerows (BH3), parks and plantations throughout most of northern Lancashire. It is not known when it was introduced to the area but today self-sown plants are frequent. Its distribution is thought to be stable or increasing locally and nationally.

Castanea sativa Mill.   Sweet Chestnut

Archaeophyte. This was introduced by the Romans and is a major constituent of coppiced woodland in south-eastern England.

Occasional (45). It was not recorded by Wheldon and Wilson (1907) in northern Lancashire but today it is scattered throughout the area, usually as an amenity tree in parks and plantations. It rarely produces fruit.

Quercus cerris L.   Turkey Oak

Neophyte. This is a native species of southern, central and south-eastern Europe and south-western Asia. It was cultivated in Britain by 1735 and reported from the wild since 1905.

Occasional (47). It was first recorded by pupils at St Michael's School (St Michael's School, 1902) from Hall Lane, St Michael's (SD44Q) but Wheldon and Wilson (1907) did not record it. Today it is scattered throughout northern Lancashire in parks and plantations. It is spreading throughout the British Isles but especially south of a line from the R. Mersey to the R. Humber where it regenerates freely.

Quercus cerris × Q. suber L. (Q. × crenata Lam.)   Lucombe Oak

Neophyte. This hybrid arose in W. Lucombe's nursery in Exeter in 1762 but was not reported from the wild until 1964.

Very rare (1). In northern Lancashire Livermore and Livermore (1991) reported it from Lancaster.

Quercus ilex L.   Evergreen Oak

Neophyte. Evergreen Oak is a native of the Mediterranean region. It has been cultivated since the sixteenth century and was widely planted from the eighteenth century but it was not recorded in the wild until 1962.

Rare (7). Q. ilex was first recorded in northern Lancashire from the banks of the R. Lune, Lancaster (SD46W) in 1986 (L.A.L.; LIV). It was subsequently recorded from six further localities all in the north-western part of the area. All records are of planted trees. It is spreading in southern Britain.

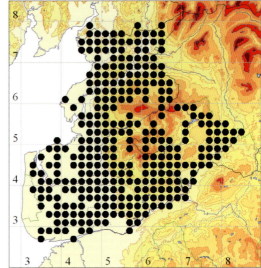

'Quercus robur like'

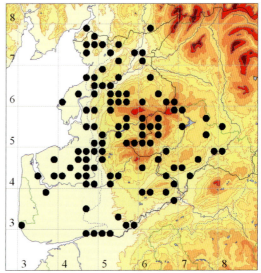

Quercus × rosacea

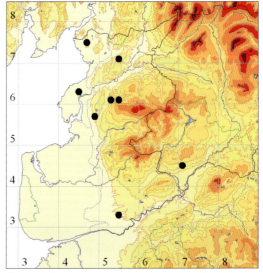

Quercus rubra

Quercus petraea (Matt.) Liebl.   Sessile Oak

Quercus robur L.   Pedunculate Oak

Quercus petraea × Q. robur (Q. × rosacea Bechst.)

European Temperate element.

Not only is there considerable variation within these two species but also it is believed that extensive hybridisation has occurred between them. This makes identification of individual trees very difficult (Rushton, 1997). Oaks are found throughout the British Isles in woodlands, parks and hedgerows (BH1, 3). They are an important constituent of most ancient woodlands.

Common or very common (321). Halliday (1997) considers both *Q. petraea* and *Q. robur* occur in Cumbria but in northern Lancashire when individual trees are examined critically most appear to be *Q. × rosacea* with at least some characters from both species. Oaks occur throughout northern Lancashire extending up the Bowland cloughs to over 300m (1000ft) but in the west of the area many trees were planted. The distribution maps of the two species are based on recorders assigning plants on the basis of being most like one or other of the two species. It seems that 'Q. petraea like' plants are more likely to be found in the north of the area including the limestone country around Morecambe Bay. Interestingly some of the trees recorded at the highest levels were 'Q. robur like' or clearly hybrids and not *Q. petraea* as might be expected. Indeed some of the oldest trees seen, often at high levels, were *Q. × rosacea* suggesting that hybridisation has taken place over a long time period. The map of *Q. × rosacea* shows a scatter of records and represents the distribution of recorders who took a more critical approach to identification. Oaks are likely to be extending their distribution as planting takes place in unwooded areas. Often recently planted trees are *Q. robur*.

Quercus rubra L.   Red Oak

Neophyte, a native of eastern North America. It has been planted widely in parks, estates, gardens and roadsides since 1724 but it was not recorded from the wild until 1942.

Rare (8). It was first recorded in northern Lancashire by Livermore and Livermore (1987). It occurs scattered across the area as planted trees.

MYRICACEAE   BOG-MYRTLE FAMILY

Myrica gale L.   Bog-myrtle

Suboceanic Boreo-temperate element.

Bog-myrtle is a fragrant and common species of mires (BH12) in western parts of the British Isles and occasionally elsewhere.

Rare (14). The map shows the distribution of the species in northern Lancashire post 1964. All the sites were remnant raised bogs or lowland wet heaths in the west of the area with an outlying locality in the east at White Moss (SD75X). It may persist on dry peat as relic bushes, e.g. on peat tracks elevated above the drained mosses around Stalmine and Out Rawcliffe. However since 1964 many sites have been lost and it is possible that only five or six remained by 2006. Formerly this must have been a common plant

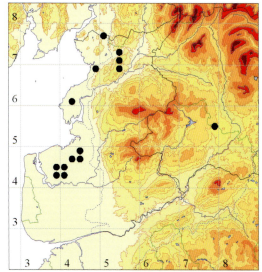
Myrica gale

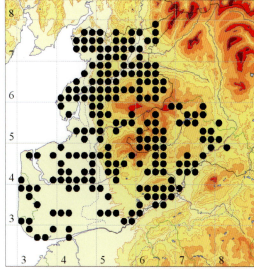
Betula pendula

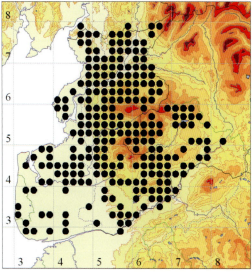
Betula pubescens

on all the lowland mosses but there are few written records or herbarium specimens before the end of the nineteenth century. Even then recorded sites included Thrang Moss, Hawes Water and Little Hawes Water in the northwest of the area whilst there is a record for the Fylde on Blundell's Moss (SD43M). Interestingly there were also records on raised bogs in the Bowland foothills, e.g. Tarnbrook (SD55X). The losses are due to the drainage and drying out of bogs and their utilization for moss litter, grazing and arable farming. In the Bowland foothills the management of the moors for grouse with regular moor burning has been an additional adverse factor. Elsewhere in the country losses have been caused by the use of peat for potting compost and horticulture. Losses throughout the country continue.

JUGLANDACEAE WALNUT FAMILY

Juglans regia L. Walnut

Neophyte. It is thought to be a native of south-western and central Asia, perhaps as far west as the Balkans but it is widely planted. It has been grown since Roman times in Britain but it was not recorded in the wild until 1836.

Rare (6). It was first recorded in northern Lancashire from Kirkham (SD43F) in 1964 (J.H.) and subsequently from Scorton (no grid reference) in 1968 (A.E.R.), Warton (SD47W) in 1999 (R.P.), Silverdale (SD47S) in 1997 (C.B.W.), whilst Livermore and Livermore (1987) recorded it from tetrads SD47M and SD57B. All records are for planted trees.

BETULACEAE BIRCH FAMILY

Betula pendula Roth Silver Birch

Eurosiberian Boreo-temperate element.

This is found throughout the British Isles in woodland especially on light, well-drained soils (BH1).

Frequent (219). Although Silver Birch is a native British species in northern Lancashire most trees appear to be introduced or derived from planted trees. Only on the limestone around Morecambe Bay do populations appear native or at least long established. It is also frequently confused with the variable *Betula pubescens* probably causing *B. pendula* to be over recorded. It is usually found in hedgerows (BH3), plantations and in built up areas (BH17).

Betula pendula × B. pubescens (B. × aurata Borkh.)

This hybrid has been recorded widely in the British Isles but probably incorrectly as it has been shown that most plants that appear intermediate are one or other of the presumed parent species, usually *B. pubescens* (Stace, 1997, Rich and Jermy, 1998).

Very rare (5). However it was confirmed in northern Lancashire at Forton (SD45Z; Kennedy and Brown, 1983). Other records that are likely to be this are from Out Rawcliffe (SD44C) where young plants were growing with both parents (E.F.G.), Tatham (SD66J; C.C. & J.O'R.) and in tetrads SD64S & 85H (Abbott, 2005).

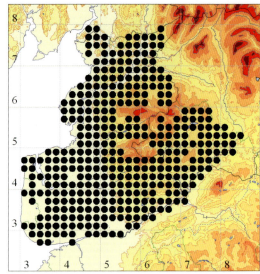
Alnus glutinosa

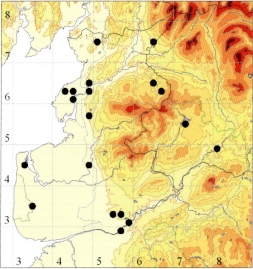
Alnus incana

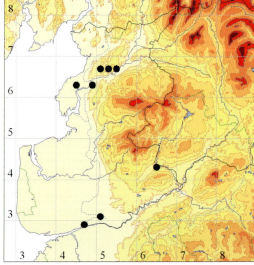
Alnus cordata

Betula pubescens Ehrh.   Downy Birch

Eurosiberian Boreo-temperate element.

This is found throughout the British Isles in woodlands and hedgerows (BH1, 3) and often reaches the highest levels in upland woodlands.

Common (253). Downy Birch occurs throughout northern Lancashire and may be the dominant tree on drying out mossland in the west of the area. It is also particularly frequent in upland woodlands on acid soils and extends to the highest levels in clough woodlands. In addition to woodlands it is frequent in hedgerows. It is believed most plants belong to *B. pubescens* ssp. *pubescens* but in the upland cloughs the nearly glabrous but glandular *B. pubescens* ssp. *tortuosa* (Ledeb.) Nyman may be frequent. Unfortunately the subspecies were rarely recorded. The distribution of *B. pubescens* is thought to be unchanged locally and nationally.

Betula utilis D. Don var. **jacquemontii** (Spach) A. Henry

Himalayan Birch

Neophyte. This is a native of the Himalayas that is increasingly being planted for amenity purposes.

Very rare (1). In northern Lancashire a few trees were noted planted at the entrance to a farm drive at Wennington (SD66J) in 2004 (E.F.G.).

Alnus glutinosa (L.) Gaertn.   Alder

Eurosiberian Temperate element.

This is found in damp woodlands and hedgerows (BH1, 3) throughout the British Isles.

Very common (377). Alder occurs throughout northern Lancashire in damp woodlands and hedgerows. It readily colonizes bare ground but it is absent from many upland areas. Its distribution locally and nationally is stable.

Alnus incana (L.) Moench   Grey Alder

Neophyte. This is a circumpolar Boreal-montane species but absent as a native from much of Europe. However it was introduced into Britain in 1780 although it was not recorded in the wild until 1922. It is widely planted particularly on wetter ground and in many reclamation schemes of old industrial sites.

Occasional (19). The first record in northern Lancashire is an unlocalised, unattributed record for the 10km square SD63 some time in the 1950s (B.R.C.). This was not followed until Livermore and Livermore (1987) published several records for the Lancaster area. Other records are scattered throughout northern Lancashire.

Alnus cordata (Loisel.) Duby   Italian Alder

Neophyte. Italian Alder is a native of Corsica, southern Italy and Albania. It was introduced into Britain in 1820 and recorded from the wild in 1935. It is increasingly planted as an ornamental tree.

Rare (8). Livermore and Livermore (1990b) recorded this planted on old railways at Heaton-with-Oxcliffe (SD46L), Quernmore (SD56C) and Caton-with-Littledale SD56H & M). It was also recorded from Lancaster (SD46W) in 2005 (M.Sh.), near Lea (SD42U) in 2006 (D.P.E.) and Preston (SD53A) in 1999 (S.B.). In Lancashire VC 64 it was found near Doeford Bridge, Bowland Forest Low (SD64L) in 2009 (P.G.)

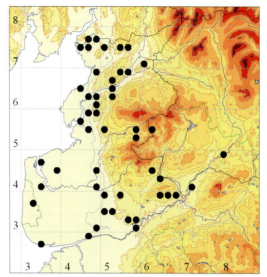
Carpinus betulus

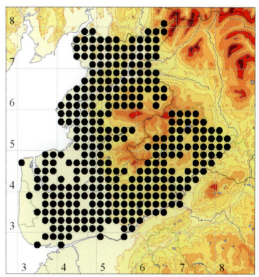
Corylus avellana

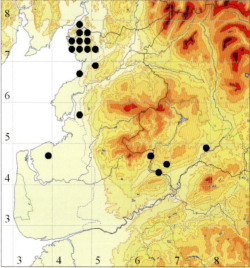
Euonymus europaeus

Carpinus betulus L.   Hornbeam

European Temperate element.

This is a native tree of woodlands (BH1) in southern England but it is not clear how far north it is native. However it is also widely planted and is found in Scotland and Ireland.

Occasional (48). Hornbeam occurs throughout northern Lancashire as single trees in parkland, and estates where it is clearly planted. It may have been planted and then coppiced at Gait Barrows, Yealand Redmayne but many of the plants are found in limestone grykes where they must be at least self-sown (R. Petley-Jones, pers. comm.). Furthermore, at Caton-with-Littledale, at least one tree grows out of rocks in a steep-sided, wooded ravine with *Tilia cordata*. Although it is not considered native in north-western England *Carpinus betulus* has a similar European distribution to *Tilia cordata*, which is native as far north as the limestone area around Morecambe Bay and in some of the Lune valley woodlands. It is suggested therefore that *Carpinus betulus* may be a very rare relic native species in northern Lancashire. In northern Lancashire it is difficult to know if its distribution as a possible native tree is declining or not but nationally it is increasing as a planted tree.

Corylus avellana L.   Hazel

European Temperate element.

This shrub is found in woodlands and hedgerows (BH1, 3) throughout the British Isles.

Common (335). Hazel occurs throughout northern Lancashire in hedgerows, scrub and in woodlands. It was frequently coppiced, especially in the Lune valley and around Morecambe Bay. However it avoids the uplands, lowland mosslands and is very rare in Fylde coastal areas. Its distribution is stable locally and nationally or possibly increasing ('Local Change').

Corylus maxima Mill.   Filbert

Neophyte. Filbert is a deciduous shrub found in gardens, parks and in amenity plantings mostly in southern Britain. It is a native of the Balkan Peninsula and Caucasia but widely planted commercially in the northern and upland Mediterranean zone. In Britain Filbert was first cultivated in 1759 and recorded in the wild in 1975. A purple leaved form is a popular garden plant.

Very rare (1). In northern Lancashire Filbert was found in plantations at Brockholes Quarry, Preston (SD53V) in 2008 (G.W. & M.Cl.).

CUCURBITACEAE   WHITE BRYONY FAMILY

Bryonia dioica Jacq.   White Bryony

Neophyte. This is native in southern Britain.

In northern Lancashire it is only known from two old records. It was recorded by W. Nicholson from near Lancaster c. 1690 (Whittaker, 1981) and from hedges at St Michael's (Ashfield, 1860).

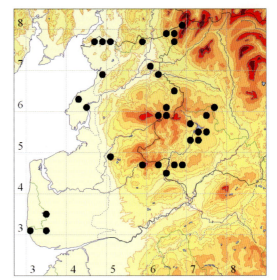
Parnassia palustris

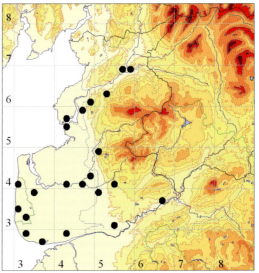
Oxalis corniculata

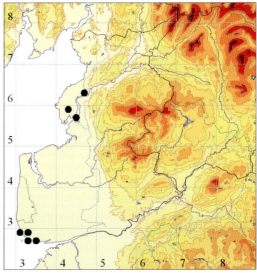
Oxalis articulata

Cucurbita pepo L. Marrow

Neophyte. This is a native of Central America and some cultivars can be confused with *C. maxima* Duchesne ex Lam. (Pumpkin). Both are grown widely and appear on rubbish tips especially where 'hot bed' conditions are provided by rotting vegetation. However they are both almost always found as casuals and are rarely recorded.

Very rare (1). In northern Lancashire *C. pepo* was recorded from Marton tip, Blackpool (SD33H) in c. 1966 (A.E.R.) but it is likely to occur elsewhere as a garden escape.

CELASTRACEAE SPINDLE FAMILY

Euonymus europaeus L. Spindle

European Temperate element.

This is a deciduous shrub or small tree found in open deciduous woodland and woodland edge habitats (BH1, 3) on calcareous soils. Spindle is found throughout the southern half of Britain and in Ireland but it also occurs further north as a planted shrub and is sometimes planted elsewhere.

Occasional (18). In northern Lancashire it is found as a presumed native in the limestone woodlands around Morecambe Bay and in woodlands on calcareous soils in the Ribble and Hodder river valleys. However there are also a few records elsewhere, where presumably it has escaped from cultivation. Although Wheldon and Wilson (1907) did not record Spindle from the Ribble and Hodder valleys Pickard (1901) found it near Slaidburn. Thus although it is now more widespread in northern Lancashire than 100 years ago this is probably due largely to better recording and escapes from gardens. A similar situation may apply nationally.

Euonymus latifolius (L.) Mill. Large-leaved Spindle

Neophyte. This is a native of southern, central and south-eastern Europe, north-western Africa and south-western Asia and was cultivated in Britain by 1730. It is a deciduous shrub planted in gardens and was recorded in the wild by 1904. It is found in scattered localities in Britain.

Very rare (1). The only northern Lancashire record is from Warton (SD57B) in 1978 (C.F. & N.J.S.; Livermore and Livermore, 1987).

Euonymus japonicus Thunb. Evergreen Spindle

Neophyte. Evergreen Spindle is a native of Japan and was introduced into cultivation in Britain in 1804. It is used widely as a hedge plant and in shrubberies, especially in coastal areas. It was found in the wild in 1897 and today is found in coastal areas of England and Wales, the Isle of Man and south-eastern Ireland.

Very rare (5). The only records for northern Lancashire are from the sand dunes at Lytham St Anne's (SD32I & J) in the 1970s (C.F. & N.J.S.) and (SD32N) in 1998 (E.F.G.), from an old

railway line near Fleetwood (SD34L) in 2008 (Anon) and by the Lancaster Canal, Preston (SD53F) in 2006 (Anon). However the B.S.B.I. 'on-line' vice-county database refers to an unpublished, post 1987 record by L.A.L., probably for Lancaster District. The origin for this has not been traced.

Celastrus orbiculatus Thunb. Staff-vine

Neophyte. This woody climber is a native of eastern Asia and was introduced into British cultivation in 1870. It was first recorded in the wild in Surrey in 1985 but there are few other records.

Very rare (1). In northern Lancashire it has been known from a roadside at Silverdale (SD47R) for many years but it was not identified until 2000 (J.Cl.).

PARNASSIACEAE
GRASS-OF-PARNASSUS FAMILY

Parnassia palustris L. Grass-of-Parnassus

Circumpolar Boreo-temperate element.

This is found in base-rich flushes in short grassland, mires and fens and also in coastal sand dune slacks (BH11, 19). It is found north of a line from North Wales to the Thames valley and in Ireland.

Occasional (33). Grass-of-Parnassus occurs scattered throughout northern Lancashire with var. *condensata* Travis and Wheldon occurring on the sand dunes at Lytham St Anne's. However Wentworth and Gornall (1996) showed that there are two cytotypes of *P. palustris* (including var. *condensata*). Material from Hawes Water, Silverdale is tetraploid ($2n = 36$) along with most material from northern England, Scotland and Ireland. Diploid plants ($2n = 18$) occur in North Wales and from the central Pennines to East Anglia and it is possible that this cytotype occurs in upland northern Lancashire. Wheldon and Wilson (1907) give no localities for Grass-of-Parnassus in VC 60 and it seems that it was a common species in suitable places indicating that some decline had taken place in the next sixty years or so. However in recent years it has become clear that the decline of this species has accelerated: by 2007 only eleven localities were known and in some of these only one plant had been seen. Amongst the remaining populations are those of var. *condensata* on the sand dunes. The 'New Atlas' noted the decline in the southern part of its range in Britain but 'Local Change' did not record further losses.

OXALIDACEAE WOOD-SORREL FAMILY

Oxalis corniculata L. Procumbent Yellow-sorrel

Neophyte. The native range of Procumbent Yellow-sorrel is not known but it is found in warm temperate and tropical regions throughout the world. It was cultivated in Britain by 1656 and it was first found in the wild in 1770. Today it is found as a weed in cultivated land and in other disturbed habitats throughout the British Isles, but it is especially common in midland and southern England.

Occasional (22). In northern Lancashire it was first recorded from Lancaster in 1834 (S.S.; OXF). It is now found in scattered localities in VC 60 but so far it has not been found in Lancashire VC 64. Var. *atropurpurea* Planch. was seen on cobblestones at Scorton, Nether Wyresdale (SD54E) in 1999 (E.F.G.) and at Churchtown (SD44W) in 1997 (C.F. & N.J.S.).

Oxalis exilis A. Cunn.   Least Yellow-sorrel

Neophyte. This is a native of Australasia and was first recorded in the wild in Britain in 1926. It is a small prostrate annual or short-lived perennial grown in gardens but escaping into ruderal habitats. It is sometimes mistaken for forms of *O. corniculata*. It is found in scattered localities in Britain and can become a troublesome weed in gardens.

Very rare (2). In northern Lancashire this was found at Pilling (SD44E) in 1999 (C.J.B.) and in Preston (SD52J) also in 1999 (P.J.).

Oxalis stricta L.   Upright Yellow-sorrel

Neophyte. This is a native of North America and eastern Asia but it is extensively naturalised in western Europe. It was first cultivated in Britain in 1658 and was recorded in the wild by 1823. It has been frequent in southern England for many years but since 1962 has spread westwards as well as into Scotland and Ireland.

Very rare (5). In northern Lancashire Upright Yellow-sorrel has been recorded from Silverdale (SD47S) in 2010 (J.Cl.), the Kirkham and Wesham area (SD43G) in 1964 (E. & J.H.), Skippool (SD34K) in 1965 (A.E.R.), St Anne's (SD32J) between 1994 and 2010 (C.F. & N.J.S.) and Singleton (SD33Z) in 1965 (A.E.R.).

Oxalis articulata Savigny   Pink-sorrel

Neophyte. This is a native of temperate South America and was introduced into Britain in 1870. It is frequently grown in gardens and was recorded in the wild by 1912. It escapes from gardens when pieces of woody rhizome are thrown out and today it is found near houses, often in coastal areas of England, Wales and the Isle of Man and more rarely elsewhere.

Rare (7). In northern Lancashire this was recorded from Glasson Dock (SD45N) in 1966 (E.H.) and since then in a few other scattered localities.

Oxalis acetosella L.   Wood-sorrel

Eurasian Boreo-temperate element.

Wood-sorrel is a familiar woodland plant but it also occurs on rock ledges and on limestone pavements (BH1, 2, 16). It is found throughout the British Isles.

Common (288). In northern Lancashire it is found in most parts of the east and north of the area with only a few records in the lowland west and here it is possibly a relic of former woodland, e.g. at Kirkham and Preesall. Its distribution in northern Lancashire is stable but there were losses in eastern England mostly before 1950 ('New Atlas') but otherwise its distribution nationally is unchanged.

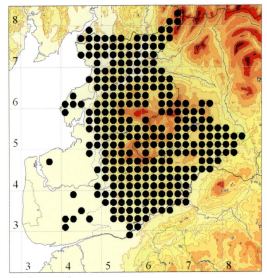

Oxalis acetosella

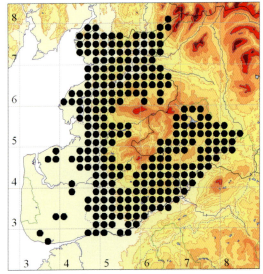

Mercurialis perennis

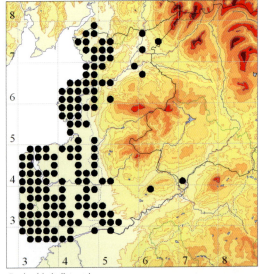

Euphorbia helioscopia

Oxalis debilis Kunth   Large-flowered Pink-sorrel

Neophyte. *Oxalis debilis* is a native of temperate South America. It was introduced into Britain in 1826 and was recorded from the wild by 1900. Today it is found in scattered localities throughout the British Isles but especially in south-eastern England.

Very rare (1). In northern Lancashire Large-flowered Pink-sorrel was found in Silverdale (SD47M) in 2010 (J.Cl.).

Oxalis incarnata L.   Pale Pink-sorrel

Neophyte. This is a native of southern Africa and was culti-vated in Britain by 1739. It was recorded in the wild by 1912 and today it is found in cultivated ground and ruderal habitats, mostly in southern and south-western England and the Isle of Man.

Very rare (3). In northern Lancashire this was recorded from Sunderland Point, Overton (SD45I) in 1974 (A.E.C.), Silverdale (SD47S) in 2008 (J.Cl.) and from Lytham boat yard (SD32Y) in 2007 (J.Cl.).

EUPHORBIACEAE   SPURGE FAMILY

Mercurialis perennis L.   Dog's Mercury

European Temperate element.

This is a rhizomatous perennial herb usually found on damp soil in woodlands (BH1). It is found throughout Britain except northern Scotland and it is also absent, except as an introduc-tion, in the Isle of Man and Ireland although it is thought to be native in the Burren.

Common (281). Dog's Mercury is found in deciduous wood-lands and hedgerows mostly in the east and north of northern Lancashire but it is absent from the fells. There are a few records in the west of the area and these may represent relics of former ancient woodlands, e.g. at Lytham, Kirkham and Preesall. There has been no change in its distribution in northern Lancashire and whilst the 'New Atlas' recorded no change nationally 'Local Change' noted a decline since 1987.

Mercurialis annua L.   Annual Mercury

Archaeophyte with a Submediterranean-Subatlantic distribution.

Annual Mercury is a plant of waste places and cultivated ground known since it was found in Viking deposits in York. Today it is a common species in south-eastern England and eastern Ireland but elsewhere it is found much more rarely.

Very rare (2). In northern Lancashire it was first recorded from near Knott End in 1902 (Wheldon and Wilson, 1907). There were also unlocalised records in the 1950s and 1960s from the 10km squares SD54 and 66 (B.R.C.). More recent localised records are from SD44W in 1964 (E. & J.H.) and from Blackpool (SD33I) in 1965 (E.H.). It may be increasing nationally.

Euphorbia platyphyllos   Broad-leaved Spurge

Archaeophyte with a European Southern-temperate distribution.

It is an annual of cultivated and waste ground usually growing on calcareous clays in south-eastern England.

Very rare (1). In northern Lancashire a few plants of Broad-leaved Spurge were found in Lea (SD42U) in 1996 (C.F. & N.J.S.). It is declining nationally.

Euphorbia stricta L.   Upright Spurge

Neophyte. This is an annual or biennial herb of open decid-uous woodland thought to be native in the lower Severn valley. It is a member of the European Southern-temperate element of the British flora and as a neophyte is found in scattered localities, mostly in southern England, where it is a garden escape.

Very rare (2). In northern Lancashire Upright Spurge was first recorded as a weed in a border at Inskip (SD43T) in 1996 (C.F. & N.J.S) and in a lane and garden at Silverdale (SD47S) in 2010 (J.Cl.) where it had been known for several years. There is no VC 60 record for the SD42 dot in the 'New Atlas'.

Euphorbia helioscopia L.   Sun Spurge

An archaeophyte with a Eurasian Southern-temperate distribution.

This is an annual weed of cultivated ground and waste places (BH4, 17), which occurs throughout the British Isles although it is rare in some upland areas.

Frequent (151). Sun Spurge is a common weed in the west of northern Lancashire with only a few records further east. Its distribution locally is unchanged but the 'New Atlas' reported a decline at the edges of its range whilst 'Local Change' reported an increase since 1987.

Euphorbia lathyris L.   Caper Spurge

An archaeophyte with a European Southern-temperate distri-bution but probably a neophyte in northern Lancashire.

Caper Spurge is found in waste places and in disturbed ground (BH3, 14, 17) mostly in the southern half of Britain with only occasional records in Scotland and Ireland.

Rare (10). This was first recorded in northern Lancashire from near Catforth (SD43S or T) in 1901 (H.B.; YRK, NMW) and about the same time from near St Michael's (Wheldon and Wilson, 1907). It was also recorded from the banks of the Artle Beck at Caton (SD56H) in 1942 (J.N.F.). Since 1964 it has been found in scattered localities in VC 60. Nationally Caper Spurge appears to be spreading whilst generally maintaining a southern distribution in Britain.

Euphorbia exigua L.   Dwarf Spurge

An archaeophyte with a European Southern-temperate distribution.

This is an annual of cultivated and disturbed ground (BH4) with a generally southern distribution in the British Isles.

Rare (6). Today this is found on limestone rocks and stones in the north-west of the area and at Lytham St Anne's. Although this has never been common in northern Lancashire it appears that 100 years ago it was more widespread usually being found as a weed of cultivated ground. The 'New Atlas' noted considerable losses before 1930 and that these had continued after 1962, but further losses since 1987 were not confirmed ('Local Change').

Euphorbia peplus L.   Petty Spurge

Archaeophyte with a European Southern-temperate distribution.

This is an annual of cultivated and disturbed ground (BH4, 17) that occurs throughout the British Isles although it is rare or absent in many upland areas, especially in Scotland.

Frequent (184). This is a common weed in the west of northern Lancashire with more occasional records elsewhere especially in the Lune, Ribble and Hodder river valleys. The distribution of Petty Spurge is unchanged in the area and nationally ('New Atlas') but 'Local Change' reported a significant increase since 1987.

Euphorbia portlandica L.   Portland Spurge

Oceanic Southern-temperate element.

Portland Spurge occurs in a range of coastal habitats (BH18, 19) in Britain from south-western Scotland to the Isle of Wight and Ireland.

Very rare (2). In northern Lancashire Portland Spurge has only been found on the sand dunes at Lytham St Anne's where it has always been rare. In recent years it has been found at two sites (SD32I & SD33A) in very small quantity. It is believed its distribution nationally is unchanged.

Euphorbia paralias L.   Sea Spurge

Mediterranean-Atlantic element.

Sea Spurge is found on coastal sand dunes (BH19) from south-western Scotland around the western and southern coasts of Britain to East Anglia. It also occurs in Ireland.

Rare (8). In northern Lancashire Sea Spurge is found on sand dunes and sandy ground by the sea at Lytham St Anne's, Rossall and Fleetwood. In places it is abundant and is an important species for stabilizing mobile dunes. It is possible that *E. paralias* has become more abundant over the last 100 years extending its range to the Rossall peninsula. The 'New Atlas' reported some losses from the south coast of England.

[Euphorbia esula L. var. **pseudocyparissias** Jord.   Leafy Spurge

This name is believed to include a number of taxa (Rich and Jermy, 1998) but the record (Whellan, 1942) from St Anne's probably refers to *E. cyparissias* or *E.* × *pseudoesula*.]

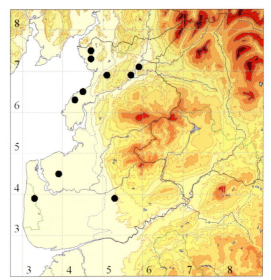
Euphorbia lathyris

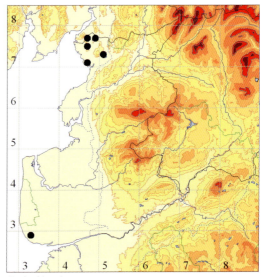
Euphorbia exigua

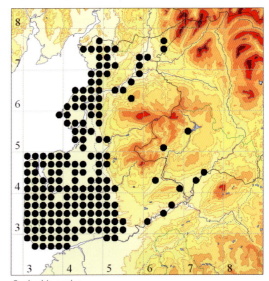
Euphorbia peplus

Euphorbia esula × E. waldsteinii (Soják) Czerep.
(**E. × pseudovirgata** (Schur) Soó)   Waldstein's or Twiggy Spurge

Neophyte. This perennial hybrid occurs with its parents in central and eastern Europe. It was probably introduced into Britain with grain or timber and was first recognised in the wild in 1937. It is found on waste ground and in other ruderal habitats in scattered localities in Britain, especially in the London area and south-eastern England.

Very rare (2). In northern Lancashire this was found at Glasson (SD45N) in 1966 (A.E.R.) and at Preston Dock (SD52E) in 1975 (C.F. & N.J.S.).

Euphorbia esula × E. cyparissias (**E. × pseudoesula** Schur)
Figert's Spurge

Neophyte. *E. × pseudoesula* is a native of Europe but it is not known when it was first cultivated in Britain. However it was reported as a garden weed in 1904. It is rarely recorded in the wild as it is difficult to distinguish from other members of the *E. esula* group (Stace, 1997).

Very rare (1). It is believed that plants on the Lytham St Anne's Local Nature Reserve (SD33A) may belong to this taxon. It was first recognised here in 1999 (E.F.G.; LIV).

Euphorbia cyparissias L.   Cyprus Spurge

Neophyte with a European Temperate distribution.

Cyprus Spurge is a rhizomatous perennial herb, which was cultivated in Britain by 1640. It was recorded in the wild by 1799 and today occurs on waste ground and sand dunes throughout the British Isles.

Rare (7). In northern Lancashire Cyprus Spurge was first recorded from a grassy field in front of Lytham Vicarage in 1897 (LIV) and it still occurs in the area and elsewhere on sand dunes at Lytham St Anne's. It also occurs in the Ribble valley and in the Lancaster area. Some records may refer to other taxa in the *E. esula* group (Stace, 1997).

Euphorbia amygdaloides L.   Wood Spurge

European Temperate element but a neophyte in northern Lancashire.

This is found in old deciduous woodlands on neutral to acidic soils in southern Britain and as a garden escape further north.

Very rare (3). This was first recorded as a garden escape by a path at Silverdale (SD47M; Livermore and Livermore, 1987), where it was still present in 2007 (E.F. & B.D.G.). It was also recorded, as ssp. *robbiae* (Turrill) Stace, from Poulton-le-Fylde (SD33P) in 2008 (D.P.E.) and as a garden escape at Forest Brecks in Lancashire VC 64 (SD75V; Abbott, 2005). Ssp. *robbiae* is a native of north-western Turkey.

SALICACEAE   WILLOW FAMILY

Populus alba L.   White Poplar

Neophyte, a native of south, central and eastern Europe eastwards to central Asia but widely naturalised elsewhere. It is thought it was brought to Britain from Holland in the sixteenth century and was recorded in the wild by 1597.

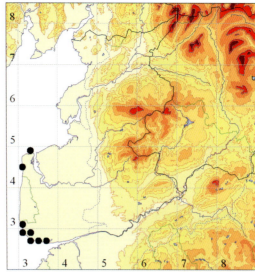
Euphorbia paralias

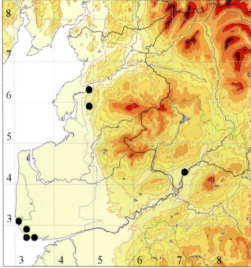
Euphorbia cyparissias

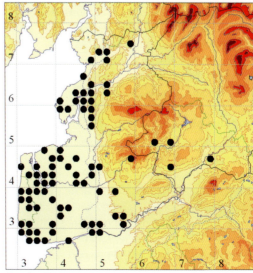
Populus alba

Frequent (82). It is found scattered throughout northern Lancashire but especially in the west of the area. It suckers freely, often forming dense thickets. However it was not recorded before 1907 (Wheldon and Wilson, 1907).

Populus alba × P. tremula (P. × canescens (Aiton) Sm.)   Grey Poplar

Neophyte. This hybrid was probably imported to Britain and was first recorded *c.* 1700. It is extensively planted for amenity but it rarely becomes naturalised.

Occasional (18). This is found scattered throughout northern Lancashire but it was not reported before 1964 when it was found in Preston (SD53G).

Populus tremula L.   Aspen

Eurasian Boreo-temperate element.

This is found throughout the British Isles in woodlands, hedgerows and on cliffs (BH1, 3, 16).

Frequent (101). It is found throughout northern Lancashire but in Bowland it can form thickets on rocky slopes and cliffs, e.g. Foxdale (SD56Q). It has also been planted for amenity and probably for this reason it has expanded its range in the area. It has also extended its range nationally.

Populus nigra L. ssp. betulifolia (Pursh) Dippel   Black-poplar

This is a native of western Europe.

Because of confusion between this and other subspecies and hybrids the distribution and native habitat for *P. nigra* ssp. *betulifolia* is only now becoming clearer (Cooper, 2006). It is probably a tree of lowland river valleys but it has often been planted.

Rare (12). In northern Lancashire it is found in scattered localities in the west of the area as far north as Lancaster (SD46K) where it was clearly planted on a river embankment. However three trees were found at the junction between salt marshes and clay banks on tidal rivers. At Sunderland Point (SD45H) the 'cotton tree' was a well-known feature and although always regarded as an introduction it grew from the base of a garden wall by the shore. It was blown down in 1996. Trees at Conder Green (SD45M) and Freckleton (SD42J) border salt marshes and other plants are found in similar situations and in old hedges. It is possible these few surviving trees are relics of more widespread riverside populations. Populations both locally and nationally appear to be stable but there is no accurate data to assess change.

Populus nigra *sensu lato*

Occasional (69). Before the complexity of poplar taxonomy was appreciated many recorders noted the occurrence of *Populus nigra* across much of VC 60 but this embraced various *P. nigra* taxa including hybrids. Amongst the taxa sometimes recorded separately was the distinctive *P. nigra* 'Italica' or Lombardy-poplar. This is frequently planted in parks and as windbreaks or for screening purposes. It originated in Italy and was introduced into Britain in 1758. However it never became naturalised although it was recorded in the 'wild' in 1886. In northern Lancashire it was recorded in

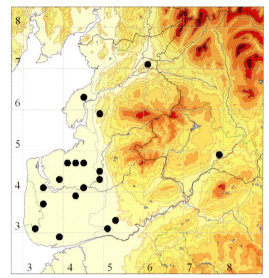

Populus × canescens

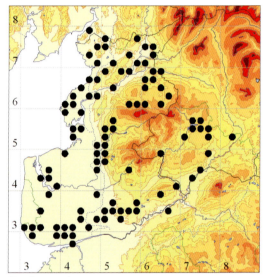

Populus tremula

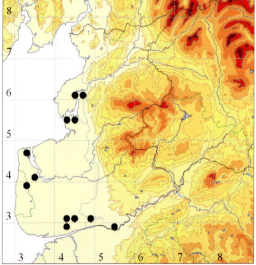

Populus nigra ssp. *betulifolia*

the Lancaster District where there are thirteen tetrad records mostly attributed to Livermore and Livermore (1987). However it is certain to occur elsewhere but as it is never truly naturalised it is largely overlooked.

Populus nigra × P. deltoides Marshall (P. × canadensis Moench)
Hybrid Black-poplar

Neophyte. This hybrid was introduced to the British Isles about 1770 and was recorded from the wild by 1799. It occurs throughout the British Isles and it is almost always planted. Numerous cultivars are involved.

Occasional (24). This hybrid is found scattered across northern Lancashire but it is likely to be more frequent than the records suggest. At least some records are probably recorded under *P. nigra sensu lato.*

Populus balsamifera L. × P. deltoides (P. × jackii Sarg.)
Balm-of-Gilead

Neophyte. This tree was introduced into Britain (as *P. × candicans*) in 1773 and was recorded in the wild in 1876. It is frequently planted in damp woods, by rivers and in parks throughout Britain.

Rare (14). *P. × jackii* occurs in scattered localities in northern Lancashire.

Populus trichocarpa Torr. & A. Gray ex Hook. Western Balsam-poplar

Neophyte. This species was introduced into Britain in 1892 and was recorded from the wild in 1935. It is planted for amenity purposes and most plants are male. It occasionally spreads by suckers.

Rare (7). The only records are from Lancaster District. It is probably under recorded.

Salix pentandra L.
Bay Willow

Eurosiberian Boreo-temperate element.

This is a large shrub or small tree that is found in damp or wet ground, sometimes forming thickets, or in hedgerows (BH1, 3). It is found throughout the British Isles but it is thought to be planted in many areas in Wales and the southern half of England.

Occasional (53). In northern Lancashire it is found in most parts of the area in hedges and very occasionally in thickets by streams, e.g. near Chipping (see Plate 2.13). It is probably native in the Bowland Fells and in the north of the area but may be planted in many parts of the west where it has become much more frequent since 1907. There is no change in its distribution nationally.

Salix fragilis L. *sensu lato*
Crack-willow

Meikle (1984) pointed out the taxonomic and nomenclatural difficulties associated with a morphologically variable taxon known in the British Isles as *Salix fragilis*. He also pointed out that continental botanists believed that *S. fragilis* was a hybrid. It now appears in a revision of the group (Belyaeva, 2009) that this is indeed the case. The parents of the hybrid are *S. alba* and what British botanists know as *S. fragilis* var. *decipiens*. (Meikle, 1984). This latter taxon is named *S. euxina* I.V. Belyaeva and the hybrid is known as *S. × fragilis* L., a morphologically variable series linking *S. alba* with *S. euxina* and includes *S. × rubens* (see below). However these revisions came too late to reassess the taxonomy, nomenclature and distribution of the taxa involved in northern Lancashire and therefore this account follows Stace (2010).

Archaeophyte with a Eurosiberian Temperate distribution.

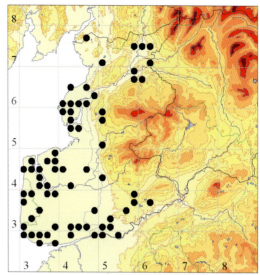
Populus nigra s.l.

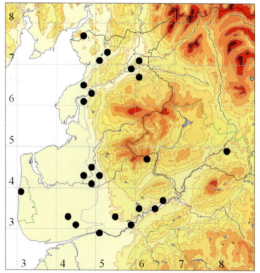
Populus × canadensis

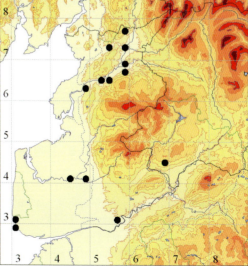
Populus × jackii

This tree is found in many parts of the British Isles although it becomes much rarer in upland areas and in western Ireland than elsewhere. It is extensively planted and is especially frequent by streams, rivers and in wet areas (BH1, 14).

Common (281). There are numerous varieties (Meikle, 1984) but generally these have not been recorded separately. However *S. fragilis* var. *decipiens* (Hoffm.) Koch and *S. fragilis* var. *russelliana* (Sm.) Koch have been recorded in VC 60 (Wheldon and Wilson, 1907; Livermore and Livermore, 1987, 1989). *Salix fragilis* is found throughout northern Lancashire but it is rare in the Bowland Fells and in Lancashire VC 64. Its distribution locally and nationally is unchanged.

Salix alba L.   White Willow

Archaeophyte with a Eurosiberian Southern-temperate distribution.

This tree usually grows in marshes, by ponds and especially by ditches, streams and rivers (BH14) where it is extensively planted. Like *S. fragilis* it occurs throughout the British Isles but it is much rarer in upland areas and in western Ireland than elsewhere.

Frequent (176). There are also numerous varieties that have not generally been identified in northern Lancashire. However *S. alba* var. *caerulea* (Sm.) Dumort. and *S. alba* var. *vitellina* (L.) Stokes have both been recorded in VC 60 (Wheldon and Wilson, 1907; Livermore and Livermore, 1990b; LIV). *Salix alba* is found throughout northern Lancashire but is much commoner in lowland areas in the west and in the Ribble valley than elsewhere. It is not thought that there has been any change in its distribution locally or nationally.

Salix alba × S. fragilis (S. × rubens Schrank)   Hybrid Crack-willow

Archaeophyte. This hybrid sometimes arises spontaneously but it is more often planted. It was originally introduced for basket making but it is now more usually planted for amenity.

Rare (11). It is found in scattered localities in VC 60 and in most cases it was almost certainly planted for amenity. However on the banks of the R. Lune at Gressingham (SD56Z) it may have escaped from the Arkholme osier beds where willows were cultivated for basket making. Garnett (2000) provides an account of this Lune valley industry but unfortunately there are no records of the taxa cultivated. *S. × rubens* nothovar. *basfordiana* (Scaling ex Salter) Meikle forma *sanguinea* Meikle was recorded from Heysham (SD45E) in 2000 (M.W. & B.A.T.) For notes on other taxa introduced at Heysham see *S. eriocephala*. Nothovar. *basfordiana* was also found at Conder Green (SD45M) in 2010 (M.W.).

Salix triandra L.   Almond Willow

Archaeophyte with a Eurosiberian Temperate distribution.

This shrub or small tree grows in damp or wet places often by streams, rivers, and ponds (BH11, 13, 14) and occurs mostly in south-eastern England and Wales.

Rare (6). It was first known in northern Lancashire from an unattributed, unlocalised record in the 10km square SD45 in 1950 (B.R.C.). Later, it was found by the R. Wyre at Garstang (SD44X) in 1968 (A.E.R.) and subsequently from a few other sites in VC 60. Probably the best known site is by the R. Lune at Arkholme (SD57V) where it was introduced for basket making. It is possibly overlooked.

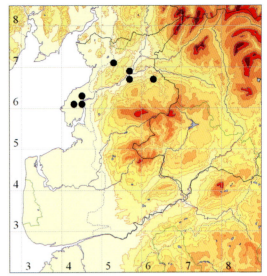

Populus trichocarpa

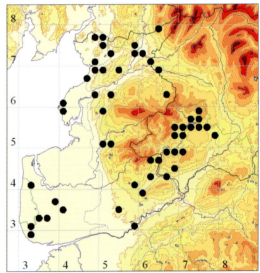

Salix pentandra

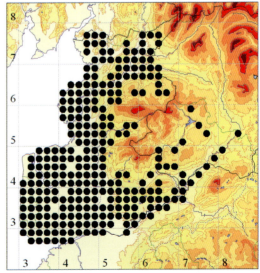

Salix fragilis s.l.

Salix triandra × S. viminalis (S. × mollissima Hoffm. ex Elwert)
Sharp-stipuled Willow

Archaeophyte. This hybrid shrub is found in damp places and was often planted for basketry especially in Northern Ireland. It is found scattered over much of the British Isles.

Very rare (4). In northern Lancashire it was first recorded from Brock Mill, Goosnargh (SD54L) in 1965 (Anon). Other records are from tetrads SD45S and SD57R (Livermore and Livermore, 1987) and from Heysham (SD45E) in 2000 (M.W. & B.A.T.). This latter record was identified as *S. × mollissima* var. *undulata* (Ehrh.) Wimm.

Salix purpurea L.   Purple Willow

Eurosiberian Temperate element.

This shrub or small tree is found on wet ground at the edge of woods, in hedgerows and by streams and rivers (BH3, 11, 14) throughout most of the British Isles. However it is rare in northern Scotland and it is often planted.

Occasional (49). *S. purpurea* is found scattered throughout northern Lancashire but it is especially common by the R. Lune in the Arkholme area where it was probably grown in the osier beds. It is believed that its distribution is unchanged locally and nationally.

Salix purpurea × S. cinerea (S. × pontederiana Willd.)

Very rare (1). This hybrid occurs in a few scattered localities in Britain and in northern Lancashire it was found on a low cliff by the R. Lune at Stodday (SD45P) in 1978 (M.J.W.).

Salix purpurea × S. viminalis (S. × rubra Huds.)
Green-leaved Willow

This spontaneous hybrid is widespread in Europe and occurs throughout the British Isles. However it has often been grown in osier beds for basketry.

Rare (6). This was first recorded in northern Lancashire from an old osier bed at Arkholme (SD57V) in 1986 (J.M.N.) and nearby on the banks of the R. Lune at Gressingham (SD56Z) in 2002 (E.F.G.; LIV). Other records are from Ireby (SD67M; Livermore and Livermore, 1987), Lancaster (SD46R; Livermore and Livermore, 1991), Heysham (SD45E) in 2000 (M.W. & B.A.T.) and near Stocks Reservoir, Easington (SD75I) in 2008 (M.W.).

Salix purpurea × S. viminalis × S. cinerea (S. × forbyana Sm.)
Fine Osier

This hybrid is used in basketry and was first collected in Norfolk in 1804. It is found scattered in England, Wales and southern Scotland but it is much more common in Northern Ireland.

Very rare (1). In northern Lancashire it was probably this that was gathered by the R. Lune at Gressingham (SD56Z) in 2002 (E.F.G.), not far from the former osier beds at Arkholme.

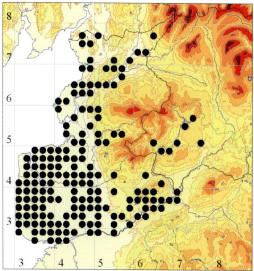

Salix alba

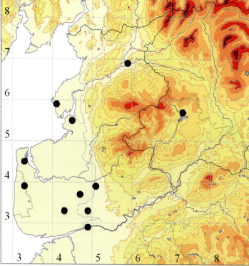

Salix × rubens

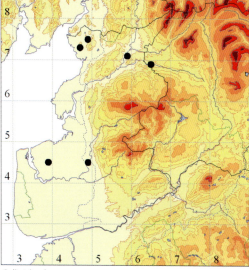

Salix triandra

Salix daphnoides Vill.   European Violet-willow

Neophyte. This species was introduced into Britain about 1829 and was known from the wild by 1905. Its violet-brown twigs, which have a dense white bloom, make it an attractive tree for amenity planting. It is found in many places in Britain but it seems to be especially frequent in the Lancashire-Yorkshire region.

Rare (11). In northern Lancashire it was first recorded from near a golf course at Blackpool (SD33I) in 1967 (J.H., A.E.R., H.S.) and has since been found in scattered localities in VC 60.

Salix viminalis L.   Osier

Archaeophyte with a Eurasian Temperate distribution. This is a frequently coppiced or pollarded tree found throughout most of the British Isles. It grows in damp places by streams and rivers (BH11, 13, 14) and has a range of economic uses.

Frequent (195). *S. viminalis* is found throughout northern Lancashire and appears to have considerably extended its range and frequency since 1907, probably due in part to plantings for various purposes. It has also extended its range nationally.

Salix viminalis × S. cinerea × S. repens (S. × angusensis Rech. f.)

The willows of the Sefton coast sand dune system (VC 59) have interested botanists for many years (P. Smith pers. comm.) and in 2000 Meikle and Robinson published an account of the occurrence of *Salix × angusensis* previously known only from the coast of Angus (VC 90). However similar and puzzling willows were also found on sand dunes from northern Wales to Cumbria including the sand dunes at Lytham St Anne's. However *S. × angusensis* is difficult to identify and in particular to distinguish from another rare willow hybrid, *S. × friesiana*. To clarify the identity of these hybrids Pauline Michell undertook a morphological study of willows on the Sefton coast (Michell, 2001) and showed that *S. × angusensis* was distinct from the hybrids *S. × friesiana* and *S. × subsericea* and the putative parents *S. cinerea*, *S. repens* and *S. viminalis*. However further studies by M. Wilcox (pers. comm.) were not so clear-cut.

Very rare (3). Meikle has looked at several gatherings from Lytham St Anne's (SD33A, SD32I, J) in northern Lancashire and has concluded that a few bushes are referable to this triple hybrid. Further observations suggest that at least one of the forms of this hybrid at Lytham St Anne's accords with the low-growing habit described for the Sefton coast by Meikle and Robinson (2000).

Salix viminalis × S. repens (S. × friesiana Andersson)

This is a slightly more frequent and widespread low growing tree found on coastal sand dunes from northern Wales to Cumbria and occasionally elsewhere in Britain. It also occurs in Europe.

Very rare (3). In northern Lancashire it was found in a few localities on the sand dunes at Lytham St Anne's (SD33A, SD32N, SD32P).

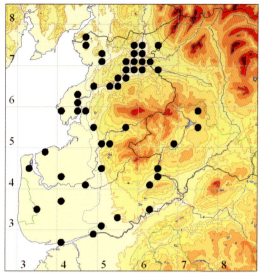

Salix purpurea

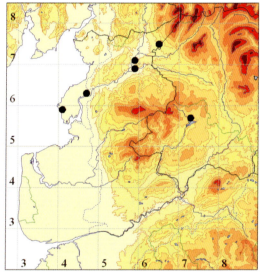

Salix × rubra

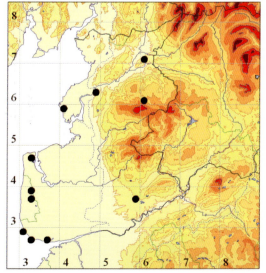

Salix daphnoides

Salix eleagnos Scop.   Olive Willow

Neophyte. This is a European Southern-temperate species and was introduced into cultivation in 1820. It was first recorded from the wild in 1928 and today it is often found in amenity plantings. It is found in scattered localities in Britain.

Very rare (5). In northern Lancashire it has been found planted on an old railway embankment at Alston (SD53Y) in 1989, by the R. Wyre at Garstang (SD44X) in 1998 and as part of amenity planting on an old tip at Blackpool (SD33M) in 1999 (all E.F.G.). It was also recorded planted at Carleton (SD33J) in 2007 (M.S.) and at Heysham power station (SD45E) in 1999 (J.M.N.).

Salix viminalis × **S. cinerea** (**S.** × **holosericea** Willd.)

Silky-leaved Osier

This spontaneous hybrid is widespread in Europe and occurs throughout the British Isles. It is one of the commonest willow hybrids. It occurs in hedges and thickets (BH3), often with the parents.

Occasional (50). *S.* × *holosericea* is found throughout northern Lancashire.

Salix viminalis × **S. caprea** × **S. cinerea**
(**S.** × **calodendron** Wimm.)   Holme Willow

Neophyte. This hybrid appears to be represented by a single female clone and is found scattered over much of the British Isles. Reasons for its introduction are not known.

Very rare (1). In northern Lancashire it was recorded from plantings at Heysham (SD45E) in 2000 (M.W. & B.A.T.).

Salix viminalis × **S. aurita** (**S.** × **fruticosa** Döll)   Shrubby Osier

This is a spontaneous hybrid found in scattered localities in the British Isles but it is also planted for basketry and more recently for biomass production. Only female shrubs are known. It occurs in hedges and in thickets (BH3).

Very rare (4). In northern Lancashire it was found in a hedge in the Bolton-le-Sands – Nether Kellet area (SD46Y; Livermore and Livermore, 1987), near Longridge Fell (SD64K) no date (Anon), Claughton (SD54B) in 1964 (Anon) and possibly also by a sea wall at Middleton (SD45D) in 2002 (E.F.G.).

Salix viminalis × **S. caprea** (**S.** × **smithiana** Willd.)

Broad-leaved Osier

This is a spontaneous hybrid that occurs in hedgerows, thickets and waste ground (BH3), often with the parents, throughout the British Isles. It is often a relic of cultivation.

Occasional (39). In northern Lancashire it is found in scattered localities in VC 60 and VC 64.

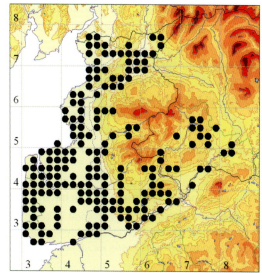
Salix viminalis

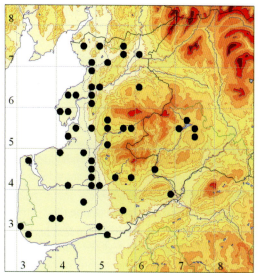
Salix × holosericea

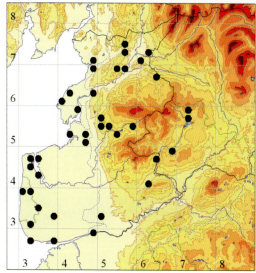
Salix × smithiana

Salix caprea L. ssp. caprea
Goat Willow

Eurasian Boreo-temperate element.

This is a shrub or small tree found in woodlands, scrub and hedgerows (BH1, 3) throughout the British Isles. However it may be over recorded as it hybridises freely with *Salix cinerea* ssp. *oleifolia* and the hybrid readily backcrosses with both parents to provide a range of intermediates between the parents. It is likely that many records for *S. caprea* are *S. caprea* with varying amounts of *S. cinerea* in their genetic composition.

Common (282). It occurs throughout northern Lancashire. Its distribution both locally and nationally is stable.

Salix caprea × S. cinerea (S. × reichardtii A. Kern.)

This is widespread in Europe and is found in woodlands, hedgerows, thickets and waste ground (BH1, 3) throughout the British Isles. However it is very much under recorded being mistaken for one or other of the parents. It is almost certainly more common than *S. caprea* and possibly as common as *S. cinerea*.

Occasional (46). In northern Lancashire *S. × reichardtii* occurs throughout the area.

Salix caprea × S. aurita (S. × capreola Jos. Kern. ex Andersson)

This hybrid is widespread in Europe and is found in woodland margins and hedgerows (BH3) in scattered localities throughout the British Isles.

Very rare (1). In northern Lancashire it was found in a hedge in the Roeburndale – Wray-with-Botton area (SD66H; Livermore and Livermore, 1987). It probably occurs elsewhere in northern Lancashire, especially in the valleys of the Bowland Fells.

Salix cinerea L. ssp. cinerea
Grey Willow

Eurosiberian Boreo-temperate element.

This subspecies is found in base-rich fens and marshes (BH11) and is largely confined to south-eastern England with only scattered records elsewhere. However it is probably under recorded and towards the western edge of its range there appear to be many intermediates with *S. cinerea* ssp. *oleifolia*.

Rare (9). In northern Lancashire it is found in the fen at Hawes Water (SD47T) where intermediates with *S. cinerea* ssp. *oleifolia* occur and in scattered localities in the west of the area. There is also a record from Gisburn Forest (SD75M; Abbott, 2005).

Salix cinerea L. ssp. oleifolia Macreight

Suboceanic Temperate element.

This shrub or small tree grows on acid to base-rich soils in wet places, in hedges, woodlands, woodland margins and waste places (BH1, 3, 11) throughout the British Isles.

Very common (375). It also occurs throughout northern Lancashire. Its distribution is stable locally and nationally.

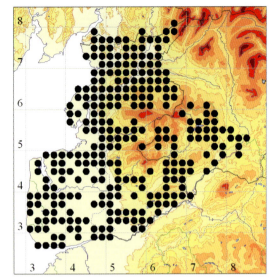

Salix caprea

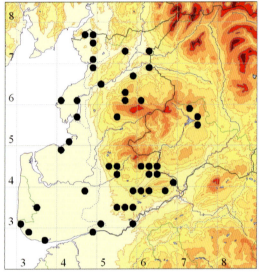

Salix × reichardtii

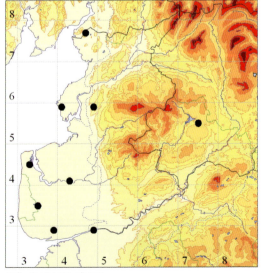

Salix cinerea ssp. *cinerea*

Salix cinerea × S. aurita (S. × multinervis Döll)

This shrub or small tree is widespread in northern and central Europe. It is found in hedgerows, scrub and in woodland margins on acidic soils (BH3, 11) throughout the British Isles.

Occasional (31). It is found in scattered localities in northern Lancashire but it is probably under recorded.

Salix cinerea × S. myrsinifolia

Very rare (1). This occurs occasionally in northern Britain and was found in hedges at Scotforth (SD45Z) in 1972 and 1973 (E.F. & B.D.G.; LIV).

Salix cinerea × S. repens (S. × subsericea Döll)

This is a rare hybrid that occurs with the parents but is found in a few British localities.

Very rare (1). In northern Lancashire there are records from the sand dunes at Lytham St Anne's (SD33A) spanning the period 1967 to 2001.

Salix cinerea × S. phylicifolia (S. × laurina Sm.)

This is a frequent hybrid where the parents grow together in northern Britain.

Very rare (5). In northern Lancashire it was found at Slaidburn (SD75B; Abbott, 2005), Gisburn Forest (SD75N & P) in 2007 (E.F. & B.D.G), near Stocks Reservoir, Easington (SD75I) in 2008 (M.W.) and probably at Carnforth (SD46Z) in 2002 (E.F.G.; LIV).

Salix cinerea × S. myrsinifolia × S. phylicifolia

Very rare (1). The identification of triple hybrids is always difficult especially where two of the parents (*S. myrsinifolia* and *S. phylicifolia*) are themselves sometimes difficult to distinguish. However this hybrid was recorded from Gisburn Forest (SD75M; Abbott, 2005).

Salix aurita L.   Eared Willow

European Boreo-temperate element.

This occurs on acid soils on heaths, in hedgerows and woodland margins (BH1, 3) over much of the British Isles.

Frequent (99). *S. aurita* is found throughout northern Lancashire. It is thought its distribution is stable but some records may have been recorded in error for *S. × multinervis*, especially in the west of the region. The 'New Atlas' showed losses in south-eastern England although continued loss was not noted by 'Local Change'.

Salix aurita × S. myrsinifolia (S. × coriacea J. Forbes)

This occurs occasionally with the parents in northern Britain.

Very rare (1). In northern Lancashire it was found by a roadside at Scotforth (SD45Z) in 1973 (E.F. & B.D.G.; LIV).

Salix aurita × S. repens (S. × ambigua Ehrh.)

This is a common hybrid where the parents grow together and is found throughout the British Isles but especially in northern Britain.

Very rare (3). In northern Lancashire it was found in a woodland at Preston (SD53L) in 1999 (S.B.); White Moss, Gisburn Forest (SD75X) in 2006 (E.F.G. & T. Bonniface) and in Gisburn Forest, Easington (SD75M; Abbott, 2005).

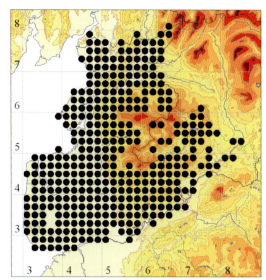

Salix cinerea ssp. *oleifolia*

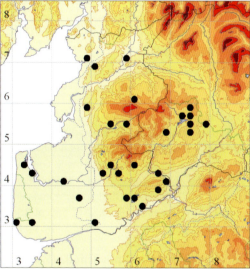

Salix × multinervis

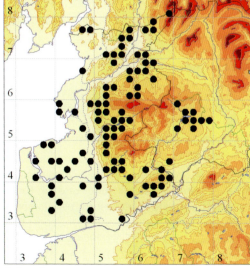

Salix aurita

Salix eriocephala Michx.   Heart-leaved Willow

Neophyte. This is a native of north-western North America and is occasionally found planted in wet places in Britain. It was introduced into British gardens in 1811 but it remains a rare cultivated plant. It was reported naturalised in eastern Sussex in 1972. According to a draft letter (L.A. Livermore to H.H. Fowkes at LIV) this was planted at Heysham (SD45E) in 1987 and subsequently recorded by Clement and Foster (1994). It was still present in 2000 (M.W. & B.A.T.).

It seems at least three other rare introductions were planted at Heysham at this time (Clement and Foster, 1994). They were **Salix hookeriana** J. Barratt, a native of western North America, **Salix lucida** Muhlenb. (Shining Willow), a native of eastern North America and **Salix microstachya** Turez. ex Trautv., a native of north-eastern Asia. In 2000 *Salix hookeriana* and *S. lucida* were re-found but not *S. microstachya* (M.W. & B.A.T.).

Salix myrsinifolia Salisb.   Dark-leaved Willow

Eurosiberian Boreal-montane element.

This is a shrub or small tree found on gravely riverbanks, in thickets and in marshy ground at the edge of woods (BH13, 14, 16). It is found in northern England, Scotland and Northern Ireland and occasionally elsewhere.

Very rare (2) or extinct. Lancashire is at the southern limit of its native distribution and former records were by the R. Lune between Kirkby Lonsdale and Nether Burrow (YRK, NMW) and near Lower Emmetts, Over Wyresdale. The voucher specimen (SYT) for a record by the R. Hodder is probably *S. × reichardtii*. Since 1964 the only records for northern Lancashire are from the banks of the R. Greta at Melling-with-Wrayton (SD67B) and at Wrayton (SD67F) in 1968 (E.F.G.; LIV). Searches of these localities in 2002 failed to find *S. myrsinifolia* and it has not been rediscovered at former localities. Because of the confusion with other taxa it is not clear if nationally the distribution of *S. myrsinifolia* has changed.

Salix myrsinifolia × S. phylicifolia (**S. × tetrapla** Walker)

This is found frequently in northern Europe and in northern Britain occurring on damp rocky banks by rivers and by lakes.

Very rare (1). In northern Lancashire it was recorded from Gisburn Forest (SD75N; Abbott, 2005).

Salix phylicifolia L.   Tea-leaved Willow

Circumpolar Boreo-arctic Montane element.

This shrub grows by ponds, streams and rivers and in damp rocky places (BH14, 16) in northern England, Scotland and in parts of western Ireland. It is similar to *S. myrsinifolia* with which it hybridises making identification sometimes difficult.

Very rare (4). In northern Lancashire former localities were on the bank of the R. Lune near Tunstall, in lower Ease Gill, Leck, between Botton and Wray, on a roadside near Marshaw, near Tarnbrook and at two sites by the R. Hodder downstream of Higher Hodder Bridge. A further record by the R. Ribble is an error. Since 1964 it has been recorded, usually as single bushes, by the R. Lune at Gressingham (SD56U), Higher Bridge Island, R. Hodder (SD64V) in 1971 (T.B.), where it is believed to have now gone and

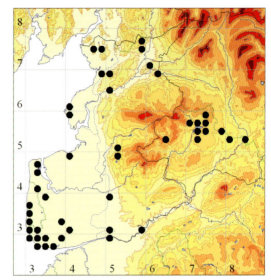

Salix repens

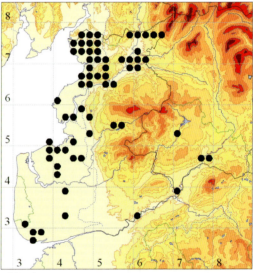

Viola odorata

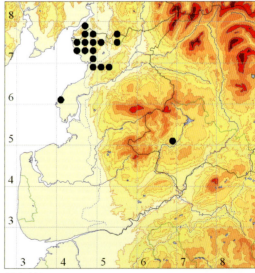

Viola hirta

from Gisburn Forest (SD75N; Abbott, 2005; SD76K in 2007 and earlier, D.Bunn). It has clearly declined in northern Lancashire and it is now critically endangered but nationally its distribution is stable.

Salix repens L.   Creeping Willow

Eurosiberian Boreo-temperate element.

This is found throughout the British Isles in a variety of habitats. Morphologically it is very variable and at least three variants are recognised but with many intermediates. Var. *repens* is a rhizomatous, procumbent shrub with nearly glabrous stems and leaves. It is typically found on damp heaths and moors in acidic, nutrient poor situations (BH10). Var. *argentea* (Sm.) Wimm. & Grab. with silky-pubescent stems and densely, silky-pubescent leaves is usually found on sand dunes but it is also found inland colonizing base-rich, post-industrial sites (BH16, 19) whilst var. *fusca* Wimm. & Grab. occurs on East Anglian fens.

Occasional (47). In northern Lancashire both var. *repens* and var. *argentea* occur but detailed analysis of their separate distributions has not been made and some inland populations are difficult to identify being intermediate between the two variants. Nevertheless var. *argentea* dominates many sand dune slacks at Lytham St Anne's and increasingly appears inland in base-rich conditions on roadsides and in quarries. On the other hand localities for var. *repens* appear to be getting fewer as general eutrophication destroys sites where it may have grown. Nevertheless it still grows on wet heaths and mires in the north and east of the area. The 'New Atlas' showed that *Salix repens* had declined in England since 1962 but no further decline was noted by 'Local Change'. There is no information on the changing status of the variants.

[**Salix babylonica** L. **'Tortuosa'** (Corkscrew Willow) was recorded from Lancaster (Livermore and Livermore, 1991) but this record is almost certainly of a recently planted tree.]

VIOLACEAE   VIOLET FAMILY

Viola odorata L.   Sweet Violet

European Temperate element.

This is found in woodland, woodland margins, hedge banks etc. on calcareous soils (BH1, 3, 7). It is thought to be native in most of England, Wales and south-eastern Ireland but introduced further north and often within its native range.

Occasional (65). In northern Lancashire it is found scattered throughout the area but it is more common in the north than elsewhere. White flowered forms are frequent but they have not been critically identified. *V. odorata* is probably native in northern woodlands and woodland edge habitats and possibly also in the Ribble and Hodder valleys but many of the other localities are probably escapes from cultivation. It has probably extended its range in northern Lancashire reflecting the national situation. Var. *subcarnea* (Jordan) Partalori was found at Warton (SD47W) in 2010 (J.Cl.).

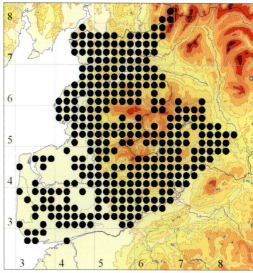

Viola riviniana

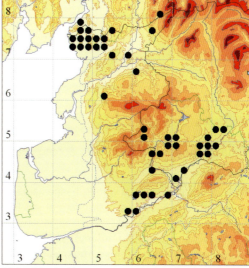

Viola reichenbachiana

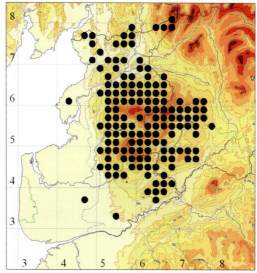

Viola palustris

Viola hirta L.   Hairy Violet

Eurosiberian Temperate element.

This occurs in short grasslands or open scrub on calcareous soils (BH7) in England, Wales, eastern Scotland and parts of Ireland.

Occasional (18). In northern Lancashire it is found on the limestone soils around Morecambe Bay and on Dalton Crags and it was rediscovered in 2008 in the Hodder valley on a roadside verge at Newton, Lancashire VC 64 after an absence of 100 years. However there are no recent records for former localities in Leck and the Lune and Ribble valleys. This decline was noted nationally by the 'New Atlas' but further loss since 1987 was not noted ('Local Change').

[**Viola odorata** × **V. hirta** (**V.** × **scabra** F. Braun) is a common hybrid and probably occurs around Morecambe Bay but has so far not been recognised.]

Viola riviniana Rchb.   Common Dog-violet

European Temperate element.

This occurs in a wide range of habitats (BH1, 7, 16) throughout the British Isles.

Common (332). In northern Lancashire it favours woodlands, woodland margins and hedgerows and occurs throughout the area. There has been no change in its distribution locally or nationally.

Viola reichenbachiana Jord. ex Boreau   Early Dog-violet

European Temperate element.

This is found in deciduous woods, hedge banks and other woodland edge habitats on calcareous or less frequently on neutral soils (BH1, 3) mostly in England, Wales and Ireland. It is not as easy to distinguish from *V. riviniana* as the literature might suggest (Rich and Jermy, 1998) and this problem may be exacerbated by hybrids.

Occasional (46). In northern Lancashire *V. reichenbachiana* is common in limestone woodlands in the north of the area but it is also frequent in the Ribble and Hodder valley woodlands. *Viola sylvestris* var. *punctata* Grey recorded from Silverdale (Wheldon and Wilson, 1925) may be this species or *V.* × *bavarica* but it is not clear to which taxon it belongs. There has been no change in the distribution of *V. reichenbachiana* locally or nationally.

Viola reichenbachiana × **V. riviniana**
(**V.** × **bavarica** Schrank)

There are differing views on the presence of this hybrid in Britain. Rich and Jermy (1998) summarised the morphological features of the two parents and the hybrid but pointed out that Valentine's work suggested that *V.* × *bavarica* was rare and largely infertile. However continental authors suggest that *V.* × *bavarica* is common and fertile. There is no doubt that in northern Lancashire there are plants (rather than populations) that are intermediate morphologically between the parents often having pale spurs (but not as pale as in *V. riviniana*), short appendages c. 1mm long and petal venation intermediate between the two parents. In Britain these plants have been regarded as belonging to a morphologically variable *V. riviniana*. C.L. O'Reilly (pers. comm.) suggests these plants are showing introgression between the sterile F1 hybrid *V.* × *bavarica* and *V. riviniana* or *V. reichenbachiana* but this has not been proved for British material. However here they have been called *V.* × *bavarica* and whilst few records have been made they occur in scattered localities on calcareous or neutral soils in woodland edge habitats, both putative parents are usually found nearby.

There is an unlocalised record (Stace, *et al.*, 2003) attributed to Whellan and Bunker (1948) but this is an error.

Viola canina L. ssp. **canina**   Heath Dog-violet

Eurosiberian-Boreo-temperate element.

This species is found on both acid and alkaline substrates on heaths, coastal sand dunes and stony riversides and lake shores (BH8, 10, 19) throughout the British Isles.

Very rare (3). In northern Lancashire it occurs on the sand dunes at Lytham St Anne's (SD32I, N, SD33A) where formerly it was more widespread and may now be confined to tetrads SD33A and SD32I. It was also recorded from sandy peat at Hawes Water (Wheldon and Wilson, 1907). *Viola canina* declined considerably after 1950 ('New Atlas') but 'Local Change' did not note further decline after 1987.

Viola canina × **V. riviniana** (**V.** × **intersita** Beck)

This sterile hybrid is widespread in Europe and occurs occasionally in the British Isles.

In northern Lancashire it was found on the sand dunes at Ansdell (Whellan and Bunker, 1948).

Viola palustris L. ssp. **palustris**   Marsh Violet

European Boreo-temperate element.

This is a plant of wet heaths, marshes and hill flushes (BH11, 14) and is found in much of the British Isles but very rarely in south-eastern England and central Ireland.

Frequent (150). In northern Lancashire it is particularly characteristic of marshes and flushes in and around the Forest of Bowland and in the north of the area. Its distribution in northern Lancashire is stable but losses in south-eastern England and central Ireland have taken place since 1950 ('New Atlas') and this decline is continuing in Britain ('Local Change').

Viola tricolor L. ssp. tricolor   Wild Pansy

European Temperate element.

This subspecies is an annual weed of cultivated and waste ground (BH4) and occurs throughout the British Isles.

Occasional (64). In northern Lancashire it was found scattered throughout VC 60 but there are few post 1987 records indicating a massive, recent decline in its distribution and frequency. It could now be very rare. A similar decline was noted by the 'New Atlas' but not by 'Local Change'.

Viola tricolor L. ssp. curtisii (E. Forst.) Syme

Suboceanic Temperate element.

This is a perennial herb found on sand dunes and coastal grassland (BH19) around many coasts of the British Isles.

Very rare (4). In northern Lancashire it is found on the sand dunes at Lytham St Anne's (SD32I, N, SD33A) where it is often abundant and until the building of the power station it was found on sandy ground at Heysham (SD45E). The 'New Atlas' reported some losses nationally, probably due to the continuing development of coastal resorts.

Viola × wittrockiana Gams ex Kappert   Garden Pansy

Neophyte. This is probably derived from *Viola tricolor* × *V. arvensis* and has been cultivated in Britain since 1816. It was first recorded in the wild in 1927 and occurs in waste places in many parts of the British Isles.

Rare (6). Livermore and Livermore (1990a, 1991) recorded it in five localities in Lancaster District and Abbott (2005) recorded it from tetrad SD74G.

Viola arvensis Murray   Field Pansy

An archaeophyte with a Eurosiberian Temperate distribution.

This is an annual of cultivated and waste ground (BH4) that occurs in much of the British Isles. It is however absent from many hilly and mountainous areas.

Frequent (91). In northern Lancashire it is found in most western areas of VC 60 where its distribution is stable. In the British Isles the 'New Atlas' reported a decline in western Scotland and in central and western Ireland. 'Local Change' noted no further decline.

LINACEAE   FLAX FAMILY

Linum bienne Mill.   Pale Flax

Mediterranean-Atlantic element but a neophyte in northern Lancashire.

Pale Flax is a native in grassy places, field margins and roadsides etc. in southern Britain and Ireland, especially in south-western England. However it also occurs as a casual in ruderal habitats elsewhere.

Very rare (1). This was found on tipped soil in a garden at Blackpool (SD34E) in 1968 (E.J.H.). The record in the 'New Atlas' for the 10km square SD53 is probably an error.

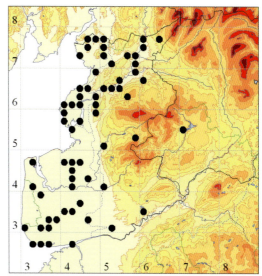

Viola tricolor ssp. *tricolor*

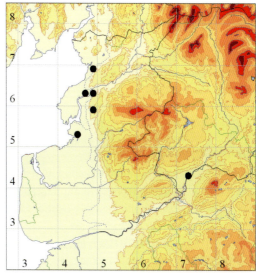

Viola × wittrockiana

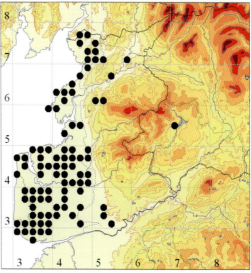

Viola arvensis

Linum usitatissimum L.   Flax

Neophyte. Flax was cultivated in Britain by 1240 and was known from the wild by 1632. It was widely used for its fibre but in recent years it has been planted for linseed oil. It is found throughout the British Isles but it is rare in northern England, Scotland, Ireland and much of Wales.

Rare (11). Flax was grown widely in northern Lancashire in the eighteenth century but as cotton became a more important fibre Flax growing declined. Today Flax is not grown in the area for its fibre but a little is cultivated for linseed oil. In northern Lancashire it was first recorded from Aldcliffe (Fielding, MS) and near Holden Clough, Bolton-by-Bowland (Milne-Redhead, 1870s) whilst Wheldon and Wilson (1907) recorded it from a further six localities. Since 1964 it has been found in a few scattered places.

[**Linum perenne** L.   Perennial Flax

Circumpolar Boreo-temperate element.

Perennial Flax is found on calcareous grassland mostly in eastern England with a few localities west of the Pennines in Cumbria and south-western Scotland. In Britain only the endemic ssp. *anglicum* (Mill.) Ockendon is found.

Very rare (1). In northern Lancashire Ashfield (1860) reported it from stubble fields near Stalmine and in 2000 (C.B.W.) it was found near the salt marsh at Warton (SD47R). Both habitats are very unlikely for *L. perenne* and until confirmed for northern Lancashire these records probably refer to *L. usitatissimum*, which was grown throughout the area.]

Linum catharticum L.   Fairy Flax

European Temperate element. It is also found in North America.

This is a small annual or biennial of dry, infertile calcareous substrates as well as in flushed sites with generally neutral soils (BH7, 11). It is found throughout the British Isles.

Frequent (169). Whilst Fairy Flax is found throughout northern Lancashire it seems to be more frequent in some parts of the area than in others, e.g. in Lancashire VC 64 and in the northwest of the area.

Radiola linoides Roth   Allseed

European Temperate element.

This is a small inconspicuous annual of damp, bare, infertile ground on acidic soils in grassland and on heaths (BH10). Allseed was found on heaths throughout the country but the 'New Atlas' shows recent records are all coastal.

Extinct, formerly very rare. To the north of the R. Lune a series of heaths on common land extended from Over Kellet to near Kirkby Lonsdale. These were mostly enclosed and drained by the middle of the nineteenth century and although the distinctive mosaic of wet and dry heath was lost, fragments remained until the early twentieth century and even today some fragments remain in Whittington. Amongst the characteristic species found on the heaths was *R. linoides* and this occurred on Arkholme Moor (SD57Q) in 1900 (A.W.) and in Lord's Lot Wood, Over Kellet (SD57K) a few years later (Wilson, 1947-49).

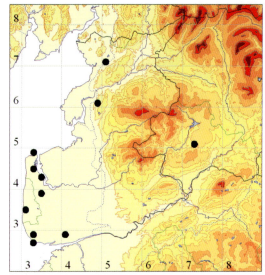
Linum usitatissimum

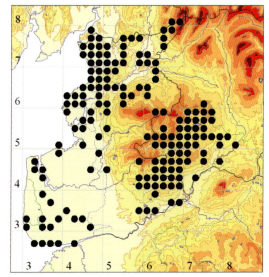
Linum catharticum

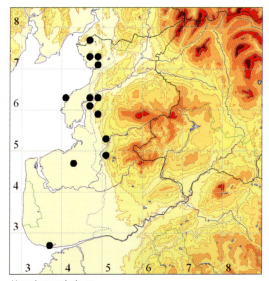
Hypericum calycinum

HYPERICACEAE   ST JOHN'S-WORT FAMILY

Hypericum calycinum L.   Rose-of-Sharon

Neophyte. This was introduced into Britain in 1676 but it was not recorded from the wild until 1809. It is a native of south-eastern Bulgaria and Turkey. All naturalised plants appear to be derived from the original introduction but despite poor seed production it is found throughout the British Isles, especially in southern England.

Rare (13). In northern Lancashire *H. calycinum* was first recorded from Warton Crag (SD47W) in 1973 (L.A.L.). Since then it has been found in scattered localities in VC 60.

Hypericum forrestii (Chitt.) N. Robson   Forrest's Tutsan

Neophyte. *H. forrestii* is a native of China, Assam and Burma and has been cultivated in Britain since 1906. It was recorded in the wild in 1987 and today it is found in scattered localities in Britain. However it is easily confused with the garden hybrid *H.* 'Hidcote' and possibly other garden plants many of which were introduced at about the same time.

Very rare (1) a single plant of what is believed to be this species was found on a steep roadside bank in Tatham (SD66M) in 2008 (E.F.G.).

[Hypericum 'Hidcote'

Neophyte. This shrub is a semi-evergreen, sterile cultivar of unknown, probably hybrid origin. It is commonly mass-planted in public places and is easily confused with other garden species, hybrids and cultivars. Consequently it is uncertain when it was first found or how widespread it is in the wild.

In northern Lancashire it was recorded from Lancaster (SD46R) in 2006 (Anon) where it was planted. It is likely to escape from amenity plantings throughout the area.]

Hypericum androsaemum L.   Tutsan

Submediterranean-Subatlantic element.

This is a shrub of shaded situations in woodlands and hedgerows (BH1, 3) but it is also widely cultivated and escapes into the wild making it difficult to define its native distribution.

Occasional (50). In northern Lancashire most records are from the northern half of VC 60 with a few scattered localities elsewhere. It is probably native in at least some woodlands and although it seems to have been lost from some woodlands recorded by Wheldon and Wilson (1907) it has considerably expanded its range in northern VC 60. At least some of this expansion is due to garden escapes and this reflects the national situation.

Hypericum hircinum L.   Stinking Tutsan

Neophyte. *H. hircinum* was grown in Britain by 1640 and was recorded in the wild by 1856. It is a native of the Mediterranean region and most records are from the southern half of the British Isles.

In northern Lancashire there is an unlocalised, unattributed post 1950 record for the 10km square SD47 (B.R.C.).

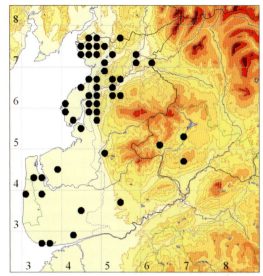
Hypericum androsaemum

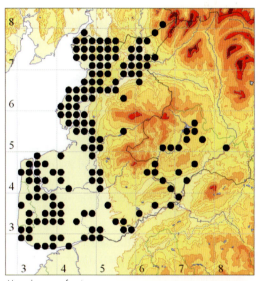
Hypericum perforatum

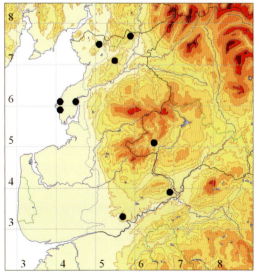
Hypericum × desetangsii

Hypericum xylosteifolium (Spach) N. Robson   Turkish Tutsan

Neophyte. This species was introduced into cultivation in Britain c. 1870 and first recorded in the wild from Eaves Wood, Silverdale in 1978 ('New Atlas' CD). Since then it has been found in a few other localities in England. It is a native of north-eastern Turkey and the Caucasus.

Very rare (1). The record from Eaves Wood (SD47S) is from a boundary hedge and probably dates from nineteenth century amenity planting (Peter, 1994). It also occurs in the nearby woods around Burton Well.

Hypericum perforatum L.   Perforate St John's-wort

Eurosiberian Southern-temperate element.

This occurs in woodland edge habitats, grasslands, hedgerows and grassy banks (BH3, 7) throughout most of the British Isles.

Frequent (161). It occurs in most of northern Lancashire but it is rare or absent in some areas. There has been no change in its distribution locally or nationally although it apparently spread along railways into Scotland during the twentieth century.

Hypericum perforatum × H. maculatum
(H. × desetangsii Lamotte)   Des Etangs' St John's-wort

Widespread in Europe.

There is a continuous series of intermediates between *H. perforatum* and *H. maculatum* often making identification of the hybrid between them very difficult. However *H. × desetangsii* has been found in most parts of England, Wales and southern Scotland as well as very rarely in Ireland.

Rare (9). In northern Lancashire it was first recognised as occurring in VC 60 from Caton by Wheldon and Wilson (1925) and since 1964 it has been found scattered in the north of VC 60 and in the Ribble and Hodder valleys. However it is probably under recorded and some records for *H. maculatum* may be this.

Hypericum maculatum Cranz
ssp. **obtusiusculum** (Tourlet) Hayek   Imperforate St John's-wort

Suboceanic Temperate element.

This occurs in woodland edge and occasionally in ruderal habitats (BH1, 3, 16) throughout most of the British Isles.

Occasional (24). In northern Lancashire it is found in the north of VC 60, near the mouth of the R. Wyre and very rarely in the Ribble and Hodder valleys. Imperforate St John's-wort's occurrence on the Wyre estuary needs confirmation as it may have been recorded erroneously. It is not thought that there has been any change in its distribution locally or nationally.

Hypericum tetrapterum Fr.   Square-stalked St John's-wort

European Temperate element.

This is found in nutrient rich, wet habitats (BH11) throughout most of the British Isles.

Frequent (206). It also occurs throughout northern Lancashire. There has been no change in its distribution locally or nationally up to 1987 ('New Atlas') but 'Local Change' reports a significant increase since 1987.

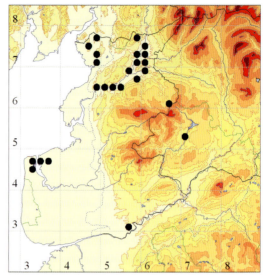

Hypericum maculatum

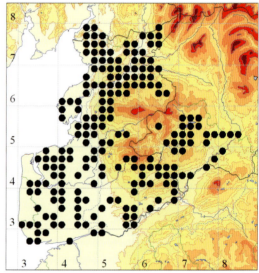

Hypericum tetrapterum

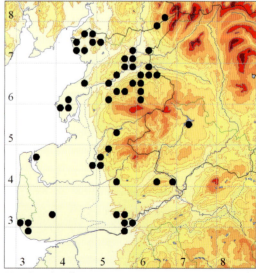

Hypericum humifusum

Hypericum humifusum L.   Trailing St John's-wort

European Temperate element.

This is found in well-drained habitats on heaths and in grassy places, usually on neutral or acid soils (BH3), but it is rarely abundant and often ephemeral in its appearance at any one site. It is found throughout the British Isles.

Occasional (51). It is found throughout northern Lancashire, especially in the north and in parts of Bowland. It is possibly overlooked but it is not thought its distribution has changed locally. Since 1950 it has declined in England and Scotland but 'Local Change' did not note further decline since 1987.

Hypericum pulchrum L.   Slender St John's-wort

Suboceanic Temperate element.

This is found on heaths and in wood margins on neutral to acid soils (BH3, 10, 16) throughout the British Isles.

Frequent (107). In northern Lancashire it is found mostly in the north and east of the area. There has been no change in its distribution locally although since 1950 it has declined in central England while 'Local Change' noted no further decline since 1987.

Hypericum hirsutum L.   Hairy St John's-wort

Eurosiberian Temperate element.

H. hirsutum is found on neutral to calcareous soils in woodland edge, scrub and rough grassland habitats (BH3, 6, 7) in England, eastern and northern Wales, eastern and central Scotland and very rarely in eastern Ireland.

Occasional (55). In northern Lancashire most records are from the north of the area and in the Ribble and Hodder valleys. There has been no change in its distribution locally or nationally.

Hypericum montanum L.   Pale St John's-wort

European Temperate element.

This is almost confined to woodland edge and rough grassland habitats (BH1, 3) on calcareous soils in England and Wales.

Rare (9). In northern Lancashire it is restricted to limestone soils around Morecambe Bay, on Dalton Crags and on calcareous soils at Heysham. There has been no change in its distribution locally but the 'New Atlas' reported losses nationally, mostly before 1930.

Hypericum elodes L.   Marsh St John's-wort

Oceanic Temperate element.

This is found on wet, nutrient poor habitats (BH11) mostly in the west of the British Isles.

Extinct. In northern Lancashire *H. elodes* was always very rare. It was recorded from Morecambe between 1850 and 1859 (LIV), Lancaster Moor in 1862 (W. H., LIV), Ribbleton Moor, Preston where it may have persisted until the end of the nineteenth century and on a boggy hillside near Scorton (France, 1931). The site was on Nicky Nook in a flush to the northeast of The Tarn, Nether Wyresdale (SD54E; C.F. & N.J.S.) where it may have persisted until at least the 1940s. There is also a record from the Trough of Bowland in Lancashire VC 64 (Anon, 1891). Nationally it has declined considerably over the last 150 years but 'Local Change' does not note further decline since 1987.

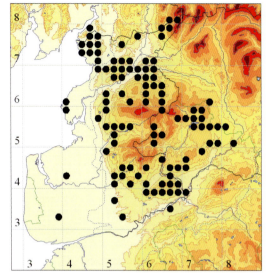
Hypericum pulchrum

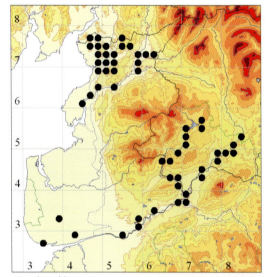
Hypericum hirsutum

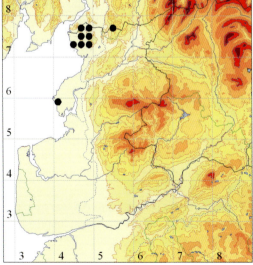
Hypericum montanum

[**Hypericum patulum** Thunb.

This was recorded from by the R. Lune, Arkholme-with-Cawood (SD57W) in 1986 (J.M.N.) but it is very rare in cultivation and there are no confirmed records from the wild. It is likely to be *H. forrestii* (Chitt.) N. Robson or *H.* 'Hidcote' – a sterile cultivar of unknown, probably hybrid origin (Stace, 1997; Clement and Foster, 1994).]

GERANIACEAE   CRANE'S-BILL FAMILY

Geranium endressii J. Gay   French Crane's-bill

Neophyte. French Crane's-bill has a very restricted native distribution in the Pyrenees. It was introduced into Britain in 1812 and has been recorded in the wild since 1906. However it is easily confused with forms of *G. × oxonianum*. Today *G. endressii* is found as a garden escape in ruderal habitats throughout the British Isles.

Occasional (28). It was first recorded in northern Lancashire from an abandoned garden in Fulwood (SD53G) in 1964 (E.H.). Today it is found in scattered localities in the area but mostly in VC 60.

Geranium endressii × G. versicolor (G. × oxonianum Yeo)
Druce's Crane's-bill

Neophyte. This is a hybrid of garden origin, often confused with *G. endressii*. It was first cultivated in Britain in 1932 and it has been found in the wild since 1954. It is morphologically variable with several cultivars. It is widely grown in gardens from which it readily escapes into ruderal habitats. It is found throughout the British Isles.

Rare (18). *G. × oxonianum* was first recognised in northern Lancashire from Silverdale (SD47) in 1962 (A.E.R.). Today it is found in scattered localities throughout the area. It is probably under recorded with at least some records for *G. endressii* belonging here.

Geranium versicolor L.   Pencilled Crane's-bill

Neophyte. This is a native of Italy, Sicily and the southern Balkans. It was cultivated in Britain by 1629 and has been known in the wild since 1820. It is a frequent garden escape in southern Britain, especially in south-western England, but occurs occasionally in Scotland and Ireland.

Very rare (3). In northern Lancashire it was found at Silverdale (SD47M) in 1979 but not since (C.B.W.), Nether Kellet (SD56D) in 1991 (Lancashire Wildlife Trust roadside verge survey) and Pilling (SD34Y) in 1999 (C.J.B.).

[**Geranium rotundifolium** L.   Round-leaved Crane's-bill

Eurosiberian Southern-temperate element but a neophyte in northern Lancashire. This is an annual of hedgerows, roadside banks and wall-tops, especially close to the sea. It is found as a native in southern England, southern Wales and south-eastern Ireland but as an introduction elsewhere.

The only northern Lancashire record was from Lytham Churchyard (SD32T; Ashfield, 1858). As it has never been found again some doubt exists as to whether this was a correct identification.]

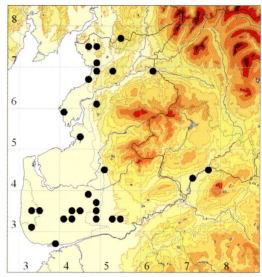
Geranium endressii

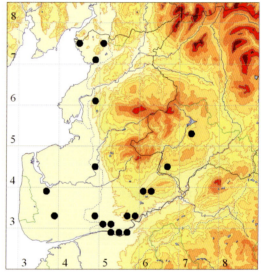
Geranium × oxonianum

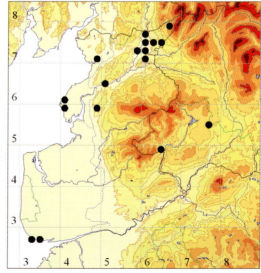
Geranium sylvaticum

Geranium sylvaticum L.   Wood Crane's-bill

Eurosiberian Boreal-montane element.

This is a characteristic herb of northern hay meadows (BH6, 16) and is found in northern England and Scotland with a few localities in Wales and Northern Ireland. It also occurs as an introduction in a few localities elsewhere.

Occasional (17). In northern Lancashire Wood Crane's-bill occurs in ruderal habitats as well as grasslands and roadside verges. Most records are from the northeast of the area but as a grassland species it has declined over the last 100 years and is now very rare. The 'New Atlas' reported some decline in its distribution and whilst overall 'Local Change' did not note significant decline, some erosion on the edges of its distribution was noted.

Geranium pratense L.   Meadow Crane's-bill

Eurasian Boreo-temperate element.

This is a perennial herb of meadows and grassland on roadsides, railway banks and stream sides (BH6) and occurs as a native species in England, Wales and Scotland, but it also occurs as an introduction in many places and in Ireland.

Frequent (188). In northern Lancashire Meadow Crane's-bill has a somewhat disjunct distribution occurring in the north of the area, in the Ribble and Hodder valleys and perhaps as an introduction in many western areas. Over the last 100 years the distribution of *G. pratense* has increased considerably with most localities in the west of northern Lancashire being new. A similar increase is reported nationally.

Geranium sanguineum L.   Bloody Crane's-bill

European Temperate element.

Bloody Crane's-bill is a perennial herb of base-rich grasslands and sand dunes (BH7, 16, 19) and occurs largely as a coastal plant. However it is also found on limestone pavements and chalk grassland. It is extensively grown in gardens from where it escapes into the wild. It is thought that most inland records from midland and southern England are introductions.

Occasional (21). In northern Lancashire most records are from limestone areas or sandy ground by the sea with only a few introduced inland localities. Whilst introductions in coastal localities are possible it is felt that most are derived from native populations. Locally populations appear largely stable but nationally Bloody Crane's-bill has become more frequent since 1962, mostly as a garden escape ('New Atlas', 'Local Change').

Geranium columbinum L.   Long-stalked Crane's-bill

European Temperate element.

This is an annual of dry grasslands and scrub usually on calcareous soils (BH3, 7). It is found particularly frequently in south-western Britain and southern Ireland but it occurs as far north as northern Scotland.

Rare (14). In northern Lancashire Long-stalked Crane's-bill is confined to the limestone in the northwest of the area. Its distribution is stable locally but nationally there was a widespread decline in northern and south-eastern England since 1950 ('New Atlas'), however further losses since 1987 were not reported by 'Local Change'.

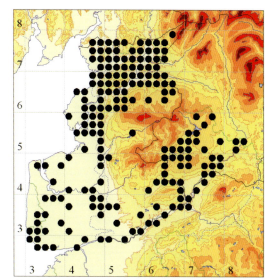
Geranium pratense

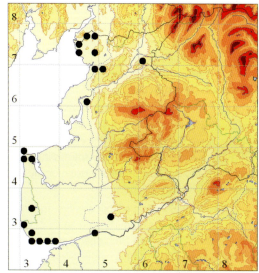
Geranium sanguineum

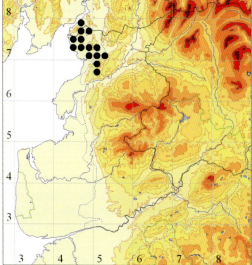
Geranium columbinum

Geranium dissectum L.   Cut-leaved Crane's-bill

Archaeophyte with a European Southern-temperate distribution.

This is an annual of grassland, hedge-banks, waste ground and as a weed of cultivated ground (BH3, 4). It is found throughout the British Isles although it is rare in north-western Scotland.

Frequent (164). In northern Lancashire *G. dissectum* is a common species of ruderal habitats in western areas with a few localities further east, especially in the Ribble and Hodder valleys. Whilst its distribution locally appears stable, nationally both the 'New Atlas' and 'Local Change' report an extension of its range particularly towards the north of Britain.

Geranium ibericum Cav. × **G. platypetalum** Fisch. & C.A. Mey.
(**G. × magnificum** Hyl.)   Purple Crane's-bill

Neophyte. This is a sterile hybrid of garden origin where both parents are natives of the Caucasus. Its showy flowers and ground-covering abilities make this a popular garden plant and wild populations are derived from garden throw-outs. It was first recorded in the wild in 1932 and today it is recorded from scattered localities in Britain.

Occasional (16). In northern Lancashire it was first recorded from Lytham St Anne's (SD32N) in the 1960s (A.E.R.) and today it continues to be found in Lytham St Anne's but it also occurs in the Lancaster area.

Geranium pyrenaicum Burm.f.   Hedgerow Crane's-bill

Neophyte. *G. pyrenaicum* is a native of the mountains of southern Europe and south-western Asia but it spread rapidly in western and central Europe in the eighteenth and nineteenth centuries. It was first recorded in Britain in 1762 and today it is a common species in much of southern Britain and eastern Ireland but it occurs more occasionally elsewhere as far north as the Moray Firth in Scotland.

Rare (13). Hedgerow Crane's-bill was first found in northern Lancashire at Lytham in 1833 (Fielding MS) and again c. 1840 (Riddelsdall, 1902). Subsequent records were from near Garstang in 1882 (A.W.; YRK), Silverdale in 1888 (Preston Scientific Society; LIV) and the Chipping area in 1917 (T.H. Timbrill school holiday collection seen by E.F.G., 2004), which is probably the same locality in Bowland-with-Leagram where it still occurs today. Other post 1964 records for *G. pyrenaicum* are in scattered localities in VC 60.

Geranium pusillum L.   Small-flowered Crane's-bill

Eurosiberian Temperate element.

This is an annual of cultivated ground and dry open habitats in grassland, roadsides and waste places (BH3). It is found throughout the British Isles but especially in south-eastern and eastern Britain.

Rare (9). Old records for *G. pusillum* were from between Caton and Halton and near Bolton-le-Sands and Lytham (Wheldon and Wilson, 1907). There were also records from Bispham in 1902 (St Michael's School) and Silverdale in 1915 (A.J.C.; LSA). Post 1964 records are from the northwest of the area and Fylde coastal areas. Whilst *G. pusillum* remains rare in northern Lancashire its distribution seems stable. However it is difficult to distinguish from *G. molle* and it may be under recorded. Nationally it may be extending its range ('Local Change').

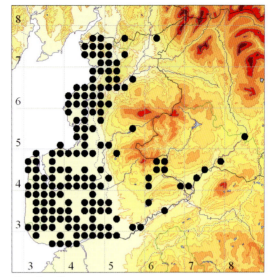
Geranium dissectum

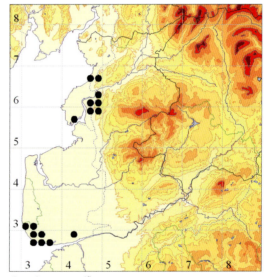
Geranium × magnificum

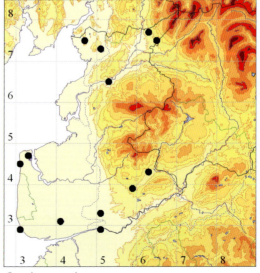
Geranium pyrenaicum

Geranium molle L.   Dove's-foot Crane's-bill

European Southern-temperate element.

This is an annual found in a variety of open habitats (BH3, 4) in generally lowland areas of the British Isles.

Frequent (138). Dove's-foot Crane's-bill is found throughout northern Lancashire but most records are from coastal localities in VC 60. Its distribution locally and nationally remains unchanged.

Geranium macrorrhizum L.   Rock Crane's-bill

Neophyte. This is a native of the mountains of southern Europe and was introduced into Britain by 1576. It is a popular garden plant and has been known in the wild since 1835. Today it is found in scattered localities in Britain.

Very rare (4). In northern Lancashire this was first found near Higher Hodder Hotel (SD64V) in 1964 (A.H.). It was later found from roadsides and waste ground at Lancaster (SD46V, W; Livermore and Livermore, 1987) and Hornby-with-Farleton (SD56Y) in 1991 (Lancashire Wildlife Trust roadside verge survey).

Geranium lucidum L.   Shining Crane's-bill

Submediterranean-Subatlantic element.

This is an annual of roadside banks, walls and rock outcrops usually on limestone (BH3, 16). It is found in most parts of the British Isles but it is rare or absent from most of highland and northern Scotland.

Frequent (84). Shining Crane's-bill is found throughout northern Lancashire but it is especially common on limestone in the northwest of the area and in the vicinity of Lytham St Anne's. This appears to have become much more common and widespread in northern Lancashire over the last 100 years reflecting the national situation.

Geranium robertianum L. ssp. **robertianum**   Herb-Robert

European Temperate element.

Herb-Robert is a shade tolerant annual or biennial herb found in a variety of woodland, woodland edge and waste ground habitats (BH1, 16). It is found throughout the British Isles.

Very common (377). This is found throughout northern Lancashire except on the fells. There has been no change in its distribution locally or nationally.

Geranium robertianum L. ssp. **maritimum** (Bab.) H.G. Baker

This subspecies has an oceanic distribution occurring along Atlantic coasts from Madeira to Norway. There are scattered records from the coasts of the British Isles although it is mostly absent from North Sea coasts of England and Scotland (Perring, 1968). It is characteristically found on stable shingle particularly at the rear of fringing beaches (Rich and Jermy, 1998).

Very rare (5). This was recorded in northern Lancashire from Bare c. 1900 (F.A.L. in Wheldon and Wilson 1907) and not far away on shingle at Hest Bank (SD46M) in 1947 (J.N.F.; LIV). Livermore and Livermore (1987) recorded it from tetrads SD47R, T, 56Z and 57D some of which refer to inland localities. A further inland record was from Lundsfield Quarry, Carnforth (SD46Z) along with other coastal species in 1980 (E.F.G.).

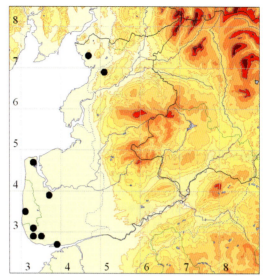
Geranium pusillum

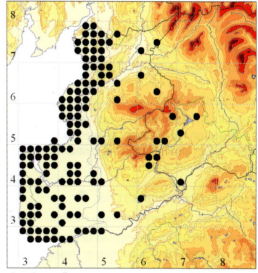
Geranium molle

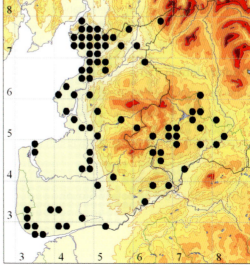
Geranium lucidum

Epilobium hirsutum × E. ciliatum (E. × novae-civitatis Smejkal)

This hybrid has been found in a few places in Britain but it is possibly overlooked.

Very rare (1). The only record from northern Lancashire is from a car park in Preston (SD52J) in 2005 (M.W.).

Epilobium parviflorum Schreb.   Hoary Willowherb

European Temperate element.

This willowherb is found in marshy and wet places but occasionally also occurs in drier places in disturbed habitats and on waste ground (BH11). It is found throughout the British Isles but it is rare or absent in many upland areas, especially in Scotland.

Frequent (155). Hoary Willowherb is found scattered throughout northern Lancashire. Its distribution is stable locally and whilst the 'New Atlas' reported no change in its distribution nationally 'Local Change' noted an increase.

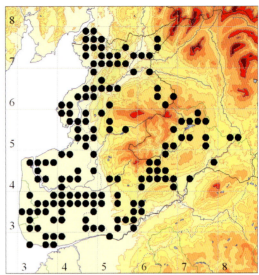
Epilobium parviflorum

Epilobium parviflorum × E. montanum (E. × limosum Schur)

This is one of the commonest willowherb hybrids and is found in scattered localities in the British Isles.

Very rare (1). This was found amongst shrubs at St Martin's College, Lancaster (SD46V) in 1997 (G.K.). It is probably overlooked.

Epilobium parviflorum × E. roseum (E. × persicinum Rchb.)

A rare hybrid found in scattered localities in the British Isles.

Very rare (1). In northern Lancashire this hybrid was found in a shrub border with the parents at Lancaster (SD46V) in 1995 (G.K.).

Epilobium parviflorum × E. palustre (E. × rivulare Wahlenb.)

Another willowherb hybrid found in scattered localities in the British Isles.

Very rare (2). In northern Lancashire this was found on Robert Hall Moor, Tatham (SD66J) in 1972 (J.M.N.) and in a marshy field at Hest Bank (SD46T) in 1998 (E.F.G.).

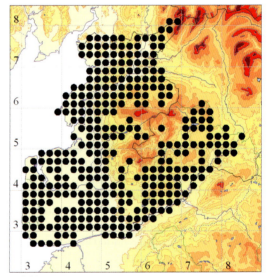
Epilobium montanum

Epilobium montanum L.   Broad-leaved Willowherb

European Temperate element.

This common species is found in a variety of wood margin and ruderal habitats (BH3, 16, 17) throughout the British Isles.

Common (341). *E. montanum* is found in most parts of northern Lancashire except on the Bowland fells. There has been no change in its distribution locally or nationally.

Epilobium montanum × E. obscurum (E. × aggregatum Čelak.)

This hybrid is found throughout the British Isles.

Very rare (1). The only record in northern Lancashire is from Gisburn Forest (SD75N; Abbott, 2005).

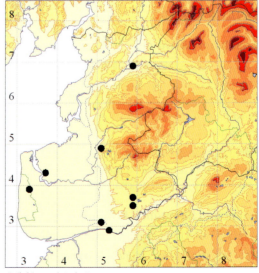
Epilobium × interjectum

Epilobium montanum × E. roseum (E. × heterocaule Borbás)

E. × heterocaule has been found in scattered localities in the British Isles.

Very rare (3). In northern Lancashire this hybrid was found in Fulwood (SD53F) in 1965 (E.H.), St Martin's College, Lancaster (SD46V) in 1997 (G.K.) and in Preston (SD52J) in 2005 (M.W.).

Epilobium montanum × E. ciliatum (E. × interjectum Smejkal)

This is a common hybrid between a native and an introduced species found in disturbed ground throughout the British Isles.

Rare (8). This was first recorded in northern Lancashire from a garden at Hornby (SD56Z) in 1987 (J.M.N.). It is found today in scattered localities in VC 60.

Epilobium montanum × E. palustre (E. × montaniforme Knaf ex Čelak.)

This is a rare hybrid found in a few places in Britain.

Very rare (1). In northern Lancashire this was reported from a river bank in the Nether Burrow and Wittington area (SD67C; Livermore and Livermore, 1987).

Epilobium tetragonum L.   Square-stalked Willowherb

Eurosiberian Temperate element.

This perennial herb is found in a variety of ruderal and wasteland habitats (BH3, 17) and is found in much of England, except the northwest and in Wales. It occurs as an introduction in Ireland.

Very rare (2). Although this is a distinctive species with long seed pods it has often been recorded in error for other species. In particular Livermore and Livermore (1987) published a map showing it to be frequent in Lancaster District. It is believed all the records are errors but for what species is unknown. However verified records have been made for this species in Preston (SD52J) in 2005 (M.W.) and from the riverside path (on tipped land) on Lea Marsh (SD42Z) in 2007 (E.F.G.). As these are the first records for *E. tetragonum* north of the R. Ribble it is suggested that this species is spreading northwards. 'Local Change' confirms this extension of its distribution in Britain since 1987.

Epilobium obscurum Schreb.   Short-fruited Willowherb

European Temperate element.

Short-fruited Willowherb is found in wet places in woodland edge habitats, on waste ground and in marshy places (BH11, 14) throughout the British Isles.

Frequent (190). *E. obscurum* is found throughout northern Lancashire but may be overlooked by some observers. This may account for why Wheldon and Wilson (1907) knew it from only nine localities. On the other hand the 'New Atlas' reported losses from parts of eastern England yet 'Local Change' noted an increase since 1987. This conflicting evidence on its status both locally and nationally suggests that observers find *E. obscurum* difficult to recognise and any changes noted in its distribution are probably unreliable.

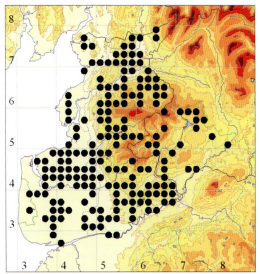

Epilobium obscurum

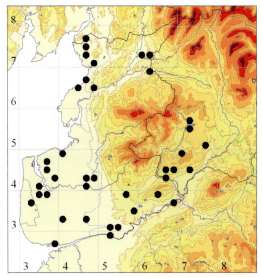

Epilobium roseum

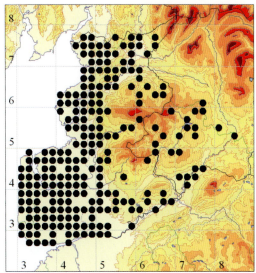

Epilobium ciliatum

Epilobium obscurum × E. ciliatum
(**E. × vicinum** Smejkal)

This is a perennial herb of disturbed ground first found in Surrey in 1934. It is found throughout the British Isles but it is often overlooked.

Very rare (3). This was first recorded in northern Lancashire from Lancaster in 1987 (SD46V; Livermore and Livermore, 1987) and again in 1997 (G.K.). It was also recorded from Brockholes Quarry, Preston (SD53V) in 2005 (P.H.S. & M.W.) and probably this from old railway ballast at Great Plumpton (SD33W) with both parents in 2010 (E.F.G.). It is likely to be under recorded.

Epilobium roseum Schreb.   Pale Willowherb

Eurosiberian Temperate element.

A perennial herb of damp disturbed places often in woodland edge habitats (BH1, 3, 14, 17). It is found in many parts of the British Isles but generally avoids upland areas.

Occasional (39). Pale Willowherb is found in scattered localities in northern Lancashire but its absence from much of northern and western Bowland may be because recorders have over-looked it. This species was unknown to Wheldon and Wilson (1907) although Watson (1883) had recorded it from VC 60. The 'New Atlas' reported losses but these were not confirmed by 'Local Change'. It appears that this is another willowherb, which has often been overlooked or wrongly identified, making it difficult to know if its distribution has changed.

Epilobium roseum × E. ciliatum
(**E. × nutantiflorum** Smejkal)

This hybrid has been found in a few localities in Britain.

Very rare (1). In northern Lancashire a single plant was found in a corner of a playing field at Lancaster (SD46V) in 1997 (G.K.).

Epilobium ciliatum Raf.   American Willowherb

Neophyte. American Willowherb is a native of North America but widely naturalised in central and northern Europe.

It was first collected in Britain in 1891 but remained unrecognised until the 1930s. It is found in disturbed ground and ruderal habitats, especially in urban areas. The 'New Atlas' reports a dramatic extension of its range since 1962 and today it occurs throughout the British Isles.

Common (242). *E. ciliatum* was first found in northern Lancashire on a tip at Kirkham (SD43G) in 1964 (E.H. & J.H.). It is found throughout the area but it is especially common in lowland western areas.

Epilobium palustre L.   Marsh Willowherb

Circumpolar Boreo-temperate element.

This is a perennial herb of wet acidic sites (BH11) both in lowland and upland areas throughout most of the British Isles.

Common (307). Marsh Willowherb is found throughout northern Lancashire where its distribution remains unchanged. However the 'New Atlas' reported a decline in south-eastern England but further decline was not noted by 'Local Change'.

Epilobium alsinifolium Vill.   Chickweed Willowherb

European Arctic-montane element.

This small plant is found in mountain flushes (BH11, 16) in England, Wales and Scotland with a single Irish record.

Extinct. The only record for this willowherb in northern Lancashire was from a calcareous flush at c. 580m (1900ft) on Green Hill, Leck (SD68V) in 1972 (E.F.G. & B.D.W.). In 2000 the flush had dried up and *E. alsinifolium* was no longer present.

Epilobium brunnescens (Cockayne) P.H. Raven & Engelhorn   New Zealand Willowherb

Neophyte. This is a native of New Zealand and was first recorded in the wild in Britain in Edinburgh in 1904. From the 1930s it spread rapidly and today it is found mostly in upland parts of northern and western areas of the British Isles. It is characteristic of wet banks, flushes and stony areas.

Frequent (93). It is not known when this species became established in northern Lancashire. There is an unlocalised specimen at OXF from the 10km square SD44 collected in the 1930s (H.E.B.) and by the time the *Atlas of the British Flora* was published (Perring and Walters, 1962) it was widespread in the area. Today it is found commonly in the upland areas of Bowland and Leck with occasional records elsewhere.

Chamerion angustifolium (L.) Holub Rosebay Willowherb

Circumpolar Boreo-temperate element.

This is a vigorous perennial herb that formerly occurred in upland areas of Britain on rock ledges and cliffs but which today is often found in large patches on waste ground, in woodland edge habitats and on railway banks. It particularly favours areas of burnt ground (BH3, 17). In the early nineteenth century this was a rare species but it is now common throughout the British Isles.

Very common (419) throughout northern Lancashire. The spread of this species was already noticeable by 1907 when Wheldon and Wilson recorded it from about 25 sites. Since then its spread has been spectacular reflecting the national situation.

Ludwigia grandiflora (Michaux) Greuter & Burdet   Water Primrose

Neophyte. This is a native of South America and although a tropical species it is apparently frost hardy. It is established in a number of European countries where it has become a pest species. It was first recorded from London in 1999 and was established in ponds in Hampshire by 2002 (Clement, 2001).

Very rare (1). In northern Lancashire Water Primrose was found covering a pond in Carleton (SD34F) in 2007 (M.S.).

Oenothera L.   Evening-primroses

The peculiar breeding system within this genus gives rise to a confusing array of species and hybrids that are found in the British Isles today (Bowra, 1998). As a consequence the difficulties of naming individual plants has been a problem over at least the last 100 years. However Rostański (1982) published a paper that described the taxonomic complexity and provided details of the species and hybrids known in the British Isles at that time. In this paper reference was made to observations on the Lancashire and Sefton coast sand dunes dating back to the early nineteenth century. Rostański also provided a key to identify the species and hybrids and Bowra (1998) provided further information. In this account the taxonomy and nomenclature follows Stace (2010) and as far as possible older records have been reinterpreted in the light of recent publications.

Oenothera glazioviana P. Micheli ex Mart.

Large-flowered Evening-primrose

Neophyte. This is a native of North America and was first cultivated in Britain about 1858. It was recorded from the wild about 1866. It is a conspicuous plant of sand dunes but it is also increasingly frequent on waste ground and today occurs throughout England and Wales and more occasionally in Scotland and Ireland.

Occasional (66). The first records of Large-flowered Evening-primrose in northern Lancashire were from St Anne's in 1904, and in the period 1904–1908 Charles Bailey distributed material to several herbaria (Rostański, 1982). However by that time it was well established and abundant on the sand dunes (Bailey, 1907). Today O. glazioviana continues to be abundant on the sand dunes at Lytham St Anne's and elsewhere in coastal areas but it also occurs more occasionally inland on waste ground.

Oenothera glazioviana × O. biennis (**O. × fallax** Renner)

Intermediate Evening-primrose

This is a spontaneous hybrid between two introduced parents. It is morphologically variable and frequently occurs where O. biennis in particular is absent and may also occur as a garden escape. It is found on sand dunes and waste ground in England, Wales and more occasionally in Scotland and Ireland. It is probably very much under recorded particularly where hybrids are similar to O. biennis.

Rare (14). Charles Bailey distributed material of this hybrid to several herbaria and the earliest specimens from St Anne's appear to be dated 1901 (MANCH) although Rostański (1982) cites specimens dated 1907. However, as with O. glazioviana, it was probably well established by then. Today it is still found on the sand dunes and in other coastal localities as well as on waste ground inland. However it is felt that it is very much under recorded.

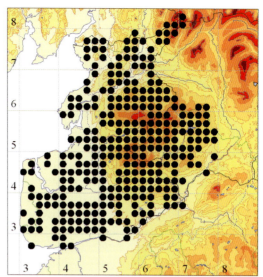

Epilobium palustre

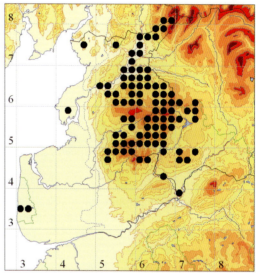

Epilobium brunnescens

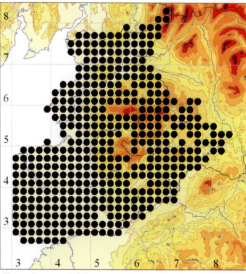

Chamerion angustifolium

Oenothera biennis L.   Common Evening-primrose

Neophyte. *O. biennis* was introduced from North America or from North America via Europe. It was cultivated in Britain by 1629 and was recorded in the wild by about 1650. It occurs in waste places and on sand dunes in England and more occasionally elsewhere.

Rare (10). This has always been rarer than *O. glazioviana* or *O. × fallax* but was nevertheless the first evening-primrose to be found in northern Lancashire having been collected from the sand dunes at St Anne's in 1898 (NMW). However this is long after it was first recorded in VC 59 when it was found on Crosby Marsh near Liverpool in 1801 (Savidge, *et al.*, 1963) and must surely have been introduced directly from North America with cargo imported into Liverpool. Today it is found on the sand dunes and in mostly coastal localities elsewhere in VC 60. Individual populations rarely last long and it appears to hybridise readily with *O. glazioviana* (Bowra, 1998). In recent years it seems new introductions are occurring as it escapes from gardens where it is often grown.

Oenothera stricta Ledeb. ex Link   Fragrant Evening-primrose

Neophyte. This is a native of Chile, was introduced into Britain in 1790 and was recorded in the wild in 1852. It does not hybridise with other *Oenothera* species and remains scarce. It is found in scattered localities, usually on sandy soils, in England and Wales and occasionally elsewhere.

Very rare (1). In northern Lancashire it was introduced as part of the landscaping works following refurbishment of the waste water treatment plant at Fairhaven (SD32I) in 1997 (C.F. & N.J.S.). The reasoning behind this introduction into a semi-natural habitat is unknown but it was still present in 2007 (E.F.G.) and had spread to nearby dunes (C.F. & N.J.S.).

Oenothera laciniata Hill   Cut-leaved Evening-primrose

Neophyte. This is a North American species with the earliest British record reported from the canal side at Ford in southern Lancashire (VC 59) in 1903 (Rostański, 1982). However it has not been recorded in the British Isles since 1928.

In northern Lancashire it was recorded from St Anne's in 1906 (C.B.; Wheldon and Wilson, 1907).

Oenothera rubricaulis Kleb.

Neophyte. Rostański (1982) regarded this as a native of sandy shores of rivers and lakes in eastern Europe but as a casual of sandy and ruderal areas elsewhere. There are few British records. Stace (2010) considers that it should be regarded as part of *O. biennis*.

Very rare (1). In northern Lancashire it was found at Lytham (SD32) in 1965 (A.E.R.; LIV).

Fuchsia magellanica Lam.   Fuchsia

Neophyte. Fuchsia is a native of Argentina and Chile and was introduced into Britain in 1788. It was first recorded from the wild in 1857 and today most records come from Ireland and western Britain where it is a common component of hedges. It is believed these hedge plants are the cultivar 'Riccartonii', which is sterile and apparently arose in a Scottish nursery before 1850.

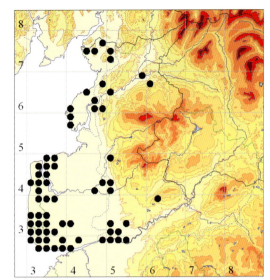

Oenothera glazioviana

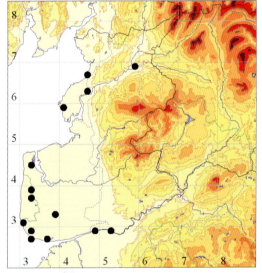

Oenothera × fallax

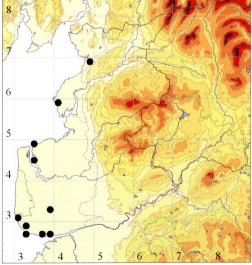

Oenothera biennis

Very rare (4). It is perhaps surprising that this is such a rare species in northern Lancashire. It does not seem to have been used in hedges and it was not recorded until 1968 (A.E.R.) when it was found on the sand dunes at Lytham St Anne's (SD32I). Other records are from Over Kellet (SD57F; Livermore and Livermore, 1987), Wyresdale Park, Nether Wyresdale (SD54E) in 1999 (E.F.G.) and from the site of the former Fleetwood Power Station (SD34I) in 2000 (C.C.).

Circaea lutetiana L.   Enchanter's-nightshade

European Temperate element.

This is a perennial herb found in moist, usually base-rich woodlands and woodland edge habitats (BH1) and more occasionally in ruderal habitats. In gardens Enchanter's-nightshade is a difficult plant to eradicate as it spreads through a network of underground rhizomes. It is found throughout the British Isles although it is rare in northern Scotland.

Frequent (224). In northern Lancashire Enchanter's-nightshade is found in woodlands throughout the area including western lowland areas of VC 60 where it may be a relic of former naturally wooded areas but it can also become established in ruderal habitats. There has been no change in its distribution locally or nationally.

Circaea lutetiana × C. alpina L. (C. × intermedia Ehrh.)
                                      Upland Enchanter's-nightshade

This is widespread in temperate Europe and it is found in upland wooded areas (BH1) of Britain and in the north of Ireland. This is a vigorous hybrid that probably arose shortly after the last glacial period when C. alpina was more frequent. Remarkably this sterile hybrid survives and spreads behaving as a species in areas where C. alpina no longer occurs.

Occasional (33). In northern Lancashire this is a frequent taxon in woodlands in Lancaster District with single records in Nether Wyresdale and more surprisingly at Singleton in the Fylde. In VC 64 the only record is from Newton (Anon, 1909). Although it is better recorded than 100 years ago it is not thought that its distribution in Lancashire has changed. A similar situation is reported nationally.

ANACARDIACEAE   SUMACH FAMILY

Rhus typhina L.   Stag's-horn Sumach

Neophyte. This is a native of eastern North America and was cultivated in Britain by 1629. It is a popular garden plant but it was not recorded in the wild until 1966. It is found commonly as a garden escape in southern England and parts of Wales but records from further north are much rarer with only a single record from Scotland.

Very rare (3). In northern Lancashire it was found by the Lancaster Canal at Slyne-with-Hest (SD46T; Livermore and Livermore, 1989) and in Lancaster (SD46R, 45U; Livermore and Livermore, 1991).

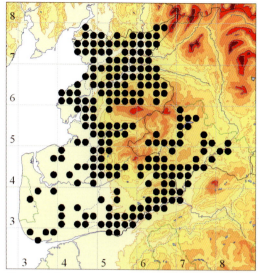
Circaea lutetiana

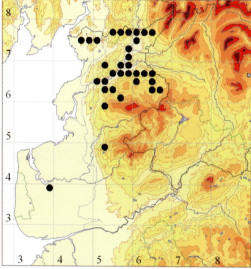
Circaea × intermedia

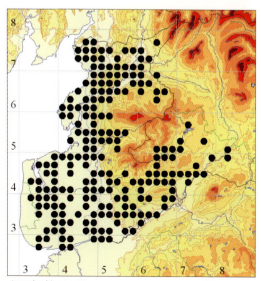
Aesculus hippocastanum

SAPINDACEAE
MAPLE FAMILY

Aesculus hippocastanum L.   Horse-chestnut

Neophyte. This is a native of the Balkan Peninsula and was introduced into British cultivation about 1612. It was recorded from the wild by 1870 and today it is found in parks, estates and in other amenity plantings throughout the British Isles. It is common in many areas and is self-sown in some places.

Frequent (215). It is not known when Horse-chestnut first grew in the wild in northern Lancashire. It was not recorded by Wheldon and Wilson (1907) but several 10km square records are noted by Perring and Walters (1962). Today it is found in most lowland areas of northern Lancashire and regenerates freely.

Aesculus carnea J. Zeyh.   Red Horse-chestnut

Neophyte. It is believed that this is of garden origin and derived from the hybrid *A. hippocastanum* × *A. pavia* L. in the nineteenth century. It has been cultivated in Britain since 1818 and was recorded in the wild by 1955. It is found in scattered localities in Britain especially in southern England.

Very rare (5). The first records of Red Horse-chestnut for northern Lancashire were from Pilling (SD44I) and Winmarleigh (SD44T) in 1995 (Anon). Subsequently it was seen at Silverdale (SD47T) in 2000 (E.F.G.) and in Lancashire VC 64 in the Waddington area (SD74C, G; Abbott, 2005).

Aesculus flava Sol.   Yellow Buckeye

Neophyte. This is a native of eastern North America, which has been recorded in Britain on a few occasions.

Very rare (1). In northern Lancashire it was reported from Yealand Conyers (SD57C; Livermore and Livermore, 1987).

Acer platanoides L.   Norway Maple

Neophyte. Norway Maple is a European Temperate species but it is absent as a native from much of western Europe. It was cultivated in Britain by 1683 and it has been known in the wild since at least 1905. It is found planted as an amenity tree in many parts of Britain but much less commonly in Ireland. It is frequently self-sown.

Occasional (41). The first known record for Norway Maple in northern Lancashire was from the edge of Tunbrook Wood, Preston (SD53W) in 1967 (E.F.G.). Today it is found in scattered localities throughout the area.

Acer cappadocicum Gled.   Cappadocian Maple

Neophyte. Cappadocian Maple is a native of south-western and central Asia and was introduced into cultivation is 1838. It was not recorded in the wild until 1977 and today it has been recorded from scattered localities in Britain. It is a fast growing deciduous tree and is planted widely for amenity purposes.

Very rare (2). In northern Lancashire it was first noted from the upper tidal reaches of the R. Wyre (SD44A) in 1991 where seeds were produced but no seedlings were seen. It was also recorded from Preston (SD52P) in 2006 where the plants were producing suckers. It was planted at both localities (Anon).

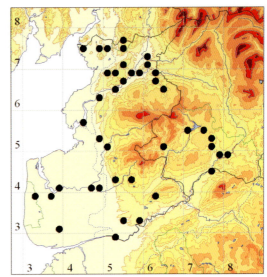

Acer platanoides

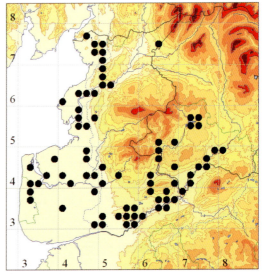

Acer campestre

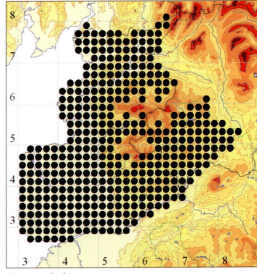

Acer pseudoplatanus

Acer campestre L.   Field Maple

European Temperate element.

This is a deciduous tree found in woodland, scrub and hedges usually on base-rich soils (BH1, 3) in England and Wales. It is also found planted in hedges and in amenity plantings. It occurs as a neophyte in western Wales, western England and in Scotland and Ireland.

Occasional (76). Northern Lancashire is at the northern edge of Field Maple's native distribution and it is therefore often difficult to assess the status of individual plants. Wheldon and Wilson (1907) knew it only as a single shrub in a hedge at Grimsargh but better recording suggests it is native in the Ribble and Hodder valleys. Here it is found in woods as well as in hedges and occasionally old trees are seen. However there is little or no regeneration. It may also be native in the woodlands on limestone around Morecambe Bay (Halliday, 1997) but this seems less certain. Elsewhere it is widely planted. Because of the extent of plantings it is difficult to know if its native range has changed either locally or nationally.

Acer pseudoplatanus L.   Sycamore

Neophyte. Sycamore is a European Temperate species found as a native in the mountains of central and southern Europe. It was introduced into Britain in the sixteenth century and was widely planted from the late eighteenth century. It was first recorded in the wild in 1632 and today occurs throughout the British Isles in a wide variety of habitats. It regenerates freely.

Very common (412). It is not known when Sycamore was first found in northern Lancashire but it was known as a plantation tree by Holt (1795) and by 1900 it was very common. Today it is found throughout the area except on the higher fells. A number of varieties and forms occur (Sell and Murrell, 2009). *A. pseudoplatanus* var. *pseudoplatanus* forma *purpureum* (Loudon) Rehder, with distinctive red or purplish lower leaf surfaces, has been recorded very rarely in northern Lancashire.

Acer villosum C. Presl   Mediterranean Sycamore

Neophyte. This sycamore with hairy undersides to the leaves has been recognised as a garden plant for a long time but often only recognised as a variety of *A. pseudoplatanus*. As a consequence it is rarely recorded and it is not mentioned in standard floras. However it is a native of Sicily, southern Italy and Dalmatia and in Britain is found by roads, in estates and in amenity plantings generally. It is common in Cambridgeshire and probably elsewhere but overlooked (Sell and Murrell, 2009).

Very rare (2) but almost certainly overlooked. Mediterranean Sycamore was found at Silverdale (SD47T) and Yealand Redmayne (SD47Y) in 2009 where it was thought to be regenerating in at least one locality (M.W.).

Acer saccharinum L.   Silver Maple

Neophyte. This is a native of eastern North America and was introduced into Britain in 1725. It is widely planted but it was not recorded in the wild until 1959. Today it is found in scattered localities in England, Wales, eastern Scotland and eastern Ireland.

Very rare (4). In northern Lancashire this was found in Lancaster (SD46Q, V, W; Livermore and Livermore, 1991) and planted at Bull Bank picnic site, Caton (SD56M) in 2002 (E.F.G.).

MALVACEAE   MALLOW FAMILY

Malva moschata L.   Musk-mallow

European Temperate element.

This is a plant of woodland margins, roadsides, and grassy waste places (BH3, 6) and occurs throughout England and Wales and in much of Scotland and Ireland as an introduction.

Occasional (67). In northern Lancashire it is plentiful in the north of the area but much rarer elsewhere and where many former localities may have been lost. Nationally the 'New Atlas' thought its range was stable but since 1987 it has become more frequent probably through garden escapes and the inclusion of seed in wildflower mixes sown for amenity.

Malva sylvestris L.   Common Mallow

Archaeophyte with a Eurosiberian Southern-temperate distribution.

This is found on roadsides, waste ground and in ruderal sites generally (BH3, 6) in England and Wales but more rarely in Scotland.

Frequent (97). In northern Lancashire *M. sylvestris* is found throughout most of the area and is more frequent than 100 years ago. The 'New Atlas' reported no change in its distribution but since 1987 there has been a marked increase ('Local Change').

Malva nicaeensis All.   French Mallow

Neophyte. This is a native of the Mediterranean region and south-western Asia but widely naturalised in Australasia. In Britain it was first recorded in the wild in 1859 and today occurs occasionally on waste ground and on rubbish tips.

In northern Lancashire it was recorded from St Anne's (C.B. in Wheldon and Wilson, 1907).

Malva parviflora L.   Least Mallow

Neophyte. This is a native of the Mediterranean region east to central Asia and was first cultivated in Britain in 1779. It was recorded as a casual in the wild in 1859 and today it is found in a few places in England and Scotland. It is usually derived from an impurity in imported goods or from birdseed.

Very rare (1). In northern Lancashire there are records from Fleetwood in 1902 (J.A.W., NMW), St Anne's in 1907 (C.B.; NMW, MANCH) and from demolition sites in Preston (SD53F) in 1966 (A.E.R., E.H.).

Malva pusilla Sm.   Small Mallow

Neophyte. This belongs to the Eurosiberian Temperate element but its distribution extends west as a native to Scandinavia, Belgium and Italy. In Britain it was first recorded in the wild in 1700 and today it is found casually on roadsides, waste ground and on tips etc. in England, Wales, Ireland and southern Scotland.

Very rare (1). In northern Lancashire it was first recorded from waste ground near Ribchester in 1883 (F.C.K.; NMW). Wheldon and Wilson (1907) recorded a further five or six localities, mostly near the coast of VC 60. (Voucher specimens for some of these records are at NMW, MANCH, YRK and LIV). The only recent record is from a tip at Lytham St Anne's (SD32Y) in 1968 (A.E.R.).

Malva neglecta Wallr.   Dwarf Mallow

Archaeophyte. *M. neglecta* was present in Britain in Roman times but today it is found as a casual in the southern half of England and more occasionally further north and in Scotland.

Rare (6). Because of confusion with *M. pusilla* it is difficult to know its former distribution. However it was found in Roman deposits at Ribchester (Huntley and Hillam, 2000), at St Anne's in 1906 and 1907 (C.B.; YRK, LIV, MANCH, NMW) and Wheldon and Wilson listed (as *M. rotundifolia* L.) six other localities, mostly from the west of VC 60. Since 1964 it has been found in a few scattered lowland localities in the south of VC 60.

Malva arborea (L.) Webb & Berthel.   Tree-mallow

Neophyte. Mediterranean-Atlantic element. This is believed to be native in coastal areas bordering the Irish Sea but many populations found elsewhere on coasts and inland are garden escapes.

Very rare (4). In northern Lancashire the distinction between *M. arborea* and *M. × clementii* (Cheek) Stace was not appreciated until recently. Nevertheless the following records are attributed to *M. arborea*, which was first noted as an unlocalised, unattributed post 1950 record from the 10km square SD47 (B.S.B.I.). Since 1964 it has been recorded from Lytham St Anne's (SD32N) in 1991, Blackpool (SD33F) in 1991 and from a disused railway line at Great Plumpton (SD33W) in 2003 all recorded by C.F. & N.J.S. A further record near allotments at Haslam Park, Preston (SD53A) was made in 1999 (E.F.G.).

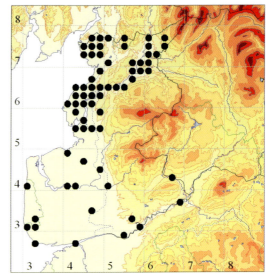

Malva moschata

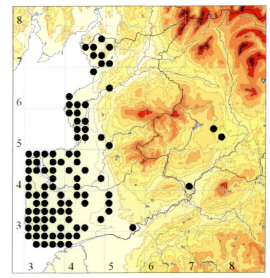

Malva sylvestris

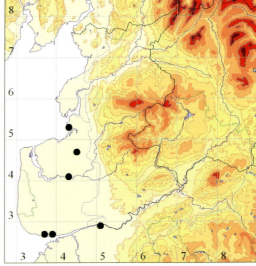

Malva neglecta

Malva olbia (L.) Alef. × **M. thuringiaca** (L.) Vis.
(**M. × clementii** (Cheek) Stace   Garden Tree-mallow

Neophyte. A native of south-eastern Europe from Italy eastwards, western and central Asia. This was cultivated in Britain by 1731 and is now extensively grown in gardens from which it escapes into the wild. It was first reported in the wild in 1862 and now occurs in much of England and Wales. Several cultivars are known.

Very rare (3). In northern Lancashire it was first recorded and distinguished from *M. arborea* from Thistleton (SD43D) and Elswick (SD43D) both in 1999 (R.W.) and from Blackpool (SD33A) in 2004 (E.F.G.).

Alcea rosea L.   Hollyhock

Neophyte. Hollyhock is a garden plant of unknown, probably hybrid origin. It was known in Britain by 1573 but not recorded in the wild until 1906 but occurrences outside gardens are usually short-lived. Most records are from south-eastern England.

Very rare (1). In northern Lancashire there is a very early record from Lytham (Anon, 1829), which, if correct, predates the existing first record for Britain by nearly 80 years. The only other record is from the sand dunes at St Anne's (SD32J) in 1969 (A.E.R.).

Sidalcea malviflora agg.   Greek Mallows

Neophyte. This includes a group of species, hybrids and cultivars of North American origin that are widely grown in gardens since 1838 and when they escape into the wild on waste ground can become established. However the first record from the wild dates only from 1940. It is now known from scattered localities in England, Scotland and the Isle of Man.

Very rare (3). In northern Lancashire it was recorded from roadsides near Rossall (SD34H) in *c.* 1984 and near Staining, Hardhorn-with-Newton (SD33M) in 1988 (both C.F. & N.J.S.). L. A. and P.D. Livermore (1989) also recorded *L. malviflora* agg. from the Lancaster Canal at Slyne-with-Hest (SD46T).

Tilia platyphyllos Scop.   Large-leaved Lime

Neophyte. European Temperate element.

This is native in parts of England and the Welsh borders but it has been cultivated since at least the sixteenth century. *Tilia platyphyllos* is found throughout much of England, Wales and eastern Scotland and occasionally elsewhere in the British Isles.

Very rare (2). In northern Lancashire there are records from Silverdale (SD47S; Livermore and Livermore, 1987) and Upper Rawcliffe-with-Tarnacre (SD44R) in 1996 (C.J.B.).

Tilia platyphyllos × **T. cordata** (**T. × europaea** L.)   Lime

Neophyte. Two clones of this hybrid, which occurs as a native taxon where the parents grow together, were widely planted in the late seventeenth and early eighteenth centuries and it remains a popular tree for amenity planting. It occurs throughout the British Isles.

Frequent (146). Lime is planted throughout northern Lancashire as an amenity tree in woodlands, parks and roadsides including urban streets.

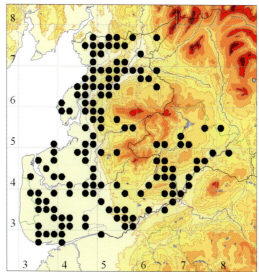

Tilia × europaea

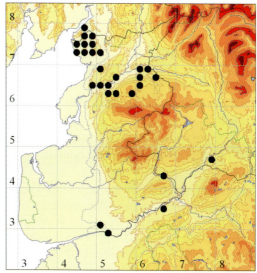

Tilia cordata

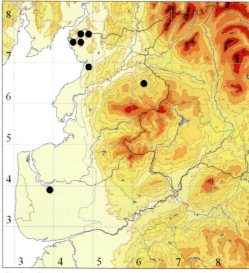

Daphne laureola

Tilia cordata Mill. Small-leaved Lime

Eurosiberian Temperate element.

This tree occurs in deciduous woodlands, often on rocky substrates, steep slopes and on cliffs (BH1) in England, Wales and parts of Scotland and Ireland. However in England it is not thought to be native north of southern Cumbria.

Occasional (28). In northern Lancashire it is found in the limestone woodlands around Morecambe Bay and in the woods in the Lune valley and on the north side of the Bowland Fells. It occurs much more rarely in the Ribble and Hodder valleys. Apart from a record at Aughton and in the woods around Morecambe Bay Wheldon and Wilson (1907) overlooked this tree. It is still probably under recorded in the Ribble and Hodder valleys. Most records are of old trees so that it is unlikely to have extended its range. Nationally 'Local Change' reports an increase in its distribution but suggests that this may be due to amenity planting and better recording rather than a real increase of the native population.

THYMELAEACEAE MEZEREON FAMILY

Daphne mezereum L. Mezereon

Eurosiberian Boreo-temperate element.

Mezereon is a deciduous shrub of calcareous woodland (BH1) and is found in parts of England and Wales but it is also found as an introduction or escape from cultivation. Its native distribution is therefore uncertain.

Very rare (2). In northern Lancashire it has been known from various places in Eaves Wood, Silverdale (SD47T) since 1966 (E.F.G.) and J.F. Pickard also found a single plant at Great Dunnow Wood near Slaidburn (SD75A) in 1897 (LDS). Although not recorded by Wheldon and Wilson (1907) it is possibly native or derived from native stock at these localities. It has also been recorded from Quernmore (SD56F) in 1997 (M.S.) where it is likely to have been bird-sown from garden stock. This has always been a rare plant in the limestone woodlands around Morecambe Bay and has also suffered from being uprooted, presumably for gardens, as occurred to two plants in Eaves Wood. Because of confusion between introduced and native populations it is unclear if there has been any change in its distribution nationally.

Daphne laureola L. Spurge-laurel

Submediterranean-Subatlantic element.

This is an evergreen shrub of neutral or basic soils in deciduous woodland (BH1) found as a native in many parts of England and Wales and as an introduction elsewhere.

Rare (7). Spurge-laurel is found in limestone woodlands around Morecambe Bay where it regenerates freely in coppiced areas. It also occurs occasionally elsewhere as an introduction. There has been no change in its native distribution locally or nationally.

CISTACEAE ROCK-ROSE FAMILY

Helianthemum nummularium (L.) Mill.

Common Rock-rose

European Temperate element.

This species occurs in short, dry, calcareous grassland (BH7) and is found in suitable situations in England, Wales and Scotland.

Occasional (18). In northern Lancashire it is found in limestone grassland around Morecambe Bay, where it is often abundant but it is absent from apparently suitable places in Leck and on Dalton Crags although it is found on the adjacent Hutton Roof in Cumbria (Halliday, 1997). In the Bowland Fells it was found on limestone near Slaidburn (SD75A) in 1908 (J.F.P.; LDS) but not since. Its distribution in northern Lancashire is unchanged but there have been losses nationally since 1950 ('New Atlas') but no further losses were reported by 'Local Change'.

TROPAEOLACEAE NASTURTIUM FAMILY

Tropaeolum peregrinum L. Canary-creeper

Neophyte. This is a native of South America, which is grown in gardens and may escape into the wild. It is found in only a few places in Britain but it can persist for many years in any one locality.

Very rare (1). It was found at St Anne's in 1965 (A.E.R.).

Tropaeolum majus L. Nasturtium

Neophyte. The plant found in Britain today is a much modified species originating from South America. *T. majus* was introduced into Britain in 1686 and became a popular garden plant. It was found in the wild by 1908 and today occurs on tips and disturbed ground in many, but especially urban, parts of the British Isles.

Rare (7). In northern Lancashire this was first recorded from Lytham tip about 1966 (A.E.R.). Subsequently it was recorded from scattered localities in western parts of the area.

LIMNANTHACEAE MEADOW-FOAM FAMILY

Limnanthes douglasii R. Br. Meadow-foam

Neophyte. This is a casual annual grown in gardens, which often escapes into the wild. It is a native of California and was first cultivated in Britain in 1833. *L. douglasii* was known from the wild by 1870 and although it rarely persists for long at any given locality it appears to be increasing. It is found throughout the British Isles.

Rare (7). In northern Lancashire Meadow-foam was first recorded (Livermore and Livermore, 1987) from Heysham (SD46A) and Tatham (SD66J). It has also been recorded from a few other scattered localities in the region.

RESEDACEAE   MIGNONETTE FAMILY

Reseda luteola L.   Weld

Archaeophyte. This has a Eurosiberian Southern-temperate distribution but it is widely naturalised outside of this range. It is found in disturbed ground (BH3, 17) in many parts of the British Isles but it is rare or absent in upland areas and in western Ireland and north-western Scotland.

Frequent (102). Weld occurs mostly in the western half of northern Lancashire and although it may be more frequent than formerly in the Fylde its distribution elsewhere is unchanged. This is in line with the situation reported by the 'New Atlas' but 'Local Change' reports an increase in its range.

Reseda lutea L.   Wild Mignonette

European Southern-temperate element.

This is found in disturbed places on waste ground and on roadsides (BH3, 17) in England, central Scotland and parts of Wales but it is rare or absent in upland areas. It occurs as an introduction in Ireland, especially near Dublin.

Occasional (48). In northern Lancashire *R. lutea* is mostly found in coastal areas and in the vicinity of Preston. This represents a considerable extension of its range since 1907 (Wheldon and Wilson) when it was only known from a road bank near Warton (Carnforth), near Churchtown, Preston Dock and St Anne's. There has been no change in its distribution nationally.

BRASSICACEAE   CABBAGE FAMILY

Erysimum cheiranthoides L.   Treacle-mustard

Archaeophyte with a Circumpolar Boreo-temperate distribution.

This is a widely naturalised species thought to have been in Britain since the Bronze Age. It grows in arable fields and on waste ground (BH3, 4) in many parts of the British Isles but especially in south-eastern England.

Very rare (5). The first reports for Treacle-mustard in northern Lancashire are unlocalised (Wheldon and Wilson, 1907; B.R.C.). Since 1964 it has been recorded from Nether Kellet (SD56D) in 1970 (E.F.G.), Thurnham (SD45M; Livermore and Livermore, 1987), Lancaster (SD46W; Livermore and Livermore, 1991), Freckleton (SD42J) in 1994 (C.F. & N.J.S.) and Catterall (SD54A) in 1989 (L.R.F.).

Erysimum cheiri (L.) Crantz   Wallflower

Archaeophyte. The wallflower is a plant of garden origin widely naturalised on cliffs, old walls and rocks (BH3, 16, 17) in western and central Europe. It has been cultivated since medieval times and recorded as a wild plant in Britain from 1548. It occurs throughout much of the British Isles.

Rare (12). It has been known as a wild plant in northern Lancashire since Fielding recorded it in his Stodday garden and on the walls of the Priory Church and Castle at Lancaster in c. 1836 (Fielding MS). It was later recorded from sea cliffs at Silverdale (Ashfield, 1864) where it still grows. Other post 1964 localities are in the Lancaster area, near the Shard Bridge on the Wyre estuary and at Lytham St Anne's.

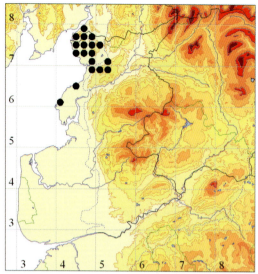
Helianthemum nummularium

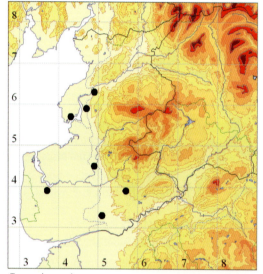
Tropaeolum majus

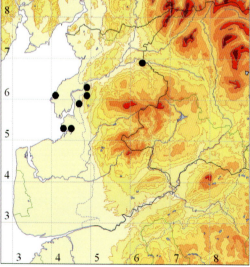
Limnanthes douglasii

Arabidopsis thaliana (L.) Heynh.   Thale Cress

Eurosiberian Temperate element.

This winter annual is found on sand dunes and open disturbed ground (BH16, 17, 19) throughout most of the British Isles.

Frequent (163). In northern Lancashire it is especially frequent in western areas but it is largely absent from upland and pastoral areas between Preston and Lancaster. There has been a considerable expansion of its range in northern Lancashire from thirteen localities noted 100 years ago (Wheldon and Wilson, 1907) and whilst the 'New Atlas' reported no change 'Local Change' noted an expansion in its distribution nationally since 1987.

Camelina sativa (L.) Crantz   Gold-of-Pleasure

Archaeophyte and cultivated in Europe since prehistoric times with an uncertain native distribution.

Formerly *C. sativa* was much more frequent than it is today occurring as an escape from cultivation in many parts of the British Isles. More recently records arise from birdseed mixtures.

Very rare (2). In northern Lancashire former records were from Preston (Ashfield, 1860), St Anne's (A.J.C.; LSA), and Kirkham (Heathcote, 1923). Post 1964 records are from a tip at Blackpool (SD33I) in 1966 (A.E.R. & J.H.) and from a tip at Lytham (SD32Y) in 1966 (A.E.R.).

Neslia paniculata (L.) Desv.   Ball Mustard

Neophyte. This has a Eurosiberian Southern-temperate distribution but is widely naturalised outside its native range. In the British Isles it appears as a casual associated with imported grain.

In northern Lancashire it was recorded from St Anne's (C.B.; Wheldon and Wilson, 1907) and from Newton-in-Bowland in 1912 (Peel, 1913).

Capsella bursa-pastoris (L.) Medik.   Shepherd's-purse

Archaeophyte with a Eurosiberian Wide-temperate distribution.

This is found in ruderal habitats (BH4, 17) throughout the British Isles.

Very common (362). It occurs in much of northern Lancashire but is absent from upland areas in the east of the area. The distribution is stable in northern Lancashire but there have been losses in north-western Scotland ('New Atlas') with further losses since 1987 confirmed by 'Local Change'.

Turritis glabra L.   Tower Mustard

Eurosiberian Temperate element but a neophyte in northern Lancashire.

The only record is from the beach at Lytham where it was found in 1830 (Fielding MS). However in 1974 it was found in Middlebarrow Quarry just over the VC 60 border in Cumbria (Halliday, 1997).

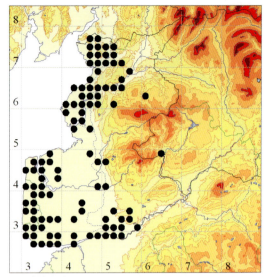
Reseda luteola

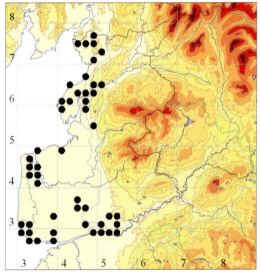
Reseda lutea

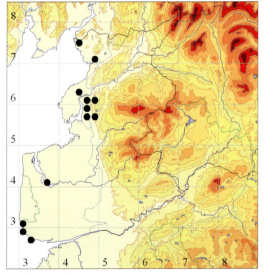
Erysimum cheiri

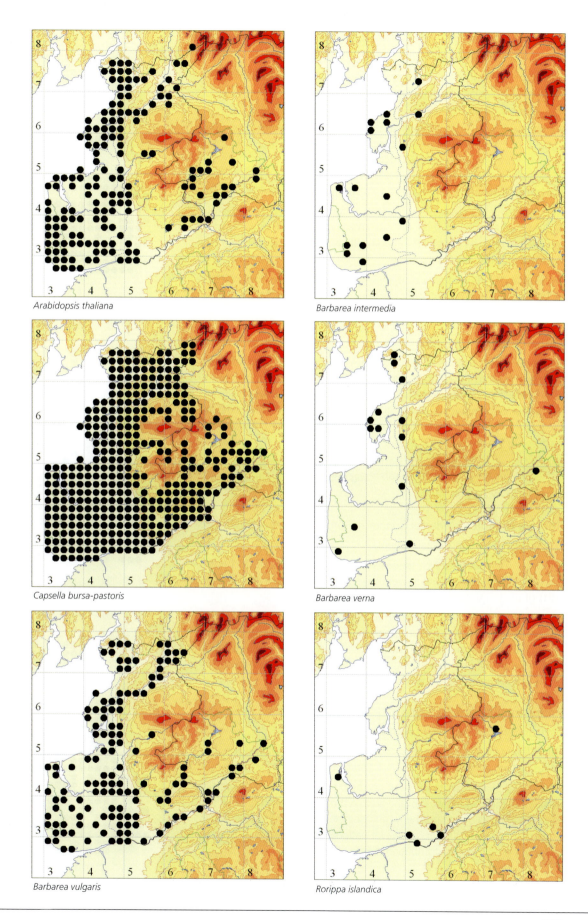

Arabidopsis thaliana

Barbarea intermedia

Capsella bursa-pastoris

Barbarea verna

Barbarea vulgaris

Rorippa islandica

Barbarea vulgaris W.T. Aiton   Winter-cress

Eurosiberian Temperate element.

This occurs throughout much of the British Isles although rarely in north-western and highland Scotland. It is found by rivers and streams, roadsides and in waste places (BH3, 14).

Frequent (135). It is found mostly in western parts of northern Lancashire but also in the Lune, Hodder and Ribble valleys. Its distribution has remained unchanged locally and nationally.

Barbarea intermedia Boreau   Medium-flowered Winter-cress

Neophyte. This is a native of north-western Africa and western Europe and is found in ruderal habitats in many parts of the British Isles. It was recorded in the wild before 1849 but its range has increased considerably since 1962 ('New Atlas').

Occasional (16). It was first recorded in northern Lancashire from Preesall in 1965 (E.J.H.) and has subsequently been found in scattered localities in western parts of VC 60.

Barbarea verna (Mill.) Asch.   American Winter-cress

Neophyte. This is a native of south-western Europe and is found scattered in ruderal habitats throughout much of the British Isles but appears to be more frequent in south-western England than elsewhere. *Barbarea verna* was grown for centuries as a substitute for water-cress and after a gap in the eighteenth and nineteenth centuries it is again cultivated. It was first recorded in the wild in 1803.

Rare (14). It was first recorded in northern Lancashire from near St Michael's (Wheldon and Wilson, 1907) and since 1964 it has been found in scattered localities in the area.

Rorippa islandica (Oeder ex Gunnerus) Borbás Northern Yellow-cress

Eurosiberian Boreal-montane element.

This was only recognised as a species separate from *R. palustris* in 1968. Since then it has been found in wet places (BH13) in western and northern parts of the British Isles.

Rare (6). The first records in northern Lancashire were from the Preston area where it was first found in a pond in Avenham Park, Preston (SD52J) in 2003 (P.J.). Subsequently it has been found in scattered localities in both VC 60 and VC 64. It is suggested that, as all the sites are of recent origin, this is a new immigrant to the Lancashire flora.

Rorippa palustris (L.) Besser   Marsh Yellow-cress

Circumpolar Boreo-temperate element.

This is found in wet and waste places (BH11, 13) throughout England, Wales, Ireland and central and eastern Scotland.

Frequent (155). It grows throughout northern Lancashire but it is especially frequent in the lowland west of the area. Although it is difficult to be certain it appears that in northern Lancashire *R. palustris* has extended its range over the last 100 years. However nationally the 'New Atlas' reports losses but since 1987 its distribution appears unchanged ('Local Change').

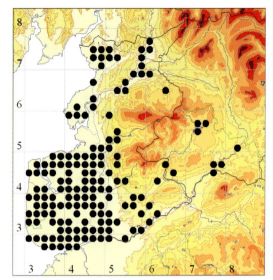
Rorippa palustris

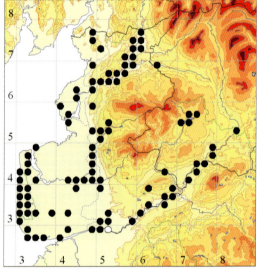
Rorippa sylvestris

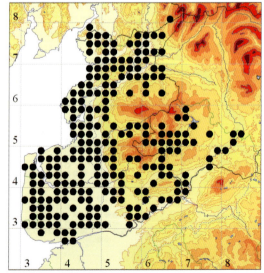
Nasturtium officinale s.l.

Rorippa sylvestris (L.) Besser   Creeping Yellow-cress

European Temperate element.

This is a plant of wet places, riversides, streams and ditches etc. (BH11, 14) and is found over much of the British Isles but it is rare in northern Scotland.

Frequent (95). In northern Lancashire it is closely associated with the Rivers Lune, Wyre and Ribble and Fylde coastal areas. This represents a considerable extension of its range from the three sites between Preston and Lytham mentioned by Wheldon and Wilson (1907). Nationally the 'New Atlas' reports an expansion of its range since 1962 but 'Local Change' reported, perhaps unexpectedly, a considerable loss of localities since 1987.

[**Rorippa amphibia** (L.) Besser   Great Yellow-cress

This was reported from the R. Wyre between St Michael's and Garstang (Stewart, *et al.*, 1994) but it is thought that this was an identification error.]

Nasturtium officinale *sensu lato*   Water-cress

Water-cresses are found throughout the British Isles and recorded here are three taxa, *N. officinale* W.T. Aiton, *N. × sterile* and *N. microphyllum*. All three taxa are found in slow moving streams, ditches and ponds (BH11, 13, 14) throughout most of the British Isles. Because of identification difficulties it is not known if the distribution of the individual taxa has changed or not.

Nasturtium officinale s.l. is common (243) and occurs throughout northern Lancashire. Unfortunately *N. officinale sensu stricto*, which has a Eurosiberian Southern-temperate distribution, was rarely distinguished from the other taxa but it is believed to be widespread.

Nasturtium officinale × N. microphyllum
(**N. × sterile** (Airy Shaw) Oefelein)   Hybrid Water-cress

This is widespread in Europe and is the taxon most widely used in growing water-cress commercially. It occurs throughout the British Isles but it is largely sterile and is overlooked.

Rare (11). In northern Lancashire it was recorded from Heysham (SD46A; Livermore and Livermore, 1987) and Hornby (SD56Z), where it was formerly cultivated, in 1999 (J.M.N.). Since then *N. × sterile* has been found in scattered localities in northern Lancashire but generally it has probably been overlooked and is likely to be widespread and common.

Nasturtium microphyllum (Boenn.) Rchb. Narrow-fruited Water-cress

The world distribution of this species is uncertain but it is widespread in Europe. It is found in most of the British Isles but is under recorded.

Occasional (62). Its distribution in northern Lancashire is uncertain but it is probably very much under recorded.

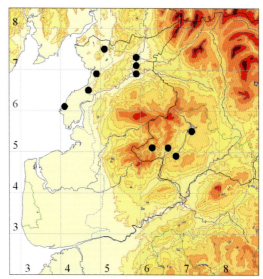

Nasturtium × sterile

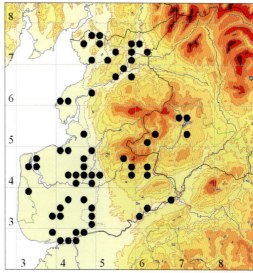

Nasturtium microphyllum

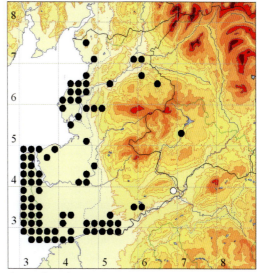

Armoracia rusticana

Armoracia rusticana P. Gaertn., B. Mey. & Scherb.　　Horse-radish

Archaeophyte although not known as a native plant anywhere it is naturalised throughout temperate Europe, North America and elsewhere.

It is grown as a vegetable for use in hot relishes and was introduced into Britain before 1500. It is found in waste places, roadsides and in old gardens (BH3) throughout most of the British Isles but it is rare in upland areas, parts of Scotland and Ireland.

Frequent (86). Wheldon and Wilson (1907) recorded it from Stonyhurst, Preston Dock and Ashton but since then it has spread to many parts of northern Lancashire. It is particularly frequent near towns and villages around Morecambe, the Fylde coast and Preston. Nationally its distribution appears stable.

Cardamine bulbifera (L.) Crantz
forma **ptarmicifolia** (DC.) O.E. Schulz　　Coralroot

Neophyte. It is probably native in scattered localities in Europe, especially the Alps and in the Caucasus. In Britain it is sometimes grown in gardens from which it may escape into the wild.

Very rare (3). It was first recorded from a nursery and nearby woodland in Silverdale (SD47S) in 1982 (A.E.C.) and in Eaves Wood, Silverdale (SD47T) in 1997 (Arnside Naturalists). Coralroot also appeared as a garden weed at Lytham (SD32T) in 2010 (K. Livesley) where it had been known for three or four years before it flowered.

Cardamine heptaphylla (Vill.) O.E. Schulz　　Pinnate Coralroot

Neophyte. This is a native of Europe and was cultivated in Britain by 1683 and recorded in the wild in 1907. There are a few localities for this species scattered across England.

Very rare (1). In northern Lancashire this was first recorded from Holden Clough (SD74U) in 1961 (V.G.; LIV). Later records are from two sites in Silverdale (SD47S) where it was first seen in 1965 (C.J.-P., LIV). The record from Holden Clough and one of the Silverdale records are from or adjacent to nursery gardens.

Cardamine amara L.　　Large Bitter-cress

European Temperate element.

This occurs in wet woodlands and by streamsides (BH1, 14), mostly in central Britain and in the north of Ireland.

Frequent (157). In northern Lancashire it is particularly characteristic of woodlands in the north and east of the area. Its distribution is stable both locally and nationally.

Cardamine pratensis L.　　Cuckooflower

Circumpolar Wide-boreal element.

This is found throughout the British Isles in wet meadows, fens, flushes and other wet places (BH6, 11). It is morphologically and cytologically variable but as yet there is no satisfactory taxonomic treatment available to reflect this variation.

Very common (422). It occurs throughout northern Lancashire. Its distribution is stable both locally and nationally.

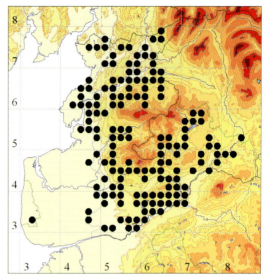
Cardamine amara

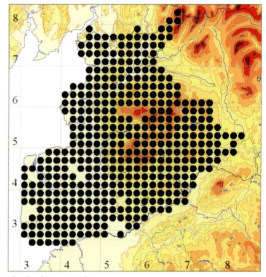
Cardamine pratensis

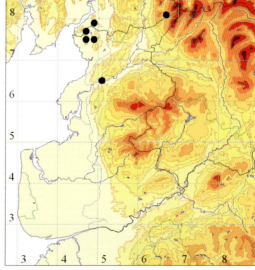
Cardamine impatiens

Cardamine impatiens L.　　　　　Narrow-leaved Bitter-cress

Eurasian Temperate element.

This is a plant of woodlands on calcareous soils including limestone pavements and by rivers (BH1, 3). It is found in many parts of England and Wales and rarely elsewhere.

Rare (6). Population sizes vary from year to year and in northern Lancashire appearances of *C. impatiens* seem to be erratic. It was first recorded in the Silverdale area in 1868 (Petty, 1902) but the record for Middlebarrow is in VC 69. Other records are from Ease Gill, Leck (SD68Q) in 1966 (E.F.G.), by the edge of a wood Hawes Water (SD47T) in 1967 (H.S.), Leighton Moss (SD47X) in 1973 (J.P.), unlocalised tetrad records (SD47P, Z) in 1974 (B.R.C.) and by the R. Lune at Halton (SD56C) in 2002 (M.S.). The overall distribution of this species nationally is stable.

Cardamine flexuosa With.　　　　　Wavy Bitter-cress

European Temperate element.

Wavy Bitter-cress is found in a wide range of wet places ranging from ponds and stream sides to woodlands (BH1, 11). It occurs throughout the British Isles.

Very common (397). It has been recorded throughout northern Lancashire. There has been no change in its distribution locally or nationally.

Cardamine hirsuta L.　　　　　Hairy Bitter-cress

Eurosiberian Southern-temperate element.

This is a winter annual favouring open habitats and is particularly common in coastal areas on sand dunes and as a weed of cultivation (BH4, 16, 19). It is found in most of the British Isles.

Common (265). It occurs throughout northern Lancashire but it is especially common in coastal areas. Its distribution in northern Lancashire is stable but whereas the 'New Atlas' reports possible losses from northern Scotland and western Ireland 'Local Change' notes an increase in its British distribution since 1987.

Lepidium sativum L.　　　　　Garden Cress

Neophyte. This is probably a native of Egypt and south-western Asia but it has been grown in gardens since 995. It was known in the wild about 1860 and has been found as a casual in many parts of the British Isles.

Rare (7). In northern Lancashire Garden Cress was first recorded from Morecambe, Preston, and St Anne's (Wheldon and Wilson, 1907). Since 1964 it has been recorded in different parts of VC 60 but always as a casual.

Lepidium campestre (L.) W.T. Aiton　　　　　Field Pepperwort

Archaeophyte with a European Temperate distribution.

This is found in many parts of the British Isles but mostly in the south-eastern half of Britain. It occurs in ruderal habitats and as weed of cultivated ground (BH3, 4, 17).

Occasional (23). In northern Lancashire it is found in a few scattered localities in VC 60. Its distribution is probably stable in northern Lancashire but nationally there were losses post 1950 ('New Atlas') but no further losses were noted since 1987 ('Local Change').

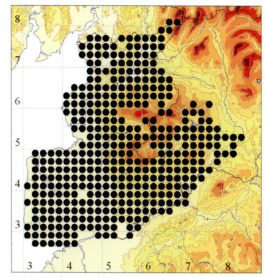

Cardamine flexuosa

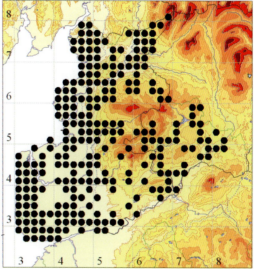

Cardamine hirsuta

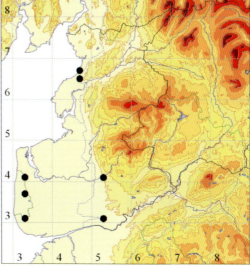

Lepidium sativum

Lepidium heterophyllum Benth.　　　　　　　Smith's Pepperwort

Oceanic Southern-temperate element.

This is a plant of dry heaths and gravely places including railway ballast (BH3) and occurs in many places in the British Isles.

Rare (10). Smith's Pepperwort has always been rare in northern Lancashire and former records were from Silverdale and Preston. Since 1964 it has been recorded in a few localities in the Lancaster and Heysham areas and in the southwest of VC 60. Its distribution nationally is stable apart from some losses in south-eastern England ('New Atlas').

Lepidium virginicum L.　　　　　　　　　　Least Pepperwort

Neophyte. This is a native of North America but it is widespread elsewhere. Although cultivated in Britain by 1713 and recorded from the wild in 1881 most records are from grain impurities.

Very rare (1). In northern Lancashire it was recorded from St Anne's in 1907 (C.B.; Wheldon and Wilson, 1907) and from Lancaster (Livermore and Livermore, 1991).

Lepidium ruderale L.　　　　　　　　Narrow-leaved Pepperwort

Archaeophyte with a Eurosiberian Temperate distribution.

This is found in ruderal habitats but increasingly as a halophyte on salt treated roads in the southern half of the British Isles (BH3, 17).

Very rare (4). In northern Lancashire it was found on the sand dunes at St Anne's and from near Preston Docks (Wheldon and Wilson, 1907). Since 1964 it has been found near Preston Dock (SD52E) in 2002, Medlar-with-Wesham (SD43C) in 2004 and Marton, Blackpool (SD33H) in 2004 (all C.F. & N.J.S.). What is believed to be this species was also found at Fleetwood (SD34J) in 2007 (P.G.).

Lepidium latifolium L.　　　　　　　　　　Dittander

Eurosiberian Southern-temperate element but a neophyte in northern Lancashire.

This is a native of brackish habitats (BH6) in south-eastern England and the Severn estuary but occurs in ruderal habitats elsewhere.

Very rare (1). In northern Lancashire it was first recorded from brackish pools at Fleetwood (SD34I) in 1994 (P.J.) where today it appears well established.

Lepidium draba L.　　　　　　　　　　　Hoary Cress

Neophyte. This is a native of southern Europe and south-western Asia but it is widely naturalised elsewhere. It was accidentally introduced to Swansea in 1802 and spread rapidly from there to other places in the nineteenth century. It grows on waste ground and now occurs in many places in the British Isles but especially in south-eastern England.

Occasional (43). In northern Lancashire it was first recorded by Wheldon and Wilson (1907) from Morecambe (1900), Fleetwood (1900) and St Anne's (1905). Today it is largely a coastal plant with occasional records elsewhere.

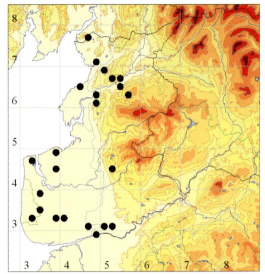

Lepidium campestre

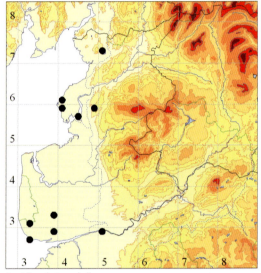

Lepidium heterophyllum

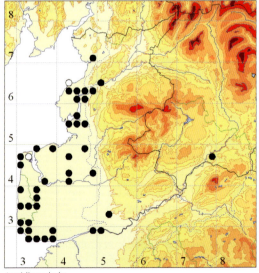

Lepidium draba

Lepidium coronopus (L.) Al-Shehbaz   Swine-cress

Archaeophyte with a European Southern-temperate distribution.

This occurs in ruderal habitats typically paths, gateways, farmyards and on waste ground (BH3, 4) and is found mostly in the south-eastern England.

Occasional (35). In northern Lancashire Wheldon and Wilson (1907) knew Swine-cress only from between Blackpool and Cleveleys, Little Bispham and near Garstang. Since 1964 it has been recorded frequently from the Fylde coast and occasionally elsewhere. Nationally it has expanded its range since 1962 and this continues post 1987.

Lepidium didymum (L.)   Lesser Swine-cress

Neophyte. The native distribution of this species is uncertain but it is widely naturalised in many parts of the world. It was first found in Britain in the early eighteenth century and was recorded in the wild in 1778. Today it is found in ruderal habitats (BH4, 17), mostly in the southern half of the British Isles but it is probably still spreading.

Frequent (78). In northern Lancashire it was first recorded from near St Michael's in 1915 (Wheldon and Wilson, 1925) and since 1964 it has been found in scattered localities in the area but seems to be especially frequent in the Heysham peninsula.

Lunaria annua L.   Honesty

Neophyte. This is a cultivated plant of unknown origin but widely naturalised in Europe and found throughout most of the British Isles, although it is rare in much of highland Scotland and Ireland. It has been cultivated since 1570 and was known from the wild by 1597.

Frequent (88). Honesty was first recorded in northern Lancashire from the Wyre estuary (France, 1931) and today it occurs throughout much of the area although it is absent from the Bowland fells.

Lunaria rediviva L.   Perennial Honesty

Neophyte. This native of Europe and western Asia is a garden plant that has occasionally escaped into the wild.

In northern Lancashire James Britten reported it from the 'sands of Morecambe Bay, Lancashire' in June 1864 (Britten, 1864). However this could have meant Furness Lancashire.

Alyssum alyssoides (L.) L.   Small Alison

Neophyte. This garden plant is a native of temperate Europe and it was first cultivated in Britain in 1740. It was recorded in the wild in 1838 and was found later in many places in Britain but today it is rarely found.

Very rare (1). The only record for northern Lancashire is as a garden weed in Lancaster (SD45Z) in c. 1990 (L.A.L.).

Aurinia saxatilis (L.) Desv.   Golden Alison

Neophyte. This is a native of central and south-eastern Europe and south-western Asia. It was first cultivated in Britain in 1710 and recorded from the wild in 1912. It is found on rocks, walls and waste ground in England and Wales and occasionally elsewhere.

Very rare (2). In northern Lancashire it was found in a quarry at Dilworth (SD63E) in 1987 (E.F.G.) and from tetrad SD74H in VC 64 in c. 2005 (P.P.A.).

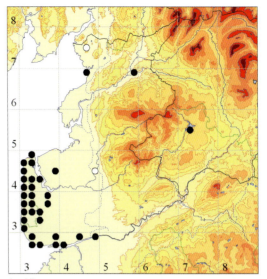
Lepidium coronopus

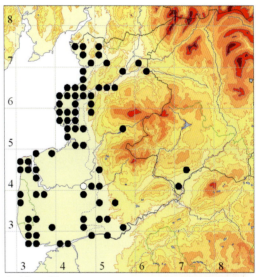
Lepidium didymum

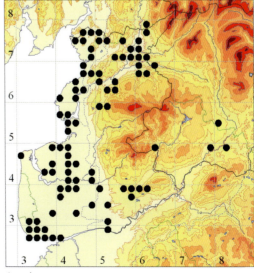
Lunaria annua

Berteroa incana (L.) DC.   Hoary Alison

Neophyte. This is a Eurosiberian Temperate species, which was cultivated in Britain by 1640 and was recorded casually in the wild by 1870. It has arisen mainly as an impurity in imported grain and whilst there are old records from much of England and Wales and occasionally elsewhere most records are confined to south-eastern England.

In northern Lancashire it was found near Preston Docks between 1897 and 1902 (Clitheroe and Robinson, 1903).

Lobularia maritima (L.) Desv.   Sweet Alison

Neophyte. This popular garden plant is a native of coastal areas of south-western Europe and the Mediterranean region. It was cultivated in Britain by 1722 and was known from the wild by 1807. Today it is found as an escape from gardens in many places in the British Isles.

Occasional (36). This was first recorded from the sand dunes at Lytham St Anne's in 1908 (C.B.; BIRM) and today Sweet Alison is found commonly in coastal areas of VC 60 and occasionally elsewhere.

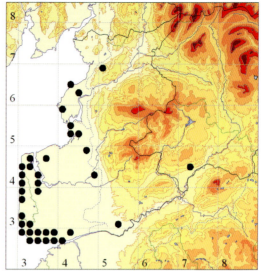
Lobularia maritima

Descurainia sophia (L.) Webb ex Prantl   Flixweed

Archaeophyte with a Eurosiberian Temperate distribution.

This is found in arable fields and waste places (BH4) in most parts of the British Isles but especially in East Anglia.

Rare (11). Flixweed was first found in northern Lancashire from Roman deposits at Ribchester (Huntley and Hillam, 2000). However apart from a locality near Leighton Hall (Jenkinson, 1775) all recent records are from coastal localities, mostly on the Fylde coast. It has always been rare in VC 60; nationally it declined before 1930 but since 1962 there has been little further change in its distribution.

Arabis caucasica Willd. ex Schltdl.   Garden Arabis

Neophyte, a native of southern Europe, northern Africa and south-western Asia. It was introduced into cultivation by 1798 and was recorded in the wild by 1855. It is found over much of the British Isles naturalised on walls, rocks and cliffs, although it is very rare in north-western Scotland and Ireland.

Rare (11). It was first recorded from northern Lancashire at St Anne's in 1946 (Whellan, 1954) and again in 1962 (SD32I, A.E.R.). Post 1964 records are concentrated in the northwest of VC 60 and in the Dunsop Bridge area of VC 64.

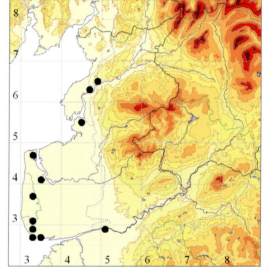
Descurainia sophia

Arabis hirsuta (L.) Scop.   Hairy Rock-cress

Circumpolar Boreo-temperate element.

This is found throughout the British Isles growing in dry sunny situations in rocky places and on basic soils (BH7, 16).

Occasional (38). In northern Lancashire most records are from the lime-stone areas in the north of VC 60 and in Bowland with occasional records elsewhere. There have been losses in its distribution in northern Lancashire but the 'New Atlas' reported a decline nationally, mostly before 1950 and 'Local Change' noted a further decline since 1987.

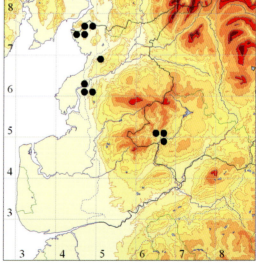
Arabis caucasica

Aubrieta deltoidea (L.) DC.   Aubretia

Neophyte. This popular garden plant, a native of Sicily and the eastern Mediterranean to south-western Asia, has been cultivated in Britain since 1710 and was reported from the wild by 1928. It is found throughout most of the British Isles, especially in south-western England, on walls, paths and waste ground.

Very rare (5). Aubretia does not appear to be naturalised in northern Lancashire but it has been recorded from Lancaster (Livermore and Livermore, 1991), on outbuildings at Higher Brock Mill (SD54K) in 1998 (E.F.G.) and in VC 64 tetrads SD64X, 74G and 85F (Abbott, 2005).

Draba incana L.   Hoary Whitlowgrass

European Boreo-arctic Montane element.

This is found on calcareous rocks and in open habitats on calcareous grasslands (BH7, 16) in the mountains of the British Isles.

Very rare (3). In northern Lancashire it has only been found on the limestone in the vicinity of Ease Gill, Leck (SD67P, 68Q & V). Its distribution in northern Lancashire is unchanged but nationally there have been some losses on the edges of its main areas of distribution.

Draba muralis L.   Wall Whitlowgrass

European Temperate element.

This is a winter annual found on limestone rocks on south facing ledges and screes (BH3, 16) in the Pennines and south-western England and as a casual throughout much of the British Isles.

Very rare (2) or extinct. In northern Lancashire there are old records for the Lune valley between Kirkby Lonsdale and Whittington, the Hodder valley (Wheldon and Wilson, 1907) and in a nursery at Silverdale in 1956 (V.G.; LIV). The only recent records are from a quarry near Eaves Wood, Silverdale (SD47T) in 1969 (C.J.-P.) and on gravel in Hornby Churchyard (SD56Z) in 1983 (J.M.N.; LIV) where it has not been seen recently. Its distribution nationally is stable.

Erophila verna (L.) DC.   Common Whitlowgrass

World range uncertain.

This is found in open habitats in sand dunes, calcareous grassland and in ruderal habitats (BH3, 16, 17, 19) and occurs throughout the British Isles.

Frequent (99). In northern Lancashire it occurs throughout the area but especially near the coast and in limestone areas. *E. verna* var. *praecox* (Steven) Diklic was recognised from sand dunes at Lytham St Anne's (SD33A) in 1991 (E.F.G.). The distribution of *E. verna* is stable locally and nationally but as the taxonomy of *E. verna sensu lato* was not elucidated until 1987 this is not certain.

Erophila glabrescens Jord.   Glabrous Whitlowgrass

World range uncertain.

This occurs in similar situations to *E. verna* (BH3, 16, 17, 19) and occurs throughout the British Isles. However as it was not recognised until 1987 it is very much under recorded.

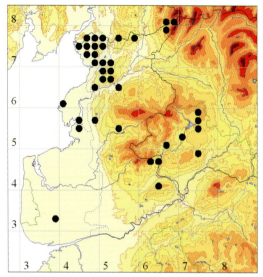
Arabis hirsuta

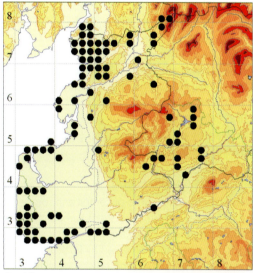
Erophila verna

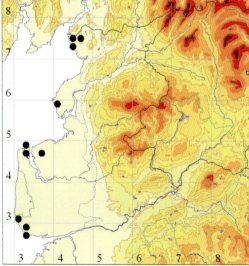
Erophila glabrescens

Rare (10). In northern Lancashire it has a more restricted distribution than *E. verna* being found in sandy areas at Lytham St Anne's, Fleetwood and Heysham and on the limestone in the Silverdale area. It is believed its distribution is stable locally and nationally.

Conringia orientalis (L.) Dumort.   Hare's-ear Mustard

Neophyte. A native of central and southern Europe first recorded in the wild in Britain in 1778. It was a contaminant of cereal and clover seed and occurred as a casual in ruderal habitats.

There are no recent records for northern Lancashire but it was found on the sand dunes at St Anne's between 1907 and 1909 (Bailey, 1910; MANCH) with other records from Fleetwood and Preston Docks (Wheldon and Wilson, 1907) and from Lancaster in 1923 (H.E.G.; LIV).

Diplotaxis tenuifolia (L.) DC.   Perennial Wall-rocket

Archaeophyte with a European Temperate distribution.

This is a plant of waste places and ruderal habitats (BH3, 16, 17) found in many parts of the British Isles although it is very rare in most of Scotland and Ireland. It is closely associated with ports.

Very rare (5). In northern Lancashire it was first recorded from waste ground at St Anne's c. 1915 (A.J.C.: LSA). Post 1964 records are from an old railway at Lancaster in 1966 (A.E.R.), railway ballast at Heysham (SD45E) in 1965, waste land, Heysham Harbour (SD46A) in 1978 (A.E.C.), Warton (SD57B) in 2010 (J.Cl.) and from Lytham St Anne's (SD32E) in 1978 where it persisted on sandy waste ground for about ten years. It was also found as a garden weed in the same tetrad in 2009 (C.F. & N.J.S.).

Diplotaxis muralis (L.) DC.   Annual Wall-rocket

Neophyte. This is a native of central and southern Europe and northern Africa but naturalised in northern Europe. It was first recorded from a field of oats raised from seeds from a wrecked ship on the Kent coast in 1778. From there, and supplemented by further introductions elsewhere, it has colonised waste ground and other ruderal habitats in many parts of the British Isles.

Occasional (61). In northern Lancashire Wheldon and Wilson (1907) recorded it from Lytham St Anne's in 1906 and subsequently also at Preston Docks. Today it is found in coastal areas of VC 60 with scattered records inland in the north of the vice-county and around Preston.

Diplotaxis erucoides (L.) DC.   White Wall-rocket

Neophyte. This is a native of the Mediterranean region and was first cultivated in Britain in 1736 and recorded in the wild in 1859. It is found as a casual on waste ground and tips etc. in a few scattered localities in England and Wales.

Very rare (1). The only northern Lancashire record is from waste land at Heysham Harbour (SD45E) in 1978 (A.E.C.).

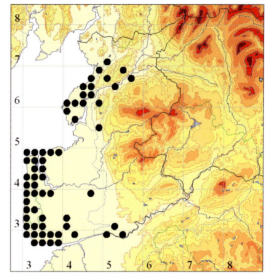
Diplotaxis muralis

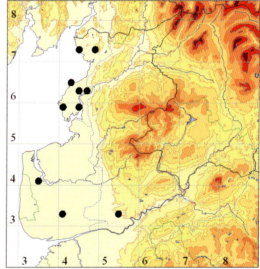
Brassica oleracea

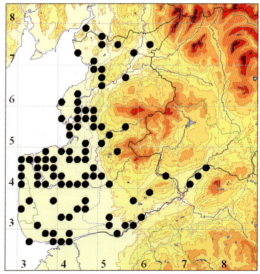
Brassica napus

Brassica oleracea L.   Cabbage

Suboceanic Southern-temperate element.

This is probably native on sea cliffs (BH18) in parts of Britain but as it is impossible to distinguish between native and plants derived from cultivated stock the native distribution is uncertain. As an escape from cultivation it is widely distributed in the British Isles (BH17).

Rare (10). In northern Lancashire it is found in scattered localities in VC 60. It was first recorded at Bolton-le-Sands in 1775 (Jenkinson, 1775) but it was not seen again until 1975 when it was found at Morecambe (SD46H; A.E.C.). Today, however, it is established on the cliff face of Warton Quarry (SD47W) although it was not seen there until 1985. Some of the records are clearly escapes from cultivation such as the summer cabbage recorded from Glasson Dock in 2010.

Brassica napus L.   Rape

Neophyte. This was derived from *B. oleracea* and is not known in the wild as a native species. It was first recorded in 1660. Two subspecies are widely cultivated but their separate distributions are not known. The species is widespread in Britain and is found in waste places and as a relic of cultivation.

Frequent (93). This is found throughout much of northern Lancashire but confined to the Ribble valley in VC 64.

Brassica rapa L.   Turnip

Archaeophyte with a Eurasian distribution.

There are three subspecies found in the British Isles but their separate distributions have not been determined. Ssp. *rapa* is a frequent relic of cultivation (BH4) whilst ssp. *oleifera* (DC.) Metzg. is a birdseed alien and ssp. *campestris* (L.) A.R. Clapham is found in semi-natural habitats often by streams and rivers. The species is found throughout the British Isles but much less frequently in upland areas than elsewhere.

Frequent (176). In northern Lancashire it is frequent in the west of the area and in the Lune, Wyre, and Ribble valleys, often as a relic of cultivation. It is absent from much of the east of the area.

Brassica juncea (L.) Czern.   Chinese Mustard

Neophyte. This species has been derived from *B. nigra* and *B. rapa* and occurs as a casual scattered throughout the northern hemisphere. It was grown in Britain in 1710 and was found in the wild c. 1876. Today it is found scattered throughout much of the British Isles.

Rare (6). In northern Lancashire it was first recorded from the sand dunes at St Anne's (Bailey, 1910). Post 1964 records are from scattered localities in VC 60.

Brassica elongata Ehrh.   Long-stalked Rape

Neophyte. This is a native of central and south-eastern Europe and western Asia but it is naturalised elsewhere. *B. elongata* was cultivated in Britain in 1801 and recorded in the wild in 1881. It formerly occurred in many places in Britain but always as a casual.

In northern Lancashire it was found at St Anne's in 1908 (C.B.; BM).

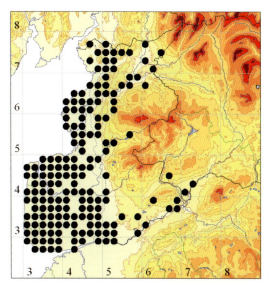

Brassica rapa

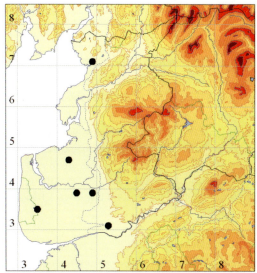

Brassica juncea

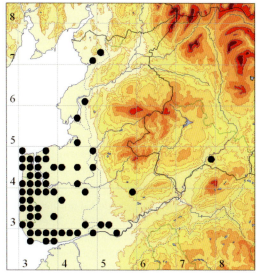

Brassica nigra

Brassica nigra (L.) W.D.J. Koch   Black Mustard

European Temperate element.

This is found by rivers and on coastal shingle and cliffs (BH3, 4) throughout England and more rarely elsewhere.

Occasional (61). In northern Lancashire it is typically found in coastal areas of the Fylde and occasionally in other parts of the area. However its present distribution is a considerable expansion on the eight localities noted by Wheldon and Wilson (1907). Nationally there were many losses after 1962 ('New Atlas') but 'Local Change' noted no further losses after 1987.

Sinapis arvensis L.   Charlock

Archaeophyte with a Eurosiberian Temperate distribution.

This is found as an arable weed and on roadsides and waste ground etc. (BH3, 4, 17) throughout most of the British Isles.

Frequent (203). In northern Lancashire it occurs mostly in the west of the area. There is no change in its distribution locally or nationally although the 'New Atlas' thought there might have been losses from arable fields.

Sinapis alba L.   White Mustard

Archaeophyte with a European Southern-temperate distribution.

This is a weed of arable land and other ruderal habitats, often on calcareous soils (BH3, 4). It occurs throughout most of the British Isles but especially in south-eastern Britain.

Occasional (19). In northern Lancashire old records are confined to Stalmine, near Garstang (Wheldon and Wilson, 1907) and St Anne's (Whellan, 1942). Post 1964 records are mostly from the west of the area. Nationally the 'New Atlas' suggests that there has been a decline in the distribution of White Mustard but 'Local Change' reports no further losses since 1987.

Eruca vesicaria (L.) Cav.   Garden Rocket

Neophyte found as a native species in the Mediterranean region and south-eastern Asia. It has been grown in gardens since at least 1200 but it was not recorded in the wild until 1859. It is found occasionally as a casual in waste places and on tips mostly in England.

Very rare (3). It was first recorded in northern Lancashire from the sand dunes at St Anne's (Bailey, 1907). It was next recorded from a waste heap at Haslam Park, Preston (SD53A) in 1965 (E.H.), St Anne's (SD32J) in 2006 (C.F. & N.J.S.) and from Fairhaven (SD32I) in 1998 (C.F. & N.J.S.).

Erucastrum gallicum (Willd.) O.E. Schulz   Hairy Rocket

Neophyte. This is a native of the Pyrenees and central Europe and was first recorded from the wild in Britain in 1863. Today it is usually found as a casual on roadsides, on waste ground and in other ruderal habitats in England, Wales, Ireland and southern Scotland.

Very rare (5). It was not recorded in northern Lancashire until it was found on a tip at Blackpool c. 1966 (A.E.R.). Other more recent records are from Lancaster (SD46R) in 1984 (D.P.E.), near Thurnham (SD45S; Livermore and Livermore, 1987), Glasson Dock (SD45M) in 1987 (T.C.G.R.) and on the A6 near Catterall (SD54A) in 1989 (L.R.F.).

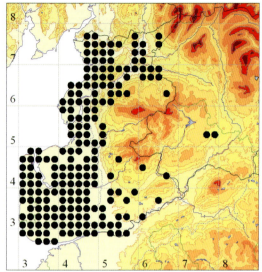

Sinapis arvensis

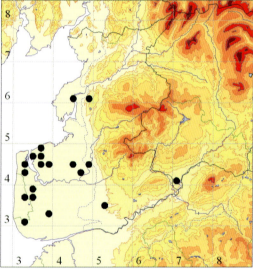

Sinapis alba

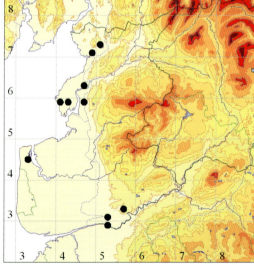

Hirshfeldia incana

Hirschfeldia incana (L.) Lagr.-Foss   Hoary Mustard

Neophyte. This is a native of south-western Europe, the Mediterranean region and south-western Asia. It was cultivated in Britain by 1771 and recorded from the wild by 1837. It occurs in waste places especially in large urban areas where it is now naturalised in several places.

Rare (10). This was first recorded in northern Lancashire from demolition sites in Preston (SD53F) in 1966 and since then it has been found in a number of places in the western half of VC 60, especially in recent years.

Coincya monensis (L.) Greuter & Burdet ssp. **monensis**
                                                   Isle of Man Cabbage

Endemic to Irish Sea coasts and southern Wales.

This is found on sand dunes and sandy ground (BH3, 17, 19) near the sea in England, Wales, Scotland and the Isle of Man. Facey, *et al.* (2007) suggest that it was formerly more widespread and that present populations are composed of genetically isolated endemic population clusters. The taxon is also the subject of a Biological Flora account (Hipkin and Facey, 2009)

Rare (9). In northern Lancashire it is confined to the Fylde coast at Lytham St Anne's, Blackpool and Fleetwood. Ashfield (1860) also reported it from Preesall. There has been no change in its distribution locally or nationally.

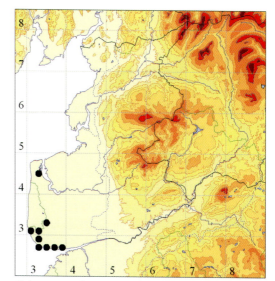

Coincya monensis ssp. *monensis*

Coincya longirostra (Boiss.) Greuter & Berdet

Neophyte. This is a native of southern Spain, which has only rarely been recorded in Britain, all before 1930.

In northern Lancashire it was recorded from Newton-in-Bowland in 1912 (Peel, 1913).

Cakile maritima Scop.   Sea Rocket

European Wide-temperate element.

This occurs on sandy seashores, fore dunes and sandy waste places (BH19) around all the coasts of the British Isles.

Occasional (38). Although Wheldon and Wilson recorded Sea Rocket from the VC 60 coast it appears to have been a rare plant. Today it occurs in sandy places along the whole VC 60 coast. Its distribution nationally is stable.

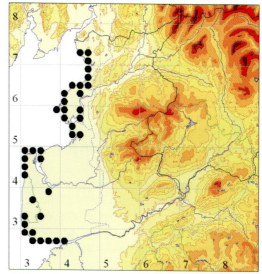

Cakile maritima

Rapistrum rugosum (L.) J.P. Bergeret   Bastard Cabbage

Neophyte. This is a native of the Mediterranean region and south-western Asia. It was introduced into cultivation in Britain by 1739 and was known from the wild by 1863. It was found mainly as a casual of waste ground mostly in England, Wales and around Dublin in Ireland. Bastard Cabbage is morphologically variable and there is disagreement as to what extent this can be recognised taxonomically (Clement and Foster, 1994).

Very rare (4). It was first recorded in northern Lancashire from the sand dunes at St Anne's in 1906 and 1907 (C.B.; MANCH). More recent records are from a tip at Lancaster in 1962 (E.H.), a tip at Blackpool (SD33I) in 1966 (A.E.R.), demolition sites at Preston (SD53F) in 1966 (E.H.), near Marton Mere, Blackpool (SDSSH) in c. 1975 (C.F. & N.J.S.) and from Glasson Dock (SD45M) in 1991 (T.C.G.R.).

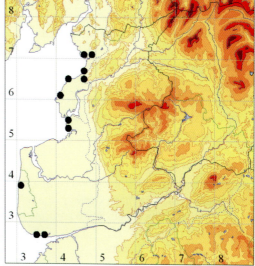

Crambe maritima

Crambe maritima L.   Sea-kale

European Temperate element.

This occurs on stony shores (BH19) around the coasts of England, Wales, Ireland and southern Scotland.

Rare (11). In northern Lancashire the only old record is that of Clitheroe and Robinson (1903) from Lytham and it was not recorded again until it was found on iron slag at Warton (SD47V) in the 1950s (H.S.). Since 1964 it has been found at various places on the VC 60 coast, usually in small numbers. Its distribution has also increased nationally.

Raphanus raphanistrum L. ssp. **raphanistrum**   Wild Radish

Archaeophyte with a European Southern-temperate distribution.

This is found as a weed in cultivated ground and in waste places (BH4) throughout much of the British Isles.

Frequent (92). In northern Lancashire this was first recorded from Roman deposits at Ribchester (Huntley and Hillam, 2000) but Wheldon and Wilson (1907) only found this in seven places in the west of the area. It still occurs mainly in the west of northern Lancashire but it is now much more frequent. Nationally the 'New Atlas' noted a considerable decline but 'Local Change' did not note further decline since 1987.

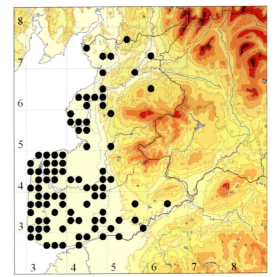

Raphanus raphanistrum ssp. *raphanistrum*

Raphanus raphanistrum L. ssp. **maritimus** (Sm.) Thell   Sea Radish

Mediterranean-Atlantic element.

This is found in open coastal grassland, sand dunes, shingle and disturbed ground by the sea (BH19) around the western coasts of England, Wales and Scotland and also on the coasts of Ireland, the Isle of Man and occasionally elsewhere.

Occasional (49). In northern Lancashire this was a rare species 100 years ago. Early records were from Lytham (Clitheroe and Robinson, 1903), Knott End in 1915 and St Annes in 1918 (Wheldon and Wilson, 1925) but by the early 1940s it was locally abundant at St Anne's (Whellan, 1942). Today it is frequent along the whole VC 60 coast. It has also spread nationally.

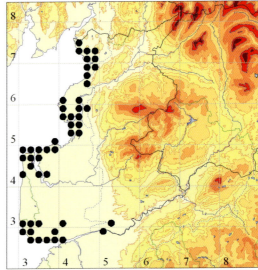

Raphanus raphanistrum ssp. *maritimus*

Raphanus sativus L.   Garden Radish

Neophyte. This is a cultivated plant probably derived from Mediterranean *Raphanus* taxa. It has been cultivated in gardens since 995 but was not reported from the wild until 1893. It is found scattered in waste places throughout much of Britain and around Dublin in Ireland but always as a casual.

Rare (9). In northern Lancashire it was first recorded from the sand dunes at St Anne's in 1907 (C.B. in Wheldon and Wilson, 1907; MANCH). Since 1964 it has been reported from scattered localities in VC 60.

[Sisymbrium irio L.   London-rocket

Neophyte. This is a native of western Europe, the Mediterranean region and western Asia. It has been known in the wild in Britain since 1650 but its abundance has fluctuated. It was particularly abundant in London after the Great Fire of 1666.

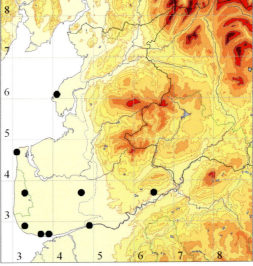

Raphanus sativus

In northern Lancashire the only records are from Blackpool (Thornber, 1837) and Cuckoo Moss, Kirkham (Heathcote, 1923). As there are no voucher specimens for these records they should be considered doubtful.]

Sisymbrium loeselii L.   False London-rocket

Neophyte. This is a native of central and eastern Europe, western and central Asia but it is widely naturalised elsewhere. It was introduced into cultivation in Britain in 1787 and recorded from the wild in 1883. It has only recently become persistent with centres of distribution based on the East Midlands and the London area.

Very rare (1). In northern Lancashire it was recorded from a tip at Blackpool in c. 1966 (A.E.R.).

Sisymbrium altissimum L.   Tall Rocket

Neophyte. Tall Rocket is a native of eastern Europe and western Asia but it is widely naturalised in temperate western Europe. It was cultivated in Britain by 1768 and recorded from the wild in 1862. Today it is found over much of England and central Scotland but more rarely elsewhere in the British Isles.

Occasional (40). In northern Lancashire it was first recorded from Fleetwood and Preston Docks (Wheldon and Wilson, 1901b). Further localities were noted by Wheldon and Wilson (1907) and both France (1931) and Whellan (1942) thought it was established at Lytham St Anne's. Today it is found in coastal areas of VC 60 and in the Preston area.

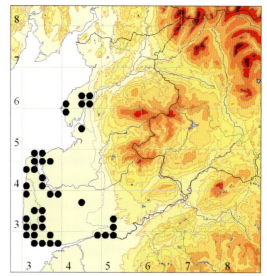

Sisymbrium altissimum

Sisymbrium orientale L.   Eastern Rocket

Neophyte. This is a native of southern Europe, the Mediterranean region and western Asia but it is widely naturalised in western Europe. It was cultivated in Britain by 1739 and was found in the wild in 1859.

Occasional (42). This was first recorded in northern Lancashire from Lytham St Anne's (Bailey, 1907; BIRM) and from Caton in 1941 (J.N.F.). Since 1964 it has been recorded mainly from coastal areas of VC 60 but occasionally elsewhere.

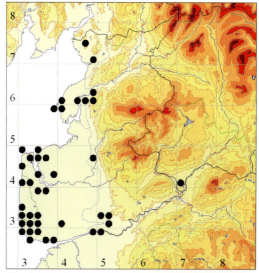

Sisymbrium orientale

[Sisymbrium austriacum Jacq.   Austrian Rocket

This was recorded from Lytham St Anne's (Bailey, 1910) but the voucher at MANCH is *S. officinale*]

Sisymbrium officinale L.   Hedge Mustard

Archaeophyte with a European Southern-temperate distribution.

This is found on roadsides and in cultivated and waste ground (BH3, 4, 17) over much of the British Isles although it is absent from many upland areas in Wales and Scotland.

Common (242). In northern Lancashire it is common in the west of the area but much rarer in the Bowland Fells and in VC 64. There has been no change in its distribution locally or nationally.

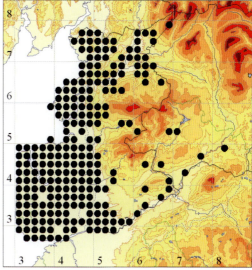

Sisymbrium officinale

Isatis tinctoria L.   Woad

Archaeophyte. This is widespread in Eurasia and was until the nineteenth century an important dye plant grown in Britain since the Iron Age. It occurred mostly in south-eastern England but it is now a rare casual.

In northern Lancashire Jenkinson (1775) knew it from several places in Yealand Conyers and Yealand Redmayne where it would have been used in the flax industry (Roberts, 1998) and had no doubt escaped from cultivation.

Alliaria petiolata (M. Bieb.) Cavara & Grande   Garlic Mustard

European Temperate element.

Garlic Mustard is found in a variety of habitats ranging from woodland margins, hedgerows and riverbanks to waste ground (BH3). It is found in most of the British Isles except parts of north-western Scotland and western Ireland.

Very common (358). It occurs throughout much of northern Lancashire but it is absent from upland areas. Its distribution is unchanged locally and nationally.

[Teesdalia nudicaulis (L.) W.T. Aiton   Shepherd's Cress

There is a record for this from Ribchester (B.R.C.; Stewart, et al., 1994) but as there is no voucher specimen and there are no other records for northern Lancashire it is probably an identification error.]

Thlaspi arvense L.   Field Penny-cress

Archaeophyte with a Eurasian Temperate distribution.

This is found as an arable weed and in other ruderal habitats (BH3, 4) in lowland areas of the British Isles.

Frequent (111). In northern Lancashire it occurs in coastal areas and occasionally elsewhere. For a time in the 1980s it was especially associated with the central reservation of the M6 motorway between Preston and Lancaster. However 100 years ago this was a very rare species only being found at Ashton and St Anne's (Wheldon and Wilson, 1907). Despite this increase in its distribution it is often erratic in its appearance. Nationally there has been an increase in its frequency in the north and west of its range ('New Atlas') but no further change was noted since 1987 ('Local Change').

Thlaspi alliaceum L.   Garlic Penny-cress

Neophyte. Garlic Penny-cress is a native of southern Europe and northern Turkey. It was cultivated in Britain by 1714 and was recorded in the wild in 1923. It is an annual species and is often naturalised. Most records are from south-eastern England,.

Very rare (1). In northern Lancashire it was found on bare clay in a clay pit at Peel (SD33K) in c. 1974 (C.F. & N.J.S.).

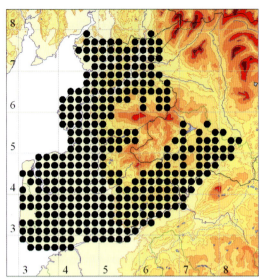

Alliaria petiolata

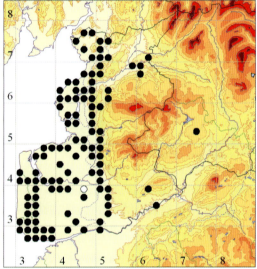

Thlaspi arvense

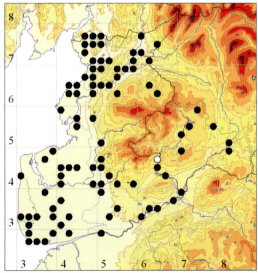

Hesperis matronalis

Hesperis matronalis L.   Dame's-violet

Neophyte. This is a native of southern Europe and western Asia but widely naturalised elsewhere. It has been cultivated in gardens since 1375 and was known in the wild from 1805. It is found in hedgerows, wood borders, riverbanks and on waste ground throughout most of the British Isles.

Frequent (91). In northern Lancashire *Hesperis matronalis* was first recorded from Hawes Water (SD47T) in 1868 (Wheldon and Wilson, 1907) but until 1964 there were only four further records scattered across VC 60. Today it is found in most parts of the area.

Bunias orientalis L.   Warty-cabbage

Neophyte. This is a native of eastern Europe and western Asia and was cultivated in Britain by 1731. It was recorded from the wild in 1739. In Britain it is mostly found in central Scotland and in the London area extending westwards to Bristol.

Very rare (1). Warty-cabbage was first seen in northern Lancashire at Fleetwood Dock in 1946 (H.E.B.) where it was reported to be established in some quantity (Whellan, 1948). No doubt it was a remnant of this colony that was found on a disused railway line at Fleetwood (SD34I) in 1990 (C.F. & N.J.S.).

Matthiola longipetala (Vert.) DC.   Night-scented Stock

Neophyte. This is a native of Greece, northern Africa and south-western Asia and was introduced into British gardens in 1818. It was reported from the wild in 1905 and it is always found as a casual in scattered localities in England, Wales, Scotland and the Isle of Man.

Very rare (2). In northern Lancashire it was recorded from near the shore at Heysham (SD45E) in 1975 (A.E.C.) and Fleetwood Docks (SD34I) in 1995 and 2006 (C.F. & N.J.S.). It probably occurs from time to time elsewhere in ruderal situations.

Malcolmia maritima (L.) W.T. Aiton   Virginia Stock

Neophyte. This species is a native of coastal areas of Italy and Greece but naturalised further west along the Mediterranean coast. It has been cultivated in Britain since 1713 and was known from the wild in 1866. However it only occurs as a casual on waste ground but may be found almost anywhere in England, Wales, Scotland and the Isle of Man. It is very rare in Ireland.

Very rare (4). In northern Lancashire it was first recorded from a tip at Blackpool (SD33I) in 1965 (E.P.) and subsequently from Heysham (SD46M) in 1974 (A.E.C.), a tip at Lytham (SD32Y) in c. 1980 (C.F. & N.J.S.) and from Blackpool (SD33H) in 1991 (C.F. & N.J.S.).

Cochlearia anglica L.   English Scurvygrass

Oceanic Temperate element.

The distribution of this species is unclear as plants around the coasts of the northern Irish Sea seem to be to some extent intermediate between *C. anglica* as seen in south-eastern England and *C. officinalis*. Yet populations seem morphologically uniform. Irish populations are sometimes named as the hybrid between *C. anglica* and *C. officinalis* (*C.* × *hollandica* Henrard). However taking a wide interpretation of the taxon, *C. anglica sensu lato* occurs around most coasts of England, Wales, Ireland and southern Scotland. It occurs on salt marshes and sea walls and occasionally on other substrates near the coast (BH21). However recent research (T. Rich, pers. comm.) suggests that material around Irish Sea coasts and western coasts of Scotland is part of *C. officinalis sensu lato* and is identifiable as **Cochlearia atlantica** Pobed. It is probably endemic to the British Isles (Rich, 1991).

Occasional (62). In northern Lancashire *C. atlantica* is found on all the coasts and salt marshes of VC 60 extending inland up the estuaries to the highest points of tidal influence. Some plants have been referred to *C.* × *hollandica*. Because of identification and taxonomic difficulties it is not possible to assess if there has been any change in the distribution of this taxon.

Cochlearia anglica *sensu lato* × C. danica

A hybrid *Cochlearia* was found on the sea wall at Thurnham (SD45H) in 1987 (T.C.G.R., L.A.L.). It is believed to be this taxon but more work is required on Irish Sea coastal Scurvygrasses to be certain.

Cochlearia pyrenaica DC. ssp. **pyrenaica**
                             Pyrenean Scurvygrass

European Arctic-montane element.

This recently described subspecies is found in damp open habitats on calcareous substrates or on heavy metal spoil heaps (BH11, 16) in upland areas of the British Isles.

Rare (8). In northern Lancashire it has been found on limestone rocks in Ease Gill and on Green Hill, Leck and on the banks of the R. Greta, although it could not be found here in 2002. Milne-Redhead (1870s) recorded *C. officinalis* from the Holden Clough area, Bolton-by-Bowland, which could be this species. Also there is a record from the Trough of Bowland (SD65G; Abbott, 2005) and an unconfirmed record from Bowland-with-Leagram (SD64L). Because of identification difficulties it is not known if its distribution has changed nationally.

Cochlearia officinalis L. ssp. **officinalis**   Common Scurvygrass

Circumpolar Wide-boreal element.

Because of confusion with other taxa and especially *C. anglica sensu lato* the distribution of this species in the British Isles is not clear. However it occurs on sea cliffs (BH18) and other rock surfaces around the coasts of the British Isles and occasionally on roadsides.

Very rare (1 or 2). In northern Lancashire there is an old 1875 record from Silverdale (LDS), which might be this, but the only confirmed records are from coastal cliffs at Heysham (SD46A) and possibly from the Heysham Harbour breakwater (SD35Z). Because of identification and taxonomic difficulties it is not possible to assess change.

Cochlearia danica L.   Danish Scurvygrass

Oceanic Temperate element.

This is a winter annual of cliff tops, coastal walls, sand dunes and latterly roadsides (BH3, 18). It occurs around the coasts of the British Isles and since *c.* 1980 inland on roadside verges in England, Wales, southern Scotland and Ireland.

Frequent (107). In northern Lancashire a similar spread was noted (Greenwood, 2004a) and it is now found in many parts of VC 60. Even the distribution on the coast has expanded considerably since Wheldon and Wilson (1907) recorded only six sites. Nationally this species has spread spectacularly across the country.

Iberis sempervirens L.   Perennial Candytuft

Neophyte. This is a native of the mountains of southern Europe, northern Africa and south-western Asia. It was first cultivated in Britain by 1731 and was recorded from the wild in 1928.

Very rare (1). The only northern Lancashire record is from Heysham (SD46A) in 1975 (A.E.C.).

Iberis umbellata L.   Garden Candytuft

Neophyte. This is a native of the European Mediterranean region but it is widely cultivated in gardens. It was first known as a garden plant in Britain in 1596 but not recorded from the wild until 1858. It occurs as a casual in many parts of the British Isles.

Rare (11). This was first recorded from Torrisholme (SD46M) in 1974 (A.E.C.) and subsequently from other localities in the north of the area and from Lytham St Anne's. It is probably under recorded and is always a casual.

SANTALACEAE   BASTARD-TOADFLAX FAMILY

Viscum album L.   Mistletoe

European Temperate element but a neophyte in northern Lancashire.

Mistletoe is a hemiparasite on a wide variety of trees growing in woodlands, parks, gardens, orchards and hedges in much of England and Wales. However at least towards the north of its British range it is probably introduced.

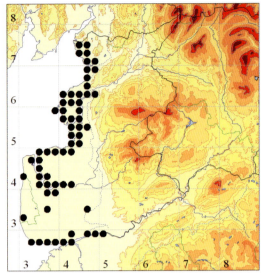
Cochlearia anglica

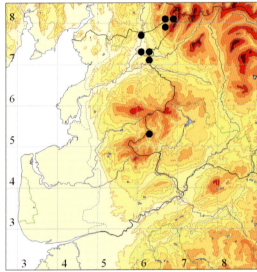
Cochlearia pyrenaica ssp. *pyrenaica*

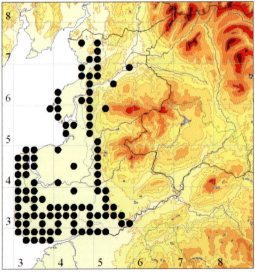
Cochlearia danica

Very rare (3). In northern Lancashire Mistletoe was known from a garden in Fulwood (SD53K) where it grew on an apple tree in the 1950s (E.F.G.). It was also found on an apple tree in Silverdale (SD47S) in 1973 (L.A.L.), which was subsequently cut down (J.M.N.). Mistletoe was found again in 2009 (P. Francis) at Bowland-with-Leagram (SD64M) and growing on *Sorbus aucuparia* at Ashton-on-Ribble (SD53F) in 2011 (J. Foran). It is believed it was deliberately introduced at most sites.

TAMARICACEAE   TAMARISK FAMILY

Tamarix gallica L.   Tamarisk

Neophyte. This species is a native of the western Mediterranean region and south-western Europe. It has been grown in British gardens since before 1597 and was known from the wild by 1796. It has been extensively planted in coastal areas in the southern half of the British Isles where it is very resistant to wind damage.

Very rare (5). This was first recorded as a garden escape at Lytham St Anne's (Bailey, 1907) and again in 1915 (A.J.C.; LSA). Post 1964 records are from old plantings by Fairhaven Lake and on sand dunes at St Anne's (SD32I) in 1994 (E.F.G.), Lytham St Anne's Local Nature Reserve (SD33A) in 2001 (Bradford Botany Group), as long established in an old garden at Knott End (SD34P) in 1999 (E.F.G.) subsequently lost to building works, old plantings at Fleetwood Cemetery (SD34D) in 2001 (E.F.G.) and more recently planted at Heysham power station (SD45E) in 1999 (J.M.N.). It is doubtful if it is naturalised at any of these localities but once planted it will persist for many years.

PLUMBAGINACEAE   THRIFT FAMILY

Limonium vulgare Mill.   Common Sea-lavender

Mediterranean-Atlantic element.

This is an attractive and characteristic plant of ungrazed salt marshes (BH21) around the coasts of England and southern Scotland. However it can be difficult to distinguish from *L. humile* and *L. × neumanii* (Dawson and Ingrouille, 1995).

Occasional (40). In VC 60 Wheldon and Wilson (1907) recorded it from the Wyre and Lune estuaries but today its range has extended to Silverdale on Morecambe Bay and Lytham St Anne's on the Ribble estuary where it was first seen in about 1968. At Barnaby's Sands on the Wyre estuary it is especially abundant (see Plate 2.64). This extension of range is probably due to a decline of marsh grazing. It is thought that nationally its distribution is stable.

Limonium vulgare × L. humile (L. × neumanii C.E. Salmon)

Dawson and Ingrouille (1995) carried out a biometric survey of *L. vulgare* and *L. humile* and showed that not only were the two species difficult to distinguish but where they occurred together intermediates were common. The Wyre estuary was amongst their sampling sites and there they recognised that both species were present and that plants showing characteristics

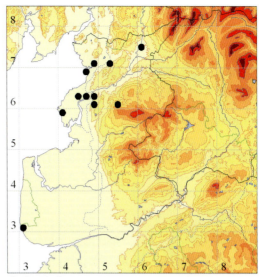
Iberis umbellata

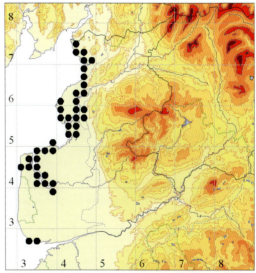
Limonium vulgare

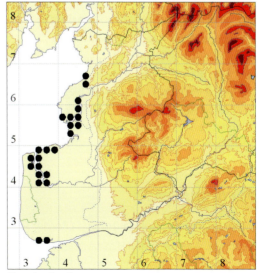
Limonium humile

of both species were also present indicating hybridisation and that the range of variation suggested that further introgression had occurred. Voucher specimens at MANCH for old records are for localities at Fleetwood in 1876 and 1887 and at Wardless in 1874. Recent records believed to be this hybrid have been from Fairhaven (SD32N) in 2007 (E.F.G.) and Glasson Dock (SD45N) in 2010 (E.F.G. & Bradford Botany Group).

Limonium humile Mill.   Lax-flowered Sea-lavender

Oceanic Temperate element.

This is found on salt marshes (BH21) along many coasts of England, Ireland and on the Solway Firth in Scotland. Mixed populations with *L. vulgare* occur (see *L .× neumanii*).

Occasional (22). In northern Lancashire *L. humile* is found on the salt marshes of the Lune and Wyre estuaries and on the shores of Morecambe Bay at Bolton-le-Sands and Hest Bank. The Morecambe Bay records represent a spread of the species since 1907 (Wheldon and Wilson, 1907) whilst in 1995 it was found at Lytham St Anne's. Nationally its distribution is unchanged.

Limonium britannicum Ingr. ssp. celticum Ingr.
                                          Western Sea-lavender

Endemic.

This rock sea-lavender is found on sea cliffs, at high elevations on salt marshes, especially if the substrate is stabilised shingle, and on sea walls (BH18, 19, 21). It is found in a restricted area of coast from northern Wales to Cumbria but may occur at other localities around the northern Irish Sea coast. Furthermore recent research (Ingrouille, 2006) suggests that *L. britannicum* ssp. *celticum* may not be distinct from other subspecies or from *L. procerum* (C.E. Salmon) Ingr., also endemic to western coasts of the British Isles.

Very rare (2). In northern Lancashire *L. britannicum* was found in a few localities on the Wyre and Lune estuaries but since 1964 only Wyre estuary colonies have been known. One site was lost when the Shard Bridge (SD34V) was re-built and the remaining colonies are now confined to stabilised shingle at the highest parts of salt marshes and on old sea walls on the east bank of the R. Wyre in the vicinity of Barnaby's Sands, Preesall-with-Hackensall (SD34N).

Armeria maritima Willd. ssp. maritima   Thrift

Circumpolar Wide-boreal element.

This is found on sea cliffs, salt marshes and other coastal habitats as well as in montane habitats and as a garden escape (BH18, 21). It occurs around all the coasts of the British Isles and on many mountains.

Occasional (58). In northern Lancashire it is a common coastal species of salt marshes and old sea walls and very rarely as a garden escape inland. There has been no change in its distribution locally or nationally.

POLYGONACEAE   KNOTWEED FAMILY

Persicaria campanulata (Hook. f.) Rouse Decr.   Lesser Knotweed

Neophyte. A native of the Himalayas introduced into Britain as a garden plant in about 1909 and reported from the wild in 1933. Although not yet common it occurs throughout the British Isles.

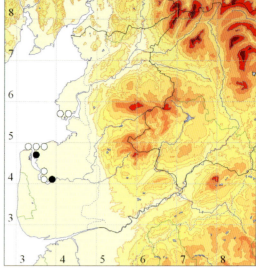
Limonium britannicum ssp. *celticum*

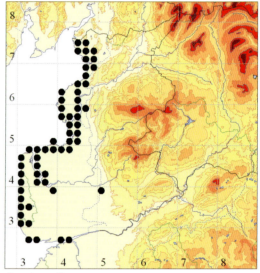
Armeria maritima

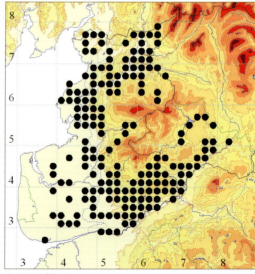
Persicaria bistorta

Very rare (2). In northern Lancashire the only records, all from VC 60, are by a stream opposite houses at Lower Lee, Over Wyresdale (SD55S) in 1999 (E.F.G.), by a roadside at Roeburndale Chapel (SD66B) in 2004 (E.F.G. & J.M.N.) and by the R. Wyre, Stoops Bridge, Abbeystead, Over Wyresdale (SD55S) in 2005 (E.F.G.; LIV), which was previously recorded as *P. wallichii.*.

Persicaria bistorta (L.) Samp.   Common Bistort

Eurasian Boreo-temperate element.

This is found in woodland edge habitats (BH3, 6) and occurs throughout much of Britain and parts of Ireland but its native distribution is obscured by escapes from cultivation.

Frequent (182). In northern Lancashire it is found mostly around the edge of the Bowland Fells, in the north of the area and in the Ribble valley becoming less frequent towards the coast. 'Local Change' suggests that native populations are centred on Lancashire and Cumbria. In the northern Pennines it was used to make dock pudding (Mabey, 1996). *P. bistorta* was lost from many sites in southern England and Ireland before 1930 but its distribution is now believed to be stable both locally and nationally.

Persicaria amplexicaulis (D. Don) Rouse Decr.   Red Bistort

Neophyte. A native of Asia from Afghanistan to south-western China introduced into cultivation in 1826. It has been known in the wild since 1908 and occurs largely in more populous parts of the British Isles.

Very rare (4). In northern Lancashire it was first recorded from waste ground at Lytham St Anne's (SD33J) in 1962 (J. M.) and subsequently from an old garden in Blackpool (SD33J) in 1965 (A.E.R., E.H.), another garden, Blackpool (SD33I) in 1997 (C.F. & N.J.S.), at Silverdale (SD47S) in 2010 (J.Cl.) and at Dolphinholme, Ellel (SD55B) in 1995 (E.F.G.).

Persicaria wallichii Greuter & Burdet   Himalayan Knotweed

Neophyte. A native of the Himalayas introduced just before 1900 and first recorded in the wild in 1917. It is found throughout the British Isles and has expanded its distribution considerably since 1962.

Very rare (3). In northern Lancashire the only records are from a wood in Nether Wyresdale (SD54E) in 1965 (E.F.G.), woods near Caton Lune Bridge (SD56H) in 1997 (P.J.) and from a wood near High Barn, Gressingham (SD56U) in 1968 (J.M.N.). It is believed there may have been some confusion in distinguishing *P. campanulata* from *P. wallichii* and as there are no voucher specimens the records should be checked.

Persicaria amphibia (L.) Gray   Amphibious Bistort

Circumpolar Boreo-temperate element.

Amphibious Bistort is found throughout the British Isles in wet places and on waste ground (BH11, 13, 14)

Frequent (201). In the west of northern Lancashire this is a common plant of ponds, marshes, dune slacks and ditches and also in drier situations on waste ground. It also occurs further inland in the Lune and Ribble valleys. Its distribution locally and nationally is stable.

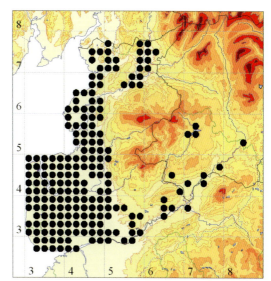

Persicaria amphibia

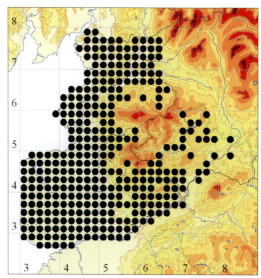

Persicaria maculosa

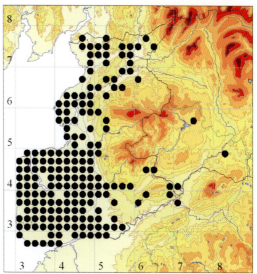

Persicaria lapathifolia

Persicaria maculosa Gray   Redshank

Eurasian Temperate element.

This is a common weed of arable farmland and in open habitats generally (BH3, 4) throughout the British Isles.

Common (341). It is found in similar habitats, particularly potato fields, throughout northern Lancashire but becomes much less frequent in Bowland and in Lancashire VC 64. There have been no changes in its distribution locally or nationally except in northern Scotland where there may have been some losses since 1962 ('New Atlas').

Persicaria lapathifolia (L.) Gray   Pale Persicaria

Circumpolar Southern-temperate element.

This occurs in similar habitats (BH3, 4) and places to *P. maculosa* and is found throughout the British Isles but it is much less frequent in northern Scotland and western Ireland.

Frequent (192). In northern Lancashire it also occurs in similar habitats and places to *P. maculosa* but is generally less frequent, especially in the east of the area.

Although Wheldon and Wilson (1907) recorded this as common in VC 60 they did not find it in the Lune valley suggesting that it has extended its distribution in northern Lancashire. Also whilst the 'New Atlas' recorded no change nationally since 1962 'Local Change' noted an increase since 1987.

Persicaria hydropiper (L.) Spach   Water-pepper

Circumpolar Temperate element.

This occurs throughout the British Isles, although it is much less frequent in the east and in central Ireland than elsewhere. It is found in marshes, by lakes, ponds and canal margins etc. (BH11, 13, 14).

Common (282). *P. hydropiper* occurs throughout northern Lancashire but it is less frequent in the east of the area than elsewhere. There has been no change in its distribution locally but the 'New Atlas' reported losses in eastern Britain. However 'Local Change' noted no further losses.

Persicaria mitis (Schrank) Opiz ex Assenov   Tasteless Water-pepper

European Temperate element.

This is found scattered in wet places (BH13, 14) in England, Wales and Ireland but it is similar to *P. hydropiper* and may be overlooked.

Very rare (5). In northern Lancashire it was recorded from Carr House Green Common (SD43T) in 1964 (J.H.), by the R. Ribble at Dutton (SD63T) in 1987 (E.F.G.), in a ditch at Pilling (SD44E) in 1988 (C.J.B.), in a ditch at Medlar (SD43H) in 1991 (Anon) and in a pond at Ribchester (SD63N) in 2003 (P.G.). Because of confusion with other species it is not known if the distribution of *P. mitis* nationally is stable or not.

Persicaria minor (Huds.) Opiz   Small Water-pepper

Eurasian Temperate element.

This is an annual plant of marshy, open habitats in scattered localities in the British Isles except northern Scotland but it is especially characteristic of ground flooded in winter (BH13, 14).

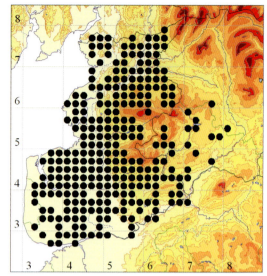
Persicaria hydropiper

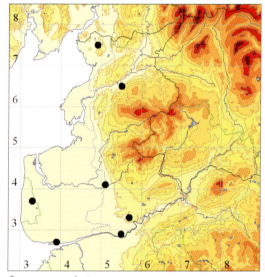
Fagopyrum esculentum

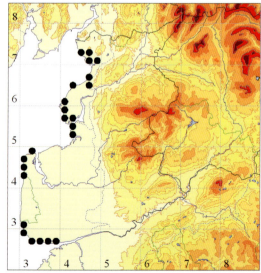
Polygonum oxyspermum ssp. raii

Very rare (4). In northern Lancashire *P. minor* is largely confined to reservoir margins with their fluctuating water levels. When water levels are low it can be abundant. In VC 60 it was first recorded from Grizedale Reservoir, Nether Wyresdale (SD54J) in 1976 and also in nearby Barnacre Reservoir (both C.F. & N.J.S.). In VC 64 it was recorded from Stocks Reservoir (SD75H, I) and in a muddy area near Dunnow Hall, Slaidburn (SD75A), both in Abbott (2005). It is not thought that there has been any change in its distribution nationally.

Fagopyrum esculentum Moench   Buckwheat

Neophyte. This is a crop plant known from ancient times probably originating in south-western China. In Britain it was first recorded in the wild in 1597 and appears today on waste ground, rubbish tips, field margins and in other open habitats (BH4) but rarely persists at any one site. It is found throughout the British Isles but particularly in the southern half of England.

Rare (7). In northern Lancashire it was first recorded from arable land at Garstang in 1883 (Wheldon and Wilson, 1907), Cuckoo Moss, Upper Rawcliffe-with-Tarnacre (St Michael's School, 1902), and from waste ground at St Anne's in 1915 (A.J.C.). Since 1964 it has been recorded casually from open habitats in widely scattered localities in the west of northern Lancashire.

Polygonum oxyspermum C.A. Mey. & Bunge ex Ledeb.
ssp. **raii** D.A. Webb & Chater   Ray's Knotgrass

European Wide-temperate element.

This occurs on strand lines (BH19) on all the coasts of the British Isles but rarely on the east coast of England and the north and east coasts of Scotland.

Occasional (23). In northern Lancashire *P. oxyspermum* is found in suitable places along the whole coast but its frequency and abundance varies from year to year. It is not thought that its distribution has changed locally or nationally.

Polygonum aviculare agg.   Knotgrasses

This aggregate includes the native *Polygonum aviculare sensu stricto* and *P. boreale* (Lange) Small and the archaeophytes *P. arenastrum* Boreau and *P. rurivagum* Jord. ex Boreau. The aggregate has a circumpolar wide-temperate distribution and is found as arable weeds, on waste ground and roadsides (BH3, 4, 17) throughout the British Isles. However whilst *P. aviculare sensu stricto* and *P. arenastrum* have similar distributions *P. boreale* is restricted to Scottish coastal localities as far south as the Solway Firth and *P. rurivagum* occurs mostly in south-eastern England but it has been found in South Lancaster (VC 59) and as far north as mid-Scotland. Whilst the treatment of this group here is that of Stace (2010) it has not been possible to reflect the range of variation of plants seen in northern Lancashire. Sell and Murrell are publishing a more detailed treatment of the group in a forthcoming volume of their *Flora of Great Britain and Ireland*, which Chater (2010) has used in his *Flora of Cardiganshire*.

Very common (379). In northern Lancashire identification problems have resulted in an imperfect knowledge of the distribution of the species within *P. aviculare* agg. It is believed that both *P. aviculare sensu stricto* and *P. arenastrum* are equally widespread but as the latter is associated with the very common habitats of trampled ground by tracks, on roadsides, by farm gates and on pavements it may be more frequent (173 tetrads)

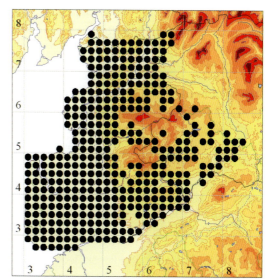

Polygonum aviculare agg.

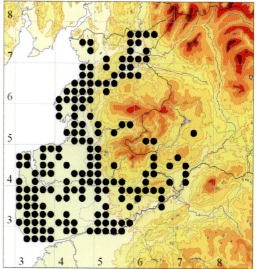

Fallopia japonica

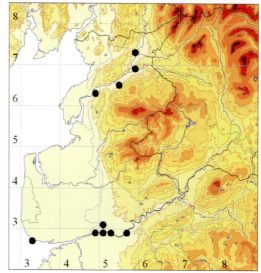

Fallopia × bohemica

than *P. aviculare sensu stricto* (123 tetrads) but with the present state of knowledge these are only tentative conclusions. The other two species of *P. aviculare* agg. have not been found in northern Lancashire but it is possible that either one or both species are present.

Polygonum patulum M. Bieb.   Red Knotgrass

Neophyte. This is a native of southern and central Europe, northern Africa and south-western Asia but it is often confused with other species. It occurs casually on tips and in waste places. In Britain it was first recorded from Middlesex in 1902.

Very rare (2). It was first recorded in northern Lancashire from a tip at Lytham (SD32Y) in 1963 (A.E.R.) and subsequently from Marton Mere tip, Blackpool (SD33I) in 1966 (A.E.R., J.H.) and from demolition sites in Preston (SD53F) in 1966 and 1967 (E.H., E.F.G.).

Fallopia japonica (Houtt.) Ronse Decr.   Japanese Knotweed

Neophyte. This is a native of eastern Asia but it is widely naturalized as a single, male-sterile clone in temperate Europe. It is often a serious pest species. *F. japonica* was first grown in British gardens in 1825 (Conolly, 1977) and was recorded in the wild in 1886 becoming well established between 1920 and 1940 on waste ground, tips and railway banks etc. (BH3, 14, 17).

Frequent (178). *F. japonica* was first recorded in northern Lancashire sometime between 1940 and 1960 (Conolly, 1977) and was present on waste ground in Fulwood (SD53K) in the 1950s (E.F.G.). Today it occurs throughout the area but is much less frequent in Bowland and in the east of the area than elsewhere.

F. japonica var. *compacta* (Hook. f.) J.P. Bailey was recorded from Blackpool (A.E.R.) in 1962 (LIV).

Fallopia japonica × F. sachalinensis
(F. × bohemica (Chrtek & Chrtková) J.P. Bailey   Bohemian Knotweed

Neophyte. This vigorous hybrid, which arose in Europe, has been known in cultivation in Britain since 1872 and was collected in the wild in 1954 although not recognised as this hybrid until the 1980s.

Rare (10). In northern Lancashire it was first recorded from Preston (SD52E) in 1977 (A.C.; LTR) and subsequently from other localities in the Preston area, the Lune valley and from sand dunes at Lytham St Anne's. It is probably under recorded, as it is morphologically similar to *F. japonica*.

Fallopia sachalinensis (F. Schmidt ex Maxim.) Ronse Decr.
                     Giant Knotweed

Neophyte. A native of eastern Asia but widely naturalized in temperate Europe. It became commercially available to British gardeners in 1869 but because of its large size it is much less widely planted than *F. japonica*. It was naturalized in Britain by 1903.

Occasional (20). *F. sachalinensis* was first recorded in northern Lancashire in Preston (SD52E) in 1963 (A.E.R.). Localities are scattered in VC 60 but it seems particularly well established in Wyresdale. Although a large plant it is not as vigorous as *F. japonica* and its spread is relatively modest. It is not known in Lancashire VC 64.

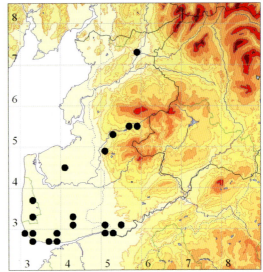
Fallopia sachalinensis

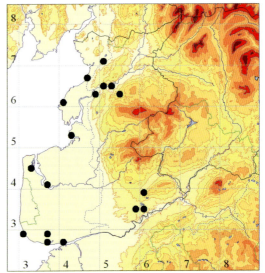
Fallopia baldschuanica

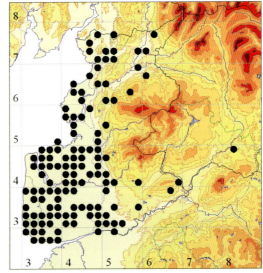
Fallopia convolvulus

Fallopia baldschuanica (Regel) Holub   Russian-vine

Neophyte. *F. baldschuanica* is a native of central Asia and was introduced into British gardens about 1894 and was first reported from the wild in 1936. It is a vigorous climbing perennial that clambers over hedges, walls and fences. It continues to be a popular garden plant, often used to screen unsightly material. It occurs throughout the British Isles but it is more frequent in southern Britain than elsewhere.

Occasional (17). In northern Lancashire it was first recorded from beside the railway at St Anne's in 1962 (A.E.R.) and is now found in scattered localities throughout much of VC 60.

Fallopia convolvulus (L.) Á. Löve   Black-bindweed

Archaeophyte with a Eurosiberian wide-temperate distribution. It is widespread and common in cultivated and waste ground (BH3, 4) throughout most of the British Isles.

Frequent (125). In northern Lancashire *F. convolvulus* is largely confined to western parts of the area. Nationally it declined in parts of northern England and Scotland before 1950 but further decline has not been noted. Its distribution in northern Lancashire remains unchanged.

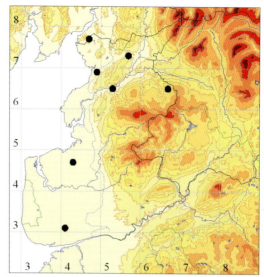
Rheum × rhabarbarum

Rheum × rhabarbarum L.   Rhubarb

Neophyte. Rhubarb is a hybrid of uncertain origin, probably arising in northern China and eastern Siberia. It has been cultivated in Britain since at least 1573 but was not recorded in the wild until 1960. It is unlikely to spread as it does not set seed and whilst rhizome fragments can be washed down streams and rivers this does not seem to occur frequently. However individual colonies are long lived.

Rare (7). This was first reported by Livermore and Livermore (1987) as a garden escape from the Silverdale (SD47T), Arkholme (SD57R) and Tatham (SD66S) areas. Since then it has also been reported from Caton-with-Littledale, Bolton-le-Sands, Ribby and Pilling but it is probably under recorded. Formerly railway workers often cultivated a patch of railway bank near stations etc. and when these were abandoned Rhubarb often survived for a number of years.

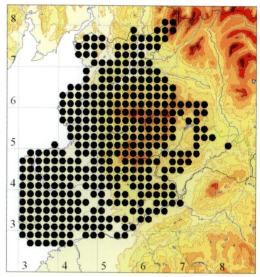
Rumex acetosella

Rumex acetosella L.   Sheep's Sorrel

Eurosiberian Wide-temperate element.

This occurs on dry acid heaths, sand dunes and grasslands (BH8, 9, 16) throughout the British Isles

Very common (383). Sheep's Sorrel is found throughout northern Lancashire where its distribution is unchanged. The 'New Atlas' reported a similar situation nationally but 'Local Change' noted a sharp decline in eastern England since 1987.

The taxonomy of *R. acetosella* has caused problems and Stace (2010) recognised ssp. *acetosella* and ssp. *pyrenaicus* (Pourr.) Akeroyd. The latter is widespread but ssp. *acetosella* is believed to replace it in northern Britain. However the subspecies were not distinguished in northern Lancashire. Also Lousley and Kent (1981) recognised *R. tenuifolius* (Wallr.) Á. Löve as a distinct species but Stace (2010) regards this as *R. acetosella* ssp. *acetosella* var. *tenuifolius* Wallr. It has very narrow leaves and is found on dry, sandy ground. This was found on Nicky Nook, Nether Wyresdale (SD54E) in 1966 (H.E.B.; LIV) and from fixed dunes at Lytham St Anne's (SD32N) in 1994 (E.F.G.) and (SD32I) in 1999 (E.F.G.; LIV).

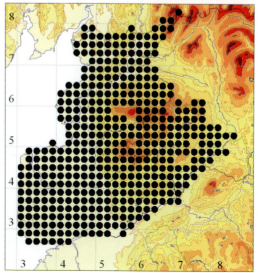
Rumex acetosa

Rumex scutatus L. — French Sorrel

Neophyte. This is a native of central and southern Europe, northern Africa and western Asia. It was cultivated in British gardens by 1596 and was recorded from the wild by c. 1800. Today it is found naturalized on walls and roadsides, mostly in England, with clusters of records in northern England and in the Bristol area.

Very rare (2). There is an unlocalised record from the 10km square SD47 (B.R.C.) but confirmed records are from a cobblestone wall at Staynall (SD34L) where it has been known since 1972 and Dunsop Bridge (SD65Q) in 1996 (A.U.).

Rumex acetosa L. — Common Sorrel

Eurosiberian Boreo-temperate element.

This occurs in a wide variety of neutral to acid woodland edge and grassland habitats (BH6) throughout the British Isles

Very common (438). Common Sorrel occurs throughout northern Lancashire where it is one of the commonest species. It is believed all plants in northern Lancashire belong to ssp. *acetosa*. There has been no change in its distribution locally or nationally.

Rumex longifolius DC. — Northern Dock

Eurasian Boreal-montane element.

This occurs in disturbed ground on roadsides, riverbanks, in fields and around farms (BH3, 13). It is a species of the Scottish borders and eastern Scotland but its distribution extends southwards in the Pennines to Cheshire and Staffordshire.

Rare (6). In northern Lancashire it was found in Roman deposits at Ribchester (Huntley and Hillam, 2000) and there are old records from beside the R. Lune near Kirkby Lonsdale; by Crowshaw Reservoir on the south side of Longridge Fell (Wheldon and Wilson, 1907) and from near Paythorne in VC 64 (Miall in Lees, 1888). Post 1964 records are confined to scattered localities in the north and east of the area. Nationally ('New Atlas') it appears to be spreading although 'Local Change' does not confirm this.

Rumex hydrolapathum Huds. — Water Dock

European Temperate element.

Water Dock is a conspicuous species of lake margins, fens and ditches (BH11) occurring in England, especially south of a line running between the R. Ribble and the Humber, Wales, Ireland and central Scotland.

Occasional (15). In northern Lancashire it is confined to coastal areas from the Wyre estuary, where it has not been seen recently, to Morecambe Bay. Nationally it appears to have extended its range northwards in Britain and Ireland ('New Atlas') but 'Local Change' notes no further change.

Rumex crispus L. ssp. crispus — Curled Dock

Eurosiberian Southern-temperate element.

This is a plant of waste ground and disturbed habitats (BH3, 6) throughout the British Isles.

Very common (353). It occurs throughout northern Lancashire except parts of peat covered Bowland. There has been no change in its distribution locally or nationally.

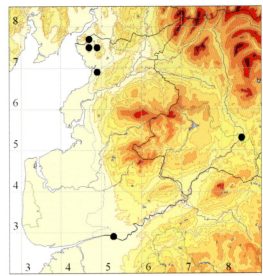

Rumex longifolius

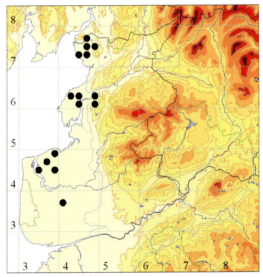

Rumex hydrolapathum

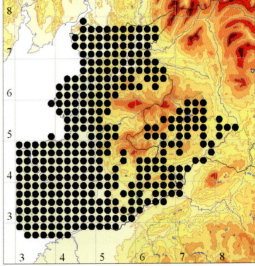

Rumex crispus

Rumex crispus L. ssp. **littoreus** (J. Hardy) Akeroyd

Oceanic Temperate element.

This is a distinctive subspecies of strand lines on beaches and salt marshes (BH19, 21) and occurs around most of the coasts of the British Isles.

Occasional (32). Although this subspecies has only been recognised recently (Stace, 1991) this was probably what Wheldon and Wilson (1907) recorded as *R. crispus* var. *trigranulatus* Syme from Heysham and Preston Docks and on the Wyre estuary. Although still probably under recorded it occurs along the whole northern Lancashire coast. Its distribution both nationally and locally is probably stable.

Rumex crispus × R. obtusifolius
(**R. × pratensis** Mert. & W.D.J. Koch)

This is a common hybrid that occurs throughout the British Isles on disturbed ground.

Rare (9). In northern Lancashire it occurs scattered across the area but it is probably very much under recorded.

Rumex crispus × R. sanguineus (**R. × sagorskii** Hausskn.)

This hybrid is fairly common in southern and central Britain (Stace, 1997).

Very rare (2). It has been recorded in northern Lancashire from the Tunstall area (SD67B; Livermore and Livermore, 1997) and from Hawes Water (SD47T) in 2000 (J.Cl.).

Rumex conglomeratus Murray   Clustered Dock

Eurosiberian Southern-temperate element.

This is a plant of wet meadows, fens, marshes, stream, river and canal banks etc. (BH11, 14) and occurs in most parts of the British Isles from central Scotland southwards.

Frequent (178). In northern Lancashire it is common in the west of the area but much rarer towards the east. There have been no changes in its distribution locally or nationally.

Rumex conglomerates × R. obtusifolius (**R. × abortivus** Ruhmer)

This hybrid occurs frequently with the parents and is found in scattered localities throughout Britain (Stace, 1997).

Very rare (2). It was found in VC 60 in 1988 in Lancaster (SD46R; Livermore and Livermore, 1989) and from near Bolton-le-Sands (SD46T) in 1988 (Anon).

Rumex sanguineus L.   Wood Dock

European Temperate element.

This occurs throughout most of the British Isles except northern Scotland in woodland margins, hedgerows and on waste ground (BH1, 3).

Common (308). In northern Lancashire it occurs in similar habitats throughout the area. There has been no change in its distribution locally but 'Local Change' notes an increase in its distribution nationally.

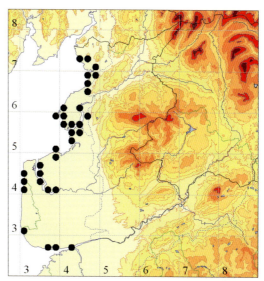

Rumex crispus ssp. *littoreus*

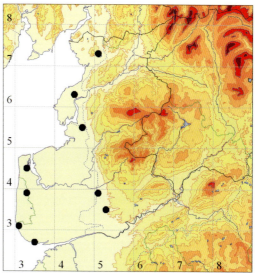

Rumex × pratensis

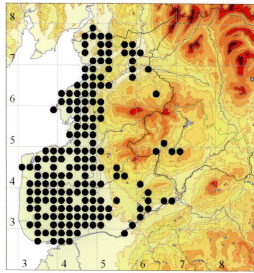

Rumex conglomeratus

Rumex obtusifolius L.   Broad-leaved Dock

European Temperate element.

Broad-leaved Dock is found in field margins, roadsides, riverbanks, ditches and on waste ground (BH3, 5, 17) throughout the British Isles.

Very common (416). It occurs throughout most of northern Lancashire. There has been no change in its distribution locally or nationally.

Rumex dentatus L.   Aegean Dock

Neophyte. A native of south-eastern Europe, north-eastern Africa and south-western Asia it was first cultivated in Britain in 1732 and was recorded in the wild in 1887. It is found occasionally on tips and waste ground in England but there are few recent records.

In northern Lancashire it was recorded from the 10km square SD33 in 1959 (B.R.C.).

Rumex maritimus L.   Golden Dock

Circumpolar Temperate element.

This occurs growing on the margins of lakes and pools where sites are usually waterlogged in winter (BH13, 14). It is found across much of the southern half of the British Isles reaching its northern limit on the west coast around Morecambe Bay.

Rare (7). In northern Lancashire occurrences have been sporadic and post 1964 records are scattered across the area. Because its appearance is sporadic it is not clear if its distribution locally has changed but as it readily colonizes new and eutrophic sites it may be increasing in the British Isles, at least in Ireland ('New Atlas').

Oxyria digyna (L.) Hill   Mountain Sorrel

Neophyte. This Circumpolar Arctic montane species, widespread on British mountains, appeared as a garden weed in Fulwood (SD53G) in 1965 (A.E.R.).

DROSERACEAE   SUNDEW FAMILY

Drosera rotundifolia L.   Round-leaved Sundew

Circumpolar Boreo-temperate element.

This insectivorous species is found in bogs and flushes (BH12) throughout the British Isles but it is becoming increasingly rare in south-eastern Britain.

Frequent (86). It occurs throughout much of northern Lancashire where suitable habitats occur but it is absent from intensively farmed areas in the Fylde and near Preston. However it has a long history of decline as bogs, flushes and heaths have been drained over at least the last 200 years, especially in lowland areas. The 'New Atlas' noted long-term decline in England but further decline since 1987 was not reported by 'Local Change'.

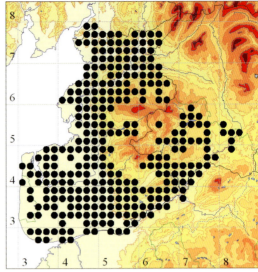

Rumex sanguineus

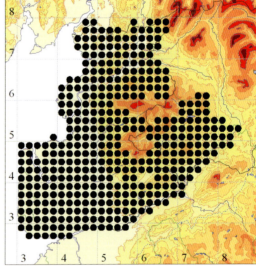

Rumex obtusifolius

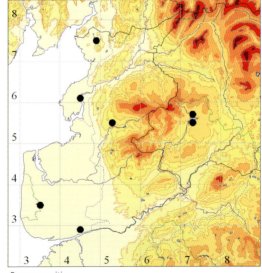

Rumex maritimus

Drosera anglica Huds.   Great Sundew

Circumpolar Boreal-montane element.

This is a plant of wet bogs in lowland areas (BH11, 12) occurring mostly in the west of the British Isles.

Extinct. In northern Lancashire this was a characteristic plant of lowland, raised bogs but even by the mid nineteenth century it had been lost from most of them. However there are observations from White Moss, Yealand Redmayne (Jenkinson, 1775); Pilling Moss (Ashfield, 1858); Heysham Moss in 1836 (OXF) and Cockerham Moss where it was extinct by 1913 (Wheldon and Wilson, 1925). This long-term decline is noted by the 'New Atlas' but not post 1987 by 'Local Change'.

Drosera intermedia Hayne   Oblong-leaved Sundew

Suboceanic Temperate element.

This is found on wet heaths and around the edges of bogs (BH12, 14) in western and southern Britain and formerly more widely in central and eastern England.

Extinct. In northern Lancashire the only record is from Pilling Moss (Ashfield, 1858) and possibly in the mid twentieth century (Whiteside, no date). However as this species is difficult to distinguish from the hybrid *Drosera rotundifolia* × *D. anglica* (*D.* × *obovata* Mert. & W.D.J. Koch) it is possible that it was the hybrid that was found. Unfortunately no voucher specimens have been located to verify these records. Nationally long-term decline of *D. intermedia* continues.

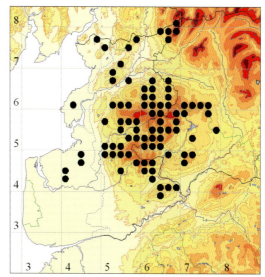
Drosera rotundifolia

CARYOPHYLLACEAE   PINK FAMILY

Arenaria serpyllifolia L. ssp. **serpyllifolia**   Thyme-leaved Sandwort

Eurosiberian Southern-temperate element.

This is found in a wide variety of rather open habitats (BH16) usually on neutral to basic soils throughout most of the British Isles.

Frequent (94). This occurs mostly on the sandy and limestone soils in the west and north of northern Lancashire and more rarely in dry open habitats elsewhere. It is not thought that there has been any change in its distribution locally, which is in line with the 'New Atlas' but 'Local Change' suggests losses might be occurring. (Note the distribution map is for *A. serpyllifolia sensu lato* as all records for this are assumed to be for ssp. *serpyllifolia*.)

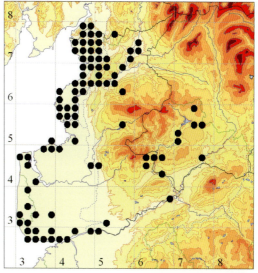
Arenaria serpyllifolia

Arenaria leptoclados (Rchb.) Guss   Slender Sandwort

Eurosiberian Southern-temperate element.

Although this belongs to the same geographical element as *A. serpyllifolia* it is much commoner in southern England than elsewhere. It is found in similar habitats (BH16) although there may be a stronger preference for waste ground, old walls and quarries.

Rare (11). This has been found scattered across VC 60 (there are no records for Lancashire VC 64) but it is possible that some of the records are errors for *A. serpyllifolia*. It has always been rare in northern Lancashire but its distribution is stable or declining. The 'New Atlas' suggests its distribution is stable nationally.

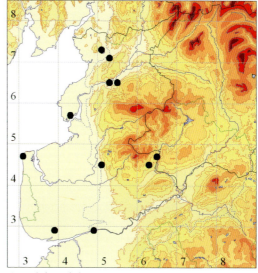
Arenaria leptoclados

Arenaria balearica L.   Mossy Sandwort

Neophyte. It has been cultivated in Britain since 1787 and was first reported from the wild in 1861. It is widely grown on walls, rockeries and paved areas in gardens and escapes from cultivation into similar areas in the wild. It is a native of the western Mediterranean islands.

Very rare (4). It was first recorded in northern Lancashire as naturalised on a wall at Silverdale (Whellan, 1942). More recent records are from Silverdale (SD47M) in 2000 (C.B.W.), Goosnargh (SD54Q) in the period 1964–1989 (E.F.G.), Lytham (SD32N) in the 1970s (C.F. & N.J.S.) and St Anne's (SD32I) in 1965 (A.E.R.).

Moehringia trinervia (L.) Clairv.   Three-nerved Sandwort

European Temperate element.

This occurs on open moist ground in woodland and shaded hedge banks (BH1, 3) throughout most of the British Isles.

Frequent (209). It occurs anywhere in northern Lancashire where there are ancient woodlands or hedge banks. It is a small, inconspicuous spring flowering plant often overlooked as it is shaded by taller vegetation. There is no evidence that it has declined locally and the 'New Atlas' suggests that there has been no change nationally since 1962 but 'Local Change' reports a significant decrease in its distribution since 1987.

Honckenya peploides (L.) Ehrh.   Sea Sandwort

Circumpolar Wide-boreal element.

This is a particularly characteristic plant of strand lines in front of fore dunes and on shingle beaches (BH19). It occurs around all coasts of the British Isles.

Occasional (38). This occurs in suitable places on the coast from Lytham to Silverdale. There does not appear to be any change in its distribution locally or nationally.

Minuartia verna (L.) Hiern   Spring Sandwort

Eurasian Boreal-montane element.

This occurs in open habitats in calcareous grassland and on base-rich rocks (BH7, 16), especially on carboniferous limestone, in disjunct areas of the British Isles. It is especially frequent in the Pennines.

Occasional (15). This occurs frequently on the limestone around Morecambe Bay and on Dalton Crags. Spring Sandwort was also found on rocks by an old lead mine at Newton-in-Bowland (SD64Z; Pickard, 1901) but it could not be found in this locality in 2008. Its distribution both locally and nationally is stable.

Stellaria nemorum L. ssp. **nemorum**   Wood Stitchwort

European Boreo-temperate element.

This occurs in damp woodlands and hedge banks (BH1, 3) in central Britain and parts of Wales.

Frequent (98). This is an especially characteristic plant of valley woodlands in the Bowland Fells as well as in the north of the area and in the Ribble valley. Its distribution both locally and nationally is stable.

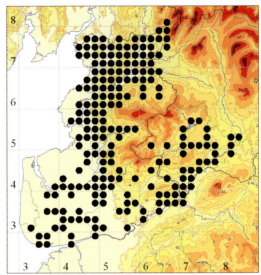
Moehringia trinervia

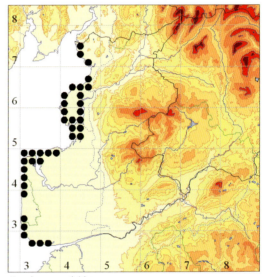
Honckenya peploides

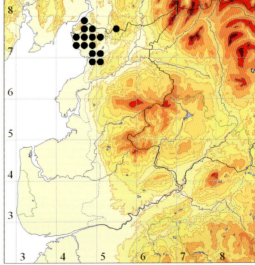
Minuartia verna

Stellaria media (L.) Vill.   Common Chickweed

Circumpolar Wide-temperate element.

This is a very common annual of disturbed habitats (e.g. BH3, 4, 17) throughout the British Isles.

Very common (427). It occurs in a variety of disturbed habitats throughout northern Lancashire only being absent from the peat covered Bowland Fells, although there are still a few tetrads in Lancashire VC 64 where it should be found. Its distribution both locally and nationally is stable.

Stellaria pallida (Dumort.) Crép.   Lesser Chickweed

Eurosiberian Southern-temperate element.

This is an early flowering plant of light, well-drained soils occurring in south-eastern England generally and in coastal areas elsewhere.

Occasional (15). This occurs in open habitats on light sandy soils (BH19) on the coast from Warton to Pilling. It is easily overlooked. As this species was not recognised by earlier botanists in northern Lancashire it is not known if its distribution has changed. Nationally it appears to have increased its range since 1962 but this may be because recorders have become more familiar with the species.

Stellaria neglecta Weihe   Greater Chickweed

European Temperate element.

This is a plant of damp shaded places, often by streams in woods (BH1, 3). It occurs in England and Wales, more especially in the west with a few scattered records in Ireland and Scotland. However it is easily mistaken for the variable *S. media*.

Rare (11). Wheldon and Wilson (1907) recorded this from near Docker and Bleasdale whilst post 1964 records are from the Ribble valley with isolated records from Heysham and Silverdale. It is likely that it is overlooked in some valley woodlands and yet others may be errors for *S. media*, so it is not possible to know if there is any change in its distribution locally. Similarly there is little evidence for change nationally.

Stellaria holostea L.   Greater Stitchwort

Eurosiberian Temperate element.

This is a characteristic spring flowering plant of hedgerows, unmanaged grassy roadsides and woodland margins (BH1, 3) throughout most of the British Isles.

Common (285). It occurs throughout most of northern Lancashire but is absent from moorland areas and much of the intensively cultivated parts in the west of the area. There has been little change in its distribution locally or nationally.

Stellaria palustris Retz   Marsh Stitchwort

Eurasian Boreo-temperate element.

This is a plant of wet places and especially marshy areas with standing water in winter. It is scattered throughout the British Isles except northern Scotland.

Extinct. In northern Lancashire Marsh Stitchwort was possibly found in Roman deposits at Ribchester (Huntley and Hillam, 2000). More recently it was gathered at Pilling in the early twentieth century (A.J.C.) and it was

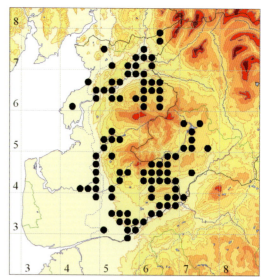

Stellaria nemorum

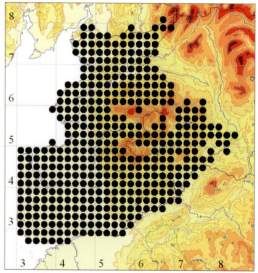

Stellaria media

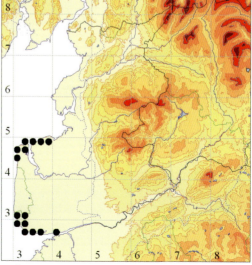

Stellaria pallida

also found in a ditch on the east side of Heysham Moss (SD46F) in 1974 (A.E.C.) but the site was destroyed shortly afterwards. It is possible that it may still occur in the Heysham peninsula. However it may be that all or some of the records refer to forms of *S. graminea*, which when growing in marshy areas have glabrous leaves, a *S. palustris* character, but otherwise conform to the descriptions for *S. graminea*. Confirmation of *S. palustris* as a northern Lancashire species is therefore required. Nationally the decline noted before 1930 for *S. palustris* has continued.

Stellaria graminea L. — Lesser Stitchwort

Eurosiberian Boreo-temperate element.

This is a common summer flowering plant of damp but free draining neutral and acid soils throughout the British Isles. It occurs in woodlands, hedge banks, neglected pastures and other grasslands (BH6) but survives with some nutrient enrichment.

Common (307). It occurs throughout northern Lancashire where its distribution is stable reflecting the national situation.

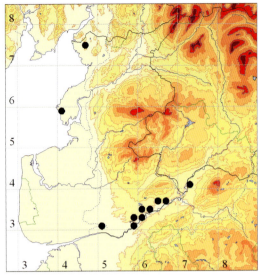
Stellaria neglecta

Stellaria alsine Grimm — Bog Stitchwort

European Temperate element.

This is one of the commonest species of wetland habitats (BH11, 14) and occurs throughout the British Isles.

Very common (355). It occurs throughout northern Lancashire and its distribution is stable. Nationally it has declined in southern and eastern England since 1962 ('New Atlas') but no further significant decline was noted since 1987 ('Local Change').

Cerastium arvense L. — Field Mouse-ear

Circumpolar Boreo-temperate element.

A species of dry, calcareous to slightly acid sandy soils often on roadside banks and sand dunes (BH8, 19) throughout the British Isles but especially in eastern Britain.

Rare (7). In northern Lancashire it is found on older sand dunes at Lytham St Anne's and in the Warton to Silverdale area. However Wheldon and Wilson (1907) only reported it from Cockerham. Although it appears to have increased its range in VC 60 over the past 100 years, nationally there has been a decline ('New Atlas', 'Local Change').

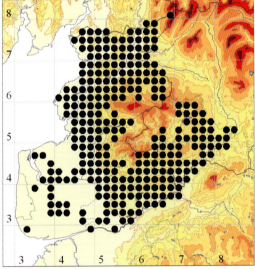
Stellaria holostea

Cerastium arvense × C. tomentosum

This has often been overlooked but may occur widely where the two parents occur near to each other. It produces some good seed.

Very rare (4). This occurs on the sand dunes at Lytham St Anne's in several places and may be more frequent than either parent but it was not recognised until 1994 and all records are by E.F.G. with vouchers at LIV.

Cerastium tomentosum L. — Snow-in-summer

Neophyte. This is a native of Italy and Sicily. It has been cultivated since 1648 and is common in rock gardens but it was not known in the wild until 1915. It is now distributed throughout the British Isles occurring in waste places, sand dunes and in other open habitats having spread considerably since 1962.

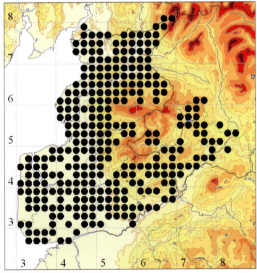
Stellaria graminea

Occasional (52). It occurs throughout northern Lancashire but especially in coastal areas where it was first recorded from St Anne's in 1931 (France, 1931; LIV).

Cerastium fontanum Baumg. — Common Mouse-ear

Eurosiberian Boreo-temperate element.

It occurs in a wide variety of habitats ranging from fertile grasslands to wet places and acid grasslands, waste places and walls (e.g. BH6, 17, 3). It is found throughout the British Isles.

Very common (450). This is the second most common species in northern Lancashire occurring in six fewer tetrads than *Poa annua*. The subspecies were not distinguished but it is believed most records are for ssp. *vulgare* (Hartm.) Greuter & Burdet. However ssp. *holosteoides* (Fr.) Salman may occur in wet places. There is no change in the distribution of Common Mouse-ear locally or nationally.

Cerastium glomeratum Thuill. — Sticky Mouse-ear

European Southern-temperate element.

This is found in disturbed areas, often in nutrient enriched soils, throughout the British Isles (BH3, 5, 17).

Very common (364). It occurs throughout northern Lancashire and is often found as the only weed in nutrient enriched *Lolium* spp. grassland. It has probably become more common over the last 100 years reflecting the national situation.

Cerastium diffusum Pers. — Sea Mouse-ear

European Temperate element.

A species of light, usually calcareous soils on sand dunes or limestone (BH18, 19) occurring throughout the British Isles but mostly in coastal areas.

Occasional (56). It is found in coastal areas of northern Lancashire and much more rarely inland. As Wheldon and Wilson (1907) recorded this species only from Bolton-le-Sands, Middleton, Ashton and the sand dunes at St Anne's, it appears that it has extended its range considerably over the last 100 years. However the 'New Atlas' reports no change in its coastal distribution since 1962 but notes a decline from inland railway sites colonised during the 1940s. 'Local Change' reports no further change since 1987.

Cerastium semidecandrum L. — Little Mouse-ear

European Temperate element.

This is a spring annual occurring in sandy or calcareous soils usually in open habitats on sand dunes and occasionally elsewhere, especially on limestone. (BH7, 18, 19). It occurs throughout most of Britain and coastal areas of Ireland.

Occasional (21). This is found in open habitats on sand dunes and on limestone in coastal areas of northern Lancashire and occasionally inland. Although still a local plant it has increased slightly since Wheldon and Wilson (1907) reported it from four sites. The 'New Atlas' reports that it was under recorded in 1962 and 'Local Change notes its distribution is stable.

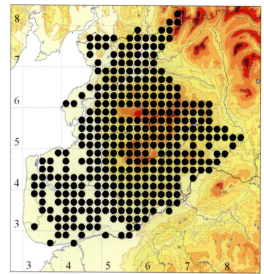
Stellaria alsine

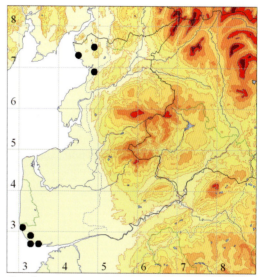
Cerastium arvense

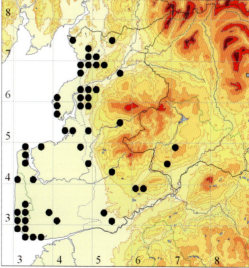
Cerastium tomentosum

Myosoton aquaticum (L.) Moench   Water Chickweed

Eurosiberian Temperate element but a neophyte in northern Lancashire.

This occurs in wet habitats in Britain south of a line between the R. Ribble and R. Tees.

Very rare (2). In northern Lancashire it was found as a casual on waste ground at Heysham (SD46A) in 1982 (L.A.L.; LIV) and near Bolton-by-Bowland (SD64U; Abbott, 2005).

Sagina nodosa (L.) Fenzl   Knotted Pearlwort

Eurosiberian Boreo-temperate element.

S. nodosa is a plant of damp habitats, e.g. flushes, and also open calcareous habitats on limestone and in sand dunes (BH11, 19). It is found throughout the British Isles.

Frequent (90). It occurs throughout northern Lancashire but it is rare or absent from more intensively cultivated areas. Locally its distribution is stable but nationally it has declined considerably in southern Britain since 1962 ('New Atlas') and this decline has continued since 1987 ('Local Change').

Sagina procumbens L.   Procumbent Pearlwort

Eurosiberian Boreo-temperate element.

A common species growing in a variety of habitats (e.g. BH6, 11, 16, 17) ranging from hill flushes to pavement cracks and garden lawns. It occurs throughout the British Isles.

Very common (421). This occurs throughout northern Lancashire and it probably grows in the few tetrads from which it remains unrecorded. Its distribution is stable locally and nationally.

Sagina apetala Ard.   Annual Pearlwort

European Southern-temperate element.

This occurs all over the British Isles and is found in open habitats in sandy places, gravely places and waste ground in the built environment (BH17).

Occasional (16). This is much rarer than *S. filicaulis* from which it is distinguished with difficulty and intermediates seem to occur. J.A. Wheldon specimens at NMW suggest that formerly it was found at Carnforth and Preesall. Post 1964 records are scattered across northern Lancashire but it seems to prefer light sandy soils.

Sagina filicaulis Jord.   Slender Pearlwort

European Southern-temperate element.

This is found in similar habitats (BH17) to *S. apetala* and occurs throughout the British Isles.

Frequent (93). In northern Lancashire this is much more frequent than *S. apetala* and although it occurs throughout it is mainly a coastal taxon. It is only in recent years that the two species were reliably distinguished in Britain making assessment of change difficult. Furthermore Abbott (2005) considers that in VC 64 there is little difference in the frequency of the two species. *S. filicaulis* has extended its range in northern Lancashire, especially in coastal areas, during the last 100 years. Nationally the 'New Atlas' reports no change since 1962 whilst 'Local Change' notes a significant extension of its range since 1987 especially on roadsides and other disturbed habitats.

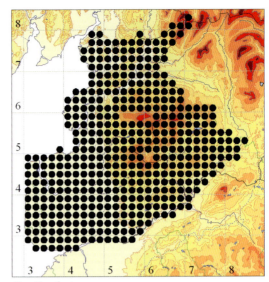

Cerastium fontanum

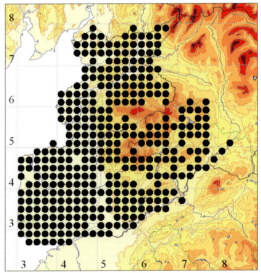

Cerastium glomeratum

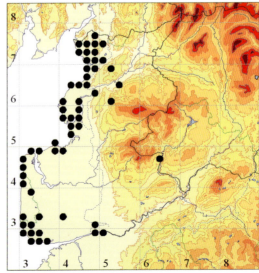

Cerastium diffusum

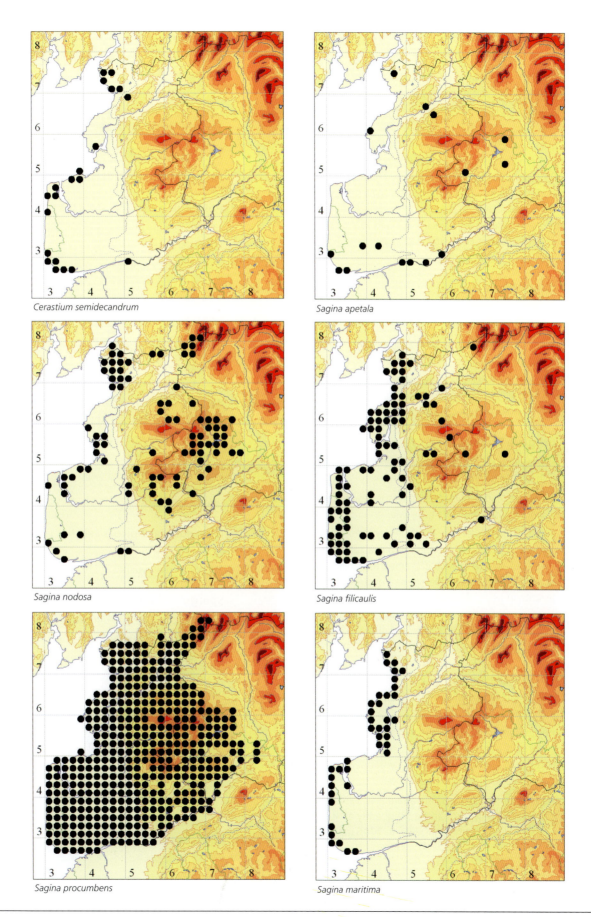

Cerastium semidecandrum

Sagina apetala

Sagina nodosa

Sagina filicaulis

Sagina procumbens

Sagina maritima

Sagina maritima Don   Sea Pearlwort

European Southern-temperate element.

This is an annual of maritime rock crevices, cliff tops, stabilized shingle, upper salt marshes and in cracks in walls and pavements etc. (BH17, 18, 19) around all the coasts of the British Isles.

Occasional (39). *S. maritima* is found along the coasts of northern Lancashire from Lytham to Silverdale. Over the last 100 years it has extended its range considerably from two Heysham peninsula localities noted by Wheldon and Wilson (1907). However the 'New Atlas' reported that its distribution had changed little since 1962 and this was confirmed by 'Local Change'. It is possible that in northern Lancashire it was overlooked 100 years ago.

Scleranthus annuus L.   Annual Knawel

European Temperate element but probably a casual neophyte in northern Lancashire.

It occurs in dry places on heaths, in arable fields and waste places (BH4, 8, 10, 16) throughout much of the British Isles.

Very rare (1) or extinct. It was recorded from a field near Garstang in 1888 (Wheldon and Wilson, 1900) and from Lancaster (SD46Q) in *c.* 1970 (A.Wa.).

Corrigiola litoralis L.   Strapwort

Suboceanic Southern-temperate element but a neophyte in northern Lancashire.

As a native plant this is a very rare species in south-western England but casual plants have been found in several English localities in open habitats, especially on railway ballast (BH19).

Very rare (3). This was found in two coastal localities on railway ballast and at each it seemed to persist for several years before industrial development destroyed the sites. It was known from Heysham (SD45E, 45A) from 1959 until the 1980s (E.F.G. & others) whilst at Fleetwood (SD34I) it was seen from 1975 until 1985 (C.F. & N.J.S.). It is possible it may still be present at one or both sites where suitable habitats still occur.

Herniaria glabra L.   Smooth Rupturewort

Eurosiberian Temperate element but a neophyte in northern Lancashire.

Smooth Rupturewort is a native plant on compacted sandy or gravely soils in eastern England. Elsewhere it occurs in a variety of disturbed areas, often seasonally flooded, in scattered localities throughout the British Isles.

Very rare (3). In northern Lancashire it was first found at Lytham (SD32T) in 1999 and subsequently at St Anne's (SD32J) in 2000 and at Blackpool (SD33D) in 2006 (all C.F. & N.J.S.).

Illecebrum verticillatum L.   Coral-necklace

Suboceanic Southern-temperate element but a neophyte in northern Lancashire.

This is a plant of periodically wet or inundated, acidic to neutral soils in gravely tracks, pool and ditch margins in southern England but also on railway ballast elsewhere (BH3, 13).

Very rare (1). It occurred as a casual on railway sidings at Fleetwood (SD34I) in 1975 (C.F. & N.J.S.; LIV).

Polycarpon tetraphyllum (L.) L.   Four-leaved Allseed

Mediterranean-Atlantic element but a neophyte in northern Lancashire.

It grows in dry places and may be native on the south coast of England but elsewhere it is found in waste places.

In northern Lancashire it was found as a casual on a tip in Lancaster in 1963 (E.H.; LANC; A.E.R.; LIV).

Spergula arvensis L.   Corn Spurrey

Eurosiberian Wide-temperate element but widely naturalised elsewhere; an archaeophyte in most of the British Isles.

It is found in open disturbed habitats including arable fields and waste places (BH4) throughout the British Isles.

Frequent (160). This is found all over northern Lancashire, especially in the west of the area. Its distribution is stable in northern Lancashire but the 'New Atlas' reported a decline nationally since 1962 but 'Local Change' noted no further significant losses since 1987.

[**Spergularia rupicola** Lebel ex Le Sol   Rock Sea-spurrey

This was reported from Bolton-le-Sands (Wheldon and Wilson, 1925) but the voucher at LIV is *S. marina*]

Spergularia media (L.) C. Presl   Greater Sea-spurrey

Eurosiberian Southern-temperate element.

It occurs on salt marshes and other maritime habitats around the coasts of the British Isles (BH21).

Occasional (52). This is found on all the salt marshes of the Ribble, Wyre and Lune estuaries, often extending inland to the highest level of tidal influence, and around Morecambe Bay. It appears that over the last 100 years *S. media* may have extended its range and become more common. Nationally the 'New Atlas' noted that since 1962 its distribution was stable but since 1987 'Local Change' reported an expansion of its range.

Spergularia marina (L.) Grisch.   Lesser Sea-spurrey

Circumpolar Southern-temperate element.

This occurs on salt marshes and other maritime habitats around the coasts of the British Isles but also inland on salt treated roadside verges (BH3, 21).

Occasional (66). This has a similar coastal distribution on salt marshes to *S. media*, with which it often occurs, but in recent years it has also been found inland on roadside verges, especially near mounds of salt kept for treating roads in winter. It has extended its range in northern Lancashire over the last 100 years and nationally its range has increased both in its coastal habitats and inland on many salt treated roads.

Spergularia rubra (L.) J. & C. Presl   Sand Spurrey

European Southern-temperate element.

Sand Spurrey is an annual herb found in open habitats on acidic soils (BH8, 17). It is found throughout the British Isles although it is rare in much of Ireland.

Occasional (15). In northern Lancashire *S. rubra* is found mostly in coastal areas with occasional records from further inland including a single locality in Lancashire VC 64. As Wheldon and Wilson (1907) only recorded it from two sites it appears that there has been a slight extension of its range in the region. Nationally there were signs *S. rubra* was declining ('New Atlas') but 'Local Change' reported a considerable resurgence. It is particularly successful in colonizing tracks in forestry plantations.

Agrostemma githago L.   Corncockle

Archaeophyte; probably a native of the eastern Mediterranean but spread with cultivation to many parts of the world. In Britain it was usually found as a weed of arable crops from which it was eradicated by the mid-twentieth century. In recent years it has been planted as part of wild flower seed mixtures.

Very rare (4). Formerly this was found as a weed of arable land in northern Lancashire, especially of cereal crops and on wasteland, often near ports, mostly in the west of the area. However it never appears to have been common and most records are probably derived from contamination of imported grain. It was first reported from Roman horse dung at Lancaster (Wilson, 1979) and from Roman deposits at Ribchester (Huntley and Hillam, 2000). Recent records are from Poulton-le-Fylde (SD33P) in 1964 (E.P.), Torrisholme (SD46L) in 1991 (K.R.), Pilling (SD44E) in 1999 (C.J.B.) and Marton, Blackpool (SD33H) in c. 1998 (C.F. & N.J.S.) but at the latter three sites it was planted. The 'New Atlas' considered it extinct as an arable weed by 1962 and since then it has occurred only as a casual or in recent years in wild flower planting schemes.

Silene nutans L.   Nottingham Catchfly

Eurosiberian Temperate element but a casual neophyte in northern Lancashire.

This is a rare native of some coastal and inland sites in Britain but in northern Lancashire the only record is from a roadside near Scorton, Nether Wyresdale in 1941 (H.E.B.).

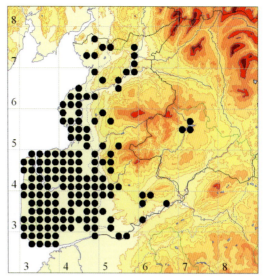

Spergula arvensis

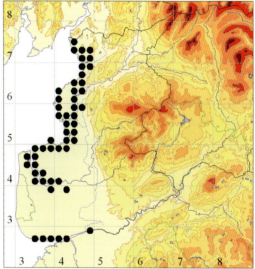

Spergularia media

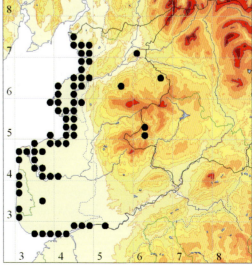

Spergularia marina

Silene vulgaris Garcke ssp. **vulgaris**　　　　Bladder Campion

Eurasian Southern-temperate element.

This is found in a variety of open and grassy habitats as well as waste ground, dry banks and other disturbed places (BH3, 6). It is found throughout most of the British Isles but it is much rarer in western Ireland, western and northern Scotland than elsewhere.

Frequent (92). It has a disjunct distribution in northern Lancashire with most records in the west of the area but with a number of records running north – south along the line of the A6 and with a cluster around Preston. Elsewhere it is rarely found. The present distribution is similar to that of 100 years ago although it may be more frequent on the Fylde coast and around Preston. Nationally the 'New Atlas' reports a decline in its distribution since 1962 with further decline since 1987 reported by 'Local Change'.

Silene uniflora Roth　　　　Sea Campion

Suboceanic Boreo-temperate element.

S. uniflora is a characteristic plant of sea cliffs, coastal walls and drift lines (BH18, 19) around most of the coasts of the British Isles.

Occasional (42). It occurs on most of the coast between Preston and Silverdale and appears to be more frequent and in more places than 100 years ago. Nationally its distribution is stable.

Silene noctiflora L.　　　　Night-flowering Catchfly

Archaeophyte, with a European Temperate distribution but widely naturalised outside this range. In the British Isles it is found mostly in south-eastern Scotland, eastern and southern England where it occurs on dry sandy, calcareous soils in cultivated and waste land (BH4).

In northern Lancashire it appeared as a casual on the Lytham and St Anne's sand dunes with other introduced species in 1903 (Wheldon and Wilson, 1907) and 1908 (C.B.; NMW). It was also found abundantly in a cultivated field near Nether Kellet in the 1930s (France, 1930s).

Silene latifolia Poir.　　　　White Campion

Archaeophyte with a Eurosiberian Southern-temperate distribution but widely naturalised elsewhere. It is found throughout much of the British Isles occurring on well-drained soils on arable land, hedge banks and waste land (BH3).

Frequent (86). It occurs throughout northern Lancashire but it is primarily a coastal species. Its distribution is probably stable but the 'New Atlas' notes a decline in the west of the British Isles, which is continuing ('Local Change').

Silene latifolia × **S. dioica** (**S. × hampeana** Meusel & K. Werner)

This hybrid is usually found on scrubby banks, hedgerows and woodland margins or wherever the parents meet. It is a common hybrid in England, Wales and eastern Scotland but much rarer elsewhere.

Occasional (17). It is scattered across VC 60 but is apparently absent from Lancashire VC 64. It is possibly under recorded.

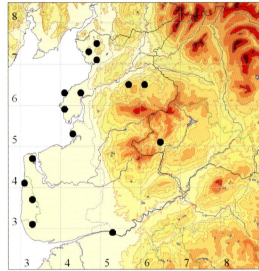

Spergularia rubra

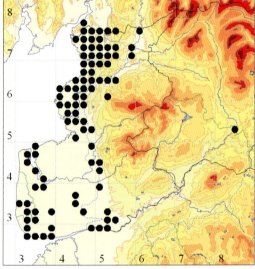

Silene vulgaris

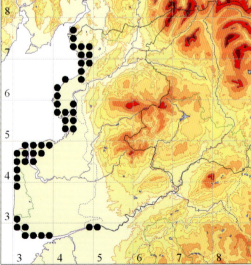

Silene uniflora

Silene dioica (L.) Clairv.   Red Campion

European Boreo-temperate element.

This is one of the most prominent species of shaded situations in hedge-rows and woodlands (BH1). It is found throughout the British Isles.

Very common (373). *S. dioica* occurs throughout northern Lancashire except in moorland areas. Its distribution is stable locally and nationally.

Silene gallica L.   Small-flowered Catchfly

Archaeophyte with a Submediterranean-Subatlantic distribution but a neophyte in northern Lancashire. It occurs on dry cliffs and banks in southern Britain.

Very rare (1). There are old records for Ashton, Preston in 1883 (F.C.K.; MANCH) and Ansdell in 1886 (M.; MANCH) but the only recent record is from a demolition site in Preston (SD53F) in 1966 (E.H.; LANC).

Silene conica L.   Sand Catchfly

Eurosiberian Southern-temperate element but widely naturalised outside its native range and a casual neophyte in VC 60. In the British Isles it is regarded as native in East Anglia, parts of southern England and Wales and the Channel Islands. It occurs on sandy, free-draining soils in open habitats (BH8, 19).

In northern Lancashire it was found in a field at the northern end of Little Hawes Water (SD47Y; Wheldon and Wilson, 1907).

Silene coronaria (L.) Clairv.   Rose Campion

Neophyte. This is a native of southern Europe and south-western Asia but it was known as a garden plant in Britain since the mid fourteenth century. By 1905 it had escaped into the wild and by 2000 was a persistent garden escape on light soils throughout much of Britain.

Very rare (4). Despite being an attractive plant and easily recognised it has only been recorded from Scorton (SD54E) in 1999, on sand dunes at St Anne's (SD32I) in 2001, on pavements in Waddington (SD74G) in 2008 (all E.F.G.) and on Lea Marsh (SD42Z) in 2000 (C.F. & N.J.S.).

Silene flos-cuculi (L.) Clairv.   Ragged-Robin

Eurosiberian Temperate element.

This is a plant of damp places found in wet grassland, rush-pasture, fen meadow, tall herb fen and damp woodland margins throughout the British Isles (BH11).

Frequent (223). It is found scattered throughout northern Lancashire (see Plate 2.30). It is believed its distribution is stable locally and nationally but some county floras record local decline and this may be the case in northern Lancashire. However for a still frequent species the tetrad system of recording is too insensitive to note very localised losses.

Silene chalcedonica (L.) E.H.L. Krause   Maltese-Cross

Neophyte. Maltese-Cross is a native of temperate eastern Europe, western and central Asia. It was cultivated in Britain by 1596 and has been known in the wild since 1902. It is a popular garden plant and occurs as a casual, or rarely naturalised, in a few scattered localities in Britain.

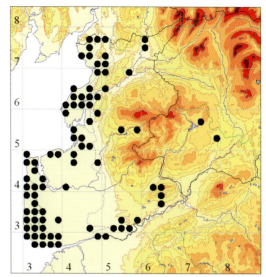

Silene latifolia

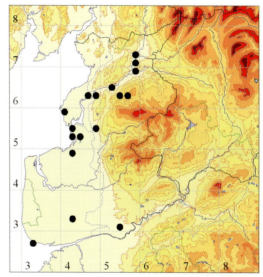

Silene × hampeana

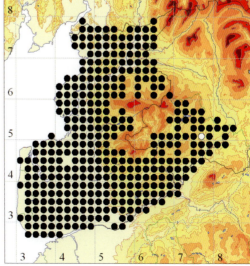

Silene dioica

Very rare (1). In northern Lancashire *L. chalcedonica* was recorded from gravel pits in Nether Wyresdale (SD55A) in 1999 (Anon).

Silene dichotoma Ehrh.   Forked Catchfly

Neophyte. This is a native of Eurasia but although it is decreasing it can be a persistent introduction. It was found amongst other introductions on the sand dunes at St Anne's in 1908 (Bailey, 1910; C.B.; MANCH).

Silene muscipula L.

Neophyte. A native of the Mediterranean formerly found as a grain and birdseed casual.

Very rare (1). Recorded from a demolition site in Preston (SD53F) in 1966 (E.H., A.E.R.; LIV).

Saponaria officinalis L.   Soapwort

Archaeophyte with a European Temperate distribution but widely naturalised outside this range. It is found in a wide range of marginal and man-made habitats (BH3, 17) and occurs throughout the British Isles.

Occasional (58). In northern Lancashire this is predominantly a coastal species but it is also conspicuous in the Lune and Ribble valleys where it is naturalised by streams and in damp woods. It has been known in northern Lancashire since records were first made in the seventeenth century and whilst it may have become more frequent its range is stable locally and nationally.

Vaccaria hispanica (Mill.) Rauschert   Cowherb

Neophyte and apparently a native of south-eastern Europe and south-western Asia but widely naturalised throughout the world. It was known as a garden plant in Britain by 1548 and recorded in the wild from 1832. It is usually found as a casual almost anywhere in the British Isles but usually in open man-made habitats.

Very rare (2). In northern Lancashire it was first recorded in 1902 from Fleetwood Docks (Wheldon and Wilson, 1902) and subsequently from several places in St Anne's in 1907 (C.B.; MANCH); in 1915 (A.J.C.) and in 1969 (A.E.R. at SD32J, LIV) and from a demolition site in Preston (SD53F) in 1966 (E.H. & J.H.).

Gypsophila paniculata L.   Baby's-breath

Neophyte. This species has been known in cultivation since 1759, is commonly grown in gardens and was recorded from the wild in 1884. It is a native of central and eastern Europe and western and central Asia.

Very rare (1). The only record is for a single plant found flowering abundantly on waste land at St Anne's (SD33F) in 1991 (C.F. & N.J.S.).

Dianthus gratianopolitanus Vill. × D. plumarius L.   A Pink

According to Stace (1997) this is one of three garden hybrids with *D. gratianopolitanus* as one parent. They occur occasionally as garden escapes on walls and waste ground mostly in central and southern Britain.

Very rare (1). A small patch of what is believed to be this hybrid was found on fixed sand dunes at Lytham St Anne's (SD33A) in 2009.

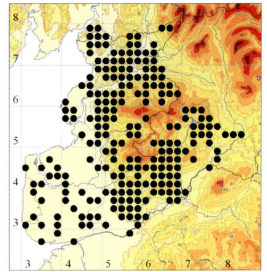

Silene flos-cuculi

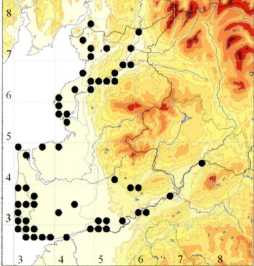

Saponaria officinalis

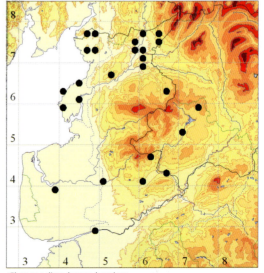

Chenopodium bonus-henricus

Dianthus plumarius L.   Pink

Neophyte. This is a native of the mountains of central and eastern Europe. It has been cultivated in Britain since 1629 and was first recorded in the wild in 1724. It is still a very common garden plant and from time to time escapes into the wild where it occasionally becomes naturalised.

Very rare (1). There is a single record from St Anne's (SD32I) in 1965 (A.E.R., LIV).

Dianthus deltoides L.   Maiden Pink

Eurosiberian Boreo-temperate element with a continental distribution in western Europe.

Maiden Pink is a perennial species of dry, usually base-rich soils, on limestone and chalk. It is found throughout Britain but especially in eastern England and Scotland.

Very rare (1). *Dianthus deltoides* was first found in northern Lancashire in a quarry on Dalton Crags (SD57N) in 2009 (A. McLay). Its origin is not clear, as there are no known colonies of Maiden Pink in the surrounding area. However it is a recent arrival in the quarry.

[Dianthus carthusianorum L.   Carthusian Pink

Neophyte. A native of central and southern Europe grown in gardens, which occasionally escapes into the wild. However Clement and Foster (1994) doubt that there are any post 1930 records

Very rare (1). Nevertheless it was reported from by the side of a lane leading to the beach at Overton (SD45I) in 1974 (A.E.C.) but was no doubt recorded in error for another taxon.]

AMARANTHACEAE   GOOSEFOOT FAMILY

Axyris amaranthoides L.   Russian Pigweed

Neophyte. A native of Russia that occurs occasionally in waste places. The only northern Lancashire record is for St Anne's (C.B.; MANCH) in 1907.

Dysphania ambrosioides (L.) Mosyakin & Clemants   Mexican-tea

Neophyte. This is a native of the warmer parts of America and appears casually in the British Isles. It was cultivated in Britain by 1640 and was known in the wild by 1876 but it is now rare.

Very rare (1). In northern Lancashire it was found on waste ground at St Anne's in 1906 and 1908 (C.B.; MANCH) and at Kirkham (SD43G) in 1964 (E.H.).

Chenopodium bonus-henricus L.   Good-King-Henry

Archaeophyte. This is a native of the mountains of central and southern Europe but was present in Britain during Roman times. It was once grown for its edible leaves. Today it is found in much of the British Isles except western Scotland.

Occasional (26). It occurs scattered throughout northern Lancashire in ruderal places often near farms and cottages or near former habitation. Wheldon and Wilson (1907) thought it too frequent to list localities and it is likely that it has declined in the last 100 years, which is consistent with the national situation.

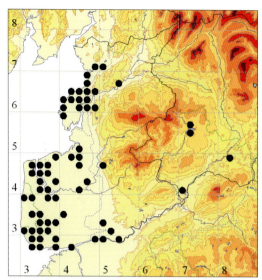
Chenopodium rubrum

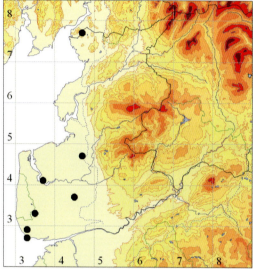
Chenopodium polyspermum

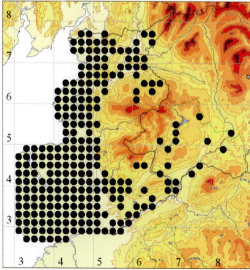
Chenopodium album

Chenopodium rubrum L. — Red Goosefoot

Eurosiberian Temperate element.

This is found in ruderal places (BH4, 17) throughout England but it is rare or absent elsewhere.

Frequent (66). Red Goosefoot is found throughout northern Lancashire but especially in coastal areas on waste tips. Its distribution in northern Lancashire is probably stable but nationally it has increased its range.

Chenopodium polyspermum L. — Many-seeded Goosefoot

Archaeophyte. Eurosiberian Temperate element but widely naturalised outside its natural range. It is found in disturbed ground (BH4) in most of England but it is rare or absent elsewhere.

Rare (7). In northern Lancashire it was first recorded in 1906 from between Heaton and Overton (Wheldon and Wilson, 1907) and today it is found as a casual in arable and waste land in the west of the area.

Chenopodium hybridum L. — Maple-leaved Goosefoot

Archaeophyte with circumpolar distribution.

It has been known in Britain since Roman times but today is found in disturbed places (BH4) mostly in south-eastern England.

Very rare (1). The first northern Lancashire record was from the sand dunes at St Anne's where it was recorded in 1906 (C.B.; MANCH). The only other record is from Kirkham (SD43G) in 1964 (E.H.).

Chenopodium urbicum L. — Upright Goosefoot

Archaeophyte with a Eurosiberian Temperate distribution.

Until about 1940 *C. urbicum* was a frequent casual in Britain but it is now rare.

In northern Lancashire it was recorded from near Morecambe and Preesall (Wheldon and Wilson, 1907).

Chenopodium murale L. — Nettle-leaved Goosefoot

Archaeophyte with a Eurosiberian Southern-temperate distribution. It has been known in Britain since Roman times but it has become much rarer since 1962.

Very rare (4). It was first recorded in northern Lancashire from Lytham in 1870 (J.W.; MANCH) and subsequently from Wyre Docks, Fleetwood and from sand dunes at St Anne's (Wheldon and Wilson, 1907). More recent records are from a waste heap at Preston (SD53A) in 1965 (E.H.), by a coastal path at Slyne-with-Hest (SD46S) in 1966 (J.Wi.), as a garden weed at Bispham (unlocalised) in 1968 (J.H.) and from a caravan site at Heysham (SD45E) in 1974 (A.E.C.).

Chenopodium leptophyllum group — Slimleaf Goosefoot

Neophyte. A group of closely related North American plants introduced with grain. First recorded in Britain (as *C. dessicatum* A. Nelson) in 1901 from East Cornwall. Also included here is *C. pratericola* Rydb.

Very rare (1). In northern Lancashire records comprise ones from St Anne's in 1901–1907 (C.B.; MANCH, NMW), Caton in 1941 (J.N.F.; LIV) and demolition sites in Preston in 1966 (E.H.; LANC).

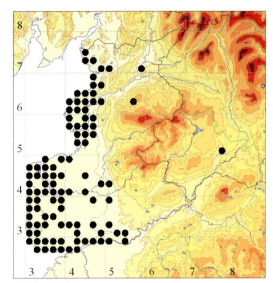

Atriplex prostrata

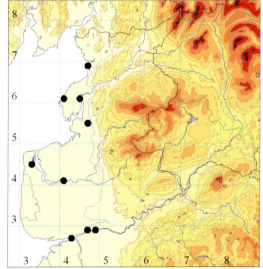

Atriplex × gustafssoniana

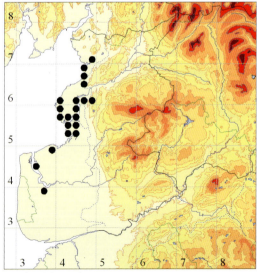

Atriplex glabriuscula

Chenopodium ficifolium Sm.   Fig-leaved Goosefoot

Archaeophyte with a Eurosiberian Temperate distribution. There is a continuous archaeological record for this species in Britain from the Iron Age onwards and whilst it remains common in disturbed ground (BH4) in much of the country southeast of a line from the Humber to the Bristol Channel it has only been known as a casual in northern Lancashire.

Very rare (5). It was first recorded from Roman horse dung at Lancaster (Wilson, 1979) and more recently from Fleetwood Docks in 1900 and from the St Anne's sand dunes in 1906 (Wheldon and Wilson, 1907). More recent records are from Preston (SD53A, 53F) in 1965 and 1966 respectively (E.H.), Upper Rawcliffe-with-Tarnacre (SD44R) in 1996 (C.J.B.), Morecambe (SD46G) in 1998 (J.K.) and Over Kellet (SD57A) in 2009. It is probably under recorded.

Chenopodium berlandieri Moq.   Pitseed Goosefoot

Neophyte, a native of North America. Formerly fairly frequent but now found as a rare casual on tips and on waste ground. It was first recorded in the wild by 1905.

Very rare (2). The only northern Lancashire records are from Blackpool (SD33I) in 1963 (A.E.R., E.H.), demolition sites in Preston (SD53F) in 1966 (E.H., J.H., E.F.G.) and from a sandy shore at Lytham (SD32T) in 1983 (E.F.G.).

Chenopodium bushianum Aellen   Soyabean Goosefoot

Neophyte, a native of North America first recorded in Britain in 1938. However it may not be distinct from *C. album* and perhaps for this reason, rather than a genuine absence, it has not been recorded since 1986. Typically it is found on tips and waste ground.

Very rare (1). In northern Lancashire it was only doubtfully recorded from a tip in Haslam Park, Preston (SD53A) in 1965 (E.H.).

Chenopodium opulifolium Schrad. ex W.D.J. Koch & Ziz Grey
     Goosefoot

Neophyte. This is a European Southern-temperate species but has been known in the wild in Britain since 1853. It is found on tips and waste ground.

Very rare (3). In northern Lancashire it was first recorded from ballast near Preston Docks in 1897, Fleetwood and St Anne's (Wheldon and Wilson, 1907). The only other records were from demolition sites in Preston (SD52J, 53A & 53F) in 1966 (A.E.R., E.H.).

Chenopodium album L.   Fat-hen

Eurasian Wide-temperate element.

This is a common species throughout most of the British Isles favouring nutrient rich, disturbed habitats including arable fields, gardens and waste places (BH4, 17).

Common (260). Fat-hen is found throughout northern Lancashire but it is especially common in lowland areas west of the M6. It can be particularly abundant in potato fields. *C. album* var. *reticulatum* (Aellen) Uotila was recorded from Roman horse dung at Lancaster (Wilson, 1979). The distribution of Fat-hen both locally and nationally is stable.

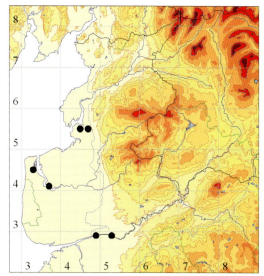

Atriplex longipes

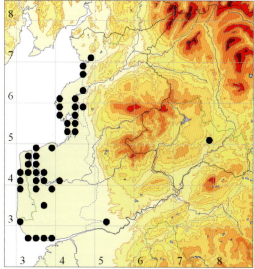

Atriplex littoralis

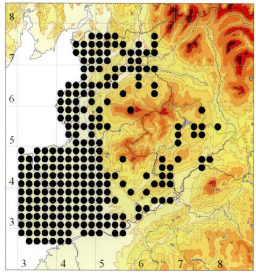

Atriplex patula

Chenopodium suecicum Murr.　　　　　Swedish Goosefoot

Neophyte. A native of northern Europe and often confused with *C. album*. It occurs occasionally on tips and waste ground in Britain and was first recorded in 1844.

Very rare (1). The only northern Lancashire record was from Preesall-with-Hackensall (SD34U) in 1970 (E.F.G., LIV).

Chenopodium probstii Aellen　　　　　Probst's Goosefoot

Neophyte. A North American introduction first recorded from the British Isles in 1930. Because of its similarity to *C. album* it has probably been overlooked.

Very rare (4). In northern Lancashire it was recorded from Lytham St Anne's (SD32Y) in 1962 (A.E.R.; LIV), from a tip at Blackpool (SD33I) in 1965 (E.P.) and from demolition sites in Preston (SD52J, 53F) in 1966 (E.H.) and possibly from a waste heap at Haslam Park, Preston (SD53A) in 1965 (E.H.).

Atriplex hortensis L.　　　　　Garden Orache

Neophyte. Possibly a native of central Asia but widely cultivated. It was introduced into Britain by 1548 and was cultivated as a food crop until the eighteenth century. It was first reported from the wild in Surrey in 1824.

Very rare (2). In northern Lancashire it was recorded from a Blackpool rock garden (SD33E) in 1968 (J.H.) and from a tip at Poulton-le-Fylde (unlocalised) in 1970 (A.E.R.).

Atriplex prostrata Boucher ex DC.　　　　　Spear-leaved Orache

Eurosiberian Wide-temperate element.

This occurs around most of the coast of the British Isles and inland in England and Wales. It is found on beaches, salt marshes and in disturbed habitats inland (BH3, 4, 19, 21).

Frequent (102). It occurs throughout northern Lancashire but it is especially frequent in the north and west of the area. Nationally *A. prostrata* appears to be extending its range and although Abbott (2005) records a considerable increase in Mid-west Yorkshire this is mostly in the east of the vice-county. In northern Lancashire it appears that there has been only a modest, if any, increase in its range over the last 100 years.

Atriplex prostrata × A. glabriuscula

This hybrid occurs rarely on beaches with both parents throughout Britain but is often recorded in error for one of the parents.

Very rare (2). In northern Lancashire there are records from Heysham (SD46A) in 1995 (B.S.B.I.) and Cockerham (SD45G) in 1998 (E.F.G.).

Atriplex prostrata × A. littoralis (A. × hulmeana Tascher.)

This hybrid is found in many places around the coasts of Britain.

Very rare (2). In northern Lancashire it was found on the banks of the R. Wyre at Preesall (SD34N) in 1974 (Taschereau, 1989; MANCH) and on the salt marsh at Conder Green (SD45M) in 2004 (E.F.G.).

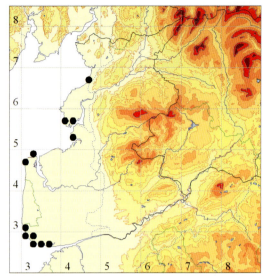

Atriplex laciniata

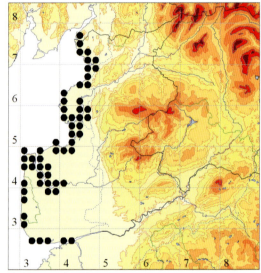

Atriplex portulacoides

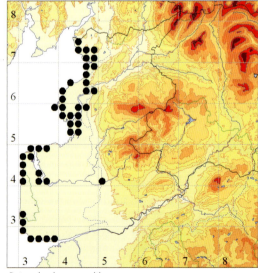

Beta vulgaris ssp. *maritima*

Atriplex prostrata × A. longipes (A. × gustafssoniana Tascher.)
Kattegat Orache

This is found scattered around the coasts of Britain in the upper salt marsh zones. It is morphologically very variable, fertile and probably overlooked as a form of *A. prostrata*.

Rare (9). This hybrid was first recognised in northern Lancashire from a salt marsh at Thurnham (SD45S) in 1977 (P.M.T., MANCH). Subsequently it has been recorded from the upper salt marsh zones from the Ribble estuary to Carnforth. It is probably more frequent than the records suggest.

Atriplex glabriuscula Edmonston
Babington's Orache

Suboceanic Boreo-temperate element.

This is found on the strand line of sand and shingle beaches (BH19) throughout the British Isles but it is difficult to identify and is easily mistaken for forms of *A. prostrata* or *A. prostrata* hybrids.

Occasional (20). This is apparently confined to strand lines from the Wyre estuary northwards. It may have been overlooked from the Fylde coast, or perhaps habitats were unsuitable. However habitats are changing and suitable conditions may be developing at Lytham St Anne's. Nationally there is probably little change in its distribution but in northern Lancashire it may have become slightly more frequent over the last 100 years.

Atriplex longipes Drejer
Long-stalked Orache

European Boreal-montane element.

This is a morphologically distinct species found occasionally around the coasts of Britain at the highest levels of salt marshes (BH21). However it was only confirmed as a British species in 1977 although it was first reported in 1957.

Rare (6). In northern Lancashire it often occurs amongst reed beds at the highest levels of salt marshes and there are confirmed records for Thurnham (SD45S) in 1977 (P.M.T.), Conder Green (SD45M) in 1988 (L.R.F), near the Shard bridge on the Wyre estuary (SD34Q), Fleetwood (SD34H) in 1996 (P.J.) and at Lea on the Ribble estuary (SD42Z) in 1995 (P.J., N.A. Bruce, A. Cox). There is also a doubtful early inland record for Preston (SD52J).

Atriplex littoralis L.
Grass-leaved Orache

Circumpolar Temperate element.

This is found on salt marshes around most of the coasts of the British Isles and increasingly inland on the sides of motorways and other salt treated roads (BH3, 19, 21).

Occasional (40). It occurs in suitable places along the coast and more occasionally on salt treated roads inland. Wheldon and Wilson (1907) recorded only seven localities yet say it is 'not uncommon'. Nevertheless it appears that it has extended its range in coastal localities during the last 100 years and it is beginning to extend its range inland. The 'New Atlas' suggests it spread rapidly along inland roads from the early 1980s, especially in eastern England and this is continuing ('Local Change').

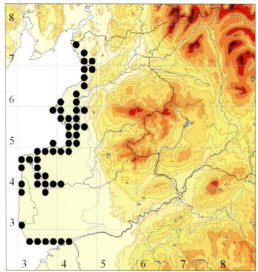

Salicornia agg.

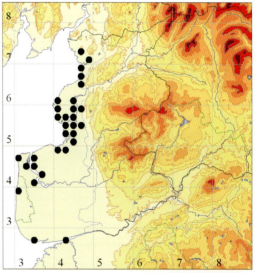

Salicornia ramosissima

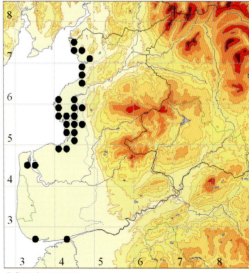

Salicornia europaea

Atriplex patula L.   Common Orache

Eurosiberian Wide-temperate element.

This is an annual of cultivated ground, waste places and tips etc. and is found commonly throughout most of the British Isles (BH3, 4, 17).

Common (259). It occurs throughout northern Lancashire but especially in the west of the area. Its distribution is stable reflecting the national situation.

Atriplex laciniata L.   Frosted Orache

Oceanic Temperate element.

This occurs occasionally on strand lines and fore dunes on shingle and sandy beaches along most of the coasts of the British Isles (BH19).

Rare (12). It is found in small quantity in suitable places along most of the northern Lancashire coast. There has been little change in its distribution during the last 100 years reflecting the national situation although it has been lost where coastal resorts have developed ('New Atlas').

Atriplex portulacoides L.   Sea-purslane

Mediterranean-Atlantic element.

This is a common and characteristic low, grey shrub of salt marshes in the southern half of the British Isles where it often lines the margins of inter-tidal pools and creeks. More occasionally it occurs on sea walls and cliffs (BH18, 21).

Occasional (57). In northern Lancashire it occurs along the whole coastline where, in some places, it dominates the vegetation, especially along the sides of creeks, on ungrazed marshes (see Plate 2.65). It is possible that it has extended its range slightly since 1907 but its distribution probably follows the changing distribution of salt marshes and changes in grazing intensity. The 'New Atlas' reports that *A. portulacoides* extended its range northwards in the British Isles and in northern Europe generally during the twentieth century but 'Local Change' reported no further change.

Beta vulgaris L. ssp. **maritima** (L.) Arcang.   Sea Beet

Mediterranean-Atlantic element.

This is a common plant of cliffs, rocks, strand lines and salt marshes (BH18, 19, 21) along the coasts of England, Wales, Ireland and southern Scotland.

Occasional (45). This occurs commonly along the coast where it is espe-cially frequent on strand lines and on the higher parts of salt marshes. Remarkably Wheldon and Wilson (1907) report only a single record from near Lytham. Despite the dramatic increase in its distribution in northern Lancashire over the last 100 years the 'New Atlas' and 'Local Change' suggest that there has been little change nationally since 1962.

Beta vulgaris L. ssp. **vulgaris**   Root Beet

Neophyte. This taxon was in cultivation in Britain by 1548 and was known in the wild from 1905. Many forms are grown as root vegetables and recording of the different forms has been inconsistent. It is presumed they arose in cultivation.

Very rare (2). Most records nationally are in south-eastern Britain and Lancashire is at the north-western limit of this distribution. Despite many forms being grown in the Fylde the only records are as casuals on a railway bank at Silverdale (Wilson, 1902), as a trackside weed at Marton, Blackpool

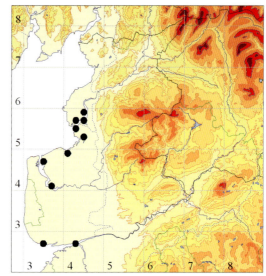
Salicornia fragilis

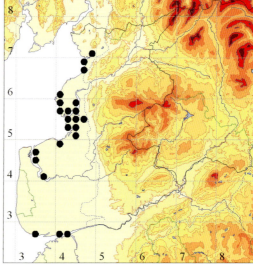
Salicornia dolichostachya

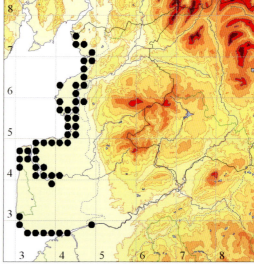
Suaeda maritima

(SD33G) in c. 1990 (C.F. & N.J.S.) and as an escape from cultivation in an arable field at Myerscough (SD54A) in 1987 (C.J.B.).

Salicornia L. — Glassworts

These annuals grow on salt marshes (BH21) around the coasts of the British Isles and throughout much of the world. They are very difficult to identify, not helped by the difficulty of obtaining a taxonomic or nomenclatural consensus amongst the different authorities in the British Isles or in north-western Europe. Identification of the species requires living material examined in September or early October and in this provisional account maps are provided showing the distribution of the genus as well as the commoner species found in northern Lancashire.

Occasional (52). The genus occurs along the whole coast of northern Lancashire and there is no reason to believe that there has been any change in its distribution in salt marshes. Pickled 'Samphire' is a Lancashire delicacy although its culinary use may have declined over the last 100 years.

Salicornia ramosissima Woods — Purple Glasswort
Suboceanic Southern-temperate element.

This species probably occurs around most coasts of the British Isles favouring the middle and upper reaches of salt marshes on firmer mud or muddy sand and shingle. It usually turns a distinctive purple colour when mature.

Occasional (30). It occurs in suitable places on the northern Lancashire coast but is less frequent in the Ribble estuary than elsewhere.

Salicornia europaea L. — Common Glasswort
Circumpolar Wide-temperate element.

This occurs throughout the British Isles at most levels of salt marshes and wherever brackish conditions occur.

Occasional (27). This is largely confined to the shores of the Lune estuary and Morecambe Bay.

Salicornia obscura P.W. Ball & Tutin — Glaucous Glasswort
Oceanic Temperate element.

This is one of the rarest species and was only described in 1959. It is found in a few widely scattered salt marshes in England but it is probably overlooked.

Very rare (3). The only records in northern Lancashire are from Conder Green (SD45N) in 1996, Hest Bank (SD46T) in 2001 and Freckleton (SD42D) in 1998 (all E.F.G.).

Salicornia emerici Duval-Jouve — Shiny Glasswort
Oceanic Southern-temperate element.

Another rare species only described in 1959 and also found in widely scattered salt marshes in southern Britain. Probably overlooked.

Rare (6). Records for this in northern Lancashire are from Carnforth (SD47V) in 1979 (L.A.L.), Freckleton (SD42I) in 1983, Lytham (SD32T) and Preesall (SD34N) in 1999; Overton (SD45H) and Hest Bank (SD46T) in 2001 (all E.F.G.).

Salicornia fragilis P.W. Ball & Tutin — Yellow Glasswort
Oceanic Temperate element.

This is found in open mud and usually at lower levels of salt marshes around most of the coast of England, Wales, Ireland and southern Scotland.

Rare (10). It is found scattered on salt marshes along most of the northern Lancashire coast. It is probably under recorded despite its distinctive yellowish colour.

Salicornia dolichostachya Moss — Long-spiked Glasswort
European Boreo-temperate element.

This is perhaps the most easily recognised species with its long, pale green terminal spike. It is found on salt marshes throughout most of the British Isles.

Occasional (22). This occurs on most salt marshes in northern Lancashire.

Suaeda maritima (L.) Dumort. — Annual Sea-blite
Eurasian Southern-temperate element.

This is found in the middle and lower parts of salt marshes (BH21) in open habitats on mud, often with *Salicornia* spp. It is found around most of the coasts of the British Isles.

Occasional (52). It occurs on all the northern Lancashire salt marshes, and in river estuaries it extends inland to the highest levels of tidal influence. There has been no change in its distribution locally or nationally.

Salsola kali L. ssp. kali — Prickly Saltwort
Eurosiberian Southern-temperate element.

This is usually found on the drift line of sand and shingle beaches often with *Atriplex laciniata*, *Cakile maritima* and *Honkenya peploides* (BH19). It is found in suitable places around the coasts of the British Isles except in parts of northern Scotland.

Rare (11). Most records in northern Lancashire are from the Heysham peninsula, Fleetwood and Lytham St Anne's where it has usually occurred in small quantity. However Fielding (Fielding MS) thought it 'frequent on the sandy sea coast' but refers only to a Lytham station. It was also found at Carnforth (Livermore and Livermore, 1987). Although there has been little change in its distribution in northern Lancashire the 'New Atlas' reports a decline nationally, especially in southern England, since 1962.

Salsola kali L. ssp. **tragus** (L.) Čelak.   Spineless Saltwort

Neophyte. This was first reported in 1857 from Oxfordshire but remains a rare casual. Its native distribution is not clear but it occurs in central and southern Europe.

Very rare (1). In northern Lancashire it was found casually on a demolition site in Preston in 1966 (E.H.; LANC).

Amaranthus retroflexus L.   Common Amaranth

Neophyte. An annual of disturbed, nutrient rich waste land known in British gardens since 1759 and in the wild since 1853. It is a native of temperate and tropical America but naturalised in many parts of the world.

Rare (6). It was first recorded in northern Lancashire from Marton Mere tip, Blackpool (SD33I) in 1961 (A.E.R.; LIV) and it persisted here until 1966. It was also recorded from a roadside at Lytham (SD32Z) in 1995 (C.F. & N.J.S.), a garden weed in Blackpool (SD33B) in 1999 (C.F. & N.J.S.), Freckleton (SD42I in c. 1985 (C.F. & N.J.S.), Fairhaven (SD32I) in 2000 (C.F. & N.J.S.), an urban roadside at Bare (SD46M) in 2010 (J.Cl.) and there is an unlocalised, unattributed record from 1965 in the 10km square SD34 (B.R.C.). However despite it appearing regularly for a few years at Blackpool it was always a casual.

Amaranthus hybridus L.   Green Amaranth

Neophyte. Another annual of disturbed, nutrient rich waste land cultivated in Britain by 1656 and recorded in the wild in 1876. It is a native of tropical and subtropical America but widely naturalised elsewhere.

Very rare (4). The first northern Lancashire record was from Marton Mere tip, Blackpool (SD33I) in 1965 (E.P.) followed by records from Lytham (SD32Y) in 1972 (A.E.R.), Silverdale (SD47M) in 1984 (B.M. Smith) and Morecambe (SD46G) in 1998 (J.K.). However there are earlier records made as *A. cruentus* L. (Purple Amaranth), which may be this species, from Marton Mere in 1961 and Lytham in 1962 (both A.E.R.).

Amaranthus caudatus L.   Love-lies-bleeding

Neophyte. A garden plant probably originating from *A. quitensis* Kunth from South America but known in British gardens since 1596.

Very rare (1). Found as a casual on waste ground at Singleton (SD33Y) in 1989 (C.F. & N.J.S.).

Amaranthus blitum L.   Guernsey Pigweed

Neophyte. *A. blitum* is a native of southern Europe, Africa and Asia and has been known in Britain since 1771. Today it is found in a few scattered localities, mostly in south-eastern England.

Very rare (1). In northern Lancashire Guernsey Pigweed was found in a nursery garden at Westby-with-Plumptons (SD33R) in 2006 (C.F. & N.J.S.).

Amaranthus graecizans L.   Short-tepalled Pigweed

Neophyte. This is a native of the Mediterranean and Africa and found as a casual in Britain. First recorded in the wild in 1905.

Material recorded by J.A.W. as *A. blitum* L. from ballast at Preston Dock in 1900 (Wheldon and Wilson, 1902) was re-identified as *A. graecizans* from a specimen at LANC.

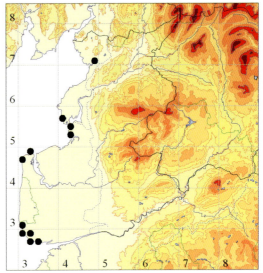

Salsola kali

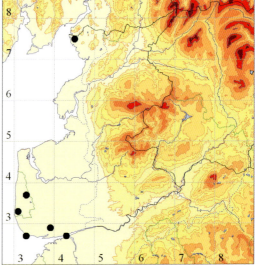

Amaranthus retroflexus

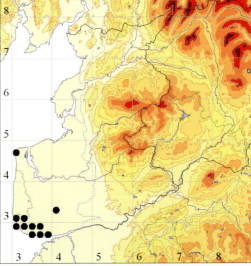

Claytonia perfoliata

AIZOACEAE   DEWPLANT FAMILY

Carpobrotus edulis (L.) N.E. Br.   Hottentot-fig

Neophyte. A native of southern Africa but cultivated in British gardens from c. 1690. It was not recorded in the wild until 1886 and today is a serious threat to native species on Cornish cliffs. However it is climatically limited.

Very rare (1). The only northern Lancashire record is from Rossall in 1968 (P.C.) where it was found as a casual.

MONTIACEAE   BLINKS FAMILY

Claytonia perfoliata Don ex Willd.   Springbeauty

Neophyte. This was introduced into cultivation in 1794 and was first recorded in the wild in 1849. It is a native of western North America. However by 1853 it was a troublesome weed in the Chelsea Physic Garden, London although it was still uncommon in Britain as a whole in 1930. Since then it has spread across the country.

Rare (11). This was not recorded in VC 60 until it was found at Lytham in 1946 (Whellan, 1954). Since then it has been found, sometimes in abundance, in sandy places on the Fylde coast, at Fleetwood and also in railway sidings at Kirkham.

Claytonia sibirica L.   Pink Purslane

Neophyte. This was cultivated in Britain by 1768 and recorded in the wild in 1838. It has spread rapidly since then especially in the west and north of Britain. It is a native of eastern Asia and western North America but widely naturalised in north-western Europe.

Frequent (84). It was first recorded in northern Lancashire from Great Eccleston in 1902 (Wheldon and Wilson, 1902). Since then it has become established over much of the area favouring damp woodland stream banks, where it can be abundant.

[Claytonia virginica L.   Virginia Springbeauty

Neophyte. There are no modern records for this garden escape and native of eastern North America.

In VC 60 it was found on a ditch bank at Marton Mere (France, 1931) but as this is the only record and there is no voucher specimen it is perhaps doubtful.]

Montia fontana L.   Blinks

This is an annual to perennial herb of acidic or neutral, seasonally or permanently wet places including springs and flushes (BH11). However there are four subspecies each of which may have different ecological requirements. As they are difficult to identify requiring microscopical examination of the seed, most recorders have only noted the species.

Frequent (204). The species occurs mostly in upland areas but there are a number of records in western, lowland areas. There has been no change in its distribution locally but the 'New Atlas' suggests there were losses in lowland England since 1962 but no further losses were reported after 1987 ('Local Change').

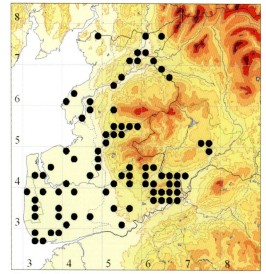

Claytonia sibirica

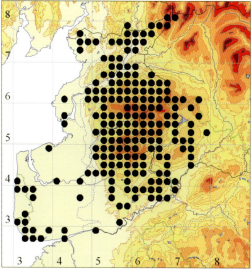

Montia fontana

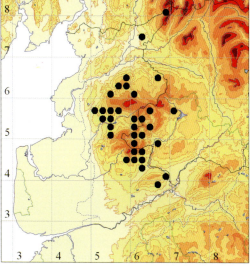

Montia fontana ssp. fontana

Montia fontana L. ssp. **fontana**

European Boreo-temperate element.

This is a plant of hill flushes and of other wet places in the uplands and occurs in northern Britain. It is often difficult to distinguish from *M. fontana* ssp. *variabilis* and intermediates occur.

Occasional (34). This occurs in flushes and wet places in the upland areas of northern Lancashire but is under recorded.

Montia fontana L. ssp. **variabilis** Walters

European Temperate element.

This occurs throughout most of western Britain but does not appear to extend as far north as ssp. *fontana*. It occupies similar habitats of springs, flushes and wet pastures.

Occasional (48). It is clear that despite under recording this is the commonest subspecies in northern Lancashire occurring in all the upland areas.

Montia fontana L. ssp. **amporitana** Senneu

European Temperate element.

Although this is perhaps the least well recorded of the subspecies its national distribution seems to have declined and is now largely confined to south-western parts of the British Isles.

Very rare (4). This is the rarest subspecies in northern Lancashire and has been found by a roadside in Bleasdale (SD54S) in 1981 (E.F. & B.D.G.) probably confirming an unlocalised record from 1873 (B.R.C.), in a wet field near Caton (unlocalised) in 1967 (A.E.R., BM), Roeburndale (SD66C; Livermore and Livermore, 1987) and west of Stocks Reservoir (SD75D; Abbott, 2005).

Montia fontana L. ssp. **chondrosperma** (Fenzl) Walters

European Temperate element.

This has a more southerly and lowland distribution in the British Isles than the other subspecies. It is distinctive appearing as tiny yellowish-green plants in early spring in open habitats, which have been at least wet during the winter. After flowering in April and early May it dies and the seeds germinate in the following spring.

Rare (9). In northern Lancashire it occurs mostly in coastal areas from Lytham to Silverdale and much more rarely inland.

Montia parvifolia (Moc.) Greene   Small-leaved Blinks

Neophyte. A native of western North America. Probably a garden escape but naturalised by the R. Cart, Lanarkshire.

In northern Lancashire it was found at Leagram Hall (SD64H) in 1913 (Bickham, 1914; BM).

PORTULACACEAE   PURSLANE FAMILY

Portulaca oleracea L.   Common Purslane

Neophyte. The native range of Common Purslane is obscure but it occurs as a weed in tropical and warm temperate areas throughout the world.

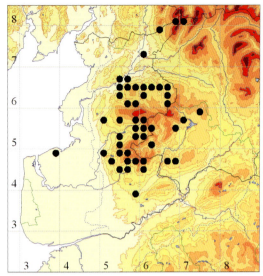

Montia fontana ssp. variabilis

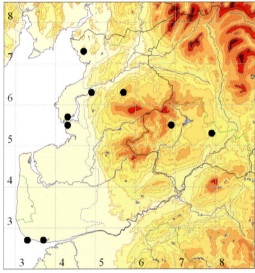

Montia fontana ssp. chondrosperma

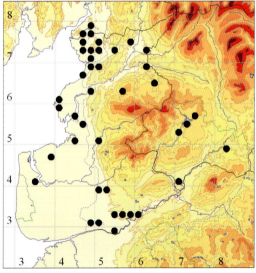

Cornus sanguinea

It has been grown in British gardens since 1200 and has been recorded in the wild since 1874. Today it is found in scattered localities, mostly in south-eastern England.

Very rare (1). In northern Lancashire it was found on bare ground in a nursery garden at Westby-with-Plumptons (SD33R) in 2006 (C.F. & N.J.S.).

CORNACEAE   DOGWOOD FAMILY

Cornus sanguinea L.   Dogwood

European Temperate element.

This is a deciduous shrub found in woodlands and woodland edge habitats (BH1, 3) on calcareous soils but it is also widely planted for amenity purposes. Native plants belong ssp. *sanguinea* but introduced plants are probably ssp. *australis* (C.A. Mey.) Jáv.

Occasional (41). In northern Lancashire Dogwood is probably native on the limestone around Morecambe Bay and in some woodlands in the Ribble and Hodder valleys. It is possibly native in a few other localities but many records probably owe their origins to garden escapes or amenity planting. Wheldon and Wilson (1907) suggested it was sometimes planted as shelter for game. It has become more widespread in the area over the last 100 years, which reflects the national situation. It is likely that both locally and nationally the increase is due to plantings.

Cornus sericea L.   Red-osier Dogwood

Neophyte. This is a native of North America and was cultivated in Britain by 1683. It was known in the wild by 1905 and today Red-osier Dogwood is found throughout the British Isles although it is absent from most of the Scottish Highlands and Western Isles. It is often found in amenity plantings.

Occasional (23). Red-osier Dogwood was first recorded in northern Lancashire from an old orchard at Newton-in-Bowland (SD65V) in 1908 (J.F.P.). Today it is found in scattered localities throughout the area.

Cornus alba L.   White Dogwood

Neophyte. *C. alba* is a native of Eurasia and was introduced into cultivation in 1741. It is a deciduous shrub found in hedges, parkland and scrub but it was not found in the wild until 1875. Today it is found in scattered localities throughout the British Isles.

Very rare (2). In northern Lancashire White Dogwood was found on the disused Preston to Longridge railway at Grimsargh (SD53X) and in Preston (SD52U) in 2007 (Anon).

Cornus mas L.   Cornelian-cherry

Neophyte. This is a native of central and south-eastern Europe and western Asia. It was cultivated in Britain by 1596 and although it is a popular garden plant it was not recorded in the wild until 1927, Cornelian-cherry remains a scarce plant but it is found in scattered localities in Britain.

Very rare (2). In northern Lancashire it was recorded from Carnforth (SD47V) in 1972 (C.F. & N.J.S.) and Garstang (SD44X) in 2009 (J. Cl.).

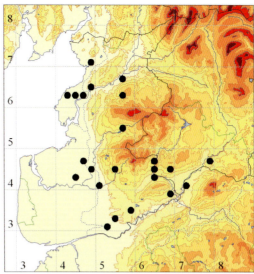
Cornus sericea

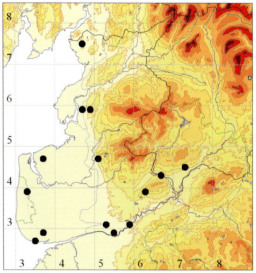
Philadelphus coronarius

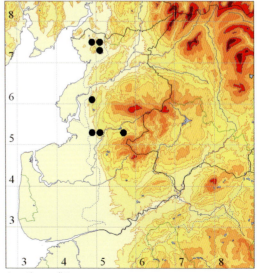
Impatiens noli-tangere

HYDRANGEACEAE   MOCK-ORANGE FAMILY

Philadelphus coronarius L.   Mock-orange

Neophyte. This is a large deciduous shrub or tree, probably native in Austria, northern Italy and the Caucasus. It was first cultivated in Britain by 1596 but not recorded from the wild until 1919. A number of other species and hybrids are grown in gardens and some may be recorded here. Mock-oranges are usually found as garden outcasts on waste ground and in woodlands.

Rare (14). This was first recorded planted in a hedge at Barnacre-with-Bonds (SD54D) in 1989 (B.S.B.I.) and subsequent records are scattered throughout northern Lancashire. However many of these may belong to *P. × virginatus* Rehder, which is believed to be more frequent.

Philadelphus 'Lemoinei' Group   Hairy Mock-orange

Neophyte. This hybrid of garden origin was raised about 1909 and is now more commonly grown in gardens than *P. coronarius*. However whilst it occurs throughout the British Isles it is not recorded as often as *P. coronarius* possibly because of confusion between the two taxa or because it has not escaped as frequently into the wild.

Very rare (3). Hairy Mock-orange or similar garden hybrid was first found in Lancaster (SD46Q; L.A.L.; LIV) in 1990 and subsequently on a bank overlooking the R. Ribble, Preston (SD42Z) in 2007 (E.F.G.). In addition there are two records for the 10km squares SD53 and 52 in the 'New Atlas'. It was also found as a relic of cultivation in the old vicarage garden (abandoned perhaps when the church was re-built in its present position in 1938) at Stocks Reservoir, Easington (SD75I) in 2007 (E.F.G.).

Philadelphus microphyllus A. Gray and hybrids

Neophyte. Included here are garden hybrids, often small shrubs with very fragrant flowers.

Very rare (1). A few bushes were found on the sand dunes at Lytham St Anne's (SD32N) in 1994 (B.S.B.I.). They were thought to belong to the cultivar 'Avalanche'.

Hydrangea macrophylla (Thunb.) Ser.   Hydrangea

Neophyte. This is a native of Japan and found as a garden escape in woodland and waste places. There are several cultivars. It was first introduced into Britain about 1788 but it was not recorded in the wild until 1982 and most records are from southern and south-western England. Nevertheless it is surprising that this common garden plant is rarely found in the wild even as a garden outcast.

Very rare (4). Hydrangea has only been found in northern Lancashire from Lancaster (SD46V) in 1988 (Livermore and Livermore, 1987), Bolton-le-Sands (SD46T) in 1988 (Livermore and Livermore, 1989), Warton, (SD57B) in 2008 (J.Cl.) and from Quernmore (SD55J) in 1998 (E.F.G.).

BALSAMINACEAE   BALSAM FAMILY

Impatiens noli-tangere L.   Touch-me-not Balsam

European Temperate element.

This is an annual plant of nutrient rich sites in damp woodland (BH1). As a native plant it is found in north-western England, especially in the English

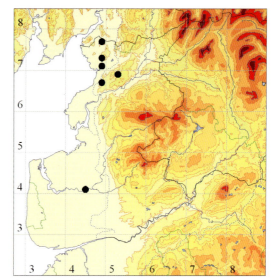
Impatiens parviflora

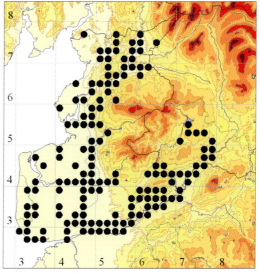
Impatiens glandulifera

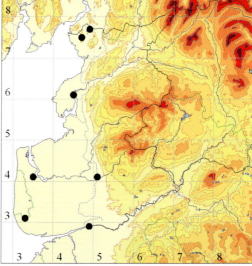
Polemonium caeruleum

Lake District and in parts of Wales. However it is also found occasionally as a short-lived casual in other parts of Britain.

Rare (7). It is difficult to know the status of *I. noli-tangere* in northern Lancashire. It has been known from the north of VC 60 since at least the middle of the nineteenth century when it was found in a ghyll near Whittington (Baker, 1885) and from a wood at Ellel Grange (SD45W) in 1862 (W.H.; LIV) and again in 1991 (A.U.). Other records are from Overton in 1927 (H.E.G.), woods by the R. Lune opposite Caton in 1941 (J.N.F.) and Scorton in 1930 (Anon). In VC 64 it was found in the wooded gorge of the R. Ribble at Bolton-by-Bowland and in Bashall Woods, Browsholme (Lees, 1888). However post 1964 records are from woods in the Yealand Conyers area, Lancaster and Wyresdale but there have been no recent records from the Ribble valley. It is probably native in woodland sites at some of which the host-specific Netted Carpet Moth (*Eustroma reticulata* Schiff.) is also found. Whilst individual localities have changed over the years the distribution in VC 60 is probably unchanged although some recent records are casuals. This situation is reflected nationally.

Impatiens capensis Meerb.   Orange Balsam

Neophyte. This is a native of North America and was probably introduced into Britain very early in the nineteenth century. Orange Balsam was recorded in the wild in 1822 in Surrey but a separate introduction occurred in Norfolk in 1927. Today it is naturalised by rivers, lakes and reservoirs etc. in southern and midland England as far north as Cheshire with occasional records outside this range.

Very rare (1). In northern Lancashire a few plants were found by the Lancaster Canal at Newton-with-Clifton (SD43R) in 1998 (E.F.G.).

Impatiens parviflora DC.   Small Balsam

Neophyte. Small Balsam is a native of central Asia and was introduced into Britain in 1823. It was recorded in the wild in Surrey in 1851 and in Scotland in 1864. It is found in semi-natural woodland and waste places in many parts of the British Isles but in Ireland it is only found in the Dublin area.

Rare (6). In northern Lancashire there is an unlocalised and unattributed record for the 10km square SD63 from the 1950s (B.R.C.). Otherwise the first record for Small Balsam is from Carnforth (SD47V) in 1966 (C.J.-P.). Other records are from a wood at Over Kellet (SD56J) in 1983 (C.F. & N.J.S.), by the Lancaster Canal (SD46Y or Z; Livermore and Livermore, 1989), in a second locality at Carnforth (SD47W) in 1997 (J.M.N.), at Thrang End, Yealand Redmayne (SD47Y) in 2001 (P.J.) and as a garden weed at Great Eccleston (SD44K) in 1996 (C.F. & N.J.S.).

Impatiens glandulifera Royle   Indian Balsam

Neophyte. This is a native of the Himalayas and was introduced into Britain in 1839. It was first recorded in the wild in Middlesex in 1855 but later it became naturalised independently in many different places in Britain. However it was not until the twentieth century that it spread rapidly and today it is found in many parts of the British Isles where it is commonly known as Himalayan Balsam. Indian Balsam grows on riverbanks and stream sides and occasionally elsewhere. It is often found in dense thickets excluding other flowering plants and ferns.

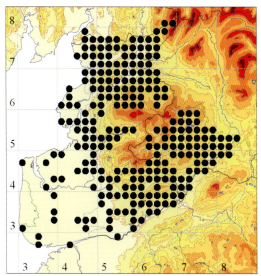

Primula vulgaris

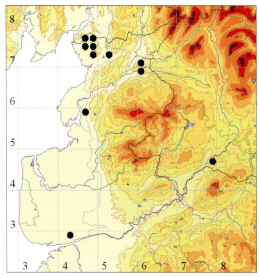

Primula × polyantha

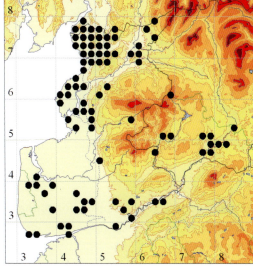

Primula veris

Frequent (153). There is an unlocalised VC 60 record from 1942 (Frankland, 1942) but the first localised record for *I. glandulifera* was in 1946 when it was found by the Lancaster Canal at Preston (J.E.D.; BM). However it is likely that it was established on the banks of the R. Ribble before this as it was found on the banks of the R. Darwen, a tributary of the R. Ribble, at Roach Bridge in South Lancashire in 1913 (Savidge, *et al.*, 1963). Today its distribution in northern Lancashire correlates with river valleys and the Lancaster Canal as well as occurring in western parts of the area.

POLEMONIACEAE   JACOB'S-LADDER FAMILY

Polemonium caeruleum L.   Jacob's-ladder

Eurosiberian Boreal-montane element but a neophyte in northern Lancashire.

As a native species this is found on calcareous screes and river cliffs in the Pennines and in Northumberland. However it is widely naturalised in Britain and more rarely in Ireland.

Rare (7). This was first recorded from Sale Wheel by the R. Ribble (SD63S) in 1887 (Anon, 1891) with further pre 1964 records from near St Michael's (c. SD44R), Stonyhurst (SD63Z), by the R. Hodder (SD64V) and near Winckley Farm, Hurst Green (SD73E). Since 1964 it has been found in a few scattered localities in the region.

Phlox paniculata L.   Phlox

Neophyte. Phlox is a native of eastern North America and was introduced into British cultivation by 1730. It is a perennial herb with scented flowers and is grown widely in the British Isles. Despite its popularity it was not recorded in the wild until 1915 and remains a scarce plant with most records from the London area. There are numerous cultivars.

Very rare (4). In northern Lancashire it was found on waste ground between Lancaster and Morecambe (SD46L; Livermore and Livermore, 1987), in tetrad SD53K in 1966 (E.F.G.), from a roadside at Dilworth (SD63J) in 2004 (E.F.G.) and from a roadside between Holden and Bolton-by-Bowland (SD74U) in 2007 (E.F.G.).

PRIMULACEAE   PRIMROSE FAMILY

Primula vulgaris Huds   Primrose

European Temperate element.

This is found in woodlands and on banks (BH1, 16) throughout the British Isles.

Common (254). The Primrose occurs throughout northern Lancashire and its distribution is stable. The 'New Atlas' reports that it has suffered in hot summers in East Anglia but no losses were reported by 'Local Change'.

Primula vulgaris × P. veris (P. × polyantha Mill.)

This hybrid occurs over much of the British Isles in woodland edge and scrub habitats but it is rare in most of Scotland and Ireland. However it is easily overlooked.

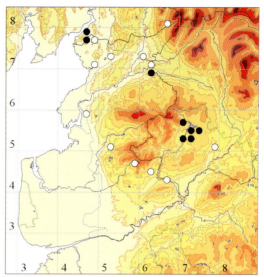
Primula farinosa

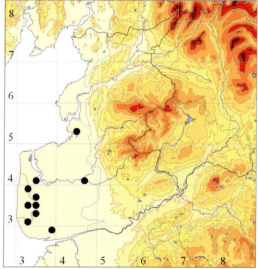
Hottonia palustris

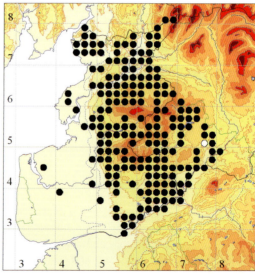
Lysimachia nemorum

Rare (11). This occurs in scattered localities but mostly in the north of VC 60 especially on the limestone in the Silverdale area where both species occur. Some records may involve garden Polyanthus.

Primula veris L.   Cowslip

Eurosiberian Temperate element.

This is a plant of well-drained, calcareous soils and is characteristic of herb-rich grasslands, scrub and woodland edge habitats (BH6, 7). It is found in much of England, Wales, Ireland and eastern Scotland.

Frequent (88). Cowslips are found throughout northern Lancashire on calcareous soils but particularly from Heysham northwards to Silverdale. There was probably a considerable decline during the twentieth century but it spread rapidly onto the newly constructed M6 motorway banks in the Warton area. Today its natural distribution is obscured by plantings on roadside and motorway banks (e.g. junction 32 of the M6 motorway at Broughton) and as amenity plantings elsewhere. Often these introductions seem to be of a more robust stock. The ability of Cowslip to colonize man-made habitats was noted by Wheldon and Wilson (1907) 100 years ago. Nationally there has been little change in its distribution although similar fluctuations to those observed in northern Lancashire have been noted elsewhere.

Primula farinosa L.   Bird's-eye Primrose

Eurasian Boreal-montane element.

This pretty pink-flowered primrose is confined to calcareous flushes (BH7, 11) in northern England.

Rare (8) decreasing to very rare (5). Wheldon and Wilson (1907) recorded eleven localities in VC 60 and literature and herbarium searches have revealed at least four other sites from where it had probably gone by 1900. In Lancashire VC 64 sites were too numerous for Pickard (1901) to list. Today sites are confined to shell marl at Hawes Water, Silverdale (SD47T), Robert Hall Moor, Tatham (SD66J), Standridge Meadow, Slaidburn (SD75G), Bottom Laithe, Gisburn Forest (SD75M) and Copped Hill Clough, Slaidburn (SD75D). It seems that inappropriate grazing management, drainage and eutrophication are causing these losses at the southern edge of its British range. Nationally it is often abundant within its main area of distribution but the pattern of losses seen in Lancashire is also reflected in losses elsewhere around the edges of its British range.

Hottonia palustris L.   Water-violet

European Temperate element.

This is found in base-rich, clear and non-eutrophic water bodies (BH13) in England and Wales. It occurs occasionally as an introduction elsewhere.

Rare (10) decreasing to very rare (4). This occurs in ponds and ditches in lowland VC 60 and between 1900 and 1964 there had been little change in its distribution. However from the late 1970s pollution of many ditches occurred and drainage in parts of the Fylde lowered the water table with the loss of several colonies. It still occurs in ponds at Bispham (SD34F), on the Cockerham/Winmarleigh border (SD44U), Poulton-le-Fylde (SD33J) and Staining, Blackpool (SD33M). At some sites it has been transplanted from nearby ponds when these have been threatened. There have also been losses nationally.

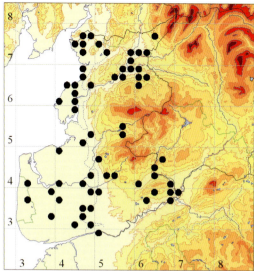

Lysimachia nummularia

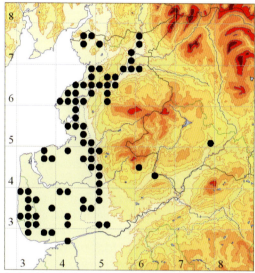

Lysimachia vulgaris

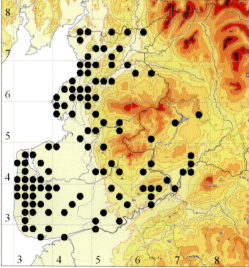

Lysimachia punctata

Lysimachia nemorum L.   Yellow Pimpernel

Suboceanic Temperate element.

This is a characteristic species of herb-rich deciduous woodland, hedge-rows, fens and marshes etc. (BH1) and is found throughout the British Isles.

Frequent (202). This is a common woodland plant in the east and north of northern Lancashire with only occasional records in the lowland west of the area. Its distribution is unchanged in northern Lancashire but nationally there have been losses in southern England ('New Atlas') but further losses since 1987 were not noted ('Local Change').

Lysimachia nummularia L.   Creeping-Jenny

European Temperate element but widely naturalised outside of its native range.

This occurs in damp places often in woodland but also in hedgerows and in waste places (BH6, 11, 14). It is found in many parts of the British Isles but it is very rare in most of northern Scotland.

Occasional (63). Wheldon and Wilson (1907) recorded this in ten locali-ties in the western half of northern Lancashire whilst Pickard (1901, 1902) recorded it in three localities in Lancashire VC 64. Today it is scattered throughout the area but whilst it is probably native in northern Lancashire it is also grown in gardens and perhaps its spread is due in part to garden escapes. Nationally it has shown an increase since 1987 ('Local Change').

Lysimachia vulgaris L.   Yellow Loosestrife

Eurasian Temperate element.

This occurs, sometimes in large patches, in wet places in fens, on river-banks and stream sides and by ponds and ditches (BH11) in England, Wales, Ireland and southern Scotland.

Frequent (80). In northern Lancashire this is found generally in lowland areas in the west of the area but it is also especially characteristic of the Lancaster Canal and the Lune valley. There are occasional records else-where. There has been no change in its distribution in northern Lancashire but the 'New Atlas' reported some losses nationally but since 1987 there have been no further losses ('Local Change').

Lysimachia ciliata L.   Fringed Loosestrife

Neophyte. This is an evergreen perennial herb native to North America. It was first cultivated in British gardens by 1732 and it was known from the wild by 1849. It is seldom grown in gardens today but it occurs in scat-tered localities in Britain.

Very rare. (1). In northern Lancashire it was recorded from rough ground at Carleton (SD34F) in 2007 (M.S.).

Lysimachia punctata L.   Dotted Loosestrife

Neophyte. This is a native of south-eastern and central Europe and western Asia. It has been cultivated in British gardens since 1658 and was recorded in the wild in 1853. However McAllister (1999) pointed out that records for *L. punctata* probably included *L. verticillaris* L. from which it is difficult to distinguish except by the presence in living material of an orange flush to the petals of *L. verticillaris* whereas the petals of *L. punctata* are uniformly pale yellow. On the other hand Richards (2002) suggests that the two taxa

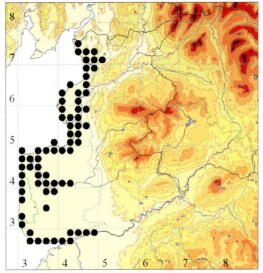

Glaux maritima

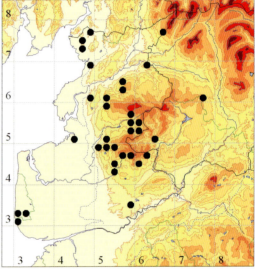

Anagallis tenella

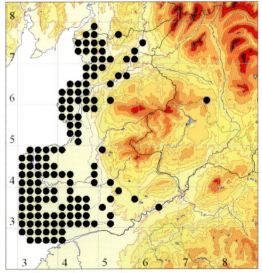

Anagallis arvensis ssp. arvensis

are not specifically distinct. *L. punctata sensu lato* is found throughout the British Isles although it is rare in some parts, e.g. highland Scotland and most of Ireland.

Frequent (111). *L. punctata sensu lato* was first recorded from waste land at Poulton-le-Fylde railway station (SD33Y) in 1966 (E.P.) and today it is found throughout northern Lancashire but especially near the Fylde coast and in the Lancaster area. All specimens examined so far have an orange flush at the base of the petals and are therefore referable to *L. verticillaris*.

Lysimachia terrestris (L.) Britton, Sterns & Poggenb.
Lake Loosestrife

Neophyte. This is a native of North America and was first cultivated in Britain in 1781. It was discovered in the wild next to Lake Windermere in 1883 but apart from a record in West Sussex in 1958 all subsequent records have been in north-western England.

Very rare (1). The only record for northern Lancashire is from marshy ground near Fleetwood (SD34I) in 1985 (C.F. & N.J.S.; LIV).

Lysimachia thyrsiflora L.
Tufted Loosestrife

Circumpolar Boreal-montane element.

This is found in shallow water in fens, on lake margins, by rivers and in ditches (BH13) in central Scotland and Yorkshire and occasionally elsewhere either as introductions or by natural spread.

Very rare (1). This was found at Marton Mere, Blackpool (SD33M) in 2006 (C.F. & N.J.S.) but it is believed it had been present for a few years prior to this. It is likely that it arrived by natural spread. [There is a record from Lancaster (LANC) but a duplicate voucher at MANCH makes it clear that it was recorded from a reservoir at Bury, VC 59.] In Scotland there has been no change in its distribution but there have been losses in Yorkshire. However it flowers infrequently and may be overlooked.

Glaux maritima L.
Sea-milkwort

Circumpolar Boreo-temperate element.

This is found on salt marshes and muddy strand lines (BH19, 21) around all the coasts of the British Isles. It is often abundant.

Frequent (70). Sea-milkwort occurs along the whole northern Lancashire coast where it is often abundant in salt marshes. Its distribution is stable both locally and nationally.

Anagallis tenella (L.) L.
Bog Pimpernel

Oceanic Southern-temperate element.

This is found in wet open and often flushed habitats (BH11) in coastal and hilly areas in many parts of the British Isles but especially in western areas.

Occasional (33). In northern Lancashire Bog Pimpernel is found in many hill flushes in the east and north of the area and more occasionally in coastal areas, especially formerly on the sand dunes at Lytham St Anne's and in damp places on the limestone in the Silverdale area. However it has not been seen on the coast for many years. There were losses before the 1970s but since then there has been no change in its distribution in northern Lancashire but the 'New Atlas' showed numerous losses in much of England especially in south-eastern areas. However 'Local Change' reported no further significant losses since 1987.

Anagallis arvensis L. ssp. **arvensis**
Scarlet Pimpernel

Eurosiberian Southern-temperate element.

This occurs as an arable and garden weed and also grows in disturbed waste places (BH4) throughout lowland parts of the British Isles.

Frequent (141). Scarlet Pimpernel is a common plant of the western half of northern Lancashire but it is rare in the upland east of the area. Occasional blue flowered forms occur, which may have been identified as ssp. *foemina*. There has been no change in its distribution in northern Lancashire but the 'New Atlas' reports losses in the north of its British range but no further losses since 1987 were noted by 'Local Change'.

Anagallis arvensis L. ssp. **foemina** (Mill.)
Schinz & Thell.
Blue Pimpernel

Archaeophyte with a Eurosiberian Southern-temperate distribution. This occurs on waste ground and as an arable weed but it is much rarer than ssp. *arvensis* and found mostly in south-eastern England. It is easily confused with blue forms of ssp. *arvensis*. For this reason there is some doubt as to whether or not it has been found in northern Lancashire as voucher material has not been checked. The following records are therefore tentative.

Very rare (1). Blue Pimpernel was recorded from Glasson Dock in 1906 (J.A.W.), from the Wyre banks near Fleetwood in 1851 (Ashfield, 1860), on the sand hills at St Anne's in 1907 (C.B.) and from demolition sites in Preston (SD53F) in 1966 (E.H.).

Trientalis europaea L.
Chickweed-wintergreen

Circumpolar Boreal-montane element.

This is found in moist, acidic and humus rich upland woodlands and moorland (BH1, 2, 9, 10) in Scotland and northern England.

Very rare (3). This occurs over an extensive area on both sides of Black Clough, Marshaw Fell, Over Wyresdale (SD55V, 65A, 65B) where it is found fringing the woodland but mostly on the Bracken covered hillsides. It also grew on Waddington Fell near the Moorcock Inn (Pickard, 1901; SD74I) where it could still grow. However in 2010 the ground appeared to have been disturbed at some time and *T. europaea* was not seen. Its distribution in Scotland is stable but there have been losses in England ('New Atlas'). The extant Black Clough locality is at the southern edge of its British distribution.

Centunculus minimus L.   Chaffweed

European Temperate element.

Chaffweed is an annual of open damp, sandy sites usually on acid soils (BH3). Today it is mostly found on or near the coasts especially along southern and western coasts of the British Isles.

Very rare (2). The only records for this in northern Lancashire are from Arkholme Moor in 1900 (A.W.; Wheldon and Wilson, 1907), Cringlebarrow Wood, Yealand Redmayne (SD47X) in 1986 (B.S.B.I.) and St Anne's Old Links Golf Course (SD33A) in 1988 (C.F. & N.J.S.). The 'New Atlas' reports that there have been many losses at inland sites in England but in coastal localities, with an easily overlooked species that appears sporadically, it is difficult to know if there is any significant change.

Cyclamen hederifolium Aiton   Sowbread

Neophyte. This is a native of southern Europe and western Turkey. It was introduced into Britain before 1596 and was recorded in the wild as early as 1597. It is frequent in woodlands and hedgerows in southern England but is rare further north and in Ireland.

Very rare (1). Sowbread was found in a hedgerow adjacent to woodland at Bailrigg, Scotforth (SD45Z) in 2008 (E.F. & B.D.G), where it appeared naturalised. Both pink and white flowered plants were found.

Samolus valerandi L.   Brookweed

Circumpolar Southern-temperate element.

This occurs in flushed sites near the sea on cliffs, salt marshes and sand dunes (BH11) and occasionally inland in somewhat saline conditions. It is found around most coasts of the British Isles except northern and eastern Scotland.

Occasional (17). Brookweed is found at several sites on the northern Lancashire coast and occasionally inland in abandoned clay pits. Only seven or eight sites had been located for this species prior to 1964 indicating that its distribution has increased over the last 100 years. However nationally the 'New Atlas' reported losses but 'Local Change' noted no significant change since 1987.

ERICACEAE   HEATHER FAMILY

Empetrum nigrum L. ssp. nigrum   Crowberry

Circumpolar Boreo-arctic Montane element.

This is found on heaths and bogs (BH10, 12, 15) in the British Isles northwest of a line from the R. Severn to the R. Humber.

Frequent (86). Crowberry occurs in all the upland areas of northern Lancashire and more rarely on the raised bogs of Cockerham and Winmarleigh, the dune heath at Lytham St Anne's and the remnants of wet heath on the north side of the Lune valley. Its distribution locally and nationally is unchanged.

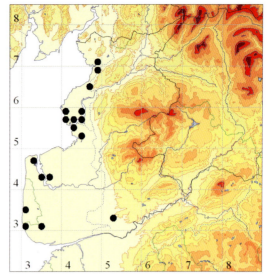

Samolus valerandi

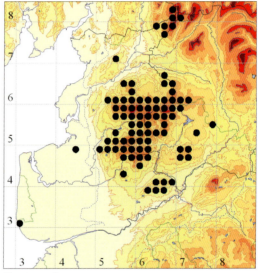

Empetrum nigrum

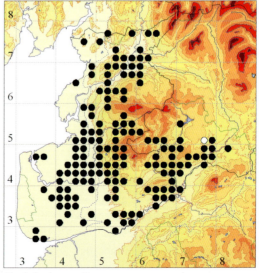

Rhododendron ponticum

Rhododendron ponticum L.   Rhododendron

Neophyte. This is a native of two disjunct areas: the Iberian Peninsula and south-eastern Europe, Lebanon, Turkey and the Caucasus. Plants from Iberia are referred to ssp. *baeticum* (Boiss. & Reuter) Hand.-Mazz., whilst material from the Near East is referred to ssp. *ponticum* (Tutin, *et al.*, 1972). *R. ponticum* was native to Ireland in the Hoxnian interglacial and in the current interglacial was introduced to cultivation in 1763 when it was described as not fully hardy. It was known in the wild by at least 1894 and has spread throughout the British Isles where it is found on heaths and in woodlands on acid soils (BH1, 10, 16). However recently it has been shown (Milne and Abbott, 2000) that *R. ponticum* in the British Isles originated from Iberia (i.e. ssp. *baeticum*) where it is rare and endangered but also half hardy. It became popular in the nineteenth century for planting as cover for game but at some stage it appears that introgression occurred with the hardy North American *R. catawbiense* Michaux, *R. maximum* L. and another North American species. Work is ongoing to elucidate the composition of what seems to be a complex series of species and hybrids involving *R. ponticum* ssp. *baeticum* as one parent. It is possible that introgression with other species has given British *R. ponticum* a competitive edge so that it has become a hardy, invasive species causing economic problems (Dehnen-Schmutz, *et al.*, 2004; Dehnen-Schmutz and Williamson, 2006). Research, particularly on the morphology of British material, to elucidate what taxa occur in the British Isles continues but it now seems clear that British material is all of hybrid origin and is endemic to the British Isles. *R. ponticum* ssp. *baeticum* is frost sensitive and does not now occur in the British Isles. British hybrid material is named *R. x superponticum* Cullen (Cullen, 2011).

Frequent (160). It was first recorded in northern Lancashire by Perring and Walters (1962) although it was probably well established by then. Unfortunately it has not been possible to discover when it was first planted in the area but this was probably in the second half of the nineteenth century. Rhododendron is found throughout northern Lancashire but the complex taxonomy was not appreciated until 2006. Then it became apparent that Lancashire *R.* 'ponticum' was morphologically variable and that one gathering of a large, vigorous, very glandular shrub at Nicky Nook, Nether Wyresdale (SD54J) probably involves or is *R. maximum*.

Rhododendron luteum Sweet   Yellow Azalea

Neophyte. This is a native of eastern Europe, Turkey and the Caucasus. It was introduced into cultivation in 1793 but not recorded in the wild until 1939. It is found in scattered localities in England, Wales and Scotland but there is only one record in Ireland.

In northern Lancashire the only record is from a wood at Winkley Hall, Stonyhurst (SD73E) in *c.* 1960 (MS at SYT).

Rhododendron groenlandicum (Oeder) Kron & Judd   Labrador-tea

Neophyte (probably). This has a circumpolar Boreo-arctic distribution although so far all the material in this country seems to have originated from northern North America with 2n = 52. It also occurs in Greenland but this appears to be a dwarf form (H.A. McAllister, pers. comm.). Labrador-tea was brought into cultivation in 1762 and reported from the wild in Stirlingshire before 1860 (Proctor, 2002). It is established in both lowland raised bogs and upland blanket bogs but as all recorded sites are remote from habitation there has been speculation as to whether or

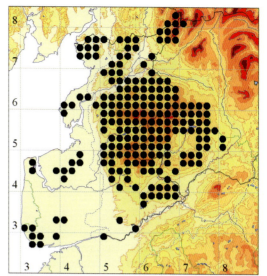
Calluna vulgaris

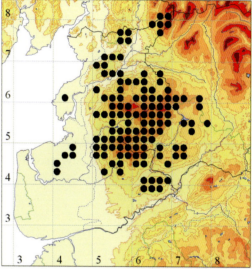
Erica tetralix

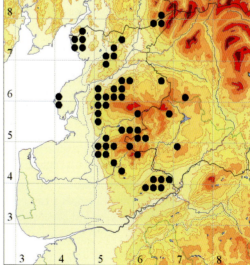
Erica cinerea

not colonisation has been by long distance dispersal. This is discussed by Yalden (1996) in the context of southern Pennine sites. Alternatively as many of the sites are on sporting estates accidental introduction in the course of land management is possible. Perhaps the most likely explanation is that natural dispersal from cultivation in central Scotland occurred in the mid nineteenth century and further natural spread then took place.

Very rare (2). In northern Lancashire this was first found on Cockerham Moss (SD44P) in 1972 (J.Wi.) and more recently on Winmarleigh Moss (SD44N) in 2005 (M.S.) where plants were transplanted from the original Cockerham colony in 1975 or 1976 (L.A.L.).

Calluna vulgaris (L.) Hull   Heather
European Boreo-temperate element.

This is found on acid soils (BH10, 12) throughout the British Isles except for parts of central and eastern England. It dominates many moors and heaths where in northern England and Scotland heather moors are carefully managed as sporting estates for grouse shoots.

Frequent (211). Heather occurs in upland areas in the east of northern Lancashire where it dominates large areas of moorland (see Plate 2.34). The moors are carefully managed by burning and grazing by sheep to maximise the production of Red Grouse (*Lagopus lagopus* L.) for sport. Heather is also found on lowland heaths and raised bogs and occasionally elsewhere. *C. vulgaris* has declined as heaths and bogs have been reclaimed for farming and in the uplands severe outbreaks of heather beetle (*Locmaea saturalis* Thomson) and over-grazing have caused the loss of some heather covered moors. Similar losses have been noted nationally.

Erica ciliaris L. × E. tetralix (E. × watsonii Benth.)
This hybrid occurs throughout the range of *E. ciliaris*, which occurs on heaths in southern England.

Very rare (1). In northern Lancashire *E. × watsonii* was found on a rough grassy area on a golf course at Fairhaven (SD32P) in 1999 (C.F. & N.J.S.).

Erica tetralix L.   Cross-leaved Heath
Suboceanic Temperate element.

This is found in a wide range of mires and wet heaths (BH10, 12) in most areas of the British Isles except parts of central and eastern England.

Frequent (125). In northern England it occurs in bogs in all the upland areas and more rarely on lowland raised bogs. It has declined as lowland mires and heaths have been drained and this loss has occurred nationally.

Erica cinerea L.   Bell Heather
Oceanic Temperate element.

This is a plant of acid, dry heaths (BH10) and is found in much of the British Isles except central and eastern England.

Occasional (54). This is found on heaths in the east of northern Lancashire and also in the Silverdale and Heysham areas. It has declined in northern Lancashire as habitats have been lost and losses have also been reported nationally.

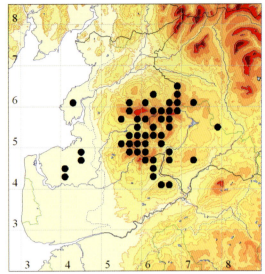
Andromeda polifolia

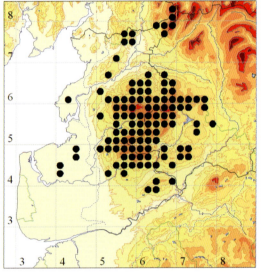
Vaccinium oxycoccus

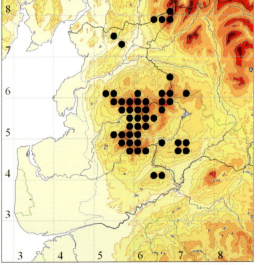
Vaccinium vitis-idaea

Andromeda polifolia L.   Bog-rosemary

Circumpolar Boreal-montane element.

This is found in bogs (BH12) in England, Wales, southern Scotland and Ireland.

Occasional (49). In northern Lancashire it occurs on the wet blanket bogs on Longridge Fell and in the Bowland Fells. It is also found on raised bogs fringing the fells and on lowland raised and valley bogs elsewhere. It does not occur in Leck. It has been lost from the wet heaths on the north side of the Lune valley and from most of the raised bogs fringing the Bowland Fells and in lowland areas in the west of the area. The 'New Atlas' also noted some losses nationally.

Gaultheria mucronata (L. f.) Hook. & Arn.   Prickly Heath

Neophyte. This dwarf shrub was introduced into Britain in 1828 and was recorded in the wild in 1903. It is a common garden plant and has been found in scattered localities throughout much of the British Isles.

Very rare (2). It was first recorded near Churchtown (SD44R) in 1964 (J.H.) and on waste ground near Lancaster Priory (SD46R) in 1984 (D.P.E.).

Vaccinium oxycoccus L.   Cranberry

Circumpolar Boreal-montane element.

Cranberry is found in bogs and wet heaths (BH12) over much of Ireland, Wales, northern England, central and southern Scotland but rarely elsewhere.

Frequent (115). This occurs in most of the upland areas in the eastern half of northern Lancashire and less frequently on lowland mires in the west of the area. It was lost from lowland mires as these were drained. Losses took place in southern and eastern England before 1930 but elsewhere its distribution is stable ('New Atlas', 'Local Change').

Vaccinium vitis-idaea L.   Cowberry

Circumpolar Boreo-arctic Montane element.

This is found on peaty heaths and moorland on acid soils in upland parts of the British Isles (BH2, 10, 15).

Occasional (49). In northern Lancashire it is found in upland areas of the north and east of the area but seems to be more frequent on the western slopes of the Bowland Fells than elsewhere. There have been no changes in its distribution locally or nationally.

Vaccinium myrtillus L.   Bilberry

Eurosiberian Boreal-montane element.

This is found on heaths and woodland on acid soils (BH1, 10, 16) throughout much of the British Isles except central and eastern England.

Frequent (189). This occurs in most of the east and north of northern Lancashire where it can dominate some of the more heavily grazed heaths, e.g. on Clougha. It is also a common component of upland, acid woodlands. In addition it is found in scattered localities in the western half of the area. There has been no change in its distribution locally but the 'New Atlas' reports losses in parts of England and central Ireland and these have continued since 1987 ('Local Change').

Pyrola minor L.   Common Wintergreen

Circumpolar Boreal-montane element.

This is found in damp woodlands throughout the British Isles but most frequently from northern England northwards.

Extinct. Davis and Lees (1878) recorded Common Wintergreen from somewhere in the VC 64 part of the Hodder valley. However the record was not repeated in Lees (1888) and no other reference to this species growing in northern Lancashire has been found. The 'New Atlas' notes a decline nationally, especially in the south of its range and mostly before 1930.

Pyrola rotundifolia L. ssp. **maritima**
(Kenyon) E.F. Warb.   Round-leaved Wintergreen

Suboceanic Temperate element.

This occurs on coastal sand dunes (BH19) especially in Wales and north-western England and occasionally inland on post-industrial sites.

Very rare (1). Since 1964 this has been found in a few places on the sand dunes at Lytham St Anne's (SD33A). Formerly it was found from Lytham to Blackpool but by 1907 Wheldon and Wilson considered it rare. Today it occurs in very small quantity in one or two localities in SD33A. The 'New Atlas' suggests that nationally it has spread over the last 100 years but that individual populations fluctuate widely.

Hypopitys monotropa Crantz.   Yellow Bird's-nest

Circumpolar Temperate element.

This is a saprophyte of leaf litter in shaded woodlands (BH1) on calcareous soils and amongst *Salix repens* on sand dunes (BH19). It occurs in scattered localities in England and Wales and more rarely elsewhere. Two subspecies are recognised but the only one identified as occurring on west coast sand dunes is ssp. *hypophegea* (Wallr.) Tzvelev whilst the distribution of ssp. *monotropa* and intermediates is less certain (Perring, 1968).

Very rare (3). This occurs sporadically at Silverdale (SD47S, T) and at Lytham St Anne's (SD33A). Although not critically determined it is believed all records are referable to ssp. *hypophegea*. It is not clear to what extent *H. monotropa* has declined in northern Lancashire because it appears only sporadically. However with the reduction of its sand dune habitat it must have declined on the Fylde coast. It has declined nationally ('New Atlas').

GARRYACEAE   SPOTTED-LAUREL FAMILY

Aucuba japonica Thunb.   Spotted-laurel

Neophyte. This is a native of eastern Asia and plants with yellow-spotted leaves were introduced into Britain from Japan in 1783. These speckled leaved plants predominate in cultivation where they are widely planted in gardens and parks. It was first recorded in the wild in 1981 and today most records are southwest of a line running between the R. Clyde and the Wash.

Rare (8). Spotted-laurel was first recorded in northern Lancashire as a garden escape in two tetrads in Lancaster District (SD46L, 56C; Livermore and Livermore, 1987). Further records were made from scattered localities in VC 60. All are garden escapes but it was regenerating at a locality in Preston (SD52J; P.J.).

RUBIACEAE   BEDSTRAW FAMILY

Sherardia arvensis L.   Field Madder

European Southern-temperate element.

This is an annual herb of dry rather open grasslands (BH7, 16) and is found in many lowland areas of the British Isles.

Occasional (33). In northern Lancashire Field Madder is found mostly in the north of the area, especially on the calcareous soils around Morecambe Bay. However there are also a few localities in the Fylde and in the Ribble and Hodder valleys. It has probably declined over the last 100 years, which is in line with the national situation reported by the 'New Atlas'. However 'Local Change' noted a marked increase. What appears to have happened is that it was lost from arable fields as weed control became more successful but that it then became more of an urban species occurring in the built environment.

Asperula cynanchica L.   Squinancywort

European Temperate element.

Squinancywort is a rhizomatous perennial herb of calcareous grassland (BH7). It occurs on limestone and chalk in southern Britain and western Ireland with occasional records as far north as mid Yorkshire. However it also occurs on the limestone around Morecambe Bay.

Rare (9). In northern Lancashire A. cynanchica is found on limestone around Morecambe Bay and on Dalton Crags. There has been no change in its distribution locally but the 'New Atlas' reported losses from eastern England and 'Local Change' noted these had continued since 1987.

Asperula arvensis L.   Blue Woodruff

Casual neophyte. This annual herb is probably a native of south-western Asia and possibly southern Europe. It was cultivated in Britain by the sixteenth century and was found in the wild in 1541. It occurs in a few scattered localities in the British Isles but mostly in England.

Very rare (2). In northern Lancashire this was found at Silverdale in the period 1964–68 (SD47M) and possibly in 1971 (B.R.C.). It was also found at Heysham (SD46B) in 1975 (A.E.C.).

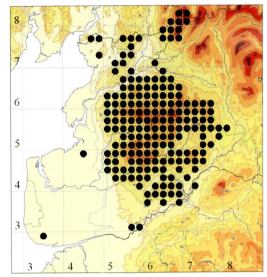

Vaccinium myrtillus

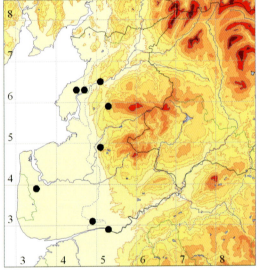

Aucuba japonica

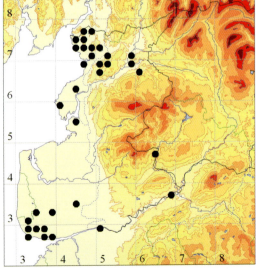

Sherardia arvensis

Galium boreale L. — Northern Bedstraw

Circumpolar Boreo-temperate element.

Northern Bedstraw is a perennial herb of base-rich substrates in rocky places, flushes and montane grasslands (BH7, 16). It is found in upland areas of Wales, Ireland, Scotland and northern England.

Very rare (1 or 2). *G. boreale* was recorded from by the R. Lune in 1903 (Wheldon and Wilson, 1907), where it was last recorded in 1932 (Whiteside, no date). However the main sites for this species at the southern limit of its English distribution are in Gait Barrows National Nature Reserve (SD47T, Y) where two colonies were known in 1967 (C.D.P.). It was last seen in 2005 (E.F.G.) where there was a single shoot. Nationally there have been losses more especially in lowland areas on the edge of its geographical range ('New Atlas', 'Local Change').

Galium odoratum (L.) Scop. — Woodruff

European Temperate element.

Woodruff is a rhizomatous perennial herb of deciduous woodland (BH1). It occurs in most parts of the British Isles, where its white scented flowers and green foliage is a delightful feature of British spring time.

Frequent (111). In northern Lancashire it occurs mostly in northern and eastern parts of the area. It is occasionally grown in gardens and some records may be of garden escapes. Locally its distribution is unchanged but nationally there is some evidence for decline especially in south-eastern England ('New Atlas', 'Local Change').

Galium uliginosum L. — Fen Bedstraw

Eurasian Boreo-temperate element.

This is a perennial herb of base-rich marshes and fens (BH11). It occurs in much of the British Isles but appears to be absent from northern Scotland.

Occasional (58). Fen Bedstraw occurs in northern and eastern areas of northern Lancashire. Wheldon and Wilson (1907) found it in only eight localities and it appears that it has become more widespread over the last 100 years. However it is possible that Wheldon and Wilson under recorded this species whilst from 1964 until at least the 1980s it was over recorded in the area. Today it seems to be a rare species. The 'New Atlas' reported a similar situation nationally but 'Local Change' suggests its distribution since 1987 has been stable.

Galium palustre L. — Common Marsh-bedstraw

Eurosiberian Boreo-temperate element.

This is a perennial herb of wetland habitats including wet meadows, ditches, ponds and marshes (BH11). It occurs throughout the British Isles. Stace (1987) recognised two subspecies; ssp. *palustre* and ssp. *elongatum* (C. Presl) Arcang. However Sell and Murrell (2006) recognised three subspecies each with different chromosome numbers and with differing morphological characters – ssp. *palustre* (2n = 24), ssp. *tetraploideum* A.R. Clapham ex Franco (2n = 48) and ssp. *elongatum* (C. Presl) Arcang (2n = 96, 144).

Very common (371). Common Marsh-bedstraw occurs throughout northern Lancashire. Unfortunately very little work has been done to record the distribution of the three subspecies, but all three occur in the

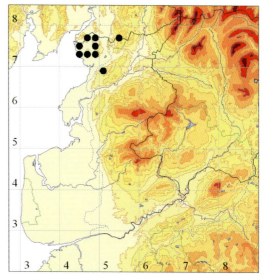

Asperula cynanchica

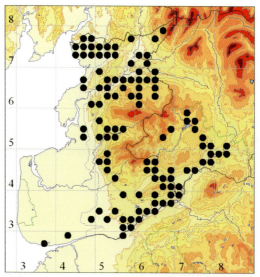

Galium odoratum

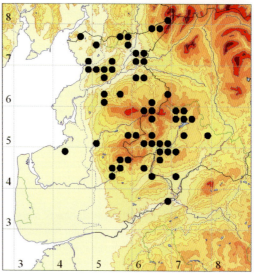

Galium uliginosum

area. Limited observations suggest ssp. *palustre* occurs all over the region and is perhaps especially characteristic of more acidic marshes. Ssp. *elongatum* may have a more limited distribution possibly being rare in Bowland and occurring in more base-rich marshes and fens further west. Sell and Murrell (2006) suggest ssp. *tetraploideum* may be the commonest subspecies in calcareous habitats. It has been found in a few widely separated localities in northern Lancashire and may well be common. It is likely that the three subspecies have differing ecological requirements and further study could be rewarding. The distribution of *G. palustre* is thought to be stable both locally and nationally.

Galium verum L. Lady's Bedstraw

Eurasian Boreo-temperate element.

Lady's Bedstraw is a perennial herb of well-drained, nutrient poor but often calcareous substrates, especially on limestone or chalk, in grassland as well as on sand dunes (BH7). It is found throughout the British Isles. Ssp. *verum* occurs throughout the range of the species while ssp. *maritimum* (DC.) Adema is thought to have a largely coastal distribution (Sell and Murrell, 2006).

Frequent (121). In northern Lancashire *G. verum* is found in coastal areas and in the Lune Ribble and Hodder valleys. The subspecies have not been identified. There has been little change in the distribution of Lady's Bedstraw either locally or nationally.

Galium verum × G. album (G. × pomeranicum Retz.)

This is a common hybrid in Europe including Britain. It is probably under recorded.

Very rare (1). In northern Lancashire it was recorded from Heysham (SD46A) in 1974 (A.E.C.).

Galium album Mill. Hedge Bedstraw

European Boreo-temperate element.

This is a stoloniferous perennial herb of well-drained, base-rich soils and occurs in rough grassland, scrub and waste places (BH7). It occurs throughout Britain but it is rare in much of Scotland, and in Ireland it is thought to be an introduction.

Frequent (85). In northern Lancashire *G. album* occurs mostly in the north of the area with records from scattered localities elsewhere. Some populations are introduced with wild flower mixtures and it is possible that these may belong to continental taxa. The distribution of Hedge Bedstraw is thought to be stable both locally and nationally although it could be increasing through its introduction in wild flower seed mixtures.

Galium sterneri Ehrend. Limestone Bedstraw

Suboceanic Boreal-montane element.

This is a perennial herb of short grassland on calcareous substrates (BH7, 16). It is found in England from the Peak District northwards, Scotland and Ireland.

Occasional (22). In northern Lancashire *G. sterneri* is often abundant on the limestone around Morecambe Bay but it also occurs on Dalton Crags, at Leck and much more rarely on limestone near Chipping and in Lancashire VC 64. Its distribution is probably stable both locally and nationally.

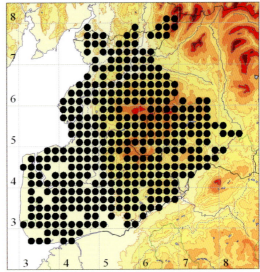
Galium palustre

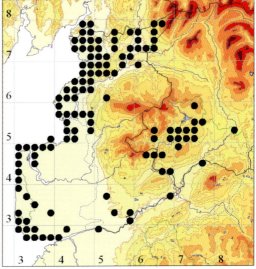
Galium verum

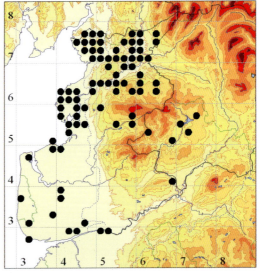
Galium album

Galium saxatile L.   Heath Bedstraw

Suboceanic Temperate element.

This is a low growing perennial herb of infertile acidic soils found in grassland and on heaths (BH8, 9) throughout the British Isles.

Common (269). Heath Bedstraw is found in most of northern Lancashire except in intensively cultivated areas, especially in the Fylde where it has probably become less frequent over the last 100 years. Nationally it has also declined in lowland areas particularly on the fringes of its British distribution ('New Atlas', 'Local Change').

Galium aparine L.   Cleavers

European Temperate element.

This is a scrambling annual herb of cultivated ground, hedgerows, waste ground and coastal shingle (BH3, 4, 17). It is found throughout the British Isles. However Sell and Murrell (2006) recognise ssp. *aparine* as the plant most commonly found in hedgerows, ssp. *agreste* P.D. Sell var. *agreste* P.D. Sell is found in arable land whilst ssp. *agreste* var. *marinum* Fr. is found on coastal shingle and sand dunes.

Very common (401). Cleavers is found throughout northern Lancashire except on the fells. It is not known what infraspecific taxa occur in the area. Its distribution locally and nationally is stable.

Cruciata laevipes Opiz   Crosswort

Eurosiberian Temperate element.

Crosswort is a perennial herb of well-drained, usually calcareous soils in ungrazed grassland, scrub, on banks and roadsides (BH6). It occurs in southern Scotland, England and Wales but is a rare introduction in Ireland.

Common (267). Crosswort is found in the north of northern Lancashire and in the Ribble and Hodder valleys. It also occurs in a broad belt from west of Preston to Lancaster but elsewhere it is rare or absent. Its distribution is thought to be stable locally and nationally.

Rubia peregrina L.   Wild Madder

Mediterranean-Atlantic element but a neophyte in northern Lancashire. This is a scrambling, evergreen perennial herb of hedge banks and scrub in mostly coastal areas of southern England, Wales and southern Ireland.

It was found at Silverdale in 1915 (A.J.C.; LSA) where it must have occurred as a garden escape although it is found as a native species as far north as the coast of northern Wales.

GENTIANACEAE   GENTIAN FAMILY

Centaurium erythraea Rafn   Common Centaury

European Southern-temperate element.

Common Centaury is found on neutral to calcareous soils in a variety of usually open habitats (BH7, 19). It occurs in lowland areas throughout much of the British Isles. Ubsdell (1976a, b) in her studies on *C. erythraea* concluded that there were five varieties and of these var. *erythraea* and var. *capitatum* (Willd. ex Cham.) Melderis are found in northern Lancashire.

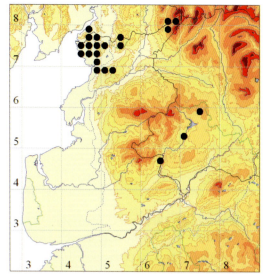
Galium sterneri

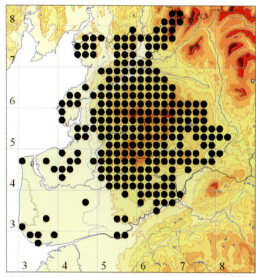
Galium saxatile

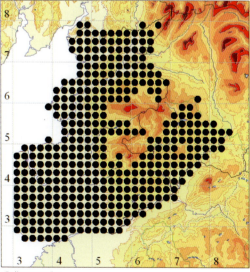
Galium aparine

Frequent (109). In northern Lancashire *C. erythraea* occurs mostly on or near the coast with occasional records elsewhere. However it is absent from Lancashire VC 64. There has been no change in its distribution locally or nationally.

Var. *capitatum* was recorded from limestone grassland on Warton Crag (SD47W) where it was seen in 1968 (E.F.G. & J.B.F.) and from Heald Brow, Silverdale (SD47R) in 1969 (E.F.G.). It was also seen in 1987 (L.A.L.), presumably on Warton Crag. The record of *C. erythraea* var. *subcapitatum* (Corb.) Gilmour from between Lytham and St Anne's made in 1895 (Marshall, 1949) is probably an error and Gilmour's taxon may not be the same as *C. erythraea* var. *subcapitatum* (Corb.) Ubsdell, which Ubsdell (1976a) suggests is confined to maritime cliff tops in southern England.

Centaurium erythraea × C. littorale
(C. × intermedium (Wheldon) Druce)

Ubsdell in her papers on *Centaurium* (Ubsdell, 1976a, b, 1979) confirmed the special position of the sand dunes on the Anglesey, Merseyside and Lancashire coasts for hybrids between *C. erythraea* and *C. littorale*. Worldwide there are only a few areas where the distribution of the two species overlap and even in these places various isolating mechanisms usually prevent hybridisation. However on the Merseyside and Lancashire coasts in particular disturbance events have occurred that have broken down the isolating barriers with the development of more or less sterile F_1 tetraploid hybrids. However backcrossing of F_1 hybrids with either parent occurs, mostly with *C. erythraea* at St Anne's, producing hybrids with increased fertility. The backcrosses with *C. littorale* do not generally show much increased fertility at the tetraploid level. Nevertheless polyploidy has occurred and hexaploid plants have been found on the Merseyside coast. These are highly fertile and form a species, *C. intermedium*, distinct from either parent from which they originated. This is a new species, possibly endemic to the Merseyside coast but it should be searched for elsewhere including the sand dunes at St Anne's.

Very rare (2). This was first recorded from between Lytham and St Anne's in 1895 (Marshall, 1949). Subsequently the F_1 hybrid was again found at Lytham St Anne's (Ubsdell, 1976a, b, 1979) and it was presumably this that was found on the sand dunes (SD33A) in 1999 and 2008 (E.F.G.; LIV). There is also a probable record at Fleetwood in 1994 (P.J.; LIV).

Centaurium erythraea × C. pulchellum

This hybrid occurs with the parents on the coasts of North Somerset (VC 6), South Essex (VC 18) and West Lancaster (VC 60). It is highly fertile and its morphological characters are intermediate between the parents.

In northern Lancashire it was found on the coast at Lytham St Anne's (Wheldon and Salmon, 1925).

Centaurium littorale (Turner ex Sm.) Gilmour   Seaside Centaury
European Temperate element.

This is a biennial herb confined to coastal sand dunes, the uppermost levels of salt marshes and other calcareous and humus-rich damp places near the sea (BH19, 21). Seaside Centaury is found on western and northern coasts of the British Isles.

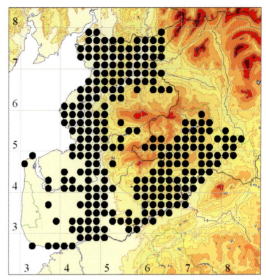
Cruciata laevipes

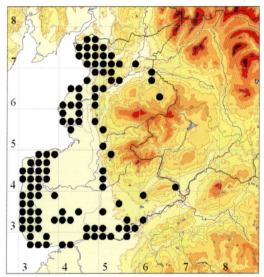
Centaurium erythraea

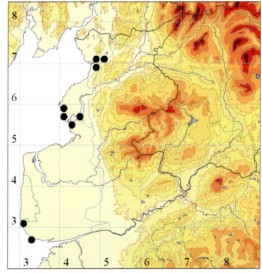
Centaurium littorale

Rare (9). In northern Lancashire *C. littorale* is found at coastal sites near Carnforth, on the Lune estuary and at Lytham St Anne's. There has been a slight extension to its range over the last 100 years with its spread into the Carnforth area but nationally there has been little change to its distribution.

Centaurium pulchellum (Sm.) Druce   Lesser Centaury

Eurosiberian Southern-temperate element.

This is an annual of neutral or calcareous soils in open grassland habitats and on sandy or muddy ground on the coast (BH21). It is found on the coasts of England and Wales and in Scotland on the shores of the Solway Firth. It also occurs at inland localities in southern England.

Occasional (15). In northern Lancashire Lesser Centaury is found in coastal sites from the Wyre estuary northwards. Wheldon and Wilson (1907) knew it only from Blackpool and Lytham St Anne's, where it hybridised with Common Centaury, so that all post 1964 records are an extension of its range. However *C. pulchellum* has not been seen at Lytham St Anne's since 1931 (France, 1931). Nationally its distribution is stable.

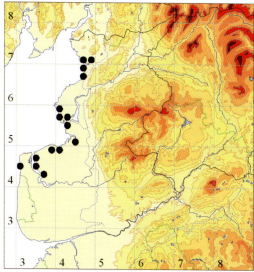
Centaurium pulchellum

Blackstonia perfoliata (L.) Huds.   Yellow-wort

Submediterranean-Subatlantic element.

This is an annual or biennial of open dry and usually calcareous habitats in grasslands on sand dunes and in waste places (BH7). It is found in England, Wales and Ireland and as an introduction in southern Scotland.

Rare (9). In northern Lancashire Yellow-wort is found in coastal sites in the Heysham peninsula, on the Wyre estuary and at Lytham St Anne's. Wheldon and Wilson (1907) considered Yellow-wort to be very rare although they knew it from the Wyre and Ribble estuaries as well as at Lytham St Anne's. Nevertheless within this area it has become much commoner and has extended its range northwards. Its Lancashire sites are on the northern edge of its native range in Britain. Nationally its distribution is largely unchanged but the 'New Atlas' notes that it had spread northwards on the east coast of England into Northumberland.

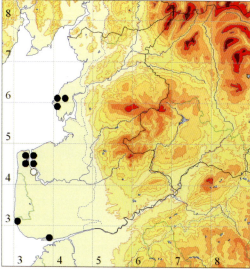
Blackstonia perfoliata

Gentianella campestris (L.) Börner   Field Gentian

European Boreo-temperate element.

This is a biennial herb of open grassland habitats on mostly neutral soils (BH7). Most records are from the northern half of the British Isles.

Very rare (5). In northern Lancashire Field Gentian has always been a rare species. Wheldon and Wilson (1907) knew of localities on limestone in the northwest of the area, on the sand dunes at Lytham St Anne's and on the south side of Longridge Fell (Anon, 1891). It persisted at Lytham St Anne's by Fairhaven Lake until 1959 (H.E.B.; LIV) and although it was known from Warton Crag, post 1964 records are confined to Silverdale (SD47L) in 2000 (E.F.G.), SD47M (Livermore and Livermore, 1987), SD47R in 1972 (C.J.-P.,), SD47T between 1964 and 1968 (Anon) and SD47Y in 1983 (A.A.). It is believed it has gone from all the Silverdale sites possibly including the SD47L site where only a few sickly plants were seen in 2000. Nationally it has suffered a sharp decline although since 1987 the decline has not been significant.

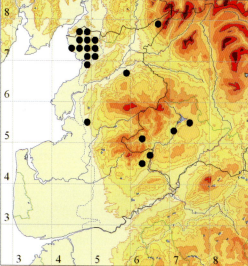
Gentianella amarella

Gentianella amarella (L.) Börner ssp. **amarella**   Autumn Gentian

European Temperate element.

Autumn Gentian is an annual or biennial herb of well-drained, calcareous soils in open grassland habitats or on spoil heaps and in quarries (BH7). It is found in suitable places in many parts of the British Isles.

Occasional (20). In northern Lancashire most records of Autumn Gentian are from the limestone in the northwest of the area with occasional records elsewhere in the north and in Bowland. Whilst its distribution appears broadly similar to that of 100 years ago it has gone from Lytham St Anne's where it was last seen in 1915 (A.J.C.) and from Dunnow, Newton-in-Bowland where it was seen in 1896 (J.F.P.). However although it may still be abundant in some localities, e.g. Trowbarrow Quarry, Silverdale (SD47Y), it is known to have gone from many localities recorded after 1964 and by 2008 may be confined to two or three localities. There is no doubt that this is a declining species in the area. The 'New Atlas' noted a decline in its distribution nationally but after 1987 the rate of this decline seems to have accelerated.

Gentiana pneumonanthe L.   Marsh Gentian

Eurosiberian Temperate element.

This is a long-lived perennial of wet heaths (BH8, 10) found in England and parts of Wales.

Extinct. Even 100 years ago there were few areas of wet heath left in northern Lancashire although at one time it might have been a frequent habitat type. It is therefore difficult to plot its former distribution but it is known to have occurred near the Yealands, Morecambe (Poulton-le-Sands), Claughton near Garstang and Ribbleton Moor, Preston. All the sites were drained for agriculture and some, e.g. Ribbleton Moor, were subsequently built on. The last extant site was at Claughton (SD54L) where the field was ploughed for the war effort in 1941 (H.E.B.). The field was still herb-rich and badly drained in the mid 1960s but by 2007 it was an improved grassland (MG6 *Lolium perenne-Cynosurus cristatus* grassland) It survives just beyond the northern Lancashire border at Keasden (SD76I) in Yorkshire but here the habitat is deteriorating and it is only a matter of time before it becomes extinct there.

APOCYNACEAE   PERIWINKLE FAMILY

Vinca minor L.   Lesser Periwinkle

Archaeophyte. It is believed that Lesser Periwinkle is a native of south, western and central Europe, central and southern Russia and the Caucasus but the limits of its native range are obscured by widespread cultivation. It was grown in British gardens by 995 and occurs in the wild in woodlands, woodland edge habitats and in waste places (BH1, 3, 17). It is found throughout most of the British Isles but especially in southern Britain.

Occasional (22). In northern Lancashire *V. minor* was first found on Ashton Marsh (SD52E; Ashfield, 1858) but then not thought to be truly wild. However it had become naturalised on a bank beside the former Ashton Marsh by 1901 (A.A. Dallman, 1901). Today it is found in scattered localities throughout the area.

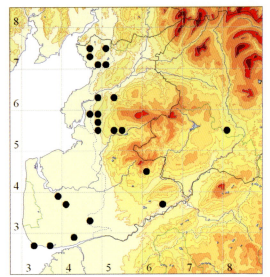
Vinca minor

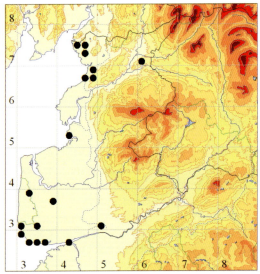
Vinca major

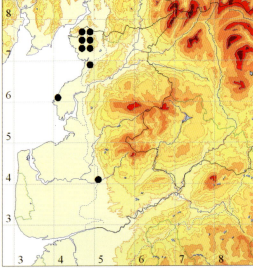
Lithospermum officinale

Vinca major L.   Greater Periwinkle

Neophyte. Greater Periwinkle is a native of the European Mediterranean region and was cultivated in Britain by 1597. It is widely grown for its ground covering properties and was recorded in the wild by 1650. Today it is found in many places in the southern half of Britain and in Ireland but it is found much more rarely in Scotland.

Occasional (18). In northern Lancashire *V. major* was first recorded from Blackpool (Thornber, 1837) and Jenny Brown's Point, Silverdale (SD47L; Kirkby, 1902 in Wheldon and Wilson, 1907). Today it is mostly found in coastal areas with an occasional inland locality.

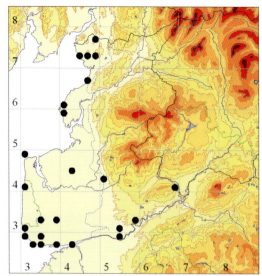
Echium vulgare

BORAGINACEAE   BORAGE FAMILY

Lithospermum officinale L.   Common Gromwell

Eurasian Temperate element.

This is a perennial herb that grows in grassland and woodland edge habitats (BH1, 3, 7), mostly on base-rich soils. It is found in lowland areas of England, Wales, Ireland and more rarely in Scotland.

Rare (9). In northern Lancashire Common Gromwell is found mainly on the calcareous soils in the northwest of the area. Formerly it occurred more widely in VC 60 but, as today, it was much commoner in the Silverdale area than elsewhere. Nationally there has been a decline in its distribution, especially in northern England ('New Atlas') but no decline since 1987 was reported by 'Local Change'.

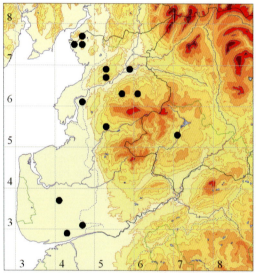
Pulmonaria officinalis

Lithospermum arvense L.   Field Gromwell

Archaeophyte with a Eurosiberian Southern-temperate distribution.

Field Gromwell is an annual herb of arable fields (BH4) known since the Bronze Age but it is also found occasionally on waste ground. It occurs mainly in south-eastern England but it also occurs occasionally in Scotland, Wales and Ireland.

Very rare or extinct (1). In northern Lancashire *L. arvense* was found between Knott End and Pilling where it was described as plentiful (Ashfield, 1864), near Carnforth in 1900 (Wheldon and Wilson, 1907), St Anne's (A.J.C., C.B.) and Upper Rawcliffe-with-Tarnacre (St Michael's School, 1902). The only recent record is from Poulton-le-Fylde (SD33P) where it occurred as a garden weed in 1967 (A.E.R.). Its distribution nationally has declined substantially since the 1950s ('New Atlas').

Echium vulgare L.   Viper's-bugloss

Eurosiberian Temperate element.

This is a biennial herb of grassy and disturbed habitats on well-drained soils (BH7). Usually it is found in lowland areas of England, Wales, Ireland and southern Scotland and as an introduction in northern Scotland.

Occasional (24). In northern Lancashire Viper's-bugloss occurs in scattered localities in VC 60 and represents an increase from the two localities at Fleetwood and St Anne's known to Wheldon and Wilson (1907). Nationally the 'New Atlas' showed a small decline in its distribution but 'Local Change' reported an unchanged distribution although some increase, that was not statistically significant, was noted.

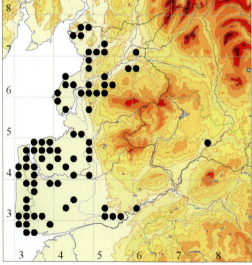
Symphytum officinale

Echium plantagineum L. Purple Viper's-bugloss

Archaeophyte with a Mediterranean-Atlantic distribution but a neophyte in northern Lancashire.

This is an annual or biennial herb found in arable fields, on cliffs and on waste ground (BH4), often near the coast. It occurs mostly in the Isle of Man and southern England with occasional records elsewhere. It is regarded by some as native in the Channel Islands and perhaps Cornwall.

Very rare (1). In northern Lancashire there is an undated anonymous specimen at BON collected at Brock. The only other record is from a tip at Lytham (SD32Y) found in 1966 (A.E.R.).

Pulmonaria officinalis L. Lungwort

Neophyte. This has a European Temperate distribution but it is absent as a native from much of western Europe. Lungwort was cultivated in Britain before 1597 and was recorded from the wild by 1793. It is found throughout Britain and in the north of Ireland.

Rare (14). *P. officinalis* was first recorded in northern Lancashire from Preston, between Warton and Yealand and near Docker (Wheldon and Wilson, 1902). Today it is found in scattered localities throughout the area.

Pulmonaria rubra Schott Red Lungwort

Neophyte. Red Lungwort is a perennial herb found in the Carpathians and the mountains of the Balkan Peninsula. It was cultivated in Britain by 1914 and was recorded in the wild by 1969. It is a popular garden plant and today it is found in a few British localities.

Very rare (2). In northern Lancashire *P. rubra* was found on a roadside near Slaidburn (SD75L) in the 1970s or earlier (J.N.F.) and was re-found in 2007 (M.W.). It was also found in a hedge bank at Silverdale (SD47S) in 2010 (J.Cl.).

Symphytum officinale L. Common Comfrey

European Temperate element.

Common Comfrey is a tall perennial herb found on the banks of streams and rivers, in fens and in other wet places including roadside verges (BH11). It occurs throughout the British Isles but confusion with other taxa and especially *S. × uplandicum* make it difficult to know its native range or if its distribution has changed. The complex taxonomic and identification problems associated with *S. officinale* and *S. × uplandicum* are discussed by Perring (1994). He pointed out that there are at least three cytotypes of *S. officinale* and whilst many have creamy white flowers (mostly 2n = 24) some have red/purple flowers (2n = 48)

Frequent (78). Common Comfrey occurs throughout northern Lancashire but mostly west of the M6 motorway and in the Lune and Ribble valleys. However, it is likely to have been mistaken for *S. × uplandicum* in many localities especially on roadside verges. Nevertheless this is a native species of former fens, riverbanks and other wetland areas and of the ten localities known to Wheldon and Wilson (1907) only one or two records seem as if they may have been misidentified. However it was also grown in gardens from which it escaped into the wild (Fielding MS). It would appear, therefore, that Common Comfrey has spread considerably in the area during the last 100 years either from native or introduced stock. Nationally identification problems prevent any assessment of change in its distribution.

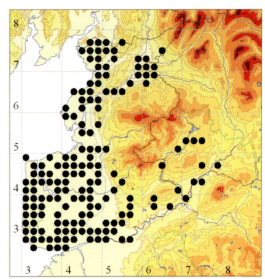
Symphytum × uplandicum

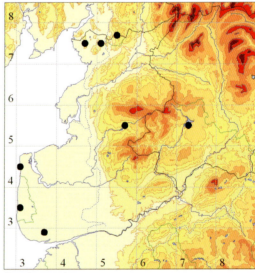
Symphytum tuberosum

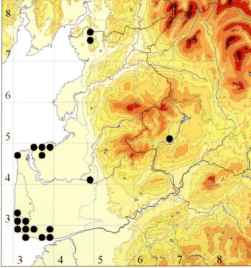
Anchusa arvensis

Symphytum officinale × S. asperum Lepech.
(S. × uplandicum Nyman)   Russian Comfrey

Neophyte. This perennial hybrid was introduced in 1871 from Sweden and it was widely cultivated in the late nineteenth and early twentieth centuries as a forage plant. It was reported from the wild in 1884 and today occurs throughout the British Isles on waste ground and in other ruderal habitats. Two cytotypes are found in the British Isles (Perring, 1994). One of these (2n = 40) has pink to violet coloured flowers whilst the other (2n = 36) and less frequent taxon has violet or violet blue flowers.

Frequent (163). Russian Comfrey was first reported in northern Lancashire from near Eaves Wood, Silverdale (SD47T) in 1901 where it is believed it had escaped from nearby culti-vation (Petty, 1902). A pink flowered form was found on a roadside near Slaidburn (SD75G) in 2007 (E.F.G.). Today Russian Comfrey occurs throughout the area but it is especially frequent in the west.

Symphytum tuberosum L.   Tuberous Comfrey

European Temperate element but probably a neophyte in northern Lancashire.

This occurs in damp woodland, by ditches and streams and in hedgerows (BH1, 3). Tuberous Comfrey is found throughout the British Isles but it is thought to be native only in Scotland and parts of northern England.

Rare (8). *S. tuberosum* was first recorded in northern Lancashire at Silverdale (SD47S) in 1968 (C. J.-P.). It has subsequently been found in scattered localities in the area and, particularly in coastal areas; it appears to be an escape from cultivation. However Lees (1888) recorded it in several places by the R. Ribble in VC 64 from Stainforth to Sawley. The plants introduced into the churchyard at Stocks-in-Bowland (SD75H) are especially low growing and were mistaken for *S. grandiflorum* (Abbott, 2005).

Symphytum grandiflorum × ?S. × uplandicum
(S. × hidcotense P.D. Sell)   Hidcote Comfrey

Neophyte. This taxon was raised at Hidcote in Gloucestershire not long before 1930. It grows aggressively in gardens and is often discarded or escapes from gardens into neighbouring areas. It was first noticed in the wild in 1979 and today it is found in various places in England and Wales.

Very rare (2). Hidcote Comfrey is probably under recorded but has been seen in the wild in Bolton-by-Bowland (SD74U) in 1996 (A.U.) and at Silverdale (SD47S) in 2007 (E.F. & B.D.G.). Here it was growing on a path side having evidently escaped from a nearby garden.

Symphytum grandiflorum DC.   Creeping Comfrey

Neophyte. This is a creeping perennial herb native to the Caucasus and was introduced into Britain at the end of the nineteenth century. Creeping Comfrey was recorded from the wild in 1898 and today it is found in many parts of Britain.

Very rare (2). In northern Lancashire *S. grandiflorum* was found at Catforth (SD43S) in 1997 (C.F. & N.J.S.) and from near Slaidburn (SD75M; Abbott, 2005). The record in Abbott (2005) for tetrad SD75H is an error for *S. tuberosum* (see above).

Symphytum orientale L.   White Comfrey

Neophyte. This is a native of southern Russia, north-western Turkey and the Caucasus. It was introduced into Britain by 1752 and was known from the wild by 1849. Today White Comfrey is found mostly in south-eastern and eastern England but there are a few records from elsewhere in England, Wales and Scotland.

Very rare (2). In northern Lancashire it was found on an old railway at Melling-with-Wrayton (SD67A) in 1979 (C.S.) and from Lytham (SD32U) in 1985 (C.F. & N.J.S.).

Anchusa ochroleuca M. Bieb.   Yellow Alkanet

Neophyte. Yellow Alkanet is a native of central and south-eastern Europe and south-western Asia. It was cultivated in Britain in 1810 and was known in the wild in Cornwall by 1922. Whilst it is naturalised at one locality in western Cornwall elsewhere it is found as a rare casual.

In northern Lancashire a large patch was found at St Anne's where it was later built on (Whellan, 1954).

Anchusa officinalis L.   Alkanet

Neophyte with a European Temperate distribution. It was introduced into British gardens by 1200 and was cultivated for fodder. Alkanet was recorded from the wild by 1799 and today it is found in scattered localities in the British Isles.

In northern Lancashire it was recorded from St Anne's in 1906 and 1907 (C.B.; MANCH).

Anchusa azurea Mill.   Garden Anchusa

Neophyte. This is a native of southern Europe, the Mediterranean region and western Asia. It was introduced into British gardens by 1597 and it was subsequently grown as a fodder plant. Garden Anchusa was found in the wild in 1866 and today occurs occasionally on waste ground in Britain and the Isle of Man.

In northern Lancashire *A. azurea* was found on the sand dunes at St Anne's in 1907 (C.B.; MANCH).

Anchusa arvensis (L.) M. Bieb. ssp. **arvensis**   Bugloss

Archaeophyte with a Eurosiberian Temperate distribution.

This is an annual herb found on well-drained soils in arable fields, on waste ground and in sandy places near the sea (BH4). Bugloss occurs in lowland areas throughout the British Isles.

Occasional (19). *A. arvensis* was first found in northern Lancashire at Lytham in the 1830s (Fielding MS) when it was described as a common weed. Today it still occurs on sandy ground on the Fylde coast and also near the mouth of the R. Wyre and occasionally elsewhere. In northern Lancashire the distribution of Bugloss is unchanged but nationally there were losses since 1950 ('New Atlas') but not since 1987 ('Local Change').

Anchusa arvensis (L.) M. Bieb. ssp. **orientalis** (L.) Nordh.

Neophyte. This is a native of south-eastern Europe, north-eastern Africa and Asia. There are a few pre 1930 records from Britain.

In northern Lancashire it was found at St Anne's in 1906 (C.B.; MANCH) and possibly from Bare (F.A.L.; KGY).

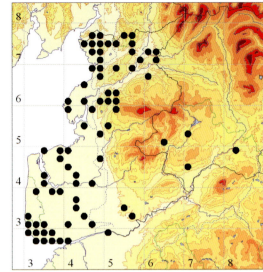
Pentaglottis sempervirens

Pentaglottis sempervirens (L.) Tausch ex L.H. Bailey   Green Alkanet

Neophyte. Green Alkanet is a native of south-western Europe and was introduced into British gardens before 1700. It was known from the wild by 1724 and today occurs in lightly shaded habitats, usually near houses, in many parts of the British Isles.

Frequent (77). In northern Lancashire Green Alkanet was first found at Ribbleton, near Preston (Ashfield, 1858). Today it is found throughout the area but with a preponderance of records west of the M6 motorway.

Borago officinalis L.   Borage

Neophyte. This is a native of the Mediterranean region that has been grown in British gardens since at least 1200. It was recorded from the wild in 1777 and today occurs throughout England and Wales but much more rarely in Scotland and Ireland.

Occasional (17). In northern Lancashire this was first recorded as a garden weed at Garstang and St Michael's (Ashfield, 1858). Today Borage is found mostly in the west of northern Lancashire with a single record for Lancashire VC 64.

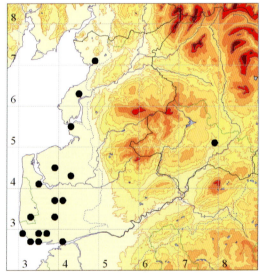
Borago officinalis

Mertensia maritima (L.) Gray   Oysterplant

European Boreo-arctic Montane element.

Oysterplant is a perennial plant of gravely and shingle beaches (BH19) found on the shores in the north of the British Isles.

Extinct. *M. maritima* was probably never established in northern Lancashire but a single plant was found near Bare (SD46M) in 1941 (J.F.N.; LIV).

Amsinckia calycina (Moris) Chater   Hairy Fiddleneck
Amsinckia lycopsoides (Lehm.) Lehm.   Scarce Fiddleneck
Amsinckia micrantha Suksd.   Common Fiddleneck

Neophytes. There has been a great deal of confusion over the identity of these three North American species. Most records in Britain are for *A.*

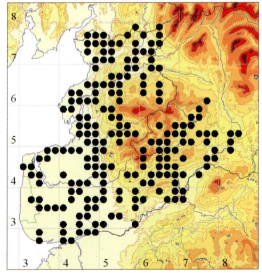
Myosotis scorpioides

micrantha, which was first cultivated in Britain in 1836; it was recorded in the wild in 1910. Today Common Fiddleneck is found mostly in eastern Britain. However E.J. Clement (pers. comm., 2008) suggests that more work is required to clarify the taxonomy of the genus worldwide and that at present it is impossible to name British material. In this account the names as given by the recorders are used.

Very rare (3). *A. micrantha* was recorded from St Anne's (SD33A, 32J) in 2001 and 1993 (C.F. & N.J.S.) and from Fleetwood (SD34D) in 1985 (N.W.). However *A. lycopsoides* and *A. calycina* were previously recorded from sand dunes at St Anne's *c.* 1907 (C.B., MANCH).

Asperugo procumbens L.   Madwort

Neophyte. The native range of this species is not known as it has spread in cultivation across Europe, western and central Asia. It was introduced into Britain with grain and wool and was known in the wild by 1660. Today it is a rare weed of arable and waste ground.

Very rare (1). In northern Lancashire Madwort was found as a garden weed at Poulton-le-Fylde in 1968 (A.E.R.).

Myosotis scorpioides L.   Water Forget-me-not

Eurosiberian Temperate element.

Water Forget-me-not is a perennial herb found in damp or wet habitats on usually neutral to calcareous, nutrient rich soils (BH11, 14). It is found throughout the British Isles.

Frequent (203). *M. scorpioides* is found throughout northern Lancashire. Its distribution locally and nationally was stable until 1987 but since then there has been a decline nationally ('Local Change').

Myosotis scorpioides × M. laxa (M. × suzae Domin)

This partially fertile hybrid is found with the parents in scattered localities in England and Wales. It is probably overlooked.

Very rare (2). In northern Lancashire *M. × suzae* was found at Cockerham (SD44J) in 1995 and at Pilling (SD34Z) in 1999 (both C.J.B.). No doubt this hybrid is much more frequent than these two records suggest.

Myosotis secunda Al. Murray   Creeping Forget-me-not

Oceanic Temperate element.

Creeping Forget-me-not is found in marshy places and flushes (BH11) in many parts of the British Isles although it is largely absent from central and south-eastern England.

Frequent (107). In northern Lancashire *M. secunda* occurs in marshy areas and flushes mostly in Bowland and Leck. Some colonies appear to be sterile and small plants are sometimes difficult to distinguish from *M. stolonifera*. Wheldon and Wilson (1907) recorded Creeping Forget-me-not from only about twelve localities and it is possible that it has become more frequent over the last 100 years. The 'New Atlas' reported its distribution was stable apart from a few losses at the edge of its range in central and southern England. On the other hand 'Local Change' recorded a significant increase in its distribution since 1987.

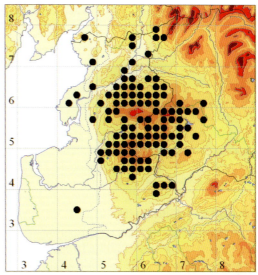
Myosotis secunda

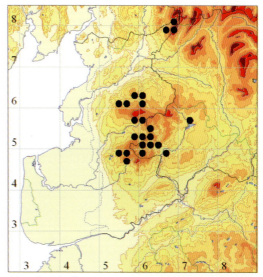
Myosotis stolonifera

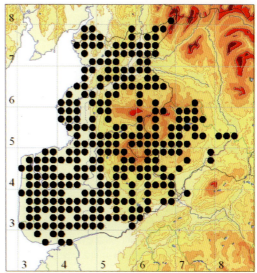
Myosotis laxa

Myosotis stolonifera (DC.) J. Gray ex Leresche & Levier

Pale Forget-me-not

Oceanic Boreal-montane element.

This small, pale flowered Forget-me-not was overlooked by botanists until recently and was not collected in Britain until 1919. It grows in hill flushes (BH11, 14) in southern Scotland and northern England and elsewhere only in Portugal and Spain.

Occasional (23). Pale Forget-me-not is easily overlooked or confused with small *M. secunda*. It is found in hill flushes in Bowland and Leck. However because of confusion with other taxa it is not known if its distribution has changed locally or nationally.

Myosotis stolonifera hybrids

The difficulty in recognising some plants of *M. stolonifera* may be due to the presence of hybrids, which so far have not been recognised. However in recent years both E.F.G. and P.J. thought that part of the problem might be that some plants were hybrids. P.J. gathered material in the Marshaw area of the R. Wyre in 2004 and subsequently in the Brennand valley, which was sterile but clearly perennial. It is believed this material is the hybrid with *M. secunda*. In 2009 E.F.G. gathered slender annual or short-lived perennial, sterile material from upper Roeburndale, which may be the hybrid with *M. laxa*. Further research is ongoing to confirm these tentative identifications.

Myosotis laxa Lehm.

Tufted Forget-me-not

Circumpolar Boreo-temperate element.

Tufted Forget-me-not grows in wet places often in open habitats (BH11) throughout the British Isles.

Common (294). *M. laxa* is found throughout northern Lancashire. There has been no change in its distribution locally or nationally.

Myosotis sylvatica Hoffm.

Wood Forget-me-not

Eurasian Temperate element.

This is a woodland and woodland edge species (BH1) found widely in England and Wales but occurs largely as a lowland species in Scotland. In Ireland it is mostly confined to the north. However it is an attractive species often grown in gardens from which it readily escapes into the wild.

Frequent (174). Wheldon and Wilson (1907) knew Wood Forget-me-not from only six woodland localities in the Lune and Ribble valleys. Today, whilst its distribution still shows an abundance of records from the Lune and Ribble valleys, it is much more widespread and it is only absent from intensively cultivated and upland areas. No doubt the increase in its distribution is due to garden escapes. This situation is also reflected nationally.

Myosotis arvensis (L.) Hill

Field Forget-me-not

Archaeophyte with a Eurosiberian Boreo-temperate distribution.

This small annual or biennial herb is found in open and disturbed habitats especially in cultivated fields (BH3, 4). It is found throughout the British Isles. However two subspecies are recognised. Ssp. *arvensis* is typical of cultivated and waste ground whilst ssp. *umbriata* (Mert. & W.D.J. Koch) O. Schwarz is larger flowered and found in woodland edge habitats. Both

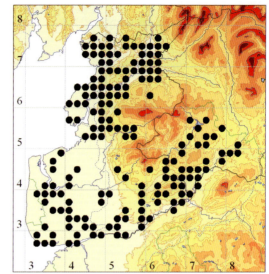
Myosotis sylvatica

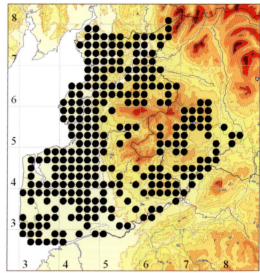
Myosotis arvensis

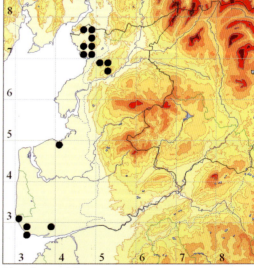
Myosotis ramosissima

subspecies are thought to be widespread but there is no data on their occurrence in northern Lancashire.

Common (291). Field Forget-me-not occurs throughout northern Lancashire except in upland areas. There has been no change in its distribution locally or nationally.

Myosotis ramosissima Rochel   Early Forget-me-not

European Southern-temperate element.

This is a winter annual flowering early in the year. It is found in open calcareous habitats (BH8, 16) in southern Britain and in coastal areas elsewhere.

Occasional (15). In northern Lancashire Early Forget-me-not is confined to calcareous soils and rocks around Morecambe Bay and to coastal sandy areas elsewhere. Whilst its distribution has remained stable in northern Lancashire there have been losses nationally ('New Atlas') but not since 1987 ('Local Change').

Myosotis discolor Pers.   Changing Forget-me-not

European Temperate element.

This is a small annual herb found in a wide variety of open habitats ranging from cultivated ground to grasslands, marshes and woodland edges (BH6). It occurs throughout the British Isles. However there are two subspecies. Ssp. *discolor* occurs on sandy or peaty ground whilst ssp. *dubia* (Arrond.) Blaise is found in damp pastures and in muddy tracks often with *Juncus bufonius*. Both subspecies are thought to be widespread.

Frequent (75). Changing Forget-me-not occurs in scattered localities throughout northern Lancashire. Information on the occurrence of the two subspecies is not generally available but ssp. *dubia* was recognised from a few damp pastures in Bowland and at Silverdale. It is not thought that there has been any change in the distribution of *M. discolor* in northern Lancashire but the 'New Atlas' reports a decline whilst 'Local Change' notes a significant increase since 1987. It is possible that the status of the two subspecies is different and that these differences remain undetected.

Myosotis verna Nutt.

Neophyte. This is a native of North America and has only been recorded in a few British localities; all before 1930.

In northern Lancashire it was found at St Anne's in 1907 and 1908 (C.B.; MANCH).

Lappula squarrosa (Retz.) Dumort.   Bur Forget-me-not

Neophyte. This has a European Temperate distribution and was cultivated in Britain by 1683. It was recorded from the wild by 1871 but today occurs as a casual in scattered localities in the British Isles, mostly in southern England.

In northern Lancashire it was found at several sites at St Anne's between 1906 and 1908 (MANCH; Bailey, 1907).

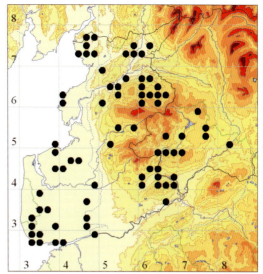

Myosotis discolor

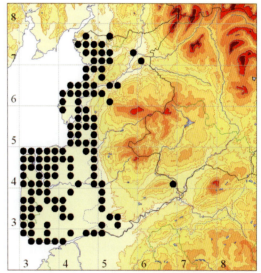

Convolvulus arvensis

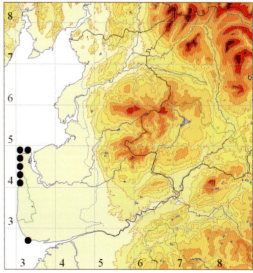

Calystegia soldanella

Omphalodes verna Moench   Blue-eyed-Mary

Neophyte. Blue-eyed-Mary is a native of the mountains of southern, central and south-eastern Europe and was cultivated in Britain by 1633. It was known from the wild by 1840. Today it is found in a few scattered localities in the British Isles.

Very rare (2). This was first recorded from St Michael's in 1902 (St Michael's School, 1902) and occurs today in and near Eaves Wood, Silverdale (SD47M, S) where it was first found in 1974 (L.A.L. & P.D.L.).

Cynoglossum officinale L.   Hound's-tongue

Eurosiberian Temperate element.

This is a biennial herb of disturbed ground often on calcareous soils in coastal sandy areas (BH7, 19). It is found in England and Wales and in coastal areas elsewhere but it is absent from western Ireland, western and northern Scotland.

Very rare (4). Wheldon and Wilson (1907) knew this from Dalton Crag, at sites near Morecambe Bay and from Lytham St Anne's. Since 1964 it has been recorded from Warton Crag (SD47W) where it was last seen in 1984 (T.C.G.R.), near Morecambe (SD46G) in 1978 (A.E.C.), Lytham (SD32N) in 1999 (C.F. & N.J.S.) and from another locality in Lytham St Anne's (SD32I) where four plants were seen in 2007 (E.F.G.). However a more thorough survey in 2008 revealed a few more colonies on the sand dunes (Skelcher, 2008). Although this was a rare species in 1907, today it is close to extinction at its remaining sites at St Anne's where it has been seen from time to time at various localities since 1964 (C.F. & N.J.S.). The 'New Atlas' reports a sharp decline nationally since the 1950s and although 'Local Change' noted a decline since 1987 it was not thought to be significant.

Phacelia tanacetifolia Benth.   Phacelia

Neophyte. This is a native of western North America and it has been cultivated in Britain since 1832. It was first recorded in the wild in 1885. It is found on waste ground and in other ruderal habitats in England and Wales and more occasionally in Scotland and Ireland.

Very rare (4). Phacelia was found in Lancaster (SD45Z; Livermore and Livermore, 1991), Fleetwood (SD34J) in 1999 (C.F. & N.J.S.), near Clifton Marsh (SD42U) in 1999 (C.F. & N.J.S.) and in the vicinity of Preston Dock (SD52E) between 1987 and 1999 (C.F. & N.J.S.).

CONVOVULACEAE   BINDWEED FAMILY

Convolvulus arvensis L.   Field Bindweed

Eurosiberian Southern-temperate element.

This trailing perennial herb is found on waste and cultivated ground (BH3, 4) in lowland areas of the British Isles. There are many colour forms of *C. arvensis*, which are illustrated in Chater (2010). It seems to particularly favour path edges.

Frequent (129). In northern Lancashire Field Bindweed is found commonly in the west of the area but elsewhere it is very rare. Notes were not made on the occurrence of the colour forms. Over the last 100 years this has become much more frequent having spread from the nine localities reported by Wheldon and Wilson (1907). However nationally the 'New

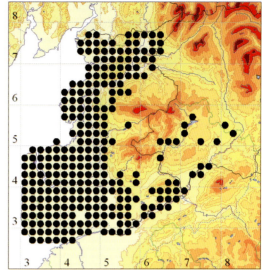
Calystegia sepium ssp. *sepium*

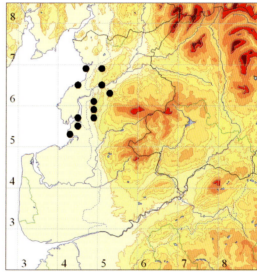
Calystegia sepium ssp. *roseata*

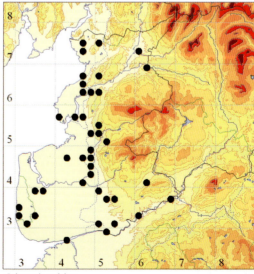
Calystegia pulchra

Atlas' noted losses in the north and west of its range since 1962 but its distribution was reported as stable since 1987 ('Local Change').

Calystegia soldanella (L.) Br.   Sea Bindweed

Mediterranean-Atlantic element.

This attractive trailing perennial is found on sandy shores (BH19) around the coasts of the British Isles except those of northern Scotland.

Rare (7). In northern Lancashire this has always been a rare species found on the sand dunes at Lytham St Anne's, on shingle and sandy shores of the Rossall peninsula and on the east bank of the Wyre estuary. There is also a mid twentieth century record for Bare (Whiteside, no date) The last remaining colony on the sand dunes at Lytham St Anne's was lost in the 1970s but Sea Bindweed is still found further north, especially in the Fleetwood area. Nationally there have been losses especially in southern and eastern England ('New Atlas').

Calystegia sepium (L.) R. Br. ssp. **sepium**

Hedge Bindweed

Circumpolar Temperate element.

This is an attractive, white-flowered climbing perennial occurring in hedges, scrub, woodland edge habitats and on waste ground (BH3, 17). However its rhizomes are easily broken off to form new plants and it can become a pernicious weed in gardens. Hedge Bindweed is found throughout the British Isles but it is rare in northern Scotland.

Common (279). *C. sepium* ssp. *sepium* is a common subspecies in the west of northern Lancashire and in the Ribble and Lune valleys but it is rare in Bowland and in eastern areas. Forma *colorata* (Lange) Dörfl. with pink flowers and white stripes is similar to, but distinct from, *C. sepium* ssp. *roseata* and has been identified from at least seven localities in the Lancaster area, mostly in hedges by the Lancaster Canal. There has been no change in the distribution of *C. sepium* ssp. *sepium* in northern Lancashire and similarly the 'New Atlas' reported no change nationally but 'Local Change' noted a significant increase in Britain since 1987.

Calystegia sepium (L.) R.Br. ssp. **roseata** Brummitt

Oceanic Temperate element.

This subspecies occurs mostly in brackish habitats at the upper edges of salt marshes, in reedbeds, in grassy places and more occasionally in hedges in western coastal areas of Britain and Ireland and more rarely inland and on the east coast of England.

Rare (11). This subspecies was first described in 1967 but in northern Lancashire it is suggested old pink-flowered records of Hedge Bindweed probably refer to this taxon. Accordingly it is likely that this was recorded in a hedge between Freckleton and the R. Ribble (Ashfield, 1862) and also by the canal near

Glasson (Wheldon and Wilson, 1907). Unfortunately in the Lancaster area its distribution overlaps with that of *C. sepium* ssp. *sepium* f. *colorata* shedding some doubt as to what was recorded. However *C. sepium* ssp. *roseata* occurs on the coast, usually in brackish habitats but it is occasionally found in hedgerows where these are close to the sea. All post 1964 records are in the northwest of the area and despite searches it has not been found on the Ribble estuary. Nevertheless it may be overlooked as usually it seems to flower in late August or September and often produces only a few flowers or remains sterile. Its distribution is probably stable both locally and nationally.

Calystegia sepium × C. silvatica
(**C. × lucana** (Ten.) G. Don)

This hybrid occurs in similar places to its parents and although it has been recorded from many parts of the British Isles most records are from southern Britain. It is poorly recorded.

Very rare (1). It is believed this hybrid was found at Fleetwood (SD34H) in 2009 (Anon). However it likely that this hybrid is more frequent than the single record suggests.

Calystegia pulchra Brummitt & Heywood Hairy Bindweed

Neophyte. The origin of this species is unknown, possibly originating in cultivation, but it is now widely naturalised in northern and central Europe. Although there are herbarium specimens dating from 1867 it was not described until 1960 (Brummitt and Heywood, 1960) and the holotype from Earlestown, near St Helens (VC 59) is deposited at LIV. Today it is found in hedges and on waste ground throughout the British Isles but mostly near houses and in urban areas.

Occasional (41). It is not known when *C. pulchra* was first found growing wild in northern Lancashire but it was not recorded by Perring and Walters (1962). Yet several unlocalised tetrad records were made from 1964 onwards, e.g. SD53B. Today it is found throughout VC 60 but so far it has not been found in Lancashire VC 64.

Calystegia silvatica (Kit.) Griseb.
ssp. **disjuncta** Brummitt   Large Bindweed

Neophyte. This is a native of the western Mediterranean region. The species was not described until 1948 but it is known that it was this that was cultivated in Britain in 1815 and collected from the wild in 1863. However the subspecies were not recognised until 1996. It is believed *C. silvatica* ssp. *disjuncta* is common and widespread in hedges and on waste ground in England, Wales, Ireland and central Scotland but it is rare or absent in upland areas and in much of Scotland.

Frequent (158). A herbarium specimen at Fleetwood Museum collected at St Anne's in the 1920s and originally named as *C. sepium* was this taxon and is probably the first record for northern Lancashire. Today *C. silvatica* ssp. *disjuncta* is found in western parts of the area with only a few records further east in the Ribble valley and in Lancashire VC 64. It is believed

C. silvatica ssp. *silvatica*, a native of the eastern Mediterranean region, was found at Staining (SD33M in 1999 (E.F.G.) and possibly at Conder Green (SD45N) in 2010 (E.F.G. & Bradford Botany Group) where it was growing with ssp. *disjuncta*. There is some doubt about both records for ssp. *silvatica* as sepals may have been distorted by insect damage or they might be hybrids. Ssp. *silvatica* tends to be found in western areas of the British Isles.

Cuscuta epithymum (L.) L.   Dodder

Eurosiberian Southern-temperate element.

This is an annual, rootless twining parasitic herb on the stems of a wide variety of shrubs and herbs. It is found on heathland and sand dune grasslands (BH10) and was found in England, Wales, Ireland and southern Scotland, but today it is mostly found in southern England and coastal areas of Ireland.

Extinct. In northern Lancashire this may never have been more than a casual but it occurred on the sand dunes between St Anne's and Fairhaven between 1901 and 1903 (C.B.; MANCH). Nationally there has been a considerable decline in its distribution ('New Atlas').

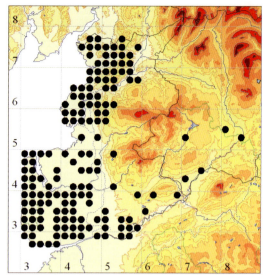
Calystegia silvatica

SOLANACEAE   NIGHTSHADE FAMILY

Lycium barbarum L. and Lycium chinense Mill.   Teaplants

Neophytes. Both species are shrubs and natives of China but are readily confused so that records of the individual species are unreliable. However the illustrations in Stace (2010) clearly show the differences between the two species and future recording should be more reliable. Teaplants were introduced before 1696 and have been recorded in the wild since 1848. Today they are found in the southern half of Britain and more rarely in Scotland and Ireland.

Occasional (35). Wheldon and Wilson (1907) acknowledged that teaplants grew in northern Lancashire, especially near the coast, but gave no localities. The first localised records were from a wood near Burton Well, Silverdale (SD47S; Petty, 1902), from a shingle beach near Glasson in 1933 (H.E.G.; LIV) and Skippool (SD34K) in the 1930s (France, 1930s). All specimens at LIV and seen in recent years are *L. barbarum*.

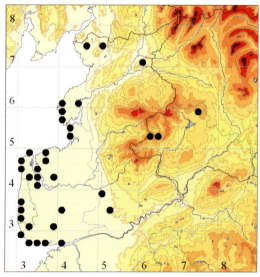
Lycium barbarum

Atropa belladonna L.   Deadly Nightshade

European Temperate element.

This is a robust perennial herb of dry disturbed, usually calcareous ground of marginal habitats (BH1, 3). It is found as a native species in the southern half of Britain but it may be introduced in some places and it is certainly introduced in Scotland and Ireland.

Rare (11). Deadly Nightshade is found occasionally on calcareous soils in the northwest of the area where it is at the northern edge of its native range in Britain. It has also occurred as an introduction and probably casually, on the coast at Poulton (Morecambe) in 1808 (Salmon, 1912) and in 1831 (Fielding MS), at Ribby Hall, Kirkham (SD43A) in 1901 (Dallman, 1901), near Leagram in 1962 (Anon, 1983), Fulwood Leisure Centre (SD53G) in 1999 (R.L.). Its native distribution appears to be stable locally but it has declined nationally ('New Atlas').

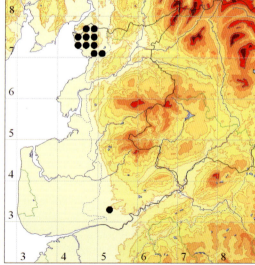
Atropa belladonna

Hyoscyamus niger L.   Henbane

Archaeophyte with a Eurosiberian Southern-temperate distribution.

There is a continuous archaeological record for Henbane in Britain since the Bronze Age and it has been found in England, Wales, Ireland and in southern and eastern Scotland. It occurs in disturbed places especially on calcareous soils (BH4).

Very rare (4). Although this has never been a common plant in northern Lancashire Henbane was found from time to time in coastal sites and more occasionally inland. The earliest record is from Roman deposits at Ribchester (Huntley and Hillam, 2000) and other pre 1964 records are from Poulton (now Morecambe) in 1808 (Salmon, 1912), Hest Bank in 1881 (Wheldon and Wilson, 1907), Lytham St Annes (several records from 1833 onwards), Kirkham in c. 1900 (Preston Scientific Society, 1903) and by the R. Hodder c. 1894 (MS at SYT). Since 1964 *H. niger* has been recorded from Hest Bank (SD46T) in 1973 (P.A.), at Cleveleys (SD34B) in 1967 (E.J.H.), St Anne's (SD32E) in 1993 (C.F. & N.J.S.) and Bryning-with-Warton (SD32Z) in 1979 (C.F. & N.J.S.). The decline in the frequency of Henbane in northern Lancashire is reflected nationally ('New Atlas').

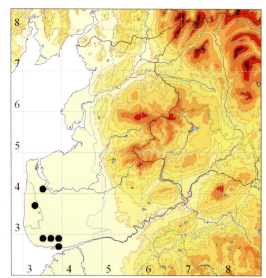
Nicandra physalodes

Nicandra physalodes (L.) Gaertn.   Apple-of-Peru

Neophyte. This is an annual native to Peru in South America. *N. physalodes* was grown in Britain by 1759 and was recorded in the wild in 1860. It is found as a garden escape in waste places in England, Wales, the Isle of Man and in the north of Ireland.

Rare (6). In northern Lancashire *N. physalodes* was first found on Marton Mere tip (SD34I) between 1961 and 1963 (A.E.R.) where it was again seen in 1966 (A.E.R. & J.H.). Other records are from a tip at Lytham St Anne's (SD32P) in 1967 (A.Wa.), on another tip at Lytham (SD32Z) in the early 1970s (C.F. & N.J.S.) and from Poulton-le-Fylde (SD34K) in 1964 (A.E.R.).

Datura stramonium L.   Thorn-apple

Neophyte. Thorn-apple is found widely in temperate and sub-tropical regions of the world but its native range is unknown. It is a species of cultivated and waste ground found in England and Wales and more rarely in Scotland and Ireland.

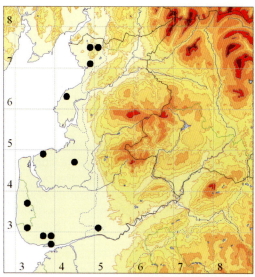
Datura stramonium

Rare (12). In northern Lancashire Thorn-apple was first found on the beach at Lytham (Ashfield, 1860). It was then not recorded again until it occurred at St Anne's (Bailey, 1910) and nearly another 50 years elapsed before it was found on a waste heap in Haslam Park, Preston (SD53A) in 1965 (E.H.). Since then it has been found in a few coastal sites from Silverdale to Lytham.

Solanum nigrum L.   Black Nightshade

Eurasian Southern-temperate element.

This is an annual herb of cultivated and waste ground (BH4) and occurs in most parts of lowland England and Wales. However it is thought to be introduced in north-eastern England, Scotland and Ireland.

Frequent (70). Wheldon and Wilson (1907) knew *S. nigrum* from only four sites in northern Lancashire and it appears it was not known before 1883. This suggests that it only spread into the area in the nineteenth century. Since 1964 it has been found in many coastal areas and more occasionally inland but it has still not been found in Lancashire VC 64. Although the

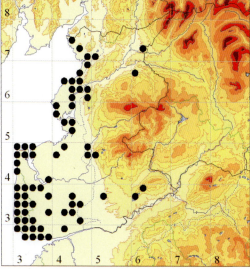
Solanum nigrum

'New Atlas' suggested some decline at the edges of Black Nightshade's distribution 'Local Change' confirms the considerable extension of its range, noted locally, in Britain as a whole.

Solanum physalifolium Rusby — Green Nightshade

Neophyte. This is a native of South America first reported from the wild in 1949. It is found in cultivated and waste ground and occurs mostly in south-eastern England with occasional records elsewhere.

In northern Lancashire it has only been recorded from waste ground at Lytham St Anne's in 1962 (A.E.R.; LIV). This was originally identified as *S. sarachoides* Sendtn., and recorded as such in the 'New Atlas'.

Solanum triflorum Nutt. — Small Nightshade

Neophyte. This is an annual native to western North America, Chile and Argentina. It was first recorded from the wild in Britain by 1876 and today it is naturalised in a few places in East Anglia. However it has been recorded in a number of other localities in Britain but these are mostly before 1970.

In northern Lancashire the only record is from St Anne's (Bailey, 1907).

Solanum dulcamara L. — Bittersweet

Circumpolar Southern-temperate element.

This is a scrambling woody perennial growing in woodland, woodland edge habitats, marshy areas and on coastal shingle (BH3, 11, 14). It is found in lowland areas of the British Isles but it is rare or absent in northern Scotland.

Common (302). In northern Lancashire Bittersweet is a common plant in lowland areas and in the Ribble valley but it is rare or absent in most of Bowland. Var. *marinum* Bab., a prostrate variety growing on coastal shingle, is probably overlooked but it was recorded from Lytham St Anne's (SD32N) in 1986 (C.F. & N.J.S.). There has been no change in its distribution locally or nationally.

Solanum tuberosum L. — Potato

Neophyte. This is a native of South America first grown in England about 1590. It became a staple food and remains an important crop plant but it was not recorded in the wild until about 1908. However, as with the Tomato, recorders often ignore it. Today it is found throughout the British Isles as a relic of cultivation or in waste places. There are numerous cultivars.

Occasional (16). Potato was first recorded in northern Lancashire at St Annes (Bailey, 1907) making this one of the earliest records for *S. tuberosum* growing wild in Britain. However it was not reported again until it was found near a garden at Poulton-le-Fylde in 1959 (Stalker, 1960). Today it is found in scattered localities in VC 60 but it is probably still under recorded.

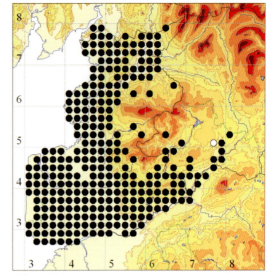

Solanum dulcamara

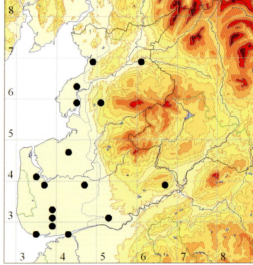

Solanum tuberosum

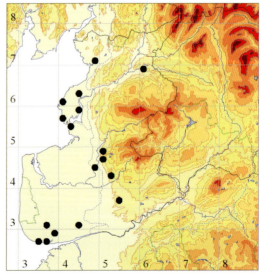

Solanum lycopersicum

Solanum lycopersicum L.   Tomato

Neophyte. Tomato is a native annual of central and South America and was introduced into Britain in 1595. There are numerous cultivars and it is widely cultivated. It was known from the wild by 1905 and today it is a common casual especially in urban areas and near sewage works. However Tomato rarely persists and, no doubt because it is a common horticultural crop, it is often ignored by recorders. It may be found anywhere in the British Isles.

Occasional (17). In northern Lancashire Tomato was first recorded from the sand dunes at Lytham St Anne's (Bailey, 1907) making this one of the earliest British records. Since 1964 it has been found at various localities mostly in the west of the area.

Solanum rostratum Dunal   Buffalo-bur

Neophyte. This is a native of south-eastern North America and Mexico. It was first grown in Britain in 1823 and recorded in the wild by 1886. It is found casually in cultivated ground and in waste places mostly in the south-eastern half of Britain but it is occasionally found elsewhere. There is some evidence that it is becoming more frequent.

Very rare (2). This was first recorded from St Anne's (Bailey, 1907) and then in a new garden at Poulton-le-Fylde in 1959 (Stalker, 1960; LIV). It was found again at St Anne's in 1963 (A.E.R.; LIV). Post 1964 records are from Freckleton sewage works (SD42P) in 1973 (M.J.) and from by the Lancaster Canal at Lancaster (SD46V) in 2006 (J.Cl.).

Nicotiana alata Link & Otto   Sweet Tobacco

Neophyte. This is a native of South America first cultivated in Britain in 1829 and recorded from the wild by 1928. It occurs casually in waste places and in cultivated ground, mostly in south-eastern and southern England.

Very rare (1). In northern Lancashire it was found on a tip at Lytham c. 1966 (A.E.R.).

OLEACEAE   ASH FAMILY

Forsythia suspensa (Thunb.) Vahl × F. viridissima Lindl.
(F. × intermedia Zabel)   Forsythia

Neophyte. This is a hybrid of garden origin raised c. 1880 in Germany. It was first grown in Britain ten years later. It is a common, popular and vigorous garden shrub, which occurs in the wild usually as a relic of cultivation in or near gardens or on rubbish tips. It is sterile but propagates easily from cuttings.

Very rare (5). Forsythia was recorded from Quernmore (SD55J; Livermore and Livermore, 1987) and from Lancaster (SD46W; Livermore and Livermore, 1991). Both records were identified as F. europaea Degan and Bald. but as there are no confirmed British records for this taxon it is assumed that the common garden Forsythia, F. × intermedia, was found. Forsythia was also found at two localities in Silverdale (SD47M & S) in 2007 (J.W.) and in Preston (SD52P) in 2008 (D.P.E.).

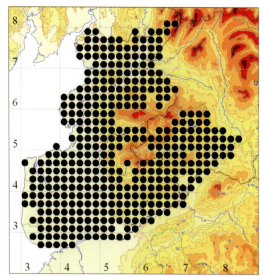

Fraxinus excelsior

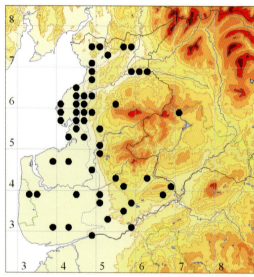

Syringa vulgaris

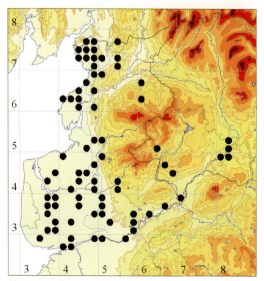

Ligustrum vulgare

Jasminum nudiflorum Lindl.   Winter Jasmine

Neophyte. Winter Jasmine is a native of China and was introduced into British cultivation in 1844. It is a common garden plant but it was not recorded in the wild until 1970. Today it is found as a relic of cultivation or thrown out with garden rubbish on tips etc., mostly in south-eastern England.

Very rare (1). In northern Lancashire it was found on a roadside at Conder Green (SD45S) in 2006 (M.W.).

Fraxinus excelsior L.   Ash

European Temperate element.

This is a deciduous tree of woodland, scrub and hedgerows (BH1) found on moist, basic soils throughout the British Isles. It is however widely planted and it is often difficult to distinguish between native populations and those of planted origin.

Very common (394). Ash is found throughout northern Lancashire except on the peat covered fells. It is not thought that its distribution has changed locally or nationally.

Fraxinus ornus L.   Manna Ash

Neophyte. This is a native of southern Europe and south-western Asia. It is occasionally grown in gardens but there are only a few reports of it in the wild.

Very rare (1). The only record for northern Lancashire is for a single tree growing in a field in the Halton or Caton areas (SD56H; Livermore and Livermore, 1987).

Syringa vulgaris L.   Lilac

Neophyte. Lilac is a native of south-eastern Europe and was cultivated in Britain by 1597. It is a common garden shrub and through selective breeding there are several horticultural cultivars. It was known from the wild by 1879 and today it is found in many parts of the British Isles, often near houses or as a relic of cultivation. Spread is usually vegetative but it can propagate by seed.

Occasional (53). It is not known when Lilac was first growing wild in northern Lancashire but from 1964 it has been found in scattered localities in the area, usually in urban areas or near houses. It is possibly under recorded.

Ligustrum vulgare L.   Wild Privet

European Temperate element.

This deciduous to semi-deciduous shrub is found as a native in hedgerows, woodland and scrub (BH1, 3), preferring well-drained base-rich soils. It is regarded as native in England and Wales but introduced in Scotland and Ireland. However, it is rare or absent in the Scottish Highlands and Islands.

Frequent (77). Wild Privet is found in scattered localities throughout northern Lancashire but native populations are probably restricted to base-rich soils in the north and west of the area and in the Ribble and Hodder valleys. Wheldon and Wilson (1907) only recorded Wild Privet from its area of native distribution indicating that its spread into other areas follows widespread introductions. Nationally its native distribution is thought to be stable but overall it has increased through introductions.

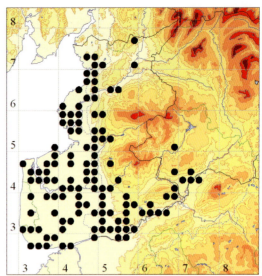
Ligustrum ovalifolium

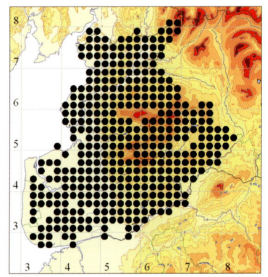
Digitalis purpurea

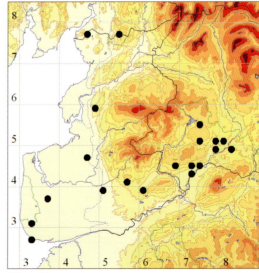
Erinus alpinus

Ligustrum ovalifolium Hassk.   Garden Privet

Neophyte. This more or less evergreen shrub is a native of Japan and was cultivated in Britain in 1842. It was first recorded in the wild in 1939. It became a popular garden hedging shrub and today it occurs throughout the British Isles as a garden relic or throw out on rubbish tips etc. Most records are from urban areas and it is absent or rare in many upland parts of the British Isles.

Frequent (123). It is not known when Garden Privet first grew wild in northern Lancashire but since 1964 it has been found mostly in the west of the area and in the Ribble valley.

VERONICACEAE   SPEEDWELL FAMILY

Hebe Comm. ex Juss.   Hedge Veronicas

Various species and hybrids of *Hebe* from the Southern Hemisphere have been planted in hedges and some have become naturalised, notably in the Isle of Man.

Very rare (1). In northern Lancashire *Hebe* sp. was recorded from a hedge by Fleetwood Golf Course (SD43D) in 1998 (E.F.G.). However Stace (2010) considers that all *Hebe* records refer to *Veronica × franciscana* Eastw.

Digitalis purpurea L.   Foxglove

Suboceanic Southern-temperate element.

This is a biennial or short-lived herb found on acidic soils on hedge banks, in open woodland and in woodland margins (BH3, 8, 9) and occurs throughout the British Isles.

Very common (388). Foxglove occurs throughout northern Lancashire. Its distribution is stable locally and nationally.

Erinus alpinus L.   Fairy Foxglove

Neophyte. This is a native of the mountains of south-western and south-central Europe. It was cultivated in British gardens by 1739 and became a popular garden species. It was known from the wild by 1867 and today it is found in many parts of the British Isles growing on walls or on basic rocks.

Occasional (20). Fairy Foxglove was first recorded in northern Lancashire from a farm wall near Goosnargh (SD54Q) in 1942 (H.E.B.). Today it occurs in scattered localities throughout the area.

Veronica officinalis L.   Heath Speedwell

European Boreo-temperate element.

Heath Speedwell is a perennial herb found on well-drained, moderately acid soils in grasslands, woods and woodland edge habitats (BH7, 8). It is found throughout the British Isles.

Frequent (135). In northern Lancashire *V. officinalis* occurs throughout the area but it is more frequent in the east and north than elsewhere. Its distribution is stable both locally and nationally.

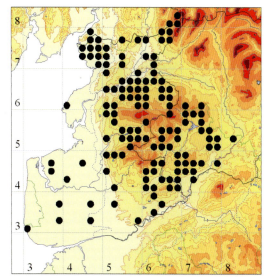

Veronica officinalis

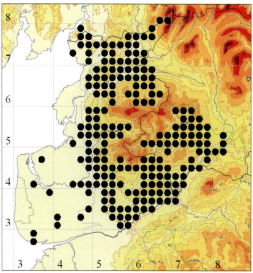

Veronica montana

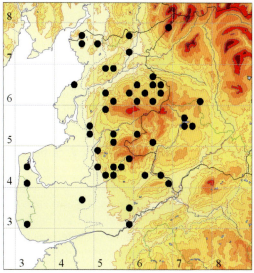

Veronica scutellata

Veronica montana L.   Wood Speedwell

European Temperate element.

Wood Speedwell is a perennial herb found on mostly neutral soils in woodlands and woodland edge habitats (BH1). It is found in most parts of the British Isles.

Frequent (211). In northern Lancashire *V. montana* is a characteristic species of woodlands and hedgerows around the Bowland Fells and in the north of the area with occasional localities in the lowland west of the region. Its distribution is stable both locally and nationally.

Veronica scutellata L.   Marsh Speedwell

Eurosiberian Boreo-temperate element.

This is a perennial herb found in a wide range of wetland habitats including ponds, lake margins, fens and marshes, wet grasslands and hill flushes (BH11, 13). It is found throughout the British Isles.

Occasional (47). In northern Lancashire Marsh Speedwell is found in scattered localities in the north and east of the area and much more rarely further west. Its distribution is probably stable locally but nationally the 'New Atlas' reported widespread losses after 1950 in central and southern England but 'Local Change' did not note further decline since 1987.

Veronica beccabunga L.   Brooklime

Eurosiberian Temperate element.

This is a robust perennial herb found in a wide variety of wetland habitats avoiding only the most infertile substrates (BH11, 14). It is found throughout the British Isles except parts of northern Scotland.

Common (345). Brooklime is found throughout northern Lancashire except in former and current peatland areas in the Pilling and Cockerham area and on the fells. Its distribution is stable both locally and nationally.

Veronica anagallis-aquatica L.   Blue Water-speedwell

Eurasian Southern-temperate element.

This is an annual herb found on fertile substrates by rivers, streams and ponds, in ditches and gravel pits (BH13, 14). It is found in many parts of the British Isles but it is absent or very rare in some areas, e.g. parts of Wales, upland Scotland, south-western and central England.

Occasional (38). In northern Lancashire Blue Water-speedwell occurs in the Lune valley and in the northwest of the area. It also occurs in scattered localities elsewhere, notably in a line, on the boulder clay, extending from Preston to Bispham. Some records from the Fylde may have been recorded in error for *V. catenata*. Its distribution is probably stable both locally and nationally.

Veronica anagallis-aquatica × V. catenata (V. × lackschewitzii J.B. Keller)

This annual or sometimes perennial hybrid is found in similar wetland habitats to its parents. It is found in central and southern parts of the British Isles but it is probably under recorded. A concentration of records in Hampshire is probably due to better recording there than elsewhere but it also seems to replace the parents in that county.

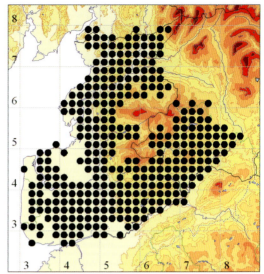

Veronica beccabunga

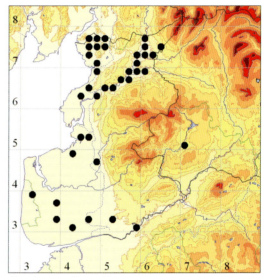

Veronica anagallis-aquatica

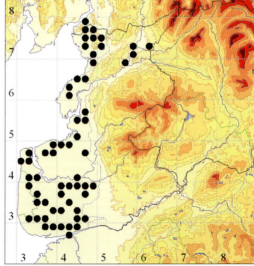

Veronica catenata

Very rare (2). This hybrid was found in a gravel pit at Borwick (SD57B) in 1986 (C.F. & N.J.S.) and in oxbows of the R. Lune at Melling-with-Wrayton (SD57V) in 1995 and since (J.M.N.).

Veronica catenata Pennell   Pink Water-speedwell

Circumpolar Temperate element.

V. catenata is usually an annual herb found in wet areas at the edge of rivers, streams, ponds and in gravel pits and sand dune slacks (BH13, 14). It is found in much of southern and central parts of the British Isles but it also occurs in the Outer Hebrides and Orkney Islands.

Occasional (60). *V. catenata* is found in western parts of northern Lancashire and in the Lune valley. Although Wheldon and Wilson (1907) did not distinguish this species from *V. anagallis-aquatica* the paucity of water-speedwell records in western parts of VC 60 known to them suggests that this species has spread into the area and become much more frequent over the last 100 years. Nationally its distribution is stable.

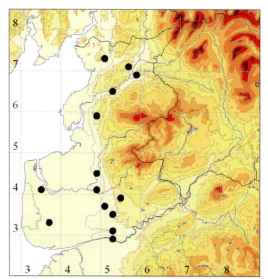
Veronica peregrina

Veronica peregrina L.   American Speedwell

Neophyte. American Speedwell is a native of North and South America. It was introduced into Britain by 1680, apparently via mainland Europe. It was first recorded in the wild in 1836 and since then it has spread slowly to many parts of the British Isles.

Rare (14). In northern Lancashire American Speedwell was first found as a garden weed at St Michael's (SD44Q) in 1902 (St Michael's School) and a few years later in 1909 (Bangerter, 1964) from Leagram Hall (SD64H). Today it is found in scattered localities in VC 60 and appears to be natural-ised in the Preston area.

Veronica serpyllifolia L. ssp. **serpyllifolia**   Thyme-leaved Speedwell

Circumpolar Boreo-temperate element.

V. serpyllifolia is a low, creeping perennial herb found in a wide variety of grasslands, flushes and on waste ground (BH3, 5, 11) and occurs throughout the British Isles.

Common (333). Thyme-leaved Speedwell is found throughout northern Lancashire. Its distribution is stable locally but despite it being a very common species nationally 'Local Change' detected some spread in East Anglia.

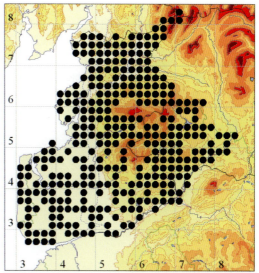
Veronica serpyllifolia

Veronica longifolia L.   Garden Speedwell

Neophyte. This has a Eurasian Boreo-temperate distribution but it is absent from western Europe. It was cultivated in Britain by 1731 and although it is a popular garden plant it was not found in the wild until 1928. Today it is found in scattered localities in Britain. However most garden plants and garden escapes are probably the hybrid *V. longifolia* × *V. spicata*.

Very rare (5). In northern Lancashire Garden Speedwell was recorded as a garden escape at Lytham St Anne's (SD32J) in 1967 (A.E.R.) and later at other localities in the Borough; SD32E in 1993, 32I in 1970s onwards and 32U in 2002 (all C.F. & N.J.S.). Also in Blackpool (SD33B) in 1969 (E.J.H.). These records suggest that it is naturalised on the coast between Lytham and Blackpool.

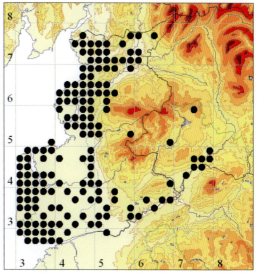
Veronica hederifolia

Veronica spicata L.   Spiked Speedwell

Eurosiberian Temperate element.

This occurs on well-drained, nutrient poor soils. In East Anglia these may
be acidic to basic but elsewhere it prefers thin calcareous soils often on
cliffs. Apart from East Anglia it occurs in a few places in Wales, northern
England and near Bristol.

Extinct. In northern Lancashire there are several records from the nineteenth century in the Silverdale and Yealand areas. It was last recorded
from near 'Hawes Tarn' in 1881 (E. Pickard; LDS). It still grows just over the
county boundary on the coast at Arnside.

Veronica hederifolia L.   Ivy-leaved Speedwell

Archaeophyte with a European Southern-temperate distribution.

This is an annual herb of cultivated and waste ground and shaded places
in woodland edge habitats (BH1, 3, 4, 17). It occurs in much of the British
Isles although it is rare or absent from many parts of western Ireland,
northern and western Scotland. However there are two subspecies that
can be difficult to distinguish. Ssp. *hederifolia* is thought to be commoner
in open habitats and cultivated ground whilst ssp. *lucorum* (Klett & Richt.)
Hartl is thought to favour more shaded places.

Frequent (163). *V. hederifolia* is found in the western half of northern
Lancashire and in the Lune and Ribble valleys with only occasional records
elsewhere in the eastern half of the region. Although some attempt has
been made to record the subspecies identification difficulties suggest
that the results may be unreliable. However initial observations suggest
that ssp. *lucorum* is much the commoner taxon and that it is widespread
as an annual weed of cultivated ground. Similar observations were made
for neighbouring counties (Halliday, 1997; Abbott, 2005). In northern
Lancashire Ivy-leaved Speedwell has spread considerably from the eight
localities mentioned by Wheldon and Wilson (1907). Nationally the 'New
Atlas' reports the distribution of *V. hederifolia* as stable but 'Local Change'
notes an increase since 1987.

Veronica filiformis Sm.   Slender Speedwell

Neophyte. This is a native of northern Turkey and the Caucasus and was
cultivated in Britain by 1808. However it was not widely grown until the
twentieth century. It was reported growing wild in 1838 but not again
until 1927. It then spread rapidly and today it is found in lawns and short
grassland in many parts of the British Isles.

Frequent (158). Slender Speedwell was first found in northern Lancashire at
Gressingham in 1941 (J.N.F.) and in 1953 from near Ribchester (Bangerter
and Kent, 1957). Since then it has been found in most parts of the area.

Veronica agrestis L.   Green Field-speedwell

Archaeophyte with a European Temperate distribution.

This is a spring germinating annual herb found in cultivated and waste
ground (BH3, 4, 17) throughout the British Isles.

Frequent (85). In northern Lancashire *V. agrestis* is found throughout
the area but more particularly in the west. Wheldon and Wilson (1907)
recorded *V. agrestis* as very common suggesting some decline in the area.
This decline was noted nationally by the 'New Atlas' but further loss since
1987 was not recorded by 'Local Change'.

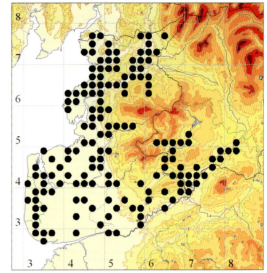
Veronica filiformis

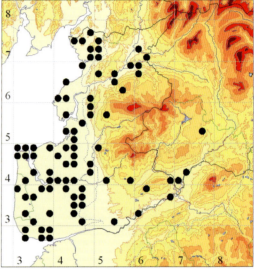
Veronica agrestis

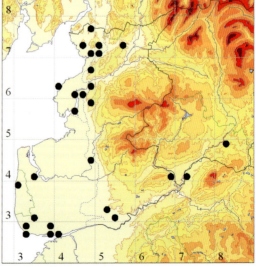
Veronica polita

Veronica polita Fr.   Grey Field-speedwell

Neophyte with a Eurosiberian Southern-temperate distribution. *V. polita* was first recorded in Britain in 1777 and today occurs as an annual herb of cultivated and waste ground. It is found in much of the British Isles but it is rare in most of Ireland and Scotland.

Occasional (27). In northern Lancashire this was first found at Ashton near Preston (Ashfield, 1858) with other early records from Stonyhurst (Anon, 1891), Garstang and Caton (Wheldon and Wilson, 1901a). However Wheldon and Wilson (1907) thought it sufficiently common to omit giving any localities. Today it is largely a coastal species with a few inland sites. It has probably declined over the last 100 years, which was also reported more generally for northern England ('New Atlas').

Veronica persica Poir.   Common Field-speedwell

Neophyte. This is probably a native of the Caucasus and northern Iran but it is now widespread in many temperate parts of the world. In Britain it was first recorded in the wild in 1826 ('New Atlas') and today it is found in many parts of the British Isles as a weed of cultivated and waste ground.

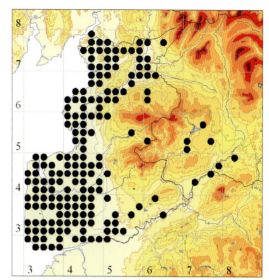
Veronica persica

Frequent (180). In northern Lancashire Common Field-speedwell was first reported from Roman deposits at Ribchester (Huntley and Hillam, 2000) pre-dating the previous earliest known British record by 1800 years. It was then not recorded again until it was found at Silverdale in 1862 (W.H.; LIV). By 1907 Wheldon and Wilson had only recorded *V. persica* from about ten localities. Today it is common in the west and north of the area but it occurs more rarely elsewhere as well.

Veronica chamaedrys L.   Germander Speedwell

Eurosiberian Boreo-temperate element.

This is a stoloniferous perennial herb of grasslands, woods and woodland edge habitats on a variety of soil types (BH1, 3, 6). It is found throughout the British Isles.

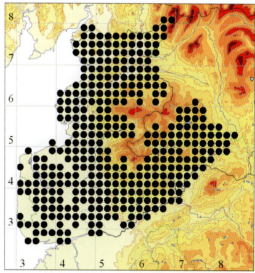
Veronica chamaedrys

Very common (369). Germander Speedwell is found throughout northern Lancashire except on the highest fells. There has been no change in its distribution either locally or nationally.

Veronica arvensis L.   Wall Speedwell

European Southern-temperate element.

This is an annual herb of cultivated land and open habitats (BH3, 4, 16). It is found throughout the British Isles.

Frequent (177). Wall Speedwell occurs throughout northern Lancashire but it is probably commoner in western areas than elsewhere. There has been no change in its distribution locally and whilst the 'New Atlas' also reported no change 'Local Change' noted a significant increase since 1987.

Antirrhinum majus L.   Snapdragon

Neophyte. This is a native of south-western Europe and the western Mediterranean region. It is a short-lived perennial herb grown in British gardens since Elizabethan times. It is a popular garden and bedding species with many cultivars first recorded in the wild in 1762. Today it is found throughout the British Isles usually in urban areas and it is rare or absent in many parts of Scotland.

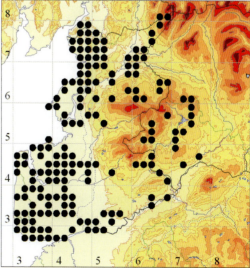
Veronica arvensis

Occasional (24). Snapdragon was first recorded in the 1830s from the walls of H.B. Fielding's garden at Stodday (SD45U; Fielding MS). It was also recorded at Halton in 1862 (W.H.; LIV). Today it is found in scattered localities in the west of the area, especially in and around Lancaster.

Antirrhinum hispanicum Chav. ssp. hispanicum

This is a dwarf shrub found on wall tops and rocks in south-eastern Spain. It has rarely been found in Britain.

Very rare (1). In northern Lancaster it was found on the top of a wall surrounding a supermarket at Carnforth (SD47V) in 2009 (J.Cl.).

Chaenorhinum origanifolium (L.) Kostel.   Malling Toadflax

Neophyte. *C. origanifolium* is a native of the western Mediterranean region and was first cultivated in Britain in 1785. It is a rare garden plant but was recorded from walls in West Malling in 1899. It has been recorded from a few other places in England.

Very rare (1). In northern Lancaster this was found on a pavement at Carnforth (SD47V) in 2001 (G.H.)

Chaenorhinum minus (L.) Lange   Small Toadflax

Archaeophyte with a European Temperate distribution.

This is a spring germinating annual herb of open, well-drained habitats. It seems to especially favour the ballast of old railways (BH3, 4, 17). It is found in many places in the British Isles but it is largely absent from the Scottish Highlands and Islands.

Occasional (55). This was first recorded in northern Lancashire from the railway between Cowan Bridge and the Yorkshire border at Ireby in 1893 (Petty, 1893). By 1907 Wheldon and Wilson knew of ten localities mostly from railways but also occasionally from river shingle. Today it is found in scattered localities in the west of the area and whilst it still occurs on old railways the former open habitats are being grassed over and today it is more likely to be found on waste ground. Nationally it has been lost as an arable weed and increasingly from railways so that a continuing decline has been noted ('New Atlas', 'Local Change').

Misopates orontium (L.) Raf.   Weasel's-snout

Archaeophyte with a Eurosiberian Southern-temperate distribution but a neophyte in northern Lancashire.

This is a spring germinating annual of light cultivated soils usually found in southern England.

In northern Lancashire it was found on a railway bank at Garstang (Wheldon and Wilson, 1902). There is also an unlocalised, unattributed record of 1971 from the 10km square SD47 (B.R.C.).

Cymbalaria muralis P. Gaertn., B. Mey & Scherb. Ivy-leaved Toadflax

Neophyte. This is a native of the mountains of south, central and south-eastern Europe and was introduced into British gardens before 1602. It was recorded from the wild by 1640 and today occurs on walls and well-drained stony places throughout most of the British Isles.

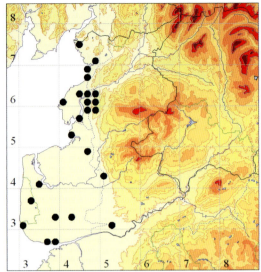

Antirrhinum majus

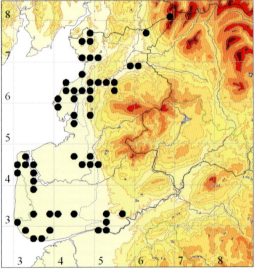

Chaenorhinum minus

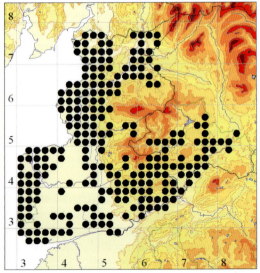

Cymbalaria muralis

Common (247). Ivy-leaved Toadflax was well established and was found throughout northern Lancashire by 1907 (Wheldon and Wilson). Today it still occurs throughout the area.

Cymbalaria pallida (Ten.) Wettst.   Italian Toadflax

Neophyte. This is a native of the mountains of central Italy and was introduced into British cultivation by 1882. It was recorded from the wild by 1924 and today occurs in scattered localities in Britain.

Rare (8). In northern Lancashire Italian Toadflax was first recorded from a church wall at Elswick (SD43J; Whellan, 1948) where it was re-found in 1987 (C.F. & N.J.S.) and was still present in 2010 (E.F.G.). Other records are from Garstang (unlocalised) in 1965 (A.E.R.), Heysham (SD46B) in 1982 (A.E.C.), Claughton (SD56T) in 1983 (J.M.N.), Lancaster (SD46Q, 45Z; Livermore and Livermore, 1991), Newton-with-Scales (SD43K) in 1999 (C.F. & N.J.S.), Scorton village (SD54E) in 2005 (C.F. & N.J.S.) and Little Thornton (SD34K) in the 1980s (N. Woods, LIV).

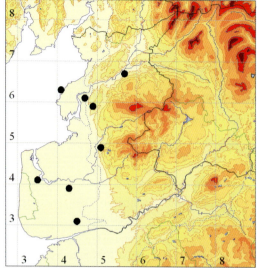
Cymbalaria pallida

Kickxia elatine (L.) Dumort.   Sharp-leaved Fluellen

Archaeophyte with a European Southern-temperate distribution but a neophyte in northern Lancashire.

This is an annual herb of basic soils found in arable fields and other cultivated ground in the southern half of the British Isles.

Very rare (1). This is a garden weed only known from Arkholme (SD56V) where it persisted for fourteen years prior to 1980 (C.D.P.).

Linaria vulgaris Mill.   Common Toadflax

Eurasian Boreo-temperate element.

This is a perennial herb found in open grassy places on waste ground, railway banks, roadside verges etc. especially on calcareous soils (BH3, 6). It is found in most of the British Isles but it is rare or absent in much of Ireland and northern Scotland.

Frequent (76). In northern Lancashire Common Toadflax occurs mostly in the west of the area. Its distribution is stable locally but nationally it has declined ('New Atlas', 'Local Change').

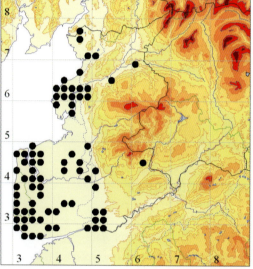
Linaria vulgaris

Linaria vulgaris × L. repens (L. × sepium G.J. Allman)

This is a spontaneous hybrid between a native and an introduced species. It occurs in open habitats on dry, calcareous soils on banks and on waste ground over much of southern Britain and occasionally in Ireland.

Very rare (2). In northern Lancashire there is a record from near Garstang (SD44N) in 1913 (A. Breakell; NMW). Other records are from cindery ground by the railway at Wesham (SD43B) in 1980 and on similar ground at Great Plumpton (SD33U) in 1992 (both C.F. & N.J.S.).

Linaria purpurea (L.) Mill.   Purple Toadflax

Neophyte. This is a native of central and southern Italy and Sicily and was introduced into British cultivation by 1648. It is a popular garden plant with several horticultural cultivars and was recorded from the wild by c. 1830. Today it occurs as a garden escape on waste ground throughout much of the British Isles.

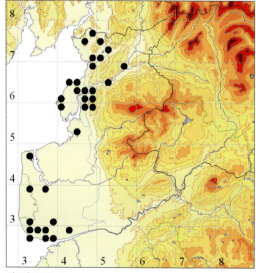
Linaria purpurea

Occasional (33). There is an unlocalised, unattributed record for the 10km square SD33 from the 1950s (B.R.C.) but the first localised record is from a roadside tip at Heaton-with-Oxcliffe (SD46L) in 1966 (J.Wi.). Today it is found in the northwest of the area and on the Fylde coast at Blackpool and Lytham St Anne's.

Linaria purpurea × L. repens (L. × dominii Druce)

This hybrid is found in a few British localities with one or both parents.

Very rare (1). This was found in a garden and adjacent road at Carnforth (SD57A) in 2001 (G.H.).

Linaria repens (L.) Mill. Pale Toadflax

Archaeophyte with a Suboceanic Temperate distribution, possibly a neophyte in northern Lancashire.

This is a rhizomatous perennial herb found in stony places and on waste ground (BH3, 7) in many parts of Britain and eastern Ireland.

Rare (9). This was first recorded from near Silverdale in 1881 (Petty, 1902). Today it still occurs in the Silverdale area and in a few scattered localities elsewhere.

Linaria maroccana Hook. f. Annual Toadflax

Casual neophyte. This is an annual herb brought into British cultivation in 1872 and recorded in the wild by 1928. It occurs in a few scattered localities in Britain.

In northern Lancashire Annual Toadflax was found on a tip at Marton Mere (SD33H) in 1961 (A.E.R.).

PLANTAGINACEAE PLANTAIN FAMILY

Plantago coronopus L. Buck's-horn Plantain

Eurosiberian Southern-temperate element.

This is a perennial herb of dry, open habitats often on the upper parts of salt marshes and on sand dunes, but it may occur in other open habitats near the coast on rocks or cracks in pavements etc. (BH3, 6, 18). It is found in coastal areas throughout the British Isles and occasionally also inland.

Occasional (64). In northern Lancashire Buck's-horn Plantain is found along the whole coastline extending inland to Preston on the Ribble estuary. Wheldon and Wilson (1907) suggested that *P. coronopus* was frequent but gave only seven localities. This suggests it has become more frequent and has extended its range in the twentieth century, and whilst the 'New Atlas' records no change in its distribution nationally 'Local Change' suggests it has extended its range since 1987, possibly because it has spread inland in some areas.

Plantago maritima L. Sea Plantain

Eurosiberian Wide-boreal element.

This is a perennial herb of the middle and upper parts of salt marshes and in other coastal habitats throughout British Isles. It also occurs inland, in upland flushes and occasionally on road sides (BH15, 21), especially in Scotland, northern England and Ireland.

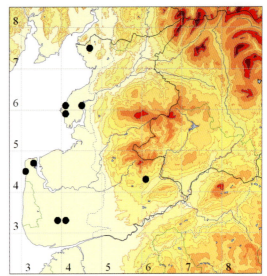

Linaria repens

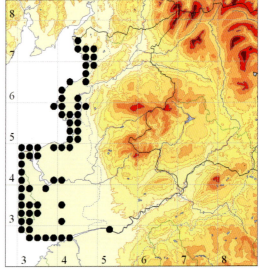

Plantago coronopus

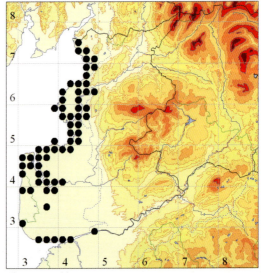

Plantago maritima

Occasional (63). In northern Lancashire Sea Plantain is found in most coastal areas but it was formerly rare in Lytham St Anne's but it has now spread into the developing salt marshes. There has been no change in its distribution locally or nationally.

Plantago major L. ssp. **major**   Greater Plantain

Eurasian Wide-temperate element.

Greater Plantain is a perennial herb of open habitats, especially by paths, tracks, and disturbed field edges and on waste ground (BH3, 5). It is found throughout the British Isles.

Very common (441). Greater Plantain occurs throughout northern Lancashire. There has been no change in its distribution locally or nationally.

Plantago major L. ssp. **intermedia** (Gilib.) Lange

Widespread in Europe but its distribution is uncertain.

This subspecies occurs in open habitats, often in somewhat saline coastal habitats but it is also found in damp places inland. However it was not recognised in Britain until 1958 (Lousley, 1958) and it is still under recorded making its distribution uncertain. *Plantago major* ssp. *intermedia* probably occurs throughout the British Isles.

Very rare (5). In northern Lancashire *Plantago major* ssp. *intermedia* was first found at the top of a salt marsh at Silverdale (SD47M) in 1993 (E.F.G.). Subsequently it was found in similar habitats in tetrads SD47W, 35Z, 34L & R but it is likely to be much more frequent than these few records suggest.

Plantago media L.   Hoary Plantain

Eurasian Temperate element.

This is a perennial herb found in calcareous grassland (BH7) in England, Wales and southern Scotland. It occurs as a rare introduction elsewhere.

Occasional (44). In northern Lancashire Hoary Plantain is found on calcareous soils in the north and east of the area with occasional records elsewhere. Formerly it seems to have been more frequent in the Ribble valley. It has also declined nationally.

Plantago lanceolata L.   Ribwort Plantain

Eurosiberian Southern-temperate element.

This is a common perennial herb found in a wide variety of habitats including grassland, sand dunes, salt marshes, upland flushes and waste ground (BH6, 7). Ribwort Plantain occurs throughout the British Isles.

Very common (430). *P. lanceolata* occurs throughout northern Lancashire. There has been no change in its distribution locally or nationally.

Littorella uniflora (L.) Asch.   Shoreweed

Suboceanic Temperate element.

This is a perennial herb of nutrient poor waters found in lakes and reservoirs etc., especially where there are fluctuating water levels (BH11, 13). It grows either submerged or on exposed gravely shores. It is found mostly in the west and north of the British Isles.

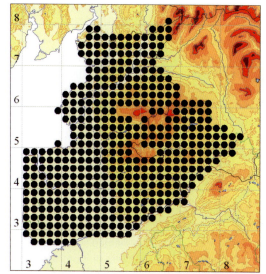
Plantago major

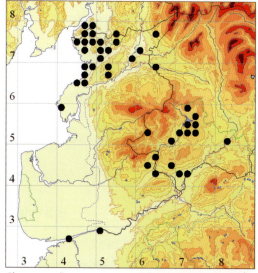
Plantago media

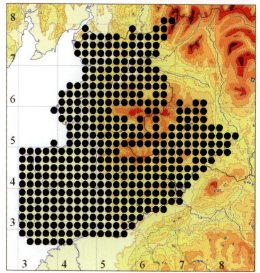
Plantago lanceolata

Rare (6). Shoreweed occurs in two areas based on the reservoirs and lakes around Nicky Nook, Nether Wyresdale and Stocks Reservoir, near Slaidburn. It particularly favours reservoir shores where water levels drop in summer and it may then dominate the vegetation over extensive areas. Formerly it occurred by the canal at Garstang (Wheldon and Wilson, 1907). Nationally Shoreweed has declined especially in south-eastern England ('New Atlas') but further decline since 1987 was not noted ('Local Change').

HIPPURIDACEAE — MARE'S-TAIL FAMILY

Hippuris vulgaris L. — Mare's-tail

Circumpolar-temperate element.

This is an emergent or submerged aquatic perennial herb (BH11, 13) found in most parts of the British Isles. It is not tolerant of eutrophic conditions, at least in northern Lancashire.

Occasional (32). Mare's-tail was found in the northern parts of VC 60 with a single locality on sandy ground at Lytham St Anne's. However most records were from the Lancaster Canal from which it had largely disappeared by 2000. Wheldon and Wilson (1907) knew Mare's-tail from twelve sites four of which were from the Canal. Thus, in northern Lancashire it appears there was an extension of its range through spread onto and along the Canal followed by a contraction, as the Canal sites were lost. It has also gone from some of its former sites on the Fylde coast and probably elsewhere. Nationally the 'New Atlas' reported no changes in its distribution but 'Local Change' reported significant losses since 1987.

CALLITRICHACEAE — WATER-STARWORT FAMILY

Callitriche hermaphroditica L. — Autumnal Water-starwort

Circumpolar Boreal-montane element.

Autumnal Water-starwort is a submerged aquatic found in mesotrophic lakes, ponds, canals and gravel pits etc. (BH13). It is found in northern and midland parts of the British Isles. In a revision of European *Callitriche* Lansdown (2006, 2008) referred to British material as *C. hermaphroditica* ssp. *macrocarpa* (Hegelm.) Lansdown and ssp. *hermaphroditica*. In northern Lancashire the few specimens that have been checked appear to belong to ssp. *hermaphroditica* with smaller fruits and probably with a more southern distribution in Britain.

Occasional (24). In northern Lancashire most records are from the Lancaster Canal, the R. Lune and in gravel pits and reservoirs giving a somewhat linear distribution from near Kirkby Lonsdale to Lancaster and Preston. Wheldon and Wilson (1907) recorded *C. hermaphroditica* mostly from the Lancaster Canal and it appears that since then it has spread into other habitats. This is consistent with the findings reported in the 'New Atlas'.

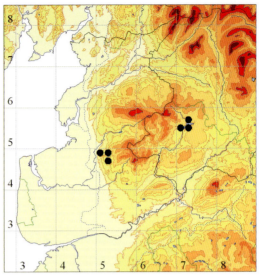
Littorella uniflora

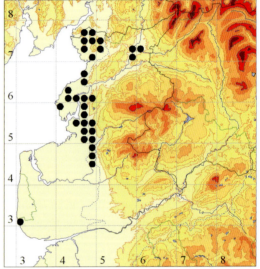
Hippuris vulgaris

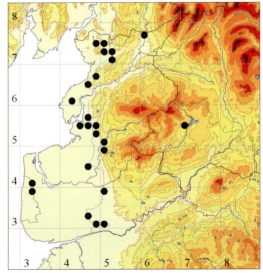
Callitriche hermaphroditica

Callitriche stagnalis *sensu lato*   Common Water-starwort

European Temperate element.

These are herbs of wet places often found at the edge of ponds or in rutted cart tracks (BH11, 13, 14) and are found throughout the British Isles. *C. stagnalis sensu lato* includes *C. stagnalis* Scop. and *C. platycarpa* but only a few recorders have distinguished between the two species.

Common (279). *C. stagnalis sensu lato* is found throughout northern Lancashire but *C. stagnalis* Scop. may be more restricted with perhaps most records occurring around the Bowland Fells. However it is much more frequent than the 18 tetrads from which it is currently recorded. Identification difficulties make it impossible to make any assessment of change.

Callitriche platycarpa Kütz.   Various-leaved Water-starwort

European Temperate element.

This occurs in wet places, often on eutrophic substrates (BH11, 13), in most parts of the British Isles but it is likely to be under recorded with many records included in *C. stagnalis sensu lato*.

Frequent (71). *C. platycarpa* occurs in scattered localities in northern Lancashire although it is rare in Lancashire VC 64. It is probably a more lowland and eutrophic species than *C. stagnalis*. Again identification difficulties make assessment of change impossible.

Callitriche obtusangula Le Gall   Blunt-fruited Water-starwort

Suboceanic Southern-temperate element.

C. obtusangula is found in ditches and ponds with mesotrophic to eutrophic waters (BH13, 14) in Ireland and the southern half of Britain.

Occasional (17). *C. obtusangula* occurs mostly in coastal areas of northern Lancashire. It was first recorded in 1913 (Wheldon and Wilson, 1925) but nationally it is believed there has been no change in its distribution.

Callitriche brutia Petagna var. **brutia**   Pedunculate Water-starwort

European Southern-temperate element.

This submerged aquatic or terrestrial plant of wet places often occurs where there are fluctuating water levels and in nutrient poor conditions (BH13). It may be found anywhere in the British Isles but seems to be abundant in some places but rare or absent in others. Lansdown (2006, 2008), following detailed taxonomic studies on European, including British, material, concluded that *C. brutia* (2n = 28) and *C. hamulata* (2n = 38) were very closely related and that they could be distinguished morphologically only by examining terrestrial plants where *C. brutia* developed peduncles. It was not possible to distinguish submerged plants. Accordingly he recognised *C. brutia* Petagna var. *brutia* and *C. brutia* var. *hamulata* (Kütz. ex W.D.J. Koch) Lansdown. In this account only plants with pedunculate fruit are referred to *C. brutia*.

Rare (9). *C. brutia* was first recorded in 1989 (Mr & Mrs M. Braithwaite) from Wyresdale Park Lake, Nether Wyresdale (SD54E). Since then it has been found in a few ponds and reservoirs in VC 60.

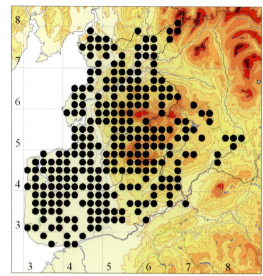
Callitriche stagnalis s.l.

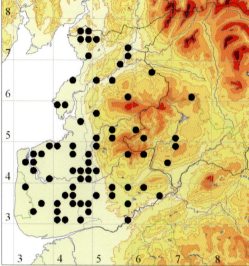
Callitriche platycarpa

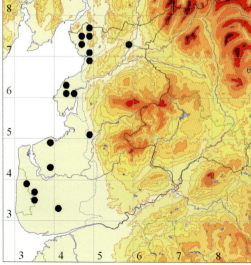
Callitriche obtusangula

Callitriche brutia Petagna var. **hamulata**
(Kűtz. ex W.D.J. Koch) Lansdown   Intermediate Water-starwort

European Wide-temperate distribution.

Because of identification difficulties associated with submerged plants it is likely that some records included here are of *C. brutia* var. *brutia*. However var. *hamulata* is found in wet places (BH11, 13, 14), usually acid and nutrient poor, throughout the British Isles.

Occasional (60). Var. *hamulata* occurs in scattered localities in northern Lancashire but very rarely in Lancashire VC 64. Wheldon and Wilson (1907) recorded it from only one locality but added two more later (Wheldon and Wilson, 1925). Apparently *C. hamulata* became much more frequent in the second half of the twentieth century before declining and since 2000 there have been no records of this species. Although the 'bicycle spanner' tips to the leaves are distinctive the bifid leaf tips of *C. hermaphroditica* have been mistaken for this species. It is possible, therefore, that var. *hamulata* was over recorded and that today it is very rare or extinct. Nationally it is believed that there has been no change in the distribution of var. *hamulata* since 1987 ('Local Change').

[Wheldon and Wilson (1907) refer to records of *C. vernalis* Koch from near Bruna Hill, Garstang and *C. polymorpha* Lőnnr. from near Middleton, but it is not known to which species recognised today they belong.]

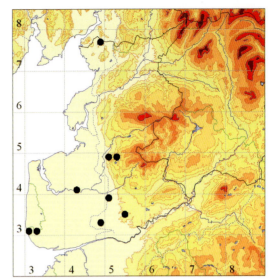
Callitriche brutia var. *brutia*

SCROPHULARIACEAE   FIGWORT FAMILY

[**Verbascum blattaria** L.   Moth Mullein

Neophyte. *V. blattaria* has a Eurosiberian Southern-temperate distribution and was cultivated in Britain by 1596. It has been known in the wild since 1629. Today it is found mostly in south-eastern Britain.

This was recorded from a hen run at Bare in 1899 (Lees, 1899) but the voucher specimen at KGY appears to be *V. virgatum*.]

Verbascum virgatum Stokes   Twiggy Mullein

Neophyte. This has a Suboceanic Southern-temperate distribution and was first recorded in the wild in 1787. However in south-western England it may be native. Today it is found in scattered places in England, Wales and more rarely in Scotland and Ireland.

Rare (8). In northern Lancashire *V. virgatum* was first recorded from Stodday south of Lancaster in 1832 (Fielding MS) with subsequent records from Silverdale, on the Wyre estuary and at St Anne's. Today it is found in scattered localities, often as single plants, along the VC 60 coast.

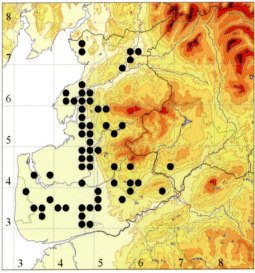
Callitriche brutia var. *hamulata*

Verbascum phoeniceum L.   Purple Mullein

Neophyte. This is a native of Europe and south-western Asia. It was introduced into British cultivation by 1796 and became a popular garden plant. Purple Mullein was recorded in the wild in 1880 and today occurs casually on waste ground in scattered localities in Britain.

Very rare (1). The only record in northern Lancashire is from brickwork by the sand dunes at Lytham St Anne's (SD32N) in 2007 (J. Cl.).

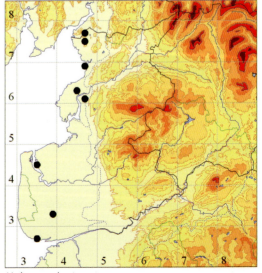
Verbascum virgatum

Verbascum phlomoides L.   Orange Mullein

Neophyte. Orange Mullein has a European Temperate distribution and was cultivated in Britain by 1739. It was known in the wild by 1838 and although rarely cultivated today it occurs naturalised in central and southern Britain and occurs more rarely in Scotland and the Isle of Man.

Very rare (2). In northern Lancashire *V. phlomoides* was found on tips at Lytham (SD32) in 1962 and at Blackpool (SD33) in 1966 (both A.E.R.). Further records were from St Anne's (SD32E) in 1996 and Marton Mere, Blackpool (SD33M) in 1997 (both C.F. & N.J.S.).

Verbascum densiflorum Bertol.   Dense-flowered Mullein

Neophyte. This has a European Temperate distribution and has been grown in British gardens since about 1825. It is a popular garden plant and has been known in the wild since 1838. Today it occurs in scattered localities in southern Britain and Ireland with a concentration of records in some areas, notably on the Lancashire and Merseyside coasts.

Rare (6). In northern Lancashire this was first recorded from the sand dunes at St Anne's in 1907 (Bailey, 1910). Post 1964 records (all C.F. & N.J.S.) are from Blackpool Airport (SD33F) in 1984, Marton (SD33H) in 1985, near Staining (SD33M) in 1988, Lytham St Anne's (SD33F) in 1998, Lytham railway station (SD32T) in 1988 and in Blackpool (SD33G) in 1989.

Verbascum thapsus L.   Great Mullein

Eurosiberian Temperate element.

This is a biennial herb of open scrub and waste ground (BH3) and is found throughout the British Isles although it becomes rare or absent from much of the Scottish Highlands and Islands.

Frequent (88). Great Mullein is found in scattered localities throughout northern Lancashire but particularly in coastal areas. It is believed there has been no change in its distribution locally or nationally.

Verbascum nigrum L.   Dark Mullein

Eurosiberian Temperate element but a neophyte in northern Lancashire.

This is a biennial or short-lived perennial herb found on roadsides and waste ground throughout the British Isles although it is very rare in Ireland and most of Scotland. However it is only thought to be native in southern Britain but it has often been grown in gardens from which it has escaped into the wild.

Very rare (5). In northern Lancashire this was first found on Warton Crag (SD47W) in *c.* 1960 and again in 1964 (H.S.). Later records were from near Dolphinholme (SD55B) in 1967 (E.F.G.), Myerscough (SD44V) in *c.* 1986 (C.J.B.), Heysham (SD46A) in 1984 and Carnforth (SD47V) in 2007 (J.M.N.).

Scrophularia nodosa L.   Common Figwort

Eurosiberian Temperate element.

Common Figwort is a perennial herb found in open or shaded habitats on damp soils in woodlands, woodland edges, hedgerows, by rivers and on waste ground (BH1, 3). It occurs throughout the British Isles.

Common (285). Whilst *S. nodosa* occurs throughout northern Lancashire it is predominantly a lowland species favouring areas covered in boulder clay or in river valleys. Its distribution is stable locally and nationally.

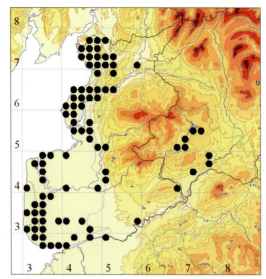
Verbascum thapsus

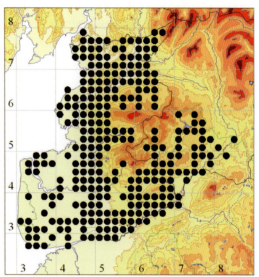
Scrophularia nodosa

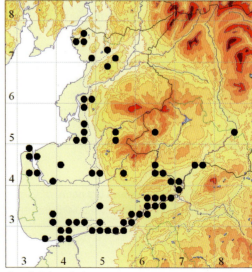
Scrophularia auriculata

Scrophularia auriculata L.   Water Figwort

Suboceanic Southern-temperate element.

This is a perennial herb of wet places by the margins of rivers, lakes, canals, in ditches and on damp roadside verges (BH11, 14). It is found mostly in the southern half of Britain, in Ireland and more rarely in Scotland.

Occasional (65). Water Figwort occurs in scattered localities in northern Lancashire but especially in the Ribble valley. Comparing the distribution of Water Figwort today in northern Lancashire with that of 100 years ago (Wheldon and Wilson, 1907) it appears that there may have been an extension of its range. The 'New Atlas' similarly reported a slight extension of its range northwards, but since 1987 this extension of its range has been more significant ('Local Change').

Scrophularia umbrosa Dumort.   Green Figwort

Eurosiberian Temperate element.

This is a perennial herb of damp places growing by streams, rivers and in damp woodland (BH1, 14). Its distribution in the British Isles is disjunct occurring in and around the central valley in Scotland; the Eden and Wye valleys, the Ribble and Wharfe river catchments and the Norfolk Broads in England and the Liffey valley in Ireland with only occasional records elsewhere.

Occasional (18). In northern Lancashire Green Figwort is confined to the Ribble valley with most records in Lancashire VC 64. Whilst there has been no change in its distribution in northern Lancashire the 'New Atlas' suggests that it may be a relatively recent colonist as it was not recorded in Britain until 1840. Since then colonies became established in different areas and at least within its present range it appears to be becoming more frequent.

Limosella aquatica L.   Mudwort

Circumpolar Boreo-temperate element.

This is an annual of the muddy edges of rivers, lakes and reservoirs especially where water levels fluctuate (BH13). It is found in England, Wales, central, eastern and southern Scotland and western Ireland.

Very rare (4) but extinct in VC 60. Today Mudwort occurs on the shores of Stocks Reservoir (SD75C, H, I; Abbott, 2005; P.G.) and near Waddington Quarries (SD74D) in 2007 (P.J.). In VC 60 it was recorded from brackish pools near Overton in 1900 (Wheldon and Wilson, 1907), near Bolton-le-Sands (Wheldon and Wilson, 1906) and at Ribbleton near Preston (Ashfield, 1858). There is also a doubtful record from dredged sand spread on Lea Marsh (SD42Z) in 1964 (Preston Scientific Society). Nationally there have been many losses in England, mostly before 1930, but since 1962 there has been an apparent increase in Scotland ('New Atlas').

Buddleja davidii Franch   Butterfly-bush

Neophyte. The Butterfly-bush is a native of China and was introduced into British cultivation in the 1890s. It quickly became a popular garden plant and was naturalised in the wild by 1922. Today it is found throughout the British Isles but it is especially abundant on waste ground in the southern half of Britain.

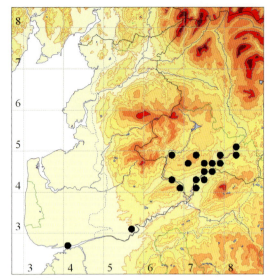

Scrophularia umbrosa

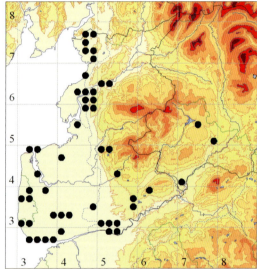

Buddleja davidii

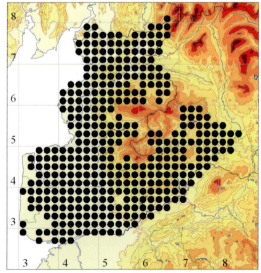

Stachys sylvatica

Occasional (49). In northern Lancashire *B. davidii* was not recorded in the wild until 1966 when it was found on rough ground in Lancaster (A.E.R.). A few years later in 1970 (E.F.G.) it was found on waste ground in Preston (SD53K). Today it is found on waste ground, especially in urban areas, in scattered localities in the area. Nationally it spread rapidly across the British Isles between 1962 and 2000 ('New Atlas').

LAMIACEAE   DEAD-NETTLE FAMILY

Dracocephalum parviflorum Nutt.   American Dragon-head

Neophyte. This is a native of North America that has been found occasionally in Britain as a birdseed or wool contaminant.

In northern Lancashire it was found on the sand dunes at St Anne's in 1907 (Bailey, 1910; MANCH).

Sideritis montana L.   Mountain Ironwort

Neophyte. This is a native of the Mediterranean region and there are a few old records for the British Isles. It was a grain contaminant.

In northern Lancashire it was found at St Anne's in 1906 (Bailey, 1907; MANCH).

Stachys byzantina K. Koch   Lamb's-ear

Neophyte. Lamb's-ear is a native of south-western Asia. It was introduced into British cultivation in 1782 and became a popular garden plant. It was first recorded in the wild in 1855 and today it is found in scattered localities in the British Isles but especially in southern England and the Isle of Man.

Very rare (2). In northern Lancashire it was found naturalised in a field at Silverdale (SD47S) in 2003 (E.F.G.) whilst a single plant was found on a river revetment wall in the Trough of Bowland (SD65F) in 2007 (E.F.G.).

Stachys sylvatica L.   Hedge Woundwort

Eurosiberian Temperate element.

This is a foetid, rhizomatous perennial herb found in hedge banks, woodland edge and ruderal habitats (BH3) throughout the British Isles.

Very common (378). In northern Lancashire Hedge Woundwort is found throughout the area except in the Bowland and Leck fells. There has been no change in its distribution locally and none was detected by the 'New Atlas' but perhaps surprisingly 'Local Change' noted a significant decline since 1987.

Stachys sylvatica × S. palustris (S. × ambigua Sm.)

Hybrid Woundwort

This hybrid is widespread in Europe and is found in the habitats of either parent but frequently in the absence of both. It is found throughout the British Isles but more especially in western Britain.

Occasional (68). In northern Lancashire *S. × ambigua* is found in scattered localities throughout the area. However it is likely to be under recorded. It is not known if its distribution has changed locally as the hybrid was not recognised by Wheldon and Wilson (1907). Similarly whilst 'Local Change' indicates an increase in its distribution nationally since 1987 this is probably due to better recording and recognition of the hybrid.

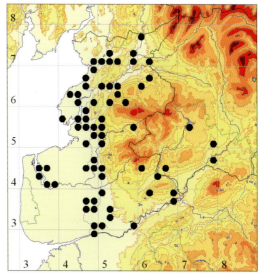

Stachys × ambigua

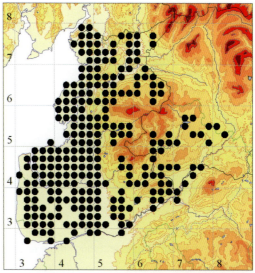

Stachys palustris

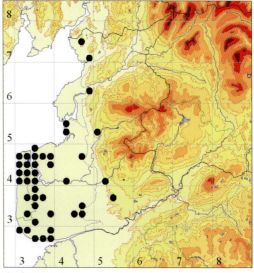

Stachys arvensis

Stachys palustris L.   Marsh Woundwort

Circumpolar Boreo-temperate element.

This is a perennial herb of damp places growing by streams, ponds and canals etc. (BH11, 14). It is found throughout British Isles.

Common (269). Marsh Woundwort is found throughout northern Lancashire but less commonly in eastern areas than elsewhere. Some records may be errors for *S. × ambigua.* Its distribution locally and nationally is stable.

Stachys arvensis (L.) L.   Field Woundwort

Archaeophyte with a Suboceanic Southern-temperate distribution.

This is a winter annual of cultivated and waste ground (BH3, 4) and occurs in many parts of the British Isles. However it is much rarer in most of Scotland and Ireland (except the southeast) than elsewhere.

Occasional (43). In northern Lancashire Field Woundwort is found mostly on sandy soils near the coast and more occasionally elsewhere in the west of VC 60. Wheldon and Wilson (1907) recorded only nine localities for Field Woundwort in VC 60, which suggests that it has become more frequent over the last 100 years. However the 'New Atlas' reported large losses nationally, yet since 1987 'Local Change' noted a reversal of its long-term trend with gains, especially in coastal areas.

Stachys cretica L.

Neophyte. This is a native of the Mediterranean region and south-western Asia. There are a few pre 1930 British records.

In northern Lancashire it was found on the sand dunes at St Anne's (Bailey, 1910).

Betonica officinalis L.   Betony

European Temperate element.

Betony is found in hedge banks, heaths and in woodland edge habitats (BH6, 7) in England, Wales and much more rarely in southern Scotland and Ireland.

Frequent (154). In northern Lancashire *S. officinalis* is found frequently in the north of VC 60 and in the Ribble valley but much more rarely in Bowland and in lowland areas in the west of the area. There has been no change in its distribution locally but there have been losses nationally ('New Atlas', 'Local Change').

Ballota nigra L.   Black Horehound

Archaeophyte with a European Southern-temperate distribution but a neophyte in northern Lancashire.

This is a perennial herb associated with human settlements since the Iron Age. It is found in hedgerows, field borders and ruderal habitats (BH3) mostly in the southern half of Britain and eastern Ireland.

Rare (11). In northern Lancashire Black Horehound was first recorded from near Preston Docks (Preston Scientific Society, 1903) and near houses at Carnforth (Wheldon and Wilson, 1907). Today it occurs in a few localities in the north of VC 60, Blackpool and Lytham St Anne's. Nationally there has been no change in its distribution.

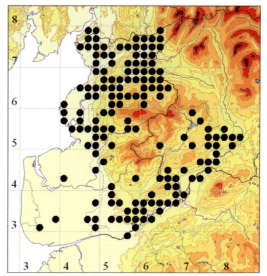
Betonica officinalis

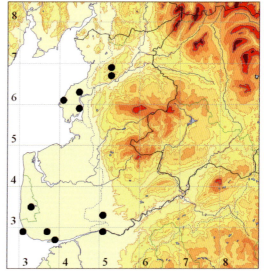
Ballota nigra

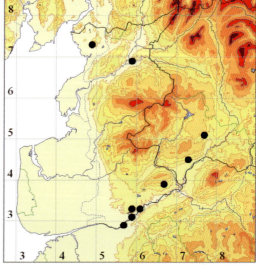
Lamiastrum galeobdolon ssp. montanum

Leonurus cardiaca L.   Motherwort

Neophyte. Motherwort is a Eurosiberian Temperate species widely culti-vated in Europe. It was introduced into Britain as a medicinal herb in the Middle Ages and recorded from the wild in 1597. It is found in scattered localities in the British Isles but mostly in England and Wales. However there was a marked contraction in its distribution in the second half of the twentieth century.

In northern Lancashire *L. cardiaca* was recorded from Poulton-by-the-Sands (Morecambe) by Jenkinson (1775); Lytham in the 1830s (Fielding MS) and near Ansdell in 1901 (Bailey, 1907). There are no recent records.

Lamiastrum galeobdolon (L.) Ehrend. & Polatschek
ssp. **montanum** (Pers.) Ehrend. & Polatschek   Yellow Archangel

European Temperate element.

This stoloniferous perennial herb is found in moist woodlands (BH1) in England, Wales and eastern Ireland and as an introduction elsewhere.

Rare (9). Yellow Archangel is a native species in the Ribble valley and occupies a narrow zone just above the winter flood levels of the river. An old record for Tarnacre near St Michael's and records in the north of the area are thought to be either introductions or errors for ssp. *argentatum*. There has been no change in its distribution locally or nationally before 1987 but since then a significant decline has been noted ('Local Change').

Lamiastrum galeobdolon (L.) Ehrend. & Polatschek
ssp. **argentatum** (Smejkal.) Stace

Neophyte. This variegated leaved herb is of uncertain origin. It was not recognised taxonomically until it was described as a new taxon in 1975. It was possibly introduced in the late 1960s and was first recorded in the wild in 1974. Today it is found in many parts of the British Isles.

Occasional (47). The history of the introduction and spread of this taxon in northern Lancashire is not known. However by the late 1980s there were several localities spread across the area and it is clear from the size of some of the colonies, e.g. near Huntingdon Hall, Dutton (SD63U) that it had been naturalised for many years.

Lamium album L.   White Dead-nettle

Archaeophyte with a Eurasian Boreo-temperate distribution.

White Dead-nettle grows in hedgerows, woodland edge and ruderal habitats (BH3, 17) in lowland areas of England, Wales, Scotland and eastern Ireland.

Frequent (158). In northern Lancashire this is frequent in the west of the area and in the Lune and Ribble valleys. It has spread considerably over the last 100 years as Wheldon and Wilson (1907) knew it at only thirteen localities in VC 60. Its distribution nationally is stable.

Lamium maculatum (L.) L.   Spotted Dead-nettle

Neophyte. This has a European Temperate distribution and was introduced into British cultivation from Italy in 1683. It is still grown in gardens and was recorded in the wild by about 1730. Today it occurs in lowland areas of England, Wales and parts of Scotland and Ireland.

Frequent (128). Spotted Dead-nettle was first recorded in northern Lancashire from near Ribchester (Ashfield, 1858) and by 1907 seven

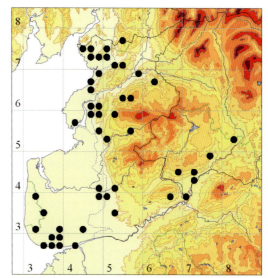
Lamiastrum galeobdolon ssp. argentatum

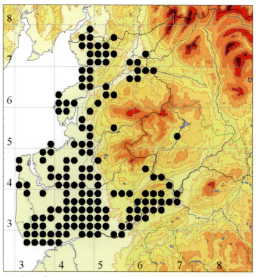
Lamium album

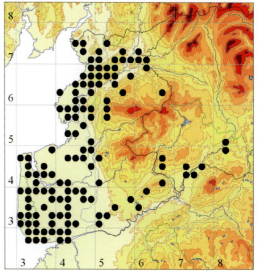
Lamium maculatum

localities were known (Wheldon and Wilson, 1907). Today it occurs frequently in the west of the area as well as in the Lune and Ribble valleys.

Lamium purpureum L.   Red Dead-nettle

Archaeophyte with a European Temperate distribution.

This is an annual herb found in cultivated and waste ground (BH3, 4, 17) throughout the British Isles.

Frequent (202). In northern Lancashire *L. purpureum* occurs in the west of the area and in the Lune valley but only occasionally elsewhere. The distribution of Red Dead-nettle is stable both locally and nationally although the 'New Atlas' reported some losses in Scotland.

Lamium hybridum Vill.   Cut-leaved Dead-nettle

Archaeophyte with a European Temperate distribution.

This is an annual herb of cultivated and waste ground (BH4). It occurs in many lowland areas of the British Isles but there are a number of areas where it is rare or absent, e.g. most of Wales and south-western Scotland.

Frequent (80). Cut-leaved Dead-nettle is found mainly in western areas of northern Lancashire. Wheldon and Wilson recorded it from sixteen localities suggesting that it has become more frequent over the last 100 years. Nationally both the 'New Atlas' and 'Local Change' report a marked expansion in the range of *L. hybridum*.

Lamium confertum Fr.   Northern Dead-nettle

Archaeophyte with a European Boreal-montane distribution.

This annual herb of cultivated and waste ground (BH4) is found largely in coastal areas of Scotland, Ireland and the Isle of Man with occasional localities elsewhere.

Very rare (1). Old records for Northern Dead-nettle in northern Lancashire are from Silverdale (Petty, 1902), near St Michael's (Wheldon and Wilson, 1907) and Barton (Preston Scientific Society, 1903). Since 1964 it was found in a field at Over Kellet (SD57A) in 2001 and again in 2009 (E.F.G.). Nationally the 'New Atlas' reported a decline but 'Local Change' considered its distribution stable.

Lamium amplexicaule L.   Henbit Dead-nettle

Archaeophyte with a Eurosiberian Southern-temperate distribution.

This is an annual of cultivated and waste ground (BH3, 4) and occurs in many lowland areas of the British Isles, especially in south-eastern and eastern Britain.

Occasional (23). Henbit Dead-nettle was first recorded in northern Lancashire from near Lytham in 1900 (Wheldon and Wilson, 1901a) and Barton (Preston Scientific Society, 1903). Today it occurs in coastal areas from Carnforth to Preston. Whilst *L. amplexicaule* has increased locally its distribution nationally is stable.

[Lamium laevigatum

The identity of this record from Lytham (Wheldon and Wilson, 1907) is not known and a voucher specimen has not been found.]

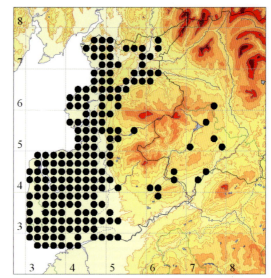
Lamium purpureum

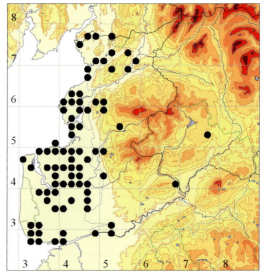
Lamium hybridum

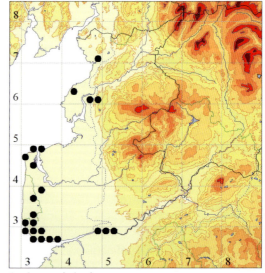
Lamium amplexicaule

Galeopsis angustifolia Ehrh. ex Hoffm.   Red Hemp-nettle

Archaeophyte with a European Temperate distribution.

This is an annual of cultivated land, ruderal and open calcareous habitats (BH4, 16). It is found mostly in the southern half of the British Isles.

Very rare (1) or extinct. Red Hemp-nettle has been known from northern Lancashire since Roman times when it was found in horse dung at Lancaster (Wilson, 1979). However it never seems to have been common and most records were from the coast at Morecambe. There is also an early, unlocalised record from Bowland in 1815 (KGY). Other records are from St Anne's (A.J.C.), Silverdale c. 1854 (Miss Williams ex J.N.F.); Garstang in 1952 (A.W.W.); Elmslack, Silverdale in 1959 (Mrs Mackie, MANCH) and on the south facing screes on Warton Crag (SD47W) in 1958 (M.J.). Since 1964 it has only been recorded from Heysham (SD46A) in 1974 (A.E.C.) despite searches on the coast between Morecambe and Carnforth and on Warton Crag. There have also been losses nationally ('New Atlas').

Galeopsis speciosa Mill.   Large-flowered Hemp-nettle

Archaeophyte with a Eurosiberian Boreo-temperate distribution.

This is a large attractive weed of cultivated and waste ground (BH4) found in lowland areas of Britain from the Midlands northwards and in the north of Ireland.

Occasional (61). In the 1960s and early 1970s G. speciosa was a conspicuous and attractive weed in arable farmland found in western parts of northern Lancashire with only occasional records elsewhere. It was particularly frequent in potato fields and on soils reclaimed from the mosses. However intensive use of herbicides easily eradicates Large-flowered Hemp-nettle so that by 2000 it had become much less frequent and was largely confined to field edges and on waste ground. This decline is reflected nationally.

Galeopsis tetrahit L.   Common Hemp-nettle

European Boreo-temperate element.

This is an annual herb of woodland edge habitats and on bank sides usually in moderately acidic heathy places (BH3). It is found throughout the British Isles.

Frequent (113). In northern Lancashire many recorders did not distinguish between G. tetrahit and G. bifida. However they grow in different habitats and have different and largely complimentary distributions. Combined, the two species are common (254) occurring throughout northern Lancashire. However G. tetrahit is apparently much more frequent in the north of the area than elsewhere but this may be due to recording bias. Because of identification difficulties it is not known if there has been any change in the distribution of Common Hemp-nettle locally or nationally.

Galeopsis tetrahit × G. bifida (G. × ludwigii Hausskn.)

This hybrid is partially fertile and intermediate between the parents. It has been recorded from various localities in England and Wales but it is very much under recorded. It is likely to be frequent.

Very rare (1). In northern Lancashire G. × ludwigii was found on Winmarleigh Moss (SD44P) in 1999 (J.M.N.). Although it is likely to be under recorded it is possible that the parent's distributions overlap in only a few places, as at Winmarleigh, where the heaths of the dryer parts of the moss are adjacent to arable fields.

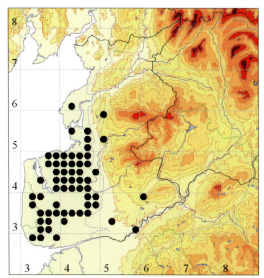
Galeopsis speciosa

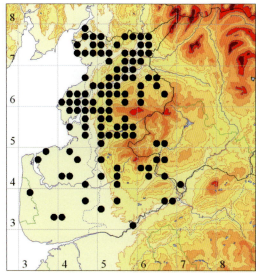
Galeopsis tetrahit s.s.

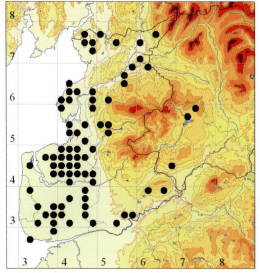
Galeopsis bifida

Galeopsis bifida Boenn.   Bifid Hemp-nettle

Eurasian Boreo-temperate element.

This is an annual species of cultivated and waste ground (BH4) and is found throughout the British Isles. It is under recorded, as it has often not been distinguished from *G. tetrahit*.

Frequent (80). This may be found anywhere in northern Lancashire although most records are from western areas. This may be commoner than *G. tetrahit* but as it has often not been distinguished from that species it is very much under recorded. Because of identification difficulties it is not known if there has been any change in its distribution locally or nationally.

Marrubium vulgare L.   White Horehound

Eurosiberian Southern-temperate element but almost certainly a neophyte in northern Lancashire.

This is a perennial herb probably only native on a few exposed limestone cliff tops in England and Wales. However it has also been grown as a herb and ornamental plant and it has escaped into the wild in many places in England and Wales as well as in parts of Scotland and Ireland.

Very rare (1). In northern Lancashire Jenkinson (1775) reported it as plentiful about Warton Lane (SD47W) and it is just possible it could have been native on the south facing cliffs and screes of nearby Warton Crag. Otherwise it has been recorded as a casual from St Anne's and Morecambe (Wheldon and Wilson, 1907), near Preston Docks (Preston Scientific Society, 1903) and there is an unlocalised record from the 10km square SD45 (Stewart, *et al.*, 1994). The only localised post 1964 record is from a tip at Blackpool (SD33I) in 1966 (A.E.R. & J.H.). Nationally native populations are stable.

Scutellaria galericulata L.   Skullcap

Eurosiberian Boreo-temperate element.

This is a perennial herb found in a variety of wetland habitats including ponds, canals, streams and marshes etc. (BH11). It is found in much of the British Isles but it is much rarer in eastern Britain and most of Ireland than elsewhere.

Frequent (80). Skullcap is found in most of northern Lancashire but seems to be much less frequent in Lancashire VC 64 than elsewhere. Whilst its distribution in northern Lancashire is stable the 'New Atlas' reported losses. On the other hand 'Local Change' noted that a possible increase was not statistically significant.

Scutellaria minor Huds.   Lesser Skullcap

Suboceanic Southern-temperate element.

This is a perennial herb of wet heaths and nutrient poor marshes (BH11). It is found in southern and western Britain and southern and western Ireland.

Very rare (3). Old records were from localities on Lancaster Moor, Whittington Moor, Arkholme Moor (Wheldon and Wilson, 1907), Thornton (St Michael's School, 1902), Winmarleigh Moss in the mid twentieth century (Whiteside, no date) and on Nicky Nook (Heathcote, 1923). Since 1964 it has been found in Lord Lot's Wood, Over Kellet (SD57K) in

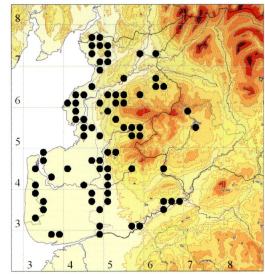

Scutellaria galericulata

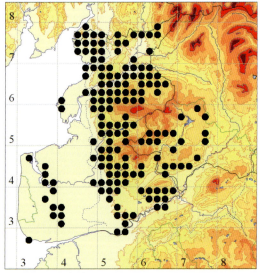

Teucrium scorodonia

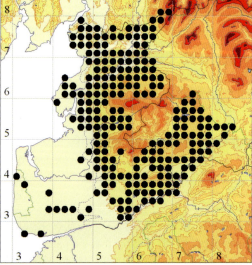

Ajuga reptans

1997 (J.M.N.), Whittington (SD57Y) in 2005 (E.F.G. & J.M.N.) and on Nicky Nook, Nether Wyresdale (SD54Z) in 2007 (C.F. & N.J.S.). The dates given are for the most recent observations. Whilst there has been a decline in the last 100 years in northern Lancashire, which is reflected nationally ('New Atlas'), no further decline was noted after 1987 ('Local Change').

Teucrium scorodonia L. — Wood Sage

Suboceanic Southern-temperate element.

Wood Sage is a rhizomatous perennial herb of well-drained, acidic, nutrient poor soils in woodland edge habitats and heaths (BH1, 9, 16). It is found throughout the British Isles although it is rare or absent in parts of eastern England and central Ireland.

Frequent (163). *T. scorodonia* occurs frequently in most of northern Lancashire but it is often absent from western areas. However some of the western records suggest that it might indicate former woodland. At present there is no quantitative evidence for a contraction of Wood Sage's distribution in northern Lancashire but recent observations suggest it has disappeared from some localities in recent years. The 'New Atlas' also reported no decline nationally but since 1987 a decline was noted by 'Local Change'.

Teucrium chamaedrys L. — Wall Germander

Neophyte with a European Southern-temperate distribution. Although there may be a native population in East Sussex it was introduced into British gardens at an early date and was first recorded in the wild by 1710. It appears to be a declining garden escape with only a few recent records in the British Isles.

In northern Lancashire it was recorded from a field at Silverdale (Wheldon and Wilson, 1907) and at Carnforth in 1908 (NMW).

Ajuga reptans L. — Bugle

European Temperate element.

This is a rhizomatous perennial herb of damp deciduous woodland and woodland edge habitats (BH1). It is found throughout the British Isles.

Common (235). In northern Lancashire Bugle occurs frequently in the north and east of the area and records further west suggest that it might indicate former woodland. However it is frequently grown in gardens and some of the localities may be garden escapes. Its distribution locally and nationally is stable.

Nepeta cataria L. — Cat-mint

Archaeophyte with a Eurosiberian Temperate distribution.

This is a perennial herb of open grassland and ruderal habitats on calcareous soils (BH3, 7). It is found mostly in the southern half of Britain with occasional records elsewhere.

Rare (7). Cat-mint was first recorded in northern Lancashire on a roadside between Lancaster and Warton in 1808 (Salmon, 1912). Other old records are from the area between Silverdale and Carnforth and at Wardleys-on-Wyre (Wheldon and Wilson, 1907). Most post 1964 records are from between Silverdale and Carnforth where a few plants were seen on a bank below Warton Crag in 2003 (E.F.G.). Other recent records are from the Fylde and Pilling. However some of these may be for *N.* × *faasenii*. The 'New Atlas' noted that nationally Cat-mint had declined considerably during the twentieth century.

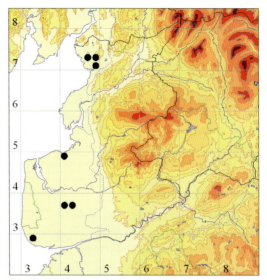

Nepeta cataria

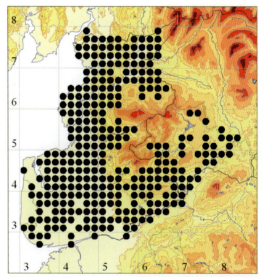

Glechoma hederacea

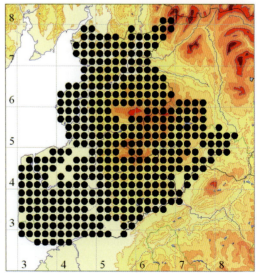

Prunella vulgaris

Nepeta racemosa Ham. × **N. nepetella** L.
(**N. × faassenii** Bergmans ex Stearn)   Garden Cat-mint

Neophyte. This is a hybrid of garden origin first raised in 1784. It is a popular garden plant but was not found in the wild until 1928. Today it is found in many parts of Britain.

Very rare (4). In northern Lancashire this was found on tipped garden refuse at Rossall (SD34C) in 1999 (C.J.B.) and naturalised on the sand dunes at Lytham St Anne's (SD33A) in 2001 and 2003 (Bradford Botany Group; E.F.G.) Other records at Lytham St Annes are from sand dunes at SD32E in 1996 and SD32I post 1990 (both C.F. & N.J.S.)

Glechoma hederacea L.   Ground-ivy

Circumpolar Boreo-temperate element.

Ground-ivy is found in woodland, woodland edges and on waste ground (BH1, 3) throughout the British Isles.

Common (312). *G. hederacea* is found throughout northern Lancashire except in the upland areas of Bowland and Leck. Its distribution is thought to be stable locally and nationally.

Prunella vulgaris L.   Selfheal

Circumpolar Wide-temperate element.

This is a perennial herb found growing in a variety of habitats ranging from woodland edges, grasslands including lawns to waste ground (BH6, 7). It occurs throughout the British Isles.

Very common (416). Selfheal is a common species throughout northern Lancashire. Its distribution locally and nationally is stable.

Melissa officinalis L.   Balm

Neophyte. Balm is a native of southern Europe, the Mediterranean region and south-western Asia. It was cultivated in British gardens by 995 and recorded in the wild by 1763. It is still a popular garden plant and today occurs on banks and roadside verges, usually close to houses and on waste ground, mostly in the southern half of the British Isles and also between Glasgow and Edinburgh in Scotland.

Rare (9). Balm was first found in northern Lancashire on Marton Mere tip, Blackpool (SD33H) in 1961 (A.E.R.). Since then it has been found in a few scattered localities in the area but most records are from Lytham St Anne's and Bryning-with-Warton.

Clinopodium ascendens (Jord.) Samp.   Common Calamint

European Temperate element but probably a neophyte in northern Lancashire.

This is a perennial herb of scrubby grassland, usually on dry base-rich soils (BH3, 16). It is found mostly in the southern half of the British Isles.

Very rare (2). Common Calamint was recorded from Yealand Hall Allotment (SD47Y) in 1973 (S.D.W.). However it has not been seen since and as there is no voucher specimen it is possible that it was wrongly identified. However there is a confirmed record from Fleetwood Dock (SD34I) where it occurred as a casual in 2004 (C.F. & N.J.S.). Both the 'New Atlas' and 'Local Change' report a decline in the distribution of this species nationally.

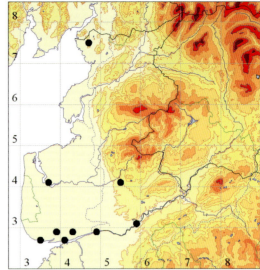

Melissa officinalis

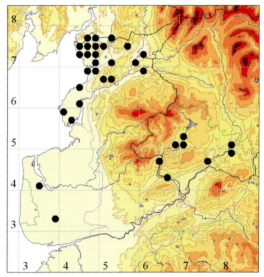

Clinopodium vulgare

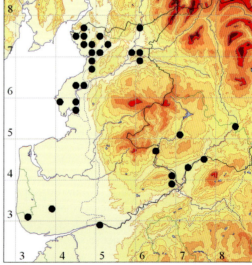

Origanum vulgare

Clinopodium vulgare L.   Wild Basil

Circumpolar Temperate element.

This is a rhizomatous perennial herb of woodland edge and grassland habitats on calcareous soils (BH7). It is found over much of England, Wales and eastern Scotland but it is rare or occurs as an introduction elsewhere in the British Isles.

Occasional (34). Wild Basil is found in scattered localities in northern Lancashire but most records are from the north or northwest of the area on calcareous soils. Although its distribution is stable in northern Lancashire and nationally since 1987 ('Local Change'), the 'New Atlas' reported losses from many parts of the country.

Clinopodium acinos (L.) Kuntze   Basil Thyme

European Temperate element.

This is an annual herb of dry open grassland and rocky habitats (BH16) found mostly in southern England but it also occurs in eastern Scotland. It is found as an introduction in Ireland.

Very rare (5). In northern Lancashire Basil Thyme is found in a few places on limestone in Silverdale, Warton and Carnforth (SD47Q, V, W, Y; SD57A). It is also found on iron slag heaps at Carnforth and Warton. Whilst its distribution in northern Lancashire is stable having found a refuge in quarries and on iron slag heaps nationally there has been a sharp decline in its distribution, which is continuing ('New Atlas', 'Local Change').

Origanum vulgare L.   Wild Marjoram

Eurasian Southern-temperate element.

Wild Marjoram is a perennial herb of dry, infertile, open calcareous scrub, grassland and rocky habitats (BH7, 16). It is found in England, Wales, Ireland, southern and eastern Scotland.

Occasional (30). In northern Lancashire *O. vulgare* is found in the north and east of the area and very rarely elsewhere. Its distribution locally and nationally is largely stable.

Thymus polytrichus A. Kern. ex Borbás   Wild Thyme

European Boreo-temperate element.

This is a perennial herb of well-drained, base-rich substrates in grassland and heath (BH7, 16). It is found in many parts of the British Isles but it is rare or absent in many central and eastern areas of England, Devon and central Ireland.

Occasional (63). In northern Lancashire Wild Thyme is found in the north and east of the area and in coastal areas of VC 60. Wheldon and Wilson (1907) suggested Wild Thyme was common throughout VC 60 but particularly in the north of the vice-county. Its absence today from most of the central and southern parts of the area suggests a contraction of its range locally during the last 100 years. This is consistent with a national decline reported by both the 'New Atlas' and 'Local Change'.

Lycopus europaeus L.   Gypsywort

Eurosiberian Temperate element.

Gypsywort is a rhizomatous perennial herb of wet habitats by streams, canals, ditches and marshes (BH11). It is found in England, Wales, Ireland and Scotland but in the north of its range it is commoner in the west than elsewhere.

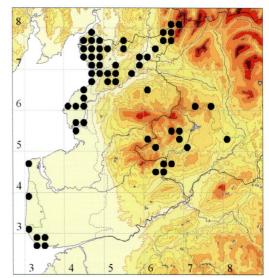
Thymus polytrichus

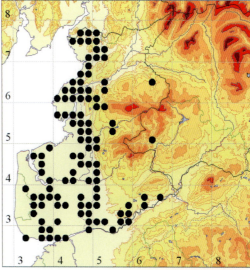
Lycopus europaeus

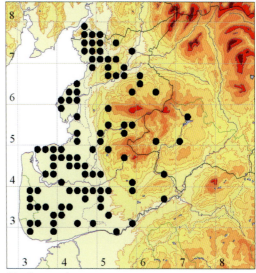
Mentha arvensis

Frequent (107). In northern Lancashire it is found in the west of the area and in the western part of the Ribble valley with few localities elsewhere. Locally Gypsywort's distribution is stable but nationally 'Local Change' reports an increase.

Mentha arvensis L.   Corn Mint

Circumpolar Boreo-temperate element.

This is a rhizomatous perennial herb found in cultivated and waste ground and occasionally in other open habitats (BH4, 11). It is found throughout the British Isles.

Frequent (100). In northern Lancashire Corn Mint is found in scattered localities throughout the area. Its distribution appears to be stable locally but nationally it has declined.

Mentha arvensis × M. aquatica (M. × verticillata L.) Whorled Mint

This is a naturally occurring but usually sterile hybrid found throughout Europe although it is rare in the Mediterranean region. It is a rhizomatous perennial herb found in a variety of habitats throughout the British Isles and is able to spread when portions of its rhizome become detached and are carried away by stream currents etc.

Frequent (79). In northern Lancashire Whorled Mint is found throughout the area but it is especially common by the Lancaster Canal and in the Lune valley. It is not known if its distribution has changed, as Wheldon and Wilson did not recognise it. Nationally the 'New Atlas' reported losses.

Mentha arvensis × M. aquatica × M. spicata
(M. × smithiana R.A. Graham)   Tall Mint

Tall Mint is a hybrid that may arise spontaneously but more usually occurs as a garden outcast. It occurs widely in Europe and in many parts of the British Isles but especially in England and Wales. It was first recorded in Britain in 1724.

Very rare (2). In northern Lancashire this was first reported from the R. Hodder (SD64V; Anon, 1891) but this could be an error for *M. × gracilis*. It was found later from the R. Lune near Lancaster (SD46W) in 1989 (B.S.B.I.) and from river and rail banks at Caton-with-Littledale (SD56C) in 1998 (B.S.B.I.). Halliday (1997) suggests that records from the R. Lune near Kirkby Lonsdale may be errors for *M. × gracilis* but material at LIV indicates that both hybrids occur on the R. Lune.

Mentha arvensis × M. spicata (M. × gracilis Sole)   Bushy Mint

This is a spontaneous hybrid found widely in Europe, including the British Isles, in damp places and on waste ground. Many records are of garden escapes.

Occasional (15). In northern Lancashire this was recorded by Wheldon and Wilson (1907) from the Lune valley below Kirkby Lonsdale, from between Caton and Aughton and on the bank of the R. Hodder 'near Mitton'. Today most records are still from the Lune and Hodder valleys. Over the last 100 years Bushy Mint may have spread a little. However nationally the situation is less certain through confusion with other taxa but the 'New Atlas' suggests it may have declined.

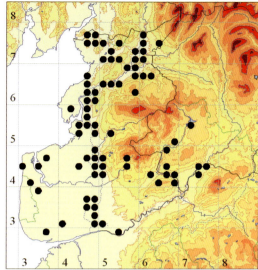

Mentha × verticillata

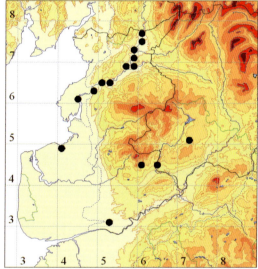

Mentha × gracilis

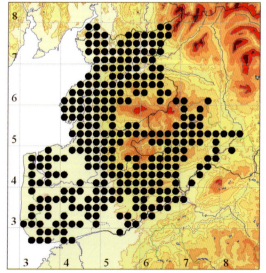

Mentha aquatica

Mentha aquatica L.   Water Mint

European Temperate element.

This is a rhizomatous perennial herb found in permanently wet places
(BH11). It is found throughout the British Isles.

Common (305). Water Mint is found throughout northern Lancashire. Its
distribution is stable locally and nationally.

Mentha aquatica × M. spicata (M. × piperita L.)   Peppermint

This is a spontaneous hybrid between a native and an introduced species.
It occurs in damp grassland and in ruderal habitats in Europe including
many parts of the British Isles.

Occasional (22). Wheldon and Wilson (1907) recorded this from at least
nine scattered localities in VC 60 and post 1964 records are also from
scattered places across northern Lancashire. It is not thought that its distribution has changed locally or nationally.

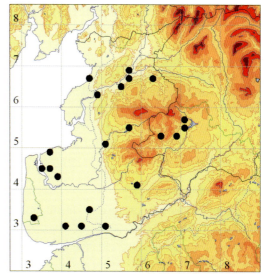

Mentha × piperita

Mentha spicata L.   Spear Mint

Archaeophyte, which has probably arisen by hybridisation in cultivation
but its origin is unknown. It is found throughout the British Isles in ruderal
habitats (BH3, 17).

Frequent (98). In northern Lancashire Spear Mint was first recorded from
near St Anne's and Halton (Wheldon and Wilson, 1907). Today it is found
throughout the area although it seems to be absent from pastoral areas to
the northeast of Preston and in parts of Bowland. Its increase in northern
Lancashire is reflected nationally.

Mentha spicata × M. longifolia (L.) Huds.
(M. × villosonervata Opiz)   Sharp-toothed Mint

Neophyte. This hybrid is commonly cultivated in gardens and was known
from the wild by 1934. It is probably widespread in Europe and although it
occurs throughout the British Isles it is probably under recorded because of
identification difficulties.

Rare (8). In northern Lancashire this was first recorded from St Anne's in
1962 (A.E.R.). Post 1964 records are from Nether Kellet and coastal localities between Fleetwood and Carnforth.

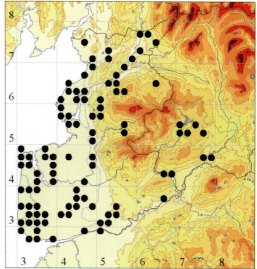

Mentha spicata

Mentha spicata × M. suaveolens Ehrh. **(M. × villosa** Huds.)
                                                          Apple Mint

Neophyte. This hybrid is a rhizomatous perennial herb naturalised in damp
ruderal habitats. It is widespread in Europe and in the British Isles, where it
was first recorded in the wild by 1882. It is a common garden taxon.

Occasional (31). In northern Lancashire it was first recorded, as var. *alope-
curoides* (Hull) Briq., from Ashton in 1883 (MANCH). It was recorded later
from Bare (SD46M) in 1960 (R.M.H.) and post 1964 records are mostly
from the northwest of the area with a few scattered localities in other
parts of northern Lancashire.

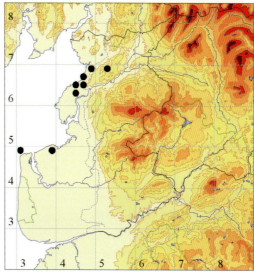

Mentha × villosonervata

Mentha longifolia × M. suaveolens
(**M. × rotundifolia** (L.) Huds.)   False Apple-mint

Neophyte. This hybrid is a rhizomatous perennial herb found in ruderal habitats. It is frequent with the parents in Europe and south-western Asia and occurs as a garden escape in scattered places in the British Isles. It was known to occur in the wild by 1900 but identification difficulties probably means that it is under recorded.

Very rare (1). The only confirmed record in northern Lancashire is from Tunstall (SD67B) in 1980 (C.F. & N.J.S.). It is also possible that it may have been seen at Heysham but this may have been *M. × villosa*.

Mentha pulegium L.   Pennyroyal

European Southern-temperate element but probably only a casual neophyte in northern Lancashire.

Pennyroyal is found in seasonally inundated grasslands (BH6, 13) in the southern half of the British Isles.

Very rare (1). In northern Lancashire the only records are from near Garstang (Preston Scientific Society, 1903), an unlocalised record from the 10km square SD65 (Stewart, *et al.*, 1994) and for a brief period in 1995 on a roadside at Gisburn (SD84J; Abbott, 2005).

Lavandula angustifolia Mill.   Garden Lavender

Neophyte. This evergreen shrub is found in the western Mediterranean region and was introduced into British cultivation in the seventeenth century. It is a popular garden plant but was not recorded in the wild until 1984. Today it is found in a few localities in southern Britain and the Isle of Man.

Very rare (1). In northern Lancashire self-sown plants were found by the boundary wall to a parish hall in Carnforth (SD47V) in 2000 (E.F.G. & J.M.N.).

Salvia verbenaca L.   Wild Clary

Mediterranean-Atlantic element.

This is an aromatic perennial herb found in well-drained calcareous grassland (BH3, 7), mostly in southern Britain but extending northwards to northern Wales and on the east coast to the Firth of Forth. In Ireland it is a coastal species.

Very rare (2). In northern Lancashire Petty (1902) found Wild Clary in two localities in Silverdale (SD47M, S). One of the localities is today a site for *Orchis morio* and *Spiranthes spiralis* and is typical of the native situations for Wild Clary in southern England. It was recorded as a casual at Fairhaven (SD32I) in 1999 and at St Anne's (SD32J) in 2000 and 2005 (both C.F. & N.J.S.). It was also doubtfully recorded from Ribchester in 1956. Nationally *S. verbenaca* has declined ('New Atlas').

[Salvia viridis L.   Annual Clary

Neophyte. Annual Clary is a native of the Mediterranean region and south-western Asia. It was introduced into British cultivation by 1596 and recorded in the wild by 1859. It occurs in scattered localities in south-eastern Britain but there have been few records since 1970.

In northern Lancashire there is an unlocalised, unattributed record from 1901 for the 10 × 10km square SD47 (B.R.C.).]

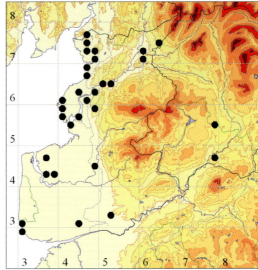

Mentha × villosa

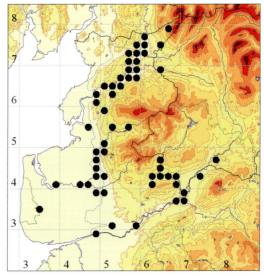

Mimulus guttatus s.l.

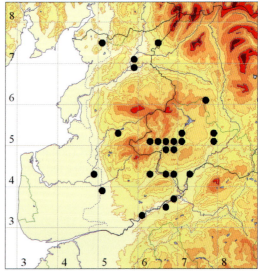

Mimulus × robertsii

Salvia verticillata L.   Whorled Clary

Neophyte. This has a European Southern-temperate distribution and was introduced into British cultivation by 1594. It was recorded in the wild by 1857 and today occurs in scattered localities in England, Wales and southern Scotland.

Very rare (2). In northern Lancashire this was found at St Anne's in 1907–8 (Bailey, 1910). Post 1964 records are from dry stony places and old iron workings at Carnforth (SD47V, 57A), where it is apparently naturalised (Livermore and Livermore, 1987; J.M.N.).

Salvia nemorosa L.   Balkan Clary

Neophyte. This is a Eurasian species imported as a grain impurity and known since 1908 from Cornwall (French, *et al.*, 2006). Otherwise it is only found as a rare alien.

In northern Lancashire Balkan Clary was found on the sand dunes at Lytham St Anne's in 1908 (C.B.; MANCH) but originally identified as *S. viridis*.

Salvia × andrzejowskii Blocki

This hybrid is a native of south-western Asia with only a few British records; all before 1930.

In northern Lancashire it was found 'plentifully' at St Anne's although few plants reached maturity (Bailey, 1910).

PHRYMACEAE   MONKEYFLOWER FAMILY

Mimulus moschatus Douglas ex Lindl.   Musk

Neophyte. This is a native of western North America that was introduced into British gardens in 1826. It was recorded from the wild in 1866. Today it occurs throughout Britain and more rarely in Ireland.

Very rare (2). Musk was first recorded in northern Lancashire by a small stream south of Woodacre Great Wood (SD54D) in 1958 (M.J.) where it was seen again in 1989 (B.S.B.I.). It was also found on a roadside verge at Tarnbrook (SD55X) in 1985 (E.F.G.) and where it was seen in 2007 (E.F.G.).

Mimulus guttatus DC.   Monkeyflower

Neophyte. This is a native of western North America and was probably introduced into British cultivation in 1812. It soon became established and was known from the wild by 1824. It spreads by seed and vegetatively but it is often confused with the hybrid *M. guttatus × M. luteus*. *M. guttatus* is found throughout the British Isles but at least some records probably belong to the hybrid.

Occasional (55). In northern Lancashire records for *M. guttatus* and *M. × robertsii* have been combined. As such *M. guttatus sensu lato* was first recorded by A. Wilson in 1887 (Wheldon

and Wilson, 1907) from near Chipping (SD64I). By 1907 Wheldon and Wilson had recorded it from several localities in the Lune, Wyre and Ribble valleys. Recent work suggests *M. guttatus sensu stricto* occurs in the Ribble valley, in the R. Hodder at Newton (SD65V), by the R. Calder (SD54B) and at Blackpool (SD33M) and may well be frequent in these southern and coastal areas.

Mimulus guttatus × M. luteus L.
(M. × robertsii Silverside)   Hybrid Monkeyflower

This is an almost sterile hybrid of garden origin. It was not recognised in Britain until 1964 and was not named until 1990. The earliest record traced is from Berwickshire in 1872 and today it is the commonest Monkeyflower of higher ground, especially in northern England, southern Scotland and in the north of Ireland.

Occasional (25). In northern Lancashire Hybrid Monkeyflower occurs in scattered localities mostly in the east of the area. It was confirmed from the Langden Brook, Trough of Bowland (SD65K) in 2010 (E.F.G.).

OROBANCHACEAE   BROOMRAPE FAMILY

Melampyrum pratense L. ssp. **pratense**
                                        Common Cow-wheat

Eurosiberian Boreo-temperate element.

This is an annual hemiparasite found on well-drained, nutrient poor acidic soils in woodlands, woodland margins and heaths (BH1, 2) over much of the British Isles. However it is rare or absent in parts of central and eastern England and parts of Ireland.

Occasional (31). In northern Lancashire Common Cow-wheat is found at mid-altitude on *Calluna* heaths of Bowland and in other heathy places in the north of the area. More rarely it is found in the west of northern Lancashire. Its distribution is probably similar to that of 100 years ago but it is possibly not as frequent. It has declined nationally over a long period and this is continuing ('New Atlas', 'Local Change').

Euphrasia L.   Eyebrights

This is a genus of annual hemiparasites found in grasslands. It is a highly critical genus with many hybrids giving rise to considerable difficulties in naming individual specimens. In this account an attempt is made to provide details of the species and hybrids found in northern Lancashire. Fortunately the relatively small number of species, some of which are extinct or very rare, limit the complexity. Nevertheless because of problems in identification it is difficult to assess change.

Euphrasia officinalis L. ssp. **pratensis** Schübl. & G. Martens
Roskov's Eyebright

European Boreo-temperate element.

This eyebright grows in damp herb-rich hay meadows and lightly grazed pastures (BH6). It occurs in Ireland, Wales, northern England, central and southern Scotland.

Very rare (4) or extinct. In northern Lancashire Wheldon and Wilson (1925) found *E. officinalis* ssp. *pratensis* near Low Gill in Hindburndale, Roeburndale and in upper Claughton near Garstang (SD54L). It was also found at Waterslack, Silverdale (SD47T) in 1957 (V.G.; LIV). Since 1964 it has been seen (Livermore and Livermore, 1987) in Caton-with-Littledale (SD56W), Roeburndale (SD66B) and Hindburndale (SD66M, N). The site near Garstang was lost to agricultural improvement in the 1940s whilst at the other sites the vegetation seems to have become more luxuriant, probably through generalised eutrophication. It was last seen in Hindburndale in 2000 (J.M.N.). The 'New Atlas' also shows losses throughout its range in the British Isles with extinction in central England.

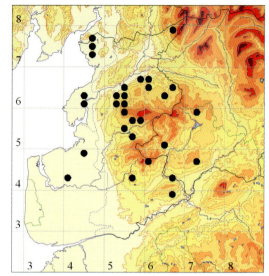
Melampyrum pratense

Euphrasia officinalis L. ssp. **anglica** (Pugsley) Silverside
English Eyebright

Endemic.

E. anglica is a difficult species to identify but it is found in heathy grassland (BH10, 16) in the southern half of the British Isles.

Extinct. In northern Lancashire this was identified from herbarium material collected in Roeburndale (SD66B) in 1975 (J.M.N.; LIV).

Euphrasia arctica Lange ex Rostrup ssp. **borealis** (F. Towns.) Yeo
Arctic Eyebright

Oceanic Boreal-temperate element.

This robust eyebright is found in damp, neutral hay meadows and on roadside verges (BH6, 11) in northern Britain, Ireland, Wales and occasionally elsewhere.

Occasional (17). In northern Lancashire *E. arctica* has been found in the north and east of the area. Qualitative evidence suggests it has become rarer in recent years and that it may be largely confined to the Slaidburn area. The 'New Atlas' shows losses throughout the British Isles.

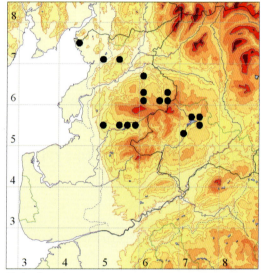
Euphrasia arctica

Euphrasia arctica × E. confusa

Because of identification difficulties the wider distribution of this hybrid is not known. In the British Isles it occurs in unimproved grassland in northern and western parts of Britain and in Ireland but it is likely to be very much under recorded.

Very rare (4). In northern Lancashire *E. arctica × E. confusa* was identified from Roeburndale (SD66H, M, S; Livermore and Livermore, 1987) and from Caton-with-Littledale (SD56W) in 1999 (J.M.N.; LIV).

Euphrasia arctica × E. nemorosa

Although likely to be widespread in unimproved grasslands where the two parents overlap in their distribution there is little information about this hybrid. Halliday (1997) suggests it is not infrequent in Cumbria.

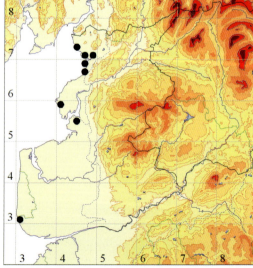
Euphrasia tetraquetra

Very rare (1). It is thought that this hybrid was found in hay meadows at Tarnbrook, Over Wyresdale (SD55X) in 1999 (E.F.G.; LIV).

Euphrasia arctica × E. tetraquetra

This is a very rare hybrid as the distributions of the parents rarely overlap. However a few inland records in Britain have been reported.

Very rare (1). In northern Lancashire Stocks Reservoir near Slaidburn attracts large numbers of wildfowl and gulls and it is possibly through their migration from coastal areas that the coastal *E. tetraquetra* was brought into contact with the upland *E. arctica*. The hybrid between the two species was found on a grassy bank by the reservoir shore (SD75C) in 2007 (E.F.G.).

Euphrasia tetraquetra (Bréb.) Arrond.   Western Eyebright

Oceanic Temperate element.

This distinctive species is found on short turf on coastal sand dunes and cliffs (BH6, 10) around many of the coasts of the British Isles. However it readily hybridises with other species so that finding examples of the species is sometimes difficult.

Rare (8). In northern Lancashire *E. tetraquetra* is found on sea cliffs at Silverdale, on iron slag at Warton, on stabilized shingle at Bolton-le-Sands and Hest Bank, Heysham, Glasson and on sand dunes at Lytham St Anne's. There is also a 1900 record from a sea bank near Little Bispham (NMW, CGE, YRK). At most sites many of the plants were hybrids and finding convincing specimens of the species is difficult.

Euphrasia tetraquetra × E. nemorosa

This is likely to be common where the distributions of the two parents overlap.

Very rare (4). This is thought to be very much under recorded but it has been identified from sites at Silverdale (SD47M), Heysham (SD45E), Glasson (SD45M) and Lytham St Anne's (SD33A).

Euphrasia tetraquetra × E. confusa

This is possibly a less frequent hybrid than the previous one but it is likely to occur where the distributions of the parents overlap.

Very rare (2). In northern Lancashire there is a 1908 record from Bolton-le-Sands (J.W. Ellis; LIV) that is thought to be this hybrid. It was also thought to occur at Silverdale (SD47M; Livermore and Livermore, 1987) and Carnforth (SD47V; Livermore and Livermore, 1990a).

Euphrasia nemorosa (Pers.) Wallr.   Common Eyebright

European Temperate element.

This is thought to be the commonest British eyebright occurring in short grasslands, in open scrub and woodland rides (BH7, 10) throughout the British Isles.

Frequent (78). In northern Lancashire *E. nemorosa* is found throughout the area but most localities are in the north, especially in the northwest, and east of the region. It is thought that as unimproved grasslands have been lost and the vegetation of banks and roadside verges has become more luxuriant the distribution and frequency of this species has declined. The 'New Atlas' shows losses all over the British Isles.

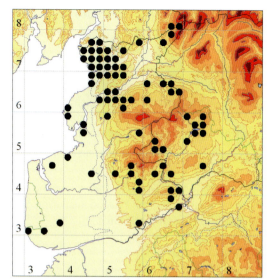

Euphrasia nemorosa

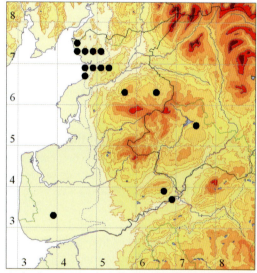

Euphrasia nemorosa × E. confusa

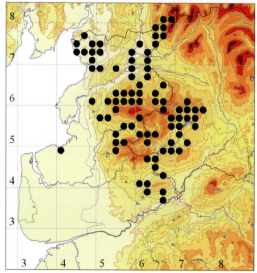

Euphrasia confusa

Euphrasia nemorosa × E. confusa

This hybrid occurs in grasslands where the distributions of the parents overlap and it is found in much of western and northern parts of the British Isles.

Rare (16). In northern Lancashire *E. nemorosa* × *E. confusa* is found in northern and eastern parts of the area.

Euphrasia nemorosa × E. scottica

This hybrid occurs in damp upland areas by flushes and tracks where the distributions of the parents overlap.

Very rare (3). In northern Lancashire this hybrid was recorded by Livermore and Livermore (1987) from Yealand Redmayne (SD47Y), Over Wyresdale (SD55M) and Quernmore (SD56F).

Euphrasia confusa Pugsley   Confused Eyebright

Oceanic Boreo-temperate element.

This eyebright is a rather small annual of grazed and heathy pastures on both acidic and calcareous soils (BH7, 8, 16). It is especially characteristic of hill pastures in northern and western Britain but it occurs occasionally elsewhere. It is mainly coastal in Ireland.

Frequent (86). *E. confusa* is found mostly in the north and east of northern Lancashire. It is the commonest species of eyebright in the area but it readily hybridises with other species and it is likely that at least some of the species records are of hybrids.

Euphrasia confusa × E. micrantha

E. confusa × *E. micrantha* is likely to occur where the distribution of the parents overlap, e.g. on heathy roadside verges in upland area. However in north-western England *E. micrantha* is very rare so that opportunities for hybridisation are rare.

Very rare (3). This hybrid was recorded by Livermore and Livermore (1987) in northern Lancashire from grassland in Leck (SD68V) and what was believed to be this from Warton Crag (SD47W) in 1999 (J.M.N.). *E. micrantha* was recorded from a heathy roadside at 420m in Easington (SD76F) in 2005 (E.F.G.) but it is believed this may be the hybrid *E. confusa* × *E. micrantha*.

Euphrasia confusa × E. scottica

The fertile hybrid *E. confusa* × *E. scottica* occurs in hill flushes and stream banks in Scotland, northern England and Wales.

Rare (10). In northern Lancashire this hybrid is found in scattered localities in the east and north of the area.

Euphrasia micrantha Rchb.   Slender Eyebright

European Temperate element.

This is a small annual eyebright characterised by its purple coloration found on acid heaths and moorlands (BH8, 10) and is found throughout the upland areas of the British Isles. However it is rare in north-western England.

Very rare (1). In northern Lancashire there are records from 1907 (A.W.; LIV) on both sides of the old Lancashire – Yorkshire border on the Tatham

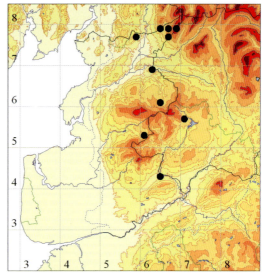
Euphrasia confusa × E. scottica

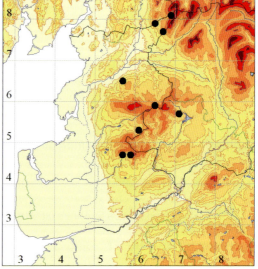
Euphrasia scottica

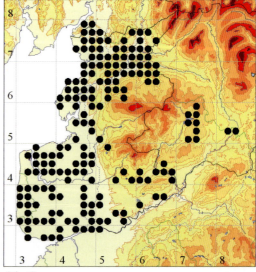
Odontites vernus

Fells and from near Hareden in the Trough of Bowland (SD65K). The only recently confirmed record is from Easington (SD65Z; Abbott, 2005). Other reports of this species are likely to be or are confirmed hybrids, e.g. from Easington (SD76F) in 2005 (E.F.G.), Silverdale in 1904 (NMW) and 1972 (G. Gorton, MANCH), Carnforth (SD47W) in 1986 (B.S.B.I.) and Warton Crag (SD47W) in 1965 (A.E.R.).

Euphrasia scottica Wettst.   Scottish Eyebright

European Boreal-montane element.

E. scottica is a small annual eyebright found in hill flushes and wet moorland areas (BH10, 11, 15) in northern and western Britain and in Ireland.

Rare (9). In northern Lancashire *E. scottica* is at the southern limit of its distribution in England and occurs in a few localities in the Bowland Fells and Leck. It readily hybridises with other species, especially *E. confusa*, and most colonies seem to be a mixture of hybrids and true species.

Odontites vernus (Bellardi) Dumort.   Red Bartsia

Eurasian Temperate element.

Red Bartsia is an annual root hemiparasite of short trampled grasslands, tracks and waste places (BH6). It is found throughout the British Isles. There are three subspecies. Ssp. *vernus* occurs all over the British Isles but it is perhaps most frequent in northern Britain. Ssp. *serotinus* (Syme) Corb. is found mostly in southern Britain and Ireland whilst ssp. *litoralis* (Fr.) Nyman is found in coastal areas of northern Britain.

Frequent (182). In northern Lancashire *O. vernus* is found throughout the area. Although a lot of populations were examined it proved difficult to assign many plants to any subspecies. Nevertheless it is clear that both ssp. *vernus* and ssp. *serotinus* are found in the area. Surprisingly few plants were thought to be ssp. *vernus* although Halliday (1997) reports that this is much more frequent than ssp. *serotinus* in Cumbria and Abbott (2005) considers that only ssp. *vernus* is found in Mid-west Yorkshire (VC 64). In northern Lancashire ssp. *serotinus* appears to have a coastal distribution, which is in line with its predominantly southern distribution in Britain. Ssp. *litoralis* has not been found in northern Lancashire but occurs on the shore at Askam-in-Furness in Cumbria (Halliday, 1997) and may occur on the shores of Morecambe Bay. It is believed the distribution of *O. vernus* is stable both locally and nationally.

Parentucellia viscosa (L.) Caruel   Yellow Bartsia

Mediterranean-Atlantic element.

This is a hemiparasitic annual herb of damp open grassy places on sandy soils and often grows in drier dune slacks and on heathy pastures (BH3, 5). Its native distribution is largely coastal in western and southern Britain and Ireland but it is also found as an introduction at many inland sites in Britain.

Rare (6). In northern Lancashire its native distribution is confined to the sand dunes at Lytham St Anne's. Post 1964 records are from SD32I and 32J in the 1960s (A.E.R., E.F.G.) but today it is probably confined to a golf course (SD33A) where it was last seen in 2008 (C.F. & N.J.S.). It was also found as a casual on a tip in Lancaster (SD46R) in 1990 (L.A.L. & P.D.L.), on the grassy margin of the crematorium at St Anne's (SD32P) in 1996 (C.F. & N.J.S.) and on West Bradford Fell in 1992 (SD74I; Abbott, 2005).

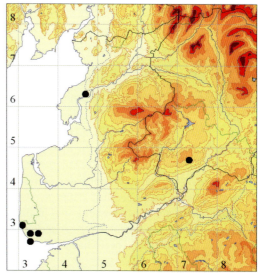

Parentucellia viscosa

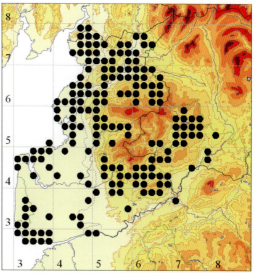

Rhinanthus minor

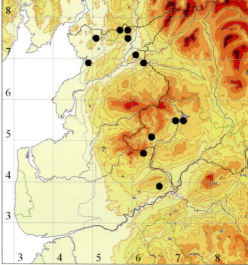

Pedicularis palustris

Rhinanthus minor L.   Yellow-rattle

European Boreo-temperate element.

This is an annual root hemiparasite of nutrient poor grasslands in a variety of habitats (BH6) and occurs throughout the British Isles. In suitable places it can be abundant. There are several subspecies but only ssp. *minor* and ssp. *stenophyllus* (Schur) O. Schwarz are thought to occur in northern Lancashire.

Frequent (187). Yellow rattle is found throughout northern Lancashire although it is rare or absent from the most intensively farmed areas and moorlands. Most populations are of ssp. *minor* but it is likely that ssp. *stenophyllus* is frequent in the north and east of the area. Yellow-rattle's distribution has probably declined in northern Lancashire although the reduction of nutrient poor grasslands may be balanced to some extent by its inclusion in amenity seed mixtures. A decline nationally noted by the 'New Atlas' is continuing ('Local Change').

Pedicularis palustris L.   Marsh Lousewort

European Boreo-temperate element.

This is an annual or biennial root hemiparasite found in a wide range of nutrient poor wet places including grasslands, fens and hill flushes (BH11). It is found throughout the British Isles.

Rare (12). In northern Lancashire Marsh Lousewort is confined to a few bogs, fens and flushes in the north and east of the area. It was recorded from at least fifteen sites 100 years ago in VC 60. It has gone from most of these and today it is only known with certainty from two sites in the vice-county. Nationally there were considerable losses in central and southern England ('New Atlas') but further losses since 1987 appear to be limited ('Local Change').

Pedicularis sylvatica L. ssp. **sylvatica**   Lousewort

European Temperate element.

Lousewort is a perennial root hemiparasite of damp grassy heaths, flushes and bogs on wet acid soil (BH10, 12, 14). It is found throughout the British Isles.

Frequent (71). *P. sylvatica* is found in northern Lancashire in many localities in the east and north of the area. Although Wheldon and Wilson (1907) recorded Lousewort as rare in the west of VC 60 it was only absent from the Fylde. Thus it appears that with losses in the west it has declined in northern Lancashire and this is consistent with the decline noted nationally by the 'New Atlas', especially for midland and eastern England, and which is continuing post 1987 ('Local Change').

Lathraea squamaria L.   Toothwort

European Temperate element.

This is an annual or perennial parasitic herb found on the roots of woody plants in woodlands and woodland edge habitats (BH1, 3) in most of the British Isles except northern Scotland.

Occasional (32). In northern Lancashire Toothwort is found in many areas of the north and east of the region. Although there is some evidence that a few sites have been lost in recent years it appears that it has become much more widespread, especially in the north of the area, over the last

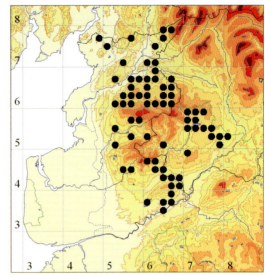
Pedicularis sylvatica

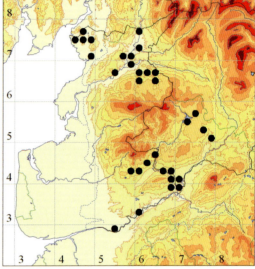
Lathraea squamaria

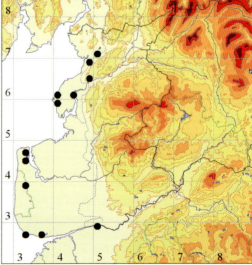
Orobanche minor

100 years. Nationally the 'New Atlas' reported losses but since 1987 'Local Change' reported no change or possibly an increase. It is not clear why these fluctuations should be taking place but it is possible that Toothwort flowers sporadically in some places.

Orobanche minor Sm.   Common Broomrape

European Southern-temperate element.

Common Broomrape is an annual root parasite found on a wide variety of hosts in grassy and waste places (BH4, 5). It is found in England, parts of Wales and as an introduced species in parts of northern England, Scotland and Ireland.

Rare (12). In northern Lancashire *O. minor* has been found at various coastal localities from Carnforth to Preston. However it rarely persists in any one locality for many years and in any single year only one or two sightings, at most, are reported. Wheldon and Wilson (1907) had records from Lytham, where it is still found from time to time, and Garstang, but its apparent increase over the last 100 years is probably not significant. Similarly it has been difficult to assess if there have been any changes in its distribution nationally.

LENTIBULARIACEAE   BLADDERWORT FAMILY

Pinguicula vulgaris L.   Common Butterwort

Circumpolar Boreal-montane element.

This is an insectivorous perennial herb of damp nutrient poor habitats, e.g. flushes and irrigated cliffs etc. (BH11, 12). It occurs throughout the British Isles.

Occasional (26). Common Butterwort is found in various localities in the east and north of the area. Wheldon and Wilson (1907) found *P. vulgaris* in all parts of VC 60 except the Fylde. It has become much scarcer over the last 100 years and in recent years further sites have been lost. Nationally the 'New Atlas' showed that Common Butterwort had been lost from much of midland and southern England and 'Local Change' reported that losses have continued since 1987.

Pinguicula grandiflora Lam.   Large-flowered Butterwort

Oceanic Temperate element but a neophyte in northern Lancashire. This is a native species in south-western Ireland but it occurs occasionally elsewhere in Ireland, England and Wales as an introduction.

Very rare (1). This conspicuous species was found in a flush on Clougha (SD56F) in 2007 (J.M.N.).

Utricularia vulgaris L.   Greater Bladderwort

Eurosiberian Temperate element.

U. vulgaris is an insectivorous species found in nutrient poor and base-rich water (BH11) in scattered localities in the British Isles.

Very rare (3 or 4). Prior to 1964 Greater Bladderwort had been found in at least nine localities in northern Lancashire. Since 1964 it has been found in Hawes Water (SD47T) where it was last seen in 1999 (R.P.-J.), Crag Bank, Carnforth (SD46Z) where it was last seen in 1999 (J.M.N.) and from a

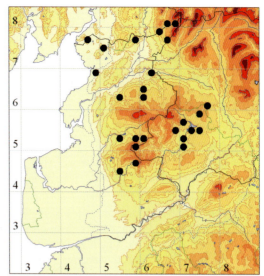
Pinguicula vulgaris

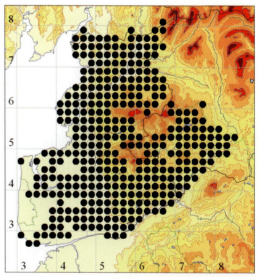
Ilex aquifolium

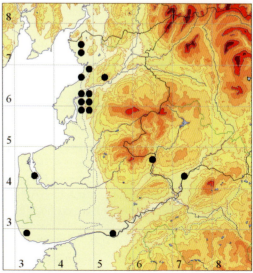
Campanula poscharskyana

pond at Stubbins Bridge near Garstang (SD54B) where it was seen in 1965 but had gone by 1999 (E.F.G.). There is also an unlocalised record from tetrad SD66M in 1969 but this seems doubtful. Nationally Greater Bladderwort has declined ('New Atlas') no doubt suffering from generalised eutrophication.

Utricularia australis R. Br.   Bladderwort
Eurasian Boreo-temperate element.

Bladderwort is an insectivorous aquatic species found in nutrient poor but often in neutral or acid water (BH11). It is found in scattered localities in the British Isles.

Very rare (1). In northern Lancashire *U. australis* has only been found in one of the pools on Storrs Moss, Yealand Redmayne (SD47X) in 2008 (R.S.P.B.). However it was probably this that was recorded on Storrs Moss by A.W. (Wheldon and Wilson, 1907) but then recorded as *U. vulgaris*.

Utricularia minor L.   Lesser Bladderwort
Circumpolar Boreo-temperate element.

This is a small insectivorous perennial herb of nutrient poor, usually acidic water in bog pools and at the edge of lakes (BH11, 12). It has been found in most parts of the British Isles but more usually in the west and north.

Extinct. In northern Lancashire this was found at Arkholme-with-Cawood (Jenkinson, 1775), Silverdale in 1864 (W.P.H.: RAMM) and at Outfield Moss, Whittington (SD57X) where it was last seen in 1944 (H.E.B.). Nationally there have been losses throughout the British Isles and it has gone from most parts of midland and eastern England ('New Atlas'). However further losses since 1987 have not occurred ('Local Change').

VERBENACEAE   VERVAIN FAMILY

Verbena officinalis L.   Vervain
Archaeophyte with a Eurasian Southern-temperate distribution.

This is a perennial herb of open habitats often on free-draining calcareous soils (BH3, 16). Vervain has been known from the vicinity of human settlements since Neolithic times and was widely cultivated in medieval gardens. It is found in the southern half of the British Isles.

Very rare (4). Most old records in northern Lancashire are from the Silverdale and Warton areas where at one time it seems to have been abundant on roadsides (e.g. Fielding MS). Other records were from Wennington, between Bolton-le-Sands and Carnforth, Woodplumpton and Ashton (Wheldon and Wilson, 1907). Post 1964 records are confined to the vicinity of Jenny Brown's Point, Silverdale (SD47R) where it was last seen in 1985 (Arnside Naturalists), Halton (SD56C) in 1976 (C.F. & N.J.S.), Preston (SD53A) in 2003 (Anon) and Carnforth (SD47W) in 2006 (J.Cl.). Localities around Morecambe Bay are at the

northern edge of its British distribution and today seems to appear only as a rare casual. Nationally there were substantial losses between 1962 and 1987 ('New Atlas') but since 1987 there have been gains ('Local Change').

Verbena bonariensis L.   Argentinian Vervain
Neophyte. This is a casual garden escape found in a few scattered places in England and the Isle of Man. It is a native of eastern South America and was introduced into British gardens by 1732. It was first recorded in the wild in 1949.

Very rare (2). A single plant of Argentinian Vervain was found at Silverdale (SD47S) in 1998 (A.U.) and several plants persisted at Warton (SD42E) between 2006 and 2008 (C.F. & N.J.S.).

AQUIFOLIACEAE   HOLLY FAMILY

Ilex aquifolium L.   Holly
Suboceanic Southern-temperate element.

This evergreen shrub or small tree is found in woodlands, hedgerows and other woodland edge habitats (BH1, 3) throughout the British Isles except on the higher mountains. However it is widely planted and there are many cultivars some of which escape into the wild.

Very common (363). In northern Lancashire Holly is only absent from the Bowland and Leck fells, coastal areas of the Fylde and peat covered areas. There has been no change in its distribution locally or nationally although managers of woodlands in northern Lancashire report that in recent years it has become increasingly common.

Ilex aquifolium × I. perado Aiton
(**I. × altaclerensis** (Loudon) Dallim.)   Highclere Holly
This is a hybrid of garden origin that arose in cultivation before 1800 but was distributed from Loddiges Nursery in Hampshire from 1836. It is widely planted and is available in numerous cultivars but can be difficult to distinguish from *Ilex aquifolium*. It is almost certainly under recorded and the patchy distribution shown in the 'New Atlas' probably reflects the distribution of recorders rather than that of the hybrid.

Very rare (5). In northern Lancashire it has been recorded from Bolton-le-Sands (SD46Z) in 1999 (M.S.), Lancaster (SD46R) and Preston (SD52P) both in 2006 (Anon) and from two localities in Lancashire VC 64 (SD64R, X; Abbott, 2005).

CAMPANULACEAE   BELLFLOWER FAMILY

Campanula persicifolia L.   Peach-leaved Bellflower
Neophyte with a European Temperate distribution. It was introduced into British cultivation before 1596 and since then it has spread to most parts of Britain.

Very rare (5). *C. persicifolia* was first found in northern Lancashire in a meadow by the R. Lune between Caton and Claughton in 1941 (J.N.F.). Post 1964 records are from Silverdale (SD47S) in 1965 (C.J.-P. & P. Newton) and at an unlocalised Silverdale site in 1967, by a roadside in Over Wyresdale (SD55S; Livermore and Livermore, 1987), Fairhaven (SD32J) in 1997 (C.F. & N.J.S.), Blackpool (SD33F) persisting from 2002 (C.F. & N.J.S.) and by the Lancaster Canal near Lancaster (SD45U or 46Q; Livermore and Livermore, 1989).

Campanula medium L.   Canterbury-bells

Neophyte. Canterbury-bells was introduced into Britain from Europe by 1597 and became a common garden plant. This species was first recorded from the wild in 1870 and although it has been found in scattered localities in Britain and the Isle of Man it usually occurs as a casual.

Very rare (2). This was first recorded in northern Lancashire from Bolton-le-Sands (SD46Y; Livermore and Livermore, 1987) and later from a car park at Waddington (SD74H; Abbott, 2005).

Campanula alliariifolia Willd.   Cornish Bellflower

Neophyte. Cornish Bellflower is a native of north-eastern Turkey and the Caucasus. It was cultivated in British gardens in 1803 but it was not recorded in the wild until 1943. Today it is found mostly in south-western and southern England.

Very rare (1). In northern Lancashire it was found on a stone wall in Silverdale (SD47S) in 2010 (P.J.).

Campanula glomerata L.   Clustered Bellflower

European Temperate element but a casual neophyte in northern Lancashire. This is a perennial herb found as a native species in southern and eastern Britain but as a casual garden escape elsewhere.

In northern Lancashire it was found at Fleetwood (SD34H) in 1956 (B.R.C.).

Campanula portenschlagiana Schult.   Adria Bellflower

Neophyte. Adria Bellflower is a native of western Yugoslavia and was introduced into British cultivation in 1835. It was first recorded in the wild in 1922. It is a popular garden plant and today it is found mostly in western Britain with occasional records elsewhere. It is easily confused with *C. poscharskyana*.

Very rare (1). In northern Lancashire this was found at Mill Brook Bridge, Browsholme (SD64X; Abbott, 2005).

Campanula poscharskyana Degen   Trailing Bellflower

Neophyte. This is a native of western Yugoslavia and was introduced into British cultivation in 1931. It is frequently grown in gardens but it was not found growing in the wild until 1957. Today it is found in many parts of England, Wales and the Isle of Man and more rarely in Scotland and Ireland.

Occasional (16). In northern Lancashire this is probably a common garden escape but because it is usually found on garden walls and rarely far from houses it is largely unrecorded. It was first found by the Lancaster Canal at Slyne-with-Hest (SD46T; Livermore and Livermore, 1989) and mostly through the observations of Livermore and Livermore many records are from the Lancaster area.

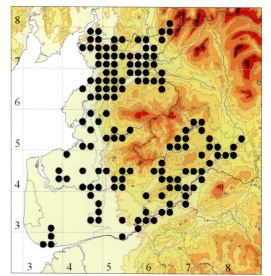
Campanula latifolia

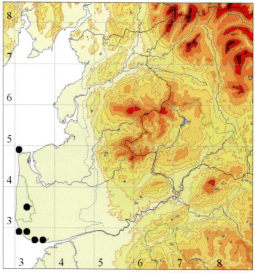
Campanula rapunculoides

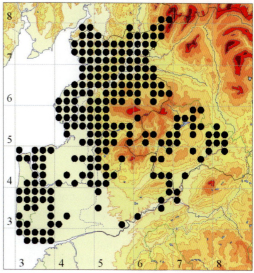
Campanula rotundifolia

Campanula latifolia L.   Giant Bellflower

European Temperate element.

This is a large perennial herb of damp woodlands and woodland edge habitats (BH1). It is found in most of Britain but as an introduction in southern England and in Ireland.

Frequent (143). Giant Bellflower is found throughout northern Lancashire but especially in the north of the area. Although there is no quantitative evidence it appears to have become less frequent in recent years particularly in the south of the region. Nationally the 'New Atlas' suggested its distribution had not changed yet showed many losses on the map. However 'Local Change' reported a considerable decline since 1987.

Campanula trachelium L.   Nettle-leaved Bellflower

European Temperate element but a neophyte in northern Lancashire. This is a large perennial herb found on dry, base-rich soils in woodlands and woodland edge habitats. It is regarded as native in central and southern parts of Britain and in south-eastern Ireland but occurs elsewhere as an introduction.

Very rare (3). In northern Lancashire it was first recorded from a roadside near Chipping (SD64G) in 1919 (T.H. Timbrill) and it is believed it has been recorded at the same site since then. It was last seen in 2004 (E.F.G.). Elsewhere it was found in a wood at Arkholme (SD57W) in 1983 (A.E.C.) and as a casual at Carnforth (SD47V; Livermore and Livermore, 1987).

Campanula rapunculoides L.   Creeping Bellflower

Neophyte. This is a European Temperate species first cultivated in Britain by 1568 and recorded from the wild by 1708. It is a common garden species and today occurs throughout Britain and more rarely in Ireland.

Rare (6). In northern Lancashire Wheldon and Wilson (1907) recorded Creeping Bellflower from Little Hawes Water, where it was first seen in 1881, between Lytham and Ansdell and near Pilling. A further locality was at St Michael's (St Michael's School, 1902). Today it occurs in a few places near the coast from Fleetwood to Lytham.

Campanula rotundifolia L. ssp. **rotundifolia**   Harebell

Circumpolar Boreo-temperate element.

This is a rhizomatous perennial herb of dry infertile habitats in grasslands and on heaths (BH7). It is found in most of the British Isles.

Common (244). This occurs in most of northern Lancashire but it is largely absent from the intensively farmed pastoral areas in the south and arable farmland reclaimed from peat mosses. It is possible that this has declined at least in the south of the area. Nationally the 'New Atlas' reported no change in its distribution but 'Local Change' reported

significant decline since 1987, at least at the edges of its distribution.

Legousia hybrida (L.) Delarbre   Venus's-looking-glass

Archaeophyte with a European Southern-temperate distribution but a neophyte in northern Lancashire. This is an annual herb of calcareous soils and cultivated ground in southern and eastern England but occasionally it occurs elsewhere.

Very rare (1). In northern Lancashire L. hybrida was found growing in the crack of paving stones on a bridge over the M6 motorway at Dalton (SD57H) in 1990 (G.H.).

Wahlenbergia hederacea (L.) Rchb.   Ivy-leaved Bellflower

Oceanic Southern-temperate element.

This is a small perennial herb found in damp or wet boggy places on acidic soils (BH11, 14). It is found in western and southern parts of the British Isles and nears the northern limit of its distribution in Lancashire.

Rare (6) but extinct in VC 60. Formerly this was found in VC 60 on Nateby Moss and by a stream in the valley at Nicky Nook, Nether Wyresdale (SD54J) but it had probably gone at both sites by or soon after 1854 (Ashfield, 1860). It was also found on Barnacre Moor (SD54I) in 1878 (YRK). Both this site and that at Nicky Nook were probably lost with the construction of reservoirs. In Lancashire VC 64 Ivy-leaved Bellflower still occurs on stabilized shingle and in flushes by the Whitendale River and River Dunsop from Whitendale Fell to about 1km from Dunsop Bridge. Curiously it does not seem to occur in the Brennand valley that joins the Whitendale valley. It also occurs in flushes by the river near Sykes in the Trough of Bowland. Nationally losses were noted at the edge of its range by the 'New Atlas' but further losses since 1987 have not occurred ('Local Change').

Phyteuma scheuchzeri All.   Oxford Rampion

Neophyte. This is a native of the southern Alps and the northern Apennines and was introduced into British gardens in 1813. In Britain it was found growing wild on the walls of St John's College, Oxford in 1951 and on limestone rocks at Inchnadamph, Sutherland in 1992.

Very rare (1 or 2). In northern Lancashire the only records are from an old garden at Blackpool (SD33I) in 1964 and on a tip at Blackpool in c. 1966 (both A.E.R.).

Jasione montana L.   Sheep's-bit

European Temperate element.

This is a biennial herb of shallow, well-drained soils on sea-cliffs, heaths and inland on dry acidic soils (BH8, 10). It is found mostly in western parts of the British Isles but it also occurs in southern and eastern England and in the Northern Isles.

Rare (14). In northern Lancashire Sheep's-bit is usually found, in small quantity, in the Lune valley and in scattered localities on the western side of the Bowland Fells with a single record from eastern Bowland at Tosside chapel (Lees, 1888). All material is likely to be *J. montana* ssp. *montana* var. *montana.* Although its distribution in northern Lancashire seems unchanged, with both losses and gains over the last 100 years, it appears that at least at some of the sites it is decreasing and on the verge of extinction. Nationally it is also decreasing.

Lobelia erinus L.   Garden Lobelia

Neophyte. Garden Lobelia is a native of South Africa and was cultivated in Britain by 1752. It is a popular garden plant with several horticultural cultivars but it was not recorded in the wild until 1913. Today it may be found anywhere in the British Isles but more often in southern Britain than elsewhere.

Very rare (1). In northern Lancashire it was found by a path at Garstang (SD44X) in 1998 (E.F.G.). It is probably more frequent than this single record suggests, especially in urban areas.

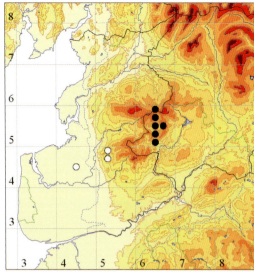
Wahlenbergia hederacea

MENYANTHACEAE   BOGBEAN FAMILY

Menyanthes trifoliata L.   Bogbean

Circumpolar Boreo-temperate element.

This is a rhizomatous perennial of wet places including canals, ponds, swamps and dune slacks etc. (BH11). It is apparently tolerant of a wide range of water chemistry and occurs throughout the British Isles.

Occasional (56). In northern Lancashire Bogbean occurs throughout the area although it is rare in lowland western areas. It was especially common in the Lancaster Canal from which it seems to have disappeared in recent years. Despite it being tolerant of a wide range of water chemistry in northern Lancashire Bogbean appears to be sensitive to nutrient enrichment. Nationally the 'New Atlas' reported a decline through drainage, although recently it had been planted as an ornamental plant, whilst 'Local Change' noted no change in its distribution since 1987.

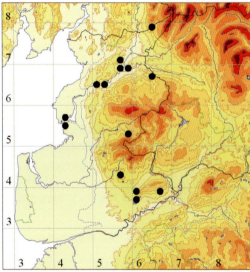
Jasione montana

Nymphoides peltata Kuntze   Fringed Water-lily

Eurasian Temperate element but a neophyte in northern Lancashire.

This is a rhizomatous perennial that grows in water 0.5–2m deep (BH13, 14) and has medium sized floating leaves. It is native in parts of south-eastern England but it occurs throughout the rest of the British Isles as an introduction and throw-out from garden ponds.

Rare (14). In northern Lancashire this was first found in an old millpond at Fleetwood (SD34I) in 1985 (C.F. & N.J.S.). Today it is found in a few localities in the northwest and southwest of the area. It has probably originated in many localities from garden throw-outs and in others it has been planted. It is an attractive but aggressive aquatic plant.

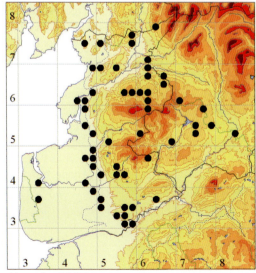
Menyanthes trifoliata

Echinops sphaerocephalus L.   Glandular Globe-thistle

Neophyte. Glandular Globe-thistle has a Eurosiberian Southern-temperate distribution and was brought into British cultivation by 1596. However it was not recorded in the wild until 1908. Today it is found as a garden escape in scattered localities in England, Wales and southern Scotland but rarely elsewhere in the British Isles.

Rare (9). This was first found in northern Lancashire from St Anne's in 1965 (A.E.R.). Subsequently it has been found in a few scattered localities in the Fylde, at Fleetwood, Carnforth and in the Lancaster area. It is possible that some of the records are one or other of the next two species or the hybrid between *E. sphaerocephalus* and *E. exaltus* (*E.* × *pellenzianus* Hügin & W. Lohmeyer).

Echinops exaltus Schrad.   Globe-thistle

Neophyte. Globe-thistle is a native of east, central and southern Europe. It was first cultivated in Britain in 1822 and recorded in the wild in 1931. Today it is found in scattered localities throughout Britain.

Very rare (2). In northern Lancashire this was found on the disused railway at Great Plumpton (SD33W) in 1987 and at Rossall (SD34C) (both C.F. & N.J.S.).

Echinops bannaticus Rochel ex Schrad.   Blue Globe-thistle

Neophyte. This is a native of south-eastern Europe as far east as the Crimea and was first brought into British cultivation in 1832. It is widely planted in gardens and today it is found in scattered localities but mostly in urban and suburban areas of the British Isles.

Rare (6). In northern Lancashire Blue Globe-thistle was first found by the Lancaster Canal near Carnforth (SD46Z; Livermore and Livermore, 1989). Subsequently it was found in a few scattered localities in the west of the region.

Carlina vulgaris L.   Carline Thistle

Eurosiberian Temperate element.

This perennial thistle grows in well grazed, dry, infertile but base-rich grasslands and in open habitats on rock ledges, in quarries and on sand dunes (BH7). It is found in suitable places in England, Wales and Ireland but in Scotland it is mostly found in coastal areas.

Occasional (22). In northern Lancashire Carline Thistle is found on limestone and other calcareous soils around Morecambe Bay and on the Fylde coast sand dunes where it is now restricted to a few places in SD33A. It occurs occasionally elsewhere but it was not found in Lancashire VC 64 until 2007 (P.G.) when it was found on limestone near Whitewell. Whilst Wheldon and Wilson (1907) recorded a similar distribution to that found today they also found it occasionally on the western side of the Bowland Fells from where it appears to have gone. Nationally the 'New Atlas' reported a widespread decline but 'Local Change' did not note significant further decline after 1987.

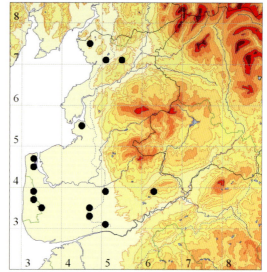

Nymphoides peltata

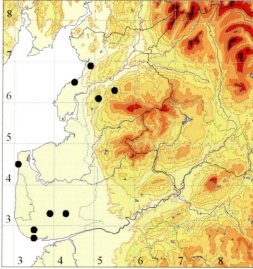

Echinops sphaerocephalus

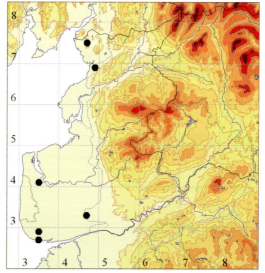

Echinops bannaticus

Arctium lappa L.   Greater Burdock

Archaeophyte. This has a Eurosiberian Temperate distribution and whilst it is common in southern and midland England it is much rarer in Wales, northern England, Ireland and Scotland.

Very rare (3). There is considerable confusion over the identity and nomenclature of this taxon (see below) and in northern Lancashire it probably only occurs as a rare casual. Confirmed records are from a tip at Lytham St Anne's (SD32Y) in 1965 (A.E.R. & E.H.), Lytham Hall grounds (SD32P) in 2001 (C.F. & N.J.S.) and from Heysham Harbour (SD46A) in 1974 (A.E.C.).

Arctium minus *sensu lato*   Lesser Burdock

European Temperate element.

The taxonomy and nomenclature of *Arctium* has caused many problems, especially for British botanists. Rich and Jermy (1998) provided two alternative treatments based on Perring (1988), who used British material, and that of Duistermaat (1996), which Stace (1997) follows but modified in 2010. Both treatments recognise *A. lappa* but whereas Perring recognises three other taxa, *A. minus* Bernh., *A. pubens* Bab. and *A. nemorosum* Lej., Duistermaat includes *A. pubens* within a variable *A. minus*. However on material from northern England Duistermaat's treatment has proved unworkable (e.g. Braithwaite, 2005). Sell and Murrell (2006) describe one species with four subspecies, *A. lappa* ssp. *lappa*, ssp. *pubens* (Bab.) P.D. Sell, ssp. *minus* (Hill) Hook. fil. and ssp. *nemorosum* (Lej.) P.D. Sell. Sell and Murrell also suggest Duistermaat's treatment is unworkable.

In this account the separate identity of *A. lappa* (= *A. lappa* ssp. *lappa*) is maintained (see above) but the remaining taxa are included in a variable *A. minus sensu lato*. Sell and Murrell narrowly define the limits of *A. lappa* ssp. *minus* and ssp. *nemorosum* recognising that ssp. *minus* with its small capitula is typical of south-western England whilst ssp. *nemorosum* with large capitula is found mostly in northern parts of the British Isles, and that the distribution of the two subspecies rarely overlap. However across the middle of Britain there is considerable variation in the morphology of *Arctium* and much of the material conforms to the broader limits of ssp. *pubens*. This is the situation in northern Lancashire although at least some plants come close to either ssp. *minus* or ssp. *nemorosum*.

Arctium minus sensu lato occurs throughout the British Isles but it is often rare in northern Scotland. It occurs in waste places, on roadsides and woodland edge habitats (BH3).

Very common (354). Lesser Burdock is found throughout northern Lancashire although it appears to be less frequent in the east of the area than elsewhere. Its distribution is stable both locally and nationally.

Carduus tenuiflorus Curtis   Slender Thistle

Suboceanic Southern-temperate element.

C. tenuiflorus is an annual or biennial species of dry, grasslands and waste places (BH3, 6). It is found in coastal areas of England, Wales, Ireland and eastern Scotland and as an introduction inland in Wales and England. It also occurs inland in Ireland where it is regarded as native.

Occasional (19). In northern Lancashire Slender Thistle is found along many parts of the coast and on the Wyre estuary as far inland as the Cartford Bridge (SD44F). There has been no change in its distribution locally or nationally.

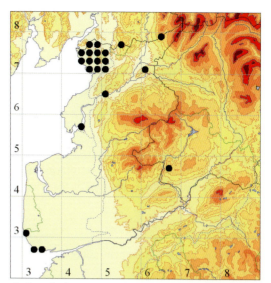
Carlina vulgaris

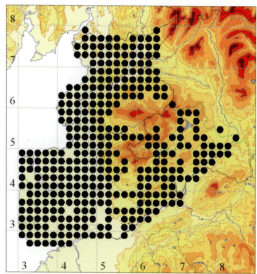
Arctium minus s.l.

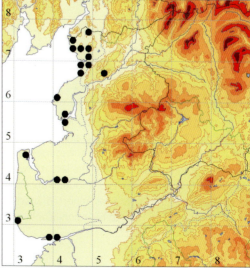
Carduus tenuiflorus

Carduus crispus L.   Welted Thistle

Eurosiberian Temperate element.

This is a biennial herb of woodland margins, tall grasslands, roadsides and
waste places (BH3). It is found in most of England, eastern Wales, eastern
Ireland, southern and eastern Scotland. It is regarded as an introduction in
some northern localities.

Frequent (91). In northern Lancashire most records of Welted Thistle are
from north-western parts of the area but there are scattered localities
elsewhere, especially in the Ribble valley. In northern Lancashire *C. crispus*
has extended its range over the last 100 years to become more widely
distributed in the region but nationally there has been no change in its
distribution.

Carduus nutans L.   Musk Thistle

Eurosiberian Temperate element but probably a neophyte in northern
Lancashire.

Musk Thistle occurs on basic soils in grassland and waste places in Wales,
southern, midland and eastern England and south-eastern Scotland.
Elsewhere it is found as an introduction.

Very rare (4). In northern Lancashire this was reported from many places
about Preston (Ashfield, 1862) but discounted by Wheldon and Wilson
(1907). However it was found from Thornton near Fleetwood in 1915
(J.Mo. in Wheldon and Wilson, 1925). It was then found from near
Lancaster (SD46X) in 1965 (Anon), near Weeton on a motorway embankment (SD33R) in 1981 (C.F. & N.J.S.), Borwick in gravel pits (SD57B) in 1986
(C.F & N.J.S.) and on waste land at Lytham (SD32T) in 2004 (Anon). Its
distribution nationally is unchanged.

Cirsium vulgare (Savi) Ten.   Spear Thistle

Eurosiberian Temperate element.

Spear Thistle is a common perennial species found in grasslands, marginal
habitats and waste ground (BH3, 5, 6, 7) throughout the British Isles.

Very common (436). This is one of the commonest species in northern
Lancashire and is found almost everywhere except on the highest fells.
There is no evidence of a change in its distribution locally or nationally.

Cirsium heterophyllum (L.) Hill   Melancholy Thistle

Eurosiberian Boreal-montane element.

Melancholy Thistle is a beautiful perennial herb found in hay meadows,
on roadsides, by streams and in woodland edge habitats (BH6, 16) in
northern Britain, northern Wales and very rarely in the north of Ireland.

Occasional (19). In northern Lancashire *C. heterophyllum* has been
recorded in the Forest of Bowland and at Hest Bank since 1964. However,
at least some of the localities in the west of the area have been lost
continuing a trend of losses over the last 100 years. In the east and especially in the Slaidburn area its distribution appears stable (see Plate 2.38).
Nationally whilst the 'New Atlas' reported losses 'Local Change' considered any losses since 1987 to be insignificant.

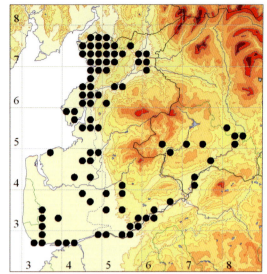

Carduus crispus

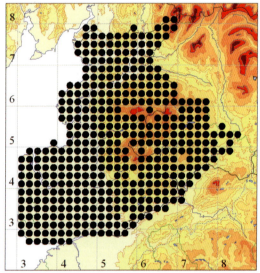

Cirsium vulgare

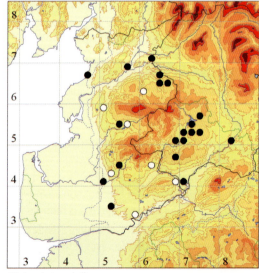

Cirsium heterophyllum

Cirsium oleraceum (L.) Scop.   Cabbage Thistle

Neophyte. *C. oleraceum* has a Eurosiberian Temperate distribution and was cultivated in Britain by 1570. It is rarely grown in gardens and was not found in the wild until 1894. Today it occurs in a few scattered localities in the British Isles.

Very rare (2). Cabbage Thistle was recorded from roadsides at Caton-with-Littledale (SD56M) and Arkholme (SD57Q) by Livermore and Livermore (1987).

Cirsium acaule (L.) Scop.   Dwarf Thistle

European Temperate element but a neophyte in northern Lancashire.

Dwarf Thistle is a rosette-forming perennial herb of short grasslands on base-rich soils (BH7). It occurs southeast of a line between northern Yorkshire and northern Wales with a few localities further north where it is believed to have been introduced.

Very rare (1). In northern Lancashire Dwarf Thistle was recorded from Nether Kellet (SD46Z) in 1999, where it had been known for some years (J.M.N.). The record for the 10km square SD45 in the 'New Atlas' is an error.

Cirsium palustre (L.) Scop.   Marsh Thistle

Eurosiberian Boreo-temperate element.

C. palustre is a perennial herb of wet places (BH11, 14) in a wide variety of habitats and is found throughout the British Isles.

Common (341). In northern Lancashire Marsh Thistle is found throughout the area but it is much rarer in the lowland west of the region than elsewhere. There has been no change in its distribution locally or nationally. Both var. *palustre* and var. *ferox* Druce occur in northern Lancashire. Var. *ferox* is an upland taxon and its unbranched stem is distinctive and contrasts with the branched stem of var. *palustre*. The distribution of the two taxa has not been recorded but in 2010 it was noted that in upper Roeburndale only var. *ferox* was found but lower down the valley near Middle Salter var. *palustre* was also seen but there were many intermediates. A similar situation was observed in the Trough of Bowland and the Harden valley.

Cirsium arvense (L.) Scop.   Creeping Thistle

Eurasian Temperate element.

Creeping Thistle is a rhizomatous perennial herb of pastures, cultivated and waste ground (BH3, 4, 6). It is found throughout the British Isles.

Very common (431). *C. arvense* is found throughout northern Lancashire except on the highest fells. There has been no change in its distribution locally or nationally.

Onopordum acanthium L.   Cotton Thistle

Archaeophyte with a Eurosiberian Temperate distribution.

There is archaeological evidence that this was found in Britain from the Iron Age onwards. It is found in marginal habitats and waste places (BH3, 17), particularly in south-eastern England. It has been recorded in much of Britain but only rarely in eastern Ireland.

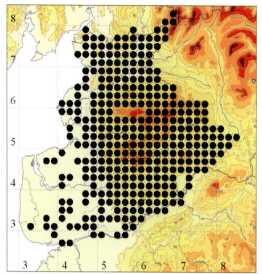
Cirsium palustre

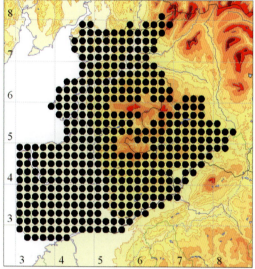
Cirsium arvense

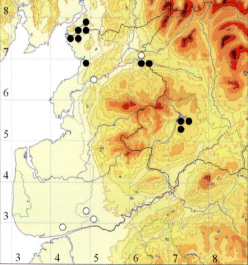
Serratula tinctoria

Very rare (5). It was first found in northern Lancashire from the sand dunes at St Anne's (Bailey, 1910). Post 1964 records are from the north side of Marton Mere, Blackpool (SD33M) in 1976 (D. Ellwood), west of Marton Mere, Blackpool (SD33H) in 1974 (M.J.), Lytham St Anne's (SD33A) in 1982 and in SD32P in c. 1990 & 2010 (C.F. & N.J.S.) and on imported soil at Myerscough (SD54H) in 1987 (C.J.B.).

Silybum marianum (L.) Gaertn.   Milk Thistle

Archaeophyte with a Mediterranean distribution.

Milk Thistle occurs in marginal habitats and on waste ground (BH3) throughout most of the British Isles but especially in south-eastern England.

Very rare (1). Milk Thistle was first recorded in northern Lancashire from Blackpool (Thornber, 1837). Later records were from the sand dunes at St Anne's (Bailey, 1910), a tip at Marton, Blackpool (SD33M; France, 1931) where it was found again in 1975 (M.J.).

Serratula tinctoria L.   Saw-wort

European Temperate element.

Saw-wort is a perennial herb found in grasslands, woodland edge habitats and waste places on calcareous soils (BH7). It is found in Britain from southern Scotland southwards.

Rare (11). In northern Lancashire *S. tinctoria* is found in small quantity on the limestone around Morecambe Bay, near Wennington and in the Slaidburn area. Although some localities have been lost near Preston the overall distribution of Saw-wort appears stable in the area. However nationally the 'New Atlas' reported losses but since 1987 losses are insignificant ('Local Change').

Centaurea scabiosa L.   Greater Knapweed

Eurosiberian Temperate element.

Greater Knapweed is a robust perennial species found in grassland, marginal habitats and on waste ground (BH7). It is found in many places in England, Wales and central Ireland but it is absent from most upland areas and most of Scotland although it occurs on the north coast and around the Firths of Forth and Tay.

Occasional (19). In northern Lancashire *C. scabiosa* is found mostly around Morecambe Bay and on the Lune estuary with only occasional records elsewhere in the area. Over the last 100 years, whilst there have been losses in some areas there have been gains in others, so that Greater Knapweed has slightly extended its range nationally ('New Atlas'), but since 1987 there has been a significant decline at the edges of its range ('Local Change').

Centaurea montana L.   Perennial Cornflower

Neophyte. This is a native of the mountains of central and southern Europe. It was introduced into British cultivation before 1596 and was known from the wild by 1888. It is widely grown in gardens and has escaped into the wild in many parts of Britain but there are only a few records from Ireland.

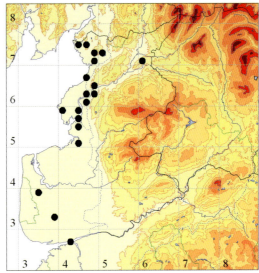

Centaurea scabiosa

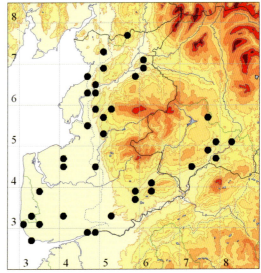

Centaurea montana

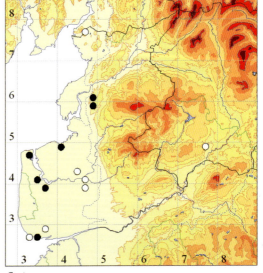

Centaurea cyanus

Occasional (37). Perennial Cornflower was first found in northern Lancashire on a roadside near Quernmore (SD55D) in 1966 (E.F.G. & J.H.). Today it occurs in scattered localities throughout the area.

Centaurea cyanus L. — Cornflower

Archaeophyte with a native distribution centred on the European Temperate region but widely naturalised outside this range.

Cornflower has been known in Britain since the Iron Age and was a serious weed of cultivated ground until seed cleaning prompted a rapid decline. There are records from cultivated and waste ground (BH3, 4, 17) from many parts of the British Isles.

Rare (7). In northern Lancashire Cornflower has been recorded since 1964 as a casual from a few coastal localities. Unlike many other parts of the country *C. cyanus* has never been common and old records are mostly from the west of the region. Whilst the 'New Atlas' reported many losses 'Local Change' reported some gains since 1987, probably because in recent years it has been included in amenity seed mixes.

Centaurea solstitialis L. — Yellow Star-thistle

Neophyte. Yellow Star-thistle is a native of southern Europe and south-western Asia but it is widely naturalised elsewhere. It was known in the wild by at least 1778 and formerly it was frequent in south-eastern England. It was even recorded as far north as eastern Scotland but today it is rarely found in the wild.

In northern Lancashire the only record is from cultivated land near Ashton, Preston (Preston Scientific Society, 1903).

Centaurea melitensis L. — Maltese Star-thistle

Neophyte. *C. melitensis* is a native of the Mediterranean region but it is widely naturalised in Australasia and North America. It was cultivated in Britain in 1710 and was recorded in the wild in 1876. It is a contaminant of many products including grain and occurs occasionally in Britain.

In northern Lancashire it was found in at least two sites on the sand dunes at St Anne's in 1907 (MANCH; Bailey, 1910).

Centaurea diluta Aiton — Lesser Star-thistle

Neophyte. *C. diluta* is a native of south-western Spain, north-western Africa and the Atlantic Islands. It was introduced into British cultivation in 1781 and was recorded from the wild in 1904. Today it occurs as a rare casual, mostly in England but it has been recorded from Wales, Scotland and the Isle of Man.

Very rare (3). In northern Lancashire Lesser Star-thistle was found on tips at Blackpool and Lytham in 1966 (SD33I; A.E.R and SD32Y; J.H) and from near St Michael's (SD44K) in 1967 (J.H.).

Centaurea nigra L. — Common Knapweed

Suboceanic Temperate element.

Common Knapweed is a common species of grasslands, woodland edge habitats and waste ground (BH6, 7). It is found throughout the British Isles although it is thought to be an introduction in Shetland. However British botanists have had considerable difficulties with the taxonomy of this taxon and have been unable to distinguish between *C. nigra* L. and *C. nemoralis* Jord. Nevertheless Sell and Murrell (2006) distinguish between *C. debeauxii* Gren. & Godr. (2n = 44), which includes ssp. *nemoralis* (Jord.) Dorstál (= *C. nemoralis* Jord.) and ssp. *thuilleri* (Dorstál) P.D. Sell, and *C. nigra* L. (2n = 22). However where both species occur hybrids may be frequent. In northern Lancashire it proved difficult to distinguish with any certainty, which taxa occurred. It appeared that *C. nigra* was a morphologically variable taxon or that both *C. debeauxii* and *C. nigra* are present with many intermediates or hybrids present. Nevertheless, a distinctive taxon, conforming to typical *C. debeauxii*, was found at Brockholes Nature Reserve, Preston (SD53V) in 2009 (E.F.G.) where it is believed it had originated from a wildflower seed mixture. Much more work is needed to elucidate the situation in the area.

Very common (399). In northern Lancashire Common Knapweed is found throughout the area except on the fells. There has been no change in its distribution locally or nationally.

Carthamus tinctorius L. — Safflower

Neophyte. This is not known as a wild plant but it has long been cultivated in southern Europe, south-western and south-central Asia and elsewhere. It was in British cultivation by 1551 but it was not found growing wild until 1899. It occurs casually on tips and waste ground in many parts of the British Isles but particularly in England.

Very rare (1). It was recorded from Blackpool tip (SD33I) in 1964 (A.E.R.).

Carthamus lanatus L. — Downy Safflower

Neophyte. This is a native of southern Europe, the Mediterranean region, south-western and central Asia but it is widely naturalised elsewhere. It was cultivated in Britain by 1596 and was recorded from the wild in 1876. It occurs casually on tips and waste ground in a few localities in England and Wales.

Very rare (1). It is believed it was found on the sand dunes at St Anne's (Bailey, 1910) and more certainly near Middleton (c. SD45J) in 1964 (A.E.R.; LIV).

Cichorium intybus L. — Chicory

Archaeophyte with a Eurosiberian Southern-temperate distribution.

Chicory is a robust perennial herb of roadsides and other marginal habitats and waste ground (BH3). It is found throughout the British Isles but it is rare in most of Scotland and Ireland.

Occasional (26). *C. intybus* is probably a neophyte in northern Lancashire although it was grown as a crop plant in the eighteenth century (Holt, 1795). However it was first recorded in the wild from Winmarleigh (J.Pe. in Ashfield, 1860) and Wheldon and Wilson (1907) recorded a further five localities. Today it is found mostly in the west of the area.

Lapsana communis L. ssp. communis   Nipplewort

European Temperate element.

Nipplewort is a common annual species of waste and cultivated ground, woodland edge and marginal habitats (BH3, 17). It is found throughout the British Isles.

Very common (364). *L. communis* is found throughout most of northern Lancashire although it is absent from many upland areas. Its distribution is stable locally and nationally.

Hypochaeris radicata L.   Cat's-ear

European Southern-temperate element.

This is a perennial herb of grasslands and waste ground in a wide range of habitats (BH6). It occurs throughout the British Isles. Sell and Murrell (2006) recognise ssp. *radicata*, the common subspecies, and a coastal ssp. *ericetorum* Van Soest.

Very common (370). *H. radicata* is found in most of northern Lancashire although it is absent in many upland areas and occasionally elsewhere. Ssp. *ericetorum* was found on sand dunes at Lytham St Anne's L.N.R. (SD33A) in 2008 (E.F.G.). Cat's-ear's distribution is stable locally and nationally.

Hypochaeris glabra L.   Smooth Cat's-ear

European Southern-temperate element.

This is an annual species of summer parched grasslands and heathy pastures, usually on acidic, nutrient poor, sandy or gravely soils (BH8). *H. glabra* is found in scattered localities in Britain, especially in eastern and southern England and northern Ireland. This is an elusive species. Perring and Walters (1962) recorded it from Merseyside where it was found on the sand dunes but the 'New Atlas' only showed pre 1970 records. Further north it was not found on the Cumbrian coast until 1968 where today several localities are known (Halliday, 1997). However despite the absence of recent records for Merseyside in the 'New Atlas', Smith (2008) demonstrated that in 2007 Smooth Cat's-ear occurred in 28 populations on the Merseyside coast.

In northern Lancashire the only record is from Roman horse dung at Lancaster (Wilson, 1979). Given the elusiveness of this species it is inconceivable that it does not or has not occurred on the Fylde coast. Nationally it has apparently declined ('New Atlas').

Scorzoneroides autumnalis (L.) Moench   Autumn Hawkbit

European Boreo-temperate element.

Autumn Hawkbit is morphologically variable and a number of infraspecific taxa have been recognised. It is found in a variety of grassland

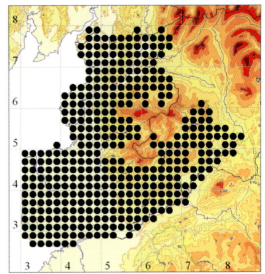
Centaurea nigra

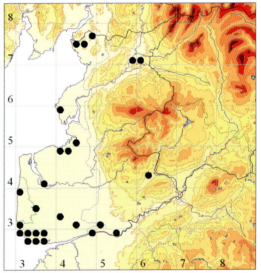
Cichorium intybus

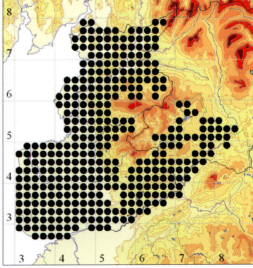
Lapsana communis

habitats (BH6) and occurs throughout the British Isles. Infraspecific taxa described by Sell and Murrell (2006) have not been recorded in northern Lancashire.

Very common (394). *S. autumnalis* is found throughout most of northern Lancashire. Its distribution is stable locally and nationally.

Leontodon hispidus L.   Rough Hawkbit

European Temperate element.

L. hispidus is a perennial herb of neutral or calcareous soils and occurs in grasslands, wasteland and marginal habitats (BH7). It is found in England, Wales, southern Scotland and central Ireland.

Frequent (219). The occurrence of Rough Hawkbit shows a complex distribution pattern in northern Lancashire probably based on the presence of neutral or basic soils. Thus it occurs on limestone soils and calcareous boulder clay in the north of the area, in river valleys around Bowland, and on limestone in the Hodder valley as well as on boulder clay in the west of the region. Whilst its distribution in northern Lancashire is probably stable 'Local Change' reports losses nationally since 1987.

Leontodon saxatilis Lam.   Lesser Hawkbit

Suboceanic Southern-temperate element.

Lesser Hawkbit is a perennial or biennial herb of grasslands, usually on well-drained basic soils (BH7). *L. saxatilis* occurs widely in England, Wales, Ireland, southern and western Scotland.

Frequent (94). *L. saxatilis* occurs in scattered localities in many parts of northern Lancashire but predominantly in western and coastal areas. Var. *arenarius* (Duby) P.D. Sell was recognised on fixed dunes at Lytham St Anne's L.N.R (SD33A) in 2008 (E.F.G.). Lesser Hawkbit's distribution in northern Lancashire is stable but the 'New Atlas' reported losses nationally. However 'Local Change' noted no further decline after 1987.

Picris hieracioides L.   Hawkweed Oxtongue

Eurasian Temperate element but a neophyte in northern Lancashire.

This occurs on calcareous soils in grasslands and marginal habitats (BH7). As a native species it occurs in southern, midland and eastern England and Wales and very occasionally elsewhere in England, Scotland and Ireland as an introduction.

Very rare (1). In northern Lancashire it was found on waste ground at Heysham Power Station (SD45E) in 1999 (S.B. comm. J.M.N.).

Helminthotheca echioides (L.) Holub   Bristly Oxtongue

Archaeophyte with a European Southern-temperate distribution.

This occurs in open grassland, marginal habitats and on waste ground on basic soils (BH3, 4). It is found mostly in England, Wales and eastern Ireland with a few records further north in Scotland.

Occasional (18). In northern Lancashire this was only known from clay banks on the Ribble estuary near Freckleton 100 years ago (Wheldon and Wilson, 1907). Today it still occurs there and in a number of other localities in and around Lytham St Anne's and Blackpool as well as in a few other scattered places. This local spread in northern Lancashire is reflected by an increase nationally ('New Atlas', 'Local Change').

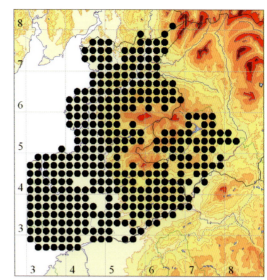
Hypochaeris radicata

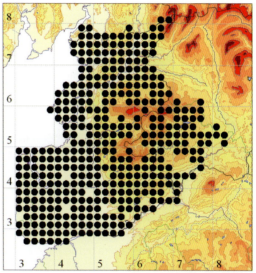
Scorzoneroides autumnalis

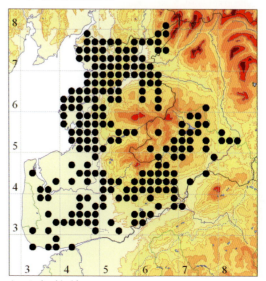
Leontodon hispidus

Tragopogon pratensis L. ssp. **minor** (Mill.) Wahlenb.   Goat's-beard

Eurosiberian Temperate element.

This perennial herb occurs in tall grassland, marginal habitats and on waste ground (BH6). It is found in lowland areas of England, Wales and Scotland and in parts of Ireland but it is absent from large areas in Wales and Scotland.

Frequent (196). Goat's-beard is a familiar species on roadsides in the west and north of northern Lancashire but it occurs less often elsewhere. Its distribution locally and nationally is stable.

Tragopogon porrifolius L.   Salsify

Neophyte. Salsify is a native of the Mediterranean region but it is widely cultivated elsewhere. It was first recorded growing wild in Britain in 1695. It is found mostly in southern Britain especially in south-eastern England.

Very rare (2). In northern Lancashire Salsify was found near the Lancaster Canal at Garstang in 1851 (J.Pe. in Ashfield, 1860), Marton, Blackpool (SD33G) in 2009 (C.F. & N.J.S.) and from near Ansdell railway station (SD32N) in 1979 (C.F. & N.J.S).

Sonchus arvensis L.   Perennial Sow-thistle

Eurosiberian Temperate element.

This is a robust perennial herb of marginal habitats, the margins of arable fields and of the upper parts of salt marshes, beaches and strand lines (BH4, 19). It is found throughout the British Isles but it is absent from much of upland Scotland. Sell and Murrell (2006) recognised ssp. *arvensis* and ssp. *uliginosus* (M. Bieb.) Nyman but suggest the ecology and distribution of ssp. *uliginosus* is unknown. Nevertheless a glabrous form of *S. arvensis* was found at Conder Green (SD45N) in 2009 (J.M.N.), which may be this latter subspecies. However within ssp. *arvensis* they suggest var. *maritimus* G.F.W. Meyer is characteristic of coastal sand dunes and shingle whilst var. *arvensis* is the widespread and common taxon. Var. *integrifolius* Bisch. is only known from Suffolk. Both var. *maritimus* and var. *arvensis* are likely to occur in northern Lancashire but so far in a limited study in the area the distinction between the two taxa was not confirmed.

Frequent (229). *S. arvensis* is a common species in western parts of northern Lancashire but it occurs occasionally in the east. Its distribution in northern Lancashire is stable but 'Local Change' notes an increase since 1987.

Sonchus oleraceus L.   Smooth Sow-thistle

European Southern-temperate element.

This is an annual herb of disturbed ground and waste places (BH3, 4). It is found in most of the British Isles but is absent from much of upland Scotland. Sell and Murrell (2006) recognised ssp. *litoralis* P.D. Sell, a coastal taxon, and the more widespread ssp. *oleraceus*.

Common (292). In northern Lancashire *S. oleraceus* is found commonly in the west of the area but it is absent from most of Bowland and Leck. No information is available about the distribution of the subspecies in the area. The distribution of *S. oleraceus* is stable in northern Lancashire, a situation reported nationally by the 'New Atlas'. However 'Local Change' noted an increase.

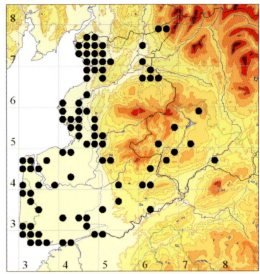
Leontodon saxatilis

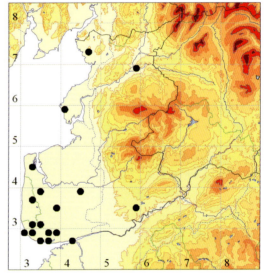
Helminthotheca echioides

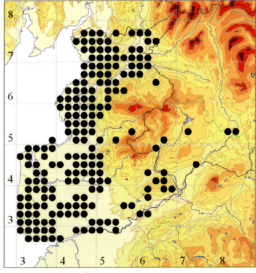
Tragopogon pratensis

Sonchus asper (L.) Hill   Prickly Sow-thistle

European Southern-temperate element.

This is an annual herb found in disturbed habitats and waste ground (BH3, 4). It occurs throughout most of the British Isles. Sell and Murrell (2006) recognise ssp. *asper* and ssp. *glaucescens* (Jord.) Ball but this latter taxon has only been seen in Cambridgeshire. *S. asper* var. *asper* is the common taxon of roadsides etc. whilst var. *sabulosus* P.D. Sell is found on coastal shingle and sand. Little is known about var. *integrifolius* Lej. but it may occur in northern Lancashire.

Common (328). *S. asper* is found throughout lowland areas of northern Lancashire but is rare in Bowland and Leck. The distribution of *S. asper* is stable in northern Lancashire but 'Local Change' reports an increase nationally since 1987.

Lactuca serriola L.   Prickly Lettuce

Archaeophyte with a Eurosiberian Southern-temperate distribution but a neophyte in northern Lancashire.

This is found in marginal habitats and waste ground (BH3, 17) and occurs commonly in England from Lancashire and Yorkshire southwards. It occurs locally in Wales but elsewhere in the British Isles it is rare.

Occasional (22). Prickly Lettuce was first found near Fleetwood Docks in 1900 (J.A.W.; NMW) and on the sand dunes at St Anne's in 1902 (C.B.; MANCH). Post 1964 records are from the Lancaster and Heysham areas, St Anne's and Preston and along the M55 corridor. *L. serriola* is apparently spreading northwards ('New Atlas'), and this has become very marked since 1987 ('Local Change'). The more recent records in northern Lancashire suggest that is now spreading into and within the area perhaps along motorways and trunk roads.

Lactuca sativa L.   Garden Lettuce

The origin of Garden Lettuce is unknown but it has been cultivated in Britain as a salad plant since at least 1200. There are numerous cultivars. However it was not recorded in the wild until 1975 and remains an occasional British casual.

Very rare (1). In northern Lancashire it was recorded from a tip at Blackpool (SD33I) in 1965 (E.P.).

Lactuca virosa L.   Great Lettuce

Suboceanic Southern-temperate element but a neophyte in northern Lancashire.

This annual or biennial herb is found as a native species on calcareous grassland and in coastal areas (BH3, 16), mostly in midland and eastern England and south-eastern Scotland.

Very rare (1). Two plants were recorded with *L. serriola* from a roadside at Heaton-with-Oxcliffe (SD46L) in 1966 (J.Wi.). The records in Wheldon and Wilson (1907) from Fleetwood and St Anne's are errors for *L. serriola*. The records for SD32 and 33 in the 'New Atlas' are also errors. Like *L. serriola* Great Lettuce is spreading northwards.

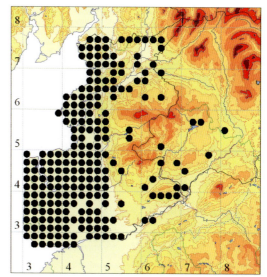
Sonchus arvensis

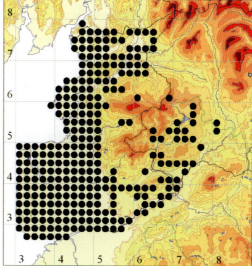
Sonchus oleraceus

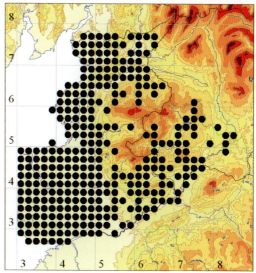
Sonchus asper

Cicerbita macrophylla (Willd.) Wallr.
ssp. **uralensis** (Rouy) P.D. Sell   Common Blue-sow-thistle

Neophyte. This tall perennial herb is a native of the Urals and was introduced into British gardens in 1823. It was first recorded in the wild in 1915. Today it occurs over most of the British Isles although it is rare in parts of Ireland, Scotland and East Anglia.

Occasional (21). In northern Lancashire *C. macrophylla* was first found by quarries at Longridge and on roadside banks at Chipping (Whellan, 1942). It still grows in the Chipping area today. It was also known from Goosnargh by the 1950s (E.F.G.) and from the Silverdale area by 1975 (L.A.L). It also occurs in a few other scattered localities.

Cicerbita plumieri (L.) Kirschl.   Hairless Blue-sow-thistle

Neophyte. This is a native of the Pyrenees and the mountains of western central Europe. It was first cultivated in Britain in 1794 and it is occasionally grown in gardens. It was first found in the wild in 1917 from Ashton-under-Lyne in Greater Manchester (VC 59). Today it is found in a few localities scattered across the British Isles.

Very rare (1). *C. plumieri* has been long established in Melling Churchyard (SD57V) where it was first reported in 1999 (J.M.N.).

Mycelis muralis (L.) Dumort.   Wall Lettuce

European Temperate element.

This is found on shaded walls, rocks, hedge banks and in woodland and woodland edge habitats (BH1, 16). It is found in suitable localities in England and Wales but more rarely in Scotland. It is thought to be an introduction in Ireland.

Frequent (135). Wall Lettuce is found frequently in the north of northern Lancashire and in the Ribble and Hodder valleys but only occasionally in most of Bowland. It also occurs occasionally elsewhere but it is absent from most lowland western areas. Its distribution locally and nationally is stable.

Taraxacum F.H. Wigg.   Dandelions

Circumpolar Wide-temperate element.

This is a genus of perennial herbs found in a wide variety of habitats, which occurs throughout the British Isles. There are at least 229 apomictic species in the British Isles of which over 40 are probably endemic and about 100 are introduced.

Very common (422). In northern Lancashire the genus occurs throughout the area except on the highest fells but in a variety of habitats. 134 species or nearly 60% of the British total have been found. Of these 11 are believed to be endemic, mostly in section Celtica, and 50, mostly belonging to section Ruderalia, are thought to be introduced.

The genus is divided into nine rather ill defined sections. Identification of plants, even to the sections, is often difficult and identification of the species involves considerable skill and expertise. Nevertheless many species are restricted to particular habitats or substrates and show distinct distribution patterns both locally and nationally. However whilst well over 1000 gatherings were identified further species can usually be found on any excursion in the area, especially in the south and east of northern Lancashire.

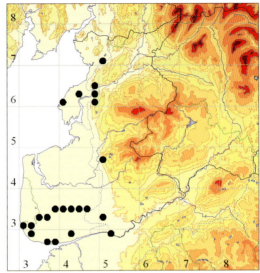

Lactuca serriola

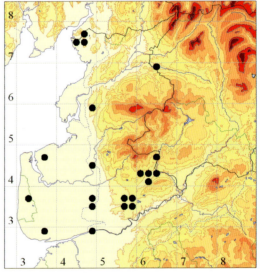

Cicerbita macrophylla

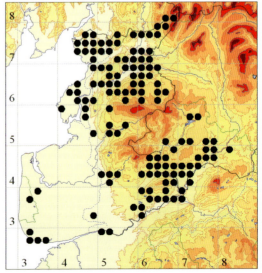

Mycelis muralis

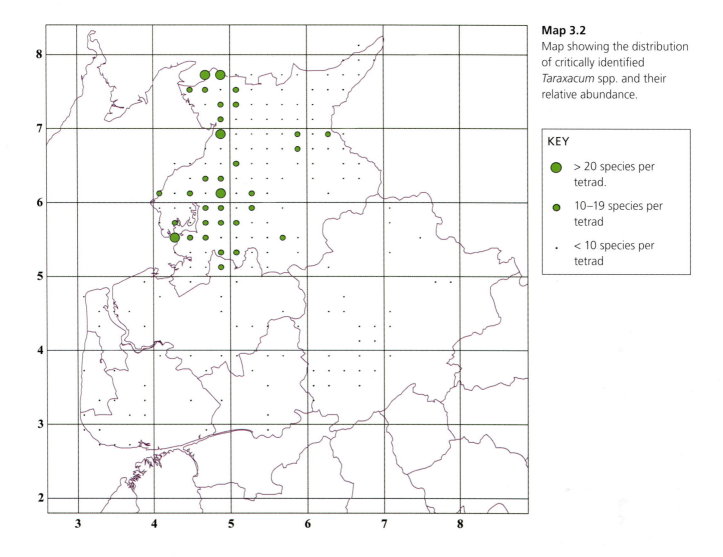

Map 3.2
Map showing the distribution of critically identified *Taraxacum* spp. and their relative abundance.

KEY

● > 20 species per tetrad.

● 10–19 species per tetrad

· < 10 species per tetrad

The total number of species found in northern Lancashire is comparable with recent accounts elsewhere, e.g. 123 in Cumbria (Halliday, 1997), 109 in Northumberland (Swann, 1993) and 138 in Monmouthshire (Evans, 2007). Map 3.2 shows the species richness of tetrads where *Taraxacum* species have been critically determined. Unfortunately it is a map showing where most work has been directed. The richest tetrads are in the north of the area where L.A. and P.D. Livermore did so much at the end of the 1980s. Here some tetrads have over 20 species and this gives an indication of the diversity that probably occurs in many places in the region. As most species belong to section Ruderalia, locations near towns, where introduced and native species can both find suitable habitats, are likely to be the richest, which with the greater intensity of study given to tetrads near the Livermore's home in Lancaster has resulted in a few tetrads in the Lancaster area being apparently the richest in northern Lancashire. However similar habitats occur near Preston where study has been limited. Nevertheless the tetrads in the Silverdale, Yealand and Warton areas have the combination

of varied habitats that give rise to a particularly rich dandelion flora. Thus the rich dandelion flora reflects the rich vascular plant flora as a whole in these areas. Overall the south and west of VC 60 and all of Lancashire VC 64 are very much under recorded. In these areas many of the species found further north will occur and recent work in Lancashire VC 64 and in the south of VC 60 has demonstrated that new species can still be added. More work in these areas may reveal further additions to the northern Lancashire dandelion flora.

Because of the unevenness of recording, frequency information is not very meaningful. In attempt to make them more meaningful the frequency categories are calculated as a percentage of the number of tetrads in which *Taraxacum* species have been recorded and critically identified (see Table 3.4). However despite this adjustment no species falls into the common or very common categories. Nevertheless whilst most species appear to be rare or very rare there are some that are frequent and they are probably common or very common. In this account localities are given for very rare and rare species and tetrad distribution maps are provided for other species.

Table 3.4 Dandelion species frequency

Frequency category	No. of tetrads in which a species was recorded	Approx. frequency as % of total No. of tetrads in which *Taraxacum* species were recorded
Extinct	0	0
Very rare	1	<1
Rare	2–6	1–3
Occasional	7–30	4–15
Frequent	31–101	16–50
Common	102–151	51–75
Very common	152–202	>75

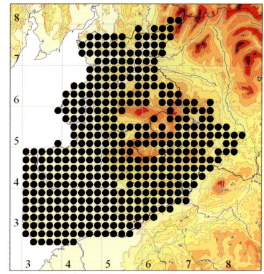

Taraxacum agg.

Similarly because of the inadequacy of the survey the distribution maps and comments on distribution within northern Lancashire are tentative. Nevertheless it is possible to make a few general remarks about both distribution and ecology.

Dandelions are so common that despite their often magnificent displays of yellow at the end of April or in early May they are usually ignored. However they are not ubiquitous avoiding peat covered areas in the hills and in lowlands. Qualitative observations suggest that most species occur in the former woodland zone on clay soils fringing the Bowland Fells and extending westwards on boulder clay in lowland areas as well as on calcareous soils in the northwest and on the sandy areas of the Fylde coast. In these places fine displays are often found on roadsides. They can also become abundant or even dominant in eutrophic grasslands, especially species belonging to sections Hamata and Ruderalia, provided they are not treated with herbicides and some plodging with animals has occurred. However these generalisations hide more specific requirements of individual species or sections. Thus Erythrospermae are found on light, well-drained and usually calcareous soils and are hardly ever found on roadsides, in woodland edges or in wet places. *T. faeroense*, the only member in Lancashire of section Spectabilia, is almost confined to neutral to base-rich hill flushes. Species belonging to sections Naevosa and Celtica are often found in damp places, in woodland edges and on shaded roadsides. They are especially characteristic of the woodland zone fringing Bowland. Species in section Hamata are found in ruderal habitats almost anywhere but by far the largest section is Ruderalia. Species in this section are often 'weedy' and are found on roadsides, waste ground and eutrophic pastures frequently with species of section Hamata. Many species of section Ruderalia are thought to be introduced.

In this tentative account of *Taraxacum* in northern Lancashire the sequence and nomenclature follows Dudman and Richards (1997). Common names were taken from Sell and Murrell (2006). All material was seen by Chris Haworth, Andrew Dudman or Professor A.J. Richards. Most gatherings were made by Len Livermore but following his death his herbarium suffered severe insect damage and most voucher specimens were lost. Fortunately labels survived and data was abstracted from them. The remains of his collection are at LIV. Other collectors included E.F & B.D.G. and C.F. & N.J.S. with a few records from other sources including Abbott (2005). Almost all records were made after 1970.

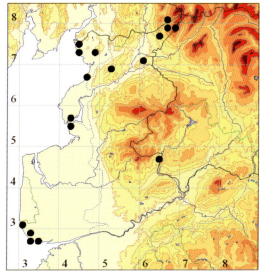

Taraxacum lacistophyllum

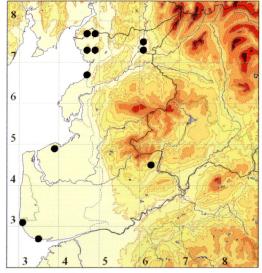

Taraxacum brachyglossum

A great deal more can be learned from a study of the dandelion flora but mastering the identification problems involved with the genus are a pre-requisite to a comprehensive study.

Section ERYTHROSPERMA (H. Lindb.) Dahlst.

These are small plants, often with dissected leaves, found on light and often calcareous soils.

Taraxacum lacistophyllum (Dahlst.) Raunk.   Cut-leaved Dandelion

Occasional (17). This is found throughout the British Isles and in Lancashire is found on calcareous soils in the north of the area, in the Hodder valley and on sand dunes at Lytham St Anne's.

Taraxacum inopinatum C.C. Haw.   Unexpected Dandelion

Very rare (1). *T. inopinatum* is found mostly in Wales and western England. In northern Lancashire it was found at Ellel (SD55B).

Taraxacum brachyglossum (Dahlst.) Raunk.

Purple-bracted Dandelion

Occasional (11). *T. brachyglossum* is one of the more readily recognisable species and is found throughout the British Isles. In northern Lancashire it was found on calcareous soils in the north of the area, in the Hodder valley and on sandy ground on the coast.

Taraxacum argutum Dahlst.   Sharp-toothed Dandelion

Rare (3). This is found in limestone areas, especially in the west although there are records from most parts of Britain. In northern Lancashire it was found at Silverdale (SD47T), Thurnham (SD45H) and Heaton-with-Oxcliffe (SD46K).

Taraxacum arenastrum A.J. Richards   Sand Dandelion

Very rare (1). This is a local and rare species of sand dunes and calcareous grasslands found mostly on the coasts of the British Isles. The northern Lancashire record is unusual in that it was found inland on a limestone pasture at Bowland-with-Leagram (SD64N).

Taraxacum rubicundum (Dahlst.) Dahlst.   Ruddy Dandelion

Occasional (8). *T. rubicundum* is a widespread species of dry, mostly calcareous places in England and more rarely in Scotland. In northern Lancashire it was found on the limestone around Morecambe Bay and in the Hodder valley.

Taraxacum parnassicum Dahlst.   Parnassus Dandelion

Rare (2). *T. parnassicum* is found in dry calcareous grassland in England. In northern Lancashire it was found at Silverdale (SD47S) and Ellel (SD55B).

Taraxacum haworthianum Dudman & A.J. Richards

Haworth's Dandelion

This is an endemic species found mostly on sand dune grassland and occasionally inland on calcareous pastures. It occurs throughout the British Isles but in northern Lancashire the only record was from Ease Gill, Leck (SD68Q) in 1899 (J.A.W. & A.W.; NMW).

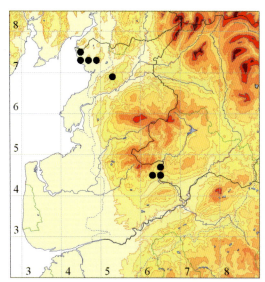

Taraxacum rubicundum

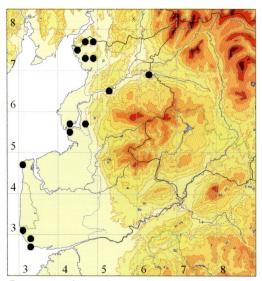

Taraxacum oxoniense

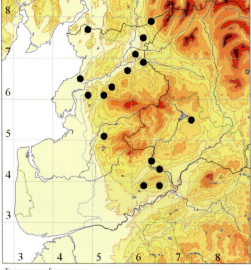

Taraxacum faeroense

Taraxacum oxoniense Dahlst.   Oxford Dandelion

Occasional (14). *T. oxoniense* is a common species of dry, neutral or calcareous grassland including sand dunes and is found in many parts of the British Isles. In northern Lancashire it was found in many coastal areas and more occasionally inland.

Taraxacum fulviforme Dahlst.   Green-bracted Dandelion

Rare (4). *T. fulviforme* is found in dry places on sand dunes and calcareous grassland throughout the British Isles. In northern Lancashire it was found in scattered localities on the Lune estuary (SD45H), Yealand (SD57C), by the R. Hodder (SD73E) and at Lytham St Anne's (SD32N).

Taraxacum fulvum Raunk.   Cinnamon-fruited Dandelion

Rare (4). This is found on light, neutral to calcareous soils and rocky places throughout the British Isles. In northern Lancashire it was found at Dalton (SD57N), Warton Crag (SD47W), Silverdale (SD47R), Roeburndale (SD66C) and at Lytham St Anne's.

Taraxacum glauciniforme Dahlst.   Many-toothed Dandelion

Very rare (1). *T. glauciniforme* is found in grassland on light, well-drained, neutral to calcareous soils and in rocky places in many localities in southern Britain. In northern Lancashire it was found at Yealand Redmayne (SD47Y).

Section **SPECTABILIA** (Dahlst.) Dahlst.

This is a small section of three British species only one of which is found in northern Lancashire.

Taraxacum faeroense (Dahlst.) Dahlst.   Faeroes Dandelion

Occasional (16). This is a small, dark green species, often with spotted and almost unlobed leaves. It is found in wet, usually flushed places, mostly in hilly and western areas but may be found anywhere in the British Isles. In northern Lancashire it was found in the north and east of the area.

Section **NAEVOSA** M.P. Christ.

This section includes species with large spotted leaves with a northern and western distribution in Britain. They are often found in woodland edge habitats.

Taraxacum naevosum Dahlst.   Squat Dandelion

Very rare (1). This is a species of damp hay meadows and is found in northern England and Scotland and occasionally elsewhere. In northern Lancashire it was found near Lower Lee, Over Wyresdale (SD55S).

Taraxacum naevosiforme Dahlst.   Wetland Dandelion

Very rare (1). *T. naevosiforme* is found in wet grassland and on cliffs etc. It occurs in Scotland, Ireland, Wales, northern and occasionally midland England. In northern Lancashire it was found in Roeburndale (SD66C).

Taraxacum europhyllum (Dahlst.) Hjelt   Wide-stalked Dandelion

Frequent (37). This is one of the commonest dandelions found in wet, rather sheltered, somewhat base-rich sites throughout Britain but it is very rare in Ireland. In northern Lancashire *T. europhyllum* was found

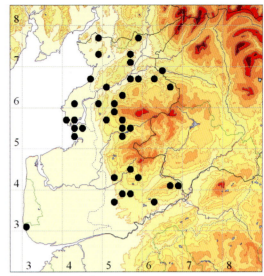
Taraxacum europhyllum

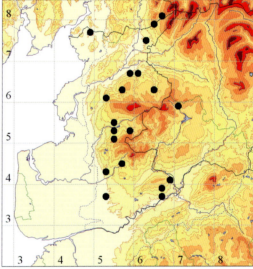
Taraxacum maculosum

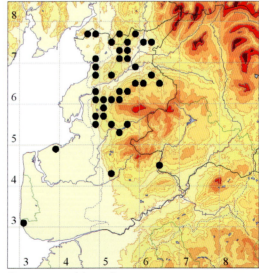
Taraxacum pseudolarssonii

in northern and western parts of VC 60 and at Lytham St Anne's. It is probably more widespread than the records suggest.

Taraxacum maculosum A.J. Richards — Spotted Dandelion

Occasional (20). *T. maculosum* is found in wet places, especially in wet wood margins on usually base-rich soils in northern parts of the British Isles with occasional records elsewhere. In northern Lancashire it was found in the north and east of the area but it is probably more widespread than the records suggest.

Taraxacum pseudolarssonii A.J. Richards
Spreading-bracted Dandelion

Frequent (39). This is a meadow and roadside species found mostly in northern England but with occasional records elsewhere, especially in Scotland. It can be abundant in some meadows. In northern Lancashire *T. pseudolarssonii* was found mostly in the north of the area and occasionally elsewhere including the sand dunes at Lytham St Anne's but it is probably found throughout the region.

Taraxacum subnaevosum A.J. Richards — Pale-bracted Dandelion

Very rare (1). *T. subnaevosum* is found in Scotland, northern England and Wales with occasional records elsewhere. In northern Lancashire it was found at Silverdale (SD47S).

Taraxacum stictophyllum Dahlst. — Stiff-leaved Dandelion

Rare (3). This is found in lowland wet shaded rocky places in northern and western Britain. In northern Lancashire there is an old record for *T. stictophyllum* from Ease Gill, Leck (*c.* SD68Q; J.A.W.; LIV). Recent records were from Over Wyresdale (SD55L), Tatham (SD66S) and Hothersall (SD63H).

Taraxacum richardsianum C.C. Haw. — Richards's Dandelion

Occasional (8). This is an endemic species found in moist grasslands mostly in western Britain with scattered records elsewhere in England. It occurs in scattered localities in northern and eastern parts of northern Lancashire and probably elsewhere as well.

Section CELTICA A.J. Richards

Species in this section are medium-sized plants often with red or bright purple leaf midribs. They generally have a western distribution occurring in woodland edge habitats including shady roadsides.

Taraxacum gelertii Raunck. — Gelert's Dandelion

Occasional (14). *T. gelertii* is found in grassy habitats on well-drained neutral to calcareous soils throughout the British Isles. In northern Lancashire it has a western distribution.

Taraxacum bracteatum Dahlst. — Dark-green Dandelion

Rare (6). This is found in damp habitats throughout the British Isles. In northern Lancashire it was found at Silverdale (SD47S), Yealand Redmayne (SD47X), Tatham (SD66I), Cockerham (SD45K), Fulwood (SD53K) and near Slaidburn (SD75F).

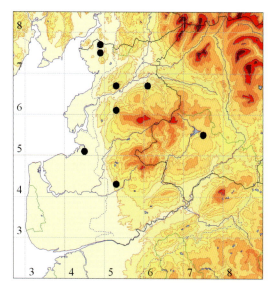

Taraxacum richardsianum

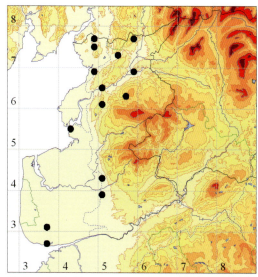

Taraxacum gelertii

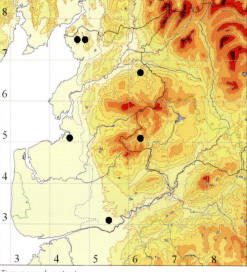

Taraxacum bracteatum

[**Taraxacum britannicum** Dahlst.

Dudman and Richards (1997) show this as occurring in VC 60 but the locality is in VC 59.]

Taraxacum subbracteatum A.J. Richards   Dark-bracted Dandelion

Rare (3). This is an endemic species found throughout Britain, particularly in the north and west. In northern Lancashire *T. subbracteatum* was found at Overton (SD45I), Lancaster (SD46V) and Halton-with-Aughton (SD56I).

Taraxacum duplidentifrons Dahlst.   Double-toothed Dandelion

Frequent (43). *T. duplidentifrons* is found throughout the British Isles, especially in grassy places on well-drained, base-rich soils. In northern Lancashire most records were from northern and eastern VC 60 but it is likely to occur throughout the area.

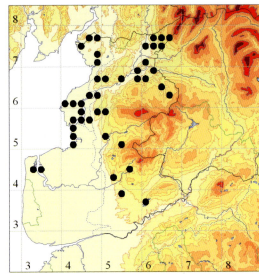
Taraxacum duplidentifrons

Taraxacum celticum A.J. Richards   Celtic Dandelion

Very rare (1). This endemic species is found on light, well-drained, neutral to calcareous soils, often in species-rich grasslands in western England and Wales. In northern Lancashire *T. celticum* was found in Over Wyresdale (SD55S).

Taraxacum hesperium C.C. Haw.   Western Dandelion

Rare (3). *T. hesperium* is an endemic species found mostly in western Britain. In northern Lancashire it occurred at Quernmore (SD56A), Hornby-with-Farleton (SD56Z) and Lancaster (SD46V).

Taraxacum excellens Dahlst.   Purple-blotched Dandelion

Occasional (11). *T. excellens* is found mostly in western Britain with occasional localities elsewhere. In northern Lancashire most records were from the north and west of the area but it probably occurs elsewhere.

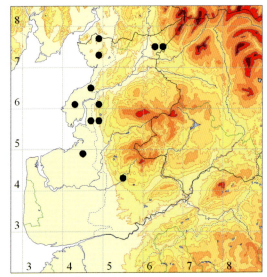
Taraxacum excellens

Taraxacum inane A.J. Richards   Pollenless Dandelion

Rare (4). This is an endemic species found mostly in Scotland, northern England and Wales. In northern Lancashire it was found at Leck (SD67N), Burrow-with-Burrow (SD67C), Yealand Redmayne (SD47T) and Over Wyresdale (SD55W).

Taraxacum fulgidum G.E. Haglund   Bright Dandelion

Very rare (1). This is found in damp hay meadows mostly in southern Britain. In northern Lancashire it was found near Ortner, Over Wyresdale (SD55H).

Taraxacum tamesense A.J. Richards   Thames Dandelion

Rare (2). This is characteristic of water meadows mown for hay in central southern England. However it is occasionally found elsewhere. In northern Lancashire *T. tamesense* was found at Yealand Redmayne (SD47X & Y).

Taraxacum texelense Hagend. ex Soest & Zevenb.   Texel Dandelion

Very rare (1). The status of this in Britain is uncertain, as the only record is from a salt marsh at Carnforth (SD47V) in 1989 (L.A.L.).

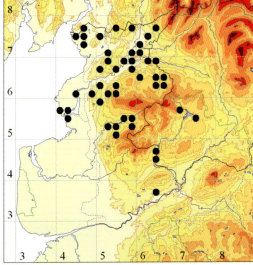
Traxacum nordstedtii

Taraxacum haematicum G.E. Haglund ex Øllg. & Wiezell
Blood-red Dandelion

Rare (3). This is a species of damp, base-rich grasslands and occurs throughout Britain with a single Irish locality. In northern Lancashire *T. haematicum* was found at Silverdale (SD47M & S) and Yealand Redmayne (SD47Y).

Taraxacum nordstedtii Dahlst.　　　　　Nordstedt's Dandelion

Frequent (47). *T. nordstedtii* is a common species of lowland wet places throughout the British Isles but it may be found in a variety of habitats in western Britain including walls and cliffs. In northern Lancashire it was found in the north and east of the area but it almost certainly occurs throughout the region.

Taraxacum pseudonordstedtii A.J. Richards　　Teesdale Dandelion

Very rare (1). This is an endemic species of calcareous flushes in north-western England. There is an unlocalised record of *T. pseudonordstedtii* in northern Lancashire from the 10km square SD56.

Taraxacum berthae C.C. Haw.　　　　　Bertha's Dandelion

Rare (2). *T. berthae* is an endemic species known only from south-western Scotland, north-western England and southern Wales. In northern Lancashire it was found at Silverdale (SD47R & S).

Taraxacum lancastriense A.J. Richards　　Lancashire Dandelion

Rare (3). This endemic species occurs in neutral to calcareous grass-lands and is found in northern England and southern Wales. It was first described from a specimen gathered on a roadside near Higher Brock Mill, Bleasdale (SD54S) in 1971 (OXF). It was also found at Wray-with-Botton (SD56Y & SD66I).

Taraxacum ostenfeldii Raunck.　　　　　Ostenfeld's Dandelion

Rare (2). *T. ostenfeldii* is found in ruderal habitats in scattered locali-ties throughout Britain. In northern Lancashire it was found at Chaigley (SD64Q) and Wray-with-Botton (SD56Y).

Taraxacum unguilobum Dahlst.　　　　　Claw-lobed Dandelion

Occasional (20). *T. unguilobum* is found in wet ruderal places, flushes and rocky places mostly in the north and west of the British Isles where it is often common. In northern Lancashire it was found in the north and east of VC 60 and on the Fylde coast. It is likely to be more widespread than the records suggest.

Taraxacum luteum C.C. Haw. & A.J. Richards　Pure Yellow Dandelion

Rare (6). *T. luteum* is an endemic species that has luminous yellow flowers without ligule stripes. It is found in damp grasslands and on walls with most records from north-western England with occasional localities else-where. In northern Lancashire it was found by the Ease Gill, Leck (SD68Q), Tatham (SD66S), Arkholme-with-Cawood (SD57R), Wray-with-Botton (SD66L), Over Wyresdale (SD55L) and Bowland-with-Leagram (SD64N).

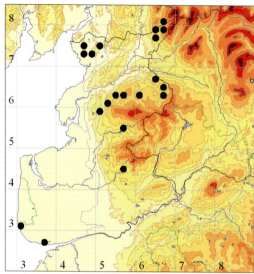

Taraxacum unguilobum

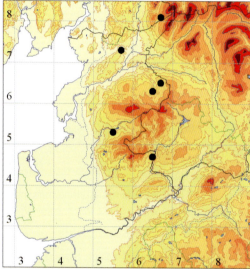

Taraxacum luteum

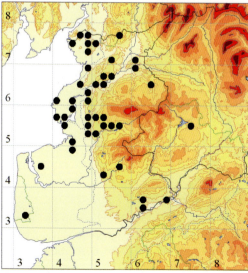

Taraxacum hamatum

Section **HAMATA** H. Øllg.

This is a small section of eighteen species found commonly on roadsides, in grasslands, woodland edges and in ruderal habitats in many parts of the British Isles.

Taraxacum hamatum Raunk.   Hook-lobed Dandelion

Frequent (44). *T. hamatum* is found in woodland edge and ruderal habitats throughout the British Isles. It is found throughout northern Lancashire although it may be rare in the intensively farmed lowland areas.

Taraxacum hamatulum Hagend., Soest & Zevenb.
                                  Slender Hook-lobed Dandelion

Rare (4). This is found in scattered localities in Britain. In northern Lancashire it was recorded from near Lancaster (SD46K), Yealand Redmayne (SD47Y), Bowland-with-Leagram (SD64N) and Bashall Eaves (SD64W).

Taraxacum subhamatum M.P. Christ.   Large Hook-lobed Dandelion

Occasional (16). *T. subhamatum* is found in grassy places, on roadsides and in other marginal and ruderal habitats in many places in the British Isles. In northern Lancashire it appears to be confined to the north and northwest of the area but it probably occurs elsewhere.

Taraxacum marklundii Palmgr.   Marklund's Dandelion

Occasional (12). This is found in grassy places and ruderal habitats throughout Britain. In northern Lancashire *T. marklundii* was found in the north and east of the area but it probably occurs elsewhere as well.

Taraxacum hamifarum Dahlst.   Dark Hook-lobed Dandelion

Occasional (7). *T. hamifarum* is found in marginal and ruderal habitats throughout Britain with a single Irish locality. In northern Lancashire it was found in northern VC 60.

Taraxacum quadrans H. Øllg.   Fleshy-lobed Dandelion

Occasional (7). *T. quadrans* is probably introduced into Britain where it occurs in ruderal habitats. It also occurs rarely in Ireland. In northern Lancashire it was found in the Lancaster area and in the Trough of Bowland.

Taraxacum pseudohamatum Dahlst.   False Hook-lobed Dandelion

Occasional (25). This is the commonest species in this section in the British Isles yet it is very rare in Europe. It is found on roadsides and in other ruderal habitats throughout the British Isles. In northern Lancashire it occurs in the north and east of the area with a single locality in the south at Blackpool. However it is likely to be more frequent than the records suggest.

Taraxacum boekmanii Borgv.   Bökman's Dandelion

Frequent (38). This is another common species of grassy places and ruderal habitats and is found throughout Britain and more rarely in Ireland. In northern Lancashire *T. boekmanii* is probably found throughout the area.

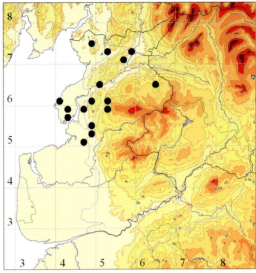
Taraxacum subhamatum

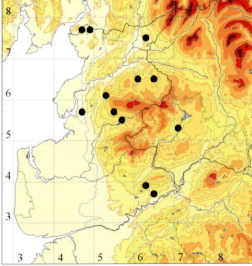
Taraxacum marklundii

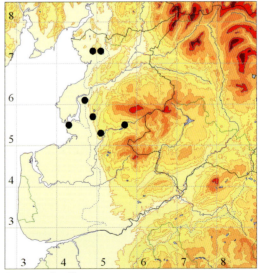
Taraxacum hamifarum

Taraxacum atactum Sahlin & Soest   Narrow-bracted Dandelion

Occasional (13). *T. atactum* is another ruderal species that is found throughout Britain and more occasionally in Ireland. In northern Lancashire it probably occurs throughout the area although it has not been recorded from southern areas except at Lytham St Anne's.

Taraxacum sahlinianum Dudman & A.J. Richards Sahlin's Dandelion

Rare (4). This endemic species of ruderal habitats is found in western and northern Britain but it has often been confused with *T. atactum*. In northern Lancashire *T. sahlinianum* was found near Carnforth (SD46Z), Lancaster (SD46V), near Dolphinholme (SD55B) and at Conder Green (SD45S).

Taraxacum hamatiforme Dahlst.
                    Asymmetrical Hook-lobed Dandelion

Occasional (24). This is found in grassy places, on roadsides and in other marginal habitats throughout the British Isles. In northern Lancashire *T. hamatiforme* was found in the northwest of VC 60 and was common there. It probably occurs elsewhere in the area.

Taraxacum spiculatum M.P. Christ.   Sagittate-lobed Dandelion

Rare (2). This is an uncommon species of ruderal habitats found in a few scattered English localities. In northern Lancashire it was found on the sand dunes at Lytham St Anne's (SD33A) and by the Lancaster Canal near Yealand Conyers (SD57C).

Taraxacum lamprophyllum M.P. Christ. Lustrous-leaved Dandelion

Occasional (12). *T. lamprophyllum* is perhaps introduced into Britain and occurs in ruderal and marginal habitats throughout the British Isles. In northern Lancashire it was found in the Lancaster, Morecambe and Heysham areas and probably occurs elsewhere, especially in urban localities.

Section **RUDERALIA** Kirschner, H. Øllg. & Stepanek

This is the largest section with over 120 species. They are typically robust, morphologically variable with complicated and multilobed leaf dentation. They are mostly 'weedy' and found in marginal and ruderal habitats, especially on roadsides often where there has been disturbance.

Taraxacum laeticolor Dahlst.   Pale-stalked Dandelion

Occasional (8). *T. laeticolor* is probably an introduction and occurs in scattered localities throughout Britain in grassy and ruderal habitats. It appears to occur mostly in western parts of northern Lancashire.

Taraxacum macrolobum Dahlst.   Incise-lobed Dandelion

Very rare (1). This is probably introduced and occurs in grassy and ruderal habitats in scattered localities in the British Isles. In northern Lancashire it was found at Melling (SD57A).

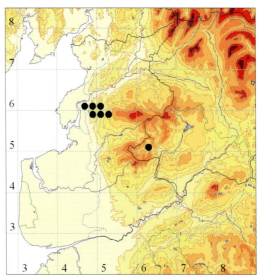
Taraxacum quadrans

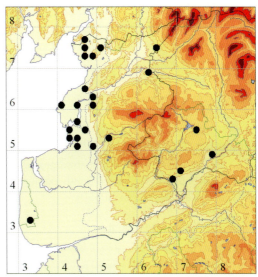
Taraxacum pseudohamatum

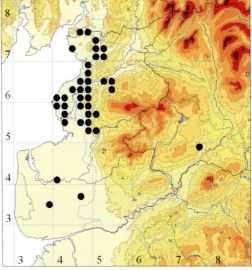
Taraxacum boekmanii

Taraxacum pannucium Dahlst.   Green-stalked Dandelion

Occasional (13). This is probably an introduction and occurs in grassy and ruderal habitats throughout the British Isles. In northern Lancashire *T. pannucium* probably occurs throughout the region although it is apparently absent from southern areas.

Taraxacum subexpallidum Dahlst.   Tongue-lobed Dandelion

Rare (5). This is probably introduced and occurs in grassy and ruderal habitats in most parts of Britain. In northern Lancashire it was found at Halton-with-Aughton (SD56C) and near Dolphinholme (SD55H). Also plants originally identified as *T. linguatum* Dahlst ex M.P. Christ. & Wiinst. were found at Over Kellet (SD57F), Nether Kellet (SD56D) and Over Wyresdale (SD55H) and probably belong to this species.

Taraxacum corynodes G.E. Haglund   Dense-lobed Dandelion

Very rare (1). This is an introduced species of grassy places and ruderal habitats. Most records are from Wales and the Welsh borders with occasional records elsewhere. In northern Lancashire it was found at Heysham Dock (SD46A).

Taraxacum undulatum H. Lindb. & Markl.   Wavy-lobed Dandelion

Rare (3). *T. undulatum* is found in grassy and ruderal habitats in scattered localities in Britain and from Dublin in Ireland. In northern Lancashire it was found at Silverdale (SD47T), Quernmore (SD56F) and probably this species from near Wray (SD67M).

Taraxacum dilaceratum M.P. Christ.   Lacerate-leaved Dandelion

Very rare (1). *T. dilaceratum* is probably introduced and occurs in grassy and ruderal habitats in scattered British localities. In northern Lancashire it was found near Quernmore (SD55D).

Taraxacum alatum H. Lindb.   Green Dandelion

Occasional (16). This is found in grassy and ruderal habitats throughout Britain and in the north of Ireland and in some areas it is very common. It probably occurs throughout northern Lancashire although so far it has only been recorded in western areas and in the Ribble valley.

Taraxacum horridifrons Rail.   Prickly-leaved Dandelion

Very rare (1). *T. horridifrons* is an introduction found on roadsides in a few areas of England and Wales. In northern Lancashire it was found at Gressingham (SD56P).

Taraxacum insigne Ekman ex M.P. Christ. & Wiinst.

Remarkable Dandelion

Occasional (8). This is found in dry grassy places and ruderal habitats throughout Britain, where it is often common, and occasionally in Ireland. *T. insigne* has been recorded from a few localities in northern Lancashire but probably occurs throughout the area.

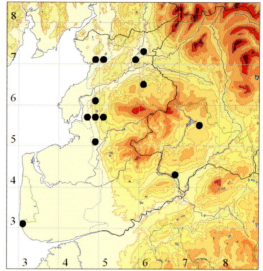

Taraxacum atactum

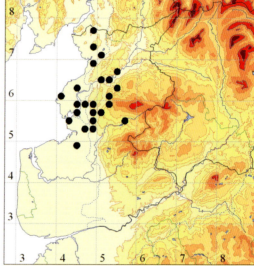

Taraxacum hamatiforme

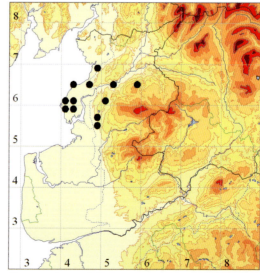

Taraxacum lamprophyllum

Taraxacum pannulatiforme Dahlst.   Tar-blotched Dandelion

Rare (4). This is found in grassy and ruderal habitats in scattered localities in the British Isles. In northern Lancashire *T. pannulatiforme* was found at Yealand Redmayne (SD47Y), near Carnforth (SD46Z), Barton (SD43Y) and near Quernmore (SD55D).

Taraxacum laticordatum Markl.   Decumbent Dandelion

Occasional (7). This occurs in grassy and ruderal habitats in Britain and eastern Ireland. In northern Lancashire *T. laticordatum* was found in a few localities in the north of the area.

Taraxacum necessarium H. Øllg.   Dark-leaved Dandelion

Rare (2). *T. necessarium* is found in grassy and ruderal habitats in scattered localities in Britain. In northern Lancashire it was found at Sunderland Point (SD45D) and near Abbeystead (SD55M).

Taraxacum sublaeticolor Dahlst.   Small-headed Dandelion

Rare (4). This is found in grassy and ruderal habitats throughout Britain. In northern Lancashire *T. sublaeticolor* was found at Arkholme-with-Cawood (SD57W), Silverdale (SD47M), near Wray (SD56Y) and near Carnforth (SD46Z).

Taraxacum lepidum M.P. Christ.   Pruinose-bracted Dandelion

Rare (3). *T. lepidum* is found in grassy places and old meadows mostly in western Britain. In northern Lancashire it was found at Morecambe (SD46M), near Warton (SD57B) and near Lancaster University (SD45Y).

Taraxacum expallidiforme Dahlst.   Broad-stalked Dandelion

Occasional (29). This is found in grassy and ruderal habitats throughout Britain, where it is often common and occasionally in Ireland. *T. expallidi-forme* is found throughout northern Lancashire.

Taraxacum subcyanolepis M.P. Christ.   Reddish-bracted Dandelion

Occasional (13). This is found in old grasslands and other grassy habitats throughout the British Isles. In northern Lancashire *T. subcyanolepis* probably occurs throughout the area.

Taraxacum pallidipes Markl.   Grey-bracted Dandelion

Rare (4). This is probably introduced and is found on roadsides and other ruderal habitats in scattered localities in Britain. In northern Lancashire *T. pallidipes* was found at Ellel (SD55A), Yealand (SD57C), Heysham (SD46A) and Ireby (SD67M).

Taraxacum croceiflorum Dahlst.   Orange-flowered Dandelion

Occasional (20). *T. croceiflorum* is found in grassy and ruderal habitats throughout the British Isles. It probably occurs throughout northern Lancashire.

Taraxacum lacerifolium G.E. Haglund   Jagged-leaved Dandelion

Very rare (1). This is probably an introduction found in scattered places on roadsides and in other grassy places. Most records are from southern England and Wales. In northern Lancashire *T. lacerifolium* was found near Carnforth (SD46Z).

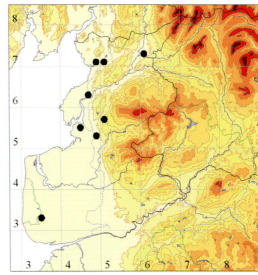

Taraxacum laeticolor

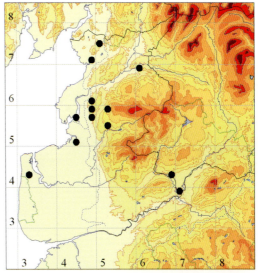

Taraxacum pannucium

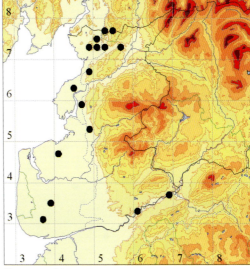

Taraxacum alatum

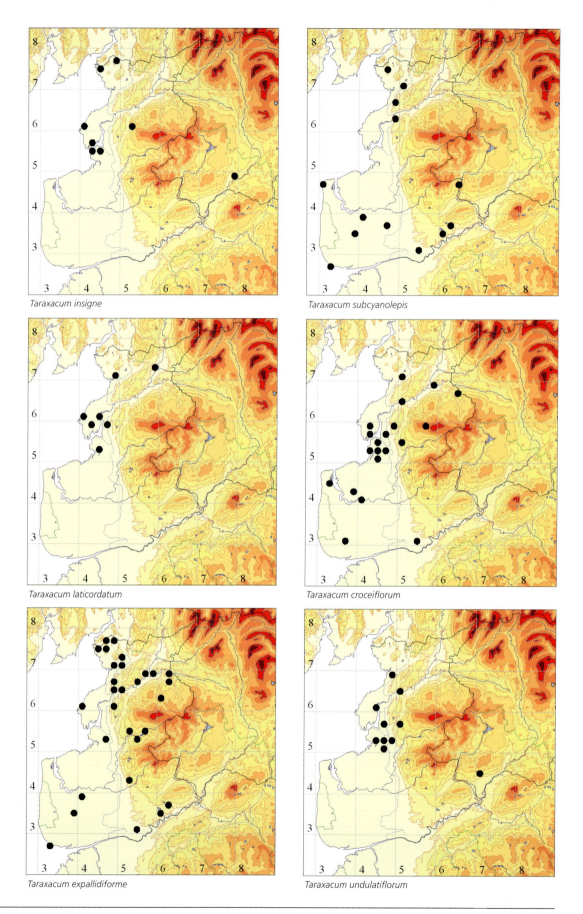

Taraxacum insigne

Taraxacum subcyanolepis

Taraxacum laticordatum

Taraxacum croceiflorum

Taraxacum expallidiforme

Taraxacum undulatiflorum

Taraxacum broddesonii G.E. Haglund *nom. nud.*

Broddeson's Dandelion

Very rare (1). This introduced species has only been recorded as a casual on waste ground on a few occasions in Britain. In northern Lancashire *T. brodesonii* was found at Cockerham (SD45R) and possibly at Over Kellet (SD57F).

Taraxacum undulatiflorum M.P. Christ. Dull-leaved Dandelion

Occasional (10). *T. undulatiflorum* is probably an introduction found on roadsides and in ruderal habitats in Britain and eastern Ireland. It probably occurs throughout northern Lancashire although most records are from the northwest of the area.

Taraxacum chloroticum Dahlst. Spiky-leaved Dandelion

Very rare (1). This is found as an introduction on a few roadsides, mostly in south-eastern England. In northern Lancashire *T. chloroticum* was found near Carnforth (SD57B).

Taraxacum piceatum Dahlst. Leaden-bracted Dandelion

Occasional (9). This is probably an introduced species found on roadsides and in ruderal habitats throughout Britain. So far this has been found in north-western areas of northern Lancashire but it is likely to be more widespread than this.

Taraxacum cyanolepis Dahlst. Bluish-bracted Dandelion

Rare (5). This is found in grasslands throughout the British Isles but especially in Scotland. It has apparently become less common since 1970 (Dudman and Richards, 1997) and is absent from large areas of Britain. In northern Lancashire *T. cyanolepis* was found near Carnforth (SD57A), Burrow-with-Burrow (SD67A), Goosnargh (SD53P), Hothersall (SD63I) and Weeton-with-Preese (SD33X).

Taraxacum acutifrons Markl. Acute-leaved Dandelion

Rare (2). This introduced species is found on roadsides and in ruderal habitats in western England and Wales. In northern Lancashire *T. acutifrons* was found at Over Kellet (SD57K) and near Carnforth (SD57A).

Taraxacum chrysophaenum Rail. Orange-toothed Dandelion

Very rare (1). *T. chrysophaenum* is a rare introduction found in a few scattered localities. In northern Lancashire it was found at Heysham (SD46A).

Taraxacum tumentilobum Markl. ex Puol. Swollen-lobed Dandelion

Rare (2). *T. tumentilobum* is probably introduced and occurs in grassy and ruderal habitats in scattered localities throughout Britain. In northern Lancashire it was found at Tatham (SD66J) and Thurnham (SD45H).

Taraxacum intumescens G.E. Haglund Red-tipped Dandelion

Very rare (1). This is an uncommon introduction of roadsides and ruderal habitats found mostly in southern England. In northern Lancashire *T. intumescens* was found at Longridge (SD63D).

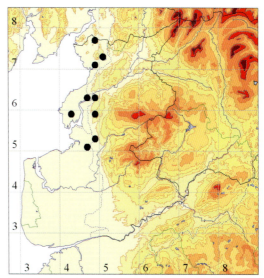

Taraxacum piceatum

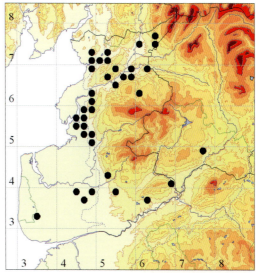

Taraxacum ancistrolobum

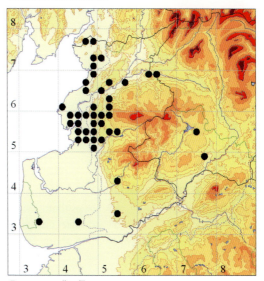

Taraxacum sellandii

Taraxacum ancistrolobum Dahlst.　　　　Few-lobed Dandelion

Frequent (37). This is found in grassy and ruderal habitats throughout Britain but it is very rare in Ireland. *T. ancistrolobum* was found throughout northern Lancashire.

Taraxacum sellandii Dahlst.　　　　Selland's Dandelion

Frequent (43). This is one of the commonest dandelions and is found in grassy and ruderal habitats throughout the British Isles. *T. sellandii* was found throughout northern Lancashire.

Taraxacum altissimum H. Lindb.　　　　Tall Dandelion

Rare (2). This is probably introduced and is found in grassy and ruderal habitats in scattered localities in Britain. It is uncommon. In northern Lancashire *T. altissimum* was found at Thurnham (SD45M) and Longridge (SD63D).

Taraxacum interveniens G.E. Haglund　　　　City Dandelion

Very rare (1). This is probably introduced and occurs in grassy and ruderal habitats in scattered localities in Britain. It is particularly associated with large urban areas. In northern Lancashire *T. interveniens* was found near Glasson Dock (SD45M).

Taraxacum angustisquamum Dahlst. ex H. Lindb.

　　　　Multilobed Dandelion

Rare (2). *T. angustisquamum* is probably introduced and is found in grassy and ruderal habitats in scattered localities in Britain. In northern Lancashire it was found near Carnforth (SD46Z) and near Blackpool (SD33L).

Taraxacum stereodes Ekman ex G.E. Haglund

　　　　Hairy-stalked Dandelion

Very rare (1). This is an introduction on major roads and found mostly in southern England. In northern Lancashire *T. stereodes* was found near Galgate (SD45X).

Taraxacum adiantifrons Ekman ex Dahlst.　　Pretty-leaved Dandelion

Rare (4). This is probably introduced and occurs in grassy and ruderal habitats throughout Britain. In northern Lancashire *T. adiantifrons* was recorded from Yealand Redmayne (SD47Y), Yealand Conyers (SD47X), Slyne-with-Hest (SD46S) and Hornby-with-Farleton (SD56Y).

Taraxacum aequilobum Dahlst.　　　　Twisted-bracted Dandelion

Occasional (12). *T. aequilobum* is probably introduced and is found in grassy and ruderal habitats throughout the British Isles. It probably occurs throughout northern Lancashire but so far it has only been found in the north of the area.

Taraxacum latissimum Palmgr.　　　　Broad-leaved Dandelion

Rare (3). This is an introduced species that is widespread in Britain in ruderal habitats. In northern Lancashire *T. latissimum* was found at Tatham (SD66I), near Carnforth (SD46Z) and on the Lune estuary (SD45H).

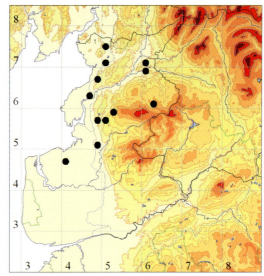

Taraxacum aequilobum

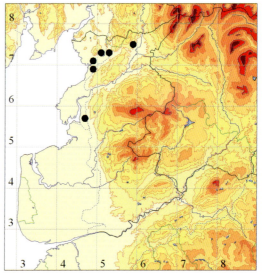

Taraxacum acroglossum

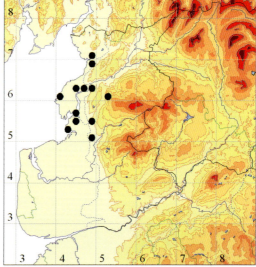

Taraxacum exacutum

Taraxacum edmondsonianum H. Øllg.   Edmondson's Dandelion

Very rare (1). So far this has only been found in the British Isles in north-western England, Monmouthshire and Midlothian. In northern Lancashire *T. edmondsonianum* was found near Scorton (SD54E).

Taraxacum acroglossum Dahlst.   Broad-bracted Dandelion

Rare (6). This is probably introduced and is found in grassy and ruderal habitats in scattered localities in Britain. In northern Lancashire it was found Whittington (SD57X), Borwick (SD57G), near Carnforth (SD47V & SD57B), Bolton-le-Sands (SD46Z) and Ashton-with-Stodday (SD45T).

Taraxacum exsertum Hagend., Soest & Zevenb. Pale-green Dandelion

Rare (2). This is an introduced species and is found in scattered localities in the British Isles. In northern Lancashire *T. exsertum* was found in Lancaster (SD46W) and near Lea (SD43W).

Taraxacum exacutum Markl.   Imbricate-bracted Dandelion

Occasional (12). *T. exacutum* is probably introduced and occurs on waste land, tips and in other ruderal habitats in most parts of Britain. So far it has only been found in north-western parts of northern Lancashire but it is likely to be widespread in the area.

Taraxacum pannulatum Dahlst.   Brown-ribbed Dandelion

Occasional (8). *T. pannulatum* is probably introduced and is found in grassy and ruderal habitats in many parts of Britain but especially in western areas. It is found in scattered localities in the north of northern Lancashire but it is probably more widespread than this suggests.

Taraxacum lingulatum Markl.   Long-bracted Dandelion

Frequent (34). This is a common species found throughout the British Isles in grassy and ruderal habitats. It was found throughout northern Lancashire.

Taraxacum macranthoides G.E. Haglund   Large-flowered Dandelion

Very rare (1). This is an introduced species found in a few British localities. In northern Lancashire *T. macranthoides* was found on a roadside at Carnforth (SD57A).

Taraxacum rhamphodes G.E. Haglund   Robust Dandelion

Occasional (8). This introduced species is found in grassy and ruderal habitats throughout Britain. *T. rhamphodes* was found in scattered localities in northern Lancashire.

Taraxacum vastisectum Markl. ex Puol.   Crowded-lobed Dandelion

Rare (6). *T. vastisectum* is an introduced species found in grassy and ruderal habitats in scattered localities in Britain. In northern Lancashire it was found near Carnforth (SD46Z), Heysham (SD46A), at Thurnham (SD45M), Ashton-with-Stodday (SD45N), Cockerham (SD45F) and near Galgate (SD45X).

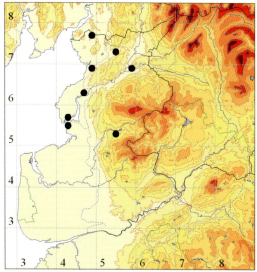

Taraxacum pannulatum

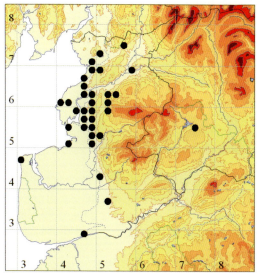

Taraxacum lingulatum

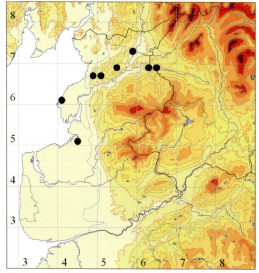

Taraxacum rhamphodes

Taraxacum cordatum Palmgr.   Entire-lobed Dandelion

Occasional (30). This is found in coastal areas, on roadsides and in ruderal habitats. It is found throughout the British Isles. In northern Lancashire *T. cordatum* was found throughout the area.

Taraxacum sagittipotens Dahlst. & Ohlsen ex G.E. Haglund
Smooth Dandelion

Rare (5). *T. sagittipotens* is found in grassy and ruderal habitats throughout Britain. In northern Lancashire it was found at Heysham (SD46F) and at various sites in and around Lancaster (SD46K, R, V & W).

Taraxacum hexhamense A.J. Richards   Hexham Dandelion

Very rare (1). This is probably an endemic species found in grassy places in a few scattered localities in Britain. In northern Lancashire *T. hexhamense* was found at Bolton-by-Bowland (SD74U).

Taraxacum ekmanii Dahlst.   Ekman's Dandelion

Frequent (35). This is found in grassy and ruderal habitats throughout the British Isles. It is one of the commonest species. *T. ekmanii* was found in many parts of northern Lancashire although it is yet to be found in Lancashire VC 64.

Taraxacum ochrochlorum G.E. Haglund ex Rail.   Winged Dandelion

Very rare (1). *T. ochrochlorum* is probably introduced and occurs in shady places as well as ruderal habitats. It is found in scattered localities in Britain and it is believed that it was this species that was found on Carr House Green Common, Inskip (SD43T).

Taraxacum aurosulum H. Lindb.   Tailed Dandelion

Occasional (7). This is probably introduced and occurs on shady roadsides and in other ruderal habitats. It is found throughout the British Isles. *T. aurosulum* was found in scattered localities in northern Lancashire.

Taraxacum lunare M.P. Christ.   Lunar-lobed Dandelion

Rare (3). There are a few British records of this introduced species. In northern Lancashire it was found at Cabus (SD44Y), in the Gressingham and Hornby areas (SD56U) and at Tatham (SD66J).

Taraxacum coartatum G.E. Haglund   Irregular-bracted Dandelion

Very rare (1). This is an introduced species found in a few localities in Britain. In northern Lancashire *T. coartatum* was found at Bashall Eaves (SD64W).

Taraxacum aberrans Hagend   Apiculate-leaved Dandelion

This is a rare introduction found in ruderal habitats in a few British localities. However there is a related plant, which is close to the Danish species *T. severum* M.P. Christ. and is found in grassy places in a number of British localities. It is probably endemic and is known by the work name *T. 'non-severum'*. It was found near Crag Bank, Carnforth (SD46Z).

Taraxacum pseudoretroflexum M.P. Christ.   Spur-lobed Dandelion

Very rare (1). This is an introduction found in a few English localities. *T. pseudoretroflexum* was found near Carnforth (SD47V).

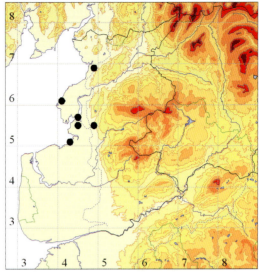

Taraxacum vastisectum

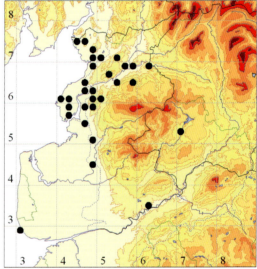

Taraxacum cordatum

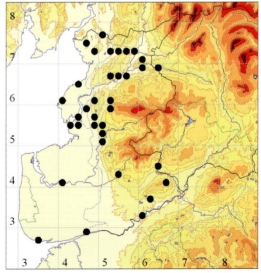

Taraxacum ekmanii

Taraxacum oblongatum Dahlst.   Oblong-leaved Dandelion

Occasional (11). *T. oblongatum* is found mostly in grassy places, including roadsides, throughout most of Britain and occasionally in Ireland. It is probably found throughout northern Lancashire.

Taraxacum cophocentrum Dahlst.   Rounded-lobed Dandelion

Rare (2). This is an endemic species found in grassy places and wood margins in Britain and more rarely in Ireland. In northern Lancashire *T. cophocentrum* was found at Hornby-with-Farleton (SD56Y) and near Abbeystead (SD55M). There is also an unlocalised record for the 10km square SD57.

Taraxacum pachymerum G.E. Haglund   Dirty-leaved Dandelion

Very rare (1). This is probably an introduced species found in grassy and ruderal habitats in Britain and eastern Ireland. In northern Lancashire *T. pachymerum* was found at Heysham (SD46A).

Taraxacum dilatatum H. Lindb.   Grassland Dandelion

Rare (2). *T. dilatatum* is found in grassy and ruderal habitats, mostly in western Britain. In northern Lancashire it was found at Yealand Conyers (SD57C) and probably at Warton (SD47W).

Taraxacum tanyphyllum Dahlst.   Spreading-lobed Dandelion

Very rare (1). This is an introduced species found as a rare plant of roadsides in a few British localities. In northern Lancashire *T. tanyphyllum* was found at Over Kellet (SD57F).

Taraxacum sinuatum Dahlst.   Sinuate-lobed Dandelion

Rare (5). *T. sinuatum* is found in grassy and ruderal habitats mostly in western Britain. In northern Lancashire it was found at Yealand Redmayne (SD47T), near Warton (SD47V), near Carnforth (SD46Z), Scotforth (SD45Y) and near Abbeystead (SD55M).

Taraxacum stenoglossum Dahlst.

(= *T. dahlstedtii* H. Lindb. in Dudman and Richards, 1997)

Occasional (17). This is found in grassy and ruderal habitats throughout the British Isles but especially near the coast, at least in northern Britain. In northern Lancashire *T. stenoglossum* was found in western areas of the region.

Taraxacum latisectum H. Lindb.   Broad-lobed Dandelion

Rare (3). This is found in grassy places, especially fertile pastures. It is widespread but local in England and Wales but rare in Scotland and Ireland. In northern Lancashire *T. latisectum* was found in Silverdale (SD47T), Ashton-with-Stodday (SD45T) and in Over Wyresdale (SD55S).

Taraxacum huelphersianum C.E. Haglund   Hülphers's Dandelion

Very rare (1). *T. huelphersianum* is probably introduced and occurs in grassy and ruderal habitats in scattered localities in Britain. In northern Lancashire it was found at Conder Green (SD45S).

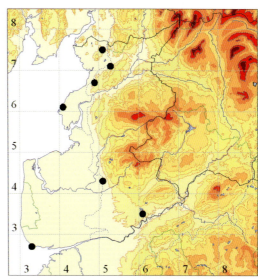

Taraxacum aurosulum

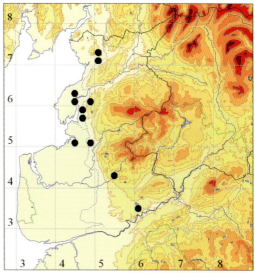

Taraxacum oblongatum

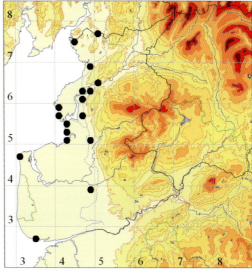

Taraxacum stenoglossum

Taraxacum fagerstroemii Såltin   Fagerström's Dandelion

Very rare (1). This is an introduced species found in grassy places and on road verges in scattered localities in Britain. In northern Lancashire *T. fagerstroemii* was found at Bolton-le-Sands (SD46Y).

Taraxacum pectinatiforme H. Lindeb.   Pectinate-leaved Dandelion

Rare (3). *T. pectinatiforme* is probably introduced and is found in grassy and ruderal habitats in scattered localities in Britain but very rarely in Ireland. In northern Lancashire it was found at Cockerham (SD45G, L) and near Carnforth (SD47V).

Taraxacum trilobatum Palmgr.   Three-lobed Dandelion

Very rare (1). This is an introduced species of grassy and ruderal habitats found in a few localities in Britain. In northern Lancashire *T. trilobatum* was found at Scotforth (SD45Z).

Taraxacum planum Raunk.   Diverse-leaved Dandelion

Very rare (1). This introduced species is found on the verges of major roads in Britain. In northern Lancashire there is an unlocalised record of *T. planum* from a trackside in the 10km square SD57.

Taraxacum polyodon Dahlst.   Common Dandelion

Rare (6). *T. polyodon* may be an introduction but it is found in grassy and ruderal habitats throughout the British Isles. In northern Lancashire it was found at Wray-with-Botton (SD56Y), in the Gressingham and Hornby areas (SD56N), Lancaster (SD46Q), on the Lune estuary (SD46K), Newton-with-Clifton (SD42U) and Ribchester (SD63N).

Taraxacum multicolorans Hagend., Soest & Zevenb.

Many-coloured Dandelion

Very rare (1). This is an introduced species found in ruderal habitats, mostly in southern England. In northern Lancashire *T. multicolorans* was found near Carnforth (SD46Z).

Taraxacum xanthostigma H. Lindb.   Ochre-styled Dandelion

Occasional (10). *T. xanthostigma* may have been introduced and is found in grassy and ruderal habitats throughout Britain and more occasionally in Ireland. So far *T. xanthostigma* has only been found in the northwest of northern Lancashire but it is probably more widespread than this. However a similar species known by the work name *T 'anceps'* H. Øllg. *in ed.* has been recorded from a number of British localities. In northern Lancashire *T. 'anceps'* was found near Carnforth (SD46Z), Ellel (SD55C) and near Longridge (SD63J).

Taraxacum longisquameum H. Lindb.   Elongate-bracted Dandelion

Occasional (7). This is found in grassy, often semi-natural habitats, throughout Britain but especially in coastal areas. It also occurs occasionally in the north of Ireland. In northern Lancashire *T. longisquameum* was found in scattered coastal localities and in the Ribble valley.

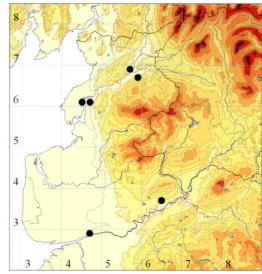

Taraxacum polyodon

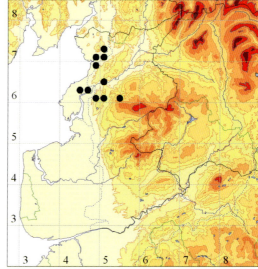

Taraxacum xanthostigma

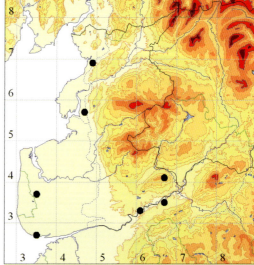

Taraxacum longisquameum

Taraxacum scotiniforme Dahlst. ex Haglund

Deltoid-lobed Dandelion

Very rare (1). This is probably introduced and is found mostly in grassy areas in southern England. *T. scotiniforme* was found in northern Lancashire on a grassy roadside by the Keer estuary near Carnforth (SD47V).

Taraxacum sublongisquameum M.P. Christ.   Roadside Dandelion

Rare (5). This is an introduced species of roadsides found in a few localities in England and Scotland. In northern Lancashire *T. sublongisquameum* was found at Over Kellet (SD57L), Ellel (SD45X & 55B), near Carnforth (SD46Z) and Lancaster SD46W).

Taraxacum fasciatum Dahlst.   Dense-bracted Dandelion

Occasional (23). This occurs mostly in grassy places on roadsides throughout Britain and occasionally in Ireland. *T. fasciatum* probably occurs throughout northern Lancashire.

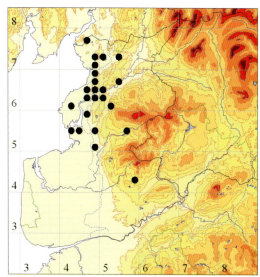
Taraxacum fasciatum

Taraxacum subxanthostigma M.P. Christ. ex Øllg.

Purple-stalked Dandelion

Rare (2). This is an introduced species found in a few scattered localities in England. In northern Lancashire *T. subxanthostigma* was found on road-sides near Galgate (SD45W) and Conder Green (SD45S).

Taraxacum acutifidum M.P. Christ.   Pointed-lobed Dandelion

Rare (2). This is an introduced species known from Wales, the West Midlands and northern England. In northern Lancashire *T. acutifidum* was found on roadsides at Melling (SD67A) and at Weeton (SD33X).

Taraxacum melanthoides Dahlst. ex M.P. Christ. & Wiinst.

Bluish-leaved Dandelion

Very rare (1). *T. melanthoides* is found in old pastures in a few localities in Britain. In northern Lancashire it was found in a wet meadow at Yealand Redmayne (SD47T).

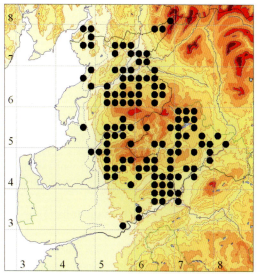
Crepis paludosa

Taraxacum lucidum Dahlst.   Large-bracted Dandelion

Very rare (1). This is probably introduced and occurs in grassy ruderal habitats in a few English localities. In northern Lancashire *T. lucidum* was found at Hothersall (SD63I).

Crepis paludosa (L.) Moench   Marsh Hawk's-beard

European Boreo-temperate element.

Marsh Hawk's-beard is a perennial herb found in wet shady places, often by streams and on rocks in woodlands (BH11, 16). It occurs in northern England, Scotland, Wales and Ireland.

Frequent (123). *C. paludosa* is found in northern and eastern parts of northern Lancashire where it is particularly characteristic of wet places in valley woodlands in Bowland. The 'New Atlas' reported losses at the southern edge of its distribution in Britain and Ireland but 'Local Change' reported no significant change. There has been no change in its distribution in northern Lancashire.

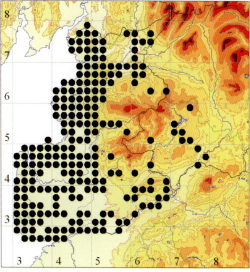
Crepis capillaris

[Crepis mollis (Jacq.) Asch.   Northern Hawk's-beard

European Temperate element.

This is a perennial herb found in herb-rich grasslands and woodland margins on base-rich soils (BH7) in northern England and Scotland.

In northern Lancashire there is an unlocalised record for VC 60 in the 10 × 10Km square SD47 made by R.A.R. Clarke in 1965 (B.R.C.). Although not impossible there are no details associated with the record and it is assumed that it is an error.]

Crepis biennis L.   Rough Hawk's-beard

European Temperate element but a neophyte in northern Lancashire.

This is thought to be a native of rough grasslands and woodland margins (BH3, 6) on chalk soils in south-eastern England. However it has spread northwards and westwards to southern Scotland, Wales and Ireland, possibly as a contaminant of grass seed.

Very rare (4). *C. biennis* was first found in northern Lancashire in a field near the Row, Silverdale (SD47S) in 1941 (H.E.B.). It still occurs on grassy roadside verges in Silverdale (SD47S & T) and in Yealand Redmayne (SD47Y). In Lancashire VC 64 it was found at Slaidburn (SD75B; Abbott, 2005).

Crepis capillaris (L.) Wallr.   Smooth Hawk's-beard

European Temperate element.

Smooth Hawk's-beard is a winter annual found in ruderal habitats and open grassland (BH7) in most parts of the British Isles.

Frequent (229). In northern Lancashire *C. capillaris* is a common species in western areas but further east it is found on roadside verges and in river valleys. There has been no change in its distribution locally or nationally.

Crepis vesicaria L. ssp. **taraxacifolia** (Thuill.) Thell.

     Beaked Hawk's-beard

Neophyte. This is a robust biennial species of ruderal habitats and is a native of the Mediterranean region and south-western Asia. It was first recorded in Britain in 1713 and spread rapidly. However whilst it is common in central and southern areas of Britain and Ireland it is rare in much of northern England and Scotland.

Rare (12). *C. vesicaria* was first found in northern Lancashire from fields near St Michael's (c. SD44Q) between 1897 and 1902 (Preston Scientific Society, 1903). It was also reported from the 10km square SD32 by Perring and Walters (1962). Today it occurs at Lytham St Anne's and more rarely further north around Halton and Warton.

Crepis setosa Haller f.   Bristly Hawk's-beard

Neophyte. *C. setosa* has a European Southern-temperate distribution and was first recorded in Britain from northern Essex in 1843 and from North Yorkshire in 1857. Today it occurs as a casual in many parts of England, Wales, southern Scotland and the north of Ireland.

Very rare (1). In northern Lancashire *C. setosa* was recorded from limestone grykes on Dalton Crags (SD57N) in 1972 (S.D.W.).

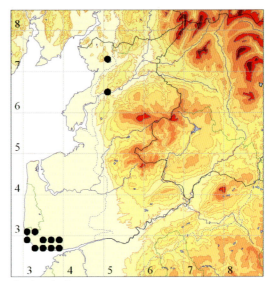
Crepis vesicaria

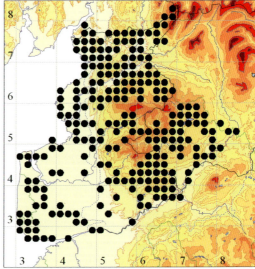
Pilosella officinarum

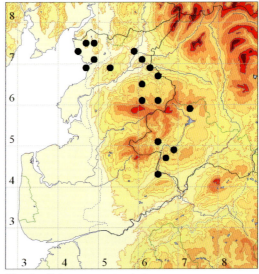
Pilosella officinarum ssp. micradenia

Pilosella officinarum F.W. Schultz & Sch. Bip.   Mouse-ear-hawkweed

European Temperate element.

Mouse-ear-hawkweed is a stoloniferous perennial herb found in dry, open habitats including grasslands, heaths, sand dunes and rocky places (BH7). It is found throughout the British Isles. Seven subspecies are recognised as occurring in the British Isles although Stace (1997) regards them as no more than varieties. However Sell and Murrell (2006) suggest that in natural habitats only one subspecies is found at any one location but in disturbed areas more than one may be present. Nevertheless intermediates occur. In this account *P. officinarum* has been well recorded but only a few observers have attempted recording the subspecies. However using the *Plant Crib 1998* (Rich and Jermy, 1998), which provided keys and illustrations, it was found that most populations could be assigned to one of the subspecies. The key was not always easy to use and identification errors may have occurred but the following account probably gives a reasonable account of their distribution in northern Lancashire. Most records are attributed to L.A. Livermore and located in the north of the area. Records from 90 tetrads were identified to subspecies and to provide a more accurate assessment frequency categories were based according to Table 3.5 (see also the account for *Taraxacum*).

Table 3.5   Frequency categories for *Pilosella officinarum*

Frequency category	No. of tetrads in which a subspecies was recorded	Approx. frequency as % of total No. of tetrads in which subspecies were recorded
Extinct	0	0
Very rare	1	<1
Rare	2–3	1–3
Occasional	4–14	4–15
Frequent	15–45	16–50
Common	46–68	51–75
Very common	69–90	>75

Common (248). In northern Lancashire *P. officinarum* is found throughout the area although it is rare in some intensively cultivated regions and absent from peat covered places. There has been no change in its distribution locally or nationally.

Pilosella officinarum F.W. Schultz & Sch. Bip.
ssp. **micradenia** (Nägeli & Peter) P.D. Sell & C. West

This is probably the commonest subspecies and is found throughout the British Isles.

Frequent (18). Whilst this has so far been recorded only in the north and east of northern Lancashire *P. officinarum* ssp. *micradenia* probably occurs throughout the area.

Pilosella officinarum F.W. Schultz & Sch. Bip.
ssp. **euronota** (Nägeli & Peter) P.D. Sell & C. West

P. officinarum ssp. *euronota* is recorded from scattered localities in western and northern Britain.

Common (51). This is one of the commonest subspecies in northern Lancashire and has been found throughout the area.

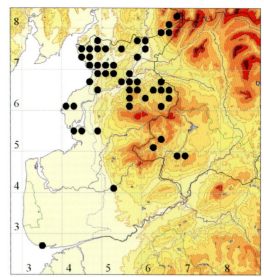

Pilosella officinarum ssp. *euronota*

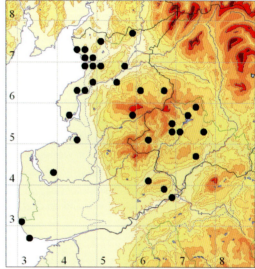

Pilosella officinarum ssp. *officinarum*

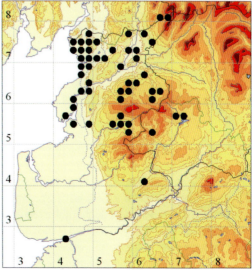

Pilosella officinarum ssp. *trichosoma*

Pilosella officinarum F.W. Schultz & Sch. Bip. ssp. **officinarum**

It is thought that *P. officinarum* ssp. *officinarum* occurs throughout the British Isles but it is mainly a plant of lowland areas. It is particularly frequent on calcareous soils.

Frequent (31). This subspecies is found in many parts of northern Lancashire but it is apparently absent from intensively cultivated and peat covered areas.

Pilosella officinarum F.W. Schultz & Sch. Bip.
ssp. **trichosoma** (Peter) P.D. Sell & C. West

P. officinarum ssp. *trichosoma* is a common subspecies in mountainous areas but occurs sparingly in other places.

Common (52). This subspecies is also one of the commonest subspecies in northern Lancashire occurring in the north of the area and in Bowland with occasional localities elsewhere.

Pilosella officinarum F.W. Schultz & Sch. Bip.
ssp. **tricholepia** (Nägeli & Peter) P.D. Sell & C. West

This subspecies occurs in scattered localities on heaths, sea cliffs and in ruderal habitats throughout the British Isles.

Frequent (17). In northern Lancashire *P. officinarum* ssp. *tricholepia* probably occurs in scattered localities throughout the area.

Pilosella officinarum F.W. Schultz & Sch. Bip.
ssp. **melanops** (Peter) P.D. Sell & C. West

This subspecies occurs in scattered localities in Britain, especially on sand dunes and sea cliffs. It also occurs in western Ireland.

Occasional (14). So far *P. officinarum* ssp. *melanops* has been found in the north of northern Lancashire, especially on calcareous soils around Morecambe Bay. It has yet to be found on coastal sandy soils further south.

Pilosella officinarum F.W. Schultz & Sch. Bip.
ssp. **trichoscapa** (Nägeli) P.D. Sell & C. West

This is a scarce subspecies found in northern Britain although it is widespread in upland areas of Europe.

Rare (2). *P. officinarum* ssp. *trichoscapa* has only been found by Livermore and Livermore (1987) in northern Lancashire from the Gressingham and Hornby areas (SD56U) and from Over Wyresdale (SD55L).

Pilosella aurantiaca (L.) F.W. Schultz & Sch. Bip.　　　Fox-and-cubs

Neophyte. Fox-and-cubs has a European Boreal-montane distribution and was first grown in British gardens by 1629 and recorded from the wild by 1793. Two subspecies occur in the British Isles and *P. aurantiaca* ssp. *aurantiaca*, a native of the Alps and Carpathians, appears to have been the first subspecies to be introduced. It is the more handsome of the two but it does not spread rapidly. *P. aurantiaca* ssp. *carpathicola* (Nägeli & Peter) P.D. Sell & C. West occurs throughout the range of the species and was probably a later introduction. Perring (1968) mapped the distribution of the two subspecies in the British Isles and demonstrated that whilst both were generally distributed *P. aurantiaca* ssp. *aurantiaca* was much less

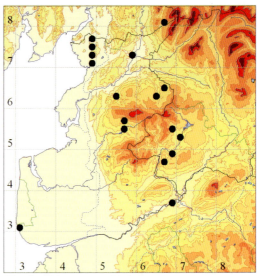

Pilosella officinarum ssp. *tricholepia*

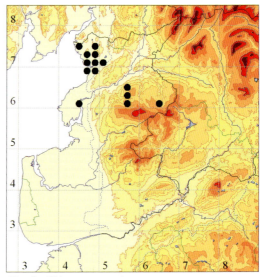

Pilosella officinarum ssp. *melanops*

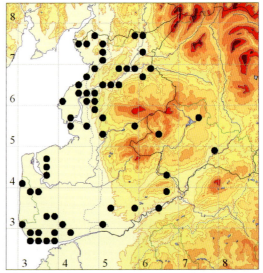

Pilosella aurantiaca

frequent than *P. aurantiaca* ssp. *carpathicola*. Little further work has been done since 1968 to plot the distribution of the two subspecies in the British Isles.

Occasional (55). Fox-and-cubs was first recorded from northern Lancashire between 1897 and 1902 from near Ashton where it was planted (Preston Scientific Society, 1903) and from the golf links east of the railway line at St Anne's in 1906 (C.B.; MANCH). Today it is found throughout the area although it appears to be absent from lowland areas in the centre of the region. So far all material that has been checked belongs to *P. aurantiaca* ssp. *carpathicola*.

Hieracium L.   Hawkweeds

Circumpolar Wide-boreal element but many species have limited distributions.

This most difficult genus of 412 apomictic species is found throughout the British Isles but whilst some are widespread others are rare, have limited distributions or occur in narrowly defined habitats. Initially considerable effort was made to record *Hieracium* species in VC 60 relying on the expertise of J.N. Mills who referred doubtful material to P.D. Sell and C. West. Nationally Sell and West published distribution maps in Perring (1968) but were conscious that a much more thorough taxonomic revision of the genus as it occurs in the British Isles was required. The deaths of J.N. Mills and C. West combined with the long illness of P.D. Sell conspired to halt work in northern Lancashire and delay the revision of *Hieracium* nationally. However Halliday published an account of *Hieracium*, including keys, in his *Flora of Cumbria* (1997). This was able to draw on the work of P.D. Sell in his revision of the genus and is especially relevant to the hawkweed flora of northern Lancashire. However despite these problems a few workers, notably Brian Burrows and Vincent Jones have been able to study hawkweeds in the north of the area. Livermore and Livermore (1987) attempted to identify hawkweeds but their account relied on their own expertise. Fortunately they collected numerous voucher specimens (LIV) some of which have been re-evaluated. Many, however, remain neither mounted nor named. The publication of Sell's revision (Sell and Murrell, 2006) has provided a fresh impetus for the study of these attractive yet most difficult species. Thus it has been possible with the help and expertise of David McCosh and others to identify and revise the northern Lancashire collections at LIV as well as in a number of other herbaria with the exception of *H. sabaudum*, *H. vagum* and *H. vulgatum*. Nevertheless there are many vouchers for these species at LIV. For all other taxa this account is based on recently identified material.

A few species are widespread but many hawkweeds are rare and have limited distributions. Many of these rare species occur in Lancashire as outliers of their main distribution centred on the limestone country of the Pennines. Some of them are endemic to Britain or even to northern England and have probably evolved here during the last 10,000 years following the retreat of the last ice cap (Sell and Murrell, 2006).

I am most grateful for all the help I have received over the years and recently I am especially indebted to Brian Burrows and David McCosh.

The account follows the sequence and nomenclature in Sell and Murrell, 2006.

Section SABAUDA (Fr.) Arv.-Touv.

This is a small section of leafy and often hairy-stemmed species that flower from mid-August to October.

Hieracium vagum Jord.   Glabrous-headed Hawkweed

This is found throughout a large part of continental Europe. In Britain *H. vagum* is found in woodland edge and ruderal habitats in central and northern England and Wales with a few localities elsewhere in Britain.

Frequent (100). In northern Lancashire *H. vagum* is found in many areas of VC 60 but especially in the north and in the valleys fringing the Bowland Fells. It is often found in woodland or former woodland areas although today it is frequently found in ruderal and marginal habitats.

Hieracium salticola (Sudre) P.D. Sell & C. West
Bluish-leaved Hawkweed

H. salticola is widespread in France and Germany but it is introduced into Britain where it is found in ruderal habitats, mostly in central areas. It is particularly frequent in the Birmingham area.

Very rare (2). In northern Lancashire it was found on a railway embankment at Warton (SD57B) in 1970 (G.H.) and possibly at Carnforth (SD47V) in 1986 (G.H.).

Hieracium virgultorum Jord.   Long-leaved Hawkweed

This is usually found in open woodland and on grassy banks in south-eastern England.

Very rare (1). *H. virgultorum* was found in railway sidings at Carnforth (SD47V) in 1995 (G.H.).

Hieracium sabaudum L.   Autumn Hawkweed

This is found in most of western and central Europe including most of the British Isles. It is characteristic of woodland edge habitats including shady hedgerows but it also occurs in some ruderal habitats.

Frequent (89). *H. sabaudum* is a common hawkweed in northern Lancashire but it is rare in lowland south-western areas and in Lancashire VC 64. Forma *bladonii* (Pugsley) P.D. Sell was recorded from Slaidburn (SD75B) and Easington (SD75P) in 2009 (E.F.G.).

Section **HIERACIOIDES** Dumort.

This is a small group of leafy hawkweeds where the leaves have recurved, minutely scabrid margins and the inflorescence is more or less umbellate.

Hieracium umbellatum L.   Umbellate Hawkweed

Several subspecies and varieties are recognised by Sell and Murrell (2006) as occurring in Britain. The species is widespread in Europe, Asia and North America and occurs in scattered localities in many parts of the British Isles.

Rare (12). In northern Lancashire post 1964 records are from sand dunes and sandy ground at Blackpool and Lytham St Anne's. They are probably all referable to ssp. *umbellatum* var. *dunense* Reyn., which is typical of these habitats. Inland Abbott (2005) refers to *H. umbellatum* occurring at Tosside (c. SD75T) but the locality may be just over the county boundary in Yorkshire. There are also old records from near Ellel (A.W.; NMW; 1906) identified as var. *commune* Fr. and near Docker (J.A.W.; 1903).

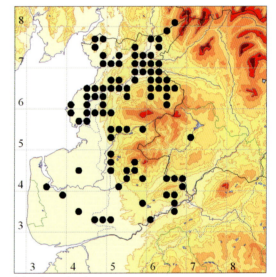
Hieracium vagum

Section **TRIDENTATA** (Fr.) Arv.-Touv.

Species in this section are found mostly on upland grassy banks in western and northern parts of the British Isles. They have fewer stem leaves than species in the previous two sections.

Hieracium ornatilorum P.D. Sell & C. West

Large-flowered Hawkweed

H. ornatilorum is endemic to Yorkshire and Lancashire where it is found in grassy places and by streams.

Very rare (1). This was found at Silverdale in 1914 (CGE, BM) and possibly also on a roadside at Dalton (SD57M) in 1970 (G.H.; LANC).

Hieracium eboracense Pugsley   Northern Hawkweed

This is endemic to Britain and occurs in woodland margins and heathy places in England and Wales.

Very rare (5). In northern Lancashire *H. eboracense* has been recorded from the banks of the R. Lune near Halton in 1903 (A.W.; NMW) and more recently from Claughton (SD54M) in 1964, Yealand (SD57C) in 1965, Yealand Redmayne in (SD57D) in 1970, Dalton (SD57S) in 1979 (G.H.; LANC) and on Warton Crag (SD47W) in 1969, all collected by E.F.G. except where noted.

Hieracium calcaricola (F. Hanb.) Roffey   Toothed Hawkweed

This is probably widespread in Europe and occurs in grassy places and heathland in scattered localities in Britain.

In northern Lancashire it was found near Wennington in 1917 (A.W.; YRK) but the voucher has not been checked recently.

[Hieracium gothicoides Pugsley   Broad-headed Hawkweed

This was recorded by Wheldon and Wilson (1907), as *H. gothicum* Backh., from Leck Fell but voucher specimens have been re-identified as *H. lissolepium*. It was also recorded from near Hawes Water in 1912 (Wheldon and Wilson, 1925) but voucher material has not been checked recently.]

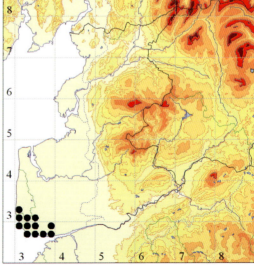
Hieracium sabaudum

Hieracium umbellatum

Hieracium placerophylloides Pugsley

Purplish-leaved Hawkweed

This is an endemic species found in rocky places on limestone in northern England and more locally in Wales.

Very rare (1). *H. placerophylloides* was found on a roadside at Warton (SD57B) in 2008 (G.H.; LANC).

Hieracium lissolepium Roffey

Hairless-bracted Hawkweed

H. lissolepium occurs in Scandinavia and central Europe. In Britain it is found on grassy slopes and rocky outcrops particularly in the northern Pennines, the Lake District and southern Scotland.

Very rare (1). In northern Lancashire *H. lissolepium* was found in a pothole on Leck Fell (SD67U) in 1904 (A.W.), in 1967 (J.N.M.; MANCH) and in 2007 (B.B.).

Section **CERINTHOIDEA** Mounier

This is a section with species found in upland and mountainous areas. Species are usually recognised by their hairy appearance, large heads and amplexicaul, cauline leaves.

Hieracium ampliatum (W.R. Linton) Ley

Shaggy-stalked Hawkweed

H. ampliatum is an endemic species of rocky and grassy places on limestone in northern England.

In northern Lancashire it was found on sea cliffs at Silverdale in 1954 (V.G.).

Section **STELLIGERA** Zahn

This section is characterised by species with numerous broad leaves but only up to one or possibly two cauline ones. They are usually found on basic rocks in western and northern parts of the British Isles as well as in Europe and south-western Asia.

[**Hieracium caledonicum** F. Hanb. Caledonian Hawkweed

This is an endemic species found on cliff ledges, by streams and on sand dunes in northern Scotland.

In northern Lancashire there are records for this species from Silverdale but voucher material has been re-identified as *H. maculoides*. Voucher material (YRK) for records from Warton and Leck has not been checked but this species is unlikely to occur in northern Lancashire.]

Hieracium decolor (W.R. Linton) Ley   Shade Hawkweed

This is an endemic species found on limestone rocks and on grassy slopes in the Pennines.

Very rare (2). It was found at Gait Barrows N.N.R. (SD47Y) in 1960 (V.G.) and again in 1996 (V.J.) and possibly this species near the village at Silverdale (SD47M) in 1968 (E.F.G.). It may occur elsewhere in the area. *Hieracium tricolorans* (Zahn) Pugsley (Three-coloured Hawkweed) and *H. subcyaneum* (W.R. Linton) Pugsley (Porrect-bracted Hawkweed) were formerly included within *H. decolor*. However, McCosh and Rich (2011), McCosh (pers. comm.) record both *H. tricolorans* (Gait Barrows N.N.R.) and *H. subcyaneum* (Barrow Scout Wood, Warton; SD47W) but not *H. decolor* in VC 60.

Hieracium stictum P.D. Sell   Lance-leaved Hawkweed

This is an endemic species of limestone rocks in northern England.

Very rare (1). It is believed this occurs on coastal rocks at Silverdale (SD47N) where it was found in 2006 (B.B. & V.J.).

Hieracium hypochaeroides S. Gibson

Cat's-ear Hawkweed

This endemic species is found on limestone rocks in Wales, northern England and Ireland.

Very rare (1). It is believed that in northern Lancashire it was found at Silverdale (SD47Y) in 1990 (L.A.L.).

[**Hieracium dicella** P.D. Sell & C. West   Forked Hawkweed

This was recorded by Livermore and Livermore (1987) but it is not known to what species their records refer.]

Section **VULGATA** (Griseb.) Willk. & Lange

This section includes some of the most frequently occurring species in northern Lancashire. They have a few basal leaves, several cauline leaves and a large panicle of small to medium sized capitula. They are found in a wide variety of habitats including rocky places, woodland margins and ruderal habitats.

Hieracium vulgatum Fr.   Common Hawkweed

This is a common and variable species found in rocky and grassy places and in ruderal habitats. It is found throughout the British Isles as well as in northern and central Europe. Several forms have been recognised.

Frequent (89). *H. vulgatum* is found throughout northern Lancashire although it is rare in the intensively farmed lowland areas in the west of the region and it is apparently rare in much of Lancashire VC 64. Of the various forms identified as occurring in the British Isles forma *vulgatum* is the commonest but forma *subfasciculare* (W.R. Linton) P.D. Sell and forma *sejunctum* (W.R. Linton) P.D. Sell are also common in Wales, northern England and Scotland. Of these forma *vulgatum* and forma *subfasciculare* have been recognised as occurring in northern Lancashire.

Hieracium cravoniense (F. Hanb.) Roffey   Craven Hawkweed

This is similar to *H. vulgatum* with which it is often confused. It is an endemic species found in rocky places and on grassy slopes in northern England and Scotland

Rare (10). This species was first recorded from Halton (A.W.) in 1896 and more recently confirmed records are from by the Leck Beck (SD67P) in 2005 (B.B. & V.J.), in a pothole on Leck Fell (SD67U) in 1967 (J.N.M. & C. West) and in Whitendale, doubtfully (SD65M) in 2008 (E.F.G.). Records from by the R. Greta (SD67G) in 1989 (J.M.N.) and Hornby Castle grounds (SD56Z) in 2008 (J.M.N.) are also probably correctly identified. However, other records have been re-identified as *H. vulgatum* but the map showing Craven Hawkweed's distribution largely confined to the Lune valley is probably accurate.

Hieracium coniops Norrl.   Grey-haired Hawkweed

H. coniops is a recently recognised species described from Finland. It is similar to *H. vulgatum* and until recently was recorded as such.

Very rare (2). So far in northern Lancashire this species has been confirmed from iron slag heaps at Warton (SD47Q) in 2006 (E.F.G.) and from Warton Crag (SD47W) also in 2006 (B.B. & V.J.).

Hieracium rubiginosum F. Hanb.   Rusty-red Hawkweed

This is an endemic species of limestone rocks found in northern England.

Very rare (1). This has only been confirmed for woodland at Abbeystead, Over Wyresdale (SD55S) in *c.* 1984 (L.A.L.).

Hieracium praesigne (Zahn) Roffey   Distinguished Hawkweed

H. praesigne is an endemic species found mostly on calcareous rocks in northern England and rarely in Scotland.

Very rare (2). This was found on Warton Crag (SD47W) in 2006 (B.B. & V.J.) and from near Whitewell (SD64N) in 2008 (E.F.G.).

Hieracium lepidulum (Stenstr.) Omang   Irregular-toothed Hawkweed

H. lepidulum is found in central and northern Europe and is found as an introduction in a number of ruderal habitats in England.

Very rare (1). It is believed this may have been found at Wray, Roeburndale (SD66D) in 1993 (L.A.L.).

Hieracium diaphanum Fr.   Dark-leaved Hawkweed

This is a native of central and northern Europe but it is believed to be introduced into the British Isles. It is found in scattered localities in Britain.

Rare (11). This is found in a few scattered localities in northern Lancashire mostly in shady habitats.

Hieracium daedalolepioides (Zahn) Roffey
                                Petite-leaved Hawkweed

This species is difficult to distinguish from *H. anglorum* with which it often grows and occurs in rocky places in the Welsh mountains and in a few other localities in Britain.

Very rare (1). In northern Lancashire it was recorded from a wall at Longridge in 1964 (E.H.; MANCH).

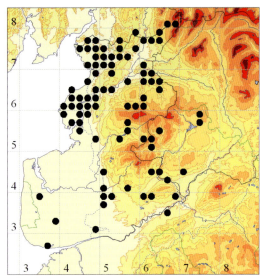
Hieracium vulgatum

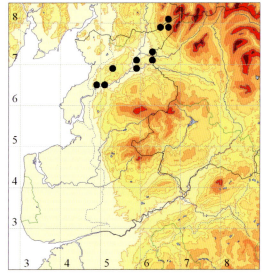
Hieracium cravoniense

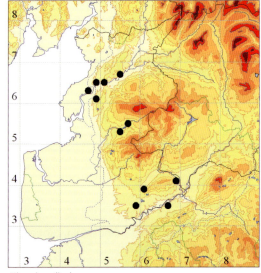
Hieracium diaphanum

Hieracium anglorum (Ley) Pugsley   Anglian Hawkweed

This is an endemic species found in rocky places in Wales and northern England.

In northern Lancashire it was found near Halton (SD56H) in 1904 (A.W.; NMW).

Hieracium diaphanoides Lindeb. Diaphanous Hawkweed

H. diaphanoides is found in central and northern Europe. In the British Isles it occurs on rocks, walls and stabilised sand dunes.

Very rare (2). In northern Lancashire this was recorded from a road bank in Nether Wyresdale (SD55G) in 1971 (E.F.G.) and from the north side of the R. Lune near Halton (SD56C) in 2007 (B.B.).

Hieracium consociatum Jord. ex Boreau

Sociable Hawkweed

H. consociatum is a native species of stream banks and rocky slopes in upland areas of England and Wales as well as in quarries, on roadside banks and in other ruderal and marginal habitats. It often grows with *H. acuminatum* and *H. argillaceum* to which it is closely related and with which it has previously been included within a variable species.

Very rare (1). This was recorded on a roadside bank near Wennington (SD67F) in 2005 (B.B.).

Hieracium argillaceum Jord.   Southern Hawkweed

This morphologically variable species occurs in a variety of often ruderal habitats throughout most of England and Wales and occasionally elsewhere. It is a native of central Europe and has probably been introduced into Britain.

Occasional (41). In northern Lancashire it was formerly recorded as *H. strumosum* (W.R. Linton) A. Ley and more recently as *H. acuminatum* Jord. but this latter species has not been confirmed for northern Lancashire. *H. argillaceum* is found in scattered, usually shaded, localities in the east and north of the region.

Hieracium aviicola Jord. ex Boreau

Many-toothed Hawkweed

This is probably an introduced species and occurs in scattered localities in England and Wales.

Very rare (3). In northern Lancashire *H. aviicola* has been found on waste ground at Inglewhite in 1956 (Betty Brennand), at Scale Hall Station near Lancaster (SD46R) in 1970 (G.H.), Wrayton (SD67B) in 1992 (L.A.L.) and Wennington (SD67A) in 1992 (L.A.L.). All specimens were previously identified as *H. acuminatum*.

Hieracium festinum Jord. ex Boreau

Hairy-leaved Hawkweed

This is probably an introduced species from central Europe and has been recorded from a few, mostly ruderal, localities in England and Wales.

Very rare (1). It is thought this species was found on a river-bank in Roeburndale (SD66D) in 1992 (L.A.L.).

Section **HIERACIUM**

Species of this section are found throughout Britain and native species occur in rocky places especially in mountainous areas. Many species are however introduced and these occur mostly in ruderal habitats.

Hieracium oistophyllum Pugsley

Sagittate-leaved Hawkweed

H. oistophyllum is found in central and northern Europe. In Britain it is found on calcareous grassy slopes and in rocky places in northern England but only in a few Scottish localities.

Very rare (3). In northern Lancashire this was found at Silverdale (SD47N) in 1961 (J.N.M.; MANCH), by the R. Hodder (SD64R) in 1970 (E.F.G.), (SD64V) in 1972 (T. B.) and from Ease Gill, Leck (SD68Q) in 2005 (B.B. & V.J.).

Hieracium lintonii Ley   Linton's Hawkweed

This endemic species is similar to *H. rubiginosum* and occurs on limestone rocks in Wales and northern England.

In northern Lancashire it was found at Silverdale in 1912 (J. Cryer; CGE).

Hieracium maculoides P.D. Sell & C. West

Small-spotted Hawkweed

This is an endemic species found on limestone in Yorkshire and in the Arnside and Silverdale area around Morecambe Bay.

Very rare (1). This was found on sea cliffs at Silverdale (SD47N) in 1965 (J.N.M. & C. West).

Hieracium silvaticoides Pugsley   Wood Hawkweed

H. silvaticoides is an endemic species found on rocky stream-sides and on grassy banks, often on limestone. It is most frequent in northern England but there are a few localities in Scotland and in the north of Ireland.

Very rare (1). In northern Lancashire it was found on rocks at Hawes Water, Silverdale (SD47T) in 1914 (J. Cryer; CGE) and more recently on Warton Crag (SD47W) in 2006 (B.B. & V.J.).

Hieracium auratiflorum Pugsley

Dark-flowered Hawkweed

This is an endemic species usually found on limestone rocks and grassy banks in the Yorkshire Dales and in Teesdale.

Very rare (1). In northern Lancashire this was found at Cantsfield (SD67F) in 1988 (J.M.N.; LANC).

Hieracium cymbifolium Purchas   Boat-leaved Hawkweed

This is an endemic species found on limestone and other basic rocks in upland areas from the Pennines northwards.

Very rare (1). There are old records for this species from Silverdale and Warton but several specimens were re-identified as *H. silvaticoides*. However it was found on Warton Crag (SD47W) in 1970 (E.F.G.).

Hieracium duriceps F. Hanb.   Hard-headed Hawkweed

H. duriceps is a locally common endemic species found on basic rocks and grassy slopes in Scotland and northern England and it also occurs in a few Irish localities.

Very rare (3). In northern Lancashire there are recent records from Ease Gill, Leck (SD68Q, V) in 2005 & 2007 (B.B. & V.J. and B.B.) and from by the River Hodder (SD64W) in 1972 (J.M.N.).

Hieracium grandidens Dahlst. Grand-toothed Hawkweed

This is an introduced hawkweed found on roadsides, railway banks and in other ruderal habitats in scattered localities in Britain with one Irish record. It is one of the commonest European species.

Very rare (1). The only record from northern Lancashire is from Abbeystead (SD55S) in 1993 (L.A.L.).

Hieracium sylvularum Jord. ex Boreau

Ample-toothed Hawkweed

This introduced species is similar to *H. grandidens* and has been recorded from ruderal habitats in scattered localities in Britain. It is widely recorded from France to the Caucasus.

Very rare (1). In northern Lancashire this was found at Leighton Moss (SD47W) in 2006 (V.J.; CGE).

Hieracium subcrassum (Almq. ex Dahlst.) Johanss.

Trackway Hawkweed

H. subcrassum is probably an introduced species found by roads and tracks in a few places in northern England. In Europe it is found in Sweden.

Very rare (2). In northern Lancashire it appears to be established in and around Eaves Wood and Waterslack, Silverdale (SD47T) where it was last recorded in 1982 (M. B.) and from Abbeystead, Over Wyresdale (SD55S) in 1992 (L.A.L.).

Hieracium subaequialtum Hyl.   Black-bracted Hawkweed

This is probably not native but occurs in scattered British localities. It was formerly regarded as a form of *H. sublepistoides*.

Very rare (2). This was found in northern Lancashire from Silverdale in 1902 (J.A.W.; NMW). Recent records are from Scale Hall, near Lancaster (SD46R) in 1970 (G.H.), Grindleton (SD74N) in 2007 (E.F.G.) and there is a possible record from Yealand Redmayne (SD47Y) in 1975 (E.F. & B.D.G.).

Hieracium sublepistoides (Zahn) Druce

Grey-bracted Hawkweed

This is an introduced species found in woods, on roadsides and on walls in England and Wales. It occurs in central Europe.

Very rare (1). Some former records are *H. subaequialtum* but a specimen from Lancaster (SD46V) collected in 1992 (L.A.L.) and formerly thought to be *H. diaphanum* has been re-identified as this species.

Hieracium severiceps Wiinst.   Strict-headed Hawkweed

H. severiceps is an introduced species found on railway banks and in quarries in scattered localities in Britain. In Europe it occurs in Denmark and Sweden.

Very rare (1). The only confirmed records in northern Lancashire are from Silverdale (SD47T) when it was seen in 1980 (D. Bevan & P.D. Sell). Livermore and Livermore (1987) recorded *H. severiceps* from a number of sites in the Silverdale area but they have not been confirmed.

Hieracium pellucidum Laest.   Pellucid-leaved Hawkweed

This species is found on cliffs and grassy banks usually on limestone in southern Wales, the Derbyshire Dales, northern England and parts of Scotland. It also occurs in Scandinavia.

Very rare (4). There are confirmed records in northern Lancashire from rocky places on limestone by Ease Gill, Leck (SD68Q) in 2005 (B.B. & V.J.), in a pothole, Leck (SD67P) in 1967 (J.N.M.), from the R. Greta, Cantsfield (SD67G) in 1968 (E.F.G.) and from a wooded bank at Halton (SD56C) in 1971 (C.P. Harris).

Hieracium exotericum Jord. ex Boreau

Jordan's Hawkweed

H. exotericum is probably introduced and is found on roadsides, railway banks, on walls and in waste places in scattered localities in Britain. It is widespread in Europe.

Very rare (2). In northern Lancashire there are confirmed records for *H. exotericum* from roadsides in Silverdale (SD47T) in 2006 (V.J.) and from Dalton Crags (SD57N) in 1970 (G.H.). However a few other records have been identified as *H. exotericum* agg. These are from Lancaster (SD45Z) in 1996, Yealand Conyers (SD57C) in 1992, Abbeystead (SD55S) in 1992, Cantsfield (SD67F) in 1986 and from Silverdale (SD47X) in 1993 (all L.A.L.).

Hieracium hjeltii Norrl.   Hjelt's Hawkweed

This is a native of Fennoscandia and is probably an introduction in Britain. It has only been recorded on one or two occasions.

In northern Lancashire it was found by the railway at Silverdale by J. Cryer in 1912 (NMW, LIV, BM).

Filago vulgaris Lam.   Common Cudweed

European Southern-temperate element.

Common Cudweed is found in open, dry and often acidic places in a variety of habitats including waste places (BH3). It occurs throughout the British Isles but reaches the northern limits of its distribution in Scotland and Jutland.

Rare (8). *F. vulgaris* has always been a rare and sporadic species in northern Lancashire. Old records were from Leagram (Anon, 1891), Bare (Wheldon and Wilson, 1907), St Anne's (A.J.C.; LSA) and Silverdale in 1912 (Wheldon and Wilson, 1925). This latter record probably refers to a site at Jenny Brown's Point (SD47R) where it was seen from time to time until about 1976. Other post 1964 records are from old gravel pits at Warton (SD57B) in 1996 (P.J.), on old railway ballast at Middleton (SD45J) & at Thornton (SD34H) both in 2005 (P.J.), Fleetwood Dock (SD34I) in 2006 & Blackpool (SD33F) in 1997 (both C.F. & N.J.S.) and at Barton (SD53I) & Lytham (SD32I) both in 2008 (P.G.). Nationally the 'New Atlas' reported a decline in its distribution especially in southern and western England. This probably reflected a decline in its native habitats of sandy or rocky pastures but towards the end of the twentieth century many sand pits, gravel workings and railways were abandoned and these have provided suitable habitats for colonisation by *F. vulgaris* (see Plate 2.75). Thus 'Local Change' noted a marked increase in its distribution after 1987 and the local situation appears to reflect the national position.

Filago minima (Sm.) Perc.   Small Cudweed

European Temperate element.

This is an annual species of open, infertile and often acidic substrates in a wide variety of habitats (BH16). It occurs throughout the British Isles and reaches the northern limit of its distribution in northern Scotland.

Very rare (2). In northern Lancashire Small Cudweed was first found in a quarry at Jenny Brown's Point, Silverdale (SD47R) in 1937 (H.E.B.). Since 1964 it has been found on old railway tracks near Fleetwood (SD34I) in 1985 (C.F. & N.J.S.) and in a sand and gravel quarry at Warton (SD47B) in 1995 (P.J.). According to the 'New Atlas' it is declining over most of its range in the British Isles but 'Local Change' reports no significant change since 1987.

Antennaria dioica (L.) Gaertn.   Mountain Everlasting

Eurasian Boreo-temperate element.

Mountain Everlasting is an attractive, stoloniferous species found on thin, usually calcareous grasslands, on heaths and on sand dunes (BH7, 10). Today it is found mostly in northern and western areas of the British Isles but it formerly also occurred in southern Britain.

Extinct. Formerly this occurred in several localities in the Silverdale and Yealand areas but 100 years ago Petty (1902) reported that 'trippers'

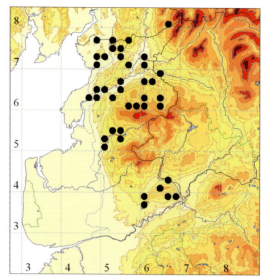
Hieracium argillaceum

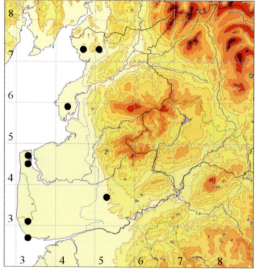
Filago vulgaris

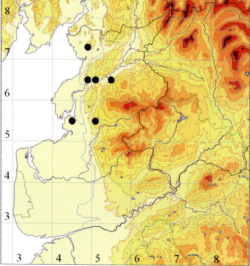
Anaphalis margaritacea

pulled up the plant causing its extinction at one Silverdale locality. It also occurred in at least two localities in Leck (Wheldon and Wilson, 1907), by the stream at Nicky Nook, Nether Wyresdale (J.P[earson], 1855) and at St Anne's in 1907 (MANCH). Nationally most losses occurred before 1962 ('New Atlas') but 'Local Change' reports no significant change since 1987.

Anaphalis margaritacea (L.) Benth.   Pearly Everlasting

Neophyte. Pearly Everlasting is a native of North America and north-eastern Asia but it is widely naturalised elsewhere. It was grown in British gardens by 1596 and was found in the wild before 1707 when it was already well established. It is found mostly in ruderal habitats throughout Britain but only rarely in Ireland.

Rare (6). *A. margaritacea* was first found in northern Lancashire on the sand dunes at St Anne's (Bailey, 1907). Since 1964 all records have been from north-western parts of the region.

Gnaphalium sylvaticum L.   Heath Cudweed

Eurosiberian Boreo-temperate element.

This is a short-lived perennial herb of open communities on dry, usually acidic and gravelly soils (BH3, 10). Formerly it occurred throughout the British Isles.

Very rare or extinct (4). Wheldon and Wilson (1907) reported *G. sylvaticum* from twelve localities in VC 60 but it has never been seen in Lancashire VC 64. Since 1964 it was recorded from a wood by the R. Hodder (SD64R) in 1965 (J. D.), Silverdale (SD47S) in 1970 (Anon), in two or three localities within Gait Barrows N.N.R. (SD47T, Y) where it was last seen in 1986 (Arnside Naturalists). The 'New Atlas' reported a considerable decline throughout its range in the British Isles but especially in Ireland, Wales and in western and midland England; however, although there have been further losses since 1987 they are not significant ('Local Change').

Gnaphalium uliginosum L.   Marsh Cudweed

Eurasian Boreo-temperate element.

Marsh Cudweed occurs in open, damp or muddy places in a variety of habitats. It is particularly characteristic of trampled field entrances, muddy pond margins and the drawdown zone of reservoirs (BH11, 13). It is found throughout the British Isles.

Frequent (214). In northern Lancashire it is particularly common in the lowland, west of the area; whilst it occurs throughout the region it is less frequent in eastern parts and in Lancashire VC 64. Whilst there appears to have been no change in its distribution locally both the 'New Atlas' and 'Local Change' report increases nationally.

Gnaphalium luteoalbum L.   Jersey Cudweed

Eurosiberian Southern-temperate element but a neophyte in northern Lancashire.

Formerly this was a native species of Breckland in East Anglia but recent records are of casual occurrences at a few widely scattered localities in Britain. It may have spread naturally into some of those in eastern England and it is believed to be native in the Channel Islands.

Very rare (1). In northern Lancashire it was found in a Preston car park (SD52J) in 2006 (P.J.).

Inula helenium L.   Elecampane

Archaeophyte. Elecampane is a native of western and central Asia but it is widely naturalised elsewhere. It has been grown in Britain for its medicinal and ornamental value since at least 995. Today it is found in marginal habitats throughout the British Isles.

Very rare (5). *I. helenium* was first found in northern Lancashire at Carnforth in c. 1690 (Whittaker, 1981) and from the Yealand area (Jenkinson, 1775) where Wheldon and Wilson (1907) also reported it. Other pre 1964 records are from woods at Leagram in the 1960s (MS at SYT) and near Warton, near Lancaster in 1932 (Whiteside, no date). Post 1964 it has been seen at Docker (SD57R) in 1974 (J.M.N.), Galgate (SD45X) in 1966 (J.H.; LANC), Glasson (c. SD45N) in 1966 (A.E.R.), Thornton (SD34L) in 1967 (E.F.G.) and Lytham (SD32Y) in 2004 (Anon).

Inula hookeri C.B. Clarke   Hooker's Fleabane

Neophyte. This is a native of the Himalayas and was introduced into British gardens in 1849. It is naturalised in a few British localities.

Very rare (1). Hooker's Fleabane was found as a garden escape on waste ground at Warton (SD57B) in 2007 (J.Cl.).

Inula conyzae (Griess.) Meikle   Ploughman's-spikenard

European Temperate element.

This is a herb of dry sites on calcareous soils in open grassy habitats and on sand dunes (BH7, 16). It occurs in England and Wales with an occasional locality in Scotland and Ireland where it is believed to be an introduction.

Occasional (23). *I. conyzae* is found in northern Lancashire on limestone in the northwest of the area and on the sand dunes at Lytham St Anne's. Apart from a former locality near Whitewell (Wheldon and Wilson, 1907) Ploughman's-spikenard's distribution is unchanged in northern Lancashire and nationally although 'Local Change' reported some losses since 1987.

Pulicaria dysenterica (L.) Bernh.   Common Fleabane

Eurosiberian Southern-temperate element.

Common Fleabane is a perennial, rhizomatous herb of wet, open places in a variety of habitats and soil types (BH6, 11). It is found in most parts of England, Wales and Ireland but it is rare towards the north of its range in northern England and southern Scotland.

Frequent (130). In northern Lancashire *P. dysenterica* occurs mostly in western areas and in the Hodder valley. Its distribution is stable locally and nationally.

Telekia speciosa (Schrieb.) Baumg.   Yellow Oxeye

Neophyte. This is a native of the mountains of eastern central Europe, the Balkan Peninsula, northern Turkey and the Caucasus. It has been cultivated in Britain since 1739 and was recorded from the wild in 1914. Today it may be found anywhere in the British Isles although it is very rare in Ireland.

Very rare (3). In northern Lancashire it was found in a woodland at Abbeystead, Over Wyresdale (SD55S) in 1988 (L.A.L.; LIV), by the River Wyre near Garstang (SD44X) in 1999 (C.F. & N.J.S.) and by a stream near Browsholme Hall (SD64X; Abbott, 2005).

Solidago virgaurea L.   Goldenrod

Eurasian Boreo-temperate element.

Goldenrod occurs on free draining, usually acidic substrates in woodlands, on heaths and in rocky places (BH10, 16) throughout the British Isles although it is rare in much of eastern England and eastern Ireland. Ssp. *virgaurea* occurs in lowland woodland and ssp. *minuta* (L.) Arcangeli occurs in exposed mountainous areas.

Frequent (75). In northern Lancashire *S. virgaurea* is characteristic of rocky cloughs both within and outside woodland. It is found in the north of the area, in Bowland and in the Ribble valley. Although the subspecies have not been recorded separately it is believed both may occur. Wheldon and Wilson (1907) reported var. *cambrica* (Huds.) Sm., which is probably ssp. *minuta,* from upper Ease Gill, Leck and by a waterfall in Whiteray Gill, Wray-with-Botton. Localities at Lytham St Anne's seem unlikely. *S. virgaurea* is not thought to have declined in northern Lancashire but there have been losses nationally ('New Atlas', 'Local Change').

Solidago canadensis L.   Canadian Goldenrod

Neophyte. This is a native of North America and was brought into British cultivation in 1648. It was recorded in the wild in 1888 but did not become widespread until 1930. It remains a popular garden plant although some populations may be of hybrid origin. It occurs mostly in urban areas anywhere in the British Isles.

Occasional (57). It is not known when *S. canadensis* first grew wild in northern Lancashire but by the late 1960s it was well established in some urban areas. Today it occurs in many parts of western northern Lancashire.

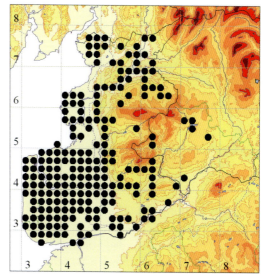
Gnaphalium uliginosum

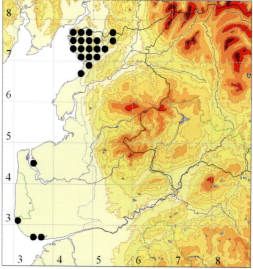
Inula conyzae

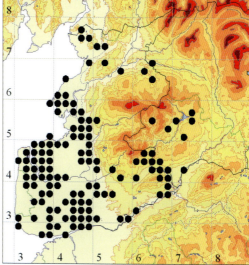
Pulicaria dysenterica

Solidago gigantea Aiton — Early Goldenrod

Neophyte. Early Goldenrod is a native of North America and was cultivated in Britain by 1758. It was known from the wild by 1916 but like *S. canadensis* it did not become widespread until after 1930. It remains a popular garden plant and occurs in England, Wales, central and southern Scotland with occasional records further north and in Ireland. It is sometimes confused with *S. canadensis*.

Frequent (80). As with Canadian Goldenrod it is not known when Early Goldenrod first grew wild in northern Lancashire but by 1971 it was found in several places. Today it is found mostly in western parts of the area and in the Ribble valley.

Solidago graminifolia (L.) Salisb. — Grass-leaved Goldenrod

Neophyte. This is a native of North America and was first cultivated in Britain in 1758. It was recorded from the wild in 1905. Grass-leaved Goldenrod is occasionally grown in gardens and it is found as a garden escape, mostly in south-western and southern England.

Very rare (4). *S. graminifolia* was first found in northern Lancashire at Fairhaven in 1958 (H.E.B.; LIV) and at Winmarleigh (SD44N) in 1967 (E.F.G.). Later it was found near Oxcliffe (SD46L) in 1974 (A.E.C.), at Heysham and Morecambe (SD46A, H; Livermore and Livermore, 1987) and Goosnargh (SD54K) in 1989 (E.F.G.).

Aster L. — Michaelmas-daisies

Neophyte. This is a group of North American species and hybrids brought into British cultivation by 1710. Since then they have escaped into the wild and today may be found anywhere in the British Isles. The various taxa are very difficult to identify and often they have been recorded as *Aster* agg. or *A. novi-belgii*, which is especially confusing as *A. novi-belgii* L. may not be one of the commoner taxa. In recent years the account by Yeo (1998) has been used to identify Michaelmas-daisies in northern Lancashire.

Occasional (57). In northern Lancashire it is not known when *Aster* agg. first occurred in the wild but it was established in several places by the late 1960s. Today Michaelmas-daisies are found mostly in western and in urban areas where colonies have become established on roadsides, waste ground and in other ruderal habitats.

Aster novae-angliae L. — Hairy Michaelmas-daisy

Neophyte. This is a native of eastern North America and was introduced into British cultivation in 1710. It was first recorded in the wild in 1915 and today occurs mostly in southern Britain.

Very rare (1). In northern Lancashire it was recorded from waste ground in Preston (unlocalised) in 1965 (A.E.R.).

Aster laevis L. × **A. novi-belgii** (**A. × versicolor** Willd.) — Late Michaelmas-daisy

Neophyte. This vigorous hybrid originated in cultivation in Britain in 1790 and was known in the wild by 1880. It is likely to occur throughout Britain but through identification difficulties it is under recorded.

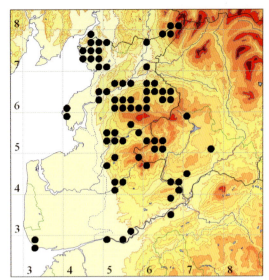

Solidago virgaurea

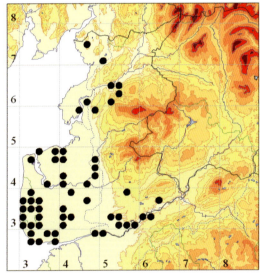

Solidago canadensis

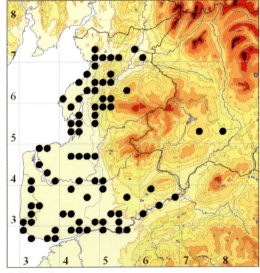

Solidago gigantea

Very rare (3). In northern Lancashire *A. × versicolor* was first found in the Carnforth area (SD47V) in 1987 (L.A.L.) where it occurs in at least two localities. It was also recorded from Bay Horse, Ellel (SD45W) in 1988 (L.A.L.) and at Lytham (SD32Y) in 1999 (E.F.G.). It is almost certainly under recorded.

Aster novi-belgii L.   Confused Michaelmas-daisy

Neophyte. *A. novi-belgii* is a native of eastern North America and was introduced into British gardens in 1710. It was recorded in the wild by 1860. It occurs throughout Britain but it is probably very much over recorded and mistaken for *A. × salignus* and *A. × versicolor*.

Rare (7). In northern Lancashire Confused Michaelmas-daisy was first recorded from the beach at Lytham (unlocalised) in 1965 (A.E.R.). Later records are scattered throughout the region.

Aster novi-belgii × A. lanceolatus (A. × salignus Willd.)
                                    Common Michaelmas-daisy

Neophyte. *A. × salignus* is a hybrid of garden origin thought to have been introduced into British cultivation in 1815. It was recorded in the wild in 1867 and today occurs throughout Britain but it is rare in Ireland. However it is readily confused with either parent, especially *A. lanceolatus*.

Rare (9). This was first recorded from waste ground between Lancaster and Morecambe (SD46L; Livermore and Livermore, 1987). Subsequent records are mostly from the west of the region. However it is likely to be much more frequent than the records suggest.

Aster lanceolatus Willd.   Narrow-leaved Michaelmas-daisy

Neophyte. This is a native of North America and has been in British cultivation since 1811. It was recorded in the wild by 1865. It may be found almost anywhere in the British Isles and is thought to be under recorded.

Very rare (3). In northern Lancashire this was first found in Fulwood (unlocalised) in 1965 (A.E.R.). Later records were from Silverdale (SD47T) in 1987 (L.A.L.), Marton, Blackpool (SD33G) in 1993 (C.F. & N.J.S.) and Warton (SD47W) in 1989 (L.A.L.).

Aster puniceus L.   Red-stalked Michaelmas-daisy

Neophyte. This is a native of eastern North America and has been found as an introduction in only a few British localities.

Very rare (1). In northern Lancashire *A. puniceus* was found by the canal at Lancaster (unlocalised) in 1966 (A.E.R.).

Aster tripolium L.   Sea Aster
Eurasian Temperate element.

This is a short-lived perennial herb found on salt marshes (BH21) around the coasts of the British Isles. It has also been found occasionally inland by salt treated roads. Var. *tripolium* with ligulate flowers occurs throughout the range of the species but var. *flosculosus* (Gray) P.D. Sell, (var. *discoideus* Rchb.) without ligulate flowers, is found mostly in southern Britain. According to Sell and Murrell (2006) var. *flosculosus* occurs on the lower parts of salt marshes.

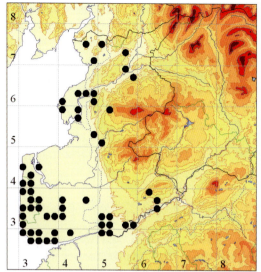
Aster agg.

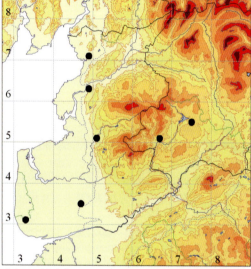
Aster novi-belgii

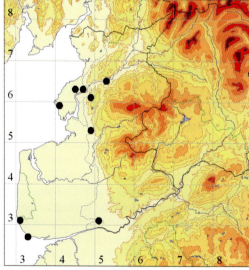
Aster × salignus

Frequent (70). In northern Lancashire Sea Aster is found around the coast where most of the plants are referable to var. *tripolium*. However var. *flosculosus* is also found occasionally. The distribution of Sea Aster is stable locally and nationally.

Erigeron glaucus Ker Gawl.   Seaside Daisy

Neophyte. Seaside Daisy is a native of North America and has been cultivated in Britain since 1812. It is commonly grown in gardens but it was not reported in the wild until 1942 when it was found on the south coast of England. Today it is found mostly on the south coast of England and more rarely elsewhere as far north as north-eastern Scotland. It is also common in the Isle of Man.

Very rare (3). In northern Lancashire it was first found on cinders by a railway at Lytham (SD32I) in 1970 (A.E.R.). Subsequent records are from sand dunes and sandy places at Lytham St Anne's (SD32I) in 1999 and 2003, Fairhaven (SD32E) in 2003 and by the tram terminal at Squires Gate, Blackpool (SD33A) in 1999 (all E.F.G.).

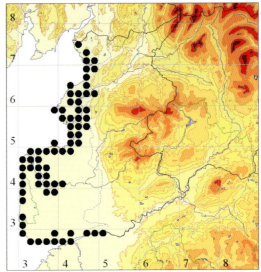
Aster tripolium

Erigeron philadelphicus L.   Robin's-plantain

Neophyte. This is a native of North America and was introduced into British gardens in 1778. It was recorded in the wild in 1928 and today occurs in a few localities in southern England and occasionally elsewhere.

In northern Lancashire *E. philadelphicus* was found in Eaves Wood, Silverdale (SD47T) in 1963 (A.E.R.).

Erigeron karvinskianus DC.   Mexican Fleabane

Neophyte. Mexican Fleabane is a native of Central America and has been cultivated in Britain since 1836. It is widely grown in frost free areas and has become established in the wild in southern parts of the British Isles, especially in south-western England. It was first found naturalised in the Channel Islands in 1860.

Very rare (5). In northern Lancashire *E. karvinskianus* was found at St Anne's (SD32J) in 1996, Ansdell (SD32N) in 2005 & Lytham (SD32T) in 2007 (all C.F. & N.J.S.); naturalised on a wall by the R. Ribble, Preston (SD52J) in 2008 and near Poulton-le-Fylde (SD33P) also in 2008 (both Anon).

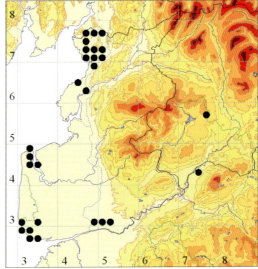
Erigeron acer

Erigeron acer L.   Blue Fleabane

Circumpolar Boreo-temperate element.

Blue Fleabane is an annual species found in open habitats on well-drained neutral or calcareous soils. It occurs on sand dunes, in stony places and in ruderal habitats (BH3, 16) in England, Wales and Ireland but in Scotland, where it is found in central areas, it is regarded as an introduction.

Occasional (28). In northern Lancashire *E. acer* is found on the calcareous soils around Morecambe Bay, on the sand dunes at Lytham St Anne's and in a few other localities in the region including ruderal habitats in and around Preston. Overall populations appear stable in Britain but in northern Lancashire it appears it may have spread a little colonizing newly created post-industrial habitats.

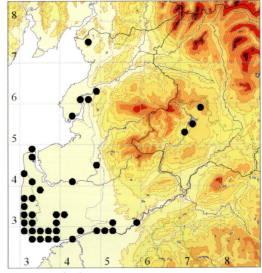
Conyza canadensis

Erigeron caucasicus Steven

This is a native of south-western Asia with only a few pre 1930 records reported from Britain.

Preston Scientific Society (1903) recorded *E. caucasicum* L., which may have referred to this species, from St Peter's churchyard, near Preston Docks.

Conyza canadensis (L.) Cronquist   Canadian Fleabane

Neophyte. This is a native of North America known in the London area since 1690 but since 1962 has spread to most parts of lowland and urban England and Wales with occasional records elsewhere.

Occasional (40). Canadian Fleabane was first found in northern Lancashire on cinders and rough ground at Fleetwood (SD34I) in 1975 (C.F. & N.J.S.) although there is an earlier unlocalised record for the 10km square SD54 (Perring and Walters, 1962). Today most records are from Lytham St Anne's with occasional records elsewhere especially on waste ground and in post-industrial sites.

Conyza sumatrensis (Retz.) E. Walker   Guernsey Fleabane

Neophyte. *C. sumatrensis* is a native of North America and was first recorded in the British Isles from Guernsey in 1961 and in Essex in 1974. Today it is especially common in the London area and occurs in many other places in southern England though only occasionally elsewhere.

Very rare (2). In northern Lancashire two colonies were found on waste ground on the newly established Lancaster Business Park (SD46W, X) in 2006 (J.Cl.).

Callistephus chinensis (L.) Nees   China Aster

Neophyte. China Aster is a native of China and was first cultivated in Britain in 1731 and recorded in the wild by 1908. It occurs casually on waste ground and on rubbish tips and, although less frequent than formerly, occurs in a few places, mostly in southern England.

Very rare (1). In northern Lancashire *C. chinensis* was found on Blackpool tip (SD33I) in *c.* 1966 (A.E.R.).

Olearia avicenniifolia (Raoul) Hook. f. × O. moschata Hook. f. (O. × haastii Hook. f.)   Daisy-bush

Neophyte. This is an evergreen shrub, which is a native of New Zealand. It has been cultivated in British gardens since 1851 and was found in the wild in 1978. So far it has been reported from a few coastal localities around the British Isles.

Very rare (1). In northern Lancashire it was reported as planted at Longridge Golf Course (SD63J) in 2003 (E.F.G.).

Olearia macrodonta Baker   New Zealand Holly

Neophyte. This evergreen shrub is a native of New Zealand. It was introduced into British gardens in 1886 and reported from the wild in 1957. It is a popular hedging plant, especially in coastal areas from where most records are reported. It is particularly common in the Isle of Man.

Very rare (2). In northern Lancashire it was found at Fleetwood Golf Course (SD34D) in 1988 and from Layton station (SD33J) in 2003 (both E.F.G.).

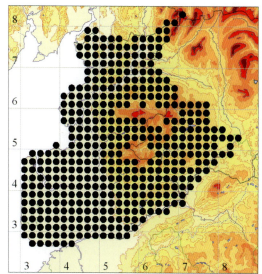
Bellis perennis

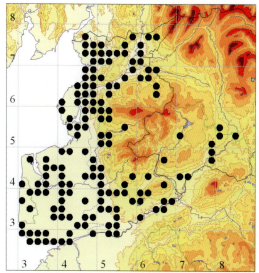
Tanacetum parthenium

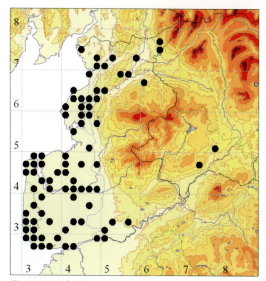
Tanacetum vulgare

Bellis perennis L.   Daisy

European Temperate element.

Daisy occurs in mown or trampled grassland but also by streams and in upland flushes (BH6). It is found throughout the British Isles.

Very common (429). *B. perennis* occurs throughout northern Lancashire except on the peat covered fells. Its distribution locally and nationally is stable.

Tanacetum parthenium (L.) Sch. Bip.   Feverfew

Archaeophyte. Apparently a native of the Balkan peninsula but it is widespread in temperate regions of the world. It was grown as a medicinal plant in Britain by 995 and today occurs in most parts of the British Isles, especially in urban areas and close to settlements.

Frequent (155). It is not clear when Feverfew first grew wild in northern Lancashire as it was widespread by the early twentieth century (Wheldon and Wilson, 1907). Today it is found throughout the area except in more rural and upland places away from habitation.

Tanacetum vulgare L.   Tansy

Eurasian Boreo-temperate element.

Tansy is an aromatic perennial herb found in grassy places by rivers, roads, railways and on waste ground (BH3). It is found throughout the British Isles but it is believed to be an introduction in Ireland. It was grown in medieval gardens as a medicinal and culinary herb and it is likely that many wild populations are of garden origin.

Frequent (82). *T. vulgare* occurs mostly in the north and west of northern Lancashire. Wheldon and Wilson (1907) reported nineteen localities suggesting that whilst its distribution remains unchanged many more localities have been found during the last 100 years. Nationally there has been no change in its distribution.

Artemisia vulgaris L.   Mugwort

Archaeophyte with a Eurosiberian Temperate distribution.

Mugwort is associated with human habitation and is found in a variety of ruderal habitats (BH3, 17). It occurs throughout the British Isles but it is rare in upland areas of Scotland, Wales and in parts of Ireland.

Frequent (230). In northern Lancashire *A. vulgaris* occurs in western areas but it also occurs in the Lune, Wyre and Ribble valleys. As Wheldon and Wilson (1907) described Mugwort as 'not very common' and did not record it from their district 7 based on the Wyre valley east of Garstang it is probable that it has extended its range and become more frequent over the last 100 years. Nationally the 'New Atlas' thought the distribution of *A. vulgaris* was stable but according to 'Local Change' it has extended its range since 1987.

Artemisia verlotiorum Lamotte   Chinese Mugwort

Neophyte. Chinese Mugwort is a native of south-western China but it is naturalised in many parts of the world. It was first collected in the wild in Britain in 1908 but it was not recognised as a distinct species until 1938/9. Today it is naturalised in south-eastern England spreading by detached pieces of rhizome. It also occurs in a few scattered localities elsewhere in Britain.

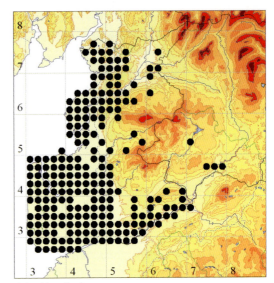
Artemisia vulgaris

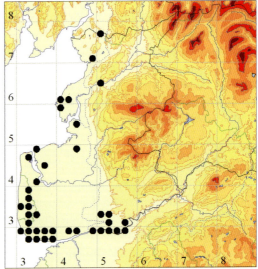
Artemisia absinthium

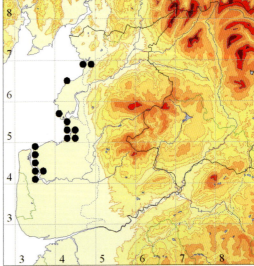
Artemisia maritima

Very rare (1). In northern Lancashire it was found as a garden weed in Blackpool (SD33D) in 2002 (C.F. & N.J.S.).

Artemisia absinthium L. — Wormwood

Archaeophyte with a Eurosiberian Temperate distribution.

This aromatic herb occurs in ruderal habitats (BH3, 16, 17) and is found in England and Wales but more rarely in Scotland and Ireland.

Occasional (39). Wheldon and Wilson (1907) did not record Wormwood in VC 60 yet Thornber (1837) recorded it from Blackpool and it was found at Halton in the Lune valley in 1862 (W.H.; LIV). Today it is found mostly in coastal areas and between Preston and Lytham. Nationally its distribution is stable.

Artemisia stelleriana Besser — Hoary Mugwort

Neophyte. This is a native of north-eastern Asia and the Aleutian Islands of North America. It was introduced into British cultivation in 1865 and was recorded from the wild in 1888. It occurs in a few British localities.

Very rare (1). Hoary Mugwort was found on Blackpool tip (SD33I) in 1966 (J.H. & A.E.R.).

Artemisia abrotanum L. — Southernwood

Neophyte. This small aromatic shrub was being grown in Britain by 995 and was reported from the wild in 1906. Its origin is uncertain but it remains a popular garden plant although it rarely if ever flowers in Britain. It is recorded from a few scattered localities in the British Isles.

Very rare (1). This was reported as a garden escape in Lancaster (SD46R; Livermore and Livermore, 1991).

Artemisia dracunculus L. — Tarragon

Neophyte. Tarragon is a native of eastern Europe, Asia and western North America. It was cultivated in British gardens by 1548 and was known in the wild in 1906. Today it occurs in a few scattered localities, mostly in south-eastern England.

Very rare (1). In northern Lancashire a single fine plant was found by a railway fence at Ansdell (SD32N) in 1977, and where it was still present in 2010 (C.F. & N.J.S.).

Artemisia maritima L. — Sea Wormwood

Suboceanic Temperate element.

Sea Wormwood is an attractive, aromatic, perennial herb found on the drier, upper part of salt marshes (BH21) around the coasts of Ireland, Wales, England and southern and eastern Scotland.

Occasional (15). In northern Lancashire S. maritima is confined to salt marshes between Carnforth and the Wyre estuary. So far as is known it has never colonised the Ribble estuary. Its distribution in northern Lancashire is unchanged but its abundance varies. Nationally the 'New Atlas' reported losses in northern and western Britain.

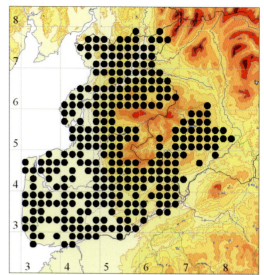
Achillea ptarmica

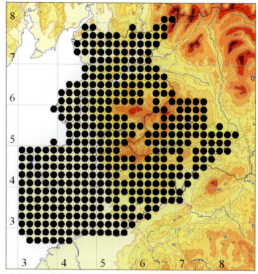
Achillea millefolium

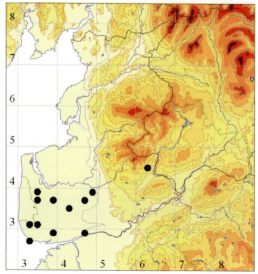
Anthemis arvensis

Santolina chamaecyparissus L.   Lavender-cotton

Neophyte. This is a native of the Mediterranean region and was cultivated in Britain by 1548. It is a popular garden plant and was found in the wild by 1905.

Very rare (2). In northern Lancashire *S. chamaecyparissus* was found as a garden escape at Morecambe (SD46M; Livermore and Livermore, 1987) and at Lancaster (SD46R; Livermore and Livermore, 1991).

Achillea ptarmica L.   Sneezewort

Eurasian Boreo-temperate element.

Sneezewort is a perennial herb of damp or wet habitats on a wide range of soils (BH11) throughout the British Isles although it is rare in south-eastern Ireland.

Common (314). *A. ptarmica* is found throughout northern Lancashire. Its distribution is stable but nationally the 'New Atlas' reported considerable losses, especially in south-eastern England but further significant losses since 1987 were not confirmed ('Local Change').

Achillea millefolium L.   Yarrow

Eurasian Boreo-temperate element.

Yarrow occurs in grasslands in a variety of habitats (BH6) throughout the British Isles. British material belongs to ssp. *millefolium* where var. *millefolium* is the common taxon. Of the other varieties found in Britain var. *compacta* Bréb may occur in northern Lancashire (Sell and Murrell, 2006).

Very common (417). Yarrow occurs throughout northern Lancashire except on peat covered fells. Its distribution is stable locally and nationally.

Chamaemelum nobile (L.) All.   Chamomile

Suboceanic Southern-temperate element but a neophyte in northern Lancashire.

Chamomile is found in acidic, seasonally wet grassland on well-drained soils (BH8). It is regarded as a native species in southern Britain and in Ireland but occurs as an introduction in northern England, Scotland and the Isle of Man.

Very rare (1). In northern Lancashire Chamomile was found in recently graded and sown banks of the New River Brock at Myerscough (SD44V) in 1987 (C.J.B.).

Anthemis arvensis L.   Corn Chamomile

Archaeophyte with a European Southern-temperate distribution.

Corn Chamomile is an annual species of light, calcareous or sandy soils found in cultivated ground and in waste places (BH3, 4) throughout the British Isles.

Rare (12). Although not recorded by Wheldon and Wilson (1907) it had been found at Stodday in 1862 (W.H.; LIV). Today it has been found in a few localities in the south of VC 60. Nationally Corn Chamomile has declined ('New Atlas', 'Local Change').

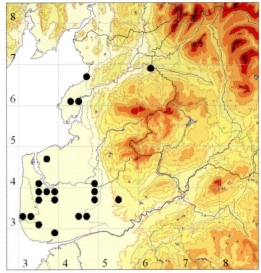

Anthemis cotula

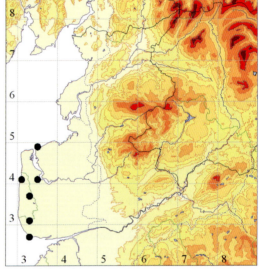

Anthemis tinctoria

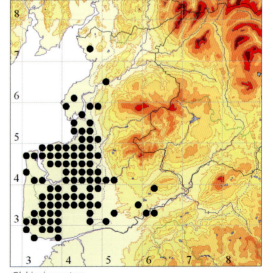

Glebionis segetum

Anthemis cotula L.   Stinking Chamomile

Archaeophyte with a European Southern-temperate distribution.

Stinking Chamomile is a foetid annual species of cultivated ground (BH4) found mostly in the southern half of the British Isles.

Occasional (21). In northern Lancashire this was found in Roman remains at Ribchester (Huntley and Hillam, 2000); at Morecambe in 1862 (W.H., LIV) and at Ribchester in 1885 (F.C.K., MANCH). Today Stinking Chamomile is found mostly in the lowland west of VC 60 but whilst its distribution is broadly similar to that of 100 years ago (Wheldon and Wilson, 1907) it is believed to be much less frequent. The 'New Atlas' reported a decline nationally and whilst this has continued it is not statistically significant ('Local Change').

Anthemis tinctoria L.   Yellow Chamomile

Neophyte with a Eurosiberian Temperate distribution. Yellow Chamomile was introduced into Britain by 1561 and was cultivated for a yellow dye. It was first noted in the wild in 1690 and today it is grown in gardens as an ornamental plant. It may be found almost anywhere in the British Isles as an escape from cultivation.

Rare (6). This was first found in northern Lancashire as a casual at Knott End (SD34P) in 1964 (E.J.H.). Subsequent records have all been near the coast between Fleetwood and Lytham St Anne's.

Glebionis segetum (L.) Fourr.   Corn Marigold

Archaeophyte with a European Southern-temperate distribution.

There is a continuous archaeological record in Britain for Corn Marigold from the Iron Age onwards. It is found as an annual species of usually light soils, often deficient in calcium, in cultivated and waste ground (BH4) throughout the British Isles. It was formerly a serious weed in grain crops.

Frequent (96). *G. segetum* was first recorded in northern Lancashire from Roman deposits at Ribchester (Huntley and Hillam, 2000) and has been found in historic times as a weed of lowland areas in the west of VC 60 and more occasionally in the Ribble valley. Until the late 1960s it particularly favoured the light soils reclaimed from former mosses where, with *Galeopsis speciosa*, it could be spectacularly colourful amongst ripening cereal crops. However with changes in agricultural practices it has become much rarer and is now usually confined to field margins and waste places and by 2010 was difficult to find anywhere in VC 60. This decline is reflected nationally ('New Atlas', 'Local Change').

Glebionis coronaria (L.) Cass. ex Spach   Crown Daisy

Neophyte. Crown Daisy is an annual species that is a native of the Mediterranean region and south-western Asia. It was cultivated in Britain by 1629 and was recorded in the wild by 1897. It is grown in gardens but occurs casually on tips and in waste places in a few scattered localities in Britain.

Very rare (1). In northern Lancashire it was found by the canal in Lancaster (SD46V) in 2006 (J. Cl.).

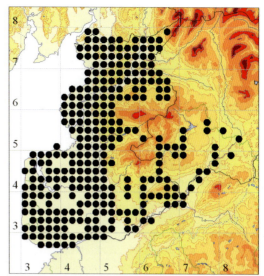

Leucanthemum vulgare

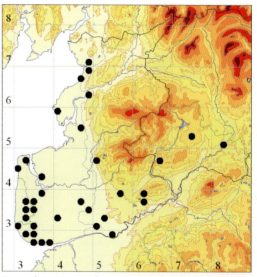

Leucanthemum × superbum

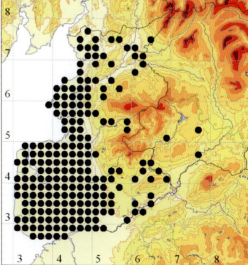

Matricaria chamomilla

Leucanthemum vulgare Lam.   Oxeye Daisy

Eurosiberian Boreo-temperate element.

This is a perennial herb of grassland and ruderal habitats (BH6, 7) throughout the British Isles.

Common (297). Oxeye Daisy is found in most parts of northern Lancashire although it is absent from many upland areas in the east of the area. Its distribution is stable locally but nationally the 'New Atlas' reported a decline in northern Scotland but 'Local Change' did not note further decline since 1987.

Leucanthemum lacustre (Brot.) Samp. × L. maximum (Ramond) DC. (L. × superbum (Bergmaus ex J.W. Ingram) D.H. Kent)

Shasta Daisy

Neophyte. This hybrid of garden origin was first introduced into British cultivation in 1816 and was recorded in the wild in 1913. It is still grown in gardens and also in amenity plantings but readily escapes into wild situations where it is found on roadside verges and in ruderal habitats generally. It is unevenly recorded but may occur anywhere in the British Isles.

Occasional (35). In northern Lancashire Shasta Daisy was first found on waste ground at Blackpool (SD33I) in 1967 (E.J.H.). Today it may be found anywhere in the area but usually occurs near habitation and most records are from coastal areas of VC 60.

Matricaria chamomilla L.   Scented Mayweed

Archaeophyte with a European Southern-temperate distribution.

Scented Mayweed is an annual species found in cultivated and waste ground (BH3, 4), mostly in England and Wales with more scattered localities in Scotland and Ireland.

Frequent (211). *M. chamomilla* is found throughout northern Lancashire but whilst it is common in the western half of the area it occurs in only scattered localities further east. Its distribution in northern Lancashire is probably stable but 'Local Change' reported an increase since 1987, possibly due to highway authorities using it in seed mixtures.

Matricaria discoidea DC.   Pineappleweed

Neophyte. Pineappleweed is probably a native of northern and southern Asia and perhaps adjacent parts of North America but in the nineteenth and twentieth centuries it spread to boreal and temperate zones throughout the northern hemisphere. It was cultivated in British gardens in 1781 and in Ireland by 1894. It then spread rapidly throughout the British Isles where it is found in ruderal habitats. It is particularly prevalent in field gateways.

Very common (396). In northern Lancashire it was first recorded from near Freckleton (Salmon and Thompson, 1902) but Wheldon and Wilson (1907) knew of only three further localities. It is possible these records owe their origin to impurities in grain imported from North America. Today Pineappleweed occurs throughout the area except on the fells.

Tripleurospermum maritimum (L.) W.A.J. Koch   Sea Mayweed

Circumpolar Wide-boreal element.

This is a perennial or biennial herb occurring in a wide variety of coastal habitats (BH18, 19) and is found around all the coasts of the British Isles.

Occasional (47). Sea Mayweed was not distinguished from Scentless

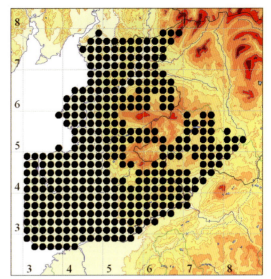

Matricaria discoidea

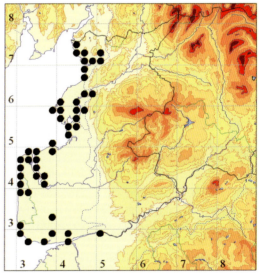

Tripleurospermum maritimum

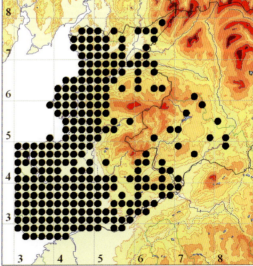

Tripleurospermum inodorum

Mayweed until 1969 and is therefore under recorded. Similarly the subspecies have not been recorded. It occurs along the entire coast of VC 60.

[Tripleurospermum maritimum × T. inodorum

This is a common hybrid but so far it has not been identified in northern Lancashire.]

Tripleurospermum inodorum (L.) Sch. Bip.   Scentless Mayweed

Archaeophyte with a Eurosiberian Temperate distribution.

There is a continuous archaeological record in Britain for Scentless Mayweed from the Bronze Age onwards. It is an annual of cultivated and waste ground occurring throughout most parts of the British Isles (BH4, 17). However it was not distinguished from *T. maritimum* until 1969 and the two species have not always been separately identified.

Common (285). In northern Lancashire *T. inodorum* is a common species in the west of the area but it is much more localised further east.

Senecio cineraria DC.   Silver Ragwort

Neophyte. This is a native of the western and central Mediterranean region and was introduced into Britain by 1633. Silver Ragwort was found in the wild by 1893 and it has become a popular garden plant. Increasingly it is found in the wild particularly in southern Britain and the Isle of Man.

Very rare (4). In northern Lancashire Silver Ragwort was found at Blackpool South railway station (SD33B) in 1998, on sand dunes at Squires Gate, Blackpool (SD33A) in 2005 and by a golf course at Lytham St Anne's (SD33A) in 1988 (all C.F. & N.J.S.). It was also found on the northern side of Fleetwood Golf Course (SD34D) in 1998 (E.F.G.).

Senecio cineraria × S. jacobaea (S. × albescens Burb. & Colgan)

This is a spontaneous hybrid between introduced and native parents. It is believed it first arose in Shropshire and then near Dublin in 1902 and in Cornwall in 1906. It occurs in scattered localities in England, Wales and eastern Ireland with a few Scottish localities. However in some areas it appears to be especially frequent including coastal areas of Cheshire, Merseyside and Lancashire.

Occasional (16). In northern Lancashire *S. × albescens* was first recorded from sandy ground at Blackpool (SD33B) in 1985 (C.F. & N.J.S.). Today it is found in coastal areas from Carnforth to Lytham St Anne's.

Senecio jacobaea L.   Common Ragwort

Eurosiberian Temperate element.

Common Ragwort is a biennial or perennial herb of neglected grasslands, sand dunes and woodland edge habitats (BH3, 6, 7, 8). It is found throughout the British Isles.

Common (349). In northern Lancashire *S. jacobaea* occurs throughout the area except in upland Bowland and parts of Lancashire VC 64. It is believed most plants belong to *S. jacobaea* ssp. *jacobaea* var. *jacobaea* but var. *condensatus* Druce was found on the sand dunes at Fairhaven (SD32I) and at Lytham St Anne's L.N.R. (SD33A) in 2008 (E.F.G.). Common Ragwort's distribution is stable locally and nationally despite it being a notifiable weed and subject to statutory control.

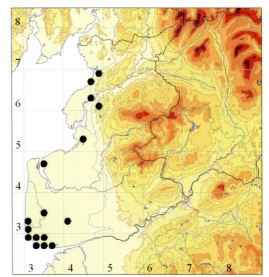

Senecio × albescens

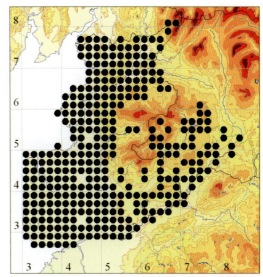

Senecio jacobaea

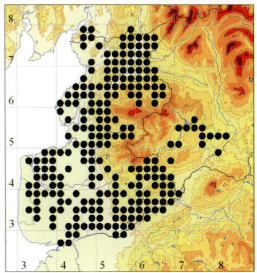

Senecio aquaticus

Senecio jacobaea × S. aquaticus (S. × ostenfeldii Druce)

This biennial or perennial hybrid grows in damp grasslands and waste places, usually with its parents. It is found throughout the British Isles but it is often overlooked.

Very rare (1). In northern Lancashire it was found at the Crook O' Lune, Caton (SD56H) in 2003 (M.Sh.). It is certain to be more widespread than this single record suggests.

Senecio aquaticus Hill   Marsh Ragwort

European Temperate element.

This biennial or perennial herb occurs in marshes, wet meadows and by streams, ditches and ponds (BH11, 14) throughout the British Isles.

Common (237). In northern Lancashire Marsh Ragwort occurs mostly in lowland areas but it is often absent from former mosses. Its distribution in northern Lancashire is probably stable but the 'New Atlas' reports losses mostly since 1950 and especially in southern and eastern England. 'Local Change' reports a continuing decline nationally since 1987.

Senecio erucifolius L.   Hoary Ragwort

Eurosiberian Temperate element.

This is a perennial herb of calcareous grassland and woodland edge habitats (BH3, 6) and is found in England, Wales and eastern Ireland. It occurs as an introduction in central Scotland.

Occasional (52). Hoary Ragwort is at the northern edge of its British range in northern Lancashire. It occurs mostly in the west of VC 60 with a few records elsewhere especially in the Ribble valley and in SD57. Records 100 years ago were more scattered than they are today in VC 60 but it is difficult to be sure to what extent there have been significant changes. Nationally the 'New Atlas' reported losses on the northern edge of its range but 'Local Change' considered its distribution stable since 1987.

Senecio inaequidens DC.   Narrow-leaved Ragwort

Neophyte. This is a native of South Africa but it is widely naturalised in Europe. It is a perennial herb naturalised in a few places, mostly in southern England. It was first recorded in the wild in Fife in 1836 but today it is found occasionally in many parts of the British Isles but mostly in southern England. However it seems to be spreading northwards.

Very rare (2). A single plant of Narrow-leaved Ragwort was found by the M6 motorway (SD53H) in 2009 (M.P.) and a few plants at St Anne's (SD32E) in 2010 (N.J.S.).

Senecio sarracenicus L.   Broad-leaved Ragwort

Neophyte with a Eurosiberian Temperate distribution. This tall and vigorous perennial herb was introduced into Britain before 1600 and was originally grown for medicinal use. It was first recorded from the wild in 1632 from Shropshire (Sinker, et al., 1985) and from Somerset in 1680 (Clement and Foster, 1994). It is grown in gardens and whilst it has become naturalised by shaded streams and rivers other colonies owe their origins to recent garden escapes. It is found in scattered localities in the British Isles but particularly in northern England and central Scotland.

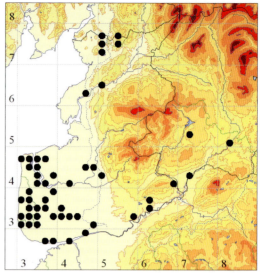

Senecio erucifolius

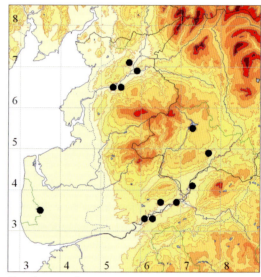

Senecio sarracenicus

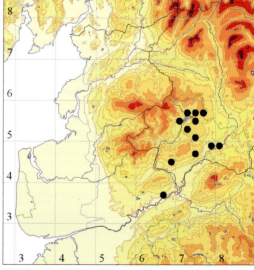

Senecio ovatus

Rare (12). There is some doubt as to when Broad-leaved Ragwort was first found in northern Lancashire (see *Tephroseris palustris*) but the first confirmed records were from the banks of the River Ribble near Redscar, Preston (Ashfield, 1858) and in the Lune valley near Melling (Wheldon and Wilson, 1901a). Today it is naturalised in both the Lune and Ribble valleys with only occasional records elsewhere. However in the Ribble valley some records may be referable to the even more vigorous but similar *S. ovatus*.

Senecio ovatus (P. Gaertn., B. Mey. & Scherb.) Willd. ssp. alpestris (Gaudin) Herborg.   Wood Ragwort

Neophyte. *S. ovatus* ssp. *alpestris* is a native of the Alps and was introduced into British gardens in 1823. It is only occasionally grown in gardens but it was recorded in the wild by 1828. All recent records are from the Ribble and Hodder valleys.

Rare (12). Until recently this was probably mistaken for *S. sarracenicus*. However it is likely that this was first recorded from Browsholme (SD64X) as *S. sarracenicus* in 1892 by Milne-Redhead (1870s) who then owned Holden Clough. In view of its subsequent history it is possible that Milne-Redhead transplanted material into his Holden Clough garden and woodland where it became naturalised. Interestingly the first confirmed record is from Bolton-by-Bowland in 1964 (J.N.F.), which is no more than 1km down stream from Holden Clough. Today it is naturalised in many parts of Lancashire VC 64 and in Gisburn Forest covers extensive areas. In VC 60 it was first found on Lytham tip (c. SD32Y) in c. 1966 (A.E.R.). It is also naturalised by the R. Ribble at Copy Scar Wood, Dutton (SD63T).

Senecio squalidus L.   Oxford Ragwort

Neophyte. It was thought that Oxford Ragwort arose in the Oxford Botanic Garden and was first recorded as an escape from the Garden in 1794. However recent research summarised by Crawford (2008) is fascinating. On the arid volcanic ash of Mt Etna in Sicily different species of *Senecio* occupy distinct altitudinal zones. Where the altitudinal range of *Senecio* species on Mt Etna overlap hybrids occur and it is believed that plants closely similar to some of these hybrids were brought to Britain. A plant morphologically similar to *S. squalidus* was collected from Mt Etna and was first grown in the British Isles in the Duchess of Beaufort's garden before being transferred to the Oxford Botanic Garden sometime before 1719. Then during a period of approximately 90 years from its introduction in the early eighteenth century until it was reported as growing on walls in Oxford a stabilized derivative developed and it is this that is known as *Senecio squalidus*. Molecular studies have shown that Oxford Ragwort is derived from the hybrid between *S. aethnensis* Jan ex DC. and *S. chrysanthemifolius* Poiret.

Occasional (67). Oxford Ragwort was first found in northern Lancashire in railway sidings at Preston (Whellan and Bunker, 1948) and by a railway bridge at Squires Gate, Blackpool (Whellan, 1948). By the mid 1960s *S. squalidus* was naturalised on the Fylde coast. Today most localities are in the west of the region particularly in coastal areas.

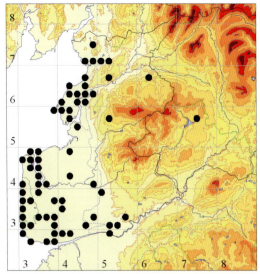

Senecio squalidus

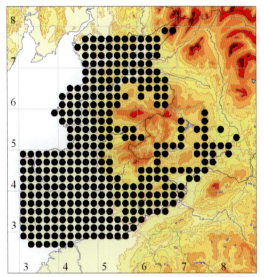

Senecio vulgaris

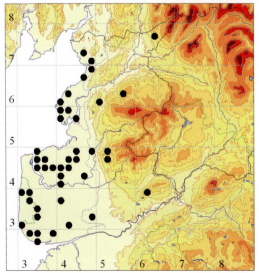

Senecio sylvaticus

Senecio squalidus × S. viscosus
(S. × subnebrodensis Simonk)

This is an annual or biennial hybrid of waste ground first found in the London area in 1944. It has been recorded in scattered localities in the British Isles but mostly in south-eastern England.

Very rare (1). In northern Lancashire S. × subnebrodensis was found in a factory forecourt at Heysham (SD46A) in 2002 (A.M. Boucher; LIV).

Senecio vulgaris L.   Groundsel

European Southern-temperate element.

Groundsel is an annual species of disturbed places in waste and cultivated ground and on sand dunes (BH3, 4, 17) throughout the British Isles. It is a variable species most notably in the presence or absence of ligulate flowers. However the variation is more complex than this simple distinction implies.

Very common (357). In northern Lancashire S. vulgaris is found throughout the area except on the fells. Plants with ligulate flowers are found occasionally and it is believed these are S. vulgaris ssp. vulgaris var. hibernicus Syme, which was found on the sand dunes at Lytham St Anne's (SD32E) in 2010 (E.F.G.). Generally records have not been kept of this or other taxa. It is possible that S. vulgaris ssp. denticulatus (O.F. Müll) P.D. Sell, also with ligulate flowers, may occur on the sand dunes. The distribution of S. vulgaris is believed to be stable in northern Lancashire but the 'New Atlas' reported a decline in northern Scotland. However, no change in its distribution nationally was reported by 'Local Change' since 1987.

Senecio sylvaticus L.   Heath Groundsel

European Temperate element.

This is an annual species of open habitats on heaths, in cleared and burnt woodland and on sandy banks, usually on acidic soils (BH2, 8, 9). It is found in most parts of the British Isles but it is rare in some areas, e.g. north-western and highland Scotland, the Pennines and much of Ireland.

Occasional (44). In northern Lancashire Heath Groundsel is found mostly in western areas. Its distribution is thought to be stable locally and nationally.

Senecio viscosus L.   Sticky Groundsel

Neophyte. This is a European Temperate species that has spread markedly in western and northern Europe in recent centuries. It was first recorded in Britain in 1660 and has spread rapidly since 1900, especially along roads and railways. Today it is found throughout the British Isles but it is rare in most of Ireland and in highland and western Scotland.

Frequent (145). In northern Lancashire Sticky Groundsel was found near Sunderland in the Heysham peninsula by Thomas Lawson in the late seventeenth century (Lankester, 1848) and at Pilling Moss (Ashfield, 1858). However Wheldon and Wilson (1907) did not know of any contemporary localities 100 years ago. It is not known when it spread into northern Lancashire in the twentieth century but it was present in VC 60 by 1962 (Perring and Walters, 1962). Today it is found in ruderal habitats mostly in the west and north of northern Lancashire and in the Ribble valley but only occasionally further east and in Bowland.

Tephroseris palustris (L.) Fourr.   Marsh Fleawort

Circumpolar Wide-boreal element.

Marsh Fleawort is a short-lived perennial herb of pond margins and fen ditches. In Holland it is known as an early colonist of bare mud on land newly reclaimed from the sea. However its seeds have a short period of viability and without bare mud habitats being continually renewed it quickly disappears. It was first recorded in Britain from Yorkshire in 1650 and whilst most records were from East Anglian fens it had a wider distribution than this implies having also been found in western Wales and Sussex (Marren, 1999). It was always known for varying in abundance but it finally became extinct in 1899.

Extinct. In northern Lancashire Marsh Fleawort was found by John Ray in 'ditches about Pillin-moss in Lancashire'. The record is quoted by Raven (1942) from Ray's book Catalogus Angliae published in 1670. However the observation was probably made in 1660 following a tour of northern England and the Isle of Man when he probably returned from the Isle of Man via the Wyre estuary (Wardleys on the east bank was then the main port on the estuary) and Garstang. This route would take him past Pilling. The record is usually regarded as an error (e.g. by Wheldon and Wilson, 1907) but Ray was familiar with the species from Cambridgeshire and elsewhere in East Anglia. Also at that time there were extensive fens near Pilling Moss. Pilling Water, which was one of the main drainage outlets from the moss, was then tidal for a considerable way inland. There is no doubt that at that time there were suitable habitats for Marsh Fleawort in lowland Lancashire.

A more puzzling record is quoted by Raven (1948) from a notebook of Thomas Lawson (1630–1691) written about 1675. Raven cites a Lawson record of Senecio paludosus from 'in Hilderston Mosse by Burton'. Wilson (1938) citing a record given by John Wilson in his A Synopsis of British Plants in Mr Ray's Method (1744) refers the record to Senecio palustris from Burton Moss and also called it Marsh Fleabane. Burton Moss and Hilderstone Moss are essentially the same bog system but the old boundary between Lancashire and Westmoreland separated the two bogs. However S. paludosus and S. palustris are two different species, which were both found in East Anglian fens but there is no suggestion that S. paludosus ever occurred in north-western England. It has been assumed that Lawson's record was for S. palustris but that it was an error for S. sarracenicus (Halliday, 1997). S.sarracenicus was found by John Dalton (1766–1844) a few miles to the north at Preston

Patrick (Wilson, 1938) in about 1790 making it one of the earliest British records for this species. A further complexity concerns a Thomas Lawson record of *S. sarracenicus* quoted by William Nicolson (1655–1727) without locality but presumably from that part of Westmorland (Whittaker, 1986). Nicolson thought it was a garden escape. Nicolson knew Lawson and this record suggests that he or both he and Lawson knew the difference between *S. sarracenicus* and *S. paludosus / palustris*.

It is suggested that Ray's record for *T. palustris* from Pilling Moss is probably correct but that there must be doubt as to what Thomas Lawson meant by his record of *S. paludosus* from Hilderstone Moss.

Brachyglottis × jubar P.D. Sell   Shrub Ragwort

Neophyte. The exact parentage of this hybrid is unknown but it originated in cultivation around 1910. It was first recorded in the wild in 1981 but probably occurred before this. Today it is established in scattered localities in the British Isles particularly along the south coast of England and in the Isle of Man.

Very rare (2). In northern Lancashire Shrub Ragwort was found by Fleetwood Golf Course (SD34D) and at Newton-with-Clifton (SD43R), both in 1998 (E.F.G.).

Brachyglottis monroi (Hook. f.) B. Nord.   Monro's Ragwort

Neophyte. This is a native of New Zealand that is occasionally grown in gardens. It was first recorded in the wild in 1985 and occurs in a few localities in Britain.

Very rare (1). In northern Lancashire Monro's Ragwort was found as a garden escape by the River Brock, Bilsborrow (SD54F) in 1998 (E.F.G.).

Sinacalia tangutica (Maxim.) B. Nord.   Chinese Ragwort

Neophyte. Chinese Ragwort is a large, rhizomatous, perennial herb, which is a native of China. It was introduced into British cultivation in 1902 and was found in the wild in 1936. Today it occurs in scattered localities throughout the British Isles.

Very rare (1). In northern Lancashire Chinese Ragwort was found by streams in Fulwood (SD53F) in 1965 (E.H.).

Ligularia dentata (A. Gray) H. Hara   Leopardplant

Neophyte. Leopardplant is a large, perennial herb, which is a native of eastern Asia. It was introduced into British cultivation in 1900 and was first recorded in the wild in 1928. It is widely grown in gardens and escapes into damp shaded or woodland habitats in scattered localities in Britain.

Very rare (1). In northern Lancashire it was found as a garden escape in the Caton area (SD56H; Livermore and Livermore, 1987).

Doronicum pardalianches L.   Leopard's-bane

Neophyte. This is a native of western Europe and has been cultivated in Britain since the sixteenth century. It was first recorded in the wild in 1633 and today occurs throughout Britain but much more rarely in Ireland.

Occasional (16). Leopard's-bane was first recorded in northern Lancashire from a roadside near Chipping in 1941 (H.E.B.) where it still occurs. Today it is found in a few scattered localities, mostly in the western half of VC 60.

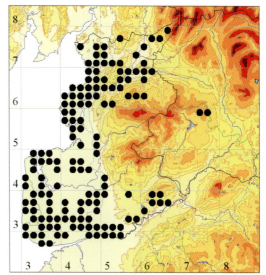

Senecio viscosus

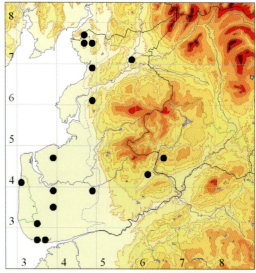

Doronicum pardalianches

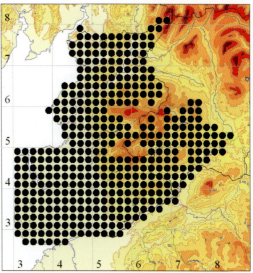

Tussilago farfara

Tussilago farfara L.   Colt's-foot

Eurosiberian Boreo-temperate element.

Colt's-foot is a rhizomatous, perennial herb found as a pioneer colonizer of moist or dry disturbed habitats (BH16) throughout the British Isles.

Very common (417). In northern Lancashire *T. farfara* is found throughout the area, except on the tops of the fells. There has been no change in its distribution locally and whilst the 'New Atlas' reported no change nationally since 1987 'Local Change' noted a significant decline. Reasons for the decline are not apparent.

Petasites hybridus (L.) P. Gaertn., B. Mey. & Scherb.   Butterbur

European Temperate element.

This is a robust and apparently dioecious, rhizomatous, perennial herb of moist fertile soils by rivers and streams, in woodlands and on roadsides (BH14). It is found in many parts of the British Isles but it is rare or absent in northern and highland Scotland and in some other upland areas. Apparently 'female' plants are frequent only in northern and central England (Perring, 1968). The sexuality of Butterbur and other issues were discussed in a series of notes in *BSBI News* (e.g. Stevens, Davies and Yeo, all 1990).

Frequent (207). Butterbur is widely distributed in northern Lancashire but it is rare in most western areas and it is absent from the fells. It is found in damp places by streams and rivers, often in shady places but it also occurs on roadsides. Only latterly were the sexes distinguished and recorded separately but as the extended growth of the 'female' inflorescences is only visible for a short period in spring ascertaining whether or not there was a difference in the distribution of the two sexes has proved difficult. It is likely that 'male' plants are more frequent (49 tetrads) than 'female' ones (30 tetrads). However ecologically it appears that 'female' plants are found largely or only by streams and rivers whilst 'male' plants also colonize roadsides away from streams and rivers. Mixed colonies by rivers and streams are frequent. A great deal more research is needed to understand the biology of this species and to investigate a theory that 'male' plants may have been introduced for medicinal and culinary purposes. The distribution of Butterbur is unchanged locally and nationally.

Petasites albus (L.) Gaertn.   White Butterbur

Neophyte. White Butterbur is a native of the mountains of Europe and south-western Asia. It was introduced into Britain by 1683 and was naturalised in western Yorkshire by 1843. Today it is found in scattered localities in Britain and in the north of Ireland but it appears to be especially frequent in central and eastern Scotland.

Very rare (3). White Butterbur was first recorded in northern Lancashire from a copse at Wrea Green in 1947 (H.E.B.; Whellan, 1948). In 1965 it was found on a roadside at Wrea Green (A.E.R.), which may be in the same area, but the exact location of the records has not been ascertained. It was also found at Carnforth (SD57A in 1971, L.A.L.) but the colony had gone by 1973, and on a roadside at Holden Clough (SD75Q; Abbott, 2005).

Petasites fragrans (Vill.) C. Presl   Winter Heliotrope

Neophyte. Winter Heliotrope is a native of the central Mediterranean region of Europe. It was introduced into Britain in 1806 and the male plant

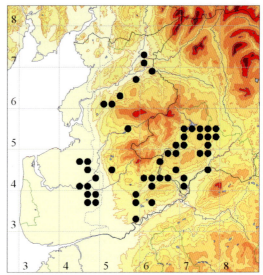
Petasites hybridus 'male'

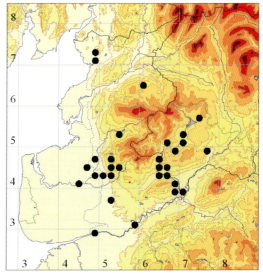
Petasites hybridus 'female'

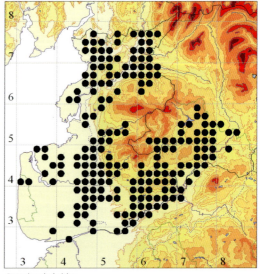
Petasites hybridus

of this dioecious species was established in the wild by the start of the twentieth century. It is naturalised by streams and on roadsides in much of the British Isles but it is rare or absent from central areas of Wales and England and most of Scotland.

Occasional (34). In northern Lancashire *P. fragrans* was first recorded from a roadside near Yealand (Wheldon and Wilson, 1907). Other pre-1964 records are from roadsides south of Lancaster and near Kirkham in 1942 (Whellan, 1948) and from a roadside near Chaigley in 1961 (Anon, 1983). Since 1964 it has been found from scattered localities, mostly in the west and south of the area.

Calendula officinalis L.   Pot Marigold

Neophyte. This attractive species was grown as a pot herb in British gardens by 995. It readily escapes from cultivation and was known in the wild by 1872 but it rarely becomes naturalised. However its origin is unknown. Today it is found throughout the British Isles although most records are from the southern half of Britain.

Occasional (37). It is not known when Pot Marigold first appeared in the wild in northern Lancashire. However by the mid 1960s it was found on tips and in waste places. Today it is found mostly in the west of the region and around Preston.

Ambrosia artemisiifolia L.   Ragweed

Neophyte. This is a native of North America and was first cultivated in Britain by 1759. It has been recorded casually in the wild since 1836 and today there are records from waste ground and tips in urban areas of Britain. For an account of *Ambrosia* spp. in Britain see Rich (1994).

Rare (9). Ragweed was first recorded in northern Lancashire from the sand dunes at St Anne's (Bailey, 1907) but it is clear from Bailey's accounts (Bailey, 1902, 1907) that most plants he called *A. artemisiifolia* were the perennial *A. psilostachya*. Nevertheless two specimens at MANCH are *A. artemisiifolia* both collected in 1906. Also it was probably *A. artemisiifolia* that was recorded from near St Michael on Wyre, Garstang, (Hornby, 1930). Since 1964 Ragweed has been found on tips, in gardens and waste places in scattered localities in the west of the area and from the old Preston to Longridge railway (D.P.E.).

Ambrosia psilostachya DC.   Perennial Ragweed

Neophyte. Perennial Ragweed is a native of North America and was first recorded in the wild in Britain from northern Lancashire in 1902 (Bailey, 1902). It was imported as a grain impurity and became naturalised on sand dunes in Lancashire but elsewhere in Britain it is a rare casual.

Very rare (2). This was first found in northern Lancashire on sand dunes at St Anne's. Early records were confused with *A. artemisiifolia* but Bailey (1902, 1907) makes it clear that his *A. artemisiifolia* was largely the perennial *A. psilostachya*, which he suggests was established on the sand dunes by at least the late 1880s. Since 1964 it has been found in at least three localities at Lytham St Anne's (SD32I, 32J) in 1966 and 1968 (A.E.R.) and also in 1983 and 1992 (SD32J; C.F. & N.J.S.) It seems to have been finally lost in 2008 (C.F. & N.J.S.). It was therefore naturalised at St Anne's for at least 100 years.

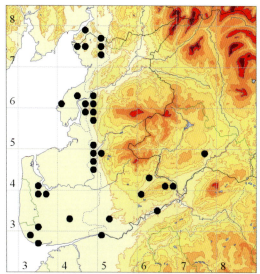
Petasites fragrans

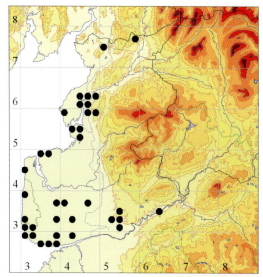
Calendula officinalis

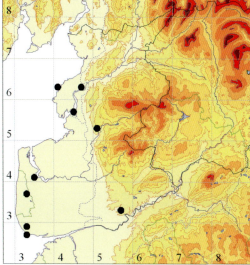
Ambrosia artemisiifolia

Ambrosia trifida L.   Giant Ragweed

Neophyte. This is a tall annual species native in North America. It was cultivated in Britain by 1699 but appeared in the wild principally as a grain contaminant when it was first recorded in 1897. It is found on waste ground and although formerly widespread in Britain it is now a rare casual.

In northern Lancashire Giant Ragweed was found on waste land at Preston Dock (Wheldon and Wilson, 1901a) and at St Anne's in 1906 (Bailey, 1907). It was last recorded near Fairhaven Lake, Ansdell in 1946 (Whellan, 1954).

[Ambrosia acanthicarpa Hook.   Hooker's Bur-ragweed

Neophyte. This is a native of North America and has only been found on a few occasions in Britain prior to 1930.

In northern Lancashire a plant found at St Anne's in 1906 (MANCH, Bailey, 1907) and named as this was identified in 2008 as *A. artemisiifolia*.]

Iva xanthiifolia Nutt.   Marsh-elder

Neophyte. This is a native of North America and was found in the wild in Britain by 1905. It occurs on waste ground in a few scattered localities.

In northern Lancashire a single plant was found at St Anne's (Bailey, 1907).

Rudbeckia hirta L.   Black-eyed-Susan

Neophyte. Black-eyed-Susan is a native of North America and was introduced into British gardens in 1714. It was recorded in the wild in 1917 and today occurs as a garden escape in scattered localities, mostly in southern Britain. It is a very common garden species.

Very rare (1). In northern Lancashire it was recorded from the towpath by the canal at Lancaster (SD46V) in 2006 (J.Cl.).

Rudbeckia laciniata L.   Coneflower

Neophyte. This is a native of North America and was cultivated in Britain by 1670. It was recorded in the wild by 1895 and today it is found in scattered localities throughout Britain. It is a popular garden plant and is found as a garden escape on waste ground and on tips.

Very rare (2). Coneflower was found at Fulwood (SD53F) in 1965 (E.H.) and at Lancaster (SD46R; Livermore and Livermore, 1991).

Helianthus annuus L.   Sunflower

Neophyte. This tall, showy, annual species was introduced into Britain by 1596. It is a native of North America and was first recorded in the wild in 1902. Besides being grown in gardens it is also grown as a field crop in southern Britain. It is found throughout the British Isles but especially in central and southern Britain.

Rare (9). In northern Lancashire this was first recorded by Bailey (1910) from sand dunes at St Anne's. Since 1964 it has been found in a few scattered localities in the west of the area.

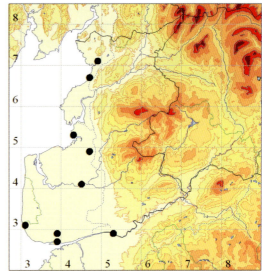
Helianthus annuus

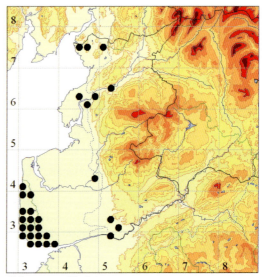
Galinsoga quadriradiata

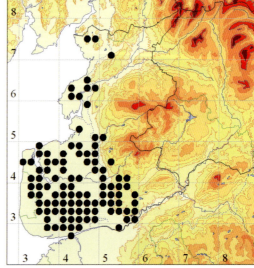
Bidens cernua

Helianthus petiolaris Nutt.   Lesser Sunflower

Neophyte. This is a native of North America that was cultivated in Britain by 1826 and was found in the wild by 1907. It is found casually on waste ground in a few scattered localities in central and southern Britain.

In northern Lancashire it was found on sand dunes at St Anne's (Bailey, 1907).

Helianthus rigidus (Cass.) Desf. × **H. tuberosus**
(**H. × laetiflorus** Pers.)   Perennial Sunflower

Neophyte. This tall, perennial hybrid was introduced into British gardens in 1815 and reported from the wild by 1902. Individual colonies can persist for many years and expand vegetatively. *H. × laetiflorus* may comprise more than one taxon and is probably of garden origin. It is a popular garden plant.

Very rare (2). In northern Lancashire Perennial Sunflower was found on waste ground between Lancaster and Morecambe (SD46L; Livermore and Livermore, 1987) and by the side of a farm track, Bolton-by-Bowland (SD75L) in 2008 (E.F.G.).

Helianthus tuberosus L.   Jerusalem Artichoke

Neophyte. Jerusalem Artichoke is a native of North America and was cultivated in Britain for its edible tubers by 1617. It rarely flowers in Britain but it survives as a garden throw out when tubers are discarded. It was first found in the wild in 1897 and occurs in scattered localities in the British Isles with most records from south-eastern England.

In northern Lancashire it was found on the sand dunes at St Anne's (Bailey, 1907).

Guizotia abyssinica (L. f.) Cass.   Niger

Neophyte. This is a casual species of waste ground and tips. It is a native of eastern Africa and was introduced into British gardens by 1806. It was known in the wild by 1876 and today it is found in scattered localities in Britain but most often in south-eastern England.

Very rare (3). It was recorded from Kirkham (unlocalised) in 1964 (J.H.), Blackpool tip (SD33I) in 1966 (J.H. & A.E.R.) and from an urban roadside at Bare (SD46M) in 2010 (J.Cl.).

Galinsoga parviflora Cav.   Gallant-soldier

Neophyte. This is a native of South America and was introduced to Kew Gardens, London in 1796 from where it had escaped into the wild by 1860. Today it is found as an annual species of cultivated ground on light soils in many parts of the British Isles but most commonly in central and southern Britain.

Very rare (3). In northern Lancashire this was first recorded from Marton Moss (SD33G) in the period 1948–1955 and Blackpool tip (SD33I; J.H. & A.E.R.), Lytham St Anne's (SD32E; A.E.R.) and Preesall-with-Hackensall (SD34U; E.J.H.) all in 1966. It is possible some of these records refer to *G. quadriradiata*.

Galinsoga quadriradiata Ruiz & Pav.   Shaggy-soldier

Neophyte. This is a native of Central and South America and was perhaps originally recorded as *G. parviflora*. It was first found in the wild in Britain in 1909 and today occurs in ruderal habitats throughout Britain but mostly in England where it seems to be becoming more frequent.

Occasional (30). Shaggy-soldier was first found in northern Lancashire from Lytham tip and St Anne's in 1962 (A.E.R.). Since then it has become common on the Fylde coast in Blackpool and Lytham St Anne's and occurs occasionally elsewhere, mostly in urban areas in the west of the region.

Hemizonia pungens Torrey & A. Gray
                                Common Spikeweed

Neophyte. Common Spikeweed is native of western North America and has been found casually in Britain in a few localities as a grain or agricultural seed contaminant.

In northern Lancashire it was found on former sand dunes at St Anne's in 1906 (C.B.; MANCH).

Bidens cernua L.   Nodding Bur-marigold

Circumpolar Temperate element.

This is an annual species of wet substrates on the margins of slow-flowing rivers and streams, by ponds and in ditches and marshes (BH13, 14). It is found throughout the British Isles but it is rare or absent from much of northern Britain.

Frequent (103). In northern Lancashire Nodding Bur-marigold is found mostly in lowland, western areas of the region. Although Wheldon and Wilson (1907) only recorded about 12 localities it is likely that it was more frequent than these records suggest. Nevertheless it appears that *B. cernua* has become more frequent over the last 100 years. Nationally the 'New Atlas' showed a marked decline, especially in eastern England but suggested that most of this occurred before 1930. Since 1987 its distribution appears unchanged ('Local Change').

Bidens tripartita L.   Trifid Bur-marigold

Eurasian Temperate element.

Trifid Bur-marigold is found in nutrient rich wet places in a wide variety of habitats but it may also occur occasionally in drier waste places (BH11, 13). It is found in Ireland, England, Wales and central and southern Scotland.

Occasional (39). In northern Lancashire *B. tripartita* has a more scattered distribution than *B. cernua* and may be found in any lowland area. Wheldon and Wilson (1907) knew Trifid Bur-marigold from only eight localities indicating that it has spread over the last 100 years. Nationally the 'New Atlas' suggests it has declined but 'Local Change' reported no significant decline since 1987.

Eupatorium cannabinum L.   Hemp-agrimony

European Temperate element.

This is a robust perennial herb of base-enriched soils found in a wide range of damp or wet habitats in both wooded and non-wooded places (BH11). Hemp-agrimony is found in England, Wales and Ireland but in Scotland appears to occur mostly in coastal areas except on the north coast and it also occurs in central Scotland between Edinburgh and Glasgow.

Frequent (93). In northern Lancashire *E. cannabinum* is found in the north and east of the region with only a few records in coastal areas of VC 60. Wheldon and Wilson (1907) described Hemp-agrimony as especially common in the west of VC 60. This is surprising in view of its present distribution and perhaps they meant it was common in the north and east of VC 60. There has been no change in its distribution nationally.

ESCALLONIACEAE   ESCALLONIA FAMILY

Escallonia rubra (Ruiz & Pav.) Pers.
var. **macrantha** (Hook. & Arn.) Reiche   Escallonia

Neophyte. This is a native of South America and was introduced into Britain about 1847. It is often planted as a hedge plant or windbreak and was recorded from the wild by 1905. Today it is found mostly in southern Ireland, south-western England and the Isle of Man but with scattered records throughout the British Isles.

Very rare (2). Included here are cultivars and hybrids of *Escallonia*. The only records in northern Lancashire are from Fleetwood (SD34D) in 1998 (E.F.G.) and from Carleton Cemetery, Blackpool (SD33J) in 2003 (M.S.).

ADOXACEAE   MOSCHATEL FAMILY

Adoxa moschatellina L.   Moschatel

Circumpolar Boreo-temperate element.

This is a small rhizomatous perennial herb that flowers early in the year on moist shady banks in woodlands and in hedgerows (BH1). It occurs in England, Wales and in southern and eastern Scotland. However it is absent from parts of eastern England and is very rare in Ireland.

Frequent (197). In northern Lancashire Moschatel is found in the north of the area, in woodlands bordering the Bowland Fells and in the Ribble valley. It is very rare in the west of the region but it occurs at Lytham and in a few localities bordering the Ribble estuary. It is believed that its distribution is stable both locally and nationally.

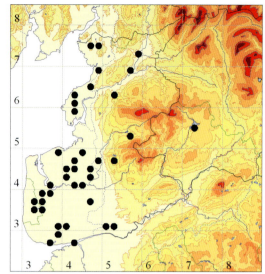
Bidens tripartita

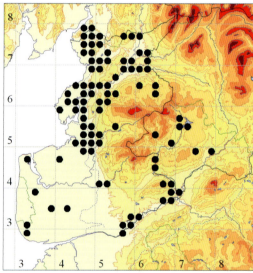
Eupatorium cannabinum

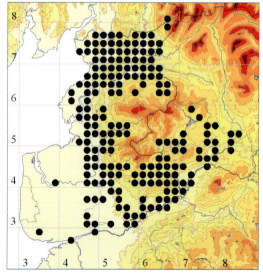
Adoxa moschatellina

CAPRIFOLIACEAE   HONEYSUCKLE FAMILY

Sambucus nigra L.   Elder

European Temperate element.

This is a deciduous shrub of fertile soils found in woodlands, hedgerows, scrub and waste places (BH3, 17) in most parts of the British Isles. However it is thought to be an introduction in parts of northern Scotland. Several forms are recognised.

Very common (387). Elder is found throughout northern Lancashire except on the fells in the east of the area. In addition to forma *nigra*, forma *aurea* (Sweet) Schwer. or Golden Elder and forma *luteovariegata* (Weston) Schwer. are found occasionally and formerly were sometimes found on railway banks. Forma *laciniata* (L.) Zabel or Parsley-leaved Elder is found very rarely but was seen for some years in the 1960s (E.F.G.) on waste ground at Fulwood (SD53K). Forma *viridis* (Weston) Schwer. with green fruits was found at Lytham St Anne's (SD32N) in 1998 (C.F. & N.J.S.). The distribution of Elder is stable locally and nationally.

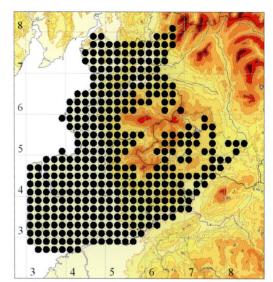
Sambucus nigra

Sambucus ebulus L.   Dwarf Elder

Archaeophyte with a European Southern-temperate distribution.

Dwarf Elder is a perennial rhizomatous herb found in hedgerows, on roadsides and on waste ground (BH3) in many parts of the British Isles.

Very rare (1). This was found naturalised by the docks at Fleetwood in 1946 (H.E.B.; Whellan, 1948). It was also found in a disused clay pit at Peel near Blackpool (SD33K) in 1978 (C.F. & N.J.S.).

Viburnum opulus L.   Guelder-rose

Circumpolar Temperate element.

This is a deciduous shrub of neutral or calcareous soils found in woodland edge habitats, scrub, hedgerows and in fen carrs (BH1). It is found throughout mainland Britain and in Ireland but it is rare in most of northern Scotland.

Frequent (187). In northern Lancashire Guelder-rose is found in wooded areas surrounding the Bowland Fells and in hedgerows on boulder clay further west. In northern Lancashire the distribution of Guelder-rose is stable and the 'New Atlas' also reported its distribution unchanged nationally. However since 1987 'Local Change' noted an increase probably because it is included in amenity planting schemes.

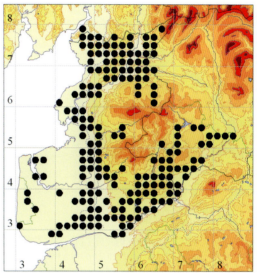
Viburnum opulus

Viburnum lantana L.   Wayfaring-tree

European Temperate element but a neophyte in northern Lancashire.

This is a deciduous shrub found in woodlands, scrub and hedgerows especially on base-rich soils. It is generally believed to be a native species in southern England and parts of southern Wales but it is found elsewhere in the British Isles as an introduction.

Rare (10). In northern Lancashire Wayfaring-tree was first found in a hedgerow near Dalton Hall (SD57H) in 1967 (C.D.P.). Since then it has been found in a few widely scattered localities.

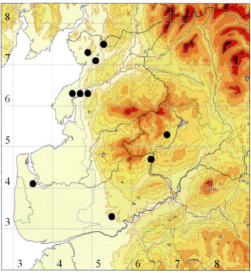
Viburnum lantana

Symphoricarpos albus (L.) S.F. Blake   Snowberry

Neophyte. This deciduous shrub is a native species of North America and was introduced into British cultivation in 1817. It has been known in the wild since 1863 and today it is found in hedgerows and as game cover in woodlands in most parts of the British Isles.

Frequent (166). In northern Lancashire it was first recorded from near Waddington (c. SD74C) in 1908 (J.F.P.; LDS) and it was well established by 1962 (Perring and Walters, 1962). Today it occurs in most lowland parts of the area.

Symphoricarpos microphyllus Kunth × **S. orbiculatus** Moench (**S. × chenaultii** Rehder)   Hybrid Coralberry

Neophyte. This hybrid arose in 1910 and is often grown in gardens and for game cover. It was not recorded in the wild until 1974 but it is easily overlooked. It reproduces by suckering and has been found throughout Britain. It fruits freely but rarely regenerates from seed. It is not as frequent as *S. albus*.

Very rare (1). In northern Lancashire *S. × chenaultii* was first found on the disused Preston to Longridge railway at Grimsargh (SD53X) in 2007 (Anon). It is believed to be overlooked and may be widespread in the Preston area.

Leycesteria formosa Wall.   Himalayan Honeysuckle

Neophyte. This is a deciduous shrub native to the Himalayas. It was introduced into British cultivation in 1824 and was known from the wild by 1905. Today it is found in many parts of the British Isles but particularly in southern England.

Rare (10). In northern Lancashire it was first found at Silverdale (SD47T) in 1965 (E.H.). Since then it has been found in a few other scattered localities.

Lonicera pileata Oliver   Box-leaved Honeysuckle

Neophyte. This is an evergreen or partially deciduous shrub, which is a native of China. It was introduced into British cultivation in 1900 and is known as a garden escape in a few English localities.

Very rare (1). In northern Lancashire it was apparently introduced with soil and was found on waste ground at Preston (SD52J) in 2005 (M.W.).

Lonicera nitida E.H. Wilson   Wilson's Honeysuckle

Neophyte. This is an evergreen shrub, which is a native of China. It was introduced into British cultivation twice. The first clone arrived in 1908 but never flowered whilst the second clone introduced in 1939 flowers freely. It was first recorded in the wild in 1955 and it is found in many parts of the British Isles but especially in Ireland, parts of Wales and in southern England.

Occasional (16). In northern Lancashire *L. nitida* was first found at Carnforth (SD47V) in 1986 (B.S.B.I.) and today most records are from the northwest of the area and more rarely elsewhere.

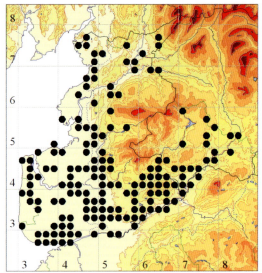
Symphoricarpus albus

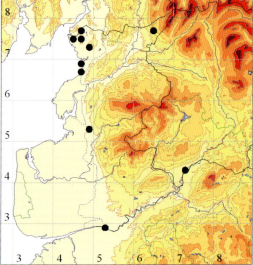
Leycesteria formosa

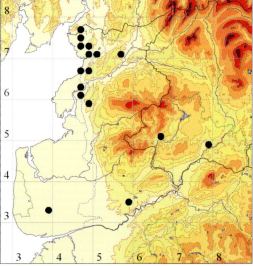
Lonicera nitida

Lonicera fragrantissima Lindley & Paxton × **L. standishii** Jacq.
(**L. × purpusii** Rehder)

Neophyte. This is a winter flowering shrub of garden origin. It has rarely been found growing wild.

Very rare (1). In northern Lancashire *L. × purpusii* was found forming thickets at Peel (SD33K) in 2010 but where it had been known for at least five years. (C.F. & N.J.S.).

Lonicera involucrata (Richardson) Banks ex Spreng.

Californian Honeysuckle

Neophyte. This deciduous shrub is a native of North America and was introduced into British cultivation in 1824. It was recorded from the wild in 1952 and today occurs in scattered localities in England, Wales and southern Scotland with a single Irish locality.

Rare (8). In northern Lancashire it was first recorded from Marton, near Blackpool in 1965 (A.E.R.). It has since then been found in a few scattered localities in VC 60.

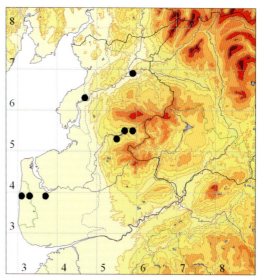

Lonicera involucrata

Lonicera xylosteum L.   Fly Honeysuckle

Neophyte with a Eurosiberian Temperate distribution. *L. xylosteum* is a deciduous shrub first cultivated in Britain by 1683 and recorded in the wild by 1770. Today it is found in scattered localities in England, Wales and southern Scotland and more rarely elsewhere and in Ireland.

Very rare (3). This was first found at Silverdale (E. Pickard) in 1875 (LDS) and Yealand in 1916 (A.J.C; LSA). Post 1964 records are from Silverdale (SD47S, T) and Lancaster (SD46U; Livermore and Livermore, 1987).

Lonicera tatarica L.   Tartarian Honeysuckle

Neophyte. This small shrub is a native of western and central Asia. It was introduced into British cultivation by 1752 and was found in the wild in 1984. Tartarian Honeysuckle occurs in a few scattered localities in Britain but it is commonly planted.

Very rare (1). *L. tatarica* was found on a roadside in Gisburn Forest (SD75R) in 2008 (E.F.G.).

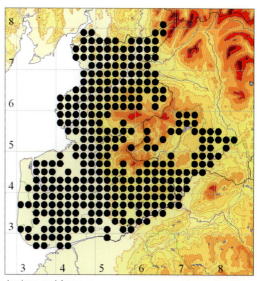

Lonicera periclymenum

Lonicera japonica Thunb. ex Murray   Japanese Honeysuckle

Neophyte. This is a semi-evergreen twining shrub, which originates from eastern Asia. It was introduced into Britain in 1806 and was recorded from the wild in 1937. Today it is found mostly in southern England and the Isle of Man with a few localities elsewhere in England and southern Ireland.

Very rare (1). In northern Lancashire it was recorded from Fleetwood Nature Park (SD34I) in 2005 (E.F.G.).

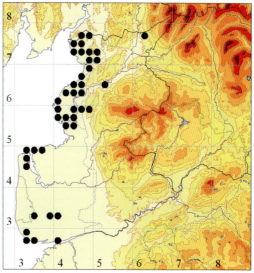

Valerianella locusta

Lonicera periclymenum L.   Honeysuckle

Suboceanic Southern-temperate element.

Honeysuckle is a deciduous twining shrub found in woodland, scrub, hedgerows and other woodland edge habitats (BH1). It is found throughout the British Isles. Sell and Murrell (2006) recognise var. *periclymenum* and var. *hirsuta* (Rouy) P.D. Sell. The former has only glandular hairs on the young shoots whereas the latter has long simple eglandular as well as glandular hairs. They suggest var. *hirsuta* is more local and possibly coastal and also occurs in France and is similar to taxa found in southern Spain and Portugal.

Common (340). *L. periclymenum* occurs over most of northern Lancashire but it is rare or absent in peat covered areas and in some urban places. Its distribution is stable both locally and nationally. The distribution of the varieties was not recorded. However in 2008 both typical var. *periclymenum* and var. *hirsuta* were found in a hedge at Tatham (SD66N). In addition to the two varieties intermediates with glandular hairs and short eglandular hairs were common.

Lonicera caprifolium L.   Perfoliate Honeysuckle

Neophyte. This is a twining glaucous shrub, which is a native of eastern, central and south-eastern Europe and south-western Asia. It was introduced into British cultivation in 1596 and recorded in the wild by 1763. Today it is rarely cultivated but it has been recorded from several localities in southern and eastern England and in Wales.

In northern Lancashire it was found at Silverdale in 1876 or 1877 (Miss K. Pickard; LDS).

VALERIANACEAE   VALERIAN FAMILY

Valerianella locusta (L.) Laterr.   Common Cornsalad

European Temperate element.

This is a winter annual, which occurs in open habitats in sandy and rocky places (BH3, 16, 19). It is found in most coastal areas of the British Isles and inland in England. Ssp. *dunensis* (D.E. Allen) P.D. Sell is found on coastal sand dunes and shingle whilst ssp. *locusta* is found throughout the range of the species.

Occasional (41). *V. locusta* ssp. *locusta* occurs in many coastal areas of northern Lancashire. Ssp. *dunensis* was found on sand dunes at Fairhaven (SD32I) in 1964 and 1965 H.E.B.; LIV) but disappeared by *c.* 1990 (C.F. & N.J.S.). The distribution of *V. locusta* is thought to be stable both locally and nationally.

Valerianella carinata Loisel.   Keeled-fruited Cornsalad

Archaeophyte with a European Southern-temperate distribution but a neophyte in northern Lancashire. This is an annual herb germinating in the autumn and is found in disturbed habitats, mostly in urban areas. It is found most frequently in southern England and south-eastern Ireland but it occurs as far north as the Tay estuary in Scotland.

Very rare (4). This was first found on a roadside at Peel near Blackpool (SD33K) in 1931 (R.S.F.; LIV). Since 1964 it has been recorded from near Skippool (SD34K) and Thornton (SD34L) both in 2008 (Anon) and from Lytham St Anne's (SD32J) in 1996 (C.F. & N.J.S.) and at another locality in the Borough (SD32I) in 1999 (M.J.).

Valerianella dentata (L.) Pollich Narrow-fruited Cornsalad

Archaeophyte with a European Temperate distribution.

This is an annual herb found on cultivated land especially on chalk (BH4). Formerly it was found throughout much of England, Wales, southern Scotland and Ireland but today it is mostly found in eastern and southern England.

Extinct. Formerly *V. dentata* was found in a few localities in western parts of northern Lancashire. It was last seen at Silverdale (SD47S) in 1957 (V.G.).

Valeriana officinalis L.   Common Valerian

Eurasian Boreo-temperate element.

Common Valerian occurs in a wide range of habitats varying from damp woodlands and marshes through dry calcareous grasslands to sand dunes (BH11). It is found throughout most of the British Isles. However three subspecies are recognised as growing in the British Isles but they are not always easy to distinguish. Ssp. *collina* (Wallr.) Nyman (2n = 28) is found in drier habitats especially in woods on boulder clay. Ssp. *dunensis* P.D. Sell (chromosome number unknown) is found on Merseyside sand dunes and on the Culbin Sands in Nairn, whilst ssp. *sambucifolia* (C.J. Mikan ex Pohl) Hayw. (2n = 56) is found in wet woodlands. Northern Lancashire material has not been examined critically and all three subspecies could occur. So far only ssp. *sambucifolia* has been confirmed and this is likely to be the common subspecies as in Cumbria (Halliday, 1997).

Frequent (218). Common Valerian occurs throughout northern Lancashire but it is much less frequent in the west than elsewhere. Its distribution in northern Lancashire is stable but the 'New Atlas' reported a decline in south-eastern England. 'Local Change' did not note further decline since 1987.

Valeriana dioica L.   Marsh Valerian

European Temperate element.

This is a perennial herb of calcareous mires, marshes and flushes (BH11). It is found in England, Wales and southern Scotland.

Frequent (94). In northern Lancashire Marsh Valerian is found in many localities in the north and east of the area with a few localities in the west. Wheldon and Wilson (1907) recorded *V. dioica* in all districts of VC 60 but its rarity in the west of VC 60 indicates that it has gone from many places in that part of Lancashire. The 'New Atlas' noted this decline nationally and 'Local Change' reported that this has continued since 1987.

Centranthus ruber (L.) DC.   Red Valerian

Neophyte. This is a perennial herb native to south-western Europe and the Mediterranean region. It was grown in Britain by 1597 and was reported from the wild by 1763. It is a popular garden plant that has escaped into the wild in many parts of England, Wales and Ireland but in Scotland it tends to have a coastal distribution. It grows on walls, calcareous rocks and waste ground.

Occasional (35). Red Valerian was first recorded in northern Lancashire from near Silverdale in 1878 (A.W.; YRK) but then not again until it was reported by Perring and Walters (1962). Today it is found in coastal areas and more occasionally inland in the Lune valley and in Lancashire VC 64.

DIPSACACEAE   TEASEL FAMILY

Dipsacus fullonum L.   Wild Teasel

European Temperate element.

Wild Teasel is a robust perennial herb found in rough grassland, wood margins on banks and in waste places (BH3, 6, 17). It is found in much of England and Wales but it is less frequent in Ireland and Scotland and it is rare or absent in northern Scotland.

Frequent (79). In northern Lancashire *D. fullonum* is found in the west of the area especially near the coast and more rarely in the Lune and Ribble valleys. Wheldon and Wilson (1907) regarded this as an introduced species and only knew it from the banks of the R. Ribble at Preston. Whatever its status it has spread dramatically over the last 100 years. Although the 'New Atlas' noted little change in Wild Teasel's national distribution it has spread considerably since 1987 ('Local Change').

Cephalaria gigantea (Ledeb.) Bobrov   Giant Scabious

Neophyte. Giant Scabious is a native of the Caucasus and was cultivated in Britain by 1759. It was recorded in the wild by 1920 and today it is a popular garden plant that has escaped into the wild in a number of British localities.

Very rare (1). In northern Lancashire it was found at Lytham (SD32Y) about 1970 (A.E.R.) and persisted until c. 2003 when the site was disturbed (C.F. & N.J.S.).

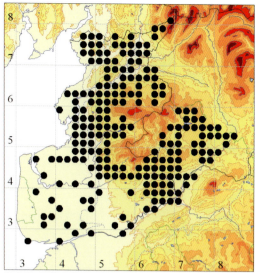
Valeriana officinalis

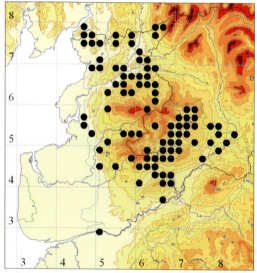
Valeriana dioica

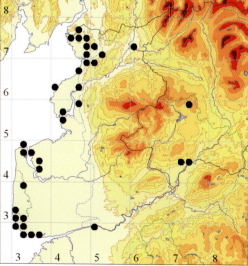
Centranthus ruber

Knautia arvensis (L.) Coult.　　　　　　Field Scabious

Eurosiberian Temperate element.

This is a perennial herb found on calcareous or neutral soils in grassland and scrub (BH6, 7). It is found in England, Wales, Ireland and eastern Scotland as far north as the north coast.

Occasional (65). In northern Lancashire most records of Field Scabious are from the northwest of the area with scattered localities elsewhere. Although its distribution locally is probably stable there have been losses nationally ('New Atlas') and these have continued since 1987 ('Local Change').

Succisa pratensis Moench　　　　　　Devil's-bit Scabious

Eurosiberian Temperate element.

Devil's-bit Scabious is a perennial herb found in a range of moist but nutrient poor, acidic soils on heaths, mires, in open woodlands and grasslands (BH6). It is found throughout the British Isles.

Frequent (191). *S. pratensis* is a common species in the east and north of northern Lancashire but it is much less frequent in western parts of the area. Its distribution in northern Lancashire is stable but the 'New Atlas' reported widespread losses since 1950 in southern and eastern England. However further significant losses nationally since 1987 were not confirmed by 'Local Change'.

Scabiosa columbaria L.　　　　　　Small Scabious

European Temperate element.

This is a perennial herb found on dry infertile calcareous soils in grassland, scrub and in rocky places (BH7). It is found in England, Wales and south-eastern Scotland.

Occasional (25). In northern Lancashire Small Scabious is found in the northwest of the area with occasional records elsewhere in the north, near Chipping and in Lancashire VC 64. In northern Lancashire its distribution is largely stable. Nationally the 'New Atlas' reported losses since 1962 whilst 'Local Change' considered that since 1987 Small Scabious was in sharp decline, especially in eastern England.

GRISELINIACEAE　　　　　　BROADLEAF FAMILY

Griselinia littoralis (Raoul) Raoul　　　New Zealand Broadleaf

Neophyte. This is a native of New Zealand and has been cultivated in Britain since 1872. It is popular in gardens and is frequently planted as a windbreak in coastal areas, especially in western Britain, the Isle of Man and Ireland. It has been known in the wild since 1957.

Very rare (2). The only northern Lancashire records for New Zealand Broadleaf are from a hedge on the seaward side of Fleetwood Golf Course (SD34D) where it was found in 1998 (E.F.G.) and planted on sand dunes at Fairhaven (SD32I) in 2008 (E.F.G.).

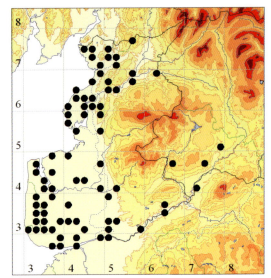

Dipsacus fullonum

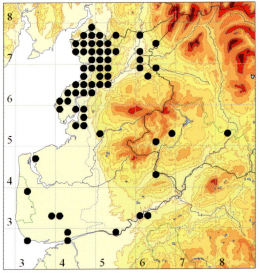

Knautia arvensis

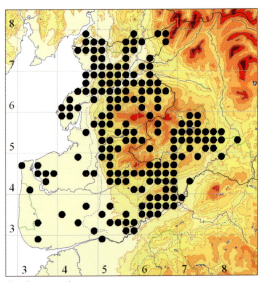

Succisa pratensis

ARALIACEAE   IVY FAMILY

Hedera colchica (K. Koch) K. Koch   Persian Ivy

Neophyte. This is a native of northern Turkey and the Caucasus. It has been cultivated in Britain since 1851 and it is popular as a ground-cover species in amenity plantings and in gardens. It was first recorded in the wild in 1959. Today it is found in woodlands, woodland edge and ruderal habitats in several places in the British Isles. However there is a concentration of records in the London and Glasgow areas, the Isle of Man and to a lesser extent in the English midlands.

Very rare (4). Persian Ivy was recorded in northern Lancashire from woodlands at Quernmore (SD55J) in 1998 (E.F.G.), Preston (SD52U) in 2006 (Anon), The Preston to Longridge railway at Grimsargh (SD53X) in 2007 (Anon) and Stonyhurst (SD63J) in 1998 (E.F.G.).

[Hedera algeriensis Hibbard   Algerian Ivy

Neophyte. Algerian Ivy is a native of northern Africa and was introduced into Britain in 1833. It is frost sensitive but occasionally escapes into the wild and may persist in sheltered areas. There are records from a few scattered localities in the British Isles but especially from the Isle of Man where many places are frost free, at least for a few years.

In northern Lancashire it may have been this species that was found escaping from a garden at Freckleton (SD42J) in 1999 (E.F.G.).]

Hedera helix L. ssp. helix   Common Ivy

European Southern-temperate element.

This evergreen climbing species is a common plant of woodland and woodland edge habitats (BH1, 3) throughout the British Isles.

Very common (372). Common Ivy is found throughout northern Lancashire except on the fells. There has been no change in its distribution locally. However whilst the 'New Atlas' also reported its distribution as stable 'Local Change' noted a significant decline in Britain since 1987. No explanation is given for this change.

Hedera helix L. ssp. hibernica (G. Kirchn.) D.C. McClint.
'Hibernica'   Irish Ivy

Neophyte. Native *Hedera helix* ssp. *hibernica* has an Oceanic Southern-temperate distribution and occurs on western coasts of Britain and Ireland. However its cultivar 'Hibernica' is widely cultivated in gardens and is found as a garden escape in many parts of Britain and occasionally in Ireland.

Occasional (9). Irish Ivy was first recorded in Lancaster District (tetrads SD46A, 46Y, 46Z and 55J; Livermore and Livermore, 1987). Subsequently it was recorded in scattered localities in western parts of northern Lancashire.

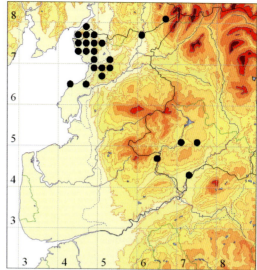
Scabiosa columbaria

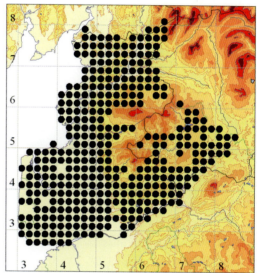
Hedera helix

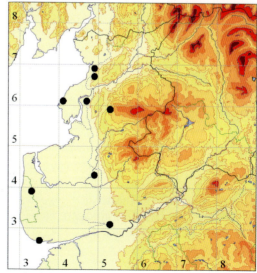
Hedera helix ssp. *hibernica*

HYDROCOTYLACEAE   PENNYWORT FAMILY

Hydrocotyle vulgaris L.   Marsh Pennywort

Suboceanic Southern-temperate element.

This is found in a wide range of damp or wet habitats ranging from
sand dune slacks and lowland ponds to hill flushes (BH11). It is found
throughout the British Isles.

Frequent (129). Whilst Marsh Pennywort may be found almost anywhere
in northern Lancashire it is most frequent in the north of the area and in
Bowland, especially in the western valleys. There has been no change in its
distribution locally but nationally the 'New Atlas' reported losses especially
in south-eastern England and these have continued since 1987 ('Local
Change').

Hydrocotyle ranunculoides L. f.   Floating Pennywort

Neophyte. This is a native of North America but it is widely sold in aquatic
plant nurseries. It was reported from the wild in Essex in 1990 and appears
to be spreading rapidly, at least in south-eastern England. It also occurs
occasionally elsewhere. It is a vigorous plant rooted in mud as well as free
floating on the surface of ponds or slow moving waters. Fragments are
easily broken off and can float away to form new colonies. It is however
frost sensitive (personal observation) although it can survive at the bottom
of a pond underneath any ice that might form above it.

Very rare (1). In northern Lancashire it was recorded from a pond at
Bispham (SD34F) in 2005 (M.S.).

APIACEAE   CARROT FAMILY

Sanicula europaea L.   Sanicle

European Temperate element.

This is a perennial herb of moist soils in deciduous woodlands (BH1) and is
found throughout the British Isles.

Frequent (127). In northern Lancashire Sanicle is found in woodlands in
the north of the area and in the wooded valleys of the rivers Calder, Wyre,
Brock, Ribble and Hodder as well as occasionally elsewhere. It is a good
indicator of ancient woodland. Whilst there has been no change in its
distribution locally the 'New Atlas' noted some losses and further losses
were reported by 'Local Change'. It is believed that Sanicle is unable to
compete with more vigorous vegetation caused by eutrophication.

Astrantia major L.   Astrantia

Neophyte. This is a native of central Europe and was introduced into
cultivation by 1596. It has been known in the wild since 1841. Astrantia is
a popular garden plant and it has escaped into the wild in many parts of
the British Isles.

Very rare (1). In northern Lancashire *A. major* was found on imported soil
at Myerscough Farm (SD54A) in 1987 (C.J.B.).

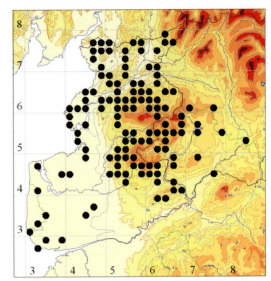
Hydrocotyle vulgaris

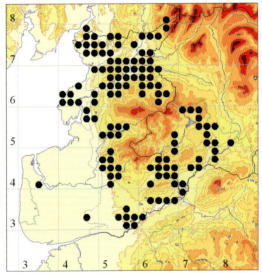
Sanicula europaea

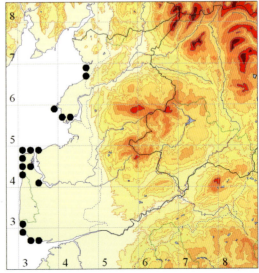
Eryngium maritimum

Eryngium giganteum M. Bieb.   Tall Eryngo

Neophyte. This is a large species, which is a native of Turkey and the Caucasus. It was introduced into British cultivation in 1820 and was recorded in the wild in 1937. It is a popular garden plant that has escaped into the wild in a few places in England.

Very rare (1). In northern Lancashire *E. giganteum* was found in a disused railway cutting at Caton-with-Littledale (SD56C) in 1998 (B.S.B.I.).

Eryngium maritimum L.   Sea-holly

European Southern-temperate element.

Sea-holly is an attractive species found on sand dunes and more occasionally on shingle (BH19) on most coasts of the British Isles except in northern Scotland.

Occasional (17). Sea-holly occurs in suitable places along the coast of northern Lancashire. Its overall distribution in northern Lancashire is unchanged although it may be more frequent today than formerly. Nationally the 'New Atlas' noted a decline in the distribution of *E. maritimum* with most sites lost in eastern Scotland and north-eastern England before 1930.

Chaerophyllum temulum L.   Rough Chervil

European Temperate element.

This is a perennial herb particularly characteristic of roadside verges and hedgerows (BH3). It is found throughout the British Isles but it is rare in much of Scotland and occurs as an introduction in Ireland.

Frequent (122). In northern Lancashire Rough Chervil is found throughout the area but it is particularly common in the north and centre of the area. Wheldon and Wilson (1907) described Rough Chervil as being very common in VC 60 suggesting that perhaps there have been some losses since then. The 'New Atlas' also suggests there may have been some decline, and further decline since 1987 was reported by 'Local Change' where it is suggested that eutrophication may have caused *Galium aparine* to have become sufficiently luxurious to outcompete *C. temulum*.

Anthriscus sylvestris (L.) Hoffm.   Cow Parsley

Eurasian Boreo-temperate element.

This is a robust and common herb of roadsides, hedgerows, woodland edges and waste ground (BH3) throughout the British Isles although it is rare in north-western Scotland. Var. *latisecta* Druce with appressed hairs on the upper surface of the leaves is thought to be frequent in southern England whilst var. *angustisecta* Druce with glabrous or nearly glabrous upper leaf surfaces is thought to be prevalent in northern England and Scotland.

Very common (386). Cow Parsley is found throughout northern Lancashire except on the fells. Records were not kept of which varieties occur but during 2006 and 2007 it was found that both, with intermediates, occur. However most plants seen appeared to be var. *angustisecta* (see Plate 2.15). There has been no change in the distribution of Cow Parsley locally or nationally.

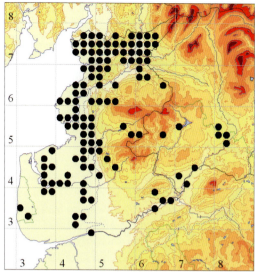
Chaerophyllum temulum

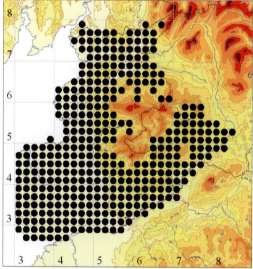
Anthriscus sylvestris

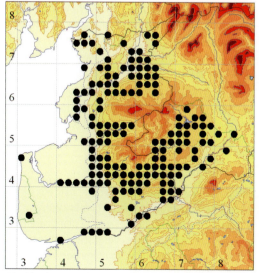
Myrrhis odorata

Anthriscus caucalis M. Bieb.   Bur Chervil

European Temperate element.

This is an annual of open habitats often on sandy or gravely substrates (BH3, 4, 8). Most records are from south-eastern England although it may be found almost anywhere in the British Isles except north-western Scotland.

Very rare (1). In northern Lancashire Wheldon and Wilson (1907) had records from Knott End, near Preesall, St Anne's and Fleetwood with the last record from St Anne's in 1905 (C.B.; OXF). It was not seen again until it was found on a sandy bank and in pavement cracks by Queen Mary's School, Fairhaven (SD32I) in 1999 (E.F.G.). It was still present in 2003 but could not be found in 2010 (E.F.G.). However it was found again on nearby sand dunes in 2007 only to have gone again by 2010 (C.F. & N.J.S.). Nationally the 'New Atlas' reported losses, particularly in southern England, but most of these occurred before 1930. Between 1962 and 1986 there was little change but since 1987 'Local Change' has reported an increase.

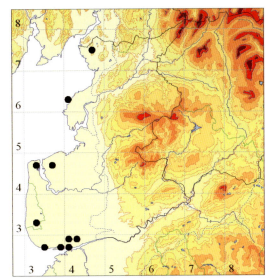
Smyrnium olusatrum

Scandix pectin-veneris L.   Shepherd's-needle

Archaeophyte with a Eurosiberian Southern-temperate distribution.

Shepherd's-needle is an annual of arable fields usually on calcareous clay soils. It formerly occurred throughout the British Isles but today it is largely confined to south-eastern England.

Very rare (1) or extinct. *S. pectin-veneris* does not appear to have ever been a common weed in northern Lancashire (Fielding MS). Old records were from Preston, St Michael's and Poulton-le-Fylde (Wheldon and Wilson, 1907). Additionally it was reported from Blackpool (Thornber, 1837) and St Anne's (France, 1930s). The only post 1964 record is from a churchyard at Claughton (SD56T) in 1983 (J.M.N.). Nationally the 'New Atlas' reported losses since 1950 although it is occasionally seen in large numbers in East Anglia.

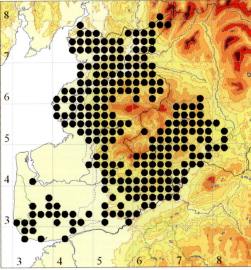
Conopodium majus

Myrrhis odorata (L.) Scop.   Sweet Cicely

Neophyte or Archaeophyte. This is a native of the mountains of central and southern Europe. It is not known when Sweet Cicely was first introduced into Britain but it was known to Gerarde (1597). It was first recorded in the wild in 1777 and today it is found throughout the British Isles but especially north of a line between the Severn and Humber estuaries. It is an attractive spring flowering, hedgerow herb usually found close to old houses and settlements.

Frequent (163). In northern Lancashire Sweet Cicely is found mostly in the north and east of the area but extends into the west by the rivers Wyre and Ribble (see Plate 2.14). It is not known when it first occurred in northern Lancashire.

Coriandrum sativum L.   Coriander

Neophyte. Coriander is a native of northern Africa and western Asia and was grown in Britain by Roman times (Wilson, 1979). Although grown as a culinary herb for centuries young plants are frost tender so limiting its spread into the wild. However it was first recorded in the wild in 1793 and today there are records from many parts of Britain but especially in south-eastern England.

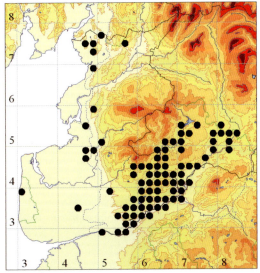
Pimpinella major

Very rare (2). This was first recorded in northern Lancashire from Roman horse dung found at Lancaster (Wilson, 1979) and from Roman deposits at Ribchester (Huntley and Hillam, 2000). More recent records were from waste ground at Ashton, Preston in 1852 (F.C.K.; LIV), Preston (SD52J) in 1941 H.E.B.; herb Bunker), from demolition sites in Preston (SD53F) in 1963 (A.E.R.) and 1966 (E.H.) and from Lancaster (SD46Q) in 2005 (M.Sh.).

Smyrnium olusatrum L.   Alexanders

Archaeophyte. This is a native of the Mediterranean region and southern Europe extending as far north as north-western France.

In Britain it was known in Roman Britain and was cultivated widely until displaced by Celery (cultivars of *Apium graveolens*) in the 15th century. It is found on roadsides and cliffs, mostly in coastal areas, throughout the British Isles but mostly in southern Britain and Ireland.

Rare (10). This is perhaps a neophyte in northern Lancashire with the first record reported from between Marton and Lytham by Ashfield (1858). It was not recorded again until 1907 when it was found at Preesall (Wheldon and Wilson, 1925). Since 1964 it has been found occasionally on the coast.

Smyrnium perfoliatum L.   Perfoliate Alexanders

Neophyte. This is a native of central and southern Europe and south-western Asia. It was known in cultivation in Britain by 1596 and was recorded in the wild in 1932. Today most records are from south-eastern England but it occurs occasionally elsewhere.

Very rare (1). In northern Lancashire it was found by a path at Morecambe (SD46M; Livermore and Livermore, 1987).

Conopodium majus (Gouan) Loret   Pignut

Oceanic Temperate element.

This is a perennial herb of shaded meadows and grasslands, hedgerows, woodland and woodland edge habitats (BH1, 6). It is found throughout the British Isles.

Common (261). In northern Lancashire Pignut is found in most parts of the east and north of the area except on the fells but it is also found in the west, mostly on boulder clay, where it possibly indicates former ancient woodland. There is no change in its distribution locally but nationally both the 'New Atlas' and 'Local Change' reported a decline.

Pimpinella major (L.) Huds.   Greater Burnet-saxifrage

European Temperate element.

This is a perennial herb found in hedgerows and woodland edge habitats (BH6) mostly on basic soils. In the British Isles it is found in a broad belt from north-eastern England, through the midlands to south-eastern England and appears to be absent from most of Cumbria, south-western England, except southern Devon and most of Wales. In Ireland it is confined to the west and south of the island. It occurs occasionally outside these limits as an introduction.

Frequent (86). In northern Lancashire Greater Burnet-saxifrage is particularly characteristic of the Ribble and Hodder river valleys. It occurs occasionally elsewhere, especially south of Lancaster and in the northwest of the area, but at some of these localities it may have been mistaken for *P. saxifraga*, especially as Wheldon and Wilson did not find *P. major*

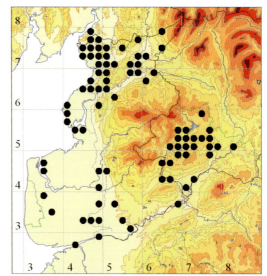
Pimpinella saxifraga

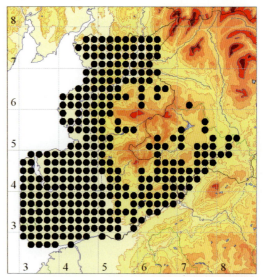
Aegopodium podagraria

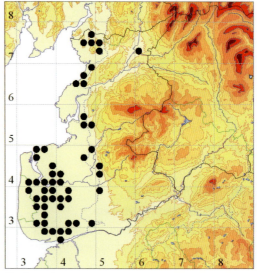
Berula erecta

in the Silverdale area. However these north-western records may represent a recent spread into the area, for whilst Halliday (1997) knew of no sites in the adjacent areas of Cumbria, he refers to a site south of Hale in VC 60 (SD57D). It is therefore possible that in northern Lancashire it has extended its range, although qualitative observations suggest that the more luxuriant vegetation of roadside verges of recent years has caused a decrease in its abundance in the Ribble and Hodder valleys. Nationally the 'New Atlas' reported a few losses before 1930. However 'Local Change' suggests that whilst Greater Burnet-saxifrage's distribution in the hilly areas of the Pennines is unchanged, in more intensively farmed areas to the south there has been a significant decline.

Pimpinella saxifraga L.   Burnet-saxifrage

Eurosiberian Temperate element.

This is a perennial herb of grassy habitats (BH7) usually on well-drained calcareous soils. It may be found almost anywhere in the British Isles but most records are from eastern and southern Scotland southwards and in eastern and central Ireland.

Frequent (83). In northern Lancashire it is found in many parts of the area with most records concentrated in the northwest and in Lancashire VC 64. As Wheldon and Wilson (1907) described Burnet-saxifrage as common in VC 60 it is possible that it has declined over the last 100 years. Nationally the 'New Atlas' reported no change in its distribution but 'Local Change' noted a significant decline since 1987. It is believed Burnet-saxifrage is intolerant of eutrophication and is uncompetitive in rank vegetation.

Aegopodium podagraria L.   Ground-elder

Archaeophyte with a Eurosiberian Temperate distribution.

Archaeological evidence suggests Ground-elder was introduced into Britain by the Romans. It is found in a variety of disturbed habitats and on waste ground (BH3, 17). It has a vigorous rhizome system and may form a monoculture over large areas. It is found throughout the British Isles.

Common (330). Ground-elder is found throughout most of northern Lancashire except on higher land at Leck and in Bowland. There has been no change in its distribution locally or nationally.

Berula erecta (Huds.) Coville   Lesser Water-parsnip

European Temperate element.

This is found by slow moving streams, rivers, in ditches and by ponds and lakes (BH11). It occurs throughout the British Isles although it is rare in much of Scotland, western Wales and parts of Ireland.

Occasional (52). In northern Lancashire this is largely confined to western areas. There has been no change in its distribution locally; however the 'New Atlas' noted a decline since 1950 but 'Local Change' recorded no further decline since 1987.

Crithmum maritimum L.   Rock Samphire

Mediterranean-Atlantic element.

This is a fleshy perennial herb of coastal rock crevices, stabilised shingle and sea walls (BH18) found on western coasts of the British Isles and on the south and south-eastern coast of England.

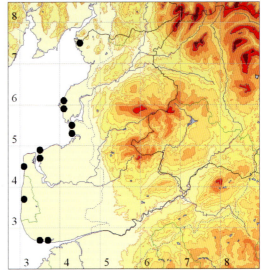
Crithmum maritimum

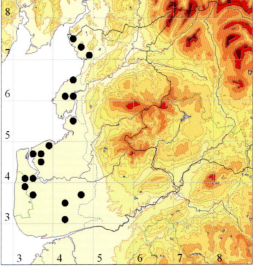
Oenanthe fistulosa

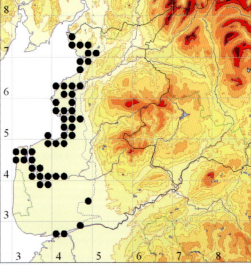
Oenanthe lachenalii

Rare (11). There are few natural habitats available for Rock Samphire in northern Lancashire but recent locations include Heysham; Cockerham; Knott End; Rossall; North Shore, Blackpool and at Lytham St Anne's. However all these are new localities since Wheldon and Wilson (1907) only knew it from Silverdale where it still occurs. Whilst these changes might suggest a spread in its distribution in northern Lancashire, nationally there has been no change.

Oenanthe fistulosa L. — Tubular Water-dropwort

European Temperate element.

This is a perennial herb of wet habitats in ponds, marshes and in areas of winter flooding (BH11). *O. fistulosa* is found in England, Wales and Ireland but very rarely in Scotland.

Occasional (18). In northern Lancashire Tubular Water-dropwort occurs mostly in coastal areas. Wheldon and Wilson (1907) knew it in only six localities indicating a modest extension of its range over the last 100 years. Nationally the 'New Atlas' reported a considerable decline since 1950 but 'Local Change' reported no further losses since 1987. However 'Local Change' also thought that some decline through eutrophication was probable.

Oenanthe lachenalii C.C. Gmel. — Parsley Water-dropwort

Suboceanic Southern-temperate element.

O. lachenalii is a perennial herb found in the uppermost parts of salt marshes (BH11). It occurs on the coast of most of the British Isles except for northern and eastern Scotland, and it also occurs occasionally inland in England.

Occasional (50). In northern Lancashire Parsley Water-dropwort is found on all the coastal salt marshes but it is less frequent on the Ribble estuary than elsewhere. There has been no change in its distribution locally but nationally there have been losses at inland sites in England ('New Atlas') with further losses noted since 1987 ('Local Change').

Oenanthe crocata L. — Hemlock Water-dropwort

Suboceanic Southern-temperate element.

This is a poisonous, tuberous perennial found in shallow water in ditches, ponds, banks of streams and canals and in other wet places (BH11, 14). It is found throughout the British Isles although it is rare or absent in many central and eastern areas of Britain and central Ireland.

Common (273). In northern Lancashire Hemlock Water-dropwort is a common species in VC 60 except in Bowland while in Lancashire VC 64 it is very rare. There has been no change in its distribution locally or nationally.

Oenanthe aquatica (L.) Poir. — Fine-leaved Water-dropwort

Eurosiberian Temperate element.

This species is found in shallow water in ponds, ditches and slow moving streams, often on deep silty and eutrophic soils (BH11). It is found in England, eastern Wales and Ireland.

Rare (9). In northern Lancashire this is confined to a few ponds in the lowland west of the area where its distribution is similar to that recorded

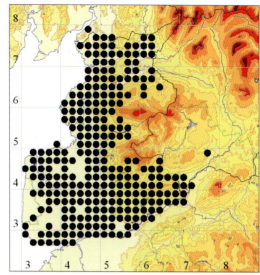

Oenanthe crocata

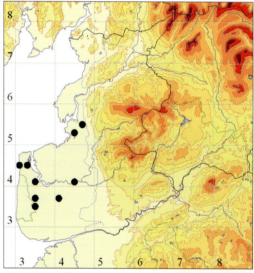

Oenanthe aquatica

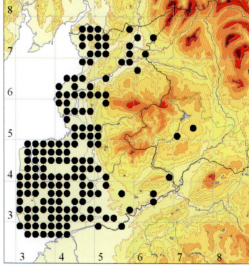

Aethusa cynapium

100 years ago. Nationally *O. aquatica* has declined substantially, especially in central England ('New Atlas'), and further decline since 1987 was noted by 'Local Change'.

Aethusa cynapium L. — Fool's Parsley

European Temperate element.

This occurs in cultivated and waste ground (BH3, 4, 17). It is thought to be a native species in southern Scotland, England and Wales and as an introduction further north in Scotland, where it is rare, and in Ireland. There are two subspecies in Britain but it is thought that most if not all plants in northern Lancashire belong to ssp. *cynapium*, the common native subspecies.

Frequent (162). In northern Lancashire Fool's Parsley occurs mostly in the west of the area with only a few records from localities in the east. There has been no change in its distribution locally, however the 'New Atlas' noted some losses nationally but 'Local Change' reported no further decline.

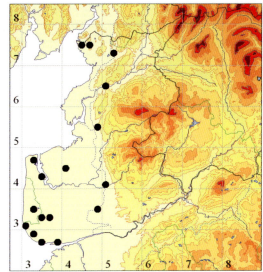
Foeniculum vulgare

Foeniculum vulgare Mill. ssp. vulgare — Fennel

Archaeophyte. *F. vulgare* ssp. *piperitum* (Ucria) Coutinho is native to the Mediterranean region but plants found in the British Isles belong to ssp. *vulgare*, which was derived from it in cultivation. *F. vulgare* ssp. *vulgare* is widely naturalised in Europe and elsewhere and it is believed it was introduced into Britain by the Romans. It is found in southern Britain and more rarely in Scotland and Ireland.

Occasional (17). Fennel is almost certainly a neophyte in northern Lancashire. It was first recorded from Ellel Grange (SD45W) in 1862 (W.H.; LIV), but Wheldon and Wilson (1907) suggested that whilst it was found on the coast from time to time it never became established. Cultivar F. 'Purpurescens' was found on the eastbound side of the M55 at Woodplumpton (SD43X) in 2009 (M.P.). Today Fennel occurs in a few localities in western parts of the area, especially in and near Lytham St Anne's.

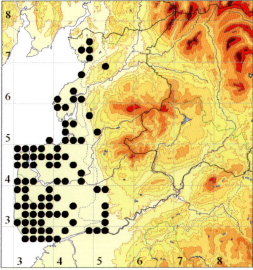
Conium maculatum

Anethum graveolens L. — Dill

Neophyte. Dill's native distribution is not known but it may have originated in warm-temperate Asia. Whilst it was grown as a herb by 995 it was not recorded in the wild until 1863. It may occur anywhere in Britain but it is always a casual.

Very rare (3). Dill was found in northern Lancashire in Roman deposits at Ribchester (Huntley and Hillam, 2000) where no doubt it was used as a culinary herb. It was next found in Preston in 1963 (A.E.R.) and again in 1965 (SD52P and 53F; E.H.), and in Blackpool (SD33I) in 1965 and 1966 (J.H. & E.H. and A.E.R.).

Silaum silaus (L.) Schinz & Thell. — Pepper-saxifrage

Eurosiberian Temperate element.

This is found in damp, unimproved grassland (BH6). It occurs in south-eastern Scotland, England and eastern Wales.

Very rare (1). This was recorded at Cantsfield (SD67G) in 1900 (A.W.; Wheldon and Wilson, 1901) where it was described as frequent, and at Silverdale *c.* 1915 (A.J.C.; LSA). It is still found in Cumbria at Beetham not

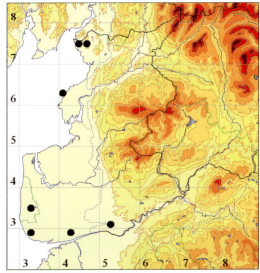
Bupleurum subovatum

far from the VC 60 border and was re-found in northern Lancashire on pastures near Wray (SD66D) in 2003 (Anon). Pepper-saxifrage has declined nationally since 1962 ('New Atlas') but there has been little further decline since 1987 ('Local Change').

Conium maculatum L.   Hemlock

Archaeophyte with a Eurosiberian Southern-temperate distribution.

Hemlock is found on banks, by rivers and ditches and on waste ground (BH3). It occurs throughout the British Isles but it is rare or absent in upland areas.

Frequent (88). The first records for Hemlock in northern Lancashire are from the remains of Roman horse dung found in Lancaster (Wilson, 1979) and from Roman deposits at Ribchester (Huntley and Hillam, 2000). It was also recorded without locality by Linton (1875) in his table of common VC 60 species. The first localised record is from Fleetwood in 1882 (J.Fr.; HLU) and Wheldon and Wilson (1907) still only knew it from about twelve localities. Today Hemlock is common in western parts of northern Lancashire and on waste ground it may be abundant, e.g. at Fleetwood.

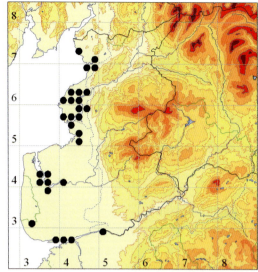
Apium graveolens

Bupleurum tenuissimum L.   Slender Hare's-ear

European Southern-temperate element.

This is a small annual of thinly vegetated coastal sites (BH3, 6) around southern Britain and occasionally inland.

Extinct. In northern Lancashire Slender Hare's-ear was found at Blackpool (Thornber, 1837) and opposite Fleetwood (possibly at Knott End) in 1841 (J.T.I.B.; BM). These localities are close to the northernmost limits of this species distribution in Britain. Nationally inland sites were lost before 1930 but since 1962 the distribution of *B. tenuissimum* appears stable ('New Atlas').

Bupleurum rotundifolium L.   Thorow-wax

Archaeophyte probably originating from south-eastern Asia.

Formerly this was an arable weed of chalk and limestone soils (BH4) but it was also introduced as an impurity in grain and other seeds. It is thought to be extinct as an arable weed and recent records are all introductions. In the nineteenth century it occurred in southern Scotland, England and eastern Wales. *B. rotundifolium* is often confused with *B. subovatum* and some records may refer to this species.

In northern Lancashire Thorow-wax was probably only a casual neophyte. It was found by the grain elevator at Fleetwood Docks in 1902 (J.A.W.; NMW) and on the sand dunes at Lytham St Anne's in 1907 (C.B.; MANCH) At both localities the seed was imported as a grain impurity.

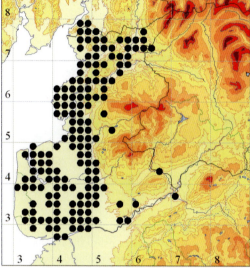
Apium nodiflorum

Bupleurum subovatum Link ex Spreng.   False Thorow-wax

Neophyte. This is a native of the Mediterranean region that was first recorded in Britain in 1859. It occurs in many parts of the British Isles, often in urban areas. It was particularly frequent in the 1950s and 1960s when it was associated with birdseed.

Rare (7). *B. subovatum* was first recorded from St Anne's in 1907 (C.B.; MANCH, NMW) and Lytham in 1963 (A.E.R.; LIV). Post 1964 records are from scattered localities in VC 60.

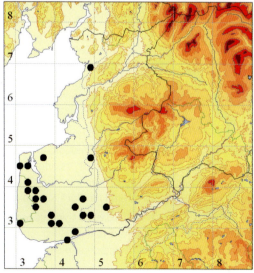
Apium inundataum

Apium graveolens L.   Wild Celery

Eurosiberian Southern-temperate element.

This biennial or perennial herb is found in brackish places, on sea walls, in ditches and on the uppermost parts of salt marshes. It also occurs in disturbed places in inland freshwater marshes (BH11). It is found on the coasts and more rarely inland in the southern half of the British Isles.

Occasional (29). In northern Lancashire Wild Celery is found in brackish marshes on the coast. Its distribution locally is unchanged but nationally there has been a decline of inland sites since 1930 ('New Atlas').

Apium nodiflorum (L.) Lag.   Fool's-water-cress

Eurosiberian Southern-temperate element.

This is found by streams, rivers, canals, ponds and in ditches and marshes (BH11, 14) in most lowland areas of England, Wales and Ireland, but in Scotland it is much more localised being found most commonly in the west of the country.

Frequent (159). Fool's-water-cress is common in lowland areas in the west of northern Lancashire but it is mostly absent from peat and soils derived from peat. There has been no change in its distribution locally but whilst the 'New Atlas' also reported no change nationally 'Local Change' noted a significant increase.

Apium inundatum (L.) Rchb. f.   Lesser Marshwort

Suboceanic Temperate element.

This perennial herb occurs in shallow water in ditches, ponds and canals etc. where the habitat is oligotrophic or meso-trophic (BH11, 13). It is found throughout the British Isles.

Occasional (22). Apart from three records from north of the R. Wyre Lesser Marshwort is confined to the lowland areas south of the R. Wyre and west of the A6. Significant changes seem to have taken place since Wheldon and Wilson (1907) recorded Lesser Marshwort in eight localities. Four of these sites were north of the R. Wyre including the Lune valley but today it is found mostly south of the river and appears to have become more widespread there. However this species is sensitive to nutrient enrichment, and whilst losses have not been observed, the loss of marl pits and general eutrophication is inevitably going to cause a decline of this species in the area. Nationally, losses are widespread.

Trachyspermum ammi (L.) Sprague   Ajowan

Neophyte. This is a casual introduced into Britain in 1773 and was recorded from the wild in 1921. Its origin is uncertain but it may have been the eastern Mediterranean region. It has been found in a few scattered localities in Britain.

Very rare (1). In northern Lancashire the only records for Ajowan are from Preston where it was first reported in 1963 (A.E.R.; LIV). It was later found on demolition sites in Preston (SD53F) in 1966 (E.H.).

Petroselinum crispum (Mill.) Nyman ex A.W. Hill
                                        Garden Parsley

Archaeophyte of uncertain origin but widely naturalised in Europe and elsewhere. It is a neophyte in northern Lancashire.

Garden Parsley is found as a casual in waste places and ruderal habitats but persists on some coastal cliffs and banks. It is found throughout the British Isles but usually in or near urban areas. It has been cultivated in British gardens since at least 995.

Very rare (4). Garden Parsley was first recorded in northern Lancashire on coastal shingle at Bolton-le-Sands in 1941 (J.N.F.). Post 1964 records are from Preesall-with-Hackensall (SD34U) in 1966 (E.J.H.), Lytham St Anne's (SD32I) in 1966 (A.E.R.) and in another locality in the Borough (SD33A) in c. 1973 (C.F. & N.J.S.) and Morecambe (SD46B; Livermore and Livermore, 1987).

Cicuta virosa L.   Cowbane

Eurasian Boreo-temperate element.

Cowbane is a perennial herb found in ditches and beside ponds and in fens (BH11, 13, 14). It is found in East Anglia, in Cheshire, Shropshire and neighbouring areas of Wales, parts of Scotland and in Ireland.

Extinct. In northern Lancashire the only record is from Roman horse dung found at Lancaster (Wilson, 1979). It belongs to a group of plants formerly found in fens and wet pastures in northern Lancashire that became extinct by the nineteenth century. Nationally Cowbane formerly grew in many areas of eastern England where it is believed drainage caused many losses ('New Atlas').

Ammi majus L.   Bullwort

Neophyte. This is a native of southern Europe, northern Africa and south-western Asia. It was introduced into Britain in 1551 and was recorded from the wild in 1845. It is found in waste places and ruderal habitats in England, Wales, the Isle of Man, eastern Ireland and southern Scotland.

Very rare (2). In northern Lancashire the only records are from a tip at Blackpool (SD33H) in c. 1966 and from Lytham St Anne's (SD32N) in 1988 (C.F. & N.J.S..).

Ammi visnaga (L.) Lam.   Toothpick-plant

Neophyte. This is a native of the Mediterranean region and south-western Asia. It was cultivated in Britain by 1596 and was recorded in the wild in 1881. It is a casual found in disturbed places, mostly in urban areas of England. It is often introduced with birdseed or as a contaminant of other materials.

Very rare (1). In northern Lancashire it was recorded from a tip at Blackpool (SD33H) in 1962 (A.E.R.; LIV) and in a garden in Lancaster (SD46Q) in 1979 (E.H.; LANC).

Carum carvi L.   Caraway

Archaeophyte apparently native in parts of Europe, western and central Asia but its range is obscured by its spread in cultivation.

It was introduced into Britain before 1375 and is found throughout the British Isles naturalised in grasslands as well as occurring in more ruderal habitats (BH3, 6, 17). It is probably a neophyte in northern Lancashire.

Very rare (2). Caraway was first recorded in northern Lancashire from Silverdale in 1863 (W.H.; LIV). Subsequently it was found near Morecambe in 1900 (F.A.L.; KGY) and near Blackpool in 1931 (R.S.F.; LIV). Post 1964 records are from a tip near Blackpool (SD33M; C.F. & N.J.S), and at Lytham St Anne's in 1969 (A.E.R.). Caraway probably occurs only as a casual in northern Lancashire.

Angelica sylvestris L.   Wild Angelica

Eurosiberian Boreo-temperate element.

This occurs in damp base-enriched soils in a variety of habitats (BH11, 16) throughout the British Isles.

Very common (365). Wild Angelica is found throughout northern Lancashire except on the higher fells. Its distribution locally is stable but 'Local Change' reports a decrease nationally since 1987.

Angelica archangelica L.   Garden Angelica

Neophyte with a Eurosiberian Boreal-montane distribution. Garden Angelica was cultivated in Britain by 1568 and was first recorded in the wild c. 1700. Although it is found occasionally in several places in the British Isles it has become naturalised and abundant in a few of them, e.g. on the banks of the R. Mersey.

Very rare (5). In northern Lancashire Garden Angelica was found at Lytham St Anne's (SD32P) in 1982, at Marton, Blackpool (SD33F) in 2005 and north of Marton Mere, Blackpool (SD33M) in c. 1988 (all C.F. & N.J.S.). It was also found by the Lancaster Canal at Cabus (SD44Y) in 2001 (E.F.G.) and on the roadside by a garden near Slaidburn (SD75G) in 2007, where it was almost certainly planted.

Levisticum officinale W.D. Koch   Lovage

Neophyte. This is a native of Afghanistan and Iran but widely naturalised. It was grown in British gardens by 995 and first recorded in the wild in 1883. It is found occasionally in scattered localities throughout the British Isles.

Very rare (1). Lovage has only been found in a hedge bank near Arkholme (SD57Q) in northern Lancashire (Livermore and Livermore, 1987).

Peucedanum officinale L.   Hog's Fennel

European Southern-temperate element.

This is a herb of brackish grassland (BH19) found today in a few places in south-eastern England.

Extinct. This was found as an archaeological record in horse-droppings in a Roman well in Lancaster (Wilson, 1979). It was also reported from Blackpool (Thornber, 1837). This is an apparently unlikely species to be found in northern Lancashire as the former brackish and freshwater fens that were once found in coastal areas of VC 60 have long since been drained. However remnants may have still occurred near Blackpool in the

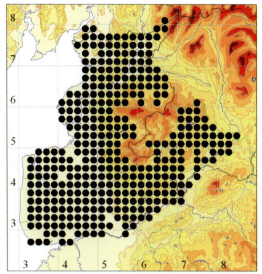
Angelica sylvestris

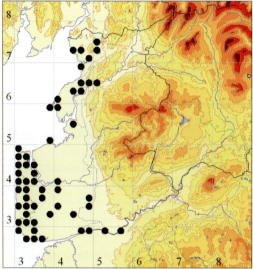
Pastinaca sativa

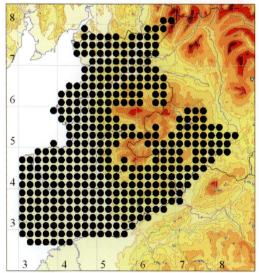
Heracleum sphondylium

early nineteenth century. Taken on its own Thornber's record could easily be dismissed as an error but evidence is accumulating that this is a record of a long lost Lancashire habitat (see also *Tephroseris palustris*).

Imperatoria ostruthium L.   Masterwort

Archaeophyte. This is a native of the mountains of central and south-western Europe.

In Britain Masterwort is found naturalised in damp grassy areas (BH3) mostly in northern Britain and northern Ireland.

Very rare (2). Wheldon and Wilson recorded Masterwort from near St Michael's; Oakenclough and Low Moor, Over Wyresdale. It was also found at Damas Gill (NMW), by the Lancaster Canal near Cottam (Blackburn Field Club, 1925) and at Blackpool (France, 1931). More recently it was doubt-fully recorded from Morecambe (SD46M) in 1967 (J.Wi.) and naturalised near the farm at Beckfoot, Gisburn Forest (SD75R; Abbott, 2005).

Pastinaca sativa L. var. **sativa**   Wild Parsnip

Eurosiberian Temperate element.

This is a biennial herb found in neutral and calcareous grassland, especially in chalk and limestone districts (BH3, 6, 7). It is found as a native species in England and southern Wales but as an introduction elsewhere.

Occasional (55). In northern Lancashire it is mostly found in coastal areas but it occurs inland in the south of the area as far east as Preston. Lancashire is close to the northern limit of its range in Britain. Wheldon and Wilson (1907) recorded this 100 years ago as a rare species with perhaps fewer than ten localities. Today its general range in the area remains unchanged but it has become much more frequent within it. However 'Local Change' reports a significant decrease in its national distri-bution since 1987.

Heracleum sphondylium L. ssp. **sphondylium**   Hogweed

Eurasian Boreo-temperate element.

This robust perennial is found in rough grassland and woodland edge habitats, especially on roadsides and waste ground (BH3, 6). It is found throughout the British Isles.

Very common (403). In northern Lancashire Hogweed is found throughout the area except on the higher hills. *H. sphondylium* var. *angustifolium* Huds. was recognised from Lancaster (SD46Q; Livermore and Livermore, 1991). There has been no change in its distribution locally or nationally.

Heracleum mantegazzianum Sommier & Levier   Giant Hogweed

Neophyte. This very large perennial herb is a native of south-western Asia. It was introduced into British gardens as a curiosity in 1820 and was planted by ponds and rivers. Giant Hogweed was first recorded in the wild in 1828 but it was not until after 1962 that it spread rapidly. It is now found by rivers and streams as well as on roadsides and on waste ground in many lowland areas of the British Isles. However Sell and Murrell (2009) refer to three species within the *H mantegazzianum* group. These are *H. grossheimii* Manden. ex Grossh., *H. lehmannianum* Bunge and *H. trachyloma* Fisch. & C.A. Mey. but not *H. mantegazzianum* itself. The three species are separated on leaf and fruit characters. No work has been done to identify these taxa in northern Lancashire.

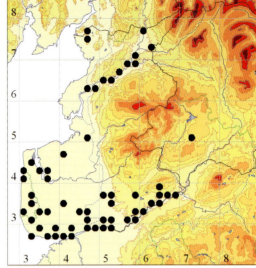
Heracleum mantegazzianum

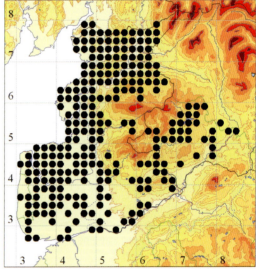
Torilis japonica

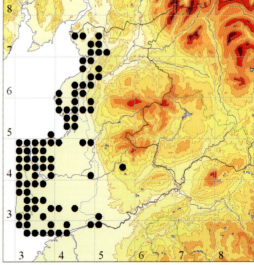
Daucus carota

Occasional (59). It is not known when this was first found in the wild in northern Lancashire. Perring and Walters (1962) show several 10km square records for the area but the first localised record is for woods near Hurst Green c. 1960 (Anon, 1983). Other early records are for the bank of the R. Ribble at Preston in 1965 (E.H.), by the Duddel Brook, Dutton (SD63M, N) in 1968 (E.F.G.) and by a stream at Woodplumpton (SD53B) in 1967 (E.F.G.). Today it is found in several places, mostly in the south and west of the area but it is especially frequent in the Lune and Ribble valleys and along the Fylde coast. Because the sap can cause severe blistering of the skin eradication measures are used to control the spread of Giant Hogweed, at least in areas to which the public has access.

Torilis japonica (Houtt.) DC. — Upright Hedge-parsley

Eurasian Temperate element.

T. japonica is an annual or biennial summer flowering herb found in hedgerows and woodland edge habitats (BH3) in most parts of the British Isles except central and northern Scotland.

Common (264). Upright Hedge-parsley is found in most parts of northern Lancashire except on the fells and it also seems to be absent from southern parts of the area, which is difficult to explain. Its distribution locally and nationally is unchanged.

Torilis nodosa (L.) Gaertn. — Knotted Hedge-parsley

Mediterranean Atlantic element.

This is an annual of dry, sparsely vegetated habitats (BH3, 6) and is found mostly in south-eastern Britain and the south-eastern half of Ireland.

Very rare (2). This has always been rare in northern Lancashire. Wheldon and Wilson (1907) recorded it from near Borwick, Carnforth, Cockersand Abbey and Lytham. Post 1964 records are from Silverdale (SD47T) in the 1970s (G.M.K. & P.J.) and on a south facing sea wall at Cockerham (SD45L) in 1993 (J.M.N.) and 1998 (P.J.). Whilst in northern Lancashire Knotted Hedge-parsley is surviving, nationally it is increasing and markedly so since 1987 ('Local Change').

Daucus carota L. ssp. carota — Wild Carrot

Eurosiberian Southern-temperate element.

This is a biennial herb of well-drained, often calcareous soils, on sand dunes, grasslands and waste ground (BH6, 7). It is found in most lowland areas of the British Isles.

Frequent (90). In northern Lancashire Wild Carrot is found in the west of the area and is largely a coastal species. Although it is difficult to be sure it appears that *D. carota* may have been more widespread 100 years ago being present in the east of VC 60 and also being especially abundant on the limestone in the northwest of the area. This is consistent with the comments in the 'New Atlas' that reports that there has been some decline on the northern fringes of its range whilst 'Local Change' notes a decline nationally since 1987.

Turgenia latifolia (L.) Hoffm. — Greater Bur-parsley

Neophyte. This is native in parts of Europe, northern Africa and south-western Asia. It has been found casually in a few places in Britain but it is rarely seen today. It is a contaminant of grain and birdseed.

In northern Lancashire it was found at Preston (Ashfield, 1858).

Caucalis platycarpos L. — Small Bur-parsley

Neophyte. This is a native of the Mediterranean region and south-western Asia. It is a grain and birdseed contaminant found occasionally in Britain. Formerly it was a persistent weed in some areas but today it is a rare casual.

In northern Lancashire it was found on the sand dunes at St Anne's in 1907 (C.B.; MANCH; Wheldon and Wilson, 1907).

MONOCOTS

Monocotyledons

ACORACEAE — SWEET-FLAG FAMILY

Acorus calamus L. — Sweet-flag

Neophyte. Diploid plants are natives of Siberia and North America whilst tetraploid plants are found in southern and eastern Asia. Only sterile triploids are found in Britain and these are naturalised elsewhere in Europe, western Asia, the Himalayas and eastern North America but their origin is unknown. Sweet-flag was introduced into England in the sixteenth century and by 1668 was established in the wild. Today it occurs most commonly in lowland areas of England but occurs in Wales, eastern Ireland and in Scotland as far north as the Moray and Dornoch Firths. It is found by the margins of streams, ponds and canals in nutrient rich, calcareous water.

Occasional (53). In northern Lancashire this sweet smelling species was first recorded from a pit near Preston Cemetery (SD53Q; Ashfield, 1858) and from the Lancaster Canal at Cottam (Preston Scientific Society, 1903). It is not known when Sweet-flag first appeared in the Canal but it was probably sometime between Ashfield's records in the late 1850s and early 1860s and the records of Preston Scientific Society made between 1897 and 1902. Its spread was probably rapid as Wheldon and Wilson (1907) reported it from numerous places on the canal. Today it occurs along the canal's whole length and also occasionally in ponds in VC 60.

ARACEAE   LORDS-AND-LADIES FAMILY

Zantedeschia aethiopica (L.) Spreng.   Altar-lily

Neophyte. Altar-lily is a native of southern Africa and was cultivated in British gardens by 1731. It is widely grown, especially in places with a mild climate and was recorded from the wild in western Kerry, Ireland in 1952. Today it is naturalised in several localities in southern, and especially south-western, Britain.

Very rare (1). In northern Lancashire it was found planted in a pond in a housing estate at Carleton (SD34F) in 2003 (M.S.).

Arum maculatum L.   Lords-and-Ladies

European Temperate element.

Lords-and-Ladies is a characteristic species of woodlands and hedgerows in moist but well-drained, fertile soils (BH1). It is found as a native species in England, Wales and Ireland but as an introduction in southern and eastern Scotland.

Common (268). *A. maculatum* is a common plant in the 'woodland belt' surrounding the Bowland Fells, in the north of the area and in major river valleys but it is much rarer in lowland areas in western VC 60. There has been no change in its distribution locally or nationally.

Arum italicum Mill. ssp. italicum   Italian Lords-and-Ladies

Neophyte. This subspecies has a Mediterranean-Atlantic distribution and was cultivated in Britain by 1683. It was known in the wild by at least 1905 and occurs in England, Wales, Ireland and southern Scotland. Native *A. italicum* ssp. *neglectum* (F. Towns.) Prime is confined to southern England.

Rare (11). Although not critically determined it is assumed all records in northern Lancashire belong to *A. italicum* ssp. *italicum*. It was first discovered in the area at Fleetwood (SD34H) in 1990 (C.F. & N.J.S) and subsequently in a few areas in the west of the region.

Pistia stratiotes L.   Water-lettuce

Neophyte. This is a native of the sub-tropics and occurs in Britain as a casual escape from gardens. It has been recorded in the wild on a few occasions.

Very rare (11). Water-lettuce was found in northern Lancashire in a pond at Carleton (SD34F) in 2007 (M.S.).

LEMNACEAE   DUCKWEED FAMILY

Spirodela polyrhiza (L.) Schleid.   Greater Duckweed

Circumpolar Southern-temperate element.

This floating leaved species occurs in still, base-rich water in ponds, canals and rivers (BH13). It occurs in England from Lancashire and Yorkshire southwards, Wales and Ireland with occasional introductions in northern England and Scotland.

Occasional (21). In northern Lancashire Greater Duckweed occurs in scattered localities, mostly in ponds and ditches, in western parts of VC 60 except where there are or were mosses. This species was formerly very

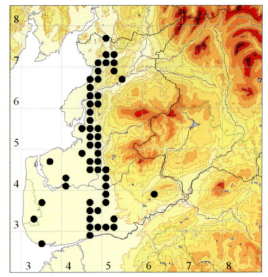

Acorus calamus

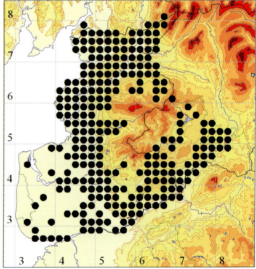

Arum maculatum

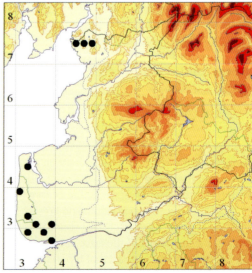

Arum italicum

rare and had only been found in the Lancaster Canal at Preston (Ashfield, 1860) and in the Glasson branch (Wheldon and Wilson, 1907), but whilst their work was in press Wheldon and Wilson added several more canal localities. Thus it appears that initially Greater Duckweed was introduced into the Lancaster Canal and subsequently spread along its whole length before spreading from this and possibly other sources into lowland western VC 60. Today it is probably absent from the canal as it does not tolerate water movement caused by powered boats. Nationally the 'New Atlas' reported some losses in England.

Lemna gibba L.   Fat Duckweed

European Southern-temperate element.

This buoyant duckweed is a plant of still or slow flowing, eutrophic water in ponds, canals and ditches etc. (BH13). It occurs in England from Lancashire southwards, Wales, Ireland and between Edinburgh and Glasgow in Scotland. In very eutrophic sites it can form dense masses but it can also disappear from locations where it was once abundant.

Occasional (37). In northern Lancashire Fat Duckweed occurs in lowland areas of western VC 60. Compared with 100 years ago, when only five sites were recorded (Wheldon and Wilson, 1907), *L. gibba* has considerably expanded its range. Nationally its distribution is largely unchanged.

Lemna minor L.   Common Duckweed

Circumpolar Southern-temperate element.

Common Duckweed is a free floating aquatic species found in a variety of still or slow moving, mesotrophic or eutrophic waters. It is found in ponds, ditches, canals, small pools and on wet mud (BH11, 13) in lowland areas throughout the British Isles.

Common (241). In northern Lancashire *L. minor* occurs in all lowland areas but it is particularly frequent in VC 60.

Lemna trisulca L.   Ivy-leaved Duckweed

Circumpolar Temperate element.

L. trisulca is a free floating but submerged aquatic species found in mesotrophic and eutrophic, still or slow moving water (BH11, 13). It is found in England, Wales, Ireland and southern Scotland but with a few localities further north.

Frequent (121). In northern Lancashire Ivy-leaved Duckweed is found mostly in western and southern parts of the area. Its distribution locally and nationally is unchanged.

Lemna minuta Kunth   Least Duckweed

Neophyte. Least Duckweed is a native of temperate and subtropical North and South America. It was first recorded in Britain from Cambridge in 1977 and since then it has spread rapidly. In Britain it is found in England and Wales with a few localities in southern and central Scotland. There are a few widely scattered localities in Ireland where it was first found in 1993.

Very rare (2). Least Duckweed was found in northern Lancashire in Moss Sluice, Lytham Moss (SD33K) in 2002 (E.F.G.) and in a pond near Bispham (SD34F) in 2008 (J.Cl.). The 'New Atlas' also shows records in the 10km squares SD56 and 57.

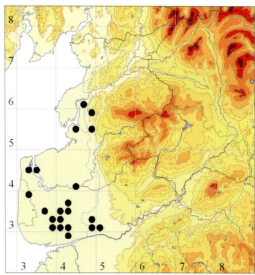

Spirodela polyrhiza

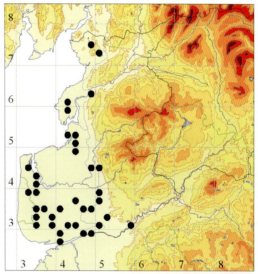

Lemna gibba

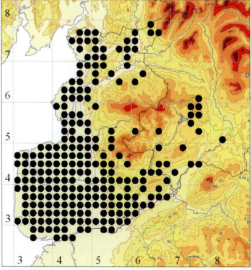

Lemna minor

ALISMATACEAE   WATER-PLANTAIN FAMILY

Sagittaria sagittifolia L.   Arrowhead

Eurosiberian Boreo-temperate element but a neophyte in northern Lancashire.

Arrowhead is a herb of shallow, still or slow flowing, calcareous and eutrophic water (BH13, 14). It is found in many parts of England, eastern Wales, Ireland and as an introduction in Scotland.

Occasional (30). *S. sagittifolia* is almost confined to the Lancaster Canal where it was first found near Preston in 1875 (Wheldon and Wilson, 1907). Its origin is unknown but it was probably introduced with goods transferred from barges on the Leeds – Liverpool Canal in South Lancaster (VC 59). Its distribution is probably stable both locally and nationally.

Baldellia ranunculoides (L.) Parl.   Lesser Water-plantain

Suboceanic Southern-temperate element.

This perennial herb is found in marshes, ditches and pond edges in open habitats. It usually grows in calcareous or brackish waters but on a range of organic and inorganic substrates (BH13, 14).

Rare (10). In northern Lancashire it has been found in a few scattered localities in lowland, western parts of the area. However it was considered frequent in lowland areas in VC 60 by Wheldon and Wilson (1907). Today it has become extinct in at least some of the localities where it was recorded in the 1960s and 1970s. It is now probably very rare perhaps being confined to a few localities between Silverdale and Carnforth. The 'New Atlas' reports a considerable decline nationally.

Alisma plantago-aquatica L.   Water-plantain

Circumpolar Wide-temperate element.

This is a perennial herb found in waterside communities in mesotrophic or eutrophic habitats (BH11, 13). Water-plantain is found in lowland areas throughout the British Isles except northern Scotland.

Frequent (210). *A. plantago-aquatica* is found in lowland areas and in river valleys in much of northern Lancashire. Its distribution locally and nationally is unchanged.

[Alisma lanceolatum With.   Narrow-leaved Water-plantain

Eurosiberian Southern-temperate element.

A. lanceolatum was not distinguished as a distinct species from *A. plantago-aquatica* until 1952 although narrow and broad leaved forms of water-plantain were known long before this. However leaf shape is not a reliable diagnostic character and it is believed that *A. lanceolatum* was then recorded erroneously in some places. It is found in similar places to *A. plantago-aquatica* (BH13) but it has a more south-easterly distribution in Britain.

Very rare (3). This is very doubtfully a northern Lancashire species. There are records from Preston, Blackpool and Hothersall in the 1950s (B.R.C.) and unlocalised records from SD44X, 44Z and 54C from the 1960s (E.H. & J.H.). Most of the records are attributed to competent botanists but none of the records are substantiated by voucher specimens. Furthermore since the 1970s unsuccessful searches have been made to find *A. lanceolatum*

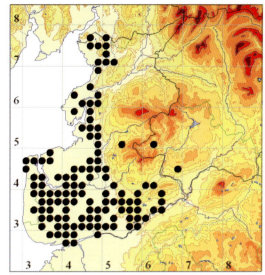

Lemna trisulca

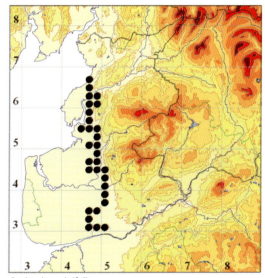

Sagittaria sagittifolia

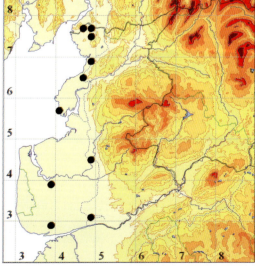

Baldellia ranunculoides

and it is suggested that narrow leaved forms of *A. plantago-aquatica*, which are frequent, have been mistaken for it. Nevertheless *A. lanceolatum* is confirmed for South Lancaster (VC 59) but until critically identified material is seen from northern Lancashire its occurrence in the region is doubtful.]

BUTOMACEAE FLOWERING-RUSH FAMILY

Butomus umbellatus L. Flowering-rush

Eurosiberian Temperate element.

Flowering-rush is an attractive, emergent marsh or aquatic species found in calcareous and often eutrophic water (BH13, 14). It rarely sets seed in Britain but occurs in many parts of England, Wales and southern Scotland. It is regarded as native in most parts of England but in much of northern England, Ireland and southern Scotland it is thought to be introduced. However it is impossible to distinguish between native and introduced populations.

Occasional (40). The status of *B. umbellatus* in northern Lancashire is uncertain. It was first recorded from Lytham in 1839 (S.S.; OXF) suggesting that it could be a relic fen species. It was then recorded from the Lancaster Canal from near Preston (Ashfield, 1858) and quickly became established along most of the Canal. Since 1964 most records are from the canal and more occasionally in marshes and ponds in lowland areas in the west of the area. Apart from the record from Lytham, where the origin is uncertain, it is thought that all subsequent populations originated from introductions. Its distribution in northern Lancashire has probably remained unchanged over the last 100 years but nationally 'Local Change' reported an increase probably as a result of introductions.

HYDROCHARITACEAE FROGBIT FAMILY

Hydrocharis morsus-ranae L. Frogbit

Eurosiberian Temperate element.

This floating perennial species is found in shallow, calcareous, mesotrophic water in ponds, ditches and other sheltered, still waters (BH13). It occurs in England, Wales and Ireland but also as an introduction in many places and in Scotland.

Very rare (4). Frogbit has always been a rare species in northern Lancashire. Pre 1964 records were from Ribbleton Moor (Ashfield, 1858), Cockerham (Ashfield, 1860), between Inskip and Kirkham in 1943 (H.E.B.) and Garstang (NMW). It is believed plants from Ribbleton Moor were transferred successively into nearby ponds over the years as old sites were filled in. Since 1964 it has been found in ponds in Grange Park, Preston (SD53Q, V). It was also found at Wesham (SD43B) in 1974 (C.F. & N.J.S.) but the lowering of the water table in the area dried out the ditch and it was gone by 2002 (E.F.G.). It was introduced into its remaining site at Bank Well, Silverdale (SD47S) where it was first found in 1998 (P.J.). Nationally the 'New Atlas' reported it had declined but that it had also been planted in the wild in recent years.

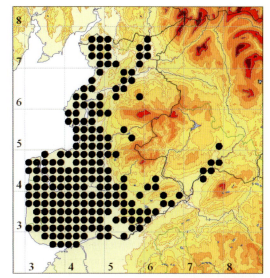

Alisma plantago-aquatica

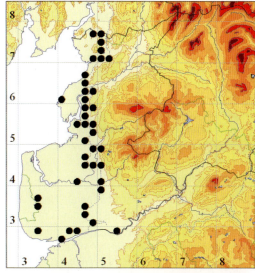

Butomus umbellatus

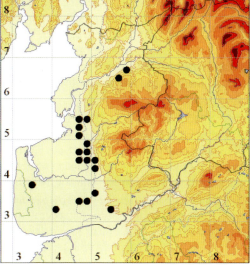

Statiotes aloides

Stratiotes aloides L.   Water-soldier

Eurosiberian Boreo-temperate element but a neophyte in northern Lancashire.

This floating perennial species is found in calcareous, mesotrophic lakes and ponds (BH13) and is found in England, Wales, Ireland and central Scotland. It is regarded as an introduction apart from localities in East Anglia.

Occasional (19). Water-soldier was first recorded from near Cadley Mill, Preston (SD53F, Ashfield, 1858). Subsequently it was found in ponds in scattered lowland localities in VC 60. However most records were from the Lancaster Canal where it was first found near Bell's Bridge (SD44T) in the 1950s (Greenwood, 1974). For a time it became abundant but quite suddenly it disappeared (Greenwood, 2005). It is believed that the chemical composition of the water where it grows is critical and that nutrient enrichment probably caused its loss from the canal.

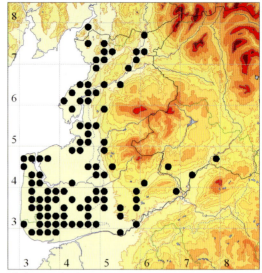
Elodea canadensis

Elodea canadensis Michx.   Canadian Waterweed

Neophyte. This is a native of temperate North America. It is an aquatic perennial first recorded in Ireland in 1836 and in Britain in 1842. Subsequently Canadian Waterweed spread rapidly and became established in lowland areas of the British Isles except northern Scotland.

Frequent (101). In northern Lancashire *E. canadensis* was first recorded from the Lancaster Canal north of Preston and was especially abundant near Nateby Hall (Ashfield, 1864). Since 1964 it has been found mostly in western areas but also in the Lune and Ribble valleys. In recent years it appears to have been replaced in many places by *E. nuttallii*, especially in the Lancaster Canal.

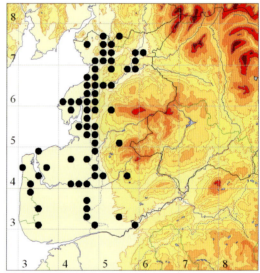
Elodea nuttallii

Elodea nuttallii (Planch.) H. St John   Nuttall's Waterweed

Neophyte. This is a native of temperate North America, which has been naturalised in Europe since 1939 and was first recorded as naturalised in Britain in 1966. It is an aquatic species found in eutrophic ponds and slow moving waters and it appears to withstand boat disturbance better than *E. canadensis*. Today it occurs in England, Wales, southern Scotland and eastern Ireland.

Occasional (66). In northern Lancashire *E. nuttallii* was first found in Pedder Potts Reservoir, Over Kellet (SD57F) in 1976 (J. Leeming) and two years later it was found in several places in the R. Lune and nearby ponds. By 1980 it was found in the Lancaster Canal in the Lancaster area. Today it occurs throughout the western part of the region although most records are still from the northern parts of the Lancaster Canal and nearby areas.

Lagarosiphon major (Ridl.) Moss   Curly Waterweed

Neophyte. Curly Waterweed is a submerged aquatic native in southern Africa. It is commonly cultivated and was first recorded as naturalised in the wild in Britain in 1944. It is found in ponds and slow moving water in England, Wales, southern Scotland and Ireland.

Rare (8). In northern Lancashire *L. major* was first found in a pond near Staining, Hardhorn-with-Newton (SD33N) in 1997 (P.B.). Today it is found in a few scattered localities in VC 60.

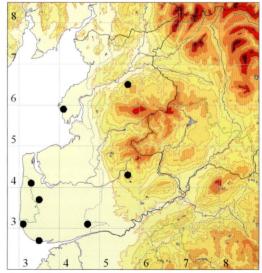
Lagarosiphon major

SCHEUCHZERIACEAE   RANNOCH-RUSH FAMILY

Scheuchzeria palustris L.   Rannoch-rush

Circumpolar Boreal-montane element.

This is a species of base-poor, wet habitats, typically found in acid runnels, pools or semi-submerged *Sphagnum* lawns at pool edges. It was formerly found in lowland areas of England and the Welsh borders and was found in central Ireland in 1951 only to be lost to peat extraction in 1960. All the English and Welsh localities were lost before 1900 to drainage and eutrophication. Today it is only found on Rannoch Moor in Scotland.

Extinct. In northern Lancashire *S. palustris* dominated the vegetation of some of the bogs in the Pilling area about 2000BC (Middleton, *et al.*, 1995) and perhaps as late as 800BC (Oldfield and Statham, 1965). However it is not known when it ceased to be part of Lancashire's bog vegetation and may have become extinct by the warmer and drier conditions of the Roman period. On the other hand it may have persisted in small quantity until the eighteenth century or later but remained unrecorded. It is thus unclear why it should have become extinct before this in view of its persistence in Cheshire at Wybundbury Moss until 1865 (De Tabley, 1899) and at Ellesmere, Shropshire until 1884 (Sinker, *et al.*, 1985).

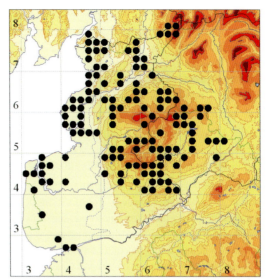

Triglochin palustris

JUNCAGINACEAE   ARROWGRASS FAMILY

Triglochin palustris L.   Marsh Arrowgrass

Circumpolar Boreo-temperate element.

Marsh Arrowgrass is a slender, perennial, rhizomatous herb found in open, damp or marshy places often with calcareous substrates (BH11). It is found throughout the British Isles.

Frequent (136). In northern Lancashire *T. palustris* is found in most of the area although it is rare or absent in lowland, southern areas of the region. Whilst its distribution in northern Lancashire is believed to be stable there has been a considerable decline nationally, especially in southern England, mostly since 1950 ('New Atlas'), which has continued since 1987 ('Local Change').

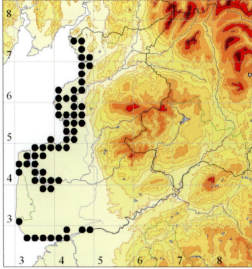

Triglochin maritima

Triglochin maritima L.   Sea Arrowgrass

Circumpolar Boreo-temperate element.

This is a rhizomatous perennial herb of saline habitats (BH21) and is found on salt marshes around the coasts of the British Isles.

Occasional (60). *T. maritimum* occurs on all the salt marshes in northern Lancashire. Its distribution locally and nationally is unchanged.

POTAMOGETONACEAE   PONDWEED FAMILY

Potamogeton natans L.   Broad-leaved Pondweed

Circumpolar Boreo-temperate element.

This rhizomatous, floating-leaved aquatic species is found in ponds and slow moving waters (BH11, 13, 14) throughout the British Isles.

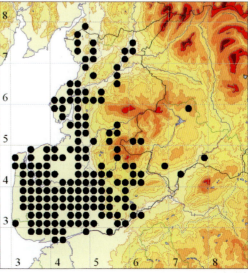

Potamogeton natans

Frequent (177). In northern Lancashire *P. natans* is found in most lowland areas in the west of the region and in the Lune valley but more rarely in the east of the region. Its distribution locally and nationally is stable.

Potamogeton polygonifolius Pourr. Bog Pondweed

Suboceanic Temperate element.

Bog Pondweed is a rhizomatous, perennial herb found in ponds, ditches and shallow water bodies but it is particularly characteristic of upland flushes. It is usually found in acidic water but may occasionally occur in highly calcareous, nutrient-poor sites (BH11, 12, 13).

Frequent (85). In northern Lancashire this is mostly found by upland ponds and in acidic flushes. However, it occurs more occasionally in the west of the area and it is then found on calcareous substrates, e.g. in the Silverdale area. Whilst its distribution in northern Lancashire is probably stable, nationally it has declined at the edges of its distribution, especially in south-eastern England and this decline is continuing ('New Atlas', 'Local Change').

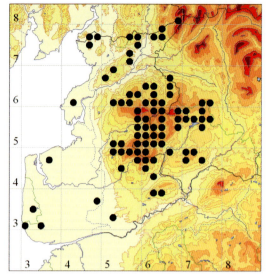
Potamogeton polygonifolius

Potamogeton coloratus Hornem. Fen Pondweed

European Southern-temperate element.

This rhizomatous, perennial herb is found in shallow, calcium-rich but nutrient-poor waters in ponds, ditches and marshes etc. (BH13). It has a disjunct distribution in the British Isles with major concentrations of records in eastern England and central Ireland.

Rare (6). This was not recognised as occurring in northern Lancashire until it was found at Silverdale 1890 (C.B.; BM) and in a ditch near the Leighton Beck in 1913 (Wheldon and Wilson, 1925). It was probably overlooked but in recent years it appears to have spread to new sites in the northwest of the region and in the Heysham peninsula. Similarly there is some evidence for recent spread nationally ('New Atlas').

Potamogeton lucens L. Shining Pondweed

Eurosiberian Temperate element.

This attractive, rhizomatous, perennial, aquatic herb is found in deep calcareous water in lakes etc. (BH13, 14). It is found mostly in south-eastern England and Ireland with occasional localities elsewhere.

Very rare (1). In northern Lancashire its only locality is Hawes Water, Silverdale (SD47T), which is probably the only suitable site in the area. It has declined nationally as waters have become more eutrophic.

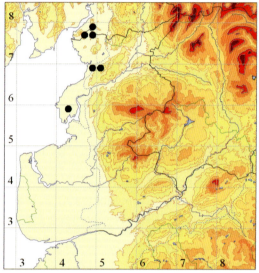
Potamogeton coloratus

Potamogeton gramineus L. Various-leaved Pondweed

Circumpolar Boreo-temperate element.

P. gramineus is found in shallow water in a variety of water bodies. Its morphology is variable and whilst it is absent from the most oligotrophic and eutrophic water it has a wide tolerance of nutrient levels (BH13, 14). It is found in northern and eastern Britain and in Ireland but it is rare or absent from most of Wales and western England.

Extinct. In northern Lancashire the only confirmed record was from a ditch by the railway at Silverdale (SD47T) in 1881 (C.B.; Wheldon and Wilson, 1925). The record from Stonyhurst Ponds (Anon, 1891) was an error for *P. alpinus* (SYT). There has been a considerable decline nationally through drainage and eutrophication ('New Atlas').

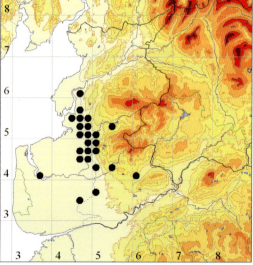
Potamogeton alpinus

Potamogeton alpinus Balb.   Red Pondweed

Circumpolar Boreal-montane element.

This is an aquatic species of still or slow moving water in lakes, ponds and canals (BH13) found in most of the British Isles although it is rare in south-western Britain and southern Ireland.

Occasional (24) but by 2008 it was believed to be very rare (3). In northern Lancashire post 1964 records for Red Pondweed are mostly from central areas of VC 60 and especially in the Lancaster Canal where it was abundant in the 1960s and early 1970s. Prior to 1964 old records suggest it was found more widely in ponds in central parts of VC 60. However by the late 1990s it was probably extinct in the canal (Greenwood, 2005) and the only recent records are from a small reservoir on Nicky Nook, Nether Wyresdale (SD54E) in 1999 (E.F.G.), a pond in Over Wyresdale (SD55L) in 1997 (P.B.) and from Arbour Quarry, Thornley-with-Wheatley (SD64A) in 1999 (E.F.G.). However in 2011 it was refound in the canal (SD45S, SD46S). Although nationally there appears to be little change in its distribution in northern parts of its range in the British Isles the 'New Atlas' suggests that it has declined markedly in England and south-eastern Scotland during the twentieth century as ponds were filled in but that further, more recent, decline was probably attributed to eutrophication.

Potamogeton perfoliatus L.   Perfoliate Pondweed

Circumpolar Boreo-temperate element.

This is an aquatic species found in still or slow moving, mesotrophic water where it grows most vigorously at depths of 1m or more (BH13, 14). It is found throughout the British Isles.

Occasional (37). In northern Lancashire most post 1964 records were from the Lancaster Canal where it was first recognised from near Garstang in 1891 (A.W.; YRK). However whilst it was still present in 2002 (SD44Y; E.F.G., P.J.) it had become very rare. Although there are few early records it also occurs in both the R. Lune and R. Ribble. Nationally there has only been local decline ('New Atlas', 'Local Change').

[Potamogeton friesii Rupr.   Flat-stalked Pondweed

This was reported from near Winmarleigh and Hawes Water, Silverdale (Wheldon and Wilson, 1907). The voucher specimen for the Winmarleigh record at NMW is *P. obtusifolius* and the Hawes Water record is also believed to be this species.]

Potamogeton friesii × P. crispus (**P. × lintonii** Fryer)

                                                 Linton's Pondweed

This hybrid pondweed is found in scattered localities in England, Wales, Ireland and southern Scotland and in Europe in Belgium, Holland and the Czech Republic. It is found in eutrophic, still and slow moving water and although sterile it is found in the absence of either or both parents. It spreads vegetatively by means of turions. However the history of its origin and spread is unclear.

Very rare (2) or extinct. Linton's Pondweed was found in the Glasson branch of the Lancaster Canal (SD45S) in 1971 and 1973 (E.F.G.; LIV) and in the Lancaster Canal at Lea (SD53A) in 1974 (V.G.; BM). It seems likely that at that time it may have been widespread in the Canal but unrecorded because of identification problems. Despite recent searches in the Glasson branch of the canal it has not been refound and it may be extinct.

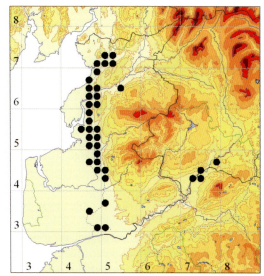
Potamogeton perfoliatus

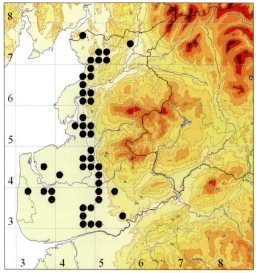
Potamogeton obtusifolius

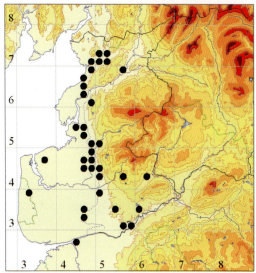
Potamogeton pusillus

Potamogeton obtusifolius Mert. & W.D. J. Koch

Blunt-leaved Pondweed

Circumpolar Boreo-temperate element.

This aquatic species is found in mesotrophic, acidic or neutral, still or slow moving waters in lakes, ponds and canals (BH13) throughout most of the British Isles.

Occasional (45). In northern Lancashire most records of *P. obtusifolius* were from the Lancaster Canal where it has declined considerably in recent years. Other localities are in lowland areas of VC 60. This local decline is reflected nationally ('New Atlas').

Potamogeton pusillus L.

Lesser Pondweed

Circumpolar Southern-temperate element.

Lesser Pondweed is a fine-leaved, aquatic species found in still or slow moving, mesotrophic or eutrophic water (BH13). It is difficult to distinguish from other fine-leaved pondweeds but is found throughout the British Isles.

Occasional (35). In northern Lancashire *P. pusillus* has been found in ponds, gravel pits and the Lancaster Canal in lowland areas of VC 60. Because of identification difficulties it is not easy to assess if the distribution of *P. pusillus* has changed. There is some evidence that it has become more widespread in northern Lancashire over the last 100 years whilst nationally 'Local Change' confirmed an increase.

Potamogeton berchtoldii Fieber

Small Pondweed

Circumpolar Boreo-temperate element.

Small Pondweed is found in still or slow flowing waters and is perhaps not found in the most eutrophic places but otherwise occurs in a variety of conditions (BH13, 14). It is a fine-leaved species and it is easily confused with similar species, especially *P. pusillus*. *P. berchtoldii* is found throughout the British Isles.

Frequent (78). Small Pondweed was found throughout VC 60 but appears to be absent from Lancashire VC 64. It was formally common in the Lancaster Canal but it seems to have largely gone from the waterway in recent years. It is difficult to assess change because of identification difficulties but it is possible that there is some decline in its distribution locally and nationally.

Potamogeton trichoides Cham. & Schltdl.

Hairlike Pondweed

Eurosiberian Southern-temperate element.

Hairlike Pondweed is a very fine-leaved pondweed found in mesotrophic or eutrophic, still and slow moving water (BH13, 14) in midland and southern Britain with a few localities between Glasgow and Edinburgh in Scotland.

Rare (6). Although old records were from the Preston area all post 1964 localities are from the Lancaster Canal in the north of VC 60 between Cabus and Lancaster. Nationally there is some evidence that this species is spreading, possibly in response to eutrophication ('New Atlas').

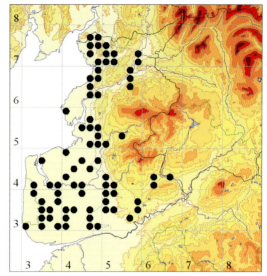

Potamogeton berchtoldii

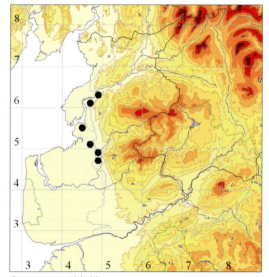

Potamogeton trichoides

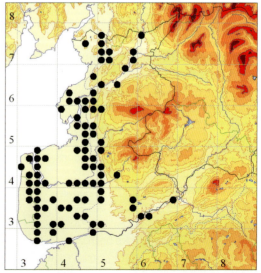

Potamogeton crispus

Potamogeton crispus L.   Curled Pondweed

Eurasian Southern-temperate element.

Curled Pondweed is perhaps the most easily identified pondweed and is found in a wide range of mesotrophic or eutrophic, still and slow flowing waters (BH13, 14). It is found in most parts of the British Isles.

Frequent (89). In northern Lancashire Curled Pondweed occurs in the west of the area and in the Lune and Ribble valleys. There has been no change in its distribution locally or nationally.

Potamogeton pectinatus L.   Fennel Pondweed

Circumpolar Boreal-montane element.

This is a linear leaved aquatic species found in eutrophic or brackish water (BH13, 14). It can become very abundant and occurs in most lowland areas of the British Isles.

Occasional (52). In northern Lancashire *P. pectinatus* occurs in the Lancaster Canal and in lowland areas of VC 60 generally as well as in the Lune and Ribble valleys. Over the last 100 years *P. pectinatus* has considerably extended its distribution in the area but nationally its distribution is unchanged.

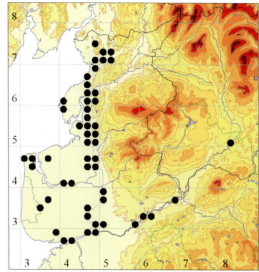
Potamogeton pectinatus

Groenlandia densa (L.) Fourr.   Opposite-leaved Pondweed

European Temperate element.

This is a perennial, aquatic herb of shallow, clear, base-rich, still or slow moving water (BH13, 14). It is mostly found in England and south-eastern Ireland.

Rare (7) or very rare (1). Prior to 1964 *G. densa* was recorded from several places in the Lancaster Canal from Preston to Carnforth. It was also found at Silverdale, Bare and Ribchester. In 1964 it was abundant in the Glasson branch of the Lancaster Canal, especially in the mill leet at Thurnham. However this was drained *c.* 1968 and it disappeared from the Canal in the 1990s. Today it is confined to oxbows of the R. Lune (SD57W) and possibly in neighbouring tetrads. The decline of *G. densa* locally is reflected nationally ('New Atlas').

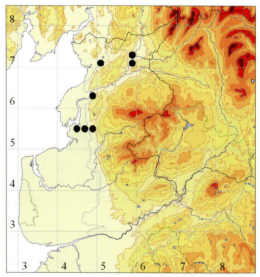
Groenlandia densa

Zannichellia palustris L.   Horned Pondweed

Circumpolar Southern-temperate element.

Horned Pondweed is a submerged, perennial, aquatic herb found in a range of shallow, often brackish, shallow water habitats (BH13, 14). It occurs in most lowland parts of the British Isles.

Occasional (29). In northern Lancashire Horned Pondweed was found in coastal areas between the Wyre estuary and the Silverdale area. Formerly it also occurred on the Ribble estuary (Wheldon and Wilson, 1907). During the 1960s and 1970s it appears as if *Z. palustris* was becoming more frequent in northern Lancashire, but in recent years there have been few records, suggesting a decline. This contradictory evidence is reflected nationally where an increase is reported in southern Scotland but a decline is noted in England ('New Atlas'). 'Local Change' reports its distribution as stable.

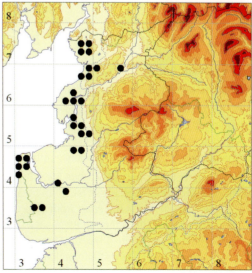
Zannichellia palustris

RUPPIACEAE   TASSELWEED FAMILY

Ruppia maritima L.   Beaked Tasselweed

Circumpolar Wide-temperate element.

This is a submerged, fine-leaved, aquatic species found in shallow, usually brackish water (BH21). It occurs around the coast of the British Isles.

Rare (12). Most of the localities for *R. maritima* in northern Lancashire are from brackish pools at the top of salt marshes and in nearby brackish ponds. It tends to be erratic in its appearance. However it has not been seen in the Ribble estuary for about 100 years. It has also gone from Fairhaven Lake (SD32I & N) where it was recorded regularly from 1946 until it was last seen in 1998 (E.F.G.). Its disappearance followed mechanical removal of the weed and a large increase in the resident wildfowl population. It was also recorded, unusually, in an inland gravel pit at Claughton (SD54B) in 1969 (E.F.G.), no doubt brought in by gulls that used the pit as a roosting site. The distribution of *R. maritima* is thought to be stable in northern Lancashire but there have been losses nationally, especially in southern Britain ('New Atlas').

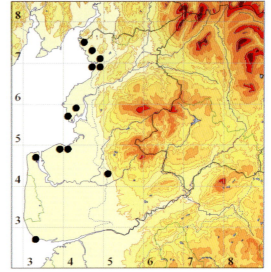
Ruppia maritima

NARTHECIACEAE   BOG ASPHODEL FAMILY

Narthecium ossifragum (L.) Huds.   Bog Asphodel

Oceanic Boreo-temperate element.

Bog Asphodel is a rhizomatous perennial herb of wet usually acid, mineral soils on a range of wet heaths, flushes and bog communities (BH12). It is found in most of the British Isles although it is rare or absent from much of lowland midland and eastern England.

Frequent (82). In northern Lancashire Bog Asphodel is found in the north and east of the region where, in some bogs and flushes, it can provide a vivid golden yellow carpet when in flower (see Plate 2.26). During the last 100 years its distribution in northern Lancashire is unchanged but prior to the drainage of bogs in the Fylde, e.g. Lytham Moss, it must also have been present in the south and west of the area. Nationally the 'New Atlas' reported losses from southern and eastern England but since 1987 'Local Change' reported no further significant losses.

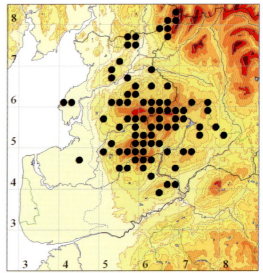
Narthecium ossifragum

DIOSCOREACEAE   BLACK BRYONY FAMILY

Tamus communis L.   Black Bryony

Submediterranean-Subatlantic element.

T. communis is a dioecious, tuberous liana found clambering over scrub and hedges usually on calcareous, well-drained soils (BH1, 3). It is found in lowland areas of Wales and England as far north as southern Cumbria and Durham. It also occurs as an occasional introduction elsewhere.

Frequent (110). In northern Lancashire Black Bryony is found mostly in the north of the region but occurs as far south as Garstang. It also occurs in the Ribble valley in VC 64 but apart from an occasional locality it is absent from the rest of the area although there are old records for Tunbrook Wood, near Preston (Ashfield, 1860), Alston and Nicky Nook (Preston Scientific Society 1903). Its distribution locally and nationally is thought to be stable although 'Local Change' reported losses since 1987.

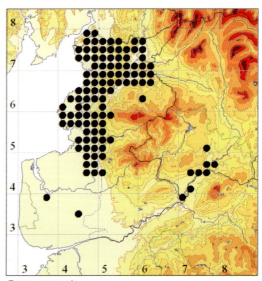
Tamus communis

MELANTHIACEAE   HERB-PARIS FAMILY

Paris quadrifolia L.   Herb-Paris

Eurosiberian Boreo-temperate element.

Herb-Paris is a rhizomatous perennial herb found in woodlands, usually on calcareous substrates. It also occurs on limestone pavements (BH1). It is found in most of Britain but it can be difficult to see as it often grows with Dog's Mercury.

Occasional (21). Wheldon and Wilson (1907) recorded *P. quadrifolia* from throughout VC 60 but remarked that it was especially frequent on limestone. However they gave no localities for the lowland areas in the west and no other sources have been found to support localities in this part of the region. Today Herb-Paris is found in the north of the region, usually on limestone. It also occurs in woodlands in the Hodder and Ribble valleys. However it is clear that *P. quadrifolia* has suffered a substantial decline in northern Lancashire over the last 100 years, which may be continuing in non-limestone areas. There have also been losses nationally ('New Atlas').

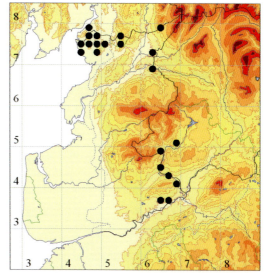

Paris quadrifolia

COLCHICACEAE   MEADOW SAFRON FAMILY

Colchicum autumnale L.   Meadow Saffron

European Temperate element but possibly an escape from cultivation in northern Lancashire.

Meadow Saffron is a perennial herb found in damp meadows, on river banks and in open areas in woodlands (BH6). It is also found as an escape from cultivation. It is very poisonous but formerly its corms were used as a remedy for gout (Mabey, 1996). It occurs throughout Britain and southern Ireland.

Very rare (1). In northern Lancashire *C. autumnale* was first found in a meadow on the south side of the R. Wyre about a mile from St Michael's church (Moss, 1912). There is an unlocalised record for a locality near Ribchester in 1956 (B.R.C.). Since 1964 the only locality noted is from a roadside at Ireby (SD67M) in 1994 (J.M.N.). Nationally its distribution is thought to be stable.

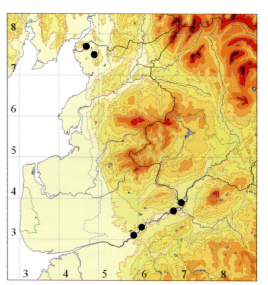

Gagea lutea

LILIACEAE   LILY FAMILY

Gagea lutea (L.) Ker Gawl.   Yellow Star-of-Bethlehem

European Temperate element.

This bulbous perennial herb is found in shady habitats and woodlands (BH1, 3, 14, 16) in England, eastern Wales, central and southern Scotland. It occurs as an introduction in north-eastern Scotland.

Rare (6). In northern Lancashire *G. lutea* is found in a few limestone woods in the north of the area and in the Ribble and lower Hodder valleys. Although it is elusive flowering early in the year and perhaps not flowering in some years, searches in recent years suggest that by 2008 only two or three colonies remain. Nationally its distribution is thought to be stable.

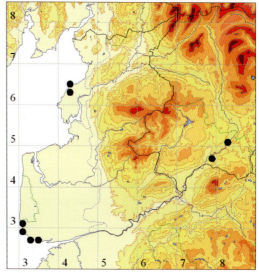

Tulipa gesneriana

Tulipa sylvestris L.   Wild Tulip

Neophyte. The native range of Wild Tulip is uncertain but at present it occurs in Europe, northern Africa and south-western Asia. It is a bulbous perennial herb found in woodlands and marginal habitats. It was cultivated in Britain by 1596 and was recorded in the wild by 1790. It was widely naturalised by the late eighteenth and nineteenth centuries but had declined dramatically by the mid twentieth century. Records are from England, eastern Wales, eastern Scotland and very rarely in Ireland.

In northern Lancashire it was found abundantly at Scale Hall (SD46R) near Lancaster in 1831 (Fielding MS) and near Whittingham, Goosnargh c. 1870 (Preston Scientific Society, 1903) but it was later lost at this site (Wheldon and Wilson, 1907).

Tulipa gesneriana L.   Garden Tulip

Neophyte. Garden Tulip is probably of garden origin. It is a bulbous perennial plant found in ruderal habitats in Britain and the Isle of Man. It was cultivated in Britain by 1577 but it was not recorded in the wild until 1955. There are numerous cultivars.

Rare (8). In northern Lancashire it was first found in an overgrown allotment at Morecambe (SD46H) in 1975 (A.E.C.). Since then it has been found in a few localities in the Lancaster area, Lytham St Anne's and in Lancashire VC 64.

Fritillaria meleagris L.   Fritillary

European Temperate element but a neophyte in northern Lancashire. Fritillary is a bulbous perennial species of damp, sometimes winter flooded, meadows but it is also planted and may become naturalised. It was first recorded in Britain by 1578 but it was not seen in the wild until 1736 casting doubt as to its native status in central and southern England. It has been found in many parts of Britain.

Very rare (3). In northern Lancashire Fritillary was found in a meadow at Stainall (Ashfield, 1860). More recently a single plant was found as a garden escape in Silverdale (SD47S; Livermore and Livermore, 1987), in a woodland at Blackpool (SD33I) in 1996 (C.F. & N.J.S.) and planted at Marton Mere, Blackpool (SD33M) c. 2000 where it is increasing (M.J.).

Lilium martagon L.   Martagon Lily

Neophyte with a Eurosiberian Temperate distribution but widely naturalised north of its natural range. It is a bulbous perennial species often found in small clumps in woodland or woodland edge habitats. It was introduced into British gardens by 1591 and was first recorded in the wild in 1782. It is found in England, Wales and southern Scotland and rarely elsewhere in the British Isles.

Rare (10). In northern Lancashire Martagon Lily was first found in a roadside coppice at Goosnargh (SD53I) in 1949 (H.E.B.). Since 1964 it has been found in a few widely scattered localities.

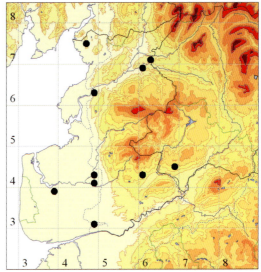
Lilium martagon

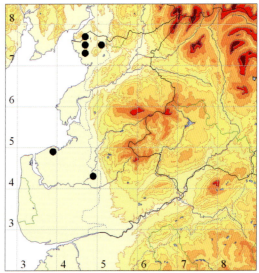
Lilium pyrenaicum

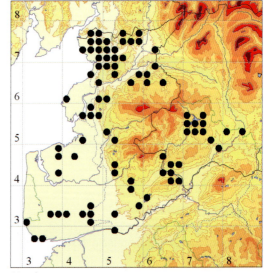
Neottia ovata

Lilium pyrenaicum Gouan   Pyrenean Lily

Neophyte. *L. pyrenaicum* is a bulbous perennial species native to the Pyrenees and was cultivated in Britain before 1596. It was recorded in the wild by 1853 and occurs in woodland and woodland edge habitats in many parts of the British Isles but it is rare or absent in most of Ireland and eastern England.

Rare (6). In northern Lancashire Pyrenean Lily was first recorded from Waterslack Wood, Silverdale in 1961 (E. Hardy in Bryant, 2008). Subsequently it was recorded from a number of sites in the Silverdale and Yealand areas (SD47R, S, T and 57C) by various recorders and it still occurs here. It was also found in Fluke Hall woods, Pilling (SD34Z) in 1999 (C.F. & N.J.S.) and at Catterall (SD44W) in the 1970s and may still be present (M.E.).

ORCHIDACEAE   ORCHID FAMILY

Nomenclature and order follows Foley and Clarke (2005).

Cypripedium calceolus L.   Lady's-slipper

Circumpolar Boreo-temperate element.

Lady's-slipper is a rhizomatous perennial species found on well-drained calcareous soils derived from limestone (BH7). In Britain its native distribution was confined to northern England and the southern Pennines. During the nineteenth century it was lost from most localities largely through collecting leaving only one surviving plant by the mid twentieth century. Since then there has been an active conservation and propagation programme and it has been re-introduced into a number of localities within its former range.

Very rare (1). The status of Lady's-slipper in northern Lancashire is uncertain. There is no doubt that it grew in the county or close to the border. A nineteenth century specimen (BM) collected by a Mrs Humble gives a locality as 'nr Lancaster' but this probably refers to an old but well-known locality at Helks Wood, Ingleton in Yorkshire. Similarly Ashfield (1864) refers to a locality 'near Milnthorpe not far from Silverdale' and this could be in Cumbria rather than Lancashire. More convincing, although reported through a third party, is the record of Robert Whiteside (c. 1866–1960) of Lancaster who, about 1890, is said to have seen Lady's-slipper in 'Gait Barrows Wood at Silverdale and in a field not far from there'. However there is no voucher specimen in his collection now at BM. Nevertheless there have been persistent rumours that it did occur in this area. The discovery in 1975 that it grew in Silverdale (SD47S) led to a belief that this was the re-discovery of a native population of this colourful orchid. Local naturalists found that it was rooted deep in a crack in the limestone seeming to rule out deliberate planting. However as part of the ongoing research programme the genetic relationship of the Silverdale plant was investigated at the Royal Botanic Gardens, Kew. Here M. Fay (pers. comm., 2005) quoted a report he had written to English Nature stating that 'Cytotype 3a found in the putatively introduced Silverdale plant was only otherwise found in Spain. These data do not prove that it is introduced, but in the light of other evidence, it appears prudent to exclude this plant from any introduction activity'. It therefore appears that the Silverdale plant is not of native British stock. However, in an attempt at its destruction in 2004 by a person unknown the deep rooting of the plant in a crack in the limestone was confirmed, but the attempt failed and the plant continued to flower in the following years. The origin of the Silverdale plant remains a mystery but perhaps it should be mentioned that *C. calceolus* was grown in a wild area of a nearby nursery garden although the origin of the plants is unknown. The possibility of natural spread from these plants should not be ignored. Further details of the occurrence of Lady's-slipper in Lancashire can be found in Greenwood (2004a).

Cephalanthera longifolia (L.) Fritsch
                    Narrow-leaved Helleborine

European Temperate element.

This rhizomatous perennial herb is found in a variety of woodland types on calcareous soils (BH1). It formerly occurred in many places in the British Isles.

Extinct. In northern Lancashire Jenkinson (1775) recorded it in two localities in the Yealand area and there is a specimen at OXF collected in Silverdale in 1898 by Rev. W.W. Mason. There is also a record identified from a non-flowering plant at Silverdale in 1958 (Henderson, 1962). Nationally it declined markedly in the eighteenth and nineteenth centuries ('New Atlas').

Neottia cordata (L.) Rich   Lesser Twayblade

European Southern-temperate element.

This is a rhizomatous herb found on moorland and on peat bogs often growing in *Sphagnum* or in the moss layer beneath *Calluna* and *Vaccinium* and always in wet acid conditions (BH2, 10, 12). Lesser Twayblade is a small, two-leaved orchid that is difficult to spot and is found in upland areas of the British Isles.

Very rare (2). *N. cordata* has always been a rare species in northern Lancashire but pre 1964 records were from Ward's Stone in 1883; Gavell's Clough, Tarnbrook and Leagram Fells all cited by Wheldon and Wilson (1907). It was also found in upper Grizedale near Garstang (Wheldon and Wilson, 1925) and there is a specimen collected by J.A.W. & A.W. in 1899 at NMW from Udale, which may be part of the Ward's Stone site. In Lancashire VC 64 it was found on Newton Fell (SD74E) in 1908 (J.F.P.; LDS) and Waddington Fell (Peel, 1913b) although these localities may refer to the same site. Since 1964 Lesser Twayblade has been seen on Marshaw Fell, Over Wyresdale extending over two tetrads (SD65B and 55W). Several plants were seen in 2005 (P.J. & E.F.G.) and a single plant was found a short distance away from the main colony in 2008 (P.G.). There is also a reference to a post 1964 site on Ward's Stone (E. Hardy in Bryant, 2008) but the exact locality has not been identified. The intensive management of moorland areas involving regular burning makes it unlikely that *N. cordata* will be found elsewhere and the present colony with other rare species on the hillside is vulnerable without positive conservation measures. Its loss locally is reflected nationally

Neottia ovata (L.) Bluff & Fingerh.   Common Twayblade
Eurosiberian Boreo-temperate element.

Common Twayblade is a rhizomatous perennial herb found on a wide range of calcareous and neutral soils and in a variety of habitats (BH1, 11). It is found in most parts of the British Isles.

Frequent (83). In northern Lancashire *N. ovata* is found throughout the area except in intensively cultivated areas and on moorland. Its distribution locally is probably stable but there have been some losses nationally ('New Atlas') and these may have continued since 1987 ('Local Change').

Neottia nidus-avis (L.) Rich.   Bird's-nest Orchid
Eurosiberian Temperate element.

Bird's-nest Orchid is a saprophytic herb found on deep humus in densely shaded woods on base-rich soils (BH1). It may be found anywhere in the British Isles but it has not been seen in most of the offshore islands.

Very rare (4). *N. nidus-avis* is another orchid that has always been rare but its sporadic appearance makes it difficult to assess change. Pre 1964 records were from near the R. Hodder, Aighton, Bailey and Chaigley; Middleton Woods, Goosnargh; Red Scar, near Preston and Tunbrook Wood all cited by Wheldon and Wilson (1907). Wheldon and Wilson (1925) also found it in woods by the R. Greta. Other pre 1964 records were from Silverdale in 1916 (A.J.C.; LSA); in the Yealand area in 1935 and 1941 (H.E.B.); near Bolton-by-Bowland (SD74U; Milne-Redhead, 1870s) and in two places on the north-eastern side of Warton Crag (Wilson, 1947–49). Since 1964 it has been recorded from an old quarry in Roeburndale (SD66D) where it was last seen 1988 (J.M.N.); Eaves Wood, Silverdale (SD47T) in 1968 (C. J.-P.); roadside copse, Yealand Redmayne (SD47X) where it was last seen in 1983 (Arnside Naturalists) and in a nearby wood where it was last seen in 2000 (C.B.W.); Kit Bill Wood, Over Kellet (SD56E) in 1976 (L.A.L.) and Gait Barrows N.N.R. (SD47T) in 1986 (C.B.W.). Despite its uncertain appearance *N. nidus-avis* is declining in northern Lancashire and these losses are reflected nationally ('New Atlas').

Epipactis palustris (L.) Crantz   Marsh Helleborine
Eurosiberian Temperate element.

Marsh Helleborine is a rhizomatous perennial herb of neutral to calcareous fens, marshes and dune slacks (BH11) and it sometimes colonizes post-industrial sites, e.g. quarries and clay pits etc. It is found in England, Wales and southern Scotland.

Rare (10). Wheldon and Wilson (1907) recorded *E. palustris* from seven localities in VC 60 but apart from the sand dunes at Lytham St Anne's these were different localities to those recorded after 1964. In addition to the localities recorded by Wheldon and Wilson other early records

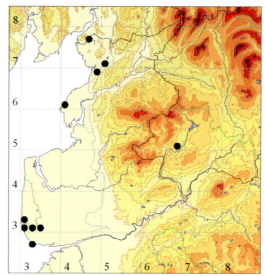
Epipactis palustris

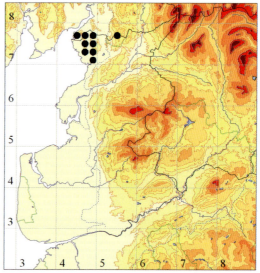
Epipactis atrorubens

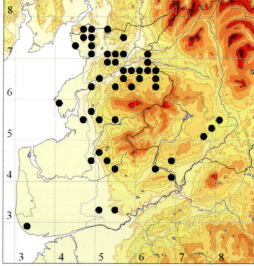
Epipactis helleborine

included sites at Stodday (Fielding MS) and Sunderland Point (Garlick, 1957a) where again there are no post 1964 records. Since 1964 it has been found in a few localities in the north of the area and on the sand dunes and in post-industrial sites in the Lytham St Anne's area. In Lancashire VC 64 it was found near Newton-in-Bowland (SD75V) in 1893 (J.F.P.) where it still occurs. Whilst never common Marsh Helleborine appears to readily colonise suitable new sites when they become available but it also disappears from sites as they become overgrown. Nevertheless where it occurs there may be a large number of plants. Overall the distribution of *E. palustris* is stable in northern Lancashire but nationally there has been a considerable decline in England ('New Atlas').

Epipactis atrorubens (Hoffm. ex Bernh.) Besser
Dark-red Helleborine

Eurosiberian Boreo-temperate element.

E. atrorubens is a perennial herb found mostly on base-rich rocks or well-drained skeletal soils overlying limestone (BH16). It is found in northern England and the southern Pennines, western Ireland, northern Wales and more rarely in highland Scotland.

Rare (9). In northern Lancashire Dark-red Helleborine is found on limestone around Morecambe Bay and occasionally on old railway ballast in the same area. It also occurs on Dalton Crags. It is often frequent on limestone pavement and rocks. Its distribution is stable locally and nationally.

Epipactis helleborine (L.) Crantz
Broad-leaved Helleborine

Eurasian Temperate element.

Broad-leaved Helleborine is a rhizomatous perennial herb found on calcareous or neutral soils in woodlands and marginal habitats (BH1, 7). It occurs in most of the British Isles although it is absent from many areas of northern and southern Scotland.

Occasional (47). In northern Lancashire *E. helleborine* is found throughout the region in woodland and former woodland areas of the region but it is absent from intensively farmed areas in the west of the region. However it rarely appears in the same locality for more than a year or so before disap-pearing only to re-appear in new sites. Although Wheldon and Wilson (1907) did not list any localities their description of its distribution suggests it has declined over the last 100 years. Its distribution nationally is stable.

Epipactis dunensis (T. & T.A. Stephenson) Godfrey
Dune Helleborine

Endemic.

Dune Helleborine was first described from populations on the Lancashire (now Sefton) coast in the early twentieth century.

However since then the identity of the taxon and of other similar plants in Britain and elsewhere has been the subject of much research and discussion (Foley and Clarke, 2005). However based on the most recent research *E. dunensis* is confined to sand dunes (BH19) where it grows with *Salix repens* or under planted pine trees in Anglesey and on the Sefton coast and in riverside communities in the Tyne valley. It may also occur in a few other English localities.

Very rare (4). In northern Lancashire Dune Helleborine was first recorded from sand dunes at Lytham St Anne's (Wheldon and Wilson, 1925); today it still occurs in small quantity here (SD33A, 32I, J, P). However it has not been seen on dunes at Fairhaven (SD32I) since 1992.

Epipactis phyllanthes G.E. Sm.
Green-flowered Helleborine

European Temperate element.

This is a rhizomatous perennial herb usually found in sparsely vegetated, shady places on acidic, humus-poor substrates (BH1). It is also found with *Salix repens* on sand dunes in north-western England. Most records are from southern England but it occurs occasionally elsewhere in England, Wales and Ireland.

Very rare (1). *E. phyllanthes* was first found on sand dunes at Lytham St Anne's in 1890 (C.B.; MANCH) although the voucher specimen was not identified until much more recently. It still occurs in very small quantity on sand dunes on either side of Clifton Drive, Lytham St Anne's (SD33A). Nationally Green-flowered Helleborine has declined in southern England ('New Atlas').

[**Hammarbya paludosa** (L.) Kuntze   Bog Orchid
Circumpolar Boreal-montane element.

This occurs in bogs in upland parts of the British Isles and at lower levels in southern and eastern England.

Perring and Walters (1962) list Bog Orchid as an omitted record for VC 60 suggesting that there was an unconfirmed record for the vice-county. Although it is possible that it did once grow in the area the basis for the record has not been ascertained.]

Spiranthes spiralis (L.) Chevall.   Autumn Lady's-tresses
European Southern-temperate element.

Autumn Lady's-tresses is a rhizomatous herb found in grazed grassland on dry calcareous soils (BH7) and is found in England as far north as the limestone area around Morecambe Bay and in Ireland.

Rare (7). Although never common *S. spiralis* was known from several sites in the Silverdale and Yealand area of northern Lancashire. However from the mid 1970s most sites suffered from nutrient enrichment and by 2002 it was confined to three sites: Thrang End, Yealand Redmayne (SD47Y), the Lots, Silverdale (SD47M) and Jack Scout, Silverdale (SD47L). In 2008 it was flourishing at the Lots and Jack Scout but at Thrang End, where it grew in small quantity in 2002 (E.F.G.), it may not have survived. Nationally there have been many losses ('New Atlas').

Orchis mascula (L.) L.   Early-purple Orchid

European Temperate element.

This tuberous perennial herb grows on a variety of neutral and calcareous soils in woodlands and marginal habitats (BH1, 7, 16). It is found throughout the British Isles.

Frequent (94). In northern Lancashire *O. mascula* grows in the wooded and former wooded parts of the region but it is absent from most of the intensively farmed areas in the west of the region. Although it is too frequent for individual localities to be recorded it is clear that it has declined or has gone from many localities where Wheldon and Wilson (1907) must have known it. More recently it seems to have gone from sites to the north and east of Preston where it occurred in the 1960s and 1970s. Losses have also been noted nationally and these have continued since 1987 ('Local Change').

Pseudorchis albida (L.) Á. & D. Löve   Small-white Orchid

European Boreal-montane element.

P. albida is a tuberous rooted perennial herb of well-drained grassland (BH7, 8). Its former range covered Scotland, Ireland, Wales, northern England and parts of south-eastern England.

Extinct. In northern Lancashire Small-white Orchid was found near Newton-in-Bowland (SD74U) in 1912 (M.N. Peel; LDS) and at Silverdale in the early twentieth century (A.J.C.; LSA).

Platanthera bifolia (L.) Rich.   Lesser Butterfly-orchid

Eurasian Boreo-temperate element.

Lesser Butterfly-orchid is found in heathy pastures, scrub and in woodland edges (BH1, 10) throughout the British Isles.

Rare (7) but probably extinct by 2008. Prior to 1964 *P. bifolia* had been recorded in at least sixteen localities scattered in the north and east of VC 60. Additionally it had been found near Newton-in-Bowland in 1912 (Peel, 1913) and near Bolton-by-Bowland in 1878 (Milne-Redhead, 1870s). Since 1964 it has been seen in a few localities in the north of the region, mostly in the Silverdale area. However during the forty years covered by tetrad recording in northern Lancashire sites were lost mostly by generalised nutrient enrichment or more rarely physical destruction of the habitat. The last known colony was found at Yealand Hall Allotment (SD47Y) where over a period of years the number of plants gradually diminished until the last record of a single plant in 1999 (Arnside Naturalists). Nationally there have been losses over a long period and these are continuing so that a once frequent species is becoming rare, even in Scotland and Ireland, whilst in England it has been lost from many parts of the country ('New Atlas').

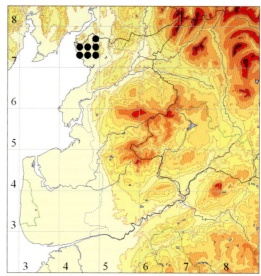
Spiranthes spiralis

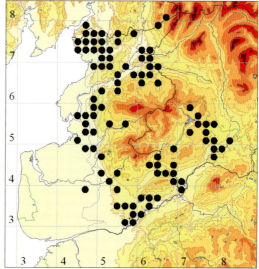
Orchis mascula

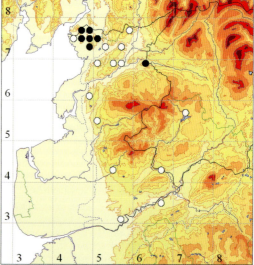
Platanthera bifolia

Platanthera chlorantha (Custer) Rchb.   Greater Butterfly-orchid

European Temperate element.

P. chlorantha is a perennial herb found in a wide variety of well-drained habitats on calcareous soils including pastures, meadows and woodland edge habitats (BH1, 6). It is found in most parts of the British Isles.

Very rare (4). This orchid must have been an abundant and common species in most meadows in Bowland and in the north of the region during the nineteenth century and extending west as far as Claughton near Garstang, and Longridge (Wheldon and Wilson, 1907; Anon, 1891). However since 1964 it has only been seen on a hedge bank at Aighton, Bailey and Chaigley (SD64R) in 1966 (E.F.G. & B. Oddie); Thrang Moss, Yealand Redmayne (SD47Y) in 1968 (C. J.-P.) and at two sites on either side of the R. Hindburn (SD66M, N). However, only one of the sites remained (SD66N) by 2010 (J.M.N.). Nationally there have been similar losses ('New Atlas') but further losses since 1987 have not been observed ('Local Change').

Gymnadenia conopsea (L.) R. Br.   Chalk Fragrant-orchid

Eurasian Boreo-temperate element.

This is a tuberous perennial herb of species rich chalk and limestone grassland and scrub (BH7, 11). Its distribution is unclear, as most recorders have not distinguished this from other fragrant orchid species. However it is believed it occurs throughout the British Isles.

Rare (9 or 10). Because the different fragrant orchids were not distinguished until recently it is difficult to know the former distribution of Chalk Fragrant-orchid. However it is believed that it was thinly distributed in northern and eastern areas of the region. The post 1964 distribution is confined to the north of the region, especially in the Silverdale area and to Lancashire VC 64. However by 2008 *G. conopsea* was only found on shell marl by Hawes Water, Silverdale (SD47T) and on roadsides at Slaidburn (SD75G, C). It is endangered at each of these localities as more vigorous species grow up and out-compete it, possibly due to generalised nutrient enrichment. The 'New Atlas' reported a decline nationally but since 1987 its distribution appears stable ('Local Change').

Gymnadenia borealis (Druce) R.M. Bateman, Pridgeon
& M.W. Chase   Heath Fragrant-orchid

This species of fragrant orchid is a tuberous, perennial herb found in hill pastures, heaths and *Molinia* grassland on base-rich or acid substrates. It is found mostly in the north and west of the British Isles. Its distribution elsewhere is unclear.

Very rare (1). The former distribution of this species in northern Lancashire is unclear. Foley and Clarke (2005) show old records for the 10 × 10km squares SD46 and 47 and it is possibly this species that Peel (1913) recorded from the upper Hodder valley. However it is believed that *G. borealis* was recorded from a pasture, with abundant *Molinia caerulea*, at Hammerton (SD75B) in 2007 (E.F.G.).

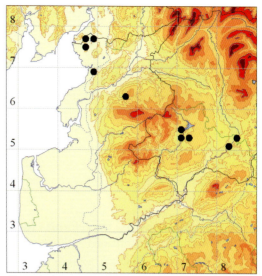
Gymnadenia conopsea s.l.

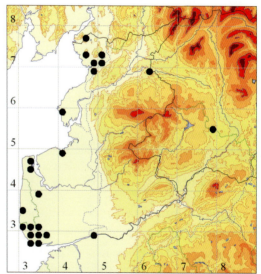
Dactylorhiza incarnata

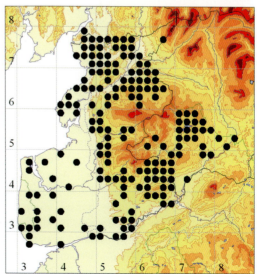
Dactylorhiza fuchsii

Gymnadenia densiflora (Wahlenb.) A. Dietr.

Marsh Fragrant-orchid

Widespread in Europe.

Marsh Fragrant-orchid is the largest of these tuberous rooted perennial fragrant orchids and is found in base-rich meadows, fens and ditches. Although it occurs throughout the British Isles most records are from south-eastern England.

Very rare (1). In northern Lancashire nineteenth century herbarium specimens collected from near Lancaster and Silverdale (BM) were identified as this species. However in 2010 M.J. & H.S. confirmed its presence at Hawes Water, Silverdale (SD47T).

Gymnadenia conopsea × Dactylorhiza fuchsii
(× Dactylodenia St.-quintinii (Godfrey) J. Duvign.)

This tuberous rooted intergeneric hybrid is found occasionally where the parents grow together. Populations usually consist of single plants and may occur in a variety of habitats. It has been found in scattered localities in many parts of the British Isles.

Very rare (1). In northern Lancashire × D. St.-quintinii was found in a field at the east end of Hawes Water, Silverdale (SD47S) in 1966 (M.J.).

Gymnadenia conopsea × Dactylorhiza incarnata
(× Dactylodenia vollmannii (M. Schulze) Peitz)

This intergeneric hybrid is rarely recorded. However, a specimen collected in a lane between Dale Head and Tosside in Lancashire VC 64 in 1909 was labelled at a later date by an unknown person as × D. vollmannii (LDS).

Dactylorhiza incarnata (L.) Soó   Early Marsh-orchid

Eurosiberian Boreo-temperate element.

Early Marsh-orchid is a tuberous rooted perennial herb found in damp places on calcareous soils in meadows, marshes and sand dunes and on more acid soils on heaths (BH11). It is found throughout the British Isles. However three subspecies occur in northern Lancashire. Ssp. *incarnata* occurs throughout the British Isles on base-rich calcareous soils but ssp. *coccinea* (Pugsley) Soó, an endemic subspecies, is found in coastal sites and especially in dune slacks whilst ssp. *pulchella* (Druce) Soó, possibly an endemic subspecies, occurs throughout the British Isles on neutral or acid soils in bogs and heaths.

Occasional (23). It appears that Early Marsh-orchid has always been a rare northern Lancashire species. Since 1964 it has been found mostly in coastal sites and more occasionally inland in northern and eastern areas. As with many orchids it often appears in post-industrial sites. Recorders have not always identified the subspecies but ssp. *incarnata* occurs throughout the range of the species. The distinctive but rare var. *gemmana* Pugsley was found in an old gravel pit at Borwick (SD57B) in 2009 (A. Gendle). Ssp. *coccinea* is confined to coastal sites on the Lytham St Anne's sand dunes

(SD33A), marshes at Fleetwood (SD34I) and in an old clay pit at Peel (SD33K). Ssp. *pulchella* was recorded by Livermore and Livermore (1987) from tetrads SD46Z, 47V and 57A and it was also known (J.M.N., pers. comm.) from Robert Hall Moor, Tatham (SD67J). It is likely that it occurred more widely inland in marshes and mires from where it has probably disappeared and may now be extinct. Overall *D. incarnata* may have become more frequent over the last 100 years with the spread mainly of ssp. *incarnata* and ssp. *coccinea*. Nationally it appears that *S. incarnata* has suffered losses ('New Atlas', 'Local Change') through the loss of inland, lowland base-rich flushes.

Dactylorhiza viridis (L.) R.M. Bateman, Pridgeon & M.W. Chase   Frog Orchid

Circumpolar Boreal-montane element.

This tuberous rooted perennial orchid is found in dry, grazed, base-rich grasslands (BH7). It is found throughout the British Isles.

Very rare (2) or extinct. In northern Lancashire Frog Orchid was known from at least 13 localities, mostly in the north of VC 60 on limestone but also in pastures elsewhere in the north of the region and in Bowland. In Lancashire VC 64 the only locality was near Newton-in-Bowland (J.F.P.; LDS). Since 1964 it has only been recorded from a pasture near Trowbarrow Quarry, Silverdale (SD47S) in 1964–68 (Anon but M.J. saw it in 1959) and from Warton Crag (SD47W) in 1965 (J. D.). As it has not been seen since the 1960s it is presumed extinct. Nationally there have been losses throughout its range but especially in England ('New Atlas'). However whilst losses have occurred since 1987 they are not significant ('Local Change').

Dactylorhiza fuchsii (Druce) Soó

Common Spotted-orchid

Eurosiberian Temperate element.

Common Spotted-orchid is a tuberous perennial herb of base-rich soils in a wide range of habitats. It readily colonizes new open and post-industrial habitats (BH11). It occurs throughout the British Isles.

Frequent (178). *D. fuchsii* is found throughout northern Lancashire although it is rare in intensively farmed areas. In Gisburn Forest it is especially abundant at the side of tracks covered with limestone chippings. *D. fuchsii* var. *rhodochila* Turner Ettl. was recognised from Heysham (SD45E) in 1992 (L.A.L.).

Dactylorhiza fuchsii × D. incarnata
(D. × kernerorum (Soó) Soó)

This hybrid is a tuberous rooted perennial herb usually found with the parents in calcareous fens and marshes, often in post-industrial sites. It is usually sterile and occurs in small numbers in scattered localities in England, Wales and Ireland.

Very rare (5). In northern Lancashire *D.* × *kernerorum* was found in grassland south of Carnforth (SD46Z; Livermore and Livermore, 1987), in a marsh at Fleetwood (SD34H) in 1968 (E.F.G.), on an old railway at Fleetwood (SD34L) in 1994 (P.J.), on sand dunes at Fairhaven (SD32I) in 1974 (B.S.B.I.) and at Lytham St Anne's L.N.R. (SD33A) in 2001 (Bradford Botany Group).

Dactylorhiza fuchsii × D. maculata (D. × transiens (Druce) Soó)

This is a tuberous rooted hybrid orchid found where base-rich and base-poor soils coexist allowing the parents to grow together. It is an uncommon hybrid and difficult to recognise but it has been found in many parts of the British Isles.

Very rare (1). In northern Lancashire it was found at Bolton-by-Bowland (SD64Z) in 1999 (Anon).

Dactylorhiza fuchsii × D. praetermissa
(D. × grandis (Druce) P.F. Hunt)

D. × *grandis* is a tuberous rooted perennial hybrid orchid found in base-rich marshes where the parents grow together. It is often found in post-industrial sites and occurs in England and Wales.

Rare (8). In northern Lancashire it is probable that *D.* × *grandis* was found near the railway at Blackpool (SD33A) in the early 1960s. However the first confirmed record was from tipped waste at Salwick (SD43Q) in 1975 (E.F.G.). Since then it has been found in a few scattered localities in lowland areas in the west of the region.

Dactylorhiza fuchsii × D. purpurella
(D. × venusta (T. & T.A. Stephenson) Soó)

D. × *venusta* is a tuberous rooted perennial hybrid orchid found frequently where the parents grow together in marshes, fens and wet grasslands, including post-industrial sites. It is found in Wales, northern England, Scotland and Ireland.

Rare (9). In northern Lancashire *D.* × *venusta* was first recorded from a railway cutting at Great Marton, Blackpool (SD33L) in 1974 (E.F.G.). Subsequently it has been found in a few scattered localities in the west of the region.

Dactylorhiza maculata (L.) Soó   Heath Spotted-orchid
Eurosiberian Boreo-temperate element.

Heath Spotted-orchid is a tuberous perennial herb found in a range of well-drained but acid soils in a variety of grasslands, flushes and heaths (BH8, 12). It occurs throughout the British Isles.

Occasional (28). In northern Lancashire *D. maculata* has been found mostly in upland areas in the north and east of the area and more rarely in coastal sites near Blackpool. However since 1987 it has only been found in five localities, at Lytham St Anne's (SD33A; C.F. & N.J.S.), Tatham (SD66D; J.M.N.), Roeburndale (SD66A & SD66C; J.M.N.) and Chipping (SD64C; P.G.). Wheldon and Wilson (1907) did not distinguish between *D. fuchsii* and *D. maculata* making it impossible to know the extent of any changes in the distribution of Heath Spotted-orchid over the last 100 years. It is suspected that there has been a considerable decline and this is confirmed for the last 50 years so that by 2008 it had become very rare. There has been a decline nationally, especially in lowland areas ('New Atlas').

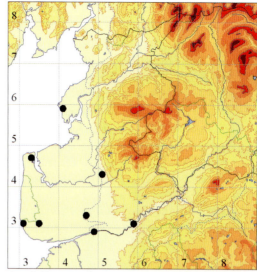

Dactylorhiza × *grandis*

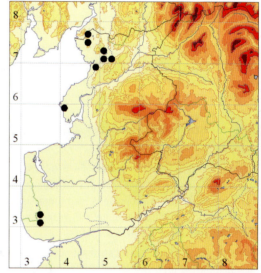

Dactylorhiza × *venusta*

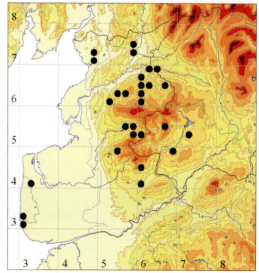

Dactylorhiza maculata

Dactylorhiza praetermissa (Druce) Soó   Southern Marsh-orchid

Oceanic temperate element.

This is a tuberous rooted perennial herb of calcareous marshes, fens and damp meadows (BH11). It readily colonizes post-industrial sites and may occur in large numbers. It is found in Wales, and in England from Lancashire and Yorkshire southwards.

Occasional (17). In northern Lancashire Southern Marsh-orchid was first found in marshy ground by Freckleton Pool (SD42I) in c. 1964 (E.F.G.). Since then it has slowly colonized new sites but has subsequently been lost from some of these, as vegetational succession has occurred. It is now found in scattered sites in the west of the area. Forma *juniales* (Vermeul.) P.D. Sell (Leopard Marsh-orchid) may occur in a gravel pit at Borwick (SD57B; A. Gendle, pers. comm., 2009). It is believed that *D. praetermissa* was introduced into a site at Claughton, near Garstang from stock at Salwick. The spread into and within northern Lancashire is reflected by a northwards spread nationally.

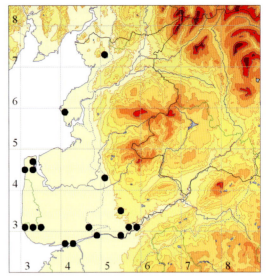

Dactylorhiza praetermissa

Dactylorhiza praetermissa × D. purpurella

(**D. × insignis** (T. & T.A. Stephenson) Soó)

This hybrid is likely to occur where the distribution of the two parent species overlap in northern England and Wales. However it is difficult to identify and it has only been recorded on a few occasions.

Very rare (2). In northern Lancashire it is believed that *D. × insignis* was found in a marsh at Middleton (SD45Z) in 2006 (J.M.N.) and probably in an old gravel pit at Borwick (SD57B) in 2009 (A. Gendle).

Dactylorhiza purpurella (T. & T.A. Stephenson) Soó

Northern Marsh-orchid

Oceanic Boreal-montane element.

Northern Marsh-orchid is a tuberous rooted perennial species found in neutral or base-rich marshes, fens, damp grasslands and dune slacks (BH11). It is found in Scotland, Ireland, Wales and northern England with a few localities further south.

Occasional (25). In northern Lancashire *D. purpurella* is found mostly in the north of the area with occasional localities elsewhere. It often grows in post-industrial sites. Wheldon and Wilson (1907) recorded Northern Marsh-orchid in fewer than ten sites in VC 60 suggesting a slight increase over the last 100 years. However although it readily colonizes post-industrial sites it then disappears as plant succession occurs. Overall its distribution is probably stable both locally and nationally.

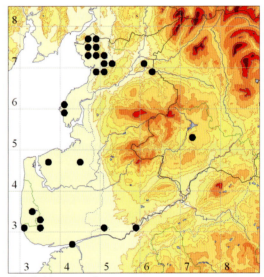

Dactylorhiza purpurella

Neotinea ustulata (L.) R.M. Bateman, Pridgeon & M.W. Chase

Burnt Orchid

European Temperate element.

Burnt Orchid is a tuberous rooted perennial herb found on grazed chalk and limestone grassland usually on south facing slopes (BH7). It is found in England and Wales.

Extinct. In northern Lancashire Burnt Orchid was found at Silverdale and in the Over Kellet neighbourhood (Wheldon and Wilson, 1907) and at Carnforth c. 1830 (Fielding MS). It was probably last seen at the east end of Kellet Seed Wood (SD56Z) in the 1930s or 1940s (France, 1930s). There have been considerable losses nationally ('New Atlas').

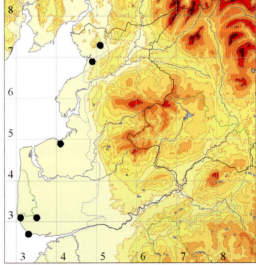

Anacamptis pyramidalis

Anacamptis pyramidalis (L.) Rich.   Pyramidal Orchid

European Southern-temperate element.

Pyramidal Orchid is a tuberous rooted perennial herb found in well-drained calcareous grasslands and on sand dunes (BH7). It occurs in England, Wales and Ireland but it is confined to coastal areas in Scotland.

Rare (6). In northern Lancashire early records were from Stodday in c. 1831 (Fielding MS), Caton in 1862 (W.H.; LIV), Blackpool (Thornber, 1837) and from the Lytham and Yealand areas (Wheldon and Wilson, 1907). Since 1964 it has been found on the sand dunes at Lytham St Anne's (SD33A) in 2007 (E.F.G.) and SD32I in 1998 & 2000 (C.F. & N.J.S.), Peel clay pits (SD33K) in 2003 (M.S.), in amenity land at Pilling (SD44E) in 2002 (B. Dyson), Fairhaven (SD32I) in 2000 (M.J.), Warton (SD57B) in 2008 (P.J. and J. Hickling) and Carnforth (SD46Z) in 2010 (B. Yorke). Overall its distribution is stable in northern Lancashire but it is often ephemeral in its appearance. Nationally whilst the 'New Atlas' considered its distribution stable 'Local Change' reported a significant increase since 1987.

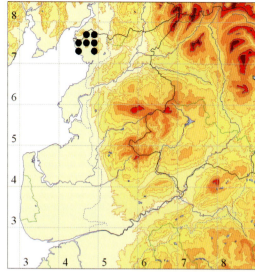
Anacamptis morio

Anacamptis morio (L.) R.M. Bateman, Pridgeon & M.W. Chase
       Green-winged Orchid

European Temperate element.

Green-winged Orchid is a tuberous rooted perennial species found in neutral or base-rich pastures and other grasslands and heaths (BH6, 7). It is found in England, Wales, Ireland and southern Scotland.

Rare (7). Since 1964 *A. morio* has been confined to limestone pastures around Morecambe Bay in northern Lancashire. However Wheldon and Wilson (1907) reported sites elsewhere including the Heysham peninsula, Pilling, near the Crook O' Lune, Cottam, Lea and Thornley. Clearly its distribution has become more restricted in northern Lancashire during the last 100 years and it has been lost from all but one of its post 1964 sites probably due to nutrient enrichment. Today it is confined to one site at Silverdale (SD47M). It has also declined nationally ('New Atlas').

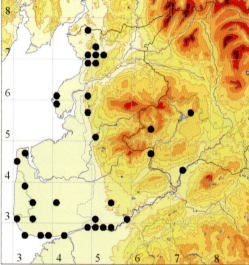
Ophrys apifera

Ophrys apifera Huds.   Bee Orchid

Submediterranean-Subatlantic element.

Bee Orchid is a tuberous rooted perennial herb found in open habitats on well-drained, calcareous soils. It occurs in a range of habitats including sand dunes and ruderal sites (BH7). It is found in England, Wales and Ireland.

Occasional (34). It is not clear when Bee Orchid was first recorded in northern Lancashire. Ashfield (1864) recorded it from Silverdale but Petty (1902) had not seen it and Wheldon and Wilson (1907) knew of no localities in VC 60. The first confirmed records were from three localities on the sand dunes in 1943 and 1946 (Whellan, 1948). Since 1964 it has become increasingly frequent although disappearing from sites as plant succession occurs and colonizing others. It is found in scattered lowland localities throughout northern Lancashire. Nationally it has increased by spreading northwards and westwards from its former centre of distribution in south-eastern England.

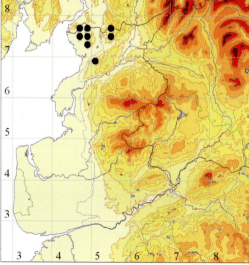
Ophrys insectifera

Ophrys insectifera L.   Fly Orchid

European Temperate element.

This is a shade tolerant, tuberous rooted herb found on calcareous soils in open deciduous woodland and woodland margins. In Ireland and Anglesey it also occurs in calcareous flushes and fens (BH1, 7, 11). Fly Orchid is found in England, Wales and Ireland.

Rare (8). In northern Lancashire it has been found on limestone around Morecambe Bay and at Dalton. However there have only been a few recent records. It was last seen at Gait Barrows N.N.R. (SD47X) in 2010 (J.M.N.), on Warton Crag (SD47W) in 2000 (Anon) and at Trowbarrow Quarry (SD47X) in 2009 (A. Kitchen). Although Fly Orchid has always been rare it is thought that it is declining and close to extinction in northern Lancashire. There have been considerable losses nationally ('New Atlas').

IRIDACEAE   IRIS FAMILY

Sisyrinchium montanum Greene

American Blue-eyed-grass

Neophyte. *S. montanum* is a native of North America but it is widely naturalised in central Europe. It has been cultivated in Britain since 1693 and was known in the wild by 1871. However it has been confused with *S. bermudiana* L., which may be a native species in Ireland as well as in North America. It is likely that most if not all material referred to this species in Britain is *S. montanum* (Stace, 1997; 'New Atlas'). It is found in scattered localities mostly in western Britain.

Very rare (3). In northern Lancashire *S. montanum* was first recorded on a railway bank near Preston in 1900 (H.B.; NMW; Preston Scientific Society, 1903) and then not until it was found in a field on sandy ground at Blackpool (SD33E) in 1966 (A.E.R.; LIV) and from a quarry at Carnforth (SD47V) in 2009 (D.P.E.). It was also found on sand dunes at Lytham St Anne's (SD33A) in the 1980s (M.J.).

Iris germanica L.   Bearded Iris

Neophyte. Bearded Iris is a rhizomatous perennial herb that is probably of hybrid origin but its parentage is obscure. It has been grown in gardens since Viking times but it was not known in the wild until 1905. There are many cultivars and it is a popular garden plant but it is often thrown out and may then become established in ruderal habitats. It is found in scattered localities in Britain and very rarely in Ireland.

Very rare (4). Bearded iris was found at Freckleton (SD42J) in 1999 (E.F.G.), on the sand dunes at Fairhaven (SD32I) in 1999 and 2003 (E.F.G.), on sand dunes at Lytham St Anne's (SD33A) in 1999 (E.F.G.) and at Silverdale (SD47S) in 2000 (C.B.W.).

Iris pseudacorus L.   Yellow Iris

European Southern-temperate element.

Yellow Iris is a rhizomatous perennial herb found in wet meadows, wet woods, fens and at the margins of lakes and ponds and in ditches etc. (BH11). It is found throughout the British Isles.

Common (261). In northern Lancashire Yellow Iris is found in the west of the region and in river valleys further east. Its distribution locally is stable but nationally it has spread since 1987 ('Local Change').

Iris foetidissima L.   Stinking Iris

Suboceanic Southern-temperate element but probably a neophyte in northern Lancashire.

Stinking Iris is a perennial herb found in hedge banks and in woodlands as a native species in southern England and parts of Wales. However it is introduced in Scotland, Ireland and in many places elsewhere in England and Wales, including northern England. It is often difficult to distinguish between native and introduced populations.

Rare (8). *I. foetidissima* was first found at Lytham (SD32T) and Peel Hill (SD33L) both in 2003 (C.F. & N.J.S.). Subsequently it has been found in a few other localities in the west of the region. Nationally there has been a considerable extension of its range ('Local Change') since 1987, which may be a combination of natural spread and garden escapes.

Crocus vernus (L.) Hill   Spring Crocus

Neophyte. Spring Crocus is a native of upland and montane areas of central and southern Europe. It was introduced into British cultivation before 1600 and was first recorded in the wild in 1763. It is found in scattered localities in Britain but it is unevenly recorded.

Rare (11). In northern Lancashire *C. vernus* was first recorded from Fulwood in 1965 (A.E.R.). Subsequently it was recorded from scattered localities in VC 60, often in churchyards. It is likely that most records are for the coloured *C. vernus* ssp. *vernus*. It is also possible that some records are for *C. tommasinianus* Herb. with which *C. vernus* is easily confused.

Crocus flavus Weston × **C. angustifolius** Weston (**C. × luteus** Lam.)   Yellow Crocus

Neophyte. Yellow Crocus is a hybrid of garden origin and is often grown in gardens as a sterile cultivar 'Golden Yellow'. Its parents have been grown in British gardens since the sixteenth century and *C. × luteus* was first recorded in the wild in 1848. It is easily confused with other taxa and was often recorded as *C. flavus*. It is found in scattered localities in Britain but it is under recorded.

Very rare (3). In northern Lancashire *C. × stellaris* (recorded as *C. flavus*) was found on waste ground in Preston in 1965 (E.H.; LANC), in Garstang (SD44W) in 1965 (A.E.R.) and in small quantity in the centre of Newton-in-Bowland village (SD65V) in 2009 (E.F. & B.D.G.).

Crocus nudiflorus Sm.   Autumn Crocus

Neophyte. Autumn Crocus is a native of south-western France and northern Spain. It was cultivated in Britain before 1600 and was first recorded in the wild in 1738. It is found in meadows, pastures, amenity grasslands and on roadsides in scattered localities in Britain but most records are from southern Lancashire and from northern parts of central England. It was sometimes grown as a substitute for saffron.

Very rare (3). In northern Lancashire *C. nudiflorus* was first recorded from near Goosnargh (Wheldon and Wilson, 1907). It was also recorded from Fairhaven (SD32N) in 1984, 1986 & 2003 (C.F. & N.J.S.), Lytham St Anne's L.N.R. (SD33A) in 2001 (M.J.) and from Barton (SD53I) in 2000 where it had been known for many years (M.E.). It is possible that this latter record is the 'near Goosnargh' reported by Wheldon and Wilson (1907).

Gladiolus communis L.   Eastern Gladiolus

Neophyte. *G. communis* is a native of the Mediterranean region and was introduced into British gardens by 1596. It was recorded in the wild by 1862 and has been found mostly in south-western England and the Isle of Man with a few scattered records from elsewhere in England and Wales. The corms are frost sensitive ensuring that it only persists in frost free areas.

Very rare (1). In northern Lancashire it is thought that it was this species that was found on waste ground between Lancaster and Morecambe (SD46L; Livermore and Livermore, 1987).

Crocosmia paniculata (Klatt) Goldblatt   Aunt-Eliza

Neophyte. Aunt-Eliza is a native of southern Africa and was cultivated in Britain by 1904. It was recorded in the wild in 1961 and today occurs in scattered localities in the British Isles but especially in western areas. However it is believed that most plants assigned to *C. paniculata* are the hybrid between this species and *C. pottsii* (Stace, 2010).

Rare (6). *C. paniculata* was first found in northern Lancashire by the Lancaster Canal at Slyne-with-Hest (SD46T) in 1988 (Livermore and Livermore, 1989). Subsequently it has been found in a few scattered localities in VC 60.

Crocosmia pottsii (Macnab ex Baker) N.E. Br. × C. aurea (Hook.) Planch. (C. × crocosmiiflora (Lemoine) N.E. Br.)   Montbretia

Neophyte. Montbretia is a hybrid between two South African parents but it is of garden origin. It was raised in France in 1880 and reached Britain the same year. It was first recorded in the wild in 1911. It is a common and vigorous garden plant that is often discarded and then becomes established in ruderal habitats. It may be found anywhere in the British Isles but mostly in lowland areas.

Frequent (106). In northern Lancashire it was not recorded by Perring and Walters (1962) but it was found frequently in 1963 and 1964 when tetrad recording started in the region. Today it is found in scattered localities throughout the area.

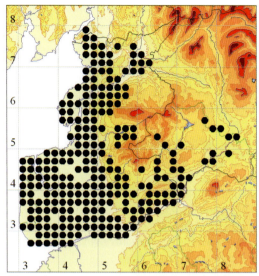

Iris pseudacorus

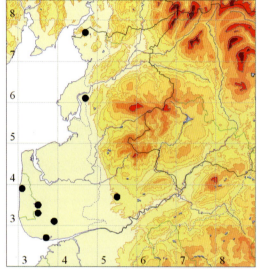

Iris foetidissima

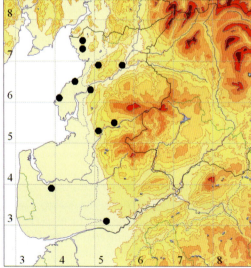

Crocus vernus

XANTHORRHOEACEAE
ASPHODEL FAMILY

Asphodelus fistulosus L.   Hollow-leaved Asphodel

Neophyte. This is a rare Mediterranean species found introduced with wool and grain into a few British localities.

In northern Lancashire Bailey (1908) found it frequently on the sand dunes at St Anne's in 1906 and 1907, where it was probably introduced with grain.

Hemerocallis fulva (L.) L.   Orange Day-lily

Neophyte. *H. fulva* is a cultivated plant of garden origin and was grown in British gardens before 1596. It was found in the wild by 1905 (but was probably present much earlier). Included within this taxon are other garden hybrids and most records are probably of a sterile triploid hybrid (Clement and Foster, 1994). Orange Day-lily is particularly frequent in southern England but there are records from scattered localities throughout Britain and the Isle of Man.

Very rare (4). In northern Lancashire Orange Day-lily was found at Silverdale (SD47S; Livermore and Livermore, 1987), Slyne-with-Hest (SD46T) and in the Middleton/Overton area (SD45D) both Livermore and Livermore (1990a) and on the banks of the R. Lune at Lancaster (SD46X) where it had been known since 1977 (K.R.).

Hemerocallis lilioasphodelus L.   Yellow Day-lily

Neophyte. Yellow Day-lily is a native of China and was introduced into British gardens by 1596. It was recorded in the wild by 1908. It is naturalised in woodlands and ruderal habitats mostly on the western side of Britain. It spreads mostly vegetatively but individual populations may be long-lived.

Very rare (1). In northern Lancashire one established plant was found near an old sand pit at Blackpool (SD33E) in 1966 (R. Kilby & E.J.H.).

Kniphofia uvaria (L.) Oken   Red-hot-poker
Kniphofia × praecox Baker   Greater Red-hot-poker

Neophytes. There has been considerable confusion between these two taxa and *K. × praecox* probably includes a range of hybrids. *K. uvaria* was cultivated in Britain by 1705 but was not recorded in the wild until 1950 whereas *K. × praecox* was first cultivated in Britain in 1862 and recorded in the wild by 1957. *K. uvaria* is a native of China but *K. × praecox* is a hybrid of garden origin. Red-hot-pokers are found in ruderal habitats and on sand dunes throughout Britain.

Very rare (4). Red-hot-pokers were recorded in northern Lancashire from Heysham (SD46A; Livermore and Livermore, 1987) and in two localities at Lytham St Anne's (SD33A, 32E) since 1996 (C.F. & N.J.S.; E.F.G.). A plant was also found at Conder Green (SD45M) in 2010 (E.F.G.). Plants on the Lytham St Anne's L.N.R. (SD33A) were identified as *K. × praecox* (Bradford Botany Group).

Phormium tenax J.R. & G. Forst.   New Zealand Flax

Neophyte. New Zealand Flax is a long-lived, evergreen perennial introduced into British cultivation in 1789. It was first recorded in the wild in 1898. It was grown as a fibre crop in a few places but today it is increasingly used in amenity planting schemes. It is mostly found in western Ireland, southern England and the Isle of Man.

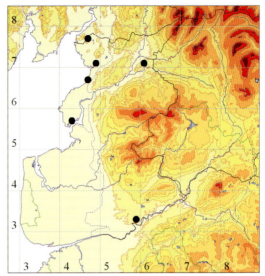
Crocosmia paniculata

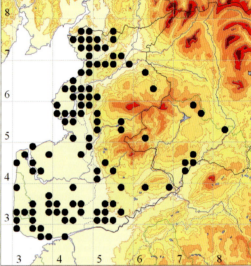
Crocosmia × crocosmiiflora

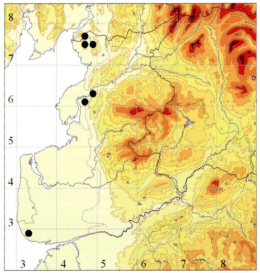
Allium schoenoprasum

Very rare (1). In northern Lancashire a few plants were found on the northern side of Fleetwood Golf Course (SD34D) in 1998 (E.F.G.).

AMARYLLIDACEAE   DAFFODIL FAMILY

Allium schoenoprasum L.   Chives

Circumpolar Boreo-arctic Montane element but a neophyte in northern Lancashire. It is found as a native species in a few British localities but most populations are derived from garden outcasts and are found in ruderal habitats. It is found in scattered localities in the British Isles.

Rare (6). In northern Lancashire Chives was first recorded from Eaves Wood, Silverdale (SD47S) in 1973 (L.A.L.). Subsequently it was found in other localities in the northwest of the area and at Lytham St Anne's.

Allium cepa L.   Onion

Neophyte. The origin of Onion is uncertain but it was known to the Ancient Egyptians. It is a bulbous perennial species and was cultivated in Britain by 995. It is a common vegetable and there are many cultivars. It was first recorded in the wild in Britain in 1927 and today it has been recorded from scattered localities in Britain but always as a casual.

Very rare (1). The only record from northern Lancashire is from Blackpool tip (SD33M) in c. 1966 (A.E.R.).

Allium neapolitanum Cirillo   Neapolitan Garlic

Neophyte. Neapolitan Garlic is a native of south-western Europe and the Mediterranean region. It was introduced into British cultivation in 1823. It is a popular garden plant and was recorded from the wild by 1864. Today it is found mostly in southern England and is probably increasing.

Very rare (1). In northern Lancashire *A. neapolitanum* was found on a roadside at Cottam (SD53B) in 2006 (C.F. & N.J.S.).

Allium triquetrum L.   Three-cornered Garlic

Neophyte. This is a native of the western and central Mediterranean region. It was introduced into British cultivation by 1759 and was established in the wild by 1849. It is naturalised in many places in southern and western Britain and eastern Ireland.

Rare (8). In northern Lancashire it was first found by a wooded path side at Freckleton (SD42J) in 1999 (E.F.G.). Subsequently it was recorded from a few other localities in the west of the region.

Allium paradoxum (M. Bieb.) G. Don   Few-flowered Garlic

Neophyte. This bulbous perennial is a native of the Caucasus and Iran and was introduced into British cultivation in 1827. It was first recorded in the wild near Edinburgh in 1863 where

today there is a concentration of recent records. It is also frequent in south-eastern England but there are scattered localities throughout the British Isles.

Very rare (4). In northern Lancashire it was first recorded from a roadside bank at Westby-with-Plumptons (SD33K) in 1989 from where it had been known for many years and from sand dunes at Fairhaven (SD32I) in 1994 where it was still present in 2011 (M.J.). It has also been recorded from other sites in Lytham St Anne's (SD32N, P) since 1996 (all C.F. & N.J.S.).

Allium ursinum L.   Ramsons

European Temperate element.

Ramsons is a perennial species found in moist woodlands and woodland edge habitats (BH1) throughout most of the British Isles.

Common (244). In northern Lancashire Ramsons is found in most of the region being absent only from intensively farmed areas and moorlands. It often carpets the woodland floor with white flowers in spring (see Plate 2.3). Its distribution in northern Lancashire is stable but nationally there has been an increase since 1987 ('Local Change').

Allium oleraceum L.   Field Garlic

European Temperate element.

Field Garlic is a bulbous perennial herb usually found on steeply sloping calcareous grasslands and on sunny banks in river flood plains (BH7). Whilst it occurs in scattered localities in England and eastern Scotland most records are from northern England and the northern midlands as well as in the Severn Valley.

Rare (7). In northern Lancashire Field Garlic was recorded from Hawes Water (SD47T) in 1814 (J.E. Bicheno; SWA) and from the banks of the R. Greta near Wrayton (SD67B) in 1901 (Wheldon and Wilson, 1901). The Wrayton material was identified by Wheldon and Wilson (1907) as var. *complanatum* Fr. Since 1964 it has been recorded in a few places in the north of the region especially on limestone, also Conder Green (SD45N) and near St Michael's (SD44Q). Apart from the Wrayton locality material has not been identified at the variety level. Field Garlic's distribution is thought to be largely stable locally and nationally although the 'New Atlas' reported some losses.

Allium carinatum L.   Keeled Garlic

Neophyte. *A. carinatum* is a native of central and south-eastern Europe. It was cultivated in Britain by 1789 and found in the wild by 1806. It is frequently grown in gardens and occurs in scattered localities throughout most of the British Isles.

Rare (8). Keeled Garlic was first found in northern Lancashire at Galgate (SD45S) in 1948 (Garlick, 1957b). Subsequently it was found in widely scattered localities in the region.

Allium paniculatum L. ssp. **paniculatum**   Pale Garlic

Neophyte. Pale Garlic is a native of the Mediterranean region and was first recorded in the British Isles, as ssp. *fuscum* Waldst. & Kit., from Cornwall in 2004 where it is naturalised. It is widely grown in gardens.

Very rare (1). In northern Lancashire *A. paniculatum* ssp. *paniculatum* was found near a road junction at Conder Green (SD45T) in 2010 (M.W. & B.A.T.). It has possibly been overlooked in previous years and possibly mistaken for *A. carinatum* that occurs in the area.

Allium sativum L.   Garlic

Neophyte. The origin of this bulbous perennial herb is unknown but it was cultivated by the Ancient Egyptians. It was first grown in Britain by 995 but it was not recorded in the wild until 1937. It has been recorded from a few scattered localities in the British Isles.

Very rare (1). In northern Lancashire Garlic was found apparently naturalised at the top of a salt marsh in Lancaster (SD46R) in 1990 (Livermore and Livermore, 1992).

[Allium ampeloprasum L. var. **babingtonii** (Borrer) Syme   Wild Leek

The record for this in the 10km square SD32 in the 'New Atlas' was an error for *A. scorodoprasum*.]

Allium scorodoprasum L.   Sand Leek

European Temperate element.

Sand Leek is a bulbous perennial species found in rough grassland (BH1, 3, 6) and ruderal habitats in northern England, central and southern Scotland with a few introductions elsewhere in the British Isles.

Occasional (20). There are very few pre 1964 records for Sand Leek in northern Lancashire. However it is believed it may have occurred in meadows near Preston in 1700 (C. Leigh in Wheldon and Wilson, 1907) and it was found at the edge of a field below Warton Crag in 1908 (Wheldon and Wilson, 1925). Since 1964 it has been found in a number of localities in the north of northern Lancashire as well as at Lytham St Anne's and in Lancashire VC 64. Its distribution is probably stable nationally.

Allium vineale L.   Wild Onion

European Temperate element.

This is a bulbous perennial herb of dry, neutral or calcareous soils and is found in grasslands and marginal habitats (BH3, 6, 7). It is found in much of the British Isles except northern Scotland and upland areas.

Occasional (29). *A. vineale* is mostly a coastal species in northern Lancashire but extends inland in the Lune and Ribble valleys. Wheldon and Wilson (1907) recognised *A. vineale* L. var. *compactum* (Thuill.) Boreau as occurring on both banks of the R. Keer near Warton. They knew of approximately six localities for Wild Onion suggesting that in northern Lancashire it has extended its range over the last 100 years. This expansion is reflected nationally since 1987 ('Local Change').

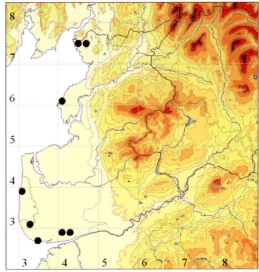

Allium triquetrum

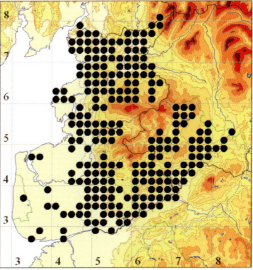

Allium ursinum

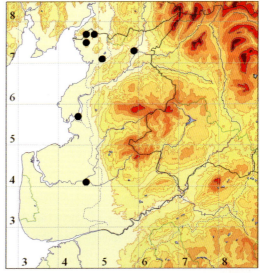

Allium oleraceum

Leucojum aestivum L.   Summer Snowflake

European Southern-temperate element but a neophyte in northern Lancashire. *L. aestivum* ssp. *aestivum* is a native species in some wet meadows in southern England and Ireland and is sometimes grown in gardens. However *L. aestivum* L. ssp. *pulchellum* (Salisb.) Briq. is a common garden plant first found in British cultivation in 1596. The two subspecies are frequently confused and it is not clear which subspecies occur as introductions in scattered localities throughout most of the British Isles.

Very rare (2). In northern Lancashire Summer Snowflake was found at Lytham St Anne's (SD33A) in 1997 (C.F. & N.J.S.) and in woodland on limestone pavement adjacent to gardens in Silverdale (SD47S) in 2007 (E.F. & B.D.G.).

Leucojum vernum L.   Spring Snowflake

Neophyte with a European Temperate distribution. Spring Snowflake was cultivated in Britain by 1596 and was recorded in the wild by 1866. It has been found in scattered localities in Britain with a single Irish locality.

In northern Lancashire it was found in the grounds of Leagram Hall (SD64H) in *c.* 1960 (Anon., 1983).

Galanthus nivalis L.   Snowdrop

Neophyte with a European Southern-temperate distribution. This is a bulbous perennial herb of moist woodlands and woodland edge habitats first cultivated in Britain by 1597. It was not recorded in the wild until 1778. Today it occurs commonly in England and Wales and in lowland areas of Scotland but it is much less frequent in Ireland. It often forms extensive carpets of white flowers in February in estate parklands and churchyards.

Frequent (145). It is not known when Snowdrop was first found in the wild in northern Lancashire, as Wheldon and Wilson (1907) knew it as a common and widespread species. Today it occurs throughout the area but especially in the more wooded parts of the region. However it is usually found near habitation and it is often planted for amenity in churchyards and on village greens etc. where it naturalises to form extensive patches. *G. nivalis* forma *pleniflorus* P.D. Sell is naturalised in woodlands on the Bailrigg estate of the University of Lancaster, Scotforth (SD45Y, Z) where it was seen in 2008 (E.F. & B.D.G.). It was also found in the centre of Newton-in-Bowland village (SD65V) in 2009 (E.F. & B.D.G.)

Narcissus poeticus L.   Pheasant's-eye Daffodil

Neophyte. It is found as a native species in the mountains of southern Europe. This bulbous perennial herb was cultivated in Britain by 1538 and was known in the wild by 1795. It is frequently grown in gardens and the bulbs are often thrown away when they may become established in ruderal habitats for a few years. Pheasant's-eye Daffodil is found in scattered localities in Britain but it is unevenly recorded.

Occasional (18). In northern Lancashire *N. poeticus* was first found in a meadow at Out Rawcliffe (Pearson, 1874). It was then not recorded until the 1940s or 1950s when it was established at Fulwood (SD53K) on waste land. The bulbs had been discarded following intensive cultivation in an adjacent nursery garden for Easter markets. Since 1964 it has been found in scattered localities mostly in the north and west of the area.

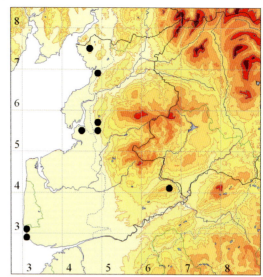
Allium carinatum

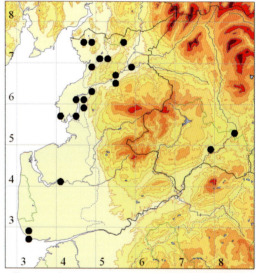
Allium scorodoprasum

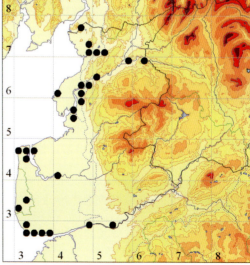
Allium vineale

Narcissus L.   Daffodils

This is a genus of bulbous perennial herbs found in a variety of woodlands, marginal and ruderal habitats. Included here are numerous species and cultivars not included in *N. poeticus* or *N. pseudonarcissus* ssp. *pseudonarcissus*. All are introduced as amenity plantings or are derived from bulbs thrown out after cultivation. The distribution of the genus is centred on the Mediterranean region and it is most diverse in south-western Europe. However its long history of cultivation and undocumented hybridisation renders its taxonomy almost intractable. Cultivated daffodils are found in the wild throughout the British Isles.

Occasional (130). It is not known when cultivated daffodils were first found wild in northern Lancashire. Although some early records for *N. pseudonarcissus* (Wheldon and Wilson, 1907) were probably for plants of garden origin it is only since 1964 that tetrad localities for garden plants growing in the wild have been noted. They usually occur in ruderal and marginal habitats and large trumpet flowered plants are found on roadsides. Recently many thousands of bulbs have been planted as part of amenity planting schemes. Daffodils are found throughout the area.

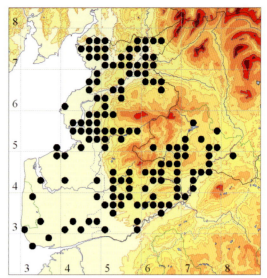

Galanthus nivalis

Narcissus pseudonarcissus L. ssp. **pseudonarcissus**   Daffodil

Suboceanic Temperate element.

Daffodil is a bulbous perennial herb found in deciduous woodlands and scrubby pastures (BH3). Its status in the British Isles is unclear but it is generally regarded as native in semi-natural woodlands in England and Wales but introduced in Ireland and Scotland. However it is also introduced in many English localities ('New Atlas'), and Anderton (2002) states that *N. pseudonarcissus* is a native of Spain and France and was introduced into Britain in Roman times becoming naturalised in a few areas including north-western England.

Occasional (38). In northern Lancashire *N. pseudonarcissus* ssp. *pseudonarcissus* has been confused with garden cultivars but during the last ten years efforts were made to elucidate more clearly its distribution. This follows the present and former distribution of ancient woodlands and within this range it may occur abundantly, e.g. in Silverdale woodlands and in parts of the Wyre and Brock valleys. Daffodil's distribution in northern Lancashire is probably stable but it can be quickly lost by inappropriate management, e.g. grazing. It is likely that there have been some losses nationally ('New Atlas').

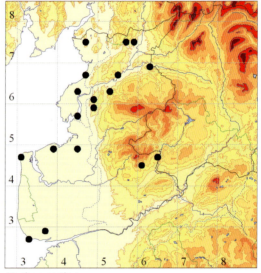

Narcissus poeticus

ASPARAGACEAE   ASPARAGUS FAMILY

Convallaria majalis L.   Lily-of-the-valley

European Boreo-temperate element.

This is a rhizomatous perennial herb found in free-draining, nutrient poor and usually calcareous soils in woodlands (BH1, 7). It is also grown in gardens from where it escapes into the wild. It occurs throughout the British Isles but it is rare in Ireland where it is thought to be introduced.

Occasional (19). In northern Lancashire records from the Lancaster area, Lytham St Anne's and Kirkham, although often naturalised, are thought to be garden escapes but all other localities are probably native populations. Nationally its native distribution is thought to be stable but it is

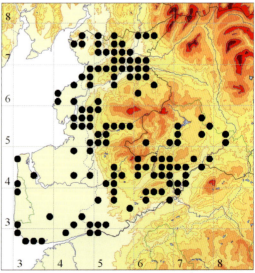

Narcissus agg.

often difficult to distinguish between native and introduced populations. In northern Lancashire the native distribution of *C. majalis* is probably stable although Wheldon and Wilson (1907) did not record the Lune valley localities.

Polygonatum multiflorum (L.) All.   Solomon's-seal

European Temperate element.

Solomon's-seal is a rhizomatous perennial herb found in woodlands and woodland edge habitats usually on calcareous substrates (BH1). It is found in England, Wales, Scotland and in the north of Ireland but many populations are thought to be garden escapes. It is also sometimes recorded in error for the hybrid *P. × hybridum*.

Occasional (23). The status of *P. multiflorum* in northern Lancashire is unclear. At least some populations are introductions, e.g. at Lytham St Anne's, whilst others in woodlands in the northwest of the region are probably mostly native. However there are a number of localities in central VC 60, which could be either relic native populations or long established introductions. Overall it is likely that the distribution of Solomon's-seal is stable locally and nationally.

Polygonatum multiflorum × P. odoratum
(P. × hybridum Brügger)   Garden Solomon's-seal

Garden Solomon's-seal is a hybrid of garden origin and has been found in the wild since at least 1867. It is a common and vigorous garden plant that is often thrown out. It is a rhizomatous herb that readily colonizes marginal and ruderal habitats. Today it is found in many parts of the British Isles.

Occasional (31). In northern Lancashire *P. × hybridum* was first recorded from a hedge bank at Barnacre-with-Bonds (SD54C) in 1966 (Preston Scientific Society). Today it is found in scattered localities throughout northern Lancashire although there are few records from Lancashire VC 64.

Polygonatum odoratum (Mill.) Druce   Angular Soloman's-seal

Eurasian Temperate element.

Angular Solomon's-seal is a rhizomatous perennial herb of ancient ash woods often growing on limestone pavements (BH1, 16). As a native species it is found in north-western England, the English Peak District and around the Severn estuary. It occurs occasionally elsewhere as an introduction.

Rare (6). In northern Lancashire Angular Solomon's-seal is confined to the limestone areas around Morecambe Bay and on Dalton Crags. Its distribution locally and nationally is stable.

Ornithogalum umbellatum L. ssp. campestre Rouy
                                        Star-of-Bethlehem

Neophyte with a European Southern-temperate distribution. This bulbous perennial species was cultivated in Britain by 1548 and was recorded in the wild by 1650. *O. umbellatum* is found in most parts of Britain and eastern Ireland. It is believed most records are for ssp. *campestre* but ssp. *umbellatum* occurs in Cambridgeshire and may occur more widely.

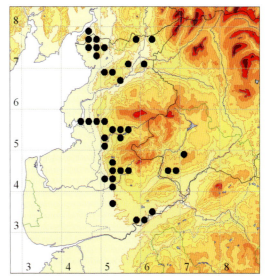

Narcissus pseudonarcissus

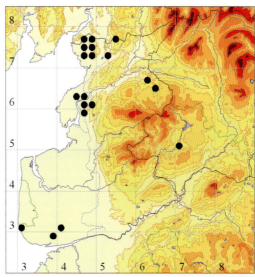

Convallaria majalis

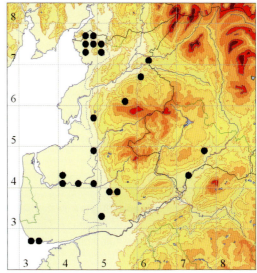

Polygonatum multiflorum

Occasional (32). In northern Lancashire Star-of-Bethlehem was first recorded near Leighton Hall, Yealand Conyers by Jenkinson (1775). Today it is found mostly in the west of northern Lancashire and it is especially frequent on sandy soils at Lytham St Anne's.

Scilla siberica Haw.   Siberian Squill

Neophyte. Siberian Squill is a native of southern Russia, Turkey and the Caucasus. It was introduced in 1796 and it is a popular garden plant. However it was not recorded from the wild until 1968 but it is now recorded from several scattered localities throughout Britain.

Very rare (1). In northern Lancashire *S. siberica* was found at two sites in Lytham St Anne's (SD32I) in 2006 (C.F. & N.J.S.).

[Scilla verna Huds.   Spring Squill

There is a record attributed to A. Hoyer from Poulton-le-Fylde in the autumn issue of the *Wildflower Magazine* for 1993. This is probably either an error or a short-lived garden escape.]

Scilla forbesii (Baker) Speta   Glory-of the-snow

Neophyte. This is a bulbous perennial herb of free-draining soils in ruderal habitats where it may become naturalised. Glory-of-the-snow is a native of the mountains of western and south-western Turkey. It has been cultivated in British gardens since 1877 but it was not recorded in the wild until 1968. Today it is found in scattered localities in Britain.

Very rare (1). In northern Lancashire *S. forbesii* was found on the coast at Silverdale (SD47M) in 1974 (Livermore and Livermore, 1987) when it was recorded as *S. luciliae*. It was still present in 2009 (J.Cl.)

Hyacinthoides non-scripta (L.) Chouard ex Rothm.   Bluebell

Oceanic Temperate element.

Bluebell is a bulbous perennial species occurring abundantly in a variety of deciduous woodlands and woodland edge habitats. It may also grow in the open on hillsides often under Bracken but in these situations it is likely to be a relic of former woodlands (BH1, 9). It is found in most of the British Isles.

Common (330). *H. non-scripta* is found throughout northern Lancashire except in intensively farmed areas and on the fells. It frequently carpets woodland floors providing a fine spectacle in spring (see Plate 2.1). However the presence of *H. non-scripta* × *H. hispanica* was not appreciated for many years and it is likely that many records in the west of the region at least are for this hybrid. Despite the confusion the distribution of Bluebell is thought to be stable locally and nationally.

Hyacinthoides non-scripta × H. hispanica (Mill.) Rothm.
(H. × massartiana Geer.)   Hybrid Bluebell

Neophyte. This bulbous perennial hybrid is fertile and it is frequently grown in gardens. It arises naturally in the Iberian Peninsula where the ranges of its parents overlap. It is not clear when it was first cultivated in Britain but it was not recorded in the wild until 1963 and it is only since 1987 that its presence was fully appreciated. It can be difficult to identify as it backcrosses with both parents and in Britain particularly with *H. non-scripta* so that plants ranging from *H. non-scripta* to *H. hispanica* may be

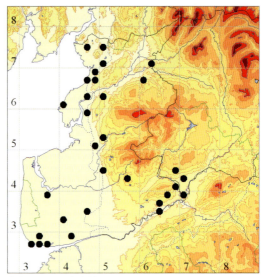

Polygonatum × hybridum

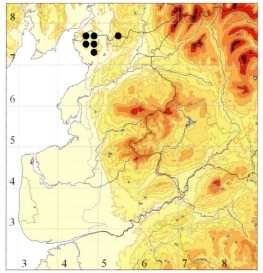

Polygonatum odoratum

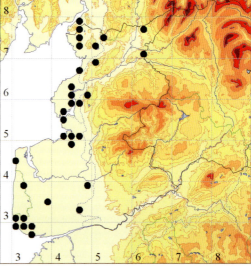

Ornithogalum umbellatum

found. In Britain wild populations of Hybrid Bluebell probably originate from garden throw outs. It occurs throughout the British Isles but it is often overlooked. However the most recent research suggests that what has been regarded as *H. hispanica* in the British Isles is not the same as the Iberian *H. hispanica,* first recorded in the wild in Britain in 1909. It now appears that *H. hispanica* does not occur in the British Isles and that all records formerly attributed to this are hybrids of some kind.

Frequent (127). Hybrid Bluebell was first recognised in northern Lancashire by Livermore and Livermore (1989) from the Lancaster Canal at Slyne-with-Hest (SD46S). However what was thought to be *H. hispanica* and now known to be *H. × massartiana* was recorded from sand dunes at Lytham in 1965 but it was probably naturalised in the area long before this. Today the hybrid is found mostly in the west of northern Lancashire and in the Lune, Ribble and Hodder valleys.

Hyacinthus orientalis L.   Hyacinth

Neophyte. Hyacinth is a native of south-western Asia but numerous cultivars have originated in cultivation. It was grown in Britain by 1596 and it is a popular garden and house plant. Although bulbs are often thrown away after flowering it was not recorded in the wild until 1957. Most records are from southern England but there are scattered records from elsewhere in Britain.

Very rare (2). Hyacinth was found at Out Rawcliffe (SD44C) in 1996 (C.F. & N.J.S.) and on the sand dunes at Lytham St Anne's (SD33A) in 2003 (E.F.G.).

Muscari armeniacum Leichtlin ex Baker   Garden Grape-hyacinth

Neophyte. Garden Grape-hyacinth is a native of the Balkans, Turkey and the Caucasus. It has been cultivated in Britain since 1878 and was recorded in the wild by 1892. It has been frequently confused with *M. neglectum* Guss. ex Ten., native in parts of East Anglia, but it is by far the commonest Grape-hyacinth in cultivation and in the wild. *M. armeniacum* is a bulbous perennial and discarded bulbs readily become naturalised; it also spreads rapidly by seed. Garden Grape-hyacinth may be found anywhere in the British Isles.

Occasional (18). In northern Lancashire *M. armeniacum* was recorded as *M. neglectum* and it is only recently that the mistake was appreciated. It is not thought that *M. neglectum* occurs in the area. *M. armeniacum* was first found in northern Lancashire at Silverdale in 1898 (Anon, BON) but it was not recorded again until Livermore and Livermore (1987) found it in several localities in Lancaster District. Most records are still from the north of the area but it probably occurs throughout the region in ruderal habitats.

Muscari comosum (L.) Mill.   Tassel Hyacinth

Neophyte. Tassel Hyacinth has a European Southern-temperate distribution and was cultivated in Britain by 1596. It was known from the wild by 1888 and today it is found in scattered localities in England and Wales. Most populations are short-lived but it may become naturalised on sand dunes.

Very rare (2). Tassel Hyacinth was found near the railway at St Anne's (SD32J) in 1965 (A.E.R. and illustrated in Clement, *et al.,* 2005) and on sand dunes at Fairhaven (SD32J) in 2003 (M.C.). It has also been recorded near Marton Mere (SD33M) in 2004 (M.J.).

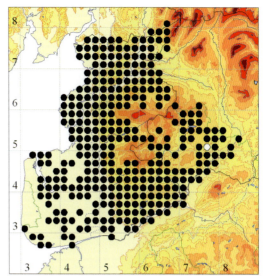

Hyacinthoides non-scripta

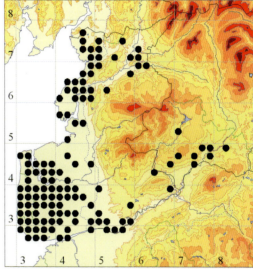

Hyacinthoides × massartiana

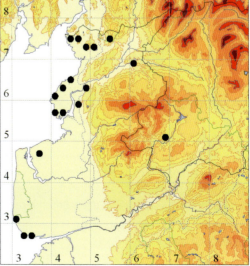

Muscari armeniacum

Asparagus officinalis L.   Garden Asparagus

Archaeophyte with a Eurosiberian Temperate distribution.

Garden Asparagus is a dioecious, rhizomatous perennial herb found in free-draining sandy soils (BH3). It was cultivated in Britain in Roman times and it readily escapes into the wild by bird-dispersed seed. It is found in England and Wales with a few records from Scotland and eastern Ireland.

Rare (8). Garden Asparagus has been grown in Lancashire for many years (Holt, 1795) and it became an important crop on the sandy soils of the Sefton coast. It was cultivated less frequently north of the R. Ribble but it was recorded growing wild on the sandy soils at Lytham St Anne's (Anon, 1829) and Blackpool (Thornber, 1837). Since 1964 it has been found occasionally in the Blackpool and Lytham St Anne's area with an inland record from near Preston. There is also an earlier inland record from Caton in 1942 (J.N.F.).

Ruscus aculeatus L.   Butcher's-broom

Submediterranean-Subatlantic element but a neophyte in northern Lancashire.

Butcher's-broom is a native species of woodlands and marginal habitats in southern England. Further north it is found as a garden escape in similar habitats but in northern England, Scotland and Ireland it is only found occasionally.

Rare (7). In northern Lancashire *R. aculeatus* was first recorded from Salwick in 1901 (H.B.; NMW). Since 1964 it has been found in a few localities in the west of the area.

Cordyline australis (G. Forst.) Endl.   Cabbage-palm

Neophyte. Cabbage-palm is an evergreen shrub or small tree, which is a native of New Zealand. It was introduced into British cultivation in 1823 and was recorded in the wild in 1965. Today it is found mostly in southern and western areas of the British Isles and appears to be increasing. In the Isle of Man, where it has been planted in many areas, it readily reproduces by seed.

Very rare (1). In northern Lancashire it was found planted at the entrance to Carleton Cemetery, Blackpool (SD33J) in 2003 (M.S.) where it readily sets seed. As its natural habitat is a temperate rain forest it is possible that *C. australis* may become established in northern Lancashire especially if winters become milder. However the very low temperatures of December 2010 killed most garden plants.

PONTEDERIACEAE   PICKERELWEED FAMILY

Eichhornia crassipes (C. Martius) Solms-Laub.   Water-Hyacinth

Neophyte. Water-Hyacinth is a native of tropical Brazil and has been introduced into Britain for tropical aquaria. It was found in the wild in the 1980s in Surrey (A.C. Leslie cited by Clement and Foster, 1994) and probably occurs as a casual in a few British localities.

Very rare (1). In northern Lancashire *E. crassipes* was found in a pond at Carleton (SD34F) in 2007 (M.S.).

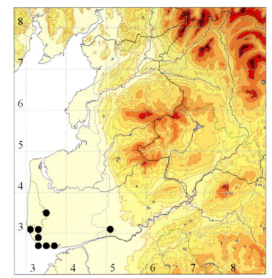

Asparagus officinalis

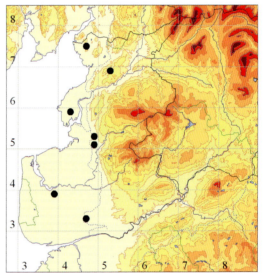

Ruscus aculeatus

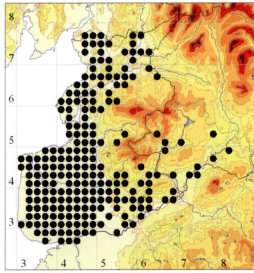

Sparganium erectum

TYPHACEAE   BULRUSH FAMILY

Sparganium erectum L.   Branched Bur-reed

Circumpolar Temperate element.

Branched Bur-reed is an emergent herb, which grows in shallow water (BH11, 13) and is tolerant of eutrophication. It is found in lowland areas of the British Isles.

Frequent (223). In northern Lancashire *S. erectum* occurs in lowland areas so that most records are in the west of the region and in river valleys. Very little work has been done on recording the subspecies as mature fruits ripening late in the season are required for identification. However most plants appear to be *S. erectum* ssp. *microcarpum* (Neuman) Domin. whilst *S. erectum* ssp. *neglectum* (Beeby) K. Richt. has been found in a few places. Although its distribution in northern Lancashire is stable nationally there has been an increase since 1987 ('Local Change').

Sparganium emersum Rehmann   Unbranched Bur-reed

Circumpolar Boreo-temperate element.

Unbranched Bur-reed is found in shallow water in similar places to *S. erectum* (BH13, 14). However whilst occurring throughout the British Isles it is usually less frequent than Branched Bur-reed.

Frequent (94). In northern Lancashire *S. emersum* occurs mostly in the west of the region and especially in the Lancaster Canal where it often fails to flower. Its distribution locally is probably unchanged but nationally the 'New Atlas' and 'Local Change' reported increases.

[Sparganium angustifolium Michx.   Floating Bur-reed

The record reported in the 'New Atlas' for the 10 × 10km square SD46 is probably an error.]

Sparganium natans L.   Least Bur-reed

Circumpolar Boreo-temperate element.

Least Bur-reed grows in shallow, sheltered water at the edges of lakes, ponds and slow moving water. It is found in mesotrophic, highly calcareous to acid waters (BH13). Formerly it was found in much of the British Isles but today it has a more restricted distribution in the west and north.

Very rare (1). In northern Lancashire Wheldon and Wilson (1907) recorded Least Bur-reed from between Carnforth and Nether Kellet; near Borwick; Bank Well, Silverdale and Little Hawes Water. It must also have occurred in Hawes Water (SD47T) where it has been seen at intervals since 1967 (C.J.-P.). Nationally the 'New Atlas' reported extensive losses but further significant losses since 1987 do not appear to have occurred ('Local Change').

Typha latifolia L.   Bulrush

Circumpolar Southern-temperate element.

This tall emergent herb is found in shallow water or on exposed mud at the edges of lakes, ponds, streams and ditches etc. (BH11) usually in nutrient rich sites. It is found in most of the British Isles but it is absent from much of northern Scotland.

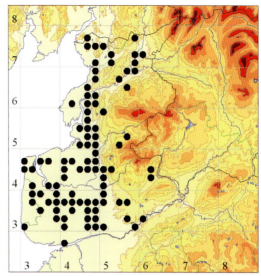

Sparganium emersum

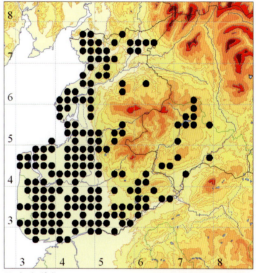

Typha latifolia

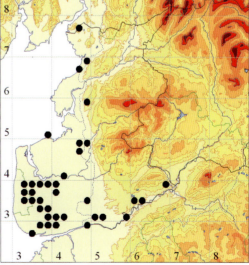

Typha angustifolia

Frequent (191). In northern Lancashire *T. latifolia* occurs mostly in lowland areas but it is also found in Lancashire VC 64 in the upper Hodder valley. Locally its distribution has probably remained stable in lowland areas but the records in Bowland may represent a significant spread. Nationally it has spread considerably since 1987 in the west and north of the British Isles ('Local Change').

Typha latifolia × T. angustifolia (T. × glauca Godr.)

Widespread in Europe and North America.

T. × glauca is a vigorous, rhizomatous perennial herb found in shallow, eutrophic water sometimes in the absence of one parent. It is frequent in England and Wales but occurs more rarely in Scotland and Ireland although it is easily overlooked.

Very rare (1). A single plant was found with both parents nearby in Brockholes Quarry, Preston (SD53Q) in 2006 (E.F.G.).

Typha angustifolia L.   Lesser Bulrush

Eurosiberian Temperate element.

This is a tall rhizomatous perennial herb found in mesotrophic to eutrophic shallow water (BH11). It is found in most of England and eastern Wales but occurs more rarely in Ireland and southern Scotland.

Occasional (37). In northern Lancashire *T. angustifolia* occurs in the west of the area and in the lower Ribble valley with most localities in the Fylde. Wheldon and Wilson (1907) knew of nine localities suggesting that Lesser Bulrush has expanded its range in northern Lancashire over the last 100 years. Nationally its distribution is stable.

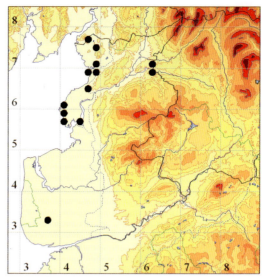
Juncus subnodulosus

JUNCACEAE   RUSH FAMILY

Juncus subnodulosus Schrank   Blunt-flowered Rush

European Southern-temperate element.

This is a rhizomatous perennial herb that often grows in dense stands in fens, marshes and wet meadows etc., usually in base-rich or occasionally brackish conditions (BH11). It is found in England, Wales, southern Scotland and Ireland.

Rare (13). In northern Lancashire *J. subnodulosus* is found mostly close to or on the coast on the Lune estuary and around Morecambe Bay with only occasional records elsewhere. All Wheldon and Wilson's records (1907) were between Carnforth and Silverdale suggesting that there has been a modest extension of its range over the last 100 years. Nationally the 'New Atlas' reported a decline in southern England before 1930 but since 1987 'Local Change' reported its distribution unchanged.

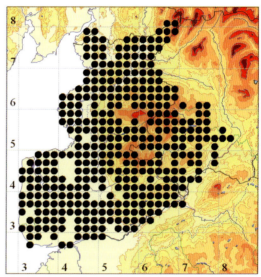
Juncus articulatus

Juncus articulatus L.   Jointed Rush

Eurosiberian Southern-temperate element.

This jointed rush is found in a variety of wet and marshy habitats usually on neutral substrates (BH11). It occurs throughout the British Isles. However some recorders may have recorded Jointed Rush in error for Sharp-flowered Rush or the hybrid between them.

Very common (369). Jointed Rush occurs throughout northern Lancashire. There has been no change in its distribution locally or nationally.

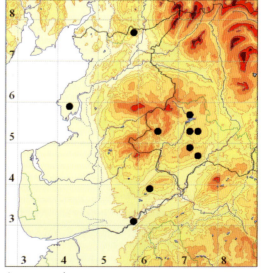
Juncus × surrejanus

Juncus articulatus × J. acutiflorus
(**J. × surrejanus** Druce ex Stace & Lambinon)

This is a common hybrid and occurs in a wide variety of habitats in the British Isles as well as elsewhere in western and central Europe. It is morphologically variable and usually sterile. It may be more frequent than either parent but it is often recorded for one or other species. Thus the map of its distribution in the 'New Atlas' plots the distribution of recorders able to recognise the hybrid rather than that of the hybrid itself.

Rare (10). *J. × surrejanus* was not recognised in northern Lancashire until it was found in a boggy field at Dilworth (SD63P) in 2003 (E.F.G.). However it is probably widespread and common and may be more frequent than *J. acutiflorus*, which may have been recorded for it (Wilcox, 2011a, 2011b). Because of the confusion meaningful comments on its distribution are not possible.

Juncus acutiflorus Ehrh. ex Hoffm.   Sharp-flowered Rush

European Temperate element.

Sharp-flowered Rush is usually a tall, erect and robust rhizomatous species found in wet and damp habitats on acid substrates (BH11). It is found throughout the British Isles. However *J. articulatus* and particularly this species have been recorded in error for the hybrid *J. × surrejanus*.

Common (258). *J. acutiflorus* occurs throughout northern Lancashire but on the one hand some recorders may have recorded *J. articulatus* in error for *J. acutiflorus* whilst most have failed to record *J. × surrejanus* but instead have recorded *J. acutiflorus*. Thus the distribution and status of *J. acutiflorus* and especially its hybrid with *J. articulatus* is uncertain. However it is likely that the distribution of *J. acutiflorus* is unchanged locally and nationally.

Juncus bulbosus L.   Bulbous Rush

European Boreo-temperate element.

This is a morphologically variable species found as a terrestrial or submerged and free floating aquatic species. It is usually found on acid substrates but in Ireland it occurs in calcareous water (BH14). It is found throughout the British Isles but it is rare in south-eastern England. Two subspecies are recognised but they have rarely been distinguished in northern Lancashire.

Frequent (154). In northern Lancashire *J. bulbosus* is a common plant of boggy places in Bowland and Leck but occurs occasionally in lowland, western areas. Only ssp. *kochii* (F.W. Schultz.) Reichg. has been recorded to date. The distribution of Bulbous Rush is stable locally and nationally.

Juncus maritimus Lam.   Sea Rush

European Southern-temperate element.

Sea Rush is a rhizomatous, clump forming perennial species found on salt marshes and in other coastal saline habitats (BH21). It is found on the coasts of the British Isles but it is rare in eastern England and Scotland and absent from northern Scotland.

Occasional (40). In northern Lancashire *J. maritimus* is found in salt marshes on the Wyre and Lune estuaries and on the shores of Morecambe Bay. In these areas it is often abundant. It occurs more sparingly on the Ribble estuary and on the sand dunes at Lytham St Anne's. The

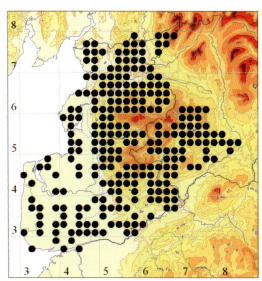
Juncus acutiflorus

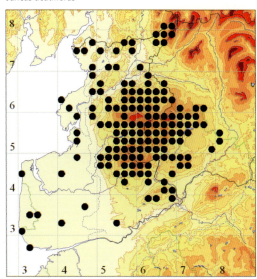
Juncus bulbosus

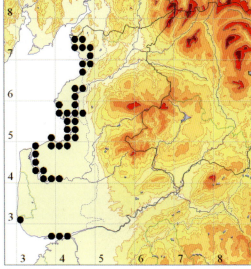
Juncus maritimus

distribution of Sea Rush is stable in northern Lancashire but nationally the 'New Atlas' reported losses from southern and eastern England. However 'Local Change' reported no further losses since 1987.

Juncus squarrosus L.   Heath Rush

Suboceanic Temperate element.

This perennial herb is characteristic of wet, peaty heaths and moorland, raised and valley mires and upland flushes on acid substrates (BH8, 12). It is found throughout the British Isles but it is rare in parts of central Ireland and southern England.

Frequent (167). In northern Lancashire Heath Rush is found in upland areas in the east of the region with a few localities on lowland mosses and near the coast at Lytham St Anne's and Blackpool in the west of the area. Surprisingly Wheldon and Wilson (1907) did not record *J. squarrosus* from the west of VC 60 but apart from losses in south-eastern England ('New Atlas') its distribution is stable nationally.

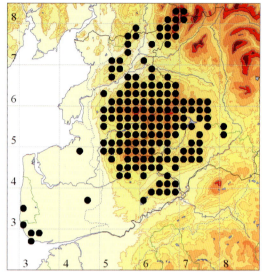
Juncus squarrosus

Juncus tenuis Willd.   Slender Rush

Neophyte. This is a native of North and South America. It was first recorded in Britain from Angus in Scotland in the 1790s but did not spread widely until the late nineteenth century. It is found in damp, open habitats, especially on paths. Today Slender Rush is found throughout the British Isles but particularly in western Britain and in coastal areas of Ireland.

Occasional (36). In northern Lancashire it was first found on Warton Crag (SD47W) in 1925 (H.E.G.; LIV). There is also an unlocalised, unattributed record from sometime after 1930 from the 10km square SD67 (B.R.C.) and it was found in the Grizedale valley (SD54) in 1947 (F.S. Hudson, annotation in copy of Wheldon and Wilson, 1907 in possession of C.F. & N.J.S.). Today it is found in scattered localities in VC 60.

Juncus compressus Jacq.   Round-fruited Rush

Eurosiberian Temperate element.

This is a shortly rhizomatous perennial species found in marshes and wet grasslands inland and near the sea where it can occur in brackish conditions with *J. gerardii*. However in these localities there is usually evidence of fresh water seepage through the marsh (BH6, 11). Round-fruited Rush is found mostly in southern and eastern Britain.

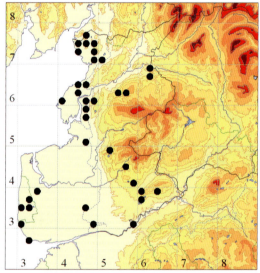
Juncus tenuis

Rare (12). In northern Lancashire it is thought that Round-fruited Rush occurs in sand dunes, in coastal ponds and marshes, at the top of salt marshes and at the base of coastal clay cliffs, which are irrigated by fresh water. However, *J. compressus* has been confused with *J. gerardii* and although they may occur in close proximity to each other they do not appear to form mixed populations. Nevertheless in 2010 doubts were raised regarding the identity of these plants with the suggestion that they were forms of *J. gerardii* (M.W., pers. comm..). This prompted a brief review of the literature and specimens at LIV. This review suggests that Lancashire coastal '*J. compressus*' is not typical of inland material either of this species or of typical Lancashire salt marsh *J. gerardii*. In addition to further morphological studies both cytological and molecular work is required to ascertain the status of these coastal plants not only in Lancashire but also elsewhere.

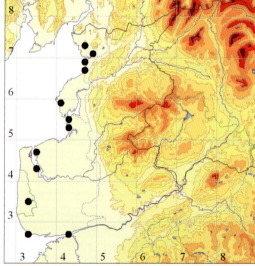
'*Juncus compressus* like'

Juncus gerardii Loisel.   Saltmarsh Rush

Circumpolar Wide-temperate element.

J. gerardii is confined to saline habitats and occurs mostly in the upper-most parts of salt marshes. However, it also occurs in other coastal, saline habitats and occasionally inland (BH21). It occurs on all the coasts around the British Isles.

Occasional (56). In northern Lancashire Saltmarsh Rush is found in all the coastal salt marshes and occasionally in other saline, coastal habitats. There has been no change in its distribution locally or nationally.

Juncus bufonius L.   Toad Rush

Circumpolar Wide-temperate element.

This is an annual species found in open habitats with seasonally high water tables. It grows in a wide variety of wetland habitats including cart tracks and muddy field entrances (BH3, 11, 13, 14). It is found throughout the British Isles.

Very common (377). Toad Rush is found throughout northern Lancashire. The taxonomy of British species of *J. bufonius sensu lato* was not eluci-dated until the 1970s and 1980s and thus most records are for *J. bufonius sensu lato*. However, unless they have been specifically identified as *J. ranarius*, most records are probably *J. bufonius sensu stricto*. There has been no change in its distribution locally or nationally.

Juncus ranarius Songeon & E.P. Perrier   Frog Rush

European Southern-temperate element.

This rush was not distinguished from *J. bufonius* until 1978 but occurs in bare, damp and brackish places, typically on mud and in sandy places above high water mark (BH19, 21) around the coasts of the British Isles. It also occurs occasionally inland.

Occasional (21). In northern Lancashire most records are from the top of salt marshes on the Wyre and Lune estuaries and around Morecambe Bay with a single record on the Ribble estuary. It is likely to be under recorded. Because of identification difficulties it is not known if there have been any changes in its distribution.

Juncus balticus Willd.   Baltic Rush

Circumpolar Boreo-arctic Montane element.

Baltic Rush occurs in damp sandy places mostly on the coast (BH19) in Scotland with a few localities on the Lancashire and Merseyside coasts.

Extinct. In northern Lancashire Baltic Rush was only known from two nearby sites at Ansdell (H.E.B., LIV; SD32I) where it was found in 1914 (Wheldon and Wilson, 1925). However it was lost about 1966 when development for local schools eradicated it. Nationally populations are stable but in VC 59, where new slacks have appeared on the 'green beach' during the last 20 years or so, it has become more frequent.

Juncus balticus × J. inflexus

Endemic. Only three completely sterile clones are known of this hybrid. Two are found in VC 59 where they are very tall up to 2m high and have interrupted pith, the other, in VC 60, is slightly taller than *J. inflexus* but has continuous pith. All three clones have 2n = 84.

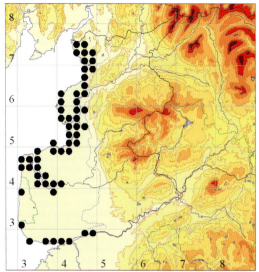

Juncus gerardii

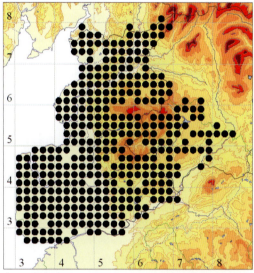

Juncus bufonius

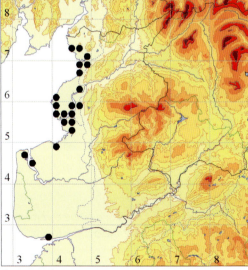

Juncus ranarius

Very rare (1). *J. balticus* × *J. inflexus* was found at Lytham St Anne's L.N.R. (SD33A) in 1966 (Stace, 1972). It was still present in 2010. Wilcox (2011a) considers that the populations in VC 59 are sufficiently distinct from the one in VC 60 to merit varietal status.

Juncus filiformis L. — Thread Rush

Circumpolar Boreal-montane element.

This is a rhizomatous perennial herb restricted in Britain to the shores of lakes and reservoirs with fluctuating water levels (BH13). It is found in England, Wales and Scotland.

Very rare (1). This rush is confined to the shores of Stocks Reservoir (SD76I; Abbott, 2005) where it has been known since at least 1978 (P.J.).

Juncus inflexus L. — Hard Rush

Eurosiberian Southern-temperate element.

Hard Rush is a clump forming perennial of wet places in a wide variety of habitats but usually on base-rich soils and often on heavy clays (BH6, 11). It is found in England, Wales, Ireland, central and southern Scotland. It is curiously absent from the Isle of Man.

Common (345). In northern Lancashire *J. inflexus* occurs throughout the area except on peaty soils and the higher parts of Leck and Bowland. Its distribution locally and nationally is stable.

Juncus inflexus × J. effusus (J. × diffusus Hoppe)

Widespread in Europe.

J. inflexus and *J. effusus* often grow together but have slightly different flowering times, which probably accounts for the scarcity of the hybrid between them. *J. × diffusus* usually occurs in small numbers but it is easily overlooked. It is not fully sterile and second or backcross generations may occur. Furthermore some populations of *J. inflexus* are sterile and floral characteristics are not reliable diagnostic features so that without anatomical examination hybrids may be exceptionally difficult to recognise. However the 'New Atlas' shows that *J. × diffusus* has been found in scattered localities in England, Wales, Ireland and southern Scotland.

Very rare (2). In northern Lancashire there were pre 1964 records from near Bare and Stonyhurst (Wheldon and Wilson, 1907b) and from between Grimsargh and Alston (Wheldon and Wilson, 1901; BIRM). There is also an undated specimen (KGY) from Hest Bank probably collected about 1900 by F.A. Lees. A post 1964 record from Thornton (SD34L) proved to be an error so that the only confirmed recent records are from Stocks Reservoir (SD75I) in 2007 (M.W.) and Gisburn Forest (SD75M) in 2010 (M.W.).

Juncus effusus L. — Soft Rush

European Southern-temperate element.

Soft Rush is found in wet places, often abundant in wet pastures, but occurs in a wide variety of habitats and is generally absent from base-rich habitats (BH8, 11). It is found throughout the British Isles.

Very common (443). This is one of the commonest species in northern Lancashire and occurs throughout the region. Its distribution is stable locally and nationally.

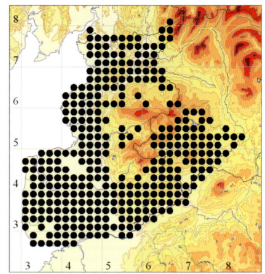

Juncus inflexus

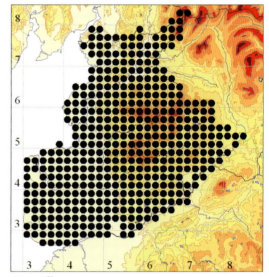

Juncus effusus

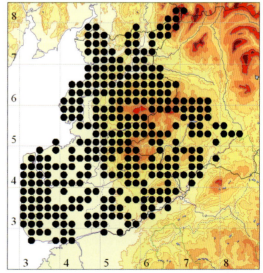

Juncus conglomeratus

Juncus effusus × J. conglomeratus

(**J. × kern-reichgeltii** Jansen & Wacht. ex Reichg.)

This hybrid, which is often fertile, is exceptionally difficult to recognise and consequently it is frequently overlooked. It is believed to be frequent, especially in western Britain

Very rare (2). *J. × kern-reichgeltii* was identified from Waddington Fell (SD74I) and from near Stocks Reservoir, Easington (SD75I) both in 2008 (M.W.).

Juncus conglomeratus L.   Compact Rush

European Temperate element.

Compact Rush occurs in similar places to *J. effusus* with which it is often confused but it generally occurs in slightly less acid places (BH11). It is found throughout the British Isles.

Common (335). *J. conglomeratus* occurs throughout northern Lancashire. Its distribution is stable locally and nationally.

Luzula pilosa (L.) Willd.   Hairy Wood-rush

Eurosiberian Boreo-temperate element.

This is a characteristic herb of damp acid woodlands (BH1, 2) and whilst it occurs throughout the British Isles it is rare or absent in much of south-eastern England and central Ireland.

Frequent (116). In northern Lancashire Hairy Wood-rush is found in woodlands in the east of the area. Its distribution locally and nationally is stable.

Luzula sylvatica (Huds.) Gaudin   Great Wood-rush

European Temperate element.

This rhizomatous, patch-forming species is found in acid woodlands but it also occurs on moorland heaths, probably surviving as a relic of former woodland (BH1, 16). It is found throughout the British Isles but it is rare or absent in much of south-eastern England and central Ireland.

Frequent (124). In northern Lancashire *L. sylvatica* is found in northern and eastern parts of the region. Its distribution is unchanged locally and nationally.

Luzula luzuloides (Lam.) Dandy & Wilmott   White Woodrush

Neophyte. This is a native of central Europe and was introduced into Britain before 1800. It was recorded in the wild by 1871 and today occurs mostly in northern England and Scotland with occasional localities elsewhere.

Very rare (1). In northern Lancashire *L. luzuloides* was found in Avenham Park, Preston, (SD52J) in 2008 (P.J.).

Luzula campestris (L.) DC.   Field Wood-rush

European Temperate element.

Field Wood-rush is found in short grassland on somewhat acid substrates (BH6). It occurs throughout the British Isles.

Very common (381). *L. campestris* occurs throughout northern Lancashire. Its distribution is unchanged locally and nationally.

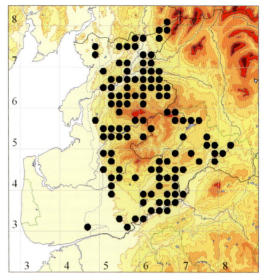

Luzula pilosa

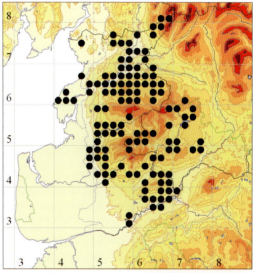

Luzula sylvatica

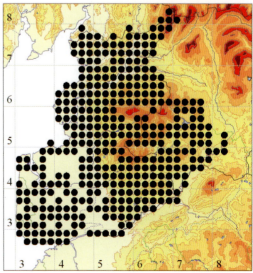

Luzula campestris

Luzula multiflora (Ehrh.) Lej.   Heath Wood-rush

Circumpolar Wide-boreal element.

This tufted but shortly rhizomatous species is found in short grassland on acid soils (BH8) but flowers slightly later than *L. campestris* with which it sometimes grows in close proximity. It occurs throughout the British Isles. Ssp. *multiflora* and ssp. *congesta* (Thuill.) Arcang. are recognised as distinct subspecies but intermediates occur making recognition not always easy. Both subspecies are believed to be widespread.

Frequent (206). *L. multiflora* occurs throughout northern Lancashire but it is much more frequent in the upland areas in the north and east than in the lowland west of the region. Both ssp. *multiflora* and ssp. *congesta* occur and whilst ssp. *congesta* seems to be more frequent, in line with findings nationally (Kirschner and Rich, 1998), no distinction could be found in their distribution in northern Lancashire. The distribution of *L. multiflora* locally is stable and apart from some losses reported by the 'New Atlas' in south-eastern England its distribution nationally is also thought to be stable.

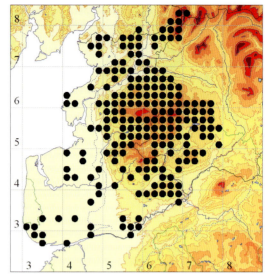
Luzula multiflora

CYPERACEAE   SEDGE FAMILY

Eriophorum angustifolium Honck.   Common Cottongrass

Circumpolar Wide-boreal element.

This is a rhizomatous perennial herb of wet peaty ground typically in acid bog pools and on the wettest parts of bogs but it may also occur in more calcareous, nutrient-poor habitats (BH12). It is found throughout the British Isles.

Frequent (154). In northern Lancashire Common Cottongrass is found in all the upland areas of the north and east of the area with scattered localities elsewhere in the region (see Plate 2.21). Before the mosses in lowland areas were drained *E. angustifolium* must have been more widespread but it was already rare in these areas 100 years ago (Wheldon and Wilson, 1907). Nationally there have been considerable losses in south-eastern England where most sites were lost in Hertfordshire by 1900 ('New Atlas'). These losses have continued since 1987 ('Local Change').

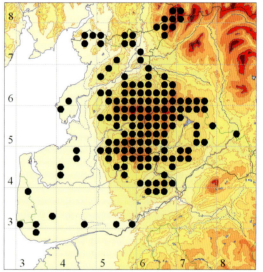
Eriophorum angustifolium

Eriophorum latifolium Hoppe   Broad-leaved Cottongrass

European Boreo-temperate element.

Broad-leaved Cottongrass is a rhizomatous perennial species of open sites growing in wet, base-rich, lowland meadows and mires and calcareous flushes in upland areas (BH11). It is found in many parts of the British Isles but especially in upland areas of the north and west.

Very rare (2). In northern Lancashire Broad-leaved Cottongrass was first found in Over Wyresdale (SD55W & 65B) in 1974 (P.J.) where it occurred in a few flushes on both sides of a valley. By 2005 it was confined to one or two flushes on one side of the valley and was present in very small quantity. Nationally there have been many losses in most of England and although 'Local Change' recorded an apparent increase since 1987 this is thought to be due to better recording.

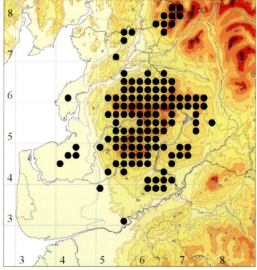
Eriophorum vaginatum

Eriophorum vaginatum L.   Hare's-tail Cottongrass

Circumpolar Boreo-arctic Montane element.

E. vaginatum is a tussock-forming, rhizomatous perennial herb of usually acid, wet heaths and mires. It is dominant or co-dominant with *Calluna vulgaris* and can cover large areas of blanket bog (BH12). It is found in most of the British Isles but it is absent from much of midland and south-eastern England.

Frequent (127). In northern Lancashire *E. vaginatum* occurs in all the upland bogs in the north and east of the area but less frequently in the remaining lowland mosses and heaths (see Plate 2.23). As with *E. angustifolium* this must have been more frequent in lowland areas of northern Lancashire before the mosses were drained. Similarly the 'New Atlas' reported losses in midland and south-eastern England but further losses since 1987 were not noted by 'Local Change'.

Trichophorum germanicum Palla   Deergrass

It is believed that *T. germanicum* has an Oceanic or Suboceanic distribution.

It is a densely tufted perennial species occurring on peaty moors and bogs on acid substrates (BH10, 12). It is found in most parts of the British Isles except midland and south-eastern England.

Frequent (85). In northern Lancashire Deergrass is found in upland areas in the north and east of the area. Formerly it also grew on the lowland mosses but it was already rare in these areas by 1900 (Wheldon and Wilson, 1907). Nationally there have been losses in midland and south-eastern England ('New Atlas', 'Local Change').

Trichophorum cespitosum (L.) Hartm. × **T. germanicum** (**T. × foersteri** (G.A. Swan) D.A. Simpson)

This sterile hybrid was identified as occurring in Britain by Swan (1999). Much of his work was done in Northumberland where the rare *T. cespitosum* with an arctic-montane distribution occurs. Since his paper the sterile hybrid between the two species has been found to be rare but with a widespread distribution in upland areas, often in the absence of one parent, *T. cespitosum*.

Very rare (4). In northern Lancashire *T. × foersteri* was first recognised from a heath on the summit of Gragareth, Leck (SD68V) in 2000 (E.F.G. & J.M.N.). Subsequently it was found in flushes in Over Wyresdale (SD65B) in 2006 (E.F.G.), in a valley bog in the Trough of Bowland (SD65K) in 2010 (E.F.G.) and at Slaidburn (SD75D) in 2004 (E.F.G.). It is difficult to spot *T. × foersteri* and it is likely that it is more frequent than the small number of records suggest. *T. cespitosum* has not been found in northern Lancashire.

Bolboschoenus maritimus (L.) Palla   Sea Club-rush

Eurosiberian Southern-temperate element.

Sea Club-rush is a rhizomatous perennial species found on the upper parts of salt marshes and in other coastal and usually brackish water (BH21). It is found around the coasts of the British Isles and occasionally inland.

Occasional (55). Sea Club-rush is found on all the salt marshes of northern Lancashire and often in adjacent coastal, usually brackish water, e.g. the Glasson branch of the Lancaster Canal. Wheldon and Wilson (1907) refer to a taxon 'Scirpus maritimus L. var. compactus Koch. (conglobatus, S. Gray)'. It is not clear to what this taxon refers and it is now no longer

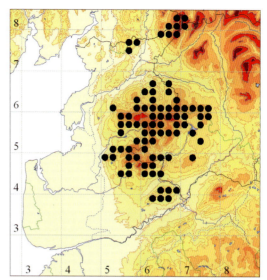
Trichophorum germanicum

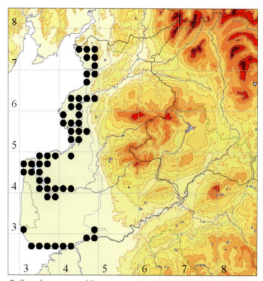
Bolboschoenus maritimus

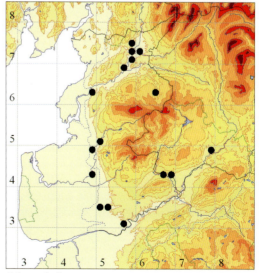
Scirpus sylvaticus

recognised. There has been no change in the distribution of *B. maritimus* locally or nationally although it may be declining in south-eastern England.

Scirpus sylvaticus L.   Wood Club-rush

Eurosiberian Temperate element.

S. sylvaticus is a robust, rhizomatous perennial species found in wet valley woodlands and on the margins of rivers, streams, lakes and ponds (BH1, 11). It is found in many parts of the British Isles but it is absent from northern Scotland and parts of eastern England. However despite its size it is often overlooked and some absences, e.g. in Ireland, may reflect poor recording.

Occasional (16). In northern Lancashire Wood Club-rush occurs in scattered localities in the north and east of the area. Its distribution is stable both locally and nationally.

Schoenoplectus lacustris (L.) Palla   Common Club-rush

Eurosiberian Wide-temperate element.

This is a tall, rhizomatous perennial herb found in standing or slow flowing water in a wide variety of conditions but tends to avoid muddy substrates (BH13, 14). It is found throughout the British Isles.

Rare (11). In northern Lancashire Common Club-rush occurs in a few localities in the north and west of the area, near Preston and in the Fylde although some records may refer to *S. tabernaemontani*. There has been no change in its distribution locally or nationally.

Schoenoplectus tabernaemontani (C.C. Gmel.) Palla Grey Club-rush

Eurasian Southern-temperate element.

Grey Club-rush is a rhizomatous perennial herb found in brackish conditions in coastal areas but it also occurs inland in ponds, lakes and gravel pits. It is characteristic of slightly more eutrophic conditions than *S. lacustris* (BH11, 13). It is found around the coasts of the British Isles and at inland sites mostly in England.

Occasional (33). In northern Lancashire Grey Club-rush is found at many coastal sites, on salt marshes, in nearby ditches and ponds but it is also a colonizer of gravel pits. In addition there are a few records from other inland localities. Wheldon and Wilson (1907) knew of only three sites at Bolton-le-Sands, Carnforth and Overton suggesting that this species has spread considerably in the last 100 years. A similar spread nationally was reported by the 'New Atlas' but since 1987 there has been little further change ('Local Change').

Eleocharis palustris (L.) Roem. & Schult.   Common Spike-rush

Eurasian Wide-temperate element.

Common Spike-rush is a rhizomatous perennial species found on the margins of ponds, lakes, slow moving rivers and in marshes etc. (BH11). Whilst it grows on a wide variety of substrates it is rarely found in acid conditions. It occurs throughout the British Isles. However it is believed another closely similar species, *E. mitracarpa* Steud., may occur in Britain (Jermy, *et al.*, 2007) and it has been tentatively recorded from Midlothian and Cardiganshire (Chater, 2010). This could occur in northern Lancashire but more work is required to elucidate the taxonomic problems associated with *E. palustris*, *E. mamillata*, *E. mitracarpa* and *E. uniglumis*.

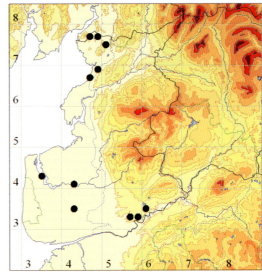
Schoenoplectus lacustris

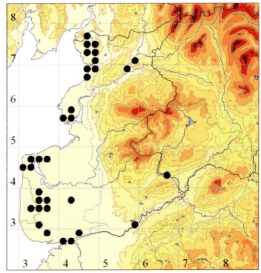
Schoenoplectus tabernaemontani

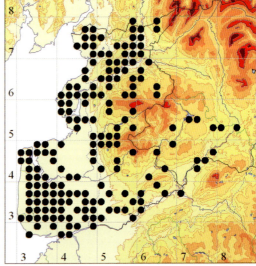
Eleocharis palustris

Frequent (182). In northern Lancashire Common Spike-rush is found in many parts of the area but it is especially common in northern and south-western parts of the region. It is believed all records are for ssp. *vulgaris* Walters. Its distribution is probably stable both locally and nationally.

[Eleocharis mamillata (H. Lindb. f.) H. Lindb. f. ssp. **austriaca** (Hayek) Strandh.   Northern Spike-rush

This Boreal-montane species has been found in the Ribble valley close to the northern Lancashire border both in Yorkshire VC 64 and South Lancaster VC 59. So far suitable habitats have not been found in northern Lancashire but it may occur in the region, especially in Lancashire VC 64.]

Eleocharis uniglumis (Link) Schult.   Slender Spike-rush

Circumpolar Temperate element.

Slender Spike-rush is a rhizomatous species found predominantly in coastal marshes, in sand dunes, at the top of salt marshes and in calcareous marshy areas near the coast but also very occasionally in inland situations (BH11). It is found throughout the British Isles.

Occasional (23). In northern Lancashire this is a coastal species and is particularly frequent on the Lune estuary and on the shores of Morecambe Bay. It also occurs inland in calcareous marshes in the northwest of the area and in Gisburn Forest (SD75N). However in a few places and especially in a meadow at Silverdale *E. palustris* and *E. uniglumis* grow in close proximity to each other. At Silverdale the two species seem to be zonally separated and at the junction intermediates seem to be present. These could be hybrids, which have been found elsewhere in the country (Stace, 2010). Assessing change in the distribution of *E. uniglumis* is difficult, as recorders have often overlooked it. Thus the apparent increase in northern Lancashire over the last 100 years and the increase recorded by the 'New Atlas' nationally are probably due to better recording. However 'Local Change' recorded significant losses, which may reflect recording bias.

Eleocharis multicaulis (Sm.) Desv.   Many-stalked Spike-rush

Suboceanic Temperate element.

This is a densely tufted perennial species found on wet heaths, valley mires and other wetland, acid habitats (BH11, 12, 13). It is found mostly in western and northern localities in the British Isles.

Very rare (1) or extinct. The status of this species in northern Lancashire is uncertain. The record from Thornley near Chipping (Wheldon and Wilson, 1907) is an error. It was also recorded from Silverdale (A.J.C.; LSA) in 1915 and from Fairhaven (SD32I; Heathcote, 1923 and H.E.B. in 1946) but both records seem to be from unlikely localities. However it was found on the northeast facing slope of Clougha (SD56F) in 1988 (J.M.N.) but the locality could not be re-found. Nationally the 'New Atlas' reported losses in many parts of eastern Scotland, eastern Wales and in England but the gains noted by 'Local Change' are probably the result of better recording.

Eleocharis quinqueflora (Hartmann) O. Schwarz
       Few-flowered Spike-rush

European Boreo-temperate element.

This is a small perennial herb of base-rich marshes, fens and calcareous flushes. It is often found in coastal areas on sand dunes and at the top of

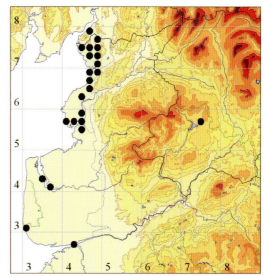

Eleocharis uniglumis

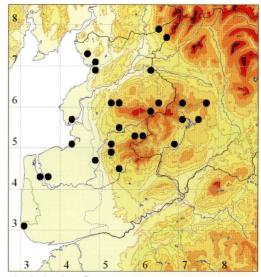

Eleocharis quinqueflora

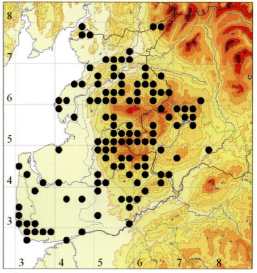

Isolepis setacea

salt marshes (BH11). It occurs in most parts of the British Isles although it is rare or absent in much of midland and eastern England.

Occasional (27). In northern Lancashire *E. quinqueflora* occurs in scattered coastal localities as well as inland in eastern and northern parts of the region. Although it appears to have become more widespread in northern Lancashire over the last 100 years this is probably due to better recording. Nationally there have been losses in England ('New Atlas') but since 1987 its distribution appears to be stable ('Local Change').

Isolepis setacea (L.) R. Br.   Bristle Club-rush

Eurosiberian Temperate element.

This small perennial herb is found in open, damp, acid habitats, especially sites that are subject to winter flooding. It is found by roadsides, on the shores of ponds and lakes, in upland runnels, on sand dunes and on the uppermost parts of salt marshes (BH11, 14). It is found throughout the British Isles.

Frequent (122). Bristle Club-rush is found in scattered localities throughout northern Lancashire. Its distribution is probably stable both locally and nationally.

Eleogiton fluitans Link.   Floating Club-rush

Oceanic Southern-temperate element.

This perennial herb is found in ponds, ditches and in other slow moving water but it requires acid and nutrient poor conditions (BH11). It is found in many coastal areas of the British Isles but it is much less frequent at inland localities.

Extinct. In northern Lancashire *E. fluitans* was only found in ditches near Morecambe and Bare (Wheldon and Wilson, 1907) and was last recorded from Lytham sometime before 1925 (Wheldon and Wilson, 1925). Nationally the 'New Atlas' reported a decline over much of Floating Club-rush's range but surprisingly 'Local Change' reported an increase since 1987. However this observation should be considered cautiously as its habitat is thought to be declining.

Cyperus longus L.   Galingale

European Southern-temperate element but a neophyte in northern Lancashire.

This perennial species is thought to be native in south-western Britain but it occurs as an introduction in many parts of England, Wales and more rarely in southern Scotland.

Rare (7). Galingale was first found in northern Lancashire at Heaton-with-Oxcliffe (SD46G) in 1991 (J.M.N.). Subsequently it was found in scattered localities in the west of northern Lancashire.

Blysmus compressus (L.) Panz. ex Link   Flat-sedge

European Temperate element.

Flat-sedge is a rhizomatous perennial herb of open areas in marshes and fens, in short damp grassland and in calcareous flushes (BH11). It is found in England, Wales and southern Scotland.

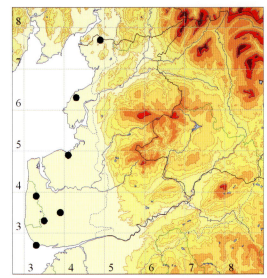

Cyperus longus

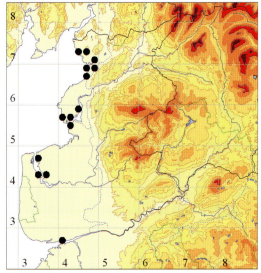

Blysmus rufus

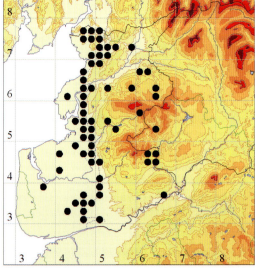

Carex paniculata

Very rare (3). In northern Lancashire Flat-sedge is found in the old oxbows of the R. Lune, Melling-with-Wrayton (SD57V, W) and at Lytham St Anne's (SD32I). It was seen in the Lune oxbows in 2009 (Lancashire Endangered Plants Group) and at Lytham St Anne's in 2008 (E.F.G.). It was also recorded from the Heysham Peninsula (Garlick, 1957a). Northern Lancashire populations are small and declining. At Lytham St Anne's the population is particularly endangered as the slack where it grows is becoming dryer and the vegetation is becoming taller and less open. Nationally it has declined considerably ('New Atlas').

Blysmus rufus (Huds.) Link — Saltmarsh Flat-sedge

European Boreal-montane element.

This is a rhizomatous perennial herb found at the top of salt marshes in generally short vegetation (BH21). It is found around the coasts of the northern half of the British Isles and in southern Wales.

Rare (14). In northern Lancashire *B. rufus* is found at the top of salt marshes. It appears to have become more widespread as Wheldon and Wilson (1907) only knew it from Bolton-le-Sands, Silverdale and near Lytham. Nationally its distribution is probably stable.

Schoenus nigricans L. — Black Bog-rush

Eurosiberian Southern-temperate element.

This is a tussock-forming perennial herb found in calcareous and other base-rich fens, dune slacks, the upper parts of salt marshes and sea cliff flushes (BH11). It has a disjunct distribution in the British Isles with most records from northern and western areas but also in East Anglia.

Very rare (5). Since 1964 Black Bog-rush has been found on shell marl at Hawes Water, Silverdale (SD47T) in 2005 (E.F.G.), Leighton Moss, Yealand Conyers (SD47X) in 2000 (C.B.W.), on the estuary of the R. Keer, Carnforth (SD47V) in 1966 (C.J.-P.) but the site was lost to road works by 1982 (E.F.G.) and it has recently appeared in Warton Quarry (SD47W) in 2005 (P.J.). There is a doubtful record for Bolton-le-Sands (SD46T) in 1965 (Anon). There are earlier records for Castlebarrow, Silverdale (SD47T; Petty, 1902), by the Leighton Beck (Wheldon and Wilson, 1907) and from Little Hawes Water (Wheldon and Wilson, 1907). Its distribution nationally is stable.

Cladium mariscus (L.) Pohl — Great Fen-sedge

Eurosiberian Southern-temperate element.

This is a vigorous, rhizomatous perennial species found in nutrient poor fens often on the margins of lakes (BH11). In England and Wales it is usually found in calcareous sites but in Ireland and Scotland it often occurs on acid substrates. It is found in many parts of the British Isles but particularly in Ireland, western Scotland and East Anglia.

Very rare (3). In northern Lancashire Great Fen-sedge occurs around Hawes Water, Silverdale and Little Hawes Water, Yealand Redmayne (SD47T) where it was seen in 2006 (E.F.G. & M.P.). In addition Livermore and Livermore (1987) recorded Great Fen-sedge from tetrad SD47Y, which is probably from the margin of Little Hawes Water and there is an unconfirmed record from tetrad SD47S, possibly from Leighton Moss about 1964. Nationally there has been a decline in the distribution of *C. mariscus* ('New Atlas').

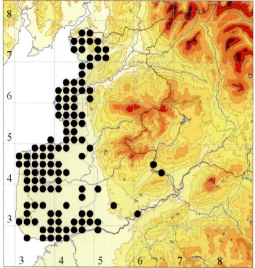
Carex otrubae

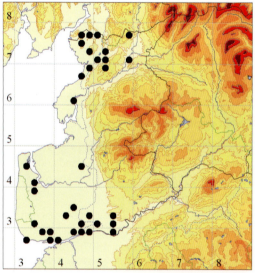
Carex spicata

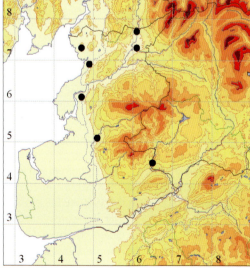
Carex muricata

Rhynchospora alba (L.) Vahl White Beak-sedge

Circumpolar Boreo-temperate element.

White Beak-sedge is a perennial herb of acid bogs and mires but it prefers open sites within them (BH12). It is found today mostly in western parts of the British Isles with occasional records elsewhere.

Very rare (2). Since 1964 *R. alba* was found near the northern edge of Cockerham Moss (SD44P) in 1973 (C.F. & N.J.S.) but it has not been seen since. It is still found on Heysham Moss (SD46F). In addition to these two localities it formerly grew on Tarnbrook Fell, Over Wyresdale at approximately 195m (Wheldon and Wilson, 1901). The 'New Atlas' reported considerable losses in England but since 1987 its distribution appears to be unchanged ('Local Change').

Carex paniculata L. Greater Tussock-sedge

European Temperate element.

Greater Tussock-sedge is a large tussock forming perennial herb occurring in fens, wet woodland and by the side of lakes, rivers and canals (BH1, 11). It is found in lowland areas throughout the British Isles.

Occasional (65). In northern Lancashire *C. paniculata* is found in lowland areas throughout the region but most records are from north-western parts and the Lancaster Canal. Its distribution locally is unchanged but whilst the 'New Atlas' shows losses nationally 'Local Change' noted no further change since 1987.

Carex paniculata × C. remota (C. × boenninghausiana Weihe)

Widespread in temperate Europe.

This sterile hybrid is found in fen-woodland and in places where there is seasonal inundation. It is found in many places in Britain and Ireland but it is often overlooked.

Very rare (2). In northern Lancashire it was first recorded from the Lancaster Canal at Brock (originally identified as *C. × pseudoaxillaris*) in 1904 (Wheldon and Wilson, 1907). Other records are from the Lancaster Canal at Garstang (Whellan, 1942) and since 1964 from the Lancaster Canal at Forton in 1967 (J.H.; LANC) and Silverdale (SD47S) in 1980 (H.J.M. Bowen).

Carex diandra Schrank Lesser Tussock-sedge

Circumpolar Boreo-temperate element.

Lesser Tussock-sedge is a perennial herb of wet peaty areas on both acid substrates and those flushed by calcareous springs (BH11). It is found mostly in lowland areas, where suitable habitats exist, throughout the British Isles.

Very rare (5). Old records for *C. diandra* in northern Lancashire are from near Winkley Hall Farm, (SD73E) and on Longridge Fell (SD64Q) both in Aighton, Bailey and Chaigley and both found in 1891 (SYT). Since 1964 it has been found at Whittington (SD57Y) in 2005 (E.F.G. & J.M.N.); Outfield Moss, Docker (SD57X) in the 1960s (E.F.G.), which was lost to nutrient enrichment of the site shortly afterwards; Gressingham (SD57Y) in 1969 (B.R.C.) and from Arbour Quarry, Thornley (SD64A, F) in 1999 (E.F.G.). Nationally the 'New Atlas' reports losses especially in midland and south-eastern England.

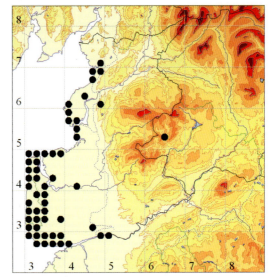

Carex arenaria

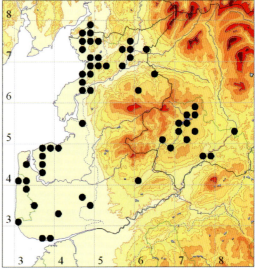

Carex disticha

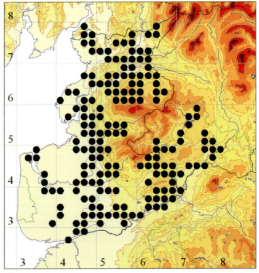

Carex remota

Carex otrubae Podp.   False Fox-sedge

Eurosiberian Southern-temperate element.

False Fox-sedge is a perennial herb of wet, usually heavy soils. It is found in ponds, ditches, wet lowland grasslands and marshes and often colonizes old clay and gravel pits (BH11). It is found in lowland areas of the British Isles.

Frequent (114). In northern Lancashire *C. otrubae* is found in lowland areas of western VC 60 and occasionally elsewhere, e.g. in the Hodder valley. Wheldon and Wilson (1907) recorded '*C. vulpina* L. var. *nemorosa* Lumn.' from two localities but it is not known to what taxon this refers. There has been no change in the distribution of *C. otrubae* locally or nationally.

Carex otrubae × C. remota (C. × pseudoaxillaris K. Richt.)

This hybrid is usually found near both parents in a range of wet habitats. It is found in England, Wales, Ireland and Scotland where there are old records from near Edinburgh.

Very rare (2). This was found by a ditch at Newton-with-Scales (SD43K) in 1997 (C.F. & N.J.S.) and with both parents in open communities on wet scrubby grassland on clay soil at Heysham (SD46A) in 2002 (P.J.). An earlier record from Brock in 1904 (A.W.; BM, NMW) is *C. × boenninghausiana*. The 'New Atlas' shows numerous old records suggesting that *C. × pseudoaxillaris* is decreasing or is overlooked.

Carex spicata Huds.   Spiked Sedge

European Temperate element.

This is an easily overlooked perennial species of open, rough grassland often colonizing ruderal habitats (BH3, 6, 7). It is found in England, Wales, Ireland and southern Scotland.

Occasional (35). In northern Lancashire *C. spicata* is found mostly in the north and south of the area with few records in central areas and it is apparently absent from the east of the region. As *C. spicata* was not distinguished from *C. muricata* 100 years ago it is not known if its distribution has changed in northern Lancashire. 'Local Change' reports an increase nationally since 1987.

Carex muricata L. ssp. pairae (F.W. Schultz) Čelak.   Prickly Sedge

European Southern-temperate element.

This is a tufted perennial herb of grasslands on well-drained, usually light and slightly acid soils (BH3, 7, 8). It is a lowland species easily confused with *C. spicata* or overlooked. It is found in England, Wales, and eastern Ireland, southern and eastern Scotland.

Rare (7). In northern Lancashire Prickly Sedge has been recognised from a few scattered localities in the north and east of the area. It is not known if its distribution in northern Lancashire has changed but 'Local Change' reports an increase nationally since 1987.

Carex arenaria L.   Sand Sedge

European Temperate element.

Sand Sedge is a rhizomatous species of open communities particularly characteristic of sand dunes (BH19). It is found around the coasts of the British Isles and occasionally inland, notably on sandy soils in eastern England.

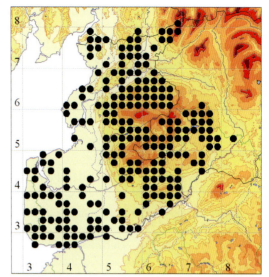
Carex leporina

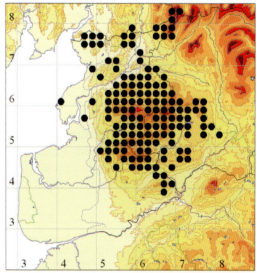
Carex echinata

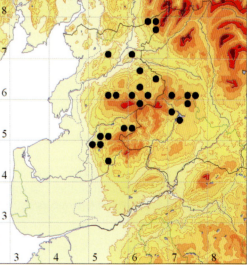
Carex dioica

Occasional (54). In northern Lancashire *C. arenaria* is found in or near the coast but occasionally it occurs inland, often in ruderal habitats. Its occurrence in a wet sandy area by the R. Dunsop in Lancashire VC 64 is unusual and may have been introduced accidentally in connection with water catchment works. The distribution of *C. arenaria* is unchanged locally and nationally.

Carex disticha Huds.   Brown Sedge

Eurosiberian Temperate element.

This is a rhizomatous species found in wet grasslands, fens, marshes, in dune slacks, by lakes and ponds (BH11). It is found in many parts of the British Isles but it is absent from most of highland Scotland.

Occasional (57). In northern Lancashire Brown Sedge is found in coastal areas, in the Lune and Hodder valleys and occasionally elsewhere. Wheldon and Wilson (1907) recorded *C. disticha* in eight localities suggesting that it has increased over the last 100 years. However nationally the 'New Atlas' suggests it had declined and whilst the decline noted by 'Local Change' was not significant both the 'New Atlas' and 'Local Change' suggest that it is easily overlooked when not flowering and that any losses may be exaggerated. In northern Lancashire it escaped notice on the Lytham St Anne's L.N.R. for many years and when it was finally recognised it covered an extensive area of one of the dune slacks.

Carex divisa Huds.   Divided Sedge

Submediterranean-Subatlantic element.

This is a rhizomatous perennial herb of brackish ditches, dune slacks and damp grassland near the sea sometimes occurring at the top of salt marshes (BH6). It is found on southern coasts of the British Isles with only occasional records further north. Unless it is in flower it is easily overlooked.

Very rare (1). This was first recognised in 2003 (E.F.G.) when a large patch was found at the top of a salt marsh at Bryning-with-Warton (SD42D). Nearby were patches of *Glyceria maxima*, *Schoenoplectus tabernaemontani* and *Phragmites australis*, which, with *C. divisa*, had been first seen as colonizers of the marsh many years earlier following cessation or reduction in grazing. However Divided Sedge had remained unidentified until it flowered. This colonization could have been as early as 1968 when *Glyceria maxima* was first recorded. Its distribution nationally is probably stable ('New Atlas').

Carex remota L.   Remote Sedge

European Temperate element.

This is a tufted perennial herb of damp woodland and woodland edge habitats (BH1, 14). It is found in most lowland areas of the British Isles.

Frequent (180). In northern Lancashire *C. remota* is found in most lowland areas although it is rare in the western Fylde and Bowland valleys. Whilst the distribution of *C. remota* in northern Lancashire is unchanged and nationally the 'New Atlas' also reported its distribution unchanged, 'Local Change' noted a significant increase.

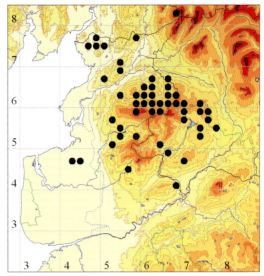

Carex canescens

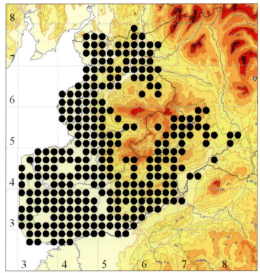

Carex hirta

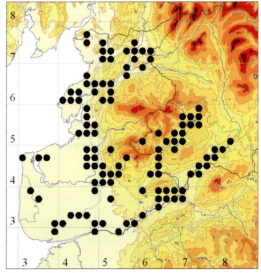

Carex acutiformis

Carex leporina L.   Oval Sedge

Eurosiberian Boreo-temperate element.

Oval Sedge is a tufted perennial herb of mostly acid grasslands where it is especially frequent in upland pastures (BH3, 10). It is found throughout the British Isles.

Frequent (235). *C. leporina* occurs throughout northern Lancashire. Its distribution is largely stable both locally and nationally.

Carex echinata Murray   Star Sedge

European Boreo-temperate element.

This is a perennial herb of wet, acid places. It is especially characteristic of acid upland flushes (BH11, 12, 14). It is found throughout the British Isles.

Frequent (146). In northern Lancashire Star Sedge occurs in northern and eastern areas and is especially frequent in acid flushes in Leck and Bowland (see Plates 2.27 and 2.35). It is believed that its distribution in northern Lancashire is stable although in lowland parts of VC 60 west of the M6 motorway it is very rare. Nationally it has been lost from many parts of midland and eastern England ('New Atlas') although since 1987 there has been little change in its distribution ('Local Change').

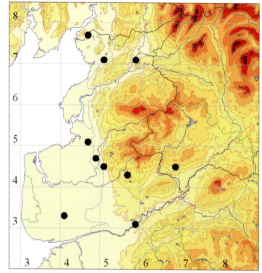

Carex riparia

Carex dioica L.   Dioecious Sedge

Circumpolar Boreo-arctic Montane element.

C. dioica is a small perennial herb of wet, neutral to base-rich mires and flushes (BH11). It is found in upland areas of the British Isles and more occasionally in some lowland areas of England.

Occasional (26). In northern Lancashire it is found in scattered localities in the north and east of the area. Although more localities are known today than 100 years ago (Wheldon and Wilson, 1907) these are in upland areas where it may have been overlooked. However there is evidence that it was more widespread in lowland areas 100 years ago than it is today, e.g. Silverdale and near Preston. Nationally there were considerable losses in lowland England before 1930 ('New Atlas') but as in northern Lancashire better recording suggests that since 1987 there may have been some increase ('Local Change').

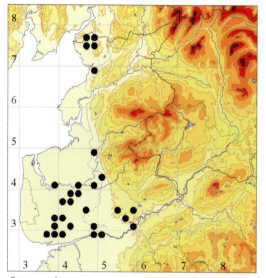

Carex pseudocyperus

Carex elongata L.   Elongated Sedge

Eurosiberian Boreal-montane element.

Elongated Sedge is a perennial herb of wet woodlands, especially those dominated by *Alnus glutinosa*, by lakes and in seasonally flooded areas (BH1). It is found in south-western Scotland, northern England and the Welsh border counties, southern England and the north of Ireland.

Extinct. This was recorded in northern Lancashire from Roman horse dung at Lancaster (Wilson, 1979). It is a member of a group of species characteristic of fens and carrs, which disappeared, almost entirely through drainage, some 500 or so years ago.

Carex canescens L.   White Sedge

Circumpolar Boreal-montane element.

This is a perennial herb of lowland bogs and nutrient poor mires in upland areas always on acid substrates (BH11). It is found in many parts of the British Isles except parts of midland England and Ireland.

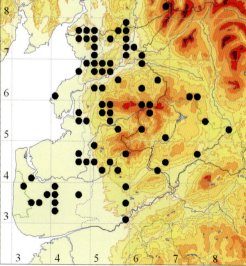

Carex rostrata

Occasional (51). In northern Lancashire *C. canescens* is found in northern and eastern areas and much more rarely in western parts of the region. Whilst its distribution in northern Lancashire is probably unchanged losses in lowland England were reported by the 'New Atlas'. However since 1987 losses seem to have become more widespread ('Local Change').

Carex hirta L.   Hairy Sedge

European Temperate element.

This rhizomatous perennial herb is found in a wide variety of damp grassy and wasteland habitats. It prefers neutral and nutrient rich habitats (BH6). It is found throughout the British Isles but it is rare in northern Scotland.

Common (305). Hairy Sedge is found throughout northern Lancashire except on the higher fells and in very acid conditions. There has been no change in its distribution in northern Lancashire and no change was noted nationally by the 'New Atlas'. However since 1987 'Local Change' reported a significant increase no doubt due to Hairy Sedge's ability to colonize partly improved damp pastures and ruderal habitats.

Carex lasiocarpa Ehrh.   Slender Sedge

Circumpolar Boreal-montane element.

This is a rhizomatous perennial herb of reed-swamps, fens and other wetland habitats. It occurs in nutrient poor water, which may be base-rich or base-poor (BH11). Slender Sedge occurs in Ireland, Scotland and Wales but in England it is now mostly confined to the northwest, East Anglia and southern areas.

Very rare (2) or extinct. In northern Lancashire this was found in a bog at Nether Kellet (SD65E) in 1968 (E.F.G.), which was lost when the wetland was converted to a pond and at Whittington (SD57Y; Livermore and Livermore, 1987). It has not been seen at the Whittington locality since its original discovery. Nationally there have been losses in England ('Local Change').

Carex acutiformis Ehrh.   Lesser Pond-sedge

Eurosiberian Temperate element.

This rhizomatous perennial species forms large patches in base-rich, mesotrophic to eutrophic waters occurring in marshes, fens, and by lakes, ponds and rivers (BH11). It is found in England, Wales, Ireland and southern Scotland but with a few localities as far north as the north coast.

Frequent (113). In northern Lancashire whilst it occurs in many lowland areas most records are from river valleys and near the Lancaster Canal. The distribution of *C. acutiformis* is stable locally and nationally.

Carex acutiformis × C. acuta (C. × subgracilis Druce)

This rare hybrid is found in marshes, mires and by rivers in a few scattered localities in Britain.

Very rare (1). This was found in northern Lancashire with both parents on both banks of the R. Lune, Halton-with-Aughton and Quernmore (SD46W) in 1990 and 1991 (K.R., L.A.L.; LIV).

Carex riparia Curtis   Greater Pond-sedge

Eurosiberian Temperate element.

This tall, rhizomatous perennial herb is found in reed swamps, fens and at the edge of ponds, lakes and slow moving rivers. It occurs in base-rich, mesotrophic or eutrophic habitats (BH11, 14) and is found in England, Wales, Ireland, southern and eastern Scotland.

Rare (10). In northern Lancashire *C. riparia* is found in a few lowland localities. Wheldon and Wilson (1907) knew of only two sites one of which had been lost suggesting that Greater Pond-sedge has spread slightly over the last 100 years. Its distribution nationally is probably unchanged.

Carex pseudocyperus L.   Cyperus Sedge

Eurosiberian Temperate element.

This attractive species is found in shallow water in ponds, fens and by the side of lakes, rivers, reservoirs etc. and readily colonizes bare mud (BH11). It is found in England, Wales and Ireland.

Occasional (29). In northern Lancashire Cyperus Sedge is found in western areas especially in the northwest of the region and in the Fylde. It has become more widespread over the last 100 years as Wheldon and Wilson (1907) reported it from only six sites. However nationally the 'New Atlas' recorded a substantial decline but since 1987 it has become more widespread ('Local Change') possibly because it has been able to colonize newly made gravel pits and other ruderal sites.

Carex pseudocyperus × C. rostrata

This very rare hybrid was found in W. Norfolk (VC 28) in 1955 but has since disappeared and in Fermanagh, Ireland (VC H33) in 1988 (Jermy and Simpson, 2007).

Very rare (1). In northern Lancashire this hybrid was discovered at Hawes Water, Silverdale (SD47T) in 2008 (M.W.).

Carex rostrata Stokes   Bottle Sedge

Circumpolar Boreo-temperate element.

Bottle Sedge is a rhizomatous perennial herb found in emergent stands at the edge of lakes, ponds, rivers, streams, in dune slacks and in alder and willow carr. It usually grows in oligotrophic or mesotrophic water (BH11) and is found throughout the British Isles.

Frequent (75). In northern Lancashire *C. rostrata* is found in scattered localities throughout much of the area including bog pools on top of the fells. Its distribution in the area is stable but nationally there have been losses in south-eastern England ('New Atlas') but since 1987 its distribution is unchanged.

Carex vesicaria L.   Bladder Sedge

Circumpolar Boreo-temperate element.

This is a perennial herb of wet mesotrophic and slightly basic habitats (BH11). It is found in most parts of the British Isles by lakes, rivers, streams, ponds and in marshes and fens etc.

Rare (8). In northern Lancashire Bladder Sedge occurs in a few scattered localities. Its distribution is largely stable locally but it has been lost from many sites in the British Isles ('New Atlas') but further decline since 1987 was not observed ('Local Change').

Carex pendula Huds.   Pendulous Sedge

European Southern-temperate element.

This is a large attractive perennial herb usually found growing on damp, base-rich clays in woodland edge habitats (BH1, 14). However it is also grown in gardens from which it escapes into the wild. Pendulous Sedge is found in England, Wales, Ireland, southern and eastern Scotland.

Frequent (85). In northern Lancashire the native habitat for *C. pendula* is valley woodland surrounding the Bowland fells, especially in the Lune and Ribble valleys. However it has also escaped from gardens and there are scattered localities throughout the area. *C. pendula* has extended its range over the last 100 years in northern Lancashire and this is reflected nationally by a northward extension of its range ('New Atlas') and a continuing general increase since 1987 ('Local Change').

Carex sylvatica Huds.   Wood-sedge

Eurasian Temperate element.

Wood-sedge is a tufted perennial herb found in woodlands and woodland edge habitats (BH1) throughout the British Isles although it is rare or absent from much of northern Scotland.

Frequent (129). In northern Lancashire Wood-sedge occurs in woodlands and woodland edge habitats in the east and north of the region. Its distribution in the region is unchanged and the 'New Atlas' similarly reported an unchanged distribution nationally. However 'Local Change' reported a significant spread of the species since 1987.

Carex strigosa Huds.   Thin-spiked Wood-sedge

Suboceanic Temperate element.

This is a perennial herb of moist, base-rich soils in deciduous woodland often near streams or seepages (BH1, 14). It is found in England and Wales from the Morecambe Bay area southwards and in Ireland. There is also a single record in southern Scotland.

Very rare (3). In northern Lancashire this was first found from a wood at Silverdale in 1965 (A.E.R.) and presumably it was this locality in SD47T that was recorded by Livermore and Livermore (1987). It was also recorded from one of the Hodder valley woods, Aighton, Bailey and Chaigley (SD64V) in 1970 (T.B.) and from Alston Wood, Grimsargh (SD63B) in 1999 (P.J.). *C. strigosa* is easily overlooked and although rare it may occur in additional localities. Nationally its distribution is stable.

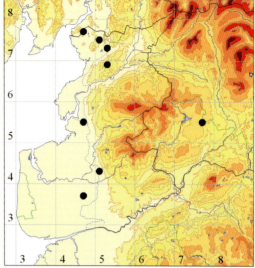
Carex vesicaria

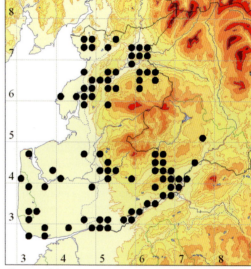
Carex pendula

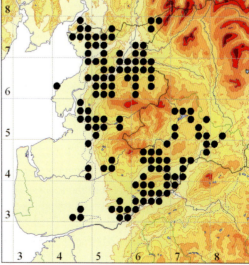
Carex sylvatica

Carex flacca Schreb.   Glaucous Sedge

European Southern-temperate element.

Glaucous Sedge is a rhizomatous perennial herb of unshaded neutral and calcareous grasslands (BH7, 11). It is found throughout the British Isles.

Common (264). *C. flacca* is found in suitable localities throughout northern Lancashire. Its distribution is unchanged locally and nationally.

Carex panicea L.   Carnation Sedge

European Boreo-temperate element.

This perennial herb occurs in a wide range of damp or wet habitats often on neutral soils in grasslands, mires and flushes etc. (BH11). It is found throughout the British Isles.

Common (234). Carnation Sedge is found throughout northern Lancashire except in peat covered areas and the most intensively cultivated parts of the region. Its distribution in northern Lancashire is stable but there has been a decline in south-eastern England ('New Atlas') but further significant decline since 1987 was not noted by 'Local Change'.

Carex laevigata Sm.   Smooth-stalked Sedge

Oceanic Temperate element.

C. laevigata is a perennial herb characteristically found in moist woodlands often flushed with base-rich water (BH1, 16). It is found in much of the British Isles but it is rare or absent from central Ireland, midland and eastern England.

Occasional (22). Smooth-stalked Sedge is found in woodlands in the north and east of VC 60. There is also a doubtful record from Gisburn Forest (SD75N) in Lancashire VC 64. Wheldon and Wilson (1907) only recorded *C. laevigata* from woods by the R. Calder near Garstang but it is easily overlooked so that the spread of this species over the last 100 years may not be a real increase but due to better recording. There has been no change in its distribution nationally.

Carex binervis Sm.   Green-ribbed Sedge

Oceanic Temperate element.

This is a perennial species of both wet and dry acid soils found in lowland and upland heaths, *Nardus* grassland and heather moors (BH8, 10, 16). It is found throughout the British Isles but it is rare in much of midland and eastern England and parts of eastern Ireland.

Frequent (78). In northern Lancashire *C. binervis* occurs in northern and eastern parts of the area. There is also a record from near Fleetwood (SD34I) but this is probably an error. The distribution of Green-ribbed Sedge is stable locally and nationally.

Carex distans L.   Distant Sedge

European Southern-temperate element.

Distant Sedge is a perennial herb found on sea cliffs, rocky shores and coastal grasslands (BH21). It occurs around the shores of the British Isles and inland in southern England.

Occasional (46). *C. distans* occurs on all the coasts of northern Lancashire but appears to be much less frequent on the Ribble estuary and on the Fylde

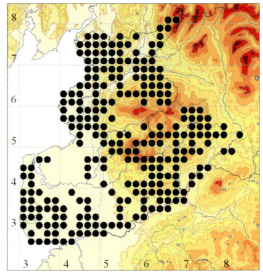

Carex flacca

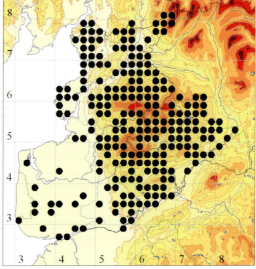

Carex panicea

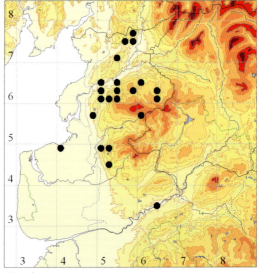

Carex laevigata

coast than elsewhere. Its distribution is stable locally and in coastal sites nationally but there has been a decline at inland sites ('New Atlas'). There have been no significant changes nationally since 1987 ('Local Change').

Carex extensa Gooden.   Long-bracted Sedge

European Southern-temperate element.

This is a perennial herb found on the uppermost parts of salt marshes, on sea cliffs and in coastal grasslands (BH21). It is found around the coasts of the British Isles but it is rare in eastern England and Ireland.

Occasional (23). In northern Lancashire *C. extensa* occurs mostly at the top of salt marshes on the Wyre and Lune estuaries and around Morecambe Bay. So far it has not been found on the Ribble estuary where it formerly occurred and may spread following expansion of its range further south. Nationally there has been little change in its distribution and whilst the extension of its range noted by 'Local Change' since 1987 is not significant it has become much more common on the Dee estuary in VC 58 and on the Merseyside coast (VC 59) in recent years.

Carex hostiana DC.   Tawny Sedge

European Temperate element.

Tawny Sedge is a perennial herb occurring in damp, base-rich grasslands and flushes (BH11). It is found throughout the British Isles but it is rare in most of midland and eastern England.

Occasional (35). In northern Lancashire *C. hostiana* is found in northern and eastern parts of the area. Although Wheldon and Wilson (1907) recorded Tawny Sedge from only twelve sites it has probably been better recorded in recent years. Nationally there have been losses, mostly since 1950, in midland and southern England ('New Atlas'), but 'Local Change' noted no further losses since 1987.

[Carex hostiana × **C. viridula** (**C.** × **fulva** Gooden.)

This is the commonest hybrid sedge occurring in many parts of northern and western areas of the British Isles usually with both parents in close proximity. It is therefore surprising that so far this hybrid has not been seen in northern Lancashire where it must surely occur.]

[Carex flava L.   Large Yellow-sedge

This was reported erroneously from a damp pasture at Tatham (SD66J) by Livermore and Livermore (1987).]

Carex flava group   Yellow-sedges

In the British Isles three species are recognised all of which occur in northern Lancashire. However this is a taxonomically difficult group and whilst it is relatively easy to recognise many plants others seem to be somewhat intermediate, especially between *C lepidocarpa* and *C. demissa*. These plants are fertile but may be hybrids. However in this account plants have been assigned to one or other species on the basis of the characters that seem to best fit a particular species.

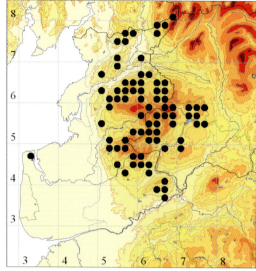
Carex birnervis

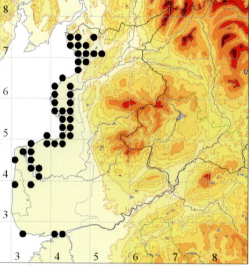
Carex distans

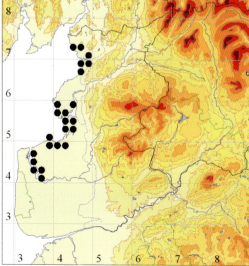
Carex extensa

Carex lepidocarpa Tausch   Long-stalked Yellow-sedge

European Temperate element.

This is a perennial herb of calcareous mires, fens and flushes (BH11, 14). It is found throughout the British Isles but it is found most commonly in northern Britain and Ireland.

Occasional (41). In northern Lancashire *C. lepidocarpa* is found in northern and eastern parts of the region. However included here are plants that fit the description by Jermy, *et al.* (2007) except that the lowest utricle is often only weakly deflexed and thus they may be more accurately considered as intermediate between this species and *C. demissa*. Because of identification problems it is not known if its distribution has changed locally. Nationally it is thought that there have been losses ('New Atlas', 'Local Change').

Carex demissa Hornem.   Common Yellow-sedge

Suboceanic Boreo-temperate element.

This perennial species occurs in wet acid or neutral substrates in open habitats ranging from sandy shores, tracksides and marshy fields to hill flushes and other places where water seeps through the ground (BH14). It is found throughout the British Isles but it is rare in south-eastern England.

Frequent (157). This species is found throughout northern Lancashire but it is rare in lowland, western areas. It is not thought that its distribution has changed significantly locally or nationally.

Carex oederi Retz.   Small-fruited Yellow-sedge

European Boreo-temperate element.

This small perennial herb occurs in open habitats on damp soils in dune slacks, on the uppermost parts of salt marshes and on the stony margins of lakes. It can grow on acid substrates but more usually they are base-rich (BH11, 19). Although there are records from many parts of the British Isles most records are from north-western Scotland.

Very rare (4). In northern Lancashire *C. oederi* was found at Coldwell, Silverdale in 1980 (L.A.L.) and on shell marl by Hawes Water, Silverdale (both SD47T) in 1983 (A.E.C.), in a dune slack at Heysham (SD45E) in 1965 (Preston Scientific Society), Lytham St Anne's Old Links Golf Course in 2002 where it had been known for many years and was still present in 2008 (C.F. & N.J.S.), Lytham St Anne's L.N.R. (both SD33A) where it was last seen in 2007 (E.F.G.) and in a damp hollow on the Royal Lytham St Anne's Golf Course (SD32J) in 1975 (C.F. & N.J.S.). At Lytham St Anne's ssp. *pulchella* (Lönnr.) Palmgr. was recognised as well as ssp. *oederi*. *C. oederi* ssp. *oederi* was lost at Heysham with the construction of the power stations and it has not been seen at the Silverdale localities for some years. It is not clear if its distribution nationally has changed or not.

Carex pallescens L.   Pale Sedge

Eurosiberian Boreo-temperate element.

Pale Sedge is a perennial herb of damp grassland, woodland rides and stream banks mostly on neutral soils but sometimes occurs in more acid situations (BH1). It is found in most parts of the British Isles.

Occasional (44). In northern Lancashire Pale Sedge is found in the north and east of the area. Its distribution locally is unchanged but nationally the

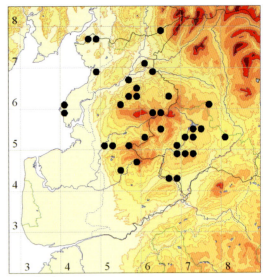

Carex hostiana

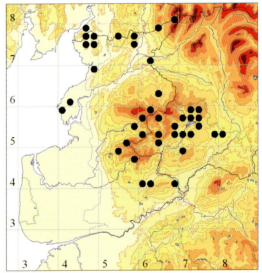

Carex lepidocarpa

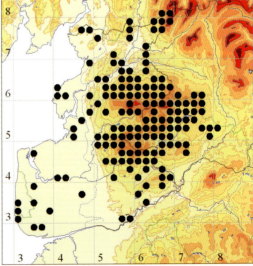

Carex demissa

'New Atlas' reported many losses since 1950. However no further significant losses were reported after 1987 ('Local Change').

Carex digitata L. — Fingered Sedge

European Boreo-temperate element.

C. digitata is a perennial herb found in open deciduous woodland on limestone and in other lightly shaded habitats. It is often found at the side of woodland paths (BH1, 16). It is found mostly in northern England and on the Severn estuary

Very rare (5). Fingered Sedge occurs in a limited area of northern Lancashire in limestone woodland in Silverdale, Yealand Conyers and Yealand Redmayne (SD47S, T, U, X, Y). Here it is frequent occurring in several localities. Its distribution is stable locally and nationally.

Carex caryophyllea Latourr. — Spring Sedge

Eurosiberian Temperate element.

This is a shortly rhizomatous perennial species found in short grassland usually on dry calcareous substrates but occasionally on grassy heaths on more acid soils (BH7). It is found throughout most of the British Isles but it is absent from most of northern Scotland.

Frequent (117). In northern Lancashire Spring Sedge is widespread in northern and eastern parts of the area but it is very rare in lowland western areas. It has probably declined in western parts of the region and the 'New Atlas' reported losses nationally since 1950 in south-western, midland and south-eastern England. 'Local Change' did not note further losses since 1987.

Carex ericetorum Pollich — Rare Spring-sedge

Eurosiberian Boreal-montane element.

This perennial herb is restricted to dry, grazed grasslands on infertile calcareous soils (BH7). It occurs in northern England, the eastern midlands and in East Anglia.

Rare (7). In northern Lancashire *C. ericetorum* was not discovered until 1951 (Bunker, 1953) when it was found near Hawes Water, Silverdale (SD47T). Since then it has been found in several localities in Silverdale, Yealand Conyers and Yealand Redmayne. Its distribution locally is thought to be stable but nationally it has declined ('New Atlas').

Carex pilulifera L. — Pill Sedge

European Temperate element.

Pill Sedge is a perennial herb of base-poor, usually acid soils on heaths, in open woodlands, upland grasslands and moorland (BH8). It is found throughout the British Isles although it is rare in midland England and central Ireland.

Frequent (84). In northern Lancashire *C. pilulifera* is found in northern and eastern parts of the area with a single record from Lytham St Anne's in the west. Wheldon and Wilson (1907) knew Pill Sedge from only seven localities suggesting that there has been a substantial extension of the range of this species. Nationally the 'New Atlas' reported no change in its distribution but 'Local Change' noted a significant increase suggesting that the increase was due to increased grazing levels as the sedge responds positively to grazing.

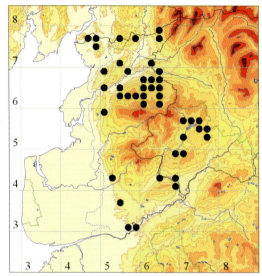

Carex pallescens

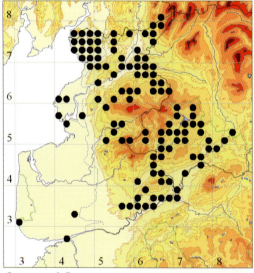

Carex caryophyllea

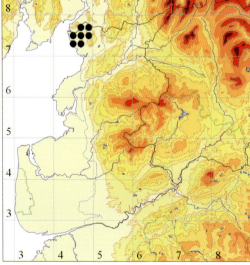

Carex ericetorum

Carex limosa L.   Bog-sedge

Circumpolar Boreal-montane element.

This is a perennial species found in *Sphagnum* dominated mires in mostly lowland areas (BH11, 12). It was found in Scotland, northern England, Wales, southern England and Ireland.

Extinct. In northern Lancashire Bog-sedge was found on Cockerham Moss in 1881 (A.W.; YRK, NMW) and Lytham Moss, probably between 1796 and 1810 (Wheldon and Wilson, 1925). Extensive peat cutting and drainage took place at Cockerham Moss in 1912 and Bog-sedge was last seen at that time. Lytham Moss was drained *c.* 1825. Nationally *C. limosa* was lost from English sites before 1930 and drainage has caused losses in Ireland ('New Atlas'). However further losses since 1987 were not noted by 'Local Change'.

Carex acuta L.   Slender Tufted-sedge

Eurosiberian Boreo-temperate element.

This is a rhizomatous perennial herb of shallow water at the edge of streams, rivers and ponds and in marshy areas. It usually grows in meso-trophic to eutrophic conditions on calcareous substrates (BH11). It is found in lowland areas of England, Wales, Ireland and southern Scotland.

Rare (14). Slender Tufted-sedge is found in scattered localities in northern Lancashire. Wheldon and Wilson (1907) recorded it from about six locali-ties, mostly by the R. Lune. Whilst it has been lost and found in other localities those on the R. Ribble appear to be new. Nationally it has declined ('New Atlas') but 'Local Change' suggests that there might be a slight increase.

Carex nigra (L.) Reichard   Common Sedge

Eurosiberian Boreo-temperate element.

Common Sedge is found in a wide range of wet habitats but it is absent from basic and very acid substrates (BH11). It is morphologically variable and may be either tussock forming or rhizomatous forming extensive patches. It occurs throughout the British Isles.

Common (286). Common Sedge is found throughout northern Lancashire but it is less frequent in lowland, western areas than elsewhere. The distri-bution of *C. nigra* is unchanged locally and nationally except perhaps in south-eastern England where there have been some losses ('New Atlas').

Carex nigra × C. elata (C. × turfosa Fr.)

This hybrid is found in a few scattered localities in Britain where the parents grow close to each other. Most records are from north-western England, northern Wales, East Anglia and Ireland.

Very rare (1). This was found in willow carr with both parents at Little Hawes Water, Yealand Redmayne (SD47T) in 2006 (E.F.G. & M.P.).

Carex elata All.   Tufted-sedge

Eurasian Temperate element.

This tussock forming perennial sedge occurs in oligotrophic or mesotrophic wetlands often in calcareous conditions (BH11). It is found in England partic-ularly in the Lake District and in eastern counties, Wales especially Anglesey and in Ireland. It has been recorded from a few sites in western Scotland.

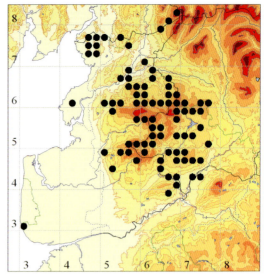
Carex pilulifera

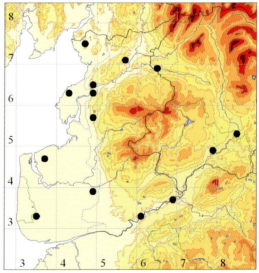
Carex acuta

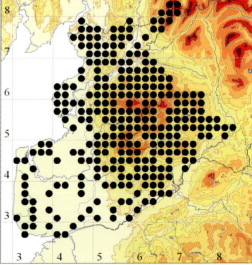
Carex nigra

Rare (11). *C. elata* has been found in a few localities in the north-western parts of the region and near Garstang. Apart from the addition of the Garstang locality the distribution of Tufted-sedge in northern Lancashire is unchanged. Nationally there have been losses particularly in East Anglia ('New Atlas'). Wheldon and Wilson (1907) referred to *Carex elata* var. *turfosa* Ar. Benn. but the only voucher specimens seen seem to be *C. elata*.

Carex bigelowii Torr. ex Schwein.   Stiff Sedge

Circumpolar Arctic-montane element.

Stiff Sedge is a perennial herb of well-drained, montane grassland and sedge-heath on open stony ground (BH15). It is found in the mountains of northern England, northern Wales, Ireland and Scotland.

Very rare (3). In northern Lancashire *C. bigelowii* has been found on the summit ridge of Gragareth and Greenhill, Leck (SD78A; Livermore and Livermore, 1987), SD67Z in 1966 (E.F.G.) and SD68U in 2000 (E.F.G. & J.M.N.). There has been no change in its distribution locally or nationally.

Carex pulicaris L.   Flea Sedge

Suboceanic Temperate element.

This is a small perennial herb of wet neutral or calcareous soils. It occurs in short-sedge mires, damp meadows, fens, wet heaths and flushes (BH11, 16) and is found throughout the British Isles.

Frequent (88). *C. pulicaris* is found in northern and eastern parts of northern Lancashire. Its distribution locally is probably stable but nationally there have been losses in midland and eastern England ('New Atlas') but no further losses since 1987 were noted by 'Local Change'.

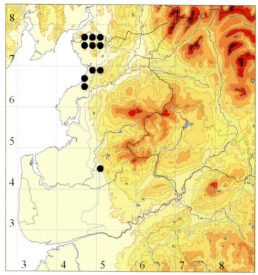
Carex elata

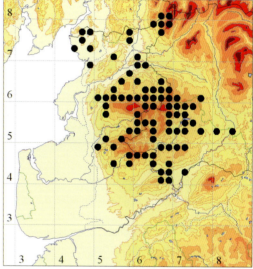
Carex pulicaris

POACEAE   GRASS FAMILY

For many years the standard monograph on British grasses was Hubbard's *Grasses* the last edition of which was published in 1984 (Hubbard, 1984). In late 2009 a new monograph was published revising Poaceae species (except bamboos) found in the British Isles (Cope and Gray, 2009). However their treatment is different to that of Stace (2010), which the following account follows.

Sasa palmata (Burb.) E.G. Camus   Broad-leaved Bamboo

Neophyte. Broad-leaved Bamboo is a native of Japan and Sakhalin and was introduced into Britain about 1889. It is commonly grown in gardens and in the grounds of country houses. It was found growing wild by 1964 and today occurs in England, Wales, Ireland and southern Scotland.

Very rare (2). *S. palmata* was found in northern Lancashire at Lancaster (SD46V; Livermore and Livermore, 1991) and in Ox Hey Wood, Bashall Eaves (SD64W; Abbott, 2005).

Sasaella ramosa (Makino) Makino   Hairy Bamboo

Neophyte. *S. ramosa* is a native of Japan and was introduced into British cultivation in 1892. It is planted in woodlands and rough grassland and is increasingly popular in gardens. It was first found growing wild in 1983 and today occurs in scattered localities in England, especially in the London area and Wales.

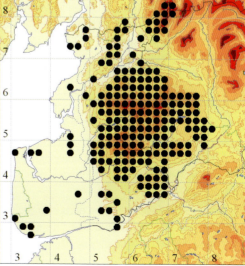
Nardus stricta

Very rare (2). In northern Lancashire Hairy Bamboo was found in woodland and waste ground between Lancaster and Morecambe (SD46L) and in the Lune valley (SD56H), both Livermore and Livermore (1987).

Pseudosasa japonica (Siebold & Zucc. ex Steud.) Makino ex Nakai
Arrow Bamboo

Neophyte. *P. japonica* is a native of Japan and Korea and has been grown in British gardens since 1850. It was first recorded in the wild in 1955 and today occurs mostly in southern England and Wales.

Very rare (5). In northern Lancashire Arrow Bamboo was first recorded from Carnforth (SD47V) in 1986 (B.S.B.I.). Other records are from Forton (SD45V) and Over Wyresdale (SD55H), both Livermore and Livermore (1987); Silverdale (SD47S) in 2000 (C.B.W.) and Warton (SD57B) in 2009 (E.F.G.).

Nardus stricta L. Mat-grass

European Boreo-temperate element.

This is a densely tufted, shortly rhizomatous perennial grass found on winter-wet, base-poor infertile and peaty soils (BH8) occurring in most parts of the British Isles. It is particularly characteristic of heavily grazed upland pastures in Wales, northern England and Scotland.

Frequent (205). Mat-grass is very common in the upland areas of Bowland and Leck but only occurs in scattered locations in western parts of northern Lancashire. Its distribution is unchanged locally but the 'New Atlas' reported local declines nationally. 'Local Change' noted a significant decrease since 1987 in southern Britain.

Milium effusum L. Wood Millet

Circumpolar Boreo-temperate element.

Wood Millet is a perennial herb found in damp deciduous woodland and in woodland edge habitats on neutral or calcareous soils (BH1). It occurs in England, Wales and Scotland but it is rare in highland and northern Scotland. It also occurs in scattered Irish localities.

Occasional (58). *M. effusum* occurs in scattered localities in northern Lancashire but especially in valley woodlands surrounding the Bowland fells and in the Lune, Ribble and Hodder valleys. Wheldon and Wilson (1907) only recorded Wood Millet from ten localities suggesting an increase in its distribution over the last 100 years. Similarly the 'New Atlas' suggested that nationally it might have spread slightly in recent years but 'Local Change' reported an unchanged distribution since 1987.

Schedonorus pratensis Huds. Meadow Fescue

Eurosiberian Boreo-temperate element.

This is a short-lived perennial species found in a wide range of neutral grasslands (BH6). It was formerly widely planted as a fodder plant and today occurs throughout the British Isles although it is rare in northern Scotland.

Common (258). Meadow Fescue occurs throughout northern Lancashire except on peat soils and on moors. Its distribution in the area is unchanged but nationally it may be decreasing ('New Atlas') as it is now rarely grown as a fodder crop and a further decline after 1987 was confirmed by 'Local Change'.

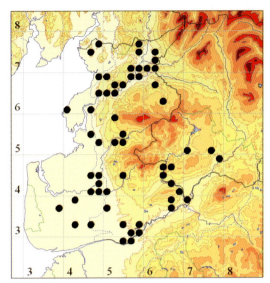

Milium effusum

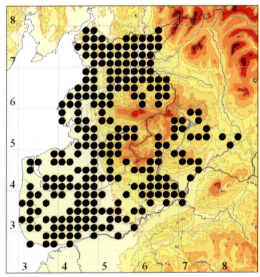

Schedonorus pratensis

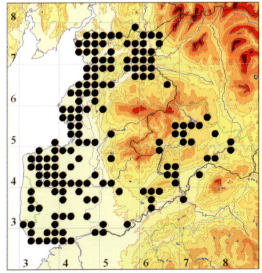

Schedonorus arundinaceus

Schedonorus arundinaceus (Schreb.) Dumort.   Tall Fescue

Eurosiberian Southern-temperate element.

Tall Fescue is a robust perennial herb of scrub, woodland margins and rough grassland (BH6, 7). It is found throughout the British Isles but it is rare in northern Scotland.

Frequent (162). In northern Lancashire *S. arundinaceus* is found in most parts of the region but it is rare in Bowland and to the north of Preston. It is particularly characteristic of coastal clay banks. Wheldon and Wilson (1907) reported thirteen localities suggesting a substantial spread of this species over the last 100 years. It has also spread nationally ('New Atlas', 'Local Change').

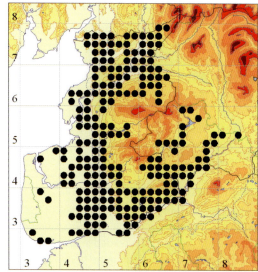
Schedonorus giganteus

Schedonorus giganteus (L.) Holub   Giant Fescue

European Temperate element.

This is a large tufted perennial grass found in moist woodlands on neutral or base-rich soils (BH1). It is found throughout the British Isles but it is rare in northern Scotland and parts of Ireland.

Frequent (228). In northern Lancashire *S. giganteus* is found in many places but it is absent from moorland areas and it is rare or absent in western areas. It is especially characteristic of wet valley woodlands on clay soils. The distribution of Great Fescue is unchanged in northern Lancashire but it is increasing nationally especially since 1987 ('New Atlas', 'Local Change'). Wheldon and Wilson (1907) recorded a var. *triflora* Sm. but it is not known to what this referred.

Schedonorus pratensis × Lolium perenne
(× Schedolium loliaceum (Huds.) Holub)   Hybrid Fescue

Widespread in Europe.

Hybrid Fescue occurs in usually damp, fertile grasslands (BH6) and is found in many parts of the British Isles although it is rare in northern Scotland.

Occasional (33). It is found in scattered localities in northern Lancashire.

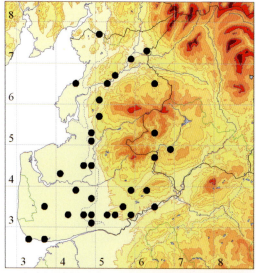
X Schedolium loliaceum

Lolium perenne L.   Perennial Rye-grass

European Southern-temperate element.

Perennial Rye-grass is predominantly a species of improved lowland grassland but it is found in a wide variety of grasslands (BH3, 5, 6). It is an important agricultural grass with numerous cultivars. It is found throughout the British Isles.

Very common (420). It is found throughout northern Lancashire except on peat. Its distribution is unchanged locally and nationally.

Lolium perenne × L. multiflorum (L. × boucheanum Kunth)

Widespread in temperate Europe.

L. × boucheanum is an annual or short-lived perennial grass found in agricultural grasslands and ruderal habitats. The hybrid is fertile and whilst populations can persist for a few years most occurrences are casual. It is found in scattered localities throughout the British Isles but most records are from southern England. It is often planted for grass production and frequently overlooked in the wild.

Rare (8). In northern Lancashire it is found in scattered western localities but it is likely to have been overlooked.

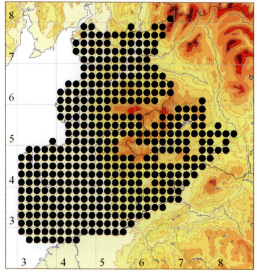
Lolium perenne

Lolium multiflorum Lam.   Italian Rye-grass

Neophyte. Italian Rye-grass is probably a native of the Mediterranean region and began to be used in agriculture about 1830. It was recorded in the wild by 1840 and today occurs throughout the British Isles. It is grown for fodder and it is an important agricultural crop.

Frequent (153). In northern Lancashire it was first found at Leck (Petty, 1893) and Wheldon and Wilson (1907) also found it at Fleetwood Docks and near Winmarleigh. Today it is particularly common in lowland areas of VC 60 but occurs as an escape from agricultural grassland in many parts of the region.

Lolium temulentum L.   Darnel

Archaeophyte. Darnel is possibly a native of the Mediterranean region and south-western Asia but it has spread with cultivation obscuring its native range. It was first recorded in Britain in 1548 and became a serious weed of arable land but had gone from this habitat by the early twentieth century. Since then it has been found as a casual of ruderal habitats.

Rare (7). In northern Lancashire Darnel was first found near Winmarleigh in 1899 (Wheldon and Wilson, 1902). Today it has been found in lowland areas of south-western VC 60.

[Lolium remotum Schrank   Flaxfield Rye-grass

The origin of this species is obscure but it was formerly an agricultural weed especially of flax fields in England and elsewhere in Europe.

In northern Lancashire there is an unlocalised, unattributed post 1950 record for the 10 × 10km square SD47 (B.R.C.) but this has not been confirmed.]

Festuca altissima All.   Wood Fescue

European Temperate element.

Wood Fescue is a perennial species of deciduous woodland on neutral or calcareous substrates (BH1, 16). It is found in Scotland, Wales, Ireland and northern England but with a few localities further south in Kent.

Occasional (25). In northern Lancashire F. altissima occurs in valley wood-lands, especially in the Lune and Hodder valleys. Wheldon and Wilson (1907) recorded only four localities in VC 60 suggesting a substantial increase but this may be due to better recording rather than a real spread of the species as it is easily overlooked. The increase noted nationally by the 'New Atlas' was also thought to be due to better recording.

Festuca heterophylla Lam.   Various-leaved Fescue

Neophyte with a European Temperate distribution. This densely tufted perennial grass became available in Britain in 1812 and was grown as an ornamental species or more rarely for fodder. It was first recorded in the wild in 1874 and today occurs in scattered localities throughout the British Isles.

Very rare (4). In northern Lancashire F. heterophylla was first recorded from somewhere in the 10 × 10km square SD63 in 1965 (B.R.C.). Later records are from Myerscough (SD43Z) in 1987 (C.J.B.), Catterall (SD44V) in 1995 (C.J.B.) and in tetrad SD44A in 1995 (Anon).

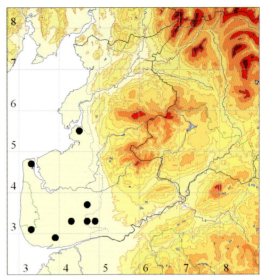

Lolium × boucheanum

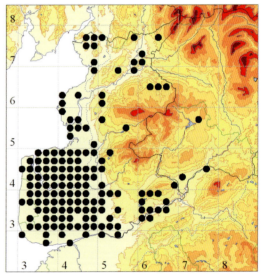

Lolium multiflorum

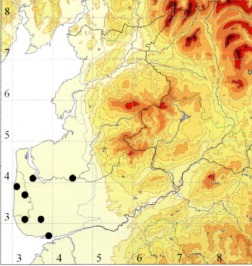

Lolium temulentum

Festuca rubra L. ssp. **rubra**   Red Fescue

Circumpolar Wide-boreal element.

This rhizomatous perennial grass is found in grassy places usually on neutral or calcareous soils (BH3, 5, 6, 21). It occurs throughout the British Isles.

Very common (441). There are several subspecies of Red Fescue and where subspecies have not been recorded it is assumed that the records are for ssp. *rubra*, which is by far the commonest subspecies. It occurs throughout northern Lancashire. However *F. rubra* was historically a rare species and 100 years ago Wheldon and Wilson (1907) recorded it mostly from sandy coastal sites. Since then it has been planted extensively in seed mixtures for amenity purposes. Nevertheless at least some of the increase is probably due to better recording. It is not thought that there has been a change in its distribution nationally – at least since 1962.

Festuca rubra L. ssp. **juncea** (Hack.) K. Richt.

Widespread in Europe but distribution uncertain.

Red Fescue taxonomy is complex but as at present understood *F. rubra* ssp. *juncea* is a densely tufted, shortly rhizomatous and often at least slightly glaucous perennial herb found mostly on sea cliffs and other coastal rocky or well-drained habitats. It is found around the coasts of the British Isles.

Occasional (19). In northern Lancashire this is a coastal subspecies of rocky places, sea-walls and other stony places near the sea. It is not known if its distribution has changed locally or nationally.

Festuca rubra L. ssp. **litoralis** (G. Mey.) Auquier

European Boreo-temperate element recorded from European Atlantic coasts and the Baltic region.

This is a rhizomatous mat-forming subspecies found on and often domi-nating large areas of the middle and upper zones of salt marshes. It occurs on salt marshes and in brackish grasslands around the coasts of the British Isles.

Very rare (5). Although *F. rubra* ssp. *litoralis* has only been certainly recorded from five localities on the shores of Morecambe Bay and on the Lune, Wyre and Ribble estuaries it is thought to be present on all the salt marshes. Where there has been intensive grazing it dominates large areas. Also it is believed that it was this subspecies that sustained a turf cutting industry on the shores of Morecambe Bay where the turf was used for making domestic lawns. It is not known if the distribution of *F. rubra* ssp. *litoralis* has changed locally or nationally.

Festuca rubra L. ssp. **commutata** Gaudin   Chewing's Fescue

European Temperate element.

Chewing's Fescue is a tufted perennial grass found in grassy places on well-drained soils. Although it is a native British taxon it was first sold as seed in New Zealand and many tons were exported to Britain for use as lawn seed. Subsequently it was imported to Britain from sources in the U.S.A. and from continental Europe. It is widely grown but it is only occa-sionally recorded in the wild probably because it is overlooked.

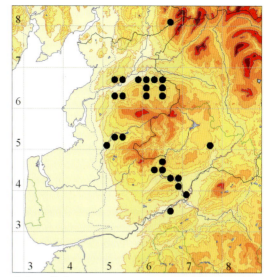
Festuca altissima

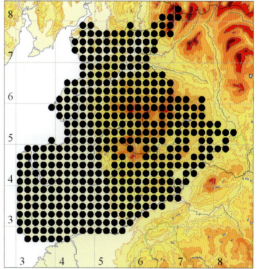
Festuca rubra

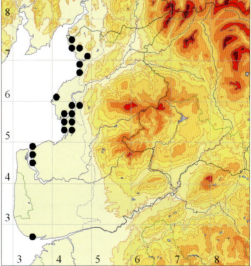
Festuca rubra ssp. juncea

Very rare (3). In northern Lancashire Chewing's Fescue was recorded from St Anne's (SD32I) in 1965 (A.E.R.), Greenhalgh-with-Thistleton (SD33Y) in 1988 (C.J.B.) and from Pilling (SD34Z) in 1998 (C.J.B.). It is almost certainly under recorded but it is not known if its distribution has changed either locally or nationally.

Festuca ovina L.   Sheep's-fescue

Eurasian Boreo-temperate element.

This is a densely tufted perennial herb occurring in a wide range of well-drained habitats. It is usually found in upland areas on acid heaths and in rocky places but it may also grow in lowland areas sometimes on calcareous substrates (BH7, 8). It is found throughout the British Isles.

Common (241). In northern Lancashire Sheep's-fescue is a common species in upland areas of the east and north of the region. It also occurs in scattered lowland, western areas particularly on the coastal heaths of the Fylde coast. Here however it may have been recorded erroneously for *F. filiformis*. Little work has been done on identifying the different taxa within *Festuca ovina* aggregate but some observations have been recorded. *Festuca ovina* L. ssp. *hirtula* (Hackel ex Travis) M.J. Wilk. is thought to be the most common and widespread taxon in the British Isles (Wilkinson and Stace, 1991) and recorded as such in Cumbria (Halliday, 1997). However although cited by Wilkinson and Stace (1991) as occurring in VC 60 no details of its occurrence are available. *Festuca ovina* L. ssp. *ovina* is apparently less frequent and occurs on acid sandy soils and was found on sandy ground at the base of Thorn Crag, Over Wyresdale (SD55Y). *Festuca ovina* L. ssp. *ophioliticola* (Kerguélen) M.J. Wilk. appears to be most frequent on calcareous soils in southern Britain and it is believed it was this that was planted on sand dunes at Fairhaven (SD32I) and found in 2001 (E.F.G.). Wheldon and Wilson (1907) record *F. ovina* L. var. *glauca* Hack. as occurring on limestone but it is not known to what this refers. Cope and Gray (2009) suggest that *F. ovina* is best regarded as a complex of intergrading cytological and ecological races where morphological characters are difficult to discern. The distribution of *F. ovina* is thought to be unchanged locally and nationally.

[Festuca vivipara (L.) Sm.   Viviparous Sheep's-fescue

Circumpolar Boreo-arctic Montane element.

This is a tufted perennial grass found on acid soils (BH15, 16) in the mountains of Scotland, Wales, Ireland and northern England.

In northern Lancashire there is an unlocalised record for VC 60 cited by Wilkinson and Stace (1991).]

Festuca filiformis Pourr.   Fine-leaved Sheep's-fescue

Suboceanic Temperate element.

This is a densely tufted fine-leaved species found on heaths, moors and in woodland edge habitats on acid well-drained soils (BH8). It probably occurs throughout the British Isles but it has often not been distinguished from *F. ovina*.

Very rare (3). *F. filiformis* is often overlooked. There is an unlocalised record (1883) from the 10 × 10km square SD55 (A.W.; BM) but otherwise the only records are from dune heath at Lytham St Anne's where it was found in 1996 (SD32J, N; P.J.) and 2002 (SD33A; E.F.G.).

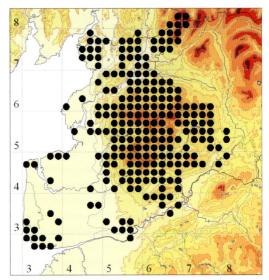
Festuca ovina

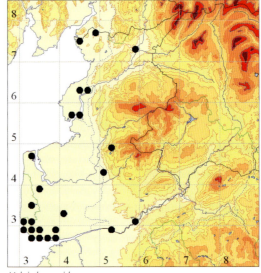
Vulpia bromoides

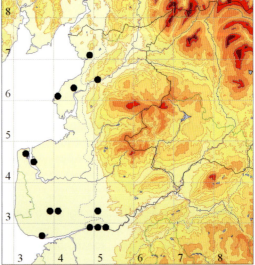
Vulpia myuros

Festuca brevipila R. Tracey   Hard Fescue

Neophyte. This is a tufted perennial species native in central Europe. It was introduced in turf and seed mixtures for amenity use and has been known in the wild since 1830. Today it is found mostly in the south-eastern half of Britain. However it is easily overlooked and it is often mistaken for *F. ovina*.

Very rare (1). It may have been this that Wheldon and Wilson called *F. ovina* L. var. *duriuscula* Fr., which they considered frequent in lowland areas of VC 60. The only confirmed record is from Fairhaven (SD32N) in 1996 (P.J.).

Festuca rubra × Vulpia fasciculata
(× Festulpia hubbardii Stace & Cotton)

This intergeneric hybrid was first described in 1974 (Stace and Cotton, 1974) and probably occurs where the parents *Festuca rubra* and *Vulpia fasciculata* are present. However it is easily overlooked and its distribution is not fully known.

Very rare (3). In northern Lancashire, following confirmation of × *Festulpia hubbardii* on sand dunes in Cheshire (VC 58), South Lancaster (VC 59) and Cumberland (VC 70), searches were successfully made for it on the West Lancaster (VC 60) coastal sand dunes. Several colonies were found at Lytham St Anne's (SD32E, I, SD33A) in 2001 (P.L. Thomas).

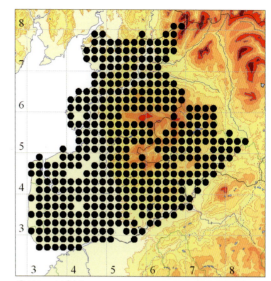
Cynosurus cristatus

Vulpia fasciculata (Forssk.) Fritsch   Dune Fescue

Mediterranean Atlantic element.

Dune Fescue is an annual species of open habitats on sand dunes (BH19) and occurs mostly on western coasts of England and Wales and on the east coast of Ireland.

Very rare (5). In northern Lancashire *V. fasciculata* occurs on the sand dunes at Lytham St Anne's where it occurs in several localities and is often abundant. Although there is some evidence that Dune Fescue has increased in East Anglia ('New Atlas') it is thought that both locally and nationally its distribution is unchanged.

Vulpia bromoides (L.) Gray   Squirreltail Fescue

Submediterranean-Subatlantic element.

V. bromoides is an annual species of open habitats often in ruderal habitats (BH3) and occurs in many lowland areas of the British Isles.

Occasional (25). In northern Lancashire *V. bromoides* occurs mostly in coastal areas, especially at Lytham St Anne's, with only occasional localities elsewhere in VC 60. Although the 'New Atlas' recorded little change in Squirreltail Fescue's distribution nationally 'Local Change' reported significant increases since 1987, especially in inland ruderal habitats. In northern Lancashire *V. bromoides* has spread considerably from the two localities noted by Wheldon and Wilson (1907).

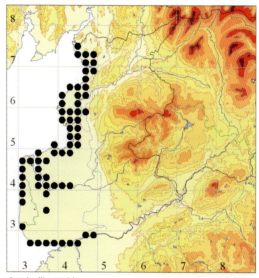
Puccinellia maritima

Vulpia myuros (L.) C.C. Gmel.   Rat's-tail Fescue

Archaeophyte with a Eurosiberian Southern-temperate distribution but a neophyte in northern Lancashire. *V. myuros* occurs in open, usually ruderal habitats, in built-up areas (BH3, 17). It is found most commonly in the southern half of the British Isles but localities occur more thinly scattered as far north as northern Scotland.

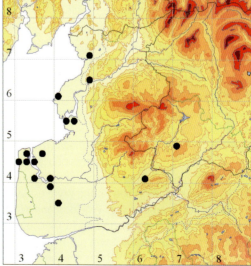
Puccinellia distans

Rare (13). In northern Lancashire *V. myuros* was first found on a tip at Lancaster (SD46L) in 1969 (E.F.G.). Today it occurs in a few coastal localities in VC 60 but more especially in Preston where it seems to be naturalised. Nationally it has spread considerably since 1962 and appears to be still spreading ('New Atlas', 'Local Change').

Cynosurus cristatus L.   Crested Dog's-tail

European Temperate element.

Crested Dog's-tail is a short-lived perennial grass occurring in neutral or calcareous, well-drained grasslands that are usually heavily grazed (BH6). It is found throughout the British Isles.

Very common (411). *C. cristatus* occurs throughout northern Lancashire except on peat substrates. There has been no change in its distribution locally or nationally.

Cynosurus echinatus L.   Rough Dog's-tail

Neophyte. This is a native of southern Europe, the Mediterranean region and south-western Asia. It is found naturalised in sandy fields in southern England but elsewhere it is a rare casual of tips and ruderal habitats.

Very rare (1). In northern Lancashire *C. echinatus* was first found in 1901 and 1902 at Fleetwood and Preston Docks (Wheldon and Wilson, 1907). It was then found at the base of a sea wall at Fairhaven (Whellan, 1948, and again in 1965 (A.E.R.)). It was last seen in the mid 1970s (C.F. & N.J.S.).

Puccinellia maritima (Huds.) Parl.   Common Saltmarsh-grass

Oceanic Boreo-temperate element.

Common Saltmarsh-grass is a stoloniferous perennial herb occurring in salt marshes and rarely in brackish places inland. It often dominates lower and mid parts of salt marshes and is tolerant of heavy grazing when it can then form a monoculture (BH21). It is found around all the coasts of the British Isles.

Occasional (64). In northern Lancashire *P. maritima* is found on all the coastal salt marshes with occasional inland localities. The coastal distribution of *P. maritima* is unchanged locally and nationally.

Puccinellia distans (Jacq.) Parl. ssp. distans Reflexed Saltmarsh-grass

Eurosiberian Boreo-temperate element.

This is a perennial herb found in open habitats in brackish conditions near the coast or inland on salt treated roads (BH3, 21). *P. distans* occurs around the coasts of the British Isles but more especially on eastern coasts of Britain and Ireland. It has also been found inland particularly in eastern Britain.

Occasional (16). In northern Lancashire Reflexed Saltmarsh-grass has been found on the estuaries of the Wyre and Lune and on the shores of Morecambe Bay. However on the Wyre estuary it was also frequent on salt mine waste heaps and occasionally inland on roadsides. It is not known when *P. distans* first appeared in northern Lancashire and, although it was established on the Wyre estuary by the mid 1960s, it was not recorded by either Wheldon and Wilson (1907) or Perring and Walters (1962). It was present further south in VC 59 in 1909 (Savidge, *et al.*, 1963) but it was not known in Cumbria to the north until 1970 (Halliday, 1997). By comparing the distribution of Reflexed

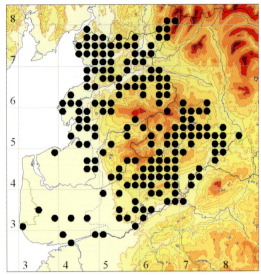

Briza media

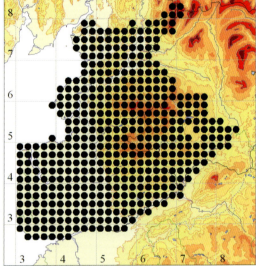

Poa annua

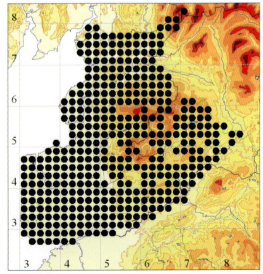

Poa trivialis

Saltmarsh-grass in Perring and Walters (1962) with that in the 'New Atlas' it is clear that there was a significant spread of this largely east coast species to coasts bordering the Irish Sea both in Ireland and Britain. However since 1962 it has also spread inland and this has continued since 1987 ('New Atlas', 'Local Change').

Briza media L. Quaking-grass

European Temperate element.

Quaking-grass is a readily recognisable perennial species found in unimproved, species-rich, grazed grasslands on infertile, calcareous soils (BH7). It is found throughout the British Isles but it is rare in northern Scotland and parts of Ireland.

Frequent (190). *B. media* is found mostly in eastern and northern parts of northern Lancashire but does occur in a few places in lowland western areas of VC 60. It has probably become less frequent in lowland areas of western VC 60 and nationally a decline is noted in its distribution both by the 'New Atlas' and since 1987 by 'Local Change'.

Briza maxima L. Greater Quaking-grass

Neophyte. *B. maxima* is a native of the Mediterranean region and was introduced into Britain by 1633. It was recorded in the wild by 1860 and today it is naturalised in south-western England but may occur as a casual or garden escape almost anywhere in the British Isles.

Very rare (4). In northern Lancashire *B. maxima* was found in Lancaster (SD46V; Livermore and Livermore, 1991), on the sand dunes at Lytham St Anne's (SD32I) in 1994 (E.F.G.) and at other sites in Lytham St Anne's (SD32J) since 2005 (C.F. & N.J.S.). It was also found at Slaidburn (SD75B) in about 2006 (P.P.A.).

Poa annua L. Annual Meadow-grass

Eurosiberian Wide-temperate element.

This is a very common annual grass found in a variety of disturbed habitats as well as in grasslands and lawns (BH3, 4, 5, 6). It is found throughout the British Isles.

Very common (456). *P. annua* is found throughout northern Lancashire and is the region's commonest species. Its distribution locally and nationally is unchanged.

Poa trivialis L. Rough Meadow-grass

Circumpolar Wide-temperate element.

Rough Meadow-grass is a perennial species found in woodland edge habitats, waste ground and other, often shady, marginal and ruderal habitats (BH1, 3, 6). It is found throughout the British Isles.

Very common (409). In northern Lancashire *P. trivialis* is found in most parts of the region being absent only from a few upland areas. Its distribution is stable both locally and nationally.

Poa humilis Ehrh. ex Hoffm. Spreading Meadow-grass

World distribution uncertain.

P. humilis is a small, rhizomatous perennial herb found in grassland, ruderal habitats and on sand dunes (BH6, 19). It probably occurs throughout

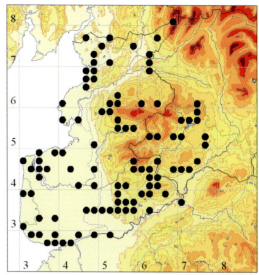
Poa humilis

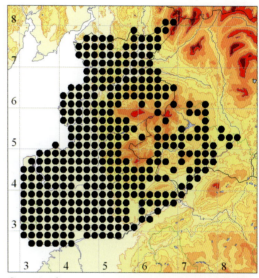
Poa pratensis

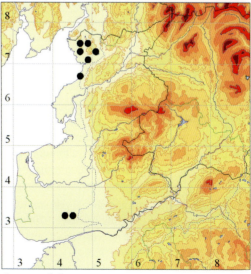
Poa angustifolia

the British Isles but recorders have not always recognised it as a distinct species.

Frequent (102). Spreading Meadow-grass is very much under recorded in northern Lancashire but occurs throughout the region. It is a characteristic species of sand dunes and in a zone at the edge of roadside verges. It is not known if its distribution has changed locally or nationally.

Poa pratensis L.   Smooth Meadow-grass

Circumpolar Wide-temperate element.

This is a rhizomatous perennial herb of meadows, roadsides and waste places (BH3, 5, 6, 7). It was formerly included in grassland seed mixtures and is still used in amenity plantings. It probably occurs throughout the British Isles but recorders often included *P. humilis* as part of *P. pratensis sensu lato*.

Very common (373). In northern Lancashire recorders have not always recorded *P. humilis* as a separate species and have included it within *P. pratensis*. However it is believed Smooth Meadow-grass occurs throughout the area. Its distribution is probably unchanged both locally and nationally although anecdotal evidence suggests that *P. pratensis* is not as common as *P. humilis* in northern Lancashire.

Poa angustifolia L.   Narrow-leaved Meadow-grass

Circumpolar Southern-temperate element.

This is a rhizomatous, narrow-leaved perennial herb of dry grassland and ruderal habitats (BH7, 8). It is found throughout Britain but most records are from south-eastern England.

Rare (8). *P. angustifolia* has been found in a few localities in the northwest of the area and in the Fylde. Because of identification problems it is not known if its distribution has changed locally or nationally.

Poa compressa L.   Flattened Meadow-grass

European Temperate element.

This rhizomatous perennial species is found in open habitats often on stony ground or in built-up areas (BH3). It is found mostly in England but it also occurs occasionally in Ireland, Wales and Scotland.

Occasional (36). In northern Lancashire most records are from western areas with only occasional records elsewhere. Wheldon and Wilson (1907) recorded four localities in VC 60 indicating a spread of this species over the last 100 years but nationally it is thought that Flattened Meadow-grass distribution is unchanged ('Local Change').

Poa palustris L.   Swamp Meadow-grass

Neophyte with a Circumpolar Boreo-temperate distribution. It is a species of marshes and wet places; although generally lowland it occurs throughout the British Isles. It is thought that it was introduced as a fodder grass in the nineteenth century and was recorded in the wild in 1879.

Very rare (3). In northern Lancashire *P. palustris* was first recorded from Roman horse dung at Lancaster (Wilson, 1979) making this the first British record. However it was not recorded again until it was found on a tip at Blackpool (SD33I) in 1966 (A.E.R. & J.H.). Other records are from Myerscough (SD54A) in 1987 (C.J.B.) and Leighton Moss (SD47X) in 2000 (R.P.).

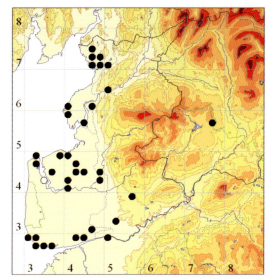

Poa compressa

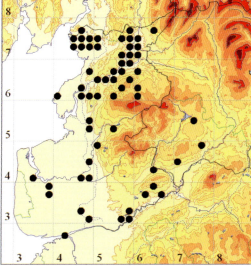

Poa nemoralis

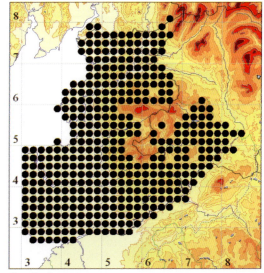

Dactylis glomerata

Poa nemoralis L.   Wood Meadow-grass

Circumpolar Boreo-temperate element.

This is a tufted perennial grass of woodlands and woodland edges (BH1). It is found throughout Britain but it is thought to be an introduction in Ireland.

Occasional (61). In northern Lancashire *P. nemoralis* is found mostly in the north of the area but occurs occasionally throughout the region. It is believed that its distribution is unchanged locally and nationally.

Poa bulbosa L.   Bulbous Meadow-grass

Eurosiberian Southern-temperate element but a neophyte in northern Lancashire.

P. bulbosa is a native species of open habitats in coastal areas of southern and eastern Britain but occurs elsewhere as a rare introduction.

Very rare (1). In northern Lancashire *P. bulbosa* was found in Miller Park, Preston (SD52J) in 1995 (P.J.).

Dactylis glomerata L.   Cock's-foot

Eurosiberian Southern-temperate element.

Cock's-foot is usually a robust, tufted perennial grass of woodland edges, grasslands and ruderal habitats on fertile, neutral or basic substrates (BH6). It is found throughout the British Isles.

Very common (411). *D. glomerata* is found throughout northern Lancashire except on moorland. Its distribution is unchanged locally and nationally.

Catabrosa aquatica (L.) P. Beauv.   Whorl-grass

European Boreo-temperate element.

This is a stoloniferous herb of muddy pond margins, ditches and canals etc. (BH13, 14) occurring in lowland areas of the British Isles.

Rare (13). In northern Lancashire Whorl-grass occurs in the Lancaster Canal and more rarely in ponds in lowland, western parts of the region. Wheldon and Wilson (1907) recorded it from five localities only one of which was in the canal. With increased boat traffic since the 1970s it is likely that *C. aquatica* will have suffered losses in recent years. Nationally it declined after 1962 ('New Atlas') but 'Local Change' suggested that being tolerant of nutrient enrichment it may have increased since 1987.

Catapodium rigidum (L.) C.E. Hubb. ssp. **rigidum**   Fern-grass

Submediterranean-Subatlantic element.

This is an annual herb of open habitats on sandy and rocky or stony places as well as in quarries and pavements, usually on calcareous substrates (BH7, 17). Fern-grass is found in England, Wales, Ireland and southern Scotland.

Occasional (36). In northern Lancashire most records are from the north-west of the area, often on limestone but it also occurs occasionally in coastal areas of the region. As 100 years ago it was known from only seven localities (Wheldon and Wilson, 1907) it appears that Fern-grass has increased in northern Lancashire. Nationally the 'New Atlas' reported little change but since 1987 'Local Change' noted an increase.

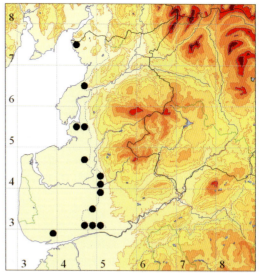
Catabrosa aquatica

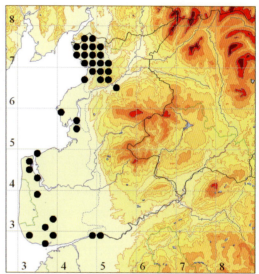
Catapodium rigidum

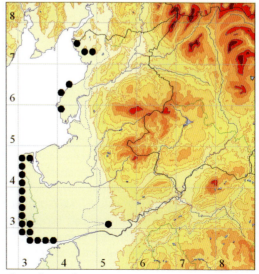
Catapodium marinum

Catapodium marinum (L.) C.E. Hubb.   Sea Fern-grass

Mediterranean-Atlantic element.

Sea Fern-grass is an annual species of coastal, open habitats on rocks, grassy banks, sand dunes, walls and pavements (BH18). It is found on most coasts of the British Isles.

Occasional (24). In northern Lancashire *C. marinum* is found on all the coasts. Wheldon and Wilson (1907) recorded it from four localities but two of these, at Ingol and Cottam, were probably errors. It is apparent, therefore, that it has increased considerably over the last 100 years. Nationally its coastal distribution is stable but the 'New Atlas' reports some spread inland in southern England. Also, whilst not significant, 'Local Change' noted some increase since 1987.

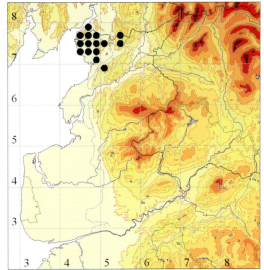

Sesleria caerulea

Sesleria caerulea (L.) Ard.   Blue Moor-grass

European Boreo-temperate element but *S. caerulea* ssp. *calcarea* is confined to western and central Europe and Iceland.

Blue Moor-grass is a tufted, rhizomatous perennial herb of well-drained, mainly open habitats on limestone (BH7, 16). It is found in northern England, western Ireland and Perthshire in Scotland.

Occasional (15). In northern Lancashire *S. caerulea* is only found on the limestone around Morecambe Bay and on Dalton Crags. Despite apparently suitable conditions occurring on Leck Fell and in Bowland it does not occur in these areas although it is abundant in the nearby Yorkshire Dales. Where it does occur in northern Lancashire it is often abundant and in some places dominates the vegetation. Its distribution is stable locally and nationally.

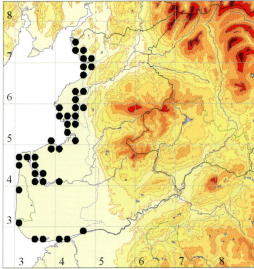

Parapholis strigosa

Parapholis strigosa (Dumort.) C.E. Hubb.   Hard-grass

Suboceanic Southern-temperate element.

Hard-grass is a small annual grass of open habitats on the upper parts of salt marshes (BH21). It is found on the coasts of England, Wales, Ireland and southern Scotland.

Occasional (41). *P. strigosa* occurs on all the salt marshes of northern Lancashire. It is easily overlooked and this probably accounts for an apparent increase over the last 100 years. The 'New Atlas' also recorded an apparent increase and attributed this to better recording.

Avenula pubescens (Huds.) Dumort.   Downy Oat-grass

European Temperate element.

Downy Oat-grass is a perennial herb found in neutral or calcareous grasslands and marginal habitats (BH6, 7). It occurs in many parts of the British Isles.

Frequent (84). In northern Lancashire *A. pubescens* is found mostly in northern and eastern areas, especially on the calcareous soils in the northwest of the area and in the Hodder valley. Occasionally it occurs elsewhere. Wheldon and Wilson (1907) may have overlooked this grass as they only recorded it from Silverdale (SD47) and Middleton (SD45). However the 'New Atlas' reported an increase nationally after 1962 but thought that there had also been some losses. 'Local Change' reported some decline and pointed out that *H. pubescens* was not a competitive species and may be adversely affected by drainage and nutrient

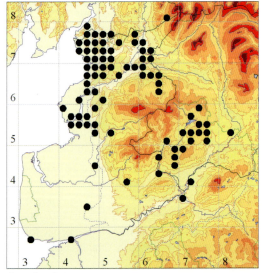

Avenula pubescens

enrichment. It seems possible, therefore, that during the first half of the twentieth century *H. pubescens* expanded its range only to suffer losses in the last decade or so.

Avenula pratensis (L.) Dumort.   Meadow Oat-grass

European Temperate element.

A. pratensis is a perennial herb of calcareous soils and is characteristic of limestone and chalk grassland (BH7). It is found in suitable places in England, Wales and Scotland but it is absent from Ireland.

Occasional (21). In northern Lancashire most records are from limestone grasslands around Morecambe Bay and on Dalton Crags with only occasional records elsewhere, more especially in other limestone grasslands in the east of the region. Wheldon and Wilson (1907) recorded only two localities suggesting that *A. pratense* has extended its range in the area. The 'New Atlas' noted some losses nationally and this decline seems to have accelerated since 1987 ('Local Change').

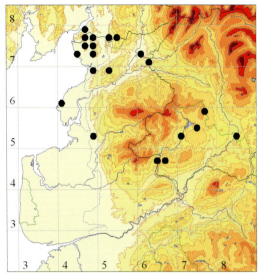
Avenula pratensis

Arrhenatherum elatius (L.) P. Beauv. ex J. & C. Presl False Oat-grass

European Temperate element.

False Oat-grass is a vigorous, tufted perennial herb found in a wide range of neutral to base-rich habitats. It is frequent in grasslands, especially in the rough grasslands of marginal and ruderal habitats (BH3, 6). It is found throughout the British Isles.

Very common (387). In northern Lancashire *A. elatius* occurs throughout the area except on the fells. The distinction between *A. elatius* ssp. *elatius* (var. *elatius*) and *A. elatius* ssp. *bulbosum* (Willd.) Hyl. (var. *bulbosum* (Willd.) Spenner) or Onion Couch was rarely recorded. Onion Couch was formerly an arable weed but in recent years it has been found in a few ruderal habitats in northern Lancashire. Both subspecies are likely to be common. Wheldon and Wilson (1907) recorded var. *nodosum* Reichb., which may refer to ssp. *bulbosum*, as frequent in dryer situations. There has been no change in the distribution of False Oat-grass either locally or nationally.

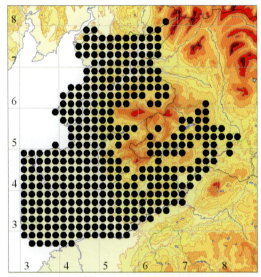
Arrhenatherum elatius

Avena fatua L.   Wild-oat

Archaeophyte, which was probably a native of the eastern Mediterranean and the Near East but has spread with cultivation throughout the world except in tropical regions.

Wild-oat is an annual grass of cultivated ground and ruderal habitats (BH3, 4). It is still a troublesome weed of cereal crops and occurs in suitable places throughout the British Isles.

Occasional (57). This was not known in northern Lancashire until it was found at Ribchester (SD63) in 1900 (Wheldon and Wilson, 1902). Today it is found mostly in western areas with a few records from further east in the region. Nationally *A. fatua* has also extended its range ('New Atlas', 'Local Change').

Avena fatua × A. sativa (A. × hybrida Peterm.)

This hybrid has been found in arable fields in a few British locations.

Very rare (1). In northern Lancashire *A. fatua* × *A. sativa* was found on waste ground in Fulwood (SD53) in 1965 (A.E.R.; LIV).

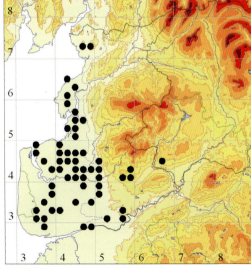
Avena fatua

Avena sterilis (L.)   Winter Wild-oat

Neophyte. *A. sterilis* is a native of the Mediterranean region, south-western and central Asia and was cultivated in Britain by 1640. It was first recorded in the wild in Oxfordshire in 1910 and has apparently spread from here into neighbouring counties. Today it occurs in winter cereal crops, mainly on clay soils, in southern England with scattered localities elsewhere in Britain.

In northern Lancashire it was found at Marton (SD33) in 1963 (A.E.R.; LIV).

Avena sativa L.   Oat

Casual archaeophyte but a neophyte in northern Lancashire. Oat probably originated in cultivation by selection from *A. fatua*. It may have evolved in Europe in the 2nd millennium BC but did not reach Britain until the Iron Age. It was an important crop plant until the second half of the twentieth century but it was not recorded in the wild until 1908. Even today it is probably under recorded. It is usually found as a casual in ruderal habitats or as a relic of cultivation.

Occasional (19). In northern Lancashire *A. sativa* was first recorded from Lytham tip (SD32) in about 1966 (A.E.R.). Since then it has been recorded from scattered localities, mostly in the west of the region.

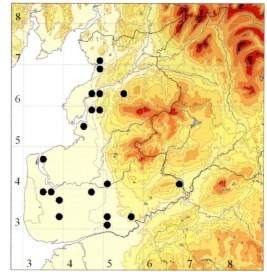
Avena sativa

Trisetum flavescens (L.) P. Beauv.   Yellow Oat-grass

European Temperate element.

This is a perennial grass of well-drained, neutral and calcareous grassland and ruderal habitats (BH6, 7) in lowland areas of England, Wales, Ireland and southern Scotland with a few localities further north.

Frequent (142). In northern Lancashire *T. flavescens* has a complex distribution pattern corresponding to the occurrence of calcareous substrates. Thus it occurs frequently in the northwest of the area as well as in the Ribble and Hodder valleys and in the south of the region on calcareous boulder clay. Its distribution is stable locally and nationally.

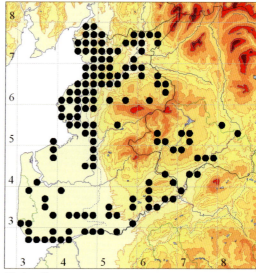
Trisetum flavescens

Koeleria macrantha (Ledeb.) Schult.   Crested Hair-grass

Circumpolar Temperate element.

Crested Hair-grass is a perennial herb of infertile grassland and heaths usually on calcareous substrates (BH7). It is found throughout the British Isles in coastal areas but also inland on chalk, limestone and other calcareous substrates.

Occasional (17). In northern Lancashire most records are from limestone areas in the northwest of the area with only occasional records elsewhere. Wheldon and Wilson (1907) found *K. macrantha* on the limestone around Morecambe Bay and also near Chipping where it has not been seen since. Although the core area of its distribution is unchanged there have been some changes elsewhere in the region. The 'New Atlas' reported losses nationally but 'Local Change' noted a possible increase since 1987.

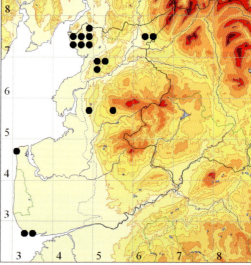
Koeleria macrantha

Deschampsia cespitosa (L.) P. Beauv.   Tufted Hair-grass

Circumpolar Wide-boreal element.

This is a tufted perennial species found in poorly drained acid, neutral or sometimes basic soils in marshy grasslands, ruderal and woodland habitats (BH1, 6). It is found throughout the British Isles.

Very common (384). In northern Lancashire *D. cespitosa* is found throughout the region except on peat. However it was only in recent years that attempts were made to distinguish between *D. cespitosa* ssp. *cespitosa* and *D. cespitosa* ssp. *parviflora*. Both subspecies are frequent or common but they occur in different habitats. *D. cespitosa* ssp. *cespitosa* is a more robust plant and is found in unshaded areas of moorland pasture, roadsides and ruderal habitats whilst *D. cespitosa* ssp. *parviflora* is a more slender taxon found mostly in woodland. There is insufficient data to map the distribution of *D. cespitosa* ssp. *cespitosa* separately but it is believed that its distribution in northern Lancashire is similar to that of *D. cespitosa* *sensu lato*, which is stable locally and nationally.

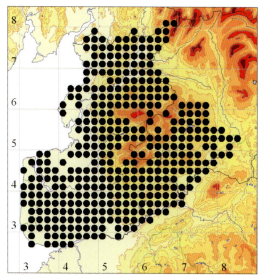
Deschampsia cespitosa

Deschampsia cespitosa (L.) P. Beauv.
ssp. **parviflora** (Thuill.) Dumort.

European distribution uncertain but it occurs in central Europe.

This subspecies is found in damp woodland and in woodland edge habitats (BH1) usually on poorly drained, heavy soils. It probably occurs in most parts of the British Isles but its distribution is not fully known.

Occasional (69). In northern Lancashire *D. cespitosa* ssp. *parviflora* is a common species of deciduous woodland mostly in the east of the area. It is not known if its distribution has changed locally or nationally.

Deschampsia flexuosa (L.) Trin.   Wavy Hair-grass
European Boreo-temperate element.

Wavy Hair-grass is a tufted perennial species of acid heaths, moorland and open woodland (BH8, 10). It is found throughout the British Isles but it is rare on the calcareous soils of southern England and Ireland.

Frequent (215). In northern Lancashire *D. flexuosa* is common in the east and north of the area but it is rare in the west although it occurs on coastal heaths at Lytham St Anne's. Formerly it was probably more frequent in lowland western areas but is likely to have disappeared as bogs were drained and commons cultivated during the first half of the nineteenth century. Nationally the 'New Atlas' reported local losses in lowland areas but 'Local Change' noted no significant decline since 1987.

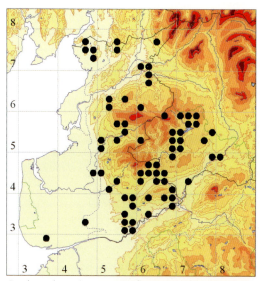
Deschampsia cespitosa ssp. *parviflora*

Holcus lanatus L.   Yorkshire-fog
European Southern-temperate element.

This is a short-lived, tufted perennial species found in a wide range of grasslands, marginal and ruderal habitats (BH3, 6). It is found throughout the British Isles.

Very common (430). *H. lanatus* is found throughout northern Lancashire except on the highest fells. Its distribution is stable locally and nationally.

Holcus mollis L.   Creeping Soft-grass
European Temperate element.

H. mollis is a creeping rhizomatous perennial grass of well-drained acidic or neutral soils found in woodlands, woodland edges and on heaths (BH1, 3, 9). It is found throughout the British Isles.

Very common (373). Creeping Soft-grass is found throughout northern Lancashire except in some urban areas and on the higher fells. Its distribution locally and nationally is unchanged.

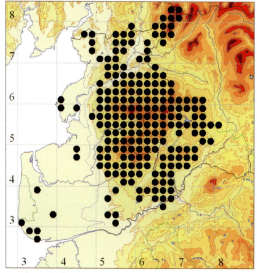
Deschampsia flexuosa

Aira caryophyllea L.   Silver Hair-grass

European Southern-temperate element.

This is an annual species of well-drained sandy and stony places (BH10, 16). It is found throughout the British Isles.

Occasional (54). In northern Lancashire Silver Hair-grass is mainly found on light soils near the coast but it also occurs occasionally elsewhere in western and northern areas. There are also a few records from the Bowland fells. Wheldon and Wilson (1907) recorded *A. caryophyllea* from nine localities in VC 60 suggesting that it has spread over the last 100 years. However nationally it has declined ('New Atlas', 'Local Change') with most losses since 1950.

Aira praecox L.   Early Hair-grass

Suboceanic Southern-temperate element.

A. praecox is an annual grass of sandy and stony places often on acidic soils but it occurs in a variety of habitats (BH8, 16). It is found throughout the British Isles.

Frequent (163). In northern Lancashire Early Hair-grass occurs in coastal areas, on gravel and sandy banks in river valleys and in the fells in the north and east of the area. Its distribution is stable in northern Lancashire but some decline was noted nationally ('New Atlas', 'Local Change').

Anthoxanthum odoratum L.   Sweet Vernal-grass

Eurosiberian Wide-temperate element.

This is a short-lived perennial herb, which occurs in a wide variety of grassland habitats usually on acid soils (BH6). When species-rich meadows are cut for hay it gives rise to the 'new mown hay' scent. It is found throughout the British Isles.

Very common (437). Sweet Vernal-grass occurs throughout northern Lancashire. There has been no change in its distribution locally or nationally.

Anthoxanthum aristatum Boiss.   Annual Vernal-grass

Neophyte. Annual Vernal-grass is a native of southern Europe and it is believed it was introduced into Britain from France as an impurity in fodder seed in the latter half of the nineteenth century. It was first recorded in the wild in 1872 and became a serious weed of cereal crops on sandy or gravely soils. However it was declining before 1930 and today is rarely recorded.

In northern Lancashire it has only been found between the railway lines on Preston Docks (SD52) in 1900 (Wheldon and Wilson, 1901b).

Phalaris arundinacea L.   Reed Canary-grass

Circumpolar Boreo-temperate element.

Reed Canary-grass is a tall, rhizomatous perennial species found in ditches, by rivers, canals, lakes and ponds and in fens (BH11, 14). It occurs throughout the British Isles although it is rare in highland Scotland.

Very common (351). *P. arundinacea* occurs throughout most of northern Lancashire but it is absent from the fells. Var. *picta* L. is a garden plant that has been planted or has escaped into the wild in a few places. The distribution of Reed Canary-grass is stable both locally and nationally.

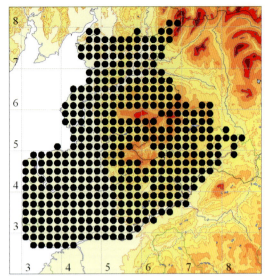

Holcus lanatus

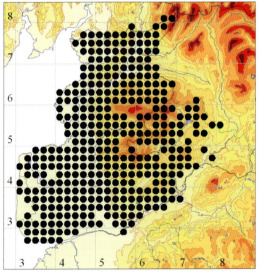

Holcus mollis

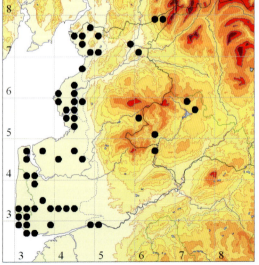

Aira caryophyllea

Phalaris canariensis L. — Canary-grass

Neophyte. This is perhaps a native of north-western Africa and the Canary Islands and was first recorded from Britain in 1632. Today it is found throughout much of the British Isles but it is rare or absent in northern Scotland and parts of Ireland.

Occasional (42). Canary-grass was first recorded in northern Lancashire from Lytham (c. 1874) by F.A.L. (Linton, 1875) and subsequently from ballast near Morecambe in 1899 (Wheldon and Wilson, 1900) and from the sand dunes at St Anne's in 1907 (C.B.). Today it has been recorded from scattered localities, mostly in the west of the area, but it rarely persists for long at any site.

[Phalaris brachystachys Link — Confused Canary-grass

In northern Lancashire *P. brachystachys* was recorded in error for *P. canariensis* from the sand dunes at St Anne's in 1907 (C.B.; Wheldon and Wilson, 1907; MANCH).]

Phalaris minor Retz. — Lesser Canary-grass

Neophyte. *P. minor* is a Mediterranean-Atlantic species and was first recorded from the Channel Islands in 1791. Today it has been recorded from scattered localities in the British Isles but mostly in midland and southern England.

In northern Lancashire Lesser Canary-grass was recorded from the sand dunes at St Anne's in 1907 and 1908 (Bailey, 1910) and from ballast at Preston Docks in 1900 (Wheldon and Wilson, 1901a).

Phalaris paradoxa L. — Awned Canary-grass

Neophyte. This is a native of the Mediterranean region and south-western Asia. It was cultivated in Britain in 1687 and recorded in the wild in Surrey in 1859. Today it occurs mostly in south-eastern England with occasional records elsewhere in Britain.

In northern Lancashire it was found at Blackpool (SD33) in 1959 (C. Goodman; B.R.C.)

Agrostis capillaris L. — Common Bent

Eurosiberian Boreo-temperate element.

Common Bent is a rhizomatous, perennial grass occurring mainly on dry, neutral to acidic soils in pastures, meadows, heaths and woodland edge habitats (BH8). It is found throughout the British Isles.

Very common (430). *A. capillaris* occurs throughout northern Lancashire. Its distribution is unchanged locally and nationally.

Agrostis capillaris × A. stolonifera (A. × murbeckii Fouill.)

This is a common sterile hybrid, which has both stolons and rhizomes and is found throughout the British Isles. In very old pastures it may persist in the absence of both parents. However it is difficult to recognise and it is often overlooked.

Very rare (1). In northern Lancashire *A. × murbeckii* was found at the top of a salt marsh at Conder Green (SD45M) in 2010 (M.W.).

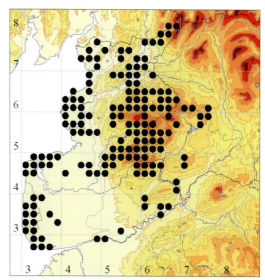

Aira praecox

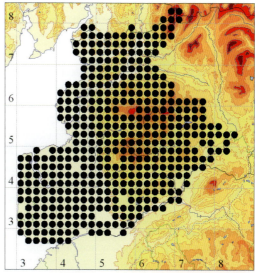

Anthoxanthum odoratum

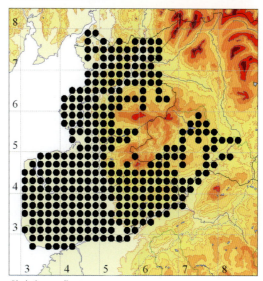

Phalaris arundinacea

Agrostis gigantea Roth   Black Bent

Archaeophyte with a Eurasian Southern-temperate distribution.

Black Bent is an easily overlooked perennial herb found in cultivated land and ruderal habitats (BH3, 4). It is found throughout the British Isles but it is thought to be under recorded.

Frequent (144). *A. gigantea* is found throughout northern Lancashire but it is especially frequent in the lowland cultivated areas in the west of VC 60. Wheldon and Wilson (1907) recorded Black Bent from cultivated fields in three localities indicating a considerable increase over the last 100 years. Nationally there has also been a marked increase since 1962 ('New Atlas') but since 1987 there may have been a slight decrease ('Local Change') possibly because of its vulnerability to more recently developed herbicides.

Agrostis stolonifera L.   Creeping Bent

Circumpolar Wide-temperate element.

Creeping Bent is a stoloniferous grass found in a variety of grassy habitats ranging from salt marshes and sand dunes to upland springs and flushes as well as many marginal and ruderal habitats (BH4, 6). *A stolonifera* is morphologically variable and several varieties have been described. It is found throughout the British Isles.

Very common (418). *A stolonifera* occurs throughout northern Lancashire except on the higher fells. Several varieties are recognised. Var. *palustris* (Huds.) Farw. was found at St Anne's (SD32) in 1965 (A.E.R.) and at Yealand Redmayne (SD47Y; Wheldon and Wilson, 1907). Var. *stolonifera* is likely to be the commonest variety and was recorded by Wheldon and Wilson (1907) as *A. alba* L. var. *coarctata* Hoffm. from Glasson and in a few other coastal sites. *A. stolonifera* var. *maritima* (Lam.) Koch occurs in sandy areas near the coast but Wheldon and Wilson (1907) recorded it as '*A. alba* L. var. *maritima* Mey.' and found it at Silverdale and St Anne's. *A. stolonifera* var. *marina* (Gray) P.D. Sell is likely to be common on salt marshes but so far it has not been recorded. The distribution of *A. stolonifera* is unchanged locally and nationally.

Agrostis canina L.   Velvet Bent

Circumpolar Boreo-temperate element.

This is a stoloniferous perennial grass of infertile, acidic and often peaty soils in fens and marshes (BH11, 13). It probably occurs throughout the British Isles and not only is it under recorded but it is also confused with *A. vinealis* although the morphological characters distinguishing the two species have been understood for a long time.

Frequent (159). Until recently *A. vinealis* was not distinguished from *A. canina* in northern Lancashire. Accordingly the distribution map is for *A. canina sensu lato*. Furthermore Wheldon and Wilson (1925) overlooked both species. However it is believed that *A. canina* is much more frequent than *A. vinealis*. *A. canina* probably occurs throughout the region but it is believed to be much more frequent in upland areas than elsewhere. It is not known if its distribution has changed locally but 'Local Change' suggests that *A. canina sensu lato* has declined nationally since 1987.

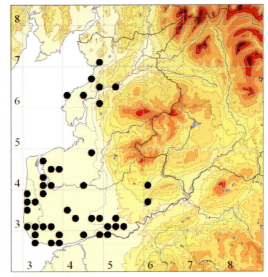

Phalaris canariensis

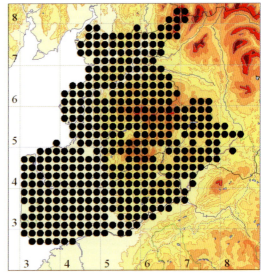

Agrostis capillaris

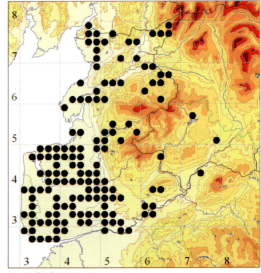

Agrostis gigantea

Agrostis vinealis Schreb.   Brown Bent

European Temperate element.

Brown Bent is a shortly rhizomatous perennial herb mainly occurring on free-draining, acidic, sandy or peaty soils in heaths and woodland edges (BH8, 10). It is also used as a drought resistant lawn grass. *A. vinealis* is found throughout the British Isles but it is under recorded through confusion with *A. canina*.

Occasional (49). In northern Lancashire *A. vinealis* has been found in scattered localities throughout the area but it is very much under recorded. It is not known if its distribution has changed locally or nationally.

Agrostis scabra Willd.   Rough Bent

Neophyte. Rough Bent is a tufted perennial or annual species native in North America and north-eastern Asia. It was probably introduced into Britain with wool shoddy or grain and was first recorded in the wild in 1896. Today it is found in a few scattered localities in the British Isles but especially in the Glasgow area, Lancashire and the Mersey basin and in the London area.

Very rare (2). In northern Lancashire it was first found on railway ballast at Preston Docks (SD52E) in 1964 (E.H.). Since then it has been found in various places in Preston (SD52J) where it seems to be established (2007).

Calamagrostis epigejos (L.) Roth   Wood Small-reed

Eurasian Boreo-temperate element.

C. epigejos is a tufted, rhizomatous perennial species found in damp woods, ditches and fens as well as on coastal cliffs and sand dunes (BH3, 11). It is also a colonist of post-industrial sites. It is found most frequently in the south-eastern half of England but may occur anywhere in the British Isles.

Occasional (23). In northern Lancashire it is mostly a coastal species where it is usually found on clay cliffs. It has probably extended its range slightly over the last 100 years. A similar increase was observed by the 'New Atlas' but since 1987 its distribution is stable ('Local Change').

Ammophila arenaria (L.) Link   Marram

European Southern-temperate element.

This rhizomatous perennial grass is found on coastal mobile sand dunes where it is an important species for the stabilisation of blowing sand (BH19). It occurs around the coasts of the British Isles.

Occasional (26). Marram is found on coastal sand dunes and on sandy soils near the coast in VC 60 (see Plate 2.59). Its distribution is stable locally and nationally.

Lagurus ovatus L.   Hare's-tail

Neophyte with a Mediterranean-Atlantic distribution. Hare's-tail was introduced into British cultivation by 1640 and was recorded in the wild in 1791. It is established on sand dunes in southern England but occurs in scattered localities in many parts of the British Isles.

Very rare (2). This was first recorded on sand dunes bordering Clifton Drive, Lytham St Anne's (SD32E, 33A) in 1996 (C.F. & N.J.S.) where it appears to have become established.

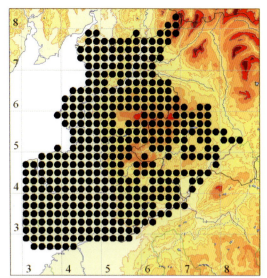

Agrostis stolonifera

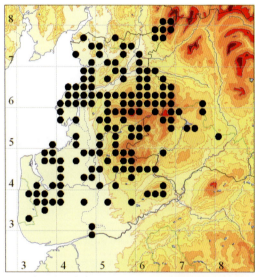

Agrostis canina s.l.

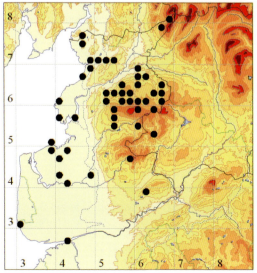

Agrostis vinealis

Apera spica-venti (L.) P. Beauv.   Loose Silky-bent

Archaeophyte with a Eurosiberian Boreo-temperate distribution but a neophyte in northern Lancashire.

This is an annual of open habitats in arable fields and ruderal habitats. It was grown in the London area in the nineteenth century as an ornamental grass and today it is naturalised in eastern and southern England. However it has been recorded from scattered localities elsewhere in the British Isles.

Very rare (1). Loose Silky-bent was recorded from Preston Docks in 1900 and from Ashton, Preston (Wheldon and Wilson, 1907). More recently it was found at Fleetwood (SD34I) in 2005 (P.J. & D.P.E.).

Apera interrupta (L.) P. Beauv.   Dense Silky-bent

Neophyte. Dense Silky-bent is a Eurosiberian Southern-temperate species first recorded wild in Britain in 1848. Most records are from eastern England where it may be increasing.

Very rare (2). In northern Lancashire *A. interrupta* was recorded from waste ground at Lytham (SD32T) in 2005 and from levelled sand dunes at St Anne's (SD32E) in 2006 (C.F. & N.J.S.).

Mibora minima (L.) Desv.   Early Sand-grass

Suboceanic Southern-temperate element.

This is a small, early flowering, annual grass found on nutrient poor, coastal sandy ground and sand dunes in Wales, especially Anglesey, and more recently on the Sefton coast. It also occurs as a rare, casual introduction elsewhere in Britain particularly in southern England. It is difficult to know, therefore, if the increase in post 1980 records is due to natural spread or not but it seems that the spread northwards to the Sefton coast and Lancashire may be a natural extension of its range.

Very rare (1). Early Sand-grass was found on stabilised sand at Fleetwood (SD34I) in 2007 (P.J.). However it did not reappear in 2008 (P.J.).

Polypogon viridis (Gouan) Breistr.   Water Bent

Neophyte. This is a native of southern Europe, south-western and central Asia and northern Africa. It was introduced into British cultivation in 1800 and was first recorded in the wild in 1876. Today it is found mostly in southern Britain with occasional records from elsewhere in the British Isles.

Rare (8). It was first recorded in northern Lancashire from a landfill site at Westby (SD33K) in 2006 (P.J.). Subsequently it has been found in scattered urban areas in the west of VC 60.

Alopecurus pratensis L.   Meadow Foxtail

Eurosiberian Boreo-temperate element.

Meadow Foxtail is a tufted perennial herb occurring in moist, fertile grasslands and marginal habitats (BH6). Up to about the 1950s it was frequently included in seed mixtures and was a valuable agricultural species. It is found throughout the British Isles.

Very common (377). *A. pratensis* is found throughout northern Lancashire except in parts of upland Bowland and Leck. Its distribution is stable both locally and nationally.

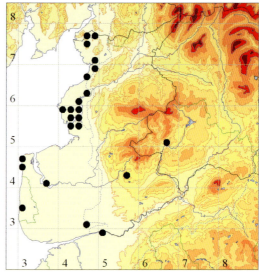

Calamagrostis epigejos

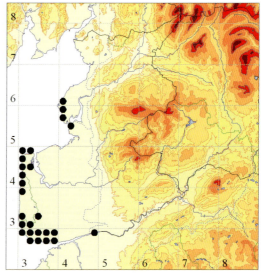

Ammophila arenaria

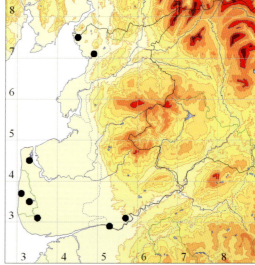

Polypogon viridis

Alopecurus geniculatus L.   Marsh Foxtail

European Boreo-temperate element.

This is a perennial herb found in wet, fertile sites around ponds, in fields and in other marshy areas (BH6) throughout the British Isles.

Very common (354). In northern Lancashire Marsh Foxtail is found throughout the area although it is absent from some upland areas. Its distribution is probably stable both locally and nationally although 'Local Change' noted some losses since 1987.

Alopecurus aequalis Sobol.   Orange Foxtail

Circumpolar Boreo-temperate element.

This is an annual species found on drying mud in wetland habitats with fluctuating water levels (BH13). It is found in southern Britain, the Isle of Man and southern Ireland.

Very rare (2). In northern Lancashire *A. aequalis* is found around the shores of Stocks Reservoir in Lancashire VC 64 (SD75H, I; Abbott, 2005).

Alopecurus myosuroides Huds.   Black-grass

Archaeophyte with a European Southern-temperate distribution.

Black-grass occurs in neglected grassland and cultivated ground (BH4) and occurs mostly in south-eastern Britain but with occasional records elsewhere in the British Isles. It is sometimes a serious weed of cereal crops.

Rare (6). In northern Lancashire *A. myosuroides* was recorded from Hothersall (SD63) in 1965 (A. Clegg; B.R.C.). Later records were from a tip at Blackpool (SD33I) in 1966; (J.H. & A.E.R.), demolition sites in Preston (SD53F) in 1966 (E.H.), Silverdale Moss (SD47R) in 1967 (C. J.-P.), Poulton-le-Fylde (SD33P) in 1968 (E.P.) and Hambleton (SD34V) in 2008 (J.Cl.).

Phleum pratense L.   Timothy

Circumpolar Temperate element.

Timothy is a perennial grass found in a range of grassy habitats (BH3, 6). It has often been sown in agricultural grasslands and occurs throughout the British Isles. However it is thought to be an introduction in some of the Scottish islands.

Very common (365). *P. pratense* occurs throughout northern Lancashire except on the fells. The distribution of *P. pratense* is thought to be unchanged locally and nationally.

Phleum bertolonii DC.   Small Cat's-tail

European Southern-temperate element.

P. bertolonii is a perennial herb of old meadows and pastures as well as marginal habitats of roadsides and scrubby places (BH3, 6). It occurs in similar places to *P. pratense* but shows a preference for thinner swards, drier and less fertile soils. However it is also grown as an agricultural grass and robust forms are morphologically indistinguishable from *P. pratense*. *P. bertolonii* is believed to occur throughout the British Isles but it has often been confused with *P. pratense*.

Frequent (77). In northern Lancashire Small Cat's-tail is found mostly in the west of the area with scattered localities elsewhere. It is often found on dry banks and pastures. It is not known if its distribution has changed locally or nationally.

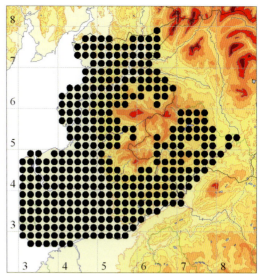
Alopecurus pratensis

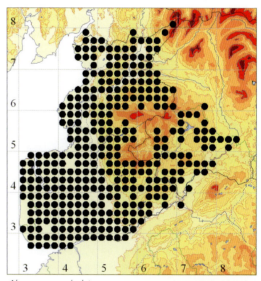
Alopecurus geniculatus

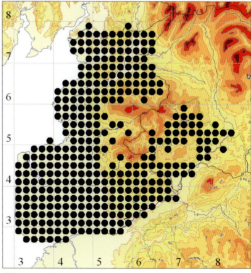
Phleum pratense

Phleum arenarium L.   Sand Cat's-tail

European Southern-temperate element.

This is an annual species of coastal sandy ground (BH19). It is found on suitable coasts around the British Isles but it is absent from western and northern Scotland.

Rare (7). *P. arenarium* is found on coastal sand dunes and sandy ground at Fleetwood, Blackpool and Lytham St Anne's. It is sometimes abundant on the sand dunes. Its distribution locally and nationally is probably stable but Wheldon and Wilson (1907) did not record *P. arenarium*.

Glyceria maxima (Hartm.) Holmb.   Reed Sweet-grass

Circumpolar Temperate element.

This is a vigorous, rhizomatous perennial grass of ditches, lakes, ponds and fens (BH11). It was formerly planted as a fodder plant and occurs mostly in lowland areas of England, Wales, Ireland and southern and eastern Scotland.

Rare (12). Reed Sweet-grass occurs in scattered localities in northern Lancashire but its status is unclear. It was first recorded from Marton, near Blackpool (SD33) in 1899 (Wheldon and Wilson, 1907) and it is likely that it was planted or is an escape from cultivation in many of the post 1964 localities. However a few localities are in fens or are at the top of salt marshes and natural spread into these habitats from native or introduced populations seems likely. Nationally the 'New Atlas' noted an increase but 'Local Change' reported its distribution as unchanged since 1987.

Glyceria fluitans (L.) R. Br.   Floating Sweet-grass

European Temperate element.

Floating Sweet-grass is a perennial herb of marshes, muddy pond margins, ditches and other nutrient rich and often disturbed wet places (BH11, 14). It is found throughout the British Isles.

Common (320). In northern Lancashire *G. fluitans* occurs throughout the area except on the higher fells. There has been no change in its distribution locally or nationally although 'Local Change' noted some losses since 1987.

Glyceria fluitans × G. notata (**G. × pedicellata** F. Towns.)
                                                          Hybrid Sweet-grass

Widespread in temperate Europe.

This sterile, stoloniferous herb occurs in similar habitats to its parents (BH11, 14). It is probably under recorded but occurs in many parts of the British Isles although it is probably rare in western Scotland and absent from Orkney and Shetland.

Occasional (35). Hybrid Sweet-grass was not recognised as occurring in northern Lancashire until it was recorded from Lytham St Anne's (SD32) in 1965 (A.E.R. & E.F.G.). Since then it has been found in scattered localities in the area. Because of identification difficulties it is not known if its distribution has changed locally or nationally.

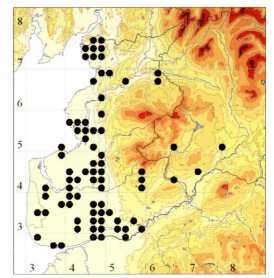

Phleum bertolonii

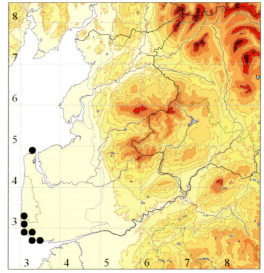

Phleum arenarium

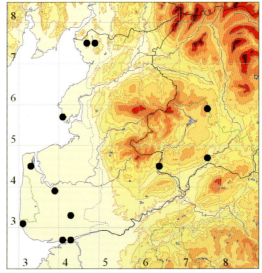

Glyceria maxima

Glyceria declinata Bréb.   Small Sweet-grass

Suboceanic Temperate element.

Small Sweet-grass is a perennial herb of pond margins, marshes and
shallow water generally (BH13, 14). It occurs throughout the British Isles
and although small it has distinctive glaucous leaves, but it has been under
recorded.

Frequent (227). *G. declinata* occurs throughout northern Lancashire and
although absent from the tops of the fells it often occurs in muddy places
by gates on the highest pastures. Surprisingly it was overlooked and not
recorded by Wheldon and Wilson (1907, 1925) but it was noted in several
10 × 10km squares by Perring and Walters (1962). It is not known if its
distribution has changed in northern Lancashire but nationally losses were
noted in eastern England ('New Atlas').

Glyceria notata Chevall.   Plicate Sweet-grass

European Temperate element.

Plicate Sweet-grass occurs in marshes, ponds, ditches and other water
bodies and is found in more calcareous water than other British *Glyceria*
species (BH11, 14). It is found throughout the British Isles but it is rare or
absent from northern and western Scotland. It is probably under recorded.

Frequent (92). *G. notata* occurs in scattered localities throughout northern
Lancashire but it is probably under-recorded. Wheldon and Wilson (1907)
recorded it from fewer than ten localities in VC 60 but the apparent
increase since then is probably due to better recording. Nationally the
'New Atlas' suggested that there were some losses in southern England
but since 1987 its distribution is stable ('Local Change').

Melica nutans L.   Mountain Melick

Eurasian Boreo-temperate element.

Mountain Melick is a rhizomatous perennial grass of basic soils, often on
limestone, in shady places in woodland margins and in grykes on limestone pavement (BH1, 7, 16). It is found in Wales, northern and midland
England and Scotland.

Very rare (4). In northern Lancashire *M. nutans* occurs in a few localities in
Silverdale (SD47T), Yealand Redmayne (SD47Y), Warton Crag (SD47W) and
on Dalton Crags (SD57N). Apart from Warton Crag most of the localities
were known to Wheldon and Wilson (1907). Nationally the 'New Atlas'
reported that the distribution of *M. nutans* was stable but 'Local Change'
noted significant losses since 1987.

Melica uniflora Retz.   Wood Melick

European Temperate element.

This is a rhizomatous perennial grass of woodland margins and shady
places on free-draining, base-rich soils (BH1). It occurs in many places in
the British Isles but it is absent from northern Scotland.

Frequent (115). In northern Lancashire *M. uniflora* occurs most commonly
in the north of the area but it is also present in many of the woodlands in
eastern parts of the region. There is a single record in the lowland west of
VC 60, where it may have been more frequent 100 years ago (Wheldon
and Wilson, 1907). Its distribution nationally is stable.

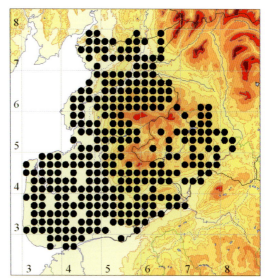

Glyceria fluitans

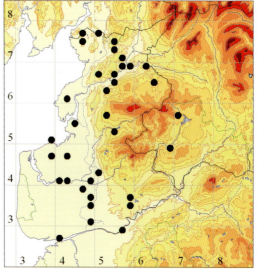

Glyceria × pedicellata

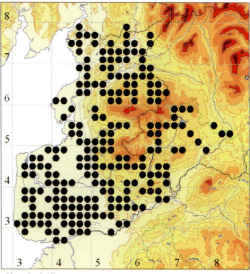

Glyceria declinata

[Bromus arvensis L.   Field Brome

Neophyte. Field Brome has an uncertain native range having spread with cultivation. Today it has a European Temperate distribution. It was first recorded in Britain in 1763 and was formerly frequent in cultivated ground. It suffered a sharp decline in the twentieth century, mostly before 1930. It occurs today only rarely but whilst there are records from many parts of Britain most are from eastern England.

In northern Lancashire the only record is from St Anne's c. 1915 (A.J.C.; LTA) but the voucher specimen needs checking.]

Bromus commutatus Schrad.   Meadow Brome

Although recognised here and elsewhere as a species recognisably distinct from *B. racemosus* Cope and Gray (2009) suggest that distinguishing characters overlap to such an extent that often the two taxa cannot be distinguished.

European Temperate element.

Meadow Brome is an annual grass of meadows and marginal habitats (BH3). It occurs in southern Britain and Ireland as a native species but it also occurs as an introduction in Scotland.

Rare (11). Until recently the morphological characters distinguishing *B. commutatus*, *B. racemosus* and some subspecies of *B. hordeaceus* were not understood. However Spalton (2001) clarified these and pointed out the existence of a new subspecies, *B. hordeaceus* ssp. *longipedicellatus* but the distinguishing features separating this taxon from *B. commutatus* and *B. racemosus* are not always readily discernible. Accordingly the accounts of these taxa in northern Lancashire are tentative. However it seems that *B. commutatus* occurs widely in the west of the region in fertile meadows, on roadsides and waste ground. There is a single record (not mapped) from Lancashire VC 64 at Slaidburn (SD75B) in 2000 (Anon). It is not known if its distribution has changed locally but nationally it has declined since 1960 ('New Atlas') although 'Local Change' suggests it has increased since 1987.

Bromus racemosus L.   Smooth Brome

European Temperate element.

Smooth Brome is an annual grass found in meadows and marginal habitats (BH3, 6) in England, Wales and Ireland. It occurs rarely in Scotland as an introduction.

Very rare (4). Wheldon and Wilson (1907) recorded *B. racemosus* from Nether Kellet and from near Fleetwood Dock but voucher specimens have not been found to confirm their identity. Confirmed post 1964 records are from roadside verges at Bartle (SD43X) and Woodplumpton (SD43Y) in 1964 (both J.H.) and from a meadow at Tarnbrook, Over Wyresdale (SD55X) in 1999 (E.F.G.). There is also an unconfirmed record from Carnforth (SD47V) in 1968 (C.J.-P.). It is not known if its distribution has changed locally but the 'New Atlas' reported a widespread decline although 'Local Change' reported an increase since 1987.

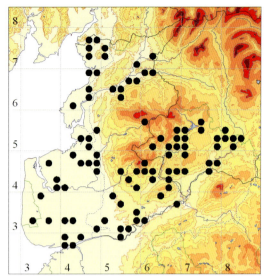
Glyceria notata

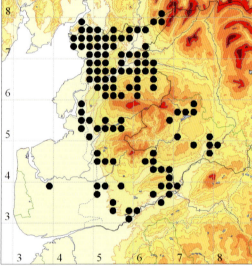
Melica uniflora

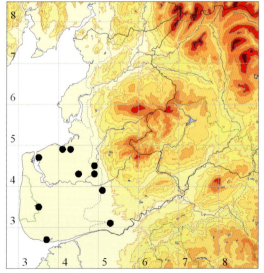
Bromus commutatus

Bromus hordeaceus L.   Soft-brome

European Southern-temperate element.

Soft-brome is a morphologically variable species and several subspecies are recognised. It occurs in disturbed, open habitats, on sand dunes, coastal cliffs, grasslands and in marginal and ruderal habitats (BH4, 6). It occurs throughout the British Isles. *B. hordeaceus* ssp. *hordeaceus* is much the commonest subspecies and probably has the same distribution as the species.

Common (306). In northern Lancashire Soft-brome occurs throughout the area but it is less frequent in eastern parts of the region and is absent from moorland areas. Its distribution in northern Lancashire is probably stable but 'Local Change' noted an increase nationally since 1987.

Bromus hordeaceus L. ssp. **thominei** (Hardouin) Braun-Blanq.

Suboceanic Temperate element.

This subspecies is found in coastal localities on sand dunes, cliffs and sandy places. It is found on the coasts of Britain. The taxon was re-defined by Smith (1968) and many early records are believed to be of other taxa, particularly *B. × pseudothominei*.

Very rare (3). In northern Lancashire all the records are pre 1968 and it has been impossible to check the voucher specimens that might be available. However as all records are from coastal localities *B. hordeaceus* ssp. *thominei* may well be a native northern Lancashire subspecies. It was recorded from St Anne's (Whellan, 1954; and in 1965, A.E.R.), Thurnham (SD45G) and on dredged sand, Lea (SD42Z) both in 1964 (J.H.).

Bromus hordeaceus L. ssp. **longipedicellatus** L.M. Spalton

This subspecies was described by Spalton (2001) and probably occurs widely in lowland areas of Britain. It is found in meadows and marginal habitats. Search of herbaria reveals that it was first found in Devon in 1926 suggesting that its origin is recent and that after 1926 it spread rapidly.

Very rare (5). In northern Lancashire *B. hordeaceus* ssp. *longipedicellatus* was found at Thornton (SD34K) in 1999 (C.J.B.), Pilling (SD44E, J) in 1999 (C.J.B. & E.F.G.), Preston (SD53F) in 1999 (C.F. & N.J.S.) and Easington (SD75P) in 2006 (E.F.G. & D. Bunn). It is likely to be much more frequent than the records suggest and at one of the Pilling sites it dominated the meadow.

Bromus hordeaceus × B. lepidus
(B. × pseudothominei P.M. Sm.)   Lesser Soft-brome

Neophyte. This hybrid was described by Smith (1968) and until then it had been included within *B. hordeaceus* ssp. *thominei*. However Cope and Gray (2009) suggest that this taxon is not a hybrid. It occurs in sown grassland and ruderal habitats and is found in many parts of the British Isles, often in the absence of the parents. It is fully fertile.

Very rare (3). This was first found in northern Lancashire on a tip at Warton in 1930 (J.N.F.; LIV). Post 1964 records are from Middleton (SD45D) in 1998 (E.F.G.), Pilling marsh (SD44E) in 1998 (C.J.B.) and Gisburn Forest (SD75N; Abbott, 2005).

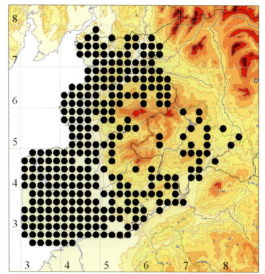
Bromus hordeaceus

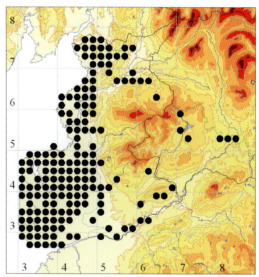
Anisantha sterilis

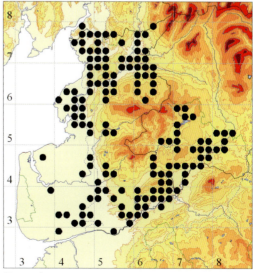
Bromopsis ramosa

Bromus lepidus Holmb.   Slender Soft-brome

Neophyte. The full distribution of *B. lepidus* is unknown but it occurs in north-western and north-central Europe and southern Scandinavia. It was first recorded in the wild in Britain in 1836. It occurs in ruderal habitats in fields sown with rye-grass seed mixtures. It is found throughout the British Isles.

Very rare (5). It was first recorded in northern Lancashire from the 10 × 10km square SD66 in 1959 (M.M. Sayer; B.R.C.). Post 1964 records are from Myerscough (SD53E) in 1965 (E.H.), Lytham St Anne's (SD32J) in 1967 (A.E.R.), Thurnham (SD45S) in 1964 (J.H.), Pilling (SD34Z) in 1999 (C.J.B. & E.F.G.) and Lea Marsh (SD42Z) in 2007 (E.F.G.).

Anisantha diandra (Roth) Tutin ex Tzvelev   Great Brome

Neophyte. Great Brome is a native of the Mediterranean region and south-western Asia. It was introduced into Britain in 1804 and was first recorded in the wild in 1835. It is found on heathland and sandy soils often occurring as a grain impurity.

Very rare (2). *A. diandra* (as *Bromus maximus* Desf., – Great Brome) was first recorded in northern Lancashire at St Anne's in 1903 (MANCH) and again in 1998 (SD32E; C.F. & N.J.S.). It was also recorded from Preston (SD52J) in 2005 (P.J.).

Anisantha rigida (Roth) Hyl.   Ripgut Brome

Neophyte. Ripgut Brome is similar to Great Brome with which it is easily confused. It is an annual found in ruderal habitats often on light soils. It is a native of the Mediterranean region and was first recorded in the wild in the British Isles in 1834. Today it is found in scattered localities in Britain, especially in south-eastern England.

Very rare (1). In northern Lancashire it was reported from St Anne's (SD32E) in 1903 (C.B.; MANCH, E) but the specimen at MANCH appears to be *A. diandra*. More recently it was found near Fairhaven, Lytham St Anne's (M.W., B.A.T. & B.K. Byrne) in 2001 (SD32I).

Anisantha sterilis (L.) Nevski   Barren Brome

Archaeophyte with a European Southern-temperate distribution.

Barren Brome is found in ruderal habitats (BH3, 4, 17) in most parts of England, Wales, eastern Ireland and eastern Scotland with a few scattered records from elsewhere.

Frequent (178). In northern Lancashire most records for *A. sterilis* are from western areas of the region but it occurs in scattered localities elsewhere. Its distribution is stable locally and nationally.

Anisantha tectorum (L.) Nevski   Drooping Brome

Neophyte. Drooping Brome has a Eurosiberian Southern-temperate distribution and was first grown in Britain in 1776. It has been known in the wild since 1863 and occurs on sandy soils often originating as an impurity with grain, wool shoddy and grass seed.

In northern Lancashire it was found on the sand dunes at St Anne's in 1907 (C.B.; MANCH).

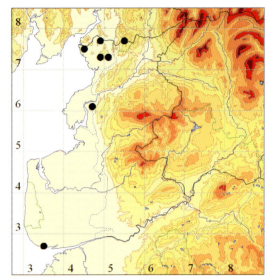
Bromopsis erecta

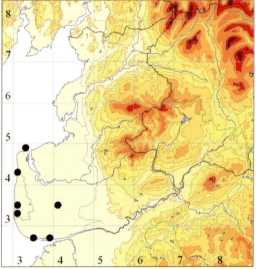
Bromopsis inermis

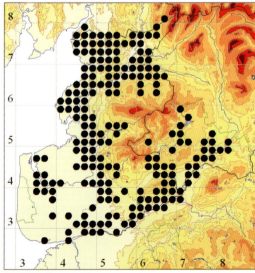
Brachypodium sylvaticum

Bromopsis ramosa (Huds.) Holub   Hairy-brome

European Temperate element.

Hairy-brome is a tufted perennial grass found in woodlands and shaded habitats (BH1) on moist, moderately base-rich soils. It is found in most of the British Isles but it is rare or absent from many places in upland Britain.

Frequent (152). In northern Lancashire Hairy-brome is found throughout the area except the extreme west of VC 60. It is especially frequent in northern areas and in the Ribble and Hodder valleys. Its distribution is unchanged locally and nationally.

Bromopsis benekenii (Lange) Holub   Lesser Hairy-brome

European Temperate element.

Lesser Hairy-brome is a tufted perennial grass found in woodland and shaded habitats (BH1) mainly on humus-rich, calcareous soils. It is found in scattered localities in Britain but particularly in beech woods in southern England.

Very rare (1). In northern Lancashire it is believed this species was found in woods in Roeburndale (SD66D) in 1994 (P.J.). It is easily mistaken for *B. ramosa*. It is not known if its distribution has changed nationally.

Bromopsis erecta (Huds.) Fourr.   Upright Brome

European Temperate element.

This is a tufted perennial herb of ungrazed or lightly grazed grasslands on infertile calcareous soils (BH7). It is found in midland and southern Britain and Ireland but occurs as an introduction in north-western England (Halliday, 1997) and in a few places in Scotland.

Rare (7). In northern Lancashire Upright Brome was recorded from a few scattered localities, mostly on limestone in the northwest of the area and occasionally elsewhere. However despite being readily recognisable some records may be errors. Confirmation of *B. erecta* as a northern Lancashire species is needed.

Bromopsis inermis (Leyss.) Holub   Hungarian Brome

Neophyte. *B. inermis* ssp. *inermis* has a Eurosiberian Temperate distribution and was first cultivated in Britain in 1794. It was formerly sown as a fodder plant but it is now found as a seed contaminant. It is found throughout Britain.

Rare (7). Hungarian Brome was first recorded in northern Lancashire from Ansdell (Whellan, 1948). Post 1964 records are from Lytham St Anne's (SD32Y) in 1966 (J.H.) and (SD32N) in 1988 and subsequently, Blackpool (SD33B, C) in 1984, Fleetwood (SD34J) in 1993, Medlar (SD43C) in 1997 and Thornton (SD34B) in 1989 (all C.F. & N.J.S.).

Ceratochloa carinata (Hook. & Arn.) Tutin

California Brome

Neophyte. *C. carinata* is a native of North America and was originally imported as a fodder grass. It was first recorded as an escape from the Royal Botanic Gardens, Kew in about 1919 but it was only after 1945 that it began to be found elsewhere. Today it is found in south-eastern England and in the Mersey Basin with scattered records from elsewhere in the British Isles.

Very rare (2). In northern Lancashire *C. carinata* was found in Lancaster (SD46V) in 1989 (V.G.) and in SD46W (Livermore and Livermore, 1991).

Brachypodium sylvaticum (Huds.) P. Beauv.   False Brome

European Temperate element.

False Brome is a tufted perennial grass found on well-drained, neutral to calcareous soils in woodland and woodland edge habitats (BH1). It is found in most of the British Isles.

Frequent (208). In northern Lancashire *B. sylvaticum* is found in the north of the area and in a central belt between Lancaster and Preston, in river valleys, especially the Hodder and Ribble and on boulder clay in the west particularly on the clay cliffs bordering the Wyre estuary. The distribution of *B. sylvaticum* is stable both locally and nationally.

Brachypodium rupestre (Host) Roem. & Schult. and
Brachypodium pinnatum (L.) P. Beauv.   Tor-grasses

Eurosiberian Temperate element.

These are rhizomatous perennial herbs of infertile, calcareous grasslands (BH7) and woodland edge habitats but the two species have only recently been distinguished from each other. It is believed *B. rupestre* is particularly characteristic of chalk and limestone grasslands in southern and central Britain whilst *B. pinnatum* favours clay soils and may extend further north.

Very rare (3). In northern Lancashire Tor-grass was recorded from Hest Bank (SD46T) in 1965 (J.Wi.) and Silverdale (SD47R; Livermore and Livermore, 1987). It is thought that both records may be errors and no voucher specimens have been seen. It was also found in the Slaidburn area of Lancashire VC 64 (SD75A; Abbott, 2005). Further work is needed to confirm these records and if correct to determine which species occur in the region.

Elymus caninus (L.) L.   Bearded Couch

Eurosiberian Boreo-temperate element.

Bearded Couch is a tufted perennial herb found in woodland and woodland edge habitats mostly on base-rich soils (BH1, 3). It is found throughout most of the British Isles.

Frequent (129). *E. caninus* is found in scattered localities in northern Lancashire with a similar distribution pattern to that of *B. sylvaticum*. However the records in SD32 and 34 are probably errors. The distribution of Bearded Couch is stable locally and nationally.

Elytrigia repens (L.) Desv. ex Nevski — Common Couch

Eurosiberian Wide-temperate element.

Common Couch is a rhizomatous perennial herb found in a wide range of fertile, disturbed habitats as well as in coastal habitats (BH3, 4, 19). It can become a troublesome weed of cultivated ground.

Common (327). *E. repens* is found throughout northern Lancashire except on moorland. It is particularly common in western areas and at the top of salt marshes. All material so far identified has been *E. repens* but some coastal plants, particularly on sandy substrates, may be *E. campestris* (Godr. & Gren.) Kerguélen. The distribution of *E. repens* is stable locally and nationally.

Elytrigia repens × E. atherica (E. × drucei Stace)

This rhizomatous sterile hybrid occurs with or in the absence of its parents in scattered places around the coasts of the British Isles, western Europe and the Baltic. It is likely to have been under recorded and there is some evidence that it is spreading along salt treated roads (Cook, 2006).

Occasional (58). In northern Lancashire *E. × drucei* was mistaken for *E. atherica*, which has not been seen in recent years. The hybrid is common on most salt marshes where it dominates the upper marsh communities often to the exclusion of almost all other taxa (see Plate 2.67). Above *E. × drucei* there is often a zone dominated by *E. repens* (Greenwood, 2004).

Elytrigia repens × E. juncea (E. × laxa (Fr.) Kerguélen)

This hybrid occurs with the parents on sandy shores and on shingle probably on most coasts of the British Isles. It is widespread on the Mediterranean and Atlantic coasts of Europe.

Rare (13). In northern Lancashire *E. × laxa* is found in a few localities on sandy shores of VC 60.

Elytrigia atherica (Link) Kerguélen — Sea Couch

European Southern-temperate element.

E. atherica grows on the margins of brackish creeks and salt marshes (BH19, 21) and probably occurs on coasts in the southern half of the British Isles. However its northern limits are unknown as it has often been identified in error for *E. × drucei*.

Extinct. In northern Lancashire the only confirmed record is from near Fleetwood in 1904 (J.A.W.; NMW). There is also an unconfirmed post 1964 record from Fleetwood (SD34I). The nearest confirmed colonies of *E. atherica* known today are on the northern bank of the Dee estuary (VC 58) but here it is sterile.

Elytrigia atherica × E. juncea (E. × acuta (DC.) Tzvelev)

E. × acuta occurs on sandy shores and shingle often in the transition zone between salt marshes and sand dunes. It may or may not be with the parents. It is widespread on European Mediterranean and Atlantic coasts and in the British Isles it is found on the coasts of England, Wales and southern Ireland.

Rare (9). In northern Lancashire it has been found in a few localities on the coast of VC 60.

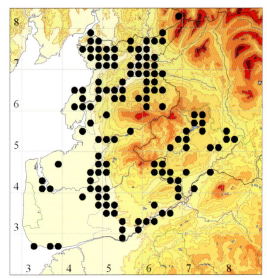
Elymus caninus

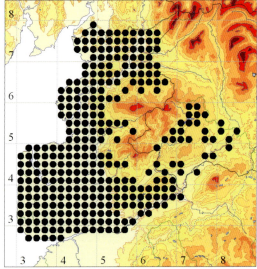
Elytrigia repens

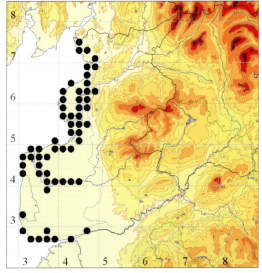
Elytrigia × drucei

Elytrigia juncea (L.) Nevski
ssp. **boreoatlantica** (Simonet & Guin.) Hyl.   Sand Couch

European Southern-temperate element.

Sand Couch is a rhizomatous perennial herb found just above the strand line in loose sand (BH19) around the coasts of the British Isles.

Occasional (36). Sand Couch is found on all the sandy shores of northern Lancashire. The distribution of *E. juncea* is stable locally and nationally.

Leymus arenarius (L.) Hochst.   Lyme-grass

European Boreo-arctic Montane element.

Lyme-grass is a rhizomatous perennial herb found on coastal sand dunes (BH19) of the British Isles.

Occasional (46). *L. arenarius* occurs on sandy shores of VC 60 and occasionally inland in post-industrial sites. Although its distribution nationally is stable there has been a considerable extension of its range over the last 100 years in northern Lancashire.

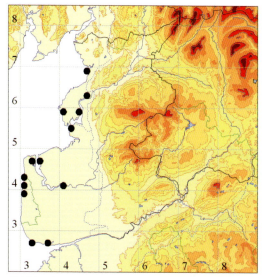

Elytrigia × laxa

Hordelymus europaeus (L.) Jess. Jess. ex Harz   Wood Barley

European Temperate element.

This is a perennial herb found in woods (BH1) on calcareous soils in England and Wales with single localities in southern Scotland and Ireland.

Very rare (3). Wood Barley was first found in VC 60 in woods by the R. Hodder, Aighton, Bailey and Chaigley (SD64R) in 1965 (E.F.G.). It was subsequently found in other woods on both sides of the river (SD64W; T.B., P.J.) and by the R. Ribble, Bolton-by-Bowland (SD74Z) in 2006 (E.F.G.). It has also been found in Middlebarrow Wood, Arnside, just over the county boundary in Cumbria (Halliday, 1997). Its distribution nationally is declining ('New Atlas').

Hordeum vulgare L.   Six-rowed Barley

Neophyte. Six-rowed Barley originated in cultivation and is grown in temperate climates worldwide. It usually occurs casually with records from throughout the British Isles but with most localities in southern England. It was first recorded in the wild in 1905.

Very rare (2). In northern Lancashire *H. vulgare* was first recorded from Roman horse dung in Lancaster (Wilson, 1979). Recent records are from near Hest Bank (SD46S; Livermore and Livermore, 1987) and from near Myerscough (SD54A) in 1987 (C.J.B.).

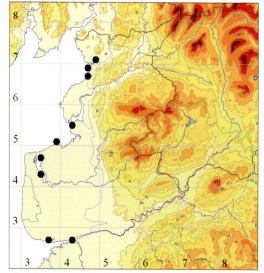

Elytrigia × acuta

Hordeum distichon L.   Two-rowed Barley

Neophyte. Two-rowed Barley is the common cultivated barley, of which there are many cultivars, but its origin is unknown. It is cultivated throughout the temperate regions of the world. Although cultivated in Britain for thousands of years it was first recorded in the wild in 1908. It occurs throughout the British Isles but it is of casual occurrence.

Occasional (22). In northern Lancashire *H. distichon* was first recorded from St Anne's in 1965 (A.E.R.) and although most records are from the north of the region it is probably just as frequent elsewhere in lowland areas.

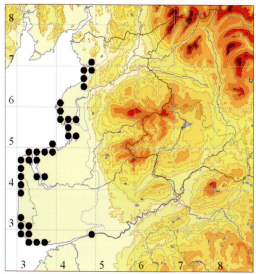

Elytrigia juncea

Hordeum murinum L.　　　　　　　　　　　　Wall Barley

Archaeophyte with a Eurosiberian Southern-temperate distribution but a neophyte in northern Lancashire.

Wall Barley occurs in ruderal habitats (BH3, 17), especially in urban areas and is found in England, Wales, eastern Scotland and eastern Ireland with occasional records elsewhere.

Frequent (89). Wall Barley was first recorded in northern Lancashire from Preston Docks in 1899 (Wheldon and Wilson, 1900) but only two further localities were noted by them by 1907. Since then it has become established in many coastal areas of VC 60 but occurs occasionally inland. It is probable that all northern Lancashire records are referable to *H. murinum* ssp. *murinum* but no material has been checked. However, *H. murinum* ssp. *leporinum* (Link) Arcang. and ssp. *glaucum* (Steud.) Tzvelev, both casuals, have been found in South Lancaster, VC 59 (Stace, *et al.*, 2003) and could occur in northern Lancashire.

Hordeum jubatum L.　　　　　　　　　　　　Foxtail Barley

Neophyte. *H. jubatum* is a native of North America and eastern Asia but it is widely naturalised in northern and western Europe. It is a short-lived perennial herb found in ruderal habitats and it was introduced into Britain as a fodder grass in 1782. It has been recorded in the wild since 1890 and has been found in many parts of Britain. It also occurs occasionally in Ireland.

Rare (7). In northern Lancashire it was recorded from disturbed ground at Fleetwood (SD34I) in 1985 (C.F. & N.J.S.) and in two localities in the same area in 2005 (P.J. & D.P.E.). It was also recorded on a slip road to the M6 motorway, Quernmore (SD46X) in 2009 (M.P.), near the motorways at Broughton (SD53M) in 2002, near Peel Hill (SD33L) in 2003, near Lower Brockholes, Preston (SD53V) in 2003, near Medlar (SD43C) in 2003 and near Weeton (SD33X) in 2004 (all C.F. & N.J.S.).

Hordeum secalinum Schreb.　　　　　　　　Meadow Barley

European Temperate element.

This is a perennial herb of meadows and pastures (BH5) and is found in England, particularly in the southeast, Wales and occasionally in Ireland. It is also recorded as an introduction in a few localities in Scotland. In coastal areas it is frequently abundant on grazed marshes.

Very rare (2). In northern Lancashire the first records were from Lea (Preston Scientific Society, 1903), Kirkham in 1950 and Lytham in 1957 (both B.R.C.). Since 1964 Meadow Barley has been found in a pasture adjacent to the salt marsh at Freckleton (SD42I) where it was first seen in 1973 and where it was last recorded in 2006 (C.F. & N.J.S.) and on waste ground at Lancaster (SD46R; Livermore and Livermore, 1987). Nationally its distribution is stable.

[Hordeum marinum Huds.　　　　　　　　　Sea Barley

Mediterranean-Atlantic element.

This is an annual species of open habitats by the sea (BH6). It occurs as a native species in southern Britain and occasionally elsewhere as an introduction.

In northern Lancashire there is an unconfirmed record for Sea Barley from Lytham (Anon, 1829) and from near Lytham in 1883 (Wheldon and Wilson, 1907). Both are believed to be errors.]

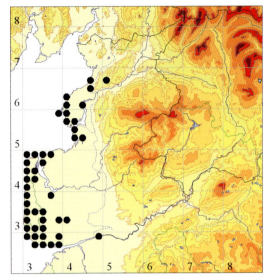

Leymus arenarius

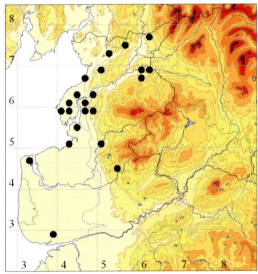

Hordeum distichon

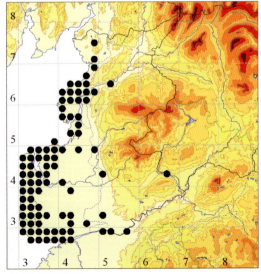

Hordeum murinum

Secale cereale L. — Rye

Neophyte or archaeophyte. Rye is only known from cultivation and is widely grown in the temperate regions of the world. It is an annual herb formerly widely cultivated in Britain but not recorded from the wild until 1865. It is now rarely grown but occurs casually in England, Wales and rarely in Scotland and Ireland.

Very rare (3). In northern Lancashire Rye was first recorded from Roman horse dung at Lancaster (Wilson, 1979) and from the sand dunes at St Anne's in 1907 (C.B.; MANCH; Wheldon and Wilson, 1907). Post 1964 records are from demolition sites in Preston (SD53F) in 1966 (J.H. & E.H.), Warton (SD57B; Livermore and Livermore, 1987) and from a roadside at Alston (SD63C) in 1987 (E.F.G.).

Triticum aestivum L. — Bread Wheat

Neophyte. Bread Wheat originated in cultivation and is grown throughout the world. It is an annual herb with numerous cultivars but it was not recorded in the wild in Britain until 1927. It occurs casually in small numbers and may be found as a relic of cultivation throughout the British Isles. Recorders often ignore it.

Rare (16). It is believed that *T. aestivum* was first found in northern Lancashire from 1st or 2nd century Roman remains at Ribchester (Huntley and Hillam, 2000). It was then not recorded until it was found at St Anne's in 1965 (A.E.R.). Since then it has been found in a few localities in VC 60.

Triticum spelta L. — Spelt

Spelt is a hybrid of obscure origin and was cultivated from Neolithic times. In Britain there have been few twentieth century records.

In northern Lancashire Spelt was found in Roman remains of the 1st and 2nd century at Ribchester (Huntley and Hillam, 2000).

Danthonia decumbens (L.) DC. — Heath-grass

European Temperate element.

Heath-grass is a tufted perennial herb occurring in heathy grassland on mildly acid soils (BH7, 8). It is found throughout the British Isles.

Frequent (167). *D. decumbens* is found in most of northern Lancashire but it is largely absent from cultivated areas in the lowland west of the region. The distribution of *D. decumbens* in northern Lancashire is stable but the 'New Atlas' reported losses nationally. However 'Local Change' reported an increase since 1987 that was attributed to better recording pointing out that Heath-grass could be easily overlooked.

Cortaderia selloana (Schult. & Schult. f.) Asch. & Graebn. — Pampas-grass

Neophyte. Pampas-grass is a native of North America. It is a large, showy, tussock-forming, dioecious perennial herb cultivated in Britain since 1848. It is commonly grown in parks and gardens and was first recorded in the wild in 1925. Most records are from southern England but there are scattered records from elsewhere in the British Isles.

Very rare (2). In northern Lancashire Pampas-grass was found at the top of a salt marsh at Singleton (SD33U) not far from two large garden plants in 1998 (E.F.G.) and on the sand dunes at Fairhaven (SD32I) in 2008.

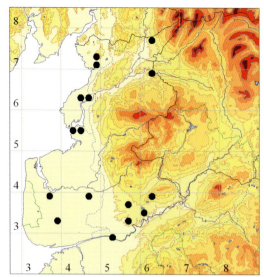

Triticum aestivum

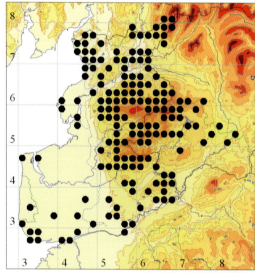

Danthonia decumbens

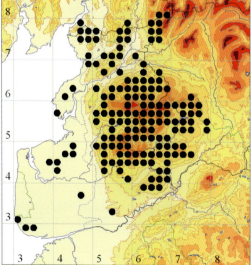

Molinia caerulea

Cortaderia richardii (Endl.) Zotov   Early Pampas-grass

Neophyte. This is a large tufted perennial herb native to South Island, New Zealand. It is naturalised on cliffs and on waste ground mostly in western Britain. It reproduces by seed and escapes from gardens. Early Pampas-grass was first found in Dorset in the 1880s and is probably under recorded as it is sometimes confused with *C. selloana*.

Very rare (1). In northern Lancashire a seedling was found at the edge of a road in Glasson Dock (SD45M) in 2010 (M.W.).

Molinia caerulea (L.) Moench   Purple Moor-grass

Eurosiberian Boreo-temperate element.

This is a perennial herb found in a wide range of habitats especially heaths, moors, bogs and fens on mildly basic to strongly acid substrates (BH12). It is found throughout the British Isles but it is rare in parts of southern and eastern England.

Frequent (163). *M. caerulea* occurs commonly in northern and eastern areas of northern Lancashire and more rarely in the west of the region. In some parts of Bowland *M. caerulea* dominates large areas of bog (see Plate 2.45), usually at lower levels of *c.* 150m (500ft.). No attempt was made to distinguish between *M. caerulea* ssp. *caerulea* and *M. caerulea* ssp. *arundinacea* (Schrank) K. Richt. but it is believed the latter was found by a river at Caton-with-Littledale (SD56R) in 1997 (B.S.B.I.). However Cope and Gray (2009) believe that there is so much overlap between the morphology of the two taxa that it is difficult to maintain their distinction. The distribution of Purple Moor-grass is stable locally and nationally although the 'New Atlas' reported some losses in lowland areas.

Phragmites australis (Cav.) Trin. ex Steud.   Common Reed

Circumpolar Wide-temperate element.

Common Reed is a tall, rhizomatous and stoloniferous herb of swamps and fens often forming large stands. It is also found in seepages on cliffs and at the top of salt marshes (BH11). It is found throughout the British Isles.

Frequent (140). *P. australis* is found mostly in western areas of northern Lancashire but with occasional localities further east. Although the distribution of Common Reed is largely unchanged in northern Lancashire it has become much more extensive and common within its range. The large reed beds at Leighton Moss are the most notable of these developments but reed beds have also formed in recent years at the top of salt marshes. 'Local Change' also noted an increase nationally since 1987 and attributed this to plantings for game cover and bird conservation whilst Common Reed also responds favourably to nutrient enrichment.

Cynodon dactylon (L.) Pers.   Bermuda-grass

Neophyte with a European Southern-temperate distribution. However it is possibly native in south-western England. Bermuda-grass is found on sandy ground on the coast and in ruderal places in England and Wales.

Very rare (1). In northern Lancashire Bermuda-grass was found on sandy ground at Lytham St Anne's (SD32J) in 1983 and survived until the mid 1990s (C.F. & N.J.S.).

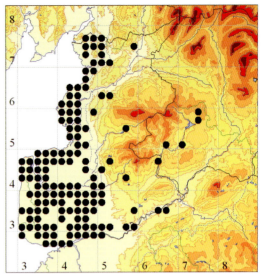
Phragmites australis

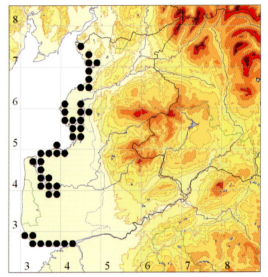
Spartina anglica

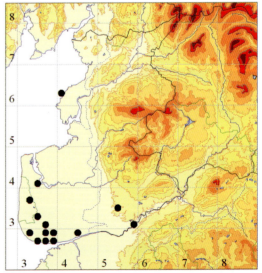
Panicum miliaceum

[Spartina maritima (Curtis) Fernald × **S. alterniflora** Loisel.
(S. × townsendii H. & J. Groves) Townsend's Cord-grass

This hybrid originated in Southampton Water in about 1870 but in about 1890 an amphidiploid derivative arose and for many years this fertile taxon, *S. anglica*, was confused with the F₁ hybrid. It appears that both may have been planted on mud flats around the shores of England and possibly Wales. The spread of the two taxa was described by Hubbard and Stebbings (1967), who indicated that a cord-grass was found on the Ribble estuary in 1932. This is amongst the earlier records in Britain following initial establishment in Hampshire.

In northern Lancashire no attempt was made to ascertain which taxon first colonized the shores of Morecambe Bay and the estuaries of the Lune and Wyre. However a cord-grass was found on the Wyre estuary near the Shard Bridge where it appeared to have colonized the muddy bank naturally (Whellan, 1942) and also at Fleetwood (E.W., 1942). Garlick (1957a) referred to cord-grass being planted at Sunderland Point on the Lune estuary in 1955 and he found it at Bolton-le-Sands also in 1955 (Garlick, 1957b). It is possible that some of these observations are for *S. × townsendii* as a plant found at Preesall, near Knott End (on the Wyre estuary opposite Fleetwood) in 1999 (SD34N; E.F.G.) appeared to be the F₁ hybrid. In 2010 an apparently sterile plant with morphological measurements fitting the F₁ hybrid proved to be fertile. Confirmation is therefore needed that *S. × townsendii* occurs in northern Lancashire.]

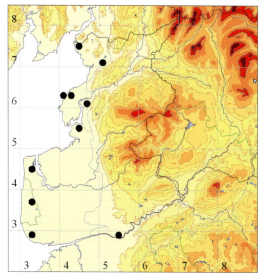
Echinochloa crus-galli

Spartina anglica C.E. Hubb. Common Cord-grass

Endemic.

This is a vigorous, rhizomatous perennial herb that occurs on salt marshes and mud flats (BH21) in England, Wales, Ireland and southern Scotland. It is impossible to distinguish between planted and native populations. It is also widely planted in western Europe.

Occasional (43). Common Cord-grass is found on all the VC 60 salt marshes where it is often a pioneer colonizer of bare mud and may cover extensive areas of the lower salt marsh (see Plate 2.62).

Panicum capillare L. Witch-grass

Neophyte. This is a native of North America but it is widely naturalised in central and southern Europe and elsewhere. It was cultivated in Britain by 1758 and was recorded in the wild by 1867. It is increasingly grown in gardens as an ornamental species but in the wild it is a rare casual. It has been found mostly in southern England but with occasional records from elsewhere in England, Wales, southern Scotland and the Isle of Man.

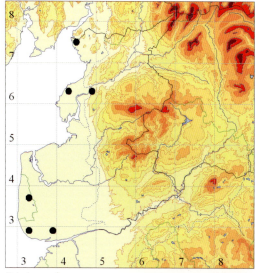
Setaria pumila

Very rare (2). Witch-grass was found in northern Lancashire on Lytham tip (SD32Z) in 1979 (C.F. & N.J.S.) and in Lancaster (SD46Q) in 2002 (A.M. Boucher).

Panicum miliaceum L. Common Millet

Neophyte. Common Millet was originally domesticated in central and eastern Asia but it is now grown in warm-temperate and tropical regions of the world. It was brought into British cultivation by 1596 and was first recorded in the wild in 1872. Today it occurs casually in many places in England and the Isle of Man but less widely in Wales, eastern Scotland and eastern Ireland.

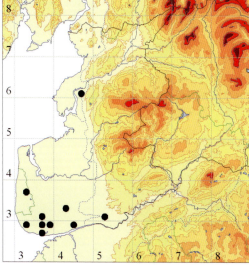
Setaria viridis

Rare (14). Common Millet was first found on the sand dunes at Lytham St Anne's where it persisted for a few years before road works destroyed the site in 1908 (Bailey, 1910). In the early 1960s it was found in the Blackpool area and since then it has been found from time to time in ruderal habitats on the coast between Freckleton and Thornton with occasional records elsewhere.

Echinochloa crus-galli (L.) P. Beauv. Cockspur

Neophyte. Cockspur is a native of warm-temperate and tropical regions of Europe, Asia and North America but it is widely introduced elsewhere as a fodder crop. It has been known in the British Isles since at least 1690 but its occurrence in the wild increased greatly after the 1940s when it was introduced with North American seed. It is found casually in many places in England and the Isle of Man but more rarely in Wales, Scotland and Ireland.

Rare (10). Cockspur was found at intervals on Blackpool tip (SD33I) between 1963 and 1966 (A.E.R., J.H.) and since then in waste ground and cultivated ground in scattered localities in the western half of VC 60.

Echinochloa esculenta (A. Braun) H. Scholz
Japanese Millet

Neophyte. Japanese Millet originated in cultivation in Japan as a derivative of *E. crus-galli*. It is not known when it first grew wild in Britain as it is easily confused with *E. crus-galli* but it was present by 1971. It is used in birdseed mixtures and as a food source for game. It is found casually mostly in England but occasionally elsewhere.

Very rare (1). In northern Lancashire *E. esculenta* was found on a tip at Lytham (SD32U) in 1971 (A.E.R.).

Setaria pumila (Poir.) Roem. & Schult. Yellow Bristle-grass

Neophyte. The native range of *S. pumila* is uncertain but it is probably centred on the Mediterranean region and south-western Asia. It is naturalised in many warm-temperate and subtropical areas of the world. It was first cultivated in Britain in 1819 and it was found in the wild by 1867. *S. pumila* has been found in ruderal habitats in England and more occasionally elsewhere in the British Isles.

Rare (6). Yellow Bristle-grass was first found in northern Lancashire from near Ashton, Preston in 1900 (Wheldon and Wilson, 1902) and from waste ground at St Anne's in 1906 (C.B.; MANCH). Post 1964 records are from tips at Blackpool (SD33I) in 1966 (A.E.R.) and Lytham (SD32Z) in 1975 (C.F. & N.J.S.), Lancaster (SD46W) in 1995 (G.H.), Morecambe (SD46G) in 1998 (J.K.), an urban roadside at Bare (SD46M) in 2010 (J.Cl.) and as a garden weed at St Anne's (SD32J) in 1997 (C.F. & N.J.S.).

Setaria viridis (L.) P. Beauv. Green Bristle-grass

Neophyte. Green Bristle-grass is a native of Eurasia but it is found in many temperate and subtropical regions of the northern hemisphere. It was first recorded in the wild in Britain in 1666 and today occurs in many places in England and southern Ireland as well as occasionally elsewhere in the British Isles.

Rare (10). In northern Lancashire Green Bristle-grass was first recorded from Wardless (SD34R; Wheldon and Wilson, 1902) and later was 'rather frequent' on waste ground at St Anne's (France, 1931). Since 1964 it has been found in a few localities near the Fylde coast and at Lancaster.

Setaria italica (L.) P. Beauv. Foxtail Bristle-grass

Neophyte. Foxtail Bristle-grass originated in cultivation and was cultivated in Britain by 1739. It was recorded from the wild by 1905 and today occurs casually in England, Wales and southern Scotland. It is mainly introduced in birdseed and as a grain contaminant.

Very rare (3). Foxtail Bristle-grass was found on Blackpool tip (SD33I) between 1961 and 1966 (A.E.R., E.P., J.H.), Lytham tip (SD32U) in 1966 (E.H.), and Blackpool (SD33H) in 1989 (C.F. & N.J.S.).

Digitaria sanguinalis (L.) Scop. Hairy Finger-grass

Neophyte. Hairy Finger-grass is a native of the Mediterranean region and south-western Asia. It was first recorded in the wild in the British Isles in 1690 and occurs today in ruderal habitats in many parts of the British Isles but especially in southern England. It is often a casual.

Very rare (2). In northern Lancashire it was found at the base of a wall behind the library in Carnforth (SD47V) in 2010 (J.Cl.) and on a pavement in Blackpool (SD33C) in 1999 (C.F. & N.J.S.).

Sorghum halepense (L.) Pers. Johnson-grass

Neophyte. *S. halepense* is probably a native of the Mediterranean region but it has spread throughout the world in warm-temperate and tropical areas in cultivation or as a weed. It was cultivated in Britain by 1691 and recorded in the wild by 1924. It has been found in scattered localities in England and Wales.

Very rare (1). In northern Lancashire it was recorded from a tip at Lytham (SD32Z) in 1971 (A.E.R.).

Zea mays L. Maize

Neophyte. The origin of Maize is unknown but it has been grown in the Americas for a long time and is now cultivated in many parts of the world. It was first grown in Britain in 1562 and was found in the wild by 1876. However it is only since the 1970s that it has been grown extensively in Britain as a fodder plant. It has been recorded casually from scattered localities in Britain and eastern Ireland.

Very rare (3). In northern Lancashire Maize was recorded from Woodplumpton (SD43X) in 1964 (J.H.), demolition sites in Preston (SD53F) in 1966 (J.H & E.H.) and from a barley field at Ballam (SD33Q) in 1967 (E.P.).

4. Characterising the northern Lancashire flora

Introduction

Chapters 1 and 2 described how the habitats found today developed and how the species were organised into plant communities (Rodwell, 1991–2000). However it was pointed out that the flora and the communities are dynamic and changing. Some communities of open habitats may last for only a few months but in contrast woodland and mire communities have stability extending over centuries or longer. Yet others do not fit a currently described community but are perhaps intermediate either in space, i.e. situated between two described communities, or time, i.e. the present community is in the process of changing from one community to another *in situ*.

The nature of the vegetation and the landscape fabric (or morphology) form a mosaic that gives rise to the character of northern Lancashire (Anon, 1997; Anon, 2008). However the individual species are the building blocks on which this character is built. But which species occur where depends upon a series of environmental factors, history and the biological characteristics of individual species.

Ever since humans travelled the world and recorded what they saw there has been an appreciation that different plants and animals were found in different places and that this seemed to be broadly related to climate (Breckle, 2002). It is now generally accepted that on the largest scale the limits of distribution are determined mainly by climate and dispersal history. At a more local level the present geographical distribution of plants is also the result of climate and dispersal history but also of habitat availability (Preston and Hill, 1997). Thus within the British Isles the only species found growing wild are ones that are adapted to a temperate, oceanic climate, i.e. cool and damp without any extremes. Nevertheless within that overall climate there is variation of temperature and rainfall, which is reflected in the distribution patterns of individual species.

However whilst climate is an overall determinant of plant occurrence, soils and other features of the environment mould the habitats. Unfortunately, whilst in the most general terms ecologists agree the terminologies for some Broad Habitats (e.g. there is little disagreement by what is meant by woodland), there are many areas where there is disagreement. These problems will be discussed below, but by looking at the climatic preferences of species and the habitats in which they grow, a picture emerges that defines the character of the native and archaeophyte flora.

At the county level species show a variety of distribution patterns many of which can be grouped together suggesting that there are other factors besides climate governing their distribution. Often environmental features can be correlated with distribution patterns but the subtleties of these may be too difficult to explain. Furthermore it has not been possible to use statistical techniques to define distribution patterns and it is likely that patterns exist that are not easily recognisable.

Because of the complex interactions taking place two further topics need to be considered. The composition of the northern Lancashire flora is in constant flux. Hybrids are continually arising or spreading into the area and whilst many of these do not persist others are highly successful and form important components of the vegetation. Also through human activity new species are constantly being introduced and some become established. In addition new habitats are created that are exploited by a variety of species providing their environmental requirements and dispersal mechanisms allow them to take advantage of the new situations.

Thus the character of the north Lancashire flora and vegetation is defined in terms of all these factors.

How many species and where they are found

In this study of northern Lancashire's flora data has been assembled from as many sources as possible in order to provide information on all the taxa that have been found in the area over the last 10,000 years. No doubt additional data exists and if and when herbaria are digitised they may provide a rich source of new information. Table 4.1 shows that approximately 2000 species and subspecies were recorded in northern Lancashire between 1964 and 2008.

Table 4.1 Total number of species and subspecies recorded in northern Lancashire between 1964 and 2008 in tetrad frequency categories.

Frequency category	No. of tetrads	No. of species
Very rare	1–5	841 (136 native)
Rare	6–14	338
Occasional	15–69	418
Frequent	70–231	307
Common	232–347	92
Very common	348–466	93
Total		2089

Note in chapters 4 and 5 the number of taxa recorded or analysed may vary because it has not been possible to ensure that at the time of analysis the numbers recorded were consistent. This is due to the constant addition of new species as work progresses and after much of the data had already been analysed and to continuing changes in taxonomic treatment.

Of these *c.* 2,000 taxa approximately 825 are thought to be native and 613 are neophytes of which only 167 are thought to be naturalised. There are also 170 hybrids of which 69 are naturalised. Until recently hybrids were not thought to be important components of vegetation but, although often sterile, many can perennate vegetatively. There are also 44 *Hieracium*, 57 *Rubus* and 134 *Taraxacum* species. Excluding these critical genera there are only eight endemic species found in northern Lancashire.

Naturalised species are ones that are reproducing or extending their range during a continuous period of 5 or more years even if they are subsequently lost. Subspecies are not included in this table.

Most native species are established members of the flora but a few have only occurred on a few occasions, e.g. *Mertensia maritima*, *Mibora minima* and *Trifolium ornithopodioides*. Similarly a number of archaeophytes do not seem to be fully established in the region. However most neophytes occur either casually or are planted trees that remain in the landscape without reproducing.

The number of species recorded in each tetrad since 1964 is shown in Map 4.2. It demonstrates that the species diversity of tetrads varies enormously. On the one hand some areas have a very diverse flora, e.g. around Morecambe Bay where over 700 taxa have been recorded from some tetrads, whilst in the upland areas totals are less than 100. With only 30 taxa found in SD65E this tetrad must be one of the least diverse in the country.

Table 4.2 Total numbers of species recorded in northern Lancashire.

Species category	Numbers	Endemic	Naturalised
Extinct	51		
Hybrids	170		69
Native	825	8	
Archaeophytes	113		70
Neophytes	613		167
Sub total	1772	8	306
Hieracium	44	16	
Rubus	57	22	
Taraxacum	134	11	
Total	2007	57	306

Notes. Extinct species are ones that have not been seen for 20 years or are known to have gone from their last known site. However some species formerly thought to be extinct have reappeared after absences of about 100 years.

Excluding critical groups (*Hieracium*, *Rubus* & *Taraxacum*) most taxa are very rare (Table 4.1). However of the 841 very rare taxa recorded only 136 are believed to be native. There are also surprisingly few common (92) or very common (93) taxa. Thus there are no species that are truly ubiquitous occurring in all the 466 tetrads from which records have been gathered. The commonest species is *Poa annua* found in 456 tetrads. It is only absent from a few coastal areas, mostly tidal mudflats, and a few of the highest upland tetrads.

However it is also surprising that of the 93 very common taxa the only neophytes or introductions are *Acer pseudoplatanus* (412 tetrads) and *Matricaria discoidea* (396 tetrads). None of the so-called invasive species, e.g. *Rhododendron ' ponticum'* (160 tetrads) or *Impatiens glandulifera* (146 tetrads) are very common or even common.

I suggest that very common taxa are particularly successful northern Lancashire species whilst very rare taxa are relatively unsuccessful and have

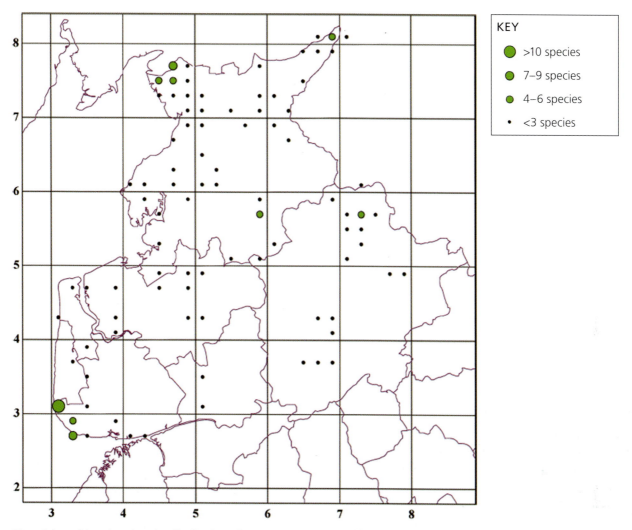

Map 4.1 Map showing the distribution of 85 rare native species (found in three or fewer tetrads) in northern Lancashire since 1964. It demonstrates that rare species tend to be concentrated in certain areas.

KEY

● >10 species

● 7–9 species

● 4–6 species

• <3 species

demanding ecological or climatological require-ments. The demanding nature of very rare taxa is further demonstrated by their distribution. Map 4.1 shows the distribution of 85 native species that have been recorded in three or fewer tetrads in northern Lancashire since 1964. Whilst there is a scattering of single records throughout most of the region there are clear clusters of tetrads where several very rare species occur. The most important of these are on the sand dunes at Lytham St Anne's where eleven very rare species were recorded in tetrad SD33A and on the limestone around Morecambe Bay where eight species were found in tetrad SD47T. Both these areas coincide with tetrads with the most diverse flora in the region. Other impor-tant areas for rare species are located at Leck, on

the Bowland Fells and around Stocks Reservoir in Lancashire VC 64.

Map 4.2 illustrates the wide species diversity in northern Lancashire. The most species diverse areas are around Morecambe Bay, Heysham, and Lytham St Anne's but examining the tetrads with 301 to 450 species suggests some interesting correlations. In particular the Lancaster Canal gives rise to a line of floristically rich tetrads running from Preston, into the Fylde (SD43) and then north through Garstang, Lancaster and to the Cumbrian border at Tewitfield. Similarly areas of greater diversity can be followed in the river valleys of the Lune, Wyre, lower Ribble, Hodder and the valleys of the northern Bowland Fells. A further group of floristically rich tetrads follows the estuary of the R. Wyre. On the other hand, apart

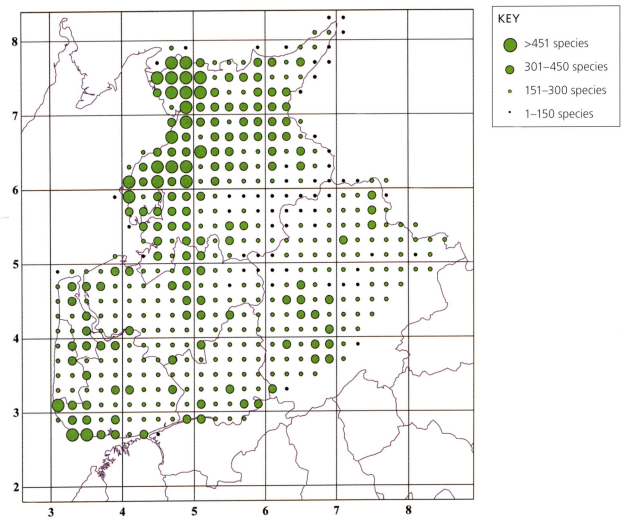

Map 4.2   Map showing the distribution of species recorded per tetrad in northern Lancashire since 1964.

KEY
- ● >451 species
- ● 301–450 species
- • 151–300 species
- · 1–150 species

from tetrads with only a fragment of land in northern Lancashire, species poor areas occur on the tops of the fells at Leck and in Bowland and to a lesser extent in the intensively farmed areas west of the A6/M6 corridor.

Climate preferences of the northern Lancashire flora

Although on a world scale the relationship between climate and vegetation is clear it has proved more difficult to demonstrate how the distribution of species is related to climate at a regional level. With the development of the vice-county system (Watson, 1883) it was possible to demonstrate that in the British Isles different species had different distributions. Then by comparing the distribution of species found in the British Isles with European distributions, Matthews

(1955) defined them in terms of broad geographical elements.

Unfortunately more accurate mapping of species distributions had to await the publication of the *Atlas of the British Flora* (Perring and Walters, 1962), other national and regional mapping projects, the development of the *Flora Europaea* project and the ongoing publication of plant distributions at the European level (Jalas and Suominen, 1972➔). Now it is possible to show increasingly accurately the distribution of plants not only in the British Isles but also in the European and wider context. Building on the work of Matthews (1955), Preston and Hill (1997) analysed the geographical relationships of all British and Irish native and archaeophyte species.

Within Europe there are three main climatic factors that determine plant distribution:

- temperature, particularly summer warmth and winter cold,
- rainfall especially summer drought,
- oceanicity, particularly the number of wet days (Averis, *et al.*, 2004).

The distribution of most species is correlated with one or more of these climatic variables and in a few cases the effects of climate have been demonstrated experimentally. Also important is Pleistocene history, and for the British Isles the severing of the land bridge with the continent of Europe about 5,000BC (e.g. Simmons, 2001) allowed fewer species to migrate northwards following the retreat of the ice than might be expected.

For the purpose of classifying plant distribution it is necessary to establish categories that reflect similarities of range. Few, if any, species have identical ranges so generalisations have to be made by grouping together species with similar distributions into floristic elements. The boundaries are somewhat arbitrary as there is a continuum between the elements but the concept recognises clusters within the distributional continuum.

Recognition of floristic elements

Preston and Hill (1997, and Hill, *et al.*, 2004) recognised nine major groupings or floristic elements based on latitudinal differences. In addition there is a small group of endemic species found only in the British Isles. The basis of these groupings is recognition of four latitudinal zones or major biomes.

1. In the north there is an Arctic-montane zone where species are largely found north of the tree line or above the tree line on mountains.
2. To the south and at lower altitudes on mountains there is the Boreal-montane zone corresponding with the distribution of coniferous forest.
3. Extending over the middle latitudes of Europe there is a broad, cool-temperate, broad-leaved deciduous forest zone (the Temperate zone).
4. Finally to the south of this lies a southern region with a Mediterranean zone characterised by summer droughts.

However some species occupy more than one zone although their distribution is usually centred in one major area. Thus the main floristic elements numbered 1 to 9 (with 10 assigned to endemic species) based on latitudinal differences are:

1. Arctic-montane. Species found north of the tree-line or (on mountains) above the tree-line or both
2. Boreo-arctic Montane. Species found in both Arctic-montane and Boreal-montane zones
3. Wide Boreal. Species found in Arctic-montane, Boreal-montane and Temperate zones
4. Boreal-montane. Species found in coniferous forest, either in northern Europe or in mountains further south or both, where the vegetation is dominated by coniferous forest (the Boreal zone)
5. Boreo-temperate. Species found in Wide Boreal, Boreal-montane, Temperate and Southern-temperate zones
6. Wide Temperate. Species found in Boreal-montane, Temperate and Southern-temperate zones
7. Temperate. Species found in the cool-temperate, broad-leaved deciduous forest zone
8. Southern-temperate. Species found more or less equally in the Temperate and the Mediterranean zones
9. Mediterranean (Southern). Species found in the warm-temperate zone south of the broad-leaved, deciduous forest zone in the Mediterranean region of Europe
10. Endemic. Only found in the British Isles (excluding the Channel Islands).

For each of these main elements there are further divisions numbered 1 to 5 based on their eastern limits with 0 assigned to hyperoceanic species found mostly in the extreme west of the Oceanic zone (Hill and Preston, 1998) and 6 to circumpolar taxa. Thus Oceanic species (1) are restricted to the Atlantic seaboards of Europe whilst Suboceanic (2) represents species that extend further eastwards to include Sweden, western central Europe and in the Mediterranean to include the Adriatic coasts of Italy. Further groups (3–5) cover species found more widely in Europe (European, Eurosiberan and Eurasian), which includes species extending across Asia to an eastern limit of 120°E. A final group includes species that are circumpolar in their distribution (6).

Tables and composite maps showing the distribution of the British flora according to floristic elements demonstrate that most species are European Temperate species (Preston and Hill, 1997; Preston, *et al.*, 2002). In this analysis for northern Lancashire emphasis is placed on the nine categories or floristic elements defined on the basis of latitudinal distribution whilst reference to the eastern limits categories is discussed when appropriate.

Table 4.3 Floristic elements in the British and northern Lancashire flora

Element	British Isles		Northern Lancashire	
	Nos.	%	Nos.	%
Arctic-montane	79	5.4	4	0.4
Boreo-arctic Montane	38	2.6	11	1.3
Wide Boreal	19	1.3	19	2.1
Boreal-montane	103	7	42	4.5
Boreo-temperate	233	15.8	194	21.0
Wide Temperate	34	2.3	31	3.4
Temperate	557	37.7	402	43.5
Southern-temperate	296	20.1	181	19.6
Mediterranean	69	4.7	33	3.7
Endemic	48	3.3	8	0.5
Total	924		1,476	
Oceanic (incl. Mediterranean-Atlantic)	159	10.8	64	6.9
Suboceanic (incl. Submediterranean-Subatlantic)	142	9.6	77	8.3
Total (Oceanic & Suboceanic)	301	20.4	141	15.2

Table 4.3 shows the results of this analysis. As might be expected northern Lancashire, in the centre of Great Britain situated in the middle latitudes of Europe, has an overwhelming majority of species from temperate latitudes but extending northwards into the Boreal zone as well as southwards into southern Europe. However there are differences. In the British Isles the north of Scotland and the south of England are over 1600km (1000 miles) apart and in Scotland and to a lesser extent in Ireland, Wales and northern England there are mountains of over 1,200m. This range of latitude and altitude enables a number of northern species (Arctic-montane, Boreo-arctic Montane, Wide Boreal and Boreal-montane) to occur (16.3% of the flora), especially in Scotland whilst 24.8% of the flora has a southern distribution. In northern Lancashire only 8.3% of the taxa found in the area had such a pronounced northern bias. On the other hand proportionately more southern taxa

(23.3%) were found in the area – very close to the proportion nationally.

The lack of mountains having cold winters and cool summers explains the absence of many northern taxa characterised by Arctic-montane species. However it is perhaps surprising that many southern species occur so far north.

Although Lancashire has a long coastline this borders the land-locked Irish Sea and not the Atlantic Ocean so lacks the extreme oceanicity of western Scotland and Ireland. Nevertheless the Oceanic species, four of which are classed as hyperoceanic, represents 15% of the British Isles total. Conversely only ten northern Lancashire species are considered 'continental' (not shown in Table 4.3) representing 9% of those that occur in the British Isles.

Further analysis of the northern Lancashire flora is confined to those species that belong to floristic elements where climatic variables might be limiting distribution. These are species with a broadly northern, southern or oceanic distribution in Europe and in order to eliminate taxa that occur throughout northern Lancashire only rare species (those occurring in 15 or fewer tetrads) are considered. They are all species on the margins of British or even European distribution. They are all likely to be particularly affected by climate change or other environmental changes (Crawford, 2008).

Northern Species

These are defined as species belonging to Arctic-montane, Boreo-arctic Montane, Wide Boreal and Boreal-montane elements. The northern Lancashire Wide Boreal species all occur in more than 15 tetrads and are not considered further. Combining the Arctic-montane and Boreo-arctic Montane elements provides a group of seven species (Table 4.4) whilst the Boreal-montane element provides a group of 24 species (Table 4.5). Maps 4.3 and 4.4 are composite maps showing the distribution of these species in northern Lancashire.

Whilst there are scattered occurrences of Arctic-montane and Boreo-arctic Montane species in upland and coastal areas the seven species are concentrated in the north-east corner of northern Lancashire in Leck. This is the highest part of the area with the summit of Gragareth at 627m. However the composite map of Boreal-montane species shows additional features. The concentration of northern species in the Leck area is confirmed but further concentrations occur

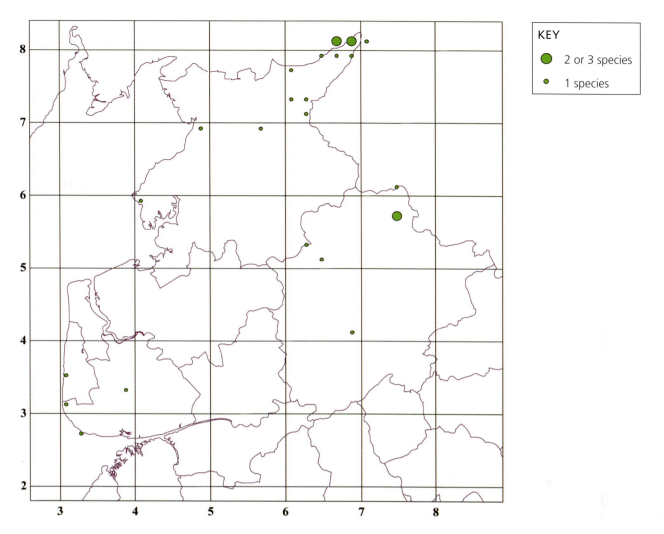

Map 4.3   Map showing the distribution of Arctic-montane and Boreo-arctic Montane species recorded in 15 or fewer tetrads in northern Lancashire since 1964.

Table 4.4   Rare Arctic-montane and Boreo-arctic Montane species recorded in northern Lancashire since 1964

Species	Jan. Mean °C	July Mean °C	Rainfall mm	N value	Summer summit max. isotherm °C
Carex bigelowii	1.8	12.1	1,800	2	25
Cochlearia pyrenaica	1.5	12.9	1,567	3	-
Diphasiastrum alpinum	1.9	12.4	1,686	2	25/27
Draba incana	2.3	12.5	1,584	2	26-27
Epilobium alsinifolium*	1.0	11.9	1,832	4	25
Equisetum variegatum	3.4	14.0	1,224	3	26
Salix phylicifolia	1.8	13.0	1,253	4	27
Mean	1.5	12.69	1,564	2.9	

Notes. * Extinct after 1964. Mean temperatures are taken from Hill, *et al.* (2004) and represent the mean temperature for where the species occur in the British Isles. Rainfall is taken from the same source and is the mean for where the species occur. The N value is the Ellenberg value for nitrogen (Hill, *et al.*, 2004; see chapter 5). The summer summit maximum isotherm is taken from Conolly and Dahl (1970) and refers to temperatures prevailing at the highest places in the landscape.

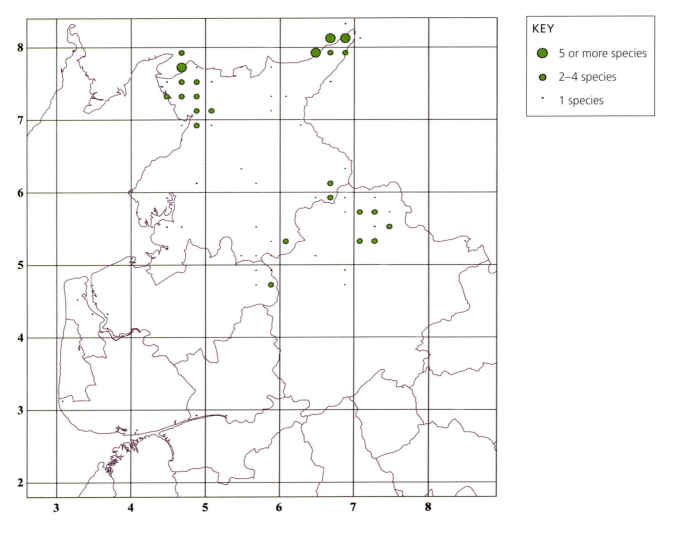

Map 4.4   Map showing the distribution of Boreal-montane species recorded in 15 or fewer tetrads in northern Lancashire since 1964.

in Bowland where the highest peak is Ward's Stone at 561m. More interestingly there is a concentration of species in the Silverdale – Carnforth area on limestone more or less at sea level.

Correlating the distribution of these northern species with climate data is not easy. Conolly and Dahl (1970) demonstrated that the distribution of a number of northern species found in upland areas was correlated with mean annual maximum summit isotherms. In Table 4.4 the more northerly Arctic-montane and Boreo-arctic Montane species appear to have their southern limits bounded by the 25°C isotherm. There are exceptions notably *Equisetum variegatum*, which occurs on sand dunes and other coastal habitats where the summer maximum isotherm is 28°C. Similarly whilst *Salix phylicifolia* is not a coastal species it is found in valleys and lowland areas with a distribution apparently limited

by the 27°C maximum isotherm. Also *Diphasiastrum alpinum* seems to have retreated from a limiting 27°C maximum isotherm to a 25°C isotherm in the last 100 years or so. All these species have broadly similar distributions in the British Isles (Preston, *et al.*, 2002).

Also shown in Tables 4.4 and 4.5 are the annual mean January and July temperatures for where these species occur today (Hill, *et al.*, 2004). These average 2.0°C for January and 13°C for July whilst the annual rainfall averages 1,500mm. In northern Lancashire the mean January temperature on the coast is 3.6°C but by applying a regression of 0.6°C per 100m of altitude the mean January temperature at 600m is 0°C. In summer the comparable figures for July are 15.6°C and 12.0°C. Rainfall varies considerably from 840mm on the coast at Blackpool to 2,260mm in parts of Bowland.

Table 4.5 Rare Boreal-montane species recorded in northern Lancashire since 1964

Species	Jan. mean °C	July mean °C	Rainfall mm	N value	Summer summit max. isotherm °C
*Actaea spicata**	2.5	14.3	1,054	6	
Alchemilla minima	1.7	13.5	1,667	3	
Alchemilla wichurae	0.9	12.0	1,992	3	
Asplenium viride	2.0	12.8	1,701	3	27
Atriplex longipes	4.2	15.6	982	7	
Blysmus rufus	3.8	13.6	1,371	4	
*Carex lasiocarpa**	3.1	13.6	1,383	3	
*Coeloglossum viride**	3.2	14.1	1,148	2	
Cryptogramma crispa	1.8	12.9	1,678	3	26/27
Dryopteris oreades	1.9	12.6	1,810	2	
Euphrasia scottica	2.5	12.8	1,575	3	
Juncus filiformis	2.3	13.6	1,530	3	
Lamium confertum	3.5	13.5	1,097	7	
Minuartia verna	2.7	13.9	1,215	1	
Neottia cordata	2.4	12.8	1,450	2	27
Primula farinosa	2.2	13.8	1,194	2	
Rubus chamaemorus	1.1	12.2	1,594	1	26
Rumex longifolius	2.3	13.0	1,174	7	
*Salix myrsinifolia**	1.8	13.0	1,253	2	27
Saxifraga hypnoides	2.0	12.8	1,697	3	27
Selaginella selaginoides	2.8	13.0	1,443	2	
Sorbus rupicola	2.9	13.6	1,405	3	
Trientalis europaea	2.2	13.0	1,517	3	
Trollius europaeus	2.2	13.0	1,517	4	27
Mean	2.4	13.3	1,435	3.3	

Notes. * Extinct after 1964. For other notes see Table 4.2.

Boreal-montane species have distributions in the British Isles that generally extend further south and at lower altitudes than Arctic-montane and Boreo-arctic Montane species (Preston, *et al.*, 2002). Where the data is available this is reflected by the limiting mean annual maximum summit isotherm being about 27°C. Similarly the January and July mean temperatures for where they are found are slightly higher and the annual rainfall is slightly less. However a number of the species are found in coastal and lowland situations where temperatures are higher and rainfall less. Thus for some of these species temperature may not be the limiting factor in northern Lancashire but rather the presence of open, base-rich and often nutrient poor habitats.

Most species of both groups of northern species reach their southern limits of distribution in the British Isles in Lancashire extending further south only in the upland areas of Wales and the southern Pennines broadly in line with mean annual maximum temperature isotherms. Thus being at their climatic limits suggests that they are vulnerable to small environmental changes.

It is more difficult to explain the incidence of more northern species in the Silverdale and other coastal areas near or at sea level. A more extreme example of this situation is found with the occurrence of Arctic-montane and other northern species at sea level in the equable climate of the Burren in western Ireland. Clearly temperature is not a limiting factor for some species in these lowland situations and at the present time their disjunct distribution is not understood (Webb and Scannell, 1983). Nevertheless Crawford (2008) pointed out that in response to warmer springs and in the absence of competition from other species *Saxifraga oppositifolia* provided fine floristic displays on the coast at Hornsund, Spitsbergen.

All the northern species are typical of nutrient poor soils especially those belonging to the Arctic-montane and Boreo-arctic Montane floristic elements.

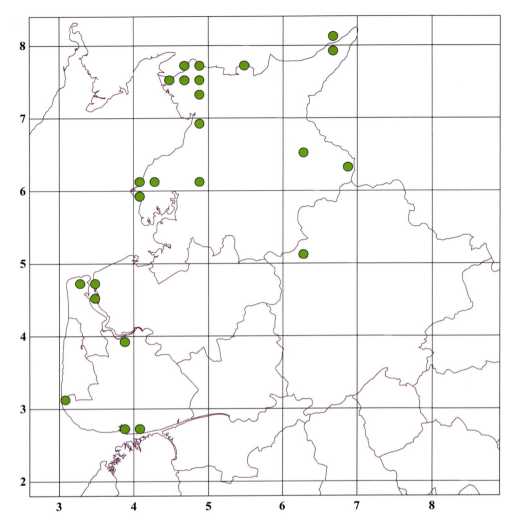

Map 4.5   Map showing the distribution of Mediterranean species recorded in 15 or fewer tetrads in northern Lancashire since 1964.

Oceanic and southern or Mediterranean Species

Species in these floristic elements have some common features. It might be expected that Oceanic species would be limited by drought/moisture characteristics whilst temperature would limit the distribution of Mediterranean species. However some Mediterranean species are also Oceanic occurring in south-western Europe.

Table 4.6 lists the rare northern Lancashire species found in 15 or fewer tetrads in northern Lancashire. It shows that there are thirteen Mediterranean and 29 Oceanic species but eleven are both Oceanic and Mediterranean. Within northern Lancashire the Mediterranean species are largely coastal with occasional records elsewhere. These latter records are of

Dryopteris submontana, which occurs in the mountains of the Mediterranean region and *Daphne laureola* found as a garden escape. Main distribution centres are concentrated in the Silverdale – Carnforth area, the Heysham peninsula, Rossall – Wyre estuary and at Lytham St Anne's (Map 4.5).

Oceanic species follow a similar pattern (Map 4.6). However, significantly there is a more generalised occurrence of species across the region with further concentrations on Leck Fell and in Bowland. Species with both a Mediterranean and Oceanic distribution are shown in Map 4.7.

Correlating the distribution of these two floristic elements of the northern Lancashire flora with climate is difficult and there is little published work in this field. It might be thought that for Mediterranean

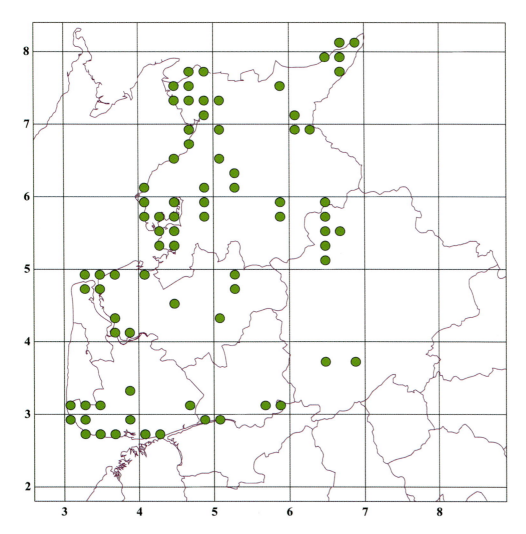

Map 4.6   Map showing the distribution of Oceanic species recorded in 15 or fewer tetrads in northern Lancashire since 1964.

species summer warmth is important but a mainly coastal distribution suggests that this is not the case as summer maximum temperatures are lower on the coast than further inland although at 15.6°C are within the range of northern Lancashire Mediterranean species. Alternatively Mediterranean species might be sensitive to winter cold but here winter temperatures on the Lancashire coast at 3.6°C are below that characteristic of Mediterranean species. A few species, e.g. *Torilis nodosa* and *Vulpia fasciculata*, reach their northern limits in Britain around Morecambe Bay and as annuals summer warmth is probably involved. Whilst the highest summer maximum temperatures do not occur on the coast but inland local warming may occur. Figures are not available for all coastal areas but Blackpool has significantly more sunshine than inland areas and this is especially important in summer when radiation is at its strongest (White and Smith, 1982). The effect of this increased insolation is to raise the temperature above ambient in sheltered localities, e.g. in dune hollows, by several degrees Celsius. However, several species extend much further north along the western coast of Scotland, e.g. *Glaucium flavum, Polypodium cambricum* etc. where winter warming is provided by the North Atlantic Drift (Gulf Stream). Also amongst species with a Mediterranean distribution is *Dryopteris submontana* but this occurs in mountainous areas and accordingly the mean January and July temperatures favoured by this species are lower than for other species in the group.

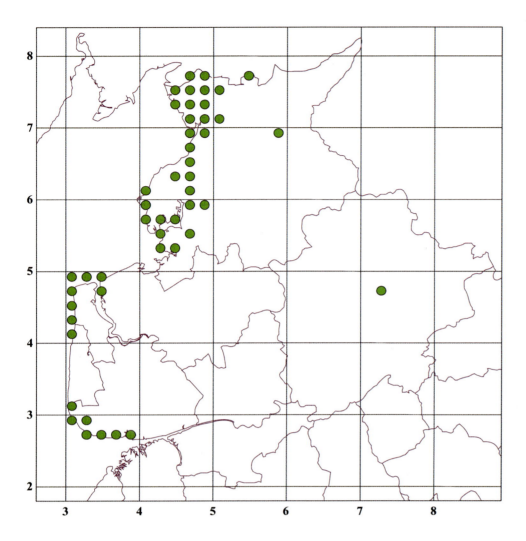

Map 4.7   Map showing species with both a Mediterranean and Oceanic distribution recorded in 15 or fewer tetrads in northern Lancashire since 1964.

Table 4.6   Oceanic and Mediterranean species recorded in northern Lancashire since 1964

Species	Oceanic	Mediterranean	Jan. Mean °C	July Mean °C	Rainfall mm	N value
Alchemilla minima	+		1.7	13.5	1,667	3
Atriplex laciniata	+		4.5	14.8	979	7
Blackstonia perfoliata		+	4.0	15.8	812	2
Calystegia sepium ssp. *roseata*	+					
Calystegia soldanella	+	+	4.8	15.4	959	4
Carex divisa		+	4.4	16.4	727	6
Crithmum maritimum	+	+	5.1	15.4	1,042	5
Dactylorhiza praetermissa	+		3.9	15.9	849	3
Daphne laureola		+	3.7	16.0	760	5
Dryopteris aemula	+		4.2	14.1	1,373	3
Dryopteris submontana		+	2.1	13.7	1,527	3
Euphorbia paralias	+	+	5.1	15.6	987	5

Species	Oceanic	Mediterranean	Jan. Mean °C	July Mean °C	Rainfall mm	N value
Euphorbia portlandica	+		5.3	15.4	1,060	3
Euphrasia anglica	+		4.1	15.3	1,081	3
Euphrasia tetraquetra	+		4.7	14.9	1,105	3
Fumaria bastardii	+	+	4.5	14.8	1,086	6
Genista anglica	+		3.0	14.6	1,019	2
Glaucium flavum	+	+	4.7	15.5	933	6
Hymenophyllum tunbrigense	+		3.1	13.1	1,685	3
Hymenophyllum wilsonii	+		3.8	14.0	1,567	3
Lepidium heterophyllum	+		3.8	14.7	1,074	4
Limonium britannicum	+		5.4	15.7	1,004	5
Parentucellia viscosa	+	+	5.1	15.4	1,129	5
Polypodium cambricum	+	+	4.4	15.1	1,102	3
Salicornia emerici	+		4.2	15.7	821	6
Salicornia fragilis	+		4.5	15.7	884	6
Salicornia obscura	+		4.1	16.4	712	6
Saxifraga hypnoides	+		2.0	12.8	1,697	3
Sorbus lancastriensis	+		3.3	14.8	1285	3
Torilis nodosa	+	+	4.1	15.9	792	6
Trichomanes speciosum	+		3.8	14.2	1,390	3
Vulpia fasciculata	+	+	5.0	15.8	911	2
Wahlenbergia hederacea	+		4.1	14.9	1,280	3
Mean Mediterranean			4.8	15.5	837	4.5
Mean Oceanic			4.2	15.0	1,124	4.1

Averis, *et al.* (2004) reproduced a map for the British Isles showing January mean temperatures and demonstrated that in the west of the British Isles the January mean temperature is above 4°C whilst on the Lancashire coast it is perhaps a little cooler and for the period 1941–1970 it was recorded as 3.6°C at Blackpool and Morecambe. However further inland at Stonyhurst in the Ribble valley the mean January temperature falls to 2.8°C although the map published by Averis, *et al.* (2004) suggests that the mean for the whole of Lancashire is above 3°C. Furthermore these figures are for mean temperature whereas what is probably more important is the mean January minimum temperature, for which figures are not available. On clear frosty nights in winter the warming influence of the Irish Sea is considerable. Manley (1952) showed that even on the East Anglian coast the cooler North Sea still raised the coastal temperature by 10°C when inland severe frost with minimum temperatures of -16°C were recorded on the night of 20 January 1940. However the sea temperature of the North Sea may only be 4°C whereas the Irish Sea may be 3°C higher with consequently an increased warming effect. In Wirral, some 48–64km (30–40 miles) to the south of northern Lancashire, the peninsula is bounded on three sides by the estuaries of the R. Dee and R. Mersey as well as the Irish Sea and here on a frosty morning temperatures of -2 to -3°C are common in the south eastern part of the peninsula towards Chester but at coastal Wallasey, at the opposite end, temperatures of +1–2°C are noted (personal observation). These local effects are immediately obvious with frost sensitive garden *Pelargonium* spp. surviving outside at Wallasey but not a mile or so to the south-east. Thus winter minimum temperatures may be raised locally on the coast in winter and in summer increased insolation provides local warming. These localised effects probably ensure that a suitable climate occurs for a few Mediterranean species at the edge of their distributional range to grow on the Lancashire coast.

It might be expected that Oceanic species are unable to tolerate drought and for the delicate filmy ferns this must be so. However some Oceanic species also belong to the Mediterranean floristic element and for these winter warmth may be important.

Hill and Preston (1998) citing Ratcliffe (1968) suggested that rainfall was an especially good predictor of Atlantic (Oceanic) bryophyte richness but atmospheric humidity and especially lack of drought are probably more important. It was concluded that the best single predictor for an oceanic climate was the annual number of wet days, i.e. the number of days in which more than 1mm of precipitation was recorded. Only regions with more than 220 wet days were moist enough to support communities of large leafy liverworts. Lack of drought is also dependent on continuity of woodland cover. The concept of oceanicity is taken further by Averis, *et al.* (2004) who developed a map of oceanicity calculated by dividing the mean annual number of wet days by the range of monthly mean temperatures (°C). Whilst maps showing wet days and oceanicity refine the concept of an oceanic climate, maps for the British Isles show that the highest rainfall, highest number of wet days and greatest oceanicity all occur on the western side of the British Isles and in the most mountainous areas. Furthermore this temperate climate of extreme oceanicity is unusual worldwide and unique in Europe. It is therefore not surprising that in western Scotland and Ireland the bryophyte flora especially reflects this unusual climate.

In northern Lancashire there are detailed records for rainfall (Meteorological Office, 1961; Meteorological Office, 1983) but wet days and degrees of oceanicity figures are not available. Nevertheless the rainfall figures show that whilst over 200 years annual rainfall is very variable from year to year and from place to place, long-term averages remain constant. These show that in coastal areas annual rainfall averages are under 1,000mm but in parts of Bowland they exceed 2,000mm. For example the long term annual average for Blackpool is *c.* 850mm whilst at White Hill in the Bowland Fells it is *c.* 2,266mm. The totals for the Bowland Fells are high and it is not surprising that maps of the number of wet days (i.e. more than 220 p.a.) and oceanicity (Averis, *et al.*, 2004) show that the Bowland Fells have a climate that could support oceanic species and communities but that they are at the southern and eastern limits of such a climate. The concept of oceanicity implies that the climate is wet and/or equable.

Temperature is an important factor in understanding the distribution of oceanic species in northern Lancashire. Along the coast winter minimum temperatures are higher than inland but summer maximum temperatures are lower. Manley (1952) pointed out that when inland temperatures are 25°C at Blackpool it might only be 18°C due to the onset of afternoon sea breezes. Thus whilst the coastal areas are not especially wet the climate is more equable than further inland. On the other hand in Bowland the potential for low temperatures and a less equable climate is considerable. However for at least some of the oceanic species, e.g. *Hymenophyllum* spp., the lowest temperatures are avoided. They are found in sheltered rock crevices on hillsides facing southwest at altitudes of *c.* 300m or lower. In this situation the lowest winter temperatures are avoided as cold air sinks to the valley below (Manley, 1952). Furthermore these cliffs were lightly wooded and this would have retained humid conditions in summer, but today the woodland has gone and the filmy ferns are confined to the deepest recesses.

In northern Lancashire the distribution of rare species with an oceanic distribution in Europe correlates with the climatic data as far as it is known. In general they are species favouring mild winters with a January mean temperature of *c.* 4°C and cool summers with a July mean temperature of *c.* 15°C. An exception to this is *Alchemilla minima*, which is a British endemic species confined to the limestone of the Craven hills. Its favoured mean temperatures are 1.7°C in January and 13.5°C in July, both well below the average for the group. However *A. minima* is perhaps taxonomically better considered as a variety of *A. filicaulis* – a Boreal-montane species that favours these lower temperatures. Whilst rainfall totals are much lower on the coast than in the Bowland fells it is possible that with a smaller difference between summer and winter temperatures the degree of oceanicity is similar.

A feature of all the rare terrestrial species with a Mediterranean or oceanic distribution is their apparent intolerance of nutrients. Their N value has a mean of *c.* 3. However several species are either salt marsh species or ones subject to salt spray and consequently their N values are much higher at *c.* 6.

Very rare and very common species

For each group of very common and very rare species found in northern Lancashire the number and percentage of species in each category of floristic element and eastern limit climatic types was plotted and compared with the values for all species occurring in the British Isles. This shows that for very rare species the proportion of species in each floristic element is the same as those for the British Isles as a whole (Figure 4.1).

For very common species the geographical limits for northern Lancashire species and for those for the British Isles as a whole are also similar but there is a tendency for northern Lancashire species to be more characteristic of northern temperate latitudes (Figure 4.2).

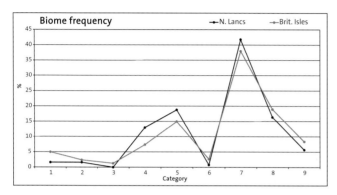

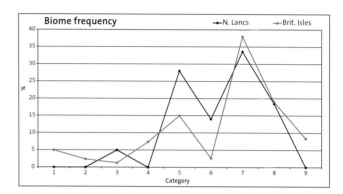

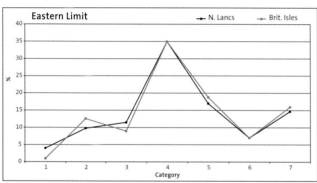

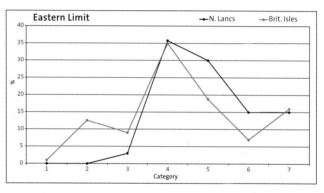

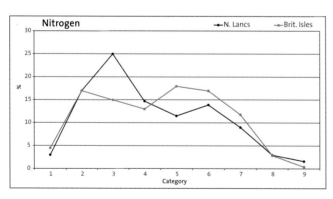

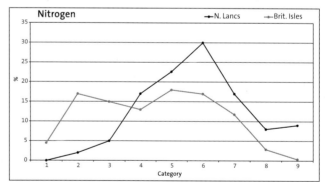

Figure 4.1 Geographical limits for very rare species in northern Lancashire and for all species found in the British Isles

Floristic element categories are: 1 = Arctic-montane; 2 = Boreo-arctic Montane; 3 = Wide Boreal; 4 = Boreal-montane 5 = Boreo-temperate; 6 = Wide Temperate; 7 = Temperate; 8 = Southern-temperate; 9 = Mediterranean.
Eastern limit categories are: 0 = Hyperoceanic; 1 = Oceanic; 2 = Sub-oceanic; 3 = European; 4 = Eurosiberian; 5 = Eurasian; 6 = Circumpolar.

Figure 4.2 Geographical limits for very common species in northern Lancashire and for all species occurring in the British Isles

For an explanation of categories see Figure 4.1
For an explanation of categories see Figure 4.1

Experimental evidence as a determinant for plant distribution

Experimental evidence linking climate to the distribution of species is limited but where available suggests that climatic variables limit plant distribution. For the Boreal-montane species, *Trientalis europaea* and *Rubus chamaemorus*, experimental data suggests that temperature limits their southern distribution. Thus for *Trientalis europaea* it was found that the optimum temperature for carbon assimilation was between 11 and 18°C, which is consistent with its southern limit coinciding with the 15.6°C July mean isotherm (Taylor, *et al.*, 2002). Similarly Taylor (1971) showed that *Rubus chamaemorus* requires continuous low temperatures for seed germination and low temperatures are also required for satisfactory bud break in the spring.

Pigott (1975) commented that many species had an eastern limit of distribution coinciding with isotherms of mean temperature during the coldest month of the year, e.g. *Ilex aquifolium*, *Hedera helix*, *Digitalis purpurea* and *Primula vulgaris*, but that others had northern limits running southwest to northeast across western Europe following the track of the isotherms for the mean and mean maximum temperature during the warmest month of the year. In particular he showed the correlation between the northern limits of *Tilia cordata* (Eurosiberian Temperate floristic element) and the 16°C isotherm for mean temperature for July. His work was taken further (Pigott and Huntley, 1978, 1980, 1981) and demonstrated that for ovule fertilization to take place temperatures over 21°C were required. Although *Tilia cordata* occurs at its northern limit around Morecambe Bay the necessary warm periods at the time of year required are infrequent so that fertile seed is not often produced. Where fertile seed is found more frequently further south this corresponds with the 20°C isotherm for mean daily maximum temperature in August.

Transplant experiments (Hunt, *et al.*, 2005) have shown that winter temperatures limit the distribution of the Suboceanic Temperate taxon, *Pyrola rotundifolia* ssp. *maritima*. Similarly the distribution of the Suboceanic Southern-temperate species *Coincya monensis* represented in Britain by the endemic ssp. *monensis* has also been shown to be limited by winter temperatures (Facey, *et al.*, 2007). In both taxa satisfactory seedling establishment is dependant on mild largely frost free winters.

Thus, whilst correlations can be made between plant distributions and climatic variables there are anomalies. Nevertheless where experiments were carried out causal relationships were demonstrated.

Habitat preferences of the northern Lancashire flora

The problem of defining what is meant by a particular habitat is probably unresolved. In this account of the vegetation of northern Lancashire, plant communities were grouped into habitats that closely follow those of the NVC (see Table 2.1). Unfortunately a major problem arises with the classification and descriptions of Broad Habitats developed as part of the UK Biodiversity Action Plan (BAP) process. The background and description of these is given by Hill, *et al.* (2004). To show how the NVC communities and Broad Habitats groups are related in northern Lancashire Table 4.7 provides a synopsis and concordance. In comparing this table with Table 2.1 summary of major north Lancashire habitat groups it is clear that there are significant discrepancies. Amongst the problems is the creation of Broad Habitats that have no counterpart in NVC, e.g. Boundary and linear features and Built-up areas and gardens etc. Further complexity with the Broad Habitat concept was introduced with its revision in 2007 (Anon, 2007).

Authors of national, regional and local Floras usually assign species to preferred habitats but there is rarely any quantitative basis for the assignments nor is the terminology standardized. Authors use a variety of terms to describe similar habitats and often the basis of assignment is an informed guess! Nevertheless a reader gets a general feeling of where a species may be expected to grow. During the development of NVC and the Countryside Survey 2000 (Haines-Young, *et al.*, 2000 cited by Hill, *et al.*, 2004) thousands of data sets of British vegetation were collated for Britain as a whole. For the first time it was possible to use the data to calculate the preferred Broad Habitats (BAP definitions) for every native and archaeophyte species. Thus Hill, *et al.* (2004) allocated every species to not more than four preferred but slightly modified Broad Habitats in which they occurred most frequently. It was necessary to limit the number of preferred habitats to four even though many species can be found in more habitats, e.g. *Poa annua*.

In this analysis only established native and archaeophyte species where the taxa were known to have persisted in at least one site for five or more years are included. Thus a few native species are excluded, e.g. *Mertensia maritima*.

Table 4.7 Concordance between Broad Habitats, UK BAP and NVC Plant Communities as they occur in northern Lancashire

Broad Habitat (See Hill, *et al.* (2004) for terminology)	UK BAP (Anon, 2007)	NVC community (Rodwell, 1991–2000)
BH1. Broad leaved mixed and yew woodland. Not included here are woodland scrub communities W21–24 included under BH3 Boundary and linear features	Traditional orchards Wood-pasture and Parkland Upland Oakwood Lowland Beech and Yew woodland Upland Mixed Ashwoods Wet Woodland Lowland Mixed Deciduous woodland Upland Birchwoods	W1 *Salix cinerea-Galium palustre* woodland W2 *Salix cinerea-Betula pubescens-Phragmites australis* woodland W3 *Salix pentandra-Carex rostrata* woodland W4 *Betula pubescens- Molinia caerulea* woodland W5 *Alnus glutinosa-Carex paniculata* woodland W6 *Alnus glutinosa-Urtica dioica* woodland W7 *Alnus glutinosa-Fraxinus excelsior-Lysimachia nemorum* woodland W8 *Fraxinus excelsior-Acer campestre-Mercurialis perennis* woodland W9 *Fraxinus excelsior-Sorbus aucuparia-Mercurialis perennis* woodland W10 *Quercus robur-Pteridium aquilinum-Rubus fruticosus* woodland W11 *Quercus petraea-Betula pubescens-Oxalis acetosella* woodland W13 *Taxus baccata* woodland W16 *Quercus* spp.-*Betula* spp.-*Deschampsia flexuosa* woodland W17 *Quercus petraea-Betula pubescens-Dicranum majus* woodland
BH2. Coniferous woodland. Native pine woods do not occur in N. Lancashire but Hill, *et al.* (2004) recognise the importance of *Dryopteris dilatata* in conifer plantations	Native Pinewoods	
BH3. Boundary and linear features. Includes woodland scrub, walls, hedges, tree-lines, earth banks, grass strips and dry ditches (roads, tracks & railways in urban areas belong to BH17).	Hedgerows	OV18 *Polygonum aviculare-Matricaria discoidea* community (Also in BH4 arable and horticultural) OV19 *Poa annua- Tripleurospermum inodorum* community (also in BH4 arable and horticultural) OV21 *Poa annua-Plantago major* community (also in BH4 Arable and Horticultural) OV22 *Poa annua-Taraxacum* spp. community (also in BH4 arable and horticultural) OV24 *Urtica dioica-Galium aparine* community (also in BH17 built-up areas and gardens) OV25 *Urtica dioica-Cirsium arvense* community (also in BH5 improved grassland) OV27 *Chamerion angustifolium* community OV39 *Asplenium trichomanes-Asplenium ruta-muraria* community (also in BH17 built-up areas and gardens. This characteristic wall community was omitted by Hill, *et al.*, 2004)
BH4. Arable and horticultural. Includes commercial horticulture and arable farmland but does not include domestic gardens and allotments, which are included in BH17, built up areas and gardens.	Arable Field Margins	OV1 *Viola arvensis-Aphanes australis* community OV4 *Glebionis segetum-Spergula arvensis* community OV7 *Veronica persica-Veronica polita* community OV9 *Tripleurospermum inodorum-Stellaria media* community OV10 *Poa annua-Senecio vulgaris* community OV11 *Poa annua-Stachys arvensis* community OV13 *Stellaria media-Capsella bursa-pastoris* community OV18 *Polygonum aviculare-Matricaria discoidea* community (also in BH3 boundary and linear features) OV19 *Poa annua-Tripleurospermum inodorum* community (also in BH3 boundary and linear features) OV21 *Poa annua-Plantago major* community (also in BH3 boundary and linear features) OV22 *Poa annua-Taraxacum* spp. community (also in BH3 boundary and linear features)

Broad Habitat (See Hill, *et al.* (2004) for terminology)	UK BAP (Anon, 2007)	NVC community (Rodwell, 1991–2000)
BH5. Improved grassland. Typically dominated by *Lolium* spp. and/or *Trifolium repens*. NVC describes OV12 *Poa annua-Myosotis arvensis* community as a disturbed element of improved pasture and is included here. However in N. Lancashire *M. arvensis* does not seem to occur in improved grassland. The nine species found in this habitat are characteristic of nutrient rich places (average Ellenberg values N = 6.2 and R = 6.2)	Improved Grassland	MG6 *Lolium perenne-Cynosurus cristatus* grassland (also in BH6 neutral grassland) MG7 *Lolium perenne* leys and neutral grasslands OV12 *Poa annua-Myosotis arvensis* community OV23 *Lolium perenne-Dactylis glomerata* community (also in BH17 built-up areas and gardens) OV25 *Urtica dioica-Cirsium arvense* community (also in BH3 boundary and linear features)
BH6. Neutral grassland. The core communities belong to mesotrophic grasslands but some coastal cliff grasslands are also included. Species are characteristic of moderately nutrient rich places (average Ellenberg values N = 4.7 and R = 6.3)	Lowland Meadows	W24 *Rubus fruticosus-Holcus lanatus* scrub (also in BH3 boundary and linear features) MG1 *Arrhenatherum elatius* grassland MG3 *Anthoxanthum odoratum-Geranium sylvaticum* grassland MG4 *Alopecurus pratensis-Sanguisorba officinalis* grassland MG5 *Cynosurus cristatus-Centaurea nigra* grassland MG6 *Lolium perenne-Cynosurus cristatus* grassland (also in BH5 improved grassland) MG8 *Cynosurus cristatus-Caltha palustris* grassland MG9 *Holcus lanatus-Deschampsia cespitosa* grassland MG10 *Holcus lanatus-Juncus effusus* rush-pasture MG11 *Festuca rubra-Agrostis stolonifera-Potentilla anserina* grassland (typically found on the uppermost parts of Lancashire salt marshes) MG12 *Festuca arundinacea* grassland MG13 *Agrostis stolonifera-Alopecuris geniculatus* grassland OV28 *Agrostis stolonifera-Ranunculus repens* community (also in BH11 fen, marsh and swamp)
BH7. Calcareous grassland. Species are generally characteristic of base-rich places (average Ellenberg value 6.8) but often nutrient poor (average Ellenberg value 3.3)	Lowland Calcareous Grassland Upland Calcareous Grassland	CG1 *Festuca ovina-Carlina vulgaris* grassland CG2 *Festuca ovina-Avenula pratensis* grassland CG9 *Sesleria caerulea-Galium sterneri* grassland CG10 *Festuca ovina- Agrostis capillaris-Thymus polytrichus* grassland
BH8. Acid grassland. Species are generally characteristic of nutrient and base poor sites (average Ellenberg values N = 3.4 and R = 4.6).	Lowland Dry Acid Grassland	U2 *Deschampsia flexuosa* grassland U4 *Festuca ovina-Agrostis capillaris-Galium saxatile* grassland U5 *Nardus stricta-Galium saxatile* grassland U6 *Juncus squarrosus-Festuca ovina* grassland U19 *Oreopteris limbosperma-Blechnum spicant* community

Broad Habitat (See Hill, *et al.* (2004) for terminology)	UK BAP (Anon, 2007)	NVC community (Rodwell, 1991–2000)
BH9. Bracken. Large areas of upland Britain including northern Lancashire have hillsides dominated by *Pteridium aquilinum*. The communities involved were originally derived from woodland but the fern often invades acid grassland.		U20 *Pteridium aquilinum-Galium saxatile* community W25 *Pteridium aquilinum-Rubus fruticosus* underscrub
BH10. Dwarf shrub heath. Includes vegetation with at least 25% Ericaceae. Dune heath is excluded (see BH19). Communities belonging to this Broad Habitat dominate large areas of Bowland. However lowland heaths have almost disappeared.	Lowland Heathland Upland Heathland	H8 *Calluna vulgaris-Ulex gallii* heath H9 *Calluna vulgaris-Deschampsia flexuosa* heath H12 *Calluna vulgaris-Vaccinium myrtillus* heath H18 *Vaccinium myrtillus-Deschampsia flexuosa* heath H21 *Calluna vulgaris-Vaccinium myrtillus-Sphagnum capillifolium* heath M16 *Erica tetralix-Sphagnum compactum* wet heath
BH11. Fen, marsh and swamp. This is a very wide category and includes reed-beds, swamps, tall-herb fens, flushes, springs, marshes, rush-pastures and wet grassland. As a consequence species characteristic of lowland nutrient and base-rich communities are included with acid, nutrient poor upland flushes. Furthermore whilst the average Ellenberg moisture value (F) is 8.6 the variation ranges from 5, a moist site indicator, to 12, submerged plants characteristic of BH13 standing water and canals.	Upland Flushes, Fens and Swamps Purple Moorgrass and Rush-Pasture Lowland Fens Reed-beds In the revised UKBAB Priority Habitat List (Anon, 2007) separate categories for river (but see BH14), oligotrophic & dystrophic lakes and ponds were recognised.	M4 *Carex rostrata-Sphagnum recurvum* mire M6 *Carex echinata-Sphagnum recurvum/auriculatum* mire M9 *Carex rostrata-Calliergonella cuspidatum/Calliergon giganteum* mire M10 *Carex dioica-Pinguicula vulgaris* mire M13 *Schoenus nigricans-Juncus subnodulosus* mire M22 *Juncus subnodulosus-Cirsium palustre* fen-meadow M23 *Juncus effusus/acutiflorus-Galium palustre* rush-pasture M25 *Molinia caerulea-Potentilla erecta* mire (also in BH12 bog) M27 *Filipendula ulmaria-Angelica sylvestris* mire M29 *Hypericum elodes-Potamogeton polygonifolius* soakway M30 Related vegetation of seasonally-inundated habitats M32 *Philonotis fontana-Saxifraga stellaris* spring M35 *Ranunculus omiophyllus-Montia fontana* rill M36 Lowland springs and streambanks of shaded situations S1 *Carex elata* swamp S2 *Cladium mariscus* swamp and sedge-beds S4 *Phragmites australis* swamp and reed-beds S5 *Glyceria maxima* swamp S7 *Carex acutiformis* swamp S8 *Schoenoplectus lacustris* swamp S9 *Carex rostrata* swamp S10 *Equisetum fluviatile* swamp S12 *Typha latifolia* swamp S13 *Typha angustifolia* swamp S14 *Sparganium erectum* swamp S15 *Acorus calamus* swamp S19 *Eleocharis palustris* swamp S20 *Schoenoplectus tabernaemontani* swamp (also in BH21 littoral sediments) S22 *Glyceria fluitans* water-margin vegetation S23 Other water-margin vegetation S25 *Phragmites australis-Eupatorium cannabinum* tall-herb fen S26 *Phragmites australis-Urtica dioica* tall-herb fen

Broad Habitat (See Hill, *et al.* (2004) for terminology)	UK BAP (Anon, 2007)	NVC community (Rodwell, 1991–2000)
		S28 *Phalaris arundinacea* tall-herb fen
		OV26 *Epilobium hirsutum* community
		OV28 *Agrostis stolonifera-Ranunculus repens* community (also in BH6 neutral grassland)
		OV29 *Alopecurus geniculatus-Rorippa palustris* community
		OV31 *Rorippa palustris-Gnaphalium uliginosum* community
		OV32 *Myosotis scorpioides-Ranunculus sceleratus* community
		OV35 *Lythrum portula-Ranunculus flammula* community
BH12. Bog. This habitat includes ombrotrophic bogs, valley mires and bog pools – all acid, more or less waterlogged, on peat.	Lowland Raised Bog Blanket Bog	M3 *Eriophorum angustifolium* bog pool community
		M17 *Trichophorum germanicum-Eriophorum vaginatum* blanket mire
		M18 *Erica tetralix-Sphagnum papillosum* raised and blanket mire
		M19 *Calluna vulgaris-Eriophorum vaginatum* blanket mire
		M20 *Eriophorum vaginatum* blanket and raised mire
		M21 *Narthecium ossifragum-Sphagnum papillosum* valley mire
		M25 *Molinia caerulea-Potentilla erecta* mire (also in BH11 fen, marsh and swamp)
BH13. Standing water and canals. Only aquatic vegetation is included with average Ellenberg moisture values of 10.3. Most species are submerged aquatics or emergent species rooted under water but a few are also found in drier conditions, e.g. *Gnaphalium uliginosum* (F = 6).	Oligotrophic and Dystrophic Lakes Ponds Mesotrophic Lakes Eutrophic Standing Waters Aquifer fed naturally fluctuating Water Bodies	A1 *Lemna gibba* community
		A2 *Lemna minor* community
		A3 *Spirodela polyrhiza-Hydrocharis morsus-ranae* community
		A4 *Hydrocharis morsus-ranae-Stratiotes aloides* community
		A5 *Ceratophyllum demersum* community
		A7 *Nymphaea alba* community
		A8 *Nuphar lutea* community (also in BH14 rivers and streams)
		A9 *Potamogeton natans* community
		A10 *Persicaria amphibia* community
		A11 *Potamogeton pectinatus-Myriophyllum spicatum* community (also in BH14 rivers and streams)
		A12 *Potamogeton pectinatus* community (also in BH14 rivers and streams)
		A13 *Potamogeton perfoliatus-Myriophyllum alterniflorum* community (also in BH14 rivers and streams)
		A15 *Elodea canadensis* community (also in BH14 rivers and streams)
		A16 *Callitriche stagnalis* community (also in BH14 rivers and streams)
		A19 *Ranunculus aquatilis* community (also in BH14 rivers and streams)
		A20 *Ranunculus peltatus* community (also in BH14 rivers and streams)
		A21 *Ranunculus baudotii* community
		A24 *Juncus bulbosus* community
BH14. Rivers and streams. Includes vegetation within the banks but bank vegetation itself is included in other habitats. Most species are aquatics tolerant of flowing water but also often in BH11 and BH13. Only *Ranunculus fluitans* and *Ranunculus penicillatus* are confined to this habitat.	Rivers	A8 *Nuphar lutea* community
		A9 *Potamogeton natans* community
		A11 *Potamogeton pectinatus-Myriophyllum spicatum* community
		A12 *Potamogeton pectinatus* community
		A13 *Potamogeton perfoliatus-Myriophyllum alterniflorum* community
		A14 *Myriophyllum alterniflorum* community
		A15 *Elodea canadensis* community
		Increasingly *E. nuttallii* is replacing *E. canadensis*.
		A16 *Callitriche stagnalis* community
		A17 *Ranunculus penicillatus* ssp. *pseudofluitans* community
		A19 *Ranunculus aquatilis* community
		With the exception of A17 all the above communities are found in BH13

Broad Habitat (See Hill, *et al.* (2004) for terminology)	UK BAP (Anon, 2007)	NVC community (Rodwell, 1991–2000)
BH15. Montane habitats. This is defined by having distinctive arctic-alpine species provided that they are not calcicolous when they are generally included in BH7. Of the small number of species found in this Broad Habitat only *Carex bigelowii* can be assigned to a typical NVC community in N. Lancashire.	Mountain Heaths and Willow Scrub	U7 *Nardus stricta-Carex bigelowii* grass-heath
BH16. Inland rock. This is a heterogeneous habitat including limestone pavement, cliffs, caves, scree, quarries and vegetation on skeletal soils over rock. Perhaps with the exception of parts of Gait Barrows most natural or semi-natural inland rock sites were developed from woodland and often a few trees remain. It also includes sites derived from human activity. Lancashire communities are described under heaths, urban and post-industrial sites and calcareous grassland.	Inland Rock Outcrops and scree habitats Calaminorian habitats Open mosaic habitats on previously developed land (formerly post-industrial sites) Limestone pavements	U21 *Cryptogramma crispa-Deschampsia flexuosa* community OV38 *Gymnocarpium robertianum-Arrhenatherum elatius* community OV39 *Asplenium trichomanes-Asplenium ruta-muraria* community OV40 *Asplenium viride-Cystopteris fragilis* community OV41 *Parietaria diffusa* community (also in BH17 built up areas and gardens)
BH17. Built-up areas and gardens. Habitats within the urban or built-up area are included. Some confusion exists with habitats that transcend rural and urban areas. Thus vegetation of walls may be in BH3 boundary and linear features and/or in this Broad Habitat. Vegetation in urban areas was covered poorly by the NVC. Also included here are the habitats occurring in post-industrial sites re-named 'Open mosaic habitats on previously developed land' (Anon, 2007)		OV20 *Poa annua-Sagina procumbens* community OV23 *Lolium perenne-Dactylis glomerata* community (also in BH5 improved grassland) OV24 *Urtica dioica-Galium aparine* community (also in BH3 boundary and linear features) OV39 *Asplenium trichomanes-Asplenium ruta-muraria* community (also in BH3 boundary and linear features. This characteristic wall community, common on old walls in built-up areas was omitted by Hill, *et al.*, 2004) OV41 *Parietaria diffusa* community (also in BH16 inland rock) OV42 *Cymbalaria muralis* community On one wall in the Fylde *C. muralis* is replaced by *C. pallida*.

Broad Habitat (See Hill, *et al.* (2004) for terminology)	UK BAP (Anon, 2007)	NVC community (Rodwell, 1991–2000)
BH18. Supralittoral rock. This habitat covers maritime cliffs but excludes maritime grassland. In N. Lancashire the maritime clay cliffs are therefore excluded.	Maritime Cliffs and slopes	MC1 *Crithmum maritimum-Spergularia rupicola* maritime rock-crevice community MC8 *Festuca rubra-Armeria maritima* grassland
BH19. Supralittoral sediment. This includes coastal strand lines, shingle and sand dunes including dune heath.	Coastal vegetated Shingle Machair Coastal sand dunes	H11 *Calluna vulgaris-Carex arenaria* heath SD1 *Rumex crispus-Glaucium flavum* shingle community SD2 *Honkenya peploides-Cakile maritima* strand line community SD3 *Tripleurospermum maritima-Galium aparine* strand line community SD4 *Elytrigia juncea* foredune community SD5 *Leymus arenarius* mobile dune community SD6 *Ammophila arenaria* mobile dune community SD7 *Ammophila arenaria-Festuca rubra* semi-fixed dune community SD8 *Festuca rubra-Galium verum* fixed dune community SD9 *Ammophila arenaria-Arrhenatherum elatius* dune grassland SD10 *Carex arenaria* dune community SD12 *Carex arenaria-Festuca ovina-Agrostis capillaris* dune grassland SD13 *Sagina nodosa-Bryum pseudotriquetrum* dune-slack community SD14 *Salix repens-Campylium stellatum* dune-slack community SD15 *Salix repens-Calliergonella cuspidata* dune-slack community SD16 *Salix repens-Holcus lanatus* dune-slack community SD17 *Potentilla anserina-Carex nigra* dune-slack community SD18 *Hippophae rhamnoides* dune scrub SD19 *Phleum arenarium-Arenaria serpyllifolia* dune annual community
BH21. Littoral sediment. This includes salt marshes and salt marsh pools. At the upper tidal limits this habitat passes into grassland and fens but only species found in places which are regularly inundated by at least spring tides are included. All species are salt tolerant with Ellenberg values of at least 2. A few species and communities that favour salt marshes in Lancashire are included here but elsewhere may be more typical of inland grasslands, e.g. *Trifolium fragiferum*.	Coastal salt marsh Intertidal mudflats Seagrass beds Sheltered muddy gravels Peat and clay exposures	S20 *Schoenoplectus tabernaemontani* swamp S21 *Bolboschoenus maritimus* swamp SM2 *Ruppia maritima* salt-marsh community SM6 *Spartina anglica* salt-marsh community SM8 Annual *Salicornia* salt-marsh community SM9 *Suaeda maritima* salt-marsh community SM10 Transitional low-marsh vegetation with *Puccinellia maritima*, annual *Salicornia* species and *Suaeda maritima*. SM12 Rayed *Aster tripolium* on salt-marshes SM13 *Puccinellia maritima* salt-marsh community SM14 *Atriplex portulacoides* salt-marsh community SM15 *Juncus maritimus-Triglochin maritima* salt-marsh community SM16 *Festuca rubra* salt-marsh community SM17 *Artemesia maritima* salt-marsh community SM18 *Juncus maritimus* salt-marsh community SM19 *Blysmus rufus* salt-marsh community SM20 *Eleocharis uniglumis* salt-marsh community SM24 *Elytrigia atherica* salt-marsh community where *E. atherica* is replaced by *E. × drucei* in N. Lancashire SM27 Ephemeral salt-marsh vegetation with *Sagina maritima* SM28 *Elytrigia repens* salt-marsh community

Also some of the national assignments are not appropriate in northern Lancashire so where preferences are known to differ habitats are added or deleted, e.g. *Trifolium fragiferum* is a salt marsh plant in northern Lancashire but nationally it is found in inland neutral grasslands.

The taxa included in the analysis include some sub-species and hybrids where their inclusion is significant, e.g. *Viola tricolor* ssp. *tricolor* and ssp. *curtisii* or where hybrids are well established, e.g. *Circaea × intermedia* and *Elytrigia × drucei*.

In northern Lancashire it was possible to assign 919 native and archaeophyte taxa to preferred Broad Habitats. This is not an exact figure and could be increased or decreased according to different assessments for a small number of 'problematical' taxa. Table 4.8 shows the results of this analysis.

It shows that nineteen Broad Habitats are recognised in northern Lancashire and additionally coniferous plantations should be added. However nationally there is no data for allocating species to this habitat.

Most species are found in Boundary and linear features (27%), Broad leaved mixed and yew woodland (18%) and Fen, marsh and swamp (17%). This is broadly in line with what might be expected from the remains of the natural habitats of 2000 years ago. At that time woodlands and wetlands covered most of the area. However today the most important Broad Habitat is Boundary and linear features. This follows the massive human interference of the natural landscape creating these features. Nevertheless many of the species involved are characteristic of woodland clearings or woodland edges.

More surprising is the apparent paucity of plants from major coastal habitats, which are such important features of the Lancashire coastline. However if the three coastal habitats are combined, comprising 109 species or nearly 12% of the total, coastal species are also significant.

Acid habitats are naturally species poor and this is reflected in the small number of species found in Acid grassland, Bracken, Dwarf shrub heath and Bog. Similarly with few areas approaching or exceeding 600 meters only six species were found in the Montane Broad Habitat.

If a number of Broad Habitats are combined on the basis of their affinities it is found that 40% of species belong to woodland and boundary habitats, 27% to wetlands including bogs and 12% to coastal communities. Thus most of the native and archaeophyte species have survived from the natural and semi-natural habitats that occurred historically in northern Lancashire. However, 26% belong to grasslands, almost all being characteristic of neutral or calcareous soils. This may be linked to the idea that species rich grasslands are derived from woodland clearings. In contrast only 11% of the flora inhabit, by preference, the expanding and relatively newly created built-up and garden habitats whilst 9% are found as Arable and horticultural weeds.

Table 4.8 Habitat preferences of North Lancashire species

Broad Habitat	No. of Taxa	% of total no. of Taxa
1. Broad leaved mixed and yew woodland	166	18
2. Boundary and linear features	245	27
4. Arable and horticultural	79	9
5. Improved grassland	9	1
6. Neutral grassland	109	12
7. Calcareous grassland	110	12
8. Acid grassland	32	4
9. Bracken	10	1
10. Dwarf shrub heath	32	4
11. Fen, marsh and swamp (includes some mires)	160	17
12. Bog	28	3
13. Standing water and canals	76	8
14. Rivers and streams	65	7
15. Montane	6	1
16. Inland rock (includes limestone pavement)	100	11
17. Built-up areas and gardens	54	11
18. Supralittoral rock (rock sea cliffs)	17	2
19. Supralittoral sediment (coastal shingle, sand dunes and dune heath)	87	10
21. Littoral sediment (salt-marshes)	47	5

Note: a total of 919 taxa assigned to 19 Broad Habitats found in northern Lancashire with some taxa assigned to more than one Broad Habitat.

Furthermore most (53%) of the species assigned to Arable and horticultural Broad Habitats are archaeophytes and 52% of the species found in built-up areas and gardens are also archaeophytes. Clearly the majority of native species were unable to colonize many habitats directly derived from human activity and most species that have been successful in these habitats are closely associated with humans and were probably introduced by them or with their crops. This conclusion is despite the fact that arable farmland and gardens in some form have existed for thousands of years. However many habitats directly created by human activity are not included within Built-up areas and gardens Broad Habitat. These include the post-industrial sites of clay pits, quarries, reservoirs and transport routes for which no separate analysis is available. Here the vegetation that has developed is often included in other Broad Habitat groups, e.g. wetlands, grasslands and inland rock. In these situations the flora is largely composed of readily dispersed native species.

ROCKS AND SOILS

Introduction

Rocks, where these come to the surface, and soils are important factors in determining the distribution of plants. Lancashire is particularly well covered through the maps of the Geological Survey of Great Britain and the Soils Survey of England and Wales (Crompton, 1966; Hall and Folland, 1970). However the Soil Survey maps were completed before local government reorganisation in 1974 and are only readily available for the old county of Lancashire. They do not cover Lancashire VC 64 but a sketch map of soils for this area is provided by Carroll (2005).

Whilst many different soil associations are recognised with relatively few rock exposures, most of the agricultural soils are derived from alluvium, till or boulder clay and lowland peat deposits. On the coast sandy soils are derived from the coastal sand dunes and loam soils are formed from reclaimed salt marshes and from alluvium deposits in the large river valleys. Overall the agricultural soils are neutral or calcareous and in the Over Wyre and the Fylde form some of the most valuable agricultural land in the country. However unreclaimed or partially reclaimed mosslands are acidic as are the bogs and exposures of millstone grit rocks in the Bowland Fells and Leck. In contrast the limestone around Morecambe Bay,

on Dalton Crags and at Leck and Ireby are highly calcareous. Similar calcareous soils are found where limestone occurs in Bowland but in places, especially to the south of Lancaster and in the Ribble valley where the boulder clay contains a substantial amount of limestone and where the clay is exposed, calcareous substrates are available for plant colonization. With a high rainfall even the most calcareous soils are often leached giving rise to acid surface soils. Thus within a few metres on Warton Crag the surface substrate can vary from calcareous to acid with consequent changes in vegetation from calcareous grassland to acid grassland or heath.

Soil reaction is only partially reflected in the Broad Habitats classification. Thus calcareous, neutral and acid grassland are recognised but there is no recognition of base status in the remaining habitats. Yet vascular plants and NVC communities often show soil and water pH preferences. The soil and water reaction preferences for British vascular plants are listed by Hill, *et al.*, 2004. Using these tables species preferring soil or water with an Ellenberg R value of 1–4 are characteristic of acid soils where 1 is indicative of extreme acidity. At the other extreme plants preferring soil or water with an Ellenberg R value of 8 or 9 are characteristic of basic soils. Values of 5–7 indicate a range of essentially neutral soils ranging from moderately or somewhat acid soils (5) to weakly basic conditions (7).

The preferences of northern Lancashire species show that they are overwhelmingly characteristic of neutral substrates. As most soils are neutral, species typical of neutral substrates are found in most parts of the area or their distributions are limited by other factors.

Of most interest are the species of acidic and calcareous substrates. Approximately 10% (111 species) of the flora are calcifuges and 10% (104 species) are calcicoles but of the calcicoles fifteen are salt marsh species where sodium rather than calcium ions provide the bases. However even if these species are excluded both calcifuge and calcicole species are found in most parts of northern Lancashire. Common calcifuges include *Holcus mollis* and common calcicoles include *Salix alba* but there are far fewer common calcicoles than calcifuges. The more or less ubiquitous distribution of these common species reflects the potential for acidic and basic soils to occur almost anywhere in the region.

On the other hand it is possible to plot the most likely areas for acid and calcareous soils and rock

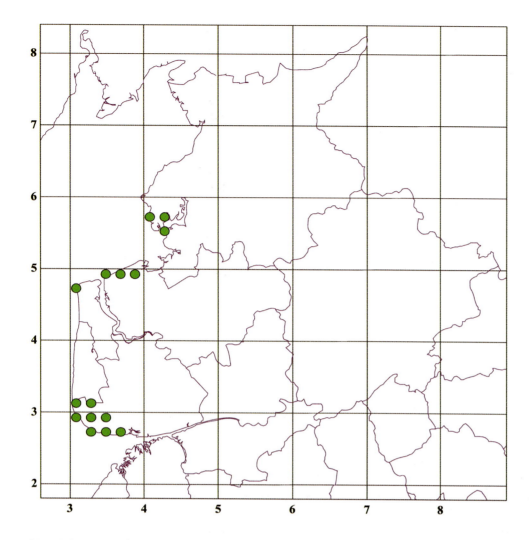

Map 4.8   Map showing the tetrad distribution of blown sand in northern Lancashire.

exposures to occur and the more demanding and rare species should be confined to these areas.

Acidic rocks and soils – Calcifuge species

Some rocks and soils are more likely to provide acid soils than others. However many acid soils can provide valuable agricultural land with heavy applications of lime and fertilizer to reduce acidity and improve fertility. There are potentially four groups of acidic soils.

1. Soils derived from blown sand near the coast. Sand from the highly calcareous coastal dunes was blown inland, often over peat bogs, to form the Formby and Ainsdale Association of soils. A few of these remain in a 'wild' state on the golf courses at Lytham St Anne's (formerly a mosaic of heath and marsh comprising Lytham

Hawes enclosed from the early seventeenth century (Shakeshaft, 2001)) and on the coast between Fleetwood and Pilling, but most were not mapped by the Soil Survey (Map 4.8).

2. Soils derived from peat or where unreclaimed peat persists. Peat bogs were formed both in lowland and upland areas but most of the former were reclaimed for agriculture and form the Altcar Association of soils. They are found extensively in the Silverdale – Warton area, Heysham (not mapped by the Soils Survey) and lowland areas of Over Wyre and the Fylde (Map 4.9.). On the top of the fells the higher altitude upland peat with a harsher climate prevented most of these areas being reclaimed and the soils are referred to the Winter Hill Association (Map 4.10.).

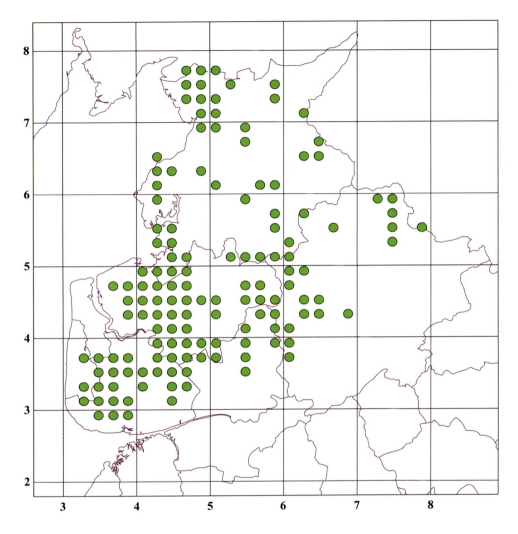

Map 4.9   Map showing the tetrad distribution of mosslands (mostly raised bogs) in northern Lancashire. Sources include Hall and Folland, 1970; place names from Ordnance Survey maps and personal notes.

3. The Pennine Drift covers a large area of the slopes and farmland surrounding the Bowland Fells. Formerly small peat bogs developed in hollows and on level ground but they are mostly drained although waterlogged acidic grassland or rush-pasture often remains. The soils involved include the Wilcocks, Rivington, Belmont and Brickfield Associations. Also belonging here are soils of the Charnock Association that extends on higher ground from south of Lancaster north-eastwards in the Lune valley towards Kirkby Lonsdale. It covers much of the area.

4. Finally in the Inskip area of the Fylde a few soils are derived from Shirdley Hill Sand forming the Astley Hall Association. Carr

House Green Common probably has soils of this association. Attempts at cultivation during the 1940s were unsuccessful and today it is a form of rush-pasture.

These potentially acidic soils cover much of VC 60. They extend eastwards covering much of Lancashire VC 64 but are not mapped. Thus it is not surprising that common calcifuge species are found in most areas but demanding species are usually limited to more natural habitats. In an effort to demonstrate that the distribution of these species is linked to the distribution of acidic soils a composite map (Map 4.11) shows the distribution of 24 species (Table 4.9) that were found in fifteen or fewer tetrads between 1964 and 2008 in northern Lancashire although some have also become extinct since then.

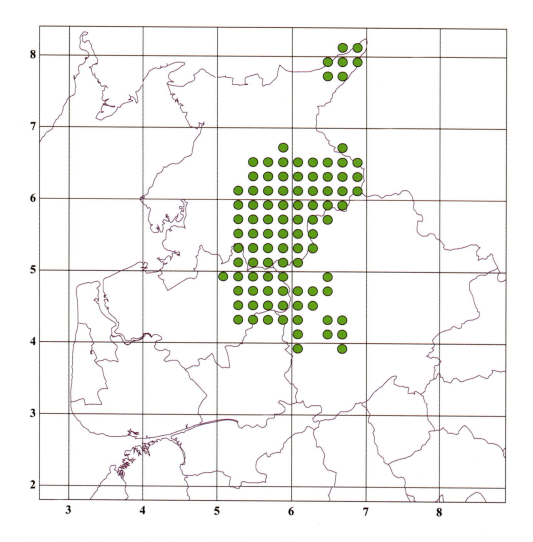

Map 4.10   Map showing the tetrad distribution of hill peat and peaty gley soils (Winter Hill and Wilcock series) often supporting blanket bogs in VC 60 (data from Lancashire VC 64 not readily available but see Carroll in Abbott, 2005)

This shows that the rarer (very rare, rare and occasional) species are found in five major groups with a number of apparently miscellaneous occurrences.

1.   Species associated with millstone grit exposures and hill peats, e.g. in Leck, Bowland and on Longridge Fell. Typical species include *Cryptogramma crispa, Hymenophyllum* spp. *Huperzia selago* and *Rubus chamaemorus*.

2.   Species associated with the mosslands of Over Wyre (Cockerham, Winmarleigh, Stalmine and Out Rawcliffe), White Moss, Yealand Redmayne and Heysham Moss. Typical species include *Myrica gale* and *Rhynchospora alba*, both also formerly found in the foothills of the Bowland Fells.

3.   Species associated with blown sand at Lytham St Anne's and between Fleetwood and Pilling.

Typical species include *Ornithopus perpusillus* and *Stellaria pallida*.

4.   Species found mostly in the Lune valley, but for reasons that are not entirely clear. However soils of the Charnock Association form a landscape of undulating hills and hollows between Lancaster and Kirkby Lonsdale (Map 4.12). On the north side of the R. Lune this land remained unenclosed until Parliamentary Enclosure about 200 years ago. At that time the vegetation was a mosaic of wet and dry heath with bog development in the deeper hollows and used as common grazing. Most of these habitats were drained and reclaimed for agriculture and forestry but sufficient remained for some of the rarer calcifuge species to survive until the mid

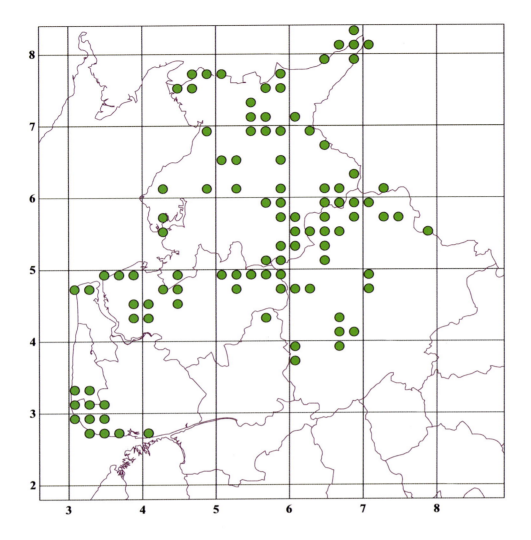

Map 4.11   Map showing the distribution of calcifuge species found in 15 or fewer tetrads in northern Lancashire since 1964.

1960s and to the present day. *Scutellaria minor* is an example of one of these species.

5. The remaining rarer calcifuge species reflect the remnants of other acidic rock outcrops and relic bogs.

Potentially acidic soils are much more extensive than the map of calcifuge species suggests. However most of the natural and semi-natural habitats were reclaimed for agriculture and other purposes. Thus there are no rare calcifuge species associated with the mosses in the Silverdale – Warton area (except *Myrica gale* now extinct at White Moss) or in the Fylde, and similarly acidic habitats on most of the Pennine drift have gone. Nevertheless if the distribution of rarer species used in this exercise along with extinct calcifuges had been done 100 or more years ago the correlation with these features would have been more clearly seen. Amongst those

Table 4.9   Calcifuge species recorded between 1964 and 2008 in 15 or fewer tetrads in northern Lancashire.

Carex bigelowii	*Hymenophyllum wilsonii*
Cryptogramma crispa	*Jasione montana*
Diphasiastrum alpinum	*Lycopodium clavatum*
Dryopteris aemula	*Myrica gale*
Dryopteris oreades	*Neottia cordata*
Eleocharis multicaulis*	*Ornithopus perpusillus*
Euphrasia micrantha	*Rhynchospora alba*
Festuca filiformis	*Rubus chamaemorus*
Filago minima	*Scutellaria minor*
Genista anglica*	*Stellaria pallida*
Gnaphalium sylvaticum*	*Trientalis europaea*
Hymenophyllum tunbrigense	*Wahlenbergia hederacea*

*Extinct after 1964

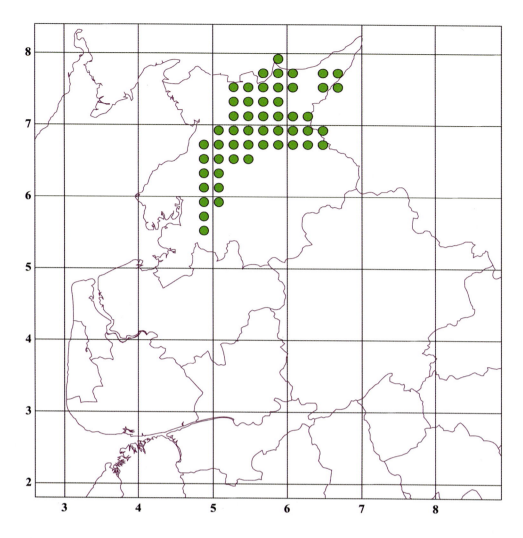

Map 4.12 Map showing the tetrad distribution of soils of the Charnock Association in northern Lancashire (data taken from Hall and Folland, 1970).

that are now extinct are *Antennaria dioica, Carex limosa, Drosera anglica, Drosera intermedia, Eleogiton fluitans, Gentiana pneumonanthe, Hypericum elodes, Pilularia globulifera, Radiola linoides, Scleranthus annuus, Sedum anglicum* (which re-appeared at St Anne's in 2007) and *Utricularia minor*. Reasons for their extinction are diverse but the removal of peat and drying out of remaining mosses accounted for *Carex limosa* and *Drosera anglica* whilst the construction of Heysham Harbour accounted for *Sedum anglicum*. Almost all the other species were found within the mosaic of mires, wet and dry heaths found throughout VC 60 including the former heaths of the north Lune valley on soils of the Charnock Association, but also elsewhere, e.g. Ribbleton Moor, Preston and Nicky Nook, Nether Wyresdale. *Scleranthus annuus* is the exception and

although a heath species the status of its only record near Garstang is doubtful.

If more commonly occurring calcifuge species are included species characteristic of peat bogs are found where they survive. These include *Andromeda polifolia, Erica tetralix, Eriophorum angustifolium, E. vaginatum, Narthecium ossifragum* and *Vaccinium oxycoccus* while in upland flushes, *Carex echinata* and *C. dioica* are found. Apparently confined to uplands are *Trichophorum germanicum* (bogs) and *Vaccinium vitis-idaea* (heaths). More generally *Carex binervis* and *Empetrum nigrum* are found on heaths mostly in the uplands but also in lowland areas.

Calcareous rocks and soils – calcicole species
Rocks and soils giving rise to potentially calcareous substrates can be divided into three main groups (Map 4.13).

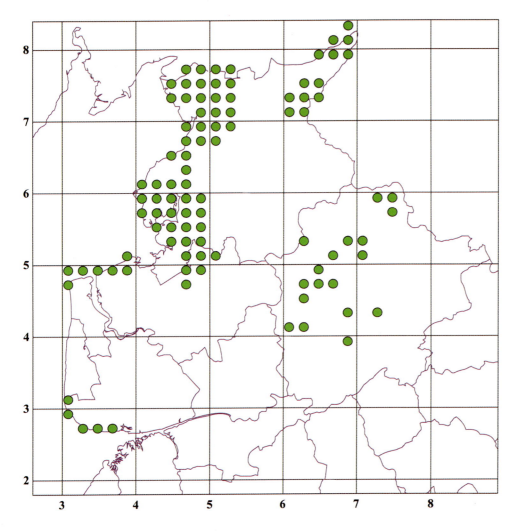

Map 4.13 Map showing the tetrad distribution of potentially calcareous substrates derived from calcareous blown sand, limestone rocks, highly calcareous till and calcareous till derived from the Northern Drift in northern Lancashire.

1. Derived from calcareous blown sand
2. Limestone rocks and highly calcareous till
3. Calcareous till soils derived from the Northern Drift.

The coastal sand dunes are rich in calcium carbonate, mainly in the form of shells and give rise to blown sand soils of the Ainsdale Association. In addition to the coastal dunes at Lytham St Anne's the Association is also found between Fleetwood and Pilling and on the Heysham peninsula at Middleton and Overton.

Soils formed directly from limestone comprise the Warton Association and closely associated with it is a very stony till soil with an abundance of limestone forming the Carnforth Association. The Carnforth Association is found from Carnforth northwards to

the Cumbrian border and overlaps with the limestone of the Warton Association. Calcareous soils are also found in Nether and Over Kellet, on Dalton Crags (now in Cumbria), Leck and Ireby and on the limestone knolls and other exposures in the Hodder and Ribble valleys. Although not mapped by the Soil Survey there are also limestone knolls in the Loud valley at Thornley. Three further Associations of the Northern Drift form other potentially calcareous soils that all contain limestone stones and boulders. These comprise the Winmarleigh Association that runs south from Carnforth to Garstang but includes the Heysham peninsula. It forms an undulating landscape and outcrops as clay cliffs in coastal areas. Further south covering much of Over Wyre, the Fylde and extending eastwards up the Ribble valley towards the

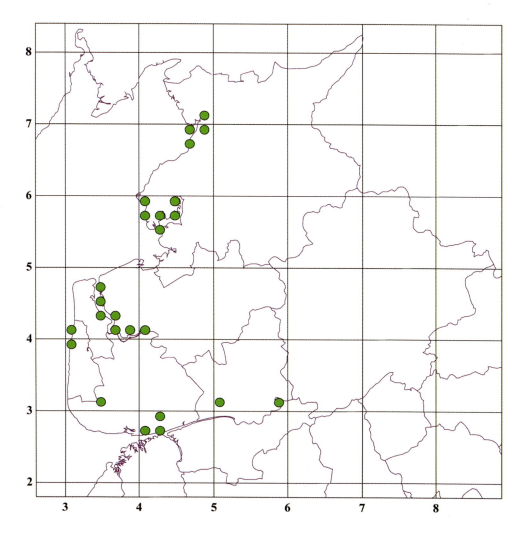

Map 4.14   Map showing the tetrad distribution of calcareous clay banks, mostly coastal, in northern Lancashire.

Hodder valley are the Salwick and Salop Associations. The former provides an undulating landscape with well-drained soils whilst the latter occurs on more level ground, is usually badly drained and formerly small bogs occurred in hollows whilst wet and dry heaths occurred elsewhere, e.g. Ribbleton Moor, Preston. Thus despite the calcareous nature of the clay, leaching and water logging produced acid soils on the surface. Neither of these Associations appears important for the distribution of calcicoles except where the clay is exposed as on coastal cliffs, in clay pits or on riverbanks, e.g. Red Scar near Preston. This is a notable feature of the Ribble valley (Map 4.14) where the calcicole *Hypericum hirsutum* is found.

In addition to calcareous and potentially calcareous soils outcrops of calcareous rocks are particularly significant for the occurrence of calcicoles. The limestone outcrops forming the pavements around Morecambe Bay and on Dalton Crags along with the cliffs, potholes and pavements etc. in Leck and Ireby are especially significant. However other calcareous rock exposures occur in quarries and in Bowland river valleys where the streams have exposed cliffs with bands of shale and limestone (Map 4.16). In these latter situations calcicoles and calcifuges grow in close proximity to each other in largely wooded situations. Some of the most important of these features are found by the River Greta near Wennington; Artle Beck and in Foxdale both in Caton-with-Littledale; by the R. Wyre in Over Wyresdale and by the R. Hodder.

A total of 104 species with an Ellenberg R value of 8 or 9 were recognised as occurring in northern

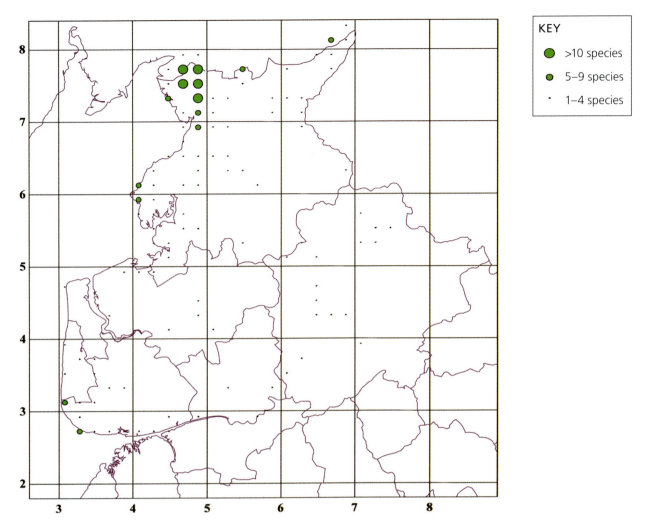

Map 4.15   Map showing the distribution of calcicole species occurring in 15 or fewer tetrads in northern Lancashire since 1964.

Lancashire but of these 15 were salt marsh species and of the remaining 89 species some were found in most parts of northern Lancashire. Nevertheless 43 calcicoles (Table 4.10) occurred in 15 or fewer tetrads and their combined distribution was mapped (Map 4.15). Interpreting this map is complex but four clusters are fairly readily discernible.

1. Three groups are clustered around the limestone and calcareous soils of Leck, Ireby, Dalton Crags and the limestones of the Silverdale – Warton and Kellet area.
2. Another group is based on the clay soils and sandy shores of the Heysham peninsula.
3. Two further clusters are based on the sandy shores of Lytham St Anne's.
4. Lesser concentrations are found along the Lune, Hodder and Ribble valleys; on the coast

near Pilling, around Garstang and in the Slaidburn area.

The features that give rise to the minor clusters are diverse. Exposures of till on river banks and clay pits are responsible for the clusters in the tidal reaches of the R. Wyre, in the western Fylde and in the Ribble valley, but in the latter area and in the Garstang area the calcicoles are often aquatics found in the Rivers Wyre, Brock, Hodder and Ribble. In the Hodder valley, Wyre valley, Caton-with-Littledale and in the Greta valley exposures of calcareous shale form a habitat for calcicole species.

Calcicole aquatic and wetland species are found in the R. Lune oxbows in the Arkholme – Melling area. In general there is no correlation between the soil reaction of rocks and soils in the immediate vicinity of the aquatics in rivers as the rock strata

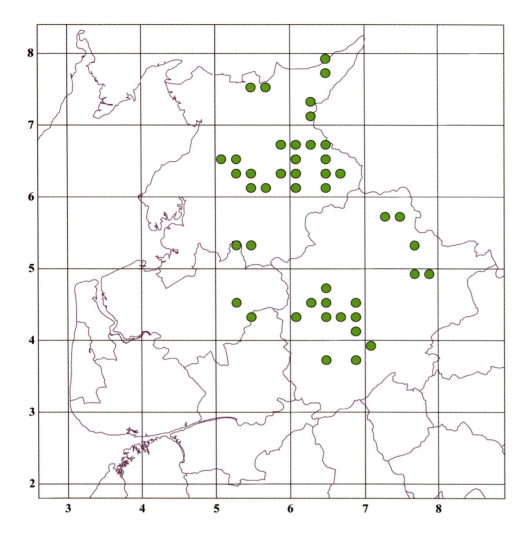

Map 4.16 Map showing the tetrad distribution of shale cliffs and banks, mostly in river gorges, in northern Lancashire.

from which the water arises determines the pH of the water. Finally the limestone reef knolls provide a calcareous habitat for surprisingly few calcicoles. This may be due to the sparse exposures of rock and relatively late removal of woodland that covered them. However *Potentilla tabernaemontani* and *Euonymus europaeus* are examples that are occasionally found on reef knolls, as well as on limestone around Morecambe Bay

Calcicoles are amongst the most interesting species in northern Lancashire because of their generally limited distribution and yet there have only been three extinctions. These are *Potentilla crantzii* that only occurred on Great Dunnow Cliff between Newton and Slaidburn, *Galeopsis angustifolia* and *Neotinea ustulata*. *Potentilla crantzii* was lost before 1900 through shading from a maturing plantation, but the reasons for the

loss of *Galeopsis angustifolia* are not known although it follows a national trend. Similarly the exact reasons for the loss of *Neotinea ustulata* at the end of the nineteenth century are not known but seem to reflect a continuing change and reduction of floristic diversity of limestone grasslands.

Amongst the most characteristic of the calcicoles are those more or less confined to the limestones of Silverdale – Warton – Kellet Seeds and to a lesser extent Dalton Crags areas. These include *Sesleria caerulea, Ophrys insectifera, Epipactis atrorubens, Asperula cynanchica, Carex digitata, Clinopodium acinos, Hippocrepis comosa, Hypericum montanum, Potentilla tabernaemontani* and *Euonymus europaeus*. Some species are found more widely extending to Leck and on shales in river valleys or even mortared walls. These include *Dryopteris submontana, Gymnocarpium robertianum* and *Asplenium viride*. Calcicoles found in flushes include *Equisetum variegatum* (also on sand dunes), and *Primula farinosa* but the latter has been lost from many of its former sites. On the coast some calcicoles are largely confined to sand dunes, e.g. *Epipactis dunensis* and *Epipactis phyllanthes* whilst others occur on shingle and tipped but basic furnace slag, e.g. *Crambe maritima* and *Glaucium flavum*. Also in this coastal group are species formerly often found on sand dunes but now more likely to be found at spring lines below clay cliffs at the head of salt marshes, including *Centaurium littorale* and *Centaurium pulchellum*. Also found on clay banks is *Ononis repens* and more rarely, *O. spinosa*. A few species that might naturally occur on sand dunes are also opportunists and being characteristic of rather open habitats take advantage of places created by human activity. These include clay pits and newly built embankments etc. In these situations *Ophrys apifera*, *Anacamptis pyramidalis* and *Orobanche minor* may be found.

There is also a diverse group of calcicole wetland species including *Blysmus compressus*, *Ceratophyllum submersum*, *Cladium mariscus*, *Juncus subnodulosus*, *Potamogeton coloratus* and *Ranunculus penicillatus*.

Table 4.10 Calcicole species recorded between 1964 and 2008 in 15 or fewer tetrads in northern Lancashire

Actaea spicata*	*Epipactis phyllanthes*
Alchemilla minima	*Equisetum variegatum*
Anacamptis pyramidalis	*Dryopteris submontana*
Asperula cynanchica	*Galeopsis angustifolia**
Asplenium viride	*Glaucium flavum*
Atropa belladonna	*Groenlandia densa*
Blackstonia perfoliata	*Gymnocarpium robertianum*
Blysmus compressus	*Helleborus foetidus*
Bromopsis erecta	*Helleborus viridis*
Bromus commutatus	*Hippocrepis comosa*
Cardamine impatiens	*Hypericum montanum*
Carex digitata	*Juncus subnodulosus*
Centaurium littorale	*Lithospermum officinale*
Centaurium pulchellum	*Ononis spinosa*
Ceratophyllum submersum	*Ophrys insectifera*
Cladium mariscus	*Orobanche minor*
Clinopodium acinos	*Potamogeton coloratus*
Cochlearia pyrenaica	*Potentilla tabernaemontani*
Crambe maritima	*Primula farinosa*
Cynoglossum officinale	*Rosa obtusifolia*
Epipactis atrorubens	*Valerianella carinata*
Epipactis dunensis	

*Extinct after 1964

A small portion of Lancashire at Leck and Ireby is geographically part of the extensive Craven limestones of Yorkshire and a few species are confined to this part of the County. They include *Actaea spicata* (possibly now extinct), *Alchemilla minima* and *Cochlearia pyrenaica*, which from time to time establish themselves on river gravels of the Rivers Greta and Lune.

Soil nutrient status

In addition to soil reaction (soil and water pH) soil nutrient status is an important determinant for plant distribution. Ellenberg's N or nitrogen value is effectively a general indicator of soil fertility and is a different measure to soil reaction value (R). Nutrient poor soils may be associated with soils of any pH. Although almost all species respond positively to increased fertility many species found in nutrient poor soils are poor competitors favouring habitats with low vegetation and often open communities.

An analysis of natives and archaeophytes shows that some 289 taxa, or approximately 31% of the flora, favour nutrient poor soils (N = 1–3). Of these 83 taxa favour acid soils (R = 1–3) whilst only 36 taxa favour base-rich soils (R = 8–9). There are 24 rarer (taxa occurring in 15 or fewer tetrads in northern Lancashire) calcifuge species (Table 4.9) and these are all nutrient poor species. Their distribution is shown in Map 4.11.

However, there are only 21 rarer nutrient poor, calcicole taxa (Table 4.11). Map 4.18 shows that they are largely found in the limestone area of Silverdale – Warton and on the sand dunes at Lytham St Anne's. Nevertheless some of the species have a more scattered distribution with a few localities in Bowland where they are found on small outcrops of calcareous rocks and soils, e.g. *Asplenium viride*, *Cochlearia pyrenaica*, *Cystopteris fragilis*, *Equisetum variegatum*, *Ophrys apifera* and *Primula farinosa*.

Perhaps the most interesting group is of species that favour nutrient poor but neutral rocks and soils. Potentially such habitats occur throughout the area. 45 taxa belong to this group (Table 4.12).

A composite map (Map 4.1) of the rarest species (found in three or fewer tetrads) includes calcicoles, calcifuges and species characteristic of neutral soils. This shows clear distribution clusters. The most important of these are in the Silverdale – Warton – Carnforth area and around Lytham St Anne's. Other important clusters are at Leck, Heysham peninsula,

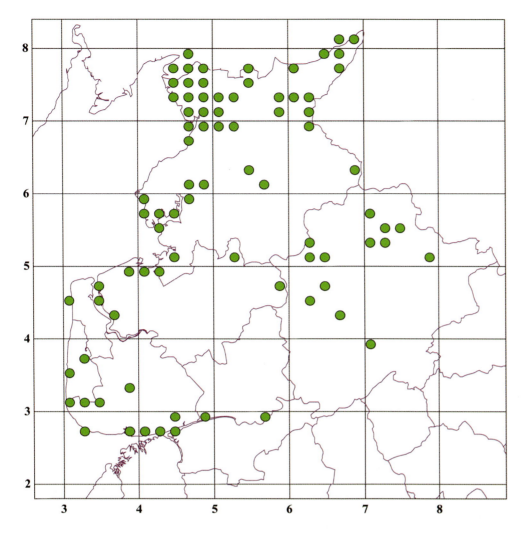

Map 4.17   Map showing the distribution of nutrient poor, neutral species found in 15 or fewer tetrads in northern Lancashire since 1964.

Bowland Fells and Lune valley. By also including Lancashire VC 64 a small cluster is also found in the Slaidburn – Stocks Reservoir area.

Explaining these clusters is difficult. A number are associated with calcareous substrates (Silverdale, Leck, Lytham St Anne's) but few are on acidic substrates as calcifuge communities are usually species poor. However the Bowland Fells are perhaps such a region. However most of the areas support species with a wide variety of soil reaction preferences, e.g. Leck, Heysham.

Map 4.17 shows a scatter of records in similar areas to those shown for the rarest species. However most records are for the limestone areas around Morecambe Bay and the sand dunes at Lytham St Anne's, so the distribution pattern shown by these species is similar to that of calcicoles.

Table 4.11   Nutrient poor, calcicole species recorded between 1964 and 2008 in 15 or fewer tetrads in VC 60

Alchemilla minima	*Equisetum variegatum*
Anacamptis pyramidalis	*Dryopteris submontana*
Asperula cynanchica	*Helleborus foetidus*
Asplenium viride	*Hippocrepis comosa*
Blysmus compressus	*Hypericum montanum*
Bromopsis erecta	*Ononis spinosa*
Centaurium littorale	*Ophrys apifera*
Centaurium pulchellum	*Ophrys insectifera*
Clinopodium acinos	*Potentilla tabernaemontani*
Cochlearia pyrenaica	*Primula farinosa*
Epipactis atrorubens	

Perhaps the clearest feature of these distributions is that in general rare species of nutrient poor, neutral substrates (Table 4.12) do not occur in the more

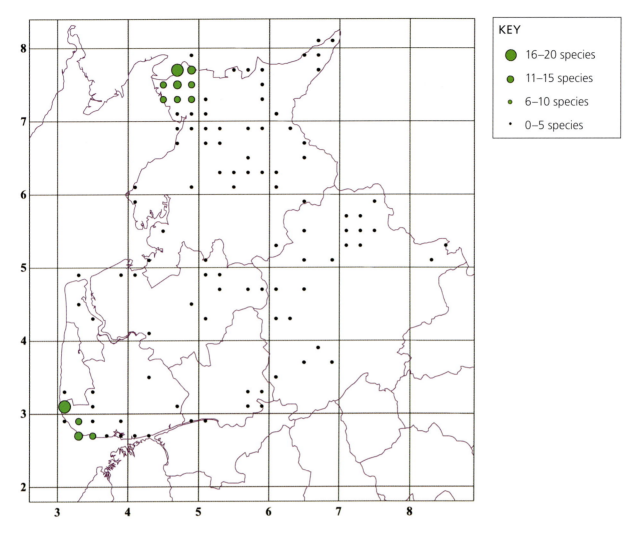

Map 4.18 Map showing the distribution of nutrient poor, calicole species found in 15 or fewer tetrads in northern Lancashire since 1964.

Table 4.12 Nutrient poor, neutral species recorded between 1964 and 2008 in 15 or fewer tetrads in VC 60

Anacamptis morio	*Eriophorum latifolium*	*Montia fontana* ssp.	*Serratula tinctoria*
Avenula pratensis	*Erodium lebelii*	*amporitana*	*Schoenoplectus lacustris*
Berberis vulgaris	*Erophila glabrescens*	*Montia fontana* ssp.	*Schoenus nigricans*
Botrychium lunaria	*Euphorbia portlandica*	*chondrosperma*	*Sparganium natans*
Carex diandra	*Euphrasia officinalis* ssp.	*Myosotis ramosissima*	*Spiranthes spiralis*
Carex ericetorum	*pratensis*	*Pedicularis palustris*	*Thalictrum minus*
Carex lasiocarpa	*Euphrasia scottica*	*Phleum arenarium*	*Trichomanes speciosum*
Carex oederi	*Euphrasia tetraquetra*	*Polygala vulgaris* ssp. *collina*	*(gametophyte)*
Centunculus minimus	*Galium boreale*	*Polygonatum odoratum*	*Trifolium ornithopodioides*
Cerastium arvense	*Gentianella campestris*	*Polypodium cambricum*	*Trifolium striatum*
Cerastium semidecandrum	*Gymnadenia conopsea*	*Pyrola rotundifolia*	*Viola canina*
Coincya monensis	*Littorella uniflora*	*Rosa spinosissima*	*Vicia lathyroides*
Dactylorhiza praetermissa	*Lythrum portula*	*Sagina apetala*	*Vulpia fasciculata*
Draba incana	*Melica nutans*	*Saxifraga hypnoides*	*Vulpia myuros*
Epipactis palustris	*Monotropa hypopitys*	*Selaginella selaginoides*	

intensively farmed and urban areas or where large areas of acid mires occur. This is also true of calcicole and calcifuge species although there is a group of rare calcifuges that are characteristic of acid mires found in Bowland and in lowland areas. However all the species are ones that favour nutrient poor substrates and avoid fertile soils.

Very rare and very common species

The nutritional preferences for very rare and very common species in northern Lancashire differ from the preferences of all species found in the British Isles as a whole. Northern Lancashire's very rare species have a preference for N values of around 3 indicating that they prefer nutrient poor substrates (Figure 4.3). However very common species in northern Lancashire have a preference for moderately nutrient rich substrates (Figure 4.4). Whilst nationally some species favour nutrient poor substrates most prefer moderately fertile soils.

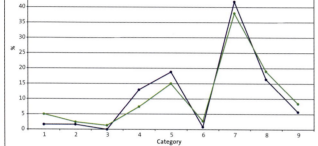

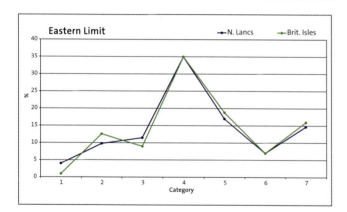

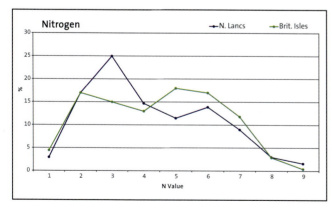

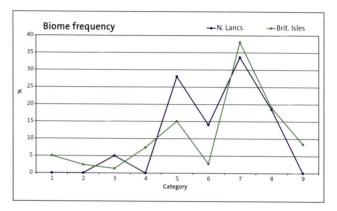

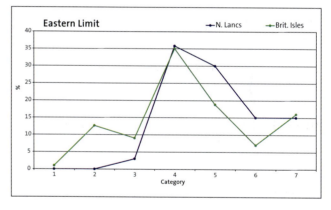

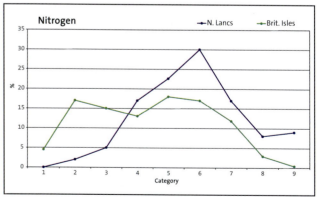

Figure 4.3 Nutritional preferences for very rare species in northern Lancashire and for all species found in the British Isles

Figure 4.4 Nutritional preferences for very common species in northern Lancashire and for all species found in the British Isles

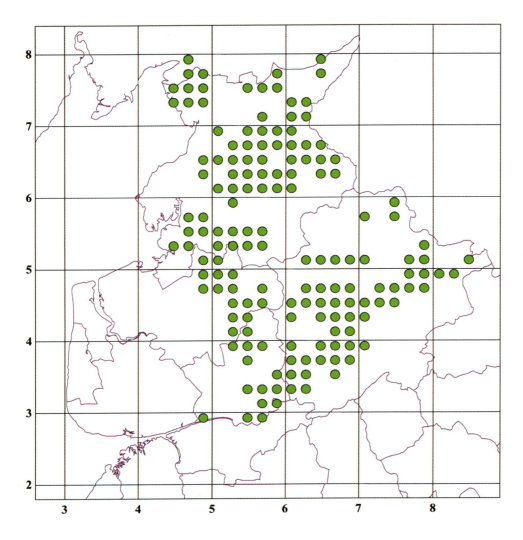

Map 4.19 Map showing the tetrad distribution of ancient semi-natural woodlands in northern Lancashire based on Backmeroff, *et al.* (1988).

Woodlands

In this chapter species distribution has been correlated with climate and soil attributes. However it is possible to correlate the distributions of species with other features or habitats. The major habitats and plant communities were described in chapter 2. It is not feasible to map the distributions of them all but amongst the most distinct are woodlands. The distribution of ancient woodlands was described in 1988 (Backmeroff, *et al.*, 1988). Map 4.19 shows their tetrad distribution.

Using Hill, *et al.* (2004) 42 of the most characteristic woodland species were selected and a composite tetrad distribution map was compiled (Map 4.20). This demonstrates that only a few parts of northern Lancashire are devoid of woodland species. They appear to be absent only from the highest hills, some

coastal areas of the Fylde and Over Wyre and in much of central lowland VC 60 extending from the Lune estuary to the Kirkham area. Ancient woodlands are absent from these areas and although the peat cover and harsh climate of the higher fells can explain this absence of woodland and woodland species, it is less easy to explain their absence from the other two areas.

However the absence of ancient woodland in the central lowland areas of VC 60 corresponds to the distribution of soils of the Altcar mossland and Astley Hall series. Formerly these areas were covered in peat bogs (of which a few remnants remain at Cockerham and Winmarleigh), fens and wet heaths. None of these areas are likely to have supported ancient woodland for at least 4000 years yet today the landscape is characterised by farmland and copses. The copses were mostly planted in the late eighteenth and nineteenth

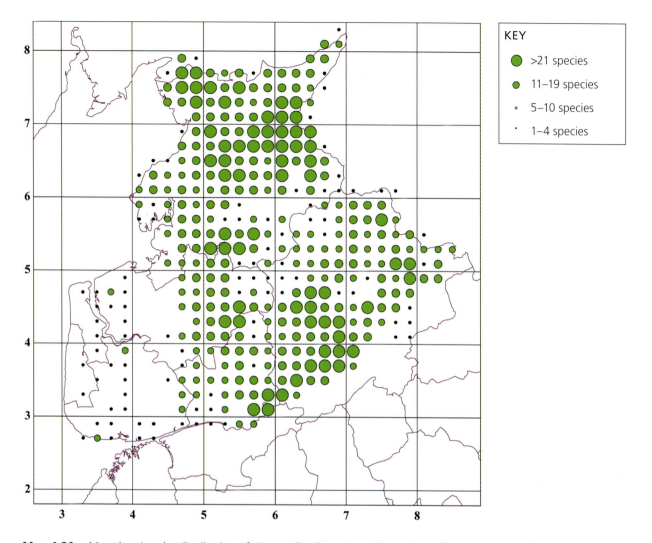

Map 4.20   Map showing the distribution of 42 woodland species with numbers of species per tetrad

KEY

● >21 species

● 11–19 species

· 5–10 species

· 1–4 species

centuries and have not been colonised by woodland species.

The absence of woodland and woodland species on the coast of the Fylde and Over Wyre corresponds to areas subject to the full force of Irish Sea storms and the presence of shifting sand dunes and salt marshes. Woodlands have not had a chance to become established in these areas.

The tetrad distribution map of woodland species has been prepared using four classes of frequency (Map 4.20). Although there are several types of woodland the most species diverse woods (with between 21 and 42 species) correspond to the distribution of ancient woodlands. The most species diverse woodlands are found in the lower Hodder valley and in the lower reaches of Roeburndale and Hindburndale.

When tetrads with eleven to twenty species are included the area covered by woodland species is extended to include a region loosely termed the woodland belt. This includes the valleys surrounding the Bowland Fells, the Ribble and Lune valleys and the limestone country around Morecambe Bay. Perhaps more surprising is the presence of woodland species in the Heysham peninsula and to the north-west of Galgate. There are no ancient woodlands remaining in the Heysham peninsula but fragments remain near Galgate. These tetrads with eleven to twenty woodland species indicate the presence of former woodlands, perhaps only cleared relatively recently but where woodland species survive in old hedges or small woodland fragments.

The species found in tetrads with 11 to 42 species vary from ones with a very limited distribution, e.g. *Gagea lutea*, to ones found more generally in the woodland zone, e.g. *Arum maculatum*, *Chrysosplenium alternifolium*, *Cardamine amara* and *Lysimachia nemorum*. However many of these woodland species with a more generalised distribution in the woodland zone also occur in a few tetrads further west in the absence of any extant ancient woodlands. For individual species these records appear anomalous. However if the distribution of tetrads with five to ten woodland species is analysed it is found that they are either on the edge of the woodland zone or are in areas where there is no ancient woodland today.

In the lowland west of the area three tetrads are noteworthy. These are SD32N (Lytham Hall), SD33Z (Singleton) and SD34T (Preesall). Today there are estate parklands or scrub in these tetrads but no ancient woodland and all three tetrads are on higher ground formed by deposits of boulder clay or other glacial deposits. Humans probably settled them, at least to some extent, by Neolithic times but amongst the cultivated ground some ancient woodland probably survived until at least 1000 years ago. At Lytham the former woodland vegetation is also suggested by the presence of four species of bramble. These are *Rubus rubritinctus*, *R. raduloides*, *R. adenanthoides* (endemic to central areas of the British Isles) and *R. pallidus*, which are all characteristic of woodland edge habitats (Edees and Newton, 1988). Further support for former wooded areas is suggested by tetrads with perhaps only one or two woodland species. The scatter of odd records for single species is possibly not significant, but when the scatter of records for several species is plotted the line of records extends westwards from Preston along a ridge of boulder clay deposits through Kirkham and then northwards to the east of Blackpool to the Wyre estuary.

The soils derived from these deposits belong to the Salwick and Salop series and produce an undulating landscape of slightly calcareous till soils (Hall and Folland, 1970). In hollows and poorly drained areas wet heath and bog probably developed but on better drained slopes the woodland that formerly covered most of the area 5000 years ago was cleared to form valuable farmland for early settlers. It is likely that most of the woodlands were cleared by the Iron Age and certainly by 1000 years ago. Nevertheless there are woodland species that have a scattered distribution on these boulder clay areas including *Bromopsis ramosa*, *Mercurialis perennis* and *Oxalis acetosella*. Today they occur in hedge banks and possibly represent the remnants of a woodland flora present in ancient forests long gone. Alternatively they could represent the early stages of recent colonization but if this were so they should have spread into copses planted since the eighteenth century, which is not the case.

A similar scatter of tetrads with one to four woodland species occurs in the higher parts of Bowland and Leck. Although peat covers the tops of the fells and bogs formed in all the poorly drained areas throughout northern Lancashire, it is thought that woodland covered all the well-drained slopes (now often covered in heath, Bracken or grassland) and extended high up the valleys. Remnants of these former ancient woodlands are found in Black Clough, Over Wyresdale (SD55W & 65B) and on the north side of Longridge Fell (SD64Q & V) where the woodland still occurs up to *c.* 300m (1000ft). However woodland species occur above the present tree line. Examples include *Chrysosplenium oppositifolium* found in flushes and *Dryopteris affinis s.l.* found on the banks of streams. This latter species also occurs in hedges on the boulder clay in the west of the area.

Thus it is concluded that plotting the distribution of woodland species not only shows the location of extant ancient woodlands but also the extent of former woodlands.

Coastal species

The distribution patterns shown by some species can be correlated with specific features or habitats. Amongst the most readily identified are the coastal habitats of salt marshes and sand dunes. Elsewhere in the British Isles many species are associated with rocky coastal cliffs but there are few of these in northern Lancashire and whilst there are several clay cliffs few if any species are uniquely associated with them.

Also found elsewhere in the British Isles are shingle beaches and spits and whilst extensive examples may have existed in northern Lancashire they have almost all been destroyed by the development of coastal towns and sea walls. It is believed the coast north of Blackpool towards Fleetwood had shingle beaches whilst at St Anne's the double stanner at Fairhaven enclosing a sheltered embayment, used as a harbour, was a well known feature (Plate 71 in Haley, 1995) until it was enclosed over 100 years ago to form Fairhaven lake. Smaller shingle spits and beaches occurred on the Wyre estuary at Barnaby's Sands and between Morecambe and Carnforth.

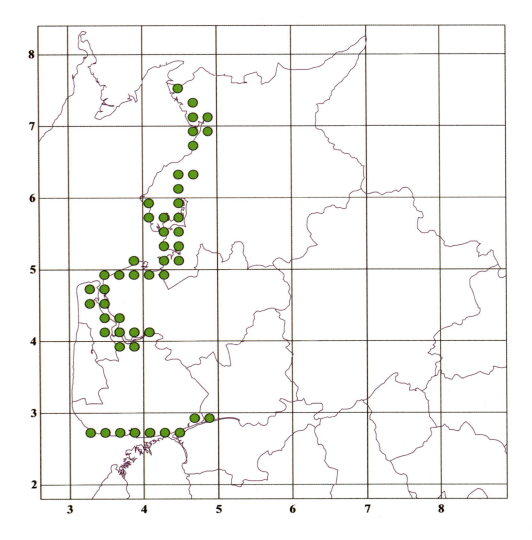

Map 4.21 Map showing the tetrad distribution of salt marshes in northern Lancashire.

The distribution of salt marshes is shown in Map 4.21 and several species are uniquely associated with them including *Salicornia* spp., *Plantago maritima*, *Triglochin maritima*, *Glaux maritima*, *Atriplex portulacoides*, *Puccinellia maritima*, *Artemisia maritima*, *Limonium humile*, *L. vulgare*, *Spergularia media*, *Blysmus rufus*, *Juncus gerardii*, *J. maritimus*, *Elytrigia* × *drucei*, *Spartina anglica* and *Oenanthe lachenalii*.

Sand dunes occur at Lytham St Anne's and Fleetwood with a small fragment at Middleton (Map 4.8). Additionally sand tipped from dredgings from the R. Ribble is found at Lea. Although the building of Lytham and especially St Anne's from the 1870s destroyed most of the sand dunes, species uniquely associated with the habitat survive. These include *Elytrigia juncea*, *Ammophila arenaria*, *Euphorbia paralias*, *E. portlandica*, *Erodium lebelii*, *Pyrola rotundifolia*,

Epipactis dunensis, *E. phyllanthes*, *Dactylorhiza incarnata* ssp. *coccinea* and *Coincya monensis* ssp. *monensis*.

A few typical sand dune species occur inland in other habitats. Associated with calcareous soils, usually on limestone, are *Inula conyza* and *Carlina vulgaris* whilst some species also occur on sandy ruderal habitats, e.g. *Erigeron acris*.

A small number of typical sand dune slack species also occur inland in base-rich wet or flushed places. Sometimes these inland sites are post-industrial quarries or sand pits etc. Characteristic of these species are *Epipactis palustris*, *Equisetum variegatum* and *Parnassia palustris* although the taxon on the sand dunes is var. *condensata*, thought only to occur here.

As there are so few rock exposures on the coast of northern Lancashire it is not surprising that only

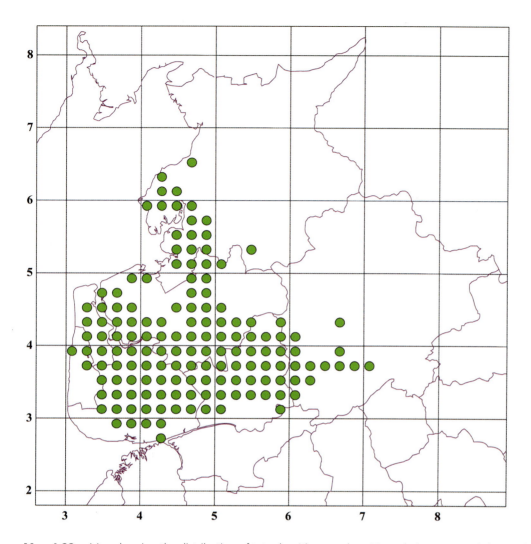

Map 4.22   Map showing the distribution of tetrads with more than 10 marl pits per tetrad. (Data abstracted from 1:25,000 Ordnance Survey maps published in 1959. As records were compiled from pits that were subsequently lost it is important to record pit distribution as found at the start of the plant recording period in 1964).

Asplenium marinum is uniquely associated with them, formerly at Silverdale but now only at Heysham. Also found at Heysham is *Cochlearia officinalis,* which does not appear to occur on the salt marshes. *Crithmum maritimum* occurs on rocky sea cliffs but it is also found on sea walls. No species is uniquely associated with coastal clay cliffs but in freshwater springs arising from the base of coastal clay cliffs 'Juncus compressus like' plants may be found, although there are also old records reported for this species.

Natural shingle exposures have almost all gone or have become stabilized by mud and vegetation. However remnants survive and on these and the iron waste at Warton on the Keer estuary suitable habitats for typical shingle species including *Crambe maritima* and *Glaucium flavum* occur. The endemic *Limonium*

britannicum occurs on the Wyre estuary on stabilized shingle at the top of salt marshes and on old sea walls.

Wetland species of mesotrophic and eutrophic still water

Mesotrophic and eutrophic wetland habitats occur in lowland areas of northern Lancashire and whilst marl pits are confined to the west of the area (Map 4.22) ponds and marshes are associated with both the R. Lune and R. Ribble. Near the coast there are brackish fens and marshes but some of the largest freshwater wetlands have been established over the last 100 years. These include the extensive fens at Leighton Moss and the numerous gravel pits but perhaps the oldest man-made features are ditches, marl pits and the Lancaster Canal.

Preparing a tetrad distribution map of all the mesotrophic and eutrophic freshwaters would show that they occur throughout the region except in peat covered areas, on the Bowland Fells and Leck. However only the commonest wetland species occur in all these habitats. An example is *Phalaris arundinacea* but whilst it is absent from the fells such small areas of lowland peat bog exist today that its absence from these is not evident at the tetrad level.

Despite the ubiquitous distribution of freshwater habitats a number of distinct distribution patterns can be identified.

A few species are only found on or near the coast, often in slightly brackish conditions. Typical of this extreme western distribution are *Apium graveolens*, *Oenanthe fistulosa* and *Bolboschoenus maritimus*.

A more generalised western distribution is shown by species which are particularly associated with marl pits (Guest, 1997; Day, *et al.*, 1982). These include *Apium inundatum*, *Bidens cernua*, *Lemna gibba*, *Spirodela polyrhiza* and *Carex pseudocyperus*. Some species show a range that goes beyond the distribution of marl pits. For example *Veronica catenata* also occurs in the Lune valley and *Alisma plantago-aquatica*, *Sparganium erectum*, *Lemna minor*, *Ranunculus sceleratus* and *Potamogeton crispus* also occur in both the Lune and Ribble valleys.

Yet other species, although being mostly found in the west of northern Lancashire, are also found more generally further east. Examples include *Phragmites australis*, *Schoenoplectus tabernaemontani*, *Typha angustifolia* and *Carex otrubae* whilst *Oenanthe crocata* is generally distributed in VC 60 except in the fells, but it is rare in Lancashire VC 64.

A few species are associated with particular river valleys. In the north *Veronica anagallis-aquatica* seems especially associated with the Lune valley and wetlands in the Silverdale and Warton area with only a few scattered localities elsewhere. Similarly *Scrophularia umbrosa* is associated with the Ribble and Hodder valleys in northern Lancashire and in other river valleys elsewhere in Britain ('New Atlas').

The Lancaster Canal is a major freshwater habitat in northern Lancashire extending from Preston to the Lancashire and Cumbria border at Tewitfield. The flora and changes to the flora were described by Greenwood (2005) who showed that a number of species are almost confined to the Canal. These include *Acorus calamus* and *Sagittaria sagittifolia*.

Despite the apparently clear-cut distinctions between the distribution patterns described here many other species have patterns that are intermediate between one or more of those noted. However what governs these patterns is mostly unknown. Correlations with marl pits or brackish conditions seem clear but insufficient is known about the biology of the species or the environmental attributes of the habitats to necessarily imply causal relationships.

In addition to still waters a number of rivers traverse the region. Many of these are swift mountain streams poor in nutrients and with little or no aquatic or marsh plants associated with them. Many of the rivers have been canalised in their middle and lower reaches and again offer few opportunities for vascular plants to grow in or adjacent to them. Only the R. Lune flows through a flood plain where the bed of former meanders has left oxbows with pools and marshes. Further problems for plant growth have been caused by pollution yet despite these difficulties some species are only found in or close by rivers. In particular *Ranunculus penicillatus* was confined to the R. Ribble but has recently colonized the R. Wyre and the R. Brock. *Myriophyllum alterniflorum* is also largely confined to rivers. Today *Ranunculus peltatus* and *Groenlandia densa* are confined to the R. Lune oxbows but formerly had a wider distribution in ponds and the Lancaster Canal. Similarly *Rorippa sylvestris* is typical of river valleys but also occurs on the Fylde coast and occasionally elsewhere.

Arable weeds (See also Arable weeds in chapter 2)

Arable farmland is mostly found in the west of the region and especially on soils derived from reclaimed peat bogs. However the extent of arable farmland has varied over the years and whilst it was never a common feature of land use in some places, particularly in the uplands, some arable fields were found throughout the farmed landscape. Even today a field of turnips or other crop may be found almost anywhere east of the M6 in an otherwise predominantly pastoral landscape.

Until the mid twentieth century many weeds were associated with arable farmland and consequently most were found west of the M6 and particularly in the Fylde and Over Wyre areas. These include *Viola arvensis*, *Urtica urens*, *Persicaria lapathifolia*, *Fallopia convolvulus*, *Euphorbia helioscopia*, *E. peplus*, *Fumaria muralis* and *Galeopsis bifida*. A few other species characteristic of

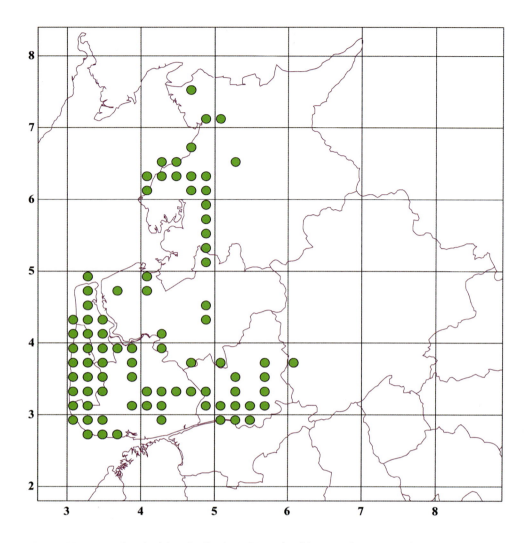

Map 4.23 Map showing the distribution of tetrads with more than 10% urban land per tetrad. (Data abstracted from 1:25,000 Ordnance Survey maps published in 1959. As records were compiled from rural areas that were subsequently built on for residential, commercial and industrial purposes it was important to record the extent of urban land at the start of the plant recording period in 1964).

arable fields occur almost anywhere in cultivated ground, e.g. *Atriplex patula, Veronica persica, Chenopodium album, Lamium hybridum* and *L. purpureum*.

Many of these species are also found as garden weeds or in any cultivated ground and so although they may occur mostly west of the M6 they occur occasionally almost anywhere. Nevertheless some of them have been especially associated with particular crops. These include *Atriplex patula* and *Chenopodium album*, which until recently, were serious pest species of potato crops.

Some weed species have a more restricted distribution. *Lamium amplexicaule* is associated with light sandy soils near the coast whilst *Stachys arvensis* also favours light sandy soils near the coast but additionally occurs occasionally further inland.

Two species that formerly provided a colourful display in cereal crops are *Galeopsis speciosa* and *Glebionis segetum*. They were particularly common on peaty soils north of the R. Wyre.

A number of arable species are conspicuous by their absence. Corncockle and Cornflower were perhaps never common in northern Lancashire and they have not been part of the arable field flora for over 100 years. More interestingly *Papaver* spp. have only occasionally featured as arable weeds in the last 50 years or so although they may appear if a portion of a cereal crop escapes herbicide treatment. However both *P. rhoeas* and *P. dubium* occur frequently in ruderal habitats.

Roads

During the last 20 years or so it has become apparent that some species are associated with motorways and A class roads (Scott and Davison, 1982, 1985; Wyse Jackson, 2000; Greenwood, 2001, 2004). Most notable has been the spread of *Cochlearia danica* in northern Lancashire from its natural coastal sites to major roads. It is thought that the spread is correlated with the winter use of salt to keep roads free of ice, which as a consequence creates open, brackish verges. Although the spread from coastal sites has not been so obvious *Spergularia marina* and *Puccinellia distans* have also been found on roadsides associated with salt treatment.

Urban areas

Historically the built landscape of northern Lancashire was confined to a few large towns and many small villages. However during the last 200 years and especially during the last 100 years an extensive urban or built landscape has developed covering large areas around Morecambe and Lancaster, the coast from Fleetwood to Lytham St Anne's, and around Preston (Map 4.23). These areas provide new habitats for plants and with the industry and commerce associated with them together with their parks and gardens many species new to northern Lancashire have been introduced to the region.

The urban landscape is nevertheless a new one and despite the many introductions few species are uniquely associated with it. Nevertheless most naturalised introductions in the British Isles are seldom found more than 10m from buildings, gardens, walls, waste ground, roadsides or railways (Crawley, *et al.*, 1996). Furthermore relatively few native species have been able to exploit the urban environment so that often species diversity may be low in built up areas, e.g. tetrads SD33C and D at Blackpool and SD53K in Preston. However species diversity in urban areas may be temporarily high if land is left vacant when buildings are demolished thus providing a habitat that can be exploited by incoming species or where dormant seeds from former commercial operations find conditions suitable for their germination, as occurred in Preston in the 1960s (tetrad SD53F).

On the other hand the most species diverse areas are either within or close to large urban areas. These species diverse areas are in the Silverdale area (tetrads SD47S, T & V) where tetrad totals are over 600, at Heysham (SD46A) with nearly 600 taxa recorded and at Lytham St Anne's (tetrads SD33A, SD32I, N, & T) where species totals are over 500 per tetrad. In all three localities there is a mixture of relatively densely populated areas (but the houses have gardens) and wilder natural areas with diverse habitats. This diversity is particularly rich around Morecambe Bay where the wilder areas are protected for their wild life or natural beauty. In these areas the naturally diverse and species rich flora is augmented by estate plantings, garden escapes and accidental introductions.

Although few species have distributions closely identified with the built environment examples include *Sisymbrium altissimum, S. orientale* and *Diplotaxis muralis.* All are accidental introductions. As an example of a garden escape found only in urban areas *Geranium* × *magnificum* has been found at Lytham St Anne's and Lancaster. Most introductions and garden escapes have a more diffuse distribution, e.g. *Senecio squalidus* and *Phalaris canariensis*, which whilst occurring commonly in the built environment may be found in any open ruderal habitat. Many however become naturalised throughout most of the region, e.g. *Epilobium ciliatum, Fallopia japonica*, or as casuals occurring on only a few occasions or have a limited distribution in one town, e.g. *Agrostis scabra* in Preston. Nevertheless urban areas are characterised by a high proportion of introduced species and nationally they are most numerous in south-eastern England and least numerous in the northwest of the British Isles reflecting a close correlation between human population density and number of introduced species (Roy, *et al.*, 1999).

Local British distributions

Newton and Randall (2004) published a map showing the distribution of six major groupings of species characteristic of certain areas of the British Isles. They called these groupings *Florulae* to distinguish them from more localised or regional assemblages, which could be recognised. However the distribution patterns or *Florulae* shown by *Rubus* spp. are not confined to the genus.

Most significant for northern Lancashire is the Irish Sea *Florula*, which comprises species that have their main British distribution centred around the shores of the Irish Sea from mid-Wales north to Loch Broom in Scotland and eastwards towards the Pennines. Northern Lancashire species occurring throughout this range are *R. dasyphyllus, R. errabundus* (E), *R. latifolius* (E), *R. lindleianus, R. nemoralis, R. plicatus, R.*

polyanthemis, *R. scissus* and *R. wirralensis* (E). Those marked by (E) are endemic to the British Isles, often with localised distributions. Although these species are considered part of the Irish Sea *Florula* most have distributions that extend beyond the area. However other species have a more limited range. Amongst these are ones that extend from northern Wales to Lancashire where they are often at their northern limits. These include *R. bartonii* (E), *R. bertramii*, *R. calvatus* (E), *R. cardiophyllus*, *R. criniger* (E), *R. griffithianus* (E), *R. painteri* (E), *R. rufescens* and *R. rubritinctus*. *R. painteri* is also part of small group that appears endemic to the Pennine foothills from near Stoke-on-Trent to Lancashire. A small group is described as submontane and includes *R. cumbrensis* (E), *R. griffithianus* (E) and *R. silurum*.

An interesting feature of *Rubus* phytogeography is the presence of linking corridors between one major group and another. For the Irish Sea *Florula* two corridors link species found on either side of the Pennines. These are formed by the Tyne Gap in the north and the Ribble Gap further south. Species characteristic of the Ribble Gap are *R. adenthoides* (E), *R. dasyphyllus*, *R. eboracensis* (E), *R. echinatoides* (E), *R. errabundus* (E), *R. furnarius* (E), *R. hylocharis* (E), *R. incurvatiformis* (E), *R. infestus*, *R. lindebergii*, *R. mucronulatus*, *R. nemoralis*, *R. newboldii* (E), *R. robiae* (E), *R. sciocharis*, *R. scissus*, *R. sprengelii* and *R. warrenii* (E) whilst *R. radula*, largely characteristic of the North Sea *Florula*, extends westwards to the west coast through the Tyne Gap. Amongst species from other genera that seem to have distributions closely correlated with the Ribble Gap are *Pimpinella major* and perhaps *Scrophularia umbrosa*.

However northern Lancashire also has *Rubus* species that are more characteristic of other *Florulae*. Amongst the more interesting are species found in the Cornubian *Florula* based on south-western England and south-eastern Ireland. Within this *Florula* are species with a predominantly western distribution in the British Isles but which are sometimes found in western France. Examples found in northern Lancashire are *R. bertramii*, *R. hylocharis* (E) and *R. rubritinctus*.

Also a number of species more characteristic of the South and Midland *Florulae* occur in northern Lancashire. These include *R. cardiophyllus*, *R. criniger* (E), *R. echinatoides* (E), *R. echinatus*, *R. lindleianus*, *R. polyanthemus*, *R. pruinosus*, *R. rhombifolius*, *R. rudis*, *R. rufescens*, *R. sprengelii*, *R. tuberculatus* and *R. ulmifolius*.

Identifying bramble distributions in terms of *Florulae* within the British Isles is a useful way of defining plant distribution. However some of the *Florulae* may be extensions of a wider European distribution pattern. Species belonging to the Cornubian *Florula* are probably oceanic species whilst many of the more widely distributed species probably belong to temperate biomes.

However the more limited *Rubus* Irish Sea *Florula*, composed largely of endemic species, has species from other genera that can also be assigned to this grouping. In particular the endemic *Limonium britannicum*, *Coincya monensis* ssp. *monensis* and possibly *Cochlearia atlantica* found on Irish Sea coasts belong to this group. The endemic *Epipactis dunensis* possibly belongs to the Irish Sea Florula but it also occurs on river gravels in the Tyne valley and perhaps elsewhere.

Similar distributions restricted to the Irish Sea region have not been found in the apomictic genera of *Taraxacum, Sorbus* or *Hieracium*. Nevertheless restricted distributions have been observed with *Sorbus* and *Hieracium* species correlated with carboniferous limestone extending from the Pennines to Morecambe Bay. In this group the endemic *Sorbus lancastriensis* is restricted to limestone around Morecambe Bay. Amongst the endemic hawkweeds in this group occurring in northern Lancashire are *Hieracium placerophylloides*, *H. rubiginosum*, *H. maculoides*, *H. silvaticoides*, *H. auratiflorum* and *H. decolor*.

In addition to these apomictic and often endemic taxa a number of other species are particularly associated with northern England and occur in northern Lancashire. Amongst these are *Myosotis stolonifera*, *Alchemilla minima*, *Primula farinosa*, *Dryopteris submontana*, *Sesleria caerulea* (also in western Ireland), female *Petasites hybridus* and perhaps *Gymnocarpium robertianum*. Most of the species in the group are found on limestone but *Myosotis stolonifera* is found on slightly base-rich flushes in Bowland and Leck whilst female *Petasites hybridus* is particularly common by rivers in southern Bowland.

Sell and Murrell (2006) describe a way in which the localised distribution of apomictic hawkweed species could arise. Citing Ostenfield (1921) and the observations of Nils Hylander and P.D. Sell in Cambridgeshire they demonstrated that mutations giving rise to morphologically different taxa to their parents are constantly arising. If these new taxa happen to arise in or close to a suitable vacant habitat niche they will continue to flourish. Furthermore these changes can take place over a relatively short time scale and it is suggested that many apomictic species have arisen since the retreat of the ice from the last glaciation about 10,000 years ago. The open habitats found on the carboniferous limestone in northern England provide plenty of vacant niches for apomictic hawk-weeds to exploit.

However hybridisation is an important process in speciation with the appearance of *Spartina anglica* a recent documented example (Cope and Gray, 2009). It is believed that hybridisation was also important in the development of apomictic species. The monograph on *Sorbus* (Rich, *et al.*, 2010) explains how hybridisation has probably given rise to several locally distributed apomictic species including *Sorbus lancastriensis*.

The distinctiveness of the flora and its post-glacial history in the northern Irish Sea region were noted by Godwin (1975) and by Innes, *et al.* (2004). Explaining its development is less easily understood. The area is surrounded on two sides by mountains or uplands, i.e. of Cumbria, northern Wales, the Pennines and the Scottish uplands, and is therefore somewhat isolated from the rest of Britain. The shifting coastline of salt marsh and sand has provided open habitats and opportunities for colonization and it is perhaps note-worthy that the Isle of Man Cabbage exploits ruderal habitats as well as sand dunes at Lytham St Anne's. However it is possible that bramble apomicts either arose or spread into the area when open scrub vege-tation was still prevalent. On the other hand some species appear to have spread from the east through the Ribble Gap although most must have spread into northern Lancashire via the low lying land of southern Lancashire and the Cheshire plain.

Explaining the distinctive distribution shown by *Tamus communis* is especially difficult. It is a member of the Submediterranean-Subatlantic element, which has a largely southern and western distri-bution in Britain reaching the northern limits in southern Cumbria and northern Yorkshire. *Tamus communis* however has a peculiarly disjunct distribu-tion at its northern limits. It is largely absent from the Pennines but it is abundant on calcareous soils of southern Cumbria and, with decreasing abundance, extends to south of Lancaster. Apart from possible introductions it does not occur in the southern half of northern Lancashire apart from the upper Ribble valley. In Mid-west Yorkshire (VC 64) it is found in the Craven district but it is rare between the Ribble valley and Craven areas in the west but in the eastern half of the vice-county it is common (Abbott, 2005).

This disjunct distribution suggests that in the post-glacial period *Tamus* spread northward from southern England through the Cheshire plain and southern Lancashire to reach southern Cumbria before climate changes and human activity eliminated suitable habitats in the southern half of northern Lancashire whilst spread from the east may have been through the Ribble Gap. Whether or not this is a plausible theory may never be known but the distribution pattern shown by Black Bryony appears unique.

Thus it is tempting to suggest that to explain the origin of the native northern Lancashire flora the main thrust of migration from the continent following the retreat of the ice 10,000 years ago was across the main land bridge connecting south-eastern England to the continent. Migration northward continued across England and into the region via the Cheshire plain. However some species may have migrated northwards on the eastern side of the Pennines before finding a way to the west through one of the gaps in the hills. However an intriguing possibility to explain the presence of the Eurosiberian and continental *Carex ericetorum* is that it took a route on the northern flange of the main route from the continent leaving a line of relic populations extending from East Anglia to Morecambe Bay. However the Cornubian and Irish Sea *Florulae* with oceanic distributions may have taken a more westerly route from refugia in north-western France and Iberia.

Support for such a hypothesis comes from analyses of post-glacial floristic history (Birks and Deacon, 1973). Throughout the Flandrian period a northwest – southeast gradient is discernible with northern species favouring cold climates always on the northern edge of the gradient whilst southern species favouring warmer climates were found on the southern edge. More interesting is the introduc-tion of oceanic species. In the late Devensian period (before 10,000BP) most records were from south-western England, Ireland and the English midlands. As might be expected at this early period following the retreat of the ice most records are from warmer south-western areas with few records from the more northern western regions of Wales, north-western England and western Scotland where they are preva-lent today. Of considerable interest was a relatively high representation of oceanic species in the English midlands. Birks and Deacon (1973) were unable to explain this finding but perhaps this is the route by which oceanic species spread into Wales and other northern western areas of Britain? As time progressed oceanic species became more abundant, especially in the late Flandrian (*c.* 4000BP), when the climate became cooler and wetter. The late arrival of most oceanic species, correlating with the change to a more oceanic climate, was noted by Godwin (1975). The establishment of their distribution in western parts of the British Isles at that time remains essentially unchanged today.

Conclusion

A variety of distribution patterns are shown by species occurring in northern Lancashire and possible explanations for them are postulated. It is likely that many more complex distribution patterns exist and remain to be detected. However, understanding the factors governing the distribution patterns is complex. Several may owe their origins to colonization and evolutionary events following the retreat of ice from the last glaciation. The routes by which species found in northern Lancashire colonised the area from continental Europe remain unknown. The presence in Lancashire of species found in Iberia and north-western France is particularly difficult to explain. Other species arrived in recent times, often as a result of human activity creating and destroying habitats. However species show different methods of dispersal and responses to environmental change. Thus the landscape with the species that clothe it is like a canvas where the artist paints and re-paints a picture leaving the original only just visible as later changes become more evident. Understanding what has happened over the millennia is therefore important in interpreting the present, in understanding changes that have occurred and attempting to predict the future.

5. The changing flora

Introduction

There has always been and there always will be changes in the flora of a particular area and its vegetation. In chapter 1 (The evolution of a landscape) the major vegetation changes up to recent times were described. However to describe changes in the species composition of the northern Lancashire flora one needs a date when there was some degree of stability in the natural vegetation as a base-line against which changes can be assessed. That date is probably between about 3000 and 2000BC when the cool damp climate that occurs today was established even though since then there have been some variations. Human interference in the natural vegetation had already occurred but it was not so great as to obliterate the main vegetation and floristic features. However knowledge of the species growing in the area 4000 years ago is poor and it is only in the last 200 years that any detail is available. Even the record for the 100 years prior to Wheldon and Wilson's Flora (1907) is relatively sketchy.

Extinctions

Nevertheless studying changes over 4000 years is revealing. Unfortunately the only changes that can be followed over such a long period are extinctions. Table 5.1 shows that of the 51 extinctions identified most have occurred since 1950. The losses before 1800 are based on written reports and archaeological remains whilst between 1800 and 1899 losses are based on herbarium and written records. For some of these species very little is known about their occurrence and it is likely that other species grew in the region about which nothing is known. On the other hand some of the species amongst these early extinctions were abundant, e.g. *Scheuchzeria palustris* on lowland bogs.

Since 1900 extinctions have continued to occur and possibly at an accelerating rate. Some were possibly always rare, e.g. *Utricularia minor*, whilst others may only have occurred casually, e.g. *Mertensia maritima*. It is also possible that some species may be rediscovered or migrate back into the area.

In addition to those listed in Table 5.1 a number of other species may also be extinct. *Euphrasia rostkoviana* has not been seen at its last known site for a few years whilst *Papaver argemone* (last seen 1979), *Neottia nidus-avis* (last seen 2000) and *Ranunculus arvensis* (last seen 1992) appear either erratically or may be only casual in northern Lancashire.

At a national level there have been few extinctions since 1970 but at the county level there have been many and the trend is accelerating (Walker, 2007). At present Walker estimates extinctions in most lowland counties are averaging six per decade. In northern Lancashire observations are not sufficiently accurate to confirm the figure. Recent observations in the region suggest that localities for formerly widespread or even frequent species are being lost, e.g. *Parnassia palustris* and *Pinguicula vulgaris*, and that if this continues losses will accelerate rapidly. Nevertheless once vulnerable species have gone, probably those most sensitive to nutrient enrichment, a period of stability may prevail.

In an effort to characterise the types of plants that have become extinct each species was scored in terms of its floristic element and eastern limit to define its climatic preferences (see chapter 4; Hill, *et al.*, 2004) and its ecological preferences were scored using Ellenberg values for light, moisture, reaction and nutrients (Hill, *et al.*, 2004). Ellenberg values for light range from 1 (plants of deep shade) to 9 (plants found in full sun); for moisture they range from 1 (extremely dry places) to 12 (submerged aquatics); for reaction they range from 1 (very acid conditions) to 9 (calcareous and other high pH soils) and for fertility or nutrient status the values range from 1 (very infertile) to 9 (very fertile or near polluted sites). Table 5.2 shows the average values for these attributes whilst Figures 5.1–5.3 demonstrate the values in which most species occur.

In general most extinct species are characteristic of temperate climates but perhaps with northerly or boreal and possibly oceanic preferences. Ecologically, extinct species show a range of preferences except that they are generally light demanding (i.e. they are found in open and non wooded habitats), grow on nutrient poor soils and are largely absent from dry places.

Table 5.1 Extinct northern Lancashire species with date of last record. (An extinct species is defined here as one that has not been seen for at least 20 years or has gone from its last known locality).

Name	Last date	Name	Last date
Extinctions from 1950		Mertensia maritima	1941
Drosera intermedia	mid twentieth	Gentiana pneumonanthe	1941
Gentianella campestris	2002	Gymnadenia densiflora*	1938
Platanthera bifolia	2000	Hypericum elodes	1931
Genista anglica	1990	Eleogiton fluitans	1925
Eleocharis multicaulis	1988	Pseudorchis albida	1913
Centunculus minimus	1988	Antennaria dioica	1907
Carex lasiocarpa	1987	Elytrigia atherica	1904
Actaea spicata	1987	Cuscuta epithymum	1903
Gnaphalium sylvaticum	1986	Potamogeton gramineus	1902
Scandix pecten-veneris	1983	Drosera anglica	1902
Draba muralis	1983	Urtica dioica ssp. galeopsifolia	1901
Stellaria palustris	1974	Salvia verbenaca	1901
Lotus tenuis	1974	**Extinctions between 1800 & 1899**	
Galeopsis angustifolia	1974	Potentilla crantzii	1897
Epilobium alsinifolium	1972	Carex limosa	1887
Salix myrsinifolia	1968	Veronica spicata	1881
Lithospermum arvense	1967	Rosa micrantha	1881
Valerianella locusta var. dunensis	1965	Bupleurum tenuissimum	1841
Juncus balticus	1965	Peucedanum officinale	1837
Coeloglossum viride	1965	Pilularia globulifera	1825
Alisma lanceolatum	1959	**Extinctions before 1800**	
Cephalanthera longifolia	1958	Tephroseris palustris	1670
Valerianella dentata	1957	Hypochaeris glabra	100
Extinctions between 1900 & 1949		Cicuta virosa	100
Utricularia minor	1944	Carex elongata	100
Radiola linoides	1940s	Scheuchzeria palustris	800BC
Neotinea ustulata	1930s		

* Rediscovered 2010

Table 5.2 Average climate and ecological values for extinct northern Lancashire species

	Floristic element	Eastern limit	Light	Moisture	Reaction	Nutrient
Average	5.5	3.6	7.1	6.4	5.3	3.0

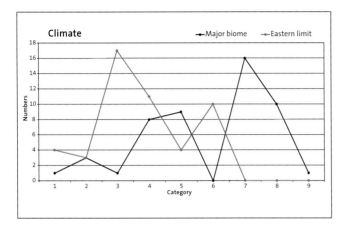

Figure 5.1 Geographical limits for extinct northern Lancashire species; (a) Major Biome and (b) Eastern limit.

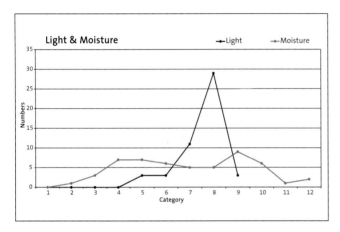

Figure 5.2 Ecological preferences for (a) Light and (b) Moisture for extinct northern Lancashire species.

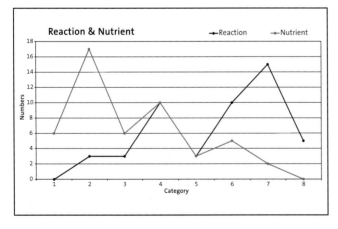

Figure 5.3 Ecological preferences (a) Reaction and (b) Nutrient for extinct northern Lancashire species.

Decreasing species

Wheldon and Wilson (1907) provided some quantitative data on the frequency of rarer species in VC 60 against which post 1964 records can be compared. In addition detailed records since 1964 have been kept for rarer species and together with other evidence it is possible to get some idea of which species are becoming less or more frequent. Despite the subjective nature of the analysis apparently meaningful results have been obtained.

Using data from the above sources a total of 95 native species (Table 5.3) and 10 archaeophytes found in northern Lancashire appear to have declined or are declining with increasingly restricted distributions. The 'New Atlas' calculated a change index (using statistical techniques) by comparing distributions of species recorded in Great Britain and the Isle of Man between 1930 and 1969 with those recorded between 1987 and 1999.

In comparing the situation in northern Lancashire with the patterns noted nationally (Great Britain and the Isle of Man) and despite the difference in time scales and methodology a similar pattern emerges. All the locally declining archaeophytes are declining nationally but 15 of the 95 locally declining native species appear to be increasing in Great Britain and the Isle of Man. However the text in the 'New Atlas' for one of these, *Scutellaria minor*, suggests a continued decline nationally. Nationally recording between 1987 and 1999 was more thorough than in the earlier period so that some species were better recorded between 1987 and 1999 and this may account for the apparent anomaly of a local decline and a national increase. Very often the narrative for individual species in the 'New Atlas' refers to losses in England despite an apparent gain nationally. Furthermore the maps themselves often show a pattern of decreasing losses extending in a line from south-eastern England to the northwest of the country.

Similarly 'Local Change' using a more selective methodology calculated a change index (using statistical techniques) when comparing the results of a species monitoring project covering England, Wales and Scotland carried out in 1987 and 1988 with a similar exercise in 2003 and 2004. However insufficient data was obtained for some rare species and these were omitted from the analysis.

Nevertheless despite the differences in methodology, timescales and geographical coverage similar results were obtained locally and nationally.

In comparing the three analyses a declining species in both national surveys was included if the change index was negative whether or not it was statistically significant. On this basis of the 95 native and 10 archaeophyte species thought to be declining in northern Lancashire 83 were found to be declining in both national surveys indicating a long-term and continuing decline for these species.

However the 'New Atlas' recorded gains for *Ophioglossum vulgatum*, *Ranunculus sardous*, *Ulex gallii* and *Zannichellia palustris* but 'Local Change' recorded declines in these four species in line with observations in northern Lancashire. A further group of four species, *Eriophorum latifolium*, *Potamogeton berchtoldii*, *Scutellaria minor* and *Vaccinium oxycoccus*, showed increases in both the 'New Atlas' and 'Local Change'. In all of these cases it is thought that recording bias with recorders better able to observe or recognise the species in later surveys may be involved. However the recorded increase for *Potamogeton berchtoldii* is possibly accounted for by better recording of fine-leaved pond-weeds generally but *P. berchtoldii* may have been over recorded in error for *P. pusillus*. Where plants are critically identified it appears that *P. berchtoldii* is less tolerant of eutrophication and is declining whilst the more nutrient tolerant *P. pusillus* is increasing (Preston and Croft, 1997). Thus even for these four species doubts remain as to whether or not they are extending their range in Great Britain and that apparent increases are perhaps attributable to better recording.

Fourteen species that appear to be declining in northern Lancashire and nationally ('New Atlas') were recorded as increasing by 'Local Change'. These are listed below

> *Cryptogramma crispa*
> *Euphorbia exigua*
> *Lithospermum officinale*
> *Malva moscata*
> *Menyanthes trifoliata*
> *Neottia cordata*
> *Rhynchospora alba*
> *Rumex hydrolapathum*
> *Salix phylicifolia*
> *Sherardia arvensis*
> *Trifolium medium*
> *Verbena officinalis*
> *Viola tricolor*
> *Wahlenbergia hederacea*

Most of the national changes are statistically insignificant or are due to better recording of some species. A few merit comment. Although the apparent increase in the distribution of *Viola tricolor* is statistically insignificant the 'New Atlas' reported it amongst the 100 species showing the most decline in the British Isles. This is an anomaly that is difficult to explain. A few species are used in amenity planting or are escapes from gardens. These include *Rumex hydrolapathum*, *Malva moschata* and *Menyanthes trifoliata*. Of the remaining species *Sherardia arvensis* and *Verbena officinalis* after showing decline nationally ('New Atlas') as their native habitats have been lost are colonising new ruderal and often urban habitats especially in southern and south-eastern England. Both species have a southern-temperate distribution and may be responding to a warmer climate as well as taking advantage of new habitats. Perhaps both species, especially *Sherardia arvensis* that is a more widespread species, may start to extend their distribution in northern Lancashire in future years.

Overall the pattern of decline noted in northern Lancashire is reflected nationally and it is likely that a number of the declining northern Lancashire species will become extinct in the region in the coming years.

In an effort to define the characteristics of northern Lancashire's declining native species the climate and ecological preferences of all the species were analysed (Table 5.4; Figures 5.4, 5.5 & 5.6). These show that declining species belong to temperate or boreo-temperate elements characteristic of infertile, neutral or basic soils. They were generally light demanding and avoided dry habitats. Thus they had similar characteristics to extinct species except that they showed less oceanic tendencies and were perhaps found on slightly more basic and less nutrient poor substrates.

Table 5.3 Species thought to be decreasing in northern Lancashire

Native species

Anacamptis morio	*Gymnocarpium dryopteris*	*Rhynchospora alba*
Andromeda polifolia*	*Hippuris vulgaris*	*Rumex hydrolapathum*
Arabis hirsuta	*Hydrochoeris morsus-ranae*	*Salix phylicifolia*
Asplenium viride	*Hymenophyllum wilsonii*	*Sanguisorba officinalis*
Baldellia ranunculoides	*Jasione montana*	*Scutellaria minor**
Blysmus compressus	*Juniperus communis*	*Selaginella selaginoides*
Botrychium lunaria	*Limonium britannicum*	*Sherardia arvensis*
Briza media	*Limosella aquatica**	*Sparganium natans*
Calluna vulgaris	*Lithospermum officinale*	*Spiranthes spiralis*
Calystegia soldanella	*Malva moschata*	*Thymus polytrichus*
Campanula latifolia	*Melica uniflora*	*Trichophorum germanicum*
Carex caryophyllea	*Menyanthes trifoliata*	*Trifolium campestre*
Carex oederi	*Monotropa hypopitys*	*Trifolium medium*
Carlina vulgaris	*Myrica gale*	*Trollius europaeus*
Chaerophyllum temulum	*Neottia cordata*	*Ulex gallii**
Cirsium heterophyllum	*Neottia nidus-avis*	*Utricularia vulgaris**
Cryptogramma crispa	*Ophioglossum vulgatum**	*Vaccinium oxycoccus**
Cynoglossum officinale	*Ophrys insectifera*	*Valeriana dioica*
Dactylorhiza maculata	*Orchis mascula*	*Viola canina*
Daucus carota	*Paris quadrifolia*	*Viola hirta*
Deschampsia flexuosa	*Parnassia palustris*	*Viola tricolor* ssp. *tricolor*
Drosera rotundifolia	*Pimpinella saxifraga*	*Wahlenbergia hederacea*
Epipactis dunensis	*Pinguicula vulgaris*	*Zannichellia palustris**
Erica cinerea	*Plantago media*	
Erica tetralix	*Platanthera chlorantha*	**Archaeophyte species**
Eriophorum latifolium*	*Potamogeton alpinus**	*Agrostemma githago*
Eupatorium cannabinum	*Potamogeton berchtoldii**	*Anthemis cotula*
Fumaria capreolata*	*Potamogeton obtusifolius**	*Chenopodium bonus-henricus*
Gagea lutea*	*Potamogeton perfoliatus*	*Glebionis segetum*
Galium boreale	*Potentilla palustris*	*Euphorbia exigua*
Genista tinctoria	*Primula farinosa*	*Galeopsis speciosa*
Gentianella amarella	*Ranunculus auricomus*	*Hyoscymus niger*
Geranium sylvaticum	*Ranunculus circinatus*	*Papaver argemone*
Groenlandia densa*	*Ranunculus peltatus*	*Verbena officinalis*
Gymnadenia conopsea s.l.	*Ranunculus sardous**	*Veronica agrestis*
	Ranunculus trichophyllus	

* Species shown as increasing in the 'New Atlas'

Table 5.4 Average climate and ecological values for decreasing northern Lancashire species.

	Floristic element	Eastern limit	Light	Moisture	Reaction	Nutrient
Average	5.8	4	6.9	6.7	5.7	3.6

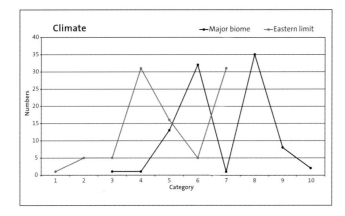

Figure 5.4 Geographical limits for decreasing northern Lancashire species; (a) Major Biome and (b) Eastern limit.

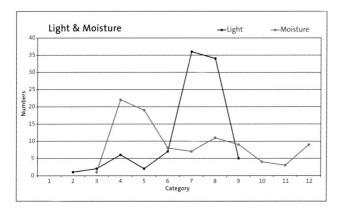

Figure 5.5 Ecological preferences for (a) Light and (b) Moisture for decreasing northern Lancashire species.

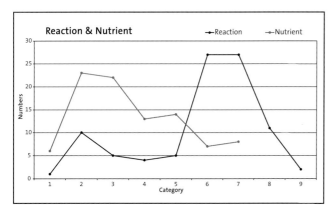

Figure 5.6 Ecological preferences (a) Reaction and (b) Nutrient for decreasing northern Lancashire species.

Increasing species

In contrast to species that have become extinct or are declining in northern Lancashire other native and archaeophyte species appear to be extending their range in the area. However whilst a majority of the species showing an increase in northern Lancashire (84 out of a total of 137 including 15 archaeophytes) also show an increase nationally, a significant minority either shows a declining pattern nationally, or the two national surveys have differing results.

Table 5.5 lists native and archaeophyte species that show an increase nationally ('New Atlas') and locally. Table 5.6 lists native and archaeophyte species that show an increase in northern Lancashire but the 'New Atlas' shows decline nationally, although 'Local Change' shows about half of these species are increasing nationally reversing the trends noted by the 'New Atlas'. Most of the discrepancies can be explained by national losses not being statistically significant. Nevertheless some require explanation. Increases in northern Lancashire for *Atriplex glabriuscula, Polygala vulgaris* and *Cerastium arvense* are probably attributable to better recording in the area whilst the colonisation of and persistence in the Lancaster Canal of *Nuphar lutea* explains its spread in the region. A number of northern Lancashire species have been able to exploit either sandy soil near the coast and/or ruderal habitats in lowland areas. These include *Saxifraga granulata* (perhaps a garden escape in coastal areas), *Trifolium arvense, Pastinaca sativa* and *Dactylorhiza incarnata*. Nationally grassland and coastal habitats favoured by these species have been lost. *Carex disticha* has colonised new wetland areas including the sand dunes at St Anne's where it remained unrecorded for many years reflecting an under recording nationally. *Oenanthe fistulosa* is at least maintaining its populations in northern Lancashire but it is possible that in the north of the region some of its localities were recorded in error. Nationally however it is amongst the 100 species showing the largest decrease ('New Atlas'). These losses nationally are explained by the drainage and re-seeding of damp grasslands in England whereas a significant number of ponds survived in northern Lancashire during the survey period. It is possible that losses have occurred in the region in recent years as ponds have been filled in but so far these have not been recorded.

Eighteen native and archaeophyte species are recorded as increasing in the 'New Atlas' and locally but decreasing in 'Local Change' (Table 5.7). Most of the changes were not statistically significant but some may reflect recent habitat changes. The decline of *Anthyllis vulneraria* and *Avenula pratensis* are thought to be due to recent losses of calcareous grassland nationally that has not occurred in northern Lancashire. Recent national losses of *Typha angustifolia* and *Myriophyllum alterniflorum* are thought to be due to eutrophication yet the former species has colonised the disused gravel pits at Brockholes, Preston and the latter the R. Wyre, along with *Ranunculus × bachii*. Of the remaining species the apparent gains for *Thalictrum minus* locally are due to garden escapes whilst native populations have probably declined in line with the national situation. Only the recent losses nationally of *Rorippa sylvestris* from its typical muddy riverbank habitat are difficult to explain. It is thought it might be uncompetitive as eutrophication favours the more robust growth of *Impatiens glandulifera*, *Phalaris arundinacea* and *Glyceria maxima* in much of England.

An analysis (Table 5.8; Figures 5.7- 5.12) of the climate and ecological preferences for native species in northern Lancashire showing an increase reveal differences to those that have become extinct or are decreasing. They tend to be species favouring a southern-temperate or even Mediterranean climate and favour more base-rich soils and less infertile soils or soils of intermediate fertility. They are still light demanding and avoid dry soils. Surprisingly they favour a more oceanic climate than decreasing species and have similar preferences for a sub-oceanic climate as extinct species. However for species showing a decline nationally ('New Atlas') there is a suggestion (Figures 5.7–5.10) that they favour a slightly warmer climate.

Table 5.5 Nationally ('New Atlas') and locally increasing native and archaeophyte species

Native species		
Allium scorodoprasum	*Festuca arundinacea*	*Reseda lutea*
Allium vineale	*Festuca rubra s.l.*	*Ribes rubrum*
Anthyllis vulneraria s.l.	*Geranium lucidum*	*Rorippa palustris*
Aquilegia vulgaris	*Geranium pratense*	*Rorippa sylvestris*
Arabidopsis thaliana	*Glyceria maxima*	*Sagina apetala s.l.*
Atriplex littoralis	*Hypericum androsaemum*	*Salix pentandra*
Atriplex portulacoides	*Juncus subnodulosus*	*Schoenoplectus tabernaemontani*
Atriplex prostrata	*Lemna gibba*	*Solanum nigrum*
Avenula pratensis	*Leymus arenarius*	*Sorbus aucuparia*
Beta vulgaris ssp. maritima	*Limonium humile*	*Spergularia marina*
Blackstonia perfoliata	*Littorella uniflora*	*Spergularia rubra*
Calamagrostis epigejos	*Lythrum portula*	*Symphytum officinale*
Callitriche hermaphroditicum	*Milium effusum*	*Taxus baccata*
Callitriche obtusangula	*Myosotis secunda*	*Trifolium micranthum*
Carex pendula	*Myosotis sylvatica*	*Typha angustifolia*
Carex riparia	*Myriophyllum alterniflorum*	*Veronica catenata*
Catapodium marinum	*Nymphaea alba*	*Vicia hirsuta*
Catapodium rigidum	*Ophrys apifera*	*Vulpia bromoides*
Centaurium erythraea	*Parietaria judaica*	
Cerastium diffusum	*Phragmites australis*	**Archaeophyte species**
Cerastium glomeratum	*Plantago coronopus*	*Agrostis gigantea*
Cerastium semidecandrum	*Poa compressa*	*Armoracia rusticana*
Cochlearia danica	*Polystichum setiferum*	*Lamium hybridum*
Crambe maritima	*Populus tremula*	*Lepidium coronopus*
Crithmum maritimum	*Potamogeton coloratus*	*Mentha spicata*
Dipsacus fullonum	*Potamogeton pectinatus*	*Reseda luteola*
Erigeron acris	*Potamogeton pusillus*	*Salix viminalis*
Euonymus europaeus	*Ranunculus lingua*	*Thlaspi arvense*
	Raphanus raphanistrum ssp. maritimus	*Veronica hederifolia s.l.*

Table 5.6 Locally increasing but nationally declining ('New Atlas') native and archaeophyte species.

Native species

Aira caryophyllea
Atriplex glabriuscula
Berberis vulgaris*
Bidens cernua*
Bidens tripartita
Blysmus rufus
Brassica nigra
Cakile maritima*
Carex acuta*
Carex disticha
Carex pilulifera*
Carex pseudocyperus*
Cerastium arvense
Chamerion angustifolia
Convolvulus arvensis
Dactylorhiza incarnata s.l.
Echium vulgare*
Erodium cicutarium*
Eryngium maritimum
Filipendula vulgaris
Hymenophyllum tunbrigense
Ilex aquifolium*
Ligustrum vulgare*
Limonium vulgare
Lysimachia nummularia*
Nuphar lutea

Oenanthe fistulosa
Ornithopus perpusillus
Pastinaca sativa
Persicaria lapathifolium*
Polygala vulgaris s.s.
Ranunculus aquatilis
Ranunculus sceleratus
Sagina maritima*
Samolus valerandi*
Saxifraga granulata
Scrophularia auriculata*
Sedum acre*
Sedum telephium*
Silene uniflora
Spergularia media*
Spirodela polyrhiza
Tanacetum vulgare*
Trifolium arvense
Trifolium striatum*
Viola odorata*

Archaeophyte species

Artemisia vulgaris*
Lamium album
Lamium amplexicaule
Malva sylvestris*
Raphanus raphanistrum*
Stachys arvensis*

Table 5.7 Locally and nationally ('New Atlas') increasing but nationally declining ('Local Change') native and archaeophyte species.

Native Species

Anthyllis vulneraria
Atriplex portulacoides
Avenula pratensis
Calamagrostis epigejos
Callitriche obtusangula
Cerastium diffusum
Littorella uniflora
Milium effusum
Myriophyllum alterniflorum
Reseda lutea

Rorippa sylvestris
Schoenoplectus tabernaemontanii
Thalictrum minus
Typha latifolia
Veronica catenata

Archaeophyte species

Agrostis gigantea
Armoracia rusticana
Thlaspi arvense

* Species showing an in increase ('Local Change').

Table 5.8 Average values for climate and ecological preferences for native increasing species.

	Floristic element	Eastern limit	Light	Moisture	Reaction	Nutrient
Average nationally & locally increasing	7.1	3.4	7.3	6.6	6.6	5.1
Average nationally declining & locally increasing	6.9	3.6	7.4	6.2	6.4	4.8

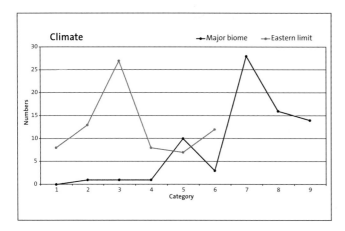

Figure 5.7 Geographical limits for increasing northern Lancashire species; (a) Major Biome and (b) Eastern limit.

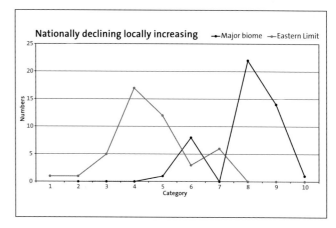

Figure 5.10 Geographical limits for nationally declining but locally increasing northern Lancashire species; (a) Major Biome and (b) Eastern limit.

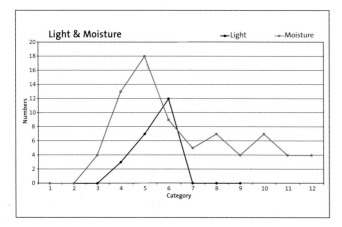

Figure 5.8 Ecological preferences for (a) Light and (b) Moisture for increasing northern Lancashire species.

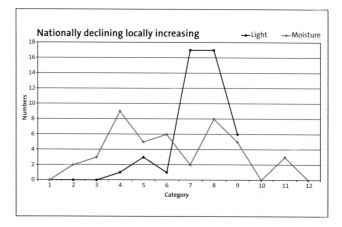

Figure 5.11 Ecological preferences for (a) Light and (b) Moisture for nationally declining but locally increasing northern Lancashire species.

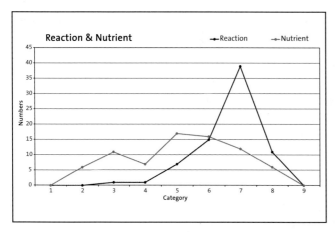

Figure 5.9 Ecological preferences (a) Reaction and (b) Nutrient for increasing northern Lancashire species.

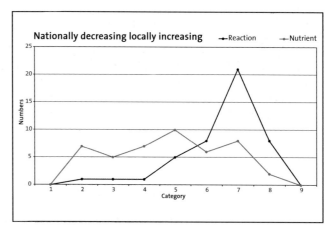

Figure 5.12 Ecological preferences (a) Reaction and (b) Nutrient for nationally declining but locally increasing northern Lancashire species.

Native and Archaeophyte species discovered in northern Lancashire since 1964 (excluding *Hieracium, Rubus* and *Taraxacum*)

A total of 33 species have been added to the native and archaeophyte flora of northern Lancashire since 1964 (Table 5.9). Most are species that were probably always present but were overlooked by earlier recorders.

The status of *Cirsium acaule* and *Brachypodium pinnatum* is unclear. *C. acaule* occurs in one locality where it may have been accidentally introduced. *B. pinnatum* is sometimes recorded in error for *B. sylvaticum* and in the absence of voucher specimens its presence should be regarded as doubtful. However in its more northerly British localities it often grows in hedgerows on clay soils and is easily overlooked.

One species, *Carex lasiocarpa*, has since been lost through habitat destruction.

Lathyrus nissolia may be spreading northwards naturally or perhaps is more likely a contaminant of grass seed used in amenity plantings and may not yet be fully established. Similarly *Trifolium ornithopodioides* and *Mibora minima* appeared casually as did *Mertensia maritima* in 1941. *Daphne mezereum* spread naturally into limestone woodlands but whether it has spread from garden plants or from native populations is unclear.

Fifteen species (marked with * in Table 5.9) have spread naturally into the region. Only for these species are date of first record, climate and ecological preferences relevant for the purposes of this analysis. There is no common factor influencing their spread. *Rorippa islandica* has spread south whilst *Carex divisa, Dactylorhiza praetermissa* and *Epilobium tetragonum* have spread north into the area. On the other hand the oceanic *Umbilicus rupestris* may have spread eastwards from Furness in Cumbria. Yet other species have exploited the fluctuating water levels of reservoirs, especially Stocks, e.g. *Persicaria minor, Juncus filiformis* and *Alopecurus aequalis*.

The climatic preferences for species that have spread naturally into the region vary from ones preferring warmer or Mediterranean climates to Boreal-montane species whilst eastern limits vary from Oceanic to Eurasian. Overall they are temperate species with tendencies towards oceanicity. Ecologically nutrient preferences vary from nutrient rich to nutrient poor but generally they prefer neutral substrates. They are fairly light demanding but moisture requirements vary considerably. In general these native immigrant species to northern Lancashire's flora are remarkable for their very small numbers and diverse climate and ecological preferences.

Table 5.9   Native species discovered in northern Lancashire since 1964

Species	Date of first record	Floristic element	Eastern limit	Light	Moisture	Reaction	Nutrient
Alchemilla minima							
*Alopecurus aequalis**	1971	5	6	8	9	4	7
Atriplex longipes							
Brachypodium pinnatum							
*Carex divisa**	2003	9	2	8	7	7	6
Carex strigosa							
Carex lasiocarpa							
*Ceratophyllum demersum**	1964	8	6	7	12	7	7
*Ceratophyllum submersum**	1966	7	4	7	12	8	8
Cirsium acaule							
*Dactylorhiza praetermissa**	1964	7	1	8	8	7	3
*Daphne mezereum**	1966	5	4	4	5	7	6
Dryopteris oreades							
*Epilobium tetragonum**	2005	7	4	6	7	5	5
Eriophorum latifolium							

Species	Date of first record	Floristic element	Eastern limit	Light	Moisture	Reaction	Nutrient
Glyceria declinata							
Gymnadenia borealis							
Hordelymus europaeus							
Juncus filiformis*	1978	4	6	7	9	6	4
Lathyrus nissolia*	1990						
Mibora minima*	2007	8	2	9	3	7	1
Myosotis stolonifera							
Persicaria minor*	1981	7	5	7	8	5	8
Persicaria mites							
Potentilla argentea*	1987	7	4	8	3	5	2
Rorippa islandica*	2003	4	4	8	8	7	6
Sorbus torminalis							
Trichomanes speciosum							
Trifolium ornithopodioides*	1999	8	2	9	6	5	3
Umbilicus rupestris*	2006	9	1	6	4	5	4
Utricularia australis							

Naturalised Introductions

The choice of species and hybrids considered as naturalised introductions in northern Lancashire is arbitrary. Generally they are taxa that have persisted for five or more years in one or more localities and appear to be reproducing or, if a single colony, it is expanding. Introductions or neophytes in northern Lancashire, which are thought to be archaeophytes or native species elsewhere in the country, are also included. These criteria give considerable scope for discussion as to what should or should not be included. Thus although it is regarded as a native or archaeophyte species in much of Britain *Conium maculatum* is included because in northern Lancashire, apart from its remains in Roman archaeological deposits, it seems to date only from 1874 and occurs in recently disturbed ruderal habitats. Other taxa have limited distributions. Thus *Lepidium latifolium* occurs in only one locality discovered in 1994 but is thriving whilst *Cyclamen hederifolium*, only found in 2008, is clearly naturalised and had been present in its single locality for many years.

Table 5.10 lists the first record of naturalised neophytes in northern Lancashire together with their geographical origin and possible means of introduction.

Table 5.10 Naturalised neophytes in northern Lancashire with date of first record, geographical origin (taken from Hill, *et al.*, 2004) and possible means of introduction to northern Lancashire.

Species	1st record	Geographical origin	How introduced to N. Lancs.
Acer platanoides	1964	Europe	Amenity
Acer pseudoplatanus	1874	Europe	Amenity
Acorus calamus	1858	Unknown	Garden, canal transport
Aesculus hippocastanum	1962	Europe	Amenity
Agrostis scabra	1964	N. America	Grain, rail transport

Species	1st record	Geographical origin	How introduced to N. Lancs.
Alchemilla conjuncta	1983	Europe	Garden
Alchemilla mollis	1981	Europe	Garden
Allium triquetrum	1999	Europe	Garden
Ambrosia psilostachya	1902	N. America	Grain
Arabis caucasica	1946	Europe	Garden
Arenaria balearica	1942	Europe	Garden
Aster novi-belgii	1965	Eastern N. America	Garden
Aster × salignus	1987	Garden origin	Garden
Astilbe chinensis	1970	Asia between 60°E & 120°E	Garden
Azolla filiculoides	1977	Western N. America, S. & central America	Garden aquatic
Ballota nigra	1903	Europe	Unknown
Barbarea intermedia	1965	Europe	Unknown
Borago officinalis	1858	Europe	Garden
Brassica napus	1874	Garden origin	Agriculture
Buddleja davidii	1966	Asia E. of 60°E	Garden
Buxus sempervirens	1902	Europe	Amenity
Calystegia pulchra	1964	Unknown	Garden
Calystegia silvatica	1920s	Europe	Garden
Campanula poscharskyana	1989	Europe	Garden
Campanula trachelium	1919	Europe	Garden
Cardamine bulbifera	1982	Europe	Garden
Centaurea montana	1966	Europe	Garden
Centranthus ruber	1878	Europe	Garden
Cicerbita macrophylla	1942	Europe	Garden
Cicerbita plumieri	1999	Europe	Garden
Claytonia perfoliata	1946	Western N. America	Garden
Claytonia sibirica	1902	Asia E. of 120°E, western N. America	Garden
Clematis vitalba	1899	Europe	Garden
Conium maculatum	1874(Roman)	Europe	Unknown
Conyza canadensis	1975	North America	Unknown
Cornus sericea	1986	North America	Amenity
Corrigiola litoralis	1965	Europe	Rail transport
Cotoneaster ascendens	1995	Asia E. 120°E	Garden
Cotoneaster bullatus	1984	Asia between 60°E & 120°E	Garden
Cotoneaster horizontalis	1967	Asia between 60°E & 120°E	Garden
Cotoneaster microphyllus	1902	Asia between 60°E & 120°E	Garden
Cotoneaster rehderi	1999	Asia E. 120°E	Garden
Cotoneaster simonsii	1967	Asia between 60°E & 120°E	Garden
Crassula helmsii	1984	Australia, New Zealand	Garden aquatic

Species	1st record	Geographical origin	How introduced to N. Lancs.
Crepis biennis	1941	Europe	Agricultural contaminant
Crepis vesicaria	1902	Europe	Unknown
Crocosmia × crocosmiiflora	1964	Garden origin	Garden
Crocus nudiflorus	1907	Europe	Garden
Cyclamen hederifolium	2008	Europe	Garden
Cymbalaria muralis	1874	Europe	Garden
Darmera peltata	1959	Western N. America	Garden
Diplotaxis muralis	1899	Europe	Grain
Doronicum pardalianches	1941	Europe	Garden
Elodea canadensis	1864	North America	Unknown
Elodea nuttallii	1976	North America	Garden aquatic
Epilobium brunnescens	1930	New Zealand	Garden
Epilobium ciliatum	1967	North America	Unknown
Eranthus hyemalis	1973	Europe	Garden
Erigeron glaucus	1970	North America	Garden
Erinus alpinus	1942	Europe	Garden
Euphorbia cyparissias	1897	Europe	Garden
Euphorbia × pseudoesula	1999	Europe	Garden
Fallopia baldschuanica	1962	Asia between 60°E & 120°E	Garden
Fallopia japonica	1962	Asia E. of 120°E	Garden
Fallopia sachalinensis	1963	Asia E. of 120°E	Garden
Fallopia × bohemica	1985	Europe	Garden
Ficus carica	1968(Roman)	Asia E. of 60°E	Unknown
Foeniculum vulgare	1862	Europe	Garden
Galanthus nivalis	1858	Europe	Garden, amenity
Galinsoga quadriradiata	1962	South America and/or Central America	Unknown
Geranium endressii	1964	Europe	Garden
Geranium phaeum	1858	Europe	Garden
Geranium pyrenaicum	1833	Europe	Garden
Geranium × oxonianum	1962	Garden origin	Garden
Heracleum mantegazzianum	1960	Europe	Garden
Hesperis matronalis	1868	Europe	Garden
Hippophae rhamnoides	1905	Europe	Amenity
Hordeum murinum	1899	Europe	Docks
Hyacinthoides × massartiana	1965	Unknown	Garden
Hypericum calycinum	1973	Europe	Garden
Hypericum xylosteifolium	1980	Garden origin	Amenity
Impatiens glandulifera	1946	Asia between 60°E & 120°E	Garden
Impatiens parviflora	1966	Asia between 60°E & 120°E	Amenity

Species	1st record	Geographical origin	How introduced to N. Lancs.
Juncus tenuis	1925	North, South and/or Central America	Unknown
Lactuca serriola	1900	Europe	Unknown
Lagarosiphon major	1997	Southern Africa	Garden aquatic
Lagurus ovatus	1998	Europe	Garden
Lamiastrum galeobdolon ssp. *argentatum*	1987	Unknown	Garden
Lamium maculatum	1858	Europe	Garden
Larix decidua	1978	Europe	Forestry/amenity
Lathyrus latifolius	1965	Europe	Garden
Lepidium didymum	1915	Unknown	Unknown
Lepidium draba	1900	Europe	Unknown
Lepidium latifolium	1994	Europe	Unknown
Leucanthemum × superbum	1967	Garden origin	Garden
Ligustrum ovalifolium	1964	Asia E. of 120°E	Garden
Lilium martagon	1949	Europe, Asia between 60°E & 120°E	Garden
Lilium pyrenaicum	1965	Europe	Garden
Linaria purpurea	1966	Europe	Garden
Linaria repens	1881	Europe	Garden
Lobularia maritima	1960s	Europe	Garden
Lonicera nitida	1986	Europe	Garden
Lonicera xylosteum	1875	Europe, Asia between 60°E & 120°E	Amenity
Lycium barbarum	1933	Asia E. of 60°E	Amenity
Lysimachia punctata	1963	Europe	Garden
Mahonia aquifolium	1967	Western N. America	Garden
Malus pumila	1888	Garden origin	Garden
Malva arborea	1991	Europe	Garden
Matricaria discoidea	1902	Asia E. of 120°E, North America	Grain, Docks
Meconopsis cambrica	1863	Europe	Garden
Medicagao sativa	1900	Europe	Agriculture
Melilotus albus	1903	Europe, Asia between 60°E & 120°E	Grain, Docks
Melilotus officinalis	1961	Europe, Asia between 60° & 120°E	Agriculture contaminant
Mimulus guttatus	1887	Western N. America	Garden
Mimulus moschatus	1958	Western N. America	Garden
Mimulus × robertsii	1978	Garden origin	Unknown
Muscari armeniacum	1987	Garden origin	Garden
Myrrhis odorata	1858	Europe	Garden
Narcissus agg.	1987	Garden origin	Garden, amenity

Species	1st record	Geographical origin	How introduced to N. Lancs.
Nymphoides peltata	1984	Europe	Garden aquatic
Oenothera biennis	1898	North America	Garden
Oenothera glazioviana	1888	North America	Garden
Oenothera stricta	1998	South America and/or Central America	Amenity
Omphalodes verna	1902	Europe	Garden
Ornithogalum umbellatum	1775	Europe	Garden
Oxalis corniculata	1834	Unknown	Garden
Parthenocissus vitacea	1988	North America	Garden
Parthenocissus quinquefolia	1965	North America	Garden
Petasites fragrans	1900	Europe	Garden
Picea abies	1978	Europe, Asia E. of 60°E	Forestry
Picea sitchensis	1987	Western N. America	Forestry
Pilosella aurantiaca	1902	Europe	Garden
Polygonatum × hybridum	1966	Garden origin	Garden
Populus alba	1907	Europe, Asia between 60°E & 120°E	Amenity
Populus × canadensis	1965	Garden origin	Amenity
Populus × canescens	1987	Europe	Amenity
Pseudofumaria lutea	1860	Europe	Garden
Pulmonaria officinalis	1901	Europe	Garden
Quercus cerris	1902	Europe	Amenity
Rhododendron 'ponticum' (hybrid origin)	1962	Britain (endemic)	Amenity
Rhododendron groenlandicum	1972	North America	Unknown
Ribes nigrum	1877	Europe, Asia between 60°E & 120°E	Garden
Ribes sanguineum	1960s	Western N. America	Garden
Ribes uva-crispa	1874	Europe	Garden
Rosa multiflora	1965	Asia E. of 120°E	Garden
Rosa rugosa	1946	Asia E. of 120°	Garden, amenity
Rubus parviflorus	1975	Western N. America	Amenity
Rumex scutatus	1972	Europe	Garden
Sagittaria sagittifolia	1875	Europe	Canal, transport
Salvia verticillata	1903	Europe	Garden
Saxifraga cymbalaria	2007	Europe	Garden
Saxifraga hirsuta	1858	Europe	Garden
Saxifraga × polita	1857	Europe	Garden
Saxifraga × urbium	1965	Garden origin	Garden
Sedum album	1891	Europe	Garden
Sedum spurium	1967	Garden origin	Garden
Sempervivum tectorum	1837	Europe	Garden
Senecio ovatus	1892	Europe	Garden

Species	1st record	Geographical origin	How introduced to N. Lancs.
Senecio sarracenicus	1857	Europe, Asia between 60°E & 120°E	Garden
Senecio squalidus	1948	Garden origin	Unknown
Senecio viscosus	1688	Europe	Unknown
Senecio × albescens	1985	Europe	Unknown
Sisymbrium altissimum	1900	Europe	Grain, Docks
Sisymbrium orientale	1907	Europe	Grain
Solidago canadensis	1960s	North America	Garden
Solidago gigantea	1971	North America	Garden
Sorbus croceocarpa	1983	Unknown	Amenity
Sorbus intermedia	1967	Europe	Amenity
Spiraea douglasii	1970	Western N. America	Garden
Spiraea japonica	1987	Japan	Garden
Stachys byzantina	2003	Garden origin	Garden
Stratiotes aloides	1858	Europe	Garden
Symphoricarpos albus	1908	North America	Amenity, game cover
Symphytum × uplandicum	1831	Europe	Garden
Tilia × europaea	1970	Europe	Amenity
Tolmiea menziesii	1957	Western N. America	Garden
Trifolium hybridum	1887	Europe	Agriculture
Verbascum virgatum	1832	Europe	Accidental
Veronica filiformis	1941	Europe	Garden
Veronica peregrina	1902	North America, South and/or Central America	Accidental
Veronica persica	1862(Roman)	Europe	Accidental
Veronica polita	1858	Europe, Asia between 60°E & 120°E	Accidental

Out of a total of 612 neophyte species recorded in the area approximately 167 are naturalised. In addition of the 170 hybrids recorded in northern Lancashire fourteen are naturalised and most are recent garden escapes.

Table 5.11. indicates that most naturalised neophyte taxa (species and hybrids) arrived in the region in the last 100 years.

Better recording in recent years has ensured that neophytes growing in the wild are recorded but additionally it is likely that increased levels of communication between Britain and other parts of the world together with a flourishing horticultural industry constantly importing new plants for British gardens has ensured an increasing potential for garden

Table 5.11 Period of first record for naturalised neophyte taxa

Period of first record	Numbers of taxa
Before 1800	2
1800–1850	5
1851–1900	41
1901–1950	37
1951–2000	92
Since 2001	3

plants to escape into the wild. Furthermore some of these garden plants have arisen by hybridisation either accidentally, e.g. *Senecio × albescens,* or deliberately synthesised by horticulturists, e.g. *Crocosmia × crocosmiiflora.*

By using the published notes in the 'New Atlas' and elsewhere it is possible to show the origin of many naturalised neophytes and how they came into the region although it is likely that many were established elsewhere in the country before spreading into northern Lancashire. Thus although most naturalised neophytes were first recorded in northern Lancashire after 1950 this may reflect an absence of recording in earlier years. Table 5.10 demonstrates that the majority were garden escapes and to a lesser extent were escapes from amenity and game plantings. However Dehnen-Schmutz and Williamson (2006) pointed out that of 348 species listed as garden escapes by Clement and Foster (1994) and Ryves, *et al.* (1996) 95% were introduced into the British Isles before 1900.

To be successful garden plant taxa must be able to cope with northern Lancashire's temperate climate and spread either vegetatively or by seed. Thus all the naturalised neophytes are from temperate climates but have come from all parts of the temperate world. Nevertheless most have originated in Europe and often from somewhat warmer climates than those found in northern Lancashire. Dehnen-Schmutz and Williamson (2006) suggested that one of the key variables explaining biological invasions and the successful establishment of neophytes is propagule pressure. This is the product of the number of introductions and the number of propagules in each introduction. These conclusions concerning the character of naturalised introductions are in line with the conclusions reached for the alien flora more generally in the British Isles (Crawley, *et al.*, 1996).

Changes in the northern Lancashire flora

The changes and trends described for the northern Lancashire flora over the last 100 years are consistent with other studies. Greenwood (2003) provided an analysis of change for the flora of VC 60 over the same period and provided further detail for habitats than is described here. However the present account covers a larger area (VC 60 and Lancashire VC 64) and with the benefit of further analysis during the last six years or so numbers will have changed. Even

so the main conclusions that the changes in the flora correlate with increasing nutrient and base status of substrates with some evidence for climate warming were confirmed. These conclusions are in line with the predictions of Sala, *et al.* (2000) who suggested that by 2100 the most important drivers for change in global diversity in descending order of importance would be: land use change, climate, nitrogen deposition, biotic exchange and atmospheric carbon dioxide concentration. Uniquely for the northern temperate biome the most important driver for change was predicted to be nitrogen deposition with climate change only marginally more important than other drivers.

Further experimental evidence is provided by Stevens, *et al.* (2004). They demonstrated that in a study of 68 acid grasslands across Great Britain longterm chronic nitrogen depositions from agriculture and fossil fuels has significantly reduced plant species richness. They showed that species adapted to infertile conditions are systematically reduced at high nitrogen depositions and at 17kg N/ha/year there is a 23% species reduction compared with grasslands receiving the lowest levels of nitrogen deposition (less than 6kg/ha/year). The higher rates of nitrogen deposition are typical of Lancashire and Bowland and suggest that atmospheric nitrogen deposition is a causal agent for species loss in the region.

However on sand dunes Plassmann, *et al.* (2009) showed that atmospheric nitrogen deposition up to 15kg/ha/year caused no change in species composition over two years although above ground biomass increased. They suggested that over a longer time scale community changes may occur and that the critical load for nitrogen deposition may be lower than 20kg/ha/year. It may be significant therefore that Smith (2009a) in his studies on the Sefton coast sand dunes in Merseyside (VC 59) found little reduction in species diversity and that some species characteristic of less eutrophic conditions were thriving, e.g. *Blysmus compressus* (Smith, 2009b).

A more robust view of extinction is taken in this review than in 2003 (Greenwood, 2003), as several species thought to be present in 2002 are now believed lost. As a consequence nearly 6% of the native flora is now thought to be extinct, an increase of nearly 2% but still below that of other northern counties, except Northumberland at 2.4% (Swann, 1993) although more species may have been lost since that Flora was written.

More detailed analysis of changes in northern Lancashire's flora suggests that climate changes may be more complex than simple warming might imply. Part of the difficulty involves distinguishing between changes that might be caused by eutrophication and changes in temperature or oceanicity. Species characteristic of nutrient poor substrates are often ones that are characteristic of oceanic climates. Thus the preferences of extinct species suggest that more oceanic species and species preferring nutrient poor soils were lost perhaps correlating with eutrophication and a less oceanic climate. Allen (1953) noted the connection with oceanicity in the Isle of Man and suggested the climate was perhaps less oceanic. However changes in oceanicity are likely to be slight. British weather is very variable on a day-to-day, month-to-month or even on an annual basis making trends in climate change difficult to observe. Nevertheless the long-term trend for Central England shows a warming of about 0.7°C over 300 years and of about 0.5°C during the twentieth century (Hulme and Jenkins, 1998). Furthermore this warming trend is greater in winter (1.1°C) than in summer (0.2°C). Whilst these trends are reflected throughout the British Isles the correlation becomes weaker to the north and west (Hulme and Barrow, 1997). Rainfall is especially variable but there is a suggestion that winter precipitation has increased in northern Britain (Hulme and Barrow, 1997; Hulme and Jenkins, 1998) whilst summer precipitation has decreased in south-eastern England. This probably means that in northern England long-term changes are minimal. Thus even if rainfall is showing little long-term change the greater warming taking place in winter relative to summer results in a slightly more oceanic climate.

Thus the correlations observed for decreasing and increasing species show a continuing trend for species susceptible to eutrophication to be lost while the correlation with climate indicates that species preferring a warmer and more oceanic climate are favoured.

The reviews on the changing flora of the British Isles in the 'New Atlas and in 'Local Change' make the same correlations with eutrophication and a warmer climate but no link with changing oceanicity was observed.

An attempt was made to assess the causes of extinction but for most species, especially those lost before 1900, the reason for the loss is unknown. It is clear, however, that for many species losses were caused by changes in farming. Reclamation of commons in the eighteenth and early nineteenth centuries caused the loss of heaths with their conversion mostly to grasslands through drainage and fertilizer applications. These changes probably account for the loss of *Pilularia globulifera*, *Radiola linoides* and *Gentiana pneumonanthe*. A few were lost with the direct destruction of their habitat for building etc., e.g. *Juncus balticus*, *Wahlenbergia hederacea* (in VC 60 only) and *Carex lasiocarpa*. For many it is believed generalised nutrient enrichment caused extinction, e.g. *Gnaphalium sylvaticum*, *Centunculus minimus*, *Platanthera bifolia*, *Antennaria dioica*, *Gentianella campestris*, *Neotinea ustulata* and *Coeloglossum viride*. For a few species the final loss was caused by a specific event. Thus *Genista anglica* succumbed to a fire on Melling Common and whilst this could not have been a unique event the recovered vegetation appeared to be lusher and in any case there was no nearby seed source for re-colonisation. However for most species the cause of extinction is not clear.

Future changes

This account of the flora of northern Lancashire demonstrates that the climate and character of the substrate on which plants grow determines what grows where. However the impact of the last ice age was to eliminate all vascular plants from the region and only a limited number of species of those that might have spread into the area from continental Europe did so as the ice retreated. It is possible that some species spread into northern Lancashire but subsequently died out but without archaeological evidence they remain unknown.

The spread of humans into the region began to have a major impact on the vegetation and the flora from the Neolithic period onwards. New species were introduced accidentally or deliberately (archaeophytes) and centuries of grazing reduced woodland cover and encouraged the development of heaths. Yet overall climate seems to have been the dominant influence even if the distribution and abundance of vegetation types and species varied enormously. It is not until the last few hundred years during a period of relative climate stability that the human influence can be seen to be the major determinant governing changes in the presence and distribution of vegetation types and species. Yet changes in native species over the last 50 years or so show that extinctions are limited (23 since 1950) whilst 15 species have spread into the region; a net loss of 8, a remarkably small number. However many native species exist in small numbers in a few localities. Perhaps a third (*c.* 300 taxa) of the flora is endangered and many of these are included in the Lancashire Biodiversity Action Plan. Despite the loss of species and the apparently large number of taxa on the brink of extinction the analysis of native species showing an increase or decrease over the last 100 years indicates that more species (122) are increasing their range than are declining (95); a net balance 27 species that are increasing rather than decreasing.

Thus the trends noted for northern Lancashire confirm the predictions of Max Walters (Walters, 1970) that the British flora would become more diverse through the naturalisation of introductions not only in northern Lancashire but nationally (Walker, 2007). In northern Lancashire at least 23% of taxa (181 out of 782) have become naturalised.

In recent years, with the appreciation that climate change might have an impact on the distribution of species, interest has developed on the significance of species at the edge of their present geographical range. Within the British Isles the decline of many species, e.g. *Primula farinosa*, at the edge of their range has been demonstrated (Preston, *et al.*, 2002). Preston (2007) showed that despite the impoverished European flora found in the British Isles the latitudinal position of the islands was pivotal with many species having a predominantly southern distribution reaching their northern limits in the British Isles.

He analysed the distribution of 1342 species occurring in the British Isles and found that 173 reached their northern European limits between 50° and 55° N corresponding to the latitudes spanned by England. A further 252 species reached their northern European limits between 55° and 60° N or equivalent to the latitudes of Scotland.

Northern Lancashire is in the centre of the British Isles and it might be expected that many of the species reaching their northern limits in the British Isles might do so in the region. Of the first group with northern limits between 50° and 55° N only 7.5% occur in the area. However 56% of the second group with their northern limits in Scotland occur in northern Lancashire. All these species are at the edge of their present natural (i.e. not introduced) European geographical range.

An analysis of northern species reaching their southern limits in the British Isles was less satisfactory as many species occurred on European mountains further south. Analysis of the eastern limits of oceanic species was also not attempted although the small group of hyperoceanic species, e.g. filmy ferns, often occur no further east than northern Lancashire. As the British Isles are on the western edge of Europe any species with a main centre of distribution in central Europe is of necessity at the western margin of its European distribution. The small group of continental species found in the British Isles are mostly found in eastern England. Nevertheless one of these, *Carex ericetorum*, is found in northern Lancashire. Most are endangered in Britain.

It may be assumed that small changes in climate would cause the extinction of species at the edge of their geographical or climate range. In a further analysis Preston (2007) found that 64% of continental, hyperoceanic, northern and southern species, which are at or near the edge of their range in the British Isles are threatened with extinction. Most of these species are found in only a few places in localised habitats where perhaps the presence of a microclimate favouring particular species may be important. This is likely to be the situation for the hyperoceanic species found on Ward's Stone in northern Lancashire: they are intolerant of both frost and drought yet in recent years they have survived both the severe winter of 1962/3 and the summer droughts of 1975 and 1976. Whilst these weather events were unusual in the context of the last 100 years they would have occurred many times over the last 6,000 years, which is the timescale that they may be presumed to have occurred on the fell. They survive in deep recesses of boulder covered cliffs, which provide a niche habitat where an equable oceanic climate persists in periods of more generalised climate stress.

Thus it is believed that many rare and endangered species at the edge of their geographical range are susceptible to minor changes in climate. However other environmental factors or habitat changes that cause stress may limit their distribution. It is possible that some declining species at the edge of their range are also declining throughout their range but because they are more abundant within their main area of distribution this decline is not apparent. Thus the northern-montane species *Cirsium heterophyllum*, *Geranium sylvaticum* and *Trollius europaeus* are declining at the southern edge of their range in Bowland but apparently are not in danger further north. However, Bradshaw (2009) showed that this is not the case and that these three species are declining in Teesdale where they were abundant and a feature of the meadows. She gives a number of causes for their loss all of which are applicable in Lancashire. It is unlikely that the small changes in the climate that have been observed so far have had any affect on their distribution. There is no doubt that the main causes for their loss are changes in agricultural practice and generalised nutrient enrichment.

Shedding further light on the hypothesis that non-climatic factors are causing changes in the distribution of many species Grime, *et al.* (2007) referred to two research projects. One series of projects showed that in densely populated European countries increasing species diversity included a high proportion of 'weedy' species or ones that favoured nutrient rich and disturbed habitats whereas declining species were stress tolerators or species that were long-lived and slow growing and were found in unproductive or nutrient poor habitats. It has been shown earlier in this work that a similar situation occurs in northern Lancashire. In another project experiments were designed to assess the importance of temperature and rainfall on two calcareous grasslands. One was upland grassland of low fertility composed of stress-tolerant species; the other, lowland grassland with soils of high fertility and with vegetation intolerant of stress. The response to variation in temperature and rainfall produced different results. At the upland site there were only minor changes in vegetation but at the lowland site there were rapid changes in species abundance. It is suggested that in soils of low fertility, where so much of the vegetation and many of the species are of high conservation value, the response to climate change is likely to be slow.

Research reported by Crawford (2008) on plants growing at the margin of their range, and particularly those in the Arctic where climate change impact is likely to be high, also showed that many species are resilient to climate change.

Although plants have geographical limits believed to be determined by climate they may nevertheless have broad tolerance limits. This could be due to the ability of some species to survive in a vegetative state. Pigott and Huntley (1978, 1980 and 1981) demonstrated that *Tilia cordata* rarely sets seed at its northern limits around Morecambe Bay. Similarly *Rubus chamaemorus* survives at its southern limits in Wales and the southern Pennines on blanket bogs yet rarely produces viable fruit. In the former species summers are rarely warm enough for seed to be produced whilst winters are rarely cold enough for Cloudberry to flower and fruit successfully. Both can survive without reproducing sexually for a very long time. Even the hyperoceanic and critically endangered *Trichomanes speciosum* survives periods of unfavourable climate. Here the strategy adopted is to grow in a niche habitat with a localised humid and equitable climate and to survive in the gametophyte generation (Loriot and Magnanon, 2006). Thus in northern Lancashire the attractive sporophyte has never been seen.

Species diversity tends to increase at marginal interfaces (Crawford, 2008) but perhaps more important species that do not normally grow in close proximity meet and may hybridise. Sand dunes provide many marginal habitats and opportunities for hybridisation and the number of *Salix* hybrids on the coast of north-western England, especially on the Sefton coast, is remarkable (Savidge, *et al.*, 1963). Until Stace (1975) drew attention to the significance of hybrids in the British flora they tended to be overlooked, yet their ecological and phytogeographical importance may be profound. The ecological significance of *Spartina anglica* formed from the hybridisation between *S. maritima* and *S. alterniflora* is well known. Equally important but much less appreciated is the presence of *Elytrigia* × *drucei*. Until recently this hybrid was confused with one of its parents, *E. atherica*. This is a southern temperate species and today probably reaches its northern limits on the Dee estuary where it is sterile. Further north the hybrid often dominates the upper parts of ungrazed salt marshes. The ability to survive and even spread vegetatively over long periods of time is illustrated by two further perennial hybrid taxa.

Circaea × *intermedia* and *Trichophorum* × *foersteri* are both sterile and have one scarce boreal-montane parent whilst the other is more widespread. In the case of *Circaea* × *intermedia* the scarce parent is *C. alpina* found in bryophyte-rich oak woodlands in mountainous areas of western Britain. It has never been found in northern Lancashire and it is probable that these habitats have not been present in the area for several thousand years. Nevertheless *C.* × *intermedia* is frequent in northern Bowland woodlands. Less is known about the scarce parent of *Trichophorum* × *foersteri*. This is *T. cespitosum*, which probably occurs in mires where there is some water movement and base enrichment. There are few habitats of this kind in northern Lancashire and it is likely that *T.* × *foersteri* has persisted for thousands of years long after the original hybridisation event(s) and the extinction of *T. cespitosum* in the area, although it is possible that the latter taxon could survive somewhere in the region. In both cases it is possible that their extinction was caused by a change in climate. Perhaps the change to a more oceanic climate in the late Flandrian some 3000 BP eradicated their preferred habitat. At that time peat bogs advanced, soils became more acid and there was increased podsolisation, all changes of which *C. alpina* and *T. cespitosum* were probably intolerant.

Because predicted climate changes over the next 100 years may be greater in south-eastern than in north-western Britain it is likely that floristic changes will be more muted in northern Lancashire. Furthermore as the present native flora in northern Lancashire has already survived major climate changes over the last 5,000 years small climatic changes are likely to have only a minimal impact on the flora. Nevertheless the historical record of the colonisation of the British Isles following the retreat of the ice (*c.* 12,000BP) shows that species can respond rapidly to a changing climate. What governs the speed of plant response to climate change is not understood.

Nevertheless whilst many species respond slowly to slow changes in climate a sudden severe weather or other event could be of considerable importance. Such was the case in 1967 when a severe storm hit Mallowdale Fell (Garnett, 2002; Kenyon, 2008). Here the Lary Syke (SD62.59.) was, in 1964, a deep-sided gully draining into the R. Roeburn with a few Juniper bushes growing on its steep banks. However the 1967 storm initiated considerable erosion on the Fell and the Juniper was lost. An earlier storm may have caused the collapse of riverside cliffs and the eradication of *Asplenium viride* in southern Bowland (Weld, *c.* 1888). A sudden change in climate could cause considerable vegetation change over a short time scale. However, most examples are palaeo-ecological (Smith, 2011). With so many northern Lancashire species occurring in small quantity at only a few sites catastrophic events of whatever kind could be highly damaging to the survival of several species.

Perhaps the most significant impact of global warming is the raising of sea levels, which could cause a re-alignment of the coastline. Even in the last 1000 years the position of the coast has fluctuated but salt marshes and sand dunes have always survived somewhere. However at some point rising sea levels will erode the present marshes and dunes so that unless they can develop on slightly higher ground further inland they will disappear.

In addition to global warming humans continue to have other profound effects on the environment. The combination of habitat destruction and creation together with pollution of varying forms, especially nitrogen, shows no sign of abating and sensitive species will disappear unless more active conservation measures are taken to ensure their survival. With continuing eutrophication robust species will flourish and those able to do so will exploit new habitats.

If new species are to become established in the region they must have vacant niches to exploit or must be more competitive than existing species. There must be a suitable propagule source that can exert sufficient propagule pressure for colonization to occur (see Naturalised Introductions, page 603). They must have a means by which they can spread, not necessarily by seed (Crawley, *et al.*, 1996). *Fallopia japonica*, an introduction, is more or less sterile in Great Britain yet spreads readily by vegetative means, presumably aided by human and other animal intervention. Thus to spread into the region new species must have a suitable vector and often this will be directly or indirectly by human intervention. A warming climate will allow further species from slightly warmer countries to become established although a severe winter every thirty years or so could reverse a medium term trend. Furthermore the pool from which to supply possible taxa is limited unless winters are frost free. Frost free winters imply a much greater warming than is currently predicted but the dark days of winter would also limit the numbers of species that might survive. However frost free winters might have profound implications for native temperate species requiring frost for successful germination, spring bud burst and flowering. These constraints for the spread of native species are considerable and may explain the small number of native species that have spread into the region in the last 100 years. Conversely the loss of species with more northerly distributions is likely to be slow unless the habitats change either by a changing climate or other causes.

If conservation measures for the existing native flora can be considerably enhanced limited climate change will have limited direct impact. Nevertheless so long as the British enjoy gardening and amenity plantings continue, the overall species diversity will increase, but as in the past some taxa will be invasive and a few will be new to science.

6. References

Abbott, P.P. (2005). *Plant atlas of Mid-west Yorkshire.* Yorkshire Naturalists' Union. Kendal.

Adam, P. (2000). Morecambe Bay saltmarshes: 25 years of change in Sherwood, B.R., Gardiner, B.G. and Harris, T., eds, *British Saltmarshes.* Forest Text for the Linnean Society of London. London.

Agricultural Statistics (No Date). Statistics for the period 1870–1980 were obtained from 'Agricultural Statistics Parish Summaries, MAF/68' at National Archives, Kew and for 1999 from 'Agricultural and Horticultural Census: 1 June 1999' at Department for Environment, Food and Rural Affairs, Peasholme Green, York.

Allen, D.E. (1953). Botanical indications of a possible climatic change in the Irish Sea area. *The Irish Naturalists' Journal,* **11**: 77–78.

Allen, D.E. and Hatfield, G. (2004). *Medicinal plants in folk tradition.* Timber Press. Portland, Oregon and Cambridge.

Anderton, S. (2002). Flashy offspring may not survive. *The Times,* March 19 2002.

Anon. (1821). Beauties of the North Wyresdale. *Lonsdale Magazine,* **2**: 201.

Anon. (1829). *History of Lytham.*

Anon. (1891). *Flora of the Stonyhurst District.* 2nd ed. Parkinson and Blacow. Clitheroe.

Anon. (1909). Newton. Yorkshire Naturalists' visit. *Clitheroe Times,* June 4 1909..

Anon. (1933). Plant notes for 1933 [Record for *Chiastophyllum oppositifolia* at Matlock]. *The Botanical Society and Exchange Club of the British Isles Report for 1933,* **10**: 468–487.

Anon. (1971). *Wildlife conservation and hill farming. Saddle Side Farm, Chipping.* Ministry of Agriculture, Fisheries and Food, Agricultural Development and Advisory Service; Lancashire Naturalists Trust in conjunction with the City of Liverpool Museum. Typescript deposited at World Museum Liverpool, National Museums Liverpool.

Anon. (1983). Handwritten notes in a copy of the 1891 *Flora of the Stonyhurst District* acquired by Stonyhurst College 8 March 1983. [Most records are from the 1960s and it is suggested these may have been written by Arthur Hitchin of Accrington.]

Anon. [1997]. *The character of England.* Countryside Commission, English Nature.

Anon. (2007). *Biodiversity reporting and information group. Report on the species and habitat review.* Joint Nature Conservation Committee UK BAP. Website Report.

Anon. (2008). *A living landscape for the north west.* Cumbria Wildlife Trust on behalf of the Wildlife Trusts in the North West.

Archer, E. (1999). A history of the stone jetty, Morecambe. *Lancashire History Quarterly,* **3**: 41–45, 117–121.

Ash, H. (1999). Man-made habitats of the Mersey Basin: what is new? In Greenwood, E.F., ed., *Ecology and landscape development: a history of the Mersey Basin.* Liverpool University Press. National Museums & Galleries on Merseyside. Liverpool.

Ashfield, C.J. (1858). On the Flora of Preston and its neighbourhood. Part 1. *Historic Society of Lancashire and Cheshire Transactions,* **10**:143 –164.

Ashfield, C.J. (1860). On the Flora of Preston and neighbourhood. Part 2. *Historic Society of Lancashire and Cheshire Transactions,* **12**: 127–134.

Ashfield, C.J. (1862). On the Flora of Preston and neighbourhood. Part 3. *Transactions of the Historic Society of Lancashire and Cheshire,* **14**: 1–6.

Ashfield, C.J. (1864). A list of Silverdale plants. *The Botanists' Chronicle,* **10**: 73–75.

Ashfield, C.J. (1865). On the Flora of Preston and the Neighbourhood. Part 4. *Transactions of the Historic Society of Lancashire and Cheshire,* **17**:181–186.

Atkinson, D. and Houston, J., eds (1993). *The sand dunes of the Sefton coast.* National Museum & Galleries on Merseyside in association with Sefton Metropolitan Borough Council. Liverpool.

Atkinson, D., Smart, R.A., Fairhurst, J., Oldfield, P. and Lageard, J.G.A. (1999). A history of woodland in the Mersey Basin in, Greenwood, E.F., ed., *Ecology and landscape development: a history of the Mersey Basin.* Liverpool University Press. National Museums & Galleries on Merseyside. Liverpool

Averis, A.M., Averis, A.B.G., Birks, H.J.B., Horsfield, D., Thompson, D.B.A. and Yeo, M.J.M. (2004). *An illustrated guide to British upland vegetation.* Joint Nature Conservation Committee. Peterborough.

Backmeroff, C., Spencer, J. and Whitehead, A. (1988). *Lancashire inventory of ancient woodlands (provisional).* Report prepared on behalf of Chief Scientist's Directorate, Nature Conservancy Council. Peterborough.

Bailey, C. (1902). 11. On the adventitious vegetation of the sandhills of St Anne's-on-the-Sea, North Lancashire (Vice-County 60). *Manchester Memoirs,* **47**: 1–8.

Bailey, C. (1907). X1. Further notes on the adventitious vegetation of the sandhills of St. Anne's-on-the-Sea,

North Lancashire (Vice-county 60). *Manchester Memoirs,* **51**: 1–16.

Bailey, C. (1908). *Asphodelus fistulosus* L. in Plant Records. *Botanical Society and Exchange Club Report for 1907,* p. 311.

Bailey, C. (1910). XV. A third list of the adventitious vegetation of the sandhills of St. Anne's-on-the-Sea, North Lancashire, vice-county 60. *Manchester Memoirs, 54*: 1–11.

Baker, J.G. (1885). *A Flora of the English Lake District.* George Bell & Sons. London.

Bangerter, E.B. (1964). Veronica peregrina L. in the British Isles. *Proceedings of the Botanical Society of the British Isles,* **5**: 303 –313.

Bangerter, E.B. and Kent, D.H. (1957). *Veronica filiformis* Sm. in the British Isles. *Proceedings of the Botanical Society of the British Isles,* **2**: 197–217.

Belyaeva, I. (2009). Nomenclature of *Salix fragilis* L. and a new species, *S. euxina* (Salicaceae). *Taxon,* **58**: 1344–1348.

Berry, W.G. (1967). Salt marsh development in the Ribble estuary in Stead, R.W. and Lawton, R., eds, *Liverpool Essays in Geography. A Jubilee Collection.* Longmans. London.

Best, R.H. and Coppock, J.T. (1962). *The changing use of land in Britain.* Faber and Faber. London.

Bickham, S.H. (1914). Record for *Montia parvifolia* at Leagram Hall in Report for 1913. *The Botanical Exchange Club and Society,* **3**: 461.

Birks, H.J.B. and Deacon, J. (1973). A numerical analysis of the past and present flora of the British Isles. *New Phytologist,* **72**: 877–902.

Blackburn Field Club (1925). Blackburn Field Club. A visit to the Preston and Kendal Canal on August 29th. *Lancashire and Cheshire Naturalist,* **17**: 267–268.

Boothby, J., ed. (1997). *British pond landscapes.* Pond *life* Project. Liverpool.

Boothby, J., ed. (2000). *A landscape worth saving. Final report of the pond diversity survey of North west England.* The Pond *Life* Project. Liverpool.

Boothby, J. and Hull, A. (1999). Ponds of the Mersey Basin: habitat, status and future in Greenwood, E.F., ed., *Ecology and landscape development. A history of the Mersey Basin.* Liverpool University Press. National Museums & Galleries on Merseyside. Liverpool.

Bowra, J.C. (1998). *Oenothera* in Rich, T.C.G. and Jermy, A.C. (1998). *Plant Crib.* Botanical Society of the British Isles. London.

Bradshaw, A.D. (1999). Urban wastelands – new niches and primary succession in Greenwood, E.F., ed., *Ecology and landscape development: a history of the Mersey Basin.* University of Liverpool. National Museum & Galleries on Merseyside. Liverpool.

Bradshaw, M.E. (2009). The decline of Lady's-mantles (*Alchemilla vulgaris* L. agg.) and other hay meadow species in Northern England since the 1950s. *Watsonia,* **27**: 315–321.

Braithwaite, M. (2005). *Arctium* – has Stace got it wrong? *BSBI News,* **98**: 23–25.

Braithwaite, M.E., Ellis, R.W. and Preston, C.D. (2006). *Change in the British Flora 1987–2004.* Botanical Society of the British Isles. London.

Braun-Blanquet, J. (1928). *Pflanzensoziologie. Grundzügeder Vegetationskunde.* Springer. Berlin.

Breckle, S-W, (2002). *Walter's Vegetation of the Earth.* 4th, completely revised and enlarged edition. Springer. Berlin

Britten, J. (1864). Spontaneous exotics. *The Naturalist,* **1864**: 201–207.

Brummitt, R.K. and Heywood, V.H. (1960). Pink-flowered Calystegiae of the Calystegia sepium complex in the British Isles. *Proceedings of the Botanical Society of the British Isles,* **3**: 384–388.

Bryant, D., ed. (2008). *In the footsteps of Eric Hardy.* Hobby Publications. Southport.

Buckley, N. (1842). List of plants in the vicinity of Lytham, Lancashire. *Phytologist,* **1**: 165–166.

Bunker, H.E. (1953). *Carex ericetorum* Poll. in Plant Records. *Watsonia,* **2**: 354.

Carroll, D. (2005). Soils in Abbott, P.P. *Plant Atlas of Mid-west Yorkshire.* Yorkshire Naturalists' Union. Kendal.

Chancellor, R.J. (1977). A preliminary survey of arable weeds in Britain. *Weed Research,* **17**: 283–287.

Chater, A.O. (2010). *Flora of Cardiganshire.* Published by the author. Aberystwyth.

Chipping Local History Society (2000). *A diary from January 1733 to March 1734 written by the Reverend Peter Walkden.* Smith Settle Ltd for Chipping Local History Society. Otley.

Clague, D. (2004). *Heysham Port a century of Manx and Irish services.* Ferry Publications Ltd. Ramsey, Isle of Man.

Clapham, A.R., Tutin, T.G. and Moore, D.M. (1987). *Flora of the British Isles.* Cambridge University Press. Cambridge.

Clement, E.J. (2001). *Ludwigia grandiflora* established at Barton-on-Sea (V.C. 11, S. Hants.). *BSBI News,* **87**: 52–54.

Clement, E.J. and Foster, M.C. (1994). *Alien Plants of the British Isles.* Botanical Society of the British Isles. London.

Clement, E.J., Smith, D.P.J. and Thirlwell, I.R. (2005). *Illustrations of Alien Plants of the British Isles.* Botanical Society of the British Isles. London.

Clitheroe, W. and Robinson, E.C., eds (1903). *Flora of Preston and Neighbourhood.* Preston Scientific Society. Preston.

Coleman, M. (2009). Elm of the Brae in Coleman, M., ed., *Wych Elm.* Royal Botanic Garden Edinburgh. Edinburgh

Conolly, A.P. (1977). The distribution and history in the British Isles of some alien species of *Polygonum* and *Reynoutria*. *Watsonia*, **11**: 291–311.

Conolly, A.P. and Dahl, E. (1970). Maximum summer temperature in relation to the modern and Quaternery distribution of certain arctic-montane species in the British Isles in Walker, D. and West, R.G., eds, *Studies in the vegetation history of the British Isles*. Cambridge University Press. Cambridge.

Cook, P.J. (2006). *Elytrigia atherica* (Sea Couch) and blue couches – a new roadside halophyte phenomenon? *BSBI News*, **102**: 33.

Cooper, F. (2006). *The Black Poplar. History, ecology and conservation*. Windgather Press Ltd. Macclesfield.

Cope, T. and Gray, A. (2009). *Grasses of the British Isles*. B.S.B.I. Handbook No. 13. Botanical Society of the British Isles. London.

Coppock, J.T. (1964). *An agricultural atlas of England and Wales*. Faber and Faber Ltd. London.

Cranfield, C. (1974). *The Parish of Chipping during the seventeenth century*. MA thesis, copy deposited at Lancashire Record Office, Preston.

Crawford, R.M.M. (2008). *Plants at the Margin*. Cambridge University Press. Cambridge.

Crawley, M.J., Harvey, P.H. and Purvis, A. (1996). Comparative ecology of the native and alien floras of the British Isles. *Philosophical Transactions of the Royal Society of London B*, **351**: 1251–1259.

Crompton, E. (1966). *The soils of the Preston District of Lancashire*. Memoirs of the Soil Survey of Great Britain. England and Wales. Agricultural Research Council. Harpenden.

Crosby, A. (1998). *A history of Lancashire*. Phillimore. Chichester.

Cullen, J. (2011). Naturalised Rhododendrons widespread in Great Britain and Ireland. *Hanburyana*, **5**: 11–29.

Curtis, M. (1990). Butterbur forms. *BSBI News*, **54**: 27–28.

Dallman, A.A. (1901). A MS 'Flora of Preston' compiled *c.* 1901 contained in box 3 of the Dallman Archives at World Museum Liverpool (LIV).

Dark, P. (2000). *The environment of Britain in the first millennium AD*. Duckworth. London.

Davies, B. (1990). More queries on Butterbur forms. *BSBI News*, **55**: 11–12.

Dawson, H.J. and Ingrouille, M.J. (1995). A biometric survey of *Limonium vulgare* Miller and *L. humile* Miller in the British Isles. *Watsonia*, **20**: 239–254.

Davies, W.J. (1961). Self-sown conifers in Short Notes. *Proceedings of the British Isles*, **4**: 198–199.

Davis, J.W. and Lees, F.A. (1878). *West Yorkshire*. L. Reeve & Co. London.

Day, P., Deadman, A.J., Greenwood, B.D. and Greenwood, E.F. (1982). A floristic appraisal of marl pits in north-western England and northern Wales. *Watsonia*, **14**: 153–165.

Dehnen-Schmutz, K., Perrings, C. and Williamson, M. (2004). Controlling *Rhododendron ponticum* in the British Isles: an economic analysis. *Journal of Environmental Management*, **70**: 323–332.

Dehnen-Schmutz, K. and Williamson, M. (2006). *Rhododendron ponticum* in Britain and Ireland: social, economic and ecological factors in its successful invasion. *Environment and History*, **12**: 325–350.

De Smidt, J.T. (1995). The imminent destruction of north-west European heaths due to atmospheric nitrogen deposition in Thompson, D.B.A., Hester, A.J. and Usher, M.B., eds., *Heaths and moorlands: cultural landscapes*. Scottish Natural Heritage. HMSO.

De Tabley, W. (1899). *The Flora of Cheshire*. Longmans, Green, and Co. London.

Dickson, R.W. (1815). *General view of the agriculture of Lancashire*.

Dines, T.D. and Bonner, J.R. (2002). A new hybrid horsetail, *Equisetum arvense × E. telmateia* (*E. × robertsii*) in Britain. *Watsonia*, **24**: 145–157.

Dudman, A.A. and Richards, A.J. (1997). *Dandelions of Great Britain and Ireland*. B.S.B.I. Handbook No. 9. Botanical Society of the British Isles. London.

Duffey, E., Morris, M.G., Sheail, J., Ward, L.K., Wells, D.A. and Wells, T.C.E. (1974). *Grassland ecology & wildlife management*. Chapman and Hall. London.

Duistermaat, H. (1996). Monograph of *Arctium* L. (Asteraceae). *Gorteria* Suppl., **3**: 1–143.

E.W. (1942). Liverpool Botanical Society [records of *Spartina townsendii*]. *The North Western Naturalist*, **17**: 413–414.

Ede, J. with Darlington, J. (2002). *Lancashire historic landscape characterisation programme*. Lancashire County Council with English Heritage published as a CD. Preston.

Edees, E.S. and Newton, A. (1988). *Brambles of the British Isles*. The Ray Society. London.

Edgington, J. (2003). Ferns of the Metropolis – a status report. *The London Naturalist*, **82**: 59–73.

Evans, T.G. (2007). *Flora of Monmouthshire*. Chepstow Society. Chepstow.

Facey, P.D., Lee, P.L.M., Smith, M.N.E. and Hipkin, C.R. (2007). Conservation of genetic diversity in British populations of the diploid endemic *Coincya monensis* ssp. *monensis* (Isle of Man Cabbage): the risk of hybridisation with the tetraploid alien, *Coincya monensis* ssp. *cheiranthos*. *Conservation Genetics*, **8**: 1029–1042.

Farrer, W., ed. (1898–1905). *The Chartulary of Cockersand Abbey* published by Chetham Society, vol. **1** Pt. 1, VIII + pp.1–160; vol. **1** pt 2. pp. 161–335; vol. **2** pt. 1 pp. 336–530; vol. **2** pt.2 pp. 531–757; vol. **3** pt.1 pp.775–924; vol. **3** pt. 2 pp. 925–1104; vol. **38NS** (1898); vol. **39NS**

(1898); vol. **40NS** (1898); vol. **43NS** (1900); vol. **56NS** (1905); vol. **57NS** (1905).

Fielding MS. MS 'English flora' collected and drawn by Mary Maria Fielding. 6 volumes. Bodleian Library, Department of Special Collections and Western Manuscripts on loan to Department of Plant Sciences, University of Oxford. (MS. Eng. D. 3357).

Fletcher, A. (2003/4). Gone shopping. *Longer Sen*, **2003/4**: 36–38. A miscellany published by Chipping Local History Society. Clitheroe.

Fletcher, T.W. (1965). The agrarian revolution in arable Lancashire. *Transactions of the Lancashire and Cheshire Antiquarian Society*, **72**:93–122.

Foley, M. and Clarke, S. (2005). *Orchids of the British Isles*. Griffin Press Publishing Limited. Cheltenham.

Ford, R. and Fuller-Maitland, J.A., eds. (1931). *John Lucas's History of Warton Parish (compiled 1710–1740)*. Titus Wilson & Son. Kendal.

France, R.S. (1931). Notes on the flora of West Lancashire. *The North Western Naturalist*, **6**: 99–100.

France, R.S. (1930s). Annotations in a copy of Wheldon and Wilson (1907) at Lancaster University believed to have belonged to R. Sharpe France.

Frankland, J.N. (1942). VC 60 record for *Impatiens glandulifera* in Wilson, A., Druce's Comital Flora: corrections and suggestions. *Botanical Society and Exchange Club Report*, **12**: 319–330.

Fraser-Jenkins, C.R. (2007). The species and subspecies in the Dryopteris affinis group. *Fern Gazette*, **18**: 1–26.

French, C., Murphy, R. and Atkinson, M. (2006). *The Flora of Cornwall*. CD-ROM version. Publisher not given.

Fryer, J. and Hylmö, B. (1997). Five new species of *Cotoneaster* Medik. (Rosaceae) naturalized in Britain. *Watsonia*, **21**: 335–340.

Fryer, J. and Hylmö, B. (2009). *Cotoneasters*. Timber Press. Portland. London.

Garlick, G.W. (1957a). A salt-marsh flora of the Heysham peninsula. *New Biologian*, **6**: 8–10.

Garlick, G.W. (1957b). *Spartina townsendii* H. & J. Groves and *Allium carianatum* in Plant Records. *Proceedings of the Botanical Society of the British Isles*, **2**: 245–268.

Garnett, E. (2000). Basket making in Winstanley, M., ed., *Rural industries of the Lune Valley*. Centre for North-West Regional Studies, University of Lancaster. Lancaster.

Garnett, E. (2002). *The Wray flood of 1967*. Centre for North-West Regional Studies, University of Lancaster. Lancaster.

Garnett, W.J. (1849). Farming of Lancashire. Prize Report. *Journal of the Royal Agricultural Society of England*, **10**: 1–51.

Geltman, D.V. (1992). *Urtica galeopsifolia* Wierzb. ex Opiz (Urticaceae) in Wicken Fen (E. England). *Watsonia* , **19**: 127–129.

Gerarde, J. (1597). *The Herball*. London.

Gil, L., Fuentes-Utrilla, P., Soto, A., Cevera, M.T. and Collada, C. (2004). English elm is a 2000-year-old Roman clone. *Nature*, **431**: 1053.

Gilbert, O.L. (1989). *The ecology of urban habitats*. Chapman and Hall. London.

Godwin, H. (1975). *The history of the British flora*. 2nd ed. Cambridge University Press.

Graham, G.G. and Primavesi, A.L. (1993). *Roses of Great Britain and Ireland*. B.S.B.I. Handbook No. 7. Botanical Society of the British Isles. London.

Gray, A.J. (1972). The ecology of Morecambe Bay V. The salt marshes of Morecambe Bay. *Journal of Applied Ecology*, **9**: 207–220.

Gray, A.J. and Scott, R. (1987). Salt marshes in Robinson, N.A. and Pringle, A.W., eds, *Morecambe Bay: an assessment of present and ecological knowledge*. Centre for North-West Regional Studies with the Morecambe Bay Study Group. Lancaster.

Greenhalgh, M. (2009). *Ribble: valley and river: A local and natural history*. Carnegie Publishing Ltd. Lancaster.

Greenwood, E.F. (1972). Coastal vegetation of Lancashire. *Nature in Lancashire*, **3**: 33–41.

Greenwood, E.F. (1974). Herbicide treatments on the Lancaster Canal. *Nature in Lancashire*, **4**: 24–36.

Greenwood, E.F., ed. (1999). *Ecology and landscape development. A history of the Mersey Basin*. Liverpool University Press. National Museum & Galleries on Merseyside. Liverpool.

Greenwood, E.F. (2001). Observations on the flora associated with street furniture. *BSBI News*, **86**: 12–15.

Greenwood, E.F. (2003). Understanding change – a Lancashire perspective. *Watsonia*, **24**: 337–350.

Greenwood, E.F. (2004). Coastal *Elytrigia* species and hybrids in north-western England and northern Wales. *BSBI News*, **95**: 15–19.

Greenwood, E.F. (2004a). Flowers and Ferns in Edmunds, M., Mitcham, T. and Morries, G., eds, *Wildlife of Lancashire*. Carnegie Publishing Ltd for the Lancashire Wildlife Trust. Preston.

Greenwood, E.F. (2005). The changing flora of the Lancaster Canal in West Lancaster (V.C. 60). *Watsonia*, **25**: 231–235.

Greenwood, E.F. and Gemmell, R.P. (1978). Derelict industrial land as a habitat for rare plants in S. Lancs. (V.C. 59) and W. Lancs. (V.C. 60). *Watsonia*, **12**: 33–40.

Greenwood, M. and Bolton, C. (2000). *Bolland Forest and the Hodder Valley. A History*. Landy Publishing. Blackpool.

Grime, J.P., Hodgson, J.G. and Hunt, R. (2007). *Comparative Plant Ecology*. Castlepoint Press. Colvend, Dalbeattie, Kirkudbrightshire.

Groves, E.W. (1958). Hippophae rhamnoides in the British Isles. *Proceedings of the Botanical Society of the British Isles*, **3**: 1–21.

Guest, J.P. (1997). Biodiversity in the ponds of lowland North-west England in Boothby, J., ed., *British pond landscapes*. The Pond *Life* Project. Liverpool

Haley, R.A. (1995). *Lytham St Anne's. A Pictorial History.* Phillimore. Chichester.

Hall, B.R. and Folland, C.J. (1970). *Soils of Lancashire.* Soil Survey of Great Britain England and Wales Bulletin No. 5. Agricultural Research Council. Harpenden.

Halliday, G. (1997). *A flora of Cumbria.* Centre for North-West Regional Studies, University of Lancaster. Lancaster.

Hanbury, F.J., ed. (1908). *The London Catalogue of British Plants.* Tenth edition. George Bell & Sons. London.

Harrison, W. (1901). Ancient forests, chases and deer parks in Lancashire. *Transactions Lancashire and Cheshire Antiquarian Society*, **19**:1–37.

Heathcote, W.H. (1923). Additions to the Flora of Preston. *Lancashire and Cheshire Naturalist*, **15**: 140.

Henderson, C.W. (1962). Northern limestones. *Bulletin of the Alpine Garden Society*, **30**: 306–310.

Hewitson, A. (1900). *Northward.* George Toulmin & Sons. Preston. Republished by S.R. Publishers Limited, 1969.

Hickling, J. (2004). Lancashire: setting the scene in Edmunds, M., Mitcham, T. and Morries, G., eds, *Wildlife of Lancashire*. Carnegie Publishing Ltd for the Lancashire Wildlife Trust. Lancaster.

Hill, M.O. and Preston, C.D. (1998). The geographical relationships of British and Irish bryophytes. Bryological Monographs. *Journal of Bryology*, **20**: 127–226.

Hill, M.O., Preston, C.D. and Roy, D.B. (2004). *PLANTATT, Atributes of British and Irish plants: status, size, life history, geography and habitats.* Biological Records Centre, NERC Centre for Ecology and Hydrology. Huntingdon.

Hindle, D. (2002). *Grimsargh.* Carnegie Publishing Ltd. Lancaster.

Hipkin, C.R. and Facey, P.D. (2009). Biological Flora of the British Isles: *Coincya monensis* (L.) Greuter & Burdet ssp. *monensis* (*Rhynchosinapis monensis* (L.) Dandy ex A.R. Clapham) and ssp. *cheiranthos* (Vill.) Aedo, Leadley & Muñoz Garm. (*Rhyncosinapis cheiranthos* (Vill.) Dandy). *Journal of Ecology*, **97**: 1101–1116.

Hodgson, E. (1965). Record for *Rosa* × *alba* L. *Wildflower Magazine*, **343**: 29.

Holden, V.J.C. (2010). The historic development of the north Sefton coast in Worsley, A.T., Lymbery, G., Holden, V. J.C. and Newton, M., eds, *Sefton's dynamic coast*. Coastal Defense: Sefton MBC Technical Service Department. Southport.

Holt, J. (1795). *General View of the agriculture of the County of Lancaster.* G. Nicol. London. David & Charles Reprints.

Hornby, P.J. (1930). *Ambrosia artemisiifolia* from near St Michael on Wyre, Garstang in Plant Records. *Botanical Society and Exchange Club Report for* 1929, **9**: 119.

Horwood, T.R. (2003). *Survey and assessment of saltmarsh Wyre estuary for Canatxx Gas Storage Ltd.* Private report.

Hoskins, W.G. (1955). *The making of the English landscape.* Hodder & Stoughton. London.

Hubbard, C.E. (1984). *Grasses.* 3rd ed. Revised by C.E. Hubbard. Penguin Books. London

Hubbard, J.C.E. and Stebbings, R.E. (1967). Distribution, dates of origin and acreage of *Spartina townsendii* (s.l.) marshes in Great Britain. *Proceedings of the Botanical Society of the British Isles*, **7**: 1–7.

Hudson, P. (1997). Industry in medieval Quernmore. *Lancashire History Quarterly*, **1**: 171–174.

Hudson, P. (2000). Quarrying and extractive industries in Winstanley, M., ed., *Rural industries of the Lune valley.* Centre for North-West Regional Studies, University of Lancaster. Lancaster.

Hudson, P.J. (1998). *Coal mining in Lunesdale.* Hudson History. Settle.

Hulme, M. and Barrow, E. (1997). *Climates of the British Isles.* Routledge. London and New York.

Hulme, M. and Jenkins, G.J. (1998). *Climate change scenarios for the United Kingdom: Scientific Report.* UKCIP Technical Report No. 1. Climatic Research Unit. Norwich

Hunt, D. (1992a). Cites J.S. Leatherbarrow, The Lancashire Elizabethan Recusants. *Chetham Society*, **111**, p. 149 (1947).

Hunt, D. (1992b). *A history of Preston.* Carnegie Publishing in conjunction with Preston Borough Council. Preston.

Hunt, R, Hope-Simpson, J.F. and Snape, J.B. (2005). Growth of the dune wintergreen (*Pyrola rotundifolia* ssp. *maritima*) at Braunton Burrows in relation to weather factors. *International Journal of Biometeorology*, **29**: 323–334.

Huntley, J. and Hillam, J. (2000). Environmental evidence in Buxton, K. and Howard-Davis, C., *BREMETENACUM excavations at Roman Ribchester 1980, 1989–1990.* Lancaster Imprints Series number 9. Lancaster University Archaeological Unit. Lancaster.

Ingrouille, M.J. (2006). What use is sex? Rock sea-lavenders (*Limonium binervosum* agg.) revisited in Bailey, J. and Ellis, G., eds, *Current taxonomic research on the British & European flora* Botanical Society of the British Isles. London.

Innes, J.B. (1992). Pollen analysis in Higgins, A.D. Speke Hall excavations in the west range, 1981-82. *Merseyside Archaeological Society Journal*, **8**: 47–84.

Innes, J.B., Chiverell, R.C., Blackford, J.J., Davey, P.J., Gonzalez, S., Rutherford, M.M. and Tomlinson, P.R. (2004). Earliest Holocene vegetation history and island biogeography of the Isle of Man, British Isles. *Journal of Biogeography*, **31**: 761–772.

Jalas, J. and Suominen, J. eds. (1972). *Atlas Florae Europaeae.* The committee for mapping the flora of Europe and Societas Biologica Fennica Vanamo. Helsinki.

Jenkinson, J. (1775). *Descriptions of British Plants....*

Jermy, A.C., Simpson, D., Foley, M. and Porter, M. (2007). *Sedges of the British Isles.* B.S.B.I. HANDBOOK No. 1, ed. 3. Botanical Society of the British Isles. London.

Jones, M. (1988). The arable field: a botanical battleground in Jones M. ed., *Archaeology and the flora of the British Isles.* Oxford University Committee for archaeology. Oxford.

J.P. [James Pearson] (1855). Notes on the Botany of North Lancashire. *The Naturalist,* **5**: 14–16.

Kay, S. (2000). Survey and audit – problems and solutions in Wilson, P. and King, M. eds, *Fields of vision a future for Britain's arable plants. Proceedings of a conference held 10th/11th July 2000 at Girton College, Cambridge.* Royal Society for the Protection of Birds and English Nature.

Kennedy, D. and Brown, I.R. (1983). The morphology of the hybrid *Betula pendula* Roth × *B. pubescens* Ehrh. *Watsonia,* **14**: 329–336.

Kent, D.H. (1956). *Senecio squalidus* L. in the British Isles – 1, early records (to 1877). *Proceedings of the Botanical Society of the British Isles,* **2**: 115–118.

Kent, D.H. (1960). *Senecio squalidus* L. in the British Isles – 2, the spread from Oxford (1879–1939). *Proceedings of the Botanical Society of the British Isles,* **3**: 375–379.

Kent, D.H. (1964). *Senecio squalidus* L. in the British Isles – 4, southern England (1940→). 5, the midlands (1940→). 6, northern England (1940→). *Proceedings of the Botanical Society of the British Isles,* **5**: 210–219.

Kent, D.H. and Allen, D.E. (1984). *British and Irish herbaria.* Botanical Society of the British Isles. London.

Kenyon, D. (2008). *Wray and District remembered.* Published privately.

Kirschner, J. and Rich, T.C.G. (1997). *Luzula campestris/ L. multiflora* group / *L. pallidula* in Rich, T.C.G. and Jermy, A.C. (1998), *Plant Crib 1998.* Botanical Society of the British Isles. London.

Lankester, E., ed. (1848). *The correspondence of John Ray.* The Ray Society. London.

Lansdown, R.V. (2006). Notes on the water-starworts (*Callitriche*) recorded in Europe. *Watsonia,* **26**: 105–120.

Lansdown, R.V. (2008). *Water-starworts* (Callitriche) *of Europe.* B.S.B.I. Handbook No. 11. Botanical Society of the British Isles. London.

Lees, F.A. (1888). *The Flora of West Yorkshire.* Lovell Reeve & Co. London.

Lees, F.A. (1899). The Florula of Bare, West Lancashire. *The Naturalist,* **1899**: 299–303.

Lees, F.A. (1900). West Lancaster Indigenes. *The Naturalist,* **1900**: 3–4.

Lewis, J.M. (2010). Archaeology and history of a changing coastline in Worsley, A.T., Lymbery, G., Holden, V.J.C. and Newton, M., eds, *Sefton's dynamic coast.* Coastal Defense: Sefton MBC Technical Services Department. Southport

Linton, E.F. (1875). Tabular list for West Lancaster, 60 in Report of the Recorder for 1874. V. tabular catalogues of common plants for Breconshire, Radnorshire, Selkirkshire, and West Lancaster. *The Botanical Record Club,* **1875**: 80–86.

Livermore, L.A. and Livermore, P.D. (1987). *The flowering plants and ferns of north Lancashire.* L.A. & P.D. Livermore. Preston.

Livermore, L.A. and Livermore, P.D. (1989). *The flowering plants, ferns & rusts of the Lancaster Canal in the Lancaster District.* L.A. & P.D. Livermore. Lancaster.

Livermore, L.A. and Livermore, P.D. (1990a). *Coastal plants and rust fungi of the North Lancashire coast.* L.A. & P.D. Livermore. Lancaster. (Copy at LIV).

Livermore, L.A. and Livermore, P.D. (1990b). *Plants & rust fungi of the dismantled railway lines in the Lancaster District.* L.A. & P.D. Livermore. Lancaster. (Copy at LIV).

Livermore, L.A. and Livermore, P.D. (1991). *Lancaster's plant life – a botanical survey.* L.A. & P.D. Livermore, Lancaster. (Copy at LIV).

Livermore, L. and Livermore, P. (1992). *Allium sativum* L. (Garlic). *BSBI News,* **60**: 11.

Lockton, A. (2004). Report on the threatened plant database. *BSBI Recorder Newsletter for BSBI Recorders.* February 2004, pp. 14–15.

Loriot, S. and Magnanon, S. (2006). The task of the Conservatoire Botanique National de Brest in the knowledge and conservation of the Armorican flora as illustrated by *Trichomanes speciosum* Willd. in Leach, S.J., Page, C.N., Peytoureau, Y and Sanford, M.N., eds, *Botanical links in the Atlantic Arc.* Botanical Society of the British Isles with financial support from English Nature. Conference report No. 24. London.

Lousley, J.E. (1958). *Plantago intermedia* in Britain? *Proceedings of the Botanical Society of the British Isles,* **3**: 33–36.

Lousley, J.E. and Kent, D.H. (1981). *Docks and Knotweeds of the British Isles.* B.S.B.I. Handbook No. 3. Botanical Society of the British Isles. London.

Lumby, J.H. (1936). *A calendar of the deeds and papers in the possession of Sir James de Hoghton, Bart. of Hoghton Tower, Lancashire.* The Record Society of Lancashire and Cheshire, vol. 88.

McCosh, D.J. and Rich, T.C.G. (2011). *Atlas of British and Irish Hawkweeds* (Pilosella *L. and* Hieracium *L.*). Botanical Society of the British Isles. London.

Mabey, R. (1996). *Flora Britannica.* Sinclair-Stevenson. London.

McAllister, H.A. (1999). *Lysimachia punctata* L. and *L. verticillaris* Sprengel (Primulaceae) naturalised in the British Isles. *Watsonia,* **22**: 279–281.

Mackay, A.W. (1993). *The recent vegetational history of the Forest of Bowland, Lancashire.* PhD thesis, University of Manchester.

Mackay, A.W. and Tallis, J.H. (1994). The recent vegetational history of the Forest of Bowland, Lancashire, UK. *New Phytologist*, **128**: 571–584.

Mackay, A.W. and Tallis, J.H. (1996). Summit-type blanket mire erosion in the Forest of Bowland, Lancashire, UK: predisposing factors and implications for conservation. *Biological Conservation*, **76**: 31–44.

Maltby, E., Legg, C.J. and Procter, M.C.F. (1990). The ecology of severe moorland fires on the North York Moors: effects of the 1976 fires and subsequent surface and vegetation development. *Journal of Ecology*, **78**: 490–518.

Manley, G. (1952). *Climate and the British scene.* The New Naturalist. Collins. London.

Marren, P. (1999). *Britain's rare flowers.* Poyser Natural History. London.

Marren, P. (2002). *Nature conservation. A review of the conservation of wildlife in Britain 1950–2001.* The New Naturalist. HarperCollins*Publishers*. London.

Marshall, B. (2001). *Cockersand Abbey.* Landy Publishing. Blackpool.

Marshall, E.S. (1949). *Centaurium umbellatum* Gilib. var. *subcapitatum* (Corb.) Gilm. and *Centaurium umbellatum* Gilib. × *C. littorale* (Turner) Gilm. in Plant Records. *Watsonia*, **1**: 48–49.

Marshall, J.D., ed. (1967). *The autobiography of William Stout of Lancaster 1665–1752.* Published for the Chetham Society by Manchester University Press. Manchester.

Matthews, J.R. (1955). *Origin and distribution of the British flora.* Hutchinson's University Library. London.

Meikle, R.D. (1984). *Willows and poplars of Great Britain and Ireland.* B.S.B.I. Handbook No 4. Botanical Society of the British Isles. London.

Meikle, R.D. and Robinson, N.A. (2000). A new record for *Salix × angusensis* (Salicaceae) Rech. f. from Ainsdale Sand Dunes National Nature Reserve, S. Lancs. v.c. 59. *Watsonia*, **23**: 327–330.

Meterological Office. (1961). *British rainfall.* Meterological Office. Bracknell.

Meterological Office. (1983). *The climate of Great Britain. Lancashire and Cheshire and Isle of Man.* Climatological Memorandum 130. Meterological Office. Bracknell.

Michell, P.E. (2001). *A morphological characterisation of the rare hybrid willows* Salix × friesiana *Anderss. and* Salix × angusensis *Rech. f. on the Sefton Coast.* A dissertation submitted in partial fulfilment of requirements for the degree of B.Sc. Edge Hill University College.

Middleton, R. (1995). The exploitation of peatlands: past and present in Cox, M., Straker, V. and Taylor, D., eds, *Wetlands, archaeology and nature conservation.* HMSO. London.

Middleton, R., Wells, C.E. and Huckerby, E. (1995). *The wetlands of North Lancashire.* North West Wetlands Survey 3. Lancaster University Archaeological Unit. Lancaster.

Milne-Redhead, R. (1870s). Annotations in Bentham, G. (1865). *Handbook of the British Flora.* Lovell Reeve & Co. London in the possession of G. Morries in 2008.

Milne, R.I. and Abbott, R.J. (2000). Origin and evolution of invasive naturalised material of *Rhododendron ponticum* L. in the British Isles. *Molecular Ecology*, **9**: 541–546.

Mitchell, A. (1974). *A field guide to the Trees of Britain and northern Europe.* Collins. London.

Mitchell, W.R. (2004). *Bowland and Pendle Hill.* Phillimore & Co. Ltd. Chichester.

Mitchell, F.J.G. (2005). How open were European primeval forests? Hypothesis testing using palaeological data. *Journal of Ecology*, **93**:168–177.

Moore, I. (1966). *Grass and grasslands.* The New Naturalist. Collins. London.

Morries, G. (1986). *Lancashire's woodland heritage.* Lancashire County Council. Preston.

Moss, J. (1912). *Colchicum autumnale* in Vice-County 59. *Lancashire and Cheshire Naturalist*, **5**: 227, 263.

Mourholme Local History Society (1998). *How it was. A north Lancashire Parish in the seventeenth century.* Mourholme Local History Society. Kendal.

Newman, J.R. (1988). *A botanical survey of limestone grassland in Lancashire.* Nature Conservancy Council. A typescript.

Newman, E. (1854). *A history of British ferns.*

Newton, A. and Randall, R.D. (2004). *Atlas of British and Irish Brambles.* Botanical Society of the British Isles. London.

Nissenbaum, D. (1989). *A management plan for the Fylde Coast sand dunes.* Unpublished MSc Thesis. Imperial College, London.

Oldfield, F. and Statham, D.C. (1965). Stratigraphy and pollen analysis on Cockerham and Pilling Mosses, North Lancashire. *Memoirs and Proceedings Manchester Literary and Philosophical Society*, **107**: 70–85.

Parker, D.M. (1979). *Saxifraga rosacea* and *S. hypnoides* in the British Isles. *BSBI News*, **21**: 22–23.

Payne, R.M. (1978). The flora of walls in south-eastern Essex. *Watsonia*, **12**: 41–46.

Pearson, J. (1874). Record for *Narcissus poeticus. Science Gossip*, **10**: 259.

Peel, A. (1913). *The Manor of Knowlmere.* Privately published.

Peel, M.N. (1913). Aliens and introduced plants of the Upper Hodder. *The Naturalist*, **1913**: 141–143.

Peel, M.N. (1913b). The orchids of the Upper Hodder valley. *The Naturalist*, **1913**: 29–32.

Perring, F.H. (1960). Report on the survey of *Arctium* L. agg. in Britain, 1959. *Proceedings of the Botanical Society of the British Isles.* **4**: 33–37.

Perring, F.H. (1994). *Symphytum* – Comfrey in Perry, A.R. and Ellis, R.G., eds, *The common ground of wild and cultivated plants*. National Museum of Wales. Cardiff.

Perring, F.H. and Walters, S.M., eds. (1962). *Atlas of the British flora*. Thomas Nelson and Sons Ltd for the Botanical Society of the British Isles. London.

Perring, F.H., ed. (1968). *Critical Supplement to the Atlas of the British Flora*. Thomas Nelson and Sons Ltd for the Botanical Society of the British Isles. London.

Peter, D. (1994). *In and around Silverdale*. Barry Ayre. Silverdale.

Peterken, G.F. (1981). *Woodland conservation and management*. Chapman and Hall. London.

Petty, L. (1893). The plants of Leck and neighbourhood, Lancashire. *The Naturalist,* **1893**: 91–102.

Petty, S.L. (1902). Some plants of Silverdale, West Lancashire. *The Naturalist*, **1902**: 33–54.

Pickard, J.F. (1901). Some rarer plants of Bowland. *The Naturalist*, **1901**: 37–41.

Pickard, J.F. (1902). Additions to the Bowland flora. *The Naturalist,* **1902**: 289–291.

Pigott, C.D. (1974). The Wild Service tree in Lancashire and Westmorland. *Nature in Lancashire*, **4**:40–43.

Pigott, C.D. (1975). Experimental studies on the influence of climate on the geographical distribution of plants. *Weather*, **30**: 82–90.

Pigott, C.D. and Huntley, J.P. (1978). Factors controlling the distribution of *Tilia cordata* at the northern limits of its geographical range. 1. Distribution in north-west England. *New Phytologist*, **81**: 429–441.

Pigott, C.D. and Huntley, J.P. (1980). Factors controlling the distribution of *Tilia cordata* at the northern limits of its geographical range. 11. History in north-west England. *New Phytologist*, **84**: 145–164.

Pigott, C.D. and Huntley, J.P. (1981). Factors controlling the distribution of *Tilia cordata* at the northern limits of its geographical range. 111. Nature and causes of seed sterility. *New Phytologist*, **87**: 817–839.

Plassmann, K., Edwards-Jones, G and Jones, M.L.M. (2009). The effects of low levels of nitrogen deposition and grazing on dune grassland. *Science of the total environment*, **407**: 1391–1404.

Plater, A.J., Lang, A.J., Huddart, D., Gonzalez, S. and Tooley, M.J. (1999). The land of the Mersey Basin: sea-level changes in Greenwood, E.F., ed., *Ecology and landscape development: a history of the Mersey Basin*. Liverpool University Press. National Museums & Galleries on Merseyside. Liverpool.

Porter, J. (1974). A forest in transition 1500–1650. *Historic Society of Lancashire and Cheshire Transactions*, **125**: 40–60.

Porter, J. (1978). Waste land reclamation in the sixteenth and seventeenth centuries: the case of south-eastern Bowland, 1550–1630. *Transactions Historic Society of Lancashire and Cheshire*, **127**: 1–23.

Porter, J. (1980). *The making of the central Pennines*. Moorland Publishing Co.

Porter, J. (1994). *The Forest of Bowland. Its landscape and history*. J. Porter. Farnborough.

Preston, C.D. (2000). Engulfed by suburbia or destroyed by the plough: the ecology of extinction in Middlesex and Cambridgeshire. *Watsonia*, **23**: 59–81.

Preston, C.D. (2007). Which vascular plants are found at the northern or southern edges of their European range in the British Isles? *Watsonia*, **26**: 271–290.

Preston, C.D. and Croft, J.M. (1997). *Aquatic plants in Britain and Ireland*. Harley Books. Colchester.

Preston, C.D. and Hill, M.O. (1997). The geographical relationships of British and Irish vascular plants. *Botanical Journal of the Linnaen Society*, **124**:1–120.

Preston, C.D., Pearman, D.A. and Dines, T.D., eds (2002). *New Atlas of the British & Irish flora*. Oxford University Press. Oxford.

Preston, C.D., Pearman, D.A. and Hall, A.R. (2004). Archaeophytes in Britain. *Botanical Journal of the Linnean Society*, **145**: 257–294.

Preston Scientific Society (1903). *Flora of Preston & Neighbourhood*. Preston Scientific Society. Preston.

Price, J.W.A. (1983). *The industrial archaeology of the Lune valley*. Occasional Paper No. 13. Centre for North-West Regional Studies, University of Lancaster. Lancaster.

Proctor, M.C.F. (2002). *Ledum palustre* in Preston, C.D., Pearman, D.A. and Dines, T.D., eds, *New Atlas of the British & Irish Flora CD-ROM*. Oxford University Press. Oxford.

Pyefinch, R. and Golborn, P. (2001). *Atlas of the breeding birds of Lancashire and north Merseyside*. Hobby Publications. Liverpool.

Rackham, O. (1999). *The history of the countryside*. Phoenix Giant. London.

Rackham, O. (2003). *Ancient woodland its history, vegetation and uses in England*. Castlepoint Press. Dalbeattie.

Radley, G.P. (1994). *Sand dune vegetation survey of Great Britain: A national inventory. Part 1. England*. Joint Nature Conservation Committee.

Radley, J. (1965). Significance of major moorland fires. *Nature*, **4978**: 1254–1259.

Ratcliffe, D.A. (1968). An ecological account of the Atlantic Bryophytes in the British Isles. *New Phytologist*, **67**: 365–439.

Ratcliffe, D. ed. (1977). *A nature conservation review*. 2 volumes. Cambridge University Press. Cambridge.

Raven, C.E. (1942). *John Ray, naturalist. His life and work*. Cambridge University Press. Cambridge.

Raven, C.E. (1948). Thomas Lawson's note-book. *Proceedings of the Linnean Society of London*, **160**: 3–5.

Rawes, M and Welch, D. (1964). Studies on sheep grazing in the northern Pennines. *Journal of the British Grassland Society,* **34**: 403–411.

Rawes, M. and Welch, D. (1969). Upland productivity of vegetation and sheep at Moor House National Nature Reserve, Westmorland, England. *Oikos Supplement,* **11**: 1–72.

Regional Biodiversity Steering group for North West England (1999). *A biodiversity audit of North West England.* 2 volumes. No publisher or ISBN number.

Rich, T.C.G. (1994). Ragweeds (*Ambrosia* L.) in Britain. *Grana,* **33**: 38–43.

Rich, T.C.G., Houston, L., Robertson, A. and Proctor, M.C.F. (2010). *Whitebeams, Rowans and Service Trees of Britain and Ireland. A monograph of British and Irish Sorbus L.* B.S.B.I. Handbook No. 14. Botanical Society of the British Isles in association with National Museum Wales. London.

Rich, T.C.G. and Jermy, A.C. (1998). *Plant Crib 1998.* Botanical Society of the British Isles. London.

Richards, A.J. (2002). *Lysimachia punctata* in Preston, C.D., Pearman, D.A. and Dines, T.D., eds, *New Atlas of the British and ℰ Irish Flora.* Oxford University Press. Oxford.

Richardson, J.A. (1957). The development of orchid populations in claypits in county Durham. *Proceedings of the Botanical Society of the British Isles,* **2**: 354–361.

Richens, R.H. (1983). *Elm.* Cambridge University Press. Cambridge.

Riddelsdall, H.J. (1902). North of England plants in the Motley Herbarium at Swansea. *The Naturalist,* **1902**: 343–351.

Roberts, E., ed. (1998). *A history of Linen in the North West.* Centre for North-West Regional Studies, University of Lancaster. Lancaster.

Robinson, N.A. and Pringle, A.W., eds. (1987). *Morecambe Bay: and assessment of present ecological knowledge.* Centre for North-West Regional Studies in conjunction with the Morecambe Bay Study Group. Lancaster.

Rodgers, H.B. (1967). Land use in Tudor Lancashire: the evidence of the final Concords, 1450–1558. MS deposited at Lancashire Record Office, Preston.

Rodwell, J.S., ed. (1991a). *British plant communities. Volume 1. Woodlands and scrub.* Cambridge University Press. Cambridge.

Rodwell, J.S., ed. (1991b). *British plant communities. Volume 2. Mires and heaths.* Cambridge University Press. Cambridge.

Rodwell, J.S., ed. (1992). *British plant communities. Volume 3. Grasslands and montane communities.* Cambridge University Press. Cambridge.

Rodwell, J.S., ed. (1995). *British plant communities. Volume 4. Aquatic communities, swamps and tall-herb fens.* Cambridge University Press. Cambridge.

Rodwell, J.S., ed. (2000). *British plant communities. Volume 5. Maritime communities and vegetation of open habitats.* Cambridge University Press.

Rogers, G. (1996). The nineteenth-century landowner as urban developer: the Clifton estate and the development of Lytham-St Anne's. *Transactions of the Historic Society of Lancashire and Cheshire for the year 1995,* **145**: 117–150.

Rostański, K. (1982). The species of *Oenothera* L. in Britain. *Watsonia,* **14**: 1–34.

Rothwell, C. (1974). *A history of Fleetwood-on-Wyre 1834–1934.* Thesis for Fellowship of the Library Association. Copy deposited at Lancashire Record Office, Preston.

Roy, D.B., Hill, M.O. and Rothery, S. (1999). Effects of urban land cover on the local species pool in Britain. *Ecography,* **22**:507–525.

Rushton, B.S. (1997). *QUERCUS* in Rich, T.C.G. and Jermy, A.C. (1998). *Plant Crib 1998.* Botanical Society of the British Isles. London.

Ryves, T.B., Clement, E.J. and Foster, M.C. (1996). *Alien grasses of the British Isles.* Botanical Society of the British Isles. London.

St. Michael's School (1902). 'A list of wild flowers which were brought to St. Michael's School by children attending school'. Handwritten list at Fleetwood Museum.

Sala, O.E., Chapin lll, F.S., Armesto, J.J., Barlow, E., Bloomfield, J., Dirzo, R., Huber-Sanwald, E., Huenneke, L.F., Jackson, R.B., Kinzig, A., Leemans, R., Lodge, D.M., Mooney, H.A., Oesterheld, M., Poff, N.L., Sykes, M.T., Walker, B.H., Walker, M. and Wall, D.H. (2000). Global biodiversity scenarios for the year 2100. *Science,* **287**: 1770–1774.

Salisbury, E. (1961). *Weeds and aliens.* The New Naturalist. Collins. London.

Salmon, C.E. (1912). Early Lancashire and Cheshire records. *The Journal of Botany,* **50**: 369–371.

Salmon, C.E. and Thompson, H.S. (1902). West Lancashire notes. *The Journal of Botany,* **40**: 293–295.

Sargent, S. (1984). *Britain's railway vegetation.* Institute of Terrestrial Ecology. Abbots Ripton.

Savidge, J.P., Heywood, V.H. and Gordon, V., eds. (1963). *Travis's Flora of South Lancashire.* Liverpool Botanical Society. Liverpool.

Scott, N.E. and Davison, A.W. (1982). De-icing salt and the invasion of road verges by maritime plants. *Watsonia,* **14**: 41–52.

Scott, N.E. and Davison, A.W. (1985). The distribution and ecology of coastal species on roadsides. *Vegetatio,* **62**: 430–440.

Sell, P. and Murrell, G. (2006). *Flora of Great Britain and Ireland. Volume 4 Campanulaceae – Asteraceae.* Cambridge University Press. Cambridge.

Shakeshaft, P. (2001). *The history of Freckleton.* Carnegie Publishing Ltd. Lancaster.

Shaw, R.C. (1956). *The Royal Forest of Lancaster.* The Guardian Press. Preston.

S[heppard], T. (1909). Yorkshire naturalists at Bowland. *The Naturalist*, **1909**: 299–302.

Simmons, I.G. (2001). *An environmental history of Great Britain*. University Press. Edinburgh.

Simmons, I.G. (2003). *The moorlands of England and Wales*. Edinburgh University Press. Edinburgh.

Simpson, S. (1843). Record for *Asplenium marinum* at Silverdale in Newman, E., County lists of the British ferns and their allies. *Phytologist*, **1**: 476–480.

Sinker, C.A., Packham, J.R., Trueman, I.C., Oswald, P.H., Perring, F.H. and Prestwood, W.V. (1985). *Ecological flora of the Shropshire region*. Shropshire Trust for Nature Conservation. Shrewsbury.

Skelcher, G. (2008). *Fylde Sand Dunes management action plan*. Unpublished report for the Fylde Sand Dunes Project Steering Group. Copy deposited with the Wildlife Trust for Lancashire, Manchester and North Merseyside, Bamber Bridge.

Smith, A.J.E. (2004). *The Moss Flora of Britain and Ireland*. 2nd ed. Cambridge University Press. Cambridge.

Smith, M.D. (2011). The ecological role of climate extremes: current understanding and future prospects. *Journal of Ecology*, **99**: 651–655.

Smith, P.H. (2008). Population explosion of *Hypochaeris glabra* L. on the Sefton Coast, Merseyside (v.c. 59). *Watsonia*, **27**: 159–166.

Smith, P.H. (2009a). *The sands of time revisited*. Amberley Publishing. Stroud.

Smith, P.H. (2009b). Distribution, status and ecology of *Blysmus compressus* (L.) Panz. ex Link on the Sefton coast sand-dunes, Merseyside. *Watsonia*, **27**: 339–353.

Smith, P.H. and Greenwood, E.F. (2009). Colonisation of the Ribble Estuary by Sea-lavenders. *BSBI News*, **111**: 15–20

Smith, P.M. (1968). The *Bromus mollis* aggregate in Britain. *Watsonia*, **6**: 327–344.

Sobee, F.J. (1997). *A history of Pilling*. Landy Publishing. Blackpool. (A reprint with an introduction by Brian Marshall of the book first published in 1953).

Spalton, L.M. (2001). A new subspecies of *Bromus hordeacus* L. (Poaceae). *Watsonia*, **23**: 525–531.

Stace, C.A. (1972). The history and occurrence in Britain of hybrids in *Juncus* subgenus Genuini. *Watsonia*, **9**: 1–11.

Stace, C.A., ed. (1975). *Hybridization and the Flora of the British Isles*. Academic Press. London.

Stace, C.A. (1991). *New Flora of the British Isles*. Cambridge University Press. Cambridge.

Stace, C.A. (2009). Notes. Eleven new combinations in the British flora. *Watsonia*, **27**: 246–248.

Stace, C. (1997). *New Flora of the British Isles*. 2nd edition. Cambridge University Press. Cambridge.

Stace, C. (2010). *New Flora of the British Isles*. 3rd edition. Cambridge University Press. Cambridge.

Stace, C.E. and Cotton, R. (1974). Hybrids between *Festuca rubra* L. *sensu lato* and *Vulpia membranacea* (L.) Dum. *Watsonia*, **10**: 119–138.

Stace, C.E., Ellis, R.G., Kent, D.H. and McCosh, D.J., eds. (2003). *Vice-county census catalogue of the vascular plants of Great Britain*. Botanical Society of the British Isles. London.

Stalker, N.M. (1960). Plant records, 1957–1960. *The Changing Scene*, **2**: 68–70.

Stevens, C.J., Dise, N.B., Mountford, J.O. and Gowing, D.J. (2004). Impact of nitrogen deposition on the species richness of grasslands. *Science*, **303**: 1876–1879.

Stevens, D.P. (1990). The distribution of gender in *Petasites hybridus* (Butterbur). *BSBI News*, **55**: 10–11.

Steward, A., Donnison, E. and Dalton, A. (1993). *Woodland surveys in North West England using National Vegetation Classification*. English Nature North-west Region.

Stewart, A., Pearman, D.A. and Preston, C.D. (1994). *Scarce Plants in Britain*. JNCC. Peterborough.

Swan, G.A. (1993). *Flora of Northumberland*. The Natural History Society of Northumbria. Newcastle upon Tyne.

Swann, G. (1999). Identification, distribution and a new nothosubspecies of *Trichophorum cespitosum* (L.) Hartman (Cyperaceae) in the British Isles and N.W. Europe. *Watsonia*, **22**: 209–233.

Tallis, J. (1997a). The southern Pennine experience: an overview of blanket mire degradation in Tallis, J.H., Meade, R and Hulme, P.D., eds. *Blanket mire degradation causes consequences and challenges*. The Macaulay Land Use Research Group on behalf of the Mires Research Group. British Ecological Society. Aberdeen.

Tallis, J. (1997b). Peat erosion in the Pennines: the badlands of Britain. *Biologist*, **44**: 277–279.

Tallis, J.H. (1999). The uplands: human influences on the plant cover in Greenwood, E.F., ed., *Ecology and landscape development: a history of the Mersey Basin*. Liverpool University Press. National Museums & Galleries on Merseyside. Liverpool.

Tansley, A.G., ed. (1911). *Types of British vegetation*. Cambridge University Press. Cambridge.

Tansley, A.G. (1939). *The British Isles and their vegetation*. Cambridge University Press. Cambridge.

Taschereau, P.M. (1989). Taxonomy, morphology and distribution of *Atriplex* hybrids in the British Isles. *Watsonia*, **17**: 247–264.

Tate, W.E. (1978). *A Domesday of English enclosure acts and awards*. The Library, University of Reading. Reading.

Taylor, I. (1986). *A botanical survey of mesotrophic grassland in Lancashire*. Nature Conservancy Council. A typescript.

Taylor, K. (1971). *Rubus chamaemorus* L. Biological Flora of the British Isles. *Journal of Ecology*, **59**: 293–306.

Taylor, K., Havitt, D.C., Pearson, J. and Woodall, J. (2002). *Trientalis europaea* L. Biological Flora of the British Isles. *Journal of Ecology*, **90**: 404–418.

Terry, A.C., Ashmore, M.R., Power, S.A., Allchin, E.A. and Heil, G.W. (2004). Modelling the impacts of atmospheric nitrogen deposition on *Calluna* – dominated ecosystems in the UK. *Journal of Applied Ecology*, **41**: 897–909.

The Nature Conservancy Council (1980). *Lancashire inventory of ancient woodland (provisional)*. Nature Conservancy Council. Peterborough. (Unpublished report).

Thompson, R.E. (1933). The Fylde. *Geography*, **18**: 307–320.

Thompson, D.B.A., Hester, A.J. and Usher, M.B., eds. (1995). *Heaths and moorland: cultural landscapes*. Scottish Natural Heritage. HMSO.

Thornber, W. (1837). *An historical and descriptive account of Blackpool and its neighbourhood.* Privately published. Poulton.

Till, J.M. (1986). The agrarian economy in theLongridge area in the 17th and 18th centuries. *Lancashire Local Historian*, **4**: 34–40.

Tipping, P. (2001). Silverdale & Gait Barrows 10th June in Field trips 2000. *Parnassia*, **Spring 2001**: 12–13.

Tooley, M.J. (1978). *Sea-level changes in North-West England during the Flandrian stage.* Oxford Research Studies in Geography. Clarendon Press. Oxford.

Tucker, G., Ash, H. and Plant, C. (2005). *Review of the coverage of urban habitats and species within the UK Biodiversity Action Plans.* English Nature Research Reports Number 651. English Nature. Peterborough.

Tutin, T.G., Heywood, V.H., Burges, N.A., Moore, D.M., Valentine, D.H., Walters, S.M. and Webb, D.A., eds. (1972). *Flora Europaea. Volume 3 Diapensiaceae to Myopporaceae.* The University Press. Cambridge.

Tüxen, R. (1937). Die Pflanzengeshellochafter Nordwestdeutschlands. *Mitteilungen der Floristsoziologischen Arbitsgemeinschaft*, **3**: 1–170.

Ubsdell, R.A.E. (1976a). Studies on variation and evolution in *Centaurium erythraea* Rafn and *C. littorale* (D. Turner) Gilmour in the British Isles, 1. Taxonomy and biometrical studies. *Watsonia*, **11**: 7–31.

Ubsdell, R.A.E. (1976b). Studies on variation and evolution in *Centaurea erythraea* Rafn and *C. littorale* (D. Turner) Gilmour, 2. Cytology. *Watsonia*, **11**: 33–43.

Ubsdell, R.A.E. (1979). Studies on variation and evolution in *Centaurium erythraea* Rafn and *C. littorale* (D. Turner) Gilmour in the British Isles, 3. Breeding systems, floral biology and general discussion. *Watsonia*, **12**: 225–232.

Uglow, J. (2002). *The lunar men.* Faber & Faber. London.

University of Liverpool, Environmental Research and Consultancy (2005). Section 3.4 Natural Environment based on a NVC survey carried out in 2002 in *The Lytham St Annes Dune Management Plan* prepared for Fylde Borough Council. Unpublished report.

Vera, F.W.M. (2000). *Grazing ecology and forest history.* CABI. Wallingford.

Vesey-Fitzgerald, B. (1946). *British Game.* The New Naturalist. Collins. London.

Wallace, E.C. (1948). Record of *Melilotus indicus* on waste land, Warton near Lytham in Plant Records. *The Botanical Society and Exchange Club of the British Isles Report for 1946-47*, **13**: 281–323.

Walker, K.J. (2007). The last thirty five years: recent changes in the flora of the British Isles. *Watsonia*, **26**: 291–302.

Walters, S.M. (1970). The next twenty five years in Perring, F., ed., *The flora of a changing Britain.* Botanical Society of the British Isles. London.

Watson, H.C. (1883). *Topographical Botany.* 2nd edition. Bernard Quaritch. London.

W[arhurst], E. (1942). Record for *Spartina Townsendii* H. & J. Groves in Liverpool Botanical Society. *North Western Naturalist*, **17**: 413–414.

Watson, R.C. and McClintock, M.E. (1979). *Traditional houses of the Fylde.* Centre for North-West Regional Studies, University of Lancaster Occasional Paper No. 6. Lancaster.

Webb, N.C. (1986). *Heathlands.* The New Naturalist. Collins. London.

Webb, D.A. and Scannell, M.J.P. (1983). *Flora of Connemara and the Burren.* Royal Dublin Society and Cambridge University Press. Cambridge.

Webster, S.D. (1990). Three natural hybrids in *Ranunculus* L. subgenus *Batrachium* (DC.) A. Gray. *Watsonia*, **18**: 139–146.

Webster, S.D. and Rich, T.C.G. (1998). 7. *Ranunculus* Subgenus *Batrachium* in Rich, T.C.G. and Jermy, A.C., eds, *Plant Crib 1998.* Botanical Society of the British Isles. London.

Weld, J. (*c.* 1888). 'Natural History of Leagram'. MS notes at the Harris Museum and Art Gallery, Preston. A typewritten copy with later notes in three volumes came into the possession of Arthur Lord of Nan Kings Farm, Chipping. His widow, Muriel, prepared a copy for the author in 2003.

Wentworth, J.E. and Gornall, R.J. (1996). Cytogenetic evidence for autoploidy in *Parnassia palustris*. *New Phytologist*, **134**: 641–648.

Wheldon, J.A. and Salmon, C.E. (1925). Notes on the genus *Erythraea*. *Journal of Botany*, **63**: 345–352.

Wheldon, J.A. and Wilson, A. (1900). Additions to the flora of West Lancashire. *The Journal of Botany*, **38**: 40–47.

Wheldon, J.A. and Wilson, A. (1901a). Notes on the flora of Over Wyresdale. *Naturalist,* **1901**: 357–362.

Wheldon, J.A. and Wilson, A. (1901b). Additions to the Flora of West Lancashire. *Journal of Botany*, **39**: 22–26.

Wheldon, J.A. and Wilson, A. (1902). West Lancashire plants. *The Journal of Botany*, **40**: 346–350.

Wheldon, J. and Wilson, A. (1906). Additions to the flora of West Lancashire. *The Journal of Botany*, **44**: 99–102.

Wheldon, J.A. and Wilson, A. (1907). *The flora of West Lancashire.* Henry Young & Sons. Liverpool.

Wheldon, J.A. and Wilson, A. (1925). West Lancashire flora: notes, additions and extinctions. *Lancashire and Cheshire Naturalist*, **17**: 117–125.

Whellan, J.A. (1942). Notes on the Flora of West Lancashire, Vice-County 60. *The North Western Naturalist*, **17**: 354–357.

Whellan, J.A. (1948). *Bromopsis inermis, Bunias orientalis, Cynosurus echinatus, Linaria pallida, Ophrys apifera, Petasites albus, Petasites fragrans* and *Sambucus ebulus* in Plant Records. *Report for 1946–47. The Botanical Society and Exchange Club of the British Isles*, **13** : 281–323.

Whellan, J.A. (1954). The present day flora of the sand-dunes at St. Annes, W. Lancs. VC 60. *The North Western Naturalist*, **2NS**: 139–141

Whellan, J.A. and Bunker, H.E. (1948). *Senecio squalidus, Viola canina × V. riviniana* in Plant Records. *Report for 1946–47, The Botanical Society and Exchange Club*, **13**: 281–323.

White, E.J. and Smith, R.I. (1982). *Climatological maps of Great Britain.* Institute of Terrestrial Ecology. Penicuik.

Whiteside, R. (no date). Annotations in a copy of Wheldon and Wilson (1907) in the possession in the 1960s of Mrs C. Jones-Parry of Silverdale.

Whittaker, E.J. (1986). *Thomas Lawson 1630–1691. North country botanist, Quaker and schoolmaster.* Sessions Book Trust. York.

Whittaker, E.J. (1981). *A seventeenth century flora of Cumbria.* Gateshead.

Whyte, I. (2003). *Transforming fell and valley. Landscape and Parliamentary Enclosure in North West England.* Centre for North-West Regional Studies, University of Lancaster. Lancaster.

Wigginton, M.J. (1995). *Mosses and liverworts of north Lancashire.* University of Lancaster. Lancaster.

Wilcox, M. (2010). A novel approach to the determination and identification of *Juncus × diffusus* Hoppe and *J. × kern-reichgeltii* Jansen & Wacht. ex Reichg. *Watsonia*, **28**: 43–56.

Wilcox, M. (2011a). Hybrid rushes in the UK – sterility and fertility. *BSBI News*, **116**: 21–27.

Wilcox, M. (2011b). *Juncus acutiflorus. BSBI News*, **116**: 37.

Wilkinson, M.J. and Stace, C.A. (1991). A new taxonomic treatment of the *Festuca ovina* L. aggregate (Poaceae) in the British Isles. *Botanical Journal of the Linnean Society*, **106**: 347–397.

Williams, A. and Martin, G.H., eds. (2003). *Domesday book. A complete translation.* Alecto Historical Editions. Penguin Books. London.

Williamson, M. (1996). *Biological invasions.* Chapman & Hall. London.

Wilson, A. (1938). *The Flora of Westmorland.* Published privately.

Wilson, A. (1947-49). 'Plants found within a radius of 3 miles of Priest Hutton'. A MS contained in box 3 of the Dallman Archives at World Museum Liverpool (LIV).

Wilson, D.G. (1979). Horse dung from Roman Lancaster: a botanical report. *Archaeo-Physica*, **8**; 331–350.

Wilson, J.P. (1991). *The ecology and conservation of rare arable weed species and communities.* PhD thesis, University of Southampton.

Winchester, A. (1993). Field. Wood and forest – landscape of medieval Lancashire in Crosby, A.G., ed., *Lancashire local studies in honour of Diana Winterbotham.* Carnegie Publishing Ltd. in conjunction with the Lancashire Local History Federation. Preston.

Winchester, A.J.L. (2000). *The harvest of the hills.* Edinburgh University Press. Edinburgh.

Winckley of Preston. Correspondence, letters, deeds and account books (unsorted) amongst which reference is made to the new plantation at Catterall (Shelley Wood SD491418) *c.* 1800. LRC.DDW (Catterall 1635 – 1831).

Winterbotham, D. (1986). Flax – a forgotten crop. *Lancashire Local Historian*, **4**: 2–5.

Wolley-Dod, A.H. (1931). *A revision of the British Roses.* Reprinted from the *Journal of Botany* 1930-31. Taylor & Francis. London.

Wright, M. (1998/9). The history of Eaves Wood, Silverdale. *The Mourholme Magazine of Local History*, **3**: 1–14.

Wyse Jackson, M. (2000). *Cochlearia danica* on Irish road-sides. *BSBI News*, **85**: 20–21.

Yalden, D.W. (1996). Labrador tea *Ledum groenlandicum* in the Peak District. *Naturalist*, **121**: 81–86.

Yeo, M. (1997). Blanket mire degradation in Wales in Tallis, J.H., Meade, R. and Hulme, P.D., eds., *Blanket mire degradation causes, consequences and challenges.* The Macaulay Land Use Research Institute on behalf of the Mires Research Group. British Ecological Society. Aberdeen.

Yeo, P. (1990). Butterbur forms – some answers. *BSBI News*, **55**: 12.

Ziegler, P. (1999). *Britain then & now.* Weidenfield & Nicholson. London.

Index

Index to plant names in Chapter 3. Page numbers for distribution maps are in bold.

Arctium lappa 375
Arctium minus 375, **375**
Arctium nemorosum 375
Arctium pubens 375
Arenaria balearica 284
Arenaria leptoclados 283, **283**
Arenaria serpyllifolia 283, **283**
Aristolochia clematitis 122
Armeria maritima 274, **274**
Armoracia rusticana 258, **257**
Arrhenatherum elatius 523, **523**
Arrowgrass, Marsh 459
Arrowgrass, Sea 459
Arrowhead 456
Artemisia abrotanum 421
Artemisia absinthium 421, **420**
Artemisia dracunculus 421
Artemisia maritima 421, **420**
Artemisia stelleriana 421
Artemisia verlotiorum 420
Artemisia vulgaris 420, **420**
Artichoke, Jerusalem 433
Arum italicum 454, **454**
Arum maculatum 454, **454**
Aruncus dioicus 166
Asarabacca 121
Asarum europaeum 121
Ash 336
Ash, Manna 336
Asparagus officinalis 486, **486**
Asparagus, Garden 486
Aspen 220
Asperugo procumbens 327
Asperula arvensis 316
Asperula cynanchica 316, **317**
Asphodel, Bog 464
Asphodel, Hollow-leaved 478
Asphodelus fistulosus 478
Asplenium adiantum-nigrum 107, **107**
Asplenium ceterach 109, **108**
Asplenium marinum 107
Asplenium ruta-muraria 108, **108**
Asplenium scolopendrium 107, **106**
Asplenium trichomanes 108, **107**
Asplenium viride 108, **108**
Aster × salignus 417, **417**
Aster × versicolor 416
Aster 416, **417**
Aster laevis × A. novi-belgii 416
Aster lanceolatus 417
Aster novae-angliae 416
Aster novi-belgii 417, **417**
Aster puniceus 417
Aster tripolium 417, **418**
Aster, China 419
Aster, Sea 417
Astilbe × arendsii 141
Astilbe chinensis 141
Astrantia 442
Astrantia major 442
Athyrium filix-femina 110, **109**
Atriplex × gustafssoniana 299, **296**
Atriplex × hulmeana 298
Atriplex glabriuscula 299, **296**
Atriplex hortensis 298

Atriplex laciniata 300, **298**
Atriplex littoralis 299, **297**
Atriplex longipes 299, **297**
Atriplex patula 300, **297**
Atriplex portulacoides 300, **298**
Atriplex prostrata 298, **296**
Atropa belladonna 332, **332**
Aubretia 263
Aubrieta deltoidea 263
Aucuba japonica 316, **316**
Aunt-Eliza 477
Aurinia saxatilis 261
Avena × hybrida 523
Avena fatua 523, **523**
Avena sativa 524, **524**
Avena sterilis 524
Avens, Water 195
Avens, Wood 195
Avenula pratensis 523, **523**
Avenula pubescens 522, **522**
Axyris amaranthoides 295
Azalea, Yellow 313
Azolla filiculoides 106, **104**
Baby's-breath 294
Baldellia ranunculoides 456, **456**
Ballota nigra 352, **352**
Balm 358
Balm-of-Gilead 221
Balsam, Indian 307
Balsam, Orange 307
Balsam, Small 307
Balsam, Touch-me-not 306
Bamboo, Arrow 512
Bamboo, Broad-leaved 511
Bamboo, Hairy 511
Baneberry 130
Barbarea intermedia 256, **255**
Barbarea verna 256, **255**
Barbarea vulgaris 256, **255**
Barberry 126
Barberry, Darwin's 126
Barberry, Hedge 127
Barley, Foxtail 540
Barley, Meadow 540
Barley, Sea 540
Barley, Six-rowed 539
Barley, Two-rowed 539
Barley, Wall 540
Barley, Wood 539
Bartsia, Red 367
Bartsia, Yellow 367
Basil, Wild 359
Beak-sedge, White 500
Bean, Broad 154
Bedstraw, Fen 317
Bedstraw, Heath 319
Bedstraw, Hedge 318
Bedstraw, Lady's 318
Bedstraw, Limestone 318
Bedstraw, Northern 317
Beech 210
Beeches, Southern 209
Beet, Root 300
Beet, Sea 300
Bellflower, Adria 371

Bellflower, Clustered 371
Bellflower, Cornish 371
Bellflower, Creeping 372
Bellflower, Giant 372
Bellflower, Ivy-leaved 372
Bellflower, Nettle-leaved 372
Bellflower, Peach-leaved 370
Bellflower, Trailing 371
Bellis perennis 420, **419**
Bent, Black 528
Bent, Brown 529
Bent, Common 527
Bent, Creeping 528
Bent, Rough 529
Bent, Velvet 528
Bent, Water 530
Berberis × stenophylla 127
Berberis aggregata × B. wilsoniae 127
Berberis darwinii 126
Berberis vulgaris 126, **128**
Bergenia × schmidtii 141
Bergenia 141
Bergenia cordifolia 141
Bergenia crassifolia 141
Bermuda-grass 542
Berteroa incana 262
Berula erecta 446, **445**
Beta vulgaris 300, **298**
Betonica officinalis 352, **352**
Betony 352
Betula × aurata 212
Betula pendula 212, **211**
Betula pubescens 213, **211**
Betula utilis 213
Bidens cernua 433, **432**
Bidens tripartita 433, **434**
Bilberry 315
Bindweed, Field 330
Bindweed, Hairy 331
Bindweed, Hedge 331
Bindweed, Large 331
Bindweed, Sea 331
Birch, Downy 213
Birch, Himalayan 213
Birch, Silver 212
Bird's-foot 150
Bird's-foot-trefoil, Common 150
Bird's-foot-trefoil, Greater 150
Bird's-foot-trefoil, Narrow-leaved 150
Bird's-nest, Yellow 315
Bird-in-a-bush 124
Birthwort 122
Bistort, Amphibious 275
Bistort, Common 275
Bistort, Red 275
Bitter-cress, Hairy 259
Bitter-cress, Large 258
Bitter-cress, Narrow-leaved 259
Bitter-cress, Wavy 259
Bittersweet 334
Bitter-vetch 154
Black-bindweed 279
Black-eyed-Susan 432
Black-grass 531
Black-poplar 220

Carduus crispus 376, **376**
Carduus nutans 376
Carduus tenuiflorus 375, **375**
Carex × boenninghausiana 500
Carex × fulva 507
Carex × pseudoaxillaris 501
Carex × subgracilis 504
Carex × turfosa 510
Carex acuta 510, **510**
Carex acutiformis 504, **502**
Carex arenaria 501, **500**
Carex bigelowii 511
Carex binervis 506, **507**
Carex canescens 503, **502**
Carex caryophyllea 509, **509**
Carex demissa 508, **508**
Carex diandra 500
Carex digitata 509
Carex dioica 503, **501**
Carex distans 506, **507**
Carex disticha 502, **500**
Carex divisa 502
Carex echinata 503, **501**
Carex elata 510, **511**
Carex elongata 503
Carex ericetorum 509, **509**
Carex extensa 507, **507**
Carex flacca 506, **506**
Carex flava 507
Carex hirta 504, **502**
Carex hostiana 507, **508**
Carex laevigata 506, **506**
Carex lasiocarpa 504
Carex lepidocarpa 508, **508**
Carex leporina 503, **501**
Carex limosa 510
Carex muricata 501, **499**
Carex nigra 510, **510**
Carex oederi 508
Carex otrubae 501, **499**
Carex pallescens 508, **509**
Carex panicea 506, **506**
Carex paniculata 500, **498**
Carex pendula 505, **505**
Carex pilulifera 509, **510**
Carex pseudocyperus 504, **503**
Carex pulicaris 511, **511**
Carex remota 502, **500**
Carex riparia 504, **503**
Carex rostrata 504, **503**
Carex spicata 501, **499**
Carex strigosa 505
Carex sylvatica 505, **505**
Carex vesicaria 505, **505**
Carlina vulgaris 374, **375**
Carpinus betulus 214, **213**
Carpobrotus edulis 303
Carrot, Wild 453
Carthamus lanatus 379
Carthamus tinctorius 379
Carum carvi 451
Castanea sativa 210, **208**
Cat's-ear 380
Cat's-ear, Smooth 380
Cat's-tail, Sand 532

Cat's-tail, Small 531
Catabrosa aquatica 521, **521**
Catapodium marinum 522, **521**
Catapodium rigidum 521, **521**
Catchfly, Forked 294
Catchfly, Night-flowering 292
Catchfly, Nottingham 291
Catchfly, Sand 293
Catchfly, Small-flowered 293
Caterpillar-plant 151
Cat-mint 357
Cat-mint, Garden 358
Caucalis platycarpos 453
Caucasian-stonecrop 146
Cedar, Atlas 117
Cedar-of-Lebanon 117
Cedrus atlantica 117
Cedrus libani 117
Celandine, Greater 124
Celandine, Lesser 136
Celastrus orbiculatus 215
Celery, Wild 450
Centaurea cyanus 379, **378**
Centaurea diluta 379
Centaurea melitensis 379
Centaurea montana 378, **378**
Centaurea nigra 379, **380**
Centaurea scabiosa 378, **378**
Centaurea solstitialis 379
Centaurium × intermedium 320
Centaurium erythraea 319, **320**
Centaurium littorale 320, **320**
Centaurium pulchellum 321, **321**
Centaury, Common 319
Centaury, Lesser 321
Centaury, Seaside 320
Centranthus ruber 439, **439**
Centunculus minimus 312
Cephalanthera longifolia 467
Cephalaria gigantea 439
Cerastium arvense 286, **287**
Cerastium diffusum 287, **288**
Cerastium fontanum 287, **288**
Cerastium glomeratum 287, **288**
Cerastium semidecandrum 287, **289**
Cerastium tomentosum 286, **287**
Ceratocapnos claviculata 125, **126**
Ceratochloa carinata 537
Ceratophyllum demersum 122, **121**
Ceratophyllum submersum 122, **123**
Chaenorhinum minus 342, **342**
Chaenorhinum origanifolium 342
Chaerophyllum temulum 443, **443**
Chaffweed 312
Chamaecyparis lawsoniana 119, **120**
Chamaemelum nobile 422
Chamerion angustifolium 244, **245**
Chamomile 422
Chamomile, Corn 422
Chamomile, Stinking 423
Chamomile, Yellow 423
Charlock 266
Chelidonium majus 124, **125**
Chenopodium album 297, **295**
Chenopodium berlandieri 297

Chenopodium bonus-henricus 295, **294**
Chenopodium bushianum 297
Chenopodium ficifolium 297
Chenopodium hybridum 296
Chenopodium leptophyllum 296
Chenopodium murale 296
Chenopodium opulifolium 297
Chenopodium polyspermum 296, **295**
Chenopodium probstii 298
Chenopodium rubrum 296, **295**
Chenopodium suecicum 298
Chenopodium urbicum 296
Cherry, Bird 167
Cherry, Dwarf 167
Cherry, Wild 167
Chervil, Bur 444
Chervil, Rough 443
Chestnut, Sweet 210
Chiastophyllum oppositifolium 145
Chickweed, Common 285
Chickweed, Greater 285
Chickweed, Lesser 285
Chickweed, Water 288
Chickweed-wintergreen 311
Chicory 379
Chives 479
Chrysosplenium alternifolium 144, **145**
Chrysosplenium oppositifolium 143, **144**
Cicely, Sweet 444
Cicerbita macrophylla 384, **384**
Cicerbita plumieri 384
Cichorium intybus 379, **380**
Cicuta virosa 450
Cinquefoil, Alpine 192
Cinquefoil, Creeping 194
Cinquefoil, Grey 192
Cinquefoil, Hoary 192
Cinquefoil, Marsh 194
Cinquefoil, Shrubby 191
Cinquefoil, Spring 193
Cinquefoil, Ternate-leaved 192
Circaea × intermedia 247, **247**
Circaea lutetiana 247, **247**
Cirsium acaule 377
Cirsium arvense 377, **377**
Cirsium heterophyllum 376, **376**
Cirsium oleraceum 377
Cirsium palustre 377, **377**
Cirsium vulgare 376, **376**
Cladium mariscus 499
Clary, Annual 362
Clary, Balkan 363
Clary, Whorled 363
Clary, Wild 362
Claytonia perfoliata 303, **302**
Claytonia sibirica 303, **303**
Claytonia virginica 303
Cleavers 319
Clematis vitalba 131, **131**
Clinopodium acinos 359
Clinopodium ascendens 358
Clinopodium vulgare 359, **358**
Cloudberry 177
Clover, Alsike 158
Clover, Bird's-foot 158

Helleborus foetidus 128, **129**
Helleborus viridis 128, **129**
Helminthotheca echioides 381, **382**
Hemerocallis fulva 478
Hemerocallis lilioasphodelus 478
Hemizonia pungens 433
Hemlock 449
Hemlock-spruce, Western 116
Hemp 207
Hemp-agrimony 434
Hemp-nettle, Bifid 356
Hemp-nettle, Common 355
Hemp-nettle, Large-flowered 355
Hemp-nettle, Red 355
Henbane 333
Heracleum grossheimii 452
Heracleum lehmannianum 452
Heracleum mantegazzianum 452, **452**
Heracleum sphondylium 452, **451**
Heracleum trachyloma 452
Herb-Paris 465
Herb-Robert 239
Herniaria glabra 290
Hesperis matronalis 271, **270**
Heuchera sanguinea 143
Hieracium 407
Hieracium ampliatum 409
Hieracium anglorum 411
Hieracium argillaceum 411, **413**
Hieracium auratiflorum 412
Hieracium aviicola 411
Hieracium calcaricola 408
Hieracium caledonicum 409
Hieracium coniops 410
Hieracium consociatum 411
Hieracium cravoniense 410, **410**
Hieracium cymbifolium 412
Hieracium daedalolepioides 410
Hieracium decolor 409
Hieracium diaphanoides 411
Hieracium diaphanum 410, **410**
Hieracium dicella 409
Hieracium duriceps 412
Hieracium eboracense 408
Hieracium exotericum 412
Hieracium festinum 411
Hieracium gothicoides 408
Hieracium grandidens 412
Hieracium hjeltii 413
Hieracium hypochaeroides 409
Hieracium lepidulum 410
Hieracium lintonii 411
Hieracium lissolepium 409
Hieracium maculoides 411
Hieracium oistophyllum 411
Hieracium ornatilorum 408
Hieracium pellucidum 412
Hieracium placerophylloides 409
Hieracium praesigne 410
Hieracium rubiginosum 410
Hieracium sabaudum 407, **408**
Hieracium salticola 407
Hieracium severiceps 412
Hieracium silvaticoides 411
Hieracium stictum 409

Hieracium subaequialtum 412
Hieracium subcrassum 412
Hieracium subcyaneum 409
Hieracium sublepistoides 412
Hieracium sylvularum 412
Hieracium tricolorans 409
Hieracium umbellatum 408, **408**
Hieracium vagum 407, **408**
Hieracium virgultorum 407
Hieracium vulgatum 409, **410**
Himalayan Giant 184
Hippocrepis comosa 151, **150**
Hippocrepis emerus 150
Hippophae rhamnoides 205, **203**
Hippuris vulgaris 346, **346**
Hirschfeldia incana 267, **266**
Hogweed 452
Hogweed, Giant 452
Holcus lanatus 525, **526**
Holcus mollis 525, **526**
Holly 370
Holly, Highclere 370
Holly, New Zealand 419
Hollyhock 251
Honckenya peploides 284, **284**
Honesty 261
Honesty, Perennial 261
Honeysuckle 438
Honeysuckle, Box-leaved 436
Honeysuckle, Californian 437
Honeysuckle, Fly 437
Honeysuckle, Himalayan 436
Honeysuckle, Japanese 437
Honeysuckle, Perfoliate 438
Honeysuckle, Tartarian 437
Honeysuckle, Wilson's 436
Hop 207
Hordelymus europaeus 539
Hordeum distichon 539, **540**
Hordeum jubatum 540
Hordeum marinum 540
Hordeum murinum 540, **540**
Hordeum secalinum 540
Hordeum vulgare 539
Horehound, Black 352
Horehound, White 356
Hornbeam 214
Horned-poppy, Yellow 124
Hornwort, Rigid 122
Hornwort, Soft 122
Horse-chestnut 248
Horse-chestnut, Red 248
Horse-radish 258
Horsetail, Field 103
Horsetail, Great 104
Horsetail, Marsh 104
Horsetail, Rough 102
Horsetail, Shore 103
Horsetail, Variegated 102
Horsetail, Water 103
Horsetail, Wood 103
Hottentot-fig 303
Hottonia palustris 309, **308**
Hound's-tongue 330
House-leek 145

Humulus lupulus 207, **206**
Huperzia selago 100, **100**
Hyacinth 485
Hyacinth, Tassel 485
Hyacinthoides × massartiana 484, **485**
Hyacinthoides hispanica 485
Hyacinthoides non-scripta 484, **485**
Hyacinthus orientalis 485
Hydrangea 306
Hydrangea macrophylla 306
Hydrocharis morsus-ranae 457
Hydrocotyle ranunculoides 442
Hydrocotyle vulgaris 442, **442**
Hymenophyllum tunbrigense 105
Hymenophyllum wilsonii 105
Hyoscyamus niger 333
Hypericum 'Hidcote' 233
Hypericum × desetangsii 234, **233**
Hypericum androsaemum 233, **233**
Hypericum calycinum 233, **232**
Hypericum elodes 235
Hypericum forrestii 233
Hypericum hircinum 233
Hypericum hirsutum 235, **235**
Hypericum humifusum 235, **234**
Hypericum maculatum 234, **234**
Hypericum montanum 235, **235**
Hypericum patulum 236
Hypericum perforatum 234, **233**
Hypericum pulchrum 235, **235**
Hypericum tetrapterum 234, **234**
Hypericum xylosteifolium 234
Hypochaeris glabra 380
Hypochaeris radicata 380, **381**
Hypopitys monotropa 315
Iberis sempervirens 272
Iberis umbellata 272, **273**
Ilex × altaclerensis 370
Ilex aquifolium 370, **369**
Illecebrum verticillatum 290
Impatiens capensis 307
Impatiens glandulifera 307, **306**
Impatiens noli-tangere 306, **305**
Impatiens parviflora 307, **306**
Imperatoria ostruthium 452
Indian-rhubarb 141
Inula conyzae 414, **415**
Inula helenium 414
Inula hookeri 414
Iris foetidissima 476, **477**
Iris germanica 476
Iris pseudacorus 476, **477**
Iris, Bearded 476
Iris, Stinking 476
Iris, Yellow 476
Ironwort, Mountain 351
Isatis tinctoria 270
Isoetes sp. 101
Isolepis setacea 498, **497**
Iva xanthiifolia 432
Ivy, Common 441
Ivy, Irish 441
Ivy, Persian 441
Ivy. Algerian 441
Jacob's-ladder 308

Rosa × involuta 201
Rosa × irregularis 200
Rosa × molletorum 202
Rosa × perthensis 204
Rosa × rothschildii 202, **201**
Rosa × suberecta 204
Rosa 200
Rosa arvensis 200, **200**
Rosa caesia 202, **201**, **202**
Rosa canina 201, **201**
Rosa ferruginea 201
Rosa micrantha 205
Rosa mollis 204, **203**
Rosa multiflora 200
Rosa obtusifolia 203
Rosa rubiginosa 204, **203**
Rosa rugosa 201, **200**
Rosa sherardii 203, **202**
Rosa spinosissima 200, **200**
Rosa tomentosa 203
Rosa villosa 204
Rosa virginiana 201
Rose, Apple 204
Rose, Burnet 200
Rose, Japanese 201
Rose, Many-flowered 200
Rose, Red-leaved 201
Rose, Virginian 201
Rose, White 201
Rose-of-Sharon 233
Roseroot 145
Rowan 169
Rubia peregrina 319
Rubus 176
Rubus adenanthoides 188, **188**
Rubus albionis 180
Rubus anisacanthos 188, **187**
Rubus armeniacus 184, **185**
Rubus bartonii 185
Rubus bertramii 179
Rubus caesius 191, **192**
Rubus calvatus 180, **180**
Rubus cardiophyllus 181
Rubus chamaemorus 177, **176**
Rubus cissburiensis 183, **182**
Rubus conjungens 190
Rubus criniger 185, **185**
Rubus cumbrensis 180, **181**
Rubus dasyphyllus 189, **189**
Rubus diversus 187
Rubus eboracensis 190, **190**
Rubus echinatoides 188, **188**
Rubus echinatus 188
Rubus elegantispinosus 183
Rubus errabundus 180, **181**
Rubus fruticosus agg 178, **177**
Rubus furnarius 183, **182**
Rubus gratus 180
Rubus griffithianus 187, **186**
Rubus hylocharis 190, **190**
Rubus idaeus 178, **177**
Rubus incurvatiformis 183, **182**
Rubus infestus 188, **187**
Rubus intensior 190
Rubus laciniatus 181, **181**

Rubus latifolius 190, **190**
Rubus leptothyrsos 181
Rubus lindebergii 183, **183**
Rubus lindleianus 181, **182**
Rubus loganobaccus 178
Rubus mucronatiformis 187, **186**
Rubus mucronulatus 187, **186**
Rubus nemoralis 183, **183**
Rubus nessensis 179
Rubus newbouldii 187, **187**
Rubus painteri 185, **186**
Rubus pallidus 189
Rubus parviflorus 177
Rubus phaeocarpus 190
Rubus pistoris 184
Rubus plicatus 179, **180**
Rubus polyanthemus 184, **183**
Rubus pruinosus 190, **191**
Rubus radula 189, **188**
Rubus raduloides 188
Rubus rhombifolius 184, **184**
Rubus robiae 181, **182**
Rubus rubritinctus 184, **184**
Rubus rudis 189
Rubus rufescens 189, **189**
Rubus saxatilis 177, **176**
Rubus sciocharis 181
Rubus scissus 180, **180**
Rubus silurum 181, **182**
Rubus spectabilis 178, **177**
Rubus sprengelii 184, **184**
Rubus subtercanens 189, **189**
Rubus tricolor 177
Rubus tuberculatus 191, **191**
Rubus ulmifolius 185, **185**
Rubus vestitus 185, **186**
Rubus warrenii 191, **191**
Rubus wirralensis 187, **186**
Rudbeckia hirta 432
Rudbeckia laciniata 432
Rumex × abortivus 281
Rumex × pratensis 281, **281**
Rumex × sagorskii 281
Rumex acetosa 280, **279**
Rumex acetosella 279, **279**
Rumex conglomeratus 281, **281**
Rumex crispus 280, **280, 281**
Rumex dentatus 282
Rumex hydrolapathum 280, **280**
Rumex longifolius 280, **280**
Rumex maritimus 282, **282**
Rumex obtusifolius 282, **282**
Rumex sanguineus 281, **282**
Rumex scutatus 280
Rumex tenuifolius 279
Ruppia maritima 464, **464**
Rupturewort, Smooth 290
Ruscus aculeatus 486, **486**
Rush, Baltic 491
Rush, Blunt-flowered 488
Rush, Bulbous 489
Rush, Compact 493
Rush, Frog 491
Rush, Hard 492
Rush, Heath 490

Rush, Jointed 488
Rush, Round-fruited 490
Rush, Saltmarsh 491
Rush, Sea 489
Rush, Sharp-flowered 489
Rush, Slender 490
Rush, Soft 492
Rush, Thread 492
Rush, Toad 491
Russian-vine 279
Rustyback 109
Rye 541
Rye-grass, Flaxfield 514
Rye-grass, Italian 514
Rye-grass, Perennial 513
Safflower 379
Safflower, Downy 379
Saffron, Meadow 465
Sage, Wood 357
Sagina apetala 288, **289**
Sagina filicaulis 288, **289**
Sagina maritima 290, **289**
Sagina nodosa 288, **289**
Sagina procumbens 288, **289**
Sagittaria sagittifolia 456, **456**
Sainfoin 149
Salicornia 301, **299**
Salicornia dolichostachya 301, **300**
Salicornia emerici 301
Salicornia europaea 301, **299**
Salicornia fragilis 301, **300**
Salicornia obscura 301
Salicornia ramosissima 301, **299**
Salix × ambigua 227
Salix × angusensis 224
Salix × calodendron 225
Salix × capreola 226
Salix × coriacea 227
Salix × forbyana 223
Salix × fragilis 221
Salix × friesiana 224
Salix × fruticosa 225
Salix × holosericea 225, **225**
Salix × laurina 227
Salix × mollissima 223
Salix × multinervis 227, **227**
Salix × pontederiana 223
Salix × reichardtii 226, **226**
Salix × rubens 222, **223**
Salix × rubra 223, **224**
Salix × smithiana 225, **225**
Salix × subsericea 227
Salix × tetrapla 228
Salix alba 222, **223**
Salix aurita 227, **227**
Salix babylonica 229
Salix caprea 226, **226**
Salix cinerea 226, **226, 227**
Salix daphnoides 224, **224**
Salix eleagnos 225
Salix eriocephala 228
Salix euxina 221
Salix fragilis 221, **222**
Salix hookeriana 228
Salix lucida 228